to success

Do you like

Choices + **Control?**

Cyclist + Entrepreneur + Connoisseur + Consultant

You're making your way in the world, passionately pursuing your own definition of success. So choose the only business school admissions test that gives you more freedom to do things your way — skip questions, change answers and control which scores schools will see. Show the world's top business schools your best.

Accepted at the world's top-ranked business schools.

Learn more at TakeTheGRE.com

Measuring the Power of Le

2018 EDITION

Best
Grad
SCHOOLS

The Wharton School at the University of Pennsylvania
BRETT ZIEGLER FOR USN&WR

CONTENTS

98

CONTENTS

⑥ The U.S. News Rankings

BE THE ONE

AT THE TOP WHO KNOWS THE *Secret* HANDSHAKE

OTHERS LOOK UP TO WHO LEADS THE PACK

You've seen others take it on, and now it's your turn. You need an MBA that takes your career to the next level. It's not just what you'll learn, but who you'll meet: instructors and classmates with the industry connections to maximize the return on your MBA.

That's why so many Colorado State Online Professional MBA grads recommended the program. Consider it our secret club. Welcome to it. **CSUonlineMBA.com**

ONLINE PROFESSIONAL MBA
COLORADO STATE UNIVERSITY

@ USNEWS.COM/EDUCATION

Prospective graduate students researching their options will find the **U.S. News** website (home of the **Best Graduate Schools** and **Best Colleges** rankings) full of tips on everything from choosing a school to landing the most generous scholarships. Here's a sampling:

MBA Admissions Blog
usnews.com/mbaadmissions
Get admissions advice from blogger Stacy Blackman, a business school specialist with degrees from Wharton and Kellogg and co-author of "The MBA Application Roadmap: The Essential Guide to Getting into a Top Business School." Learn how to master those application essays, prepare for your interviews, and find the money for business school.

Online Education
usnews.com/online
Want to get that MBA without spending time in the classroom? See our rankings of the best online degree programs in business, education, engineering, computer information technology, criminal justice and nursing. And read time-management and funding tips from students who have completed online degree programs.

Law Admissions Blog
usnews.com/lawadmissions
Get the lowdown on getting in from bloggers at Stratus Admissions Counseling, a global admissions advising firm based in New York City. Learn how to do your best on the LSAT, determine the value of a dual J.D./MBA degree, and examine potential career paths.

Medical School Admissions Blog
usnews.com/medadmissions
Wade through the medical school admissions process with tips from experts and students in the field. Learn how to choose the right undergrad major for med school, avoid MCAT prep mistakes, decide between an M.D. and a D.O. degree, and submit a winning application.

Morse Code Blog
usnews.com/morsecode
Get an insider's view of the rankings from Chief Data Strategist Bob Morse, the mastermind behind them. Morse explains the methods we use to rank graduate programs and keeps you up to date on all the commentary and controversy.

Paying for Graduate School
usnews.com/payforgrad
Find tips and tools for financing your education, including guidance on scholarships, grants and loans. Read about your borrowing options, including loan forgiveness and repayment assistance programs for people who work in public service, nonprofits or underserved areas.

U.S. News Graduate School Compass
usnews.com/gradcompass
Gain access to the U.S. News Graduate School Compass, a wealth of searchable data with tools and an expanded directory of programs. (Subscribe at usnews.com/compassdiscount to get a 25 percent discount.) Are you curious about how much you could make coming out of law school? Or which medical residency programs are the most popular? Check the Graduate School Compass.

BEST GRADUATE SCHOOLS
2018 EDITION

Executive Committee Chairman and Editor-in-Chief Mortimer B. Zuckerman
Co-Chairman Eric Gertler
Editor and Chief Content Officer Brian Kelly
Executive Editor Margaret Mannix
Managing Editor Anne McGrath
Chief Data Strategist Robert J. Morse
Data Analyst Kenneth Hines
Data Collection Manager Matthew Mason
Art Director Rebecca Pajak
Director of Photography Avijit Gupta
Photography Editor Brett Ziegler
News Editor Elizabeth Whitehead
Senior Editor Michael Morella
Publications Associate Lindsay Cates
Contributors Kaitlyn Chamberlain, Linda Childers, Cathie Gandel, Elizabeth Gardner, Katherine Hobson, Beth Howard, Margaret Loftus, Linda Marsa, Peter Rathmell, Courtney Rubin, Arlene Weintraub
Research Manager Myke Freeman
Directory Janie S. Price

USNEWS.COM/EDUCATION
Vice President and General Manager Michael Nolan
Managing Editor Anita Narayan
Senior Editors Allison Gualtieri, Joy Metcalf
Reporters/Writers Jordan Friedman, Ilana Kowarski, Farran Powell, Kelly Mae Ross, Delece Smith-Barrow
Digital Producers Briana Boyington, Alexandra Pannoni
Product Managers Amanda Gustafson, Amanda Grace Johnson

ACADEMIC INSIGHTS
Vice President Evan Jones
Product Manager Cale Gosnell
Product Marketing Specialist Taylor Suggs

INFORMATION SERVICES
Vice President, Data and Information Strategy Stephanie Salmon
Senior Data Analyst Eric Brooks
Data Analysts Alexis Krivian, Andrew Jackwin
Data Collection Jessica Benenson, Kaylah Denis, Kelsey Page-Campbell

TECHNOLOGY
Senior Director of Engineering Matt Kupferman
Director of Software Development Dan Brown
Senior Systems Manager Cathy Cacho
Software Technical Leads David Jessup, Alex Blum
Developers Joshua Brown, William Garcia, Rob Miller, Stefanie Zhou, Alan Weinstein
Project Manager Sangeetha Sharma
Quality Assurance Sandy Sathyanarayanan
Digital Production Michael A. Brooks, Manager; Michael Fingerhuth

President and Chief Executive Officer William D. Holiber

ADVERTISING
Publisher and Chief Advertising Officer Kerry Dyer
Vice President, Advertising Ed Hannigan
Vice President, Marketing and Advertising Strategy Alexandra Kalaf
Senior Sales Director, Strategic Accounts Rob Holiber
Director, Integrated Media Solutions Peter Bowes
Financial Sales Manager Heather Levine
Health Care Manager Colin Hamilton
Senior Account Executives Anthony Patterson, Michelle Rosen, Brian Roy, Shannon Tkach
Account Executives Julie Izzo, Taylor Kiefer, Samantha Stefanacci, Pranita Tiwari, Ivy Zenati
Account Executive, Integrated Media Solutions Dustin Hill
Managing Editor, BrandFuse Jada Graves
Audience Development Manager, BrandFuse Alicia Roda
Web Designer, Branded Content Sara Hampt
Director of Programmatic, Data and Revenue Partnerships Joseph Hayden
Programmatic Analyst Liam Kristinnsson
Senior Manager of Ad Technology and Platforms Teron Samuel
Senior Managers, Sales Strategy Tina Lopez, Riki Smolen
Sales Planners Gary DeNardis, Spencer Vastoler, Michael Zee
Marketing Coordinator Brielle Schwartz
Director of Advertising Operations Cory Nesser
Account Managers Jennifer Fass, Katie Harper, Brunilda Hasa, Jane Marchetti
Ad Operations Samantha Seigerman
Director of Advertising Services Phyllis Panza
Business Operations Karolee Jarnecki
Administration Judy David, Anny Lasso, Carmen Caraballo

Vice President, Specialty Marketing Mark W. White
Director of Specialty Marketing Abbe Weintraub

Chief Operating Officer Karen S. Chevalier
Chief Product Officer Chad Smolinski
Chief Financial Officer Neil Maheshwari
Senior Vice President, Education, News/Opinion and B-2-B Insights Chris DiCosmo
Senior Vice President, Technology Yingjie Shu
Senior Vice President, Strategic Development and General Counsel Peter M. Dwoskin
Senior Vice President, Human Resources Jeff Zomper
Senior Vice President Planning Thomas H. Peck

Additional copies of U.S. News & World Report's **Best Graduate Schools 2018** guidebook are available for purchase at (800) 836-6397 or online at usnews.com/gradguide. To order custom reprints, call (877) 652-5295 or email usnews@wrightsmedia.com. For all other permissions, email permissions@usnews.com.

We know NURSING.

Take your career to the next level at Wayne State University. When you become a College of Nursing graduate student, you'll grow as a leader, scholar and practitioner. Wayne State M.S.N. and D.N.P. students apply evidence in practice to improve the health of individuals, families and communities in a range of health care settings. Ph.D. students advance nursing knowledge and build the science on which practice is based.

Located in the heart of Detroit and surrounded by world-class health care institutions, Wayne State University's College of Nursing is committed to diversity and excellence.

Join us to make a lasting impact on urban health.

nursing.wayne.edu

Master of Science in Nursing
- Clinical specialties:
  - Neonatal Nurse Practitioner
  - Nurse-Midwife
  - Pediatric Nurse Practitioner-Acute Care
  - Pediatric Nurse Practitioner-Primary Care
  - Psychiatric-Mental Health Nurse Practitioner
- M.S.N. in Advanced Public Health Nursing

Doctor of Nursing Practice
Pathways:
- B.S.N. to D.N.P.
- M.S.N. to D.N.P. *(APRN certified)*
- M.S.N. to D.N.P. *(need certification)*

Clinical specialties:
- Adult-Gerontology Acute Care Nurse Practitioner
- Adult-Gerontology Primary Care Nurse Practitioner
- Family Nurse Practitioner
- Nurse-Midwife
- Neonatal Nurse Practitioner
- Pediatric Nurse Practitioner-Acute Care
- Pediatric Nurse Practitioner-Primary Care
- Psychiatric-Mental Health Nurse Practitioner

Doctor of Philosophy in Nursing
Pathways:
- M.S.N. to Ph.D.
- B.S.N. to Ph.D.

Graduate Certificates
- Nursing Education
- Clinical specialties:
  - Adult-Gerontology Acute Care Nurse Practitioner
  - Nurse-Midwife
  - Pediatric Nurse Practitioner-Acute Care
  - Pediatric Nurse Practitioner-Primary Care

Is Grad School the Right MOVE?

The answer will depend on your field, your career goals and the cost of an advanced degree

BY BETH HOWARD

A fellowship paid for Susanna Kohler, 30, to study astrophysics at the University of Colorado in Boulder, where she earned a doctoral degree in 2014 without taking out any grad school loans. "In my field, and other hard sciences, you get paid to go to graduate school," says Kohler. Without that financial burden, she was free to choose among a myriad of job opportunities. Kohler now works as an editor and writer for the American Astronomical Society, though her specialty could also lead to academia, industry or a government agency.

Not everyone is so fortunate. In other fields, the math is often trickier, with the cost of an advanced degree weighing on students' own shoulders and indebtedness on the rise. The median debt for someone earning a master of arts rose from $38,000 in 2004 to $59,000 a mere eight years later, according to a study from the nonprofit

A MASTER'S IN HISTORY HELPED MANDY GIBSON LAND
AN EDUCATION JOB AT A HISTORIC PARK IN NORTH CAROLINA.

New America, a nonpartisan public policy institute.

Meanwhile, enhanced job requirements and the desire to stand out among other applicants have been an impetus toward further study. According to the Council of Graduate Schools, enrollment in master's and doctoral programs reached more than a half million in 2015, a record high.

So it's important to assess whether a graduate degree really is worthwhile before sacrificing a salary for an extended period and piling on debt. Generally speaking, yes, "graduate degrees provide substantial returns, on average, irrespective of the field," says Andrew Hanson, a senior research analyst at the Georgetown University Center on Education and the Workforce. Overall, people with a master's degree earn an average of about $2.7 million over their lifetimes, compared to $2.3 million for people with a bachelor's, for example. And they tend to enjoy greater employment security. In 2015 the unemployment rate for workers with a master's was 2.4 percent, compared to 2.8 for those with a bachelor's and 5.4 for those with just a high school diploma. Less than 2 percent of people with a doctoral or professional degree were out of work.

Still, the spoils can vary widely depending on your chosen path. A financial services professional with a master's, for example, makes $80,000 more per year on average than a colleague with a bachelor's. People with a bachelor's in communications, on the other hand, average the same as those with a master's: $56,000. Students heading into hot fields like health care, engineering and the STEM disciplines can expect a much greater earnings boost and more opportunities than a Ph.D. in the humanities hoping to teach at a university.

Experience and personal factors come into play, too. Georgetown research also shows that 40 percent of bachelor's degree holders make more than the median pay of workers with a master's.

The decision doesn't hinge solely on the return on investment of a diploma, of course. Graduate school is also "about gaining additional expertise to help you do what you love," says Elizabeth Venturini, founder of CollegeCareerResults.com, a college and career advising service. That said, it pays to weigh the financials carefully. Start with these questions:

DO YOU NEED A DEGREE?

Advanced degrees are increasingly viewed as important to getting jobs and advancing, even in traditionally modestly paying careers such as library science and school and career counseling. Jobs for social workers, historians, survey researchers, curators, archivists, anthropologists, rehabilitation counselors, marriage and family therapists, and mental health counselors typically now require an advanced degree, though they rarely pay more than the household median income of $51,085 a year, according to Graphiq, an online data research firm.

In some fields, the education goals for licensure are ratcheting up due to the evolution in skills required, notes Hanson. Advanced practice nurses, for instance, now have job descriptions that include many of the tasks that used to be done only by anesthesiologists or other doctors, and there's been a push to raise the entry bar from a master's to a doctor of nursing practice degree.

On the other hand, science-focused students interested in research may not need to go all the way to a doctorate. According to Sean Gallagher, executive director of the Center for the Future of Higher Education and Talent Strategy at Northeastern University, an industry-oriented "professional science master's" can equip them to work in a lab for many types of companies.

The "credential creep" may seem like an arbitrary measure to screen out job candidates, but some employers regard that master's as a measure of "soft skills – like grit, determination and persistence," Hanson says.

"All the jobs I applied for said bachelor's required, master's preferred," says Mandy Gibson, 26, an education park aide at Historic Oak View County Park in Raleigh, North Carolina. So she got a master's in history from Virginia Commonwealth University. In a survey by job search firm CareerBuilder.com, 57 percent of hiring managers who had upgraded their educational requirements associated a master's degree with higher quality work and 43 percent with increased productivity.

Sometimes your portfolio will be the key credential. With her sights set on working in theater, Megan Savage considered grad school after finishing up at Harvard in 2010 with an English degree. But "everybody said this field is a meritocracy," says Savage, 29, now director of programs and operations for the America-Israel Cultural Foundation in New York, as well as co-producer of three Broadway shows. "They want to see that you can do the work," she says. "Every year that you haven't done the work is another year that people have not heard of you."

If grad school isn't a must, it might be more efficient to consider alternative ways to up your game – to add know-how in data analysis, say, or public speaking chops. "If you're looking for skills and coursework that have impact on the job, it may be that there's a short-term certificate program," suggests Gallagher. Over 38,000 people earned graduate certificates, the fastest-growing segment of higher education, in 2015. Northeastern offers more than 100 graduate certificates in everything from mutual fund management to sports administration. George Washington Uni-

"OVER 38,000 PEOPLE EARNED GRADUATE CERTIFICATES IN 2015."

#RadyMade
Engineer ➤ Co-Founder & CEO

> I knew I could make a difference through my work, but didn't know where to begin. It didn't take long for the Rady School to inspire me to start our company, Aira, an operating system that enables blind individuals to connect with a network of certified agents. The Rady School and StartR Accelerator gave me the tools and confidence I needed to make Aira happen, and positively impact the lives of others.
>
> **Suman Kanuganti, MBA '14**
> Co-Founder & CEO, Aira
>
> —— I am RadyMade ——

Rady | School of Management
UNIVERSITY OF CALIFORNIA SAN DIEGO

To see more stories:
rady.ucsd.edu/radymade

MBA | MFIN | MSBA | Ph.D. | ExecEd

versity's 87 graduate certificate programs include healthcare corporate compliance and museum collections management and care. If you're interested in software development, a coding boot camp might open up new job opportunities.

And it's certainly not a good idea to opt for a pricey degree now if more school is just a way of avoiding a tough job market.

WHAT WILL IT COST?

The tab may not be as burdensome as you think. "Many of us have in our heads the sticker price of $30,000 to $40,000 per year for undergraduate education," says Gallagher. "So we say, 'OK, it's two years for a graduate degree, so it's going to cost me $70,000 or $80,000 or more.' And while there are certainly programs at that price point, there are many programs where you can get the entire graduate degree for between $20,000 and $40,000."

Investigate multiple sources of funding – scholarships, fellowships, teaching and research assistantships, financial help from employers – to lessen the need to borrow (story, Page 22). "A good rule of thumb is that the total debt you take on to finance the program should be less than or equal to your expected annual earnings when you graduate," Hanson says. Many Ph.D. programs not only waive tuition and fees, but also pay a stipend for living expenses.

And check out how helpful a program (or the government) might be in the future. Loan forgiveness or repayment assistance is available in a number of fields, such as education, law and medicine, for people who go into public service.

Keep in mind that there are a widening array of part-time options and online programs that both offer flexibility and can limit the need to take on debt (story, Page 16). One-third of all graduate education in the U.S. today is via online education or blended learning, Gallagher says, and many of the programs are offered by reputable and even prestigious universities. It shouldn't be hard, he says,

Why I Picked

CARNEGIE MELLON
Pittsburgh

Brendan Meeder, '15
SENIOR SOFTWARE ENGINEER, UBER

➤ CMU's School of Computer Science has strengths everywhere and encourages students to be cross-disciplinary. Computer scientists can collaborate with researchers in different departments like robotics or computational biology, with advisers in each. These were real advantages for me as my interests have always been broad and deep.

Another plus: Everyone gets to focus on research. The computer science department will support you financially even if your adviser can't, without forcing you to TA every semester. The culture is both academic and entrepreneurial. In fact, students and professors sometimes form startups together. My adviser pulled me into a project that became the language-learning app Duolingo. I took time off to help build the product and company and eventually integrated this work into my Ph.D. thesis on understanding user behavior in social networks. Today, I work with many alumni on Uber's self-driving car project, which Uber chose to base in Pittsburgh largely because of CMU.

to find a program "that works for your schedule and your price point."

WILL A DEGREE BOOST YOUR EARNING POTENTIAL?

Besides obvious fields like law and medicine, career paths in STEM, business and health care tend to get the biggest financial boost from a master's or doctorate, says Hanson. Advanced degrees in English, communication, psychology, education and social sciences are the least financially rewarding.

Georgetown data show that in engineering, for instance, a bachelor's degree returns $83,000 a year on average while a master's pays $120,000; a doctorate pays $150,000. A master's in information technology pays $110,000 a year compared to $76,000 for a bachelor's; a doctorate pays $165,000. Workers with master's degrees in health fields average $89,000, some $32,000 more than people with a bachelor's only; M.D.s average $167,000. People with a master's degree in education receive about $23,000 more than those with a bachelor's. And special education instructors with the extra credential will see only about $6,200 more.

A good source to use to gauge whether a graduate degree in a chosen field will be worth the time and expense is the Occupational Outlook Handbook put out by the government's Bureau of Labor Statistics. It provides an overview on hundreds of jobs, explaining daily job tasks, education, training and projected salary.

Stephen Mangum, dean of the Haslam College of Business at the University of Tennessee, sums up the key factors in the value calculation: your likely earnings stream if you do not pursue an advanced degree versus your earnings stream if you do obtain one, the direct costs of the additional education, and the earnings you'll forgo while in school. Add to the mix your concept of your life's work and "what constitutes success." If the bottom line favors graduate school, he says, then go for it. ●

The Online Advantage

Virtual education is jump-starting careers with an array of new options

BY COURTNEY RUBIN

Mike Szalkowski, 51, always wanted an MBA but could never work out the timing around demanding jobs and a heavy travel schedule, first as a senior manager with Ernst & Young and most recently handling investments for a wealthy family. Szalkowski, who lives in Atlanta, watched the development of online graduate degrees hopefully, but wondered if employers would have the dismissive view that "you got it at some fly-by-night university." Then he saw that the University of North Carolina's Kenan-Flagler Business School – a top-20 program – was offering an online option. Szalkowski immediately knew it was "a degree that people would recognize." In 2015, he collected the degree in person in a ceremony at Chapel Hill.

Online graduate education, once a caveat emptor Wild West of questionable quality, has come a long way. "The online degree market is pretty well established, especially in terms of acceptance in the employer community," says Sean Gallagher, executive director of the Center for the Future of Higher Education and Talent Strategy at Northeastern University and author of "The Future of University Credentials," published last year. The ability to deliver instruction online has opened up a world of possibility beyond traditional degrees. Both for-profit companies and universities (including elite ones) are racing to market with a range of options, from traditional academic degrees to occupational credentialing and professional development.

A growing acceptance. According to the National Center for Education Statistics, students enrolled in fully online courses represented 25 percent of all graduate-level enrollment in 2014, the last year for which figures are available. When you include hybrid or blended programs – a mix of online and tra-

ditional classes – that figure goes up to 33 percent. One key reason for the acceptance of online graduate study is that other elite institutions have entered the market with UNC, including Johns Hopkins, Columbia, Georgetown and Harvard, the last of which offers master's degrees that can be earned more than half online in some two dozen fields ranging from sustainability to software engineering.

At Johns Hopkins, dozens of degree programs can be earned completely online; others require some in-person coursework. Museum studies, for example, mandates a two-week intensive seminar in Washington, D.C., or another specified location. At Columbia, the School of Engineering and Applied Science offers 22 fully online masters degrees, and the School of Social Work allows all coursework to be completed online, though fieldwork must also be conducted in the city where the student resides. At Georgetown, students will find that a number of master's programs – like those in applied intelligence, real estate and project management – offer the choice of learning either exclusively online or on campus, or doing a mix of both.

In general, programs at elite schools are rigorous, and admission is competitive. Harvard, for example, requires applicants to complete three courses – usually including a difficult "gatekeeper" course – and get at least a B in each before submitting a traditional application. But the online cost is attractive: Less than $31,000 compared to the roughly $90,000 price tag for the traditional de-

PHOTO ILLUSTRATION BY WILLIAM DUKE FOR USN&WR,
PHOTO BY BRETT ZIEGLER FOR USN&WR

STUDENTS "MEET" WITH PROFESSOR DAVE ROBERTS
(TOP LEFT) FOR A CLASS IN SALES THAT IS PART OF THE
UNC KENAN-FLAGLER ONLINE MBA PROGRAM.

gree. Meanwhile, at UNC Kenan-Flagler, where "Online is not a B-tier program," says Douglas Shackelford, the school's dean, the fees reflect it. The school is the rare example whose online degree costs just as much (roughly $115,000 to $120,000) as the residential one.

Students going the online route may give up a few job-search advantages unless they happen to live near enough to campus to attend recruiting or information sessions, but they don't have to sacrifice a network of classmates. Most degrees require some face-to-face time to bond, and Facebook groups and online forums make possible "online" happy hours. (The happy hours also sometimes occur in person when students visit cities where other classmates live.) Adam Brown, a physician who earned his MBA in UNC's online program, says he became close enough with classmates that they attend his holiday parties.

A focus on job skills. For those looking to expand their career options without such a heavy commitment of time or money, more offerings are opening up. Though some may have the word "degree" in their name (like for-profit online education provider Udacity's "Nanodegree programs"), they are actually credentials or certificates. While degrees involve faculty engagement and assessment and take at least a year to complete, these new programs often can be completed in months or even weeks.

Employers generally view them favorably, since they demonstrate motivation. "They put them in a category with continuing education and gaining new skills," Gallagher says. There isn't much networking attached to the shorter, more-targeted credentials as the focus is on job skills.

Some of Columbia's schools have expanded their online offerings to include certificates of professional achievement; two examples are those in health information technology and actuarial science. Typically, these certificates are made up of four courses. Udacity's Nanodegrees in such areas as virtual reality and artificial intelligence are recognized by and were built with input from partners like Google, AT&T and Facebook. The company, which was founded by Sebastian Thrun, a Stanford University AI specialist and founder of Google X, offers a full refund to any student who isn't hired within six months of completing a Nanodegree. Each typically takes 10 hours a week over six to nine months, and students generally complete six to eight courses and six projects, which showcase their abilities to employers.

Lauren Smith, 28, of Providence, Rhode Island, was processing invoices in accounts receivable in 2014 when she signed up for a front-end web developer Nanodegree from Udacity. She liked both that she could cancel the $200-per-month course at any time if she couldn't handle it and that there was an online community that could help her if she struggled, for example, with JavaScript. "I wasn't sure if anything was going to come of it," she said of the then brand-new Nanodegree program.

But within weeks of finishing, she was hired as a web developer at a small e-commerce company. She was so pleased she's since earned another Nanodegree in "full stack" – aka development involving both front- and back-end work – and a pay raise for her efforts. Udacity offers a 50 percent tuition refund to students who complete the degree within a year.

Introducing the MicroMasters. Another new credential is Massachusetts Institute of Technology's "MITx MicroMasters," an online program in in-demand subjects such as supply chain management that covers roughly a semester's worth of material of a typical master's degree. Thirteen other schools are also offering this type of credential through edX, the MIT- and Harvard-backed online education platform. Columbia, for example, is offering the credential in artificial intelligence, and Roch-

ester Institute of Technology in project management. There is no admissions process – anyone can sign up – but classes are fittingly rigorous, the participating institutions say. Students take proctored exams to verify what they've learned.

No one has yet completed the MicroMasters, which debuted last year. But there is good reason to believe it will be well received by employers, in part because of the quality of the institutions

"SOME PROGRAMS TAKE JUST MONTHS OR EVEN WEEKS."

offering it. MIT's MicroMasters has another potential upside: Students who are very successful with their credential coursework and exams can be admitted, with a semester's credit, to the MIT master's program and complete that degree on campus.

Is an online degree, credential or certificate right for you? Marty Gustafson, the assistant dean for academic planning and assessment at the University of Wisconsin-Madison's graduate school, says students often underestimate the amount of time school will take. "We recommend students plan three hours per credit minimum, so roughly 10 hours per week per three-credit class, and put that time on their schedule," she says. "That way they'll understand when they can fit it in and what will have to give."

Other things to consider: What kind of chat rooms or forums are available for you to "meet" fellow

students and share concerns and problems? Are there team projects that will facilitate your meeting other students, even if only electronically? And, how accessible will the instructor or professor be if you need help?

Keep in mind that online flexibility is not infinite. Many degree programs, in particular, have strict attendance requirements and a zero-tolerance policy for no-shows. So you'll want to make sure the program you choose has classes during times you're available.

Gallagher urges prospective students to "do your due diligence" with employers or hiring managers. Can you feel confident that the degree or credential you choose will help you advance? How will it be viewed if you want to change jobs?

Online degrees are well accepted in the education field, where many of the initial online graduate programs were developed, for example. They are much less accepted in pockets of health care and in the scientific community, where clinical experience is required. Still, a 2014 Duke University/RTI International study found that 73 percent of employers said that job seekers who took job-related MOOCs would be perceived positively. A company's "tuition support for multiple students in a particular program" is one gauge of employer interest, Gallagher points out.

Consider, too, the pace of change in your field. In fast-moving sectors like technology, data science and software engineering where you need a specific technical skill, short, targeted programs may be the way to go. See if the program offers job guarantees and if you can speak to former students to see how their credentials were received. And weigh the cost. Your studies may be cheaper if conducted online, but there's also the time and the effort. ●

There are Over 2,500 Universities in the U.S. Find the One That's Right for You.

U.S. News Global Education helps international students navigate higher education in the U.S. and connect with other students from around the world. Our trusted analysis, student-focused insights and thorough support will help you quickly research thousands of universities, simplifying your decision-making process.

To get started, visit usnewsglobaleducation.com

A Review of the Tests

Here's a brief look at what you can expect – and how much scores matter

BY LINDSAY CATES

To prepare for the Law School Admission Test the summer before senior year at the University at Buffalo, James Ingram hired a tutor, worked through prep books, and even acquired a special LSAT Watch to practice keeping track of the exam's six strict 35-minute time intervals, five devoted to testing his ability to comprehend and analyze complex material and one to an (unscored but important) essay. Not satisfied with his score of 158, Ingram doubled down on doing practice tests and took the LSAT again. His 166 impressed several top law schools, including those at Boston University, the University of Iowa, Emory, and George Washington University Law School, where he is a first-year student.

Ingram's belief that a strong LSAT score is essential to "get your foot in the door" at the best schools has long been true. But people pondering a law degree now stand to benefit by an across-the-board softening in scores accepted, says Anna Ivey, former dean of admissions at the University of Chicago Law School and founder of Ivey Consulting, an admissions advising company. The top schools do remain extremely competitive, but overall the number of applicants is down considerably since law jobs began disappearing during the recession. At GW Law, applications are off 21 percent since 2011, prompting a drop in median LSAT scores from 167 to 165. Boston College Law School and the University of North Carolina School of Law, both of which accepted Ingram, have seen decreases in applications of 36 percent and 44 percent, respectively, and a similar drop in median scores.

There's little doubt that your test scores can have a big impact on your competitiveness in many disciplines, experts say; graduate programs still use scores as their top indicator of an applicant's likelihood to succeed. And great scores improve your odds of landing scholarships: Ingram earned a merit scholarship at GW that covers half of his $56,000 annual tuition. How much scores count is the No. 1 question applicants ask him, says Stanley Dunn, vice provost and dean of graduate education at Rensselaer Polytechnic Institute. (RPI looks at test scores as a starting point, Dunn says, and if scores are on the low side, checks to see if the applicant makes up for it in other ways.) Grad school advisers say it's essential to get to know the test you are taking and to prep for it carefully. Here's what to expect of the various other exams:

The Medical College Admission Test. Future doctors need the ability to master new information rapidly and the communication skills to succeed in a patient-centered system. Thus the MCAT overhaul in 2015, which added questions on sociology and psychology as well as biochemistry and now tests skills in scientific reasoning and problem-solving, research design and data analysis. The test nearly doubled in length, with four multiple-choice sections each lasting 90 or 95 minutes. Instead of zeroing in just on scores and grades, reviewers also are increasingly doing a holistic review, looking at applicants' backgrounds and experiences.

The Graduate Record Examination. This exam tests verbal, quantitative reasoning and writing skills and is required for most programs in the arts and sciences. The three sections last 30 or 35 minutes each. Many graduate programs look for balanced verbal and quantitative scores. Alexander Wiseman, associate professor at Lehigh University's college of education, says many applicants have strong verbal scores, but students who also show strength on the quantitative side have an edge. Engineering schools typically look for strong quantitative scores. But given the need for engineers with communication skills, a low verbal score can really hurt, Dunn notes.

The Graduate Management Admission Test. Students weighing business school generally take the GMAT, a 3 1/2-hour online exam with writing, integrated reasoning, verbal and quantitative sections. B-schools are continuing to track very high GMAT scores for incoming classes. The Massachusetts Institute of Technology Sloan School of Management saw an 8-point increase in its 2016 average, and among the top 10 business schools there was a 3.4-point average increase, according to the latest U.S. News data. Most business schools also accept the GRE.

It's important to know, too, Dunn says, that reviewers look for signs that the program and applicant are a good "fit." He wishes more people obsessed with the tests would focus first on whether a program is the right match. ●

Plot Out a Payment Plan

There are ways to cover tuition and repay those loans

BY **MICHAEL MORELLA** AND **LINDSAY CATES**

After graduating from the University of Houston Law Center in 2006 with some $100,000 in debt, Dustin Rynders, 37, took a job as an attorney at a state agency in Houston representing children with disabilities in education matters. Under a standard 10-year loan repayment plan, he owed about $1,100 a month from his $38,000 starting salary. That would have been "a pretty insurmountable barrier" to a public service career, he says, if not for an "indispensable" combination of state, federal and legal sector funding that helped slash his loan burden.

A fellowship from Equal Justice Works, a nonprofit that sponsors dozens of public interest lawyers nationwide, covered most of Rynders' payments for two years. Then he found additional aid from the Texas Access to Justice Foundation, which gives about 150 public interest lawyers in the state as much as $400 a month toward their loans for up to 10 years. And thanks to the federal income-based repayment program, Rynders could adjust his loan payments to a percentage of his salary, keeping his monthly bill no higher than $450. His tip for students starting a graduate degree now: Pursue those dreams while keeping your debt "as low as possible."

Devising that kind of multipronged payment strategy can help keep graduate school affordable, whether you plan to be a doctor or lawyer or are destined for a teaching career. Prospective students should keep their costs, job and salary potential, and repayment options top of mind from the start of the application process, rather than as "the last piece of the puzzle," says David Sheridan, director of financial aid at Columbia University's School of International and Public Affairs.

The Council of Graduate Schools offers a budget calculator and other resources that can help you do the research (GradSense. org). A science teacher-to-be, for example, can see that graduates of education master's degree programs come out with a median debt load of $33,250 and command a median salary of about $62,000. If those loans carry a typical 5.31 percent interest rate, it would cost just over $350 a month to pay back the balance over 10 years.

Nationwide, about 70 percent of grad students receive financial aid in the form of grants, teaching or research assistantships, and loans. Here are several potential ways to get your share:

Find a sponsor.
Fifty-two percent of companies offer tuition assistance for

job-related courses, according to the Society for Human Resource Management. More typical in fields like business and education, employer-sponsored funding helps about 15 percent of grad students pay for school, and up to $5,250 annually of such aid qualifies as a tax-free benefit. Most university employees have access to discounted coursework, too.

Apply for fellowships and scholarships. At the graduate level, scholarships tend to be awarded based on a student's credentials or course of study rather than on financial need. Awards can come from government agencies, foundations and schools themselves. Fellowships, in addition to covering costs for one or more years of graduate study, work or research, sometimes include extra funding for living expenses or attending academic conferences. Becoming part of a network of scholars and getting those other specialized opportunities can be as valuable as the monetary benefits, says Kyle Mox, vice president of the National Association of Fellowships Advisors.

Hundreds of programs exist in the U.S. and abroad, and many are highly selective. The Fulbright Program, for instance, receives more than 10,000 U.S. student and teaching assistantship applications each year, and about 20 percent of candidates earn the State Department-funded award. Some fellowships are based at particular schools, while others are targeted at people in certain disciplines. The Rhodes Scholarship is exclusive to the University of Oxford in the U.K., while the Mitchell applies to a number of schools in Ireland and Northern Ireland. The Schwarzman Scholars program sends up to 200 students to study at Tsinghua University in Beijing.

In addition, "there's just a whole alphabet soup" of offerings in the sciences, notes Suzanne McCray, vice provost for enrollment management and director of the Office of Nationally Competitive Awards at the University of Arkansas. In 2016, the National Science Foundation, for instance, awarded $138,000 each to 2,000 individuals to pursue grad degrees across a range of scientific disciplines as part of its Graduate Research Fellowship program. A number of opportunities are earmarked for students from underrepresented minority groups, such as the GEM Fellowship in science and engineering and the National Academies Ford Foundation Fellowship.

To help students sort through their options, many universities have dedicated fellowship advisers and detailed databases of offerings. Schools like Cornell (gradschool.cornell.edu/fellowships) and UCLA (grad.ucla.edu/funding) offer publicly searchable collections of fellowships. Mox suggests working with advisers to find programs whose goals align with your interests and to check specific requirements and deadlines.

As a junior at the University of Illinois at Urbana-Champaign, Jacob Calvert, 23, worked with an adviser to seek out fellowships that could help him pay for an advanced math degree. He applied for and earned the Marshall Scholarship, which funds up to 40 American students each year who are pursuing graduate degrees in the U.K. Calvert's scholarship covers tuition, fees, travel and living expenses for two yearlong graduate programs – a master's in complex systems mathematics at the University of Bristol and a master's in theoretical physics at the University of Oxford. "I really got to choose my own experience," says Calvert, who will complete his physics degree this year.

Work for the school. Teaching or research assistantships are often awarded to Ph.D. students, many of whom will go on to become faculty members or researchers. Awards typically include tuition plus a stipend for other expenses and entail 20 or so hours of work a week. At many institutions, assistantships are viewed "not first and foremost as employment but as part of their training," says W. Jeffrey Hughes, associate dean of the graduate school of arts and sciences at Boston University.

Obtaining an assistantship can be competitive, so students should "make sure that they are marketing skill sets" that they would bring to the table, says Carol Shanklin, dean of the graduate school at Kansas State University. For instance, an aspiring Shakespeare scholar who has taught high school English might have the edge for a coveted TA position over an applicant with equal academic credentials who is arriving straight out of college.

Borrow carefully. Nearly half of all grad students take out loans. Currently, grad students can borrow up to $20,500 per year in federal loans at a 5.31 percent interest rate. That rate is fixed for the life of the loan, but the interest figure for new loans is adjusted each summer based on the 10-year U.S. Treasury note. For those who need to borrow more, federal PLUS loans are available up to the cost of attendance at 6.31 percent interest.

Federal loans have a range of flexible repayment options that allow borrowers to adjust monthly payments based on their salary or have their loan balances forgiven after a certain period of consistent payments. Teachers who work in qualifying high-need schools for five years can have up to $17,500 in federal loans forgiven, while those in certain government or public interest jobs can have their loans fully expunged after 10 years of payments. Rynders is on track to have his loans forgiven in late 2018.

Some government agencies, states and graduate schools also offer loan forgiveness or repayment assistance programs for public servants. (Borrowers should pay attention to any changes in federal student loan policies that may occur under the new administration.) Private loans tend to carry variable interest rates and have fewer repayment safeguards. The rate on loans at several private lenders, for instance, can swing by about 6 percentage points depending on market conditions. ●

How We Rank Schools

Objective measures are important, as are the opinions of experts

BY ROBERT J. MORSE

Each year, U.S. News ranks programs in business, education, engineering, law, nursing and medicine. The rankings in these six areas are based on two types of data: expert opinions about program excellence and statistical indicators that measure the quality of a school's faculty, research and students. The data come from statistical surveys sent to administrators at more than 1,970 graduate programs and from reputation surveys sent to more than 16,500 academics and professionals in the disciplines. The surveys were conducted during the fall of 2016 and in early 2017. In each field, we also present rankings of programs in various specialty areas based on reputation data alone.

As you research course offerings and weigh schools' intangible attributes, the data in these pages can help you compare concrete factors such as faculty-student ratio and placement success upon graduation. It's important that you use the rankings to supplement, not substitute for, careful thought and your own research. In each of the six major disciplines, the ranking tables show approximately the top half of the schools that were eligible to be ranked; longer lists and more complete data can be found at usnews.com/grad. Detailed information about the various methodologies can be found on the website, too; methodology summaries appear with each ranking in these pages.

Beyond the six disciplines ranked annually, we also periodically rank programs in the sciences, social sciences, humanities, the health arena and many other areas based solely on the ratings of academic experts. This year, U.S. News is publishing fresh rankings of doctoral programs in economics, English, history, political science, psychology and sociology. These rankings, based solely on academic experts' ratings, were last updated in 2013. Rankings of doctoral programs in the sciences, master's programs in public affairs and fine arts, and graduate programs in health-related fields are republished. Full rankings in all categories are available at usnews.com/grad. It's a good idea to check the site every now and then, as U.S. News occasionally adds content when additional data we think useful become available – whether on job placement, GPA, test scores or other factors – or new information changes the data.

To gather the peer assessment data, we asked deans, program directors and senior faculty to judge the academic quality of programs in their field on a scale of 1 (marginal) to 5 (outstanding). In business, education, engineering, law and medicine, we also surveyed professionals who hire new graduates and have used their three most recent years' responses to calculate the results.

Statistical indicators fall into two categories: inputs, or measures of the qualities that students and faculty bring to the educational experience, and outputs, measures of graduates' achievements linked to their degrees. As inputs, for example, we use admission test scores. Output measures for business include starting salaries and grads' ability to find jobs; in law, employment rates at graduation and 10 months later and bar exam pass rates.

We made some small changes this year: For the medical school ranking, we used scores on the new MCAT in combination with scores on the old, and in law we used GRE scores in combination with those on the LSAT. Also, our analysis of the data for several indicators (medical faculty-to-student ratio and education and nursing student-to-faculty ratios, for example) revealed a few extreme outliers. So we applied a standard statistical technique – logarithmic transformation of the original values – to avoid giving those institutions a distorted amount of credit.

Scoring system. We examined the data for individual indicators and standardized the value of each one about its mean. The weight applied to each reflects our judgment about its relative importance, as determined in consultation with experts in the field. Final scores were rescaled so the highest-scoring institution was assigned 100; the others' scores were recalculated as a percentage of that top score. Scores were then rounded to the nearest whole number. Schools with a score of 100 accumulated the highest composite score. An institution's rank reflects the number of schools that sit above it; if three are tied at No. 1, for example, the next will be ranked 4. Tied schools are listed alphabetically. ●

> ## "USE THE RANKINGS TO SUPPLEMENT YOUR OWN RESEARCH."

New jobs, New industries.

See which jobs are in-demand in the following industries:

BEST JOBS

U.S.News & WORLD REPORT

RANKINGS

- 📊 **Business**
- 🏠 **Construction**
- 🎨 **Creative & Media**
- ✏️ **Education**
- ⚙️ **Engineering**
- 🩺 **Health Care**
- 🏥 **Health Care Support**
- 🔧 **Maintenance & Repair**

- 🏷️ **Sales & Marketing**
- ⚗️ **Science**
- 📖 **Social Services**
- 〰️ **STEM**
- 🖥️ **Technology**

FIND
THE BEST
ONLINE
PROGRAM
FOR YOU

Search more than 1,200 online education programs to find one that best fits your needs.

Bachelor's
MBA
Graduate Business
Graduate Criminal Justice
Graduate Education
Graduate Engineering
Graduate Information Technology
Graduate Nursing

Engineering

SYDNEY GIBSON, LEFT, A RICE UNIVERSITY DOCTORAL STUDENT IN BIOENGINEERING, AT WORK IN THE LAB

THE U.S. NEWS RANKINGS

Masters of the Computer

Computer engineers, whose work underpins every aspect of modern life, are in great demand

BY LINDA MARSA

Even when she was in grade school, Tara Thomas was intensely curious about how computers worked. By high school, she was writing rudimentary software programs. Her undergraduate studies in her native India, a blend of electrical engineering and computer science, gave Thomas a "holistic picture" of the workings of both hardware and software. Now pursuing her master's in computer engineering at Purdue University, she has found a discipline that requires the same blend of skills. Thomas, 25, has already put her "foot in the door of a real career" by working on projects for General Electric Co. and Apple, where she has a job waiting after graduation in May.

Thomas entered computer engineering at an opportune moment, during a rapid surge in interest in advanced manufacturing, or in using sophisticated technologies to re-energize the country's manufacturing sector. At the same time, academic institutions around the country have made drastic changes in the way they teach engineering students, arming them for the workplace with an emphasis on action rather than just classroom lectures, on acquiring much-in-demand professional skills through teamwork, design projects, case studies, internships and entrepreneurial courses.

"Engineering education is undergoing a revolution," says Jelena Kovacevic, head of the electrical and computer engineering department at Carnegie Mellon University. "At the center of meeting today's challenges is an age-old idea: Learn by making, doing and experimenting. We can do this by imbuing real-world problems into our curricula through projects, internships and collaboration with companies."

Thomas has taken full advantage of the hands-on opportunities offered at Purdue.
She's currently working within a $10 million collaboration between Purdue and General Electric aimed at devising new ways to boost factory output and lower production costs. Her particular focus: helping devise a system of embedded sensors that communicate wirelessly in real time to identify production bottlenecks and reveal ways to smooth work flow. She also spent last summer interning at Apple, where she devised a prototype for an easier-to-use keyboard. "It was fun to work on an actual product," says Thomas, whose job with the tech giant will involve developing sensor systems.

The supersonic pace of technological innovation "is creating an unprecedented set of opportunities" for these young engineers, notes Kovacevic. The field has undergone tremendous growth, experts say, because it underpins virtually all of the products and processes of modern life, from video games and cool software apps to health care instrumentation and rocket deployments to Mars. While computer science generally focuses on programming and software development, computer engineers both design the components and systems and program the software that operates these systems.

A smartphone and the software apps that run on it provide a good illustration of how computer engineers put their expertise to use. Students become better programmers when they fully understand the hardware, experts say. They have a much better sense of what happens "under the covers than someone who just knows how to program," points out George Riley, associate chair

ENGINEERING STUDENT TARA THOMAS, CENTER, STUDIES WITH A GROUP OF HER PURDUE PEERS.

for graduate affairs in the electrical and computer engineering department at Georgia Institute of Technology.

Career options range well beyond straightforward information technology. They include designing high-tech hardware for the defense and aerospace industry, devising cybersecurity encryption and data protection systems, working in robotics and health care analytics, and, of course, feeding the hunger for new and better consumer electronics.

Engineering schools are scrambling to expand the pipeline. While engineering enrollment overall continues to experience healthy growth, the heftiest increase by far has been in computer engineering and computer science. At the graduate level, enrollment in computer engineering programs has mushroomed between 12 and 20 percent annually for the last several years. Between 2014 and 2015, the number of master's degrees earned by computer engineers swelled by 20 percent and doctorates rose by 19 percent, according to the American Society for Engineering Education. That same period, computer science programs based in engineering schools saw a 33 percent jump.

In contrast to traditional instructional methods, which often were aimed at thinning the ranks of engineering students, anyone shopping for a program today can expect an array of initiatives designed to deeply engage students in their academics while preparing them to succeed in the workplace. Internships and projects that entail solving community or societal problems have become an essential part of the curriculum, for example. "There's much more emphasis on active learning," says David Meyer, a professor of electrical and computer engineering at Purdue. "Creativity as well as learning blossoms when [students are] challenged with an open-ended design experience."

"STUDENTS LEARN BY MAKING, DOING AND EXPERIMENTING."

The University of California–Santa Barbara, for instance, not only offers internships at places like Hewlett-Packard in Silicon Valley but also partners with community organizations to get students into the field. Young engineers at one UCSB lab focusing on an engineering technology known as haptics – which recreates the sense of touch in robotics, virtual reality and biomedical applications – has teamed

up with the local diabetes research institute to work on a particular medical problem: an early way to detect sensory neuropathy, the nerve damage in diabetics that causes a loss of feeling in the limbs.

At Carnegie Mellon's California campus in Silicon Valley, students are encouraged to connect with the more than 9,000 CMU grads in the Bay Area, many of whom are in leadership positions at tech outfits like Google, Apple, Facebook, Oracle and Cisco. These ties generate internships, mentoring relationships and networking opportunities.

Research partnerships with industry and government are increasingly key. UCSB, for example, is the West Coast headquarters for AIM Photonics, a collaboration between academia, industry and the public sector to mainstream the use of photonics, the science of light

Why I Picked... UNIVERSITY OF MICHIGAN Ann Arbor

Frank Sedlar, '15
OWNER, VELA AERIAL

➤ Michigan's College of Engineering had several strengths that appealed to me. In my area, civil engineering, professors are often professionals actively carrying on projects, many with an international focus – a particular interest of mine. The experiential learning opportunities are superb. Instead of a formal thesis, students are encouraged to engage in independent research. For example, I studied how precipitation into Lake Superior af-

fects the availability of water in the region. I prototyped a low-cost water sensor to measure the rise of water levels in connecting rivers and canals. My prototype later became the basis of a successful Fulbright scholarship application for me to devise an early flood-warning system in Jakarta, Indonesia.

The school gave me an engineering grant after my first year to study flooding in Indonesia more closely, and it helped me build language studies into my master's program. All of these experiences gave me a great foundation to start my own drone and aerial mapping company and to continue my engineering work in Indonesia.

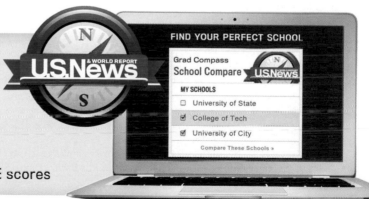

that is used in fiber optics. The group is devising the software tools and models for photonic devices and integrated circuits, which allow for a much more rapid transfer of data than electronic ones.

"This is the next generation of the electronic circuit technology," says Rui Wu, a Ph.D. candidate who works at AIM Photonics on fiber optical communications systems used at huge data centers like Facebook and Google. (Wu has also completed three internships at HP.) Major tech companies like Cadence, Synopsis and Mentor Graphics are part of the collaboration along with several other universities, says John Bowers, a professor of electrical and computer engineering at UCSB and deputy chief executive officer of AIM Photonics. UCSB faculty and students do research alongside their corporate counterparts.

Across the country at Georgia Tech, computer

engineering students work on a smorgasbord of projects, ranging from sensor networks at the football stadium that feed real-time data to enhance the safety of fans to devising technology to monitor the upper reaches of Earth's atmosphere. First-year grad student Michael Capone, 25, had a chance to work on Prox-1, a tiny 60-kilogram satellite that will eventually be deployed to help explore the potential of light-reflecting "solar sails" as a method of propulsion in space. Jay Danner, 24, who will finish his master's this May, works half time on a sensor network for the city of Atlanta that will collect data on traffic flow, air pollution and pedestrian patterns in order to improve air quality and traffic efficiencies.

Danner's project is part of an industry-academic collaboration that has been underway since 1934 through the Georgia Tech Research Institute, which is headquartered on the university's campus in Atlanta. In 2014 alone, faculty and student researchers at the GTRI labs on campus and in 19 field offices around the nation conducted $300 million of research in electronics and optics, information and cybersecurity, and sensors and intelligent systems.

The Prox-1 project "gave me exposure to satellite equipment and a real appreciation for what goes into designing satellites," says Capone. Danner, a third-generation Georgia Tech engineer, says the "real world projects are invaluable. I've actually learned 80 percent of what I know from projects like these, and not from classes."

Some programs cultivate entrepreneurship, teaching students what it takes to commercialize their research. The University of Pennsylva-

An Elite (But Cheap) Degree

When Wayne Moore saw the price of Georgia Institute of Technology's online master's degree in computer science, he thought it was a typo. "A program that's less than $7,000 – that's unheard of," says Moore, 44, a vendor manager at AT&T in Atlanta. Unable to resist the draw of a low-cost degree from a highly ranked school, he applied. Now he's one of nearly 4,000 students participating in the first accredited master's in computer science that can be earned exclusively through a formal combination of MOOCs ("massive open online courses" that are available individually to the public free of charge) at a fraction of the cost of most programs.

Georgia Tech teamed up with AT&T and Udacity, an online learning platform, to launch the program in January 2014. All courses are taught by Georgia Tech professors, and the program's large scale keeps costs low: Students pay $510 per three-credit course (plus $301 per term in fees). Like Moore, most work full time, completing assignments around their schedules. "It's tough," he says. But having these older professionals in the program is an advantage, says Zvi Galil, dean of computing and a professor, because they bring to the table their life experiences as doctors or teachers or people who already have a grounding in tech. And as an AT&T employee, Moore's tuition is reimbursed by the

nia offers a certificate in entrepreneurship that students can earn along with their degree. The highly popular four-course curriculum – classes have huge waiting lists – gives students a grounding in patent and copyright law, product development and marketing, creating positive company cultures, and raising venture capital.

"That way, when an innovative idea does cross their path, they'll have the tools to recognize it and grab it," says Tom Cassel, director of the Engineering Entrepreneurship Program in Penn's School of Engineering and Applied Science. "But it's invaluable whether or not they want to be an entrepre-

now 66 study groups on Google+.

A 2016 Harvard study suggests that Georgia Tech has discovered an untapped market of adults seeking affordable degrees from prestigious colleges: 80 percent of those accepted enrolled, and the majority of those denied did not pursue a different program. Galil says that Georgia Tech is able to accept a higher proportion of applicants for the online format – about 60 percent, compared to 15 percent for on-campus admission. If everybody finishes, Georgia Tech's program will boost the number of American computer science master's degrees each year by 8 percent, according to Harvard's study.

The recent rise of iMBA and MicroMasters programs (story, Page 16) suggests that other schools are following Georgia Tech's lead. And in January Georgia Tech announced another program launching this year that will follow the same model: an online master's in analytics for less than $10,000. The program, which will have tracks in big data, analytical tools, and eventually business analytics, is a collaboration between the College of Engineering, College of Computing and Scheller College of Business. *–By Lindsay Cates*

company if he passes the course.

Students watch video lectures and do coding assignments; course content, homework, projects and exams are all the same as in the on-campus course, although lecturing via video allows extra creativity. Charles Isbell, senior associate dean and professor in the college of computing, has created wildly popular music video parodies and "podcast-like" lectures with colleague Michael Littman at Brown University to get across the principles of machine learning, for example.

The format has also proven conducive to communication, notes Isbell, who says he uses the discussion platform to engage with the online program participants 24/7. When a student posts a question, it's typically answered within five to 10 minutes by a student, teaching assistant or the professor. And the online student communities that have sprung up across the country have come as a surprise to the program's creators; there are

neur, and adds a dimension to their engineering education. We find the grad certificate really is an added plus for employers."

Georgia Tech also offers a graduate certificate in engineering entrepreneurship, and its VentureLab is an incubator for startups based on research done on campus. The program has served as a launching pad for many success stories, including software apps to help cardiologists evaluate heart conditions and Pindrop, a cybersecurity startup that blocks phone fraud. That company's CEO created the technology while he was a Ph.D. student.

Increasingly, opportunities for future engineers to study overseas are broadening both horizons and career options. The University of Minnesota's College of Science and Engineering has partnered with Taiwan's National Tsing Hua University to offer a summer research internship for students interested in working at top research laboratories in Taiwan. The university also offers three-week seminars in India or Nicaragua in which students apply their skills on projects that address challenges particularly affecting developing nations, like climate change, food insecurity, poor sanitation and lack of access to clean water. Carnegie Mellon has two overseas satellite centers in Rwanda and Portugal. In Portugal, students can receive a combined M.S. from Carnegie Mellon and MBA from the University of Porto, that nation's leading educational institution. The added credential creates a pathway beyond systems and software development into technology management. ●

The Job Market

SPOTLIGHT ON:
quantitative research analysis

Eric Liu
Stanford University School
of Engineering, 2016

Engineering a Profit

As a preschooler, math whiz Eric Liu could compare packages on supermarket shelves and determine the best value by estimating the price-to-volume ratio. "That's not too different than what I do now with stocks," says Liu, 26. As a quantitative research analyst at Cubist Systematic Strategies, a division of the hedge fund Point72 Asset Management in New York City, Liu analyzes data sets to forecast trends in stocks, bonds, currencies and other financial derivatives in today's increasingly complex financial market.

Improving the odds. Banks and hedge funds need people to guide their investing who both understand finance and who can also use big data, computer science, statistical analysis and computational modeling to spot and anticipate what's ahead. Engineering grads are uniquely qualified for the job. Liu, who grew up in Vancouver, spent three years developing startups with friends after graduating from the University of British Columbia with a combined bachelor's in mathematics and economics, then entered the Stanford University School of Engineering's new two-year master's program in computational math and finance. After a summer 2015 internship at a hedge

fund, he was hooked on data science and modeling in finance, where analysts typically work with everything from satellite images of parking lots to data on retail store openings. Liu ended up at Point72, where he is tasked with developing "the story behind the models" so as to boost the odds of upping profits. More often than not, he says, the models get it right.

Now that big data has begun influencing the financial world in a big way, says Emanuel Derman, director of Columbia University's master's in financial engineering program, grads are increasingly taking their data analysis and modeling skills to hedge funds. Another popular landing spot is the financial technology "fintech" sector, where technology is driving innovation in financial services with companies and apps like PayPal, Venmo and Mint.

Jobs for quantitative analysts are projected to grow 12 percent in the next several years as investment portfolios and securities become more complex. Due to the unique blend of math, finance and computer skills needed, quantitative analysts command high salaries. Entry-level positions usually require a master's and average starting salaries top $100,000. –By Lindsay Cates

··· More Hot Jobs

··· BIOMEDICAL ENGINEER

Combining engineering with the medical sciences, these cutting-edge designers help create artificial organs and prosthetic limbs, often working closely with doctors to replicate biological systems. An aging population (in need of hip and knee replacements) and rapid innovations in medical technology like 3-D printing are driving demand for talent. Employment is expected to grow 23 percent from 2014 to 2024. Median salary in 2015 was $86,220.

··· COMPUTER SOFTWARE ENGINEER

In the quickly evolving software sector, engineering graduates with mobile and cybersecurity skills are highly sought after. Companies are developing new systems and apps and are relying more on cloud and mobile computing, spurring the need for skilled professionals. Expert projections estimate 10-year job growth will be 32 percent, especially in the health care and security industries. Median salary was $105,570 in 2015.

··· MECHANICAL ENGINEER

These pros help develop engines, products and machines using the latest design tools and technology. Opportunities abound in a range of expanding sectors like hybrid-electric car design, alternative energy and nanotechnology. While job growth may not be as dramatic as in other fields, a solid increase of 5 percent is expected from 2014 to 2024. Median salary in 2015 was $83,590.

Schools of Engineering

THE TOP SCHOOLS

Rank School	Overall score	Peer assessment score (5.0=highest)	Recruiter assessment score (5.0=highest)	'16 average quantitative GRE score[1]	'16 accept-ance rate	'16 Ph.D. students/ faculty	'16 faculty membership in National Academy of Engineering	'16 engineering school research expenditures (in millions)	'16 research expenditures per faculty member (in thousands)	Ph.D.s granted 2015-2016	'16 total graduate engineering enrollment
1. Massachusetts Institute of Technology	100	4.9	4.8	166	13.4%	5.5	13.0%	$448.3	$1,192.4	334	3,124
2. Stanford University (CA)	87	4.8	4.6	167	15.4%	7.1	18.8%	$201.2	$811.1	321	3,675
3. University of California–Berkeley	80	4.8	4.6	165	17.0%	5.1	14.9%	$208.9	$819.1	235	2,076
4. California Institute of Technology	74	4.7	4.6	169	9.1%	5.0	15.8%	$106.0	$1,092.6	93	543
5. Carnegie Mellon University (PA)	72	4.3	4.4	166	19.7%	4.3	11.2%	$195.8	$736.0	228	3,737
5. University of Michigan–Ann Arbor	72	4.4	4.2	166	26.6%	4.3	3.6%	$295.6	$782.1	255	3,570
7. Georgia Institute of Technology	71	4.6	4.4	164	32.7%	4.7	3.4%	$223.1	$446.1	398	8,850
8. Purdue University–West Lafayette (IN)	69	4.2	4.2	164	30.6%	4.9	4.5%	$259.1	$683.7	305	3,744
9. University of Illinois–Urbana-Champaign	67	4.4	4.2	166	30.2%	4.3	3.4%	$227.6	$530.5	245	3,806
9. University of Texas–Austin (Cockrell)	67	4.1	4.1	165	16.1%	5.1	6.9%	$204.3	$676.6	265	2,362
11. Texas A&M University–College Station	66	3.8	3.9	164	22.6%	3.6	4.6%	$282.8	$701.7	245	3,469
11. University of Southern California (Viterbi)	66	3.6	3.7	166	20.1%	5.3	9.7%	$192.1	$1,038.5	167	5,497
13. Columbia University (Fu Foundation) (NY)	64	3.8	3.9	167	23.7%	4.8	12.5%	$147.0	$966.9	142	3,350
13. Cornell University (NY)	64	4.2	4.2	165	26.8%	4.5	11.5%	$118.3	$568.5	170	2,069
13. University of California–San Diego (Jacobs)	64	3.7	4.0	166	26.2%	5.4	11.0%	$168.0	$823.6	160	2,635
16. University of California–Los Angeles (Samueli)	63	3.8	3.9	166	26.5%	5.6	18.9%	$97.0	$610.0	163	2,187
17. Princeton University (NJ)	62	4.1	4.2	167	13.3%	4.4	20.2%	$63.0	$484.5	83	615
18. University of Wisconsin–Madison	59	3.9	4.0	164	20.1%	4.2	3.9%	$141.9	$622.5	169	1,821
19. Johns Hopkins University (Whiting) (MD)	55	4.0	4.1	166	35.3%	4.2	1.5%	$121.1	$752.4	117	3,692
19. Northwestern University (McCormick) (IL)	55	3.9	3.9	166	23.3%	4.9	4.9%	$114.1	$616.7	123	2,088
19. University of California–Santa Barbara	55	3.6	3.8	165	14.3%	4.1	13.0%	$106.6	$696.4	84	721
19. University of Pennsylvania	55	3.6	3.8	165	23.4%	4.1	8.5%	$103.5	$892.6	75	1,674
23. Harvard University (MA)	54	3.7	4.1	166	11.2%	4.9	13.6%	$50.1	$625.7	48	478
24. University of Maryland–College Park (Clark)	53	3.6	3.7	164	33.8%	3.8	5.2%	$161.9	$627.4	171	2,371
25. North Carolina State University	52	3.4	3.5	164	15.2%	3.5	4.5%	$189.0	$562.4	181	3,303
25. University of Washington	52	3.7	3.8	163	28.0%	3.7	4.3%	$151.2	$588.4	121	2,416
27. University of Minnesota–Twin Cities	51	3.6	3.9	164	30.3%	3.8	4.2%	$122.2	$513.4	180	1,923
27. Virginia Tech	51	3.7	3.8	162	19.3%	3.2	0.9%	$128.3	$367.6	200	2,338
29. Duke University (Pratt) (NC)	50	3.5	3.7	164	27.0%	4.1	4.5%	$97.2	$753.5	96	1,093
29. Rice University (Brown) (TX)	50	3.6	3.9	166	23.7%	5.3	5.8%	$69.6	$595.0	100	949
31. Ohio State University	49	3.5	3.6	164	16.6%	4.0	2.4%	$128.8	$511.3	167	1,849
32. Pennsylvania State University–University Park	47	3.6	3.9	163	20.9%	3.2	1.4%	$100.1	$294.4	200	2,029
32. University of Colorado–Boulder	47	3.4	3.4	162	26.6%	4.8	3.8%	$97.6	$602.2	139	1,900
34. Boston University (MA)	46	3.1	3.5	164	28.4%	4.1	5.7%	$95.6	$796.8	82	1,121
34. University of California–Davis	46	3.4	3.8	163	21.7%	3.9	3.4%	$83.9	$473.8	118	1,090
36. Vanderbilt University (TN)	45	3.3	3.7	163	15.0%	4.5	2.2%	$66.7	$741.3	56	514
37. University of California–Irvine (Samueli)	44	3.3	3.6	164	18.3%	4.2	3.2%	$90.0	$478.8	100	1,442
38. Yale University (CT)	43	3.4	3.8	168	18.0%	3.5	5.3%	$32.3	$441.8	33	300
39. Northeastern University (MA)	41	3.1	3.4	162	42.0%	3.8	1.8%	$71.4	$460.7	82	4,259
39. Rensselaer Polytechnic Institute (NY)	41	3.4	3.8	164	26.8%	3.4	2.1%	$53.9	$369.1	92	646
39. University of Virginia	41	3.3	3.6	164	29.0%	3.4	3.4%	$70.9	$517.6	57	786
42. Arizona State University (Fulton)	40	3.3	3.2	162	46.9%	2.9	1.7%	$103.3	$370.3	152	3,636
42. University of Florida	40	3.4	3.5	163	46.2%	3.2	0.4%	$69.3	$247.7	172	3,067
42. University of Pittsburgh (Swanson) (PA)	40	3.1	3.5	162	36.8%	3.3	0.7%	$88.2	$604.1	88	1,029
45. Iowa State University	39	3.2	3.4	167	18.0%	2.9	N/A	$94.5	$367.8	104	1,337
45. New York University (Tandon)	39	2.7	3.3	164	33.5%	3.6	10.0%	$33.9	$458.4	38	2,685
45. University of Rochester (NY)	39	2.7	3.2	165	38.0%	3.5	3.3%	$89.3	$1,002.9	45	590
48. University of Delaware	38	2.9	3.5	169	36.3%	4.2	5.4%	$46.4	$354.5	96	931
48. University of Notre Dame (IN)	38	3.1	3.6	163	21.1%	3.8	3.1%	$46.7	$376.7	71	520
50. Case Western Reserve University (OH)	37	3.2	3.6	164	34.1%	3.1	1.8%	$42.1	$379.7	70	702
50. Washington University in St. Louis (MO)	37	3.2	3.7	165	39.7%	4.3	1.1%	$24.6	$276.0	50	1,256
52. Brown University (RI)	36	3.1	3.6	165	25.4%	2.8	5.0%	$24.0	$300.1	34	427
52. Dartmouth College (Thayer) (NH)	36	3.0	3.7	164	19.5%	2.6	3.5%	$25.5	$463.4	23	313
54. Rutgers, The State Univ. of N.J.–New Brunswick	35	3.0	3.3	163	22.6%	2.2	3.2%	$69.4	$363.3	83	1,395
54. University of Arizona	35	3.1	3.2	162	47.2%	2.6	4.5%	$50.3	$301.1	115	1,081
56. Colorado School of Mines	34	2.9	3.6	160	44.4%	2.7	1.6%	$51.4	$274.9	115	1,227

[1]GRE scores displayed are for master's and Ph.D. students and are only for those GRE exams taken during or after August 2011 using the new 130-170 score scale.
N/A=Data were not provided by the school. Sources: U.S. News and the schools. Assessment data collected by Ipsos Public Affairs.

THE TOP SCHOOLS continued

Rank School	Overall score	Peer assessment score (5.0=highest)	Recruiter assessment score (5.0=highest)	'16 average quantitative GRE score[1]	'16 acceptance rate	'16 Ph.D. students/ faculty	'16 faculty membership in National Academy of Engineering	'16 engineering school research expenditures (in millions)	'16 research expenditures per faculty member (in thousands)	Ph.D.s granted 2015-2016	'16 total graduate engineering enrollment
56. Michigan State University	34	3.0	3.4	162	9.0%	2.7	2.5%	$44.7	$249.7	75	735
56. University of Dayton (OH)	34	2.2	2.8	157	16.9%	2.3	N/A	$109.5	$2,190.1	24	609
56. University of Massachusetts–Amherst	34	2.9	3.4	163	33.3%	3.2	1.2%	$54.5	$336.6	79	983
60. Lehigh University (Rossin) (PA)	33	3.0	3.4	165	32.4%	3.6	2.5%	$19.8	$166.4	66	829
60. University of Tennessee–Knoxville	33	2.9	3.1	160	34.7%	3.4	2.8%	$70.7	$388.4	90	1,118
60. University of Utah	33	2.8	3.0	161	34.8%	2.8	2.6%	$79.4	$446.0	88	1,259
63. University of Illinois–Chicago	32	2.7	3.4	160	16.0%	3.7	0.9%	$26.6	$255.9	71	1,428
63. University of Texas–Dallas (Jonsson)	32	2.5	3.3	162	22.2%	2.7	3.7%	$51.1	$329.6	80	2,408
65. Auburn University (Ginn) (AL)	31	2.8	3.3	163	46.3%	1.7	N/A	$61.7	$440.6	75	897
65. University of Connecticut	31	2.8	3.0	163	25.7%	3.4	1.4%	$47.3	$333.0	72	841
67. Colorado State University	30	2.6	3.1	167	46.6%	1.0	1.7%	$70.3	$650.6	50	807
67. Stony Brook University–SUNY (NY)	30	2.7	3.1	165	36.7%	3.8	1.2%	$32.2	$192.8	92	1,503
67. Tufts University (MA)	30	2.8	3.3	162	42.4%	2.6	3.6%	$26.4	$321.6	31	688
67. University at Buffalo–SUNY (NY)	30	2.6	3.1	162	33.0%	2.8	1.2%	$59.0	$360.0	64	1,859
67. University of California–Riverside (Bourns)	30	2.4	2.8	162	28.6%	4.8	1.7%	$61.9	$583.8	63	851
67. University of Iowa	30	2.8	3.1	161	22.0%	1.9	1.0%	$45.6	$512.6	41	398
73. University of Houston (Cullen) (TX)	29	2.5	3.0	161	31.7%	3.4	5.4%	$31.5	$217.0	108	1,448
73. University of Texas–Arlington	29	2.5	3.0	158	49.5%	3.0	1.5%	$45.3	$345.5	98	3,246
75. Clemson University (SC)	28	2.8	3.2	158	31.8%	2.6	0.5%	$36.2	$175.1	97	1,415
75. Drexel University (PA)	28	2.8	3.3	160	54.0%	2.7	0.7%	$24.9	$170.5	79	1,194
75. University of Central Florida	28	2.5	3.1	160	48.2%	4.2	0.7%	$37.3	$280.1	89	1,427
78. Illinois Institute of Technology (Armour)	27	2.6	3.1	160	71.3%	3.1	3.0%	$18.8	$195.9	49	1,885
78. Oregon State University	27	2.7	3.0	160	22.0%	3.0	0.6%	$42.4	$251.1	45	1,248
78. Syracuse University (NY)	27	2.6	3.3	162	39.4%	2.8	1.3%	$12.4	$170.3	24	1,090
81. Rochester Institute of Technology (Gleason) (NY)	26	2.6	3.5	160	38.2%	1.0	N/A	$34.7	$278.0	9	1,197
81. Stevens Institute of Technology (Schaefer) (NJ)	26	2.5	3.2	161	56.2%	2.0	1.1%	$21.2	$252.7	39	2,041
81. University of North Carolina–Chapel Hill	26	2.8	3.5	159	35.5%	1.7	N/A	$7.7	$257.5	17	90
81. Washington State University	26	2.6	3.0	161	24.5%	2.8	0.7%	$33.0	$235.7	72	763
85. Michigan Technological University	25	2.6	3.2	162	25.1%	1.7	N/A	$29.6	$208.6	42	1,008
85. University of California–Santa Cruz (Baskin)	25	2.4	3.0	164	39.1%	3.1	N/A	$28.7	$334.3	35	590
87. New Jersey Institute of Technology	24	2.4	3.0	159	50.9%	1.7	N/A	$56.1	$378.7	38	2,450
87. University of Cincinnati (OH)	24	2.4	3.0	161	19.4%	2.6	N/A	$19.9	$159.3	61	782
89. George Washington University (DC)	23	2.5	3.2	163	45.1%	1.1	N/A	$13.3	$160.8	69	1,821
89. Missouri University of Science & Technology	23	2.6	3.5	156	53.5%	2.4	N/A	$25.0	$138.0	82	1,127
89. University of Alabama–Huntsville	23	2.3	2.8	157	70.8%	1.4	N/A	$49.9	$639.8	25	781
89. University of Missouri	23	2.4	2.9	161	23.1%	3.2	N/A	$21.4	$209.5	40	613
89. University of South Florida	23	2.3	2.8	158	47.1%	3.0	0.9%	$33.3	$297.1	62	1,216
94. Texas Tech University (Whitacre)	22	2.3	3.0	159	33.6%	2.6	2.9%	$17.5	$134.7	54	896
94. University of Kansas	22	2.5	3.1	161	44.0%	1.8	0.8%	$15.3	$132.6	31	640
94. University of Kentucky	22	2.4	2.9	160	44.1%	1.6	0.7%	$37.4	$261.3	54	474
94. University of Nebraska–Lincoln	22	2.5	2.9	161	34.1%	1.8	N/A	$32.8	$173.8	59	644
94. Worcester Polytechnic Institute (MA)	22	2.5	3.3	164	54.3%	1.5	0.9%	$24.7	$213.2	25	1,203
99. Louisiana State University–Baton Rouge	21	2.4	2.9	159	36.0%	2.4	N/A	$22.0	$160.4	63	619
99. University of New Mexico	21	2.4	2.8	145	44.1%	4.3	1.0%	$33.0	$343.3	50	787
99. University of Oklahoma	21	2.4	3.0	161	33.4%	1.2	N/A	$27.3	$189.8	48	710

SPECIALTIES

PROGRAMS RANKED BEST BY ENGINEERING SCHOOL DEPARTMENT HEADS

Rank School	Average assessment score (5.0=highest)
AEROSPACE/AERONAUTICAL/ASTRONAUTICAL	
1. Stanford University (CA)	4.8
2. Georgia Institute of Technology	4.7
2. Massachusetts Institute of Technology	4.7
4. California Institute of Technology	4.6
5. University of Michigan–Ann Arbor	4.5
6. Purdue University–West Lafayette (IN)	4.4
7. Texas A&M University–College Station	4.2
8. University of Texas–Austin (Cockrell)	4.1
9. University of Illinois–Urbana-Champaign	4.0
10. Princeton University (NJ)	3.9
10. University of Colorado–Boulder	3.9

Rank School	Average assessment score (5.0=highest)
BIOLOGICAL/AGRICULTURAL	
1. Iowa State University	4.6
2. Purdue University–West Lafayette (IN)	4.4
2. Texas A&M University–College Station	4.4
4. Cornell University (NY)	4.1
4. University of Florida	4.1
4. University of Illinois–Urbana-Champaign	4.1
7. University of Nebraska–Lincoln	3.9
8. University of California–Davis	3.8
9. Pennsylvania State University–University Park	3.7
10. North Carolina State University	3.6

Rank School	Average assessment score (5.0=highest)
BIOMEDICAL/BIOENGINEERING	
1. Johns Hopkins University (Whiting) (MD)	4.6
1. Massachusetts Institute of Technology	4.6
3. Georgia Institute of Technology	4.4
3. Stanford University (CA)	4.4
3. University of California–San Diego (Jacobs)	4.4
6. Duke University (Pratt) (NC)	4.3
6. University of California–Berkeley	4.3
8. University of Pennsylvania	4.2
9. Rice University (Brown) (TX)	4.0
10. University of Michigan–Ann Arbor	3.9
10. University of Washington	3.9

Rank School	Average assessment score (5.0=highest)
CHEMICAL	
1. Massachusetts Institute of Technology	4.9
2. California Institute of Technology	4.7
2. University of California–Berkeley	4.7
4. Stanford University (CA)	4.5
5. University of Minnesota–Twin Cities	4.4
6. Georgia Institute of Technology	4.3
6. Princeton University (NJ)	4.3
6. University of Delaware	4.3
6. University of Texas–Austin (Cockrell)	4.3
6. University of Wisconsin–Madison	4.3
CIVIL	
1. University of California–Berkeley	4.8
2. Georgia Institute of Technology	4.7
2. University of Illinois–Urbana-Champaign	4.7
4. Stanford University (CA)	4.6
4. University of Texas–Austin (Cockrell)	4.6
6. Purdue University–West Lafayette (IN)	4.3
7. Massachusetts Institute of Technology	4.2
7. Virginia Tech	4.2
9. University of Michigan–Ann Arbor	4.1
10. Carnegie Mellon University (PA)	4.0
10. Cornell University (NY)	4.0
COMPUTER	
1. Massachusetts Institute of Technology	5.0
2. Carnegie Mellon University (PA)	4.7
2. University of California–Berkeley	4.7
2. University of Illinois–Urbana-Champaign	4.7
5. Georgia Institute of Technology	4.5
6. University of Michigan–Ann Arbor	4.4
7. Cornell University (NY)	4.2
7. University of Texas–Austin (Cockrell)	4.2
9. California Institute of Technology	4.1
9. Princeton University (NJ)	4.1
9. Purdue University–West Lafayette (IN)	4.1
9. University of Washington	4.1
9. University of Wisconsin–Madison	4.1
ELECTRICAL/ELECTRONIC/COMMUNICATIONS	
1. Massachusetts Institute of Technology	5.0

Rank School	Average assessment score (5.0=highest)
2. Stanford University (CA)	4.9
3. University of California–Berkeley	4.8
4. California Institute of Technology	4.7
4. University of Illinois–Urbana-Champaign	4.7
6. Georgia Institute of Technology	4.6
7. University of Michigan–Ann Arbor	4.5
8. University of Texas–Austin (Cockrell)	4.3
9. Carnegie Mellon University (PA)	4.2
9. Purdue University–West Lafayette (IN)	4.2
ENVIRONMENTAL/ENVIRONMENTAL HEALTH	
1. University of California–Berkeley	4.6
2. University of Illinois–Urbana-Champaign	4.4
3. Stanford University (CA)	4.3
4. University of Michigan–Ann Arbor	4.1
4. University of Texas–Austin (Cockrell)	4.1
6. Virginia Tech	4.0
7. Georgia Institute of Technology	3.9
8. Carnegie Mellon University (PA)	3.8
9. University of Colorado–Boulder	3.7
10. Massachusetts Institute of Technology	3.6
10. Yale University (CT)	3.6
INDUSTRIAL/MANUFACTURING/SYSTEMS	
1. Georgia Institute of Technology	4.7
2. University of Michigan–Ann Arbor	4.4
3. Northwestern University (McCormick) (IL)	4.2
3. University of California–Berkeley	4.2
5. Massachusetts Institute of Technology	4.1
6. Purdue University–West Lafayette (IN)	4.0
6. Virginia Tech	4.0
8. Columbia University (Fu Foundation) (NY)	3.9
8. Cornell University (NY)	3.9
8. Pennsylvania State University–University Park	3.9
8. University of Wisconsin–Madison	3.9
MATERIALS	
1. Massachusetts Institute of Technology	4.8
2. Northwestern University (McCormick) (IL)	4.7
3. University of California–Santa Barbara	4.6
4. Stanford University (CA)	4.5
5. California Institute of Technology	4.4

Rank School	Average assessment score (5.0=highest)
5. University of California–Berkeley	4.4
5. University of Illinois–Urbana-Champaign	4.4
8. Georgia Institute of Technology	4.1
9. Cornell University (NY)	4.0
9. University of Michigan–Ann Arbor	4.0
MECHANICAL	
1. Massachusetts Institute of Technology	4.9
1. Stanford University (CA)	4.9
3. University of California–Berkeley	4.8
4. California Institute of Technology	4.6
4. University of Illinois–Urbana-Champaign	4.6
6. Georgia Institute of Technology	4.5
6. University of Michigan–Ann Arbor	4.5
8. Cornell University (NY)	4.2
8. Princeton University (NJ)	4.2
8. Purdue University–West Lafayette (IN)	4.2
NUCLEAR	
1. University of Michigan–Ann Arbor	4.7
2. Massachusetts Institute of Technology	4.6
3. University of Wisconsin–Madison	4.1
4. Texas A&M University–College Station	3.9
5. North Carolina State University	3.8
5. University of California–Berkeley	3.8
7. University of Tennessee–Knoxville	3.7
8. Pennsylvania State University–University Park	3.5
9. Georgia Institute of Technology	3.4
9. University of Illinois–Urbana-Champaign	3.4
PETROLEUM ENGINEERING	
1. University of Texas–Austin (Cockrell)	5.0
2. Stanford University (CA)	4.6
3. Texas A&M University–College Station	4.4
4. University of Tulsa (OK)	4.0
5. Colorado School of Mines	3.8
6. Pennsylvania State University–University Park	3.3
6. University of Oklahoma	3.3
6. University of Southern California (Viterbi)	3.3
9. Texas Tech University (Whitacre)	2.5
10. Louisiana State University–Baton Rouge	2.4

METHODOLOGY

Programs at the 214 engineering schools that grant doctoral degrees were surveyed; 198 responded and were eligible to be ranked based on a weighted average of 10 indicators described below.

Quality assessment: Two surveys were conducted in the fall of 2016. In one, engineering school deans and deans of graduate studies at engineering schools were asked to rate program quality from marginal (1) to outstanding (5); 51 percent responded. The average peer assessment score is weighted by .25 in the overall score. Corporate recruiters and company contacts (names

were supplied by the schools) who hire engineers from previously ranked engineering schools were also asked to rate programs. The three most recent years' results were averaged and are weighted by .15.

Student selectivity (.10): The strength of master's and Ph.D. students entering in fall 2016 was measured by their mean GRE quantitative score (67.5 percent of this measure) and acceptance rate (32.5 percent). Only scores from the new GRE were used in the rankings and are displayed.

Faculty resources (.25): This score is based on the 2016 ratio of full-time doctoral students to

full-time faculty (30 percent) and full-time master's students to full-time faculty (15 percent); the proportion of full-time faculty who were members of the National Academy of Engineering in 2016 (30 percent); and the number of engineering doctoral degrees granted in the past school year (25 percent).

Research activity (.25): Based on total externally funded engineering research expenditures (60 percent) and research dollars per full-time tenured and tenure-track faculty member (40 percent). Expenditures refer to separately funded research, public and private,

averaged over fiscal years 2015 and 2016.

Overall rank: Data were standardized about their means, and standardized scores were weighted, totaled and rescaled so the top-scoring school received 100; others received their percentage of the top score.

Specialty rankings: Rankings are based solely on assessments by department heads in the specialty who rated other schools on a 5-point scale. The top-rated schools appear here. Names of department heads and Ph.D. departments surveyed were supplied to U.S. News by the schools in the summer of 2016.

American University of the Caribbean
School of Medicine

WE CHOSE AUC FOR OUR MD

Choosing the best medical school for you is just as important as the MD you'll earn.

Here's what we believe: The best medical school is one that empowers you to be your best. It isn't defined by numbers, statistics, or percentages—those are just part of the story. It's about finding a perfect mix of culture, collaboration, and academic rigor for you. And with a consistently strong residency attainment rate, we should know.

Is American University of the Caribbean School of Medicine the right school for you? Only you can answer that question. So let's see if we can find that answer together.

Choose the school that makes you the priority. Choose AUC.

AUCMED

Health &Medicine

AT THE MAGEE-
WOMENS
RESEARCH
INSTITUTE
OF THE
UNIVERSITY OF
PITTSBURGH

THE U.S. NEWS RANKINGS

Training for the Future

A score of new medical schools are rewriting the ways that doctors-to-be learn

BY BETH HOWARD

Jeanne Wigant was leery the first time she visited a homeless shelter two years ago. But for Wigant, 37, then a second-year student at Oakland University William Beaumont School of Medicine in Rochester, Michigan, taking blood pressure readings and bandaging the wounds of shelter residents marked a turning point. "Just putting my hand on their shoulder or taking the time to listen to their stories was moving," she says of the experience, part of a required course in which med students spend time with different marginalized populations each week over a semester. "It felt like something I was meant to do." Now eyeing a career in family medicine, Wigant observes that, "at OUWB, the culture of giving back and being involved in the community is ingrained from the beginning."

Wigant could be a poster child for the crop of new medical schools that have opened their doors in the past decade or so. More than 20 new colleges of medicine have been launched and at least two more are on the drawing board, partly a response to an expected shortage of doctors that could reach 94,700 by 2025. Starting from scratch gives the schools unique opportunities to prepare doctors-to-be for a rapidly changing health care landscape. The traditional model of medical education, which has students memorizing the key science and rotating through weeks of exposure to various specialties in the hospital, has historically given scant attention to concepts and skills now viewed as vital: communication, problem-solving, teamwork, population health, empathy, and circumstances like poverty and culture that affect well-being and access to care. While many established medical schools now are adjusting their curricula, too, this is a chance "to rethink everything," says Claiborne Johnston, dean and vice president of medical affairs at just-launched Dell Medical School at the University of Texas–Austin. Says Susan Skochelak, vice president for medical education at the American Medical Association: "These schools can take the best ideas out there and build on them." Here are a few:

A 21ST-CENTURY CURRICULUM

The traditional curriculum features two years of biomedical sciences – physiology, cell biology, pathology – taught sequentially in lecture format, followed by brief rotations, or clerkships, in various specialties. Until fairly recently, students typically wouldn't see patients until their third year.

The format is quite different at the new schools. During their first eight weeks at the University of South Carolina School of Medicine Greenville and at New York's Hofstra Northwell School of Medicine, for instance, students interact with patients

constantly interacting with patients," says Devora Lichtman, 28, now in her second year at Hofstra Northwell. At Dell, students start seeing patients in their second year.

The science is imparted differently, too. Instead of tackling each scientific discipline in isolation, the new schools typically champion an integrated approach that explores how the body's organ systems work and ties basic science to clinical education. The Hofstra science curriculum, for example, assigns each week a theme – metabolic syndrome or anemia, say. With guidance from a faculty member, students discuss problem-based patient cases in small groups, determine what they need to know about the patient's predicament, then go and find the answers, reconvening to share what they've found.

It's a similar story at Dell, where the science-heavy first year is oriented toward problem-solving rather than rote memorization, which is impractical in an age when medical knowledge is expanding explosively and is easily accessible by smartphone. "We don't even have a lecture hall," Johnston says.

At the University of Central Florida College of Medicine, anatomy class "goes way beyond the memorization of body parts and mastery of dissection," says Deborah German, the school's founding dean. Students spend 16 weeks doing a "forensic investigation," discovering their cadaver's cause of death, studying pathologies, and examining evidence of the patient's quality of life. Science lessons are supplemented by training in the simulation center, where students learn to take patient histories and hone their other skills through interactions with "standardized patients" (actors playing the role), computerized mannequins and virtual patients.

● ● ●

SECOND-YEAR OAKLAND STUDENT MERRYLEES DERSCH EXAMINES A PATIENT AT A FREE CLINIC IN PONTIAC, MICHIGAN.

Similarly, Virginia Tech Carilion School of Medicine gets students considering the workings of the shoulder through the prism of a patient with a gunshot wound. "For basic science, students will dissect the shoulder in anatomy lab, analyzing the muscles, tendons, ligaments and bones in the area that could be impacted by this type of injury," says Cynda Johnson, president and founding dean. "In clinical science, the students will learn how to do a physical exam on the shoulder area." They also meet a patient who dealt with such a wound and his or her physician.

right away on ambulance runs. And they're not just along for the ride – all end up certified as EMTs.

The lessons remembered for life "are learned in the emotionally charged situation of taking care of patients," says Lawrence Smith, dean of Hofstra Northwell. "We thought, why not teach all of medicine in the context of real patient cases?" In addition to their EMT training, first- and second-year students at both schools spend time each week working with doctors out in the community or at the hospital. "From the beginning, we were

Traditional monthlong hospital rotations are no longer thought to be the best way to understand disease or the patient journey. At Central Michigan University College of Medicine, third-year students get a much fuller picture during a six-month "longitudinal clerkship" that requires them to "live in a community, work with one preceptor, and follow patients throughout the continuum of care," says George Kikano, the school's dean. Most students at Florida State University College of Medicine spend their third year in doctors' offices seeing patients. "Our students work one-on-one with their preceptor and go with them wherever they go – to same-day surgery, to labor and delivery, to the nursing home," says John Fogarty, dean of the college. Dell students do traditional hospital rotations but also undertake a two-year longitudinal clerkship at a community clinic.

A FOCUS ON RESEARCH

Given that future doctors will need to be lifelong learners, one clear priority is to foster "an ability to ask why and then find out," says German. UCF and the new med schools at Western Michigan University, Texas Tech University Health Sciences Center, and the University of Arizona are among those requiring students to complete a significant research project. At Dell, the third year is dedicated to an independent health improvement project on topics such as innovation and design or population health, though some students use the time to pursue a dual degree in public health, business administration, biomedical engineering or educational psychology.

For his project at the Frank H. Netter School of Medicine at Quinnipiac University in Connecticut, fourth-year student Edward Kobayashi, 28, focused on health care management. He completed classwork in the business school on ways organizations can increase efficiency, then measured attitudes among physicians in a large health system undergoing such upheaval in their work flow. Based on his findings, he was able to suggest ways to overcome doctors' resistance to the changes. "It was a neat experience to be part of that process," he says.

A TEAM-BASED APPROACH TO LEARNING

Medicine is increasingly a team sport, with doctors working alongside nurses, therapists, social workers and other health professionals to ensure the best outcomes. So training is increasingly "interprofessional," too.

Netter students, for instance, analyze video case studies with nursing and health sciences students and work with them on simulations to learn to avoid medical errors and to do a better job of listening to patients. At the Herbert Wertheim College of Medicine at Florida International University, medical students collaborate with law, biomedical engineering, nursing, physician assistant, social work, education and public health students to help families in underserved communi-

"COMMUNITY ENGAGEMENT ISN'T JUST A PROGRAM HERE. IT'S A MINDSET."

ties get needed care and avoid the emergency room.

"I learned there was a lot of overlapping training and more things that nurses and even pharmacists can do than I thought," says Audrey Han, 25, a first-year student at Dell who met regularly with her small group – also representing the UT schools of nursing, pharmacy and social work – to work on their assignment: finding ways to address a community health challenge. Their work, which focused on male HIV patients in Austin, resulted in a possible app that would provide information on medication, an insurance directory, and access to case workers able to offer help with getting care.

TAKING ON A SOCIAL MISSION

Reaching out to the community for clinical training opportunities furthers a couple of the new schools' priorities. One is a commitment to filling the primary care pipeline supplying their region or state, given that half of the physician shortage is expected to be in those primary-care specialties. The new New York Institute of Technology College of Osteopathic Medicine at Arkansas State University, for example, expects 60 percent of its future doctors to practice primary care in Arkansas. About 45 percent of the graduates of the City University of New York School of Medicine wind up in primary care.

Why I Picked... UNIVERSITY OF _____ ALABAMA–BIRMINGHAM

Stacey Watkins, '13
RESIDENT, UAB, INTERNAL MEDICINE

➤ I was accepted to the National Institute of General Medical Sciences' Medical Scientist Training Program that fully funds the M.D.-Ph.D. programs of future researchers at various medical schools. After going through two days of rigorous interviews at UAB's med and graduate schools, I was sure it was a great fit as it seemed strong in every research area

OAKLAND STUDENTS DISCUSS MEDICATIONS AT THE COMMUNITY CLINIC.

families in underserved areas whose health they monitor over all four years. Students make regular house calls and handle everything from taking vitals to assisting families with getting medications. By helping deliver appropriate care, the first two cohorts of students reduced emergency department use by their patients by 60 percent, says Pedro J. Greer, Jr., professor and founding chair of the department of Humanities, Health and Society. By requiring that students master conversational and medical Spanish, Texas Tech University Health Sciences Center Paul L. Foster School of Medicine is doing its best to make sure grads will be able to serve everybody in the El Paso area.

That sense of responsibility imbues the new institutions with a heightened idealism. "Our students came here because they wanted to be part of creating a different kind of student culture," says Koeppen of the Netter School of Medicine. "They are all risk takers." That goes for faculty, too. In a scenario that's typical for emergent medical colleges, nearly 1,000 people applied for 20 full-time positions at Netter.

Building a like-minded student population starts with the admissions process, which is also undergoing a transformation. Rather than zero in exclusively on grades and test scores, as historically has been the case, there's a trend toward holistic review, assessing academic performance in the context of life and work experiences and attitudes. "The type of student we seek is one who is well-rounded and focused on making a difference in the world they live in," says Kenneth S. Ramos, interim dean of the University of Arizona College of Medicine–Phoenix. A diverse student body is often a priority.

While the new schools obviously have much in common, each also "has a unique flavor," notes Skochelak. At the University of South Carolina, which builds nutrition and exercise extensively into the curriculum, students become evangelists for a healthy lifestyle. At Oakland, the spirit of compassion "is palpable," says John Prescott, chief academic officer of the Association of American Medical Colleges. And at Dell Medical School, which aims to turn out tomorrow's "physician leaders" by equipping students with the tools and mindset to help transform health delivery, there's a distinct premium on challenging the status quo. "Our students will be questioning their attending quite a bit," promises Johnston. They'll be "looking at the system and asking, 'Why are we doing it that way?'" Says Prescott: "It's an exciting time to be in medical education." ●

The other priority is to address factors such as race and poverty that so affect individuals' health. "Community engagement isn't just a program here. It's a mindset," says Robert Folberg, founding dean of the Oakland University medical school, whose curriculum is sprinkled with evidence. Besides the class that inspired Jeanne Wigant by introducing her to shelter residents, another required two-year course called the Art and Practice of Medicine includes time for future physicians to teach K-12 students about nutrition and exercise. Med students also receive credit for running health fairs, volunteering at food banks, and staffing after-school programs.

Florida International University's NeighborhoodHELP program assigns medical students to from microbiology to immunology to neurobiology.

The first two years of med school, UAB has students cycle through different labs each summer to choose a specialty. After stints in pathology and microbiology, I found my "family" in the neurobiology lab, where I spent four years looking at how malignant brain cancer spreads.

I always found colleagues willing to collaborate and to help me get the resources I needed for my research, because people at UAB are so committed to advancing treatments and techniques. I plan to pursue a fellowship in hematology/oncology and eventually hope to work at an academic institution where I can see firsthand the problems patients struggle with and then go back to the lab to solve those problems. UAB has prepared me to do just that.

FROM LEFT: HARDY MOORE PHOTOGRAPHY; RACHEL WOOLF FOR USN&WR

USN&WR • BEST GRADUATE SCHOOLS **43**

New Paths Into Health Care

All sorts of specialized degrees are springing up to respond to the field's varied challenges

BY ARLENE WEINTRAUB

After Sonia Sen earned her computer science degree at the University of Arizona in 2014, she looked for a graduate program that would apply her programming skills to the brave new world of digital health care delivery. She found the degrees springing up in health care informatics to be too narrowly focused on developing technology for hospitals. And straight computer science didn't include health training. Then Sen discovered a just-right combo: a dual Master of Science in Health Tech (one degree in health information systems and one in applied information science) launched jointly last year by Cornell University and the Technion Institute of Israel.

Much of Sen's time in the two-year program, which has been based in Google's New York building until the new Cornell Tech campus opens on Roosevelt Island this year, has been spent working on projects for health companies and nonprofits, doing exactly what she hopes to do in the future. She built an iPhone app for health insurer Aetna that uses 3-D motion-tracking technology to help people recovering from shoulder surgery do their rehab exercises. Now she's teamed up with City Health Works, a Harlem-based group of community health coaches, to develop technology that digitizes notes they take during patient visits so reports can be created for clients' physicians.

"Entrepreneurship, computer science, health care delivery – we learn all of that," says Sen, 24. Graduates are finding jobs in arenas ranging from software development at digital health companies to data mining for health care organizations.

The ever-growing pressure on doctors and hospitals to deliver better, safer care as cost-efficiently as possible – and to emphasize prevention in an effort to keep people well – has greatly increased the demand for workers with all sorts of highly specialized skills. A whole array of graduate programs are being introduced that prepare students to tackle health care's biggest challenges. Besides digital health, topics include population health (the new practice model of being compensated for keeping a patient population as healthy as possible), health care delivery science, and the effect of climate change on disease.

Some of these programs were created in response to the Affordable Care Act, whose provisions may disappear or change under President Donald Trump. But experts at the universities offering them believe the trends set in motion by advances in technology and a dire need to improve care and bring costs down will continue regardless of the political environment.

Enduring issues. "The fundamental questions in health policy have been the same for many years now," says Rainu Kaushal, chair of the department of healthcare policy and research at Weill Cornell Medicine in New York. "The answers are agnostic to who is in the White House or controlling Congress." Weill Cornell and Cornell's school of management will launch an executive MBA/M.S. program in healthcare leadership this fall that will prepare working professionals to run, say, hospitals or health systems or insurance companies.

Below the top executive rank, people with specialized health degrees are finding a multitude of opportunities as managers, ranging from running physician groups to developing cost-cutting plans in hospitals and implementing electronic health records. Such positions are expected to

SONIA SEN, CENTER LEFT, IN A STARTUP IDEAS CLASS THAT'S PART OF HER DUAL MASTER'S PROGRAM AT CORNELL TECH

jump by 17 percent from 2014 to 2024, much faster than the average overall job growth of 7 percent, according to government projections. Median pay for these health managers is $94,500.

For Jena Simon, advanced training in health care delivery science provided an immediate career boost. Simon, who graduated a year ago from the two-year-old master's program at the Icahn School of Medicine at Mount Sinai, completed the 21-month online program while working as a nurse practitioner in the hospital's Comprehensive Program for Sickle Cell Disease, which offers patients a mix of social and medical services as well as the opportunity to participate in clinical trials. She wanted the know-how to expand the program to the system's other hospitals, and the classes gave her the skills to build a business plan and apply for a $5 million grant. She won the grant and was named co-director of the new project. "That wouldn't have been possible without this degree," Simon says.

Students who are accepted into Mount Sinai's program are already working in a health profession; they take all their classes online and come together for two weeks for in-person seminars. The program is largely focused on health management and strategic planning, and it can change quickly to respond to new legislation. During a class in health care finance last fall, several students requested training in the just-passed Medicare Access and CHIP Reauthorization Act, which is widely expected to be preserved by the Trump administration. So the school added a module on the legislation to one of its online classes, bringing in a guest lecturer to teach it. "We can immediately add content and reorient courses," says Brian Nickerson, a professor in the department of population health science and policy.

Dartmouth College's online master's in health care delivery science is also designed for professionals with experience. It includes management and leadership training from the university's Tuck School of Business and coursework on health care and policy from the medical school, with 35 days of on-campus seminars throughout the 18-month program.

Lehigh University caters to both full-time and part-time students with its master's in health systems engineering, which launched in 2011. The curriculum, designed for people with a science, business, math or engineering background, includes a mix of health care management courses and technical training in such topics as using mathematical modeling to solve operational challenges.

Lehigh students work individually or in groups to complete a capstone project, putting their technical skills to work for providers and other health care organizations. One group, for example, worked with a hospital to predict the heaviest patient traffic into the emergency room each day and to adjust work shifts to reduce wait times. Full-time students can complete the program in as little as one year, while part-timers can take up to three-and-a-half years.

The search for care models focused on keeping people well has also created a need for those well-versed in the growing effort to better manage and improve health outcomes in specific populations. Among the schools that have been expanding their advanced degree programs in population health (typically as a master's in public health concentration) are Harvard, the University of Wisconsin and Thomas Jefferson University in Philadelphia.

Thomas Jefferson's program is offered online and targets people working full time, a majority of whom arrive with a plan to tackle a challenge that their employer has asked them to solve during the program. Students have worked on projects ranging from improving mental health services for adolescents living along the Texas-Mexico border to developing an educational program on Alzheimer's disease for African-Americans living in the Delaware Valley.

Some institutions are building entire graduate degrees around emerging health challenges. Yale, Berkeley and the University of Washington are among those that allow grad students in public health to specialize in climate change, for example, completing classes, projects and internships centered around studying the impact of extreme weather, drought, environmental contaminants and other variables on health. In the summer of 2016, one Yale student interned with local health department officials studying the impact of bacterial contamination on beaches, for example. Another assessed the impact of air pollution and extreme temperatures on pregnant women and their infants.

Robert Dubrow, faculty director of the Climate Change and Health

Why I Picked

CASE WESTERN RESERVE UNIVERSITY
Cleveland

Maureen Sweeney, '12

ASSOCIATE MEDICAL DIRECTOR

➤ **Cleveland has a world-class health care system, and one of the nursing school's strengths is that it finds amazing clinical placements for students. Many schools require you to find your own. I wanted to go into mental health and was able to do psychiatric rotations at the Cleveland Clinic and the Department of Veterans Affairs.**

Case works closely with each student's preceptor, or clinical instructor, to ensure you get great feedback as you gain real-world experience. The program also goes beyond the basics of treatment and medications. It taught me how to be a leader, whether supervising a team or helping direct a health care system.

The school ensures students are prepared for changes in nursing requirements and is vocal about the need for national uniformity in nursing education. Case gave me exactly the prep I needed for my current role as associate medical director of a community mental health facility.

Initiative at Yale, says he expects demand for such expertise to grow even if the new administration doesn't prioritize climate concerns. "More and more nongovernment organizations are doing work related to climate change and health," as are state governments, Dubrow notes. "California has one of the most advanced climate-change programs in the country looking at the health effects of heat waves and droughts," he says.

Drilling down. Drexel University has seen such demand from students to drill down that it has redesigned its MPH program to encourage specialization. Starting this fall, students will pick majors and minors that prepare them to work on particular issues or with defined populations. For example, a student could major in community health and prevention and minor in infectious disease prevention and control, says Yvonne Michael, associate dean for academic and faculty affairs at Drexel's Dorsife School of Public Health. Other minors in development include substance use and misuse; Latino and immigrant health; and lesbian, gay, bisexual and transgender health. Drexel offers both full-time and part-time degrees and joint M.D./MPH and J.D./MPH programs. Students are expected to complete at least 120 hours of work in the field related to their specialties.

Daniel Kinder, 23, says his stint with Children's Hospital of Philadelphia has been the most rewarding part of his master's program in community health and prevention, which he'll complete this spring. For his first-year project, Kinder helped create a strategy to measure the impact of the hospital's new Community Health and Literacy Center in South Philadelphia. In his second year, he helped gather input on the program and develop strategies for adding new services.

"I get to attend community meetings and meet with stakeholders," Kinder says. It's been a great way to gain insights into the fast-evolving world he will enter. ●

The Job Market

SPOTLIGHT ON:

biomedical informatics

Daniel K. Putnam
Vanderbilt University
School of Medicine, 2016

Going After Cancer

Daniel Putnam always wanted to be a scientist. And watching his mother struggle with mental illness and the debilitating side effects of her medications before she died helped decide his course. That experience, coupled with his growing fascination with computers, left Putnam with "a strong desire to find a career where I could combine computer science with biology, chemistry and mathematics to improve medicine."

So Putnam earned his bachelor's in bioengineering at the University of Utah in 2007. While working at a genomics company, he grew interested in biomedical informatics, a young field where computer science and medicine meet. The goal is to collect and analyze health-related data that can be used to improve health care, says Doug Fridsma, president and CEO of the American Medical Informatics Association. These pros might use data from electronic health records to help clinicians and policymakers develop strategies to reduce diabetes in a community, say. Or they might develop software to offer real-time support to doctors hoping to avoid dangerous drug interactions in their patients, or model what is occurring within the body at the

genetic level to advance cancer research.

Putnam was drawn to the latter path. After earning his Ph.D. in biomedical informatics at Vanderbilt, Putnam joined St. Jude Children's Research Hospital in Memphis, where he works with doctors and other scientists involved in the hospital's cutting-edge genomic research. The team sequences hundreds of patients' genomes to search for the mutations underlying their diseases and, eventually, targeted treatments. Putnam focuses on developing algorithms and advanced software tools to identify chromosomal variations that increase a person's likelihood to develop cancer. "We want to identify why these variations are occurring, what the patterns are, and in which cancer types. We can then more effectively diagnose and treat them," says Putnam. Already, the team has helped find critical mutations driving the growth of rare brain cancers.

Pharmaceutical and insurance companies, hospitals, health centers and tech startups are helping create demand for biomedical informatics professionals, notes Fridsma, who says starting salaries can run from $90,000 to $110,000 and exceed $300,000 for those in leadership roles. *–Kaitlyn Chamberlin*

More Hot Jobs

NURSE ANESTHETIST

Nurse anesthetists provide pain management and anesthesia before, during and after surgery. They work in operating and emergency rooms, military settings and private clinics, often in place of doctors specializing in anesthesiology. Today the job requires a master of science in nurse anesthesia. Beginning in 2025, Certified Registered Nurse Anesthetists must earn a Doctor of Nurse Anesthesia Practice. Over 2,400 new CRNAs enter the workforce annually. Median salary runs about $157,000.

SPEECH-LANGUAGE PATHOLOGIST

Patients who have difficulty speaking or swallowing due to conditions such as stroke, brain injury and autism head to speech-language pathologists for help. These experts generally work in health care facilities, private clinics and schools. The government estimates that almost 30,000 jobs will come on line during the decade ending in 2024 to serve aging baby boomers and children benefiting from increased early identification of language difficulties. The American Speech-Language-Hearing Association notes the median annual salary is $75,000.

PEDIATRICIAN

A shortage of primary care doctors should help spur growth in demand for pediatricians to the tune of some 3,600 new positions by 2024, especially as diagnosis of special needs in children increases. In 2015, median annual salary was $170,300.
–Cathie Gandel

Schools of Medicine

THE TOP SCHOOLS - RESEARCH

Rank School	Overall score	Peer assessment score (5.0=highest)	Assessment score, residency directors (5.0=highest)	'16 median undergrad GPA	'16 median total MCAT score	'16 acceptance rate	'16 NIH research grants (in millions)	'16 NIH research grants per faculty member (in thousands)	'16 faculty/ student ratio	'16 out-of-state tuition and fees	'16 total medical school enrollment
1. Harvard University (MA)	100	4.8	4.7	3.91	517	3.3%	$1,430.4	$154.9	12.8	$59,731	720
2. Stanford University (CA)	86	4.7	4.5	3.90	518	2.5%	$383.3	$391.1	2.0	$55,314	487
3. Johns Hopkins University (MD)	84	4.8	4.7	3.90	518	5.8%	$564.9	$254.5	4.7	$55,266	471
4. University of California–San Francisco	83	4.8	4.7	3.84	514	3.4%	$577.4	$238.4	3.8	$50,764	633
5. University of Pennsylvania (Perelman)	80	4.5	4.7	3.86	517	4.7%	$535.0	$176.4	4.8	$58,809	629
6. Columbia University (NY)	76	4.3	4.4	3.87	520	4.1%	$461.1	$220.1	3.2	$63,890	660
7. Duke University (NC)	75	4.5	4.4	3.80	513	3.5%	$369.6	$255.9	3.0	$59,072	478
7. Washington University in St. Louis (MO)	75	4.5	4.5	3.85	521	8.8%	$374.0	$192.4	3.8	$60,798	507
9. University of Michigan–Ann Arbor	74	4.4	4.4	3.82	514	6.3%	$402.2	$215.1	2.6	$52,708	719
9. Yale University (CT)	74	4.3	4.2	3.82	517	5.9%	$359.6	$240.8	3.6	$58,644	411
11. University of California–Los Angeles (Geffen)	73	4.1	4.4	3.72	505	2.7%	$600.2	$241.4	3.4	$50,169	737
12. New York University (Langone)	72	3.8	3.9	3.91	520	5.4%	$310.8	$285.4	1.9	$55,110	571
12. University of Washington	72	4.4	4.1	3.69	506	3.7%	$638.8	$224.1	2.8	$64,387	1,022
14. Vanderbilt University (TN)	71	4.3	4.2	3.87	520	4.1%	$353.3	$128.2	7.2	$53,604	384
15. University of Chicago (Pritzker) (IL)	70	4.0	4.1	3.88	520	4.1%	$222.1	$237.8	2.6	$57,050	362
15. University of Pittsburgh (PA)	70	4.0	4.1	3.82	514	6.1%	$476.7	$212.3	3.7	$54,908	601
17. Northwestern University (Feinberg) (IL)	69	4.1	4.2	3.87	518	6.7%	$331.4	$187.7	2.7	$60,680	648
18. Cornell University (Weill) (NY)	67	4.1	4.3	3.84	518	5.1%	$303.8	$115.3	6.4	$56,335	409
18. University of California–San Diego	67	3.9	3.8	3.82	517	3.0%	$329.9	$225.0	2.9	$50,043	507
20. Mayo Clinic School of Medicine (MN)	66	3.8	4.0	3.80	513	1.8%	$308.7	$379.3	3.9	$49,900	207
21. Baylor College of Medicine (TX)	64	3.7	4.1	3.86	515	4.1%	$301.0	$145.5	2.9	$32,663	718
22. Icahn School of Medicine at Mount Sinai (NY)	63	3.6	3.6	3.77	518	7.2%	$348.2	$233.7	2.7	$54,731	561
23. Emory University (GA)	61	3.9	4.1	3.70	514	5.4%	$256.1	$128.2	3.5	$51,100	575
24. University of North Carolina–Chapel Hill	60	4.0	3.8	3.76	509	3.8%	$278.0	$177.1	1.9	$53,661	834
25. Case Western Reserve University (OH)	58	3.5	3.7	3.76	517	8.3%	$310.7	$111.3	3.1	$61,386	896
25. U. of Texas Southwestern Medical Center	58	4.0	3.9	3.85	513	8.2%	$202.8	$89.3	2.4	$33,023	939
27. University of Virginia	56	3.6	3.8	3.88	517	9.9%	$135.0	$125.9	1.6	$58,238	650
28. University of Wisconsin–Madison	55	3.6	3.6	3.77	512	5.1%	$200.7	$161.3	1.7	$39,761	725
29. Oregon Health and Science University	54	3.7	3.7	3.69	509	3.5%	$234.3	$106.6	3.8	$63,415	578
30. Boston University (MA)	53	3.4	3.5	3.75	515	6.8%	$192.0	$113.5	2.4	$58,198	698
31. Brown University (Alpert) (RI)	52	3.4	3.7	3.78	514	2.7%	$102.0	$137.1	1.4	$60,028	544
31. Ohio State University	52	3.4	3.4	3.80	514	6.2%	$172.0	$87.5	2.6	$37,345	770
33. University of Rochester (NY)	51	3.5	3.6	3.71	512	4.2%	$137.3	$87.7	3.6	$54,830	431
33. University of Southern California (Keck)	51	3.3	3.6	3.70	512	5.0%	$167.2	$100.5	2.2	$61,689	762
35. Dartmouth College (Geisel) (NH)	50	3.4	3.7	3.69	512	4.1%	$100.2	$126.9	2.2	$61,753	365
35. University of Alabama–Birmingham	50	3.7	3.5	3.77	507	6.9%	$186.0	$134.3	1.7	$64,214	792
35. University of Colorado	50	3.6	3.6	3.71	511	4.0%	$173.0*	$46.2*	5.4	$63,098	697
35. University of Iowa (Carver)	50	3.6	3.6	3.74	511	7.4%	$117.2	$122.5	1.6	$54,003	603
35. Yeshiva University (Einstein) (NY)	50	3.2	3.3	3.82	515	4.0%	$162.1	$85.3	2.5	$55,394	762
40. University of Cincinnati (OH)	48	3.0	3.2	3.76	513	8.5%	$196.6	$107.3	2.7	$48,895	678
40. University of Florida	48	3.2	3.2	3.86	513	5.0%	$121.0	$89.1	2.5	$49,385	550
40. University of Maryland	48	3.3	3.2	3.79	511	6.9%	$129.9*	$103.7*	2.0	$63,139	638
40. University of Utah	48	3.4	3.6	3.70	509	4.2%	$141.6	$85.7	3.8	$70,002	440
44. University of Minnesota	47	3.4	3.6	3.73	508	6.0%	$158.8	$80.5	2.0	$54,619	982
45. Georgetown University (DC)	46	3.2	3.8	3.63	512	2.5%	$119.6	$67.8	2.2	$58,246	785
45. Indiana University–Indianapolis	46	3.4	3.6	3.80	509	7.8%	$126.1	$54.6	1.7	$57,438	1,395
45. University of California–Davis	46	3.2	3.3	3.64	506	2.7%	$142.8	$171.0	1.9	$50,943	438

N/A=Data were not provided by the school. *The medical school's National Institutes of Health grants do not include any grants to affiliated hospitals.
Sources: U.S. News and the schools. Peer assessment data collected by Ipsos Public Affairs.

More @ usnews.com/grad

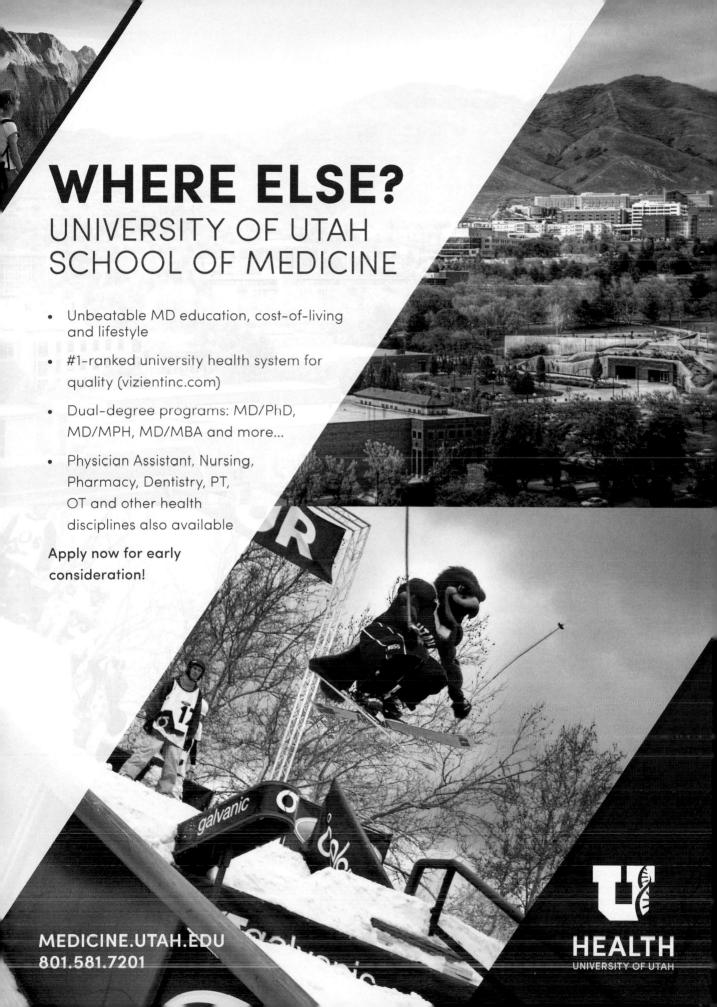

THE TOP SCHOOLS - RESEARCH continued

Rank School	Overall score	Peer assessment score (5.0=highest)	Assessment score, residency directors (5.0=highest)	'16 median undergrad GPA	'16 median total MCAT score	'16 acceptance rate	'16 NIH research grants (in millions)	'16 NIH research grants per faculty member (in thousands)	'16 faculty/student ratio	'16 out-of-state tuition and fees	'16 total medical school enrollment
48. University of California–Irvine	45	2.8	3.1	3.70	511	3.9%	$113.1	$136.5	2.0	$50,952	410
48. University of Miami (Miller) (FL)	45	3.1	3.3	3.71	512	4.4%	$114.8	$76.8	1.9	$42,642	806
50. Tufts University (MA)	44	3.3	3.6	3.67	511	5.6%	$72.7	$48.4	1.8	$60,258	846
50. University of Massachusetts–Worcester	44	3.1	3.0	3.70	510	7.8%	$148.5	$112.2	2.4	$61,457	543
52. University of Illinois	43	3.0	3.2	3.68	511	7.8%	$114.5	$122.0	0.7	$77,678	1,336
53. Thomas Jefferson University (Kimmel) (PA)	42	3.1	3.4	3.72	511	4.3%	$72.5	$22.4	3.0	$55,247	1,070
53. Wake Forest University (NC)	42	3.2	3.3	3.58	508	2.6%	$99.9	$92.6	2.3	$53,354	479
55. Temple University (Katz) (PA)	41	2.8	2.9	3.73	511	4.8%	$95.1	$114.2	1.0	$54,591	870
56. University of Connecticut	40	2.8	3.1	3.77	509	6.7%	$69.8	$67.0	2.6	$67,922	403
56. University of South Florida	40	2.5	2.7	3.57	513	5.3%	$115.2	$201.0	0.8	$54,915	707
56. University of Vermont	40	2.9	3.2	3.73	510	5.0%	$46.4	$65.5	1.5	$62,448	469
59. George Washington University (DC)	39	2.9	3.3	3.70	511	2.6%	$53.1	$47.2	1.6	$57,258	725
59. Rush University (IL)	39	2.9	3.1	3.68	511	4.5%	$60.1	$86.3	1.4	$51,306	515
59. Stony Brook University–SUNY (NY)	39	2.7	3.1	3.70	511	8.3%	$69.2	$86.6	1.5	$68,176	522
59. University of Kentucky	39	2.8	3.0	3.75	511	7.4%	$66.4	$69.3	1.8	$65,861	547
59. University of Nebraska Medical Center	39	3.0	3.1	3.73	509	8.8%	$53.3*	$72.5*	1.4	$76,405	509
59. Univ. of Texas Health Science Center–Houston	39	3.0	3.3	3.78	509	13.9%	$65.9*	$49.7*	1.4	$31,396	968

THE TOP SCHOOLS - PRIMARY CARE

Rank School	Overall score	Peer assessment score (5.0=highest)	Assessment score, residency directors (5.0=highest)	Selectivity rank	'16 median undergrad GPA	'16 median total MCAT score	'16 acceptance rate	% '14–'16 graduates entering primary care	'16 faculty/student ratio	'16 out-of-state tuition and fees	'16 total medical school enrollment
1. University of Washington	100	4.3	4.4	80	3.69	506	3.7%	53.0%	2.8	$64,387	1,022
2. University of North Carolina–Chapel Hill	99	3.9	4.2	50	3.76	509	3.8%	61.0%	1.9	$53,661	834
3. University of California–San Francisco	89	3.8	4.7	16	3.84	514	3.4%	42.5%	3.8	$50,764	633
4. Oregon Health and Science University	84	3.9	4.1	65	3.69	509	3.5%	46.3%	3.8	$63,415	578
5. University of Michigan–Ann Arbor	83	3.5	4.5	18	3.82	514	6.3%	46.1%	2.6	$52,708	719
6. University of California–Los Angeles (Geffen)	79	3.3	4.2	38	3.72	505	2.7%	50.0%	3.4	$50,169	737
7. University of Minnesota	77	3.6	3.8	63	3.73	508	6.0%	49.7%	2.0	$54,619	982
8. Baylor College of Medicine (TX)	75	3.0	4.1	11	3.86	515	4.1%	49.0%	2.9	$32,663	718
8. University of Colorado	75	3.7	3.9	55	3.71	511	4.0%	41.2%	5.4	$63,098	697
8. University of Pennsylvania (Perelman)	75	3.3	4.5	8	3.86	517	4.7%	38.0%	4.8	$58,809	629
8. U. of Texas Southwestern Medical Center	75	3.4	3.9	18	3.85	513	8.2%	46.0%	2.4	$33,023	939
12. University of California–San Diego	73	3.3	3.8	16	3.82	517	3.0%	45.2%	2.9	$50,043	507
13. University of Pittsburgh (PA)	72	3.3	4.1	27	3.82	514	6.1%	42.0%	3.7	$54,908	601
14. University of Massachusetts–Worcester	71	3.2	3.4	50	3.70	510	7.8%	52.9%	2.4	$61,457	543
14. University of Wisconsin–Madison	71	3.7	3.9	34	3.77	512	5.1%	40.1%	1.7	$39,761	725
16. Harvard University (MA)	70	2.9	4.6	3	3.91	517	3.3%	36.0%	12.8	$59,731	720
17. University of Nebraska Medical Center	69	3.3	3.3	65	3.73	509	8.8%	54.0%	1.4	$76,405	509
18. University of California–Davis	68	3.2	3.7	87	3.64	506	2.7%	52.4%	1.9	$50,943	438
18. University of New Mexico	68	3.6	3.2	92	3.71	505	7.7%	49.6%	2.3	$48,852	420
20. East Carolina University (Brody) (NC)	67	3.2	2.9	92	3.65	506	13.1%	61.0%	1.3	N/A	315
21. Brown University (Alpert) (RI)	65	3.2	4.0	25	3.78	514	2.7%	42.0%	1.4	$60,028	544
21. University of Iowa (Carver)	65	3.5	3.7	43	3.74	511	7.4%	41.0%	1.6	$54,003	603
21. University of Rochester (NY)	65	3.5	3.8	36	3.71	512	4.2%	36.8%	3.6	$54,830	431
24. Northwestern University (Feinberg) (IL)	64	3.0	4.2	9	3.87	518	6.7%	38.5%	2.7	$60,680	648
24. University of Virginia	64	3.3	3.9	11	3.88	517	9.9%	38.0%	1.6	$58,238	650
24. Washington University in St. Louis (MO)	64	3.1	4.3	10	3.85	521	8.8%	35.0%	3.8	$60,798	507
27. Dartmouth College (Geisel) (NH)	63	3.1	3.8	38	3.69	512	4.1%	43.8%	2.2	$61,753	365
27. Johns Hopkins University (MD)	63	3.1	4.6	3	3.90	518	5.8%	30.0%	4.7	$55,266	471
27. Ohio State University	63	3.1	3.6	25	3.80	514	6.2%	42.9%	2.6	$37,345	770
27. Vanderbilt University (TN)	63	3.1	4.1	3	3.87	520	4.1%	32.5%	7.2	$53,604	384
31. Mayo Clinic School of Medicine (MN)	61	3.0	4.2	29	3.80	513	1.8%	37.0%	3.9	$49,900	207
31. University of Alabama–Birmingham	61	3.3	3.8	72	3.77	507	6.9%	42.0%	1.7	$64,214	792

FOR SOME OF OUR MOST ELITE SOLDIERS, THIS IS FIELD TRAINING.

Becoming a doctor and officer on the U.S. Army health care team is an opportunity like no other. You can gain the skills and training to be a medical professional through the U.S. Army's Health Professions Scholarship Program, which offers full tuition for qualified medical students. With this elite team, you will be a leader—not just of Soldiers, but in health care.

To see the benefits of being at the forefront of Army medicine call 800-431-6691 or visit healthcare.goarmy.com/ha84.

U.S.ARMY

THE TOP SCHOOLS - PRIMARY CARE continued

Rank School	Overall score	Peer assessment score (5.0=highest)	Assessment score, residency directors (5.0=highest)	Selectivity rank	'16 median undergrad GPA	'16 median total MCAT score	'16 acceptance rate	% '14-'16 graduates entering primary care	'16 faculty/ student ratio	'16 out-of-state tuition and fees	'16 total medical school enrollment
33. Michigan State U. (College of Osteopathic Medicine)	60	2.6	3.0	107	3.62	503	8.8%	76.0%	0.2	$86,948	1,263
34. Boston University (MA)	59	3.0	3.7	27	3.75	515	6.8%	41.0%	2.4	$58,198	698
34. Duke University (NC)	59	3.2	4.4	18	3.80	513	3.5%	30.0%	3.0	$59,072	478
34. Emory University (GA)	59	3.0	4.0	32	3.70	514	5.4%	37.7%	3.5	$51,100	575
34. University of Chicago (Pritzker) (IL)	59	2.8	4.1	3	3.88	520	4.1%	38.0%	2.6	$57,050	362
34. University of Connecticut	59	2.8	3.3	41	3.77	509	6.7%	49.0%	2.6	$67,922	403
34. University of Utah	59	3.4	3.8	72	3.70	509	4.2%	35.2%	3.8	$70,002	440
34. Yeshiva University (Einstein) (NY)	59	2.8	3.4	15	3.82	515	4.0%	45.0%	2.5	$55,394	762
41. Cornell University (Weill) (NY)	58	2.5	4.1	13	3.84	518	5.1%	40.0%	6.4	$56,335	409
41. Indiana University–Indianapolis	58	3.3	3.6	55	3.80	509	7.8%	40.0%	1.7	$57,438	1,395
41. Stanford University (CA)	58	2.9	4.5	2	3.90	518	2.5%	33.0%	2.0	$55,314	487
44. New York University (Langone)	57	2.8	3.9	1	3.91	520	5.4%	39.0%	1.9	$55,110	571
44. University of Maryland	57	3.2	3.4	34	3.79	511	6.9%	40.0%	2.0	$63,139	638
44. Yale University (CT)	57	2.8	4.2	14	3.82	517	5.9%	35.0%	3.6	$58,644	411
47. University of Southern California (Keck)	56	3.0	3.8	31	3.70	512	5.0%	38.5%	2.2	$61,689	762
47. University of Vermont	56	3.3	3.5	65	3.73	510	5.0%	40.0%	1.5	$62,448	469
49. St. Louis University (MO)	55	2.8	3.3	22	3.90	512	7.1%	47.1%	0.9	$52,340	727
49. University of Kansas Medical Center	55	3.0	3.5	55	3.82	508	6.6%	45.0%	1.1	$63,471	843
51. Columbia University (NY)	54	2.7	4.3	3	3.87	520	4.1%	33.4%	3.2	$63,890	660
51. Rowan University (NJ)	54	2.3	2.5	100	3.62	503	9.6%	76.3%	0.2	$67,796	676
51. Thomas Jefferson University (Kimmel) (PA)	54	2.8	3.5	43	3.72	511	4.3%	42.9%	3.0	$55,247	1,070
51. University of Illinois	54	3.0	3.4	46	3.68	511	7.8%	46.0%	0.7	$77,678	1,336
55. Eastern Virginia Medical School	53	2.8	2.8	65	3.60	510	4.9%	54.6%	0.8	$58,554	593
55. Hofstra University (NY)	53	2.8	2.6	30	3.74	514	5.8%	45.0%	5.3	$49,500	362
55. Icahn School of Medicine at Mount Sinai (NY)	53	2.8	3.6	18	3.77	518	7.2%	38.5%	2.7	$54,731	561
55. Tufts University (MA)	53	2.7	3.6	55	3.67	511	5.6%	45.6%	1.8	$60,258	846
55. University of Missouri	53	3.0	3.4	50	3.84	508	7.7%	42.7%	1.6	$59,314	417

SPECIALTIES
MEDICAL SCHOOL DEANS AND SENIOR FACULTY SELECT THE BEST PROGRAMS

DRUG/ALCOHOL ABUSE
1. Harvard University (MA)
1. Johns Hopkins University (MD)
3. Yale University (CT)
4. Columbia University (NY)
4. University of California–San Francisco
6. University of Pennsylvania (Perelman)

FAMILY MEDICINE
1. University of Washington
2. Oregon Health and Science University
3. University of Colorado
4. University of California–San Francisco
4. University of Michigan–Ann Arbor
6. University of North Carolina–Chapel Hill
7. University of Missouri
7. University of Wisconsin–Madison
9. Duke University (NC)

GERIATRICS
1. Johns Hopkins University (MD)
2. Harvard University (MA)
3. Icahn School of Medicine at Mount Sinai (NY)
3. University of California–Los Angeles (Geffen)
5. Duke University (NC)
5. University of California–San Francisco
7. University of Washington
8. University of Michigan–Ann Arbor

INTERNAL MEDICINE
1. University of California–San Francisco
2. Johns Hopkins University (MD)
3. Harvard University (MA)
4. University of Pennsylvania (Perelman)
5. Duke University (NC)
6. University of Michigan–Ann Arbor
6. University of Washington
8. Columbia University (NY)

9. Washington University in St. Louis (MO)
10. Vanderbilt University (TN)
11. Stanford University (CA)

PEDIATRICS
1. University of Pennsylvania (Perelman)
2. Harvard University (MA)
3. University of Cincinnati (OH)
4. Johns Hopkins University (MD)
5. University of Washington
6. University of Colorado
7. University of California–San Francisco
8. University of Pittsburgh (PA)
9. Baylor College of Medicine (TX)
9. Washington University in St. Louis (MO)

RURAL MEDICINE
1. University of Washington
2. Oregon Health and Science University

3. University of Minnesota
3. University of New Mexico
5. University of North Carolina–Chapel Hill
6. University of Colorado
7. East Tennessee State University (Quillen)
7. University of North Dakota
7. University of Pikeville (KY)

WOMEN'S HEALTH
1. Harvard University (MA)
2. University of California–San Francisco
3. University of Pennsylvania (Perelman)
4. Johns Hopkins University (MD)
5. Columbia University (NY)
6. University of Pittsburgh (PA)
6. Washington University in St. Louis (MO)
8. Northwestern University (Feinberg) (IL)

99%

OR **638 out of 644** 2014-2015 Ross graduates who passed their USMLE exams on the first attempt attained a residency by April 2016.

YOUR ROAD TO RESIDENCY.

ROSS UNIVERSITY
SCHOOL OF MEDICINE

LEARN MORE AT: ROSSU.EDU

METHODOLOGY

The 140 medical schools fully accredited in 2016 by the Liaison Committee on Medical Education and the 30 schools of osteopathic medicine fully accredited in 2016 by the American Osteopathic Association were surveyed for the rankings of research- and primary care-oriented medical schools; 118 schools provided the data needed to calculate the two rankings. The research model is based on a weighted average of eight indicators; the primary care model is based on seven indicators. Most are the same for both. The research model factors in NIH research activity; the primary care model uses proportion of graduates entering primary care.

Quality assessment: Three assessment surveys were conducted in the fall of 2016. In a peer survey, medical and osteopathic school deans, deans of academic affairs, and heads of internal medicine or the directors of admissions were asked to rate program quality on a scale of marginal (1) to outstanding (5). Respondents were asked to rate research and primary care programs separately. The response rate was 32 percent. Average peer assessment score in the research model is weighted by .20; average score in the primary care model, by .25. In two separate surveys, residency program directors were asked to rate programs using the same 5-point scale. One survey dealt with research and was sent to a sample of residency program directors designated by the medical schools as being involved in non-primary residencies. The other survey was sent to residency directors designated by the medical schools as being involved in primary care. Residency directors' ratings for the three most recent years were averaged and weighted .20 for research and .15 for primary care. Schools supplied U.S. News names of residency program directors who were sent either of the surveys.

Research activity (.30 in the research model only): Research was measured as the total dollar amount of National Institutes of Health research grants awarded to the medical school and its affiliated hospitals (50 percent of this measure) and the average amount of those grants per full-time medical school science or clinical faculty member (50 percent); for the rankings, both factors were averaged for fiscal years 2015 and 2016. An asterisk indicates schools that reported only NIH research grants going to their medical school in 2016. The NIH figures published are for fiscal year 2016 only.

Primary care rate (.30 in primary care model only): The percentage of medical or osteopathic school graduates entering primary care residencies in the fields of family practice, pediatrics and internal medicine was averaged over the 2014, 2015 and 2016 graduating classes.

Student selectivity (.20 in research, .15 in primary care): Based on three measures describing the class entering in fall 2016, median Medical College Admission Test total score (65 percent of this measure), median undergraduate GPA (30 percent), and the acceptance rate (5 percent).

Faculty resources (.10 in research, .15 in primary care): Faculty resources were measured as the ratio of full-time science and clinical faculty to total medical or osteopathic students in 2016.

Overall rank: Indicators were standardized about their means, and standardized scores were weighted, totaled and rescaled so the top school received 100; other schools received their percentage of the top school's score.

Specialty rankings: Based solely on ratings by medical school deans and senior faculty at peer schools, who identified up to 10 schools offering the best programs in each specialty. The top half of programs (by number of nominations) appear.

HATTANAS KUMCHAI/GETTY IMAGES

HARVARD, TOPS IN RESEARCH AND NO. 16 IN PRIMARY CARE

BEYOND ORDINARY.

At Ross University School of Veterinary Medicine, our passion is training students to join our network of 4,000+ alumni and become the next generation of career-ready, compassionate veterinarians and researchers. Discover a world of possibilities in veterinary medicine.

EDUCATION THROUGH EXPERIENCE

Our immersive curriculum is taught by a diverse faculty from all over the globe. You'll experience hands-on animal interaction early on, including real world clinical experience at our AAHA-accredited campus veterinary clinic.

THE WORLD IS YOUR CLASSROOM

Global learning opportunities include externship programs and clinical training sites at 32 AVMA accredited schools in the US, UK, Canada, Australia, New Zealand and Ireland.

A COMMITMENT TO ONE HEALTH

Go beyond your DVM and explore the complex interplay of altered environments and infectious diseases as an increasing threat to agriculture, public health and endangered species, on a global basis through our online MSc One Health degree program.

Learn More: veterinary.rossu.edu/beyond

ROSS UNIVERSITY
SCHOOL OF VETERINARY MEDICINE

Schools of Nursing

THE TOP SCHOOLS - MASTER'S

Rank School	Overall score	Peer assessment score (5.0=highest)	'16 master's acceptance rate	'16 mean full-time undergrad GPA (master's)	'16 master's student/ faculty ratio	'16 percent of faculty in active nursing practice†	'16 master's degrees awarded	'16 NIH and all other research grants (in thousands)†	'16 NIH and all other teaching and practice grants (in thousands)†	'16 out-of-state tuition and fees	'16 master's program enrollment full-/part-time
1. Duke University (NC)	100	4.4	50.9%	3.61	1.9	92.2%	210	$20,660.5	$4,351.1	$1,639*	82/404
2. Johns Hopkins University (MD)	98	4.5	67.3%	3.40	6.6	66.3%	93	$31,058.6	$4,844.4	$38,031	396/251
3. University of Pennsylvania	93	4.4	55.9%	3.63	1.9	58.0%	320	$14,950.9	$4,552.5	$43,662	183/431
4. Emory University (GA)	91	4.2	55.7%	3.49	2.6	64.5%	74	$17,117.8	$4,831.3	$1,817*	268/46
5. Ohio State University	89	4.1	58.3%	3.51	8.1	62.8%	185	$11,055.0	$8,136.3	$1,940*	531/155
6. University of Washington	88	4.3	83.3%	3.61	0.2	65.4%	21	$11,851.7	$2,088.8	$39,641	18/51
6. Yale University (CT)	88	4.2	36.7%	3.62	5.6	94.6%	80	$4,420.2	$1,091.3	$41,046	285/12
8. Columbia University (NY)	87	4.2	34.8%	3.48	4.9	75.4%	227	$7,428.2	$1,656.6	$1,450*	340/314
8. University of Pittsburgh (PA)	87	4.2	31.9%	3.77	1.5	57.9%	61	$5,817.4	$2,135.5	$988*	136/47
10. University of Maryland–Baltimore	86	4.1	47.9%	3.31	1.4	96.9%	262	$5,460.1	$5,182.2	$1,324*	242/261
11. Case Western Reserve University (OH)	85	4.1	63.9%	3.51	2.0	99.0%	105	$5,402.2	$1,149.5	$1,952*	137/164
11. University of Michigan–Ann Arbor	85	4.2	49.6%	3.62	2.7	70.8%	75	$11,773.7	$550.5	$45,054	192/121
13. New York University (Meyers)	84	4.0	67.7%	3.50	3.3	43.5%	171	$8,475.0	$2,991.1	$41,726	42/551
13. University of Alabama–Birmingham	84	4.0	59.7%	3.43	5.1	65.2%	451	$3,696.5	$6,045.8	$510*	261/1,191
15. University of California–Los Angeles	83	4.0	45.7%	3.50	6.4	37.7%	134	$3,759.6	$2,876.0	$35,538	352/N/A
15. Vanderbilt University (TN)	83	4.2	66.5%	3.70	3.4	48.3%	330	$2,598.8	$2,310.0	$1,359*	432/201
17. U. of North Carolina–Chapel Hill	82	4.2	34.1%	3.62	1.9	60.9%	78	$3,813.7	$1,004.3	$34,124	167/67
18. Rush University (IL)	81	4.1	30.1%	3.50	2.6	66.1%	164	$1,387.1	$2,406.0	$995*	280/49
19. University of Virginia	80	4.0	58.5%	3.53	1.9	66.7%	140	$1,661.7	$1,467.5	$27,920	110/124
20. Penn. State University–University Park	78	3.7	45.2%	3.53	3.0	51.4%	49	$3,184.9	$3,302.5	$29,508	51/100
20. Rutgers University–Newark (NJ)	78	3.5	78.3%	N/A	0.4	98.0%	202	$2,215.6	$39,388.4	$1,169*	3/165
20. University of Illinois–Chicago	78	4.0	51.4%	3.37	2.5	60.4%	201	$5,057.4	$1,049.1	$35,452	277/99
23. University of Iowa	76	4.0	100.0%	N/A	0.1	34.2%	4	$2,608.0	$1,699.2	N/A	N/A/16
23. University of Texas–Austin	76	3.8	52.3%	3.48	2.8	97.4%	78	$3,197.6	$1,145.5	$21,749	197/34
23. U. of Texas Health Sci. Ctr.–Houston	76	3.7	72.7%	3.30	2.5	93.4%	129	$3,480.3	$2,114.1	$1,010*	136/479
26. Medical University of South Carolina	75	3.7	24.6%	3.70	0.4	48.1%	17	$6,597.4	$1,508.1	$31,949	14/12
26. U. of Colorado Anschutz Medical Campus	75	3.8	37.5%	3.30	4.2	88.1%	140	$645.3	$5,744.5	$1,020*	497/118
28. Georgetown University (DC)	74	3.8	42.6%	3.45	9.0	86.3%	377	$1,817.1	$387.5	$1,928*	214/603
28. Indiana Univ.–Purdue Univ.–Indianapolis	74	3.8	77.5%	3.41	0.9	71.4%	137	$6,030.1	$1,063.0	$1,499*	21/238
28. University of San Diego (CA)	74	3.7	21.9%	3.52	3.8	58.2%	82	$4,212.7	$1,143.9	$1,425*	155/47
31. Arizona State University	72	3.6	100.0%	3.53	0.1	88.3%	8	$7,329.1	$1,446.6	$23,328	12/13
31. Boston College (MA)	72	3.9	52.2%	3.55	3.6	71.7%	93	$433.0	$370.0	$1,298*	170/64
31. The Catholic University of America (DC)	72	3.6	71.4%	3.38	1.5	39.0%	24	$3,871.8	$6,223.7	$43,450	17/100
31. George Washington University (DC)	72	3.7	64.9%	3.31	3.8	70.2%	213	$1,254.2	$737.1	$1,155*	48/406
31. University of Utah	72	3.8	90.0%	3.56	0.2	33.7%	26	$2,841.4	$1,896.6	$39,658	15/13
36. Oregon Health and Science University	71	4.1	39.6%	3.54	0.9	20.9%	85	$2,101.6	$1,053.4	$755*	156/27
36. University of Rochester (NY)	71	3.8	80.3%	3.52	0.9	81.1%	42	$2,774.8	$551.6	$25,784	7/221
38. University of Cincinnati (OH)	70	3.6	64.0%	3.30	4.2	78.9%	674	$1,383.2	$1,901.4	$26,917	166/1,075
38. University of Miami (FL)	70	3.5	38.0%	3.40	1.4	81.4%	112	$2,461.7	$1,160.3	$46,037	47/110
38. University of Missouri	70	3.7	100.0%	3.76	0.2	31.2%	20	$4,848.5	$1,186.0	$422*	2/35
41. University of Arizona	69	3.7	65.6%	3.37	2.2	8.1%	296	$3,154.2	$1,616.8	$1,729*	142/258
41. Washington State University	69	3.4	70.6%	3.30	0.1	87.3%	23	$5,603.9	$1,560.0	$33,252	2/29
43. University of Connecticut	68	3.6	56.6%	3.47	0.8	69.0%	43	$568.9	$1,952.7	$37,032	31/92
43. University of Missouri–Kansas City	68	3.4	83.7%	3.57	1.3	43.2%	28	$6,247.0	$6,484.4	$450*	23/155
45. Florida Atlantic University (Lynn)	67	3.2	79.2%	3.50	2.7	81.8%	156	$2,731.0	$2,353.5	$928*	10/379
45. University of Massachusetts–Amherst	67	3.7	89.5%	3.50	0.3	58.0%	6	$379.8	$1,873.4	$750*	N/A/37
45. University of South Florida	67	3.5	39.4%	N/A	4.1	30.6%	317	$16,190.4	$1,202.0	$772*	101/535
48. University of Alabama	66	3.6	42.9%	3.33	1.5	56.8%	38	$396.4	$2,831.6	$367*	81/51
48. University of Tennessee–Knoxville	66	3.5	48.4%	3.80	1.9	100.0%	55	$93.9	$1,798.9	$1,626*	114/19
48. Virginia Commonwealth University	66	3.7	59.7%	3.62	1.7	59.6%	89	$1,235.5	$407.0	$33,921	48/175

N/A=Data were not provided by the school. †This data is common to and factors into both master's and DNP rankings. *Tuition is reported on a per-credit-hour basis.
Sources: U.S. News and the schools. Peer assessment data collected by Ipsos Public Affairs.

▶ More @ usnews.com/grad

Rank School	Overall score	Peer assessment score (5.0=highest)	'16 master's acceptance rate	'16 mean full-time undergrad GPA (master's)	'16 master's student/ faculty ratio	'16 percent of faculty in active nursing practice†	'16 master's degrees awarded	'16 NIH and all other research grants (in thousands)†	'16 NIH and all other teaching and practice grants (in thousands)†	'16 out-of-state tuition and fees	'16 master's program enrollment full-/part-time
48. Wayne State University (MI)	66	3.5	39.3%	3.60	1.5	39.1%	74	$639.4	$4,370.8	$1,555*	62/90
52. Loyola University Chicago (IL)	65	3.6	75.9%	3.46	2.1	66.1%	78	$1,120.8	$890.4	$1,081*	148/197
52. University of California–Davis	65	3.6	30.8%	3.47	3.4	9.7%	32	$1,368.5	$901.0	$36,012	97/N/A
52. University of Colorado–Colorado Springs	65	3.5	57.3%	N/A	4.0	75.0%	36	$336.4	$759.0	$771*	6/167
52. Univ. of South Carolina	65	3.5	65.6%	3.50	2.8	81.4%	30	$2,027.5	$649.0	$1,340*	132/216
56. Baylor University (TX)	64	3.5	57.1%	3.56	0.6	66.7%	10	$662.8	$564.9	$1,583*	12/2
56. Florida International University	64	3.1	52.6%	3.24	3.2	84.8%	181	$4,765.0	$2,535.6	$1,133*	208/63
56. Stony Brook University–SUNY (NY)	64	3.3	61.2%	N/A	7.2	80.0%	229	$288.7	$2,168.1	$23,906	10/787
59. University of Massachusetts–Boston	63	3.5	80.0%	3.12	1.3	54.3%	56	$1,193.3	$672.5	$1,371*	49/119
59. University of Nebraska Medical Center	63	3.8	58.9%	3.38	1.5	14.4%	73	$1,020.2	$798.9	$957*	138/128
59. University of North Carolina–Greensboro	63	3.3	67.7%	3.60	0.9	72.5%	95	$596.1	$1,654.7	$17,837	40/68
59. Villanova University (PA)	63	3.7	61.3%	3.63	2.6	91.9%	44	$439.3	$596.9	$862*	141/126
63. Marquette University (WI)	62	3.5	56.7%	3.54	3.1	63.2%	118	$576.3	$1,084.2	$1,075*	149/133
63. MGH Inst. of Health Professions (MA)	62	3.4	54.6%	3.40	5.7	59.3%	116	$1,036.1	$906.9	$56,790	276/28
63. Michigan State University	62	3.5	43.3%	3.62	1.7	44.9%	57	$1,208.2	$363.1	$1,373*	72/102
63. U. of Oklahoma Health Sciences Center	62	3.5	42.9%	3.45	1.4	26.0%	53	$782.0	$4,680.1	$877*	49/161
67. Duquesne University (PA)	61	3.5	79.1%	3.54	1.5	71.3%	38	$677.2	$371.8	$1,264*	95/60
67. Frontier Nursing University (KY)	61	3.4	50.3%	3.63	16.3	100.0%	447	N/A	$681.7	$550*	1,343/220
67. St. Louis University (MO)	61	3.6	73.2%	3.60	3.7	100.0%	114	$28.7	$630.0	$1,105*	217/201
67. SUNY Downstate Medical Center (NY)	61	3.1	41.4%	3.50	14.2	85.7%	62	$813.7	$966.7	$11,245	157/41
67. University of Kansas	61	3.7	100.0%	N/A	0.4	33.3%	87	$1,570.0	$127.9	$637*	N/A/70
67. University of Wisconsin–Milwaukee	61	3.6	72.7%	3.40	1.0	24.3%	23	$1,054.9	$1,574.9	$26,225	84/7
73. George Mason University (VA)	60	3.3	86.1%	3.47	1.2	71.2%	33	$150.0	$2,310.0	$1,425*	24/89
73. Texas Tech U. Health Sciences Center	60	3.3	42.4%	3.56	1.3	16.1%	169	$3,773.4	$3,619.5	$10,171	11/552
73. U. of Texas Medical Branch–Galveston	60	3.3	19.8%	N/A	3.4	16.1%	165	$2,332.3	$2,332.3	$693*	43/488
76. North Dakota State University	59	3.0	N/A	N/A	0.0	N/A	N/A	$571.3	$790.7	N/A	N/A/1
76. Seton Hall University (NJ)	59	3.2	78.2%	3.50	1.3	62.4%	51	$475.0	$450.0	$1,171*	39/124
76. University of Louisville (KY)	59	3.5	20.0%	N/A	1.3	55.8%	47	$754.6	$336.0	$25,682	79/6
79. Northeastern University (MA)	58	3.4	100.0%	3.60	2.9	9.4%	125	$2,459.5	$1,815.6	$1,338*	225/106
79. University of Massachusetts–Worcester	58	3.6	N/A	N/A	2.4	60.5%	48	N/A	$744.9	$825*	63/N/A
79. University of Rhode Island	58	3.4	68.0%	N/A	1.4	25.8%	52	$602.9	$761.9	$25,752	24/46
82. CUNY–Hunter College (NY)	57	3.1	44.8%	3.52	3.5	91.5%	123	$238.0	$553.5	$21,188	18/539
82. Purdue University–West Lafayette (IN)	57	3.3	85.3%	3.52	1.1	39.6%	14	$1,278.7	$2,005.7	$29,598	44/13
82. Texas Christian University	57	3.4	81.8%	3.54	0.8	63.3%	16	$150.0	$1,050.6	$1,480*	46/14
82. University of California–Irvine	57	3.4	48.8%	3.75	1.9	50.0%	16	$544.0	$160.0	$39,760	32/N/A
82. University of Central Florida	57	3.2	43.0%	3.59	1.4	53.8%	100	$1,346.5	$666.6	$1,152*	37/228
87. University of Hawaii–Manoa	56	3.2	63.8%	3.45	1.5	49.3%	71	$247.9	$2,744.6	$1,896*	73/45
88. Fairfield University (CT)	55	3.2	66.1%	N/A	0.9	82.1%	20	$135.2	$816.8	$850*	N/A/91
88. Texas Woman's University	55	3.4	68.8%	N/A	1.7	N/A	252	$419.8	$1,706.3	$714*	15/754
88. University of Missouri–St. Louis	55	3.3	N/A	N/A	0.7	69.3%	63	$142.5	$1,214.6	N/A	N/A/107
88. University of San Francisco (CA)	55	3.6	32.0%	N/A	6.0	N/A	232	$175.2	$206.1	$1,295*	409/157
92. Auburn University (AL)	54	3.3	62.6%	3.54	1.9	100.0%	49	N/A	N/A	$28,840	2/124
92. Samford University (AL)	54	3.2	42.6%	3.20	5.1	70.8%	124	N/A	$2,474.6	$809*	268/N/A
92. Seattle University (WA)	54	3.3	18.4%	N/A	3.0	99.1%	54	N/A	$528.0	$775*	190/N/A
92. University of Texas–Arlington	54	3.1	53.3%	3.51	49.1	49.5%	368	$406.8	$1,146.9	$12,807	2,294/731
92. U. of Texas Health Sci. Ctr.–San Antonio	54	3.6	73.5%	3.40	1.5	12.5%	83	$5.0	$2,339.7	$23,740	93/97
97. Brigham Young University (UT)	53	3.4	29.8%	3.86	0.7	71.7%	15	N/A	N/A	$786*	29/N/A
97. East Carolina University (NC)	53	3.2	63.6%	3.22	1.7	28.7%	174	$4,834.1	$364.6	$985*	63/289
97. Mercer University (GA)	53	3.2	52.4%	3.40	1.6	35.3%	49	$472.4	$665.0	$35,375	46/23
97. Texas A&M University–Corpus Christi	53	3.0	40.7%	N/A	2.4	55.5%	99	$254.0	$5,000.0	$780*	N/A/511
97. University at Buffalo–SUNY (NY)	53	3.3	66.7%	N/A	0.1	51.8%	2	$29.4	$1,021.9	$27,164	N/A/8
97. University of Vermont	53	3.4	80.0%	N/A	0.6	66.7%	21	N/A	$647.2	$1,130*	19/8
103. Florida State University	52	3.2	85.7%	N/A	0.3	32.3%	6	$423.0	$265.6	$1,175*	N/A/23
103. Loyola University New Orleans (LA)	52	3.3	81.1%	3.21	9.7	100.0%	164	$172.4	$20.0	$818*	188/58
103. University of North Carolina–Charlotte	52	3.3	40.1%	3.51	3.4	24.6%	79	$495.3	$705.8	$20,446	126/77
103. West Virginia University	52	3.2	91.1%	3.30	0.5	53.8%	37	$411.9	$895.7	$25,074	14/63
107. Shenandoah University (VA)	51	2.8	85.3%	3.40	3.9	91.7%	26	N/A	$310.4	$846*	24/30
108. Pace University (NY)	50	3.3	73.2%	N/A	1.8	82.7%	119	$102.6	$96.8	$1,190*	N/A/361
108. South Dakota State University	50	3.2	83.1%	N/A	1.4	22.9%	11	$663.7	$792.6	$602*	18/74

THE TOP SCHOOLS - MASTER'S continued

Rank School	Overall score	Peer assessment score (5.0=highest)	'16 master's acceptance rate	'16 mean full-time undergrad GPA (master's)	'16 master's student/ faculty ratio	'16 percent of faculty in active nursing practice†	'16 master's degrees awarded	'16 NIH and all other research grants (in thousands)†	'16 NIH and all other teaching and practice grants (in thousands)†	'16 out-of-state tuition and fees	'16 master's program enrollment full-/part-time
108. University of Portland (OR)	50	3.6	N/A	N/A	0.5	60.0%	3	$5.0	N/A	N/A	5/N/A
108. University of Southern Indiana	50	2.9	54.2%	3.70	4.8	90.9%	105	N/A	$1,306.7	$354*	97/286
112. Georgia State University	49	3.1	67.0%	3.50	3.1	51.2%	83	$92.6	$721.1	$1,249*	73/150
112. Pacific Lutheran University (WA)	49	3.1	30.9%	3.60	2.1	93.8%	26	N/A	$350.0	$1,000*	45/N/A
112. University of Indianapolis (IN)	49	3.4	50.9%	N/A	1.8	62.4%	88	N/A	N/A	$692*	12/254
115. Drexel University (PA)	48	3.3	53.1%	N/A	4.6	44.1%	328	$39.4	$220.6	$913*	35/1,200
115. East Tennessee State University	48	2.9	84.6%	3.00	1.8	100.0%	110	N/A	$2,887.0	$1,323*	42/250
115. Illinois State University	48	3.0	83.1%	3.77	0.7	59.5%	30	$746.1	$351.8	$808*	7/79
115. Mississippi University for Women	48	2.8	36.5%	3.63	4.1	100.0%	37	N/A	$204.0	N/A	30/1
115. Montana State University	48	3.0	100.0%	3.50	0.1	N/A	4	$835.6	$913.5	$934*	N/A/15
115. Robert Morris University (PA)	48	2.9	68.9%	N/A	0.2	83.3%	10	$75.0	$339.5	N/A	N/A/27
115. Simmons College (MA)	48	3.3	71.1%	3.25	5.0	59.9%	265	$306.0	$125.0	$1,315*	221/1,001
115. University of Arkansas	48	3.1	N/A	N/A	0.5	63.6%	3	N/A	$568.0	$1,047*	1/10
115. University of Maine	48	3.0	55.6%	N/A	0.4	92.2%	3	$63.0	$324.3	$648*	N/A/35
115. University of Southern Mississippi	48	2.9	75.3%	3.47	2.4	44.8%	40	N/A	$1,811.8	$24,958	100/51
115. University of Wisconsin–Eau Claire	48	3.3	100.0%	N/A	0.0	38.8%	1	$24.5	$350.0	$18,042	N/A/5
115. Wright State University (OH)	48	3.1	45.3%	3.24	3.4	21.3%	75	$490.5	$474.0	$22,892	118/90
115. Xavier University (OH)	48	3.1	52.4%	N/A	2.4	74.8%	95	N/A	$831.9	N/A	85/146
128. California State University–Los Angeles	47	3.0	52.3%	N/A	9.0	93.0%	47	N/A	$340.0	$16,830	184/35
128. Howard University (DC)	47	3.2	100.0%	3.14	0.3	25.0%	12	N/A	$1,250.0	$32,798	1/17
128. University of Michigan–Flint	47	3.2	N/A	N/A	0.8	31.9%	N/A	$150.0	$1,480.0	$15,354	47/2
131. California State University–Fullerton	46	2.9	32.3%	3.60	2.8	65.2%	83	$475.0	$250.0	N/A	125/62
131. Georgia College & State University	46	3.1	89.6%	3.51	2.9	56.8%	39	N/A	$359.7	$373*	70/27
131. James Madison University (VA)	46	3.1	55.9%	3.30	0.8	60.4%	21	$75.0	$375.0	$1,269*	17/60
131. University of Alabama–Huntsville	46	3.4	88.0%	3.51	4.2	31.0%	111	N/A	N/A	$1,530*	159/150
131. University of Massachusetts–Lowell	46	3.3	69.8%	3.42	1.2	54.6%	22	$35.4	N/A	$26,228	22/48
136. Alverno College (WI)	45	3.2	100.0%	3.12	13.6	78.6%	47	N/A	N/A	N/A	95/96
136. Binghamton University–SUNY (NY)	45	3.0	93.7%	3.46	1.9	49.3%	39	$15.0	$515.0	$24,261	83/73
136. Indiana State University	45	3.0	78.2%	N/A	2.0	96.8%	70	N/A	N/A	$499*	N/A/255
136. St. John Fisher College (NY)	45	3.0	45.2%	N/A	2.2	82.1%	39	$1.5	$729.4	$885*	5/153
136. University of Detroit Mercy (MI)	45	3.1	99.0%	3.37	2.8	53.5%	62	N/A	$374.6	$955*	76/130
136. Winston-Salem State University (NC)	45	2.6	55.7%	N/A	1.0	96.8%	39	$1,157.5	$841.0	N/A	57/21
142. Gonzaga University (WA)	44	3.4	53.9%	3.50	24.3	42.9%	131	$17.2	$28.5	$975*	418/182
142. Kent State University (OH)	44	3.1	87.9%	N/A	2.8	100.0%	123	N/A	$167.7	$881*	89/391
142. Ohio University	44	2.9	41.7%	3.00	2.1	49.2%	162	N/A	$2,226.1	$596*	4/250
142. University of the Incarnate Word (TX)	44	3.0	80.0%	N/A	0.6	N/A	8	N/A	$840.0	$885*	6/20
142. Western Kentucky University	44	2.8	55.6%	3.11	2.5	60.0%	58	$126.9	$272.6	$679*	9/62

THE TOP SCHOOLS - DOCTOR OF NURSING PRACTICE

Rank School	Overall score	Peer assessment score (5.0=highest)	'16 DNP acceptance rate	'16 mean full-time undergrad GPA (DNP)	'16 DNP student/ faculty ratio	'16 DNP enrollment as percent of graduate nursing enrollment	'16 DNP degrees awarded	'16 percent of full-time faculty with doctoral degree†	'16 percent of faculty with distinguished memberships/ fellows†	'16 out-of-state tuition and fees	'16 DNP program enrollment full-/part-time
1. Duke University (NC)	100	4.3	42.2%	3.58	1.1	30.8%	65	98.9%	24.6%	$1,639*	76/157
2. Johns Hopkins University (MD)	98	4.4	62.2%	3.33	0.3	7.6%	21	96.7%	29.6%	$38,281	9/48
3. University of Washington	97	4.4	54.5%	3.68	1.5	70.0%	84	98.3%	3.9%	$39,641	244/59
4. Rush University (IL)	92	4.2	60.4%	N/A	2.8	67.5%	175	82.7%	17.8%	$1,050*	99/635
5. Ohio State University	89	4.1	91.2%	3.56	0.5	10.4%	22	83.6%	28.7%	$723*	18/64
5. Columbia University (NY)	89	4.3	51.4%	3.68	0.3	7.1%	17	88.4%	14.9%	$1,874*	18/34
7. University of Pittsburgh (PA)	88	4.1	53.4%	3.60	0.8	39.2%	47	100.0%	21.1%	$988*	44/94
8. Yale University (CT)	87	4.2	62.9%	N/A	0.3	13.4%	11	90.0%	24.3%	N/A	N/A/48
8. Case Western Reserve University (OH)	87	4.1	87.3%	3.54	1.0	26.6%	43	79.8%	28.4%	$1,952*	75/56
10. University of Maryland–Baltimore	86	4.1	35.1%	3.39	1.0	40.2%	24	82.4%	N/A	$1,324*	194/171
11. Vanderbilt University (TN)	83	4.2	82.0%	3.70	0.6	20.9%	43	74.4%	20.4%	$1,359*	37/138
12. New York University (Meyers)	82	4.0	50.9%	N/A	0.2	6.2%	9	97.1%	26.1%	$41,726	N/A/42
13. University of Iowa	81	4.0	60.4%	3.49	2.5	83.8%	32	79.0%	26.8%	$40,124	145/56
13. University of Minnesota–Twin Cities	81	4.1	66.1%	3.54	3.9	89.8%	94	96.4%	29.1%	$20,730	320/34
15. University of Michigan–Ann Arbor	80	4.1	56.4%	3.52	0.5	13.3%	5	83.9%	39.3%	$45,054	35/19

Rank	School	Overall score	Peer assessment score (5.0=highest)	'16 DNP acceptance rate	'16 mean full-time undergrad GPA (DNP)	'16 DNP student/ faculty ratio	'16 DNP enrollment as percent of graduate nursing enrollment	'16 DNP degrees awarded	'16 percent of full-time faculty with doctoral degree†	'16 percent faculty with distinguished memberships/ fellows†	'16 out-of-state tuition and fees	'16 DNP program enrollment full-/part-time
15.	University of Virginia	80	4.1	75.0%	3.48	0.6	22.0%	15	92.2%	16.3%	$27,920	29/48
15.	University of Illinois–Chicago	80	4.1	94.8%	3.49	2.0	47.7%	26	84.3%	14.8%	$37,812	172/230
18.	Rutgers University–Newark (NJ)	79	3.4	45.5%	N/A	1.7	72.3%	55	80.4%	4.9%	$1,169*	143/340
19.	Arizona State University	78	3.6	56.1%	3.51	1.4	78.6%	46	77.8%	12.7%	$25,828	143/81
20.	Medical University of South Carolina	77	3.6	84.6%	3.60	3.8	74.3%	47	95.2%	15.4%	$32,589	148/66
20.	U. of North Carolina–Chapel Hill	77	4.1	42.0%	3.70	0.7	21.7%	6	76.4%	14.1%	$34,124	66/10
22.	University of Utah	74	3.7	50.2%	3.65	2.2	75.3%	61	75.0%	11.5%	$45,378	204/16
23.	U. of Texas Health Sci. Ctr.–Houston	73	3.6	83.8%	3.70	0.8	18.8%	26	83.7%	13.3%	$1,010*	62/91
23.	Indiana Univ.-Purdue Univ.–Indianapolis	73	3.8	50.0%	3.61	0.1	9.1%	18	59.8%	7.7%	$1,000*	11/19
23.	University of Alabama–Birmingham	73	3.9	100.0%	3.65	0.6	11.6%	20	80.6%	18.2%	$510*	13/183
26.	University of Arizona	71	3.8	53.8%	3.52	2.9	43.1%	45	46.3%	68.9%	$975*	271/93
26.	University of Kentucky	71	3.8	72.4%	3.40	1.7	85.0%	33	73.1%	18.5%	$40,519	109/124
26.	University of Wisconsin–Madison	71	3.9	54.2%	3.78	1.6	82.1%	7	71.8%	13.1%	$28,469	54/56
26.	George Washington University (DC)	71	3.6	73.6%	3.35	0.6	16.1%	36	88.6%	31.6%	$1,155*	3/84
26.	The Catholic University of America (DC)	71	3.6	78.6%	3.35	0.4	14.8%	3	90.5%	15.3%	$43,450	2/33
31.	University of Missouri–Kansas City	70	3.4	87.5%	3.56	1.8	43.3%	25	67.4%	21.6%	$450*	65/106
31.	Oregon Health and Science University	70	4.1	57.7%	3.36	0.2	16.4%	33	39.1%	3.8%	$740*	29/12
31.	Washington State University	70	3.4	61.1%	3.66	1.0	69.4%	28	59.5%	4.2%	$33,252	57/86
34.	U. of Colorado Anschutz Medical Campus	68	3.5	71.4%	3.50	0.4	10.9%	16	58.5%	21.6%	$1,020*	36/45
34.	University of Alabama	68	3.4	45.9%	3.35	1.5	57.3%	65	77.6%	8.6%	$367*	55/122
34.	Uniformed Svces U. of the Hlth. Sci. (MD)	68	3.6	58.8%	3.29	3.6	89.9%	45	95.2%	36.4%	N/A*	152/N/A

KEVIN D. LILES FOR USN&WR

THE UNIVERSITY OF
ALABAMA–BIRMINGHAM

THE TOP SCHOOLS - DOCTOR OF NURSING PRACTICE continued

Rank School	Overall score	Peer assessment score (5.0=highest)	'16 DNP acceptance rate	'16 mean full-time undergrad GPA (DNP)	'16 DNP student/ faculty ratio	'16 DNP enrollment as percent of graduate nursing enrollment	'16 DNP degrees awarded	'16 percent of full-time faculty with doctoral degree†	'16 percent faculty with distinguished memberships/ fellows†	'16 out-of-state tuition and fees	'16 DNP program enrollment full-/part-time
34. Loyola University Chicago (IL)	68	3.9	100.0%	N/A	0.2	8.7%	12	77.9%	6.1%	$1,081*	16/20
38. University of Rochester (NY)	67	3.7	100.0%	N/A	0.1	8.0%	5	67.1%	10.5%	$25,784	N/A/21
38. North Dakota State University	67	3.2	36.8%	3.61	3.4	97.9%	10	100.0%	78.6%	$24,033	45/2
38. Wayne State University (MI)	67	3.6	44.2%	3.40	1.1	36.0%	15	71.4%	14.5%	$1,555*	51/51
38. University of Massachusetts–Amherst	67	3.5	66.0%	3.50	3.0	71.0%	35	62.5%	18.0%	$750*	86/129
38. University of San Diego (CA)	67	3.4	53.3%	3.50	1.5	21.3%	18	100.0%	16.4%	$1,455*	64/9
38. University of Missouri	67	3.4	84.0%	3.40	1.6	70.8%	34	71.2%	23.0%	$422*	32/172
44. Florida Atlantic University (Lynn)	66	3.2	61.3%	3.61	1.5	18.6%	20	87.5%	23.6%	$928*	64/35
44. University of Florida	66	3.5	50.0%	3.54	2.9	87.8%	41	85.7%	21.3%	$1,255*	122/136
46. University of Miami (FL)	65	3.4	40.8%	3.48	1.2	36.4%	10	83.3%	8.1%	$50,867	56/47
47. Baylor University (TX)	64	3.5	59.1%	3.43	1.8	76.3%	5	94.7%	N/A	$1,583*	39/6
47. University of Cincinnati (OH)	64	3.5	76.9%	3.34	0.4	6.1%	19	70.3%	3.6%	$26,917	36/46
47. Villanova University (PA)	64	3.7	100.0%	3.14	0.2	4.9%	7	74.5%	10.8%	$1,375*	13/4
50. Stony Brook University–SUNY (NY)	63	3.3	69.0%	N/A	0.9	5.7%	28	83.8%	12.5%	$44,576	26/22
50. MGH Inst. of Health Professions (MA)	63	3.5	83.3%	3.42	0.4	14.1%	14	77.8%	10.2%	$1,136*	6/44
52. Florida International University	62	3.1	54.1%	3.58	1.5	29.4%	14	83.3%	9.3%	$1,133*	101/20
52. University of Wisconsin–Milwaukee	62	3.5	93.9%	3.53	0.8	46.5%	30	55.1%	15.5%	$26,225	22/129
54. University of San Francisco (CA)	61	3.9	91.9%	N/A	1.8	25.5%	51	100.0%	N/A	$1,295*	111/83
54. University of Colorado–Colorado Springs	61	3.4	42.9%	N/A	0.8	13.1%	5	90.9%	8.3%	$771*	6/20
54. George Mason University (VA)	61	3.3	95.5%	3.37	1.0	37.6%	26	86.7%	4.1%	$1,425*	27/55
57. Northeastern University (MA)	60	3.3	40.0%	3.60	1.3	28.9%	66	73.3%	5.0%	$1,338*	99/43
57. University of Connecticut	60	3.5	100.0%	3.90	0.4	26.2%	1	77.1%	9.3%	$37,032	15/40
59. Texas Christian University	59	3.2	44.9%	3.41	3.6	79.0%	66	65.0%	6.7%	$1,480*	213/13
59. Fairfield University (CT)	59	3.2	50.5%	3.49	2.0	57.9%	28	88.0%	N/A	$950*	43/82
59. University of Kansas	59	3.6	100.0%	3.63	1.6	67.8%	15	66.0%	18.3%	$637*	30/172
62. Univ. of South Carolina	57	3.3	57.1%	3.52	0.6	19.7%	3	78.4%	9.3%	$1,340*	25/64
62. Marquette University (WI)	57	3.4	92.3%	N/A	0.3	8.8%	17	63.2%	3.5%	$1,075*	11/19
62. University of Massachusetts–Boston	57	3.4	81.0%	N/A	0.2	15.7%	9	83.3%	10.0%	$1,371*	N/A/39
62. Michigan State University	57	3.5	100.0%	3.80	0.2	7.8%	5	81.6%	12.4%	$1,373*	11/5
66. University at Buffalo–SUNY (NY)	56	3.2	71.2%	3.50	2.3	83.7%	29	95.2%	12.5%	$45,357	75/94
66. Purdue University–West Lafayette (IN)	56	3.3	100.0%	N/A	0.2	27.8%	6	45.2%	6.3%	$950*	N/A/22
68. Loyola University New Orleans (LA)	55	3.3	85.0%	3.55	3.4	24.5%	37	100.0%	6.7%	$818*	69/11
68. Texas Tech U. Health Sciences Center	55	3.2	75.0%	N/A	0.3	8.6%	31	42.0%	11.7%	$10,171	41/12
68. University of Tennessee–Knoxville	55	3.2	57.1%	N/A	0.1	9.9%	2	70.5%	9.9%	$1,626*	N/A/18
68. University of Nebraska Medical Center	55	3.6	76.9%	3.42	0.8	28.4%	7	57.8%	10.1%	$957*	87/27
72. University of South Florida	54	3.1	56.4%	N/A	1.5	19.3%	17	75.4%	16.7%	$772*	77/80
72. Seton Hall University (NJ)	54	3.1	66.7%	N/A	0.2	13.4%	8	78.3%	67.7%	N/A	N/A/30
72. University of Portland (OR)	54	3.5	25.0%	3.73	2.7	85.7%	7	100.0%	6.7%	$1,170*	30/N/A
72. U. of Oklahoma Health Sciences Center	54	3.4	92.9%	3.07	0.1	9.1%	4	45.1%	6.5%	$1,125*	5/17
76. University of Central Florida	53	3.1	27.0%	3.52	0.3	13.9%	14	69.5%	8.4%	$1,152*	7/39
76. U. of Texas Medical Branch–Galveston	53	3.2	27.8%	N/A	0.2	6.9%	4	62.7%	8.1%	$693*	N/A/42
76. University of Arkansas	53	3.0	62.7%	3.47	6.3	88.3%	11	100.0%	N/A	$1,047*	37/46
79. St. Louis University (MO)	52	3.4	81.3%	3.60	0.5	9.6%	6	62.3%	4.8%	$1,105*	31/18
79. University of Wisconsin–Eau Claire	52	3.3	61.4%	3.60	1.0	94.0%	24	70.3%	2.0%	$27,371	25/53
81. Idaho State University	51	3.0	42.9%	3.81	2.0	77.4%	8	54.6%	4.0%	N/A	44/4
81. Florida State University	51	3.1	74.3%	3.30	2.7	76.8%	20	92.3%	N/A	$1,111*	74/2
81. Samford University (AL)	51	3.1	73.9%	N/A	0.6	22.1%	32	60.9%	4.6%	$809*	13/63
81. East Tennessee State University	51	3.0	61.1%	3.59	0.7	18.1%	16	54.1%	4.9%	$1,323*	41/29
85. East Carolina University (NC)	50	3.2	58.4%	3.31	1.2	29.9%	18	62.7%	7.4%	$985*	89/76
85. South Dakota State University	50	3.1	84.2%	3.24	1.8	49.3%	21	65.5%	5.7%	$602*	31/76
85. University of Michigan–Flint	50	3.0	84.0%	3.60	2.6	81.4%	34	61.3%	1.8%	$15,354	118/96
88. CUNY–Hunter College (NY)	49	3.0	93.8%	3.60	0.3	6.5%	5	88.5%	11.0%	$22,148	10/29
88. University of North Carolina–Charlotte	49	3.4	85.7%	3.36	0.4	8.6%	5	46.0%	6.6%	$25,248	15/4
88. University of Hawaii–Manoa	49	3.0	22.3%	3.43	1.0	30.6%	8	58.5%	6.7%	$1,896*	60/6
88. Creighton University (NE)	49	3.5	76.0%	3.35	2.8	86.1%	39	71.7%	1.9%	$820*	117/198
88. Montana State University	49	3.0	38.9%	3.60	0.9	85.0%	8	54.8%	1.9%	$934*	44/41
93. Texas Woman's University	48	3.3	90.9%	N/A	0.1	5.6%	10	54.8%	1.2%	$739*	6/46
93. Seattle University (WA)	48	3.4	76.5%	N/A	0.3	11.6%	1	66.7%	8.9%	$796*	20/5
93. Robert Morris University (PA)	48	2.7	63.2%	N/A	1.8	88.3%	30	91.7%	7.6%	$27,375	N/A/203

SPECIALTIES

ADMINISTRATION
1. **Johns Hopkins University** (MD)
1. **University of Pennsylvania**
3. **University of Maryland–Baltimore**
4. **University of Pittsburgh** (PA)
5. **University of Michigan–Ann Arbor**
6. **University of Alabama–Birmingham**
6. **University of Iowa**

CLINICAL NURSE LEADER
1. **University of Maryland–Baltimore**
2. **University of Virginia**
3. **University of Pittsburgh** (PA)
4. **Rush University** (IL)

INFORMATICS
1. **University of Maryland–Baltimore**
2. **University of Minnesota–Twin Cities**
3. **Duke University** (NC)
4. **Vanderbilt University** (TN)
5. **New York University** (Meyers)

NURSE PRACTITIONER
ADULT GERONTOLOGY: ACUTE CARE
1. **Johns Hopkins University** (MD)
2. **Vanderbilt University** (TN)
3. **University of Pennsylvania**
4. **Rush University** (IL)
5. **Duke University** (NC)
6. **University of Maryland–Baltimore**
6. **University of Pittsburgh** (PA)
8. **Columbia University** (NY)
8. **University of California–San Francisco**
10. **Yale University** (CT)

NURSE PRACTITIONER
ADULT GERONTOLOGY: PRIMARY CARE
1. **University of Pennsylvania**
2. **Johns Hopkins University** (MD)
3. **New York University** (Meyers)
3. **University of California–San Francisco**
5. **Columbia University** (NY)

6. **Rush University** (IL)
7. **University of Washington**
7. **Vanderbilt University** (TN)
9. **University of Maryland–Baltimore**

NURSE PRACTITIONER
FAMILY
1. **Johns Hopkins University** (MD)
2. **University of Pennsylvania**
3. **University of Washington**
4. **Duke University** (NC)
4. **University of California–San Francisco**
6. **Vanderbilt University** (TN)
7. **University of Maryland–Baltimore**
8. **Emory University** (GA)
9. **Columbia University** (NY)
10. **Rush University** (IL)
11. **University of Illinois–Chicago**
11. **University of North Carolina–Chapel Hill**
11. **Yale University** (CT)

NURSE PRACTITIONER
PEDIATRIC: PRIMARY CARE
1. **University of Pennsylvania**
2. **Duke University** (NC)
3. **Vanderbilt University** (TN)
4. **Johns Hopkins University** (MD)
5. **Rush University** (IL)
6. **U. of California–San Francisco**
7. **University of Washington**
8. **Yale University** (CT)

NURSE PRACTITIONER
PSYCHIATRIC MENTAL HEALTH: ACROSS THE LIFESPAN
1. **University of Pennsylvania**
2. **Rush University** (IL)
2. **Vanderbilt University** (TN)
4. **Yale University** (CT)
5. **Johns Hopkins University** (MD)
6. **U. of California–San Francisco**
7. **University of Virginia**
8. **University of Washington**

METHODOLOGY

The 532 nursing schools with master's or doctoral programs accredited in late summer 2016 by either the Commission on Collegiate Nursing Education or the Accreditation Commission for Education in Nursing were surveyed in late 2016 and early 2017. Of those, 292 provided enough data to be included in the rankings of nursing master's programs and 186 provided enough data to be included in a ranking of Doctor of Nursing Practice programs. Both rankings are based on a weighted average of 14 indicators in several categories, described below. Seven statistical indicators refer to the nursing school as a whole and are common to both the master's and DNP ranking models (although weighted somewhat differently): the four measures of research activity plus those related to faculty credentials, achievements and participation in nursing practice. Data for the other indicators, such as students' undergraduate GPA and the program's acceptance rate, are specific to each degree type. In addition, both rankings take into account the opinions of academic experts; nursing school deans and deans of graduate studies were asked to rate separately the academic quality of both master's and DNP programs with which they are familiar.

Quality assessment (weighted by .40 in both rankings): In the fall of 2016, nursing school deans and deans of graduate studies at nursing schools were asked to rate the quality of accredited master's and DNP programs on a scale from marginal (1) to outstanding (5). Those individuals who did not know enough about a school to evaluate it fairly were asked to mark "don't know." A school's score is the average of all the respondents who rated its program. Responses of "don't know" counted neither for nor against a school. Thirty-eight percent of those surveyed responded. Assessment data were collected by Ipsos Public Affairs.

Student selectivity and program size (.1125 for master's programs; .1875 for DNP programs): The strength of full-time and part-time students entering either type of degree program in the fall of 2016 was based on their mean undergraduate GPA (.05 for both rankings) and the acceptance rate of applicants (.0125 for both rankings). Size was measured by the percentage of the fall 2016 total full-time and part-time graduate nursing program enrollment that was pursuing either a master's or DNP (.0125 and .06 respectively); and by the number of master's or DNP degrees awarded to the 2016 graduating class (.0375 for master's; .065 for DNP).

Faculty resources (.2375 for master's, .2625 for DNP): Based on the 2016 ratio of full-time-equivalent master's or DNP students to full-time-equivalent faculty members (.05 for master's; .04 for DNP); the proportion of 2016 full-time faculty members holding doctoral degrees (.05 for both rankings); percentage of faculty in fall 2016 who were recognized for academic achievements with an array of honors identified by the American Association of Colleges of Nursing, such as Fellow of the American Academy of Nursing, Fellow of the National Institutes of Health, and Fellow of the American Psychological Association (.0375 for both rankings); the proportion of 2016 full-time and part-time faculty members who were in active nursing practice as defined by the American Association of Colleges of Nursing (.075 for both rankings); and the number of master's or DNP degrees awarded per full-time-equivalent faculty member in 2016 (.025 for master's; .06 for DNP).

Research activity (.25 for master's; .15 for DNP): Based on total grants to the nursing school from the National Institutes of Health, other federal agencies and non-federal sources (.075 for master's; .04 for DNP); total educational and practical initiative grants to the nursing school in fiscal year 2016 from the NIH and non-NIH sources (.075 for master's; .04 for DNP); average grants from the NIH, other federal agencies and nonfederal sources per full-time-equivalent nursing faculty member (.05 for master's; .035 for DNP); and average NIH and non-NIH sources of federal educational and practical initiative grants for fiscal year 2016 per full-time-equivalent nursing faculty member (.05 for master's; .035 for DNP).

Overall rank: Data for both rankings were standardized about their means, and standardized scores were weighted, totaled and rescaled so that the top-scoring school received 100; others received their percentage of the top score. Schools were then numerically ranked in descending order based on their scores. Our analysis of the data for several indicators revealed a number of extreme outliers, so we applied a standard statistical technique – a logarithmic transformation of the original values – to avoid giving those institutions a distorted amount of credit. Measures affected were all four of the research activity indicators and, for the first time this year, the number of master's degrees and DNP degrees awarded and the student-to-faculty ratios. After these indicators were normalized using a log value, each indicator's z-score was calculated to represent the different types of data on a common scale.

Specialty rankings: These rankings are based solely on assessments by nursing school deans and deans of graduate studies who identified up to 10 schools offering the best programs in each specialty area. Those schools receiving the most votes in each specialty are numerically ranked in descending order based on the number of nominations they received.

Health Disciplines

SCHOOLS RANKED BEST BY PROGRAM DIRECTORS AND FACULTY

AUDIOLOGY

DOCTORATE Ranked in 2016

Rank School	Average assessment score (5.0=highest)
1. Vanderbilt University (TN)	4.6
2. University of Iowa	4.3
3. Washington University in St. Louis (MO)	4.1
4. University of North Carolina–Chapel Hill	4.0
4. University of Texas–Dallas	4.0
4. University of Washington	4.0
7. Northwestern University (IL)	3.7
7. University of Pittsburgh (PA)	3.7
9. Arizona State University	3.6
9. Ohio State University	3.6
9. Rush University Medical Center (IL)	3.6
9. University of Arizona	3.6
13. Indiana University–Bloomington	3.5
13. Purdue University–West Lafayette (IN)	3.5
13. University of Minnesota–Twin Cities	3.5
13. University of Texas–Austin	3.5
17. James Madison University (VA)	3.4
17. University at Buffalo–SUNY (NY)	3.4
17. University of Colorado–Boulder	3.4
17. University of Maryland–College Park	3.4
17. University of Memphis (TN)	3.4
17. University of South Florida	3.4
17. University of Wisconsin AuD Consortium	3.4

CLINICAL PSYCHOLOGY

DOCTORATE Ranked in 2016

Rank School	Average assessment score (5.0=highest)
1. University of California–Los Angeles	4.7
2. University of California–Berkeley	4.5
2. University of North Carolina–Chapel Hill	4.5
4. Stony Brook University–SUNY (NY)	4.4
4. University of Minnesota–Twin Cities	4.4
4. University of Wisconsin–Madison	4.4
4. Yale University (CT)	4.4
8. University of Texas–Austin	4.3
8. University of Virginia	4.3
8. University of Washington	4.3
11. Duke University (NC)	4.2
11. Emory University (GA)	4.2
11. Univ. of Illinois–Urbana-Champaign	4.2
11. University of Pennsylvania	4.2
11. University of Pittsburgh (PA)	4.2
16. Harvard University (MA)	4.1
16. Indiana University–Bloomington	4.1

Rank School	Average assessment score (5.0=highest)
16. Northwestern University (IL)	4.1
16. University of Colorado–Boulder	4.1
16. University of Michigan–Ann Arbor	4.1
16. University of Southern California	4.1
16. U. of Kansas (Clin. Child Psych. Prog.)	4.1
16. Vanderbilt University (TN)	4.1
16. Washington University in St. Louis	4.1
25. Penn. State University–University Park	4.0
25. San Diego State Univ. - U. of Calif.–SD (CA)	4.0
25. Temple University (PA)	4.0
25. University of Iowa	4.0
25. University of Miami (FL)	4.0
25. University of Oregon	4.0
31. Boston University (MA)	3.9
31. University of Arizona	3.9
31. University of Florida	3.9
31. University of Kansas	3.9
31. University of Maryland–College Park	3.9

HEALTH CARE MANAGEMENT

MASTER'S Ranked in 2015

Rank School	Average assessment score (5.0=highest)
1. University of Michigan–Ann Arbor	4.4
2. University of Alabama–Birmingham	4.3
3. University of Minnesota–Twin Cities	4.2
3. Virginia Commonwealth University	4.2
5. Rush University (IL)	4.0
5. University of North Carolina–Chapel Hill	4.0
7. Johns Hopkins University (MD)	3.6
7. St. Louis University	3.6
7. U.S. Army-Baylor University (TX)	3.6
10. Northwestern University (Kellogg) (IL)	3.5
10. Ohio State University	3.5
10. Trinity University (TX)	3.5
10. University of Iowa	3.5
10. University of Washington	3.5
15. Cornell University (Sloan) (NY)	3.4
15. University of California–Los Angeles	3.4
17. George Washington University (DC)	3.3
18. Baylor University (TX)	3.2
18. Boston University	3.2
18. Medical University of South Carolina	3.2
18. New York University	3.2
18. U. of Col.–Denver/Network for Hlthcare Mgmt.	3.2
23. Columbia University (NY)	3.1
23. Georgetown University (DC)	3.1

Rank School	Average assessment score (5.0=highest)
23. Tulane University (LA)	3.1
23. University of Colorado–Denver	3.1
23. University of Southern California	3.1

NURSE ANESTHESIA

MASTER'S/DOCTORATE Ranked in 2016

Rank School	Average assessment score (5.0=highest)
1. Virginia Commonwealth University	4.0
2. Baylor College of Medicine (TX)	3.8
3. Duke University (NC)	3.7
4. Kaiser Perm. Sch. of Anesth.-Cal. St. U.–Fullerton	3.6
4. Rush University (IL)	3.6
4. Uniformed Svces U. of the Hlth. Sci. (MD)	3.6
4. University of Pittsburgh (PA)	3.6
8. U. of Texas Health Science Ctr.–Houston	3.5
8. U.S. Army Grad Prog., Anesth. Nursing (TX)	3.5
10. Georgetown University (DC)	3.4
10. Mayo Clinic School of Health Sci. (MN)	3.4
10. University at Buffalo–SUNY (NY)	3.4
10. University of Detroit Mercy (MI)	3.4
10. University of Iowa	3.4
10. University of Maryland–Baltimore	3.4
10. University of Southern California	3.4
10. Wake Forest Baptist Hlth.-WF Sch. of Med.(NC)	3.4
18. Goldfarb Sch. of Nursing, Barnes-Jewish	3.3
18. Oakland University–Beaumont (MI)	3.3
18. Sacred Heart Medical Ctr. - Gonzaga U (WA)	3.3
18. Samuel Merritt University (CA)	3.3

Note: All schools have either a master's or a doctoral program.

NURSE MIDWIFERY

MASTER'S/DOCTORATE Ranked in 2016

Rank School	Average assessment score (5.0=highest)
1. UC–San Francisco/S.F. General Hospital	4.2
1. University of Michigan–Ann Arbor	4.2
1. Vanderbilt University (TN)	4.2
4. Oregon Health and Science University	4.0
4. University of Minnesota–Twin Cities	4.0
4. Yale University (CT)	4.0
7. University of New Mexico	3.9
7. University of Pennsylvania	3.9
9. University of Utah	3.8
10. Baylor University (TX)	3.7
10. University of Illinois–Chicago	3.7

Note: All schools have either a master's or a doctoral program; some have both.

OCCUPATIONAL THERAPY

MASTER'S/DOCTORATE **Ranked in 2016**

Rank School	Average assessment score (5.0=highest)
1. Boston University (Sargent) (MA)	4.6
1. Washington University in St. Louis	4.6
3. University of Southern California	4.5
4. University of Illinois–Chicago	4.3
4. University of Pittsburgh (PA)	4.3
6. Colorado State University	4.1
6. Thomas Jefferson University (PA)	4.1
6. Tufts U.-Boston Sch. of Occup. Therapy (MA)	4.1
9. University of Kansas Medical Center	4.0
9. University of North Carolina–Chapel Hill	4.0
11. Columbia University (NY)	3.9
12. New York University	3.8
12. Ohio State University	3.8
14. University of Washington	3.7
14. University of Wisconsin–Madison	3.7
14. U. of Texas Medical Branch–Galveston	3.7
17. Medical University of South Carolina	3.6
17. Texas Woman's University	3.6
17. University of Florida	3.6
17. University of Wisconsin–Milwaukee	3.6
17. Virginia Commonwealth University	3.6

Note: All schools listed have master's programs; some may not have doctoral programs.

PHARMACY

PHARM.D. **Ranked in 2016**

Rank School	Average assessment score (5.0=highest)
1. University of North Carolina–Chapel Hill	4.7
2. University of Minnesota	4.5
3. University of California–San Francisco	4.4
3. University of Michigan–Ann Arbor	4.4
3. University of Texas–Austin	4.4
6. Ohio State University	4.2
6. University of Illinois–Chicago	4.2
6. University of Kentucky	4.2
9. Purdue University (IN)	4.1
9. University of Florida	4.1
9. University of Maryland–Baltimore	4.1
9. University of Pittsburgh (PA)	4.1
9. University of Southern California	4.1
9. University of Washington	4.1
9. University of Wisconsin–Madison	4.1
16. University of Arizona	4.0
17. University of Iowa	3.9
17. University of Utah	3.9
17. U. of Tennessee Health Science Center	3.9
17. Virginia Commonwealth University	3.9
21. University of Kansas	3.8
22. University at Buffalo–SUNY (NY)	3.7
22. University of Colorado–Denver	3.7

PHYSICAL THERAPY

MASTER'S/DOCTORATE **Ranked in 2016**

Rank School	Average assessment score (5.0=highest)
1. University of Delaware	4.3
1. University of Pittsburgh (PA)	4.3
1. University of Southern California	4.3
1. Washington University in St. Louis	4.3
5. Emory University (GA)	4.1
6. Northwestern University (IL)	4.0
6. University of Iowa	4.0
8. MGH Inst. of Health Professions (MA)	3.8
8. U.S. Army-Baylor University (TX)	3.8
10. Duke University (NC)	3.7
10. Ohio State University	3.7
10. University of Florida	3.7
10. University of Miami (FL)	3.7
14. Boston University (MA)	3.6
15. Creighton University (NE)	3.5
15. Marquette University (WI)	3.5
15. University of Colorado–Denver	3.5
15. University of Illinois–Chicago	3.5
15. University of North Carolina–Chapel Hill	3.5
20. Arcadia University (PA)	3.4
20. Mayo Clinic School of Health Sci. (MN)	3.4
20. University of Alabama–Birmingham	3.4
20. University of Kansas Medical Center	3.4
20. University of Minnesota–Twin Cities	3.4
20. University of Utah	3.4
20. Univ. of Calif.–San Francisco - SF State U.	3.4
20. Virginia Commonwealth University	3.4

Note: All schools have a doctoral program and may have a master's.

PHYSICIAN ASSISTANT

MASTER'S **Ranked in 2015**

Rank School	Average assessment score (5.0=highest)
1. Duke University (NC)	4.4
2. University of Iowa	4.3
3. Emory University (GA)	4.1
3. George Washington University (DC)	4.1
5. Oregon Health and Sciences University	4.0
5. Quinnipiac University (CT)	4.0
5. University of Colorado–Denver	4.0
5. University of Utah	4.0
9. University of Nebraska Medical Center	3.9
9. Wake Forest University (NC)	3.9
11. Interservice Physician Asst. Prog. (TX)	3.8
11. University of Washington	3.8
13. Baylor College of Medicine (TX)	3.7
13. Drexel University (PA)	3.7
15. U. of Texas Southwest. Med. Ctr.–Dallas	3.6
16. Rutgers Biomedical and Health Sci. (NJ)	3.5
16. Shenandoah University (VA)	3.5
16. Stony Brook University–SUNY	3.5

Rank School	Average assessment score (5.0=highest)
16. University of Alabama–Birmingham	3.5
20. Midwestern University (IL)	3.4
20. Midwestern University (AZ)	3.4
20. Northeastern University (MA)	3.4
20. Rosalind Franklin U. of Med. and Sci. (IL)	3.4
20. University of Southern California (Keck)	3.4
20. Yale University (CT)	3.4

PUBLIC HEALTH

MASTER'S/DOCTORATE **Ranked in 2015**

Rank School	Average assessment score (5.0=highest)
1. Johns Hopkins University (MD)	4.8
2. Harvard University (MA)	4.7
2. University of North Carolina–Chapel Hill	4.7
4. University of Michigan–Ann Arbor	4.5
5. Columbia University (NY)	4.4
6. University of Washington	4.2
7. Emory University (GA)	4.1
8. University of Minnesota–Twin Cities	4.0
9. University of California–Berkeley	3.9
10. Boston University	3.6
10. University of California–Los Angeles	3.6
12. Tulane University (LA)	3.5
13. University of Pittsburgh	3.4
14. George Washington University (DC)	3.2
14. Yale University (CT)	3.2
16. University of South Florida	3.1
17. University of Illinois–Chicago	3.0
17. University of Iowa	3.0
19. Ohio State University	2.9
19. University of Alabama–Birmingham	2.9
21. U. of Texas–Houston Health Sciences Ctr.	2.8
22. University of Maryland–College Park	2.7
23. St. Louis University	2.6
23. University of South Carolina	2.6

Note: All schools listed have master's programs; some may not have doctoral programs.

REHABILITATION COUNSELING

MASTER'S/DOCTORATE **Ranked in 2015**

Rank School	Average assessment score (5.0=highest)
1. Michigan State University	4.5
1. University of Wisconsin–Madison	4.5
3. University of Iowa	4.2
4. Southern Illinois University–Carbondale	4.0
4. Virginia Commonwealth University	4.0
6. George Washington University (DC)	3.8
6. Penn. State University University Park	3.8
6. University of Arizona	3.8
6. University of Kentucky	3.8
10. San Diego State University	3.7

REHABILITATION COUNSELING Continued

Rank School	Average assessment score (5.0=highest)
10. University of Wisconsin–Stout	3.7
10. Utah State University	3.7
13. Illinois Institute of Technology	3.5
13. University of Arkansas–Fayetteville	3.5
15. University of Northern Colorado	3.4
15. University of North Texas	3.4
15. University of Texas–Pan American	3.4
18. East Carolina University (NC)	3.3
18. Portland State University (OR)	3.3
18. University of Pittsburgh	3.3
21. University at Buffalo–SUNY	3.2
21. University of Memphis	3.2
21. University of North Carolina–Chapel Hill	3.2

Note: All schools listed have master's programs; some may not have doctoral programs.

SOCIAL WORK
MASTER'S Ranked in 2016

Rank School	Average assessment score (5.0=highest)
1. University of Michigan–Ann Arbor	4.5
2. Washington University in St. Louis	4.4
3. University of California–Berkeley	4.3
3. University of Chicago (IL)	4.3
3. University of Washington	4.3
6. Columbia University (NY)	4.2
7. University of North Carolina–Chapel Hill	4.1
7. University of Texas–Austin	4.1
9. Case Western Reserve University (OH)	4.0
10. Boston College (MA)	3.9
10. University of Pittsburgh (PA)	3.9
12. Boston University (MA)	3.8
12. University of California–Los Angeles	3.8
12. University of Pennsylvania	3.8
12. University of Southern California	3.8

Rank School	Average assessment score (5.0=highest)
12. University of Wisconsin–Madison	3.8
17. New York University	3.7
17. Ohio State University	3.7
17. University of Denver (CO)	3.7
17. Univ. of Illinois–Urbana-Champaign	3.7
17. University of Maryland–Baltimore	3.7
22. Fordham University (NY)	3.6
22. Rutgers University–New Brunswick (NJ)	3.6
22. Smith College (MA)	3.6
22. University of Kansas	3.6
22. Virginia Commonwealth University	3.6

SPEECH–LANGUAGE PATHOLOGY
MASTER'S Ranked in 2016

Rank School	Average assessment score (5.0=highest)
1. University of Iowa	4.5
1. Vanderbilt University (TN)	4.5
3. University of Washington	4.4
3. University of Wisconsin–Madison	4.4
5. Northwestern University (IL)	4.3
5. Purdue University–West Lafayette (IN)	4.3
7. MGH Institute of Health Professions (MA)	4.1
7. University of Arizona	4.1
7. University of Kansas	4.1
7. University of Pittsburgh (PA)	4.1
7. University of Texas–Austin	4.1
12. Boston University (MA)	4.0
12. Indiana University	4.0
12. University of North Carolina–Chapel Hill	4.0
12. University of Texas–Dallas	4.0
16. University of Minnesota–Twin Cities	3.9
17. Arizona State University	3.8
17. Ohio State University	3.8
17. Univ. of Illinois–Urbana-Champaign	3.8
20. Emerson College (MA)	3.7

Rank School	Average assessment score (5.0=highest)
20. Penn. State University–University Park	3.7
20. University of Maryland–College Park	3.7
20. University of Nebraska–Lincoln	3.7
24. Rush University Medical Center (IL)	3.6
24. San Diego State University (CA)	3.6
24. University of Colorado–Boulder	3.6
24. University of Memphis (TN)	3.6
28. Florida State University	3.5
28. University of Florida	3.5
30. Northeastern University (MA)	3.4
30. Syracuse University (NY)	3.4
30. Teachers College, Columbia Univ. (NY)	3.4
30. Temple University (PA)	3.4
30. University at Buffalo–SUNY (NY)	3.4
30. University of Connecticut	3.4
30. University of North Carolina–Greensboro	3.4
30. University of South Carolina	3.4
30. University of Utah	3.4

VETERINARY MEDICINE
DOCTOR OF VETERINARY MEDICINE Ranked in 2015

Rank School	Average assessment score (5.0=highest)
1. University of California–Davis	4.5
2. Cornell University (NY)	4.1
3. Colorado State University	3.9
3. North Carolina State University	3.9
5. Ohio State University	3.7
5. University of Wisconsin–Madison	3.7
7. Texas A&M University–College Station	3.6
7. University of Pennsylvania	3.6
9. University of Minnesota–Twin Cities	3.4
10. Tufts University (MA)	3.3
10. University of Georgia	3.3
12. Michigan State University	3.2
13. Iowa State University	3.1

METHODOLOGY

The health rankings are based solely on the results of peer assessment surveys sent to deans, other administrators, and/or faculty at accredited degree programs or schools in each discipline. Respondents rated the academic quality of programs on a 5-point scale: outstanding (5 points), strong (4), good (3), adequate (2), or marginal (1). They were instructed to select "don't know" if they did not have enough knowledge to rate a program.

Only fully accredited programs in good standing during the survey period are ranked. Those with the highest average scores appear.

In the fall of 2015, surveys were conducted for the 2016 rankings of doctor of pharmacy programs accredited by the Accreditation Council for Pharmacy Education (response rate: 40 percent); doctoral programs in clinical psychology accredited by the American Psychological Association (21 percent); graduate programs in occupational therapy accredited by the American Occupational Therapy Association (42 percent); audiology programs and speech-language pathology programs accredited by the American Speech-Language-Hearing Association (58 percent and 33 percent, respectively); physical therapy programs accredited by the Commission on Accreditation in Physical Therapy Education (39 percent); master of social work programs accredited by the Commission on Accreditation of the Council on Social Work Education (51 percent); graduate programs in nurse midwifery accredited by the Accreditation Commission for Midwifery Education (62 percent); and graduate programs in nurse anesthesia accredited by the Council on Accreditation of Nurse Anesthesia Educational Programs (54 percent).

In the fall of 2014, surveys were conducted for 2015 rankings of schools of public health accredited by the Council on Education for Public Health (response rate: 59 percent); health care management programs accredited by the Commission on Accreditation of Healthcare Management Education (57 percent); physician assistant programs accredited by the Accreditation Review Commission on Education for the Physician Assistant (50 percent); rehabilitation counselor education programs accredited by the Commission on Standards and Accreditation: Council on Rehabilitation Education (38 percent); and veterinary schools accredited by the American Veterinary Medical Association (49 percent).

Surveys for both sets of rankings were conducted by research firm Ipsos Public Affairs.

Law

IN A CLASS
ON CRIMINAL
LAW AT THE
UNIVERSITY OF
MICHIGAN LAW
SCHOOL

THE U.S. NEWS RANKINGS

Is It Time to Apply?

With the legal job market still uncertain, competition to get in has eased at many schools

BY MICHAEL MORELLA

Just a few weeks into law school at the University of California–Irvine, Nora Cassidy, 25, was already interviewing domestic violence survivors and helping them write legal declarations in an Orange County courthouse. Second semester, she researched and wrote legal memos about potential litigation for the American Civil Liberties Union of Southern California. Her first-year Legal Profession course featured weekly panels of practicing attorneys, while a Lawyering Skills class blended lessons in legal research and writing with practice in oral arguments, client interviews and negotiations.

Interested in a career in public service, Cassidy defended deportees in a second-year immigrant rights clinic, and as a third-year student, tackled employment discrimination during an externship at the Equal Employment Opportunity Commission in Washington, D.C. The sustained practical training helped Cassidy "directly apply what I was learning in the classroom," she says. After she

graduates, she has two judicial clerkships lined up.

That kind of hands-on approach is critical to getting the most out of law school (and finding work) in today's steadier but still uncertain legal job market. Since the Great Recession, law firms have shed thousands of attorneys. The latest data from the National Association for Law Placement showed that 86.7 percent of 2015 grads had secured jobs 10 months after graduation, the same as the class of 2014, which represented an uptick after six years of declines. But only slightly more than half of 2015 hires were in private practice, and just two-thirds of graduates found positions that required passage of a bar exam. "It's not all bad news," says Charlotte Wager, a partner and chief talent officer at Jenner & Block, a firm with more than 500 lawyers in five offices in the U.S. and London. But there are "a limited number of opportunities in private practice now, and that environment is very competitive."

The flip side of the coin is that this may be a good time to apply to law school. As the employment picture darkened, applications dropped sharply; they now seem to be stabilizing at about 40 percent below where they were a decade ago, according to the Law School Admission Council. Even many

extremely competitive top schools have seen fewer applicants and have accepted more of them in recent years, according to U.S. News data. And students are "not just getting in, but getting scholarship offers," says Rodia Vance, university pre-law advisor and associate director of the career center at Emory University. Meanwhile, many schools are rethinking their game so as to graduate the skilled, practice-ready lawyers that employers are demanding.

With these realities in mind, students should be "proactive in trying to figure out what it is that they need out of law school," says Michele Pistone, a professor of law at Villanova University's Charles Widger School of Law and co-author of a 2016 report by the Clayton Christensen Institute outlining how schools facing "dramatic declines in enrollment, revenue, and student quality" can adapt to an evolving legal industry. By carefully weighing your job prospects, looking closely at academic and experiential offerings, and coming up with a savvy payment – and loan repayment – strategy, you greatly increase the odds of finding the right path for you. Consider:

UNIVERSITY OF DENVER PROFESSOR ROBIN WALKER STERLING PLAYS THE JUDGE IN A CRIMINAL COURT SIMULATION.

WHAT DOES THE JOB MARKET LOOK LIKE LONG TERM?

The fact that the class of 2015, which totaled 39,980, was nearly 9 percent smaller than the 2014 crop has brought the output of new attorneys more even with the number of new openings. But even though the entry-level landscape has improved, significant questions remain. The "ongoing changes facing the industry make it all but certain that the job market will continue to change for new law school graduates in the years ahead," wrote James Leipold, executive director of NALP, in a 2016 report by the organization. The Clayton Christensen Institute and NALP point to such factors as technology that makes document review much more efficient and affordable, client belt-tightening, and increased competition from online legal services providers like LegalZoom and Rocket Lawyer as forces likely to, in Leipold's words, "put downward pressure on overall law firm lawyer headcount."

Median starting salaries have been ticking up since 2011 and are now at $64,800 for all jobs and $100,000 at law firms. But those figures are still down considerably from where they stood in 2009: $72,000 and $130,000. Notably, many of the nation's biggest firms made waves last summer when they increased starting salaries in major markets from $160,000 to $180,000, the first such bump in nearly a decade.

Government and public interest opportunities have stayed essentially flat, together accounting for about 1 in 5 entry-level jobs. "The competition is fierce," says Douglas Sylvester, dean of Arizona State University's Sandra Day O'Connor College of Law. Students who can demonstrate a track record of public service are best positioned for these slots, experts say. With median entry-level public sector salaries at only $52,000, anyone intent on taking this path needs "a real focus on keeping debt low," Sylvester says.

As it happens, prospective students have more information than ever before to help them get a sense of how particular law schools will affect their prospects. For starters, they can dig into the detailed reports that the American Bar Association now requires of schools at employmentsummary.abaquestionnaire.org. There, they can find a wide range of data about recent grads, such as how many are still unemployed, are in jobs that require a J.D., are in temporary or long-term positions, are working at private firms of different sizes, in clerkships or in government, or have taken positions funded by the law school.

Keep in mind, too, that location can make a big difference in terms of opportunities. At more than 80 percent of schools, at least half of 2015 grads who found positions landed in the state where they got their J.D. By attending a school where you want to practice, you get "three years to be building relationships with the local bar, establishing community roots, and that type of thing," says David Montoya, assistant dean for career services at the University of Texas School of Law. Make location "a key consideration," advises Vance, if you are not headed to one of the top schools with a national reputation "whose banners are going to carry from sea to shining sea."

These days, your eventual employability – and your attractiveness as a law school applicant, too – may be boosted by work experience after college, which indicates an extra level of maturity and skills. At the University of Michigan and New York University, for instance, more than 70 percent of the most recent entering classes had one or more years of experience. Before UC–Irvine, Nora Cassidy worked for a year as a grant writer at the Rhode Island Free Clinic in Providence, which she says strengthened her grounding in the nonprofit sector as well as her writing skills.

WHAT'S IMPORTANT IN A PROGRAM?

As new hires, "the faster people can get up to speed, the better," says Jane Aiken, associate dean for experiential education and vice dean at Georgetown University Law Center. Georgetown Law and many other schools have greatly expanded their real-world experiential learning opportunities, even during the first year, and are also giving students more chances to practice in mock legal disputes.

At Georgetown, first-year students can take one-week courses that have them simulating negotiations, client counseling, legal document drafting and resolving conflicts. Yale Law School allows 1Ls in their second semester to enroll in one of about two-dozen legal clinics that entail work

Help With Going Solo

Taking a page from the business school practice of nurturing startups in on-campus incubators, a growing number of law schools are establishing legal incubators to launch recent grads into solo or small-firm practice.

New attorneys get access to office space, business training and mentoring while they provide affordable legal services to needy clients in the community. It's sort of "a low-bono program," says Fred Rooney, who helped start the first legal incuba-

● ● ●

NORA CASSIDY SPENT PART OF HER THIRD YEAR WORKING AT THE EQUAL EMPLOYMENT OPPORTUNITY COMMISSION.

for actual clients – homeowners in foreclosure disputes, for example, or Connecticut veterans with legal needs. Yale also offers a number of business-oriented simulation courses in which students negotiate mock corporate merger agreements or work through intellectual property and financing issues that might affect tech startups.

At UC–Irvine, the University of Denver, Lewis & Clark Law School and the University of Maryland, tor at the CUNY School of Law in 2007. There are now more than 60 legal incubators, according to a 2016 American Bar Association survey. The economic downturn accelerated the growth, as recent grads struggled to find jobs. Now, says Rooney, "it's a national movement."

The law schools at Seattle University, Hofstra University, Loyola University New Orleans and the University of Missouri–Kansas City are among those that have established incubators. Last year, five Georgia law schools – Georgia State, Emory, John Marshall, Mercer and the University of Georgia – partnered with the state bar and the Supreme Court of Georgia to form a joint incubator in Atlanta where grads can benefit from shared resources. Select recent grads of Arizona State University's law school can join the ASU Alumni Law Group, a nonprofit firm where they "are like in-residence lawyers," says Dean Douglas Sylvester. Experienced attorneys run the firm "like a teaching hospital." The firm employs half a dozen recent grads for two-year stints, at between $42,500 and $47,500 yearly. Participants have served more than 800 clients in the Phoenix area, handling everything from family law to employment law to real-estate transactions.

Before starting her own firm in 2015, Mariana Karampelas spent a year in the incubator at Chicago-Kent College of Law, where she earned her J.D. in 2011. The program gave her training in marketing, accounting, malpractice insurance and other topics relevant to running a small firm, as well as a professional network. Says Karampelas: "The incubator took a lot of terror out" of striking out on her own. –M.M.

incoming students can connect with practicing attorneys who serve as academic and professional mentors. "We do everything we can to bring the bench and the bar into our building," says Viva Moffat, associate dean of academic affairs at Denver's Sturm College of Law, which recently retooled its curriculum to allow a full year's worth of hands-on opportunities over the course of law school. The possibilities range from externships at the Rocky Mountain Children's Law Center or the Denver City Attorney's Office to clinics offering service to real clients and skills-focused courses involving role-playing.

"We basically had to be lawyers and just think for the client," says Moayad Al-Suwaidan, 25, a second-year student at Northeastern University School of Law, recalling the required course his first year in which small "law offices" of about a dozen students tackle a public service project for a government agency or nonprofit. His group produced an advisory report for a public defender agency on the drug court process and the constitutional arguments for ensuring that defendants have adequate access to counsel.

In a range of teamwork and "lab" courses, Stanford Law students work alongside graduate students in other disciplines on multifaceted projects. Students in psychology, medicine and law might tackle an organ donation dispute together, say. Biology, African studies and law students might work on a wildlife trafficking assignment.

A number of schools, including the University of Dayton, the University of Kansas, Pepperdine and Brooklyn Law School, offer accelerated degree options. Students take courses in the summers and earn their degree in two years for the same tuition and credit requirements. The accelerated J.D. is "not an easier path, but it's a more user-friendly path," says Nick Allard, dean of Brooklyn Law School.

In its own flexible alternative, Mitchell Hamline School of Law offers a part-time, hybrid online/on-campus J.D. program in which students take courses remotely for about 12 weeks each semester and visit the Minnesota campus periodically for weeklong lawyering simulations. The hybrid four-year program costs the same ($29,320 annually) as the school's traditional part-time program and enrolls about a third of the student body. "We're trying to find a way to make [law school] more accessible," says Gregory Duhl, associate dean for strategic initiatives.

HOW CAN YOU SAVE MONEY?

Applicants can find detailed data on how many students receive scholarships and what the typical amounts are by examining a school's standard 509 report, which is available at www.abarequireddisclosures.org. (These reports also include stats on an institution's J.D. attrition, bar passage rates, and diversity.) Such information can be a useful tool in negotiating a financial aid package.

Attending a public law school, of course, can be a cost-effective move for in-state students. Tuition at the University of Iowa's law school, for example, runs about $23,700 for Iowans compared to the $45,500 average at private schools, while costs are roughly $22,800 in-state at the University of Alabama. Illinois native Christina Briggs, 28, was able to secure a scholarship to the University of Wisconsin Law School that cut her tuition payment to the roughly $21,450 in-state rate. A biology major in college, Briggs also found a position as a zoology teaching assistant for undergraduates, which eliminated her tuition costs for her second and third years and provided a monthly stipend. "Set a strict budget," Briggs advises, and "come up with creative solutions to reduce your costs."

Though attending a part-time law school program typically costs about the same overall as going full time, students can lower their annual costs by spreading them over four years; by working, they can reduce their overall debt load. "I know I could not have gone to school and not worked," says Paula Collins, 53, who is in her fourth year of the part-time J.D. program at Brooklyn Law School. The program costs about $35,600 on average annually compared to roughly $47,500 for the three-year option, and Collins helps offset the tab with her salary as a special education teacher.

Why I Picked

PEPPERDINE UNIVERSITY
Malibu, California

Jeffrey Majors, '13
OPERATIONS ATTORNEY

➤ Before law school, I served in the military and earned my master's in crisis and emergency management, where I learned how critical it was to solve problems before they deteriorate into conflicts. That's something Pepperdine, through its Straus Institute for Dispute Resolution, excels at teaching. Through Straus, Pepperdine trains future lawyers to be peacemakers, negotiators and problem solvers – rare and in-demand skills. Offerings range from negotiation to specialized courses in securities arbitration. Students can combine a J.D. with a certificate or a master's in dispute resolution. I chose the latter.

Pepperdine provides plenty of clinical experience, like the Investor Advocacy Clinic, where I argued cases for low-income investors against broker-dealers. Straus gave me a better understanding of how to manage disputes, reduce risk, and find leverage points in negotiations. I use these skills every day now as an operations attorney for Schlumberger, a global oilfield services company, to avoid crises before they occur and mitigate them when they arise.

The average indebtedness of 2015 graduates who had to borrow – as the vast majority of law students do – was about $92,700 for public school grads and $127,700 for those who chose private institutions, according to U.S. News data. With federal loans, graduates in lower-paying jobs can adjust monthly payments to a percentage of their income and increase the terms of repayment from 10 to 25 years, while those working in certain public interest or government positions can have their remaining loan balances forgiven after 10 years of steady payments. Students considering such programs should carefully research all the terms and verify whether a particular employer qualifies. You can make sure of that by completing an employer certification form from the Department of Education, which encourages borrowers to resubmit annually and whenever they change jobs.

Roughly half of the states and more than 100 law schools have established their own loan repayment assistance programs for grads in qualifying jobs. Caroline Jackson, 32, was impressed by Stanford Law School's LRAP, which she considered "retroactive financial aid" that would kick in after her 2011 graduation.

Stanford graduates who earn under $50,000 receive coverage for 100 percent of their loan payments for up to 10 years, and higher earners get partial contributions. Jackson, a staff attorney for the National Association of the Deaf in Silver Spring, Maryland, carried close to $250,000 in student loans from both college and law school; she receives between $25,000 and $28,000 each year from Stanford to help toward monthly loan payments of about $2,400.

Financial experts strongly advise borrowing only as much as you truly will need; limiting yourself to $20,000 instead of $25,000 in PLUS loans, say, would mean monthly bills of about $225 instead of $280 over the standard 10 years. That kind of strategizing upfront will feel really savvy when your payments come due. ●

The Job Market

SPOTLIGHT ON:

intellectual property law

Brendan Haberle
University of Arizona,
James E. Rogers College of Law, 2015

Guarding the Cutting Edge

After graduating with a B.S. in physics from Harvey Mudd College, Brendan Haberle worked on plasma research at the Los Alamos National Laboratory in New Mexico. But "doing basic science as a laboratory researcher just wasn't a good fit for me," says Haberle, who wanted to work in a range of scientific areas, not just one. After stints in consulting and developing intelligence systems for the U.S. Army, Haberle did some research and realized the fast-growing sector of intellectual property law offered the varied exposure to science and technology that he sought.

Helping startups grow. He headed to the University of Arizona's James E. Rogers College of Law and graduated in 2015. Hired as an IP attorney at a local Tucson firm, he assisted startups innovating in fields ranging from biotechnology to medical devices. Haberle relished his clients' "energy, optimism, and vibrancy," but as soon as a company took off, he says, the entrepreneurs moved to a larger firm that "could help them get to the next level." So a year later, Haberle joined the national full-service firm of Dinsmore & Shohl LLP in San Diego, which had a strong IP practice along with

the expertise in disciplines like tax and securities law needed to help startups grow.

A technical background and "the ability and desire to remain immersed in new technology" are essential for IP attorneys, says Haberle, 34, who continues to focus on biotechnology as well as the optics, electronics, automotive and other sectors. He engages extensively with clients to understand the technology behind each innovation, the "space" it will operate in, and the kinds of patent, copyright, trademark and other IP protections it will need, particularly if it's multiuse – for example, an optical device that has both medical and industrial applications.

The rapid pace of innovation is helping drive the need for IP attorneys. The U.S. Patent and Trademark Office reported that more than twice as many patents were granted in 2015 as a decade ago. Last year, roughly 15 percent of all jobs placed by BCG Attorney Search, one of the country's largest legal recruiting firms, were in intellectual property. While salaries vary widely across sectors, median annual pay for entry-level IP attorneys typically ranges from about $125,000 to $148,000, according to salary.com. *–By Peter Rathmell*

... ESTATE PLANNING/ ELDER LAW ATTORNEY

As more baby boomers retire, more lawyers are needed to advise clients on estate planning, probate administration and asset protection. Kaplan Test Prep's Law School Insider rates the practice, which also includes health care and family law, among the top-10 fastest-growing legal sectors. Average salary for associates is $82,000, according to indeed.com.

... CIVIL LITIGATION LAWYER

For 2016, staffing agency Robert Half Legal reported that up to a third of lawyers surveyed said that civil litigation would create the most law jobs. Legal news site Law360 attributes the growth to an increase in securities and class-action lawsuits, antitrust litigation by the Department of Justice and patent litigation, among other factors. According to payscale.com, the median salary for civil litigators is $90,647 per year.

... REAL ESTATE LAWYER

A booming housing market is spurring the need for real estate attorneys. Robert Half Legal estimates that real estate law firms, which navigate state and local zoning laws and negotiate contracts between buyers and sellers, will create 6 percent of new legal jobs over the next two years. These attorneys can expect to earn between about $117,000 and $150,000 annually, according to salary.com.

Schools of Law

THE TOP SCHOOLS

Rank School	Overall score	Peer assessment score (5.0=highest)	Assessment score by lawyers/ judges (5.0=highest)	'16 undergrad GPA 25th-75th percentile	'16 LSAT score 25th-75th percentile	'16 acceptance rate	'16 student/ faculty ratio	'15 grads employed at graduation[†]	Employed 10 months after graduation[†]	School's bar passage rate in jurisdiction	Jurisdiction's overall bar passage rate
1. Yale University (CT)	100	4.8	4.7	3.79-3.97	170-175	9%	6.8	84.5%	84.5%	97.1%/NY	68%
2. Stanford University (CA)	98	4.8	4.8	3.75-3.95	168-173	11%	7.3	88.2%	89.2%	87.5%/CA	57%
3. Harvard University (MA)	96	4.8	4.8	3.76-3.94	170-175	17%	11.6	87.3%	91.0%	97.2%/NY	68%
4. University of Chicago (IL)	94	4.6	4.6	3.73-3.95	166-172	21%	7.5	90.3%	90.8%	98.8%/IL	80%
5. Columbia University (NY)	93	4.6	4.6	3.56-3.81	168-174	20%	6.7	87.2%	89.6%	92.7%/NY	68%
6. New York University	90	4.5	4.4	3.65-3.89	166-171	30%	8.2	88.9%	90.3%	96.2%/NY	68%
7. University of Pennsylvania	88	4.3	4.4	3.57-3.95	163-170	17%	9.8	92.3%	93.9%	90.6%/NY	68%
8. University of Michigan–Ann Arbor	85	4.4	4.5	3.56-3.87	164-169	24%	10.2	83.1%	87.6%	95.0%/NY	68%
8. University of Virginia	85	4.4	4.5	3.48-3.94	164-170	20%	9.3	82.0%	87.2%	95.9%/NY	68%
10. Duke University (NC)	84	4.2	4.4	3.59-3.84	167-170	20%	8.3	88.0%	92.3%	87.0%/NY	68%
10. Northwestern University (Pritzker) (IL)	84	4.2	4.3	3.43-3.89	163-170	18%	6.4	79.5%	88.5%	90.7%/IL	80%
12. University of California–Berkeley	82	4.4	4.5	3.65-3.89	163-169	23%	13.8	80.2%	87.1%	85.1%/CA	57%
13. Cornell University (NY)	81	4.2	4.3	3.6-3.81	163-168	24%	9.2	86.9%	91.3%	95.4%/NY	68%
14. University of Texas–Austin	75	4.1	4.1	3.41-3.84	162-168	27%	8.9	65.0%	81.4%	88.3%/TX	72%
15. Georgetown University (DC)	74	4.1	4.3	3.52-3.86	162-168	26%	9.2	70.4%	75.4%	88.7%/NY	68%
15. University of California–Los Angeles	74	3.9	4.1	3.49-3.84	163-168	28%	10.6	61.8%	81.2%	85.1%/CA	57%
17. Vanderbilt University (TN)	73	3.9	4.1	3.5-3.85	162-168	32%	11.4	69.7%	83.2%	86.0%/TN	72%
18. Washington University in St. Louis (MO)	72	3.6	3.9	3.15-3.81	160-169	32%	9.3	61.1%	85.6%	93.6%/MO	87%
19. University of Southern California (Gould)	70	3.5	3.8	3.56-3.85	162-166	30%	11.3	69.5%	77.0%	87.2%/CA	57%
20. University of Iowa	67	3.4	3.6	3.44-3.79	157-163	46%	10.2	68.5%	84.9%	98.2%/IA	89%
20. University of Notre Dame (IN)	67	3.5	3.9	3.41-3.82	158-165	30%	10.6	60.9%	79.3%	96.2%/IL	80%
22. Emory University (GA)	66	3.5	3.8	3.4-3.87	157-166	37%	11.4	55.2%	81.8%	82.0%/GA	76%
23. Boston University (MA)	65	3.4	3.5	3.52-3.77	161-165	29%	11.1	56.7%	78.4%	91.4%/MA	77%
23. University of Minnesota	65	3.5	3.7	3.48-3.87	159-166	45%	8.8	64.8%	72.5%	86.4%/MN	81%
25. Arizona State University (O'Connor)	64	3.2	3.2	3.34-3.8	158-163	42%	10.8	66.8%	85.2%	84.8%/AZ	66%
26. Boston College (MA)	63	3.3	3.7	3.32-3.65	161-163	37%	10.4	66.4%	83.4%	88.7%/MA	77%
26. University of Alabama	63	3.2	3.2	3.45-3.92	157-165	31%	8.7	43.1%	81.3%	92.9%/AL	71%
28. University of California–Irvine	62	3.3	3.4	3.32-3.68	160-165	27%	6.8	55.5%	66.4%	80.6%/CA	57%
28. Washington and Lee University (VA)	62	3.1	3.7	3.16-3.67	155-161	47%	8.7	63.2%	81.6%	91.7%/VA	74%
30. George Washington University (DC)	61	3.4	3.7	3.35-3.81	158-166	39%	15.5	58.9%	76.6%	81.6%/NY	68%
30. Indiana University–Bloomington (Maurer)	61	3.3	3.6	3.36-3.82	153-163	42%	8.3	44.9%	78.8%	88.2%/IN	79%
30. Ohio State University (Moritz)	61	3.3	3.5	3.43-3.79	156-161	49%	10.3	55.7%	85.8%	90.3%/OH	78%
30. University of Georgia	61	3.2	3.4	3.47-3.86	158-163	30%	12.1	53.9%	83.2%	90.0%/GA	76%
30. University of Washington	61	3.2	3.4	3.43-3.8	157-165	27%	7.7	50.8%	77.0%	90.4%/WA	79%
30. University of Wisconsin–Madison	61	3.4	3.6	3.3-3.72	156-163	46%	7.7	48.9%	78.1%	100.0%/WI	77%
36. Fordham University (NY)	60	3.3	3.4	3.37-3.67	159-165	37%	11.0	56.3%	75.9%	84.7%/NY	68%
36. University of Colorado–Boulder	60	3.2	3.3	3.37-3.79	156-164	34%	10.0	53.5%	81.1%	87.6%/CO	76%
36. Wake Forest University (NC)	60	3.1	3.5	3.35-3.7	156-162	45%	10.4	45.7%	81.9%	81.9%/NC	65%
39. University of California–Davis	58	3.4	3.6	3.31-3.72	158-164	33%	10.2	49.2%	72.4%	74.2%/CA	57%
39. University of North Carolina–Chapel Hill	58	3.5	3.8	3.31-3.7	158-163	44%	11.3	47.0%	78.4%	82.9%/NC	65%
41. Col. of William and Mary (Marshall-Wythe) (VA)	57	3.2	3.6	3.49-3.88	157-164	41%	10.0	48.9%	75.8%	88.9%/VA	74%
41. George Mason University (VA)	57	2.7	3.1	3.32-3.73	158-164	26%	11.4	56.6%	83.6%	76.4%/VA	74%

For top schools and second tier: [†]Represents the percentage of all graduates who had a full-time job (not including those with jobs funded by their school or university) lasting at least a year for which bar passage was required or a J.D. degree was an advantage. These employment rates are part of the data on placement success used to determine a school's ranking. N/A=Data were not provided by the school. Numbers appearing with an * are from the fall 2016 entering class or school year and 2015 graduating class as reported to the American Bar Association. Concordia University in Idaho, Lincoln Memorial University in Tennessee, and Indiana Tech Law School are unranked because as of February 2017 they were only provisionally approved by the American Bar Association. Charlotte School of Law in North Carolina was unranked because it was on probation status as of February 2017. Also unranked are Inter-American University in Puerto Rico, University of Puerto Rico, and Pontifical Catholic University of Puerto Rico. The state bar examination pass rates for first-time test-takers in summer 2015 and winter 2016 were provided by the National Conference of Bar Examiners.
Sources: U.S. News and the schools. Assessment data collected by Ipsos Public Affairs.

● **More @ usnews.com/grad**

THE TOP SCHOOLS continued

Rank School	Overall score	Peer assessment score (5.0=highest)	Assessment score by lawyers/ judges (5.0=highest)	'16 undergrad GPA 25th-75th percentile	'16 LSAT score 25th-75th percentile	'16 acceptance rate	'16 student/ faculty ratio	'15 grads employed at graduation[†]	Employed 10 months after graduation[†]	School's bar passage rate in jurisdiction	Jurisdiction's overall bar passage rate
41. University of Florida (Levin)	57	3.1	3.4	3.33-3.77	156-161	36%	12.1	48.2%	81.5%	87.0%/FL	68%
44. University of Illinois–Urbana-Champaign	56	3.3	3.4	3.32-3.7	154-162	46%	11.0	51.4%	72.9%	86.8%/IL	80%
44. University of Utah (Quinney)	56	2.9	3.4	3.33-3.7	156-161	49%	7.3	54.8%	76.2%	81.4%/UT	79%
46. Brigham Young University (Clark) (UT)	55	2.9	3.3	3.55-3.89	157-164	44%	12.3	46.6%	65.4%	87.7%/UT	79%
46. Southern Methodist University (Dedman) (TX)	55	2.6	3.3	3.39-3.78	155-163	45%	13.3	58.6%	83.7%	84.5%/TX	72%
48. Florida State University	54	3.0	3.0	3.32-3.72	157-160	34%	10.4	42.9%	81.7%	80.0%/FL	68%
48. University of Arizona (Rogers)	54	3.1	3.2	3.19-3.75	155-163	34%	9.8	29.9%	69.4%	80.6%/AZ	66%
48. University of Maryland (Carey)	54	3.0	3.2	3.26-3.64	154-159	52%	10.0	59.0%	74.9%	76.0%/MD	65%
51. Baylor University (TX)	53	2.4	3.4	3.29-3.76	155-161	33%	10.8	45.4%	86.1%	81.1%/TX	72%
51. Tulane University (LA)	53	3.1	3.5	3.22-3.62	155-160	57%	11.8	50.6%	72.2%	75.7%/LA	68%
53. Temple University (Beasley) (PA)	52	2.7	3.1	3.2-3.7	156-162	42%	9.8	54.5%	75.5%	81.3%/PA	77%
54. University of California (Hastings)	50	3.1	3.6	3.18-3.64	156-161	47%	14.3	33.8%	65.6%	67.5%/CA	57%
54. University of Connecticut	50	2.8	3.0	3.08-3.62	154-158	47%	7.1	42.1%	80.3%	88.3%/CT	82%
54. University of Houston (TX)	50	2.7	3.0	3.24-3.68	156-162	32%	9.3	49.5%	77.7%	73.8%/TX	72%
57. Seton Hall University (NJ)	49	2.4	2.9	3.07-3.69	153-159	52%	11.2	72.2%	87.1%	87.5%/NJ	71%
57. University of Kentucky	49	2.6	3.2	3.24-3.74	151-157	66%	11.4	59.1%	92.1%	79.6%/KY	77%
57. University of Nebraska–Lincoln	49	2.5	2.9	3.41-3.91	154-159	57%	9.7	54.4%	84.0%	88.9%/NE	82%
57. University of Richmond (VA)	49	2.5	3.0	3.23-3.68	154-163	31%	7.7	39.0%	74.2%	79.6%/VA	74%
57. University of Tennessee–Knoxville	49	2.7	2.9	3.3-3.77	154-160	36%	7.2	37.5%	73.4%	85.3%/TN	72%
62. Case Western Reserve University (OH)	48	2.6	3.1	3.25-3.69	155-161	43%	9.3	34.0%	70.8%	84.3%/OH	78%
62. Rutgers, The State University of New Jersey	48	2.5	3.0	3.07-3.65	152-157	51%	8.6	59.1%	79.2%	74.0%/NJ	71%
62. University of Nevada–Las Vegas	48	2.5	2.6	3.21-3.71	153-159	34%	9.6	56.5%	77.1%	76.7%/NV	71%
65. Georgia State University	47	2.6	2.8	3.28-3.61	155-160	27%	8.6	41.7%	72.9%	75.7%/GA	76%
65. Loyola Marymount University (CA)	47	2.6	3.1	3.2-3.68	156-161	40%	12.8	33.1%	73.8%	77.2%/CA	57%
65. Northeastern University (MA)	47	2.4	2.8	3.3-3.69	154-163	38%	13.5	35.3%	74.3%	81.9%/MA	77%
65. Pennsylvania State U.–Carlisle (Dickinson)	47	2.0	2.9	3.07-3.71	156-160	36%	9.3	36.8%	70.2%	84.8%/PA	77%
65. University of Kansas	47	2.7	3.3	3.17-3.7	151-159	57%	12.2	40.0%	80.0%	96.0%/MO	87%
65. University of Missouri	47	2.6	3.0	3.17-3.72	153-160	55%	9.3	38.5%	77.7%	89.5%/MO	87%
65. Yeshiva University (Cardozo) (NY)	47	2.7	3.0	3.15-3.66	155-161	57%	12.8	47.0%	76.8%	78.1%/NY	68%
72. Pepperdine University (CA)	46	2.6	3.3	3.3-3.71	154-162	47%	11.3	28.4%	63.5%	68.9%/CA	57%
72. St. John's University (NY)	46	2.2	2.9	3.16-3.72	152-160	43%	12.9	44.8%	81.5%	81.3%/NY	68%
72. University of Cincinnati (OH)	46	2.4	3.0	3.24-3.76	153-158	53%	8.0	48.6%	80.7%	85.9%/OH	78%
72. University of Oklahoma	46	2.5	3.2	3.17-3.74	154-159	50%	13.8	38.7%	78.7%	90.9%/OK	75%
76. University of Denver (Sturm) (CO)	45	2.7	3.1	3.11-3.6	154-158	53%	8.4	37.6%	71.7%	83.6%/CO	76%
77. University of Arkansas–Fayetteville	44	2.4	2.7	3.19-3.71	151-157	54%	11.7	46.9%	83.8%	80.0%/AR	77%
77. University of Miami (FL)	44	2.7	3.1	3.17-3.59	155-160	58%	11.6	36.7%	71.2%	69.3%/FL	68%
77. University of New Mexico	44	2.3	2.9	3.2-3.67	150-157	43%	11.0	51.8%	81.3%	84.4%/NM	82%
77. University of San Diego (CA)	44	2.7	3.0	3.17-3.67	154-160	40%	9.9	37.7%	62.3%	70.2%/CA	57%
77. Villanova University (PA)	44	2.4	3.2	3.24-3.7	153-159	43%	13.6	46.0%	75.6%	86.4%/PA	77%
82. Loyola University Chicago (IL)	43	2.5	3.2	3.02-3.53	154-160	60%	11.4	43.7%	64.8%	79.4%/IL	80%
82. Pennsylvania State University–University Park	43	2.3	2.8	3.15-3.69	156-159	40%	9.4	31.6%	68.4%	84.6%/PA	77%
82. University of Pittsburgh (PA)	43	2.6	3.2	3.12-3.64	152-159	36%	8.4	34.2%	67.9%	77.9%/PA	77%
82. University of Tulsa (OK)	43	2.0	2.7	3.11-3.65	151-157	40%	9.3	45.7%	83.0%	78.3%/OK	75%
86. American University (Washington) (DC)	42	2.8	3.2	3.1-3.59	152-159	53%	12.0	45.7%	60.6%	58.9%/NY	68%
86. University of Oregon	42	2.8	3.1	3.2-3.64	154-159	54%	10.6	32.3%	63.7%	64.0%/OR	68%
88. Brooklyn Law School (NY)	41	2.5	2.8	3.12-3.55	154-159	49%	13.0	44.6%	73.2%	80.6%/NY	68%
88. Indiana University–Indianapolis (McKinney)	41	2.5	3.0	3.13-3.62	149-156	58%	15.4	40.9%	82.9%	79.5%/IN	79%
88. St. Louis University (MO)	41	2.3	2.9	3.13-3.62	151-158	64%	12.9	45.5%	78.2%	84.2%/MO	87%
88. University of South Carolina	41	2.4	2.9	3.17-3.64	151-157	58%	11.2	36.5%	73.9%	81.0%/SC	73%
92. Illinois Institute of Technology (Chicago-Kent)	40	2.4	2.6	3.05-3.6	151-158	64%	10.3	30.3%	66.1%	84.0%/IL	80%
92. Syracuse University (NY)	40	2.3	3.0	3.12-3.58	152-157	51%	9.2	42.9%	65.6%	85.6%/NY	68%
92. Texas A&M University	40	2.2	2.6	3.17-3.6	155-158	24%	8.4	25.1%	67.8%	75.2%/TX	72%
92. University of Louisville (Brandeis) (KY)	40	2.3	2.9	2.95-3.47	150-155	68%	8.7	40.6%	78.9%	84.8%/KY	77%

THE TOP SCHOOLS continued

Rank School	Overall score	Peer assessment score (5.0=highest)	Assessment score by lawyers/ judges (5.0=highest)	'16 undergrad GPA 25th-75th percentile	'16 LSAT score 25th-75th percentile	'16 acceptance rate	'16 student/ faculty ratio	'15 grads employed at graduation†	Employed 10 months after graduation†	School's bar passage rate in jurisdiction	Jurisdiction's overall bar passage rate
96. Louisiana State U.–Baton Rouge (Hebert)	39	2.2	3.0	3.08-3.66	152-158	60%	20.7	35.3%	80.7%	82.3%/LA	68%
96. Michigan State University	39	2.3	3.0	3.16-3.72	150-156	45%	13.4	28.2%	70.4%	79.9%/MI	72%
96. Stetson University (FL)	39	2.1	2.6	3.07-3.59	152-156	51%	12.8	43.5%	80.1%	72.6%/FL	68%
96. West Virginia University	39	2.2	2.7	3.06-3.6	151-156	60%	7.8	45.6%	80.0%	72.5%/WV	78%
100. Florida International University	38	1.8	1.7	3.16-3.78	151-157	29%	11.7	N/A	81.6%	87.1%/FL	68%
100. Lewis & Clark College (Northwestern) (OR)	38	2.4	3.1	3.05-3.62	154-161	59%	11.5	30.3%	61.7%	68.9%/OR	68%
100. Marquette University (WI)	38	2.3	3.0	3.08-3.54	149-156	66%	15.0	39.7%	76.0%	100.0%/WI	77%
100. University of Hawaii–Manoa (Richardson)	38	2.5	2.7	2.89-3.6	150-156	44%	7.6	38.4%	63.4%	78.6%/HI	76%
100. University of New Hampshire School of Law	38	2.0	2.6	3.06-3.68	154-159	52%	10.0	38.6%	67.1%	76.7%/NH	70%
100. Wayne State University (MI)	38	1.9	2.7	3.31-3.67	152-159	54%	9.9	34.8%	68.9%	80.7%/MI	72%
106. The Catholic University of America (DC)	37	2.2	2.9	3.1-3.49	150-155	51%	10.5	52.1%	70.4%	50.0%/MD	65%
106. Drake University (IA)	37	1.9	2.8	3-3.62	150-156	63%	10.5	41.9%	80.3%	85.9%/IA	89%
106. University at Buffalo–SUNY (NY)	37	2.2	2.7	3.13-3.7	150-157	51%	13.5	30.7%	72.9%	71.7%/NY	68%
109. Albany Law School (NY)	36	2.0	2.5	3.01-3.55	149-154	57%	9.7	46.4%	78.7%	67.8%/NY	68%
109. University of Idaho	36	2.1	2.7	2.87-3.55	148-154	55%	9.2	N/A	81.7%	66.2%/ID	72%
109. University of Mississippi	36	2.2	2.7	3.18-3.61	150-157	45%	11.0	22.0%	66.7%	84.0%/MS	84%
112. Drexel University (Kline) (PA)	35	2.1	2.4	3.04-3.56	152-156	52%	9.8	26.6%	78.9%	80.2%/PA	77%
112. Gonzaga University (WA)	35	2.1	3.0	3.01-3.42	151-155	57%	15.0	26.4%	69.4%	84.4%/WA	79%
112. New York Law School	35	1.9	2.5	3.02-3.54	149-155	56%	14.0	36.9%	68.8%	59.1%/NY	68%
112. University of Baltimore (MD)	35	2.1	2.5	2.82-3.47	149-155	58%	11.1	51.7%	74.2%	66.1%/MD	65%
112. University of Missouri–Kansas City	35	2.2	2.5	3.08-3.64	149-154	54%	9.7	21.3%	77.3%	84.8%/MO	87%
112. University of Wyoming	35	2.1	2.6	3.25-3.65	150-157	58%	9.9	38.4%	69.9%	73.7%/WY	77%
118. Hofstra University (Deane) (NY)	34	2.3	2.7	3.09-3.6	146-154	55%	14.4	31.2%	72.4%	66.4%/NY	68%
118. Texas Tech University	34	1.9	2.9	3.03-3.56	151-156	53%	12.4	34.6%	73.5%	81.7%/TX	72%
120. Creighton University (NE)	33	2.0	3.0	3.02-3.55	149-155	76%	11.3	35.5%	73.6%	74.6%/NE	82%
120. DePaul University (IL)	33	2.3	2.9	2.81-3.38	149-154	69%	13.1	34.6%	68.9%	81.4%/IL	80%
120. Howard University (DC)	33	2.4	2.9	2.98-3.46	148-153	39%	10.1	45.8%	60.2%	59.3%/MD	65%
120. Pace University (NY)	33	1.9	2.2	2.99-3.57	148-153	56%	12.5	N/A	74.8%	70.4%/NY	68%
120. Seattle University (WA)	33	2.4	2.7	3.11-3.54	151-158	64%	10.6	N/A	53.9%	75.7%/WA	79%
120. University of Montana	33	2.1	2.6	3.04-3.65	151-158	59%	13.1	51.2%	75.6%	67.5%/MT	70%
120. University of St. Thomas (MN)	33	1.8	2.6	3.15-3.62	149-156	71%	12.6	37.0%	77.5%	81.5%/MN	81%
127. Cleveland State U. (Cleveland-Marshall) (OH)	32	1.8	2.4	3.04-3.54	151-155	55%	8.4	33.0%	66.1%	83.0%/OH	78%
127. CUNY (NY)	32	2.2	2.4	2.96-3.57	149-155	46%	10.4	N/A	64.0%	81.1%/NY	68%
127. Duquesne University (PA)	32	1.8	2.6	3.14-3.64	150-155	61%	11.4	40.7%	65.5%	75.5%/PA	77%
127. Quinnipiac University (CT)	32	1.9	2.4	3.09-3.67	149-155	53%	10.6	24.8%	70.8%	89.4%/CT	82%
127. Washburn University (KS)	32	1.9	2.7	2.88-3.71	149-155	61%	9.9	44.2%	70.0%	73.1%/KS	82%
132. Santa Clara University (CA)	31	2.4	2.9	2.93-3.41	151-157	70%	10.4	28.3%	53.9%	68.3%/CA	57%
132. University of Toledo (OH)	31	1.8	2.1	3-3.68	149-155	57%	9.1	38.1%	65.7%	67.6%/OH	78%
134. Chapman University (Fowler) (CA)	29	1.9	1.9	3.03-3.48	152-157	50%	10.3	29.5%	64.4%	71.4%/CA	57%
134. Mercer University (George) (GA)	29	2.0	2.5	3-3.52	149-153	59%	12.2	27.8%	70.4%	74.5%/GA	76%
134. University of Akron (OH)	29	1.8	2.3	3.02-3.54	149-155	51%	14.1	30.3%	63.4%	85.1%/OH	78%
134. University of Arkansas–Little Rock (Bowen)	29	2.2	2.5	3-3.5	147-155	62%	15.0	14.3%	71.4%	76.3%/AR	77%
134. Vermont Law School	29	2.2	2.8	2.77-3.5	145-156	81%	16.8	27.8%	66.0%	76.0%/NY	68%
139. University of Maine	28	2.3	2.7	2.96-3.46	147-155	66%	10.2	35.1%	58.4%	66.7%/ME	69%
140. Suffolk University (MA)	27	2.0	2.6	2.97-3.53	146-154	64%	14.6	29.7%	64.2%	73.0%/MA	77%
140. University of Memphis (Humphreys) (TN)	27	1.9	2.3	3.01-3.54	149-154	55%	12.4	N/A	67.6%	74.7%/TN	72%
142. Loyola University New Orleans (LA)	26	2.1	3.0	2.9-3.41	146-152	85%	9.9	23.0%	52.5%	71.2%/LA	68%
142. University of North Dakota	26	2.0	2.4	2.96-3.62	146-152	64%	13.6	N/A	60.8%	76.5%/ND	80%
142. University of South Dakota	26	1.9	2.3	3.04-3.66	144-152	60%	13.5	52.5%	73.8%	57.6%/SD	70%
142. University of the Pacific (McGeorge) (CA)	26	1.9	2.4	2.95-3.44	149-155	61%	10.4	29.4%	58.8%	69.0%/CA	57%
142. Willamette University (Collins) (OR)	26	2.0	2.5	2.77-3.57	148-155	74%	8.7	28.2%	63.1%	65.1%/OR	68%
147. Samford University (Cumberland) (AL)	25	1.7	2.3	2.92-3.59	149-155	68%	15.7	33.9%	70.5%	77.8%/AL	71%
148. Northern Illinois University	24	1.7	2.3	2.79-3.33	145-151	61%	11.2	N/A	74.3%	73.6%/IL	80%
148. Widener University (Commonwealth) (PA)	24	1.6	1.9	2.87-3.45	145-150	68%	10.8	26.9%	65.4%	74.6%/PA	77%

Other Schools to Consider

The country's other law schools can be considered broadly similar in quality. To be included in the ranking, a law school had to be accredited and fully approved by the American Bar Association, and it had to draw most of its students from the United States.

Remember, as you weigh your options, that you should look not only at a law school's position in the ranking, but also at its many other key characteristics, both tangible and intangible – location, the cost of spending three years there, faculty expertise, and the breadth of the course offerings, to name a few – and certainly your prospects of being offered a job upon graduation. More information on all of the law schools is available in the directory at the back of the book as well as at usnews.com/lawschools.

SCHOOLS RANKED 150 THROUGH 197 ARE LISTED ALPHABETICALLY

School	Peer assessment score (5.0=highest)	Assessment score by lawyers/ judges (5.0=highest)	'16 undergrad GPA 25th-75th percentile	'16 LSAT score 25th-75th percentile	'16 acceptance rate	'16 student/ faculty ratio	'15 grads employed at graduation[1]	Employed 10 months after graduation[1]	School's bar passage rate in jurisdiction	Jurisdiction's overall bar passage rate
Appalachian School of Law (VA)	1.2	1.5	2.6-3.1	140-147	28%	N/A	N/A	56.7%	63.2%/VA	74%
Arizona Summit Law School[1]	1.1	1.3	2.55-3.31*	140-148*	64%*	N/A	N/A	52.7%*	41.6%/AZ*	66%
Atlanta's John Marshall Law School[1] (GA)	1.4	1.8	2.7-3.3*	145-149*	54%*	N/A	N/A	56.0%*	50.5%/GA*	76%
Ave Maria School of Law (FL)	1.2	1.6	2.84-3.38	143-151	54%	13.7	N/A	47.7%	55.6%/FL	68%
Barry University (FL)	1.2	1.3	2.62-3.31	146-151	57%	N/A	N/A	48.7%	50.5%/FL	68%
Belmont University (TN)	1.3	2.0	3.19-3.67	152-158	60%	12.1	31.8%	69.3%	92.9%/TN	72%
California Western School of Law	1.6	1.8	2.8-3.4	146-152	70%	16.0	N/A	57.6%	58.9%/CA	57%
Campbell University (NC)	1.5	2.4	2.94-3.55	150-156	60%	13.6	18.6%	62.1%	77.7%/NC	65%
Capital University (OH)	1.5	1.9	2.85-3.5	144-152	79%	11.9	29.7%	54.1%	71.4%/OH	78%
Charleston School of Law (SC)	1.3	1.9	2.7-3.31	141-149	78%	18.4	N/A	53.4%	62.5%/SC	73%
Elon University (NC)	1.6	2.3	2.92-3.48	145-152	45%	9.0	16.9%	54.5%	71.4%/NC	65%
Faulkner University (Jones) (AL)	1.3	1.3	2.5-3.44	142-148	N/A	12.7	46.3%	75.8%	68.3%/AL	71%
Florida A&M University	1.4	1.5	2.76-3.32	144-148	51%	11.0	8.8%	50.3%	66.4%/FL	68%
Florida Coastal School of Law	1.2	1.6	2.57-3.27	141-149	59%	18.1	N/A	41.3%	61.6%/FL	68%
Golden Gate University (CA)	1.6	1.8	2.56-3.33	146-152	64%	10.4	N/A	41.1%	38.9%/CA	57%
The John Marshall Law School (IL)	1.7	2.5	2.79-3.37	145-151	65%	14.2	36.0%	64.6%	76.2%/IL	80%
Liberty University (VA)	1.2	1.5	2.9-3.8	150-155	51%	8.0	4.9%	52.5%	87.5%/VA	74%
Mississippi College	1.5	1.8	2.75-3.34	144-149	64%	15.4	11.5%	76.9%	83.2%/MS	84%
Mitchell Hamline School of Law (MN)	1.7	2.2	2.94-3.49	145-154	73%	18.9	17.9%	68.8%	78.7%/MN	81%
New England Law Boston (MA)	1.5	1.9	2.85-3.49	146-153	68%	N/A	N/A	60.9%	67.9%/MA	77%
North Carolina Central University	1.5	2.2	3.04-3.53	141-149	52%	13.3	N/A	43.9%	63.1%/NC	65%
Northern Kentucky University (Chase)	1.6	2.0	2.96-3.49	145-151	78%	13.7	N/A	63.8%	62.9%/KY	77%
Nova Southeastern University (Broad) (FL)	1.6	1.8	2.89-3.36	146-152	49%	13.7	14.0%	64.0%	65.1%/FL	68%
Ohio Northern University (Pettit)	1.5	2.2	2.98-3.61	143-152	59%	9.3	N/A	50.8%	68.4%/OH	78%
Oklahoma City University	1.5	2.1	2.7-3.4	144-151	64%	13.8	N/A	73.9%	60.2%/OK	75%
Regent University (VA)	1.2	1.5	3.08-3.66	149-154	44%	10.1	21.2%	65.3%	80.3%/VA	74%
Roger Williams University (RI)	1.7	2.3	2.83-3.47	145-153	69%	15.1	N/A	66.9%	80.0%/MA	77%
South Texas College of Law Houston	1.6	2.3	2.82-3.34	148-154	58%	18.6	N/A	62.5%	70.6%/TX	72%
Southern Illinois University–Carbondale	1.7	2.4	2.55-3.27	145-150	70%	12.0	N/A	64.6%	67.2%/IL	80%
Southern University Law Center (LA)	1.4	2.0	2.52-3.16	141-146	66%	14.0	N/A	53.6%	53.2%/LA	68%
Southwestern Law School (CA)	1.9	2.1	3-3.46	149-155	52%	13.0	11.6%	48.2%	50.6%/CA	57%
St. Mary's University (TX)	1.6	2.2	2.68-3.34	147-152	65%	11.2	25.5%	61.6%	61.1%/TX	72%
St. Thomas University[1] (FL)	1.4	1.7	2.72-3.3*	144-151*	60%*	N/A	N/A	50.9%*	55.6%/FL*	68%
Texas Southern University (Marshall)[1]	1.5	1.7	2.78-3.38*	142-147*	47%*	N/A	N/A	42.9%*	58.0%/TX*	72%
Thomas Jefferson School of Law (CA)	1.3	1.6	2.63-3.14	141-147	83%	12.1	6.6%	39.4%	46.8%/CA	57%
Touro College (Fuchsberg) (NY)	1.5	1.8	2.73-3.35	146-150	50%	17.0	N/A	60.4%	54.9%/NY	68%
University of Dayton (OH)	1.7	2.6	2.83-3.41	145-152	60%	16.1	16.1%	63.4%	71.7%/OH	78%
University of Detroit Mercy (MI)	1.5	2.1	2.95-3.44	147-155	57%	13.2	N/A	51.4%	64.3%/MI	72%
University of La Verne[1] (CA)	1.2	1.3	2.68-3.21*	144-149*	52%*	N/A	N/A	51.3%*	56.4%/CA*	57%
University of Massachusetts–Dartmouth	1.5	2.5	2.81-3.36	146-152	60%	9.6	N/A	53.4%	53.7%/MA	77%
University of San Francisco (CA)	2.0	2.8	2.78-3.37	148-154	63%	11.7	27.7%	49.4%	46.4%/CA	57%
University of the District of Columbia (Clarke)	1.5	1.6	2.59-3.22	145-150	40%	8.5	32.4%	50.0%	44.0%/MD	65%
Valparaiso University (IN)	1.6	2.7	2.66-3.36	145-151	58%	13.3	55.7%	55.7%	65.5%/IN	79%
Western Michigan U. Thomas M. Cooley Law Sch.	1.2	1.7	2.6-3.2	138-147	86%	N/A	N/A	41.9%	59.7%/MI	72%
Western New England University (MA)	1.4	1.8	2.68-3.45	146-150	55%	10.0	N/A	55.6%	71.2%/CT	82%
Western State Col. of Law at Argosy U. (CA)	1.2	1.3	2.81-3.26	145-151	59%	15.4	N/A	50.9%	50.5%/CA	57%
Whittier College (CA)	1.4	1.9	2.62-3.09	144-149	66%	10.8	N/A	42.6%	37.1%/CA	57%
Widener University Delaware	1.7	2.1	2.8-3.33	146-150	64%	12.5	25.9%	57.6%	80.6%/PA	77%

Note: Key to footnotes, Page 72.

GEORGETOWN UNIVERSITY, TIED AT NO. 15

BRETT ZIEGLER FOR USN&WR

SPECIALTIES
PROGRAMS RANKED BEST BY FACULTY WHO TEACH IN THE FIELD

CLINICAL TRAINING
1. Georgetown University (DC)
2. American U. (Washington) (DC)
3. CUNY (NY)
4. New York University
5. Yale University (CT)
6. University of the District of Columbia (Clarke)
7. University of Maryland (Carey)
8. Washington University in St. Louis (MO)
9. University of Michigan–Ann Arbor
10. Stanford University (CA)
11. Northwestern U. (Pritzker) (IL)
12. University of Baltimore (MD)
13. University of Denver (Sturm) (CO)
14. University of New Mexico
15. University of California–Irvine
16. University of California–Berkeley
17. Suffolk University (MA)
18. Seattle University (WA)

DISPUTE RESOLUTION
1. Pepperdine University (CA)
2. Ohio State University (Moritz)
3. Harvard University (MA)
3. University of Missouri
5. Mitchell Hamline School of Law (MN)
6. University of Oregon
7. Marquette University (WI)
8. Yeshiva University (Cardozo) (NY)
9. University of Nevada–Las Vegas
10. Arizona State University (O'Connor)
11. Northwestern U. (Pritzker) (IL)
12. University of California (Hastings)

ENVIRONMENTAL LAW
1. Vermont Law School
2. Lewis & Clark College (Northwestern) (OR)

3. Pace University (NY)
4. University of California–Berkeley
5. University of California–Los Angeles
6. Georgetown University (DC)
6. University of Colorado–Boulder
8. Duke University (NC)
9. University of Utah (Quinney)
10. New York University
11. Harvard University (MA)
12. George Washington University (DC)
12. University of Oregon
14. Florida State University
14. University of Maryland (Carey)

HEALTH LAW
1. St. Louis University (MO)
2. University of Maryland (Carey)
3. Boston University (MA)
3. University of Houston (TX)
5. Harvard University (MA)
6. Loyola University Chicago (IL)
7. Georgia State University
8. Georgetown University (DC)
9. Case Western Reserve University (OH)
10. Seton Hall University (NJ)
11. Mitchell Hamline School of Law (MN)
12. Indiana University–Indianapolis (McKinney)

INTELLECTUAL PROPERTY LAW
1. University of California–Berkeley
2. Stanford University (CA)
3. New York University
4. George Washington University (DC)
4. Santa Clara University (CA)
6. University of New Hampshire School of Law
7. Texas A&M University
8. University of Houston (TX)
9. Boston University (MA)

10. University of Washington
11. American U. (Washington) (DC)
12. Duke University (NC)
12. University of Pennsylvania
12. Yeshiva University (Cardozo) (NY)
15. Georgetown University (DC)
16. Harvard University (MA)
17. Columbia University (NY)
17. University of California–Irvine

INTERNATIONAL LAW
1. New York University
2. Georgetown University (DC)
3. Harvard University (MA)
4. Columbia University (NY)
5. Yale University (CT)
6. University of Michigan–Ann Arbor
7. George Washington University (DC)
8. American U. (Washington) (DC)
9. University of California–Berkeley
10. Duke University (NC)
11. University of Virginia
12. Case Western Reserve University (OH)
12. Temple University (Beasley) (PA)
14. Fordham University (NY)
14. Stanford University (CA)
14. University of California–Los Angeles

LEGAL WRITING
1. Seattle University (WA)
2. University of Nevada–Las Vegas
3. University of Oregon
4. Stetson University (FL)
5. The John Marshall Law School (IL)
6. Arizona State University (O'Connor)
6. Suffolk University (MA)
8. University of Denver (Sturm) (CO)
9. Mercer University (George) (GA)
10. Marquette University (WI)
11. Ohio State University (Moritz)

12. Lewis & Clark College (Northwestern) (OR)
13. Georgetown University (DC)
13. Temple University (Beasley) (PA)
15. Indiana University–Indianapolis (McKinney)
15. Northwestern U. (Pritzker) (IL)
15. Washburn University (KS)

TAX LAW
1. New York University
2. Georgetown University (DC)
3. University of Florida (Levin)
4. Northwestern U. (Pritzker) (IL)
5. University of Virginia
6. Loyola Marymount University (CA)
7. University of California–Los Angeles
8. Boston University (MA)
8. Harvard University (MA)
10. Columbia University (NY)
11. University of San Diego (CA)
12. University of Miami (FL)
12. University of Texas–Austin

TRIAL ADVOCACY
1. Stetson University (FL)
2. Temple University (Beasley) (PA)
3. Baylor University (TX)
4. American U. (Washington) (DC)
4. Illinois Institute of Technology (Chicago-Kent)
6. Georgetown University (DC)
6. Loyola Marymount University (CA)
6. Loyola University Chicago (IL)
6. Samford University (Cumberland) (AL)
10. University of the Pacific (McGeorge) (CA)
11. South Texas College of Law Houston
11. University of Denver (Sturm) (CO)
13. The John Marshall Law School (IL)
13. Northwestern U. (Pritzker) (IL)

METHODOLOGY

Our annual rankings of 197 accredited law schools are based on a weighted average of 12 factors, described below. With rare exception, a law school official at each school – in many cases the dean – verified the data submitted on the U.S. News statistical survey.

Quality assessment: Quality was measured by two surveys conducted in the fall of 2016. The dean and three faculty members at each school were asked to rate schools from marginal (1) to outstanding (5); 66 percent voted. Their average rating is weighted by .25 in the overall ranking. Lawyers, recruiters and judges whose names were provided by the law schools also rated schools. Their three most recent years of responses were averaged and weighted by .15.

Selectivity (weighted at .25): This measure combines the following fall 2016 data for all full-time and part-time entering J.D. students: median LSAT and (for the first time) GRE scores (50 percent of this indicator), median undergrad GPA (40 percent), and the acceptance rate (10 percent).

Placement success (.20): Success is determined by calculating employment rates for 2015 grads at graduation (20 percent) and 10 months after (70 percent) as well as their bar passage rate (10 percent). For ranking purposes only, the placement measure was calculated by assigning various weights to the number of grads employed in up to 45 different types and durations of jobs as defined by the American Bar Association. Full weight was given for graduates who had a full-time job not funded by their school lasting at least a year for which bar passage was required or a J.D. degree was an advantage; less weight went to full-time long-term jobs that were professional or nonprofessional and did not require bar passage, to pursuit of an additional advanced degree, and to positions whose start dates were deferred. The least weight was applied to jobs categorized as part-time and short-term. (Employment rates published in the tables reflect all full-time jobs not school or university funded lasting at least a year for which bar passage was required or a J.D. degree was an advantage). U.S. News continues to not fully weight all jobs that were funded by the law school or university (compared to nonschool funded jobs) even if the positions were full-time, lasted at least a year, and required bar passage or were jobs for which a J.D. was a benefit. All other types of school-funded jobs were further discounted compared to nonschool-funded jobs. The bar passage indicator is the ratio of a school's pass rate in the cited jurisdiction to the overall state rate for first-time test-takers in summer and winter 2015. The jurisdiction is the state where the largest number of 2015 grads first took the test.

Faculty resources (.15): Resources are based on average fiscal year 2015 and 2016 expenditures per student for instruction, library and supporting services (65 percent), and on all other items, including financial aid (10 percent). Also: 2016 student/teacher ratio (20 percent) and total number of volumes and titles in the library (5 percent).

Overall rank: Scores on each indicator were standardized about their means. Then scores were weighted, totaled and rescaled so that the top school received 100 and other schools received a percentage of the top score.

Specialty rankings: Results are based solely on votes by faculty who were surveyed in the fall of 2016 and asked to identify up to 15 top schools in the particular field. Names of those surveyed were supplied by the law schools. Those with the most votes were ranked. Half of schools receiving a statistically significant number of votes appear.

Best Part-Time J.D. Programs

Data from the American Bar Association show that 13,736 students – about 12.3 percent of the country's 111,327 J.D. students – were enrolled part-time during the 2016-2017 academic year. For many working adults, part-time study is the only way to afford a law degree and still meet other commitments. Fewer than half of the country's law schools offer these programs, which generally require four years to complete. Below, U.S. News presents the top half of accredited law schools offering a part-time pathway. The ranking is based on four factors as described in the methodology below: reputation among deans and faculty at peer schools, LSAT scores and undergraduate GPAs of students entering in the fall of 2016, and the breadth of each school's part-time program.

THE TOP PART-TIME PROGRAMS

Rank School	Overall score	Peer assessment score (5.0=highest)	'16 part-time LSAT score 25th-75th percentile	'16 part-time acceptance rate	'16 part-time enrollment
1. Georgetown University (DC)	100	4.2	157-168	5.8%	242
2. George Washington University (DC)	80	3.6	152-163	23.6%	209
3. Fordham University (NY)	76	3.3	156-164	28.2%	169
4. George Mason University (VA)	66	2.8	157-163	14.4%	153
4. University of Maryland (Carey)	66	3.0	154-161	33.2%	112
6. American University (Washington) (DC)	62	2.9	151-158	47.2%	242
6. Temple University (Beasley) (PA)	62	2.8	155-161	34.9%	153
6. University of Houston (TX)	62	2.8	152-159	15.0%	100
9. Loyola Marymount University (CA)	59	2.7	155-160	26.3%	167
10. University of Denver (Sturm) (CO)	58	2.8	152-158	52.9%	107
11. Georgia State University	57	2.6	153-158	21.0%	179
11. Lewis & Clark College (Northwestern) (OR)	57	2.5	149-160	54.3%	132
11. University of Connecticut	57	2.7	152-158	33.1%	104
14. Loyola University Chicago (IL)	56	2.6	151-160	40.0%	86
14. University of San Diego (CA)	56	2.7	152-160	33.1%	98
16. Brooklyn Law School (NY)	53	2.6	153-159	26.4%	284
16. Rutgers, The State University of New Jersey	53	2.5	150-157	33.1%	237
16. Texas A&M University	53	2.2	156-161	11.4%	129
19. University of Nevada–Las Vegas	52	2.5	152-157	27.8%	93
19. Yeshiva University (Cardozo) (NY)	52	2.7	151-157	52.3%	78
21. Seattle University (WA)	50	2.5	150-159	52.9%	134
22. Illinois Institute of Technology (Chicago-Kent)	49	2.6	150-158	51.1%	131
22. Seton Hall University (NJ)	49	2.4	147-157	44.6%	156
24. New York Law School	46	2.2	148-152	40.5%	242
24. St. Louis University (MO)	46	2.3	150-154	40.4%	69
24. Stetson University (FL)	46	2.1	150-157	39.6%	133
24. Suffolk University (MA)	46	2.2	147-155	57.0%	346
24. The Catholic University of America (DC)	46	2.3	151-157	46.7%	119
29. DePaul University (IL)	45	2.3	149-153	50.8%	141
29. University of Baltimore (MD)	45	2.1	147-154	46.0%	247
29. University of Hawaii–Manoa (Richardson)	45	2.4	151-155	40.4%	65
32. Indiana University–Indianapolis (McKinney)	44	2.5	149-156	72.1%	240
32. Santa Clara University (CA)	44	2.4	152-164	44.6%	121
34. University of the Pacific (McGeorge) (CA)	43	2.0	147-155	69.9%	115
34. Wayne State University (MI)	43	1.9	153-161	40.6%	49
36. St. John's University (NY)	42	2.2	148-157	32.6%	114
37. Florida International University	41	1.8	148-156	22.3%	86
38. Chapman University (Fowler) (CA)	40	1.9	156-159	21.6%	26
38. Michigan State University	40	2.5	144-153	54.5%	82
38. Mitchell Hamline School of Law (MN)	40	2.0	145-154	60.4%	510
38. Southwestern Law School (CA)	40	1.9	149-154	39.2%	258
38. University of Arkansas–Little Rock (Bowen)	40	2.1	145-156	22.5%	101

METHODOLOGY

The ranking of 81 part-time law programs is based on a weighted average of four measures of quality. For a school's program to be eligible for the part-time ranking, it had to have reported at least 20 part-time students enrolled in the fall of 2016, supplied data on fall 2016 applications and acceptances to its part-time program, and still have an active part-time program for fall 2017.

Quality assessment (weighted by .50): In the fall of 2016, deans and three faculty members at each school were asked to rate programs from marginal (1) to outstanding (5); 59 percent responded, and scores for each school were averaged.

Selectivity (.275): For part-time students entering in 2016, this measure combines median LSAT scores (81.8 percent of this indicator) and undergraduate GPAs (18.2 percent).

Part-time focus (.225): An index was created from data reported by the schools about their 2016 part-time J.D. programs. Factors used in the creation of this index include the size of part-time first-year sections; the size of part-time first-year small sections; and the number of positions filled by part-time students in seminars, simulation courses, field placements, law journals, interschool skills competitions and independent study. Schools received credit for reporting data and additional credit for surpassing a threshold value in the various factors used.

Overall rank: Schools' scores on each indicator were standardized, weighted, totaled and rescaled so that the top school received 100, and other schools received a percentage of the top score.

Note: The data listed for acceptance rate and enrollment are for informational purposes only and are not used in the computation of the part-time J.D. program ranking. Only part-time J.D. programs ranked in the top half appear. Sources: U.S. News and the schools. Assessment data collected by Ipsos Public Affairs.

CHAPTER 4

Business

TAKING ADVANTAGE OF QUIET TIME AT THE UNIVERSITY OF PENNSYLVANIA'S WHARTON SCHOOL

THE U.S. NEWS RANKINGS

Good Business

Want to change the world? Many B schools now are teaching MBA students how to have a social impact

BY ELIZABETH GARDNER

Sarah Millar spent her first years out of college doing stock market research for a New York City financial firm. In her spare time, she taught English as a second language and fostered homeless dogs. "I was getting a lot more fulfillment from those things," she says, "than from work." Hoping to change that, Millar headed off to the University of Pennsylvania's Wharton School, drawn by its "Social Impact Initiative." Along with the usual grounding in finance and business strategies, she could focus on ways to make a difference in society. Today Millar works in social-impact investing at City Light Capital, a venture capital firm in New York that invests in startups aimed at doing good. Examples: ShotSpotter, whose technology helps police and the military

pinpoint the location of gunfire, and Arcadia Power, a platform that facilitates the purchasing of renewable energy across utilities in all 50 states. "I would do it again for twice the cost," says Millar, 27, who paid for her $200,000 education with loans.

"Our students want to make the world go round in a different way," says Sherryl Kuhlman, managing director of the Social Impact Initiative. Wharton MBA students have access to more than 30 social-impact courses along with extracurricular opportunities to explore nonprofit roles, pro bono consulting, and entrepreneurial activities with a change-the-world bent. Students who choose this path, she says, are no longer willing to "take a job they don't like so they can give their money away later. They want to merge the money and the purpose."

B school is certainly still about getting a career

ADVANCE WITH A SPECIALIZED, INDUSTRY FOCUS

BE RECRUITED BY MORE THAN 500 TOP COMPANIES

EXPERIENCE IMMERSIVE, REAL-WORLD LEARNING

Go farther, faster with a top-ranked Wisconsin MBA. Get the career you want, with skills to compete in the fast-paced, dynamic world of business. You'll join a collaborative community of professionals dedicated to your success. Let's begin.

go.wisc.edu/WSB

WISCONSIN
SCHOOL OF BUSINESS
UNIVERSITY OF WISCONSIN–MADISON

TOGETHER FORWARD®

boost in finance or consulting or management. But increasingly it's also about learning to apply private sector strategies to public concerns. Dozens of schools now allow students to pursue an MBA focused on sustainability or social impact or social responsibility. The nonprofit organization Net Impact, which promotes socially responsible business careers and has 100,000 members in 300 chapters at colleges, universities and business schools, lists 75 programs in its "Guide to Business Schools for Social and Environmental Impact."

A few schools, including the University of Vermont and Presidio Graduate School (with campuses in San Francisco and Seattle), offer formal "green MBA" curricula entirely focused on sustainability and/or social justice or responsibility. Other schools offer a standard MBA curriculum enriched with electives that allow a concentration.

In three worlds. The aim is to foster "tri-sector leadership" in tackling the "incredibly complex problems" where for-profit, nonprofit and government worlds intersect, says Erin Worsham, executive director of the Center for the Advancement of Social Entrepreneurship at Duke University's Fuqua School of Business. Knowing how to navigate in all three is an essential skill, she says. The programs also typically emphasize a "triple bottom line," defining success not just by profit realized but also by social impact and environmental sustainability.

Beyond the tailored coursework, extracurricular opportunities frequently include helping to manage social-impact investing funds; participants evaluate business proposals and award seed money to deserving social entrepreneurs. It's also common for students to team up with corporations, government agencies or nonprofit organizations to work on problems as part of their classwork or during internships. At Duke, for instance, MBA students can earn credit by doing consulting for social ventures around the world, from tiny African nonprofits to multinational corporations.

Why I Picked

UNIVERSITY OF VIRGINIA
Charlottesville

Annie Medaglia, '15
CO-FOUNDER OF DREAMWAKERS

> After working at the State Department, I sought a business school that combined public and private sector thinking to more innovatively address 21st-century policy challenges. I chose Darden because it emphasizes general management, teaching quality, entrepreneurial thinking and community. Through Darden's case method – students solve a company's problems with a product launch, for example – I've developed the problem-solving skills to start a business or to innovate from within.

Initiative is encouraged. When I proposed the Tri-Sector Leadership Fellows program to bring law, public policy and business students together to learn from distinguished leaders, the school and classmates moved mountains to make it happen. The i.Lab, Darden's startup incubator, provides students with advice and connections that enabled a friend and me to launch DreamWakers, a nonprofit that uses technology to connect students in high-need schools with professionals to discuss different careers. Through Darden, I feel that I can have a transformative impact on any environment.

They also collaborate with peers at other B schools, including those at North Carolina State University and the University of North Carolina–Chapel Hill, to certify companies as B Corporations, an indication that they include sustainability and social responsibility in their business plans and practices. (There are more than 2,000 B Corporations so far, including Warby Parker and Ben & Jerry's.) The students learn consulting skills along with the criteria that make a business socially responsible, says Tracy Triggs-Matthews, associate director of the Center for Sustainable Enterprise at UNC.

"I can't stand on the sidelines," says Thomas Crowley, 37, an architect who is pursuing a three-year joint MBA and Master of Public Administration at Presidio's San Francisco campus. Presidio's 200 students pursue their MBA or MPA in a low-residency format, and all of the coursework is focused on the triple bottom line and sustainable business practices, says President Mark Schulman. For example, a class in accounting might teach students how to weigh the environmental impact of a product or service in calculating its overall profitability. Crowley expects the program to allow him to focus on "human use patterns and disposability in our society." Its structure lets him work to cover his living expenses, and he's financing the $99,000 tuition with loans.

Getting a taste. Students can easily sample socially responsible practices without committing to a focused degree or concentration. Kuhlman estimates that about a third of each Wharton class takes advantage of at least some social-impact classes or extracurricular activities. At Haas School of Business at the University of California–Berkeley, roughly 80 percent of MBA students get at least some exposure through the Center for Social Sector Leadership. Ben Mangan, the center's executive director, co-teaches one popular course that's a launch pad for social-impact startups. One student team created a marketplace where disabled people can find caregivers; another developed a platform to connect small and medium-sized businesses with low-cost recycling collectors.

Lyndsey Wilson, 26, describes herself as a "social-impact lifer" who was drawn to the MBA program at Haas because of its reach into the Silicon Valley entrepreneurial and investing ecosystem. Wilson worked after college for an attorney who helps immigrants and the homeless, then did a stint at the Gates Foundation studying health problems in the developing world. "I just want to understand how it all works," she says. Haas awarded Wilson a fellowship that covers most of her tuition, and she has taken out loans for the balance of her costs.

Wilson says she may pay off her loans by spending at least a few years in the private sector. Or if she pursues her ambition of entering the nonprofit world, she'll take advantage of the Haas policy of subsidizing loan payments for graduates who opt for public service. Varying degrees of loan forgiveness or subsidy are often available for B-school grads who take government or nonprofit jobs. Wharton has an endowed fund that contributes up to $20,000 per year for five years to selected students pursuing public or nonprofit careers. Fuqua's Loan Assistance Program offers up to $8,000 annually. If you think a social-impact business degree might be right for you otherwise, loan forgiveness or assistance may make it a practical financial choice as well. ●

The Executive MBA Edge

How to boost your career – and work, too

Tiffany Willis saw the writing on the wall. She had plenty of corporate experience in accounting, auditing and consulting, but knew she would need more if she hoped to lead a team: Job listings for positions she wanted said "MBA preferred." And she admired how colleagues who had the degree approached problems. "I was missing out," she says. So she enrolled in a program at Emory University's Goizueta Business School that put her in class every other weekend. When Willis graduated in 2015, she had multiple job offers and landed at financial services technology company Fiserv as head of operational audit and advisory services.

BERKELEY EMBA STUDENTS WORK TOGETHER IN AN APPLIED INNOVATION COURSE DURING A WEEK ON CAMPUS.

Willis, now in her early 40s, is a prime example of the kind of person likely to benefit from an executive MBA program, which offers the same credential as a traditional full-time program but is formatted for professionals who want to keep their day jobs. She was at a crossroads in her career, clear on what she wanted to get out of her investment of time and money, and motivated to work hard. While the Great Recession slowed applications to EMBA programs, demand has come back. In 2016, more than half of those surveyed by the Graduate Management Admission Council reported an increase in applications.

The structure varies, but EMBA programs are typically about 20 months long and designed so classes take place in a concentrated fashion. Students spend all day Friday on campus one week and all day Saturday the next, for example, or a few days at a stretch once a month. The common ground: "No one is quitting their job and going to live on campus," says Michael Desiderio, executive director of the EMBA Council, which represents the industry.

Indeed, targeted students are in the middle of their careers; the average age of participants is about 38. The goal is to equip people with knowledge that they can parlay into greater responsibility and a bigger paycheck.

That paycheck may be more key than ever. Employers used to be willing to pay for all or most of the tuition. No longer. An EMBAC survey found that just 23 percent of students were fully funded by their employer in 2016, with another 36 percent getting some help.

More choice, please. As students have picked up more of the check, they've demanded an experience more finely tailored to their goals and interests. "Nowadays, the demand for choice is much greater," says Richard Daniels, director of executive and professional MBA programs at the University of Georgia's Terry College of Business. At the University of California–Berkeley's Haas School of Business, for example, students can take electives in entrepreneurship, leadership and strategy on top of the nuts and bolts. George Mason University in Virginia offers an EMBA focused on national security; the University of Pittsburgh Katz Graduate School of Business will launch a 19-month program for health care professionals this spring in which each class will be customized to cover health care topics, from pharmaceutical development to insurance. At St.

Mary's College of California, the Trans-Global Executive MBA focuses on corporate social responsibility and ethics.

As with a traditional MBA, face time with professors and teamwork with fellow students – and the networking opportunities both create – are considered crucial. And many programs include blocks of travel time to give students international experience as a group. But mindful of the difficulties of balancing a full-time job and family life with academics, a

"THE GOAL: GREATER RESPONSIBILITY AND A BIGGER PAYCHECK"

number of schools now broadcast some classes online so participants can occasionally skip the commute. At St. Mary's, for example, one EMBA program involves 50 percent in-person classes and 50 percent live videoconferencing. "We try to use technology to replicate the traditional face-to-face experience," explains Zhan Li, dean of the school of economics and business administration.

When employers were footing the bill – and, in return, expecting their newly minted MBAs to stay on for some period – career services for EMBA students weren't essential. That, too, has changed. Many people intend a job switch or career change. So prospective students should ask about services such as executive coaching, help with résumés and positioning, and access to the alumni and student networks. And it's best to be clear about what career outcomes

they're expecting, advises Joan Coonrod, senior director of the MBA career management center for working professionals at Goizueta. Willis credits Coonrod and her colleagues – her "career board of directors" – for pushing her to consider what skills she would need to rise to the C-suite as well as to hold out for a job that would make use of her new degree.

Anyone contemplating an EMBA should realize that it's not a magic bullet, advises Hallie Crawford, an Atlanta-based certified career coach. It's important to take stock of what you hope to gain. Does the job band above you require an MBA? Are you looking to fill gaps in your experience so you can make a lateral move in your company, such as from technology to the business side?

Once enrolled in a program, you can improve the odds of achieving your goal by staying tightly focused on it, says Crawford. Load up on classes that address gaps in your experience. Some kind of independent or team project will be required, such as consulting work for a local business; pick projects relevant to your job plans. And if you are aiming for a pivot into a new industry, prepare to be patient and possibly make multiple job moves to get there.

"I had years of experience behind me, but not the degree," says Melinda Franks, 46, who graduated from Katz's EMBA program in 2008. She found that "once I had the degree, I could leverage both." Eighteen months after graduating, Franks got a director-level position at her then-employer and today is clinical administrator for otolaryngology at Emory Healthcare in Atlanta. Her annual salary boost from that move almost equaled the cost of her MBA. ●

BY KATHERINE HOBSON

The Job Market

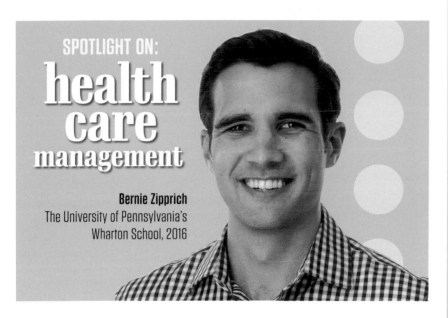

SPOTLIGHT ON:
health care management

Bernie Zipprich
The University of Pennsylvania's
Wharton School, 2016

Promoting Prevention

After Bernie Zipprich graduated from Harvard with a bachelor's in economics, he worked for a consulting firm as a member of its health care strategy team. As his interest in health grew, Zipprich decided to go on for an MBA focused on the field, a growing B-school offering. "I liked the intellectual complexity of the business challenges," he says, "as well as the opportunity for social impact."

His degree, the MBA in Health Care Management offered at the University of Pennsylvania's Wharton School, emphasizes topics like policy, financial management of health care organizations, and regulation of medical devices. After graduation, Zipprich went to work for Welltok, Inc., a Massachusetts-based technology company in the relatively new field of health optimization. Welltok assists health plans, health systems and large employers in designing benefits programs that help individuals manage their health better, "saving money and time in the process," says Zipprich. For one large client, the team reorganized the company's health benefits program to include "behavioral rewards and personalized nudges" to encourage workers to focus more on preventive care. Employees earn everything from reduced insurance premiums to gift cards or even cash for meeting diet, exercise and other health-related goals. As part of the program, Welltok designed digital apps and other resources so employees could tailor their personal wellness plans and goals to fit their needs. As the company's director of solutions strategy and value, Zipprich tracks market trends and customer needs, translating them into strategic insights to help internal teams devise new solutions – like a heart-healthy program for men in their 30s battling hypertension who can't get to the gym – and determines value and pricing for clients.

Opportunities in health care management go beyond the traditional job description of managing a hospital or clinic, says June Kinney, associate director of the graduate program in Health Care Management at Wharton. "Graduates find jobs in digital health, insurance, finance, pharmabiotech, venture capital, medical devices and entrepreneurship," she notes. And don't forget government agencies and nonprofit organizations. The Bureau of Labor Statistics projects job growth will be 17 percent from 2014 to 2024, which translates to some 56,300 more jobs. –Cathie Gandel

...More Hot Jobs

...HUMAN RESOURCE MANAGER

These pros are needed in a wide range of industries, from health care to information services to finance. Besides helping organizations with recruitment, hiring and training, many also evaluate benefits and compensation and manage labor relations. Almost 11,000 jobs are expected to be added from 2014 to 2024, a growth of 9 percent, thanks to corporate expansion and changing labor laws. Median annual pay is over $104,000, but top salaries can exceed $187,000.

...STATISTICIAN

Using mathematics to evaluate and translate data into insights, statisticians are being called upon to solve problems in diverse fields, including business, government, engineering, health care and sports. The government projects that employment for statisticians will grow 34 percent in the decade ending in 2024, as the need for this expertise moves beyond the accounting department to areas like human resources, marketing and sales. Median salaries run just over $80,000.

...MANAGEMENT ANALYST

As companies redouble their efforts to cut costs and make their operations more efficient and profitable, the need for top-level analysts is increasing. Job growth is expected to jump 14 percent by 2024 for management analysts, translating to roughly 103,000 new jobs. Median salary was about $81,000 in 2015.

Schools of Business

THE TOP MBA PROGRAMS

Rank School	Overall score	Peer assessment score (5.0=highest)	Recruiter assessment score (5.0=highest)	'16 full-time average undergrad GPA	'16 full-time average GMAT score	'16 full-time acceptance rate	'16 average starting salary and bonus	'16 graduates employed at graduation	'16 Employed 3 months after graduation	'16 out-of-state tuition and fees	'16 total full-time enrollment
1. Harvard University (MA)	100	4.8	4.5	3.67	729	10.7%	$153,830	79.3%	90.6%	$75,353	1,871
1. University of Pennsylvania (Wharton)	100	4.7	4.5	3.60	730	19.6%	$155,058	85.8%	95.5%	$73,634	1,708
3. University of Chicago (Booth) (IL)	98	4.7	4.5	3.58	726	23.6%	$147,475	84.9%	95.2%	$67,668	1,185
4. Massachusetts Institute of Technology (Sloan)	96	4.7	4.4	3.58	724	11.7%	$143,565	81.2%	92.5%	$68,250	809
4. Northwestern University (Kellogg) (IL)	96	4.6	4.4	3.60	728	20.1%	$141,694	82.8%	95.0%	$67,792	1,301
4. Stanford University (CA)	96	4.8	4.4	3.73	737	6.0%	$153,553	62.8%	82.4%	$66,540	833
7. University of California–Berkeley (Haas)	93	4.6	4.3	3.64	717	12.0%	$140,067	68.6%	89.7%	$57,560	502
8. Dartmouth College (Tuck) (NH)	92	4.3	4.2	3.53	717	22.4%	$148,997	86.8%	95.6%	$69,690	567
9. Columbia University (NY)	90	4.4	4.1	3.50	720	14.1%	$150,229	77.3%	92.3%	$71,624	1,326
9. Yale University (CT)	90	4.3	4.3	3.63	725	19.0%	$135,988	76.0%	89.9%	$66,160	694
11. University of Michigan–Ann Arbor (Ross)	89	4.4	4.2	3.44	708	26.3%	$145,926	85.6%	91.8%	$64,678	801
12. Duke University (Fuqua) (NC)	87	4.3	4.1	3.47	695	22.1%	$144,799	83.1%	91.6%	$65,760	896
12. New York University (Stern)	87	4.2	4.0	3.51	710	23.1%	$145,413	82.1%	91.8%	$69,110	790
14. University of Virginia (Darden)	85	4.1	4.0	3.50	712	26.5%	$150,823	80.7%	90.2%	$63,500	678
15. University of California–Los Angeles (Anderson)	84	4.1	4.0	3.52	715	20.7%	$140,457	73.8%	87.7%	$59,290	734
16. Cornell University (Johnson) (NY)	82	4.1	4.0	3.37	700	27.6%	$146,252	79.8%	90.1%	$64,584	580
17. University of Texas–Austin (McCombs)	79	3.9	4.0	3.42	699	28.0%	$135,194	77.5%	89.2%	$51,146	521
18. U. of North Carolina–Chapel Hill (Kenan-Flagler)	77	3.9	3.9	3.37	700	36.4%	$131,908	75.1%	90.4%	$59,574	574
19. Carnegie Mellon University (Tepper) (PA)	75	4.0	3.8	3.30	686	30.3%	$140,289	76.0%	85.2%	$62,230	428
20. Emory University (Goizueta) (GA)	74	3.7	3.7	3.30	683	33.1%	$138,864	84.0%	93.1%	$57,580	350
21. Georgetown University (McDonough) (DC)	73	3.7	3.9	3.40	692	44.6%	$124,417	69.1%	90.3%	$55,550	546
21. Indiana University (Kelley)	73	3.8	3.5	3.34	670	31.4%	$128,637	83.9%	94.0%	$46,561	370
21. Washington University in St. Louis (Olin) (MO)	73	3.6	3.6	3.46	688	29.7%	$115,830	78.5%	96.3%	$56,200	268
24. University of Southern California (Marshall)	72	3.7	3.5	3.37	692	33.3%	$126,932	75.2%	91.5%	$61,915	441
25. Arizona State University (Carey)	71	3.5	3.3	3.54	682	14.3%	$116,575	78.7%	95.1%	$43,882	203
25. Vanderbilt University (Owen) (TN)	71	3.5	3.6	3.40	691	45.5%	$129,587	80.3%	90.1%	$52,368	341
27. Ohio State University (Fisher)	70	3.6	3.2	3.52	671	31.7%	$114,643	80.0%	93.3%	$51,587	206
27. University of Washington (Foster)	70	3.4	3.0	3.38	691	23.9%	$133,299	85.3%	98.0%	$47,214	253
29. Georgia Institute of Technology (Scheller)	68	3.3	3.4	3.39	680	32.1%	$122,303	83.6%	94.5%	$41,684	143
29. Rice University (Jones) (TX)	68	3.4	3.6	3.42	690	26.6%	$131,829	75.2%	81.2%	$56,097	226
29. University of Notre Dame (Mendoza) (IN)	68	3.5	3.5	3.37	683	41.0%	$122,791	75.7%	89.7%	$50,976	304
32. Temple University (Fox) (PA)	67	3.1	3.7	3.61	639	36.9%	$92,828	91.9%	100.0%	$45,113	89
32. University of Minnesota–Twin Cities (Carlson)	67	3.4	3.0	3.43	675	45.2%	$126,217	77.4%	93.5%	$52,034	193
34. Brigham Young University (Marriott) (UT)	66	3.1	3.5	3.54	672	49.1%	$121,960	75.8%	89.1%	$24,620	325
34. University of Wisconsin–Madison	66	3.5	3.3	3.42	669	26.3%	$110,756	76.3%	88.2%	$33,379	196
36. Pennsylvania State University–University Park (Smeal)	65	3.3	3.4	3.37	659	18.1%	$123,095	81.0%	88.9%	$40,506	125
37. Michigan State University (Broad)	64	3.3	3.2	3.30	670	33.3%	$119,424	76.1%	95.5%	$46,701	144
38. Texas A&M University–College Station (Mays)	63	3.3	3.4	3.32	649	27.0%	$115,666	77.1%	93.8%	$44,078	139
38. University of Texas–Dallas	63	2.8	4.3	3.50	670	19.5%	$90,631	64.7%	92.2%	$29,106	103
40. University of Florida (Hough)	62	3.3	2.3	3.43	685	16.0%	$111,311	84.7%	93.2%	$31,130	100
40. University of Illinois–Urbana-Champaign	62	3.4	3.0	3.40	665	25.7%	$104,487	64.9%	93.0%	$36,422	134
42. University of California–Davis	61	3.2	3.0	3.41	679	15.8%	$110,206	64.7%	91.2%	$52,741	99
43. University of Rochester (Simon) (NY)	60	3.1	2.7	3.40	665	33.6%	$113,515	78.6%	95.2%	$47,089	204
44. Boston College (Carroll) (MA)	59	3.3	3.3	3.20	667	38.2%	$109,267	75.3%	87.7%	$47,450	174
44. Boston University (Questrom) (MA)	59	3.2	2.9	3.30	682	37.1%	$111,165	65.7%	91.4%	$49,900	303
44. University of California–Irvine (Merage)	59	3.2	3.1	3.43	649	28.6%	$101,991	67.2%	91.4%	$50,092	173
47. University of Maryland–College Park (Smith)	58	3.4	3.4	3.28	657	36.7%	$109,921	61.3%	80.0%	$56,134	197
48. University of Georgia (Terry)	57	3.3	2.6	3.30	647	35.5%	$104,900	75.0%	92.5%	$33,780	102
49. University of Arizona (Eller)	56	3.4	2.7	3.40	656	61.0%	$99,539	58.6%	86.2%	$48,149	87
50. Purdue University–West Lafayette (Krannert) (IN)	55	3.4	3.1	3.39	636	35.5%	$99,396	60.0%	81.5%	$42,184	147

*Tuition is reported on a per-credit-hour basis. †Total program costs, which may or may not include required fees.
Sources: U.S. News and the schools. Assessment data collected by Ipsos Public Affairs.

More @ usnews.com/grad

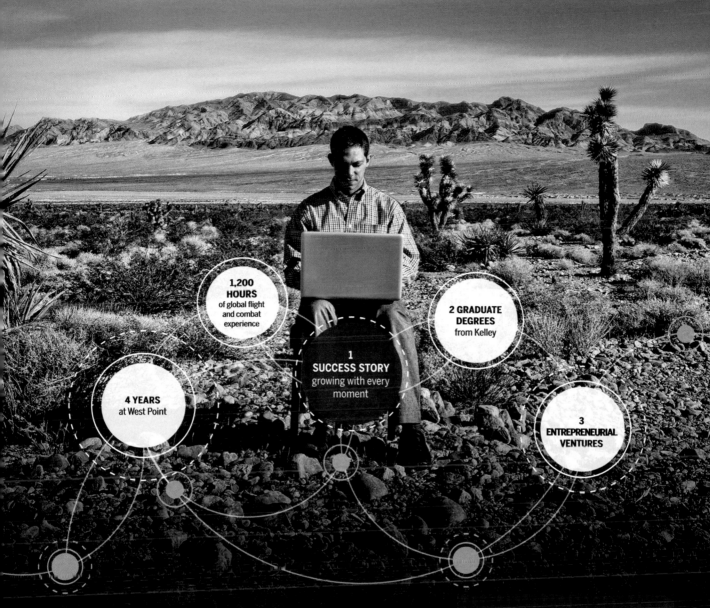

1,200
HOURS
of global flight
and combat
experience

**2 GRADUATE
DEGREES**
from Kelley

4 YEARS
at West Point

**1
SUCCESS STORY**
growing with every
moment

**3
ENTREPRENEURIAL
VENTURES**

The pivotal moments in Tony's life mean a lot more than
most. Each one starts a chain reaction of new paths,
connections and opportunities. Tony earned his MBA and
MS from Kelley online, so his moments go much farther.

Start building your momentum
gokelley.iu.edu/EarnYourMBAOnline

KELLEY
SCHOOL OF BUSINESS
GO FROM MOMENT TO MOMENTUM

THE TOP MBA PROGRAMS continued

Rank	School	Overall score	Peer assessment score (5.0=highest)	Recruiter assessment score (5.0=highest)	'16 full-time average undergrad GPA	'16 full-time average GMAT score	'16 full-time acceptance rate	'16 average starting salary and bonus	'16 graduates employed at graduation	Employed 3 months after graduation	'16 out-of-state tuition and fees	'16 total full-time enrollment
50.	Rutgers, The State U. of N.J.–Newark & New Brunswick	55	2.9	3.0	3.23	659	45.1%	$98,814	75.9%	96.3%	$47,537	139
52.	Southern Methodist University (Cox) (TX)	54	3.1	3.0	3.31	662	38.6%	$108,347	60.7%	83.3%	$45,976	238
53.	University of Pittsburgh (Katz) (PA)	53	3.2	3.2	3.29	613	30.0%	$89,382	81.6%	89.5%	$66,900†	153
54.	Northeastern University (MA)	52	3.0	3.3	3.28	632	27.4%	$82,849	58.8%	96.1%	$1,513*	169
54.	University of Alabama (Manderson)	52	2.8	2.5	3.57	677	59.4%	$75,647	77.8%	88.9%	$29,780	225
54.	University of Tennessee–Knoxville (Haslam)	52	2.9	3.5	3.36	627	59.0%	$84,212	57.7%	92.3%	$44,252	133
57.	College of William and Mary (Mason) (VA)	50	3.0	3.7	3.30	622	54.3%	$92,809	59.7%	80.6%	$44,123	179
57.	CUNY Bernard M. Baruch College (Zicklin) (NY)	50	2.7	3.1	3.33	632	31.6%	$83,579	78.4%	94.6%	$29,809	98
57.	See note below											
57.	North Carolina State University (Jenkins)	50	2.7	2.7	3.46	655	38.0%	$87,632	58.3%	91.7%	$38,704	95
57.	University of Massachusetts–Amherst (Isenberg)	50	2.8	3.1	3.50	639	31.4%	$69,858	66.7%	90.5%	$32,090	45
57.	University of Miami (FL)	50	2.9	2.6	3.32	654	22.9%	$76,302	72.4%	94.8%	$1,900*	138
57.	University of Utah (Eccles)	50	2.8	3.1	3.40	629	53.9%	$81,539	75.5%	89.8%	$60,000†	136
64.	University of Iowa (Tippie)	49	3.1	2.7	3.26	677	35.5%	$96,229	51.8%	80.4%	$40,134	110
65.	Baylor University (Hankamer) (TX)	48	2.9	2.8	3.50	621	40.0%	$80,517	63.6%	86.4%	$42,606	90
65.	Iowa State University	48	2.7	2.6	3.59	622	60.5%	$72,054	80.6%	90.3%	$24,716	79
65.	Pepperdine University (Graziadio) (CA)	48	3.0	3.2	3.33	642	55.3%	$80,249	56.5%	82.3%	$47,880	152
65.	University of Connecticut	48	2.8	2.7	3.50	623	30.4%	$103,476	65.6%	81.3%	$35,588	109

Note: George Washington University has changed from being ranked No. 57 in the 2018 edition of Best Business Schools to being an unranked school for that ranking, based on a data reporting error. This change will also be reflected on usnews.com.

SPECIALTIES

PROGRAMS RANKED BEST BY BUSINESS SCHOOL DEANS AND MBA PROGRAM DIRECTORS

ACCOUNTING
1. **University of Texas–Austin** (McCombs)
2. **University of Pennsylvania** (Wharton)
3. **University of Illinois–Urbana-Champaign**
4. **University of Chicago** (Booth) (IL)
5. **University of Michigan–Ann Arbor** (Ross)
6. **Stanford University** (CA)
7. **Brigham Young University** (Marriott) (UT)
8. **University of Southern California** (Marshall)
9. **New York University** (Stern)
9. **University of North Carolina–Chapel Hill** (Kenan-Flagler)
11. **Indiana University** (Kelley)
12. **University of California–Berkeley** (Haas)
12. **University of Notre Dame** (Mendoza) (IN)
14. **Ohio State University** (Fisher)
14. **Seattle University** (Albers) (WA)
16. **Loyola Marymount University** (CA)
17. **Columbia University** (NY)

ENTREPRENEURSHIP
1. **Babson College** (Olin) (MA)
2. **Stanford University** (CA)
3. **Harvard University** (MA)
3. **Massachusetts Institute of Technology** (Sloan)
5. **University of California–Berkeley** (Haas)

6. **University of Michigan–Ann Arbor** (Ross)
7. **University of Pennsylvania** (Wharton)
8. **Indiana University** (Kelley)
9. **University of Texas–Austin** (McCombs)
10. **University of Southern California** (Marshall)
11. **Rice University** (Jones) (TX)
12. **Loyola Marymount University** (CA)

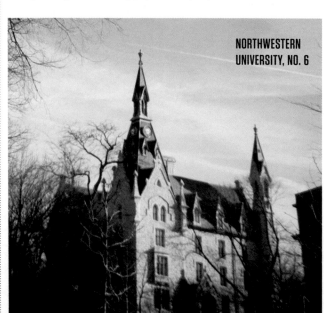

NORTHWESTERN UNIVERSITY, NO. 6

BRETT ZIEGLER FOR USN&WR

EXECUTIVE MBA
1. **University of Pennsylvania** (Wharton)
2. **University of Chicago** (Booth) (IL)
3. **Northwestern University** (Kellogg) (IL)
4. **Duke University** (Fuqua) (NC)
4. **New York University** (Stern)
6. **University of Michigan–Ann Arbor** (Ross)

7. **Columbia University** (NY)
8. **University of California–Los Angeles** (Anderson)
9. **University of California–Berkeley** (Haas)
10. **Massachusetts Institute of Technology** (Sloan)
11. **University of North Carolina–Chapel Hill** (Kenan-Flagler)
12. **Seattle University** (Albers) (WA)
12. **St. Joseph's University** (Haub) (PA)

FINANCE
1. **University of Pennsylvania** (Wharton)
2. **University of Chicago** (Booth) (IL)
3. **New York University** (Stern)
4. **Columbia University** (NY)
5. **Stanford University** (CA)
6. **Massachusetts Institute of Technology** (Sloan)
7. **University of California–Berkeley** (Haas)
8. **Harvard University** (MA)
9. **University of Michigan–Ann Arbor** (Ross)
10. **University of California–Los Angeles** (Anderson)
11. **Northwestern University** (Kellogg) (IL)
12. **Duke University** (Fuqua) (NC)
13. **University of Rochester** (Simon) (NY)

INFORMATION SYSTEMS
1. **Massachusetts Institute of Technology** (Sloan)

METHODOLOGY

The 471 master's programs in business administration accredited by the Association to Advance Collegiate Schools of Business were surveyed; 377 responded, with 131 MBA programs providing the data needed to calculate rankings based on a weighted average of eight indicators:

Quality assessment: Two surveys were conducted in the fall of 2016. Business school deans and directors of accredited MBA programs were asked to rate the overall academic quality of the MBA programs at each school on a scale from marginal (1) to outstanding (5); 43 percent responded. The average score is weighted by .25 in the ranking model. Corporate recruiters and company contacts who hired MBA grads, whose names were supplied by previously ranked MBA programs, also were asked to rate the programs. The last three years' recruiter responses were averaged and are weighted by .15 in the model.

Placement success (.35): Based on average starting salary and bonus (40 percent of this measure) and employment rates for full-time 2016 graduates at graduation (20 percent) and at three months later (40 percent). Calculations for MBA placement rates exclude those not seeking jobs and those for whom the school has no information. To be included in the full-time MBA rankings, a program needed 20 or more of its 2016 full-time graduates to be seeking employment. Salary is based on the number of graduates reporting data. Signing bonus is weighted by the proportion of graduates reporting salaries who received a bonus, since not everyone with a base salary received a signing bonus.

Student selectivity (.25): The strength of full-time students entering in the fall of 2016 was measured by the average GMAT and GRE scores (65 percent), the average undergraduate grade-point average (30 percent), and the proportion of applicants who were accepted (5 percent).

Overall rank: Data were standardized about their means, and standardized scores were weighted, totaled and rescaled so that the top school received 100; others received their percentage of the top score.

Specialty rankings: Based solely on ratings by educators at peer schools. B-school deans and MBA program heads were asked to nominate up to 10 programs for excellence. Those receiving the most nominations are listed.

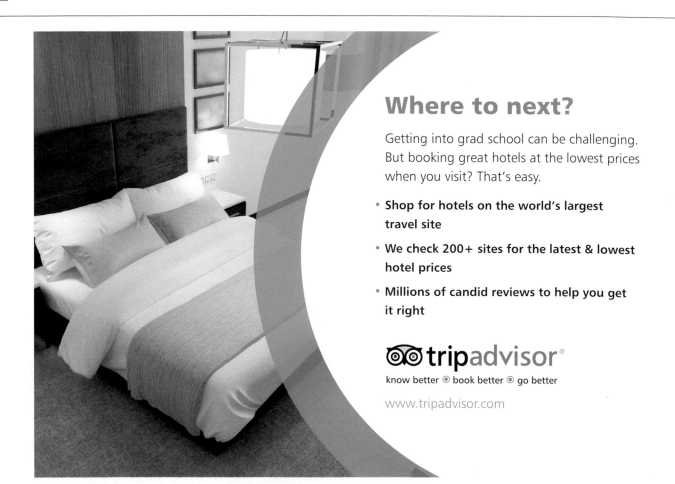

Best Part-Time MBA Programs

Part-time business programs play a vital role for working people who can't go to school full time because of family or financial reasons. The U.S. News part-time MBA ranking is based on five factors: average peer assessment score (50 percent of the overall score); average GMAT score and GRE scores of part-time MBA students entering in the fall of 2016 (15 percent); average undergraduate GPA (5 percent); average number of years of work experience (15 percent); and the percentage of the fall 2016 total MBA program enrollment that is in the part-time MBA program (15 percent). The average peer assessment score is calculated from a fall 2016 survey that asked business school deans and MBA program directors at each of the nation's 360 part-time MBA programs to rate the other part-time programs on a 5-point scale, from marginal (1) to outstanding (5); 45 percent responded. Those unfamiliar with a program were asked to indicate "don't know." To be eligible for the part-time ranking, a program had to be accredited by the Association to Advance Collegiate Schools of Business and have at least 20 students enrolled part time in the fall of 2016; 301 programs met those criteria and were ranked.

THE TOP PART-TIME PROGRAMS

Rank	School	Overall score	Peer assessment score (5.0=highest)	'16 part-time average GMAT score	'16 part-time acceptance rate	'16 total part-time enrollment
1.	University of California–Berkeley (Haas)	100	4.5	694	47.4%	802
2.	University of Chicago (Booth) (IL)	98	4.7	678	N/A	1,366
3.	New York University (Stern)	90	4.3	669	58.8%	1,381
3.	University of California–Los Angeles (Anderson)	90	4.2	678	62.6%	986
5.	Northwestern University (Kellogg) (IL)	87	4.5	674	N/A	704
6.	University of Michigan–Ann Arbor (Ross)	80	4.3	650	74.4%	430
7.	Temple University (Fox) (PA)	77	3.2	593	60.1%	847
7.	Virginia Tech (Pamplin)	77	2.9	626	91.8%	163
9.	Ohio State University (Fisher)	76	3.7	604	75.2%	323
10.	University of Texas–Austin (McCombs)	74	3.9	634	67.8%	459
11.	Indiana University (Kelley)	73	3.7	661	52.7%	294
11.	University of Minnesota–Twin Cities (Carlson)	73	3.6	604	85.7%	1,005
13.	University of Massachusetts–Amherst (Isenberg)	72	2.9	588	85.5%	1,290
13.	Wake Forest University (NC)	72	3.2	605	86.7%	305
15.	Carnegie Mellon University (Tepper) (PA)	71	4.0	646	67.6%	143
16.	College of William and Mary (Mason) (VA)	70	3.1	673	97.8%	183
16.	University of South Carolina (Moore)	70	3.0	624	89.2%	446
18.	Georgetown University (McDonough) (DC)	68	3.7	653	75.7%	427
18.	University of Washington (Foster)	68	3.5	623	69.9%	377
20.	Lehigh University (PA)	67	2.6	636	76.6%	162
20.	University of Florida (Hough)	67	3.4	591	63.2%	373
20.	University of Southern California (Marshall)	67	3.8	614	79.9%	440
20.	University of Texas–Dallas	67	3.0	640	50.5%	728
24.	Rice University (Jones) (TX)	66	3.5	618	72.8%	310
25.	Emory University (Goizueta) (GA)	65	3.7	632	69.5%	256
25.	Miami University (Farmer) (OH)	65	2.6	623	75.0%	127
25.	Santa Clara University (Leavey) (CA)	65	2.9	620	54.1%	377
28.	Kennesaw State University (Coles) (GA)	64	2.4	565	41.2%	163
29.	Pepperdine University (Graziadio) (CA)	63	3.1	561	74.3%	1,000
30.	Georgia Institute of Technology (Scheller)	62	3.3	603	76.8%	365
30.	University of Maryland–College Park (Smith)	62	3.4	600	86.8%	567
30.	Washington University in St. Louis (Olin) (MO)	62	3.7	571	83.3%	297
33.	Arizona State University (Carey)	61	3.5	585	78.3%	208
33.	University of Georgia (Terry)	61	3.4	566	88.7%	298
33.	University of Richmond (Robins) (VA)	61	2.8	614	91.8%	88
33.	University of Wisconsin–Madison	61	3.6	592	90.4%	167
33.	Xavier University (Williams) (OH)	61	2.8	563	52.2%	481
38.	Rutgers, The State U. of N.J.–Newark and New Brunswick	60	3.0	583	77.1%	1,007
38.	University of Iowa (Tippie)	60	3.1	568	93.1%	780
38.	Villanova University (PA)	60	2.9	592	88.4%	127

Note. The data listed for acceptance rate and enrollment are for informational purposes only and are not used in the computation of the part-time MBA program rankings. N/A=Data were not provided by the school. Sources: U.S. News and the schools. Assessment data collected by Ipsos Public Affairs.

THE TOP PART-TIME PROGRAMS continued

Rank	School	Overall score	Peer assessment score (5.0=highest)	'16 part-time average GMAT score	'16 part-time acceptance rate	'16 total part-time enrollment
41.	University of California–Davis	59	3.2	581	21.8%	352
42.	Boston University (Questrom) (MA)	58	3.2	596	93.0%	643
42.	Purdue University–West Lafayette (Krannert) (IN)	58	3.3	609	90.8%	85
42.	University of California–Irvine (Merage)	58	3.3	580	77.6%	327
42.	University of North Carolina–Charlotte (Belk)	58	2.8	583	70.3%	271
46.	Boston College (Carroll) (MA)	57	3.4	575	95.5%	378
46.	Georgia State University (Robinson)	57	2.9	604	51.1%	359
46.	Rutgers, The State University of New Jersey–Camden	57	2.7	540	69.6%	152
46.	University of Alabama–Birmingham	57	2.6	554	80.9%	295
46.	University of Arizona (Eller)	57	3.3	539	91.3%	198
46.	University of Colorado–Boulder (Leeds)	57	3.1	618	92.2%	128
46.	University of Colorado–Colorado Springs	57	2.3	570	66.0%	287
53.	Clemson University (SC)	56	2.9	588	95.5%	296
53.	George Mason University (VA)	56	2.8	560	75.3%	245
53.	See note below					
53.	North Carolina State University (Jenkins)	56	2.7	593	71.2%	250
57.	Loyola University Chicago (Quinlan) (IL)	55	2.9	562	55.6%	562
57.	Seton Hall University (Stillman) (NJ)	55	2.6	552	52.6%	208
57.	University of Rochester (Simon) (NY)	55	3.3	560	93.0%	161
60.	DePaul University (Kellstadt) (IL)	54	2.8	573	69.3%	825
60.	Loyola Marymount University (CA)	54	2.9	563	59.2%	143
60.	Texas A&M University–College Station (Mays)	54	3.3	604	88.0%	96
63.	Case Western Reserve University (Weatherhead) (OH)	53	3.2	583	91.4%	133
63.	Colorado State University	53	2.6	494	96.3%	734
63.	Fordham University (Gabelli) (NY)	53	3.0	550	62.8%	252
66.	Southern Methodist University (Cox) (TX)	52	3.2	596	62.2%	225
66.	University of Cincinnati (Lindner) (OH)	52	2.7	655	71.1%	136
66.	University of Connecticut	52	2.8	538	62.0%	977
66.	University of Illinois–Chicago (Liautaud)	52	2.6	574	52.2%	238
66.	University of Nebraska–Lincoln	52	2.9	595	66.7%	54
71.	Babson College (Olin) (MA)	51	3.2	562	98.4%	258
71.	Florida State University	51	2.9	550	74.0%	84
71.	Northeastern University (MA)	51	2.8	573	91.2%	345
71.	University of Pittsburgh (Katz) (PA)	51	3.3	540	87.7%	342
75.	Elon University (Love) (NC)	50	2.4	555	72.3%	133
75.	Seattle University (Albers) (WA)	50	2.6	591	55.9%	581
75.	University of California–San Diego (Rady)	50	3.0	596	88.6%	102
78.	CUNY Bernard M. Baruch College (Zicklin) (NY)	49	2.7	593	50.8%	496
78.	University of Kansas	49	2.9	579	70.4%	145
80.	St. Louis University (Cook) (MO)	48	2.9	540	80.3%	201
80.	University of Houston (Bauer) (TX)	48	2.8	584	63.7%	327
80.	University of Oklahoma (Price)	48	2.8	597	77.9%	122
80.	Virginia Commonwealth University	48	2.6	546	59.1%	141
84.	James Madison University (VA)	47	2.6	525	94.7%	26
84.	University of Colorado–Denver	47	2.6	588	74.9%	501
84.	University of Louisville (KY)	47	2.7	546	74.6%	173
84.	University of Portland (Pamplin) (OR)	47	2.3	582	64.9%	119
84.	University of Wisconsin–Milwaukee (Lubar)	47	2.7	541	81.1%	400
89.	Gonzaga University (WA)	46	2.8	540	71.9%	121
89.	Hofstra University (Zarb) (NY)	46	2.6	543	78.3%	812
89.	University of Wyoming	46	2.3	600	93.8%	88
92.	Creighton University (NE)	45	2.6	548	40.9%	96
92.	Marquette University (WI)	45	2.8	578	89.1%	211
92.	University of South Florida	45	2.4	567	33.6%	238
95.	Butler University (IN)	44	2.2	575	78.7%	141

Note: George Washington University has changed from being ranked No. 53 in the 2018 edition of Best Part-time MBA Programs to being an unranked school for that ranking, based on a data reporting error. This change will also be reflected on usnews.com.

Rank	School	Overall score	Peer assessment score (5.0=highest)	'16 part-time average GMAT score	'16 part-time acceptance rate	'16 total part-time enrollment
95.	Fairfield University (Dolan) (CT)	44	2.6	520	59.3%	60
95.	Northern Illinois University	44	2.2	487	96.3%	488
95.	San Diego State University (CA)	44	2.6	618	32.2%	247
95.	Texas Christian University (Neeley)	44	2.7	551	95.3%	141
95.	University of Nevada–Las Vegas	44	2.2	566	49.2%	171
95.	University of New Hampshire (Paul)	44	2.3	556	96.2%	200
95.	University of Wisconsin–Eau Claire	44	2.1	551	79.8%	268
103.	American University (Kogod) (DC)	43	2.8	527	80.0%	70
103.	Florida International University	43	2.3	N/A	55.4%	536
103.	Loyola University Maryland (Sellinger)	43	2.6	558	91.7%	324
103.	Oregon State University	43	2.4	598	84.6%	82
103.	University of Michigan–Flint	43	2.1	522	45.3%	160
108.	Ohio University	42	2.3	N/A	75.9%	93
108.	Old Dominion University (VA)	42	2.4	536	67.8%	131
108.	University of Central Florida	42	2.4	N/A	55.4%	378
108.	University of Delaware (Lerner)	42	2.6	N/A	86.4%	186
108.	University of San Diego (CA)	42	2.6	602	91.3%	84
108.	University of Utah (Eccles)	42	2.8	540	73.1%	293
108.	University of Wisconsin–Oshkosh	42	1.9	590	100.0%	312
115.	Drexel University (LeBow) (PA)	41	2.6	541	92.7%	160
115.	Pennsylvania State University–Harrisburg	41	2.2	543	74.6%	143

THE TOP PART-TIME PROGRAMS continued

Rank School	Overall score	Peer assessment score (5.0=highest)	'16 part-time average GMAT score	'16 part-time acceptance rate	'16 total part-time enrollment
115. Samford University (Brock) (AL)	41	2.2	586	64.7%	123
115. University of Kentucky (Gatton)	41	2.8	580	93.5%	149
115. University of Massachusetts–Lowell	41	2.1	513	88.8%	644
115. University of Nebraska–Omaha	41	2.3	574	63.4%	243
115. University of Washington–Bothell	41	2.1	529	68.5%	109
122. Bentley University (MA)	40	2.9	N/A	87.5%	212
122. Iowa State University	40	2.6	534	92.7%	63
122. Stevens Institute of Technology (NJ)	40	2.2	585	84.6%	392
122. University of Michigan–Dearborn	40	2.2	595	62.8%	119
122. University of North Carolina–Greensboro (Bryan)	40	2.3	549	80.0%	86
122. University of Scranton (PA)	40	2.3	541	36.8%	116
122. University of St. Thomas (MN)	40	2.4	513	98.3%	575
122. University of Texas–Arlington	40	2.5	496	60.6%	466
130. Portland State University (OR)	39	2.3	556	59.4%	51
130. University of Akron (OH)	39	2.1	551	62.7%	405
130. University of Denver (Daniels) (CO)	39	2.7	N/A	91.1%	107
133. California State University–Fullerton (Mihaylo)	38	2.3	550	57.6%	303
133. La Salle University (PA)	38	2.2	551	100.0%	205
133. Rockhurst University (Helzberg) (MO)	38	2.4	490	80.1%	376
133. University of Northern Iowa	38	2.1	558	43.1%	55
137. Bradley University (Foster) (IL)	37	2.2	540	87.1%	53
137. Minnesota State University–Mankato	37	1.8	553	87.0%	56
137. Oklahoma State University (Spears)	37	2.7	551	83.3%	83
137. St. Joseph's University (Haub) (PA)	37	2.7	549	64.4%	904
137. University of Washington–Tacoma Milgard	37	2.2	516	96.6%	50
137. University of Wisconsin–Whitewater	37	2.0	507	70.0%	462
143. Auburn University–Montgomery (AL)	36	2.7	N/A	N/A	59
143. California State University–Northridge (Nazarian)	36	2.2	558	18.5%	125
143. Fayetteville State University (NC)	36	1.5	481	93.2%	120
143. Illinois State University	36	2.1	546	74.6%	103
143. Louisiana State University–Baton Rouge (Ourso)	36	2.7	576	92.1%	57
143. University of Missouri–Kansas City (Bloch)	36	2.4	582	51.1%	159
143. University of Tennessee–Chattanooga	36	2.3	515	90.1%	280
143. West Chester University of Pennsylvania	36	1.8	535	85.6%	255
151. Belmont University (Massey) (TN)	35	2.2	557	91.7%	116
151. Boise State University (ID)	35	2.2	537	74.2%	73
151. California State University–San Bernardino	35	2.0	528	46.3%	228
151. Loyola University New Orleans (Butt) (LA)	35	2.5	497	100.0%	59
151. Pennsylvania State U.–Erie, The Behrend College (Black)	35	2.2	511	90.0%	116
151. SUNY–Oswego (NY)	35	1.9	555	93.2%	173
151. University at Albany–SUNY (NY)	35	2.3	540	90.0%	192
151. University of Hawaii–Manoa (Shidler)	35	2.6	N/A	85.7%	86
151. University of South Dakota	35	1.8	552	90.9%	248
151. Valparaiso University (IN)	35	2.1	542	95.8%	57

Education

IN THE
LEARNING
TECHNOLOGY
CLASSROOM
AT TEACHERS
COLLEGE,
COLUMBIA
UNIVERSITY

THE U.S. NEWS RANKINGS

Fast Track Into the Classroom

Aspiring educators get a master's and hands-on prep with a teacher residency

BY MARGARET LOFTUS

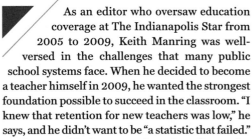

As an editor who oversaw education coverage at The Indianapolis Star from 2005 to 2009, Keith Manring was well-versed in the challenges that many public school systems face. When he decided to become a teacher himself in 2009, he wanted the strongest foundation possible to succeed in the classroom. "I knew that retention for new teachers was low," he says, and he didn't want to be "a statistic that failed."

After considering a number of teacher training programs geared toward career-switchers, Manring, 54, applied to the Woodrow Wilson National Fellowship Foundation, which offers support to about 180 aspiring educators each year to pursue graduate teaching degrees in science, technology, engineering and math fields. Manring enrolled at the nearby University of Indianapolis, where he took a series of intensive summer courses before he was placed in a classroom alongside a veteran teacher; by late winter, he was teaching on his own. Working first at a local high school before moving to a middle school, Manring sharpened his skills teaching eighth-grade science while also completing his master's coursework. As part of the deal, he also received a stipend of $30,000 toward tuition and living expenses while at UIndy in return for agreeing to teach at a high-need school in the state for at least three years after his graduation in 2011.

The Wilson program's approach is based on the teacher residency model, an alternative and increasingly popular path to becoming an educator that is often especially appealing to nontraditional students like Manring. Similar to the medical school residency, where physicians are trained in hospitals alongside practicing clinicians, these teacher prep programs give participants almost immediate exposure to

leading a K-12 classroom instead of holding off and providing a shorter student-teaching stint just before they earn a degree. "The best place to train a teacher is in a school," says Mark Neal, the director of Project Inspire, a teacher residency in Chattanooga, Tennessee. "Everything you're learning is being applied in a classroom."

Residencies are typically comprised of a partnership between a high-need school district, a graduate school that offers master's coursework, and a coordinating nonprofit. Project Inspire, for instance, teams up the private Lee University, the local Hamilton County Department of Education, and a nonprofit called the Public Education Foundation. Residents take an initial load of classes in the summer and then jump right into co-teaching for a full school year while completing graduate coursework in the evenings and on weekends. Stanford, DePaul University and the University

EMILY POWERS LEADS A FIFTH-GRADE CLASS AS PART OF HER TEACHER RESIDENCY IN VIRGINIA.

of Denver are among those that have partnered on teacher residencies.

The goal is to staff positions that are most in demand at underserved schools and in hard-to-fill subject areas, such as math and science. "Traditionally, schools will train a teacher, and they land where they will. With a residency, they're looking to fill specific, demonstrated needs," explains Tamara Azar, chief external relations officer at the National Center for Teacher Residencies, a Chicago-based network that supports 32 such programs nationwide. "The district uses its student achievement data and works with the teacher preparation provider to train teachers to fit those needs." For instance, Chattanooga schools recently identified third-grade literacy achievement as foundational to success in other content areas and asked Project Inspire to recruit and prepare elementary teachers with a specific focus on the abilities needed to foster reading and writing skills.

The linchpin of the model is the mentor teacher, a seasoned

veteran trained to coach and co-teach with residents and gradually ease them into more responsibilities throughout the school year. At Virginia's Richmond Teacher Residency, a partnership between the city's public school system and Virginia Commonwealth University, instructional coaches are carefully selected through a competitive application process, trained, and matched with residents. For many residency programs, the hope is that residents will go on to be mentors, Azar says.

The screening process can be rigorous. Candidates for the Richmond program, for instance, must present a sample classroom lesson to K-12 students and lead a group discussion on an urban issue with other applicants. "We give them feedback and ask them how to redesign and reteach a lesson," says Therese Dozier, the program's director.

IF YOU CAN HALT TURNOVER, "THE ACHIEVEMENT WILL FOLLOW."

"If you don't embrace feedback, you're not going to work well in an urban school." The program recruits heavily from the local community, and the diversity of participants has increased significantly in recent years; 43 percent of the 2016-2017 class is African-American, Hispanic or Asian compared to 22 percent in 2011-2012, the first cohort. Grads commit to teaching in a Richmond public school for at least three more years.

Chattanooga's Project Inspire has focused on preparing middle

and high school math and science teachers, occasionally tapping tech-savvy engineers and scientists from the nearby Tennessee Valley Authority, for instance, who are interested in changing careers. (The program recently added an elementary pathway.) The Wilson fellowship, also geared toward the STEM fields, has found success in recruiting midcareer professionals and former military personnel, who have many skills that make them adept at managing a classroom, says Patrick Riccards, chief communications and strategy officer for the Woodrow Wilson Foundation.

Teacher residencies aren't for everyone. Regardless of their experience, residents say the workload makes for a demanding year, though the benefits

are real. Richmond participants, for instance, kick off with 18 to 21 credit hours in the summer, and they continue coursework at VCU evenings and weekends during their co-teaching in the fall and spring. "You're basically working and going to school full time," says Emily Powers, 32, a resident co-teaching fifth grade at Bellevue Elementary School. After a stint doing customer service for a small software company, Powers decided she wanted to teach at-risk children to read and applied to the program.

"It's very demanding and difficult, but I wouldn't have wanted it any other way," says Powers, who thinks that she'll "have a leg up over other first-year teachers who have not been exposed to every minute detail that teaching involves." Plus, she gets a $24,000 stipend and a special tuition rate to VCU during the residency. And there's the potential of a job: The program boasts a 100 percent placement rate to date for its five completed cohorts, which have ranged in size from nine to 30 residents.

So far, retention rates are promising. While federal data indicate that about 1 in 6 public school teachers leave the profession within the first five years, other estimates suggest that the figure might be as high as 50 percent. In 2015-2016, the five-year retention rate across NCTR programs was 70 percent. More than 80 percent of Wilson program residents stay in teaching in a high-need school for four years or more.

Administrators say that better retention translates to stronger student performance. In Chattanooga, about 70 percent of Project Inspire grads are teaching past their four-year obligation. Until the program started in 2010, there were as many as eight to 12 secondary math teacher vacancies at the beginning of the academic year, which meant the school had to increase class sizes and hire long-term substitutes to teach those subjects. If you can halt turnover, "the achievement will follow," says Neal. Project Inspire data show the program's grads are "outperforming traditional teachers when you compare their teacher effectiveness score, which includes a student achievement measure and observation by the principal," he says.

Even before they set foot in an elementary, middle or high school, participants take classes and field trips that shed light on the low-income communities in which they'll be placed. In Richmond, residents are encouraged to go to community events and connect with families of students. At UIndy, Manring says the class that had the biggest impact on him was on equity in education. "Some of the lessons," he says, "were about checking your assumptions at the door and really trying to see [the students] as people."

Class material is also often geared toward helping residents who have professional experience in writing or science, say, learn techniques to pass on that knowledge. "Just because you know something doesn't mean you're good at teaching it. They trust you with the content and teach you how to teach it," says Josh Bearman, 39, who ran education programs for the Chesapeake Bay Foundation in Annapolis, Maryland, and toured as a bluegrass musician before enrolling in the Richmond Teacher Residency. Five years later, he's teaching earth science at the city's Lucille M. Brown Middle School. He credits seminars on life skills – how to control your energy, for instance, and organizational strategies – with helping him learn to pace himself that first year and to further expand his science knowledge.

Many residents say that co-teaching and feedback from mentor teachers has been invaluable in

"THE LINCHPIN OF THE RESIDENCY MODEL IS THE MENTOR TEACHER."

helping them get their bearings in the classroom. Bearman, who became a coach after his residency, says the dialogue allows residents to constantly reassess their performance. Richmond coaches observe participants during the week and share insights to help them sharpen their approaches. Even after residents earn their degrees, career coaches are available to help.

For Manring, who is still teaching some three years after fulfilling his commitment, that blend of trust and assistance is vital. "You're getting some scaffolding and support," he says, "without the stress of being dropped into the deep end of the pool." ●

Why I Picked... UNIVERSITY OF WASHINGTON Seattle

Christy Harris, '12
ELEMENTARY SCHOOL TEACHER

➤ When I decided to pursue teaching, I knew I wanted to work in a Title I school. UW's College of Education was ideal for me as it emphasizes preparing teachers to serve disadvantaged communities and partners up with many area schools. UW's pipeline program allows students to learn theory and then apply it immediately. Starting in the summer, I was trained to do reading assessments and then to tutor individual students.

In the fall my classmates and I took courses four days a week and began teaching classes once a week. Guided by mentor teachers, we learned to evaluate and instruct kids with diverse abilities. By January we had moved to full-time teaching, while still meeting regularly with our mentors.

UW also matched us with after-school programs so we could understand the life challenges of many students – for example, kids whose parents worked night shifts or who had a language barrier that prevented them from helping with homework. I learned to apply these insights, discussing new concepts in class and using homework solely for review. Now with my master's, I still take advantage of UW's excellent summer programs for teachers to keep up with best practices.

The Job Market

SPOTLIGHT ON:

school
psychology

Elaine Chen
San Diego State University
College of Education, 2016

Smoothing the Path to Success

In third grade, after Elaine Chen had been falling behind in her work for a while, teachers at her San Francisco Bay Area school assessed her and recommended she be placed in a special education program. "I remember going through many cognitive tests, only to have them determine my struggles weren't caused by a learning disability but rather a language barrier," says Chen, whose first language was Mandarin and who didn't learn English until kindergarten. By fifth grade, thanks to private tutoring and her own perseverance, Chen's language and academic skills were back on track. The experience inspired her to pursue a career helping other children overcome learning challenges.

A critical resource. Today Chen, 28, is a school psychologist and behaviorist in the San Mateo-Foster City School District in California. She meets with elementary school students who are struggling to try to understand why. "It may be due to a learning disability, a behavioral issue, or some other obstacle," she notes. After pinpointing the problem, she works with the kids' "families and teachers to identify resources that can help," she says, such as counsel-ing or new learning strategies.

School psychologists typically focus on students with special needs and learning challenges. Trained in both psychology and education, they help students manage a range of complex academic and behav-ioral issues, including anxiety, depression and other mental health conditions. Job growth in the field is expected to be nearly 20 percent from 2014 to 2024, according to government projections. Salaries aver-age around $76,000 annually.

Chen earned a master's and education specialist degree from San Diego State University last spring. She took advantage of several hands-on opportunities, includ-ing fieldwork in San Diego schools focus-ing on English-language learners. She also designed literacy strategies for parents to use to help their kids improve their read-ing skills. Other grad students specialize in working with children in foster care, for instance, or with those on the autism spectrum, says Tonika Green, director of SDSU's school psychology program.

For Chen, looking at each child "holisti-cally" and developing a personalized plan with teachers and parents ensures a start on the path to success. –*Linda Childers*

... More Hot Jobs

... HEALTH EDUCATOR
Professionals who teach people about good health habits and disease prevention are employed by hospitals, physicians' offices, nonprofits and colleges. As organizations make an effort to reduce health care costs by teaching individuals about improving their lifestyle choices, the field is expected to grow 13 percent over the next decade, nearly twice the average for all jobs. Median annual pay is about $43,800.

... CURRICULUM DESIGNER
As classroom technology evolves and federal and state education standards continue to change, these education administrators work behind the scenes to help teachers keep pace and improve educational methods. Also known as instructional coordinators, these specialists develop curricula in specific school subjects and help colleagues implement lessons in the classroom. Curriculum designers command a median salary of about $62,300, compared to $54,600 for elementary school teachers and $57,200 for high school educators.

... SCHOOL COUNSELOR
These pros help students with academic and career planning, provide guidance and referrals related to bullying, family problems and grief counseling, and assist with disciplinary matters. The field is expected to grow slightly faster than average over the next decade and offers a median salary of roughly $53,700.

Schools of Education

THE TOP SCHOOLS

Rank School	Overall score	Peer assessment score (5.0=highest)	Administrator/ expert assessment score (5.0=highest)	'16 mean GRE scores (verbal/ quantitative)[1]	'16 doctoral acceptance rate	'16 doctoral students/ faculty[2]	Doctorates granted/ faculty 2015-16	'16 funded research (in millions)	'16 funded research/faculty member (in thousands)	'16 total graduate education enrollment
1. Harvard University (MA)	100	4.4	4.6	163/159	4.5%	3.8	0.9	$33.6	$764.7	866
2. Stanford University (CA)	99	4.6	4.8	162/160	6.1%	3.1	0.6	$32.0	$603.2	339
3. University of California–Los Angeles	96	4.2	4.3	156/152	29.1%	7.7	1.4	$52.0	$1,239.1	674
3. University of Pennsylvania	96	4.1	4.5	163/157	5.0%	1.4	0.3	$46.4	$663.1	1,106
3. University of Wisconsin–Madison	96	4.3	4.5	155/153	26.1%	3.1	0.4	$78.6	$491.1	1,080
6. Johns Hopkins University (MD)	95	4.1	4.1	164/162	27.4%	1.4	0.2	$42.8	$620.6	2,393
7. Teachers College, Columbia University (NY)	94	4.3	4.5	159/156	11.4%	4.4	1.2	$60.1	$401.0	4,892
7. Vanderbilt University (Peabody) (TN)	94	4.5	4.6	162/159	4.9%	2.2	0.6	$35.6	$423.7	902
9. University of Washington	92	4.0	4.4	155/152	23.7%	3.6	0.9	$42.4	$831.5	1,019
10. Northwestern University (IL)	89	3.9	4.3	162/158	8.3%	1.9	0.3	$23.4	$709.3	329
11. Arizona State University	88	3.6	3.8	157/150	20.1%	1.7	0.5	$60.1	$607.2	2,778
11. University of Texas–Austin	88	4.0	4.3	155/153	26.5%	5.0	0.7	$57.0	$527.8	1,052
13. New York University (Steinhardt)	86	3.9	4.3	158/152	7.3%	2.7	0.7	$43.2	$591.6	1,431
14. University of Oregon	85	3.6	4.0	156/153	16.5%	3.8	1.0	$37.5	$915.2	544
15. University of Michigan–Ann Arbor	81	4.4	4.6	154/152	15.1%	4.6	0.7	$18.9	$378.0	526
15. University of Southern California (Rossier)	81	3.9	4.3	161/157	13.2%	11.7	8.4	$25.1	$1,196.8	1,598
17. University of Kansas	78	3.8	4.2	156/150	46.1%	4.8	0.7	$41.0	$532.7	1,390
18. Ohio State University	77	3.8	4.3	157/155	41.0%	3.4	0.5	$30.0	$248.3	1,174
18. University of California–Berkeley	77	4.2	4.6	157/154	8.4%	7.4	1.0	$11.6	$446.5	303
18. University of Virginia (Curry)	77	4.0	4.3	159/154	16.4%	2.3	0.7	$22.3	$323.7	983
21. Michigan State University	76	4.2	4.5	156/152	37.4%	4.7	1.1	$28.7	$263.2	1,639
21. University of Minnesota–Twin Cities	76	3.7	3.9	157/153	27.6%	3.7	1.3	$46.4	$383.8	2,164
23. Boston College (Lynch) (MA)	72	3.7	4.2	159/156	8.0%	2.7	0.9	$17.6	$319.4	769
24. University of Illinois–Urbana-Champaign	70	4.0	4.1	155/160	24.8%	4.4	1.0	$14.5	$190.3	809
25. University of California–Irvine	68	3.5	3.8	156/155	17.8%	3.0	0.6	$12.3	$492.6	190
26. Utah State University	67	2.9	3.2	155/153	25.2%	1.1	0.3	$46.7	$362.0	876
27. University of Connecticut (Neag)	66	3.6	4.1	157/155	42.6%	2.1	0.3	$15.2	$226.4	759
27. University of Pittsburgh (PA)	66	3.6	3.8	152/147	50.0%	4.8	0.7	$26.1	$457.8	987
29. University of Colorado–Boulder	65	3.6	3.9	161/154	17.2%	2.5	0.6	$7.7	$239.8	355
29. University of Florida	65	3.7	3.8	155/153	56.5%	4.5	1.3	$25.1	$380.4	1,146
31. University of North Carolina–Chapel Hill	64	3.9	4.3	160/155	27.8%	4.7	0.9	$6.2	$155.0	398
32. Indiana University–Bloomington	63	3.8	4.1	153/150	47.2%	3.1	0.9	$18.6	$208.9	869
32. University of Delaware	63	3.5	3.4	155/156	40.0%	1.8	0.4	$14.7	$407.2	274
32. University of Maryland–College Park	63	3.9	4.0	159/155	23.9%	4.1	0.8	$8.1	$96.2	905
35. University of Georgia	61	3.7	4.2	154/152	33.7%	3.0	0.7	$13.0	$80.1	1,614
36. Boston University (MA)	60	3.6	3.8	163/156	25.4%	2.4	0.7	$3.7	$146.1	561
36. University of California–Davis	60	3.6	4.1	154/149	35.0%	4.2	0.9	$8.7	$311.4	423
38. George Washington University (DC)	59	3.4	4.0	164/158	58.8%	4.3	1.5	$9.3	$175.5	1,514
38. Pennsylvania State University–University Park	59	3.9	4.4	154/154	46.3%	3.6	1.0	$3.4	$28.8	1,656
38. Texas A&M University–College Station	59	3.5	4.0	151/152	54.5%	3.5	1.0	$22.9	$212.1	1,643
41. University of Massachusetts–Amherst	58	3.5	3.8	156/155	49.1%	3.5	0.3	$8.0	$131.4	549
41. Virginia Commonwealth University	58	3.0	3.6	154/148	65.4%	2.4	0.8	$24.7	$588.8	807
43. University of Iowa	57	3.5	4.0	153/153	44.9%	5.0	0.9	$11.9	$198.0	631
43. University of Missouri	57	3.4	3.7	153/151	22.2%	4.9	1.0	$16.2	$215.7	1,373
43. University of Nebraska–Lincoln	57	3.5	3.5	154/150	25.8%	2.6	1.0	$16.8	$212.5	978
46. College of William and Mary (VA)	56	3.4	4.0	156/152	56.5%	2.3	0.8	$6.7	$171.0	536
46. Purdue University–West Lafayette (IN)	56	3.5	3.8	153/151	50.9%	2.0	0.3	$10.9	$141.0	750
48. Fordham University (NY)	55	3.0	3.4	166/167	38.1%	4.6	2.0	$7.2	$247.0	850

[1]GRE scores are for doctoral students only, and all those displayed are for exams taken during or after August 2011 using the new 130-170 score scale.
[2]Student/faculty ratio is for all full-time-equivalent doctoral students and full-time faculty.
N/A–Data were not provided by the school. Sources: U.S. News and the schools. Assessment data collected by Ipsos Public Affairs.

THE TOP SCHOOLS continued

Rank School	Overall score	Peer assessment score (5.0=highest)	Administrator/ expert assessment score (5.0=highest)	'16 mean GRE scores (verbal/ quantitative)[1]	'16 doctoral acceptance rate	'16 doctoral students/ faculty[2]	Doctorates granted/ faculty 2015-16	'16 funded research (in millions)	'16 funded research/faculty member (in thousands)	'16 total graduate education enrollment
48. Georgia State University	55	3.0	3.5	156/151	17.3%	2.4	0.6	$22.5	$198.7	1,327
48. Temple University (PA)	55	3.3	3.6	155/150	30.3%	4.3	1.2	$12.4	$287.8	1,004
48. University of Illinois–Chicago	55	3.5	3.6	151/148	36.7%	3.2	1.0	$11.4	$270.3	659
52. Florida State University	54	3.3	3.7	150/151	37.9%	4.1	0.9	$13.3	$181.9	1,062
52. Rutgers, The State Univ. of N.J.–New Brunswick	54	3.5	3.8	153/148	55.0%	2.5	0.9	$8.5	$188.9	1,068
52. University of California–Santa Barbara (Gevirtz)	54	3.4	3.8	156/152	17.3%	4.1	1.2	$3.8	$87.1	273
55. North Carolina State University–Raleigh	53	3.3	3.4	154/151	42.1%	2.7	0.7	$14.6	$196.8	1,034
55. Washington University in St. Louis (MO)	53	3.4	3.7	155/155	13.0%	1.2	0.3	$0.1	$5.7	29
57. Boise State University (ID)	52	2.7	3.3	159/152	23.2%	0.9	0.2	$9.7	$201.9	1,801
57. San Diego State University (CA)	52	3.2	3.4	149/143	54.1%	1.1	0.4	$22.5	$341.4	1,378
57. Syracuse University (NY)	52	3.4	3.8	153/150	33.3%	2.5	0.6	$5.0	$92.2	567
57. University of Arizona	52	3.7	3.9	153/147	72.6%	3.6	0.8	$7.1	$122.0	757
57. University of Vermont	52	3.2	3.4	157/151	60.0%	1.0	0.3	$7.6	$210.6	276
62. George Mason University (VA)	51	3.2	3.6	154/150	64.1%	2.6	0.6	$12.9	$179.4	2,286
62. Loyola Marymount University (CA)	51	2.9	3.7	155/152	29.0%	2.1	0.8	$6.7	$216.0	1,375
62. University of Kentucky	51	3.2	3.3	154/149	49.0%	3.2	0.5	$19.9	$223.9	807
62. University of Tennessee–Knoxville	51	3.2	3.8	155/150	51.1%	1.5	0.5	$10.1	$98.2	782
66. University at Albany–SUNY (NY)	50	3.2	3.6	153/153	35.2%	2.3	0.7	$5.7	$98.2	852
66. University of Arkansas–Fayetteville	50	2.8	3.1	154/150	17.0%	2.8	0.5	$21.0	$239.0	612
66. University of Utah	50	3.3	3.6	152/151	38.8%	3.5	0.6	$7.7	$140.7	671
69. University of California–San Diego	49	3.5	3.8	153/145	26.9%	3.7	1.5	$1.0	$73.0	147
69. University of Hawaii–Manoa	49	3.0	3.2	152/149	66.4%	0.9	0.2	$17.5	$157.5	888
69. University of North Carolina–Charlotte	49	3.2	3.6	155/149	58.6%	1.4	0.3	$8.5	$96.4	1,409
72. Southern Illinois University–Carbondale	48	2.6	3.1	150/151	34.2%	2.2	0.6	$19.4	$299.2	835
72. University of California–Riverside	48	3.4	3.4	153/150	21.6%	2.7	0.6	$1.0	$53.7	259

AT VANDERBILT UNIVERSITY, TIED AT NO. 7

Rank	School	Overall score	Peer assessment score (5.0=highest)	Administrator/ expert assessment score (5.0=highest)	'16 mean GRE scores (verbal/ quantitative)[1]	'16 doctoral acceptance rate	'16 doctoral students/ faculty[2]	Doctorates granted/ faculty 2015-16	'16 funded research (in millions)	'16 funded research/faculty member (in thousands)	'16 total graduate education enrollment
74.	Clemson University (SC)	47	3.1	3.7	153/147	51.5%	1.5	0.4	$4.9	$85.2	576
74.	Lehigh University (PA)	47	2.7	3.3	156/150	18.3%	3.4	0.8	$6.1	$209.8	503
74.	University of Massachusetts–Boston	47	3.1	3.1	155/151	36.5%	1.7	0.3	$4.9	$102.7	835
77.	University of Northern Iowa	46	2.7	3.1	161/162	68.8%	0.3	0.0	$0.5	$3.9	556
77.	University of Oklahoma (Rainbolt)	46	3.1	3.6	152/145	39.4%	3.8	0.5	$7.1	$117.9	765
77.	University of Wisconsin–Milwaukee	46	3.1	3.6	154/151	31.4%	2.1	0.3	$2.8	$46.1	635
80.	Brigham Young University–Provo (McKay) (UT)	45	2.9	3.3	157/153	28.2%	1.4	0.2	$1.0	$11.7	326
80.	Iowa State University	45	3.1	3.9	152/146	48.1%	1.5	0.5	$1.8	$40.3	324
80.	University at Buffalo–SUNY (NY)	45	3.1	3.6	151/150	53.6%	4.8	1.0	$3.5	$77.2	1,010
80.	University of Miami (FL)	45	3.1	3.6	153/147	26.3%	3.9	0.6	$3.3	$103.0	490
80.	University of North Carolina–Greensboro	45	3.1	3.5	155/149	31.2%	3.0	0.6	$3.8	$54.4	914
85.	Kansas State University	44	2.9	3.5	153/147	82.9%	2.3	0.5	$7.7	$174.8	943
85.	Loyola University Chicago (IL)	44	3.1	3.3	155/152	23.9%	5.1	1.4	$2.5	$72.9	664
85.	University of Louisville (KY)	44	3.0	3.3	154/149	38.4%	1.8	0.3	$4.4	$63.1	1,322
85.	Virginia Tech	44	3.1	3.9	152/149	69.0%	4.4	1.3	$4.8	$100.8	671
89.	Auburn University (AL)	43	3.3	3.4	149/147	45.0%	3.1	0.8	$5.5	$61.7	972
89.	Baylor University (TX)	43	2.9	3.5	156/150	35.7%	1.4	0.4	$0.4	$13.4	174
89.	University of Cincinnati (OH)	43	2.9	3.2	153/150	38.1%	1.8	0.5	$6.8	$90.9	1,439
89.	University of San Diego (CA)	43	2.9	3.3	155/149	49.3%	1.9	0.7	$4.3	$135.9	825
93.	Montclair State University (NJ)	42	2.8	3.4	152/145	42.9%	0.6	0.1	$5.5	$47.8	2,212
93.	St. John's University (NY)	42	2.7	3.0	163/165	92.7%	2.5	1.1	$2.4	$55.0	1,352
93.	University of Alabama	42	3.2	3.2	152/148	52.1%	3.4	0.8	$5.2	$60.9	962
93.	University of Houston (TX)	42	3.0	3.2	153/148	31.2%	3.9	1.5	$5.6	$104.2	655
93.	University of South Carolina	42	3.1	3.6	151/148	51.6%	3.0	0.7	$3.0	$38.6	1,281
93.	University of South Florida	42	2.9	3.0	150/147	69.8%	3.6	0.7	$14.9	$163.6	1,159
99.	Kent State University (OH)	41	2.9	3.4	151/149	41.8%	3.1	0.5	$5.8	$51.9	1,607
99.	University of Central Florida	41	2.9	3.0	154/150	43.1%	2.6	1.1	$5.7	$79.7	1,646
101.	Ball State University (IN)	40	2.9	3.2	153/149	56.6%	1.7	0.5	$3.5	$41.2	3,303
101.	Marquette University (WI)	40	2.9	3.2	158/148	75.0%	0.9	0.1	$0.1	$9.0	141
101.	Miami University (OH)	40	3.1	3.7	N/A	44.7%	1.5	N/A	$1.2	$15.7	722
101.	New Mexico State University	40	2.6	2.4	156/152	47.1%	2.4	0.5	$13.3	$221.1	705
101.	Portland State University (OR)	40	2.9	3.0	N/A	62.5%	1.0	0.4	$7.4	$163.4	1,226
101.	University of Alabama–Birmingham	40	2.9	2.9	149/144	65.4%	0.9	0.3	$4.8	$110.5	730
101.	University of California–Santa Cruz	40	2.7	3.1	157/147	42.4%	2.8	0.6	$1.4	$117.9	111
101.	University of Dayton (OH)	40	2.7	3.1	157/144	33.3%	1.5	0.2	$3.5	$68.0	613
101.	University of Maine	40	3.0	3.1	154/147	86.4%	1.0	0.3	$0.9	$36.3	414
101.	University of Mississippi	40	2.8	3.3	148/145	70.4%	2.0	0.3	$9.1	$190.0	603
101.	University of Missouri–Kansas City	40	2.9	3.3	N/A	20.2%	1.6	0.4	N/A	N/A	434
112.	Appalachian State University (NC)	39	2.5	3.1	156/147	81.8%	0.0	0.0	$2.1	$2.9	881
112.	Louisiana State University–Baton Rouge	39	3.1	3.5	149/142	64.4%	2.4	0.7	N/A	N/A	725
112.	Old Dominion University (Darden) (VA)	39	2.7	3.1	150/147	71.2%	1.7	0.5	$12.1	$124.7	1,514
112.	Texas Tech University	39	2.8	3.4	151/146	51.2%	4.5	1.2	$9.4	$153.5	1,426
112.	University of Nevada–Reno	39	2.6	2.8	154/147	81.8%	1.4	0.5	$9.1	$228.4	540
112.	University of Texas–Arlington	39	2.8	3.4	150/146	48.6%	1.2	0.2	$0.6	$19.9	2,004
112.	University of Wyoming	39	2.8	3.3	156/149	70.0%	1.7	0.4	$2.8	$52.4	563
112.	Wayne State University (MI)	39	2.7	2.9	152/150	12.9%	3.2	0.8	$4.0	$82.7	1,419
120.	Claremont Graduate University (CA)	38	3.1	3.7	152/145	67.0%	11.3	2.7	$1.7	$130.8	383
120.	Howard University (DC)	38	3.0	3.3	148/142	48.9%	3.3	0.6	$2.2	$76.1	231
120.	Illinois State University	38	2.7	3.1	150/148	84.2%	0.8	0.2	$8.8	$62.2	881
120.	Mills College (CA)	38	2.7	3.4	N/A	85.2%	3.3	0.5	$2.7	$248.4	202
120.	Ohio University	38	3.0	3.4	149/145	43.0%	1.7	0.6	$1.4	$21.9	826
120.	Pennsylvania State University–Harrisburg	38	2.8	3.3	N/A	100.0%	1.8	0.3	$1.8	$252.0	130
120.	University of Colorado–Denver	38	3.1	3.1	N/A	75.0%	5.1	0.6	$5.5	$142.2	1,323
120.	University of South Dakota	38	2.8	3.3	150/146	47.6%	1.6	0.9	$2.6	$79.9	484
120.	Western Michigan University	38	2.8	3.0	152/147	34.0%	1.7	0.4	$3.7	$38.4	1,371
120.	West Virginia University	38	2.8	3.0	152/148	39.8%	1.8	0.7	$3.1	$58.5	788

SPECIALTIES
PROGRAMS RANKED BEST BY EDUCATION SCHOOL DEANS

ADMINISTRATION/SUPERVISION
1. Vanderbilt University (Peabody) (TN)
2. University of Wisconsin–Madison
3. Harvard University (MA)
4. Michigan State University
5. Teachers College, Columbia University (NY)
6. University of Texas–Austin
7. Stanford University (CA)
7. University of Washington
9. Pennsylvania State University–University Park
10. University of Virginia (Curry)
11. Ohio State University
11. University of Michigan–Ann Arbor

COUNSELING/PERSONNEL SERVICES
1. University of Maryland–College Park
2. University of Georgia
3. University of Missouri
4. Ohio State University
4. University of North Carolina–Greensboro
4. University of Wisconsin–Madison
7. University of Central Florida

CURRICULUM/INSTRUCTION
1. University of Wisconsin–Madison
2. Michigan State University
3. Teachers College, Columbia University (NY)
3. Vanderbilt University (Peabody) (TN)

5. Stanford University (CA)
6. University of Michigan–Ann Arbor
7. Ohio State University
8. University of Texas–Austin
9. Indiana University–Bloomington
9. University of Georgia
9. University of Washington

EDUCATION POLICY
1. Stanford University (CA)
2. Harvard University (MA)
3. Vanderbilt University (Peabody) (TN)
4. University of Wisconsin–Madison
5. University of Michigan–Ann Arbor
6. Teachers College, Columbia University (NY)
7. University of Pennsylvania
8. University of California–Los Angeles
9. Michigan State University
10. Pennsylvania State University–University Park
10. University of California–Berkeley
10. University of Virginia (Curry)
10. University of Washington

EDUCATIONAL PSYCHOLOGY
1. University of Wisconsin–Madison
2. University of Michigan–Ann Arbor
3. Stanford University (CA)
4. Vanderbilt University (Peabody) (TN)
5. Michigan State University
5. University of Illinois–Urbana-Champaign

5. University of Maryland–College Park
8. University of Texas–Austin
9. University of California–Berkeley
9. University of Minnesota–Twin Cities

ELEMENTARY EDUCATION
1. Michigan State University
2. University of Michigan–Ann Arbor
3. Teachers College, Columbia University (NY)
4. University of Wisconsin–Madison
5. Vanderbilt University (Peabody) (TN)
6. University of Virginia (Curry)
7. University of Georgia
7. University of Washington
9. Ohio State University
10. Indiana University–Bloomington

HIGHER EDUCATION ADMINISTRATION
1. University of Michigan–Ann Arbor
2. University of Pennsylvania
3. Michigan State University
4. University of California–Los Angeles
5. Vanderbilt University (Peabody) (TN)
6. Pennsylvania State University–University Park
7. University of Georgia
7. University of Southern California (Rossier)
9. Indiana University–Bloomington
10. University of Maryland–College Park

SECONDARY EDUCATION
1. Michigan State University
2. University of Michigan–Ann Arbor
3. University of Wisconsin–Madison
4. Stanford University (CA)
4. Teachers College, Columbia University (NY)
6. University of Georgia
7. University of Washington
8. Vanderbilt University (Peabody) (TN)
9. University of Virginia (Curry)
10. Indiana University–Bloomington
11. University of California–Los Angeles
11. University of Texas–Austin

SPECIAL EDUCATION
1. Vanderbilt University (Peabody) (TN)
2. University of Kansas
3. University of Oregon
4. University of Virginia (Curry)
5. University of Florida
5. University of Texas–Austin
7. University of Wisconsin–Madison
8. University of Minnesota–Twin Cities
9. University of Washington
10. University of Illinois–Urbana-Champaign
11. University of Maryland–College Park

VOCATIONAL/TECHNICAL
1. Ohio State University
2. Pennsylvania State University–University Park

METHODOLOGY

Graduate programs at 379 schools granting education doctoral degrees were surveyed; 256 responded and provided data needed to calculate rankings based on 10 measures:

Quality assessment: Two surveys were conducted in the fall of 2016. Education school deans and deans of graduate studies were asked to rate program quality from marginal (1) to outstanding (5); 32 percent responded. The resulting score is weighted by .25. Education schools provided names of superintendents, people who hire graduates, and education experts familiar with them,

who were also asked to rate programs. The three most recent years' results were averaged and weighted by .15.

Student selectivity (.18): Combines mean verbal and quantitative GRE scores of doctoral students entering in fall 2016 and the acceptance rate of doctoral applicants for the 2016-2017 academic year (each accounts for one-third of the measure). Where scores are not available for doctoral students, mean GRE scores for all entering students may be substituted. Only scores for the new GRE were used in the rankings; only new scores are displayed.

Faculty resources (.12): Resources include the 2016 ratio of full-time-equivalent doctoral students to full-time faculty (37.5 percent); average percentage of full-time faculty holding awards or editorships at selected education journals in 2015 and 2016 (20.8 percent); and ratio of doctoral degrees granted to full-time faculty in the 2015-2016 school year (41.7 percent).

Research activity (.30): This measure uses average total education school research expenditures (50 percent) and average expenditures per full-time faculty member (50

percent). Expenditures refer to separately funded research, public and private, averaged over fiscal years 2015 and 2016.

Overall rank: Data were standardized about their means, and standardized scores were weighted, totaled and rescaled so that the top school received 100; other schools received their percentage of the top score.

Specialty rankings: These ratings are based solely on nominations by deans and deans of graduate studies, who were asked to choose up to 10 programs for excellence in each specialty. The top ones are listed.

The Rest of the Rankings

SCULPTURE STUDENTS AT VIRGINIA COMMONWEALTH, WORKING ON A METAL POUR

THE U.S. NEWS RANKINGS

Social Sciences & Humanities

PH.D. PROGRAMS RANKED BEST BY DEPARTMENT CHAIRS AND SENIOR FACULTY

ECONOMICS Ranked in 2017

Rank	School	Average assessment score (5.0=highest)
1	Harvard University (MA)	5.0
1	Massachusetts Institute of Technology	5.0
1	Princeton University (NJ)	5.0
1	Stanford University (CA)	5.0
1	University of California–Berkeley	5.0
1	Yale University (CT)	5.0
7	Northwestern University (IL)	4.9
7	University of Chicago (IL)	4.9
9	Columbia University (NY)	4.8
10	University of Pennsylvania	4.7
11	New York University	4.5
12	University of California–Los Angeles	4.4
12	University of California–San Diego	4.4
12	University of Michigan–Ann Arbor	4.4
12	University of Wisconsin–Madison	4.4
16	Cornell University (NY)	4.3
16	Duke University (NC)	4.3
16	University of Minnesota–Twin Cities	4.3
19	Brown University (RI)	4.1
20	Carnegie Mellon University (Tepper) (PA)	4.0
21	University of Maryland–College Park	3.9
21	University of Rochester (NY)	3.9
23	Boston University (MA)	3.8
23	Johns Hopkins University (MD)	3.8
25	Boston College (MA)	3.7
25	Penn. State University–University Park	3.7
27	University of Texas–Austin	3.6
27	Washington University in St. Louis (MO)	3.6
29	Michigan State University	3.5
29	Ohio State University	3.5
29	University of California–Davis	3.5
29	University of Illinois–Urbana-Champaign	3.5
29	University of North Carolina–Chapel Hill	3.5
29	University of Virginia	3.5
35	University of Washington	3.4
35	Vanderbilt University (TN)	3.4
37	University of California–Santa Barbara	3.3
37	University of Southern California	3.3
39	Indiana University–Bloomington	3.2
39	Texas A&M University–College Station	3.2
39	University of Pittsburgh (PA)	3.2
42	Arizona State University	3.1
42	Purdue–West Lafayette (Krannert) (IN)	3.1
42	Rice University (TX)	3.1
42	University of Arizona	3.1
42	University of Iowa (Tippie)	3.1
47	Rutgers, The State U. of N.J.–New Bruns.	3.0
47	University of California–Irvine	3.0
47	University of Notre Dame (IN)	3.0
50	Georgetown University (DC)	2.9
50	Syracuse University (NY)	2.9
50	University of Colorado–Boulder	2.9

ECONOMICS SPECIALTIES

DEVELOPMENT ECONOMICS
1 Harvard University (MA)
1 Massachusetts Institute of Tech.
3 Yale University (CT)
4 University of California–Berkeley
5 Stanford University (CA)
6 Brown University (RI)

ECONOMETRICS
1 Massachusetts Institute of Tech.
2 Yale University (CT)
3 University of California–Berkeley
4 Harvard University (MA)
4 University of California–San Diego
6 Princeton University (NJ)
6 Stanford University (CA)

INDUSTRIAL ORGANIZATION
1 Massachusetts Institute of Tech.
1 Stanford University (CA)
3 Harvard University (MA)
3 Yale University (CT)
5 Northwestern University (IL)

INTERNATIONAL ECONOMICS
1 Harvard University (MA)
2 Massachusetts Institute of Tech.
3 University of California–Berkeley
4 Princeton University (NJ)
5 Yale University (CT)
6 Columbia University (NY)

LABOR ECONOMICS
1 Harvard University (MA)
2 Massachusetts Institute of Tech.
3 Princeton University (NJ)
3 University of Chicago (IL)
5 University of California–Berkeley

MACROECONOMICS
1 Harvard University (MA)
2 Massachusetts Institute of Tech.
3 Princeton University (NJ)
4 Stanford University (CA)
5 University of Pennsylvania
6 University of Minnesota–Twin Cities

MICROECONOMICS
1 Harvard University (MA)
1 Massachusetts Institute of Tech.
3 Stanford University (CA)
4 Princeton University (NJ)
5 Northwestern University (IL)
6 Yale University (CT)

PUBLIC FINANCE
1 Harvard University (MA)
2 Massachusetts Institute of Tech.
3 University of California–Berkeley
4 Stanford University (CA)
4 University of Michigan–Ann Arbor
6 Princeton University (NJ)
6 University of Chicago (IL)

ENGLISH Ranked in 2017

Rank	School	Average assessment score (5.0=highest)
1	University of California–Berkeley	4.9
1	University of Chicago (IL)	4.9
3	Columbia University (NY)	4.8
3	Stanford University (CA)	4.8
3	University of Pennsylvania	4.8
6	University of California–Los Angeles	4.7
6	University of Virginia	4.7
8	Cornell University (NY)	4.6
8	Harvard University (MA)	4.6
8	Princeton University (NJ)	4.6
8	University of Michigan–Ann Arbor	4.6
8	Yale University (CT)	4.6
13	Brown University (RI)	4.5
13	Duke University (NC)	4.5
15	Johns Hopkins University (MD)	4.4
15	Rutgers, The State U. of N.J.–New Bruns.	4.4
17	University of California–Irvine	4.3
18	Northwestern University (IL)	4.2
18	University of North Carolina–Chapel Hill	4.2
20	CUNY Grad School and U. Ctr. (NY)	4.1
20	Indiana University–Bloomington	4.1
20	New York University	4.1
20	University of California–Davis	4.1
20	University of Texas–Austin	4.1
20	University of Wisconsin–Madison	4.1
26	University of Illinois–Urbana-Champaign	4.0
27	Penn. State University–University Park	3.9
27	University of California–Santa Barbara	3.9
27	Vanderbilt University (TN)	3.9
30	Emory University (GA)	3.8
30	Ohio State University	3.8
30	University of Maryland–College Park	3.8
33	University of Notre Dame (IN)	3.7

Rank	School	Average assessment score (5.0=highest)
33	University of Southern California	3.7
35	Rice University (TX)	3.6
35	University of California–Santa Cruz	3.6
35	University of Colorado–Boulder	3.6
35	University of Illinois–Chicago	3.6
35	University of Pittsburgh (PA)	3.6

Rank	School	Average assessment score (5.0=highest)
35	University of Washington	3.6
35	Washington University in St. Louis (MO)	3.6
42	Boston University (MA)	3.5
42	University at Buffalo–SUNY (NY)	3.5
42	University of California–San Diego	3.5
42	University of Iowa	3.5

Rank	School	Average assessment score (5.0=highest)
42	University of Minnesota–Twin Cities	3.5
47	Brandeis University (MA)	3.4
47	Claremont Graduate University (CA)	3.4
47	University of California–Riverside	3.4
47	University of Oregon	3.4

ENGLISH SPECIALTIES

AFRICAN-AMERICAN LITERATURE
1 Columbia University (NY)
1 Harvard University (MA)
1 University of California–Berkeley

AMERICAN LITERATURE BEFORE 1865
1 University of California–Berkeley
2 University of Pennsylvania
3 University of California–Los Angeles
4 Stanford University (CA)

5 Columbia University (NY)
5 Cornell University (NY)
5 Harvard University (MA)
5 University of Virginia
5 Yale University (CT)

AMERICAN LITERATURE AFTER 1865
1 Stanford University (CA)
2 University of Chicago (IL)
3 University of California–Berkeley

18TH- THROUGH 20TH-CENTURY BRITISH LITERATURE
1 University of California–Berkeley
2 Columbia University (NY)
2 Stanford University (CA)
4 University of Chicago (IL)
5 University of California–Los Angeles
5 Yale University (CT)

GENDER AND LITERATURE
1 University of California–Berkeley

LITERARY CRITICISM AND THEORY
1 University of California–Irvine
1 University of Chicago (IL)

MEDIEVAL/RENAISSANCE LITERATURE
1 University of California–Berkeley
2 Yale University (CT)
3 Harvard University (MA)
4 Stanford University (CA)
5 University of Pennsylvania

HISTORY Ranked in 2017

Rank	School	Average assessment score (5.0=highest)
1	Princeton University (NJ)	4.8
1	Stanford University (CA)	4.8
1	Yale University (CT)	4.8
4	Harvard University (MA)	4.7
4	University of California–Berkeley	4.7
6	Columbia University (NY)	4.6
6	University of Chicago (IL)	4.6
6	University of Michigan–Ann Arbor	4.6
9	University of California–Los Angeles	4.5
9	University of Wisconsin–Madison	4.5
11	Cornell University (NY)	4.4
11	Johns Hopkins University (MD)	4.4
11	Northwestern University (IL)	4.4

Rank	School	Average assessment score (5.0=highest)
11	University of North Carolina–Chapel Hill	4.4
11	University of Pennsylvania	4.4
16	Brown University (RI)	4.3
16	University of Texas–Austin	4.3
18	Duke University (NC)	4.2
18	University of Virginia (Corcoran)	4.2
20	Indiana University–Bloomington	4.1
21	Georgetown University (DC)	4.0
21	Rutgers, The State U. of N.J.–New Bruns.	4.0
23	New York University	3.9
23	University of Illinois–Urbana-Champaign	3.9
23	University of Washington	3.9
23	Vanderbilt University (TN)	3.9

Rank	School	Average assessment score (5.0=highest)
27	College of William and Mary (Tyler) (VA)	3.8
27	Emory University (GA)	3.8
27	Ohio State University	3.8
27	University of Maryland–College Park	3.8
27	University of Notre Dame (IN)	3.8
32	University of California–Davis	3.7
32	University of Minnesota–Twin Cities	3.7
34	Brandeis University (MA)	3.6
34	CUNY Grad School and U. Ctr. (NY)	3.6
34	Rice University (TX)	3.6
34	University of California–Irvine	3.6

HISTORY SPECIALTIES

AFRICAN HISTORY
1 Michigan State University
1 Northwestern University (IL)

AFRICAN-AMERICAN HISTORY
1 Rutgers, The State U. of N.J.–New Bruns.
2 Duke University (NC)
2 University of Maryland–College Park
2 University of North Carolina–Chapel Hill
2 Yale University (CT)

ASIAN HISTORY
1 University of California–Berkeley
2 Harvard University (MA)
2 Princeton University (NJ)
4 Yale University (CT)

CULTURAL HISTORY
1 University of California–Berkeley

EUROPEAN HISTORY
1 Yale University (CT)
2 University of California–Berkeley
3 Harvard University (MA)
3 Princeton University (NJ)
5 University of Chicago (IL)

6 Columbia University (NY)
6 University of California–Los Angeles
6 University of Michigan–Ann Arbor

LATIN AMERICAN HISTORY
1 University of Texas–Austin
2 University of California–Los Angeles
2 University of Chicago (IL)
2 University of Wisconsin–Madison

MODERN U.S. HISTORY
1 Yale University (CT)
2 University of California–Berkeley
3 Columbia University (NY)
4 Harvard University (MA)

5 Princeton University (NJ)
5 Stanford University (CA)
5 University of Michigan–Ann Arbor
5 University of Wisconsin–Madison

U.S. COLONIAL HISTORY
1 Harvard University (MA)
1 University of Virginia (Corcoran)
3 College of William and Mary (Tyler) (VA)

WOMEN'S HISTORY
1 Rutgers, The State U. of N.J.–New Bruns.

POLITICAL SCIENCE Ranked in 2017

Rank	School	Average assessment score (5.0=highest)
1	Harvard University (MA)	4.9
1	Stanford University (CA)	4.9
3	Princeton University (NJ)	4.8
4	University of California–Berkeley	4.7
4	University of Michigan–Ann Arbor	4.7
4	Yale University (CT)	4.7
7	Columbia University (NY)	4.5
7	Duke University (NC)	4.5
9	Massachusetts Institute of Technology	4.3
9	University of California–San Diego	4.3
11	University of North Carolina–Chapel Hill	4.2
12	New York University	4.1
12	University of California–Los Angeles	4.1
12	University of Chicago (IL)	4.1
15	Ohio State University	4.0

Rank	School	Average assessment score (5.0=highest)
15	University of Wisconsin–Madison	4.0
17	University of California–Davis	3.9
17	University of Rochester (NY)	3.9
19	Cornell University (NY)	3.8
19	University of Pennsylvania	3.8
19	University of Texas–Austin	3.8
19	Washington University in St. Louis (MO)	3.8
23	Northwestern University (IL)	3.7
24	Emory University (GA)	3.5
24	Texas A&M University–College Station	3.5
24	University of Illinois–Urbana-Champaign	3.5
24	University of Minnesota–Twin Cities	3.5
24	Vanderbilt University (TN)	3.5
29	Indiana University–Bloomington	3.4
29	Michigan State University	3.4

Rank	School	Average assessment score (5.0=highest)
29	Stony Brook University–SUNY (NY)	3.4
29	University of Maryland–College Park	3.4
33	Georgetown University (DC)	3.3
33	Penn. State University–University Park	3.3
33	Rice University (TX)	3.3
33	University of Washington	3.3
37	University of Iowa	3.2
37	University of Notre Dame (IN)	3.2
37	University of Virginia	3.2
40	Brown University (RI)	3.1
40	Florida State University	3.1
40	George Washington University (DC)	3.1
40	University of Colorado–Boulder	3.1
40	University of Pittsburgh (PA)	3.1

POLITICAL SCIENCE SPECIALTIES

AMERICAN POLITICS
1 Stanford University (CA)
2 Princeton University (NJ)
3 Harvard University (MA)
4 University of California–Berkeley
5 University of Michigan–Ann Arbor
6 Duke University (NC)
7 Columbia University (NY)
7 Yale University (CT)

COMPARATIVE POLITICS
1 Harvard University (MA)

2 Princeton University (NJ)
2 Stanford University (CA)
4 Yale University (CT)
5 University of California–Berkeley
6 University of Michigan–Ann Arbor
7 Columbia University (NY)

INTERNATIONAL POLITICS
1 Princeton University (NJ)
1 Stanford University (CA)
3 Harvard University (MA)
4 University of California–San Diego

5 Columbia University (NY)
5 University of Michigan–Ann Arbor
7 New York University
8 Ohio State University
8 University of California–Berkeley

POLITICAL METHODOLOGY
1 Harvard University (MA)
1 Stanford University (CA)
3 Princeton University (NJ)
4 University of Rochester (NY)
5 New York University

5 University of Michigan–Ann Arbor
7 University of California–Berkeley
7 Washington University in St. Louis (MO)

POLITICAL THEORY
1 Princeton University (NJ)
2 Harvard University (MA)
3 Yale University (CT)
4 University of Chicago (IL)
5 University of California–Berkeley
6 Duke University (NC)

PSYCHOLOGY Ranked in 2017

Rank	School	Average assessment score (5.0=highest)
1	Stanford University (CA)	4.8
1	University of California–Berkeley	4.8
3	Harvard University (MA)	4.7
3	University of California–Los Angeles	4.7
3	University of Michigan–Ann Arbor	4.7
3	Yale University (CT)	4.7
7	University of Illinois–Urbana-Champaign	4.5
8	Massachusetts Institute of Technology	4.4
8	Princeton University (NJ)	4.4
8	University of Minnesota–Twin Cities	4.4
8	University of Pennsylvania	4.4
8	University of Texas–Austin	4.4
13	University of California–San Diego	4.3
13	University of North Carolina–Chapel Hill	4.3
13	University of Wisconsin–Madison	4.3
13	Washington University in St. Louis (MO)	4.3
17	Carnegie Mellon University (PA)	4.2
17	Columbia University (NY)	4.2
17	Duke University (NC)	4.2
17	Indiana University–Bloomington	4.2
17	Northwestern University (IL)	4.2
17	University of Chicago (IL)	4.2
17	University of Virginia	4.2
24	Cornell University (NY)	4.1
24	Ohio State University	4.1
26	Brown University (RI)	4.0
26	Johns Hopkins University (MD)	4.0

Rank	School	Average assessment score (5.0=highest)
26	Penn. State University–University Park	4.0
26	University of California–Davis	4.0
26	University of Colorado–Boulder	4.0
26	University of Iowa	4.0
26	University of Pittsburgh (PA)	4.0
26	University of Southern California	4.0
26	University of Washington	4.0
26	Vanderbilt University (TN)	4.0
36	Emory University (GA)	3.9
36	New York University	3.9
36	University of California–Irvine	3.9
39	Arizona State University	3.8
39	Boston University (MA)	3.8
39	Purdue University–West Lafayette (IN)	3.8
39	Stony Brook University–SUNY (NY)	3.8
39	University of Florida	3.8
39	University of Maryland–College Park	3.8
45	Georgia Institute of Technology	3.7
45	Michigan State University	3.7
45	University of Arizona	3.7
45	University of Missouri	3.7
45	University of Oregon	3.7
50	Rice University (TX)	3.6
50	University of Kansas	3.6
50	University of Rochester (NY)	3.6
53	Boston College (MA)	3.5
53	Dartmouth College (NH)	3.5

Rank	School	Average assessment score (5.0=highest)
53	Georgetown University (DC)	3.5
53	Rutgers, The State U. of N.J.–New Bruns.	3.5
53	University of California–Santa Barbara	3.5
53	University of Connecticut	3.5
53	University of Massachusetts–Amherst	3.5
60	Florida State University	3.4
60	Teachers College, Columbia U. (NY)	3.4
60	Temple University (PA)	3.4
60	University of Miami (FL)	3.4
60	University of Notre Dame (IN)	3.4
60	Virginia Commonwealth University	3.4
66	Northeastern University (MA)	3.3
66	Oregon Health and Science University	3.3
66	Texas A&M University–College Station	3.3
66	University of California–Riverside	3.3
66	University of Delaware	3.3
66	University of Nebraska–Lincoln	3.3
66	U. of Oklahoma Health Sciences Center	3.3
66	U. of Texas Southwestern Medical Ctr.–Dallas	3.3
66	University of Vermont	3.3
75	Brandeis University (MA)	3.2
75	University at Buffalo–SUNY (NY)	3.2
75	University of Georgia	3.2
75	University of Illinois–Chicago	3.2
75	University of Kentucky	3.2
75	University of Utah	3.2

PSYCHOLOGY SPECIALTIES

BEHAVIORAL NEUROSCIENCE
1 University of Michigan–Ann Arbor
2 Harvard University (MA)
2 Stanford University (CA)

COGNITIVE PSYCHOLOGY
1 Stanford University (CA)
1 University of California–Berkeley
3 Harvard University (MA)
3 Massachusetts Institute of Tech.

5 Carnegie Mellon University (PA)
5 Yale University (CT)
7 University of Illinois–Urbana-Champaign

DEVELOPMENTAL PSYCHOLOGY
1 University of Minnesota–Twin Cities
2 University of Michigan–Ann Arbor
3 Stanford University (CA)

EXPERIMENTAL PSYCHOLOGY
1 University of Michigan–Ann Arbor
2 Harvard University (MA)
2 Yale University (CT)

INDUSTRIAL AND ORGANIZATIONAL PSYCHOLOGY
1 Michigan State University
2 Bowling Green State University (OH)

2 Georgia Institute of Technology
2 University of Minnesota–Twin Cities
2 University of South Florida

SOCIAL PSYCHOLOGY
1 Stanford University (CA)
2 University of Michigan–Ann Arbor
3 Ohio State University
4 University of California–Los Angeles
4 Yale University (CT)

SOCIOLOGY Ranked in 2017

Rank	School	Average assessment score (5.0=highest)
1	Harvard University (MA)	4.7
1	Princeton University (NJ)	4.7
1	University of California–Berkeley	4.7
1	University of Michigan–Ann Arbor	4.7
5	Stanford University (CA)	4.6
6	University of North Carolina–Chapel Hill	4.5
6	University of Wisconsin–Madison	4.5
8	University of California–Los Angeles	4.4
8	University of Chicago (IL)	4.4
10	Northwestern University (IL)	4.3
11	Columbia University (NY)	4.2
11	New York University	4.2
11	University of Pennsylvania	4.2
11	University of Texas–Austin	4.2
15	Duke University (NC)	4.1
15	Indiana University–Bloomington	4.1
17	Cornell University (NY)	4.0
17	Ohio State University	4.0
17	Penn. State University–University Park	4.0
17	University of Minnesota–Twin Cities	4.0
17	University of Washington	4.0
22	Yale University (CT)	3.9
23	University of California–Irvine	3.8
24	Brown University (RI)	3.7
24	University of Arizona	3.7
24	University of Maryland–College Park	3.7
27	Johns Hopkins University (MD)	3.6
28	CUNY Grad School and U. Ctr. (NY)	3.5
28	Rutgers, The State U. of N.J.–New Bruns.	3.5
30	University of California–Davis	3.4
30	University of Massachusetts–Amherst	3.4
32	University of California–Santa Barbara	3.3
32	University of Notre Dame (IN)	3.3
32	University of Virginia	3.3
32	Vanderbilt University (TN)	3.3
36	Emory University (GA)	3.2
36	University at Albany–SUNY (NY)	3.2
36	University of California–San Diego	3.2
36	University of Iowa	3.2
40	Stony Brook University–SUNY (NY)	3.1
40	University of Southern California	3.1

SOCIOLOGY SPECIALTIES

ECONOMIC SOCIOLOGY
1 University of California–Berkeley
2 Harvard University (MA)
3 Princeton University (NJ)
3 Stanford University (CA)

HISTORICAL SOCIOLOGY
1 Harvard University (MA)
1 Yale University (CT)

SEX AND GENDER
1 Stanford University (CA)
2 New York University

3 University of California–Berkeley
4 University of California–Santa Barbara

SOCIAL PSYCHOLOGY
1 Stanford University (CA)
2 Indiana University–Bloomington
3 University of Iowa

SOCIAL STRATIFICATION
1 University of Wisconsin–Madison
2 Stanford University (CA)
3 Harvard University (MA)

4 University of Michigan–Ann Arbor
5 University of California–Los Angeles
6 Princeton University (NJ)
7 New York University

SOCIOLOGY OF CULTURE
1 Princeton University (NJ)
2 Harvard University (MA)
2 University of California–Berkeley
4 Northwestern University (IL)
5 Yale University (CT)

SOCIOLOGY OF POPULATION
1 University of Texas–Austin
2 University of Wisconsin–Madison
3 University of North Carolina–Chapel Hill
4 University of Michigan–Ann Arbor
5 University of California–Berkeley
6 University of Pennsylvania
7 New York University
7 Penn. State University–University Park
7 Stanford University (CA)

METHODOLOGY

Rankings of doctoral programs in the social sciences and humanities are based solely on the results of peer assessment surveys sent to academics in each discipline. Each school offering a doctoral program was sent two surveys. The questionnaires asked respondents to rate the academic quality of the program at each institution on a 5-point scale: outstanding (5), strong (4), good (3), adequate (2), or marginal (1). Individuals who were unfamiliar with a

particular school's programs were asked to select "don't know." Scores for each school were determined by computing a trimmed mean (eliminating the two highest and two lowest responses) of the ratings of all respondents who rated that school; average scores were then sorted in descending order.

Surveys were conducted in the fall of 2016 by Ipsos Public Affairs. Questionnaires were sent to department heads and directors of graduate studies (or alternatively a senior faculty

member who teaches graduate students) at schools that had granted a total of five or more doctorates in each discipline during the five-year period 2011-2015 as indicated by the National Center for Education Statistics' IPEDS Completions survey. The surveys asked about Ph.D. programs in economics (response rate: 23 percent), English (14 percent), history (15 percent), political science (24 percent), psychology (14 percent), and sociology (33 percent).

In psychology, a school was listed once on the survey even if it grants a doctoral degree in psychology in multiple departments. Programs in clinical psychology are ranked separately in the health professions section. Specialty rankings are based solely on nominations by department heads and directors of graduate studies at peer schools from the list of schools surveyed. They named up to 10 programs in each area. Those with the most votes appear.

The Sciences

PH.D. PROGRAMS RANKED BEST BY DEANS AND DEPARTMENT CHAIRS

BIOLOGICAL SCIENCES Ranked in 2014

Listed schools may have multiple programs.

Rank	School	Average assessment score (5.0=highest)
1.	Harvard University (MA)	4.9
1.	Massachusetts Institute of Technology	4.9
1.	Stanford University (CA)	4.9
4.	University of California–Berkeley	4.8
5.	California Institute of Technology	4.7
5.	Johns Hopkins University (MD)	4.7
7.	University of California–San Francisco	4.6
7.	Yale University (CT)	4.6
9.	Princeton University (NJ)	4.5
9.	Scripps Research Institute (CA)	4.5
11.	Cornell University (NY)	4.4
11.	Duke University (NC)	4.4
11.	Washington University in St. Louis	4.4
14.	Columbia University (NY)	4.3
14.	Rockefeller University (NY)	4.3
14.	University of California–San Diego	4.3
14.	University of Chicago	4.3
18.	University of Wisconsin–Madison	4.2
19.	University of California–Davis	4.1
19.	University of California–Los Angeles	4.1
19.	University of Michigan–Ann Arbor	4.1
19.	University of Pennsylvania	4.1
19.	University of Washington	4.1
19.	U. of Texas Southwest. Med. Ctr.–Dallas	4.1
25.	Baylor College of Medicine (TX)	4.0
26.	Cornell University (Weill) (NY)	3.9
26.	Northwestern University (IL)	3.9
26.	University of North Carolina–Chapel Hill	3.9
26.	Vanderbilt University (TN)	3.9
30.	Emory University (GA)	3.8
30.	University of Colorado–Boulder	3.8
30.	University of Illinois–Urbana-Champaign	3.8
30.	University of Texas–Austin	3.8
34.	Brown University (RI)	3.7
34.	Indiana University–Bloomington	3.7
34.	University of California–Irvine	3.7
34.	University of Minnesota–Twin Cities	3.7
38.	Case Western Reserve University (OH)	3.6
38.	Dartmouth College (NH)	3.6
38.	Mayo Medical School (MN)	3.6
38.	University of Arizona	3.6
42.	Carnegie Mellon University (PA)	3.5
42.	Icahn Sch. of Medicine at Mt. Sinai (NY)	3.5
42.	Ohio State University	3.5
42.	Penn. State University–University Park	3.5
42.	Rice University (TX)	3.5
42.	University of Alabama–Birmingham	3.5
42.	University of Georgia	3.5
42.	University of Pittsburgh	3.5
50.	Michigan State University	3.4
50.	University of California–Santa Barbara	3.4
50.	University of Virginia	3.4
50.	U. of Mass. Medical Center–Worcester	3.4
50.	Yeshiva University (Einstein) (NY)	3.4
55.	Arizona State University	3.3
55.	Brandeis University (MA)	3.3
55.	Georgia Institute of Technology	3.3
55.	Purdue University–West Lafayette (IN)	3.3
55.	Stony Brook University–SUNY	3.3
55.	University of California–Santa Cruz	3.3
55.	University of Florida	3.3
55.	University of Iowa	3.3
55.	University of Maryland–College Park	3.3
55.	University of Massachusetts–Amherst	3.3
55.	University of Oregon	3.3
55.	University of Southern California	3.3
55.	University of Utah	3.3
68.	New York University	3.2
68.	Oregon Health and Science University	3.2
68.	Rutgers, the State U. of N.J.–New Bruns.	3.2
68.	Tufts University (MA)	3.2
68.	University of California–Riverside	3.2
68.	University of Kansas	3.2
68.	University of Rochester (NY)	3.2
75.	Colorado State University	3.1
75.	Iowa State University	3.1
75.	North Carolina State University	3.1
75.	Oregon State University	3.1
75.	Texas A&M University–College Station	3.1
75.	University of Colorado–Denver	3.1
75.	University of Connecticut	3.1
75.	University of Illinois–Chicago	3.1
75.	U. of Texas Health Sci. Ctr.–Houston	3.1

BIOLOGICAL SCIENCES SPECIALTIES

BIOCHEMISTRY/BIOPHYSICS/ STRUCTURAL BIOLOGY
1. Harvard University (MA)
1. Stanford University (CA)
3. California Institute of Technology
3. Yale University (CT)

CELL BIOLOGY
1. Yale University (CT)
2. Stanford University (CA)
3. Harvard University (MA)
3. Johns Hopkins University (MD)

ECOLOGY/EVOLUTIONARY BIOLOGY
1. University of California–Berkeley
2. Cornell University (NY)
3. University of California–Davis
4. Stanford University (CA)
4. University of Chicago

GENETICS/GENOMICS/ BIOINFORMATICS
1. Harvard University (MA)
1. Stanford University (CA)
3. University of California–Berkeley
3. University of Washington

IMMUNOLOGY/INFECTIOUS DISEASE
1. Johns Hopkins University (MD)
2. University of California–San Francisco
3. Harvard University (MA)

MICROBIOLOGY
1. Harvard University (MA)
2. Stanford University (CA)

MOLECULAR BIOLOGY
1. Harvard University (MA)

1. University of California–Berkeley
3. Johns Hopkins University (MD)
4. Massachusetts Institute of Technology
4. Stanford University (CA)

NEUROSCIENCE/NEUROBIOLOGY
1. Stanford University (CA)
2. University of California– San Diego
3. California Institute of Technology
3. Johns Hopkins University (MD)

More @ usnews.com/grad

CHEMISTRY Ranked in 2014

Rank	School	Average assessment score (5.0=highest)
1.	California Institute of Technology	5.0
1.	Massachusetts Institute of Technology	5.0
1.	University of California–Berkeley	5.0
4.	Harvard University (MA)	4.9
4.	Stanford University (CA)	4.9
6.	University of Illinois–Urbana-Champaign	4.7
7.	Northwestern University (IL)	4.6
7.	Scripps Research Institute (CA)	4.6
9.	University of Wisconsin–Madison	4.5
10.	Columbia University (NY)	4.4
10.	Cornell University (NY)	4.4
12.	University of Chicago	4.3
12.	University of Texas–Austin	4.3
12.	Yale University (CT)	4.3
15.	Princeton University (NJ)	4.2
15.	University of California–Los Angeles	4.2
15.	University of Michigan–Ann Arbor	4.2
15.	University of North Carolina–Chapel Hill	4.2
19.	Texas A&M University–College Station	4.0
19.	University of Pennsylvania	4.0
21.	Penn. State University–University Park	3.9
21.	Purdue University–West Lafayette (IN)	3.9
21.	University of California–San Diego	3.9
24.	Georgia Institute of Technology	3.8
24.	Indiana University–Bloomington	3.8
24.	Johns Hopkins University (MD)	3.8
24.	University of California–Irvine	3.8
24.	University of Colorado–Boulder	3.8
24.	University of Minnesota–Twin Cities	3.8
24.	University of Washington	3.8
31.	Ohio State University	3.7
31.	University of California–San Francisco	3.7
33.	Rice University (TX)	3.6
33.	University of California–Santa Barbara	3.6
35.	Emory University (GA)	3.5
35.	University of California–Davis	3.5
35.	University of Florida	3.5
35.	University of Pittsburgh	3.5
35.	University of Utah	3.5
35.	Washington University in St. Louis	3.5
41.	Duke University (NC)	3.4
41.	University of Arizona	3.4
41.	University of Maryland–College Park	3.4
41.	U. of Texas Southwest. Med. Ct.–Dallas	3.4
45.	Carnegie Mellon University (PA)	3.3
45.	Iowa State University	3.3
45.	Michigan State University	3.3
45.	Vanderbilt University (TN)	3.3
49.	Boston College	3.2
49.	Colorado State University	3.2
49.	Florida State University	3.2
49.	Rockefeller University (NY)	3.2
49.	University of Rochester (NY)	3.2
49.	University of Southern California	3.2
49.	University of Virginia	3.2
56.	North Carolina State University	3.1
56.	Stony Brook University–SUNY	3.1
56.	University of Georgia	3.1
56.	University of Massachusetts–Amherst	3.1
60.	Arizona State University	3.0
60.	Boston University	3.0
60.	Brown University (RI)	3.0
60.	New York University	3.0
60.	Rutgers, the State U. of N.J.–New Bruns.	3.0
60.	University of California–Riverside	3.0
60.	University of Delaware	3.0
60.	University of Iowa	3.0
60.	University of Notre Dame (IN)	3.0
60.	University of Oregon	3.0
60.	Virginia Tech	3.0

CHEMISTRY SPECIALTIES

ANALYTICAL
1. Purdue Univ.–West Lafayette (IN)
2. University of North Carolina–Chapel Hill
3. University of Illinois–Urbana-Champaign
4. University of Texas–Austin
5. Indiana University–Bloomington
6. University of Wisconsin–Madison

BIOCHEMISTRY
1. University of California–Berkeley
2. Scripps Research Institute (CA)
2. University of Wisconsin–Madison
4. Harvard University (MA)
5. University of California–San Francisco
6. Stanford University (CA)
7. Mass. Institute of Technology

INORGANIC
1. Mass. Institute of Technology
2. California Institute of Technology
3. University of California–Berkeley
4. Northwestern University (IL)
5. Texas A&M University–College Station
6. University of Wisconsin–Madison

ORGANIC
1. Harvard University (MA)
2. California Institute of Technology
3. University of California–Berkeley
4. Mass. Institute of Technology
5. Stanford University (CA)
6. Scripps Research Institute (CA)
7. Princeton University (NJ)
8. University of Wisconsin–Madison

PHYSICAL
1. University of California–Berkeley
2. California Institute of Technology
3. Mass. Institute of Technology
4. Stanford University (CA)
5. Northwestern University (IL)
6. University of Chicago

THEORETICAL
1. University of California–Berkeley
2. California Institute of Technology
3. Harvard University (MA)
3. University of Chicago
5. Columbia University (NY)
5. Yale University (CT)
7. Mass. Institute of Technology
7. Stanford University (CA)

GETTY IMAGES

COMPUTER SCIENCE Ranked in 2014

Rank	School	Average assessment score (5.0=highest)
1.	Carnegie Mellon University (PA)	5.0
1.	Massachusetts Institute of Technology	5.0
1.	Stanford University (CA)	5.0
1.	University of California–Berkeley	5.0
5.	University of Illinois–Urbana-Champaign	4.6
6.	Cornell University (NY)	4.5
6.	University of Washington	4.5
8.	Princeton University (NJ)	4.4
9.	Georgia Institute of Technology	4.3
9.	University of Texas–Austin	4.3
11.	California Institute of Technology	4.2
11.	University of Wisconsin–Madison	4.2
13.	University of California–Los Angeles	4.1
13.	University of Michigan–Ann Arbor	4.1
15.	Columbia University (NY)	4.0
15.	University of California–San Diego	4.0
15.	University of Maryland–College Park	4.0
18.	Harvard University (MA)	3.9
19.	University of Pennsylvania	3.8
20.	Brown University (RI)	3.7
20.	Purdue University–West Lafayette (IN)	3.7
20.	Rice University (TX)	3.7
20.	University of Southern California	3.7
20.	Yale University (CT)	3.7
25.	Duke University (NC)	3.6
25.	University of Massachusetts–Amherst	3.6
25.	University of North Carolina–Chapel Hill	3.6
28.	Johns Hopkins University (MD)	3.5
29.	New York University	3.4
29.	Penn. State University–University Park	3.4
29.	University of California–Irvine	3.4
29.	University of Minnesota–Twin Cities	3.4
29.	University of Virginia	3.4
34.	Northwestern University (IL)	3.3
34.	Ohio State University	3.3
34.	Rutgers, the State U. of N.J.–New Bruns.	3.3
34.	University of California–Davis	3.3
34.	University of California–Santa Barbara	3.3
34.	University of Chicago	3.3
40.	Dartmouth College (NH)	3.1
40.	Stony Brook University–SUNY	3.1
40.	Texas A&M University–College Station	3.1
40.	University of Arizona	3.1
40.	University of Colorado–Boulder	3.1
40.	University of Utah	3.1
40.	Virginia Tech	3.1
40.	Washington University in St. Louis	3.1
48.	Arizona State University	3.0
48.	Boston University	3.0
48.	North Carolina State University	3.0
48.	University of Florida	3.0

COMPUTER SCIENCE SPECIALTIES

ARTIFICIAL INTELLIGENCE
1. Stanford University (CA)
2. Carnegie Mellon University (PA)
3. Mass. Institute of Technology
4. University of California–Berkeley
5. University of Washington
6. Georgia Institute of Technology
7. University of Illinois–Urbana-Champaign
7. University of Texas–Austin
9. Cornell University (NY)
9. University of California–Los Angeles

PROGRAMMING LANGUAGE
1. Carnegie Mellon University (PA)
2. University of California–Berkeley
3. Stanford University (CA)
4. Mass. Institute of Technology
5. Princeton University (NJ)
6. Cornell University (NY)
7. University of Pennsylvania
8. University of Texas–Austin
9. University of Illinois–Urbana-Champaign
10. University of Wisconsin–Madison

SYSTEMS
1. University of California–Berkeley
2. Mass. Institute of Technology
3. Stanford University (CA)
4. Carnegie Mellon University (PA)
5. University of Washington
6. Georgia Institute of Technology
7. University of Illinois–Urbana-Champaign
8. University of Texas–Austin
8. University of Wisconsin–Madison
10. University of Michigan–Ann Arbor

THEORY
1. University of California–Berkeley
2. Mass. Institute of Technology
3. Stanford University (CA)
4. Princeton University (NJ)
5. Carnegie Mellon University (PA)
6. Cornell University (NY)
7. Harvard University (MA)
8. Georgia Institute of Technology
9. University of Washington

EARTH SCIENCES Ranked in 2014

Rank	School	Average assessment score (5.0=highest)
1.	California Institute of Technology	4.9
2.	Massachusetts Institute of Technology	4.8
3.	Stanford University (CA)	4.6
3.	University of California–Berkeley	4.6
5.	Columbia University (NY)	4.5
6.	Penn. State University–University Park	4.4
7.	University of Arizona	4.3
8.	Harvard University (MA)	4.2
8.	University of Michigan–Ann Arbor	4.2
8.	University of Texas–Austin	4.2
11.	Princeton University (NJ)	4.1
11.	University of Washington	4.1
13.	University of California–Los Angeles	4.0
13.	University of Wisconsin–Madison	4.0
13.	Yale University (CT)	4.0
16.	Brown University (RI)	3.9
16.	Cornell University (NY)	3.9
16.	University of California–San Diego	3.9
16.	University of California–Santa Cruz	3.9
20.	Arizona State University	3.8
20.	University of California–Davis	3.8
20.	University of Chicago	3.8
23.	University of California–Santa Barbara	3.7
23.	University of Colorado–Boulder	3.7
25.	Colorado School of Mines	3.6
25.	Rice University (TX)	3.6
25.	University of Minnesota–Twin Cities	3.6
25.	University of Southern California	3.6
25.	Washington University in St. Louis	3.6
30.	Johns Hopkins University (MD)	3.5
30.	Virginia Tech	3.5
32.	Texas A&M University–College Station	3.4
32.	University of Maryland–College Park	3.4
34.	Northwestern University (IL)	3.3
34.	Ohio State University	3.3
34.	Oregon State University	3.3
34.	Stony Brook University–SUNY	3.3
34.	University of California–Irvine	3.3
34.	University of Hawaii–Manoa	3.3
34.	University of Illinois–Urbana-Champaign	3.3
34.	University of Oregon	3.3

EARTH SCIENCES SPECIALTIES

ENVIRONMENTAL SCIENCES
1. Stanford University (CA)
2. Pennsylvania State University–University Park
3. Columbia University (NY)
3. University of California–Berkeley
5. University of Michigan–Ann Arbor
5. University of Wisconsin–Madison

GEOCHEMISTRY
1. California Institute of Technology
2. Pennsylvania State University–University Park

GEOLOGY
1. Pennsylvania State University–University Park
2. University of Michigan–Ann Arbor
3. Stanford University (CA)
3. University of Arizona
5. California Institute of Technology
5. University of Texas–Austin

GEOPHYSICS AND SEISMOLOGY
1. University of California–Berkeley
2. California Institute of Technology
3. Stanford University (CA)
4. Massachusetts Institute of Technology

PALEONTOLOGY
1. University of Chicago
2. University of California–Berkeley

MATHEMATICS Ranked in 2014

Rank	School	Average assessment score (5.0=highest)
1.	Massachusetts Institute of Technology	5.0
1.	Princeton University (NJ)	5.0
3.	Harvard University (MA)	4.9
3.	University of California–Berkeley	4.9
5.	Stanford University (CA)	4.8
5.	University of Chicago	4.8
7.	California Institute of Technology	4.6
7.	University of California–Los Angeles	4.6
9.	Columbia University (NY)	4.5
9.	New York University	4.5
9.	University of Michigan–Ann Arbor	4.5
9.	Yale University (CT)	4.5
13.	Cornell University (NY)	4.3
14.	Brown University (RI)	4.2
14.	University of Texas–Austin	4.2
14.	University of Wisconsin–Madison	4.2
17.	Duke University (NC)	4.0
17.	Northwestern University (IL)	4.0
17.	University of Illinois–Urbana-Champaign	4.0
17.	University of Maryland–College Park	4.0
17.	University of Minnesota–Twin Cities	4.0
17.	University of Pennsylvania	4.0
23.	Rutgers, the State U. of N.J.–New Bruns.	3.9
23.	University of California–San Diego	3.9
25.	Johns Hopkins University (MD)	3.8
25.	Stony Brook University–SUNY	3.8
25.	University of Washington	3.8
28.	Georgia Institute of Technology	3.7
28.	Ohio State University	3.7
28.	Penn. State University–University Park	3.7
28.	Purdue University–West Lafayette (IN)	3.7
28.	Rice University (TX)	3.7
28.	University of North Carolina–Chapel Hill	3.7
34.	Carnegie Mellon University (PA)	3.6
34.	Indiana University–Bloomington	3.6
34.	University of California–Davis	3.6
34.	University of Illinois–Chicago	3.6
34.	University of Utah	3.6
39.	CUNY Grad School and University Ctr.	3.5
39.	Washington University in St. Louis	3.5
41.	Brandeis University (MA)	3.4
41.	Texas A&M University–College Station	3.4
41.	University of Arizona	3.4
41.	University of California–Irvine	3.4
41.	University of Notre Dame (IN)	3.4
46.	Boston University	3.3
46.	Michigan State University	3.3
46.	University of California–Santa Barbara	3.3
46.	University of Colorado–Boulder	3.3
46.	University of Southern California	3.3
46.	Vanderbilt University (TN)	3.3
52.	Dartmouth College (NH)	3.2
52.	North Carolina State University	3.2
52.	University of Georgia	3.2
52.	University of Virginia	3.2
56.	Rensselaer Polytechnic Institute (NY)	3.1
56.	University of Florida	3.1
56.	University of Iowa	3.1
56.	University of Oregon	3.1

MATHEMATICS SPECIALTIES

ALGEBRA/NUMBER THEORY/ALGEBRAIC GEOMETRY
1. Harvard University (MA)
2. Princeton University (NJ)
3. University of California–Berkeley
4. University of Chicago
5. Mass. Institute of Technology
5. University of California–Los Angeles

ANALYSIS
1. University of California–Los Angeles
2. University of California–Berkeley
3. Princeton University (NJ)
4. University of Chicago
5. Mass. Institute of Technology

6. New York University
6. Stanford University (CA)
8. University of Texas–Austin

APPLIED MATH
1. New York University
2. University of California–Los Angeles
3. California Institute of Technology
4. Mass. Institute of Technology
5. Brown University (RI)
5. University of Minnesota–Twin Cities
7. Princeton University (NJ)

DISCRETE MATHEMATICS AND COMBINATIONS
1. Mass. Institute of Technology

2. Princeton University (NJ)
3. University of California–San Diego
4. Georgia Institute of Technology
5. University of Michigan–Ann Arbor
6. University of California–Berkeley
6. University of California–Los Angeles

GEOMETRY
1. Harvard University (MA)
2. Mass. Institute of Technology
3. Stanford University (CA)
4. Stony Brook University–SUNY
4. University of California–Berkeley
6. Princeton University (NJ)

LOGIC
1. University of California–Berkeley
2. University of California–Los Angeles
3. University of Notre Dame (IN)
4. University of Illinois–Urbana-Champaign
4. University of Wisconsin–Madison

TOPOLOGY
1. University of California–Berkeley
2. Stanford University (CA)
3. Princeton University (NJ)
4. Harvard University (MA)
4. Mass. Institute of Technology
6. University of Chicago

PHYSICS Ranked in 2014

Rank	School	Average assessment score (5.0=highest)
1.	Massachusetts Institute of Technology	5.0
2.	California Institute of Technology	4.9
2.	Harvard University (MA)	4.9
2.	Princeton University (NJ)	4.9
2.	Stanford University (CA)	4.9
2.	University of California–Berkeley	4.9
7.	Cornell University (NY)	4.7
7.	University of Chicago	4.7
9.	University of Illinois–Urbana-Champaign	4.6
10.	University of California–Santa Barbara	4.5
11.	Columbia University (NY)	4.3
11.	University of Michigan–Ann Arbor	4.3
11.	Yale University (CT)	4.3
14.	University of Maryland–College Park	4.2
14.	University of Texas–Austin	4.2
16.	University of California–San Diego	4.1
16.	University of Pennsylvania	4.1
18.	Johns Hopkins University (MD)	4.0
18.	University of California–Los Angeles	4.0
18.	University of Colorado–Boulder	4.0
18.	University of Wisconsin–Madison	4.0
22.	University of Washington	3.9
23.	Ohio State University	3.8
23.	Penn. State University–University Park	3.8
23.	Stony Brook University–SUNY	3.8
26.	Northwestern University (IL)	3.7
26.	Rice University (TX)	3.7
26.	University of Minnesota–Twin Cities	3.7
29.	Brown University (RI)	3.6
29.	Duke University (NC)	3.6
29.	Georgia Institute of Technology	3.6
29.	Michigan State University	3.6
29.	Rutgers, the State U. of N.J.–New Bruns.	3.6
29.	University of California–Davis	3.6
29.	University of California–Irvine	3.6
36.	Carnegie Mellon University (PA)	3.5
36.	New York University	3.5
36.	University of Florida	3.5
39.	Boston University	3.4
39.	Indiana University–Bloomington	3.4
39.	University of Arizona	3.4
39.	University of California–Santa Cruz	3.4
39.	University of North Carolina–Chapel Hill	3.4
44.	Florida State University	3.3
44.	Purdue University–West Lafayette (IN)	3.3
44.	Texas A&M University–College Station	3.3
44.	University of Rochester (NY)	3.3
44.	University of Virginia	3.3
44.	Washington University in St. Louis	3.3
50.	Arizona State University	3.2
50.	Iowa State University	3.2
50.	University of Massachusetts–Amherst	3.2
50.	University of Pittsburgh	3.2

PHYSICS SPECIALTIES

ATOMIC/MOLECULAR/OPTICAL
1. University of Colorado–Boulder
2. Massachusetts Institute of Technology
3. Harvard University (MA)
4. Stanford University (CA)
5. University of California–Berkeley
6. University of Maryland–College Park
6. University of Rochester (NY)
8. California Institute of Technology

CONDENSED MATTER
1. University of Illinois–Urbana-Champaign
2. Stanford University (CA)
3. Massachusetts Institute of Technology

3. University of California–Berkeley
5. University of California–Santa Barbara
6. Cornell University (NY)
7. Harvard University (MA)
8. Princeton University (NJ)
9. California Institute of Technology

COSMOLOGY/RELATIVITY/GRAVITY
1. Princeton University (NJ)
2. California Institute of Technology
3. University of Chicago
4. Harvard University (MA)
5. Stanford University (CA)
5. University of California–Berkeley
7. Massachusetts Institute of Technology
8. University of California–Santa Barbara

ELEMENTARY PARTICLES/FIELDS/STRING THEORY
1. Princeton University (NJ)
2. Harvard University (MA)
3. Stanford University (CA)
4. University of California–Berkeley
5. Massachusetts Institute of Technology
6. California Institute of Technology
7. University of California–Santa Barbara

NUCLEAR
1. Michigan State University
2. University of Washington
3. Massachusetts Institute of Technology
4. Stony Brook University–SUNY
5. Indiana University–Bloomington
6. California Institute of Technology

6. Duke University (NC)
6. University of California–Berkeley
6. Yale University (CT)

PLASMA
1. Princeton University (NJ)
2. University of California–Los Angeles
3. Massachusetts Institute of Technology
3. University of Maryland–College Park
3. University of Texas–Austin
3. University of Wisconsin–Madison

QUANTUM
1. California Institute of Technology
2. Stanford University (CA)
3. Harvard University (MA)
3. Massachusetts Institute of Technology
5. Princeton University (NJ)

STATISTICS Ranked in 2014

Rank	School	Average assessment score (5.0=highest)
1.	Stanford University (CA)	4.9
2.	University of California–Berkeley	4.7
3.	Harvard University (MA)*	4.6
3.	University of Washington*	4.6
5.	Johns Hopkins University (MD)*	4.4
5.	University of Chicago	4.4
7.	Harvard University (MA)	4.3
7.	University of Washington	4.3
9.	Carnegie Mellon University (PA)	4.2
10.	Duke University (NC)	4.1

Rank	School	Average assessment score (5.0=highest)
10.	University of Pennsylvania	4.1
12.	University of Michigan–Ann Arbor*	4.0
12.	University of North Carolina–Chapel Hill*	4.0
12.	University of Wisconsin–Madison	4.0
15.	North Carolina State University	3.9
15.	Texas A&M University–College Station	3.9
15.	University of California–Berkeley*	3.9
15.	University of Michigan–Ann Arbor	3.9
19.	Iowa State University	3.8
20.	Columbia University (NY)	3.7

Rank	School	Average assessment score (5.0=highest)
20.	Pennsylvania State University	3.7
20.	University of Minnesota–Twin Cities	3.7
20.	University of North Carolina–Chapel Hill	3.7
24.	Cornell University (NY)	3.6
24.	Purdue University–West Lafayette (IN)	3.6
24.	University of Minnesota–Twin Cities*	3.6
27.	Ohio State University	3.5
27.	University of California–Davis	3.5
27.	University of Pennsylvania (Perelman)*	3.5

*Denotes a department of biostatistics

METHODOLOGY

Rankings of doctoral programs in the sciences are based on the results of surveys sent to academics in the biological sciences, chemistry, computer science, earth sciences, mathematics, physics and statistics during the fall of 2013. The individuals rated the quality of the program at each institution from marginal (1) to outstanding (5). Individuals who were unfamiliar with a particular school's programs were asked to select "don't know." The schools with the highest average scores were sorted in descending order and appear here. Results from fall 2009 and fall 2013 were averaged to compute the scores; programs had to be rated by at least 10 respondents to be ranked. Surveys were conducted by Ipsos Public Affairs. The universe surveyed in the biological sciences, chemistry, computer science, earth sciences, mathematics and physics consisted of schools that awarded at least five doctoral degrees in 2006 through 2010, according to the National Science Foundation report "Science and Engineering Doctorate Awards." The American Statistical Association provided U.S. News with eligible programs for statistics. In the biological sciences, programs may be offered in a university's medical school or college of arts and sciences. In statistics, programs may be offered through a biostatistics or statistics department. Questionnaires were sent to the department heads and directors of graduate studies at each program in each discipline. Response rates were: for biological sciences, 9 percent; chemistry, 18 percent; computer science, 35 percent; earth sciences, 17 percent; mathematics, 24 percent; physics, 29 percent; and statistics, 39 percent.

Specialty rankings are based solely on nominations by department heads and directors of graduate studies at peer schools. These respondents ranked up to 10 programs in each area. Those with the most votes appear here.

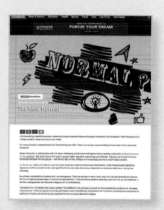

Public Affairs

ACADEMICS AT PEER INSTITUTIONS WEIGH IN ON PROGRAM EXCELLENCE

THE TOP SCHOOLS Ranked in 2016

Rank	School	Average assessment score (5.0=highest)
1.	Indiana University–Bloomington	4.4
1.	Syracuse University (Maxwell) (NY)	4.4
3.	Harvard University (Kennedy) (MA)	4.2
4.	Princeton University (Wilson) (NJ)	4.1
4.	University of Georgia	4.1
4.	University of Southern California (Price)	4.1
4.	University of Washington (Evans)	4.1
8.	Univ. of California–Berkeley (Goldman)	4.0
8.	University of Michigan–Ann Arbor (Ford)	4.0
8.	U. of Minnesota–Twin Cities (Humphrey)	4.0
11.	New York University (Wagner)	3.9
11.	University of Texas–Austin (LBJ)	3.9
13.	Arizona State University	3.8
13.	Carnegie Mellon University (Heinz) (PA)	3.8
13.	Duke University (Sanford) (NC)	3.8
13.	George Washington U. (Trachtenberg) (DC)	3.8
13.	University of Chicago (Harris) (IL)	3.8
13.	U. of Wisconsin–Madison (La Follette)	3.8
19.	American University (DC)	3.7

Rank	School	Average assessment score (5.0=highest)
19.	Columbia University (SIPA) (NY)	3.7
19.	Florida State University (Askew)	3.7
19.	Univ. at Albany–SUNY (Rockefeller) (NY)	3.7
19.	Univ. of California–Los Angeles (Luskin)	3.7
19.	University of Kansas	3.7
25.	Georgetown University (McCourt) (DC)	3.6
25.	Georgia State University (Young)	3.6
25.	Ohio State University (Glenn)	3.6
25.	University of Kentucky (Martin)	3.6
25.	University of Nebraska–Omaha	3.6
25.	University of North Carolina–Chapel Hill	3.6
31.	Texas A&M U.–College Station (Bush)	3.5
31.	University of Maryland–College Park	3.5
33.	University of Missouri (Truman)	3.4
34.	Johns Hopkins University (DC)	3.3
34.	Rutgers, The State U. of N.J.–Newark	3.3
34.	Stanford University (CA)	3.3
34.	University of Arizona	3.3
34.	University of Colorado–Denver	3.3

Rank	School	Average assessment score (5.0=highest)
34.	University of Pittsburgh (PA)	3.3
34.	Virginia Tech	3.3
41.	Cornell University (NY)	3.2
41.	George Mason University (VA)	3.2
41.	Indiana Univ.-Purdue Univ.–Indianapolis	3.2
41.	University of Virginia (Batten)	3.2
45.	Brandeis University (Heller) (MA)	3.1
45.	Cleveland State University (Levin) (OH)	3.1
45.	CUNY–Baruch College (NY)	3.1
45.	Georgia Institute of Technology	3.1
45.	North Carolina State University	3.1
45.	Northern Illinois University	3.1
45.	Portland State University (Hatfield) (OR)	3.1
45.	University of Connecticut	3.1
45.	University of Delaware	3.1
45.	University of Illinois–Chicago	3.1
45.	University of Pennsylvania (Fels)	3.1

PUBLIC AFFAIRS SPECIALTIES

CITY MANAGEMENT
1 University of Kansas
2 New York University (Wagner)
3 University of Southern California (Price)
4 Arizona State University

ENVIRONMENTAL POLICY & MANAGEMENT
1 Indiana University–Bloomington
2 University of Washington (Evans)
3 Duke University (Sanford) (NC)
3 University of California–Berkeley (Goldman)

HEALTH POLICY & MANAGEMENT
1 Harvard University (Kennedy) (MA)

2 New York University (Wagner)
3 Duke University (Sanford) (NC)
3 University of Southern California (Price)

INFORMATION & TECHNOLOGY MANAGEMENT
1 Carnegie Mellon Univ. (Heinz) (PA)
2 Georgia Institute of Technology
3 Syracuse University (Maxwell) (NY)
3 University at Albany–SUNY (Rockefeller) (NY)

NONPROFIT MANAGEMENT
1 Indiana University–Bloomington
2 University of Minnesota–Twin Cities (Humphrey)

3 Syracuse University (Maxwell) (NY)
4 Indiana University-Purdue University–Indianapolis

PUBLIC FINANCE & BUDGETING
1 Indiana University–Bloomington
2 University of Georgia
3 Syracuse University (Maxwell) (NY)
4 University of Kentucky (Martin)

PUBLIC MANAGEMENT/ADMIN.
1 Syracuse University (Maxwell) (NY)
2 University of Georgia
3 Indiana University–Bloomington
4 University of Southern California (Price)
5 American University (DC)

PUBLIC POLICY ANALYSIS
1 University of California–Berkeley (Goldman)
2 Harvard University (Kennedy) (MA)
3 University of Michigan–Ann Arbor (Ford)
4 Duke University (Sanford) (NC)

SOCIAL POLICY
1 University of Michigan–Ann Arbor (Ford)
2 Harvard University (Kennedy) (MA)
2 University of Wisconsin–Madison (La Follette)
4 University of California–Berkeley (Goldman)

METHODOLOGY

Rankings are based solely on results of a peer assessment survey conducted in the fall of 2015. Deans, directors and department chairs representing 272 master's programs in public affairs and administration were surveyed; two surveys were sent to each school. Respondents were asked to rate the academic quality of master's programs on a scale of 1 (marginal) to 5 (outstanding). Scores for each school were totaled and divided by the number of respondents who rated that school and sorted in descending order. The response rate was 43 percent. The lists of schools and individuals surveyed were provided by NASPAA (Network of Schools of Public Policy, Affairs and Administration) and the Association for Public Policy Analysis and Management. For the specialty rankings, deans and other academics at public affairs schools were asked to nominate up to 10 programs for excellence in each specialty. Those with the most nominations appear. Assessment survey data were collected by Ipsos Public Affairs.

More @ usnews.com/grad

The Fine Arts

MASTER'S PROGRAMS RANKED BEST BY DEANS AND DEPARTMENT CHAIRS

THE TOP SCHOOLS Ranked in 2016

Rank	School	Average assessment score (5.0=highest)	Rank	School	Average assessment score (5.0=highest)	Rank	School	Average assessment score (5.0=highest)
1.	Yale University (CT)	4.6	20.	Art Center College of Design (CA)	3.7	33.	University of California–Irvine	3.5
2.	University of California–Los Angeles	4.4	20.	CUNY–Hunter College (NY)	3.7	33.	University of Chicago (IL)	3.5
2.	Virginia Commonwealth University	4.4	20.	Rutgers, The State U. of N.J.–New Brunswick	3.7	33.	University of Illinois–Chicago	3.5
4.	Rhode Island School of Design	4.3	20.	School of Visual Arts (NY)	3.7	33.	University of Illinois–Urbana-Champaign	3.5
4.	School of the Art Inst. of Chicago (IL)	4.3	20.	University of Michigan	3.7	33.	University of Iowa	3.5
6.	Carnegie Mellon University (PA)	4.2	20.	University of Washington	3.7	33.	University of Pennsylvania	3.5
6.	Columbia University (NY)	4.2	27.	Cornell University (NY)	3.6	33.	University of Tennessee–Knoxville	3.5
6.	Cranbrook Academy of Art (MI)	4.2	27.	New School–Parsons Sch. of Design (NY)	3.6	48.	College for Creative Studies (MI)	3.4
9.	Alfred U.–N.Y. State College of Ceramics	4.1	27.	Purchase College–SUNY (NY)	3.6	48.	Massachusetts College of Art	3.4
9.	California Institute of the Arts	4.1	27.	University of California–Berkeley	3.6	48.	Minneapolis Coll. of Art and Design (MN)	3.4
9.	Maryland Institute College of Art	4.1	27.	University of California–Davis	3.6	48.	New York University	3.4
12.	Washington University in St. Louis	4.0	27.	University of Texas–Austin	3.6	48.	Northwestern University (IL)	3.4
13.	Bard College (NY)	3.9	33.	Indiana University Bloomington	3.5	48.	University of Georgia	3.4
13.	University of California–San Diego	3.9	33.	Ohio State University	3.5	48.	University of New Mexico	3.4
15.	California College of the Arts	3.8	33.	Ohio University	3.5	55.	California State University–Los Angeles	3.3
15.	Pratt Institute (NY)	3.8	33.	Otis College of Art and Design (CA)	3.5	55.	University of Arizona	3.3
15.	Stanford University (CA)	3.8	33.	Rensselaer Polytechnic Institute (NY)	3.5	55.	University of Cincinnati (OH)	3.3
15.	Temple University (PA)	3.8	33.	Rochester Institute of Technology (NY)	3.5	55.	University of Minnesota–Twin Cities	3.3
15.	University of Wisconsin–Madison	3.8	33.	San Francisco Art Institute (CA)	3.5			
20.	Arizona State University	3.7	33.	Syracuse University (NY)	3.5			

FINE ARTS SPECIALTIES

CERAMICS
1 Alfred University–New York State College of Ceramics
2 Cranbrook Academy of Art (MI)
3 Ohio University
4 Ohio State University
5 Rhode Island School of Design
5 University of Colorado–Boulder

FIBER ARTS
1 Cranbrook Academy of Art (MI)
1 School of the Art Institute of Chicago (IL)

GLASS
1 Rhode Island School of Design
2 Temple University (PA)

GRAPHIC DESIGN
1 Rhode Island School of Design
2 Yale University (CT)
3 Maryland Institute College of Art
4 Cranbrook Academy of Art (MI)

METALS/JEWELRY
1 Cranbrook Academy of Art (MI)
1 Rhode Island School of Design

PAINTING/DRAWING
1 Yale University (CT)
2 Rhode Island School of Design
2 School of the Art Institute of Chicago (IL)
4 Maryland Institute College of Art
5 Columbia University (NY)

PHOTOGRAPHY
1 Yale University (CT)
2 School of the Art Institute of Chicago (IL)
3 University of California–Los Angeles
4 Rochester Institute of Technology (NY)
5 School of Visual Arts (NY)
5 University of New Mexico

PRINTMAKING
1 University of Wisconsin–Madison
2 University of Tennessee–Knoxville
3 Rhode Island School of Design
4 School of the Art Institute of Chicago (IL)

5 Arizona State University
5 University of Iowa

SCULPTURE
1 Virginia Commonwealth University
2 Yale University (CT)
3 Maryland Institute College of Art
4 School of the Art Institute of Chicago (IL)
5 Rhode Island School of Design
5 University of California–Los Angeles

TIME-BASED/NEW MEDIA
1 Carnegie Mellon University (PA)
2 University of California–Los Angeles
3 University of California–San Diego

METHODOLOGY

The Master of Fine Arts rankings are based solely on the results of a peer assessment survey conducted in the fall of 2015. Art school deans or department chairs at 229 MFA programs in art and design were surveyed; one survey was sent to each school. Respondents were asked to rate the academic quality of programs on a scale of 1 (marginal) to 5 (outstanding). Scores for each school were totaled and divided by the number of respondents who rated that school and sorted in descending order. The response rate was 29 percent. The lists of schools and individuals surveyed and specialty concentrations spotlighted were developed in cooperation with the Department of Art and Visual Technology at the College of Visual and Performing Arts at George Mason University in Virginia. Institutions listed in the specialty rankings received the most nominations from respondents at peer institutions for excellence in the specialty. Assessment surveys were conducted by Ipsos Public Affairs.

▶ **More @ usnews.com/grad**

Best Online Programs

For our rankings of online graduate degree programs in business, computer information technology, criminal justice, education, engineering and nursing, U.S. News started by surveying more than 1,000 master's programs at regionally accredited colleges that deliver all required classes predominantly online. Programs were ranked based on their success at promoting student engagement, the training and credentials of their faculty, the selectivity of their admissions processes, the services and technologies available to distance learners, and the opinions of deans and other academics at peer distance-education programs in their disciplines. Although the methodologies used in each discipline rely on varying criteria, individual ranking factors common to all include retention rates, student indebtedness at graduation, the average undergraduate GPAs of new entrants, proportion of faculty members with terminal degrees, proportion of full-time faculty who are tenured or tenure-track, and whether the program offers support services like mentoring and academic advising so they are accessible to students remotely. The top programs are listed below; to see the full rankings plus an additional ranking of non-MBA business programs, as well as more detail on the methodologies, visit usnews.com/online.

BUSINESS (MBA PROGRAMS)

Rank	School	Overall score	Average peer assessment score (5.0=highest)	'16 total enrollment	'16-'17 total program cost¹	Entrance test required	'16 average undergrad GPA	'16 acceptance rate	'16 full-time faculty with terminal degree	'16 tenured or tenure-track faculty²	'16 retention rate	'16 three-year graduation rate
1.	Temple University (Fox) (PA)	100	3.5	351	$59,760	GMAT or GRE	3.4	45%	100%	82%	100%	97%
2.	Carnegie Mellon University (Tepper) (PA)	98	4.1	117	$122,880	GMAT or GRE	3.3	64%	91%	77%	100%	N/A
3.	Indiana University–Bloomington (Kelley)	95	4.2	788	N/A	GMAT or GRE	3.4	83%	90%	61%	99%	79%
4.	U. of North Carolina–Chapel Hill (Kenan-Flagler)	93	4.2	1,047	$104,610	N/A	3.2	45%	86%	72%	98%	94%
5.	Arizona State University (Carey)	89	3.9	408	N/A	GMAT or GRE	3.2	64%	87%	47%	95%	92%
5.	University of Florida (Hough)	89	3.7	433	$53,440	GMAT or GRE	3.3	54%	96%	65%	99%	88%
7.	University of Texas–Dallas	87	3.2	325	$75,701	GMAT or GRE	3.6	39%	71%	42%	99%	40%
8.	Pennsylvania State University–World Campus	86	3.3	290	N/A	GMAT or GRE	3.3	89%	100%	91%	84%	97%
9.	University of Maryland–College Park (Smith)	82	3.5	147	$79,974	GMAT or GRE	3.2	68%	95%	47%	98%	N/A
10.	Arkansas State University–Jonesboro	81	2.1	144	$19,371	GMAT or GRE	3.7	76%	100%	100%	95%	94%
10.	Auburn University (Harbert) (AL)	81	3.3	304	$33,450	GMAT or GRE	3.4	70%	96%	100%	93%	61%
12.	Ball State University (Miller) (IN)	79	2.7	288	$17,700	GMAT or GRE	3.4	78%	100%	93%	94%	57%
12.	University of Massachusetts–Amherst (Isenberg)	79	3.3	1,289	$32,175	GMAT or GRE	3.4	83%	94%	56%	93%	59%
12.	University of Southern California (Marshall)	79	3.7	64	N/A	GMAT or GRE	3.2	46%	93%	29%	N/A	N/A
12.	University of Wisconsin MBA Consortium	79	2.6	268	$20,250	GMAT or GRE	3.3	80%	89%	89%	91%	65%
16.	Florida State University	78	3.1	170	N/A	GMAT or GRE	3.5	64%	100%	88%	76%	79%
16.	University of Wisconsin–Whitewater	78	2.6	300	$22,968	GMAT or GRE	3.3	70%	100%	100%	93%	79%
18.	Mississippi State University	76	3.0	249	$12,787	GMAT or GRE	3.3	71%	100%	100%	86%	48%
18.	North Carolina State University (Jenkins)	76	2.9	245	$66,360	N/A	3.3	69%	92%	84%	94%	93%
18.	U. of South Florida–St. Petersburg (Tiedemann)	76	2.4	284	$32,664	N/A	3.4	47%	100%	79%	82%	77%
21.	James Madison University (VA)	75	2.9	46	$37,800	GMAT or GRE	3.2	96%	100%	100%	100%	100%
21.	Kennesaw State University (Coles) (GA)	75	2.8	117	$22,170	GMAT or GRE	3.2	68%	100%	100%	96%	96%
21.	Lehigh University (PA)	75	2.9	187	$39,075	GMAT or GRE	3.3	81%	90%	60%	93%	36%
21.	Pepperdine University (Graziadio) (CA)	75	3.4	296	$86,840	GMAT or GRE	3.2	71%	75%	42%	97%	66%
21.	University of Mississippi	75	3.0	111	$24,093	GMAT or GRE	3.2	39%	91%	73%	86%	43%
21.	University of Nebraska–Lincoln	75	3.2	369	$28,800	GMAT or GRE	3.4	89%	90%	100%	88%	38%
27.	SUNY–Oswego (NY)	74	2.4	170	$36,576	GMAT	3.3	83%	86%	86%	89%	71%
27.	Washington State University	74	3.0	801	N/A	GMAT	3.5	58%	88%	75%	83%	74%
29.	George Washington University (DC)	73	3.3	338	$93,795	GMAT or GRE	3.1	69%	100%	82%	91%	68%
29.	Oklahoma State University (Spears)	73	3.0	363	$34,652	GMAT or GRE	3.1	92%	97%	80%	92%	60%
29.	University of North Dakota	73	2.6	77	$13,946	GMAT or GRE	3.4	61%	92%	85%	95%	63%
33.	Columbus State University (Turner) (GA)	72	2.2	17	N/A	GMAT or GRE	3.1	61%	100%	100%	100%	95%
33.	Georgia College & State University (Bunting)	72	2.5	52	$22,170	GMAT or GRE	3.0	84%	100%	100%	94%	92%
33.	Rochester Institute of Tech. (Saunders) (NY)	72	3.0	29	N/A	None	3.2	66%	83%	75%	94%	78%
36.	Georgia Southern University	71	2.5	115	$13,302	GMAT or GRE	3.1	77%	100%	100%	91%	94%
36.	Hofstra University (Zarb) (NY)	71	2.7	47	N/A	GMAT or GRE	3.1	86%	100%	100%	91%	100%
36.	Southern Illinois University–Carbondale	71	2.7	128	$35,868	GMAT or GRE	3.3	63%	100%	100%	90%	85%
36.	University of Michigan–Dearborn	71	2.8	91	N/A	GMAT or GRE	3.4	38%	100%	95%	60%	52%

N/A=Data were not provided by the school; programs that received insufficient numbers of ratings do not have their peer-assessment scores published.
¹Tuition is reported for part-time, out-of-state students. ²Percentage reported of full-time faculty.
One school previously tied at 29 in business is no longer ranked based on communication between the school and U.S. News.

More @ usnews.com/grad

Rank	School	Overall score	Average peer assessment score (5.0=highest)	'16 total enrollment	'16-'17 total program cost[1]	Entrance test required	'16 average undergrad GPA	'16 acceptance rate	'16 full-time faculty with terminal degree	'16 tenured or tenure-track faculty[2]	'16 retention rate	'16 three-year graduation rate
36.	University of Nevada–Reno	71	2.4	74	$30,000	GMAT or GRE	3.2	79%	91%	91%	90%	100%
36.	University of Tennessee–Martin	71	2.4	80	N/A	GMAT or GRE	3.2	88%	100%	100%	92%	86%
42.	Central Michigan University	69	2.5	193	N/A	GMAT	3.2	46%	94%	75%	83%	70%
42.	Clarkson University (NY)	69	2.4	189	$52,800	GMAT or GRE	3.0	61%	87%	65%	90%	87%
42.	Florida International University	69	2.5	805	$42,000	None	3.3	54%	73%	42%	87%	82%
42.	Northeastern University (MA)	69	3.2	869	$75,650	None	3.2	87%	95%	79%	86%	44%
42.	University of Utah (Eccles)	69	3.0	88	N/A	GMAT or GRE	3.4	68%	100%	53%	97%	N/A
47.	Cleveland State University (Ahuja) (OH)	68	2.3	36	$37,500	GMAT or GRE	3.2	87%	100%	83%	93%	N/A
47.	Creighton University (NE)	68	2.7	44	$33,825	GMAT or GRE	3.2	60%	89%	67%	100%	N/A
47.	Louisiana State U.–Baton Rouge (Ourso)	68	2.9	120	$45,360	None	3.4	48%	N/A	N/A	85%	70%
47.	Syracuse University (Whitman) (NY)	68	3.3	754	$77,922	N/A	3.1	77%	91%	23%	94%	49%
47.	University of Colorado–Colorado Springs	68	2.8	99	N/A	GMAT or GRE	3.3	75%	100%	93%	79%	50%
47.	University of Massachusetts–Lowell	68	2.7	487	$18,900	GMAT or GRE	3.3	90%	81%	81%	99%	57%
47.	West Texas A&M University	68	1.9	650	$16,035	None	3.6	61%	98%	85%	88%	80%
47.	West Virginia University	68	2.7	91	$44,736	GMAT or GRE	3.2	89%	96%	79%	93%	89%
55.	Old Dominion University (VA)	67	2.7	43	$20,640	GMAT or GRE	3.2	67%	91%	96%	85%	N/A
55.	Robert Morris University (PA)	67	1.9	78	N/A	GMAT	3.3	34%	100%	100%	89%	71%
55.	University of Arizona (Eller)	67	3.4	194	$27,000	GMAT	3.3	78%	100%	100%	82%	N/A
55.	University of North Texas	67	2.6	189	$25,560	GMAT	3.3	54%	96%	81%	91%	58%
59.	Southern Utah University	66	1.8	38	$13,995	GMAT or GRE	3.4	86%	100%	100%	N/A	91%
59.	University of Louisiana–Monroe	66	2.1	82	$17,500	GMAT or GRE	3.2	72%	82%	82%	82%	48%
61.	Drexel University (LeBow) (PA)	65	2.7	202	$64,000	GMAT or GRE	3.1	89%	97%	50%	97%	80%
61.	Marist College (NY)	65	2.3	230	$23,400	GMAT or GRE	3.3	42%	93%	93%	72%	47%
61.	University of Miami (FL)	65	3.1	76	$79,800	GMAT	3.5	48%	100%	100%	N/A	N/A
61.	Western Kentucky University (Ford)	65	2.3	77	$23,570	GMAT	3.4	95%	100%	100%	82%	55%
65.	Portland State University (OR)	64	2.7	119	$41,400	N/A	3.3	64%	75%	75%	N/A	86%
65.	Tennessee Technological University	64	2.2	227	$21,180	GMAT or GRE	3.3	46%	100%	100%	87%	52%
65.	University of Cincinnati (OH)	64	2.9	124	$35,303	GMAT or GRE	3.3	82%	83%	75%	90%	N/A
65.	University of Delaware (Lerner)	64	2.8	231	$35,750	GMAT or GRE	3.3	72%	100%	96%	N/A	68%
65.	University of South Dakota	64	2.4	193	$14,588	GMAT	3.1	90%	100%	71%	93%	46%
65.	University of West Georgia	64	2.4	129	N/A	GMAT or GRE	3.2	93%	100%	100%	99%	88%
71.	Kansas State University	63	2.9	43	$32,500	GMAT	3.4	100%	100%	100%	100%	100%
72.	Baylor University (Hankamer) (TX)	62	3.2	230	$49,296	None	3.1	68%	85%	77%	24%	N/A
72.	Boise State University (ID)	62	2.5	167	$36,750	GMAT or GRE	3.4	93%	82%	82%	91%	N/A
72.	Fayetteville State University (NC)	62	1.8	120	$14,871	GMAT or GRE	3.3	37%	100%	100%	75%	57%
72.	Ohio University	62	2.8	824	$35,805	None	3.2	71%	79%	74%	94%	69%
72.	Samford University (Brock) (AL)	62	2.2	123	$37,500	GMAT or GRE	3.3	88%	100%	100%	87%	87%
72.	University of Tennessee–Chattanooga	62	2.7	147	$28,488	GMAT or GRE	3.3	48%	91%	91%	N/A	N/A
78.	Mercer University–Atlanta (Stetson) (GA)	60	N/A	24	$26,172	GMAT or GRE	3.2	55%	100%	90%	95%	N/A
78.	Stevens Institute of Technology (NJ)	60	2.4	87	$66,656	GMAT or GRE	3.1	83%	94%	63%	86%	N/A
78.	University of Kansas	60	3.0	53	$32,550	GMAT or GRE	3.3	70%	100%	75%	N/A	N/A
78.	University of New Hampshire	60	2.7	50	$42,240	GMAT	3.4	100%	89%	78%	94%	47%
82.	DeSales University (PA)	59	1.5	613	N/A	None	3.3	87%	100%	100%	96%	75%
82.	Rutgers, the State U. of New Jersey–Camden	59	2.9	99	$52,752	GMAT or GRE	3.3	63%	89%	67%	N/A	N/A
82.	Southeast Missouri State University (Harrison)	59	2.0	81	N/A	GMAT or GRE	3.4	86%	100%	100%	86%	52%
82.	West Chester University of Pennsylvania	59	1.8	182	$14,790	GMAT or GRE	3.4	92%	100%	100%	81%	60%
86.	Campbellsville University (KY)	58	1.4	82	$17,964	GMAT or GRE	3.3	49%	100%	100%	87%	71%
86.	Clarion University of Pennsylvania	58	1.8	136	$17,226	GMAT or GRE	3.4	95%	100%	100%	96%	60%
86.	East Carolina University (NC)	58	2.4	825	$53,190	GMAT or GRE	3.2	80%	96%	95%	77%	48%
86.	Sam Houston State University (TX)	58	2.0	300	$10,278	GMAT	3.4	78%	100%	94%	76%	34%
86.	Texas Southern University (Jones)	58	2.0	77	N/A	None	2.9	65%	100%	100%	90%	N/A
91.	California State University–San Bernardino	57	2.2	153	$36,000	None	3.1	95%	92%	92%	89%	N/A
91.	Missouri University of Science & Technology	57	2.2	95	$44,292	GMAT or GRE	N/A	74%	88%	88%	83%	70%
91.	St. Joseph's University (Haub) (PA)	57	2.6	339	N/A	GMAT or GRE	3.3	83%	92%	81%	58%	45%
91.	University of Scranton (PA)	57	2.3	463	$34,740	None	3.2	84%	93%	96%	88%	49%
95.	Baldwin Wallace University (OH)	56	1.6	53	N/A	GMAT	3.4	100%	90%	90%	100%	82%
95.	California Baptist University	56	1.8	76	$23,148	None	3.3	85%	86%	100%	78%	79%

BUSINESS (MBA PROGRAMS) continued

Rank	School	Overall score	Average peer assessment score (5.0=highest)	'16 total enrollment	'16-'17 total program cost[1]	Entrance test required	'16 average undergrad GPA	'16 acceptance rate	'16 full-time faculty with terminal degree	'16 tenured or tenure-track faculty[2]	'16 retention rate	'16 three-year graduation rate
95.	California State University–Fresno (Craig)	56	2.2	85	$37,700	GMAT or GRE	3.3	47%	100%	100%	N/A	N/A
95.	University of Memphis (Fogelman) (TN)	56	2.8	109	N/A	GMAT or GRE	3.2	78%	100%	100%	N/A	52%
95.	University of Wisconsin–Oshkosh	56	2.5	388	$31,845	GMAT or GRE	3.0	100%	83%	44%	N/A	N/A
100.	Embry-Riddle Aeronautical U.–Worldwide (FL)	55	2.1	946	N/A	None	3.1	74%	100%	44%	80%	49%
100.	Florida Atlantic University	55	2.4	128	$32,000	None	3.1	68%	100%	40%	N/A	N/A
100.	Fort Hays State University (KS)	55	2.0	133	$12,455	GMAT or GRE	3.3	68%	89%	89%	88%	23%
100.	Longwood University (VA)	55	1.7	33	$32,652	GMAT or GRE	3.2	81%	100%	91%	100%	80%
100.	Stetson University (FL)	55	2.4	27	$24,150	None	3.4	80%	100%	100%	60%	64%
105.	Concordia University Wisconsin	54	1.8	166	N/A	None	3.0	40%	N/A	N/A	76%	39%
105.	Louisiana Tech University	54	2.4	29	N/A	GMAT or GRE	2.9	38%	100%	100%	80%	N/A
105.	University of Bridgeport (CT)	54	2.0	130	N/A	None	3.2	46%	100%	100%	78%	N/A
105.	U. of Massachusetts–Dartmouth (Charlton)	54	3.0	43	N/A	GMAT	3.3	84%	100%	100%	29%	N/A
109.	University of Baltimore (MD)	53	2.1	593	N/A	GMAT	3.3	83%	100%	100%	89%	N/A
109.	University of Houston–Clear Lake (TX)	53	2.3	97	$33,012	N/A	N/A	43%	100%	100%	61%	58%
111.	Ashland University (OH)	52	N/A	244	$22,860	None	3.0	84%	89%	95%	97%	56%
111.	Regent University (VA)	52	1.6	413	$27,300	None	3.0	43%	100%	100%	79%	41%
111.	Texas A&M University–Kingsville	52	2.1	119	$16,241	GMAT or GRE	3.1	96%	100%	100%	83%	76%
111.	University of Texas–Tyler	52	1.8	1,145	$30,948	GMAT or GRE	3.2	87%	100%	95%	97%	81%
115.	Emporia State University (KS)	51	1.9	59	$13,356	GMAT or GRE	3.4	44%	100%	100%	84%	N/A
115.	Ferris State University (MI)	51	1.7	109	$26,016	GMAT or GRE	3.5	71%	100%	100%	91%	58%
115.	Shippensburg U. of Pennsylvania (Grove)	51	1.9	182	$18,210	None	3.2	92%	100%	100%	91%	34%
115.	University of North Alabama	51	2.1	651	$14,450	GMAT or GRE	3.0	98%	90%	90%	90%	59%
119.	Florida Institute of Technology	50	1.9	1,145	N/A	None	3.1	43%	100%	0%	82%	47%
119.	Gardner-Webb University (NC)	50	1.8	255	$18,900	GMAT or GRE	3.2	74%	88%	76%	N/A	N/A
119.	Queens University of Charlotte (McColl) (NC)	50	2.0	87	$35,830	None	3.0	89%	90%	80%	89%	N/A
119.	SUNY Polytechnic Institute (NY)	50	2.3	124	N/A	GMAT or GRE	N/A	60%	100%	75%	75%	41%
119.	University of St. Francis (IL)	50	1.6	137	N/A	None	3.4	56%	83%	83%	79%	39%

COMPUTER INFORMATION TECHNOLOGY

Rank	School	Overall score	Average peer assessment score (5.0=highest)	'16 total enrollment	'16-'17 total program cost[1]	Entrance test required	'16 average undergrad GPA	'16 acceptance rate	'16 full-time faculty with terminal degree	'16 tenured or tenure-track faculty[2]	'16 retention rate	'16 three-year graduation rate
1.	University of Southern California	100	4.0	124	N/A	GRE	3.5	50%	100%	50%	95%	100%
2.	Virginia Tech	84	3.7	445	$29,700	None	3.4	90%	100%	83%	94%	81%
3.	New York University	83	3.7	100	N/A	None	3.5	37%	87%	80%	70%	48%
4.	Boston University (MA)	77	3.8	925	$33,200	None	3.2	73%	100%	0%	86%	64%
5.	Pennsylvania State University–World Campus	71	3.1	469	N/A	None	3.4	69%	92%	50%	78%	58%
6.	Johns Hopkins University (Whiting) (MD)	68	3.7	780	N/A	None	3.4	35%	N/A	N/A	85%	40%
6.	Missouri University of Science & Technology	68	2.6	72	$36,910	GRE	3.0	91%	93%	79%	53%	46%
6.	North Carolina State University	68	3.4	47	$38,037	GRE	3.5	55%	100%	100%	100%	43%
6.	Texas Tech University (Whitacre)	68	3.0	15	N/A	GRE	3.6	42%	100%	100%	75%	N/A
10.	West Virginia University	67	2.6	50	N/A	None	3.4	82%	75%	75%	N/A	100%
11.	Drexel University (PA)	66	3.4	156	$53,640	GRE	3.5	59%	97%	63%	93%	40%
11.	Florida State University	66	2.9	62	N/A	GRE	3.4	95%	100%	78%	86%	N/A
11.	Sam Houston State University (TX)	66	2.4	49	$10,278	GRE	3.4	56%	100%	100%	93%	35%
11.	University of Arizona	66	N/A	105	$39,960	None	3.3	76%	100%	78%	94%	71%
15.	George Washington University (DC)	64	3.2	18	$52,800	None	3.1	56%	100%	100%	60%	N/A
15.	Stevens Institute of Technology (Schaefer) (NJ)	64	2.9	84	$49,992	GRE	3.1	60%	85%	40%	100%	64%
17.	Syracuse University (NY)	63	3.5	53	$51,948	None	3.2	84%	74%	61%	83%	57%
18.	Robert Morris University (PA)	61	2.0	115	N/A	None	3.2	58%	100%	100%	79%	58%
19.	University of Alabama–Birmingham	60	2.4	112	$32,640	None	2.8	94%	83%	83%	80%	N/A
19.	University of Maryland–Baltimore County	60	3.0	212	N/A	None	N/A	82%	100%	100%	74%	47%
21.	Florida Institute of Technology	58	2.5	488	N/A	None	3.1	48%	100%	0%	85%	52%
21.	Georgia Southern University	58	2.8	32	N/A	GRE	3.2	48%	100%	100%	43%	26%
21.	Marquette University (WI)	58	2.3	74	$38,700	None	3.2	80%	100%	100%	92%	67%
21.	Pace University (NY)	58	2.5	95	N/A	None	3.1	96%	100%	91%	83%	38%
25.	University of Louisville (KY)	57	2.9	35	$21,420	GRE	3.2	70%	92%	92%	90%	N/A

CRIMINAL JUSTICE

Rank	School	Overall score	Average peer assessment score (5.0=highest)	'16 total enrollment	'16-'17 total program cost[1]	Entrance test required	'16 average undergrad GPA	'16 acceptance rate	'16 full-time faculty with terminal degree	'16 tenured or tenure-track faculty[2]	'16 retention rate	'16 three-year graduation rate
1.	Sam Houston State University (TX)	100	3.6	238	$10,278	None	3.3	85%	95%	92%	79%	69%
2.	University of Nebraska–Omaha	99	3.7	123	$20,016	None	3.4	89%	100%	100%	74%	100%
3.	University of California–Irvine	96	3.9	106	N/A	None	3.2	75%	100%	100%	95%	77%
4.	Boston University (MA)	92	3.1	482	$33,200	None	3.2	69%	100%	0%	85%	70%
5.	Arizona State University	90	3.7	586	$16,566	None	3.4	88%	78%	56%	88%	69%
5.	University of Oklahoma	90	N/A	150	$26,109	None	3.3	97%	100%	58%	84%	N/A
7.	Florida State University	86	3.9	164	$22,500	GRE	3.3	84%	100%	100%	80%	68%
8.	Bowling Green State University (OH)	85	3.0	36	$14,619	None	3.2	77%	100%	100%	N/A	N/A
9.	Indiana University of Pennsylvania (PA)	84	3.3	26	N/A	None	3.1	71%	100%	100%	64%	67%
10.	Michigan State University	81	3.8	160	$20,640	N/A	3.4	82%	100%	75%	95%	85%
11.	University of Cincinnati	79	4.1	731	$21,120	None	3.1	74%	100%	100%	90%	67%
11.	University of the Cumberlands (KY)	79	N/A	85	N/A	None	3.1	59%	100%	50%	N/A	N/A
13.	University of Colorado–Denver	77	2.6	64	$22,500	GMAT or GRE	3.5	77%	100%	78%	88%	63%
14.	Colorado State University–Global Campus	76	N/A	131	$18,000	None	3.0	99%	100%	0%	70%	55%
15.	Columbia College (MO)	75	N/A	210	N/A	None	2.7	90%	100%	100%	92%	46%
15.	East Carolina University (NC)	75	3.3	48	N/A	GRE	3.2	96%	100%	100%	91%	100%
15.	National University (CA)	75	N/A	69	$7,488	None	3.0	100%	100%	0%	72%	69%
15.	Pace University (NY)	75	N/A	18	$35,928	None	3.2	60%	100%	100%	78%	45%
15.	Western Kentucky University	75	2.9	25	N/A	GRE	2.7	65%	100%	100%	29%	N/A
20.	California University of Pennsylvania (PA)	74	N/A	167	$20,916	None	3.3	70%	82%	82%	89%	79%
20.	Faulkner University (AL)	74	N/A	96	$15,000	None	N/A	55%	100%	100%	71%	72%
20.	University of Louisville (KY)	74	3.3	94	$25,704	GRE	3.4	67%	100%	100%	85%	N/A
20.	University of Wisconsin–Platteville	74	2.5	159	$19,500	None	N/A	100%	100%	100%	75%	56%
24.	University of New Haven (CT)	72	2.5	82	N/A	None	N/A	93%	100%	0%	78%	N/A
25.	College of St. Elizabeth (NJ)	70	N/A	27	N/A	None	3.3	90%	100%	100%	25%	38%
26.	Nova Southeastern University (FL)	69	1.6	172	N/A	None	N/A	93%	100%	0%	85%	65%
27.	California State University–San Bernardino	68	2.8	24	$20,925	None	3.1	75%	100%	100%	70%	50%
28.	Colorado Technical University	67	1.7	679	$24,740	None	N/A	100%	100%	0%	94%	60%

EDUCATION

Rank	School	Overall score	Average peer assessment score (5.0=highest)	'16 total enrollment	'16-'17 total program cost[1]	Entrance test required	'16 average undergrad GPA	'16 acceptance rate	'16 full-time faculty with terminal degree	'16 tenured or tenure-track faculty[2]	'16 retention rate	'16 three-year graduation rate
1.	University of Florida	100	3.4	174	$24,840	GRE	3.5	65%	100%	48%	100%	78%
2.	University of Houston (TX)	98	2.8	61	N/A	GRE	3.3	53%	100%	68%	96%	N/A
3.	Florida State University	95	3.3	124	N/A	GRE	3.6	61%	100%	77%	87%	74%
4.	Northern Illinois University	94	2.9	165	N/A	GRE	3.2	95%	100%	100%	88%	75%
4.	University of Nebraska–Lincoln	94	3.3	100	$21,924	GRE	3.5	85%	98%	70%	93%	49%
6.	University at Albany–SUNY (NY)	93	3.1	245	N/A	None	3.4	83%	100%	94%	88%	78%
6.	University of Georgia	93	3.5	107	$22,277	GRE	3.5	88%	100%	89%	94%	60%
8.	Michigan State University	91	3.8	735	$23,940	None	3.5	85%	95%	79%	89%	68%
9.	Pennsylvania State University–World Campus	90	3.6	546	N/A	GRE	3.5	84%	100%	55%	78%	63%
10.	Auburn University (AL)	89	3.2	201	$17,760	GRE	3.4	74%	100%	90%	85%	59%
10.	Clemson University (Moore) (SC)	89	N/A	21	$12,840	GRE	3.2	69%	100%	71%	N/A	N/A
10.	Ohio University	89	2.8	440	$21,240	None	3.0	88%	89%	33%	79%	78%
10.	University at Buffalo–SUNY (NY)	89	3.2	82	$33,300	None	3.1	100%	100%	83%	84%	55%
10.	University of Illinois–Urbana-Champaign	89	3.4	223	$11,232	None	3.5	95%	100%	74%	93%	82%
15.	University of Dayton (OH)	88	2.6	402	$18,600	N/A	3.6	34%	86%	77%	72%	57%
16.	Ball State University (IN)	87	3.2	3,002	$17,700	None	3.3	89%	99%	83%	89%	54%
16.	East Carolina University (NC)	87	2.8	320	N/A	None	3.3	93%	100%	93%	93%	72%
16.	George Washington University (DC)	87	3.5	185	$28,800	None	3.2	80%	100%	40%	92%	61%
16.	University of Iowa	87	3.2	34	$20,916	GRE	3.2	44%	100%	75%	100%	89%
16.	University of Massachusetts–Lowell	87	3.0	264	$14,100	None	3.4	94%	100%	73%	95%	65%
16.	University of North Texas	87	3.1	626	$23,152	None	3.7	81%	100%	49%	48%	58%
22.	Indiana University–Bloomington	86	3.6	278	$18,180	GRE	3.4	84%	100%	100%	94%	41%
22.	New York Institute of Technology	86	2.3	223	N/A	GRE	3.3	71%	88%	100%	83%	63%
22.	Sam Houston State University (TX)	86	2.5	925	$10,278	N/A	3.2	92%	100%	87%	84%	66%
22.	San Diego State University (CA)	86	2.8	85	N/A	GRE	3.3	95%	100%	100%	100%	N/A

Rank	School	Overall score	Average peer assessment score (5.0=highest)	'16 total enrollment	'16-'17 total program cost[1]	Entrance test required	'16 average undergrad GPA	'16 acceptance rate	'16 full-time faculty with terminal degree	'16 tenured or tenure-track faculty[2]	'16 retention rate	'16 three-year graduation rate
22.	St. John's University (NY)	86	2.8	44	N/A	GRE	3.2	83%	100%	94%	81%	60%
22.	University of North Carolina–Greensboro	86	3.3	315	$32,760	GRE	3.4	93%	90%	69%	87%	73%
22.	University of San Diego (CA)	86	3.3	202	$21,300	None	3.2	94%	100%	100%	86%	N/A
29.	Central Michigan University	85	2.7	700	N/A	None	3.3	81%	91%	82%	84%	58%
29.	North Carolina State University–Raleigh	85	3.0	116	$29,760	GRE	3.2	72%	100%	62%	94%	65%
29.	University of Alabama–Birmingham	85	2.7	44	N/A	None	3.0	94%	100%	73%	80%	N/A
29.	University of South Florida	85	3.1	224	N/A	None	3.4	59%	100%	94%	76%	70%
29.	University of St. Francis (IL)	85	2.2	195	N/A	None	3.5	58%	100%	100%	93%	82%
29.	William Carey University (MS)	85	1.5	305	$10,500	None	3.4	89%	100%	100%	95%	96%
35.	Purdue University–West Lafayette (IN)	84	3.4	373	N/A	None	3.4	81%	88%	59%	96%	78%
35.	Robert Morris University (PA)	84	1.9	42	N/A	None	3.3	29%	100%	100%	89%	77%
35.	Stony Brook University–SUNY (NY)	84	3.2	306	N/A	GRE	3.3	97%	100%	100%	91%	62%
35.	University of Nebraska–Kearney	84	2.6	857	$16,461	None	3.4	92%	81%	77%	95%	51%
35.	Western Kentucky University	84	2.7	301	$22,407	GRE	3.1	62%	97%	97%	71%	43%
40.	Arizona State University	83	3.5	2,514	$16,950	None	3.4	92%	100%	65%	93%	77%
40.	Emporia State University (KS)	83	2.3	1,461	$13,356	None	3.4	45%	96%	92%	85%	74%
40.	University of South Carolina	83	2.9	576	$19,939	GRE	3.2	75%	100%	65%	94%	N/A
43.	Georgia State University	82	3.0	96	$13,860	GRE	3.3	75%	100%	76%	85%	70%
43.	University of Cincinnati (OH)	82	2.9	957	$19,650	None	3.4	75%	76%	59%	94%	67%
43.	University of Mississippi	82	2.8	114	N/A	None	3.4	91%	100%	100%	100%	N/A
43.	Wright State University (OH)	82	2.4	268	$31,800	None	3.3	98%	86%	71%	95%	62%
47.	California State University–Fullerton	81	2.8	588	$21,930	None	3.3	94%	95%	78%	88%	70%
47.	College of St. Scholastica (MN)	81	1.4	128	$13,365	None	3.5	99%	83%	100%	92%	78%
47.	Graceland University (IA)	81	1.5	150	N/A	None	N/A	61%	100%	100%	N/A	N/A
47.	Montclair State University (NJ)	81	2.3	156	$20,688	N/A	3.5	78%	100%	25%	90%	68%
47.	Pittsburg State University (KS)	81	2.5	389	N/A	None	3.4	100%	92%	83%	88%	78%
47.	University of Arkansas–Fayetteville	81	3.0	266	$13,530	GRE	3.4	42%	96%	70%	79%	40%
47.	University of Colorado–Denver	81	3.0	186	N/A	None	3.7	92%	100%	100%	87%	58%
47.	University of Pittsburgh (PA)	81	3.1	65	$52,848	None	3.3	93%	88%	25%	96%	86%
47.	Valley City State University (ND)	81	2.0	200	$10,548	None	3.3	89%	88%	96%	86%	62%
56.	Angelo State University (TX)	80	1.8	1,242	N/A	None	3.3	97%	64%	64%	95%	100%
56.	Hofstra University (NY)	80	2.6	48	N/A	None	3.1	94%	100%	100%	77%	N/A
56.	North Carolina Central University	80	N/A	20	$47,205	None	2.9	67%	100%	100%	75%	N/A
56.	Regent University (VA)	80	1.9	894	$18,975	None	3.1	57%	100%	88%	89%	52%
56.	University of Texas–Arlington	80	2.6	2,175	$9,840	GRE	3.4	90%	95%	59%	86%	80%
61.	Creighton University (NE)	79	2.7	191	N/A	None	N/A	90%	100%	100%	98%	55%
61.	Kansas State University	79	3.0	516	$17,000	None	3.4	98%	100%	94%	89%	67%
61.	Queens University of Charlotte (NC)	79	2.1	141	$12,870	None	3.1	99%	100%	100%	97%	N/A
61.	University of Colorado–Colorado Springs	79	2.5	148	N/A	None	3.2	89%	73%	60%	84%	53%
61.	University of Missouri	79	3.4	696	N/A	GRE	N/A	91%	100%	59%	89%	N/A
66.	Appalachian State University (NC)	78	2.6	183	N/A	GRE	3.4	44%	100%	94%	91%	56%
66.	Concordia University (IL)	78	1.8	1,528	$14,310	None	N/A	84%	86%	64%	85%	86%
66.	Florida International University	78	2.3	129	$18,300	None	3.5	60%	89%	53%	86%	N/A
66.	Towson University (MD)	78	3.0	151	$28,260	None	3.5	77%	100%	71%	89%	23%
66.	University of North Carolina–Pembroke	78	2.4	18	N/A	None	3.3	90%	100%	100%	100%	N/A
66.	Utah State University	78	2.8	166	$16,160	GRE	3.5	88%	23%	31%	81%	75%
72.	Brenau University (GA)	77	1.7	113	$23,472	None	3.5	35%	100%	0%	91%	94%
72.	Georgetown College (KY)	77	2.2	370	$12,600	None	3.3	79%	100%	82%	91%	50%
72.	Kent State University (OH)	77	2.8	94	N/A	None	3.5	77%	100%	73%	87%	52%
72.	Texas A&M University–College Station	77	3.3	806	N/A	None	3.3	79%	100%	60%	96%	76%
72.	University of Central Missouri	77	N/A	542	N/A	None	3.4	81%	88%	100%	81%	86%
77.	Augustana University (SD)	76	1.9	313	N/A	None	N/A	92%	100%	75%	100%	90%
77.	California University of Pennsylvania (PA)	76	1.8	636	$14,790	None	3.5	81%	81%	81%	94%	84%
77.	Fort Hays State University (KS)	76	2.4	1,349	N/A	None	3.3	99%	65%	50%	90%	46%
77.	Georgia Southern University	76	2.8	706	$7,380	GRE	3.3	95%	97%	97%	87%	68%
77.	Lamar University (TX)	76	2.0	4,909	N/A	N/A	3.1	72%	94%	52%	81%	79%
77.	Old Dominion University (Darden) (VA)	76	2.5	569	$20,590	GRE	N/A	N/A	79%	70%	88%	75%
77.	Roosevelt University (IL)	76	2.3	59	$11,850	None	3.3	66%	100%	89%	63%	N/A
84.	Drexel University (PA)	75	2.7	763	N/A	None	3.3	88%	100%	38%	83%	55%

EDUCATION continued

Rank	School	Overall score	Average peer assessment score (5.0=highest)	'16 total enrollment	'16-'17 total program cost[1]	Entrance test required	'16 average undergrad GPA	'16 acceptance rate	'16 full-time faculty with terminal degree	'16 tenured or tenure-track faculty[2]	'16 retention rate	'16 three-year graduation rate
84.	Edinboro University of Pennsylvania (PA)	75	1.6	677	N/A	None	3.5	95%	100%	92%	86%	N/A
84.	Mississippi State University (MS)	75	2.5	208	N/A	N/A	3.3	64%	96%	92%	77%	42%
84.	Nova Southeastern University (Fischler) (FL)	75	1.7	1,727	$33,840	GRE	3.1	72%	100%	0%	77%	53%
84.	Southeast Missouri State University (MO)	75	2.2	214	N/A	None	3.5	98%	95%	86%	91%	48%
84.	Texas A&M University–Kingsville	75	2.2	169	N/A	GRE	3.2	95%	100%	100%	60%	47%
84.	University of Louisville (KY)	75	3.0	229	$25,704	None	3.2	74%	94%	65%	84%	N/A
84.	University of West Georgia	75	2.7	443	N/A	None	3.3	93%	96%	96%	76%	65%
92.	Campbellsville University (KY)	74	1.6	235	$19,152	N/A	3.2	65%	79%	100%	76%	57%
92.	Eastern Kentucky University	74	2.6	778	N/A	None	3.2	98%	97%	92%	N/A	53%
92.	Friends University (KS)	74	N/A	29	$13,518	None	N/A	N/A	100%	100%	93%	93%
92.	Grand Valley State University (MI)	74	2.3	77	$20,724	None	3.3	100%	71%	79%	81%	25%
92.	University of the Cumberlands (KY)	74	1.2	2,356	N/A	GRE	3.2	89%	100%	29%	90%	N/A
92.	Western Michigan University	74	2.8	178	N/A	None	3.3	83%	89%	89%	80%	36%
98.	McKendree University (IL)	73	1.7	66	$16,740	None	N/A	75%	100%	100%	97%	86%
98.	St. Joseph's University (PA)	73	2.6	842	N/A	None	3.2	87%	81%	81%	85%	57%
98.	University of New England (ME)	73	1.8	348	N/A	None	3.3	89%	100%	50%	88%	86%
101.	Boise State University (ID)	72	3.1	550	$14,396	None	3.5	58%	76%	52%	88%	39%
101.	Bowling Green State University (OH)	72	2.7	335	N/A	None	3.3	N/A	76%	70%	87%	55%
101.	Brandman University (CA)	72	1.8	184	N/A	None	3.7	100%	94%	0%	90%	55%
101.	California Baptist University	72	1.9	243	$18,450	None	3.4	71%	100%	100%	95%	77%
101.	Cedarville University (OH)	72	1.4	68	$15,266	None	3.3	41%	88%	88%	85%	23%
101.	South Dakota State University	72	2.4	17	N/A	None	3.5	100%	100%	58%	98%	N/A
101.	University of Massachusetts–Amherst	72	3.3	24	$16,374	None	3.3	64%	100%	100%	100%	N/A
101.	University of New Mexico	72	2.7	47	N/A	None	3.4	76%	100%	79%	86%	N/A
109.	Texas Tech University	71	3.0	905	N/A	None	N/A	89%	100%	70%	92%	N/A
109.	University of North Carolina–Wilmington	71	2.7	338	$26,961	N/A	N/A	N/A	100%	100%	N/A	N/A
109.	University of Toledo (OH)	71	2.3	200	$35,208	None	3.2	85%	95%	81%	90%	48%
109.	Wheeling Jesuit University (WV)	71	2.0	66	$17,490	GRE	3.5	100%	100%	50%	97%	N/A
113.	Concord University (WV)	70	N/A	203	N/A	GRE	3.5	92%	100%	100%	N/A	63%
113.	Concordia University Wisconsin	70	1.5	1,490	N/A	None	N/A	74%	100%	0%	78%	N/A
113.	Concordia University–St. Paul (MN)	70	2.1	962	N/A	None	N/A	89%	73%	45%	88%	82%
113.	Eastern Michigan University	70	2.6	230	$21,120	None	3.3	73%	100%	100%	59%	36%
113.	Indiana State University	70	3.0	22	N/A	None	3.2	67%	91%	82%	100%	N/A
113.	Lindenwood University (MO)	70	1.5	78	$14,949	None	3.4	72%	50%	0%	70%	38%
113.	Northern Arizona University	70	2.4	795	$34,920	None	3.4	92%	90%	68%	63%	51%
113.	Southwestern College (KS)	70	1.6	125	N/A	None	N/A	68%	100%	50%	93%	67%
113.	University of Scranton (PA)	70	2.3	425	$19,890	None	N/A	85%	86%	86%	N/A	66%
113.	University of Wisconsin–Stout	70	2.3	96	N/A	None	3.4	92%	75%	69%	N/A	55%
123.	Ashland University (Schar) (OH)	69	N/A	77	N/A	None	N/A	87%	100%	100%	76%	N/A
123.	Colorado State University–Global Campus	69	2.8	310	$18,000	None	3.2	98%	100%	0%	76%	51%
123.	George Mason University (VA)	69	3.2	175	$23,160	Entrance	N/A	N/A	94%	31%	93%	N/A
123.	Northwest Nazarene University (ID)	69	N/A	255	$14,815	None	3.7	96%	100%	100%	75%	100%
123.	University of Illinois–Springfield	69	2.6	80	N/A	None	3.3	86%	100%	86%	85%	47%
123.	University of Maine	69	N/A	129	$18,828	None	N/A	76%	86%	71%	100%	N/A
123.	University of Minnesota–Twin Cities	69	3.0	52	N/A	None	3.5	96%	100%	50%	10%	80%
123.	University of Northern Colorado	69	3.1	693	N/A	None	3.5	71%	0%	95%	95%	61%
123.	Valdosta State University (GA)	69	2.6	560	$13,860	GRE	N/A	96%	93%	86%	73%	69%
123.	West Virginia University	69	2.8	427	N/A	None	3.4	81%	100%	76%	N/A	N/A

ENGINEERING

Rank	School	Overall score	Average peer assessment score (5.0=highest)	'16 total enrollment	'16-'17 total program cost[1]	Entrance test required	'16 average undergrad GPA	'16 acceptance rate	'16 full-time faculty with terminal degree	'16 tenured or tenure-track faculty[2]	'16 retention rate	'16 three-year graduation rate
1.	University of California–Los Angeles (Samueli)	100	3.6	384	$34,650	GRE	3.5	41%	100%	92%	90%	84%
1.	University of Southern California (Viterbi)	100	4.0	932	N/A	GRE	3.4	49%	98%	57%	93%	83%
3.	Columbia University (Fu Foundation) (NY)	93	3.6	306	N/A	GRE	3.7	87%	100%	75%	95%	88%
4.	Pennsylvania State University–World Campus	88	3.6	781	N/A	None	3.3	74%	98%	80%	89%	82%

Rank	School	Overall score	Average peer assessment score (5.0=highest)	'16 total enrollment	'16-'17 total program cost[1]	Entrance test required	'16 average undergrad GPA	'16 acceptance rate	'16 full-time faculty with terminal degree	'16 tenured or tenure-track faculty[2]	'16 retention rate	'16 three-year graduation rate
5.	Purdue University–West Lafayette (IN)	87	3.9	745	$35,940	None	3.4	70%	100%	91%	91%	51%
6.	University of Wisconsin–Madison	82	3.9	218	$48,000	None	3.2	63%	74%	74%	97%	54%
7.	Cornell University (NY)	76	3.6	108	N/A	GRE	N/A	87%	100%	67%	85%	73%
7.	University of Michigan–Ann Arbor	76	3.8	363	$48,150	GRE	3.4	86%	95%	67%	90%	22%
9.	North Carolina State University	73	3.4	654	$29,760	GRE	3.3	72%	100%	96%	90%	46%
9.	University of Illinois–Urbana-Champaign	73	3.6	187	N/A	GRE	3.6	50%	100%	94%	86%	44%
11.	Louisiana State University–Baton Rouge	72	N/A	68	$29,064	GRE	3.1	68%	100%	100%	90%	N/A
11.	New York University	72	3.0	130	N/A	None	3.3	40%	89%	74%	75%	53%
13.	Arizona State University (Fulton)	71	3.4	362	N/A	None	3.3	58%	98%	84%	79%	30%
13.	Virginia Tech	71	3.7	41	N/A	GRE	3.2	62%	100%	91%	100%	N/A
15.	University of Virginia	70	2.9	46	$31,620	GRE	3.3	81%	100%	83%	86%	67%
16.	Missouri University of Science & Technology	69	2.8	964	N/A	GRE	3.5	87%	96%	88%	85%	67%
17.	Texas Tech University (Whitacre)	68	2.5	116	N/A	GRF	3.2	27%	100%	100%	83%	47%
18.	Ohio State University	67	3.1	67	N/A	None	3.3	78%	89%	79%	80%	N/A
18.	University of Nebraska–Lincoln	67	2.3	42	$27,000	None	3.3	68%	100%	100%	90%	N/A
20.	Auburn University (AL)	66	3.1	117	N/A	GRE	3.2	86%	98%	96%	89%	38%
21.	Johns Hopkins University (Whiting) (MD)	65	3.4	2,385	N/A	None	3.4	49%	100%	0%	90%	48%
21.	University of North Carolina–Charlotte (Lee)	65	2.6	65	$29,427	GRE	3.3	91%	100%	89%	82%	70%
23.	University of Maryland–College Park (Clark)	64	3.5	409	$32,940	None	3.3	74%	100%	76%	69%	32%
24.	Duke University (Pratt) (NC)	63	3.2	74	$50,472	GRE	3.4	72%	88%	25%	100%	91%
24.	Mississippi State University (Bagley)	63	2.7	174	N/A	GRE	3.1	92%	100%	88%	98%	25%
26.	California State University–Fullerton	62	2.5	190	$21,930	None	3.3	89%	100%	100%	81%	82%
26.	Drexel University (PA)	62	2.9	349	N/A	None	3.1	69%	100%	33%	77%	34%
28.	Oregon State University	61	2.8	18	$25,920	GRE	3.2	100%	100%	50%	100%	N/A
28.	University of Alabama–Birmingham	61	2.1	347	N/A	None	3.1	96%	100%	57%	79%	75%
28.	Washington State University	61	2.8	96	$44,000	None	3.5	81%	100%	0%	62%	33%
31.	Clemson University (SC)	59	2.8	111	N/A	GRE	N/A	N/A	100%	100%	86%	100%
31.	Colorado State University	59	2.5	213	$31,050	GRE	3.3	97%	96%	96%	54%	35%
31.	Ohio University (Russ)	59	2.4	276	$21,522	None	3.2	92%	97%	97%	89%	54%
31.	Oklahoma State University	59	2.4	239	$26,401	None	3.2	84%	100%	97%	86%	49%
35.	Kansas State University	58	2.6	166	$24,780	None	3.4	83%	100%	100%	81%	46%
35.	Rochester Institute of Tech. (Gleason) (NY)	58	2.9	16	N/A	None	3.4	76%	100%	83%	100%	N/A
35.	Syracuse University (NY)	58	2.6	74	N/A	GRE	3.4	76%	100%	70%	80%	N/A
35.	Villanova University (PA)	58	2.4	421	$39,600	None	3.4	74%	98%	90%	93%	74%
39.	Stevens Institute of Technology (Schaefer) (NJ)	57	2.6	355	$49,992	GRE	3.2	75%	88%	37%	91%	61%
40.	California Polytechnic State U.–San Luis Obispo	56	2.6	68	$24,750	None	3.1	97%	100%	80%	84%	66%
40.	University of Arkansas–Fayetteville	56	2.3	170	$8,269	None	3.2	59%	91%	78%	85%	47%
40.	University of South Florida	56	2.4	160	$27,390	GRE	3.4	61%	100%	77%	98%	73%
40.	Worcester Polytechnic Institute (MA)	56	2.7	310	N/A	None	3.3	90%	95%	65%	78%	65%
44.	Lehigh University (Rossin) (PA)	54	2.8	104	$42,600	None	3.2	78%	96%	93%	78%	N/A

NURSING

Rank	School	Overall score	Average peer assessment score (5.0=highest)	'16 total enrollment	'16-'17 total program cost[1]	Entrance test required	'16 average undergrad GPA	'16 acceptance rate	'16 full-time faculty with terminal degree	'16 tenured or tenure-track faculty[2]	'16 retention rate	'16 three-year graduation rate
1.	St. Xavier University (IL)	100	3.4	225	N/A	None	3.6	57%	90%	100%	98%	97%
2.	Medical University of South Carolina	95	3.6	408	$59,100	None	3.7	56%	88%	96%	97%	100%
3.	Duke University (NC)	92	4.1	524	$68,838	GRE	3.6	46%	96%	40%	95%	84%
3.	Ohio State University	92	3.8	127	$41,748	None	3.6	48%	79%	31%	100%	79%
5.	Johns Hopkins University (MD)	91	4.1	51	N/A	None	3.6	45%	100%	34%	100%	35%
5.	University of Cincinnati (OH)	91	3.8	1,605	$28,820	None	3.4	60%	82%	82%	91%	71%
7.	Catholic University of America (DC)	90	3.6	64	$41,630	None	3.3	73%	100%	83%	86%	N/A
7.	Rush University (IL)	90	4.0	704	N/A	GRE	3.3	79%	84%	46%	92%	78%
9.	University of Colorado	89	3.5	108	$20,130	None	3.5	85%	75%	63%	90%	94%
9.	University of Colorado–Colorado Springs	89	3.4	222	N/A	None	3.4	60%	70%	40%	87%	55%
9.	University of South Carolina	89	3.3	436	N/A	None	3.5	80%	92%	50%	100%	72%
12.	University of Pittsburgh (PA)	88	3.7	106	$50,862	N/A	3.7	75%	100%	63%	83%	33%

NURSING continued

Rank	School	Overall score	Average peer assessment score (5.0=highest)	'16 total enrollment	'16-'17 total program cost[1]	Entrance test required	'16 average undergrad GPA	'16 acceptance rate	'16 full-time faculty with terminal degree	'16 tenured or tenure-track faculty[2]	'16 retention rate	'16 three-year graduation rate
13.	Ball State University (IN)	87	3.3	436	$27,730	None	3.5	71%	90%	62%	95%	54%
13.	University of Massachusetts–Amherst	87	3.5	273	$27,780	None	3.4	57%	100%	65%	85%	55%
13.	University of Texas–Tyler	87	3.3	407	$21,984	None	3.5	91%	100%	96%	99%	51%
16.	University of Alabama–Birmingham	86	3.6	2,125	$24,342	GRE	3.5	68%	84%	26%	96%	76%
16.	University of Michigan–Flint	86	3.0	295	N/A	None	3.7	65%	92%	92%	88%	58%
16.	University of Texas Medical Branch–Galveston	86	3.3	510	$49,721	None	3.3	38%	75%	29%	97%	97%
19.	University of Kansas	85	3.7	94	N/A	None	3.5	74%	90%	41%	86%	29%
20.	University of Nevada–Las Vegas	84	3.5	89	$33,350	None	3.5	48%	69%	46%	100%	76%
21.	Indiana University-Purdue U.–Indianapolis	83	3.8	117	$62,958	None	3.5	55%	100%	65%	76%	42%
21.	Stony Brook University–SUNY (NY)	83	3.3	753	$11,881	None	3.4	56%	87%	18%	96%	82%
21.	University of Missouri–Kansas City	83	3.4	177	$20,739	None	3.6	85%	95%	16%	96%	91%
21.	University of Southern Indiana	83	3.1	422	N/A	None	3.7	56%	100%	100%	84%	30%
21.	Western Kentucky University	83	3.0	138	N/A	None	2.4	51%	85%	85%	90%	47%
26.	Duquesne University (PA)	82	3.6	192	N/A	None	3.5	79%	85%	50%	97%	77%
26.	George Washington University (DC)	82	3.6	596	$55,440	None	3.4	64%	96%	56%	94%	77%
26.	Michigan State University	82	3.7	42	$36,237	None	3.6	84%	85%	46%	88%	91%
29.	Fort Hays State University (KS)	81	2.9	138	N/A	None	3.5	90%	100%	88%	89%	24%
29.	Texas A&M University–Corpus Christi	81	3.2	416	$58,016	None	3.6	60%	100%	100%	N/A	53%
29.	University of St. Francis (IL)	81	2.9	438	N/A	None	3.4	42%	58%	75%	80%	25%
29.	University of West Georgia	81	3.1	90	$22,212	None	3.5	92%	100%	100%	73%	88%
33.	Oregon Health and Science University	80	3.9	49	$37,740	None	3.4	97%	100%	17%	100%	68%
33.	Samford University (AL)	80	3.1	297	N/A	None	3.5	81%	95%	86%	93%	87%
35.	Drexel University (PA)	79	3.3	1,578	N/A	None	3.4	51%	94%	12%	91%	27%
35.	East Carolina University (NC)	79	3.4	521	N/A	GRE	3.3	78%	63%	44%	94%	60%
35.	Robert Morris University (PA)	79	2.7	134	N/A	None	3.3	35%	89%	100%	97%	72%
35.	St. Louis University (MO)	79	3.6	416	$39,780	None	3.5	82%	62%	51%	90%	90%
39.	Baylor University (TX)	77	3.4	11	$15,830	None	3.5	75%	100%	25%	N/A	N/A
39.	Clarkson College (NE)	77	3.0	375	$25,166	None	3.5	46%	100%	0%	90%	47%
39.	Eastern Kentucky University	77	3.1	385	$23,790	None	3.5	61%	89%	83%	N/A	93%
39.	Loyola University New Orleans (LA)	77	3.2	582	$29,448	None	3.3	89%	100%	79%	78%	60%
43.	Clarion U. of Pennsylvania/Edinboro U. of Penn.	76	2.7	144	$25,830	None	3.6	85%	100%	100%	95%	60%
43.	Florida Atlantic University	76	3.3	163	$30,624	None	3.5	83%	100%	80%	98%	57%
43.	Florida State University	76	3.3	23	N/A	N/A	3.8	100%	100%	100%	70%	N/A
43.	University of Arizona	76	3.4	899	$30,000	None	3.4	62%	84%	16%	87%	N/A
47.	Georgia College & State University	75	2.9	124	$14,920	GRE	3.5	89%	87%	93%	100%	74%
47.	Nova Southeastern University (FL)	75	2.6	108	N/A	None	3.3	43%	78%	0%	83%	85%
47.	Texas Christian University	75	3.4	69	$59,200	GRE	3.3	100%	93%	73%	N/A	100%
50.	Angelo State University (TX)	74	2.9	82	N/A	None	3.4	69%	60%	60%	97%	93%
50.	Frontier Nursing University (KY)	74	3.5	1,978	$35,200	None	3.7	54%	83%	0%	N/A	83%
50.	University of Alabama–Huntsville	74	3.3	21	$15,240	None	3.4	100%	100%	50%	100%	100%
50.	University of Connecticut	74	3.1	19	$33,000	None	3.7	94%	100%	92%	N/A	N/A
54.	Boise State University (ID)	73	3.1	118	N/A	None	3.5	43%	86%	93%	88%	29%
54.	Graceland University (MO)	73	2.6	605	N/A	None	3.6	66%	75%	67%	85%	87%
54.	Northern Kentucky University	73	2.8	405	$23,500	None	3.4	79%	69%	56%	N/A	N/A
57.	University of Central Florida	72	3.3	196	$27,627	None	3.4	79%	96%	69%	98%	66%
57.	University of Oklahoma Health Sciences Center	72	3.4	38	N/A	None	3.9	93%	100%	63%	84%	100%
57.	University of Southern Mississippi	72	3.5	111	$22,080	GRE	3.3	66%	100%	70%	N/A	75%
60.	Simmons College (MA)	71	3.4	1,609	$63,120	None	3.2	63%	91%	36%	81%	N/A
61.	East Tennessee State University	70	3.0	432	$35,742	None	N/A	80%	100%	100%	89%	69%
61.	Lamar University (TX)	70	2.5	98	N/A	None	3.3	48%	100%	64%	75%	40%
61.	Old Dominion University (VA)	70	3.2	38	$24,768	GRE	3.4	77%	100%	60%	64%	77%
61.	St. Francis Medical Ctr. College of Nursing (IL)	70	2.9	300	N/A	None	3.4	83%	79%	0%	89%	9%
61.	University of Hawaii–Manoa	70	3.2	31	$56,880	None	3.4	87%	67%	67%	95%	86%
61.	University of Nebraska Medical Center	70	3.6	324	$45,912	None	3.4	66%	98%	73%	89%	85%
61.	West Virginia University	70	3.2	198	N/A	None	3.5	82%	84%	44%	92%	83%
68.	Ferris State University (MI)	69	2.4	97	$30,451	None	3.2	81%	100%	100%	N/A	78%
68.	Georgetown University (DC)	69	3.6	820	$84,832	None	3.5	40%	67%	0%	81%	83%
68.	Northwestern State University of Louisiana (LA)	69	2.8	197	$19,950	GRE	3.2	72%	65%	94%	96%	86%
68.	Texas Tech University Health Sciences Center	69	3.4	749	N/A	None	3.6	52%	86%	31%	N/A	75%

DIRECTORY OF GRADUATE SCHOOLS

Schools are listed alphabetically by state within each discipline; data are accurate as of late February 2017. A key to the terminology used in the directory can be found at the beginning of each area of study.

BUSINESS

The business directory lists all 471 U.S. schools offering master's programs in business accredited by AACSB International–the Association to Advance Collegiate Schools of Business, as of summer 2016. Most offer the MBA degree; a few offer the master of business. Three hundred and seventy-seven schools responded to the U.S. News survey conducted in the fall of 2016 and early 2017. Schools that did not respond to the survey have abbreviated entries.

KEY TO THE TERMINOLOGY

1. A school whose name is footnoted with the numeral 1 did not return the U.S. News statistical survey; limited data appear in its entry.

N/A. Not available from the school or not applicable.

Email. The address of the admissions office. If instead of an email address a website is given in this field, the website will automatically present an email screen programmed to reach the admissions office.

Application deadline. For fall 2018 enrollment. "Rolling" means there is no application deadline; the school acts on applications as they are received. "Varies" means deadlines vary according to department or whether applicants are U.S. citizens or foreign nationals.

Tuition. For the 2016-17 academic year or for the cost of the total graduate business degree program, if specified. Includes required annual student fees.

Credit hour. The cost per credit hour for the 2016-17 academic year.

Room/board/expenses. For the 2016-17 academic year.

College-funded aid and international student aid. "Yes" means the school provides its own financial aid to students.

Average indebtedness. Computed for 2016 graduates who incurred business school debt.

Enrollment. Full-time and part-time program totals are for fall 2016.

Minorities. For fall 2016, percentage of students who are black or African-American, Asian, American Indian or Alaska Native, Native Hawaiian or other Pacific Islander, Hispanic/Latino, or two or more races. The minority numbers were reported by each school.

Acceptance rate. Percentage of applicants to the full-time program who were accepted for fall 2016.

Average Graduate Management Admission Test (GMAT) score. Calculated separately for full-time and part-time students who entered in fall 2016.

Average undergraduate grade point average (1.0 to 4.0). For full-time program applicants who entered in fall 2016.

Average age of entrants. Calculated for full-time students who entered in fall 2016.

Average months of work experience. Calculated only for full-time program students who entered in fall 2016. Refers to post-baccalaureate work experience only.

TOEFL requirement. "Yes" means that students from non-English-speaking countries must submit scores for the Test of English as a Foreign Language.

Minimum TOEFL score. The lowest score on the paper TOEFL accepted for admission. (The computer-administered TOEFL is graded on a different scale.)

Most popular departments. Based on highest student demand in the 2016-17 academic year.

Mean starting base salary for 2016 graduates. Calculated only for graduates who were full-time students, had accepted full-time job offers, and reported salary data. Excludes employer-sponsored students, signing bonuses of any kind and other forms of guaranteed compensation, such as stock options.

Employment locations. For the 2016 graduating class. Calculated only for full-time students who had accepted job offers. Abbreviations: **Intl.,** international; **N.E.,** Northeast (Conn., Maine, Mass., N.H., N.J., N.Y., R.I., Vt.); **M.A.,** Middle Atlantic (Del., D.C., Md., Pa., Va., W.Va.); **S.,** South (Ala., Ark., Fla., Ga., Ky., La., Miss., N.C., S.C., Tenn.); **M.W.,** Midwest (Ill., Ind., Iowa, Kan., Mich., Minn., Mo., Neb., N.D., Ohio, S.D., Wis.); **S.W.,** Southwest (Ariz., Colo., N.M., Okla., Texas); **W.,** West (Alaska, Calif., Hawaii, Idaho, Mont., Nev., Ore., Utah, Wash., Wyo.).

ALABAMA

Auburn University (Harbert)
415 W. Magnolia, Suite 503
Auburn, AL 36849-5240
www.business.auburn.edu/mba
Public
Admissions: (334) 844-4060
Email: mbadmis@auburn.edu
Financial aid: (334) 844-4367
Application deadline: 02/01
In-state tuition: total program: $24,044 (full time); part time: N/A
Out-of-state tuition: total program: $51,260 (full time)
Room/board/expenses: $23,844
College-funded aid: Yes
International student aid: Yes
Average student indebtedness at graduation: $32,628
Full-time enrollment: 81
men: 64%; women: 36%;
minorities: 10%; international: 19%
Part-time enrollment: N/A
men: N/A; women: N/A;
minorities: N/A; international: N/A
Acceptance rate (full time): 52%
Average GMAT (full time): 590
Average GPA (full time): 3.40
Average age of entrants to full-time program: 24
Average months of prior work experience (full time): 59
TOEFL requirement: Yes
Minimum TOEFL score: 550
Most popular departments: finance, human resources management, management information systems, supply chain management/logistics, quantitative analysis/statistics and operations research
Mean starting base salary for 2016 full-time graduates: $60,464
Employment location for 2016 class: Intl. N/A; N.E. N/A; M.A. 4%; S. 87%; M.W. 4%; S.W. 4%; W. N/A

Auburn University-Montgomery
7300 East Drive
Montgomery, AL 36117
www.aum.edu
Public
Admissions: (334) 244-3623
Email: awarren3@aum.edu
Financial aid: (334) 244-3571
Application deadline: 08/01
In-state tuition: full time: $374/credit hour; part time: $374/credit hour
Out-of-state tuition: full time: $841/credit hour
Room/board/expenses: N/A
College-funded aid: Yes
International student aid: Yes
Full-time enrollment: 36
men: 53%; women: 47%;
minorities: 14%; international: 56%
Part-time enrollment: 59
men: 37%; women: 63%;
minorities: 27%; international: 7%
Acceptance rate (full time): 74%

Average GMAT (full time): 458
TOEFL requirement: Yes
Minimum TOEFL score: 500

Jacksonville State University[1]
700 Pelham Road N
Jacksonville, AL 36265
www.jsu.edu/ccba/
Public
Admissions: (256) 782-5268
Email: info@jsu.edu
Financial aid: N/A
Tuition: N/A
Room/board/expenses: N/A
Enrollment: N/A

Samford University (Brock)
800 Lakeshore Drive
Birmingham, AL 35229
www.samford.edu/business/
Private
Admissions: (205) 726-2040
Email: gradbusi@samford.edu
Financial aid: (205) 726-2905
Application deadline: 07/01
Tuition: full time: N/A; part time: $789/credit hour
Room/board/expenses: N/A
College-funded aid: Yes
International student aid: No
Full-time enrollment: N/A
men: N/A; women: N/A;
minorities: N/A; international: N/A
Part-time enrollment: 123
men: 58%; women: 42%;
minorities: 12%; international: 6%
Average GMAT (part time): 586
TOEFL requirement: Yes
Minimum TOEFL score: N/A

University of Alabama-Birmingham
1720 2nd Avenue South
Birmingham, AL 35294-4460
www.uab.edu/mba
Public
Admissions: (205) 934-8817
Email: cmanning@uab.edu
Financial aid: (205) 934-8223
Application deadline: 07/01
In-state tuition: full time: N/A; part time: $472/credit hour
Out-of-state tuition: full time: N/A
Room/board/expenses: N/A
College-funded aid: Yes
International student aid: No
Full-time enrollment: N/A
men: N/A; women: N/A;
minorities: N/A; international: N/A
Part-time enrollment: 295
men: 56%; women: 44%;
minorities: 29%; international: 10%
Average GMAT (part time): 554
TOEFL requirement: Yes
Minimum TOEFL score: 550
Most popular departments: finance, health care administration, marketing, management information systems

University of Alabama-Huntsville

BAB 202
Huntsville, AL 35899
cba.uah.edu/
Public
Admissions: (256) 824-6681
Email: gradbiz@uah.edu
Financial aid: (256) 824-2754
Application deadline: 06/01
In-state tuition: full time: $9,834;
part time: $702/credit hour
Out-of-state tuition: full time:
$21,830
Room/board/expenses: $14,076
College-funded aid: Yes
International student aid: Yes
**Average student indebtedness at
graduation:** $21,680
Full-time enrollment: 50
men: 68%; women: 32%;
minorities: 14%; international:
18%
Part-time enrollment: 104
men: 56%; women: 44%;
minorities: 13%; international:
5%
Acceptance rate (full time): 86%
Average GMAT (full time): 450
Average GMAT (part time): 492
Average GPA (full time): 3.30
**Average age of entrants to full-
time program:** 26
**Average months of prior work
experience (full time):** 37
TOEFL requirement: Yes
Minimum TOEFL score: 550
Most popular departments:
accounting, general
management, manufacturing and
technology management, supply
chain management/logistics,
technology
**Employment location for 2016
class:** Intl. N/A; N.E. N/A; M.A.
N/A; S. 100%; M.W. N/A; S.W.
N/A; W. N/A

University of Alabama (Manderson)

Box 870223
Tuscaloosa, AL 35487
www.cba.ua.edu/~mba
Public
Admissions: (888) 863-2622
Email: mba@cba.ua.edu
Financial aid: (205) 348-6517
Application deadline: 04/15
In-state tuition: full time: $13,300;
part time: N/A
Out-of-state tuition: full time:
$29,780
Room/board/expenses: N/A
College-funded aid: Yes
International student aid: Yes
Full-time enrollment: 225
men: 73%; women: 27%;
minorities: 11%; international: 4%
Part-time enrollment: N/A
men: N/A; women: N/A;
minorities: N/A; international: N/A
Acceptance rate (full time): 59%
Average GMAT (full time): 677
Average GPA (full time): 3.57
**Average age of entrants to full-
time program:** 22
**Average months of prior work
experience (full time):** 28
TOEFL requirement: Yes
Minimum TOEFL score: 550
Most popular departments:
consulting, management
information systems, production/
operations management, supply
chain management/logistics,

quantitative analysis/statistics
and operations research
**Mean starting base salary for 2016
full-time graduates:** $72,217
**Employment location for 2016
class:** Intl. 0%; N.E. 4%; M.A.
4%; S. 79%; M.W. 11%; S.W. 2%;
W. 2%

University of Montevallo

Morgan Hall 201
Station 6540
Montevallo, AL 35115
www.montevallo.edu/mba/
Public
Admissions: (205) 665-6544
Email: mba@montevallo.edu
Financial aid: (205) 665-6050
Application deadline: 07/01
In-state tuition: full time: $414/
credit hour; part time: $414/
credit hour
Out-of-state tuition: full time:
$858/credit hour
Room/board/expenses: N/A
College-funded aid: Yes
Full-time enrollment: N/A
men: N/A; women: N/A;
minorities: N/A; international: N/A
Part-time enrollment: 35
men: 51%; women: 49%;
minorities: 31%; international:
N/A
TOEFL requirement: Yes
Minimum TOEFL score: 525
Most popular departments:
general management

University of North Alabama[1]

UNA Box 5077
Florence, AL 35632
www.una.edu/mba/
Private
Admissions: (256) 765-4103
Email: mbainfo@una.edu
Financial aid: N/A
Tuition: N/A
Room/board/expenses: N/A
Enrollment: N/A

University of South Alabama (Mitchell)[1]

307 N. University Boulevard
Mobile, AL 36688
mcob.usouthal.edu
Public
Admissions: (251) 460-6418
Financial aid: N/A
Tuition: N/A
Room/board/expenses: N/A
Enrollment: N/A

ALASKA

University of Alaska-Anchorage[1]

3211 Providence Drive
Anchorage, AK 99508
www.uaa.alaska.edu/cbpp/
Public
Admissions: (907) 786-1480
Email:
admissions@uaa.alaska.edu
Financial aid: N/A
Tuition: N/A
Room/board/expenses: N/A
Enrollment: N/A

University of Alaska-Fairbanks

PO Box 756080
Fairbanks, AK 99775-6080
www.uaf.edu/index.html
Public
Admissions: (800) 478-1823
Email: admissions@uaf.edu
Financial aid: (888) 474-7256
Application deadline: 08/01
In-state tuition: full time: $533/
credit hour; part time: $533/
credit hour
Out-of-state tuition: full time:
$1,088/credit hour
Room/board/expenses: $13,340
College-funded aid: Yes
International student aid: Yes
Full-time enrollment: 32
men: 44%; women: 56%;
minorities: 25%; international:
13%
Part-time enrollment: 55
men: 49%; women: 51%;
minorities: 24%; international:
5%
Average GMAT (full time): 440
**Average age of entrants to full-
time program:** 27
TOEFL requirement: Yes
Minimum TOEFL score: N/A
Most popular departments:
finance, general management

ARIZONA

Arizona State University (Carey)

PO Box 874906
Tempe, AZ 85287-4906
wpcarey.asu.edu/mba-programs
Public
Admissions: (480) 965-3332
Email:
wpcareymasters@asu.edu
Financial aid: (480) 965-6890
Application deadline: 04/03
In-state tuition: full time: $26,776;
part time: $28,026
Out-of-state tuition: full time:
$43,882
Room/board/expenses: $19,044
College-funded aid: Yes
International student aid: Yes
**Average student indebtedness at
graduation:** $49,859
Full-time enrollment: 203
men: 63%; women: 37%;
minorities: 18%; international:
29%
Part-time enrollment: 208
men: 72%; women: 28%;
minorities: 24%; international:
6%
Acceptance rate (full time): 14%
Average GMAT (full time): 682
Average GMAT (part time): 585
Average GPA (full time): 3.54
**Average age of entrants to full-
time program:** 29
**Average months of prior work
experience (full time):** 72
TOEFL requirement: Yes
Minimum TOEFL score: 550
Most popular departments:
entrepreneurship, finance,
marketing, supply chain
management/logistics, other
**Mean starting base salary for 2016
full-time graduates:** $102,578
**Employment location for 2016
class:** Intl. 0%; N.E. 9%; M.A.
0%; S. 9%; M.W. 3%; S.W. 50%;
W. 29%

Northern Arizona University (Franke)

PO Box 15066
Flagstaff, AZ 86011-5066
www.franke.nau.edu/
graduateprograms
Public
Admissions: (928) 523-7342
Email: fcb-gradprog@nau.edu
Financial aid: (928) 523-4951
Application deadline: rolling
In-state tuition: total program:
$18,428 (full time); part time: N/A
Out-of-state tuition: total
program: $30,414 (full time)
Room/board/expenses: N/A
College-funded aid: Yes
International student aid: Yes
Full-time enrollment: 31
men: 61%; women: 39%;
minorities: 13%; international:
N/A
Part-time enrollment: N/A
men: N/A; women: N/A;
minorities: N/A; international: N/A
Acceptance rate (full time): 91%
Average GMAT (full time): 526
Average GPA (full time): 3.50
**Average age of entrants to full-
time program:** 24
**Average months of prior work
experience (full time):** 19
TOEFL requirement: Yes
Minimum TOEFL score: 550
**Mean starting base salary for 2016
full-time graduates:** $51,256

Thunderbird School of Global Management

1 Global Place
Glendale, AZ 85306-6000
www.thunderbird.edu
Public
Admissions: (602) 978-7100
Email:
admissions@thunderbird.edu
Financial aid: (602) 978-7130
Application deadline: 05/10
In-state tuition: total program:
$70,000 (full time); part time: N/A
Out-of-state tuition: total
program: $70,000 (full time)
Room/board/expenses: $5,265
College-funded aid: Yes
International student aid: Yes
Full-time enrollment: 129
men: 61%; women: 39%;
minorities: 20%; international:
50%
Part-time enrollment: N/A
men: N/A; women: N/A;
minorities: N/A; international: N/A
Acceptance rate (full time): 76%
Average GPA (full time): 3.44
**Average age of entrants to full-
time program:** 29
**Average months of prior work
experience (full time):** 56
TOEFL requirement: Yes
Minimum TOEFL score: 600
Most popular departments:
accounting, finance, general
management, international
business, marketing
**Mean starting base salary for 2016
full-time graduates:** $79,870
**Employment location for 2016
class:** Intl. 21%; N.E. 4%; M.A.
10%; S. 4%; M.W. 16%; S.W.
33%; W. 11%

University of Arizona (Eller)

McClelland Hall, Room 417
Tucson, AZ 85721-0108
ellermba.arizona.edu
Public
Admissions: (520) 621-6227
Email: mba_admissions@
eller.arizona.edu
Financial aid: (520) 621-1858
Application deadline: 05/01
In-state tuition: full time: $23,897;
part time: $25,500
Out-of-state tuition: full time:
$43,649
Room/board/expenses: $13,200
College-funded aid: Yes
International student aid: Yes
**Average student indebtedness at
graduation:** $44,654
Full-time enrollment: 87
men: 68%; women: 32%;
minorities: 21%; international:
45%
Part-time enrollment: 198
men: 59%; women: 41%;
minorities: 33%; international:
4%
Acceptance rate (full time): 61%
Average GMAT (full time): 656
Average GMAT (part time): 539
Average GPA (full time): 3.40
**Average age of entrants to full-
time program:** 28
**Average months of prior work
experience (full time):** 50
TOEFL requirement: Yes
Minimum TOEFL score: 600
Most popular departments:
entrepreneurship, finance,
health care administration,
marketing, management
information systems
**Mean starting base salary for 2016
full-time graduates:** $89,859
**Employment location for 2016
class:** Intl. 0%; N.E. 4%; M.A. 0%;
S. 16%; M.W. 12%; S.W. 32%;
W. 36%

ARKANSAS

Arkansas State University-Jonesboro

PO Box 970
State University, AR 72467
www2.astate.edu/business/
Public
Admissions: (870) 972-3029
Email: gradsch@astate.edu
Financial aid: (870) 972-2310
Application deadline: 06/01
In-state tuition: full time: $374/
credit hour; part time: N/A
Out-of-state tuition: full time:
$636/credit hour
Room/board/expenses: $15,389
College-funded aid: Yes
International student aid: Yes
**Average student indebtedness at
graduation:** $38,000
Full-time enrollment: 188
men: 56%; women: 44%;
minorities: 26%; international:
36%
Part-time enrollment: N/A
men: N/A; women: N/A;
minorities: N/A; international: N/A
Acceptance rate (full time): 86%
Average GMAT (full time): 556
Average GPA (full time): 3.42
**Average age of entrants to full-
time program:** 28
**Average months of prior work
experience (full time):** 25
TOEFL requirement: Yes

Minimum TOEFL score: 550
Most popular departments: finance, health care administration, international business, management information systems, supply chain management/logistics
Mean starting base salary for 2016 full-time graduates: $68,250
Employment location for 2016 class: Intl. 31%; N.E. 4%; M.A. N/A; S. 38%; M.W. 4%; S.W. 15%; W. 8%

Arkansas Tech University[1]
1605 North Coliseum Drive
Russellville, AR 72801
www.atu.edu/business/
Public
Admissions: (479) 968-0398
Email: gradcollege@atu.edu
Financial aid: N/A
Tuition: N/A
Room/board/expenses: N/A
Enrollment: N/A

Henderson State University
1100 Henderson Street
Box 7801
Arkadelphia, AR 71999-0001
www.hsu.edu/Academics/GraduateSchool/index.html
Public
Admissions: (870) 230-5126
Email: grad@hsu.edu
Financial aid: (870) 230-5148
Application deadline: rolling
In-state tuition: full time: $262/credit hour; part time: $262/credit hour
Out-of-state tuition: full time: $537/credit hour
Room/board/expenses: $7,200
Full-time enrollment: 14
men: 57%; women: 43%; minorities: 29%; international: 14%
Part-time enrollment: 36
men: 50%; women: 50%; minorities: 31%; international: 3%
Acceptance rate (full time): 100%
Average GPA (full time): 3.35
Average age of entrants to full-time program: 24
TOEFL requirement: Yes
Minimum TOEFL score: 550

Southern Arkansas University
100 E. University
Magnolia, AR 71753
web.saumag.edu/graduate/programs/mba/
Public
Admissions: (870) 235-4150
Email: gradstudies@saumag.edu
Financial aid: (870) 235-4023
Application deadline: 07/01
In-state tuition: full time: $279/credit hour; part time: $279/credit hour
Out-of-state tuition: full time: $414/credit hour
Room/board/expenses: N/A
College-funded aid: Yes
International student aid: Yes
Full-time enrollment: 15
men: 47%; women: 53%; minorities: 13%; international: 53%

Part-time enrollment: 58
men: 45%; women: 55%; minorities: 21%; international: 3%
Acceptance rate (full time): 75%
Average GMAT (full time): 442
Average GMAT (part time): 442
TOEFL requirement: Yes
Minimum TOEFL score: 550

University of Arkansas-Fayetteville (Walton)
310 Williard J. Walker Hall
Fayetteville, AR 72701
gsb.uark.edu
Public
Admissions: (479) 575-2851
Email: gsb@walton.uark.edu
Financial aid: (479) 575-2711
Application deadline: 04/15
In-state tuition: full time: $543/credit hour; part time: N/A
Out-of-state tuition: full time: $1,387/credit hour
Room/board/expenses: $25,152
College-funded aid: Yes
International student aid: Yes
Full-time enrollment: 98
men: 57%; women: 43%; minorities: 18%; international: 19%
Part-time enrollment: N/A
men: N/A; women: N/A; minorities: N/A; international: N/A
Acceptance rate (full time): 63%
Average GMAT (full time): 637
Average GPA (full time): 3.54
Average age of entrants to full-time program: 25
Average months of prior work experience (full time): 37
TOEFL requirement: Yes
Minimum TOEFL score: 550
Most popular departments: entrepreneurship, finance, marketing, management information systems, supply chain management/logistics
Mean starting base salary for 2016 full-time graduates: $62,963

University of Arkansas-Little Rock
2801 S. University Avenue
Little Rock, AR 72204
ualr.edu/cob
Public
Admissions: (501) 569-3356
Email: mbaadvising@ualr.edu
Financial aid: (501) 569-3035
Application deadline: 07/15
In-state tuition: full time: $345/credit hour; part time: $345/credit hour
Out-of-state tuition: full time: $740/credit hour
Room/board/expenses: $7,320
College-funded aid: Yes
International student aid: Yes
Average student indebtedness at graduation: $25,752
Full-time enrollment: 16
men: 63%; women: 38%; minorities: N/A; international: N/A
Part-time enrollment: 161
men: 57%; women: 43%; minorities: N/A; international: N/A
Acceptance rate (full time): 21%
Average GMAT (full time): 481
Average GMAT (part time): 490
Average age of entrants to full-time program: 26
TOEFL requirement: Yes
Minimum TOEFL score: 550

Most popular departments: human resources management, other

University of Central Arkansas
201 Donaghey
Conway, AR 72035
www.uca.edu/mba
Public
Admissions: (501) 450-5316
Email: mrubach@uca.edu
Financial aid: (501) 450-3140
Application deadline: 07/15
In-state tuition: full time: $255/credit hour; part time: $255/credit hour
Out-of-state tuition: full time: $510/credit hour
Room/board/expenses: $17,510
College-funded aid: Yes
International student aid: No
Average student indebtedness at graduation: $18,978
Full-time enrollment: 50
men: 44%; women: 56%; minorities: 14%; international: 36%
Part-time enrollment: 47
men: 49%; women: 51%; minorities: 26%; international: 4%
Acceptance rate (full time): 92%
Average age of entrants to full-time program: 25
TOEFL requirement: Yes
Minimum TOEFL score: 550
Most popular departments: finance, health care administration, international business

CALIFORNIA

California Polytechnic State University-San Luis Obispo (Orfalea)[1]
1 Grand Avenue
San Luis Obispo, CA 93407
www.cob.calpoly.edu/gradbusiness/
Public
Admissions: (805) 756-2311
Email: admissions@calpoly.edu
Financial aid: (805) 756-2927
Application deadline: 04/01
In-state tuition: full time: $24,384; part time: N/A
Out-of-state tuition: full time: $36,288
Room/board/expenses: $15,765
College-funded aid: Yes
International student aid: Yes
Full-time enrollment: 35
men: 31%; women: 69%; minorities: N/A; international: N/A
Part-time enrollment: N/A
men: N/A; women: N/A; minorities: N/A; international: N/A
Acceptance rate (full time): 70%
Average GMAT (full time): 539
Average GPA (full time): 3.40
TOEFL requirement: Yes
Minimum TOEFL score: 550
Most popular departments: accounting, economics, general management, tax, other

California State Polytechnic University-Pomona
3801 W. Temple Avenue
Pomona, CA 91768
www.cpp.edu/cba/grad
Public
Admissions: (909) 869-3210
Email: admissions@cpp.edu
Financial aid: (909) 869-3700
Application deadline: 06/01
In-state tuition: full time: $12,374; part time: $7,364
Out-of-state tuition: full time: $18,326
Room/board/expenses: N/A
College-funded aid: Yes
International student aid: Yes
Full-time enrollment: 55
men: 64%; women: 36%; minorities: 47%; international: 20%
Part-time enrollment: 9
men: 11%; women: 89%; minorities: 44%; international: 33%
Acceptance rate (full time): 41%
Average GMAT (full time): 495
Average GPA (full time): 3.12
Average age of entrants to full-time program: 29
TOEFL requirement: Yes
Minimum TOEFL score: 580

California State University-Bakersfield[1]
9001 Stockdale Highway
Bakersfield, CA 93311-1099
www.csub.edu/BPA
Public
Admissions: (661) 664-3036
Email: admissions@csub.edu
Financial aid: N/A
Tuition: N/A
Room/board/expenses: N/A
Enrollment: N/A

California State University-Chico
Tehama Hall 301
Chico, CA 95929-0001
www.csuchico.edu/MBA
Public
Admissions: (530) 898-6880
Email: graduatestudies@csuchico.edu
Financial aid: (530) 898-6451
Application deadline: 03/21
In-state tuition: full time: N/A; part time: N/A
Out-of-state tuition: full time: N/A
Room/board/expenses: N/A
College-funded aid: Yes
International student aid: Yes
Full-time enrollment: 79
men: 59%; women: 41%; minorities: N/A; international: N/A
Part-time enrollment: N/A
men: N/A; women: N/A; minorities: N/A; international: N/A
Acceptance rate (full time): 70%
Average GPA (full time): 3.20
Average age of entrants to full-time program: 27
Average months of prior work experience (full time): 32
TOEFL requirement: Yes
Minimum TOEFL score: 550

California State University-East Bay
25800 Carlos Bee Boulevard
Hayward, CA 94542
www.csueastbay.edu
Public
Admissions: (510) 885-3973
Email: admissions@csueastbay.edu
Financial aid: (510) 885-2784
Application deadline: 05/15
In-state tuition: total program: $21,256 (full time); $31,696 (part time)
Out-of-state tuition: total program: $37,128 (full time)
Room/board/expenses: $15,000
College-funded aid: Yes
International student aid: No
Average student indebtedness at graduation: $2,154
Full-time enrollment: 26
men: 38%; women: 62%; minorities: 27%; international: 65%
Part-time enrollment: 321
men: 49%; women: 51%; minorities: 51%; international: 31%
Acceptance rate (full time): 94%
Average GMAT (full time): 530
Average GMAT (part time): 550
Average GPA (full time): 3.06
Average age of entrants to full-time program: 25
TOEFL requirement: Yes
Minimum TOEFL score: 550
Most popular departments: finance, human resources management, international business, marketing, supply chain management/logistics

California State University-Fresno (Craig)[1]
5245 N. Backer Avenue
Fresno, CA 93740-8001
www.craig.csufresno.edu/mba
Public
Admissions: (559) 278-2107
Email: mbainfo@csufresno.edu
Financial aid: N/A
Tuition: N/A
Room/board/expenses: N/A
Enrollment: N/A

California State University-Fullerton (Mihaylo)
PO Box 6848
Fullerton, CA 92834-6848
business.fullerton.edu
Public
Admissions: (657) 278-4035
Email: mba@fullerton.edu
Financial aid: (657) 278-3125
Application deadline: 04/01
In-state tuition: full time: N/A; part time: $6,522
Out-of-state tuition: full time: N/A
Room/board/expenses: N/A
College-funded aid: Yes
International student aid: Yes
Full-time enrollment: N/A
men: N/A; women: N/A; minorities: N/A; international: N/A
Part-time enrollment: 303
men: 65%; women: 35%; minorities: 27%; international: 31%
Average GMAT (part time): 550

TOEFL requirement: Yes
Minimum TOEFL score: 570
Most popular departments: finance, general management, leadership, management information systems, quantitative analysis/statistics and operations research

California State University-Long Beach[1]

1250 Bellflower Boulevard
Long Beach, CA 90840-8501
www.csulb.edu/colleges/cba/mba
Public
Admissions: (562) 985-8627
Email: mba@csulb.edu
Financial aid: (562) 985-4141
Tuition: N/A
Room/board/expenses: N/A
Enrollment: N/A

California State University-Los Angeles[1]

5151 State University Drive
Los Angeles, CA 90032-8120
www.calstatela.edu/business/graddprog
Public
Admissions: (323) 343-2800
Email: ehsieh@calstatela.edu
Financial aid: (323) 343-6260
Tuition: N/A
Room/board/expenses: N/A
Enrollment: N/A

California State University-Northridge (Nazarian)

18111 Nordhoff Street
Northridge, CA 91330-8380
www.csun.edu/mba/
Public
Admissions: (818) 677-2467
Email: MBA@csun.edu
Financial aid: (818) 677-4085
Application deadline: 05/01
In-state tuition: full time: $12,420; part time: $8,064
Out-of-state tuition: full time: $19,116
Room/board/expenses: $15,966
College-funded aid: Yes
International student aid: Yes
Full-time enrollment: N/A
men: N/A; women: N/A;
minorities: N/A; international: N/A
Part-time enrollment: 125
men: 51%; women: 49%;
minorities: 41%; international: 6%
Average GMAT (part time): 558
TOEFL requirement: Yes
Minimum TOEFL score: 550
Most popular departments: accounting, finance, general management, human resources management, marketing

California State University-Sacramento

6000 J Street
Sacramento, CA 95819-6088
www.csus.edu/cba/graduate/index.html
Public
Admissions: (910) 270-0772

Email: CBA-MBAAdmissions@csus.edu
Financial aid: (916) 278-6980
Application deadline: N/A
In-state tuition: full time: $8,166; part time: $5,334
Out-of-state tuition: full time: $13,374
Room/board/expenses: N/A
College-funded aid: No
International student aid: No
Full-time enrollment: 26
men: 58%; women: 42%;
minorities: 35%; international: 8%
Part-time enrollment: 57
men: 54%; women: 46%;
minorities: 39%; international: 7%
TOEFL requirement: Yes
Minimum TOEFL score: N/A

California State University-San Bernardino

5500 University Parkway
San Bernardino, CA 92407
www.cpba.csusb.edu/mba_program/welcome
Public
Admissions: (909) 537-5703
Email: mba@csusb.edu
Financial aid: (909) 537-5227
Application deadline: 07/20
In-state tuition: full time: $7,867; part time: $2,035
Out-of-state tuition: full time: $16,795
Room/board/expenses: $18,219
College-funded aid: Yes
International student aid: Yes
Full-time enrollment: N/A
men: N/A; women: N/A;
minorities: N/A; international: N/A
Part-time enrollment: 228
men: 65%; women: 35%;
minorities: 43%; international: 32%
Average GMAT (part time): 528
TOEFL requirement: Yes
Minimum TOEFL score: 550
Most popular departments: accounting, entrepreneurship, finance, general management, other

California State University-Stanislaus[1]

1 University Circle
Turlock, CA 95382
www.csustan.edu/cba
Public
Admissions: (209) 667-3288
Email: graduate_school@csustan.edu
Financial aid: N/A
Tuition: N/A
Room/board/expenses: N/A
Enrollment: N/A

Chapman University (Argyros)

1 University Drive
Orange, CA 92866
www.chapman.edu/argyros
Private
Admissions: (714) 997-6596
Email: mba@chapman.edu
Financial aid: (714) 997-6741
Application deadline: 06/01

Tuition: full time: $1,530/credit hour; part time: $1,530/credit hour
Room/board/expenses: $20,100
College-funded aid: Yes
International student aid: Yes
Average student indebtedness at graduation: $66,870
Full-time enrollment: 59
men: 64%; women: 36%;
minorities: 10%; international: 47%
Part-time enrollment: 143
men: 50%; women: 50%;
minorities: 31%; international: 28%
Acceptance rate (full time): 48%
Average GMAT (full time): 634
Average GMAT (part time): 562
Average GPA (full time): 3.23
Average age of entrants to full-time program: 25
Average months of prior work experience (full time): 27
TOEFL requirement: Yes
Minimum TOEFL score: N/A
Most popular departments: entrepreneurship, finance, general management, international business, marketing
Mean starting base salary for 2016 full-time graduates: $70,125
Employment location for 2016 class: Intl. N/A; N.E. N/A; M.A. N/A; S. 8%; M.W. N/A; S.W. N/A; W. 92%

Claremont Graduate University (Drucker)[1]

1021 N. Dartmouth Avenue
Claremont, CA 91711-6184
www.drucker.cgu.edu
Private
Admissions: (800) 944-4312
Email: drucker@cgu.edu
Financial aid: (909) 621-8337
Tuition: N/A
Room/board/expenses: N/A
Enrollment: N/A

Loyola Marymount University

1 LMU Drive, MS 8387
Los Angeles, CA 90045-2659
mba.lmu.edu
Private
Admissions: (310) 338-2848
Email: Mba.office@lmu.edu
Financial aid: (310) 338-2753
Application deadline: 06/01
Tuition: full time: N/A; total program: $88,500 (part time)
Room/board/expenses: N/A
College-funded aid: Yes
International student aid: Yes
Full-time enrollment: N/A
men: N/A; women: N/A;
minorities: N/A; international: N/A
Part-time enrollment: 143
men: 62%; women: 38%;
minorities: N/A; international: N/A
Average GMAT (part time): 563
TOEFL requirement: Yes
Minimum TOEFL score: 600
Most popular departments: entrepreneurship, finance, general management, international business, marketing

Middlebury Institute of International Studies (Fisher)[1]

460 Pierce Street
Monterey, CA 93940
www.miis.edu/academics/programs/mba
Private
Admissions: (831) 647-4123
Email: admit@miis.edu
Financial aid: N/A
Tuition: N/A
Room/board/expenses: N/A
Enrollment: N/A

Naval Postgraduate School[1]

555 Dyer Road
Monterey, CA 93943
www.nps.edu/academics/schools/GSBPP/
Public
Admissions: N/A
Financial aid: N/A
Tuition: N/A
Room/board/expenses: N/A
Enrollment: N/A

Pepperdine University (Graziadio)

24255 Pacific Coast Highway
Malibu, CA 90263-4100
bschool.pepperdine.edu
Private
Admissions: (310) 568-5530
Email: gsbmadm@pepperdine.edu
Financial aid: (310) 568-5530
Application deadline: 05/01
Tuition: full time: $47,880; part time: $1,670/credit hour
Room/board/expenses: $9,800
College-funded aid: Yes
International student aid: Yes
Average student indebtedness at graduation: $91,686
Full-time enrollment: 152
men: 64%; women: 36%;
minorities: 15%; international: 41%
Part-time enrollment: 1,000
men: 54%; women: 46%;
minorities: 33%; international: 3%
Acceptance rate (full time): 55%
Average GMAT (full time): 642
Average GMAT (part time): 561
Average GPA (full time): 3.33
Average age of entrants to full-time program: 27
Average months of prior work experience (full time): 48
TOEFL requirement: Yes
Minimum TOEFL score: 600
Most popular departments: finance, general management, leadership, marketing, management information systems
Mean starting base salary for 2016 full-time graduates: $75,233
Employment location for 2016 class: Intl. 6%; N.E. N/A; M.A. 6%; S. 10%; M.W. 6%; S.W. 4%; W. 67%

San Diego State University

5500 Campanile Drive
San Diego, CA 92182-8228
www.sdsu.edu/business
Public
Admissions: (619) 594-6336
Email: admissions@sdsu.edu
Financial aid: (619) 594-6323
Application deadline: 03/01
In-state tuition: full time: $14,446; part time: $11,614
Out-of-state tuition: full time: $23,374
Room/board/expenses: $16,562
College-funded aid: Yes
International student aid: Yes
Average student indebtedness at graduation: $29,066
Full-time enrollment: 264
men: 51%; women: 49%;
minorities: 13%; international: 60%
Part-time enrollment: 247
men: 59%; women: 41%;
minorities: 31%; international: 15%
Acceptance rate (full time): 32%
Average GMAT (full time): 608
Average GMAT (part time): 618
Average GPA (full time): 3.35
Average age of entrants to full-time program: 28
Average months of prior work experience (full time): 65
TOEFL requirement: Yes
Minimum TOEFL score: N/A
Most popular departments: accounting, entrepreneurship, finance, marketing, management information systems
Mean starting base salary for 2016 full-time graduates: $55,881

San Francisco State University

835 Market Street, Suite 600
San Francisco, CA 94103
mba.sfsu.edu
Public
Admissions: (415) 817-4300
Email: mba@sfsu.edu
Financial aid: (415) 338-1581
Application deadline: 05/31
In-state tuition: full time: $16,238; part time: $10,358
Out-of-state tuition: full time: $25,166
Room/board/expenses: $32,000
College-funded aid: Yes
International student aid: Yes
Full-time enrollment: 88
men: 51%; women: 40%;
minorities: 27%; international: 45%
Part-time enrollment: 81
men: 57%; women: 43%;
minorities: 52%; international: 10%
Acceptance rate (full time): 46%
Average GMAT (full time): 557
Average GMAT (part time): 573
Average GPA (full time): 3.52
Average age of entrants to full-time program: 28
Average months of prior work experience (full time): 54
TOEFL requirement: Yes
Minimum TOEFL score: 590
Most popular departments: accounting, finance, marketing, management information systems, quantitative analysis/statistics and operations research

San Jose State University (Lucas)

1 Washington Square
San Jose, CA 95192-0162
www.sjsu.edu/lucasgsb
Public
Admissions: (408) 924-3420
Email: lucas-school@sjsu.edu
Financial aid: (408) 283-7500
Application deadline: 05/01
In-state tuition: total program:
$30,339 (full time); $35,700
(part time)
Out-of-state tuition: total
program: $45,963 (full time)
Room/board/expenses: N/A
College-funded aid: Yes
International student aid: No
Full-time enrollment: 117
men: 44%; women: 56%;
minorities: N/A; international: N/A
Part-time enrollment: 45
men: 67%; women: 33%;
minorities: N/A; international: N/A
Acceptance rate (full time): 50%
Average GMAT (full time): 596
Average GMAT (part time): 547
Average GPA (full time): 3.46
Average age of entrants to full-
time program: 28
TOEFL requirement: Yes
Minimum TOEFL score: N/A
Most popular departments:
general management

Santa Clara University (Leavey)

Lucas Hall
Santa Clara, CA 95053
www.scu.edu/business
Private
Admissions: (408) 554-4539
Email: gradbusiness@scu.edu
Financial aid: (408) 554-4505
Application deadline: N/A
Tuition: full time: N/A; part time:
$1,022/credit hour
Room/board/expenses: N/A
College-funded aid: Yes
International student aid: Yes
Average student indebtedness at
graduation: $60,346
Full-time enrollment: N/A
men: N/A; women: N/A;
minorities: N/A; international: N/A
Part-time enrollment: 377
men: 54%; women: 46%;
minorities: 40%; international:
27%
Average GMAT (part time): 620
TOEFL requirement: Yes
Minimum TOEFL score: N/A
Most popular departments:
entrepreneurship, finance,
leadership, marketing, other

Sonoma State University

1801 E. Cotati Avenue
Rohnert Park, CA 94928
www.sonoma.edu/admissions
Public
Admissions: (707) 664-2252
Email:
rosanna.kelley@sonoma.edu
Financial aid: (707) 664-2389
Application deadline: 04/30
In-state tuition: total program:
$21,581 (full time); $22,655 (part
time)
Out-of-state tuition: total
program: $30,509 (full time)
Room/board/expenses: $18,850
College-funded aid: Yes

International student aid: Yes
Full-time enrollment: 6
men: 33%; women: 67%;
minorities: 0%; international:
100%
Part-time enrollment: 59
men: 47%; women: 53%;
minorities: 34%; international:
N/A
Average GMAT (part time): 492
TOEFL requirement: Yes
Minimum TOEFL score: N/A

Stanford University

655 Knight Way
Stanford, CA 94305-7298
www.gsb.stanford.edu/mba
Private
Admissions: (650) 723-2766
Email: mba.admissions@
gsb.stanford.edu
Financial aid: (650) 723-3282
Application deadline: N/A
Tuition: full time: $66,540; part
time: N/A
Room/board/expenses: $42,678
College-funded aid: Yes
International student aid: Yes
Average student indebtedness at
graduation: $80,091
Full-time enrollment: 833
men: 60%; women: 40%;
minorities: N/A; international: N/A
Part-time enrollment: N/A
men: N/A; women: N/A;
minorities: N/A; international: N/A
Acceptance rate (full time): 6%
Average GMAT (full time): 737
Average GPA (full time): 3.73
Average months of prior work
experience (full time): 49
TOEFL requirement: Yes
Minimum TOEFL score: 600
Most popular departments:
entrepreneurship, finance,
general management, leadership,
organizational behavior
Mean starting base salary for 2016
full-time graduates: $140,553
Employment location for 2016
class: Intl. 10%; N.E. 17%; M.A.
0%; S. 1%; M.W. 2%; S.W. 6%;
W. 65%

St. Mary's College of California

1928 Saint Marys Road
Moraga, CA 94556
www.smcmba.com
Private
Admissions: (925) 631-4888
Email: smcmba@stmarys-ca.edu
Financial aid: N/A
Application deadline: N/A
Tuition: full time: N/A; part time:
$3,150/credit hour
Room/board/expenses: N/A
College-funded aid: Yes
International student aid: Yes
Full-time enrollment: N/A
men: N/A; women: N/A;
minorities: N/A; international: N/A
Part-time enrollment: 158
men: 67%; women: 33%;
minorities: 43%; international:
5%
Average GMAT (part time): 530
TOEFL requirement: Yes
Minimum TOEFL score: N/A
Most popular departments:
entrepreneurship, finance,
international business, marketing

University of California-Berkeley (Haas)

545 Student Services Building
Berkeley, CA 94720-1900
mba.haas.berkeley.edu
Public
Admissions: (510) 642-1405
Email:
mbaadm@haas.berkeley.edu
Financial aid: (510) 643-0183
Application deadline: N/A
In-state tuition: full time: $56,009;
part time: $3,169/credit hour
Out-of-state tuition: full time:
$57,560
Room/board/expenses: $25,656
College-funded aid: Yes
International student aid: Yes
Average student indebtedness at
graduation: $87,546
Full-time enrollment: 502
men: 60%; women: 40%;
minorities: 22%; international:
36%
Part-time enrollment: 802
men: 72%; women: 28%;
minorities: N/A; international: N/A
Acceptance rate (full time): 12%
Average GMAT (full time): 717
Average GMAT (part time): 694
Average GPA (full time): 3.64
Average age of entrants to full-
time program: 29
Average months of prior work
experience (full time): 65
TOEFL requirement: Yes
Minimum TOEFL score: 570
Most popular departments:
entrepreneurship, finance,
leadership, marketing,
technology
Mean starting base salary for 2016
full-time graduates: $122,488
Employment location for 2016
class: Intl. 8%; N.E. 3%; M.A.
1%; S. 1%; M.W. 1%; S.W. 6%;
W. 80%

University of California-Davis

1 Shields Avenue
Davis, CA 95616-8609
gsm.ucdavis.edu
Public
Admissions: (530) 752-7658
Email:
admissions@gsm.ucdavis.edu
Financial aid: (530) 752-7658
Application deadline: 11/08
In-state tuition: full time: $40,496;
total program: $89,640 (part
time)
Out-of-state tuition: full time:
$52,741
Room/board/expenses: $23,770
College-funded aid: Yes
International student aid: Yes
Average student indebtedness at
graduation: $52,039
Full-time enrollment: 99
men: 70%; women: 30%;
minorities: 18%; international:
35%
Part-time enrollment: 352
men: 61%; women: 39%;
minorities: 49%; international:
7%
Acceptance rate (full time): 16%
Average GMAT (full time): 679
Average GMAT (part time): 581
Average GPA (full time): 3.41
Average age of entrants to full-
time program: 29

Average months of prior work
experience (full time): 61
TOEFL requirement: Yes
Minimum TOEFL score: 600
Most popular departments:
entrepreneurship, finance,
marketing, organizational
behavior, technology
Mean starting base salary for 2016
full-time graduates: $97,426
Employment location for 2016
class: Intl. 6%; N.E. N/A; M.A.
N/A; S. 3%; M.W. 3%; S.W. 6%;
W. 81%

University of California-Irvine (Merage)

5300 SB1
4293 Pereira Drive
Irvine, CA 92697-3125
www.merage.uci.edu
Public
Admissions: (949) 824-4622
Email: mba@merage.uci.edu
Financial aid: (949) 824-7967
Application deadline: 04/01
In-state tuition: full time: $42,224;
total program: $98,703 (part
time)
Out-of-state tuition: full time:
$50,092
Room/board/expenses: $29,904
College-funded aid: Yes
International student aid: Yes
Average student indebtedness at
graduation: $83,740
Full-time enrollment: 173
men: 70%; women: 30%;
minorities: 18%; international:
53%
Part-time enrollment: 327
men: 65%; women: 35%;
minorities: 57%; international:
3%
Acceptance rate (full time): 29%
Average GMAT (full time): 649
Average GMAT (part time): 580
Average GPA (full time): 3.43
Average age of entrants to full-
time program: 29
Average months of prior work
experience (full time): 68
TOEFL requirement: Yes
Minimum TOEFL score: 600
Most popular departments:
finance, marketing,
organizational behavior,
quantitative analysis/statistics
and operations research, other
Mean starting base salary for 2016
full-time graduates: $96,606
Employment location for 2016
class: Intl. 4%; N.E. 4%; M.A.
0%; S. 2%; M.W. 4%; S.W. 2%;
W. 85%

University of California-Los Angeles (Anderson)

110 Westwood Plaza
Box 951481
Los Angeles, CA 90095-1481
www.anderson.ucla.edu
Public
Admissions: (310) 825-6944
Email: mba.admissions@
anderson.ucla.edu
Financial aid: (310) 825-2746
Application deadline: 04/12
In-state tuition: full time: $56,403;
part time: $43,983

Out-of-state tuition: full time:
$59,290
Room/board/expenses: $34,203
College-funded aid: Yes
International student aid: Yes
Average student indebtedness at
graduation: $80,806
Full-time enrollment: 734
men: 69%; women: 31%;
minorities: 25%; international:
31%
Part-time enrollment: 986
men: 71%; women: 29%;
minorities: 44%; international:
9%
Acceptance rate (full time): 21%
Average GMAT (full time): 715
Average GMAT (part time): 678
Average GPA (full time): 3.52
Average age of entrants to full-
time program: 28
Average months of prior work
experience (full time): 62
TOEFL requirement: Yes
Minimum TOEFL score: 560
Most popular departments:
accounting, consulting, finance,
marketing, technology
Mean starting base salary for 2016
full-time graduates: $118,150
Employment location for 2016
class: Intl. 10%; N.E. 7%; M.A.
1%; S. 1%; M.W. 2%; S.W. 2%;
W. 78%

University of California-Riverside (Anderson)

900 University Avenue
Riverside, CA 92521-0203
www.agsm.ucr.edu/mba/
Public
Admissions: (951) 827-6200
Email: ucr_agsm@ucr.edu
Financial aid: (951) 827-3878
Application deadline: 09/01
In-state tuition: full time: $41,941;
part time: $1,313/credit hour
Out-of-state tuition: full time:
$54,187
Room/board/expenses: $15,045
College-funded aid: Yes
International student aid: Yes
Average student indebtedness at
graduation: $41,805
Full-time enrollment: 111
men: 56%; women: 44%;
minorities: 22%; international:
66%
Part-time enrollment: 79
men: 53%; women: 47%;
minorities: 27%; international:
61%
Acceptance rate (full time): 63%
Average GMAT (full time): 581
Average GMAT (part time): 518
Average GPA (full time): 3.16
Average age of entrants to full-
time program: 26
Average months of prior work
experience (full time): 45
TOEFL requirement: Yes
Minimum TOEFL score: 550
Most popular departments:
accounting, finance, general
management, marketing, supply
chain management/logistics
Mean starting base salary for 2016
full-time graduates: $83,375
Employment location for 2016
class: Intl. 38%; N.E. 0%; M.A.
4%; S. 0%; M.W. 4%; S.W. 0%;
W. 53%

University of California-San Diego (Rady)

9500 Gilman Drive, #0553
San Diego, CA 92093-0553
www.rady.ucsd.edu/mba/
Public
Admissions: (858) 534-0864
Email: RadyGradAdmissions@
ucsd.edu
Financial aid: (858) 534-4480
Application deadline: 06/01
In-state tuition: full time: $52,435;
part time: $1,152/credit hour
Out-of-state tuition: full time:
$56,569
Room/board/expenses: $23,870
College-funded aid: Yes
International student aid: Yes
Full-time enrollment: 119
men: 71%; women: 29%;
minorities: N/A; international: N/A
Part-time enrollment: 102
men: 63%; women: 37%;
minorities: N/A; international: N/A
Acceptance rate (full time): 46%
Average GMAT (full time): 665
Average GMAT (part time): 596
Average GPA (full time): 3.39
Average age of entrants to full-time program: 28
Average months of prior work experience (full time): 58
TOEFL requirement: Yes
Minimum TOEFL score: 550
Most popular departments:
entrepreneurship, finance,
general management, marketing,
technology
Mean starting base salary for 2016 full-time graduates: $66,335
Employment location for 2016 class: Intl. 39%; N.E. 0%; M.A.
0%; S. 0%; M.W. 0%; S.W. 0%;
W. 61%

University of San Diego

5998 Alcala Park
San Diego, CA 92110-2492
www.sandiego.edu/mba
Private
Admissions: (619) 260-4860
Email: mba@sandiego.edu
Financial aid: (619) 260-4514
Application deadline: 05/01
Tuition: full time: $1,420/credit
hour; part time: $1,420/credit
hour
Room/board/expenses: $18,450
College-funded aid: Yes
International student aid: Yes
Average student indebtedness at graduation: $09,302
Full-time enrollment: 79
men: 63%; women: 37%;
minorities: 15%; international:
57%
Part-time enrollment: 84
men: 61%; women: 39%;
minorities: 24%; international:
11%
Acceptance rate (full time): 60%
Average GMAT (full time): 608
Average GMAT (part time): 602
Average GPA (full time): 3.08
Average age of entrants to full-time program: 27
Average months of prior work experience (full time): 52
TOEFL requirement: Yes
Minimum TOEFL score: 580

Most popular departments:
entrepreneurship, finance,
general management, marketing,
supply chain management/
logistics
Mean starting base salary for 2016 full-time graduates: $78,083
Employment location for 2016 class: Intl. N/A; N.E. 7%; M.A.
N/A; S. N/A; M.W. N/A; S.W. N/A;
W. 93%

University of San Francisco

101 Howard Street, Suite 500
San Francisco, CA 94105-1080
www.usfca.edu/management/
graduate/
Private
Admissions: (415) 422-2221
Email: management@usfca.edu
Financial aid: (415) 422-2020
Application deadline: 06/15
Tuition: full time: $1,380/credit
hour; part time: $1,380/credit
hour
Room/board/expenses: N/A
College-funded aid: Yes
International student aid: Yes
Average student indebtedness at graduation: $116,454
Full-time enrollment: 105
men: 60%; women: 40%;
minorities: 24%; international:
50%
Part-time enrollment: 70
men: 49%; women: 51%;
minorities: 53%; international:
3%
Acceptance rate (full time): 66%
Average GMAT (full time): 570
Average GMAT (part time): 509
Average GPA (full time): 3.19
Average age of entrants to full-time program: 28
Average months of prior work experience (full time): 47
TOEFL requirement: Yes
Minimum TOEFL score: 580
Most popular departments:
entrepreneurship, finance,
marketing, organizational
behavior, quantitative analysis/
statistics and operations
research
Mean starting base salary for 2016 full-time graduates: $98,617
Employment location for 2016 class: Intl. 5%; N.E. N/A; M.A.
N/A; S. N/A; M.W. N/A; S.W. 9%;
W. 86%

University of Southern California (Marshall)

University Park
Los Angeles, CA 90089-1421
www.marshall.usc.edu
Private
Admissions: (213) 740-7846
Email: marshallmba@
marshall.usc.edu
Financial aid: (213) 740-1111
Application deadline: 04/15
Tuition: full time: $61,915; part
time: $1,778/credit hour
Room/board/expenses: $23,320
College-funded aid: Yes
International student aid: Yes
Full-time enrollment: 441
men: 68%; women: 32%;
minorities: 31%; international:
28%

Part-time enrollment: 440
men: 68%; women: 32%;
minorities: 50%; international:
2%
Acceptance rate (full time): 33%
Average GMAT (full time): 692
Average GMAT (part time): 614
Average GPA (full time): 3.37
Average age of entrants to full-time program: 29
Average months of prior work experience (full time): 66
TOEFL requirement: Yes
Minimum TOEFL score: 600
Mean starting base salary for 2016 full-time graduates: $115,309
Employment location for 2016 class: Intl. 3%; N.E. 7%; M.A.
N/A; S. 1%; M.W. N/A; S.W. 3%;
W. 85%

University of the Pacific (Eberhardt)

3601 Pacific Avenue
Stockton, CA 95211
www.pacific.edu/mba
Private
Admissions: (209) 946-2629
Email: mba@pacific.edu
Financial aid: (209) 946-2421
Application deadline: 03/01
Tuition: total program: $67,670
(full time); part time: $1,377/
credit hour
Room/board/expenses: $28,287
College-funded aid: Yes
International student aid: Yes
Full-time enrollment: 23
men: 43%; women: 57%;
minorities: 65%; international:
13%
Part-time enrollment: 11
men: 55%; women: 45%;
minorities: 55%; international:
0%
Acceptance rate (full time): 65%
Average GMAT (full time): 541
Average GPA (full time): 3.44
Average age of entrants to full-time program: 23
Average months of prior work experience (full time): 7
TOEFL requirement: Yes
Minimum TOEFL score: 550
Most popular departments:
general management, health
care administration

Woodbury University[1]

7500 N. Glenoaks Boulevard
Burbank, CA 91504
woodbury.edu/
Private
Admissions: (818) 252-5221
Email: admissions@woodbury.
edu
Financial aid: (818) 252-5273
Tuition: N/A
Room/board/expenses: N/A
Enrollment: N/A

COLORADO

Colorado State University

110 Rockwell Hall West
Fort Collins, CO 80523-1270
biz.colostate.edu/Academics/
Graduate-Programs/Master-
of-Business-Administration
Public
Admissions: (970) 491-3704
Email: gradadmissions@
business.colostate.edu

Financial aid: (970) 491-6321
Application deadline: 07/01
In-state tuition: full time: $736/
credit hour; part time: $946/
credit hour
Out-of-state tuition: full time:
$1,513/credit hour
Room/board/expenses: $10,018
College-funded aid: Yes
International student aid: Yes
Average student indebtedness at graduation: $41,183
Full-time enrollment: 105
men: 52%; women: 48%;
minorities: 4%; international:
46%
Part-time enrollment: 734
men: 68%; women: 32%;
minorities: 21%; international: 1%
Acceptance rate (full time): 72%
Average GMAT (full time): 528
Average GMAT (part time): 494
Average GPA (full time): 3.34
Average age of entrants to full-time program: 26
Average months of prior work experience (full time): 41
TOEFL requirement: Yes
Minimum TOEFL score: N/A
Most popular departments:
general management, marketing,
management information
systems, production/operations
management, technology

Colorado State University-Pueblo[1]

2200 Bonforte Boulevard
Pueblo, CO 81001
hsb.colostate-pueblo.edu
Public
Admissions: (719) 549-2461
Email:
info@colostate-pueblo.edu
Financial aid: N/A
Tuition: N/A
Room/board/expenses: N/A
Enrollment: N/A

University of Colorado-Boulder (Leeds)

995 Regent Drive
419 UCB
Boulder, CO 80309
www.colorado.edu/business
Public
Admissions: (303) 492-8397
Email: leedsmba@Colorado.edu
Financial aid: (303) 492-8223
Application deadline: 04/15
In-state tuition: full time: $19,666;
total program: $49,800 (part
time)
Out-of-state tuition: full time:
$35,074
Room/board/expenses: $21,590
College-funded aid: Yes
International student aid: Yes
Average student indebtedness at graduation: $53,492
Full-time enrollment: 175
men: 66%; women: 34%;
minorities: N/A; international: N/A
Part-time enrollment: 128
men: 66%; women: 34%;
minorities: N/A; international: N/A
Acceptance rate (full time): 75%
Average GMAT (full time): 599
Average GMAT (part time): 618
Average GPA (full time): 3.34
Average age of entrants to full-time program: 28

Average months of prior work experience (full time): 61
TOEFL requirement: Yes
Minimum TOEFL score: N/A
Most popular departments:
entrepreneurship, finance,
general management, real
estate, other
Mean starting base salary for 2016 full-time graduates: $80,123
Employment location for 2016 class: Intl. 4%; N.E. 2%; M.A.
0%; S. 0%; M.W. 2%; S.W. 81%;
W. 10%

University of Colorado-Colorado Springs

1420 Austin Bluffs Parkway
Colorado Springs, CO 80918
www.uccs.edu/mba
Public
Admissions: (719) 255-3122
Email: cobgrad@uccs.edu
Financial aid: (719) 255-3460
Application deadline: 06/01
In-state tuition: full time: N/A; part
time: $700/credit hour
Out-of-state tuition: full time: N/A
Room/board/expenses: N/A
College-funded aid: Yes
International student aid: Yes
Full-time enrollment: N/A
men: N/A; women: N/A;
minorities: N/A; international: N/A
Part-time enrollment: 287
men: 56%; women: 44%;
minorities: 19%; international:
5%
Average GMAT (part time): 570
TOEFL requirement: Yes
Minimum TOEFL score: 550
Most popular departments:
accounting, finance, general
management, marketing, other

University of Colorado-Denver

Campus Box 165
PO Box 173364
Denver, CO 80217-3364
www.ucdenver.edu/business/
Public
Admissions: (303) 315-8200
Email: bschool.admissions@
ucdenver.edu
Financial aid: (303) 315-1850
Application deadline: 04/16
In-state tuition: full time: $44,650;
part time: $571/credit hour
Out-of-state tuition: full time:
$44,650
Room/board/expenses: $25,487
College-funded aid: Yes
International student aid: Yes
Full-time enrollment: 26
men: 50%; women: 50%;
minorities: 4%; international: 8%
Part-time enrollment: 501
men: 63%; women: 37%;
minorities: 14%; international: 4%
Acceptance rate (full time): 61%
Average GMAT (full time): 600
Average GMAT (part time): 588
Average GPA (full time): 3.30
Average age of entrants to full-time program: 28
Average months of prior work experience (full time): 31
TOEFL requirement: Yes
Minimum TOEFL score: 560

University of Denver (Daniels)

2101 S. University Boulevard
Denver, CO 80208
www.daniels.du.edu/
Private
Admissions: (303) 871-3416
Email: daniels@du.edu
Financial aid: (303) 871-7860
Application deadline: 05/15
Tuition: total program: $83,691
(full time); $87,635 (part time)
Room/board/expenses: $17,526
College-funded aid: Yes
International student aid: Yes
Full-time enrollment: 85
men: 64%; women: 36%;
minorities: 15%; international:
12%
Part-time enrollment: 107
men: 62%; women: 38%;
minorities: 18%; international: 1%
Acceptance rate (full time): 68%
Average GMAT (full time): 576
Average GPA (full time): 3.30
**Average age of entrants to full-
time program:** 27
**Average months of prior work
experience (full time):** 51
TOEFL requirement: Yes
Minimum TOEFL score: 587
**Mean starting base salary for 2016
full-time graduates:** $69,842
**Employment location for 2016
class:** Intl. 10%; N.E. 5%; M.A.
N/A; S. N/A; M.W. 5%; S.W. 70%;
W. 10%

University of Northern Colorado (Monfort)[1]

800 17th Street
Greeley, CO 80639
mcb.unco.edu/MBA/
information.cfm
Public
Admissions: N/A
Financial aid: N/A
Tuition: N/A
Room/board/expenses: N/A
Enrollment: N/A

CONNECTICUT

Central Connecticut State University

1615 Stanley Street
New Britain, CT 06050
www.ccsu.edu/mba
Public
Admissions: (860) 832-2350
Financial aid: (860) 832-2200
Application deadline: 06/10
In-state tuition: full time: N/A; part
time: $606/credit hour
Out-of-state tuition: full time: N/A
Room/board/expenses: N/A
College-funded aid: Yes
Full-time enrollment: N/A
men: N/A; women: N/A;
minorities: N/A; international: N/A
Part-time enrollment: 187
men: 59%; women: 41%;
minorities: 28%; international: 1%
TOEFL requirement: Yes
Minimum TOEFL score: N/A
Most popular departments:
accounting, finance, other

Fairfield University (Dolan)

1073 N. Benson Road
Fairfield, CT 06824
www.fairfield.edu/dsb/
graduateprograms/mba/
Private
Admissions: (203) 254-4000
Email: dsbgrad@fairfield.edu
Financial aid: (203) 254-4125
Application deadline: 08/01
Tuition: full time: N/A; part time:
$875/credit hour
Room/board/expenses: N/A
College-funded aid: Yes
International student aid: No
Full-time enrollment: N/A
men: N/A; women: N/A;
minorities: N/A; international: N/A
Part-time enrollment: 60
men: 68%; women: 32%;
minorities: 10%; international:
10%
Average GMAT (part time): 520
TOEFL requirement: Yes
Minimum TOEFL score: 550
Most popular departments:
accounting, finance, general
management, marketing, tax

Quinnipiac University

275 Mount Carmel Avenue
Hamden, CT 06518
www.quinnipiac.edu/
Private
Admissions: (800) 462-1944
Email: graduate@quinnipiac.edu
Financial aid: (203) 582-8384
Application deadline: 08/10
Tuition: full time: $985/credit
hour; part time: $985/credit hour
Room/board/expenses: $21,846
College-funded aid: Yes
International student aid: Yes
**Average student indebtedness at
graduation:** $36,430
Full-time enrollment: 173
men: 54%; women: 46%;
minorities: 20%; international:
3%
Part-time enrollment: 30
men: 53%; women: 47%;
minorities: 33%; international:
0%
Acceptance rate (full time): 87%
**Average age of entrants to full-
time program:** 22
TOEFL requirement: Yes
Minimum TOEFL score: 575
Most popular departments:
finance, general management,
health care administration,
marketing, supply chain
management/logistics

Sacred Heart University (Welch)

5151 Park Avenue
Fairfield, CT 06825
www.sacredheart.edu/
johnfwelchcob.cfm
Private
Admissions: (203) 365-7619
Email:
gradstudies@sacredheart.edu
Financial aid: (203) 371-7980
Application deadline: N/A
Tuition: full time: N/A; part time:
$875/credit hour
Room/board/expenses: N/A
College-funded aid: No
International student aid: No
Full-time enrollment: N/A
men: N/A; women: N/A;
minorities: N/A; international: N/A

Part-time enrollment: 144
men: 58%; women: 42%;
minorities: 24%; international:
6%
Average GMAT (part time): 485
TOEFL requirement: Yes
Minimum TOEFL score: 570

University of Connecticut

2100 Hillside Road, Unit 1041
Storrs, CT 06269-1041
www.business.uconn.edu
Public
Admissions: (860) 728-2440
Email: uconnmba@
business.uconn.edu
Financial aid: (860) 486-2819
Application deadline: 06/01
In-state tuition: full time: $14,552;
part time: $825/credit hour
Out-of-state tuition: full time:
$35,588
Room/board/expenses: $26,000
College-funded aid: Yes
International student aid: Yes
**Average student indebtedness at
graduation:** $34,161
Full-time enrollment: 109
men: 66%; women: 34%;
minorities: 7%; international: 61%
Part-time enrollment: 977
men: 68%; women: 32%;
minorities: 37%; international: 1%
Acceptance rate (full time): 30%
Average GMAT (full time): 623
Average GMAT (part time): 538
Average GPA (full time): 3.50
**Average age of entrants to full-
time program:** 29
**Average months of prior work
experience (full time):** 70
TOEFL requirement: Yes
Minimum TOEFL score: 575
Most popular departments:
finance, general management,
marketing, portfolio
management, other
**Mean starting base salary for 2016
full-time graduates:** $96,000
**Employment location for 2016
class:** Intl. N/A; N.E. 90%; M.A.
N/A; S. 5%; M.W. N/A; S.W. 5%;
W. N/A

University of Hartford (Barney)

200 Bloomfield Avenue
West Hartford, CT 06117
www.hartford.edu/barney/
Private
Admissions: (860) 768-5003
Email: knight@hartford.edu
Financial aid: (860) 768-4296
Application deadline: rolling
Tuition: full time: N/A; part time:
$670/credit hour
Room/board/expenses: N/A
Full-time enrollment: N/A
men: N/A; women: N/A;
minorities: N/A; international: N/A
Part-time enrollment: 405
men: 52%; women: 48%;
minorities: 23%; international:
6%
Average GMAT (part time): 522
TOEFL requirement: Yes
Minimum TOEFL score: 550

University of New Haven

300 Boston Post Road
West Haven, CT 06516
newhaven.edu
Private
Admissions: (203) 932-7440
Email: gradinfo@newhaven.edu
Financial aid: (203) 932-7315
Application deadline: rolling
Tuition: full time: $870/credit
hour; part time: $870/credit hour
Room/board/expenses: N/A
College-funded aid: Yes
International student aid: Yes
Full-time enrollment: 124
men: 53%; women: 47%;
minorities: 22%; international:
39%
Part-time enrollment: 78
men: 60%; women: 40%;
minorities: 29%; international:
13%
Acceptance rate (full time): 78%
Average GMAT (full time): 393
Average GMAT (part time): 600
Average GPA (full time): 3.21
**Average age of entrants to full-
time program:** 25
TOEFL requirement: Yes
Minimum TOEFL score: N/A
Most popular departments:
accounting, finance, human
resources management,
marketing, sports business

Yale University

165 Whitney Avenue
New Haven, CT 06511-3729
som.yale.edu
Private
Admissions: (203) 432-5635
Email: mba.admissions@yale.edu
Financial aid: (203) 432-5875
Application deadline: 04/19
Tuition: full time: $66,160; part
time: N/A
Room/board/expenses: $25,240
College-funded aid: Yes
International student aid: Yes
**Average student indebtedness at
graduation:** $107,339
Full-time enrollment: 694
men: 58%; women: 42%;
minorities: 24%; international:
37%
Part-time enrollment: N/A
men: N/A; women: N/A;
minorities: N/A; international: N/A
Acceptance rate (full time): 19%
Average GMAT (full time): 725
Average GPA (full time): 3.63
**Average age of entrants to full-
time program:** 28
**Average months of prior work
experience (full time):** 63
TOEFL requirement: No
Minimum TOEFL score: N/A
Most popular departments:
economics, entrepreneurship,
finance, general management,
marketing
**Mean starting base salary for 2016
full-time graduates:** $119,146
**Employment location for 2016
class:** Intl. 15%; N.E. 46%; M.A.
7%; S. 1%; M.W. 3%; S.W. 5%;
W. 22%

Delaware State University[1]

1200 DuPont Highway
Dover, DE 19901
www.desu.edu/business-
administration-mba-program
Public
Admissions: (302) 857-6978
Email: dkim@desu.edu
Financial aid: (302) 857-6250
Tuition: N/A
Room/board/expenses: N/A
Enrollment: N/A

University of Delaware (Lerner)

103 Alfred Lerner Hall
Newark, DE 19716
www.mba.udel.edu
Public
Admissions: (302) 831-2221
Email: mbaprogram@udel.edu
Financial aid: (302) 831-8761
Application deadline: 07/01
In-state tuition: full time: $780/
credit hour; part time: $780/
credit hour
Out-of-state tuition: full time:
$1,000/credit hour
Room/board/expenses: $8,979
College-funded aid: Yes
International student aid: Yes
Full-time enrollment: 117
men: 57%; women: 43%;
minorities: 13%; international:
56%
Part-time enrollment: 186
men: 59%; women: 41%;
minorities: 28%; international:
5%
Acceptance rate (full time): 45%
**Average age of entrants to full-
time program:** 28
**Average months of prior work
experience (full time):** 45
TOEFL requirement: Yes
Minimum TOEFL score: 600
Most popular departments:
entrepreneurship, finance,
international business,
marketing, technology
**Mean starting base salary for 2016
full-time graduates:** $53,115
**Employment location for 2016
class:** Intl. 4%; N.E. 20%; M.A.
67%; S. 7%; M.W. 2%; S.W. N/A;
W. N/A

American University (Kogod)

4400 Massachusetts Avenue NW
Washington, DC 20016
kogod.american.edu
Private
Admissions: (202) 885-1913
Email: kogodgrad@american.edu
Financial aid: (202) 885-1907
Application deadline: 05/01
Tuition: full time: $1,579/credit
hour; total program: $75,024
(part time)
Room/board/expenses: $19,440
College-funded aid: Yes
International student aid: Yes
Full-time enrollment: 60
men: 55%; women: 45%;
minorities: 32%; international:
13%

Part-time enrollment: 70
men: 46%; women: 54%;
minorities: 31%; international:
6%
Acceptance rate (full time): 60%
Average GMAT (full time): 558
Average GMAT (part time): 527
Average GPA (full time): 3.15
Average age of entrants to full-time program: 28
Average months of prior work experience (full time): 47
TOEFL requirement: Yes
Minimum TOEFL score: N/A
Most popular departments:
consulting, finance, international
business, marketing,
management information
systems
Mean starting base salary for 2016 full-time graduates: $84,725

Georgetown University (McDonough)

Rafik B. Hariri Building
37th and O Streets NW
Washington, DC 20057
msb.georgetown.edu
Private
Admissions: (202) 687-4200
Email: georgetownmba@
georgetown.edu
Financial aid: (202) 687-4547
Application deadline: N/A
Tuition: full time: $55,550; part
time: $1,795/credit hour
Room/board/expenses: $25,760
College-funded aid: Yes
International student aid: Yes
Full-time enrollment: 546
men: 67%; women: 33%;
minorities: 17%; international:
34%
Part-time enrollment: 427
men: 65%; women: 35%;
minorities: 19%; international:
8%
Acceptance rate (full time): 45%
Average GMAT (full time): 692
Average GMAT (part time): 653
Average GPA (full time): 3.40
Average age of entrants to full-time program: 28
Average months of prior work experience (full time): 65
TOEFL requirement: Yes
Minimum TOEFL score: 600
Most popular departments:
consulting, finance, general
management, international
business, marketing
Mean starting base salary for 2016 full-time graduates: $108,081

George Washington University

2201 G Street NW
Washington, DC 20052
business.gwu.edu/programs/
masters-of-business-
administration/global-mba/
Private
Admissions: (202) 994-1212
Email: gwmba@gwu.edu
Financial aid: (202) 994-7850
Application deadline: 05/01
Tuition: total program: $100,799
(full time); part time: $1,690/
credit hour
Room/board/expenses: $24,700
College-funded aid: Yes
International student aid: Yes
Average student indebtedness at graduation: $83,174

Full-time enrollment: 216
men: 58%; women: 42%;
minorities: 21%; international:
42%
Part-time enrollment: 202
men: 60%; women: 40%;
minorities: 37%; international:
4%
Acceptance rate (full time): 51%
Average GMAT (full time): 671
Average GMAT (part time): 611
Average GPA (full time): 3.30
Average age of entrants to full-time program: 28
Average months of prior work experience (full time): 60
TOEFL requirement: Yes
Minimum TOEFL score: 600
Most popular departments:
consulting, finance, international
business, marketing, other
Mean starting base salary for 2016 full-time graduates: $82,895
Employment location for 2016 class: Intl. 9%; N.E. 15%; M.A.
59%; S. 4%; M.W. 6%; S.W. 2%;
W. 6%

Howard University

2600 Sixth Street NW, Suite 236
Washington, DC 20059
www.bschool.howard.edu
Private
Admissions: (202) 806-1725
Email:
MBA_bschool@howard.edu
Financial aid: (202) 806-2820
Application deadline: 04/01
Tuition: full time: $35,485; part
time: $1,840/credit hour
Room/board/expenses: $26,518
College-funded aid: Yes
International student aid: Yes
Average student indebtedness at graduation: $47,221
Full-time enrollment: 57
men: 54%; women: 46%;
minorities: 89%; international:
11%
Part-time enrollment: 20
men: 50%; women: 50%;
minorities: 100%; international:
N/A
Acceptance rate (full time): 34%
Average GMAT (full time): 498
Average GPA (full time): 3.00
Average age of entrants to full-time program: 29
Average months of prior work experience (full time): 39
TOEFL requirement: Yes
Minimum TOEFL score: 550
Most popular departments:
finance, general management,
international business,
marketing, supply chain
management/logistics
Mean starting base salary for 2016 full-time graduates: $91,084
Employment location for 2016 class: Intl. 5%; N.E. 26%; M.A.
53%; S. 5%; M.W. 5%; S.W. N/A;
W. 5%

FLORIDA

Barry University[1]

11300 N.E. Second Avenue
Miami Shores, FL 33161-6695
www.barry.edu/mba
Private
Admissions: (305) 899-3146
Email: dfletcher@mail.barry.edu
Financial aid: (305) 899-3673
Tuition: N/A

Room/board/expenses: N/A
Enrollment: N/A

Florida Atlantic University

777 Glades Road
Boca Raton, FL 33431
www.business.fau.edu
Public
Admissions: (561) 297-3624
Email: graduatecollege@fau.edu
Financial aid: (561) 297-3530
Application deadline: N/A
In-state tuition: full time: $304/
credit hour; part time: $304/
credit hour
Out-of-state tuition: full time:
$928/credit hour
Room/board/expenses: $17,814
College-funded aid: Yes
International student aid: Yes
Full-time enrollment: N/A
men: N/A; women: N/A;
minorities: N/A; international: N/A
Part-time enrollment: 111
men: 57%; women: 43%;
minorities: 43%; international:
11%
Average GMAT (part time): 524
TOEFL requirement: Yes
Minimum TOEFL score: 600
Most popular departments:
accounting, general
management, health care
administration, international
business, tax

Florida Gulf Coast University (Lutgert)

10501 FGCU Boulevard S
Fort Myers, FL 33965-6565
lutgert.fgcu.edu
Public
Admissions: (239) 590-7988
Email: graduate@fgcu.edu
Financial aid: (239) 590-7920
Application deadline: 06/01
In-state tuition: full time: $373/
credit hour; part time: $373/
credit hour
Out-of-state tuition: full time:
$1,301/credit hour
Room/board/expenses: $11,259
College-funded aid: Yes
International student aid: Yes
Average student indebtedness at graduation: $20,642
Full-time enrollment: 22
men: 59%; women: 41%;
minorities: 18%; international:
18%
Part-time enrollment: 76
men: 58%; women: 42%;
minorities: 14%; international:
0%
Average GMAT (full time): 540
Average GMAT (part time): 510
Average GPA (full time): 3.05
Average age of entrants to full-time program: 24
TOEFL requirement: Yes
Minimum TOEFL score: 550
Most popular departments:
general management,
management information
systems

Florida International University

1050 S.W. 112th Avenue
CBC 300
Miami, FL 33199-0001
business.fiu.edu
Public
Admissions: (305) 348-7398
Email: chapman@fiu.edu
Financial aid: (305) 348-7272
Application deadline: 07/01
In-state tuition: total program:
$37,000 (full time); $48,000
(part time)
Out-of-state tuition: total
program: $45,000 (full time)
Room/board/expenses: $18,000
College-funded aid: Yes
International student aid: Yes
Full-time enrollment: 42
men: 50%; women: 50%;
minorities: 31%; international:
50%
Part-time enrollment: 536
men: 40%; women: 60%;
minorities: 80%; international:
7%
Acceptance rate (full time): 25%
Average GMAT (full time): 562
Average GPA (full time): 3.45
Average age of entrants to full-time program: 25
Average months of prior work experience (full time): 36
TOEFL requirement: Yes
Minimum TOEFL score: 550
Most popular departments:
finance, general management,
health care administration,
international business,
management information
systems
Mean starting base salary for 2016 full-time graduates: $60,000
Employment location for 2016 class: Intl. 0%; N.E. 0%; M.A.
0%; S. 100%; M.W. 0%; S.W.
0%; W. 0%

Florida Southern College

111 Lake Hollingsworth Drive
Lakeland, FL 33801
www.flsouthern.edu/
Private
Admissions: (863) 680-4205
Financial aid: (863) 680-4140
Application deadline: 07/01
Tuition: total program: $27,500
(full time); part time: N/A
Room/board/expenses: N/A
College-funded aid: Yes
International student aid: Yes
Average student indebtedness at graduation: $33,467
Full-time enrollment: 77
men: 48%; women: 52%;
minorities: 23%; international:
10%
Part-time enrollment: N/A
men: N/A; women: N/A;
minorities: N/A; international: N/A
Acceptance rate (full time): 47%
Average GMAT (full time): 465
Average GPA (full time): 3.36
Average age of entrants to full-time program: 29
Average months of prior work experience (full time): 61
Minimum TOEFL score: N/A

Most popular departments:
accounting, general
management, health care
administration, supply chain
management/logistics

Florida State University

Graduate Programs
233 Rovetta Building
Tallahassee, FL 32306-1110
business.fsu.edu/academics/
graduate-programs/
masters-degrees
Public
Admissions: (850) 644-6455
Email: gradprograms@
business.fsu.edu
Financial aid: (850) 644-5716
Application deadline: 06/01
In-state tuition: full time: $480/
credit hour; part time: $480/
credit hour
Out-of-state tuition: full time:
$1,110/credit hour
Room/board/expenses: $18,766
College-funded aid: Yes
International student aid: Yes
Average student indebtedness at graduation: $14,379
Full-time enrollment: 36
men: 58%; women: 42%;
minorities: 25%; international:
11%
Part-time enrollment: 84
men: 37%; women: 63%;
minorities: 27%; international:
N/A
Acceptance rate (full time): 67%
Average GMAT (full time): 558
Average GMAT (part time): 550
Average GPA (full time): 3.25
Average age of entrants to full-time program: 25
Average months of prior work experience (full time): 45
TOEFL requirement: Yes
Minimum TOEFL score: 600
Most popular departments:
accounting, finance, general
management, insurance,
marketing
Mean starting base salary for 2016 full-time graduates: $60,933
Employment location for 2016 class: Intl. 7%; N.E. 7%; M.A. 7%;
S. 67%; M.W. 13%; S.W. N/A;
W. N/A

Jacksonville University

2800 University Boulevard N
Jacksonville, FL 32211
www.ju.edu
Private
Admissions: (904) 256-7000
Email: admiss@ju.edu
Financial aid: (904) 256-7956
Application deadline: 08/01
Tuition: full time: $740/credit
hour; part time: $740/credit hour
Room/board/expenses: $14,298
College-funded aid: Yes
International student aid: Yes
Average student indebtedness at graduation: $30,334
Full-time enrollment: 47
men: 66%; women: 34%;
minorities: 32%; international:
30%
Part-time enrollment: 132
men: 56%; women: 44%;
minorities: 44%; international:
3%

Acceptance rate (full time): 53%
Average GMAT (full time): 441
Average GMAT (part time): 502
Average GPA (full time): 3.29
Average age of entrants to full-time program: 24
Average months of prior work experience (full time): 66
TOEFL requirement: Yes
Minimum TOEFL score: 500
Most popular departments: accounting, finance, general management, leadership, marketing
Mean starting base salary for 2016 full-time graduates: $51,071
Employment location for 2016 class: Intl. 0%; N.E. 0%; M.A. 0%; S. 100%; M.W. 0%; S.W. 0%; W. 0%

Rollins College (Crummer)
1000 Holt Avenue
Winter Park, FL 32789-4499
www.rollins.edu/business/
Private
Admissions: (407) 628-2405
Email: MBAADMISSIONS@rollins.edu
Financial aid: (407) 646-2395
Application deadline: 07/01
Tuition: total program: $73,740 (full time); $55,240 (part time)
Room/board/expenses: $63,727
College-funded aid: Yes
International student aid: Yes
Average student indebtedness at graduation: $51,952
Full-time enrollment: 140
men: 57%; women: 43%; minorities: 29%; international: 29%
Part-time enrollment: 155
men: 55%; women: 45%; minorities: 36%; international: 1%
Acceptance rate (full time): 51%
Average GMAT (full time): 565
Average GPA (full time): 3.29
Average age of entrants to full-time program: 23
Average months of prior work experience (full time): 32
TOEFL requirement: Yes
Minimum TOEFL score: N/A
Most popular departments: entrepreneurship, finance, general management, international business, marketing
Mean starting base salary for 2016 full-time graduates: $54,553
Employment location for 2016 class: Intl. 2%; N.E. 5%; M.A. 3%; S. 85%; M.W. 2%; S.W. 0%; W. 3%

Stetson University
421 N. Woodland Boulevard
Unit 8398
DeLand, FL 32723
www.stetson.edu/graduate
Private
Admissions: (386) 822-7100
Email: gradadmissions@stetson.edu
Financial aid: (800) 688-7120
Application deadline: rolling
Tuition: full time: $981/credit hour; part time: $981/credit hour
Room/board/expenses: N/A
College-funded aid: Yes
International student aid: Yes
Average student indebtedness at graduation: $28,757

Full-time enrollment: 73
men: 53%; women: 47%; minorities: 15%; international: 12%
Part-time enrollment: 36
men: 28%; women: 72%; minorities: 25%; international: 0%
Acceptance rate (full time): 63%
Average GMAT (full time): 555
Average GPA (full time): 3.39
Average age of entrants to full-time program: 27
TOEFL requirement: Yes
Minimum TOEFL score: N/A
Mean starting base salary for 2016 full-time graduates: $72,500
Employment location for 2016 class: Intl. N/A; N.E. N/A; M.A. N/A; S. 100%; M.W. N/A; S.W. N/A; W. N/A

University of Central Florida
PO Box 161400
Orlando, FL 32816-1400
www.ucf.edu
Public
Admissions: (407) 235-3917
Email: cbagrad@ucf.edu
Financial aid: (407) 823-2827
Application deadline: 07/01
In-state tuition: total program: $39,000 (full time); part time: $5,550
Out-of-state tuition: total program: $39,000 (full time)
Room/board/expenses: $15,886
College-funded aid: Yes
International student aid: Yes
Average student indebtedness at graduation: $44,559
Full-time enrollment: 26
men: 65%; women: 35%; minorities: 27%; international: 4%
Part-time enrollment: 378
men: 53%; women: 47%; minorities: 42%; international: 2%
Acceptance rate (full time): 36%
Average GMAT (full time): 3.30
Average age of entrants to full-time program: 26
Average months of prior work experience (full time): 55
TOEFL requirement: Yes
Minimum TOEFL score: 577
Most popular departments: accounting, entrepreneurship, general management, human resources management, sports business

University of Florida (Hough)
Hough Hall 310
Gainesville, FL 32611-7152
www.floridamba.ufl.edu
Public
Admissions: (352) 392-7992
Email: floridamba@warrington.ufl.edu
Financial aid: (352) 392-1275
Application deadline: 03/15
In-state tuition: full time: $12,737; part time: $25,545
Out-of-state tuition: full time: $30,130
Room/board/expenses: $17,150
College-funded aid: Yes
International student aid: Yes
Average student indebtedness at graduation: $34,426

Full-time enrollment: 100
men: 66%; women: 34%; minorities: 23%; international: 14%
Part-time enrollment: 373
men: 73%; women: 27%; minorities: 28%; international: 9%
Acceptance rate (full time): 16%
Average GMAT (full time): 685
Average GPA (full time): 3.43
Average age of entrants to full-time program: 26
Average months of prior work experience (full time): 54
TOEFL requirement: Yes
Minimum TOEFL score: 550
Most popular departments: consulting, finance, human resources management, marketing, supply chain management/logistics
Mean starting base salary for 2016 full-time graduates: $98,331
Employment location for 2016 class: Intl. 5%; N.E. 9%; M.A. 4%; S. 47%; M.W. 15%; S.W. 15%; W. 5%

University of Miami
PO Box 248027
Coral Gables, FL 33124-6520
www.bus.miami.edu/grad
Private
Admissions: (305) 284-2510
Email: mba@miami.edu
Financial aid: (305) 284-5212
Application deadline: 05/15
Tuition: full time: $1,900/credit hour; part time: N/A
Room/board/expenses: $22,652
College-funded aid: Yes
International student aid: Yes
Average student indebtedness at graduation: $79,445
Full-time enrollment: 138
men: 68%; women: 32%; minorities: 30%; international: 33%
Part-time enrollment: N/A
men: N/A; women: N/A; minorities: N/A; international: N/A
Acceptance rate (full time): 23%
Average GMAT (full time): 654
Average GPA (full time): 3.32
Average age of entrants to full-time program: 26
Average months of prior work experience (full time): 48
TOEFL requirement: Yes
Minimum TOEFL score: 587
Most popular departments: finance, marketing, real estate, quantitative analysis/statistics and operations research, other
Mean starting base salary for 2016 full-time graduates: $71,210
Employment location for 2016 class: Intl. 2%; N.E. 2%; M.A. 0%; S. 91%; M.W. 2%; S.W. 0%; W. 4%

University of North Florida (Coggin)
1 UNF Drive
Jacksonville, FL 32224-2645
www.unf.edu/coggin
Public
Admissions: (904) 620-1360
Email: l.reigger@unf.edu
Financial aid: (904) 620-5555
Application deadline: 08/01

In-state tuition: full time: $11,848; part time: $494/credit hour
Out-of-state tuition: full time: $25,066
Room/board/expenses: $20,314
College-funded aid: Yes
International student aid: Yes
Average student indebtedness at graduation: $33,365
Full-time enrollment: 95
men: 52%; women: 48%; minorities: 16%; international: 37%
Part-time enrollment: 170
men: 58%; women: 42%; minorities: 24%; international: 4%
Average GMAT (part time): 551
TOEFL requirement: Yes
Minimum TOEFL score: 550
Most popular departments: accounting, e-commerce, finance, general management, supply chain management/logistics

University of South Florida
4202 Fowler Avenue
BSN 3404
Tampa, FL 33620
www.mba.usf.edu
Public
Admissions: (813) 974-3335
Email: bsn-mba@usf.edu
Financial aid: (813) 974-4700
Application deadline: 07/01
In-state tuition: full time: $467/credit hour; part time: $467/credit hour
Out-of-state tuition: full time: $913/credit hour
Room/board/expenses: $27,000
College-funded aid: Yes
International student aid: Yes
Average student indebtedness at graduation: $54,900
Full-time enrollment: 52
men: 69%; women: 31%; minorities: 17%; international: 15%
Part-time enrollment: 238
men: 68%; women: 32%; minorities: 17%; international: 29%
Acceptance rate (full time): 36%
Average GMAT (full time): 541
Average GMAT (part time): 567
Average GPA (full time): 3.46
Average age of entrants to full-time program: 23
Average months of prior work experience (full time): 22
TOEFL requirement: Yes
Minimum TOEFL score: 550
Most popular departments: entrepreneurship, finance, leadership, marketing, other
Mean starting base salary for 2016 full-time graduates: $42,000
Employment location for 2016 class: Intl. 4%; N.E. 24%; M.A. N/A; S. 52%; M.W. 12%; S.W. 4%; W. 4%

University of South Florida-Sarasota-Manatee
8350 N. Tamiami Trail
Sarasota, FL 34243
usfsm.edu/college-of-business
Public
Admissions: (941) 359-4331
Email: admissions@sar.usf.edu
Financial aid: (941) 359-4200

Application deadline: 07/01
In-state tuition: full time: N/A; part time: $380/credit hour
Out-of-state tuition: full time: N/A
Room/board/expenses: N/A
College-funded aid: Yes
International student aid: Yes
Full-time enrollment: N/A
men: N/A; women: N/A; minorities: N/A; international: N/A
Part-time enrollment: 89
men: 55%; women: 45%; minorities: 29%; international: 0%
Average GMAT (part time): 480
TOEFL requirement: Yes
Minimum TOEFL score: 550

University of South Florida-St. Petersburg[1]
140 7th Avnue S, BAY III
St. Petersburg, FL 33701
www.usfsp.edu/ktcob
Public
Admissions: (727) 873-4567
Email: applygrad@usfsp.edu
Financial aid: (727) 873-4128
Tuition: N/A
Room/board/expenses: N/A
Enrollment: N/A

University of Tampa (Sykes)
401 W. Kennedy Boulevard
Tampa, FL 33606-1490
grad.ut.edu
Private
Admissions: (813) 257-3642
Email: utgrad@ut.edu
Financial aid: (813) 253-6219
Application deadline: rolling
Tuition: full time: $588/credit hour; part time: $588/credit hour
Room/board/expenses: $12,233
College-funded aid: Yes
International student aid: Yes
Average student indebtedness at graduation: $41,517
Full-time enrollment: 469
men: 57%; women: 43%; minorities: 6%; international: 42%
Part-time enrollment: 145
men: 51%; women: 49%; minorities: 9%; international: 10%
Acceptance rate (full time): 35%
Average GMAT (full time): 540
Average GMAT (part time): 540
Average GPA (full time): 3.50
Average age of entrants to full-time program: 25
Average months of prior work experience (full time): 60
TOEFL requirement: Yes
Minimum TOEFL score: 577
Most popular departments: accounting, entrepreneurship, finance, marketing, technology
Mean starting base salary for 2016 full-time graduates: $66,696
Employment location for 2016 class: Intl. 3%; N.E. 6%; M.A. 0%; S. 87%; M.W. 3%; S.W. 0%; W. 0%

University of West Florida[1]

11000 University Parkway
Pensacola, FL 32514
uwf.edu
Public
Admissions: (850) 474-2230
Email: mba@uwf.edu
Financial aid: N/A
Tuition: N/A
Room/board/expenses: N/A
Enrollment: N/A

GEORGIA

Augusta University[1]

1120 15th Street
Augusta, GA 30912
www.gru.edu/hull/grad/mba.php
Public
Admissions: (706) 737-1418
Email: hull@gru.edu
Financial aid: N/A
Tuition: N/A
Room/board/expenses: N/A
Enrollment: N/A

Berry College (Campbell)

PO Box 495024
Mount Berry, GA 30149-5024
www.berry.edu/academics/campbell/
Private
Admissions: (706) 236-2215
Email: admissions@berry.edu
Financial aid: (706) 236-1714
Application deadline: 07/20
Tuition: full time: $605/credit hour; part time: $605/credit hour
Room/board/expenses: N/A
College-funded aid: Yes
International student aid: Yes
Full-time enrollment: 1
men: 100%; women: 0%;
minorities: N/A; international: N/A
Part-time enrollment: 20
men: 60%; women: 40%;
minorities: N/A; international: N/A
TOEFL requirement: Yes
Minimum TOEFL score: N/A

Clark Atlanta University

223 James P. Brawley Drive SW
Atlanta, GA 30314
www.cau.edu
Private
Admissions: (404) 880-8443
Email: mbaadmissions@cau.edu
Financial aid: (404) 880-6265
Application deadline: N/A
Tuition: full time: $861/credit hour; part time: $861/credit hour
Room/board/expenses: $16,100
College-funded aid: Yes
International student aid: No
Full-time enrollment: 62
men: 34%; women: 66%;
minorities: 61%; international: 21%
Part-time enrollment: 9
men: 44%; women: 56%;
minorities: 67%; international: 11%
Acceptance rate (full time): 56%
Average GPA (full time): 3.05
Average age of entrants to full-time program: 24
TOEFL requirement: Yes
Minimum TOEFL score: N/A
Most popular departments:
accounting, marketing

Clayton State University

2000 Clayton State Boulevard
Morrow, GA 30260-0285
www.clayton.edu/mba
Public
Admissions: (678) 466-4113
Email: graduate@clayton.edu
Financial aid: (678) 466-4185
Application deadline: 07/15
In-state tuition: full time: $335/credit hour; part time: $335/credit hour
Out-of-state tuition: full time: $1,335/credit hour
Room/board/expenses: N/A
College-funded aid: Yes
International student aid: No
Full-time enrollment: 41
men: 83%; women: 17%;
minorities: 0%; international: 100%
Part-time enrollment: 149
men: 46%; women: 54%;
minorities: 81%; international: N/A
Acceptance rate (full time): 100%
Average GMAT (full time): 400
Average GMAT (part time): 420
Average GPA (full time): 2.90
TOEFL requirement: Yes
Minimum TOEFL score: 550
Most popular departments:
accounting, human resources management, international business, supply chain management/logistics, other

Columbus State University (Turner)

4225 University Avenue
Columbus, GA 31907
cobcs.columbusstate.edu
Public
Admissions: (706) 507-8800
Email: alexander_viola@columbusstate.edu
Financial aid: (706) 507-8807
Application deadline: 06/30
In-state tuition: full time: $250/credit hour; part time: $250/credit hour
Out-of-state tuition: full time: $1,000/credit hour
Room/board/expenses: N/A
College-funded aid: Yes
International student aid: Yes
Full-time enrollment: N/A
men: N/A; women: N/A;
minorities: N/A; international: N/A
Part-time enrollment: 37
men: 62%; women: 38%;
minorities: 30%; international: 3%
Average GMAT (part time): 484
TOEFL requirement: Yes
Minimum TOEFL score: 550

Emory University (Goizueta)

1300 Clifton Road NE
Atlanta, GA 30322
www.goizueta.emory.edu
Private
Admissions: (404) 727-6311
Email:
mbaadmissions@emory.edu
Financial aid: (404) 727-6039
Application deadline: 03/10
Tuition: full time: $57,580; total program: $73,600 (part time)
Room/board/expenses: $24,546
College-funded aid: Yes
International student aid: Yes

Average student indebtedness at graduation: $73,178
Full-time enrollment: 350
men: 71%; women: 29%;
minorities: 22%; international: 33%
Part-time enrollment: 256
men: 68%; women: 32%;
minorities: 29%; international: 9%
Acceptance rate (full time): 33%
Average GMAT (full time): 683
Average GMAT (part time): 632
Average GPA (full time): 3.30
Average age of entrants to full-time program: 29
Average months of prior work experience (full time): 66
TOEFL requirement: Yes
Minimum TOEFL score: N/A
Most popular departments:
consulting, finance, general management, marketing, production/operations management
Mean starting base salary for 2016 full-time graduates: $116,658
Employment location for 2016 class: Intl. 3%; N.E. 21%; M.A. 3%; S. 47%; M.W. 6%; S.W. 6%; W. 14%

Georgia College & State University (Bunting)

Campus Box 019
Milledgeville, GA 31061
mba.gcsu.edu
Public
Admissions: (478) 445-6283
Email: grad-admit@gcsu.edu
Financial aid: (478) 445-5149
Application deadline: 07/01
In-state tuition: full time: N/A; part time: $288/credit hour
Out-of-state tuition: full time: N/A
Room/board/expenses: N/A
College-funded aid: Yes
International student aid: Yes
Full-time enrollment: N/A
men: N/A; women: N/A;
minorities: N/A; international: N/A
Part-time enrollment: 183
men: 62%; women: 38%;
minorities: 27%; international: 0%
Average GMAT (part time): 534
TOEFL requirement: Yes
Minimum TOEFL score: 550

Georgia Institute of Technology (Scheller)

800 W. Peachtree Street NW
Atlanta, GA 30332-0520
scheller.gatech.edu
Public
Admissions: (404) 894-8722
Email: mba@scheller.gatech.edu
Financial aid: (404) 894-4160
Application deadline: 05/15
In-state tuition: full time: $31,096; part time: $1,107/credit hour
Out-of-state tuition: full time: $41,684
Room/board/expenses: $17,840
College-funded aid: Yes
International student aid: Yes
Average student indebtedness at graduation: $52,738
Full-time enrollment: 143
men: 78%; women: 22%;
minorities: 14%; international: 28%

Part-time enrollment: 365
men: 71%; women: 29%;
minorities: 28%; international: 5%
Acceptance rate (full time): 32%
Average GMAT (full time): 680
Average GMAT (part time): 603
Average GPA (full time): 3.39
Average age of entrants to full-time program: 28
Average months of prior work experience (full time): 59
TOEFL requirement: Yes
Minimum TOEFL score: 600
Most popular departments:
consulting, entrepreneurship, production/operations management, supply chain management/logistics, technology
Mean starting base salary for 2016 full-time graduates: $108,088
Employment location for 2016 class: Intl. N/A; N.E. 6%; M.A. 4%; S. 81%; M.W. 2%; S.W. 0%; W. 8%

Georgia Southern University

PO Box 8002
Statesboro, GA 30460-8050
coba.georgiasouthern.edu/mba
Public
Admissions: (912) 478-2357
Email:
mba@georgiasouthern.edu
Financial aid: (912) 478-5413
Application deadline: 07/31
In-state tuition: full time: N/A; part time: $410/credit hour
Out-of-state tuition: full time: N/A
Room/board/expenses: N/A
College-funded aid: Yes
International student aid: Yes
Full-time enrollment: N/A
men: N/A; women: N/A;
minorities: N/A; international: N/A
Part-time enrollment: 100
men: 57%; women: 43%;
minorities: 20%; international: 9%
Average GMAT (part time): 470
TOEFL requirement: Yes
Minimum TOEFL score: 550

Georgia Southwestern State University[1]

800 Georgia Southwestern
State University Drive
Americus, GA 31709
gsw.edu/
Public
Admissions: N/A
Financial aid: N/A
Tuition: N/A
Room/board/expenses: N/A
Enrollment: N/A

Georgia State University (Robinson)

PO Box 3989
Atlanta, GA 30302-3989
robinson.gsu.edu/
Public
Admissions: (404) 413-7167
Email: rcbgradadmissions@gsu.edu
Financial aid: (404) 413-2400
Application deadline: 05/01
In-state tuition: full time: N/A; part time: $483/credit hour
Out-of-state tuition: full time: N/A
Room/board/expenses: N/A
College-funded aid: Yes

International student aid: Yes
Full-time enrollment: N/A
men: N/A; women: N/A;
minorities: N/A; international: N/A
Part-time enrollment: 359
men: 57%; women: 43%;
minorities: 40%; international: 10%
Average GMAT (part time): 604
TOEFL requirement: Yes
Minimum TOEFL score: 610
Most popular departments:
finance, general management, health care administration, marketing, quantitative analysis/statistics and operations research

Kennesaw State University (Coles)

MD 3306
Kennesaw, GA 30144-5591
www.kennesaw.edu/graduate/admissions
Public
Admissions: (470) 578-4377
Email: ksugrad@kennesaw.edu
Financial aid: (770) 423-6074
Application deadline: 07/01
In-state tuition: full time: N/A; part time: $339/credit hour
Out-of-state tuition: full time: N/A
Room/board/expenses: N/A
College-funded aid: Yes
International student aid: Yes
Full-time enrollment: N/A
men: N/A; women: N/A;
minorities: N/A; international: N/A
Part-time enrollment: 163
men: 54%; women: 46%;
minorities: 36%; international: N/A
Average GMAT (part time): 565
TOEFL requirement: Yes
Minimum TOEFL score: N/A
Most popular departments:
accounting, economics, general management, international business, marketing

Mercer University-Atlanta (Stetson)

3001 Mercer University Drive
Atlanta, GA 30341-4155
business.mercer.edu
Private
Admissions: (678) 547-6300
Email: business.admissions@mercer.edu
Financial aid: (678) 547-6444
Application deadline: 06/15
Tuition: full time: $795/credit hour; part time: $727/credit hour
Room/board/expenses: N/A
College-funded aid: No
International student aid: No
Average student indebtedness at graduation: $17,172
Full-time enrollment: 18
men: 56%; women: 44%;
minorities: 89%; international: 11%
Part-time enrollment: 398
men: 52%; women: 48%;
minorities: 48%; international: 11%
Acceptance rate (full time): 55%
Average GMAT (full time): 515
Average GMAT (part time): 538
Average GPA (full time): 3.25
Average age of entrants to full-time program: 27
Average months of prior work experience (full time): 36
TOEFL requirement: Yes

Minimum TOEFL score: 550
Most popular departments: accounting, economics, finance, health care administration, marketing
Mean starting base salary for 2016 full-time graduates: $57,500

Savannah State University

PO Box 20359
Savannah, GA 31404
www.savannahstate.edu/coba/programs-mba.shtml
Public
Admissions: (912) 358-3393
Email: mba@savannahstate.edu
Financial aid: (912) 358-4162
Application deadline: rolling
In-state tuition: full time: N/A; total program: $10,275 (part time)
Out-of-state tuition: full time: N/A
Room/board/expenses: N/A
College-funded aid: Yes
Full-time enrollment: N/A
men: N/A; women: N/A;
minorities: N/A; international: N/A
Part-time enrollment: 67
men: 25%; women: 75%;
minorities: 78%; international: 1%
TOEFL requirement: Yes
Minimum TOEFL score: N/A

University of Georgia (Terry)

335 Brooks Hall
Athens, GA 30602-6251
terry.uga.edu/mba
Public
Admissions: (706) 542-5671
Email: ugamba@uga.edu
Financial aid: (706) 542-6147
Application deadline: 03/08
In-state tuition: full time: $15,462; total program: $56,400 (part time)
Out-of-state tuition: full time: $33,780
Room/board/expenses: $23,950
College-funded aid: Yes
International student aid: Yes
Average student indebtedness at graduation: $34,025
Full-time enrollment: 102
men: 66%; women: 34%;
minorities: 16%; international: 34%
Part-time enrollment: 298
men: 62%; women: 38%;
minorities: 39%; international: 0%
Acceptance rate (full time): 36%
Average GMAT (full time): 647
Average GMAT (part time): 566
Average GPA (full time): 3.30
Average age of entrants to full-time program: 28
Average months of prior work experience (full time): 52
TOEFL requirement: Yes
Minimum TOEFL score: N/A
Most popular departments: finance, human resources management, marketing, management information systems, production/operations management
Mean starting base salary for 2016 full-time graduates: $91,217
Employment location for 2016 class: Intl. 5%; N.E. 8%; M.A. 3%; S. 70%; M.W. 5%; S.W. 8%; W. N/A

University of North Georgia

82 College Circle
Dahlonega, GA 30597
ung.edu/mike-cottrell-college-of-business/academic-programs/the-cottrell-mba.php
Public
Admissions: (470) 239-3030
Email: mba@ung.edu
Financial aid: (706) 864-1412
Application deadline: 04/01
In-state tuition: full time: N/A; part time: $520/credit hour
Out-of-state tuition: full time: N/A
Room/board/expenses: N/A
College-funded aid: Yes
International student aid: Yes
Full-time enrollment: N/A
men: N/A; women: N/A;
minorities: N/A; international: N/A
Part-time enrollment: 56
men: 55%; women: 45%;
minorities: 23%; international: 5%
Average GMAT (part time): 491
TOEFL requirement: Yes
Minimum TOEFL score: 550
Most popular departments: technology

University of West Georgia (Richards)

1601 Maple Street
Carrollton, GA 30118-3000
www.westga.edu/academics/business/index.php
Public
Admissions: (678) 839-5355
Email: hudombon@westga.edu
Financial aid: (678) 839-6421
Application deadline: 07/15
In-state tuition: full time: $9,292; part time: $306/credit hour
Out-of-state tuition: full time: $26,976
Room/board/expenses: N/A
College-funded aid: Yes
International student aid: Yes
Full-time enrollment: N/A
men: N/A; women: N/A;
minorities: N/A; international: N/A
Part-time enrollment: 94
men: 53%; women: 47%;
minorities: N/A; international: N/A
Average GMAT (part time): 431
TOEFL requirement: Yes
Minimum TOEFL score: 550
Most popular departments: accounting, economics, finance, general management

Valdosta State University (Langdale)

1500 N. Patterson Street
Valdosta, GA 31698
www.valdosta.edu/lcoba/grad/
Public
Admissions: (229) 245-3822
Email: mschnake@valdosta.edu
Financial aid: (229) 333-5935
Application deadline: 07/15
In-state tuition: full time: $243/credit hour; part time: $243/credit hour
Out-of-state tuition: full time: $875/credit hour
Room/board/expenses: N/A
College-funded aid: Yes
International student aid: Yes
Full-time enrollment: N/A
men: N/A; women: N/A;
minorities: N/A; international: N/A

Part-time enrollment: 32
men: 53%; women: 47%;
minorities: N/A; international: N/A
TOEFL requirement: Yes
Minimum TOEFL score: 523

HAWAII

University of Hawaii-Manoa (Shidler)

2404 Maile Way
Business Administration C-204
Honolulu, HI 96822
www.shidler.hawaii.edu
Public
Admissions: (808) 956-8266
Email: mba@hawaii.edu
Financial aid: (808) 956-7251
Application deadline: N/A
In-state tuition: full time: $21,288; part time: $887/credit hour
Out-of-state tuition: full time: $38,352
Room/board/expenses: $20,000
College-funded aid: Yes
International student aid: Yes
Full-time enrollment: 40
men: 55%; women: 45%;
minorities: N/A; international: N/A
Part-time enrollment: 86
men: 53%; women: 47%;
minorities: N/A; international: N/A
Acceptance rate (full time): 50%
TOEFL requirement: Yes
Minimum TOEFL score: N/A
Most popular departments: accounting, entrepreneurship, finance, health care administration, international business

IDAHO

Boise State University

1910 University Drive
MBEB4101
Boise, ID 83725-1600
cobe.boisestate.edu/graduate
Public
Admissions: (208) 426-3116
Email: graduatebusiness@boisestate.edu
Financial aid: (208) 426-1664
Application deadline: N/A
In-state tuition: full time: $8,440; part time: $382/credit hour
Out-of-state tuition: full time: $22,890
Room/board/expenses: $14,204
College-funded aid: Yes
International student aid: Yes
Average student indebtedness at graduation: $39,533
Full-time enrollment: 67
men: 51%; women: 49%;
minorities: 12%; international: 18%
Part-time enrollment: 73
men: 63%; women: 37%;
minorities: 11%; international: 4%
Acceptance rate (full time): 57%
Average GMAT (full time): 566
Average GMAT (part time): 537
Average GPA (full time): 3.50
Average age of entrants to full-time program: 25
Average months of prior work experience (full time): 24
TOEFL requirement: Yes
Minimum TOEFL score: 587

Idaho State University[1]

921 S. 8th Avenue
Stop 8020
Pocatello, ID 83209
www.isu.edu/cob/mba.shtml
Public
Admissions: (208) 282-2966
Email: mba@isu.edu
Financial aid: N/A
Tuition: N/A
Room/board/expenses: N/A
Enrollment: N/A

University of Idaho[1]

PO Box 443161
Moscow, ID 83844-3161
www.uidaho.edu
Public
Admissions: (800) 885-4001
Email: graduateadmissions@uidaho.edu
Financial aid: N/A
Tuition: N/A
Room/board/expenses: N/A
Enrollment: N/A

ILLINOIS

Bradley University (Foster)

1501 W. Bradley Avenue
Peoria, IL 61625
www.bradley.edu/mba
Private
Admissions: (309) 677-3714
Email: mba@bradley.edu
Financial aid: (309) 677-3085
Application deadline: 08/01
Tuition: full time: N/A/credit hour; part time: $850/credit hour
Room/board/expenses: N/A
College-funded aid: Yes
International student aid: Yes
Full-time enrollment: N/A
men: N/A; women: N/A;
minorities: N/A; international: N/A
Part-time enrollment: 53
men: 57%; women: 43%;
minorities: 17%; international: 21%
Average GMAT (part time): 540
TOEFL requirement: Yes
Minimum TOEFL score: N/A
Most popular departments: finance, general management

DePaul University (Kellstadt)

1 E. Jackson Boulevard
Chicago, IL 60604-2287
www.kellstadt.depaul.edu/
Private
Admissions: (312) 362-8810
Email: kgsb@depaul.edu
Financial aid: (312) 362-8091
Application deadline: 08/01
Tuition: full time: $1,020/credit hour; part time: $1,020/credit hour
Room/board/expenses: $15,000
College-funded aid: Yes
International student aid: Yes
Average student indebtedness at graduation: $65,274
Full-time enrollment: 47
men: 62%; women: 38%;
minorities: 9%; international: 17%
Part-time enrollment: 825
men: 60%; women: 40%;
minorities: 27%; international: 3%
Acceptance rate (full time): 49%

Average GMAT (full time): 595
Average GMAT (part time): 573
Average GPA (full time): 3.14
Average age of entrants to full-time program: 27
Average months of prior work experience (full time): 49
TOEFL requirement: Yes
Minimum TOEFL score: 550
Mean starting base salary for 2016 full-time graduates: $73,460
Employment location for 2016 class: Intl. N/A; N.E. N/A; M.A. 5%; S. N/A; M.W. 95%; S.W. N/A; W. N/A

Dominican University (Brennan)

7900 West Division Street
River Forest, IL 60305
business.dom.edu/
Private
Admissions: (708) 524-6571
Email: lhancock@dom.edu
Financial aid: (708) 524-6950
Application deadline: rolling
Tuition: full time: N/A; part time: $950/credit hour
Room/board/expenses: N/A
College-funded aid: Yes
International student aid: Yes
Full-time enrollment: N/A
men: N/A; women: N/A;
minorities: N/A; international: N/A
Part-time enrollment: 163
men: 34%; women: 66%;
minorities: 15%; international: 15%
Average GMAT (part time): 408
TOEFL requirement: Yes
Minimum TOEFL score: N/A
Most popular departments: finance, general management, health care administration, international business, marketing

Eastern Illinois University (Lumpkin)

600 Lincoln Avenue
Charleston, IL 61920-3099
www.eiu.edu/mba/
Public
Admissions: (217) 581-3028
Email: mba@eiu.edu
Financial aid: (217) 581-7812
Application deadline: 08/01
In-state tuition: full time: $289/credit hour; part time: $289/credit hour
Out-of-state tuition: full time: $694/credit hour
Room/board/expenses: $11,863
College-funded aid: Yes
International student aid: Yes
Full-time enrollment: 41
men: 44%; women: 56%;
minorities: 12%; international: 27%
Part-time enrollment: 51
men: 41%; women: 59%;
minorities: 14%; international: N/A
Acceptance rate (full time): 33%
Average GMAT (full time): 507
Average GMAT (part time): 445
Average GPA (full time): 3.58
Average age of entrants to full-time program: 24
TOEFL requirement: Yes
Minimum TOEFL score: 550
Most popular departments: accounting, general management, other

Illinois Institute of Technology (Stuart)[1]

10 W. 35th Street
Chicago, IL 60616
www.stuart.iit.edu
Private
Admissions: (312) 567-3020
Email: admission@stuart.iit.edu
Financial aid: (312) 567-7219
Tuition: N/A
Room/board/expenses: N/A
Enrollment: N/A

Illinois State University

MBA Program
Campus Box 5570
Normal, IL 61790-5570
business.illinoisstate.edu/mba/
Public
Admissions: (309) 438-8388
Email: admissions@ilstu.edu
Financial aid: (309) 438-2231
Application deadline: 07/01
In-state tuition: full time: $389/credit hour; part time: $389/credit hour
Out-of-state tuition: full time: $808/credit hour
Room/board/expenses: $16,562
College-funded aid: Yes
International student aid: Yes
Full-time enrollment: N/A
men: N/A; women: N/A;
minorities: N/A; international: N/A
Part-time enrollment: 103
men: 60%; women: 40%;
minorities: N/A; international: N/A
Average GMAT (part time): 546
TOEFL requirement: Yes
Minimum TOEFL score: 600
Most popular departments:
finance, human resources management, insurance, leadership, marketing

Loyola University Chicago (Quinlan)

820 N. Michigan Avenue
Chicago, IL 60611
www.luc.edu/quinlan/
Private
Admissions: (312) 915-8908
Email: quinlangrad@luc.edu
Financial aid: (773) 508-7704
Application deadline: 07/15
Tuition: full time: $1,496/credit hour; part time: $1,496/credit hour
Room/board/expenses: $22,023
College-funded aid: Yes
International student aid: Yes
Full-time enrollment: N/A
men: N/A; women: N/A;
minorities: N/A; international: N/A
Part-time enrollment: 562
men: 44%; women: 56%;
minorities: 17%; international: 32%
Average GMAT (part time): 562
TOEFL requirement: Yes
Minimum TOEFL score: 550
Most popular departments:
accounting, finance, health care administration, human resources management, marketing

Northeastern Illinois University[1]

5500 North St. Louis Avenue
Chicago, IL 60625-4699
www.neiu.edu/academics/college-of-business-and-management/graduate-programs-business/master-business-administration
Private
Admissions: (773) 442-6114
Email: cobm-grad@neiu.edu
Financial aid: N/A
Tuition: N/A
Room/board/expenses: N/A
Enrollment: N/A

Northern Illinois University

Office of MBA Programs
Barsema Hall 203
De Kalb, IL 60115-2897
cob.niu.edu/departments/mba-programs/index.shtml
Public
Admissions: (866) 648-6221
Email: mba@niu.edu
Financial aid: (815) 753-1300
Application deadline: 07/15
In-state tuition: total program: $50,500 (full time); part time: $894/credit hour
Out-of-state tuition: total program: $63,500 (full time)
Room/board/expenses: $15,000
College-funded aid: Yes
International student aid: Yes
Full-time enrollment: 18
men: 50%; women: 50%;
minorities: 33%; international: 17%
Part-time enrollment: 488
men: 67%; women: 33%;
minorities: 35%; international: 3%
Acceptance rate (full time): 92%
Average GMAT (full time): 454
Average GMAT (part time): 487
Average GPA (full time): 3.04
Average age of entrants to full-time program: 24
Average months of prior work experience (full time): 23
TOEFL requirement: Yes
Minimum TOEFL score: N/A
Most popular departments:
finance, international business, leadership, marketing, management information systems

Northwestern University (Kellogg)

2001 Sheridan Road
Evanston, IL 60208-2001
www.kellogg.northwestern.edu
Private
Admissions: (847) 491-3308
Email: mbaadmissions@kellogg.northwestern.edu
Financial aid: (847) 491-3308
Application deadline: 04/05
Tuition: full time: $67,792; part time: $6,441/credit hour
Room/board/expenses: $21,108
College-funded aid: Yes
International student aid: Yes
Full-time enrollment: 1,301
men: 59%; women: 41%;
minorities: N/A; international: N/A
Part-time enrollment: 704
men: 73%; women: 27%;
minorities: N/A; international: N/A

Acceptance rate (full time): 20%
Average GMAT (full time): 728
Average GMAT (part time): 674
Average GPA (full time): 3.60
Average age of entrants to full-time program: 28
Average months of prior work experience (full time): 62
TOEFL requirement: Yes
Minimum TOEFL score: N/A
Most popular departments:
entrepreneurship, finance, general management, marketing, organizational behavior
Mean starting base salary for 2016 full-time graduates: $123,998
Employment location for 2016 class: Intl. 12%; N.E. 18%; M.A. 3%; S. 3%; M.W. 29%; S.W. 7%; W. 28%

Purdue University-Calumet[1]

2200 169th Street
Hammond, IN 46323
academics.pnw.edu/business/mba/
Public
Admissions: N/A
Financial aid: N/A
Tuition: N/A
Room/board/expenses: N/A
Enrollment: N/A

Southern Illinois University-Carbondale

133 Rehn Hall
Carbondale, IL 62901-4625
business.siu.edu/academics/mba/
Public
Admissions: (618) 453-3030
Email: gradprograms@business.siu.edu
Financial aid: (618) 453-4334
Application deadline: 07/31
In-state tuition: full time: $504/credit hour; part time: $504/credit hour
Out-of-state tuition: full time: $1,162/credit hour
Room/board/expenses: N/A
College-funded aid: Yes
International student aid: Yes
Full-time enrollment: 45
men: 42%; women: 58%;
minorities: 18%; international: 38%
Part-time enrollment: N/A
men: N/A; women: N/A;
minorities: N/A; international: N/A
Acceptance rate (full time): 39%
Average GMAT (full time): 574
Average GPA (full time): 3.51
Average age of entrants to full-time program: 28
Average months of prior work experience (full time): 73
TOEFL requirement: Yes
Minimum TOEFL score: 550
Most popular departments:
finance, general management, marketing, other

Southern Illinois University-Edwardsville

Box 1051
Edwardsville, IL 62026-1051
www.siue.edu/business
Public
Admissions: (618) 650-3840
Email: mba@siue.edu

Financial aid: (618) 650-3880
Application deadline: rolling
In-state tuition: full time: N/A/credit hour; part time: $305/credit hour
Out-of-state tuition: full time: N/A/credit hour
Room/board/expenses: N/A
College-funded aid: Yes
International student aid: Yes
Full-time enrollment: N/A
men: N/A; women: N/A;
minorities: N/A; international: N/A
Part-time enrollment: 130
men: 55%; women: 45%;
minorities: 10%; international: 4%
Average GMAT (part time): 480
TOEFL requirement: Yes
Minimum TOEFL score: 550
Most popular departments:
accounting, finance, general management, management information systems

St. Xavier University

3700 West 103rd Street
Chicago, IL 60655
www.sxu.edu/academics/colleges_schools/gsm/
Private
Admissions: (773) 298-3053
Email: graduateadmission@sxu.edu
Financial aid: (773) 398-3070
Application deadline: rolling
Tuition: full time: $950/credit hour; part time: $950/credit hour
Room/board/expenses: $37,050
College-funded aid: Yes
International student aid: Yes
Average student indebtedness at graduation: $44,528
Full-time enrollment: 96
men: 49%; women: 51%;
minorities: N/A; international: N/A
Part-time enrollment: 285
men: 51%; women: 49%;
minorities: N/A; international: N/A
Acceptance rate (full time): 56%
Average age of entrants to full-time program: 33
TOEFL requirement: Yes
Minimum TOEFL score: 550
Most popular departments:
accounting, general management, human resources management, marketing, other

University of Chicago (Booth)

5807 S. Woodlawn Avenue
Chicago, IL 60637
ChicagoBooth.edu
Private
Admissions: (773) 702-7369
Email: admissions@ChicagoBooth.edu
Financial aid: (773) 702-7369
Application deadline: 04/03
Tuition: full time: $67,668; part time: $6,590/credit hour
Room/board/expenses: $25,870
College-funded aid: Yes
International student aid: Yes
Full-time enrollment: 1,185
men: 58%; women: 42%;
minorities: 26%; international: 35%
Part-time enrollment: 1,366
men: 75%; women: 25%;
minorities: 26%; international: 18%
Acceptance rate (full time): 24%

Financial aid: (618) 650-3880
Average GMAT (full time): 726
Average GMAT (part time): 678
Average GPA (full time): 3.58
Average age of entrants to full-time program: 27
Average months of prior work experience (full time): 58
TOEFL requirement: Yes
Minimum TOEFL score: 600
Most popular departments:
economics, entrepreneurship, finance, organizational behavior, other
Mean starting base salary for 2016 full-time graduates: $126,937
Employment location for 2016 class: Intl. 13%; N.E. 23%; M.A. 2%; S. 2%; M.W. 31%; S.W. 5%; W. 23%

University of Illinois-Chicago (Liautaud)

601 South Morgan Street
University Hall, 11th Floor
Chicago, IL 60607
www.mba.uic.edu/
Public
Admissions: (312) 996-4573
Email: mba@uic.edu
Financial aid: (312) 996-3126
Application deadline: 06/15
In-state tuition: full time: $24,912; part time: $18,020
Out-of-state tuition: full time: $37,152
Room/board/expenses: N/A
College-funded aid: Yes
International student aid: Yes
Full-time enrollment: N/A
men: N/A; women: N/A;
minorities: N/A; international: N/A
Part-time enrollment: 238
men: 59%; women: 41%;
minorities: 28%; international: 14%
Average GMAT (part time): 574
TOEFL requirement: Yes
Minimum TOEFL score: 550
Most popular departments:
accounting, entrepreneurship, finance, general management, marketing

University of Illinois-Springfield

1 University Plaza
MS UHB 4000
Springfield, IL 62703
www.uis.edu/admissions
Public
Admissions: (888) 977-4847
Email: admissions@uis.edu
Financial aid: (217) 206-6724
Application deadline: N/A
In-state tuition: full time: $329/credit hour; part time: $329/credit hour
Out-of-state tuition: full time: $675/credit hour
Room/board/expenses: N/A
College-funded aid: Yes
International student aid: Yes
Full-time enrollment: N/A
men: N/A; women: N/A;
minorities: N/A; international: N/A
Part-time enrollment: 102
men: 56%; women: 44%;
minorities: 13%; international: 12%
Average GMAT (part time): 497
TOEFL requirement: Yes
Minimum TOEFL score: 550

University of Illinois-Urbana-Champaign

515 E. Gregory Drive
3019 BIF, MC 520
Champaign, IL 61820
www.mba.illinois.edu
Public
Admissions: (217) 244-7602
Email: mba@illinois.edu
Financial aid: (217) 333-0100
Application deadline: 03/05
In-state tuition: full time: $23,072;
part time: $22,889
Out-of-state tuition: full time:
$34,622
Room/board/expenses: $22,690
College-funded aid: Yes
International student aid: Yes
**Average student indebtedness at
graduation:** $56,491
Full-time enrollment: 134
men: 72%; women: 28%;
minorities: 18%; international:
37%
Part-time enrollment: 98
men: 59%; women: 41%;
minorities: 35%; international:
9%
Acceptance rate (full time): 26%
Average GMAT (full time): 665
Average GMAT (part time): 627
Average GPA (full time): 3.40
**Average age of entrants to full-
time program:** 27
**Average months of prior work
experience (full time):** 49
TOEFL requirement: Yes
Minimum TOEFL score: 610
Most popular departments:
consulting, finance, general
management, marketing,
technology
**Mean starting base salary for 2016
full-time graduates:** $94,688
**Employment location for 2016
class:** Intl. 11%; N.E. 2%; M.A.
2%; S. 4%; M.W. 57%; S.W. 4%;
W. 21%

Western Illinois University

1 University Circle
Macomb, IL 61455
www.wiu.edu/cbt
Public
Admissions: (309) 298-2442
Email: wj-polley@wiu.edu
Financial aid: (309) 298-2446
Application deadline: rolling
In-state tuition: full time: $324/
credit hour; part time: $324/
credit hour
Out-of-state tuition: full time:
$485/credit hour
Room/board/expenses: N/A
College-funded aid: Yes
International student aid: Yes
Full-time enrollment: 49
men: 59%; women: 41%;
minorities: N/A; international: N/A
Part-time enrollment: 31
men: 55%; women: 45%;
minorities: N/A; international: N/A
Acceptance rate (full time): 67%
Average GMAT (full time): 517
Average GMAT (part time): 515
Average GPA (full time): 3.45
TOEFL requirement: Yes
Minimum TOEFL score: 550
Most popular departments:
accounting, economics, finance,
general management, supply
chain management/logistics

INDIANA

Ball State University (Miller)[1]

Whitinger Building, 147
Muncie, IN 47306
www.bsu.edu/mba/
Public
Admissions: (765) 285-1931
Email: mba@bsu.edu
Financial aid: (765) 285-5600
Tuition: N/A
Room/board/expenses: N/A
Enrollment: N/A

Butler University

4600 Sunset Avenue
Indianapolis, IN 46208-3485
www.butlermba.com
Private
Admissions: (317) 940-9842
Email: mba@butler.edu
Financial aid: (317) 940-8200
Application deadline: 08/01
Tuition: full time: N/A; part time:
$790/credit hour
Room/board/expenses: N/A
College-funded aid: No
International student aid: No
Full-time enrollment: N/A
men: N/A; women: N/A;
minorities: N/A; international: N/A
Part-time enrollment: 141
men: 30%; women: 70%;
minorities: N/A; international: N/A
Average GMAT (part time): 575
TOEFL requirement: Yes
Minimum TOEFL score: 550

Indiana State University[1]

MBA Program
30 N 7th Street
Terre Haute, IN 47809
www.indstate.edu/mba/
Public
Admissions: (812) 237-2002
Email:
ISU-MBA@mail.indstate.edu
Financial aid: (800) 841-4744
Tuition: N/A
Room/board/expenses: N/A
Enrollment: N/A

Indiana University (Kelley)

1275 E. 10th Street, Suite 2010
Bloomington, IN 47405-1703
kelley.iu.edu/programs/
full-time-mba
Public
Admissions: (812) 855-8006
Email: iumba@indiana.edu
Financial aid: (812) 855-1618
Application deadline: 04/15
In-state tuition: full time: $27,601;
part time: $772/credit hour
Out-of-state tuition: full time:
$46,561
Room/board/expenses: $18,554
College-funded aid: Yes
International student aid: Yes
**Average student indebtedness at
graduation:** $70,146
Full-time enrollment: 370
men: 71%; women: 29%;
minorities: 16%; international:
36%
Part-time enrollment: 294
men: 84%; women: 16%;
minorities: 14%; international:
36%
Acceptance rate (full time): 31%

Average GMAT (full time): 670
Average GMAT (part time): 661
Average GPA (full time): 3.34
**Average age of entrants to full-
time program:** 28
**Average months of prior work
experience (full time):** 63
TOEFL requirement: Yes
Minimum TOEFL score: 600
Most popular departments:
finance, general management,
marketing, supply chain
management/logistics, other
**Mean starting base salary for 2016
full-time graduates:** $109,744
**Employment location for 2016
class:** Intl. 4%; N.E. 13%; M.A.
3%; S. 12%; M.W. 46%; S.W. 6%;
W. 15%

Indiana University-Kokomo[1]

2300 S. Washington Street
Kokomo, IN 46904-9003
www.iuk.edu/index.php
Public
Admissions: (765) 455-9275
Financial aid: N/A
Tuition: N/A
Room/board/expenses: N/A
Enrollment: N/A

Indiana University Northwest

3400 Broadway
Gary, IN 46408-1197
www.iun.edu/business/index.htm
Public
Admissions: (219) 980-6635
Email: iunbiz@iun.edu
Financial aid: (219) 980-6778
Application deadline: 08/01
In-state tuition: full time: N/A; part
time: $330/credit hour
Out-of-state tuition: full time: N/A
Room/board/expenses: N/A
College-funded aid: Yes
International student aid: No
Full-time enrollment: N/A
men: N/A; women: N/A;
minorities: N/A; international: N/A
Part-time enrollment: 63
men: 52%; women: 48%;
minorities: 44%; international:
3%
TOEFL requirement: Yes
Minimum TOEFL score: 550

Indiana University-Purdue University-Fort Wayne (Doermer)[1]

2101 E. Coliseum Boulevard
Fort Wayne, IN 46805-1499
www.ipfw.edu/mba
Public
Admissions: (260) 481-6498
Email: mba@ipfw.edu
Financial aid: (260) 481-6820
Tuition: N/A
Room/board/expenses: N/A
Enrollment: N/A

Indiana University-South Bend[1]

1700 Mishawaka Avenue
PO Box 7111
South Bend, IN 46634-7111
www.iusb.edu/buse
Public
Admissions: (574) 520-4497
Email: graduate@iusb.edu
Financial aid: N/A

Tuition: N/A
Room/board/expenses: N/A
Enrollment: N/A

Indiana University-Southeast

4201 Grant Line Road
New Albany, IN 47150
www.ius.edu/graduatebusiness
Public
Admissions: (812) 941-2364
Email: iusmba@ius.edu
Financial aid: (812) 941-2246
Application deadline: 07/20
In-state tuition: full time: N/A; part
time: $402/credit hour
Out-of-state tuition: full time: N/A
Room/board/expenses: N/A
College-funded aid: Yes
International student aid: Yes
Full-time enrollment: N/A
men: N/A; women: N/A;
minorities: N/A; international: N/A
Part-time enrollment: 182
men: 66%; women: 34%;
minorities: 12%; international: 1%
Average GMAT (part time): 525
TOEFL requirement: Yes
Minimum TOEFL score: 550

Purdue University-West Lafayette (Krannert)

100 S. Grant Street
Rawls Hall, Room 2020
West Lafayette, IN 47907-2076
www.krannert.purdue.edu/
masters/home.php
Public
Admissions: (765) 494-0773
Email:
krannertmasters@purdue.edu
Financial aid: (765) 494-0998
Application deadline: 05/01
In-state tuition: full time: $22,418;
part time: $24,870
Out-of-state tuition: full time:
$42,184
Room/board/expenses: $13,030
College-funded aid: Yes
International student aid: Yes
**Average student indebtedness at
graduation:** $43,355
Full-time enrollment: 147
men: 72%; women: 28%;
minorities: 16%; international:
40%
Part-time enrollment: 85
men: 74%; women: 26%;
minorities: 18%; international: 7%
Acceptance rate (full time): 36%
Average GMAT (full time): 636
Average GMAT (part time): 609
Average GPA (full time): 3.39
**Average age of entrants to full-
time program:** 26
**Average months of prior work
experience (full time):** 50
TOEFL requirement: Yes
Minimum TOEFL score: 600
Most popular departments:
finance, human resources
management, marketing,
production/operations
management, supply chain
management/logistics
**Mean starting base salary for 2016
full-time graduates:** $90,884
**Employment location for 2016
class:** Intl. 6%; N.E. 9%; M.A. 4%;
S. 13%; M.W. 36%; S.W. 11%;
W. 21%

University of Notre Dame (Mendoza)

204 Mendoza College
of Business
Notre Dame, IN 46556
mendoza.nd.edu/programs/
mba-programs/two-year-mba/
Private
Admissions: (574) 631-8488
Email: mba.business@nd.edu
Financial aid: (574) 631-6436
Application deadline: 03/28
Tuition: full time: $50,976; part
time: N/A
Room/board/expenses: $20,250
College-funded aid: Yes
International student aid: Yes
**Average student indebtedness at
graduation:** $74,068
Full-time enrollment: 304
men: 74%; women: 26%;
minorities: 13%; international:
26%
Part-time enrollment: N/A
men: N/A; women: N/A;
minorities: N/A; international: N/A
Acceptance rate (full time): 41%
Average GMAT (full time): 683
Average GPA (full time): 3.37
**Average age of entrants to full-
time program:** 27
**Average months of prior work
experience (full time):** 61
TOEFL requirement: Yes
Minimum TOEFL score: 600
Most popular departments:
consulting, finance, leadership,
marketing, other
**Mean starting base salary for 2016
full-time graduates:** $103,679
**Employment location for 2016
class:** Intl. 3%; N.E. 20%; M.A.
9%; S. 4%; M.W. 42%; S.W. 9%;
W. 13%

University of Southern Indiana

8600 University Boulevard
Evansville, IN 47712
www.usi.edu/graduatestudies
Public
Admissions: (812) 465-7015
Email: graduate.studies@usi.edu
Financial aid: (812) 464-1767
Application deadline: N/A
In-state tuition: full time: $354/
credit hour; part time: $354/
credit hour
Out-of-state tuition: full time:
$695/credit hour
Room/board/expenses: $11,198
College-funded aid: Yes
International student aid: Yes
**Average student indebtedness at
graduation:** $49,887
Full-time enrollment: 150
men: 53%; women: 47%;
minorities: 14%; international:
3%
Part-time enrollment: 64
men: 55%; women: 45%;
minorities: 8%; international: 2%
Acceptance rate (full time): 97%
Average GPA (full time): 3.21
**Average age of entrants to full-
time program:** 33
TOEFL requirement: Yes
Minimum TOEFL score: 550
Most popular departments:
general management, human
resources management,
quantitative analysis/statistics
and operations research, other

Valparaiso University

Urschel Hall
1909 Chapel Drive
Valparaiso, IN 46383
www.valpo.edu/mba/
Private
Admissions: (219) 465-7952
Email: mba@valpo.edu
Financial aid: (219) 464-5015
Application deadline: 06/30
Tuition: full time: $833/credit hour; part time: $833/credit hour
Room/board/expenses: $20,756
College-funded aid: No
International student aid: No
Average student indebtedness at graduation: $27,115
Full-time enrollment: 5
men: 40%; women: 60%; minorities: 0%; international: 0%
Part-time enrollment: 57
men: 65%; women: 35%; minorities: 11%; international: 4%
Acceptance rate (full time): 56%
Average GMAT (full time): 544
Average GMAT (part time): 542
Average GPA (full time): 3.27
Average age of entrants to full-time program: 22
Average months of prior work experience (full time): 20
TOEFL requirement: Yes
Minimum TOEFL score: 575
Most popular departments: finance, general management, manufacturing and technology management, marketing, quantitative analysis/statistics and operations research

IOWA

Iowa State University

1360 Gerdin Business Building
Ames, IA 50011-1350
www.business.iastate.edu
Public
Admissions: (515) 294-8118
Email: busgrad@iastate.edu
Financial aid: N/A
Application deadline: 06/01
In-state tuition: full time: $11,404; part time: $572/credit hour
Out-of-state tuition: full time: $24,716
Room/board/expenses: N/A
College-funded aid: Yes
International student aid: Yes
Full-time enrollment: 79
men: 62%; women: 38%; minorities: 8%; international: 29%
Part-time enrollment: 63
men: 68%; women: 32%; minorities: 14%; international: 2%
Acceptance rate (full time): 60%
Average GMAT (full time): 622
Average GMAT (part time): 534
Average GPA (full time): 3.50
Average age of entrants to full-time program: 24
Average months of prior work experience (full time): 23
TOEFL requirement: Yes
Minimum TOEFL score: 600
Most popular departments: accounting, finance, marketing, supply chain management/logistics, technology
Mean starting base salary for 2016 full-time graduates: $68,179
Employment location for 2016 class: Intl. 0%; N.E. 4%; M.A. 4%; S. 7%; M.W. 75%; S.W. 4%; W. 7%

University of Iowa (Tippie)

108 John Pappajohn Business Building, Suite W160
Iowa City, IA 52242-1000
tippie.uiowa.edu/mba
Public
Admissions: (319) 335-0864
Email: iowamba@uiowa.edu
Financial aid: (319) 335-0684
Application deadline: 07/30
In-state tuition: full time: $23,234; part time: $665/credit hour
Out-of-state tuition: full time: $40,134
Room/board/expenses: $18,732
College-funded aid: Yes
International student aid: Yes
Average student indebtedness at graduation: $44,583
Full-time enrollment: 110
men: 77%; women: 23%; minorities: 12%; international: 35%
Part-time enrollment: 780
men: 67%; women: 33%; minorities: 12%; international: 4%
Acceptance rate (full time): 36%
Average GMAT (full time): 677
Average GMAT (part time): 568
Average GPA (full time): 3.26
Average age of entrants to full-time program: 27
Average months of prior work experience (full time): 52
TOEFL requirement: Yes
Minimum TOEFL score: 600
Most popular departments: finance, general management, marketing, portfolio management, quantitative analysis/statistics and operations research
Mean starting base salary for 2016 full-time graduates: $86,492
Employment location for 2016 class: Intl. N/A; N.E. 11%; M.A. 9%; S. 13%; M.W. 60%; S.W. 2%; W. 4%

University of Northern Iowa

Curris Business Building 325
Cedar Falls, IA 50614-0123
www.cba.uni.edu/mba/
Public
Admissions: (319) 273-6243
Email: mba@uni.edu
Financial aid: (319) 273-2700
Application deadline: 05/30
In-state tuition: full time: $11,463; part time: $571/credit hour
Out-of-state tuition: full time: $21,937
Room/board/expenses: $11,929
College-funded aid: Yes
International student aid: No
Full-time enrollment: N/A
men: N/A; women: N/A; minorities: N/A; international: N/A
Part-time enrollment: 55
men: 62%; women: 38%; minorities: N/A; international: N/A
Average GMAT (part time): 558
TOEFL requirement: Yes
Minimum TOEFL score: 550
Most popular departments: general management

KANSAS

Emporia State University[1]

1 Kellogg Circle
ESU Box 4039
Emporia, KS 66801-5087
emporia.edu/business/programs/mba
Public
Admissions: (800) 950-4723
Email: gradinfo@emporia.edu
Financial aid: (620) 341-5457
Tuition: N/A
Room/board/expenses: N/A
Enrollment: N/A

Kansas State University

112 Calvin Hall
Manhattan, KS 66506-0501
www.cba.ksu.edu/cba/
Public
Admissions: (785) 532-7190
Email: gradbusiness@ksu.edu
Financial aid: (785) 532-6420
Application deadline: 02/01
In-state tuition: full time: $403/credit hour; part time: $403/credit hour
Out-of-state tuition: full time: $909/credit hour
Room/board/expenses: $22,000
College-funded aid: Yes
International student aid: Yes
Full-time enrollment: 65
men: 62%; women: 38%; minorities: 26%; international: 22%
Part-time enrollment: 30
men: 43%; women: 57%; minorities: N/A; international: N/A
Acceptance rate (full time): 87%
Average GMAT (full time): 520
Average GPA (full time): 3.51
Average age of entrants to full-time program: 30
Average months of prior work experience (full time): 96
TOEFL requirement: Yes
Minimum TOEFL score: 550
Most popular departments: finance, general management, management information systems, supply chain management/logistics

Pittsburg State University (Kelce)

1701 S. Broadway
Pittsburg, KS 66762
www.pittstate.edu/business/departments-programs/mba/
Public
Admissions: (620) 235-4180
Email: jsmiller@pittstate.edu
Financial aid: (620) 235-4240
Application deadline: 07/15
In-state tuition: full time: $9,076; part time: $323/credit hour
Out-of-state tuition: full time: $19,160
Room/board/expenses: $7,734
College-funded aid: Yes
International student aid: Yes
Full-time enrollment: 71
men: 51%; women: 49%; minorities: N/A; international: N/A
Part-time enrollment: 18
men: 56%; women: 44%; minorities: N/A; international: N/A
Acceptance rate (full time): 87%
Average GMAT (full time): 470

Average GMAT (part time): 540
Average GPA (full time): 3.36
TOEFL requirement: Yes
Minimum TOEFL score: 550

University of Kansas

1654 Naismith Drive
Lawrence, KS 66045-7585
www.mba.ku.edu
Public
Admissions: (913) 897-8617
Email: bschoolmba@ku.edu
Financial aid: (785) 864-7596
Application deadline: 06/01
In-state tuition: full time: $395/credit hour; part time: $446/credit hour
Out-of-state tuition: full time: $924/credit hour
Room/board/expenses: $14,000
College-funded aid: Yes
International student aid: Yes
Full-time enrollment: 47
men: 81%; women: 19%; minorities: 28%; international: 17%
Part-time enrollment: 145
men: 72%; women: 28%; minorities: 15%; international: 3%
Acceptance rate (full time): 55%
Average GMAT (full time): 600
Average GMAT (part time): 579
Average GPA (full time): 3.33
Average age of entrants to full-time program: 27
Average months of prior work experience (full time): 34
TOEFL requirement: Yes
Minimum TOEFL score: N/A
Most popular departments: finance, general management, international business, marketing, supply chain management/logistics
Mean starting base salary for 2016 full-time graduates: $60,571
Employment location for 2016 class: Intl. 20%; N.E. 20%; M.A. 40%; S. N/A; M.W. N/A; S.W. 10%; W. 10%

Washburn University[1]

1700 S.W. College Avenue
Topeka, KS 66621
www.washburn.edu/business
Public
Admissions: N/A
Financial aid: N/A
Tuition: N/A
Room/board/expenses: N/A
Enrollment: N/A

Wichita State University (Barton)

1845 N. Fairmount
Box 48
Wichita, KS 67260-0048
www.wichita.edu/mba
Public
Admissions: (316) 978-3230
Email: grad.business@wichita.edu
Financial aid: (316) 978-3430
Application deadline: 07/01
In-state tuition: total program: $17,220 (full time); part time: $424/credit hour
Out-of-state tuition: total program: $17,220 (full time)
Room/board/expenses: N/A
College-funded aid: Yes
International student aid: Yes

Full-time enrollment: N/A
men: N/A; women: N/A; minorities: N/A; international: N/A
Part-time enrollment: 190
men: 69%; women: 31%; minorities: 14%; international: N/A
Average GMAT (part time): 529
TOEFL requirement: Yes
Minimum TOEFL score: 570
Most popular departments: economics, finance, health care administration, management information systems, other

KENTUCKY

Bellarmine University (Rubel)

2001 Newburg Road
Louisville, KY 40205-0671
www.bellarmine.edu/mba/
Private
Admissions: (502) 272-7200
Email: gradadmissions@bellarmine.edu
Financial aid: (502) 452-8124
Application deadline: rolling
Tuition: total program: $36,140 (full time); part time: $730/credit hour
Room/board/expenses: $792
College-funded aid: Yes
International student aid: Yes
Full-time enrollment: 44
men: 59%; women: 41%; minorities: 14%; international: 2%
Part-time enrollment: 35
men: 46%; women: 54%; minorities: 9%; international: 3%
Acceptance rate (full time): 100%
Average GMAT (full time): 378
Average GMAT (part time): 425
Average GPA (full time): 3.25
Average age of entrants to full-time program: 28
TOEFL requirement: Yes
Minimum TOEFL score: 550
Most popular departments: consulting, finance, health care administration, marketing, tax

Eastern Kentucky University[1]

521 Lancaster Avenue
Richmond, KY 40475
cbt.eku.edu/
Public
Admissions: (859) 622-1742
Email: graduateschool@eku.edu
Financial aid: N/A
Tuition: N/A
Room/board/expenses: N/A
Enrollment: N/A

Morehead State University[1]

Combs Building 214
Morehead, KY 40351
www.moreheadstate.edu/mba
Public
Admissions: (606) 783-2000
Email: admissions@moreheadstate.edu
Financial aid: N/A
Tuition: N/A
Room/board/expenses: N/A
Enrollment: N/A

Murray State University (Bauernfeind)[1]

109 Business Building
Murray, KY 42071
murraystate.edu/business.aspx
Public
Admissions: (270) 809-3779
Email: Msu.graduateadmissions@
murraystate.edu
Financial aid: (270) 809-2546
Tuition: N/A
Room/board/expenses: N/A
Enrollment: N/A

Northern Kentucky University[1]

Suite 401, BEP Center
Highland Heights, KY 41099
cob.nku.edu/
graduatedegrees.html
Public
Admissions: (859) 572-6336
Email: mbusiness@nku.edu
Financial aid: N/A
Tuition: N/A
Room/board/expenses: N/A
Enrollment: N/A

University of Kentucky (Gatton)

359 Gatton College of
Business and Economics
Lexington, KY 40506-0034
gatton.uky.edu
Public
Admissions: (859) 257-1306
Email: ukmba@uky.edu
Financial aid: (859) 257-3172
Application deadline: 05/11
In-state tuition: total program:
$32,000 (full time); part time:
$889/credit hour
Out-of-state tuition: total
program: $37,000 (full time)
Room/board/expenses: $13,500
College-funded aid: Yes
International student aid: Yes
Full-time enrollment: 67
men: 72%; women: 28%;
minorities: 15%; international: 7%
Part-time enrollment: 149
men: 63%; women: 37%;
minorities: 13%; international:
3%
Acceptance rate (full time): 89%
Average GMAT (full time): 604
Average GMAT (part time): 580
Average GPA (full time): 3.46
**Average age of entrants to full-
time program:** 23
**Average months of prior work
experience (full time):** 8
TOEFL requirement: Yes
Minimum TOEFL score: 550
Most popular departments:
entrepreneurship, finance,
general management, marketing,
supply chain management/
logistics
**Mean starting base salary for 2016
full-time graduates:** $56,332
**Employment location for 2016
class:** Intl. 0%; N.E. 3%; M.A.
11%; S. 63%; M.W. 20%; S.W.
0%; W. 3%

University of Louisville

Belknap Campus
Louisville, KY 40292
business.louisville.edu/uoflmba
Public
Admissions: (502) 852-7257
Email: mba@louisville.edu
Financial aid: (502) 852-5517
Application deadline: 07/01
In-state tuition: total program:
$32,202 (full time); $32,202
(part time)
Out-of-state tuition: total
program: $32,202 (full time)
Room/board/expenses: $13,000
College-funded aid: Yes
International student aid: Yes
**Average student indebtedness at
graduation:** $28,058
Full-time enrollment: 52
men: 71%; women: 29%;
minorities: 17%; international:
10%
Part-time enrollment: 173
men: 70%; women: 30%;
minorities: 9%; international: 8%
Acceptance rate (full time): 43%
Average GMAT (full time): 623
Average GMAT (part time): 546
Average GPA (full time): 3.30
**Average age of entrants to full-
time program:** 28
**Average months of prior work
experience (full time):** 60
TOEFL requirement: Yes
Minimum TOEFL score: 550
Most popular departments:
entrepreneurship, finance,
health care administration,
marketing, quantitative analysis/
statistics and operations
research
**Mean starting base salary for 2016
full-time graduates:** $57,100
**Employment location for 2016
class:** Intl. 4%; N.E. N/A; M.A.
4%; S. 93%; M.W. N/A; S.W. N/A;
W. N/A

Western Kentucky University (Ford)

434 A. Grise Hall
Bowling Green, KY 42101-1056
www.wku.edu/mba/
Public
Admissions: (270) 745-2446
Email: mba@wku.edu
Financial aid: (270) 745-2755
Application deadline: 03/15
In-state tuition: full time: $570/
credit hour; part time: N/A
Out-of-state tuition: full time:
$816/credit hour
Room/board/expenses: $8,213
College-funded aid: Yes
International student aid: No
**Average student indebtedness at
graduation:** $16,735
Full-time enrollment: 32
men: 75%; women: 25%;
minorities: 6%; international:
19%
Part-time enrollment: 48
men: 63%; women: 38%;
minorities: 2%; international:
10%
Acceptance rate (full time): 39%
Average GMAT (full time): 514
Average GMAT (part time): 523
Average GPA (full time): 3.28
**Average age of entrants to full-
time program:** 24
TOEFL requirement: Yes
Minimum TOEFL score: 550

Most popular departments:
accounting, economics, general
management

LOUISIANA

Louisiana State University-Baton Rouge (Ourso)

4000 Business Education
Complex
Baton Rouge, LA 70803
mba.lsu.edu
Public
Admissions: (225) 578-8867
Email: busmba@lsu.edu
Financial aid: (225) 578-3103
Application deadline: 05/15
In-state tuition: total program:
$33,019 (full time); $52,979
(part time)
Out-of-state tuition: total
program: $68,903 (full time)
Room/board/expenses: $20,000
College-funded aid: Yes
International student aid: Yes
**Average student indebtedness at
graduation:** $17,900
Full-time enrollment: 102
men: 57%; women: 43%;
minorities: 13%; international:
18%
Part-time enrollment: 57
men: 68%; women: 32%;
minorities: 21%; international:
0%
Acceptance rate (full time): 55%
Average GMAT (full time): 649
Average GMAT (part time): 576
Average GPA (full time): 3.40
**Average age of entrants to full-
time program:** 24
**Average months of prior work
experience (full time):** 24
TOEFL requirement: Yes
Minimum TOEFL score: 550
Most popular departments:
entrepreneurship, human
resources management,
management information
systems, supply chain
management/logistics,
quantitative analysis/statistics
and operations research
**Mean starting base salary for 2016
full-time graduates:** $65,152
**Employment location for 2016
class:** Intl. 0%; N.E. 6%; M.A. 6%;
S. 47%; M.W. 3%; S.W. 38%;
W. 0%

Louisiana State University-Shreveport[1]

1 University Place
Shreveport, LA 71115
www.lsus.edu/ba/mba
Public
Admissions: (318) 797-5213
Email: bill.bigler@lsus.edu
Financial aid: (318) 797-5363
Tuition: N/A
Room/board/expenses: N/A
Enrollment: N/A

Louisiana Tech University

PO Box 10318
Ruston, LA 71272
www.latech.edu/graduate_school
Public
Admissions: (318) 257-2924
Email: gschool@latech.edu

Financial aid: (318) 257-2641
Application deadline: 08/01
In-state tuition: full time: $6,439;
part time: $5,925
Out-of-state tuition: full time:
$18,057
Room/board/expenses: $10,695
College-funded aid: Yes
International student aid: Yes
**Average student indebtedness at
graduation:** $20,012
Full-time enrollment: 81
men: 58%; women: 42%;
minorities: 12%; international:
25%
Part-time enrollment: 20
men: 70%; women: 30%;
minorities: 5%; international:
15%
Acceptance rate (full time): 65%
Average GMAT (full time): 545
Average GPA (full time): 3.42
TOEFL requirement: Yes
Minimum TOEFL score: 550
Most popular departments:
accounting, finance, marketing,
management information
systems

Loyola University New Orleans (Butt)

6363 St. Charles Avenue
Campus Box 15
New Orleans, LA 70118
www.business.loyno.edu
Private
Admissions: (504) 864-7953
Email: mba@loyno.edu
Financial aid: (504) 865-3231
Application deadline: 06/30
Tuition: full time: $1,005/credit
hour; part time: $1,005/credit
hour
Room/board/expenses: N/A
College-funded aid: Yes
International student aid: Yes
Full-time enrollment: 24
men: 46%; women: 54%;
minorities: 42%; international:
4%
Part-time enrollment: 59
men: 46%; women: 54%;
minorities: 29%; international:
3%
Acceptance rate (full time): 95%
Average GMAT (full time): 480
Average GMAT (part time): 497
**Average age of entrants to full-
time program:** 28
TOEFL requirement: Yes
Minimum TOEFL score: 580
Most popular departments:
entrepreneurship, finance,
marketing, production/
operations management,
quantitative analysis/statistics
and operations research

McNeese State University[1]

PO Box 91660
Lake Charles, LA 70609
www.mcneese.edu/colleges/bus
Public
Admissions: (337) 475-5576
Email: mba@mcneese.edu
Financial aid: (337) 475-5065
Tuition: N/A
Room/board/expenses: N/A
Enrollment: N/A

Nicholls State University[1]

PO Box 2015
Thibodaux, LA 70310
www.nicholls.edu/business/
Public
Admissions: (985) 448-4507
Email: becky.leblanc-durocher@
nicholls.edu
Financial aid: (985) 448-4048
Tuition: N/A
Room/board/expenses: N/A
Enrollment: N/A

Southeastern Louisiana University

SLU 10735
Hammond, LA 70402
www.selu.edu/acad_research/
programs/grad_bus
Public
Admissions: (985) 549-5637
Email: admissions@selu.edu
Financial aid: (985) 549-2244
Application deadline: 07/15
In-state tuition: full time: $8,369;
part time: $465/credit hour
Out-of-state tuition: full time:
$20,846
Room/board/expenses: $12,802
College-funded aid: Yes
International student aid: No
Full-time enrollment: 69
men: 54%; women: 46%;
minorities: 16%; international:
14%
Part-time enrollment: 10
men: 60%; women: 40%;
minorities: 30%; international:
10%
Acceptance rate (full time): 100%
Average GMAT (full time): 460
Average GPA (full time): 3.90
**Average age of entrants to full-
time program:** 24
TOEFL requirement: Yes
Minimum TOEFL score: 500
Most popular departments:
general management

Southern University and A&M College[1]

PO Box 9723
Baton Rouge, LA 70813
www.subr.edu/index.cfm/
page/121
Public
Admissions: (225) 771-5390
Email: gradschool@subr.edu
Financial aid: N/A
Tuition: N/A
Room/board/expenses: N/A
Enrollment: N/A

Tulane University (Freeman)

7 McAlister Drive
New Orleans, LA 70118-5669
freeman.tulane.edu
Private
Admissions: (504) 865-5410
Email: freeman.admissions@
tulane.edu
Financial aid: (504) 865-5410
Application deadline: 05/01
Tuition: full time: $54,689; part
time: $1,638/credit hour
Room/board/expenses: $19,053
College-funded aid: Yes
International student aid: Yes

Full-time enrollment: 88
men: 63%; women: 38%;
minorities: 14%; international:
18%
Part-time enrollment: 132
men: 53%; women: 47%;
minorities: 23%; international:
5%
Acceptance rate (full time): 63%
Average GMAT (full time): 651
Average GPA (full time): 3.24
Average age of entrants to full-
time program: 24
Average months of prior work
experience (full time): 70
TOEFL requirement: Yes
Minimum TOEFL score: N/A
Most popular departments:
entrepreneurship, finance,
general management,
international business, other
Mean starting base salary for 2016
full-time graduates: $74,163
Employment location for 2016
class: Intl. 4%; N.E. 4%; M.A.
4%; S. 67%; M.W. 8%; S.W. 8%;
W. 4%

University of
Louisiana-Lafayette
(Moody)

USL Box 44568
Lafayette, LA 70504-4568
gradschool.louisiana.edu/
Public
Admissions: (337) 482-0905
Email: gradschool@louisiana.edu
Financial aid: (337) 482-6506
Application deadline: 06/30
In-state tuition: full time: $9,450;
part time: $6,518
Out-of-state tuition: full time:
$23,178
Room/board/expenses: $10,300
College-funded aid: Yes
International student aid: Yes
Full-time enrollment: N/A
men: N/A; women: N/A;
minorities: N/A; international: N/A
Part-time enrollment: 170
men: 43%; women: 57%;
minorities: 14%; international:
11%
Average GMAT (part time): 440
TOEFL requirement: Yes
Minimum TOEFL score: N/A
Most popular departments:
accounting, finance, health care
administration, international
business, marketing

University of
Louisiana-Monroe[1]

700 University Avenue
Monroe, LA 71209
www.ulm.edu/cbss/
Public
Admissions: N/A
Financial aid: N/A
Tuition: N/A
Room/board/expenses: N/A
Enrollment: N/A

University of
New Orleans[1]

2000 Lakeshore Drive
New Orleans, LA 70148
www.uno.edu/admissions/
contact.aspx
Public
Admissions: (504) 280-6595
Email: pec@uno.edu
Financial aid: (504) 280-6603

Tuition: N/A
Room/board/expenses: N/A
Enrollment: N/A

MAINE

University of Maine[1]

Donald P. Corbett Business
Building
Orono, ME 04469-5723
www.umaine.edu/business/mba
Public
Admissions: (207) 581-1971
Email: mba@maine.edu
Financial aid: (207) 581-1324
Tuition: N/A
Room/board/expenses: N/A
Enrollment: N/A

University of
Southern Maine

PO Box 9300
Portland, ME 04104
www.usm.maine.edu/sb
Public
Admissions: (207) 780-4184
Email: mba@usm.maine.edu
Financial aid: (207) 780-5250
Application deadline: N/A
In-state tuition: full time: $380/
credit hour; part time: $380/
credit hour
Out-of-state tuition: full time:
$1,026/credit hour
Room/board/expenses: $21,250
College-funded aid: Yes
International student aid: Yes
Full-time enrollment: N/A
men: N/A; women: N/A;
minorities: N/A; international: N/A
Part-time enrollment: 65
men: 52%; women: 48%;
minorities: 6%; international: N/A
TOEFL requirement: Yes
Minimum TOEFL score: 550

MARYLAND

Frostburg State
University[1]

125 Guild Center
101 Braddock Road
Frostburg, MD 21532-2303
www.frostburg.edu/colleges/
cob/mba/
Public
Admissions: (301) 687-7053
Email:
gradservices@frostburg.edu
Financial aid: (301) 687-4301
Tuition: N/A
Room/board/expenses: N/A
Enrollment: N/A

Loyola University
Maryland (Sellinger)

4501 N. Charles Street
Baltimore, MD 21210-2699
www.loyola.edu/sellinger/
Private
Admissions: (410) 617-5020
Email: graduate@loyola.edu
Financial aid: (410) 617-2576
Application deadline: 08/20
Tuition: total program: $58,000
(full time); part time: $925/credit
hour
Room/board/expenses: N/A
College-funded aid: Yes
International student aid: Yes

Full-time enrollment: 20
men: 50%; women: 50%;
minorities: 45%; international:
5%
Part-time enrollment: 324
men: 61%; women: 39%;
minorities: 14%; international: 1%
Acceptance rate (full time): 84%
Average GMAT (full time): 587
Average GMAT (part time): 558
Average GPA (full time): 3.25
Average age of entrants to full-
time program: 24
TOEFL requirement: Yes
Minimum TOEFL score: 550

Morgan State
University (Graves)[1]

1700 E. Cold Spring Lane
Baltimore, MD 21251
www.morgan.edu/sbm
Public
Admissions: (443) 885-3185
Financial aid: N/A
Tuition: N/A
Room/board/expenses: N/A
Enrollment: N/A

Salisbury
University (Perdue)

1101 Camden Avenue
Salisbury, MD 21801-6860
www.salisbury.edu/Schools/
perdue/welcome.html
Public
Admissions: (410) 543-6161
Email: admissions@salisbury.edu
Financial aid: N/A
Application deadline: 03/01
In-state tuition: full time: $381/
credit hour; part time: $381/
credit hour
Out-of-state tuition: full time:
$670/credit hour
Room/board/expenses: N/A
College-funded aid: Yes
International student aid: Yes
Full-time enrollment: 38
men: 61%; women: 39%;
minorities: 16%; international:
8%
Part-time enrollment: 25
men: 48%; women: 52%;
minorities: 8%; international: 8%
Acceptance rate (full time): 64%
Average age of entrants to full-
time program: 27
TOEFL requirement: Yes
Minimum TOEFL score: 550

University of
Baltimore

11 W. Mt. Royal Avenue
Baltimore, MD 21201
www.ubalt.edu/mba
Private
Admissions: (410) 837-6565
Email: gradadmission@ubalt.edu
Financial aid: (410) 837-4763
Application deadline: 08/17
Tuition: full time: $824/credit
hour; part time: $824/credit hour
Room/board/expenses: $18,000
College-funded aid: Yes
International student aid: Yes
Full-time enrollment: N/A
men: N/A; women: N/A;
minorities: N/A; international: N/A
Part-time enrollment: 462
men: 49%; women: 51%;
minorities: 35%; international:
8%
Average GMAT (part time): 487

TOEFL requirement: Yes
Minimum TOEFL score: 550
Most popular departments:
general management, leadership,
marketing, other

University of
Maryland-
College Park (Smith)

2308 Van Munching Hall
College Park, MD 20742
www.rhsmith.umd.edu
Public
Admissions: (301) 405-0202
Email:
mba_info@rhsmith.umd.edu
Financial aid: (301) 405-2301
Application deadline: 03/01
In-state tuition: full time: $46,954;
part time: $15,068
Out-of-state tuition: full time:
$56,134
Room/board/expenses: N/A
College-funded aid: Yes
International student aid: Yes
Full-time enrollment: 197
men: 63%; women: 37%;
minorities: 14%; international:
37%
Part-time enrollment: 567
men: 61%; women: 39%;
minorities: 30%; international:
9%
Acceptance rate (full time): 37%
Average GMAT (full time): 657
Average GMAT (part time): 600
Average GPA (full time): 3.28
Average age of entrants to full-
time program: 29
Average months of prior work
experience (full time): 64
TOEFL requirement: Yes
Minimum TOEFL score: 600
Most popular departments:
consulting, entrepreneurship,
finance, general management,
marketing
Mean starting base salary for 2016
full-time graduates: $96,647

MASSACHUSETTS

Babson College (Olin)

231 Forest Street
Babson Park, MA 02457-0310
www.babson.edu/graduate
Private
Admissions: (781) 239-4317
Email:
gradadmissions@babson.edu
Financial aid: (781) 239-4219
Application deadline: rolling
Tuition: total program: $105,118
(full time); part time: $1,660/
credit hour
Room/board/expenses: $52,818
College-funded aid: Yes
International student aid: Yes
Average student indebtedness at
graduation: $68,328
Full-time enrollment: 319
men: 70%; women: 30%;
minorities: 8%; international:
68%
Part-time enrollment: 258
men: 67%; women: 33%;
minorities: 13%; international:
9%
Acceptance rate (full time): 70%
Average GMAT (full time): 632
Average GMAT (part time): 562
Average GPA (full time): 3.26
Average age of entrants to full-
time program: 28

Average months of prior work
experience (full time): 65
TOEFL requirement: Yes
Minimum TOEFL score: N/A
Most popular departments:
entrepreneurship, finance,
marketing, technology, other
Mean starting base salary for 2016
full-time graduates: $77,510
Employment location for 2016
class: Intl. 29%; N.E. 56%; M.A.
1%; S. 10%; M.W. 0%; S.W. 0%;
W. 4%

Bentley University

175 Forest Street
Waltham, MA 02452-4705
www.bentley.edu/graduate/
admission-financial-aid
Private
Admissions: (781) 891-2108
Email:
bentleygraduateadmissions@
bentley.edu
Financial aid: (781) 891-3441
Application deadline: 03/15
Tuition: full time: $39,445; part
time: $1,408/credit hour
Room/board/expenses: $20,160
College-funded aid: Yes
International student aid: Yes
Average student indebtedness at
graduation: $46,407
Full-time enrollment: 134
men: 55%; women: 45%;
minorities: 11%; international:
63%
Part-time enrollment: 212
men: 56%; women: 44%;
minorities: 21%; international: 2%
Acceptance rate (full time): 68%
Average age of entrants to full-
time program: 27
TOEFL requirement: Yes
Minimum TOEFL score: 600
Most popular departments:
accounting, finance, marketing,
management information
systems, quantitative analysis/
statistics and operations
research

Boston College
(Carroll)

140 Commonwealth Avenue
Fulton Hall 320
Chestnut Hill, MA 02467
www.bc.edu/mba
Private
Admissions: (617) 552-3920
Email: bcmba@bc.edu
Financial aid: (800) 294-0294
Application deadline: 04/15
Tuition: full time: $47,450; part
time: $1,612/credit hour
Room/board/expenses: $22,335
College-funded aid: Yes
International student aid: Yes
Average student indebtedness at
graduation: $63,081
Full-time enrollment: 174
men: 66%; women: 34%;
minorities: 13%; international:
34%
Part-time enrollment: 378
men: 63%; women: 37%;
minorities: 19%; international:
3%
Acceptance rate (full time): 38%
Average GMAT (full time): 667
Average GMAT (part time): 575
Average GPA (full time): 3.20
Average age of entrants to full-
time program: 28

Average months of prior work experience (full time): 55
TOEFL requirement: Yes
Minimum TOEFL score: 600
Most popular departments: accounting, finance, general management, marketing, quantitative analysis/statistics and operations research
Mean starting base salary for 2016 full-time graduates: $98,088
Employment location for 2016 class: Intl. 3%; N.E. 77%; M.A. 6%; S. 6%; M.W. 2%; S.W. 2%; W. 5%

Boston University (Questrom)

595 Commonwealth Avenue
Boston, MA 02215-1704
www.bu.edu/questrom
Private
Admissions: (617) 353-2670
Email: mba@bu.edu
Financial aid: (617) 353-2670
Application deadline: 03/22
Tuition: full time: $49,900; part time: $1,556/credit hour
Room/board/expenses: $18,794
College-funded aid: Yes
International student aid: Yes
Full-time enrollment: 303
men: 59%; women: 41%; minorities: 35%; international: 32%
Part-time enrollment: 643
men: 56%; women: 44%; minorities: 22%; international: 4%
Acceptance rate (full time): 37%
Average GMAT (full time): 682
Average GMAT (part time): 596
Average GPA (full time): 3.30
Average age of entrants to full-time program: 27
Average months of prior work experience (full time): 54
TOEFL requirement: Yes
Minimum TOEFL score: 600
Most popular departments: finance, health care administration, marketing, not-for-profit management, other
Mean starting base salary for 2016 full-time graduates: $100,820
Employment location for 2016 class: Intl. 7%; N.E. 71%; M.A. 2%; S. 5%; M.W. 2%; S.W. 1%; W. 11%

Brandeis University[1]

415 South Street
Waltham, MA 02454-9110
www.brandeis.edu/global
Private
Admissions: (781) 736-4829
Email: admissions@lembergbrandeis.edu
Financial aid: N/A
Tuition: N/A
Room/board/expenses: N/A
Enrollment: N/A

Clark University

950 Main Street
Worcester, MA 01610
www.clarku.edu/gsom
Private
Admissions: (508) 793-7559
Email: ebernstein@clarku.edu
Financial aid: (508) 793-7559
Application deadline: rolling
Tuition: total program: $57,037 (full time); $57,037 (part time)

Room/board/expenses: $12,000
College-funded aid: Yes
International student aid: Yes
Full-time enrollment: 102
men: 52%; women: 48%; minorities: 9%; international: 50%
Part-time enrollment: 104
men: 52%; women: 48%; minorities: 11%; international: 1%
Acceptance rate (full time): 73%
Average GMAT (full time): 506
Average GMAT (part time): 530
Average GPA (full time): 3.49
Average age of entrants to full-time program: 25
Average months of prior work experience (full time): 49
TOEFL requirement: Yes
Minimum TOEFL score: N/A
Mean starting base salary for 2016 full-time graduates: $53,466

Harvard University

Soldiers Field
Boston, MA 02163
www.hbs.edu
Private
Admissions: (617) 495-6128
Email: admissions@hbs.edu
Financial aid: (617) 495-6640
Application deadline: 04/03
Tuition: full time: $75,353; part time: N/A
Room/board/expenses: $26,747
College-funded aid: Yes
International student aid: Yes
Average student indebtedness at graduation: $86,375
Full-time enrollment: 1,871
men: 58%; women: 42%; minorities: N/A; international: N/A
Part-time enrollment: N/A
men: N/A; women: N/A; minorities: N/A; international: N/A
Acceptance rate (full time): 11%
Average GMAT (full time): 729
Average GPA (full time): 3.67
Average age of entrants to full-time program: 27
Average months of prior work experience (full time): 53
TOEFL requirement: Yes
Minimum TOEFL score: N/A
Mean starting base salary for 2016 full-time graduates: $134,071
Employment location for 2016 class: Intl. 14%; N.E. 43%; M.A. 5%; S. 3%; M.W. 6%; S.W. 5%; W. 24%

Massachusetts Institute of Technology (Sloan)

100 Main Street
Building E62
Cambridge, MA 02142
mitsloan.mit.edu/mba
Private
Admissions: (617) 258-5434
Email: mbaadmissions@sloan.mit.edu
Financial aid: (617) 253-4971
Application deadline: 04/10
Tuition: full time: $68,250; part time: N/A
Room/board/expenses: $33,798
College-funded aid: Yes
International student aid: Yes
Average student indebtedness at graduation: $121,822
Full-time enrollment: 809
men: 59%; women: 41%; minorities: 18%; international: 39%

Part-time enrollment: N/A
men: N/A; women: N/A; minorities: N/A; international: N/A
Acceptance rate (full time): 12%
Average GMAT (full time): 724
Average GPA (full time): 3.58
Average age of entrants to full-time program: 28
Average months of prior work experience (full time): 58
TOEFL requirement: No
Minimum TOEFL score: N/A
Most popular departments: entrepreneurship, finance, international business, manufacturing and technology management, production/operations management
Mean starting base salary for 2016 full-time graduates: $125,036
Employment location for 2016 class: Intl. 10%; N.E. 42%; M.A. 3%; S. 4%; M.W. 3%; S.W. 4%; W. 34%

Northeastern University

360 Huntington Avenue
350 Dodge Hall
Boston, MA 02115
www.mba.northeastern.edu
Private
Admissions: (617) 373-5992
Email: gradbusiness@neu.edu
Financial aid: (617) 373-5899
Application deadline: 04/18
Tuition: full time: $1,513/credit hour; part time: $1,513/credit hour
Room/board/expenses: $25,350
College-funded aid: Yes
International student aid: Yes
Full-time enrollment: 169
men: 61%; women: 39%; minorities: 15%; international: 38%
Part-time enrollment: 345
men: 57%; women: 43%; minorities: 20%; international: 3%
Acceptance rate (full time): 27%
Average GMAT (full time): 632
Average GMAT (part time): 573
Average GPA (full time): 3.28
Average age of entrants to full-time program: 26
Average months of prior work experience (full time): 39
TOEFL requirement: Yes
Minimum TOEFL score: 600
Most popular departments: entrepreneurship, finance, international business, marketing, supply chain management/logistics
Mean starting base salary for 2016 full-time graduates: $81,087
Employment location for 2016 class: Intl. N/A; N.E. 88%; M.A. 4%; S. 4%; M.W. N/A; S.W. 2%; W. 2%

Simmons College[1]

300 The Fenway
Boston, MA 02115
www.simmons.edu/som
Private
Admissions: N/A
Financial aid: N/A
Tuition: N/A
Room/board/expenses: N/A
Enrollment: N/A

Suffolk University (Sawyer)

8 Ashburton Place
Boston, MA 02108
www.suffolk.edu/business
Private
Admissions: (617) 573-8302
Email: grad.admission@suffolk.edu
Financial aid: (617) 573-8470
Application deadline: 03/15
Tuition: full time: $41,542; part time: $1,383/credit hour
Room/board/expenses: $20,400
College-funded aid: Yes
International student aid: Yes
Average student indebtedness at graduation: $67,408
Full-time enrollment: 119
men: 47%; women: 53%; minorities: 14%; international: 34%
Part-time enrollment: 268
men: 48%; women: 52%; minorities: 23%; international: 1%
Acceptance rate (full time): 59%
Average GMAT (full time): 486
Average GMAT (part time): 456
Average GPA (full time): 3.33
Average age of entrants to full-time program: 26
Average months of prior work experience (full time): 31
TOEFL requirement: Yes
Minimum TOEFL score: 550
Most popular departments: accounting, finance, marketing, tax
Mean starting base salary for 2016 full-time graduates: $80,000

University of Massachusetts-Amherst (Isenberg)

121 Presidents Drive
Amherst, MA 01003
www.isenberg.umass.edu/programs/masters/mba
Public
Admissions: (413) 545-5608
Email: mba@isenberg.umass.edu
Financial aid: (413) 577-0555
Application deadline: 04/01
In-state tuition: full time: $13,524; part time: $825/credit hour
Out-of-state tuition: full time: $29,644
Room/board/expenses: $13,904
College-funded aid: Yes
International student aid: Yes
Average student indebtedness at graduation: $30,464
Full-time enrollment: 45
men: 53%; women: 47%; minorities: 16%; international: 22%
Part-time enrollment: 1,290
men: 70%; women: 30%; minorities: 23%; international: 6%
Acceptance rate (full time): 31%
Average GMAT (full time): 639
Average GMAT (part time): 588
Average GPA (full time): 3.50
Average age of entrants to full-time program: 29
Average months of prior work experience (full time): 94
TOEFL requirement: Yes
Minimum TOEFL score: 600
Most popular departments: entrepreneurship, finance, health care administration, marketing, sports business

Mean starting base salary for 2016 full-time graduates: $67,884
Employment location for 2016 class: Intl. 5%; N.E. 74%; M.A. 11%; S. 5%; M.W. 0%; S.W. 5%; W. 0%

University of Massachusetts-Boston

100 Morrissey Boulevard
Boston, MA 02125-3393
www.umb.edu/cmgrad
Public
Admissions: (617) 287-7720
Email: gradcm@umb.edu
Financial aid: (617) 287-6300
Application deadline: 06/01
In-state tuition: full time: $717/credit hour; part time: $717/credit hour
Out-of-state tuition: full time: $1,386/credit hour
Room/board/expenses: N/A
College-funded aid: Yes
International student aid: Yes
Full-time enrollment: 268
men: 53%; women: 47%; minorities: 15%; international: 55%
Part-time enrollment: 239
men: 56%; women: 44%; minorities: 25%; international: 8%
Acceptance rate (full time): 56%
Average GMAT (full time): 522
Average GMAT (part time): 535
Average GPA (full time): 3.25
Average age of entrants to full-time program: 27
Average months of prior work experience (full time): 22
TOEFL requirement: Yes
Minimum TOEFL score: 600
Most popular departments: accounting, finance, general management, marketing, management information systems
Mean starting base salary for 2016 full-time graduates: $63,333

University of Massachusetts-Dartmouth

285 Old Westport Road
North Dartmouth, MA 02747
www.umassd.edu/charlton/programs/graduate
Public
Admissions: (508) 999-8604
Email: graduate@umassd.edu
Financial aid: (508) 999-8643
Application deadline: 07/01
In-state tuition: full time: $15,399; part time: $625/credit hour
Out-of-state tuition: full time: $27,473
Room/board/expenses: $15,324
College-funded aid: Yes
International student aid: Yes
Average student indebtedness at graduation: $31,824
Full-time enrollment: 261
men: 54%; women: 46%; minorities: 15%; international: 44%
Part-time enrollment: 50
men: 42%; women: 58%; minorities: 12%; international: 2%
Acceptance rate (full time): 87%
Average GMAT (full time): 466
Average GPA (full time): 3.08

Average age of entrants to full-time program: 30
TOEFL requirement: Yes
Minimum TOEFL score: 550
Most popular departments: finance, general management, marketing, supply chain management/logistics, technology
Mean starting base salary for 2016 full-time graduates: $40,800
Employment location for 2016 class: Intl. N/A; N.E. 100%; M.A. N/A; S. N/A; M.W. N/A; S.W. N/A; W. N/A

University of Massachusetts-Lowell
1 University Avenue
Lowell, MA 01854
www.uml.edu/grad
Public
Admissions: (978) 934-2390
Email: graduate_admissions@uml.edu
Financial aid: (978) 934-4220
Application deadline: rolling
In-state tuition: full time: $794/credit hour; part time: $794/credit hour
Out-of-state tuition: full time: $1,436/credit hour
Room/board/expenses: $18,200
College-funded aid: Yes
International student aid: Yes
Average student indebtedness at graduation: $32,268
Full-time enrollment: 78
men: 60%; women: 40%; minorities: 22%; international: 42%
Part-time enrollment: 644
men: 66%; women: 34%; minorities: 20%; international: 5%
Acceptance rate (full time): 91%
Average GMAT (full time): 523
Average GMAT (part time): 513
Average GPA (full time): 3.18
Average age of entrants to full-time program: 27
Average months of prior work experience (full time): 48
TOEFL requirement: Yes
Minimum TOEFL score: 600
Most popular departments: accounting, finance, general management, marketing, management information systems

Western New England University
1215 Wilbraham Road
Springfield, MA 01119-2684
www1.wne.edu/business/
Private
Admissions: (800) 325-1122
Email: study@wne.edu
Financial aid: (413) 796-2080
Application deadline: rolling
Tuition: full time: N/A; part time: $804/credit hour
Room/board/expenses: N/A
College-funded aid: No
International student aid: No
Full-time enrollment: N/A
men: N/A; women: N/A; minorities: N/A; international: N/A
Part-time enrollment: 134
men: 57%; women: 43%; minorities: 10%; international: 3%

Average GMAT (part time): 500
TOEFL requirement: Yes
Minimum TOEFL score: N/A
Most popular departments: accounting, general management, leadership

Worcester Polytechnic Institute
100 Institute Road
Worcester, MA 01609
business.wpi.edu
Private
Admissions: (508) 831-6345
Email: business@wpi.edu
Financial aid: (508) 831-5469
Application deadline: rolling
Tuition: full time: $1,408/credit hour; part time: $1,408/credit hour
Room/board/expenses: $23,707
College-funded aid: Yes
International student aid: Yes
Full-time enrollment: 179
men: 42%; women: 58%; minorities: 2%; international: 92%
Part-time enrollment: 221
men: 59%; women: 41%; minorities: 13%; international: 23%
Acceptance rate (full time): 60%
Average GMAT (full time): 621
Average GMAT (part time): 590
Average age of entrants to full-time program: 25
Average months of prior work experience (full time): 2
TOEFL requirement: Yes
Minimum TOEFL score: 577
Most popular departments: manufacturing and technology management, marketing, management information systems, production/operations management, technology

MICHIGAN

Central Michigan University[1]
252 ABSC-Grawn Hall
Mount Pleasant, MI 48859
www.cmich.edu/colleges/cba/Pages/default.aspx
Public
Admissions: (989) 774-4723
Email: grad@cmich.edu
Financial aid: N/A
Tuition: N/A
Room/board/expenses: N/A
Enrollment: N/A

Eastern Michigan University
404 Gary M. Owen Building
Ypsilanti, MI 48197
www.cob.emich.edu
Public
Admissions: (734) 487-4444
Email: cob.graduate@emich.edu
Financial aid: (734) 487-0455
Application deadline: 05/15
In-state tuition: full time: $630/credit hour; part time: $630/credit hour
Out-of-state tuition: full time: $1,160/credit hour
Room/board/expenses: $13,100
College-funded aid: Yes
International student aid: Yes
Average student indebtedness at graduation: $31,900

Full-time enrollment: 167
men: 49%; women: 51%; minorities: 34%; international: 25%
Part-time enrollment: 280
men: 43%; women: 57%; minorities: 24%; international: 8%
Average GMAT (part time): 507
TOEFL requirement: Yes
Minimum TOEFL score: 550
Most popular departments: accounting, finance, general management, management information systems, supply chain management/logistics

Grand Valley State University (Seidman)
50 Front Avenue SW
Grand Rapids, MI 49504-6424
www.gvsu.edu/Seidman
Public
Admissions: (616) 331-7400
Email: go2gvmba@gvsu.edu
Financial aid: (616) 331-3234
Application deadline: rolling
In-state tuition: full time: $646/credit hour; part time: $646/credit hour
Out-of-state tuition: full time: $646/credit hour
Room/board/expenses: $12,490
College-funded aid: Yes
International student aid: Yes
Full-time enrollment: N/A
men: N/A; women: N/A; minorities: N/A; international: N/A
Part-time enrollment: 310
men: 62%; women: 38%; minorities: 5%; international: 4%
Average GMAT (part time): 540
TOEFL requirement: Yes
Minimum TOEFL score: N/A
Most popular departments: accounting, finance, health care administration, international business, manufacturing and technology management

Michigan State University (Broad)
Eppley Center
645 N. Shaw Lane, Room 211
East Lansing, MI 48824-1121
www.mba.msu.edu
Public
Admissions: (517) 355-7604
Email: mba@msu.edu
Financial aid: (517) 355-7604
Application deadline: rolling
In-state tuition: full time: $29,441; part time: N/A
Out-of-state tuition: full time: $46,701
Room/board/expenses: $21,016
College-funded aid: Yes
International student aid: Yes
Average student indebtedness at graduation: $55,666
Full-time enrollment: 144
men: 61%; women: 39%; minorities: 13%; international: 43%
Part-time enrollment: N/A
men: N/A; women: N/A; minorities: N/A; international: N/A
Acceptance rate (full time): 33%
Average GMAT (full time): 670
Average GPA (full time): 3.30
Average age of entrants to full-time program: 28
Average months of prior work experience (full time): 50

TOEFL requirement: Yes
Minimum TOEFL score: N/A
Most popular departments: finance, general management, human resources management, marketing, supply chain management/logistics
Mean starting base salary for 2016 full-time graduates: $103,306
Employment location for 2016 class: Intl. 5%; N.E. 6%; M.A. 3%; S. 9%; M.W. 50%; S.W. 8%; W. 19%

Michigan Technological University
1400 Townsend Drive
Houghton, MI 49931-1295
www.mtu.edu/business/graduate/techmba/
Public
Admissions: (906) 487-3055
Email: techmba@mtu.edu
Financial aid: (906) 487-3055
Application deadline: 07/01
In-state tuition: full time: $905/credit hour; part time: $905/credit hour
Out-of-state tuition: full time: $905/credit hour
Room/board/expenses: $14,355
College-funded aid: Yes
International student aid: Yes
Full-time enrollment: 28
men: 50%; women: 50%; minorities: 11%; international: 18%
Part-time enrollment: N/A
men: N/A; women: N/A; minorities: N/A; international: N/A
Acceptance rate (full time): 23%
Average GMAT (full time): 503
Average GPA (full time): 3.05
Average age of entrants to full-time program: 28
Average months of prior work experience (full time): 53
TOEFL requirement: Yes
Minimum TOEFL score: 590
Most popular departments: entrepreneurship, manufacturing and technology management, technology

Northern Michigan University[1]
1401 Presque Isle Avenue
Marquette, MI 49855
www.nmu.edu/graduatestudies
Public
Admissions: (906) 227-2300
Email: gradapp@nmu.edu
Financial aid: (906) 227-2327
Tuition: N/A
Room/board/expenses: N/A
Enrollment: N/A

Oakland University
238 Elliott Hall
275 Varner Drive
Rochester, MI 48309-4493
www.oakland.edu/business/grad
Public
Admissions: (248) 370-3287
Email: OUGradBusiness@oakland.edu
Financial aid: (248) 370-2550
Application deadline: 07/15
In-state tuition: full time: N/A; part time: $681/credit hour
Out-of-state tuition: full time: N/A
Room/board/expenses: N/A
College-funded aid: Yes

International student aid: Yes
Full-time enrollment: N/A
men: N/A; women: N/A; minorities: N/A; international: N/A
Part-time enrollment: 294
men: 63%; women: 37%; minorities: 12%; international: 12%
Average GMAT (part time): 505
TOEFL requirement: Yes
Minimum TOEFL score: 550
Most popular departments: finance, human resources management, international business, marketing, management information systems

Saginaw Valley State University
7400 Bay Road
University Center, MI 48710
www.svsu.edu/mba/
Public
Admissions: (989) 964-6096
Email: gradadm@svsu.edu
Financial aid: (989) 964-4103
Application deadline: rolling
In-state tuition: full time: N/A; part time: $536/credit hour
Out-of-state tuition: full time: N/A
Room/board/expenses: N/A
College-funded aid: Yes
International student aid: Yes
Full-time enrollment: N/A
men: N/A; women: N/A; minorities: N/A; international: N/A
Part-time enrollment: 66
men: 68%; women: 32%; minorities: 5%; international: 55%
TOEFL requirement: Yes
Minimum TOEFL score: 550

University of Detroit Mercy
4001 W. McNichols Road
Detroit, MI 48221-3038
business.udmercy.edu
Private
Admissions: (800) 635-5020
Email: admissions@udmercy.edu
Financial aid: (313) 993-3350
Application deadline: rolling
Tuition: full time: $1,537/credit hour; part time: $1,537/credit hour
Room/board/expenses: N/A
College-funded aid: Yes
International student aid: Yes
Average student indebtedness at graduation: $58,829
Full-time enrollment: 34
men: 59%; women: 41%; minorities: 21%; international: 12%
Part-time enrollment: 76
men: 46%; women: 54%; minorities: 39%; international: 4%
Acceptance rate (full time): 91%
Average GMAT (part time): 393
Average GPA (full time): 3.69
Average age of entrants to full-time program: 24
TOEFL requirement: No
Minimum TOEFL score: N/A
Mean starting base salary for 2016 full-time graduates: $66,667

University of Michigan-Ann Arbor (Ross)

701 Tappan Street
Ann Arbor, MI 48109-1234
michiganross.umich.edu/
Public
Admissions: (734) 763-5796
Email:
rossadmissions@umich.edu
Financial aid: (734) 764-5139
Application deadline: 03/20
In-state tuition: full time: $59,678;
part time: $1,958/credit hour
Out-of-state tuition: full time:
$64,678
Room/board/expenses: $22,312
College-funded aid: Yes
International student aid: Yes
Average student indebtedness at
graduation: $102,665
Full-time enrollment: 801
men: 63%; women: 37%;
minorities: 25%; international:
32%
Part-time enrollment: 430
men: 79%; women: 21%;
minorities: 20%; international:
17%
Acceptance rate (full time): 26%
Average GMAT (full time): 708
Average GMAT (part time): 650
Average GPA (full time): 3.44
Average age of entrants to full-
time program: 27
Average months of prior work
experience (full time): 64
TOEFL requirement: Yes
Minimum TOEFL score: N/A
Most popular departments:
consulting, finance, marketing,
production/operations
management, technology
Mean starting base salary for 2016
full-time graduates: $119,959
Employment location for 2016
class: Intl. 8%; N.E. 21%; M.A.
3%; S. 4%; M.W. 36%; S.W. 5%;
W. 24%

University of Michigan-Dearborn

19000 Hubbard Drive
Dearborn, MI 48126-2638
umdearborn.edu/cob
Public
Admissions: (313) 593-5460
Email: umd-gradbusiness@
umich.edu
Financial aid: (313) 593-5300
Application deadline: 08/01
In-state tuition: full time: N/A; part
time: $659/credit hour
Out-of-state tuition: full time: N/A
Room/board/expenses: N/A
College-funded aid: Yes
International student aid: Yes
Full-time enrollment: N/A
men: N/A; women: N/A;
minorities: N/A; international: N/A
Part-time enrollment: 119
men: 69%; women: 31%;
minorities: 12%; international:
10%
Average GMAT (part time): 595
TOEFL requirement: Yes
Minimum TOEFL score: 560
Most popular departments:
finance, general management,
industrial management,
management information
systems, supply chain
management/logistics

University of Michigan-Flint

303 E. Kearsley Street
Flint, MI 48502-1950
www.umflint.edu/som/
graduate-business-programs
Public
Admissions: (810) 762-3171
Email: graduate@umflint.edu
Financial aid: (810) 762-3444
Application deadline: 08/01
In-state tuition: full time: $12,456;
part time: $668/credit hour
Out-of-state tuition: full time:
$15,354
Room/board/expenses: $11,326
College-funded aid: Yes
International student aid: Yes
Full-time enrollment: N/A
men: N/A; women: N/A;
minorities: N/A; international: N/A
Part-time enrollment: 160
men: 63%; women: 38%;
minorities: 21%; international:
10%
Average GMAT (part time): 522
TOEFL requirement: Yes
Minimum TOEFL score: 560
Most popular departments:
accounting, finance, health care
administration, international
business, leadership

Wayne State University

5201 Cass Avenue
Prentis Building
Detroit, MI 48202
www.ilitchbusiness.wayne.edu
Public
Admissions: (313) 577-4511
Email: gradbusiness@wayne.edu
Financial aid: (313) 577-2100
Application deadline: 07/01
In-state tuition: full time: $713/
credit hour; part time: $713/
credit hour
Out-of-state tuition: full time:
$1,430/credit hour
Room/board/expenses: $16,452
College-funded aid: Yes
International student aid: Yes
Full-time enrollment: N/A
men: N/A; women: N/A;
minorities: N/A; international: N/A
Part-time enrollment: 1,063
men: 57%; women: 43%;
minorities: 28%; international:
6%
TOEFL requirement: Yes
Minimum TOEFL score: 550
Most popular departments:
finance, general management,
marketing, management
information systems, supply
chain management/logistics

Western Michigan University (Haworth)

1903 W. Michigan Avenue
Kalamazoo, MI 49008-5480
wmich.edu/mba
Public
Admissions: (269) 387-5133
Email: mba-advising@wmich.edu
Financial aid: (269) 387-6000
Application deadline: 07/15
In-state tuition: full time: N/A; part
time: $555/credit hour
Out-of-state tuition: full time: N/A
Room/board/expenses: N/A
College-funded aid: Yes
International student aid: No
Full-time enrollment: N/A
men: N/A; women: N/A;
minorities: N/A; international: N/A
Part-time enrollment: 305
men: 69%; women: 31%;
minorities: 10%; international:
15%
Average GMAT (part time): 531
TOEFL requirement: Yes
Minimum TOEFL score: 550
Most popular departments:
finance, general management,
marketing, management
information systems, other

MINNESOTA

Minnesota State University-Mankato

120 Morris Hall
Mankato, MN 56001
grad.mnsu.edu
Public
Admissions: (507) 389-2321
Financial aid: (507) 389-1419
Application deadline: 06/01
In-state tuition: full time: $588/
credit hour; part time: $588/
credit hour
Out-of-state tuition: full time:
$588/credit hour
Room/board/expenses: N/A
College-funded aid: Yes
International student aid: Yes
Full-time enrollment: N/A
men: N/A; women: N/A;
minorities: N/A; international: N/A
Part-time enrollment: 56
men: 71%; women: 29%;
minorities: N/A; international: N/A
Average GMAT (part time): 553
TOEFL requirement: Yes
Minimum TOEFL score: 500
Most popular departments: health
care administration, international
business, leadership

Minnesota State University-Moorhead

1104 7th Ave South
Moorhead, MN 56563
www.mnstate.edu/graduate/
programs
Public
Admissions: (218) 477-2134
Email: graduate@mnstate.edu
Financial aid: (218) 477-2251
Application deadline: 06/15
In-state tuition: full time: $375/
credit hour; part time: $375/
credit hour
Out-of-state tuition: full time:
$750/credit hour
Room/board/expenses: N/A
College-funded aid: Yes
Full-time enrollment: 15
men: 47%; women: 53%;
minorities: N/A; international: N/A
Part-time enrollment: 26
men: 58%; women: 42%;
minorities: N/A; international: N/A
Minimum TOEFL score: N/A
Most popular departments:
accounting, finance, general
management, health care
administration

St. Cloud State University (Herberger)[1]

720 Fourth Avenue S
St. Cloud, MN 56301-4498
www.stcloudstate.edu/mba
Public
Admissions: (320) 308-3212
Email: mba@stcloudstate.edu
Financial aid: N/A
Tuition: N/A
Room/board/expenses: N/A
Enrollment: N/A

University of Minnesota-Duluth (Labovitz)

1318 Kirby Drive
Duluth, MN 55812-2496
lsbe.d.umn.edu/mba
Public
Admissions: (218) 726-8839
Email: grad@d.umn.edu
Financial aid: (218) 726-8000
Application deadline: 07/15
In-state tuition: full time: N/A; part
time: $922/credit hour
Out-of-state tuition: full time: N/A
Room/board/expenses: N/A
College-funded aid: Yes
International student aid: Yes
Full-time enrollment: N/A
men: N/A; women: N/A;
minorities: N/A; international: N/A
Part-time enrollment: 39
men: 64%; women: 36%;
minorities: 15%; international:
5%
Average GMAT (part time): 574
TOEFL requirement: Yes
Minimum TOEFL score: 550

University of Minnesota-Twin Cities (Carlson)

321 19th Avenue S, Office 4-300
Minneapolis, MN 55455
www.carlsonschool.umn.edu/
degrees/master-business-
administration
Public
Admissions: (612) 625-5555
Email: mba@umn.edu
Financial aid: (612) 624-1111
Application deadline: 04/01
In-state tuition: full time: $41,634;
part time: $1,335/credit hour
Out-of-state tuition: full time:
$52,034
Room/board/expenses: $17,000
College-funded aid: Yes
International student aid: Yes
Average student indebtedness at
graduation: $63,028
Full-time enrollment: 193
men: 69%; women: 31%;
minorities: 12%; international:
16%
Part-time enrollment: 1,005
men: 68%; women: 32%;
minorities: 11%; international: 6%
Acceptance rate (full time): 45%
Average GMAT (full time): 675
Average GMAT (part time): 604
Average GPA (full time): 3.43
Average age of entrants to full-
time program: 29
Average months of prior work
experience (full time): 58
TOEFL requirement: Yes
Minimum TOEFL score: 580

Most popular departments:
finance, general management,
health care administration,
marketing, supply chain
management/logistics
Mean starting base salary for 2016
full-time graduates: $108,720
Employment location for 2016
class: Intl. 6%; N.E. 5%; M.A.
1%; S. 1%; M.W. 70%; S.W. 5%;
W. 13%

University of St. Thomas

1000 LaSalle Avenue
SCH200
Minneapolis, MN 55403
www.stthomas.edu/business
Private
Admissions: (651) 962-8800
Email: ustmba@stthomas.edu
Financial aid: (651) 962-6550
Application deadline: 08/01
Tuition: total program: $68,721
(full time); part time: $1,085/
credit hour
Room/board/expenses: N/A
College-funded aid: Yes
International student aid: Yes
Average student indebtedness at
graduation: $48,971
Full-time enrollment: 69
men: 58%; women: 42%;
minorities: 17%; international:
19%
Part-time enrollment: 575
men: 56%; women: 44%;
minorities: 5%; international: 1%
Acceptance rate (full time): 82%
Average GMAT (full time): 552
Average GMAT (part time): 513
Average GPA (full time): 3.20
Average age of entrants to full-
time program: 29
Average months of prior work
experience (full time): 60
TOEFL requirement: Yes
Minimum TOEFL score: 550
Most popular departments:
accounting, entrepreneurship,
finance, general management,
marketing

MISSISSIPPI

Jackson State University[1]

1400 J.R. Lynch Street
Jackson, MS 39217
www.jsums.edu/business
Public
Admissions: N/A
Financial aid: N/A
Tuition: N/A
Room/board/expenses: N/A
Enrollment: N/A

Millsaps College (Else)[1]

1701 N. State Street
Jackson, MS 39210
millsaps.edu/esom
Private
Admissions: N/A
Financial aid: N/A
Tuition: N/A
Room/board/expenses: N/A
Enrollment: N/A

Mississippi State University

PO Box 5288
Mississippi State, MS 39762
www.business.msstate.edu/gsb
Public
Admissions: (662) 325-1891
Email:
gsb@business.msstate.edu
Financial aid: (662) 325-2450
Application deadline: 03/01
In-state tuition: total program:
$11,805 (full time); part time: N/A
Out-of-state tuition: total
program: $31,485 (full time)
Room/board/expenses: $19,500
College-funded aid: Yes
International student aid: Yes
Full-time enrollment: 22
men: 59%; women: 41%;
minorities: 0%; international:
18%
Part-time enrollment: N/A
men: N/A; women: N/A;
minorities: N/A; international: N/A
Acceptance rate (full time): 68%
Average GMAT (full time): 558
Average GPA (full time): 3.60
**Average age of entrants to full-
time program:** 23
**Average months of prior work
experience (full time):** 36
TOEFL requirement: Yes
Minimum TOEFL score: 575
Most popular departments:
accounting, marketing,
management information
systems, other
**Mean starting base salary for 2016
full-time graduates:** $48,508
**Employment location for 2016
class:** Intl. N/A; N.E. 7%; M.A.
N/A; S. 93%; M.W. N/A; S.W. N/A;
W. N/A

University of Mississippi

253 Holman Hall
University, MS 38677
www.olemissbusiness.com/mba
Public
Admissions: (662) 915-5483
Email: ajones@bus.olemiss.edu
Financial aid: (800) 891-4596
Application deadline: 07/01
In-state tuition: total program:
$20,201 (full time); part time:
$669/credit hour
Out-of-state tuition: total
program: $49,415 (full time)
Room/board/expenses: $17,260
College-funded aid: Yes
International student aid: Yes
**Average student indebtedness at
graduation:** $24,806
Full-time enrollment: 58
men: 67%; women: 33%;
minorities: 14%; international:
5%
Part-time enrollment: N/A
men: N/A; women: N/A;
minorities: N/A; international: N/A
Acceptance rate (full time): 32%
Average GMAT (full time): 568
Average GPA (full time): 3.33
**Average age of entrants to full-
time program:** 25
**Average months of prior work
experience (full time):** 14
TOEFL requirement: Yes
Minimum TOEFL score: 600
**Mean starting base salary for 2016
full-time graduates:** $00,000

University of Southern Mississippi

118 College Drive, #5096
Hattiesburg, MS 39406-5096
choose.usm.edu/mba.html
Public
Admissions: (601) 266-4369
Email: gc-business@usm.edu
Financial aid: (601) 266-4774
Application deadline: 04/01
In-state tuition: full time: $420/
credit hour; part time: $420/
credit hour
Out-of-state tuition: full time:
$913/credit hour
Room/board/expenses: N/A
College-funded aid: Yes
International student aid: Yes
Full-time enrollment: 26
men: 58%; women: 42%;
minorities: 12%; international:
19%
Part-time enrollment: 42
men: 50%; women: 50%;
minorities: 14%; international:
N/A
Acceptance rate (full time): 61%
Average GMAT (full time): 505
Average GMAT (part time): 506
Average GPA (full time): 3.47
**Average age of entrants to full-
time program:** 26
**Average months of prior work
experience (full time):** 43
TOEFL requirement: Yes
Minimum TOEFL score: N/A
Most popular departments:
accounting, international
business, marketing, sports
business, other

MISSOURI

Drury University

900 North Benton Avenue
Springfield, MO 65802
www.drury.edu/mba/
Private
Admissions: (417) 873-6948
Email: grad@drury.edu
Financial aid: (417) 873-7312
Application deadline: 07/15
Tuition: full time: $695/credit
hour; part time: N/A
Room/board/expenses: $12,000
College-funded aid: Yes
International student aid: Yes
Full-time enrollment: 48
men: 58%; women: 42%;
minorities: 6%; international:
21%
Part-time enrollment: N/A
men: N/A; women: N/A;
minorities: N/A; international: N/A
Acceptance rate (full time): 56%
Average GMAT (full time): 530
Average GPA (full time): 3.30
**Average months of prior work
experience (full time):** 6
TOEFL requirement: Yes
Minimum TOEFL score: 500

Missouri State University

901 S. National Avenue
Glass Hall 400
Springfield, MO 65897
www.mba.missouristate.edu
Public
Admissions: (417) 836-5616
Email: MBAProgram@
MissouriState.edu
Financial aid: (417) 836-5262
Application deadline: 08/17

In-state tuition: full time: $303/
credit hour; part time: $303/
credit hour
Out-of-state tuition: full time:
$563/credit hour
Room/board/expenses: $9,288
College-funded aid: Yes
International student aid: Yes
Full-time enrollment: 360
men: 53%; women: 47%;
minorities: 10%; international:
31%
Part-time enrollment: N/A
men: N/A; women: N/A;
minorities: N/A; international: N/A
Acceptance rate (full time): 83%
Average GMAT (full time): 532
Average GPA (full time): 3.40
**Average age of entrants to full-
time program:** 27
TOEFL requirement: Yes
Minimum TOEFL score: 550
Most popular departments:
finance, general management,
international business,
marketing, management
information systems

Missouri University of Science & Technology

1870 Miner Circle
Rolla, MO 65409
bit.mst.edu/
Public
Admissions: (573) 341-4165
Email: admissions@mst.edu
Financial aid: (573) 341-4282
Application deadline: rolling
In-state tuition: full time: $676/
credit hour; part time: $676/
credit hour
Out-of-state tuition: full time:
$1,196/credit hour
Room/board/expenses: $8,604
College-funded aid: Yes
International student aid: Yes
**Average student indebtedness at
graduation:** $11,386
Full-time enrollment: 54
men: 44%; women: 56%;
minorities: 7%; international: 81%
Part-time enrollment: 40
men: 78%; women: 23%;
minorities: 8%; international:
35%
Acceptance rate (full time): 62%
Average GMAT (full time): 620
Average GPA (full time): 3.25
**Average age of entrants to full-
time program:** 26
**Average months of prior work
experience (full time):** 36
TOEFL requirement: Yes
Minimum TOEFL score: 570
Most popular departments:
general management, leadership,
management information
systems, quantitative analysis/
statistics and operations
research, technology
**Mean starting base salary for 2016
full-time graduates:** $66,250

Rockhurst University (Helzberg)

1100 Rockhurst Road
Kansas City, MO 64110
www.rockhurst.edu/helzberg
Private
Admissions: (816) 501-4632
Email: mba@rockhurst.edu
Financial aid: (816) 501-4600
Application deadline: rolling
Tuition: full time: N/A; part time:
$660/credit hour

Room/board/expenses: N/A
College-funded aid: Yes
International student aid: Yes
Full-time enrollment: N/A
men: N/A; women: N/A;
minorities: N/A; international: N/A
Part-time enrollment: 376
men: 65%; women: 35%;
minorities: 16%; international: 1%
Average GMAT (part time): 490
TOEFL requirement: Yes
Minimum TOEFL score: 550
Most popular departments:
accounting, finance, general
management, health care
administration, quantitative
analysis/statistics and
operations research

Southeast Missouri State University (Harrison)

1 University Plaza, MS 5890
Cape Girardeau, MO 63701
www.semo.edu/mba
Public
Admissions: (573) 651-2590
Email: mba@semo.edu
Financial aid: (573) 651-2039
Application deadline: 08/01
In-state tuition: full time: $263/
credit hour; part time: $263/
credit hour
Out-of-state tuition: full time:
$490/credit hour
Room/board/expenses: $11,618
College-funded aid: Yes
International student aid: Yes
**Average student indebtedness at
graduation:** $4,661
Full-time enrollment: 72
men: 46%; women: 54%;
minorities: 8%; international:
69%
Part-time enrollment: 109
men: 62%; women: 38%;
minorities: 13%; international:
12%
Acceptance rate (full time): 69%
Average GMAT (full time): 516
Average GMAT (part time): 537
Average GPA (full time): 3.27
**Average age of entrants to full-
time program:** 25
TOEFL requirement: Yes
Minimum TOEFL score: 550
Most popular departments:
accounting, finance, general
management, health care
administration, international
business

St. Louis University (Cook)

3674 Lindell Boulevard
St. Louis, MO 63108
business.slu.edu
Private
Admissions: (314) 977-6221
Email: gradbiz@slu.edu
Financial aid: (314) 977-2350
Application deadline: 08/15
Tuition: full time: $57,206; part
time: $1,015/credit hour
Room/board/expenses: $18,540
College-funded aid: Yes
International student aid: Yes
**Average student indebtedness at
graduation:** $53,231
Full-time enrollment: 40
men: 50%; women: 50%;
minorities: 23%; international:
18%

Part-time enrollment: 201
men: 59%; women: 41%;
minorities: 11%; international: 6%
Acceptance rate (full time): 75%
Average GMAT (full time): 578
Average GMAT (part time): 540
Average GPA (full time): 3.30
**Average age of entrants to full-
time program:** 26
**Average months of prior work
experience (full time):** 27
TOEFL requirement: Yes
Minimum TOEFL score: 570
Most popular departments:
finance, general management,
international business,
marketing, supply chain
management/logistics
**Mean starting base salary for 2016
full-time graduates:** $55,891

Truman State University[1]

100 E. Normal
Kirksville, MO 63501
gradstudies.truman.edu
Public
Admissions: (660) 785-4109
Email: gradinfo@truman.edu
Financial aid: (660) 785-4130
Tuition: N/A
Room/board/expenses: N/A
Enrollment: N/A

University of Central Missouri (Harmon)

Ward Edwards 1600
Warrensburg, MO 64093
www.ucmo.edu/mba
Public
Admissions: (660) 543-8617
Email: mba@ucmo.edu
Financial aid: (800) 729-2678
Application deadline: 07/14
In-state tuition: full time: $278/
credit hour; part time: $278/
credit hour
Out-of-state tuition: full time:
$557/credit hour
Room/board/expenses: $8,318
College-funded aid: Yes
International student aid: Yes
Full-time enrollment: 30
men: 57%; women: 43%;
minorities: 7%; international: 17%
Part-time enrollment: 39
men: 44%; women: 56%;
minorities: 26%; international:
3%
Average GPA (full time): 3.20
TOEFL requirement: Yes
Minimum TOEFL score: 550
Most popular departments: ethics,
finance, general management,
marketing

University of Missouri-Kansas City (Bloch)

5100 Rockhill Road
Kansas City, MO 64110
www.bloch.umkc.edu/
graduate-program/mba
Public
Admissions: (816) 235-5254
Email: bloch@umkc.edu
Financial aid: (816) 235-1154
Application deadline: 06/15
In-state tuition: full time: $359/
credit hour; part time: $359/
credit hour
Out-of-state tuition: full time:
$926/credit hour

Room/board/expenses: $20,004
College-funded aid: Yes
International student aid: Yes
Full-time enrollment: 57
men: 61%; women: 39%;
minorities: 5%; international:
28%
Part-time enrollment: 159
men: 58%; women: 42%;
minorities: 10%; international:
4%
Average GMAT (part time): 582
TOEFL requirement: Yes
Minimum TOEFL score: 550

University of
Missouri-St. Louis[1]
1 University Boulevard
St. Louis, MO 63121
mba.umsl.edu
Public
Admissions: N/A
Financial aid: N/A
Tuition: N/A
Room/board/expenses: N/A
Enrollment: N/A

University of
Missouri (Trulaske)
213 Cornell Hall
Columbia, MO 65211
mba.missouri.edu
Public
Admissions: (573) 882-2750
Email: mba@missouri.edu
Financial aid: (573) 882-2750
Application deadline: 07/01
In-state tuition: full time: $353/
credit hour; part time: $353/
credit hour
Out-of-state tuition: full time:
$966/credit hour
Room/board/expenses: $18,806
College-funded aid: Yes
International student aid: Yes
Average student indebtedness at
graduation: $20,495
Full-time enrollment: 120
men: 58%; women: 43%;
minorities: 6%; international:
31%
Part-time enrollment: N/A
men: N/A; women: N/A;
minorities: N/A; international: N/A
Acceptance rate (full time): 37%
Average GMAT (full time): 637
Average GPA (full time): 3.54
Average age of entrants to full-
time program: 25
Average months of prior work
experience (full time): 24
TOEFL requirement: Yes
Minimum TOEFL score: N/A
Most popular departments:
entrepreneurship, finance,
general management, marketing,
quantitative analysis/statistics
and operations research
Mean starting base salary for 2016
full-time graduates: $64,252
Employment location for 2016
class: Intl. 3%; N.E. 5%; M.A.
5%; S. 3%; M.W. 69%; S.W. 8%;
W. 8%

Washington
University in
St. Louis (Olin)
1 Brookings Drive
Campus Box 1133
St. Louis, MO 63130-4899
www.olin.wustl.edu/
academicprograms/MBA/Pages/
default.aspx
Private
Admissions: (314) 935-7301
Email: mba@wustl.edu
Financial aid: (314) 935-7301
Application deadline: 04/03
Tuition: full time: $56,200; part
time: $1,620/credit hour
Room/board/expenses: $25,746
College-funded aid: Yes
International student aid: Yes
Average student indebtedness at
graduation: $72,194
Full-time enrollment: 268
men: 68%; women: 32%;
minorities: 23%; international:
37%
Part-time enrollment: 297
men: 69%; women: 31%;
minorities: 21%; international: 5%
Acceptance rate (full time): 30%
Average GMAT (full time): 688
Average GMAT (part time): 571
Average GPA (full time): 3.46
Average age of entrants to full-
time program: 28
Average months of prior work
experience (full time): 60
TOEFL requirement: Yes
Minimum TOEFL score: N/A
Most popular departments:
consulting, entrepreneurship,
finance, marketing, supply chain
management/logistics
Mean starting base salary for 2016
full-time graduates: $103,295
Employment location for 2016
class: Intl. 2%; N.E. 12%; M.A.
7%; S. 6%; M.W. 55%; S.W. 11%;
W. 8%

MONTANA

University of Montana[1]
32 Campus Drive
Missoula, MT 59812-6808
www.business.umt.edu/
Public
Admissions: N/A
Email: mba@business.umt.edu
Financial aid: N/A
Tuition: N/A
Room/board/expenses: N/A
Enrollment: N/A

NEBRASKA

Creighton University
2500 California Plaza
Omaha, NE 68178-0130
business.creighton.edu
Private
Admissions: (402) 280-2703
Email: GraduateSchool@
creighton.edu
Financial aid: (402) 280-2731
Application deadline: rolling
Tuition: full time: N/A; part time:
$820/credit hour
Room/board/expenses: N/A
College-funded aid: Yes
International student aid: Yes
Full-time enrollment: N/A
men: N/A; women: N/A;
minorities: N/A; international: N/A

Part-time enrollment: 96
men: 67%; women: 33%;
minorities: 9%; international: 3%
Average GMAT (part time): 548
TOEFL requirement: Yes
Minimum TOEFL score: 577
Most popular departments:
accounting, finance, leadership,
management information
systems, portfolio management

University of
Nebraska-Kearney[1]
905 West 25th Street
Kearney, NE 68849
www.unk.edu
Public
Admissions: (800) 717-7881
Email: gradstudies@unk.edu
Financial aid: N/A
Tuition: N/A
Room/board/expenses: N/A
Enrollment: N/A

University of
Nebraska-Lincoln
P.O. Box 880405
Lincoln, NE 68588-0405
www.mba.unl.edu
Public
Admissions: (402) 472-2338
Email: businessgrad@unl.edu
Financial aid: (402) 472-2030
Application deadline: 07/01
In-state tuition: full time: N/A; part
time: $368/credit hour
Out-of-state tuition: full time: N/A
Room/board/expenses: N/A
College-funded aid: Yes
International student aid: Yes
Full-time enrollment: N/A
men: N/A; women: N/A;
minorities: N/A; international: N/A
Part-time enrollment: 54
men: 65%; women: 35%;
minorities: 4%; international:
24%
Average GMAT (part time): 595
TOEFL requirement: Yes
Minimum TOEFL score: 550
Most popular departments:
finance, international
business, marketing, supply
chain management/logistics,
quantitative analysis/statistics
and operations research

University of
Nebraska-Omaha
6708 Pine Street
Omaha, NE 68182-0048
mba.unomaha.edu
Public
Admissions: (402) 554-4836
Email: mba@unomaha.edu
Financial aid: (402) 554-2327
Application deadline: 07/01
In-state tuition: full time: N/A; part
time: $333/credit hour
Out-of-state tuition: full time: N/A
Room/board/expenses: N/A
College-funded aid: Yes
International student aid: Yes
Full-time enrollment: N/A
men: N/A; women: N/A;
minorities: N/A; international: N/A
Part-time enrollment: 243
men: 65%; women: 35%;
minorities: 9%; international:
12%
Average GMAT (part time): 574
TOEFL requirement: Yes

Minimum TOEFL score: 550
Most popular departments:
finance, health care
administration, human resources
management, international
business, supply chain
management/logistics

NEVADA

University of
Nevada-Las Vegas
4505 Maryland Parkway
PO Box 456031
Las Vegas, NV 89154-6031
business.unlv.edu
Public
Admissions: (702) 895-3655
Email: lbsmba@unlv.edu
Financial aid: (702) 895-3682
Application deadline: 07/15
In-state tuition: full time: $364/
credit hour; part time: $364/
credit hour
Out-of-state tuition: full time:
$22,646
Room/board/expenses: N/A
College-funded aid: Yes
International student aid: Yes
Full-time enrollment: N/A
men: N/A; women: N/A;
minorities: N/A; international: N/A
Part-time enrollment: 171
men: 65%; women: 35%;
minorities: 35%; international:
8%
Average GMAT (part time): 566
TOEFL requirement: Yes
Minimum TOEFL score: 550
Most popular departments:
entrepreneurship, finance,
hotel administration, marketing,
management information
systems

University of
Nevada-Reno
1664 N. Virginia Street
Reno, NV 89557
www.mba.unr.edu
Public
Admissions: (775) 682-9142
Email: vkrentz@unr.edu
Financial aid: (775) 784-4666
Application deadline: 03/15
In-state tuition: full time: N/A; part
time: $365/credit hour
Out-of-state tuition: full time: N/A
Room/board/expenses: N/A
College-funded aid: Yes
International student aid: Yes
Full-time enrollment: N/A
men: N/A; women: N/A;
minorities: N/A; international: N/A
Part-time enrollment: 227
men: 61%; women: 39%;
minorities: 21%; international: 5%
Average GMAT (part time): 526
TOEFL requirement: Yes
Minimum TOEFL score: 550
Most popular departments:
entrepreneurship, finance,
general management, marketing

NEW HAMPSHIRE

Dartmouth
College (Tuck)
100 Tuck Hall
Hanover, NH 03755-9000
www.tuck.dartmouth.edu
Private
Admissions: (603) 646-3162

Email: tuck.admissions@tuck.
dartmouth.edu
Financial aid: (603) 646-0640
Application deadline: 04/03
Tuition: full time: $69,690; part
time: N/A
Room/board/expenses: $31,910
College-funded aid: Yes
International student aid: Yes
Full-time enrollment: 567
men: 58%; women: 42%;
minorities: 20%; international:
30%
Part-time enrollment: N/A
men: N/A; women: N/A;
minorities: N/A; international: N/A
Acceptance rate (full time): 22%
Average GMAT (full time): 717
Average GPA (full time): 3.53
Average age of entrants to full-
time program: 28
Average months of prior work
experience (full time): 63
TOEFL requirement: Yes
Minimum TOEFL score: N/A
Mean starting base salary for 2016
full-time graduates: $123,934
Employment location for 2016
class: Intl. 11%; N.E. 51%; M.A.
5%; S. 4%; M.W. 8%; S.W. 5%;
W. 15%

University of
New Hampshire (Paul)
10 Garrison Avenue
Durham, NH 03824
www.mba.unh.edu
Public
Admissions: (603) 862-1367
Email: cynthia.traver@unh.edu
Financial aid: (603) 862-3600
Application deadline: 06/01
In-state tuition: full time: $30,280;
part time: $800/credit hour
Out-of-state tuition: full time:
$44,280
Room/board/expenses: $15,000
College-funded aid: Yes
International student aid: Yes
Full-time enrollment: 27
men: 67%; women: 33%;
minorities: 0%; international:
30%
Part-time enrollment: 200
men: 64%; women: 36%;
minorities: 0%; international: 5%
Acceptance rate (full time): 93%
Average GMAT (full time): 520
Average GMAT (part time): 556
Average GPA (full time): 3.16
Average age of entrants to full-
time program: 29
Average months of prior work
experience (full time): 72
TOEFL requirement: Yes
Minimum TOEFL score: 550
Most popular departments:
entrepreneurship, finance,
general management, marketing,
organizational behavior
Mean starting base salary for 2016
full-time graduates: $54,375
Employment location for 2016
class: Intl. 8%; N.E. 58%; M.A.
8%; S. 8%; M.W. 0%; S.W. 0%;
W. 17%

NEW JERSEY

Fairleigh Dickinson University (Silberman)

1000 River Road
Teaneck, NJ 07666
view2.fdu.edu/academics/
silberman-college/
Private
Admissions: (201) 692-2554
Email: grad@fdu.edu
Financial aid: (973) 443-7304
Application deadline: 08/22
Tuition: full time: $1,256/credit hour; part time: $1,256/credit hour
Room/board/expenses: N/A
College-funded aid: Yes
International student aid: Yes
Full-time enrollment: 288
men: 55%; women: 45%;
minorities: 15%; international: 33%
Part-time enrollment: 218
men: 55%; women: 45%;
minorities: 15%; international: 0%
Acceptance rate (full time): 70%
TOEFL requirement: Yes
Minimum TOEFL score: 550
Most popular departments: accounting, finance, marketing, organizational behavior, other

Monmouth University

400 Cedar Avenue
West Long Branch, NJ 07764
www.monmouth.edu
Private
Admissions: (732) 571-3452
Email: gradadm@monmouth.edu
Financial aid: (732) 571-3463
Application deadline: 07/15
Tuition: full time: $1,098/credit hour; part time: $1,098/credit hour
Room/board/expenses: $45,293
College-funded aid: Yes
International student aid: Yes
Average student indebtedness at graduation: $16,958
Full-time enrollment: 23
men: 65%; women: 35%;
minorities: 13%; international: 0%
Part-time enrollment: 145
men: 51%; women: 49%;
minorities: 9%; international: 0%
Acceptance rate (full time): 91%
Average GMAT (part time): 463
Average GPA (full time): 3.63
Average age of entrants to full-time program: 22
TOEFL requirement: Yes
Minimum TOEFL score: 550

Montclair State University (Feliciano)

Feliciano School of Business
1 Normal Avenue
Montclair, NJ 07043
www.montclair.edu/mba
Public
Admissions: (973) 655-5147
Email: graduate.school@montclair.edu
Financial aid: (973) 655-4461
Application deadline: rolling
In-state tuition: full time: $671/credit hour; part time: $671/credit hour
Out-of-state tuition: full time: $671/credit hour
Room/board/expenses: $19,910
College-funded aid: Yes

International student aid: Yes
Average student indebtedness at graduation: $33,002
Full-time enrollment: N/A
men: N/A; women: N/A;
minorities: N/A; international: N/A
Part-time enrollment: 401
men: 50%; women: 50%;
minorities: 41%; international: 15%
TOEFL requirement: Yes
Minimum TOEFL score: 550

New Jersey Institute of Technology

University Heights
Newark, NJ 07102
management.njit.edu/
Public
Admissions: (973) 596-3300
Email: admissions@njit.edu
Financial aid: (973) 596-3479
Application deadline: N/A
In-state tuition: full time: $21,814; part time: $1,034/credit hour
Out-of-state tuition: full time: $30,898
Room/board/expenses: $18,700
College-funded aid: Yes
International student aid: Yes
Average student indebtedness at graduation: $29,637
Full-time enrollment: 76
men: 62%; women: 38%;
minorities: 24%; international: 67%
Part-time enrollment: 134
men: 65%; women: 35%;
minorities: 57%; international: 1%
Acceptance rate (full time): 65%
Average GMAT (full time): 521
Average GMAT (part time): 485
Average age of entrants to full-time program: 25
TOEFL requirement: Yes
Minimum TOEFL score: 550
Most popular departments: entrepreneurship, finance, management information systems, technology, other
Mean starting base salary for 2016 full-time graduates: $78,167
Employment location for 2016 class: Intl. 20%; N.E. 80%; M.A. N/A; S. N/A; M.W. N/A; S.W. N/A; W. N/A

Ramapo College of New Jersey

505 Ramapo Valley Road
Mahwah, NJ 07430
www.ramapo.edu/admissions/
Public
Admissions: (201) 684-7300
Email: admissions@ramapo.edu
Financial aid: (201) 684-7549
Application deadline: 05/01
In-state tuition: full time: N/A; part time: $836/credit hour
Out-of-state tuition: full time: N/A
Room/board/expenses: N/A
College-funded aid: Yes
International student aid: Yes
Full-time enrollment: N/A
men: N/A; women: N/A;
minorities: N/A; international: N/A
Part-time enrollment: 66
men: 56%; women: 44%;
minorities: 26%; international: 0%
TOEFL requirement: Yes
Minimum TOEFL score: 550

Rider University

2083 Lawrenceville Road
Lawrenceville, NJ 08648-3099
www.rider.edu/mba
Private
Admissions: (609) 896-5036
Email: gradadm@rider.edu
Financial aid: (609) 896-5360
Application deadline: rolling
Tuition: full time: N/A; part time: $1,020/credit hour
Room/board/expenses: N/A
College-funded aid: Yes
International student aid: Yes
Full-time enrollment: N/A
men: N/A; women: N/A;
minorities: N/A; international: N/A
Part-time enrollment: 161
men: 54%; women: 46%;
minorities: 16%; international: 10%
Average GMAT (part time): 486
TOEFL requirement: Yes
Minimum TOEFL score: 550
Most popular departments: accounting, finance, international business, quantitative analysis/statistics and operations research

Rowan University (Rohrer)

201 Mullica Hill Road
Glassboro, NJ 08028
www.rowanu.com
Public
Admissions: (856) 256-5435
Email: cgceadmissions@rowan.edu
Financial aid: (856) 256-5141
Application deadline: 07/01
In-state tuition: full time: $720/credit hour; part time: $720/credit hour
Out-of-state tuition: full time: $720/credit hour
Room/board/expenses: $17,496
College-funded aid: Yes
International student aid: No
Average student indebtedness at graduation: $39,875
Full-time enrollment: 44
men: 52%; women: 48%;
minorities: 23%; international: 5%
Part-time enrollment: 92
men: 60%; women: 40%;
minorities: 22%; international: 2%
Average GMAT (part time): 510
TOEFL requirement: Yes
Minimum TOEFL score: 550
Most popular departments: accounting, finance, general management, marketing, management information systems

Rutgers, The State University of New Jersey-Camden

227 Penn Street
Camden, NJ 08102
business.camden.rutgers.edu/
Public
Admissions: (856) 225-6452
Email: Rsbemba@camden.rutgers.edu
Financial aid: (856) 225-6039
Application deadline: 08/01
In-state tuition: full time: $956/credit hour; part time: $956/credit hour

Out-of-state tuition: full time: $1,620/credit hour
Room/board/expenses: N/A
College-funded aid: Yes
International student aid: Yes
Full-time enrollment: N/A
men: N/A; women: N/A;
minorities: N/A; international: N/A
Part-time enrollment: 152
men: 59%; women: 41%;
minorities: 37%; international: 5%
Average GMAT (part time): 540
TOEFL requirement: Yes
Minimum TOEFL score: 550

Rutgers, The State University of New Jersey-Newark and New Brunswick

1 Washington Park
Newark, NJ 07102-3122
www.business.rutgers.edu
Public
Admissions: (973) 353-1234
Email: admit@business.rutgers.edu
Financial aid: (973) 353-5151
Application deadline: 05/01
In-state tuition: full time: $28,517; part time: $1,077/credit hour
Out-of-state tuition: full time: $47,537
Room/board/expenses: $22,400
College-funded aid: Yes
International student aid: No
Average student indebtedness at graduation: $45,388
Full-time enrollment: 139
men: 64%; women: 36%;
minorities: 29%; international: 40%
Part-time enrollment: 1,007
men: 64%; women: 36%;
minorities: 45%; international: 3%
Acceptance rate (full time): 45%
Average GMAT (full time): 659
Average GMAT (part time): 583
Average GPA (full time): 3.23
Average age of entrants to full-time program: 28
Average months of prior work experience (full time): 55
TOEFL requirement: Yes
Minimum TOEFL score: 600
Most popular departments: entrepreneurship, finance, leadership, marketing, supply chain management/logistics
Mean starting base salary for 2016 full-time graduates: $89,436
Employment location for 2016 class: Intl. 2%; N.E. 73%; M.A. 6%; S. 2%; M.W. 6%; S.W. 10%; W. 0%

Seton Hall University (Stillman)

400 S. Orange Avenue
South Orange, NJ 07079
www.shu.edu/academics/business/
Private
Admissions: (973) 761-9262
Email: mba@shu.edu
Financial aid: (973) 761-9350
Application deadline: 05/31
Tuition: full time: N/A; part time: $1,261/credit hour
Room/board/expenses: N/A
College-funded aid: Yes
International student aid: Yes

Full-time enrollment: N/A
men: N/A; women: N/A;
minorities: N/A; international: N/A
Part-time enrollment: 208
men: 63%; women: 37%;
minorities: 31%; international: 25%
Average GMAT (part time): 552
TOEFL requirement: Yes
Minimum TOEFL score: 607
Most popular departments: accounting, finance, general management, international business, marketing

Stevens Institute of Technology

1 Castle Point Terrace
Hoboken, NJ 07030
www.stevens.edu/admissions/graduate-admissions
Private
Admissions: (888) 783-8367
Email: graduate@stevens.edu
Financial aid: (201) 216-5555
Application deadline: 06/01
Tuition: full time: $34,514; part time: $1,501/credit hour
Room/board/expenses: $16,150
College-funded aid: Yes
International student aid: Yes
Full-time enrollment: 590
men: 64%; women: 36%;
minorities: 2%; international: 95%
Part-time enrollment: 392
men: 65%; women: 35%;
minorities: 27%; international: 2%
Acceptance rate (full time): 58%
Average GMAT (full time): 623
Average GMAT (part time): 585
Average GPA (full time): 3.20
Average age of entrants to full-time program: 24
Average months of prior work experience (full time): 35
TOEFL requirement: Yes
Minimum TOEFL score: 537
Most popular departments: finance, general management, management information systems, quantitative analysis/statistics and operations research, other
Mean starting base salary for 2016 full-time graduates: $70,846

Stockton University[1]

101 Vera King Farris Drive
Galloway, NJ 08205
stockton.edu/graduate/business-administration.html
Private
Admissions: (609) 626-3640
Email: gradschool@stockton.edu
Financial aid: N/A
Tuition: N/A
Room/board/expenses: N/A
Enrollment: N/A

William Paterson University (Cotsakos)

1600 Valley Road
Wayne, NJ 07470
www.wpunj.edu/MBA
Public
Admissions: (973) 720-3601
Email: graduate@wpunj.edu
Financial aid: (973) 720-3945
Application deadline: rolling
In-state tuition: full time: $900/credit hour; part time: $688/credit hour

Out-of-state tuition: full time: $831/credit hour
Room/board/expenses: $11,572
College-funded aid: Yes
International student aid: Yes
Full-time enrollment: 74
men: 50%; women: 50%; minorities: N/A; international: N/A
Part-time enrollment: 161
men: 52%; women: 48%; minorities: N/A; international: N/A
TOEFL requirement: Yes
Minimum TOEFL score: 550

NEW MEXICO

New Mexico State University

PO Box 30001, MSC 3GSP
Las Cruces, NM 88003
business.nmsu.edu/mba
Public
Admissions: (505) 646-8003
Email: mbaprog@nmsu.edu
Financial aid: (505) 646-4105
Application deadline: 07/15
In-state tuition: full time: $4,941; part time: $227/credit hour
Out-of-state tuition: full time: $15,107
Room/board/expenses: $13,050
College-funded aid: Yes
International student aid: Yes
Full-time enrollment: N/A
men: N/A; women: N/A; minorities: N/A; international: N/A
Part-time enrollment: 176
men: 49%; women: 51%; minorities: N/A; international: N/A
Average GMAT (part time): 490
TOEFL requirement: Yes
Minimum TOEFL score: 550
Most popular departments: finance, general management, management information systems, other

University of New Mexico (Anderson)

MSC05 3090
1 University of New Mexico
Albuquerque, NM 87131-0001
www.mgt.unm.edu
Public
Admissions: (505) 277-3290
Email: andersonadvising@unm.edu
Financial aid: (505) 277-8900
Application deadline: 04/01
In-state tuition: full time: $508/credit hour; part time: $508/credit hour
Out-of-state tuition: full time: $1,134/credit hour
Room/board/expenses: N/A
College-funded aid: Yes
International student aid: Yes
Average student indebtedness at graduation: $27,329
Full-time enrollment: 153
men: 58%; women: 42%; minorities: 46%; international: 12%
Part-time enrollment: 141
men: 53%; women: 47%; minorities: 48%; international: 6%
Average GMAT (full time): 547
Average GMAT (part time): 588
Average GPA (full time): 3.57
Average age of entrants to full-time program: 26
TOEFL requirement: Yes
Minimum TOEFL score: 550

Most popular departments: accounting, finance, marketing, organizational behavior, technology

NEW YORK

Adelphi University

1 South Avenue
Garden City, NY 11530
www.adelphi.edu
Private
Admissions: (516) 877-3050
Email: admissions@adelphi.edu
Financial aid: (516) 877-3080
Application deadline: rolling
Tuition: full time: N/A; part time: $1,165/credit hour
Room/board/expenses: N/A
College-funded aid: Yes
International student aid: Yes
Full-time enrollment: N/A
men: N/A; women: N/A; minorities: N/A; international: N/A
Part-time enrollment: 306
men: 54%; women: 46%; minorities: 29%; international: 29%
Average GMAT (part time): 481
TOEFL requirement: Yes
Minimum TOEFL score: N/A
Most popular departments: accounting, finance, health care administration, marketing

Alfred University

Saxon Drive
Alfred, NY 14802
business.alfred.edu/mba.html
Private
Admissions: (800) 541-9229
Email: gradinquiry@alfred.edu
Financial aid: (607) 871-2159
Application deadline: 08/01
Tuition: full time: $38,990; part time: $810/credit hour
Room/board/expenses: $15,670
College-funded aid: Yes
International student aid: Yes
Full-time enrollment: 28
men: 61%; women: 39%; minorities: 14%; international: 0%
Part-time enrollment: 20
men: 60%; women: 40%; minorities: 20%; international: 0%
Acceptance rate (full time): 92%
Average GPA (full time): 3.35
Average age of entrants to full-time program: 23
TOEFL requirement: Yes
Minimum TOEFL score: 550
Most popular departments: accounting, general management

Binghamton University-SUNY

PO Box 6000
Binghamton, NY 13902-6000
www.binghamton.edu/som/graduate/index.html
Public
Admissions: (607) 777-2012
Email: awheeler@binghamton.edu
Financial aid: (607) 777-2428
Application deadline: 03/01
In-state tuition: full time: $16,711; part time: $600/credit hour
Out-of-state tuition: full time: $26,691
Room/board/expenses: $19,309
College-funded aid: Yes

International student aid: Yes
Average student indebtedness at graduation: $24,779
Full-time enrollment: 95
men: 67%; women: 33%; minorities: 12%; international: 28%
Part-time enrollment: N/A
men: N/A; women: N/A; minorities: N/A; international: N/A
Acceptance rate (full time): 58%
Average GMAT (full time): 615
Average GPA (full time): 3.52
Average age of entrants to full-time program: 23
Average months of prior work experience (full time): 18
TOEFL requirement: Yes
Minimum TOEFL score: 575
Most popular departments: finance, leadership, marketing, management information systems, supply chain management/logistics
Mean starting base salary for 2016 full-time graduates: $63,808
Employment location for 2016 class: Intl. 0%; N.E. 90%; M.A. 0%; S. 3%; M.W. 3%; S.W. 0%; W. 3%

Canisius College (Wehle)

2001 Main Street
Buffalo, NY 14208
www.canisius.edu/business/graduate_programs.asp
Public
Admissions: (800) 950-2505
Email: gradubus@canisius.edu
Financial aid: (716) 888-2300
Application deadline: rolling
In-state tuition: total program: $39,483 (full time); part time: $795/credit hour
Out-of-state tuition: total program: $39,483 (full time)
Room/board/expenses: $15,522
College-funded aid: Yes
International student aid: Yes
Average student indebtedness at graduation: $24,456
Full-time enrollment: 23
men: 70%; women: 30%; minorities: 22%; international: N/A
Part-time enrollment: 262
men: 61%; women: 39%; minorities: 11%; international: 11%
Acceptance rate (full time): 44%
Average GMAT (full time): 508
Average GMAT (part time): 329
Average GPA (full time): 3.10
Average age of entrants to full-time program: 24
TOEFL requirement: Yes
Minimum TOEFL score: 550
Most popular departments: accounting, general management
Mean starting base salary for 2016 full-time graduates: $45,525
Employment location for 2016 class: Intl. N/A; N.E. 100%; M.A. N/A; S. N/A; M.W. N/A; S.W. N/A; W. N/A

Clarkson University

Snell Hall 322E, Box 5770
Potsdam, NY 13699-5770
www.clarkson.edu/mba
Private
Admissions: (315) 268-6613
Email: busgrad@clarkson.edu
Financial aid: (315) 268-7699

Application deadline: rolling
Tuition: full time: $50,050; part time: $1,100/credit hour
Room/board/expenses: $15,188
College-funded aid: Yes
International student aid: Yes
Average student indebtedness at graduation: $44,679
Full-time enrollment: 60
men: 63%; women: 37%; minorities: 7%; international: 20%
Part-time enrollment: 213
men: 46%; women: 54%; minorities: 16%; international: 1%
Acceptance rate (full time): 83%
Average GMAT (full time): 567
Average GMAT (part time): 512
Average GPA (full time): 3.37
Average age of entrants to full-time program: 25
Average months of prior work experience (full time): 34
TOEFL requirement: Yes
Minimum TOEFL score: 550
Most popular departments: accounting, entrepreneurship, health care administration, supply chain management/logistics, other
Mean starting base salary for 2016 full-time graduates: $63,558
Employment location for 2016 class: Intl. N/A; N.E. 59%; M.A. 6%; S. 0%; M.W. 35%; S.W. N/A; W. N/A

College at Brockport-SUNY[1]

119 Hartwell Hall
Brockport, NY 14420
www.brockport.edu/business
Public
Admissions: N/A
Financial aid: N/A
Tuition: N/A
Room/board/expenses: N/A
Enrollment: N/A

Columbia University

3022 Broadway
216 Uris Hall
New York, NY 10027
www.gsb.columbia.edu
Private
Admissions: (212) 854-1961
Email: apply@gsb.columbia.edu
Financial aid: (212) 854-4057
Application deadline: 04/11
Tuition: full time: $71,624; part time: N/A
Room/board/expenses: $28,301
College-funded aid: Yes
International student aid: Yes
Full-time enrollment: 1,326
men: 63%; women: 37%; minorities: N/A; international: N/A
Part-time enrollment: N/A
men: N/A; women: N/A; minorities: N/A; international: N/A
Acceptance rate (full time): 14%
Average GMAT (full time): 720
Average GPA (full time): 3.50
Average age of entrants to full-time program: 28
Average months of prior work experience (full time): 63
TOEFL requirement: Yes
Minimum TOEFL score: N/A
Most popular departments: consulting, entrepreneurship, finance, health care administration, leadership
Mean starting base salary for 2016 full-time graduates: $129,379

Cornell University (Johnson)

Sage Hall, Cornell University
Ithaca, NY 14853-6201
www.johnson.cornell.edu
Private
Admissions: (607) 255-0600
Email: mba@cornell.edu
Financial aid: (607) 255-6116
Application deadline: 03/15
Tuition: full time: $64,584; part time: N/A
Room/board/expenses: $22,860
College-funded aid: Yes
International student aid: Yes
Full-time enrollment: 580
men: 70%; women: 30%; minorities: 24%; international: 33%
Part-time enrollment: N/A
men: N/A; women: N/A; minorities: N/A; international: N/A
Acceptance rate (full time): 28%
Average GMAT (full time): 700
Average GPA (full time): 3.37
Average age of entrants to full-time program: 28
Average months of prior work experience (full time): 58
TOEFL requirement: Yes
Minimum TOEFL score: 600
Most popular departments: consulting, finance, leadership, marketing, technology
Mean starting base salary for 2016 full-time graduates: $121,228
Employment location for 2016 class: Intl. 8%; N.E. 53%; M.A. 4%; S. 4%; M.W. 8%; S.W. 5%; W. 18%

CUNY Bernard M. Baruch College (Zicklin)

1 Bernard Baruch Way
New York, NY 10010
zicklin.baruch.cuny.edu
Public
Admissions: (646) 312-1300
Email: zicklingradadmissions@baruch.cuny.edu
Financial aid: (646) 312-1370
Application deadline: 04/15
In-state tuition: full time: $17,259; part time: $665/credit hour
Out-of-state tuition: full time: $29,809
Room/board/expenses: N/A
College-funded aid: Yes
International student aid: Yes
Full-time enrollment: 98
men: 59%; women: 41%; minorities: 22%; international: 43%
Part-time enrollment: 496
men: 58%; women: 42%; minorities: 31%; international: 4%
Acceptance rate (full time): 32%
Average GMAT (full time): 632
Average GMAT (part time): 593
Average GPA (full time): 3.33
Average age of entrants to full-time program: 29
Average months of prior work experience (full time): 57
TOEFL requirement: Yes
Minimum TOEFL score: N/A
Most popular departments: accounting, entrepreneurship, finance, general management, marketing
Mean starting base salary for 2016 full-time graduates: $78,161

Employment location for 2016 class: Intl. N/A; N.E. 91%; M.A. N/A; S. 6%; M.W. 3%; S.W. N/A; W. N/A

Fordham University (Gabelli)
140 W. 62nd Street
New York, NY 10023
www.fordham.edu/gabelli
Private
Admissions: (212) 636-6200
Email: admissionsgb@fordham.edu
Financial aid: (212) 636-6700
Application deadline: 06/01
Tuition: full time: $1,397/credit hour; part time: $1,397/credit hour
Room/board/expenses: $29,945
College-funded aid: Yes
International student aid: Yes
Average student indebtedness at graduation: $51,870
Full-time enrollment: 78
men: 64%; women: 36%; minorities: 18%; international: 38%
Part-time enrollment: 252
men: 56%; women: 44%; minorities: 24%; international: 11%
Acceptance rate (full time): 47%
Average GMAT (full time): 621
Average GMAT (part time): 550
Average GPA (full time): 3.16
Average age of entrants to full-time program: 30
Average months of prior work experience (full time): 80
TOEFL requirement: Yes
Minimum TOEFL score: N/A
Most popular departments: finance, general management, marketing, management information systems, other
Mean starting base salary for 2016 full-time graduates: $97,404
Employment location for 2016 class: Intl. 6%; N.E. 88%; M.A. 3%; S. 3%; M.W. N/A; S.W. N/A; W. N/A

Hofstra University (Zarb)
300 Weller Hall
Hempstead, NY 11549
www.hofstra.edu/graduate
Private
Admissions: (516) 463-4723
Email: graduateadmission@hofstra.edu
Financial aid: (516) 463-0000
Application deadline: rolling
Tuition: full time: $1,268/credit hour; part time: $1,268/credit hour
Room/board/expenses: $22,690
College-funded aid: Yes
International student aid: Yes
Full-time enrollment: 80
men: 59%; women: 41%; minorities: 11%; international: 61%
Part-time enrollment: 812
men: 51%; women: 49%; minorities: 17%; international: 50%
Acceptance rate (full time): 45%
Average GMAT (full time): 573
Average GMAT (part time): 543
Average GPA (full time): 3.27
Average age of entrants to full-time program: 25

Average months of prior work experience (full time): 39
TOEFL requirement: Yes
Minimum TOEFL score: 550
Most popular departments: accounting, finance, general management, health care administration, marketing
Mean starting base salary for 2016 full-time graduates: $57,545
Employment location for 2016 class: Intl. 0%; N.E. 100%; M.A. 0%; S. 0%; M.W. 0%; S.W. 0%; W. 0%

Iona College (Hagan)
715 North Avenue
New Rochelle, NY 10801
www.iona.edu/hagan
Private
Admissions: (800) 231-4662
Email: gradadmissions@iona.edu
Financial aid: (914) 633-2497
Application deadline: rolling
Tuition: full time: N/A; part time: $1,062/credit hour
Room/board/expenses: N/A
College-funded aid: Yes
International student aid: Yes
Full-time enrollment: N/A
men: N/A; women: N/A; minorities: N/A; international: N/A
Part-time enrollment: 292
men: 53%; women: 47%; minorities: 27%; international: 15%
Average GMAT (part time): 434
TOEFL requirement: Yes
Minimum TOEFL score: 550
Most popular departments: accounting, finance, general management, marketing, management information systems

Ithaca College
953 Danby Road
Ithaca, NY 14850-7000
www.ithaca.edu/gradadmission
Private
Admissions: (607) 274-3124
Email: admission@ithaca.edu
Financial aid: (607) 274-3131
Application deadline: 05/15
Tuition: full time: $927/credit hour; part time: $927/credit hour
Room/board/expenses: N/A
College-funded aid: Yes
International student aid: Yes
Full-time enrollment: 20
men: 70%; women: 30%; minorities: 15%; international: 5%
Part-time enrollment: 1
men: 100%; women: 0%; minorities: 0%; international: 0%
Acceptance rate (full time): 87%
Average age of entrants to full-time program: 22
TOEFL requirement: Yes
Minimum TOEFL score: 550

Le Moyne College
1419 Salt Springs Road
Syracuse, NY 13214-1301
www.lemoyne.edu/madden
Private
Admissions: (315) 445-5444
Email: business@lemoyne.edu
Financial aid: (315) 445-4400
Application deadline: 07/01
Tuition: full time: $797/credit hour; part time: $797/credit hour

Room/board/expenses: N/A
College-funded aid: Yes
International student aid: Yes
Average student indebtedness at graduation: $6,765
Full-time enrollment: 43
men: 56%; women: 44%; minorities: 7%; international: 2%
Part-time enrollment: 65
men: 60%; women: 40%; minorities: 9%; international: 0%
Acceptance rate (full time): 96%
Average GMAT (full time): 432
Average GMAT (part time): 480
Average GPA (full time): 3.20
Average age of entrants to full-time program: 24
Average months of prior work experience (full time): 24
TOEFL requirement: Yes
Minimum TOEFL score: 550

LIU Post
720 Northern Boulevard
Brookville, NY 11548-1300
www.liu.edu/postmba
Private
Admissions: (516) 299-2900
Email: post-enroll@liu.edu
Financial aid: (516) 299-2338
Application deadline: 08/18
Tuition: full time: $1,178/credit hour; part time: $1,178/credit hour
Room/board/expenses: $19,726
College-funded aid: Yes
International student aid: Yes
Full-time enrollment: 101
men: 59%; women: 41%; minorities: 16%; international: 39%
Part-time enrollment: 37
men: 70%; women: 30%; minorities: 27%; international: 0%
Acceptance rate (full time): 62%
Average GMAT (full time): 460
Average GMAT (part time): 472
Average GPA (full time): 3.24
Average age of entrants to full-time program: 24
Average months of prior work experience (full time): 33
TOEFL requirement: Yes
Minimum TOEFL score: N/A

Manhattan College
4513 Manhattan College Parkway
Riverdale, NY 10471
manhattan.edu/
Private
Admissions: (718) 862-8200
Email: gradadmit@manhattan.edu
Financial aid: (718) 862-7178
Application deadline: rolling
Tuition: full time: $1,025/credit hour; part time: $1,025/credit hour
Room/board/expenses: N/A
College-funded aid: Yes
International student aid: Yes
Full-time enrollment: 75
men: 56%; women: 44%; minorities: 25%; international: 11%
Part-time enrollment: 4
men: 25%; women: 75%; minorities: 0%; international: N/A
Minimum TOEFL score: N/A
Most popular departments: accounting, economics, entrepreneurship, ethics, leadership

Marist College
127 Dyson Center
Poughkeepsie, NY 12601
www.marist.edu/admission/graduate/businessadministration/
Private
Admissions: (845) 575-3800
Email: graduate@marist.edu
Financial aid: (845) 575-3000
Application deadline: rolling
Tuition: full time: N/A; part time: $780/credit hour
Room/board/expenses: N/A
College-funded aid: Yes
International student aid: No
Full-time enrollment: N/A
men: N/A; women: N/A; minorities: N/A; international: N/A
Part-time enrollment: 185
men: 57%; women: 43%; minorities: 17%; international: 0%
Average GMAT (part time): 539
TOEFL requirement: Yes
Minimum TOEFL score: 550
Most popular departments: finance, general management, health care administration, leadership

New York Institute of Technology[1]
1855 Broadway
New York, NY 10023
www.nyit.edu/degrees/management_mba
Private
Admissions: (516) 686-7520
Email: nyitgrad@nyit.edu
Financial aid: N/A
Tuition: N/A
Room/board/expenses: N/A
Enrollment: N/A

New York University (Stern)
44 W. Fourth Street
New York, NY 10012-1126
www.stern.nyu.edu
Private
Admissions: (212) 998-0600
Email: sternmba@stern.nyu.edu
Financial aid: (212) 998-0790
Application deadline: 03/15
Tuition: full time: $69,110; part time: $2,090/credit hour
Room/board/expenses: $37,086
College-funded aid: Yes
International student aid: Yes
Average student indebtedness at graduation: $115,861
Full-time enrollment: 790
men: 64%; women: 36%; minorities: N/A; international: N/A
Part-time enrollment: 1,381
men: 63%; women: 37%; minorities: N/A; international: N/A
Acceptance rate (full time): 23%
Average GMAT (full time): 710
Average GMAT (part time): 669
Average GPA (full time): 3.51
Average age of entrants to full-time program: 27
Average months of prior work experience (full time): 59
TOEFL requirement: Yes
Minimum TOEFL score: N/A
Most popular departments: consulting, entrepreneurship, finance, general management, marketing
Mean starting base salary for 2016 full-time graduates: $120,924

Employment location for 2016 class: Intl. 7%; N.E. 79%; M.A. 3%; S. 1%; M.W. 2%; S.W. 2%; W. 7%

Niagara University
PO Box 1909
Niagara University, NY 14109
mba.niagara.edu
Private
Admissions: (716) 286-8051
Email: mbadirector@niagara.edu
Financial aid: (716) 286-8686
Application deadline: rolling
Tuition: full time: $870/credit hour; part time: $870/credit hour
Room/board/expenses: $14,570
College-funded aid: Yes
International student aid: Yes
Full-time enrollment: 172
men: 60%; women: 40%; minorities: 11%; international: 34%
Part-time enrollment: 67
men: 45%; women: 55%; minorities: 9%; international: 25%
Average age of entrants to full-time program: 23
TOEFL requirement: Yes
Minimum TOEFL score: 550
Most popular departments: accounting, finance, general management, health care administration, marketing

Pace University (Lubin)
1 Pace Plaza
New York, NY 10038
www.pace.edu/lubin/sections/explore-programs/graduate-programs
Private
Admissions: (212) 346-1531
Email: graduateadmission@pace.edu
Financial aid: (914) 773-3751
Application deadline: 08/01
Tuition: full time: $1,195/credit hour; part time: $1,195/credit hour
Room/board/expenses: $21,250
College-funded aid: Yes
International student aid: Yes
Average student indebtedness at graduation: $44,076
Full-time enrollment: 234
men: 53%; women: 47%; minorities: 24%; international: 56%
Part-time enrollment: 122
men: 45%; women: 55%; minorities: 36%; international: 20%
Acceptance rate (full time): 61%
Average GMAT (full time): 552
Average GMAT (part time): 545
Average GPA (full time): 3.50
Average age of entrants to full-time program: 25
TOEFL requirement: Yes
Minimum TOEFL score: 577
Most popular departments: accounting, finance, general management, human resources management, marketing
Mean starting base salary for 2016 full-time graduates: $64,425
Employment location for 2016 class: Intl. 4%; N.E. 94%; M.A. N/A; S. N/A; M.W. 1%; S.W. N/A; W. 1%

Rensselaer Polytechnic Institute (Lally)[1]

110 Eighth Street
Pittsburgh Building 5202
Troy, NY 12180-3590
lallyschool.rpi.edu
Private
Admissions: (518) 276-6565
Email: lallymba@rpi.edu
Financial aid: (518) 276-6565
Tuition: N/A
Room/board/expenses: N/A
Enrollment: N/A

Rochester Institute of Technology (Saunders)

105 Lomb Memorial Drive
Rochester, NY 14623-5608
saunders.rit.edu
Private
Admissions: (585) 475-7284
Email: gradinfo@rit.edu
Financial aid: (585) 475-2186
Application deadline: rolling
Tuition: full time: $42,078; part time: $1,742/credit hour
Room/board/expenses: $14,300
College-funded aid: Yes
International student aid: Yes
Full-time enrollment: 182
men: 55%; women: 45%;
minorities: 8%; international: 59%
Part-time enrollment: 52
men: 50%; women: 50%;
minorities: 6%; international: 12%
Acceptance rate (full time): 52%
Average GMAT (full time): 558
Average GMAT (part time): 542
Average GPA (full time): 3.40
Average age of entrants to full-time program: 26
Average months of prior work experience (full time): 53
TOEFL requirement: Yes
Minimum TOEFL score: 580
Most popular departments:
finance, leadership, marketing, management information systems, technology
Mean starting base salary for 2016 full-time graduates: $51,912
Employment location for 2016 class: Intl. 20%; N.E. 62%; M.A. 3%; S. 3%; M.W. 3%; S.W. 6%; W. 3%

St. Bonaventure University

3261 West State Road
St. Bonaventure, NY 14778
www.sbu.edu/admission-aid/graduate-admissions
Private
Admissions: (716) 375-2021
Email: gradsch@sbu.edu
Financial aid: (716) 375-2528
Application deadline: 10/08
Tuition: full time: $733/credit hour; part time: $733/credit hour
Room/board/expenses: $25,639
College-funded aid: Yes
International student aid: Yes
Average student indebtedness at graduation: $19,455
Full-time enrollment: 60
men: 68%; women: 32%;
minorities: 17%; international: 3%

Part-time enrollment: 58
men: 50%; women: 50%;
minorities: 16%; international: 2%
Acceptance rate (full time): 91%
Average GMAT (full time): 441
Average GMAT (part time): 406
Average GPA (full time): 3.46
Average age of entrants to full-time program: 23
TOEFL requirement: Yes
Minimum TOEFL score: 550
Most popular departments:
accounting, finance, general management, marketing
Mean starting base salary for 2016 full-time graduates: $50,000
Employment location for 2016 class: Intl. N/A; N.E. 95%; M.A. N/A; S. 3%; M.W. 3%; S.W. N/A; W. N/A

St. John Fisher College

3690 East Avenue
Rochester, NY 14618
www.sjfc.edu/academics/business/about/index.dot
Private
Admissions: (585) 385-8161
Email: grad@sjfc.edu
Financial aid: (585) 385-8042
Application deadline: rolling
Tuition: full time: $1,050/credit hour; part time: $1,050/credit hour
Room/board/expenses: N/A
College-funded aid: Yes
International student aid: Yes
Full-time enrollment: 47
men: 60%; women: 40%;
minorities: 4%; international: 0%
Part-time enrollment: 83
men: 51%; women: 49%;
minorities: 13%; international: 2%
Acceptance rate (full time): 83%
Average GMAT (full time): 555
Average GMAT (part time): 500
Average GPA (full time): 3.39
Average age of entrants to full-time program: 25
TOEFL requirement: Yes
Minimum TOEFL score: 575

St. John's University (Tobin)

8000 Utopia Parkway
Queens, NY 11439
www.stjohns.edu/tobin
Private
Admissions: (718) 990-3060
Email: tobingradnyc@stjohns.edu
Financial aid: (718) 990-2000
Application deadline: 11/01
Tuition: full time: $1,180/credit hour; part time: $1,180/credit hour
Room/board/expenses: $23,016
College-funded aid: Yes
International student aid: Yes
Average student indebtedness at graduation: $28,291
Full-time enrollment: 397
men: 52%; women: 48%;
minorities: 25%; international: 45%
Part-time enrollment: 238
men: 60%; women: 40%;
minorities: 33%; international: 16%
Acceptance rate (full time): 72%
Average GMAT (full time): 542
Average GMAT (part time): 517
Average GPA (full time): 3.26

Part-time enrollment: 173
men: 63%; women: 37%;
minorities: 18%; international: 1%
Acceptance rate (full time): 88%
Average GMAT (full time): 514
Average GMAT (part time): 555
Average GPA (full time): 3.32
Average age of entrants to full-time program: 24
Average months of prior work experience (full time): 53
TOEFL requirement: Yes
Minimum TOEFL score: 560
Most popular departments:
accounting, general management, health care administration, marketing, tax
Mean starting base salary for 2016 full-time graduates: $48,000

SUNY-Geneseo[1]

1 College Circle
Geneseo, NY 14454
www.geneseo.edu/business
Public
Admissions: N/A
Financial aid: N/A
Tuition: N/A
Room/board/expenses: N/A
Enrollment: N/A

SUNY-New Paltz

1 Hawk Drive
New Paltz, NY
www.newpaltz.edu/graduate
Public
Admissions: (845) 257-3947
Email: gradschool@newpaltz.edu
Financial aid: (845) 257-3250
Application deadline: rolling
In-state tuition: full time: $15,677; part time: $600/credit hour
Out-of-state tuition: full time: $25,657
Room/board/expenses: N/A
College-funded aid: Yes
International student aid: No
Full-time enrollment: 41
men: 59%; women: 41%;
minorities: 27%; international: 20%
Part-time enrollment: 39
men: 41%; women: 59%;
minorities: 31%; international: 10%
Acceptance rate (full time): 93%
Average GMAT (full time): 447
Average GPA (full time): 3.43
Average age of entrants to full-time program: 26
TOEFL requirement: Yes
Minimum TOEFL score: N/A
Most popular departments:
accounting, general management

SUNY-Oswego

138 Rich Hall
Oswego, NY 13126
www.oswego.edu/graduate/
Public
Admissions: (315) 312-3152
Email: gradstudies@oswego.edu
Financial aid: (315) 312-2248
Application deadline: rolling
In-state tuition: full time: $15,068; part time: $600/credit hour
Out-of-state tuition: full time: $25,048
Room/board/expenses: $18,190
College-funded aid: Yes
International student aid: Yes
Average student indebtedness at graduation: $16,677
Full-time enrollment: 76
men: 47%; women: 53%;
minorities: 14%; international: 14%

SUNY Polytechnic Institute[1]

100 Seymour Road
Utica, NY 13502
www.sunypoly.edu/graduate/mbatm/
Public
Admissions: (315) 792-7347
Email: gradcenter@sunyit.edu
Financial aid: (315) 792-7210
Tuition: N/A
Room/board/expenses: N/A
Enrollment: N/A

Syracuse University (Whitman)

721 University Avenue, Suite 315
Syracuse, NY 13244-2450
whitman.syr.edu/mba/fulltime
Private
Admissions: (315) 443-9214
Email: busgrad@syr.edu
Financial aid: (315) 443-9214
Application deadline: 04/19
Tuition: full time: $44,492; part time: $1,443/credit hour
Room/board/expenses: $17,602
College-funded aid: Yes
International student aid: Yes
Average student indebtedness at graduation: $41,419
Full-time enrollment: 58
men: 69%; women: 31%;
minorities: 2%; international: 76%
Part-time enrollment: N/A
men: N/A; women: N/A;
minorities: N/A; international: N/A
Acceptance rate (full time): 56%
Average GMAT (full time): 622
Average GPA (full time): 3.58
Average age of entrants to full-time program: 26
Average months of prior work experience (full time): 38
TOEFL requirement: Yes
Minimum TOEFL score: 600
Most popular departments:
entrepreneurship, finance, general management, marketing, supply chain management/logistics
Mean starting base salary for 2016 full-time graduates: $75,879
Employment location for 2016 class: Intl. N/A; N.E. 52%; M.A. 4%; S. 9%; M.W. 9%; S.W. 9%; W. 17%

University at Albany-SUNY

1400 Washington Avenue
Massry Center for Business
Albany, NY 12222
graduatebusiness.albany.edu
Public
Admissions: (518) 442-3980
Email: graduate@albany.edu
Financial aid: (518) 442-5757
Application deadline: 05/01
In-state tuition: full time: $16,274; part time: $600/credit hour
Out-of-state tuition: full time: $26,254
Room/board/expenses: $12,942
College-funded aid: Yes
International student aid: Yes
Full-time enrollment: 92
men: 58%; women: 42%;
minorities: 23%; international: 17%
Part-time enrollment: 192
men: 60%; women: 40%;
minorities: 22%; international: 6%
Acceptance rate (full time): 63%
Average GMAT (full time): 580
Average GMAT (part time): 540
Average GPA (full time): 3.50
Average months of prior work experience (full time): 36
TOEFL requirement: Yes
Minimum TOEFL score: 600
Most popular departments:
finance, human resources management, marketing, management information systems, other
Mean starting base salary for 2016 full-time graduates: $62,000
Employment location for 2016 class: Intl. N/A; N.E. 100%; M.A. N/A; S. N/A; M.W. N/A; S.W. N/A; W. N/A

University at Buffalo-SUNY

203 Alfiero Center
Buffalo, NY 14260-4010
mgt.buffalo.edu/mba
Public
Admissions: (716) 645-3204
Email: som-apps@buffalo.edu
Financial aid: (716) 645-8232
Application deadline: 06/01
In-state tuition: full time: $18,857; part time: $760/credit hour
Out-of-state tuition: full time: $28,837
Room/board/expenses: $22,000
College-funded aid: Yes
International student aid: Yes
Full-time enrollment: 241
men: 62%; women: 38%;
minorities: 15%; international: 23%
Part-time enrollment: 196
men: 68%; women: 32%;
minorities: 11%; international: 2%
Acceptance rate (full time): 63%
Average GMAT (full time): 602
Average GMAT (part time): 554
Average GPA (full time): 3.40
Average age of entrants to full-time program: 24
Average months of prior work experience (full time): 15
TOEFL requirement: Yes
Minimum TOEFL score: 570
Most popular departments:
consulting, finance, health care administration, marketing, other
Mean starting base salary for 2016 full-time graduates: $61,779

Employment location for 2016 class: Intl. 5%; N.E. 75%; M.A. 3%; S. 10%; M.W. 3%; S.W. 2%; W. 2%

University of Rochester (Simon)

Schlegel Hall
Rochester, NY 14627
www.simon.rochester.edu
Private
Admissions: (585) 275-3533
Email: admissions@
simon.rochester.edu
Financial aid: (585) 275-3533
Application deadline: 05/15
Tuition: full time: $47,089; part time: $1,800/credit hour
Room/board/expenses: $17,740
College-funded aid: Yes
International student aid: Yes
Average student indebtedness at graduation: $62,717
Full-time enrollment: 204
men: 62%; women: 38%; minorities: 26%; international: 50%
Part-time enrollment: 161
men: 64%; women: 36%; minorities: 16%; international: 3%
Acceptance rate (full time): 34%
Average GMAT (full time): 665
Average GMAT (part time): 560
Average GPA (full time): 3.40
Average age of entrants to full-time program: 28
Average months of prior work experience (full time): 64
TOEFL requirement: Yes
Minimum TOEFL score: N/A
Most popular departments: accounting, consulting, finance, marketing, other
Mean starting base salary for 2016 full-time graduates: $98,640
Employment location for 2016 class: Intl. 5%; N.E. 46%; M.A. 9%; S. 8%; M.W. 10%; S.W. 4%; W. 18%

Yeshiva University (Syms)[1]

500 West 185th Street
New York, NY 10033
www.yu.edu/syms/
Private
Admissions: N/A
Financial aid: N/A
Tuition: N/A
Room/board/expenses: N/A
Enrollment: N/A

NORTH CAROLINA

Appalachian State University (Walker)

Box 32037
Boone, NC 28608-2037
www.business.appstate.edu/mba
Public
Admissions: (828) 262-2130
Email: mba@appstate.edu
Financial aid: (828) 262-2190
Application deadline: 07/01
In-state tuition: total program: $15,671 (full time); $18,109 (part time)
Out-of-state tuition: total program: $32,680 (full time)
Room/board/expenses: N/A
College-funded aid: Yes
International student aid: Yes

Full-time enrollment: 74
men: 61%; women: 39%; minorities: 9%; international: 8%
Part-time enrollment: 41
men: 56%; women: 44%; minorities: 15%; international: N/A
Acceptance rate (full time): 86%
Average GPA (full time): 3.34
Average age of entrants to full-time program: 24
Average months of prior work experience (full time): 60
TOEFL requirement: Yes
Minimum TOEFL score: N/A
Most popular departments: economics, general management, international business, management information systems, supply chain management/logistics

Duke University (Fuqua)

100 Fuqua Drive
Box 90120
Durham, NC 27708-0120
www.fuqua.duke.edu
Private
Admissions: (919) 257-9913
Email: admissions-info@
fuqua.duke.edu
Financial aid: (919) 660-7687
Application deadline: 03/20
Tuition: full time: $65,760; part time: N/A
Room/board/expenses: $21,699
College-funded aid: Yes
International student aid: Yes
Average student indebtedness at graduation: $109,960
Full-time enrollment: 896
men: 65%; women: 35%; minorities: 19%; international: 38%
Part-time enrollment: N/A
men: N/A; women: N/A; minorities: N/A; international: N/A
Acceptance rate (full time): 22%
Average GMAT (full time): 695
Average GPA (full time): 3.47
Average age of entrants to full-time program: 29
Average months of prior work experience (full time): 66
TOEFL requirement: No
Minimum TOEFL score: N/A
Most popular departments: consulting, finance, health care administration, marketing, quantitative analysis/statistics and operations research
Mean starting base salary for 2016 full-time graduates: $121,283
Employment location for 2016 class: Intl. 10%; N.E. 21%; M.A. 9%; S. 20%; M.W. 10%; S.W. 9%; W. 22%

East Carolina University

3203 Bate Building
Greenville, NC 27858-4353
www.business.ecu.edu/grad/
Public
Admissions: (252) 328-6970
Email: gradbus@ecu.edu
Financial aid: (252) 328-6610
Application deadline: 06/01
In-state tuition: full time: $353/credit hour; part time: $353/credit hour
Out-of-state tuition: full time: $985/credit hour
Room/board/expenses: $19,062

College-funded aid: Yes
International student aid: Yes
Average student indebtedness at graduation: $34,240
Full-time enrollment: 185
men: 62%; women: 38%; minorities: 24%; international: 4%
Part-time enrollment: 612
men: 52%; women: 48%; minorities: 21%; international: 2%
Acceptance rate (full time): 79%
Average GMAT (full time): 493
Average GMAT (part time): 503
Average GPA (full time): 3.40
Average age of entrants to full-time program: 27
TOEFL requirement: Yes
Minimum TOEFL score: 550
Most popular departments: finance, health care administration, marketing, management information systems, sports business

Elon University (Love)

100 Campus Drive
Elon, NC 27244-2010
elon.edu/mba
Private
Admissions: (336) 278-7600
Email: gradadm@elon.edu
Financial aid: (336) 278-7600
Application deadline: rolling
Tuition: full time: N/A; part time: $878/credit hour
Room/board/expenses: N/A
College-funded aid: No
International student aid: No
Full-time enrollment: N/A
men: N/A; women: N/A; minorities: N/A; international: N/A
Part-time enrollment: 133
men: 59%; women: 41%; minorities: N/A; international: N/A
Average GMAT (part time): 555
TOEFL requirement: Yes
Minimum TOEFL score: 550
Most popular departments: entrepreneurship, general management, human resources management, leadership, marketing

Fayetteville State University

1200 Murchison Road
Newbold Station
Fayetteville, NC 28301-1033
mba.uncfsu.edu/
Public
Admissions: (910) 672-1197
Email: mbaprogram@uncfsu.edu
Financial aid: (910) 672-1325
Application deadline: 06/30
In-state tuition: full time: $4,119; part time: $211/credit hour
Out-of-state tuition: full time: $9,328
Room/board/expenses: N/A
College-funded aid: Yes
International student aid: Yes
Full-time enrollment: N/A
men: N/A; women: N/A; minorities: N/A; international: N/A
Part-time enrollment: 120
men: 56%; women: 44%; minorities: 42%; international: 2%
Average GMAT (part time): 481
TOEFL requirement: Yes
Minimum TOEFL score: 550

Most popular departments: entrepreneurship, finance, general management, health care administration, production/operations management

Meredith College

3800 Hillsborough Street
Raleigh, NC 27607
www.meredith.edu/mba
Private
Admissions: (919) 760-2281
Email: mba@meredith.edu
Financial aid: (919) 760-8565
Application deadline: 06/01
Tuition: full time: $900/credit hour; part time: $900/credit hour
Room/board/expenses: $12,890
College-funded aid: Yes
International student aid: Yes
Average student indebtedness at graduation: $48,263
Full-time enrollment: 68
men: 15%; women: 85%; minorities: 29%; international: 6%
Part-time enrollment: 29
men: 14%; women: 86%; minorities: 24%; international: N/A
Acceptance rate (full time): 90%
Average GMAT (full time): 530
Average GPA (full time): 3.35
Average age of entrants to full-time program: 31
Average months of prior work experience (full time): 133
TOEFL requirement: Yes
Minimum TOEFL score: 550
Most popular departments: general management, human resources management
Mean starting base salary for 2016 full-time graduates: $79,000
Employment location for 2016 class: Intl. 33%; N.E. N/A; M.A. N/A; S. 67%; M.W. N/A; S.W. N/A; W. N/A

North Carolina A&T State University

1601 E. Market Street
Greensboro, NC 27411
www.ncat.edu/~business/
Public
Admissions: (336) 334-7920
Email: jjtaylor@ncat.edu
Financial aid: (336) 334-7973
Application deadline: 05/01
In-state tuition: full time: $7,446; part time: $252/credit hour
Out-of-state tuition: full time: $10,052
Room/board/expenses: $9,668
College-funded aid: Yes
International student aid: Yes
Average student indebtedness at graduation: $35,000
Full-time enrollment: 74
men: 42%; women: 58%; minorities: 93%; international: 4%
Part-time enrollment: N/A
men: N/A; women: N/A; minorities: N/A; international: N/A
Acceptance rate (full time): 64%
Average GMAT (full time): 470
Average GPA (full time): 3.52
Average age of entrants to full-time program: 28
Average months of prior work experience (full time): 36
TOEFL requirement: Yes
Minimum TOEFL score: 550

Most popular departments: human resources management, supply chain management/logistics

North Carolina Central University[1]

1801 Fayetteville Street
Durham, NC 27707
www.nccu.edu/academics/
business/index.cfm
Public
Admissions: (919) 530-6405
Email: mba@nccu.edu
Financial aid: N/A
Tuition: N/A
Room/board/expenses: N/A
Enrollment: N/A

North Carolina State University (Jenkins)

2130 Nelson Hall
Campus Box 8114
Raleigh, NC 27695-8114
www.mba.ncsu.edu
Public
Admissions: (919) 515-5584
Email: mba@ncsu.edu
Financial aid: (919) 515-2866
Application deadline: 03/01
In-state tuition: full time: $23,697; part time: $1,039/credit hour
Out-of-state tuition: full time: $38,704
Room/board/expenses: $17,813
College-funded aid: Yes
International student aid: Yes
Average student indebtedness at graduation: $40,473
Full-time enrollment: 95
men: 66%; women: 34%; minorities: 21%; international: 21%
Part-time enrollment: 250
men: 62%; women: 38%; minorities: 31%; international: 10%
Acceptance rate (full time): 38%
Average GMAT (full time): 655
Average GMAT (part time): 593
Average GPA (full time): 3.46
Average age of entrants to full-time program: 30
Average months of prior work experience (full time): 69
TOEFL requirement: Yes
Minimum TOEFL score: 650
Most popular departments: entrepreneurship, marketing, supply chain management/logistics, technology, other
Mean starting base salary for 2016 full-time graduates: $90,416
Employment location for 2016 class: Intl. 0%; N.E. 5%; M.A. 0%; S. 71%; M.W. 14%; S.W. 10%; W. 0%

Queens University of Charlotte (McColl)[1]

1900 Selwyn Avenue
Charlotte, NC 28274
mccoll.queens.edu/
Private
Admissions: (704) 337-2224
Email: MBA@Queens.edu
Financial aid: (704) 337-2225
Tuition: N/A
Room/board/expenses: N/A
Enrollment: N/A

University of North Carolina-Chapel Hill (Kenan-Flagler)

CB 3490, McColl Building
Chapel Hill, NC 27599-3490
www.kenan-flagler.unc.edu
Public
Admissions: (919) 962-3236
Email: mba_info@unc.edu
Financial aid: (919) 962-9096
Application deadline: N/A
In-state tuition: full time: $43,451;
part time: N/A
Out-of-state tuition: full time:
$59,574
Room/board/expenses: $24,424
College-funded aid: Yes
International student aid: Yes
**Average student indebtedness at
graduation:** $95,582
Full-time enrollment: 574
men: 70%; women: 30%;
minorities: 19%; international:
29%
Part-time enrollment: N/A
men: N/A; women: N/A;
minorities: N/A; international: N/A
Acceptance rate (full time): 36%
Average GMAT (full time): 700
Average GPA (full time): 3.37
**Average age of entrants to full-
time program:** 28
TOEFL requirement: Yes
Minimum TOEFL score: N/A
Most popular departments:
consulting, entrepreneurship,
finance, marketing, real estate
**Mean starting base salary for 2016
full-time graduates:** $111,922
**Employment location for 2016
class:** Intl. 2%; N.E. 15%; M.A.
9%; S. 40%; M.W. 9%; S.W. 8%;
W. 16%

University of North Carolina-Charlotte (Belk)

9201 University City Boulevard
Charlotte, NC 28223
www.mba.uncc.edu
Public
Admissions: (704) 687-7566
Email: mba@uncc.edu
Financial aid: (704) 687-7010
Application deadline: rolling
In-state tuition: full time: $13,278;
part time: $9,822
Out-of-state tuition: full time:
$26,449
Room/board/expenses: N/A
College-funded aid: Yes
International student aid: Yes
Full-time enrollment: N/A
men: N/A; women: N/A;
minorities: N/A; international: N/A
Part-time enrollment: 271
men: 68%; women: 32%;
minorities: 18%; international:
14%
Average GMAT (part time): 583
TOEFL requirement: Yes
Minimum TOEFL score: 557

University of North Carolina-Greensboro (Bryan)

PO Box 26170
Greensboro, NC 27402-6170
mba.uncg.edu
Public
Admissions: (336) 334-5390
Email: mba@uncg.edu

Financial aid: (336) 334-5702
Application deadline: 07/01
In-state tuition: full time: $10,576;
part time: $519/credit hour
Out-of-state tuition: full time:
$26,547
Room/board/expenses: $12,222
College-funded aid: Yes
International student aid: Yes
Full-time enrollment: 44
men: 64%; women: 36%;
minorities: 18%; international:
27%
Part-time enrollment: 86
men: 66%; women: 34%;
minorities: 19%; international: 1%
Acceptance rate (full time): 54%
Average GMAT (full time): 560
Average GMAT (part time): 549
Average GPA (full time): 3.40
**Average age of entrants to full-
time program:** 25
**Average months of prior work
experience (full time):** 26
TOEFL requirement: Yes
Minimum TOEFL score: 550
Most popular departments:
finance, general management,
marketing, management
information systems, supply
chain management/logistics
**Mean starting base salary for 2016
full-time graduates:** $61,000
**Employment location for 2016
class:** Intl. N/A; N.E. 0%; M.A.
5%; S. 77%; M.W. 9%; S.W. 0%;
W. 9%

University of North Carolina-Pembroke

PO Box 1510
One University Drive
Pembroke, NC 28372
www.uncp.edu/grad
Public
Admissions: (910) 521-6271
Email: grad@uncp.edu
Financial aid: (910) 521-6255
Application deadline: 08/15
In-state tuition: full time: $5,924;
part time: $4,104
Out-of-state tuition: full time:
$16,181
Room/board/expenses: $13,469
College-funded aid: Yes
International student aid: Yes
**Average student indebtedness at
graduation:** $20,935
Full-time enrollment: 76
men: 38%; women: 62%;
minorities: 47%; international:
3%
Part-time enrollment: 36
men: 33%; women: 67%;
minorities: 47%; international:
N/A
Acceptance rate (full time): 98%
Average GMAT (full time): 435
Average GMAT (part time): 410
Average GPA (full time): 3.27
**Average age of entrants to full-
time program:** 29
TOEFL requirement: Yes
Minimum TOEFL score: 580

University of North Carolina-Wilmington (Cameron)

601 S. College Road
Wilmington, NC 28403-5680
www.csb.uncw.edu/
gradprograms
Public

Admissions: (910) 962-3903
Email: wilhelmc@uncw.edu
Financial aid: (910) 962-3177
Application deadline: 06/01
In-state tuition: total program:
$18,900 (full time); $11,605 (part
time)
Out-of-state tuition: total
program: $18,900 (full time)
Room/board/expenses: $17,297
College-funded aid: Yes
International student aid: Yes
Full-time enrollment: 33
men: 30%; women: 70%;
minorities: N/A; international: N/A
Part-time enrollment: 69
men: 64%; women: 36%;
minorities: N/A; international: N/A
Acceptance rate (full time): 95%
Average GPA (full time): 3.12
**Average age of entrants to full-
time program:** 26
**Average months of prior work
experience (full time):** 139
TOEFL requirement: Yes
Minimum TOEFL score: 550
Most popular departments:
consulting, finance, general
management, marketing

Wake Forest University

PO Box 7659
Winston-Salem, NC 27109-7659
www.business.wfu.edu
Private
Admissions: (336) 758-5422
Email: busadmissions@wfu.edu
Financial aid: (336) 758-4424
Application deadline: rolling
Tuition: full time: N/A; part time:
$38,415
Room/board/expenses: N/A
College-funded aid: Yes
International student aid: Yes
Full-time enrollment: N/A
men: N/A; women: N/A;
minorities: N/A; international: N/A
Part-time enrollment: 305
men: 65%; women: 35%;
minorities: 22%; international: 1%
Average GMAT (part time): 605
TOEFL requirement: Yes
Minimum TOEFL score: N/A

Western Carolina University

Forsyth Building
Cullowhee, NC 28723
businessgrad.wcu.edu
Public
Admissions: (828) 227-3174
Email: gradadmissions@
email.wcu.edu
Financial aid: (828) 227-7290
Application deadline: 07/15
In-state tuition: full time: $5,157;
part time: $4,501
Out-of-state tuition: full time:
$10,810
Room/board/expenses: $12,357
College-funded aid: Yes
International student aid: Yes
Full-time enrollment: 68
men: 56%; women: 44%;
minorities: 26%; international:
4%
Part-time enrollment: 200
men: 58%; women: 42%;
minorities: 26%; international:
2%
Acceptance rate (full time): 89%
Average GMAT (full time): 490
Average GMAT (part time): 460
Average GPA (full time): 3.30

**Average age of entrants to full-
time program:** 27
TOEFL requirement: Yes
Minimum TOEFL score: 550

Winston-Salem State University[1]

RJR Center Suite 109
Winston-Salem, NC 27110
www.wssu.edu/
Public
Admissions: (336) 750-3045
Email: graduate@wssu.edu
Financial aid: N/A
Tuition: N/A
Room/board/expenses: N/A
Enrollment: N/A

NORTH DAKOTA

North Dakota State University

NDSU Department 2400
PO Box 6050
Fargo, ND 58108-6050
www.ndsu.edu/business/
programs/graduate/mba/
Public
Admissions: (701) 231-7681
Email: paul.brown@ndsu.edu
Financial aid: N/A
Application deadline: rolling
In-state tuition: full time: $310/
credit hour; part time: $310/
credit hour
Out-of-state tuition: full time:
$827/credit hour
Room/board/expenses: N/A
College-funded aid: Yes
International student aid: Yes
Full-time enrollment: 22
men: 55%; women: 45%;
minorities: 27%; international:
55%
Part-time enrollment: 44
men: 55%; women: 45%;
minorities: 27%; international:
N/A
Acceptance rate (full time): 80%
Average GMAT (full time): 530
Average GMAT (part time): 530
Average GPA (full time): 3.30
**Average age of entrants to full-
time program:** 25
TOEFL requirement: Yes
Minimum TOEFL score: N/A
Most popular departments:
general management

University of North Dakota[1]

293 Centennial Drive
Stop 8098
Grand Forks, ND 58202-8098
business.und.edu/
Public
Admissions: N/A
Financial aid: N/A
Tuition: N/A
Room/board/expenses: N/A
Enrollment: N/A

OHIO

Bowling Green State University

371 Business Administration
Building
Bowling Green, OH 43403-0001
www.bgsumba.com
Public
Admissions: (800) 247-8622
Email: mba@bgsu.edu

Financial aid: (419) 372-2651
Application deadline: 03/01
In-state tuition: total program:
$18,696 (full time); $24,835
(part time)
Out-of-state tuition: total
program: $30,000 (full time)
Room/board/expenses: N/A
College-funded aid: Yes
International student aid: Yes
Full-time enrollment: 40
men: 55%; women: 45%;
minorities: N/A; international: N/A
Part-time enrollment: 90
men: 64%; women: 36%;
minorities: N/A; international: N/A
Acceptance rate (full time): 50%
Average GMAT (full time): 500
Average GPA (full time): 3.36
**Average age of entrants to full-
time program:** 24
**Average months of prior work
experience (full time):** 35
TOEFL requirement: Yes
Minimum TOEFL score: 550
Most popular departments:
accounting, finance, supply
chain management/logistics
**Mean starting base salary for 2016
full-time graduates:** $54,166

Case Western Reserve University (Weatherhead)

Peter B. Lewis Building
10900 Euclid Avenue
Cleveland, OH 44106-7235
www.weatherhead.case.edu
Private
Admissions: (216) 368-6702
Email:
wsomadmissions@case.edu
Financial aid: (216) 368-8907
Application deadline: 05/28
Tuition: full time: $38,450; part
time: $30,721
Room/board/expenses: $22,302
College-funded aid: Yes
International student aid: Yes
**Average student indebtedness at
graduation:** $51,408
Full-time enrollment: 125
men: 58%; women: 42%;
minorities: 18%; international:
44%
Part-time enrollment: 133
men: 63%; women: 37%;
minorities: 16%; international:
8%
Acceptance rate (full time): 64%
Average GMAT (full time): 632
Average GMAT (part time): 583
Average GPA (full time): 3.14
**Average age of entrants to full-
time program:** 28
**Average months of prior work
experience (full time):** 50
TOEFL requirement: Yes
Minimum TOEFL score: 600
Most popular departments:
accounting, finance, leadership,
marketing, quantitative analysis/
statistics and operations
research
**Mean starting base salary for 2016
full-time graduates:** $82,290
**Employment location for 2016
class:** Intl. 3%; N.E. 0%; M.A.
3%; S. 3%; M.W. 72%; S.W. 8%;
W. 11%

Cleveland State University (Ahuja)

1860 E. 18th Street, BU420
Cleveland, OH 44115
www.csuohio.edu/mba
Public
Admissions: (216) 687-5599
Email: cbacsu@csuohio.edu
Financial aid: (216) 687-5411
Application deadline: 08/18
In-state tuition: full time: $569/credit hour; part time: $569/credit hour
Out-of-state tuition: full time: $1,074/credit hour
Room/board/expenses: $15,818
College-funded aid: Yes
International student aid: Yes
Average student indebtedness at graduation: $35,562
Full-time enrollment: 192
men: 47%; women: 53%;
minorities: 18%; international: 36%
Part-time enrollment: 331
men: 55%; women: 45%;
minorities: 18%; international: 5%
Acceptance rate (full time): 71%
Average GMAT (full time): 455
Average GMAT (part time): 512
Average GPA (full time): 3.20
Average age of entrants to full-time program: 30
TOEFL requirement: Yes
Minimum TOEFL score: 550
Most popular departments:
accounting, finance, health care administration, marketing, supply chain management/logistics

John Carroll University (Boler)

1 John Carroll Boulevard
University Heights, OH 44118
www.jcu.edu/mba
Private
Admissions: (216) 397-1970
Email: gradbusiness@jcu.edu
Financial aid: (216) 397-4248
Application deadline: 07/15
Tuition: full time: N/A; part time: $855/credit hour
Room/board/expenses: N/A
College-funded aid: Yes
International student aid: Yes
Full-time enrollment: N/A
men: N/A; women: N/A;
minorities: N/A; international: N/A
Part-time enrollment: 111
men: 57%; women: 43%;
minorities: 0%; international: 14%
Average GMAT (part time): 517
TOEFL requirement: Yes
Minimum TOEFL score: 550
Most popular departments:
accounting, finance, human resources management, international business, marketing

Kent State University

PO Box 5190
Kent, OH 44242-0001
www.kent.edu/business/grad
Public
Admissions: (330) 672-2282
Email: gradbus@kent.edu
Financial aid: (330) 672-2972
Application deadline: 03/15
In-state tuition: full time: $12,290; part time: $505/credit hour

Out-of-state tuition: full time: $20,562
Room/board/expenses: $12,720
College-funded aid: Yes
International student aid: Yes
Full-time enrollment: 54
men: 57%; women: 43%;
minorities: 2%; international: 37%
Part-time enrollment: 67
men: 58%; women: 42%;
minorities: 4%; international: 1%
Acceptance rate (full time): 63%
Average GMAT (full time): 533
Average GMAT (part time): 534
Average GPA (full time): 3.38
Average age of entrants to full-time program: 24
Average months of prior work experience (full time): 7
TOEFL requirement: Yes
Minimum TOEFL score: 550
Most popular departments:
accounting, finance, general management, international business, supply chain management/logistics
Mean starting base salary for 2016 full-time graduates: $58,916

Miami University (Farmer)

800 E. High Street
Oxford, OH 45056
miamioh.edu/fsb/mba/
Public
Admissions: (513) 895-8876
Email: mba@miamioh.edu
Financial aid: (513) 529-8710
Application deadline: rolling
In-state tuition: full time: N/A; total program: $37,800 (part time)
Out-of-state tuition: full time: N/A
Room/board/expenses: N/A
College-funded aid: No
International student aid: No
Full-time enrollment: N/A
men: N/A; women: N/A;
minorities: N/A; international: N/A
Part-time enrollment: 127
men: 68%; women: 32%;
minorities: 21%; international: 3%
Average GMAT (part time): 623
TOEFL requirement: Yes
Minimum TOEFL score: 550
Most popular departments:
finance, general management, marketing

Ohio State University (Fisher)

100 Gerlach Hall
2108 Neil Avenue
Columbus, OH 43210-1144
fisher.osu.edu/graduate/ftmba
Public
Admissions: (614) 292-8511
Email: mba@fisher.osu.edu
Financial aid: (614) 292-8511
Application deadline: 04/15
In-state tuition: full time: $31,139; part time: $1,574/credit hour
Out-of-state tuition: full time: $51,587
Room/board/expenses: $18,305
College-funded aid: Yes
International student aid: Yes
Average student indebtedness at graduation: $64,145
Full-time enrollment: 206
men: 76%; women: 24%;
minorities: 15%; international: 30%

Part-time enrollment: 323
men: 70%; women: 30%;
minorities: 18%; international: 7%
Acceptance rate (full time): 32%
Average GMAT (full time): 671
Average GMAT (part time): 604
Average GPA (full time): 3.52
Average age of entrants to full-time program: 28
Average months of prior work experience (full time): 64
TOEFL requirement: Yes
Minimum TOEFL score: 600
Most popular departments:
consulting, finance, marketing, production/operations management, supply chain management/logistics
Mean starting base salary for 2016 full-time graduates: $100,830
Employment location for 2016 class: Intl. 4%; N.E. 8%; M.A. 2%; S. 5%; M.W. 60%; S.W. 8%; W. 13%

Ohio University

1 Ohio University
College of Business Annex, 351
Athens, OH 45701
www.business.ohio.edu
Public
Admissions: (740) 597-9067
Email: hankins@ohio.edu
Financial aid: (740) 593-4141
Application deadline: 03/01
In-state tuition: total program: $19,677 (full time); $39,630 (part time)
Out-of-state tuition: total program: $31,665 (full time)
Room/board/expenses: $15,700
College-funded aid: Yes
International student aid: Yes
Average student indebtedness at graduation: $24,692
Full-time enrollment: 40
men: 55%; women: 45%;
minorities: 15%; international: 15%
Part-time enrollment: 93
men: 58%; women: 42%;
minorities: 17%; international: 4%
Acceptance rate (full time): 49%
Average GMAT (full time): 572
Average GPA (full time): 3.39
Average age of entrants to full-time program: 24
Average months of prior work experience (full time): 17
TOEFL requirement: Yes
Minimum TOEFL score: 550

University of Akron

CBA 412
Akron, OH 44325-4805
mba.uakron.edu
Public
Admissions: (330) 972-7043
Email: gradcba@uakron.edu
Financial aid: (330) 972-7032
Application deadline: 07/15
In-state tuition: full time: N/A; part time: $461/credit hour
Out-of-state tuition: full time: N/A
Room/board/expenses: N/A
College-funded aid: Yes
International student aid: Yes
Full-time enrollment: N/A
men: N/A; women: N/A;
minorities: N/A; international: N/A
Part-time enrollment: 405
men: 59%; women: 41%;
minorities: 10%; international: 30%
Average GMAT (part time): 551

TOEFL requirement: Yes
Minimum TOEFL score: 550
Most popular departments:
accounting, general management, management information systems, tax, other

University of Cincinnati (Lindner)

606 Lindner Hall
Cincinnati, OH 45221-0020
www.business.uc.edu/mba
Public
Admissions: (513) 556-7024
Email: graduate@uc.edu
Financial aid: (513) 556-6982
Application deadline: 08/01
In-state tuition: total program: $31,437 (full time); part time: $890/credit hour
Out-of-state tuition: total program: $43,194 (full time)
Room/board/expenses: $25,000
College-funded aid: Yes
International student aid: Yes
Average student indebtedness at graduation: $29,437
Full-time enrollment: 81
men: 68%; women: 32%;
minorities: 12%; international: 35%
Part-time enrollment: 136
men: 63%; women: 38%;
minorities: 17%; international: 9%
Acceptance rate (full time): 45%
Average GMAT (full time): 649
Average GMAT (part time): 655
Average GPA (full time): 3.42
Average age of entrants to full-time program: 26
Average months of prior work experience (full time): 21
TOEFL requirement: Yes
Minimum TOEFL score: 600
Most popular departments:
entrepreneurship, health care administration, marketing, real estate, quantitative analysis/statistics and operations research
Mean starting base salary for 2016 full-time graduates: $72,856
Employment location for 2016 class: Intl. 0%; N.E. 3%; M.A. 3%; S. 3%; M.W. 85%; S.W. 3%; W. 5%

University of Dayton

300 College Park Avenue
Dayton, OH 45469-2234
business.udayton.edu/mba
Private
Admissions: (937) 229-3733
Email: mba@udayton.edu
Financial aid: (937) 229-4311
Application deadline: rolling
Tuition: full time: $970/credit hour; part time: $970/credit hour
Room/board/expenses: N/A
College-funded aid: Yes
International student aid: Yes
Full-time enrollment: 107
men: 70%; women: 30%;
minorities: N/A; international: N/A
Part-time enrollment: 92
men: 59%; women: 41%;
minorities: N/A; international: N/A
Acceptance rate (full time): 34%
Average GMAT (full time): 540
Average GMAT (part time): 540
Average GPA (full time): 3.32
Average age of entrants to full-time program: 23
TOEFL requirement: Yes
Minimum TOEFL score: 550

University of Toledo

Stranahan Hall North
Room 3130
Toledo, OH 43606-3390
utoledo.edu/business/graduate
Public
Admissions: (419) 530-5689
Email: COBIGradPrograms@utoledo.edu
Financial aid: (419) 530-8700
Application deadline: 08/01
In-state tuition: full time: $527/credit hour; part time: N/A
Out-of-state tuition: full time: $943/credit hour
Room/board/expenses: N/A
College-funded aid: Yes
International student aid: Yes
Full-time enrollment: 359
men: 53%; women: 47%;
minorities: 8%; international: 52%
Part-time enrollment: N/A
men: N/A; women: N/A;
minorities: N/A; international: N/A
Acceptance rate (full time): 83%
Average GMAT (full time): 483
Average GPA (full time): 3.46
Average age of entrants to full-time program: 26
TOEFL requirement: Yes
Minimum TOEFL score: 550

Wright State University (Soin)[1]

3640 Colonel Glenn Highway
Dayton, OH 45435-0001
www.wright.edu/business
Public
Admissions: (937) 775-2437
Email: mba@wright.edu
Financial aid: N/A
Tuition: N/A
Room/board/expenses: N/A
Enrollment: N/A

Xavier University (Williams)

1002 Francis Xavier Way
Cincinnati, OH 45207-1221
www.xavier.edu/MBA
Private
Admissions: (513) 745-4800
Email: mbaadmit@xavier.edu
Financial aid: (513) 745-3142
Application deadline: 08/01
Tuition: full time: $799/credit hour; part time: $799/credit hour
Room/board/expenses: $15,200
College-funded aid: Yes
International student aid: Yes
Average student indebtedness at graduation: $28,646
Full-time enrollment: 34
men: 53%; women: 47%;
minorities: 15%; international: 29%
Part-time enrollment: 481
men: 65%; women: 35%;
minorities: 18%; international: 5%
Acceptance rate (full time): 73%
Average GMAT (full time): 542
Average GMAT (part time): 563
Average GPA (full time): 3.30
Average age of entrants to full-time program: 25
Average months of prior work experience (full time): 36
TOEFL requirement: Yes
Minimum TOEFL score: 550

Most popular departments: finance, general management, marketing, quantitative analysis/ statistics and operations research, other
Mean starting base salary for 2016 full-time graduates: $58,777
Employment location for 2016 class: Intl. 14%; N.E. N/A; M.A. N/A; S. N/A; M.W. 71%; S.W. N/A; W. 14%

Youngstown State University (Williamson)[1]

1 University Plaza
Youngstown, OH 44555
web.ysu.edu/mba
Public
Admissions: N/A
Email: graduateschool@ysu.edu
Financial aid: N/A
Tuition: N/A
Room/board/expenses: N/A
Enrollment: N/A

OKLAHOMA

Oklahoma City University

2501 N Blackwelder
Oklahoma City, OK 73106
www.okcu.edu/mba/
Private
Admissions: (405) 208-5351
Email: gadmissions@okcu.edu
Financial aid: (405) 208-5211
Application deadline: rolling
Tuition: full time: $590/credit hour; part time: $590/credit hour
Room/board/expenses: $11,124
College-funded aid: Yes
International student aid: No
Average student indebtedness at graduation: $11,331
Full-time enrollment: 25 men: 76%; women: 24%; minorities: 32%; international: 36%
Part-time enrollment: 78 men: 46%; women: 54%; minorities: 31%; international: N/A
Acceptance rate (full time): 75%
Average GMAT (full time): 523
Average GMAT (part time): 385
Average GPA (full time): 3.20
Average age of entrants to full-time program: 26
TOEFL requirement: Yes
Minimum TOEFL score: N/A
Mean starting base salary for 2016 full-time graduates: $71,090

Oklahoma State University (Spears)

102 Gundersen
Stillwater, OK 74078-4022
spears.okstate.edu/
Public
Admissions: (405) 744-2951
Email: spearsmasters@okstate.edu
Financial aid: (405) 744-6604
Application deadline: 04/15
In-state tuition: full time: $209/ credit hour; part time: $209/ credit hour
Out-of-state tuition: full time: $825/credit hour
Room/board/expenses: $14,530
College-funded aid: Yes
International student aid: Yes

Average student indebtedness at graduation: $18,728
Full-time enrollment: 75 men: 61%; women: 39%; minorities: 5%; international: 36%
Part-time enrollment: 83 men: 71%; women: 29%; minorities: 6%; international: 5%
Acceptance rate (full time): 79%
Average GMAT (full time): 552
Average GMAT (part time): 551
Average GPA (full time): 3.43
Average age of entrants to full-time program: 25
Average months of prior work experience (full time): 65
TOEFL requirement: Yes
Minimum TOEFL score: 575
Most popular departments: entrepreneurship, finance, human resources management, not-for-profit management, other
Mean starting base salary for 2016 full-time graduates: $60,910
Employment location for 2016 class: Intl. 5%; N.E. 5%; M.A. N/A; S. 5%; M.W. 11%; S.W. 68%; W. 5%

Southeastern Oklahoma State University

1405 N. Fourth Avenue
PMB 4205
Durant, OK 74701-0609
www.se.edu/bus/
Public
Admissions: (580) 745-2176
Email: kluke@se.edu
Financial aid: (580) 745-2186
Application deadline: N/A
In-state tuition: full time: $230/ credit hour; part time: $230/ credit hour
Out-of-state tuition: full time: $551/credit hour
Room/board/expenses: N/A
College-funded aid: Yes
International student aid: Yes
Full-time enrollment: 107 men: 53%; women: 47%; minorities: 50%; international: 4%
Part-time enrollment: N/A men: N/A; women: N/A; minorities: N/A; international: N/A
Acceptance rate (full time): 100%
Average GPA (full time): 3.40
Average age of entrants to full-time program: 30
TOEFL requirement: Yes
Minimum TOEFL score: N/A
Most popular departments: entrepreneurship, finance, general management, human resources management, marketing

University of Oklahoma (Price)

Adams Hall
307 West Brooks
Norman, OK 73019-4004
ou.edu/mba
Public
Admissions: (405) 325-5623
Email: rebecca_watts@ou.edu
Financial aid: (405) 325-4521
Application deadline: 05/15
In-state tuition: total program: $26,100 (full time); $20,300 (part time)

Out-of-state tuition: total program: $53,300 (full time)
Room/board/expenses: $15,000
College-funded aid: Yes
International student aid: Yes
Full-time enrollment: 86 men: 72%; women: 28%; minorities: 17%; international: 22%
Part-time enrollment: 122 men: 82%; women: 18%; minorities: 11%; international: 2%
Acceptance rate (full time): 59%
Average GMAT (full time): 637
Average GMAT (part time): 597
Average GPA (full time): 3.43
Average age of entrants to full-time program: 25
Average months of prior work experience (full time): 21
TOEFL requirement: Yes
Minimum TOEFL score: 600
Most popular departments: entrepreneurship, finance, health care administration, management information systems, other
Mean starting base salary for 2016 full-time graduates: $72,731
Employment location for 2016 class: Intl. 14%; N.E. N/A; M.A. 5%; S. 5%; M.W. N/A; S.W. 77%; W. N/A

University of Tulsa (Collins)

800 S. Tucker Drive
Tulsa, OK 74104-9700
www.utulsa.edu/graduate/ business
Private
Admissions: (918) 631-2242
Email: graduate-business@ utulsa.edu
Financial aid: (918) 631-2526
Application deadline: 07/01
Tuition: full time: $1,235/credit hour; part time: $1,235/credit hour
Room/board/expenses: $16,278
College-funded aid: Yes
International student aid: Yes
Full-time enrollment: 39 men: 59%; women: 41%; minorities: 13%; international: 21%
Part-time enrollment: 48 men: 63%; women: 38%; minorities: 13%; international: 10%
Acceptance rate (full time): 49%
Average GMAT (full time): 561
Average GMAT (part time): 593
Average GPA (full time): 3.56
Average age of entrants to full-time program: 26
TOEFL requirement: Yes
Minimum TOEFL score: 575
Most popular departments: accounting, finance, general management, marketing, other
Mean starting base salary for 2016 full-time graduates: $100,600

OREGON

Oregon State University

443 Austin Hall
Corvallis, OR 97331
business.oregonstate.edu/mba/
Public
Admissions: (541) 737-5510
Email: mba.info@oregonstate.edu

Financial aid: (541) 737-2241
Application deadline: 08/20
In-state tuition: full time: $21,063; part time: $699/credit hour
Out-of-state tuition: full time: $34,536
Room/board/expenses: $15,975
College-funded aid: Yes
International student aid: Yes
Full-time enrollment: 135 men: 56%; women: 44%; minorities: 4%; international: 68%
Part-time enrollment: 82 men: 60%; women: 40%; minorities: 23%; international: 6%
Acceptance rate (full time): 51%
Average GMAT (full time): 590
Average GMAT (part time): 598
Average GPA (full time): 3.32
Average age of entrants to full-time program: 26
Average months of prior work experience (full time): 75
TOEFL requirement: Yes
Minimum TOEFL score: 575
Most popular departments: entrepreneurship, finance, leadership, supply chain management/logistics, quantitative analysis/statistics and operations research
Mean starting base salary for 2016 full-time graduates: $76,167

Portland State University

PO Box 751
Portland, OR 97207-0751
www.pdx.edu/sba/ the-portland-mba
Public
Admissions: (503) 725-8190
Email: gradinfo.sba@pdx.edu
Financial aid: (503) 725-5446
Application deadline: 05/02
In-state tuition: full time: $600/ credit hour; part time: $600/ credit hour
Out-of-state tuition: full time: $735/credit hour
Room/board/expenses: $20,000
College-funded aid: Yes
International student aid: Yes
Full-time enrollment: 31 men: 45%; women: 55%; minorities: 13%; international: 42%
Part-time enrollment: 51 men: 65%; women: 35%; minorities: 25%; international: 6%
Acceptance rate (full time): 42%
Average GMAT (full time): 601
Average GMAT (part time): 556
Average GPA (full time): 3.26
Average age of entrants to full-time program: 30
Average months of prior work experience (full time): 64
TOEFL requirement: Yes
Minimum TOEFL score: 550
Most popular departments: entrepreneurship, finance, sports business, supply chain management/logistics, other
Mean starting base salary for 2016 full-time graduates: $69,313
Employment location for 2016 class: Intl. 0%; N.E. 0%; M.A. 0%; S. 0%; M.W. 0%; S.W. 0%; W. 100%

University of Oregon (Lundquist)

1208 University of Oregon
Eugene, OR 97403-1208
business.uoregon.edu/mba/
Public
Admissions: (541) 346-3306
Email: mbainfo@uoregon.edu
Financial aid: (541) 346-3221
Application deadline: N/A
In-state tuition: full time: $30,701; part time: N/A
Out-of-state tuition: full time: $41,228
Room/board/expenses: $15,058
College-funded aid: Yes
International student aid: Yes
Average student indebtedness at graduation: $53,783
Full-time enrollment: 112 men: 70%; women: 30%; minorities: N/A; international: N/A
Part-time enrollment: N/A men: N/A; women: N/A; minorities: N/A; international: N/A
Acceptance rate (full time): 53%
Average GMAT (full time): 624
Average GPA (full time): 3.23
Average age of entrants to full-time program: 28
Average months of prior work experience (full time): 65
TOEFL requirement: Yes
Minimum TOEFL score: 600
Most popular departments: accounting, entrepreneurship, finance, sports business, other
Mean starting base salary for 2016 full-time graduates: $63,967
Employment location for 2016 class: Intl. 12%; N.E. 6%; M.A. N/A; S. N/A; M.W. 18%; S.W. N/A; W. 65%

University of Portland (Pamplin)

5000 N. Willamette Boulevard
Portland, OR 97203-5798
business.up.edu
Private
Admissions: (503) 943-7224
Email: bus-grad@up.edu
Financial aid: (503) 943-7311
Application deadline: 07/15
Tuition: full time: $1,220/credit hour; part time: $1,220/credit hour
Room/board/expenses: $10,500
College-funded aid: Yes
International student aid: Yes
Average student indebtedness at graduation: $60,956
Full-time enrollment: 39 men: 74%; women: 26%; minorities: 13%; international: 44%
Part-time enrollment: 119 men: 66%; women: 34%; minorities: 21%; international: 8%
Acceptance rate (full time): 55%
Average GMAT (full time): 548
Average GMAT (part time): 582
Average GPA (full time): 3.60
Average age of entrants to full-time program: 28
Average months of prior work experience (full time): 53
TOEFL requirement: Yes
Minimum TOEFL score: 570
Most popular departments: finance, manufacturing and technology management, marketing, production/ operations management, other

Willamette University (Atkinson)

900 State Street
Salem, OR 97301-3922
www.willamette.edu/mba
Private
Admissions: (503) 370-6167
Email: mba-admission@
willamette.edu
Financial aid: (503) 370-6273
Application deadline: 05/01
Tuition: full time: $39,280; total
program: $69,200 (part time)
Room/board/expenses: $13,078
College-funded aid: Yes
International student aid: Yes
Average student indebtedness at
graduation: $66,302
Full-time enrollment: 155
men: 55%; women: 45%;
minorities: 11%; international:
43%
Part-time enrollment: 120
men: 44%; women: 56%;
minorities: 18%; international:
0%
Acceptance rate (full time): 95%
Average GMAT (full time): 545
Average GMAT (part time): 479
Average GPA (full time): 3.22
Average age of entrants to full-
time program: 25
Average months of prior work
experience (full time): 13
TOEFL requirement: Yes
Minimum TOEFL score: 580
Most popular departments:
accounting, entrepreneurship,
finance, marketing, production/
operations management
Mean starting base salary for 2016
full-time graduates: $53,848
Employment location for 2016
class: Intl. 15%; N.E. 6%; M.A.
0%; S. 0%; M.W. 2%; S.W. 0%;
W. 77%

PENNSYLVANIA

Bloomsburg University of Pennsylvania

Sutliff Hall, Room 212
400 Second Street
Bloomsburg, PA 17815-1301
cob.bloomu.edu/
Public
Admissions: (570) 389-4394
Email: sawan@bloomu.edu
Financial aid: (570) 389-4297
Application deadline: 06/01
In-state tuition: full time: N/A; part
time: $483/credit hour
Out-of-state tuition: full time: N/A
Room/board/expenses: N/A
College-funded aid: Yes
International student aid: Yes
Full-time enrollment: N/A
men: N/A; women: N/A;
minorities: N/A; international: N/A
Part-time enrollment: 62
men: 60%; women: 40%;
minorities: 16%; international:
3%
Average GMAT (part time): 490
TOEFL requirement: Yes
Minimum TOEFL score: 590

Carnegie Mellon University (Tepper)

5000 Forbes Avenue
Pittsburgh, PA 15213
www.tepper.cmu.edu
Private
Admissions: (412) 268-2272

Email: mba-admissions@
andrew.cmu.edu
Financial aid: (412) 268-7581
Application deadline: 03/13
Tuition: full time: $62,230; part
time: $1,920/credit hour
Room/board/expenses: $21,916
College-funded aid: Yes
International student aid: Yes
Average student indebtedness at
graduation: $101,667
Full-time enrollment: 428
men: 74%; women: 26%;
minorities: 21%; international:
34%
Part-time enrollment: 143
men: 78%; women: 22%;
minorities: 18%; international:
8%
Acceptance rate (full time): 30%
Average GMAT (full time): 686
Average GMAT (part time): 646
Average GPA (full time): 3.30
Average age of entrants to full-
time program: 28
Average months of prior work
experience (full time): 63
TOEFL requirement: Yes
Minimum TOEFL score: 600
Most popular departments:
entrepreneurship, finance,
marketing, management
information systems,
organizational behavior
Mean starting base salary for 2016
full-time graduates: $117,717
Employment location for 2016
class: Intl. 5%; N.E. 31%; M.A.
13%; S. 5%; M.W. 15%; S.W. 2%;
W. 28%

Clarion University of Pennsylvania

840 Wood Street
Clarion, PA 16214
www.clarion.edu/admissions/
graduate
Public
Admissions: (814) 393-2337
Email: gradstudies@clarion.edu
Financial aid: (800) 672-7171
Application deadline: 07/15
In-state tuition: full time: $483/
credit hour; part time: $483/
credit hour
Out-of-state tuition: full time:
$522/credit hour
Room/board/expenses: $26,204
College-funded aid: Yes
International student aid: Yes
Average student indebtedness at
graduation: $25,563
Full-time enrollment: 30
men: 47%; women: 53%;
minorities: 20%; international:
10%
Part-time enrollment: 74
men: 53%; women: 47%;
minorities: 9%; international: N/A
Acceptance rate (full time): 79%
Average GMAT (full time): 550
Average GMAT (part time): 420
Average GPA (full time): 3.25
Average age of entrants to full-
time program: 27
Average months of prior work
experience (full time): 79
TOEFL requirement: Yes
Minimum TOEFL score: 550
Most popular departments:
accounting, entrepreneurship,
finance, general management,
health care administration

Drexel University (LeBow)

3141 Chestnut Street
Philadelphia, PA 19104
www.lebow.drexel.edu/
Private
Admissions: (215) 895-6804
Email: mba@drexel.edu
Financial aid: (215) 571-4545
Application deadline: 09/01
Tuition: total program: $64,000
(full time); part time: $1,106/
credit hour
Room/board/expenses: N/A
College-funded aid: Yes
International student aid: Yes
Average student indebtedness at
graduation: $42,830
Full-time enrollment: 57
men: 60%; women: 40%;
minorities: 9%; international:
47%
Part-time enrollment: 160
men: 54%; women: 46%;
minorities: 26%; international:
6%
Acceptance rate (full time): 45%
Average GMAT (full time): 597
Average GMAT (part time): 541
Average GPA (full time): 3.20
Average age of entrants to full-
time program: 28
Average months of prior work
experience (full time): 60
TOEFL requirement: Yes
Minimum TOEFL score: 577
Most popular departments:
entrepreneurship, finance,
health care administration,
marketing, other
Mean starting base salary for 2016
full-time graduates: $84,080

Duquesne University (Donahue)

600 Forbes Avenue
704 Rockwell Hall
Pittsburgh, PA 15282
www.duq.edu/business/grad
Private
Admissions: (412) 396-6276
Email: grad-bus@duq.edu
Financial aid: (412) 396-6607
Application deadline: 07/01
Tuition: total program: $54,831
(full time); part time: $1,234/
credit hour
Room/board/expenses: $15,360
College-funded aid: Yes
International student aid: Yes
Average student indebtedness at
graduation: $41,783
Full-time enrollment: 17
men: 35%; women: 65%;
minorities: 6%; international:
24%
Part-time enrollment: 224
men: 60%; women: 40%;
minorities: 7%; international: 14%
Acceptance rate (full time): 86%
Average GMAT (full time): 526
Average GMAT (part time): 542
Average GPA (full time): 3.30
Average age of entrants to full-
time program: 25
Average months of prior work
experience (full time): 27
TOEFL requirement: Yes
Minimum TOEFL score: 577
Most popular departments:
finance, general management,
marketing, supply chain
management/logistics

Employment location for 2016
class: Intl. N/A; N.E. N/A; M.A.
67%; S. N/A; M.W. N/A; S.W. N/A;
W. 33%

Indiana University of Pennsylvania (Eberly)

664 Pratt Drive, Room 402
Indiana, PA 15705
www.eberly.iup.edu/mba
Public
Admissions: (724) 357-2522
Email: iup-mba@iup.edu
Financial aid: (724) 357-2218
Application deadline: rolling
In-state tuition: full time: $508/
credit hour; part time: $508/
credit hour
Out-of-state tuition: full time:
$763/credit hour
Room/board/expenses: $15,014
College-funded aid: Yes
International student aid: Yes
Average student indebtedness at
graduation: $34,739
Full-time enrollment: 224
men: 69%; women: 31%;
minorities: 1%; international: 91%
Part-time enrollment: 17
men: 71%; women: 29%;
minorities: 6%; international:
47%
Acceptance rate (full time): 71%
Average GMAT (full time): 494
Average GMAT (part time): 380
Average age of entrants to full-
time program: 23
TOEFL requirement: Yes
Minimum TOEFL score: 540

King's College (McGowan)[1]

133 N. River Street
Wilkes-Barre, PA 18711
www.kings.edu/academics/
colleges_and_programs/business
Private
Admissions: (570) 208-5991
Email: gradprograms@kings.edu
Financial aid: N/A
Tuition: N/A
Room/board/expenses: N/A
Enrollment: N/A

Kutztown University of Pennsylvania

PO Box 730
Kutztown, PA 19530
www.kutztown.edu/admissions/
graduate-admissions.htm
Public
Admissions: (610) 683-4200
Email: graduate@kutztown.edu
Financial aid: (610) 683-4077
Application deadline: 08/01
In-state tuition: full time: $483/
credit hour; part time: $483/
credit hour
Out-of-state tuition: full time:
$725/credit hour
Room/board/expenses: N/A
College-funded aid: Yes
International student aid: Yes
Full-time enrollment: 16
men: 63%; women: 38%;
minorities: 13%; international:
13%
Part-time enrollment: 18
men: 61%; women: 39%;
minorities: 6%; international: 11%
Acceptance rate (full time): 70%
Average GMAT (full time): 423
Average GMAT (part time): 435
Average GPA (full time): 3.36

Average age of entrants to full-
time program: 25
Average months of prior work
experience (full time): 24
TOEFL requirement: Yes
Minimum TOEFL score: 550
Most popular departments:
marketing, production/
operations management

La Salle University

1900 W. Olney Avenue
Philadelphia, PA 19141
www.lasalle.edu/mba
Private
Admissions: (215) 951-1057
Email: mba@lasalle.edu
Financial aid: (215) 951-1070
Application deadline: rolling
Tuition: full time: $23,590; part
time: $970/credit hour
Room/board/expenses: N/A
College-funded aid: Yes
International student aid: Yes
Average student indebtedness at
graduation: $21,429
Full-time enrollment: 59
men: 61%; women: 39%;
minorities: 31%; international:
29%
Part-time enrollment: 205
men: 53%; women: 47%;
minorities: 23%; international:
0%
Acceptance rate (full time): 90%
Average GMAT (full time): 482
Average GMAT (part time): 551
Average GPA (full time): 3.22
Average age of entrants to full-
time program: 24
Average months of prior work
experience (full time): 45
TOEFL requirement: Yes
Minimum TOEFL score: 573
Most popular departments:
accounting, finance, general
management, marketing, other
Mean starting base salary for 2016
full-time graduates: $55,867
Employment location for 2016
class: Intl. 8%; N.E. 14%; M.A.
76%; S. N/A; M.W. N/A; S.W. 2%;
W. N/A

Lehigh University

621 Taylor Street
Bethlehem, PA 18015
www.lehigh.edu/mba
Private
Admissions: (610) 758-3418
Email:
mba.admissions@lehigh.edu
Financial aid: (610) 758-4450
Application deadline: 08/01
Tuition: full time: $1,075/credit
hour; part time: $1,075/credit
hour
Room/board/expenses: $18,170
College-funded aid: Yes
International student aid: Yes
Average student indebtedness at
graduation: $0
Full-time enrollment: 17
men: 41%; women: 59%;
minorities: 6%; international:
65%
Part-time enrollment: 162
men: 75%; women: 25%;
minorities: 14%; international: 4%
Acceptance rate (full time): 46%
Average GMAT (full time): 595
Average GMAT (part time): 636
Average GPA (full time): 3.13
Average age of entrants to full-
time program: 27

Average months of prior work experience (full time): 57
TOEFL requirement: Yes
Minimum TOEFL score: 600
Most popular departments: entrepreneurship, finance, marketing, supply chain management/logistics, other
Mean starting base salary for 2016 full-time graduates: $86,667

Pennsylvania State University-Erie, The Behrend College (Black)

5101 Jordan Road
Erie, PA 16563
www.pennstatebehrend.psu.edu
Public
Admissions: (814) 898-7255
Email: behrend.admissions@psu.edu
Financial aid: (814) 898-6162
Application deadline: N/A
In-state tuition: full time: $842/credit hour; part time: $842/credit hour
Out-of-state tuition: full time: $1,315/credit hour
Room/board/expenses: $26,458
College-funded aid: Yes
International student aid: Yes
Average student indebtedness at graduation: $34,706
Full-time enrollment: N/A
men: N/A; women: N/A; minorities: N/A; international: N/A
Part-time enrollment: 116
men: 74%; women: 26%; minorities: N/A; international: N/A
Average GMAT (part time): 511
TOEFL requirement: Yes
Minimum TOEFL score: 550
Mean starting base salary for 2016 full-time graduates: $0
Employment location for 2016 class: Intl. N/A; N.E. N/A; M.A. 100%; S. N/A; M.W. N/A; S.W. N/A; W. N/A

Pennsylvania State University-Great Valley[1]

30 E. Swedesford Road
Malvern, PA 19355
www.sgps.psu.edu
Public
Admissions: (610) 648-3242
Email: gvadmiss@psu.edu
Financial aid: N/A
Tuition: N/A
Room/board/expenses: N/A
Enrollment: N/A

Pennsylvania State University-Harrisburg

777 W. Harrisburg Pike
Middletown, PA 17057-4898
harrisburg.psu.edu/business-administration/mba-and-business-administration/master-business-administration
Public
Admissions: (717) 948-6250
Email: mbahbg@psu.edu
Financial aid: (717) 948-6307
Application deadline: 07/18
In-state tuition: full time: N/A; part time: $842/credit hour
Out-of-state tuition: full time: N/A
Room/board/expenses: N/A
College-funded aid: Yes

International student aid: Yes
Full-time enrollment: N/A
men: N/A; women: N/A; minorities: N/A; international: N/A
Part-time enrollment: 143
men: 70%; women: 30%; minorities: 12%; international: 8%
Average GMAT (part time): 543
TOEFL requirement: Yes
Minimum TOEFL score: 550
Most popular departments: accounting, finance, general management, management information systems, supply chain management/logistics

Pennsylvania State University-University Park (Smeal)

220 Business Building
University Park, PA 16802-3000
www.smeal.psu.edu/mba
Public
Admissions: (814) 863-0474
Email: smealmba@psu.edu
Financial aid: (814) 865-6301
Application deadline: 04/01
In-state tuition: full time: $25,636; part time: N/A
Out-of-state tuition: full time: $40,506
Room/board/expenses: $21,950
College-funded aid: Yes
International student aid: Yes
Full-time enrollment: 125
men: 71%; women: 29%; minorities: 16%; international: 39%
Part-time enrollment: N/A
men: N/A; women: N/A; minorities: N/A; international: N/A
Acceptance rate (full time): 18%
Average GMAT (full time): 659
Average GPA (full time): 3.37
Average age of entrants to full-time program: 28
Average months of prior work experience (full time): 55
TOEFL requirement: Yes
Minimum TOEFL score: 600
Most popular departments: consulting, finance, leadership, marketing, supply chain management/logistics
Mean starting base salary for 2016 full-time graduates: $105,675
Employment location for 2016 class: Intl. 4%; N.E. 16%; M.A. 23%; S. 9%; M.W. 14%; S.W. 21%; W. 13%

Robert Morris University

6001 University Boulevard
Moon Township, PA 15108-1189
admissions.rmu.edu/onlinehome/mba-and-business
Private
Admissions: (800) 762-0097
Email: enrollmentoffice@rmu.edu
Financial aid: (412) 397-6250
Application deadline: N/A
Tuition: full time: N/A; part time: $900/credit hour
Room/board/expenses: N/A
College-funded aid: Yes
International student aid: Yes
Full-time enrollment: N/A
men: N/A; women: N/A; minorities: N/A; international: N/A
Part-time enrollment: 145
men: 57%; women: 43%; minorities: 6%; international: 1%

Average GMAT (part time): 515
TOEFL requirement: Yes
Minimum TOEFL score: 550
Most popular departments: general management, human resources management, tax

Shippensburg University of Pennsylvania (Grove)

1871 Old Main Drive
Shippensburg, PA 17257
www.ship.edu/mba
Public
Admissions: (717) 477-1231
Email: admiss@ship.edu
Financial aid: (717) 477-1131
Application deadline: N/A
In-state tuition: full time: $483/credit hour; part time: $483/credit hour
Out-of-state tuition: full time: $725/credit hour
Room/board/expenses: $9,572
College-funded aid: Yes
International student aid: Yes
Full-time enrollment: 72
men: 75%; women: 25%; minorities: 4%; international: 40%
Part-time enrollment: 154
men: 65%; women: 35%; minorities: 13%; international: N/A
Acceptance rate (full time): 86%
Average GMAT (full time): 546
Average GMAT (part time): 514
Average GPA (full time): 3.11
Average age of entrants to full-time program: 27
Average months of prior work experience (full time): 65
TOEFL requirement: Yes
Minimum TOEFL score: 500
Most popular departments: finance, health care administration, management information systems, supply chain management/logistics

St. Joseph's University (Haub)

5600 City Avenue
Philadelphia, PA 19131
www.sju.edu/haubmba
Private
Admissions: (610) 660-1690
Email: sjumba@sju.edu
Financial aid: (610) 660-2000
Application deadline: 07/15
Tuition: full time: $1,003/credit hour; part time: $1,003/credit hour
Room/board/expenses: N/A
College-funded aid: Yes
International student aid: Yes
Full-time enrollment: N/A
men: N/A; women: N/A; minorities: N/A; international: N/A
Part-time enrollment: 904
men: 58%; women: 42%; minorities: 18%; international: 23%
Average GMAT (part time): 549
TOEFL requirement: Yes
Minimum TOEFL score: 550
Most popular departments: finance, general management, human resources management, marketing, management information systems

Temple University (Fox)

Alter Hall
1801 Liacouras Walk, Suite A701
Philadelphia, PA 19122-6083
sbm.temple.edu/
Public
Admissions: (215) 204-7678
Email: foxinfo@temple.edu
Financial aid: (215) 204-7678
Application deadline: 12/10
In-state tuition: full time: $32,558; part time: $1,159/credit hour
Out-of-state tuition: full time: $45,113
Room/board/expenses: $19,712
College-funded aid: Yes
International student aid: Yes
Average student indebtedness at graduation: $27,770
Full-time enrollment: 89
men: 45%; women: 55%; minorities: 0%; international: 26%
Part-time enrollment: 847
men: 63%; women: 37%; minorities: 0%; international: 10%
Acceptance rate (full time): 37%
Average GMAT (full time): 639
Average GMAT (part time): 593
Average GPA (full time): 3.61
Average age of entrants to full-time program: 27
Average months of prior work experience (full time): 55
TOEFL requirement: Yes
Minimum TOEFL score: 600
Most popular departments: finance, general management, international business, marketing, management information systems
Mean starting base salary for 2016 full-time graduates: $85,278
Employment location for 2016 class: Intl. 8%; N.E. 5%; M.A. 68%; S. 3%; M.W. 5%; S.W. 5%; W. 5%

University of Pennsylvania (Wharton)

420 Jon M. Huntsman Hall
3730 Walnut Street
Philadelphia, PA 19104
www.wharton.edu
Private
Admissions: (215) 898-6183
Email: mbaadmiss@wharton.upenn.edu
Financial aid: (215) 898-8728
Application deadline: 03/28
Tuition: full time: $73,634; part time: N/A
Room/board/expenses: $31,631
College-funded aid: Yes
International student aid: Yes
Full-time enrollment: 1,708
men: 57%; women: 43%; minorities: 31%; international: 30%
Part-time enrollment: N/A
men: N/A; women: N/A; minorities: N/A; international: N/A
Acceptance rate (full time): 20%
Average GMAT (full time): 730
Average GPA (full time): 3.60
Average age of entrants to full-time program: 28
Average months of prior work experience (full time): 60
TOEFL requirement: No
Minimum TOEFL score: N/A

Most popular departments: entrepreneurship, finance, general management, health care administration, other
Mean starting base salary for 2016 full-time graduates: $130,161
Employment location for 2016 class: Intl. 12%; N.E. 45%; M.A. 12%; S. 3%; M.W. 3%; S.W. 3%; W. 21%

University of Pittsburgh (Katz)

372 Mervis Hall
Pittsburgh, PA 15260
www.business.pitt.edu/katz
Public
Admissions: (412) 648-1700
Email: mba@katz.pitt.edu
Financial aid: (412) 648-1700
Application deadline: 04/01
In-state tuition: total program: $58,688 (full time); part time: $1,246/credit hour
Out-of-state tuition: total program: $74,560 (full time)
Room/board/expenses: $34,220
College-funded aid: Yes
International student aid: Yes
Full-time enrollment: 153
men: 65%; women: 35%; minorities: 17%; international: 43%
Part-time enrollment: 342
men: 68%; women: 32%; minorities: 13%; international: 2%
Acceptance rate (full time): 30%
Average GMAT (full time): 613
Average GMAT (part time): 540
Average GPA (full time): 3.29
Average age of entrants to full-time program: 28
Average months of prior work experience (full time): 52
TOEFL requirement: Yes
Minimum TOEFL score: N/A
Most popular departments: finance, marketing, management information systems, production/operations management, supply chain management/logistics
Mean starting base salary for 2016 full-time graduates: $82,794
Employment location for 2016 class: Intl. 0%; N.E. 9%; M.A. 53%; S. 9%; M.W. 15%; S.W. 6%; W. 9%

University of Scranton

800 Linden Street
Scranton, PA 18510-4632
www.scranton.edu
Private
Admissions: (570) 941-7540
Email: robackj2@scranton.edu
Financial aid: (570) 941-7700
Application deadline: rolling
Tuition: full time: $965/credit hour; part time: $965/credit hour
Room/board/expenses: N/A
College-funded aid: Yes
International student aid: Yes
Full-time enrollment: N/A
men: N/A; women: N/A; minorities: N/A; international: N/A
Part-time enrollment: 116
men: 66%; women: 34%; minorities: 6%; international: 25%
Average GMAT (part time): 541
TOEFL requirement: Yes
Minimum TOEFL score: 550

Most popular departments:
accounting, finance, general management, management information systems, production/operations management
Mean starting base salary for 2016 full-time graduates: $56,400
Employment location for 2016 class: Intl. 5%; N.E. 40%; M.A. 45%; S. 0%; M.W. 0%; S.W. 10%; W. 0%

Villanova University

Bartley Hall
800 Lancaster Avenue
Villanova, PA 19085
mba.villanova.edu
Private
Admissions: (610) 519-4336
Email: claire.bruno@villanova.edu
Financial aid: (610) 519-4010
Application deadline: 06/30
Tuition: full time: N/A; part time: $1,095/credit hour
Room/board/expenses: N/A
College-funded aid: Yes
International student aid: Yes
Full-time enrollment: N/A
men: N/A; women: N/A;
minorities: N/A; international: N/A
Part-time enrollment: 127
men: 54%; women: 46%;
minorities: 13%; international: 2%
Average GMAT (part time): 592
TOEFL requirement: Yes
Minimum TOEFL score: 550
Most popular departments:
finance, general management, international business, marketing

West Chester University of Pennsylvania

1160 McDermott Drive
West Chester, PA 19383
www.wcupa.edu/mba
Public
Admissions: (610) 436-2943
Email: gradstudy@wcupa.edu
Financial aid: (610) 436-2627
Application deadline: rolling
In-state tuition: full time: N/A; part time: $483/credit hour
Out-of-state tuition: full time: N/A
Room/board/expenses: N/A
College-funded aid: Yes
International student aid: Yes
Full-time enrollment: N/A
men: N/A; women: N/A;
minorities: N/A; international: N/A
Part-time enrollment: 255
men: 59%; women: 41%;
minorities: 14%; international: N/A
Average GMAT (part time): 535
TOEFL requirement: Yes
Minimum TOEFL score: 550
Most popular departments:
entrepreneurship, general management, leadership, production/operations management, quantitative analysis/statistics and operations research

Widener University[1]

1 University Place
Chester, PA 19013
www.widener.edu/sba
Private
Admissions: (610) 499-4306
Email: sbagradv@mail.widener.edu

Financial aid: (610) 499-4174
Tuition: N/A
Room/board/expenses: N/A
Enrollment: N/A

RHODE ISLAND

Bryant University

1150 Douglas Pike
Smithfield, RI 02917
www.bryant.edu/
Private
Admissions: (401) 232-6707
Email: gradprog@bryant.edu
Financial aid: (401) 232-6020
Application deadline: 04/15
Tuition: full time: $1,118/credit hour; part time: $1,118/credit hour
Room/board/expenses: N/A
College-funded aid: Yes
International student aid: Yes
Full-time enrollment: 26
men: 73%; women: 27%;
minorities: 19%; international: 27%
Part-time enrollment: 58
men: 57%; women: 43%;
minorities: 9%; international: 5%
Acceptance rate (full time): 65%
Average GMAT (full time): 460
Average GMAT (part time): 525
Average GPA (full time): 3.15
Average age of entrants to full-time program: 24
TOEFL requirement: Yes
Minimum TOEFL score: N/A
Most popular departments:
finance, general management, international business, supply chain management/logistics, quantitative analysis/statistics and operations research

Providence College

One Cunningham Square
Providence, RI 02918
business.providence.edu/mba/
Private
Admissions: (401) 865-2294
Email: mba@providence.edu
Financial aid: (401) 865-2286
Application deadline: 07/01
Tuition: full time: N/A; part time: $7,800
Room/board/expenses: N/A
College-funded aid: Yes
International student aid: Yes
Full-time enrollment: N/A
men: N/A; women: N/A;
minorities: N/A; international: N/A
Part-time enrollment: 150
men: 59%; women: 41%;
minorities: 10%; international: 3%
Average GMAT (part time): 514
TOEFL requirement: Yes
Minimum TOEFL score: 577
Most popular departments:
accounting, finance, general management, international business, marketing

University of Rhode Island[1]

7 Lippitt Road
Kingston, RI 02881
web.uri.edu/business/
Public
Admissions: (401) 874-2842
Email: gradadm@etal.uri.edu
Financial aid: N/A
Tuition: N/A
Room/board/expenses: N/A
Enrollment: N/A

The Citadel

171 Moultrie Street
Charleston, SC 29409
www.citadel.edu/csba/
Public
Admissions: (843) 953-5336
Email: cgc@citadel.edu
Financial aid: (843) 953-5187
Application deadline: N/A
In-state tuition: full time: $569/credit hour; part time: $569/credit hour
Out-of-state tuition: full time: $957/credit hour
Room/board/expenses: $23,168
College-funded aid: Yes
International student aid: Yes
Average student indebtedness at graduation: $32,846
Full-time enrollment: 27
men: 63%; women: 37%;
minorities: 19%; international: 7%
Part-time enrollment: 137
men: 63%; women: 37%;
minorities: 9%; international: 1%
Average GMAT (part time): 321
Average GPA (full time): 3.17
Average age of entrants to full-time program: 24
TOEFL requirement: Yes
Minimum TOEFL score: N/A

Clemson University

1 North Main Street
Greenville, SC 29601
www.clemson.edu/cbbs/departments/mba
Public
Admissions: (864) 656-8173
Email: mba@clemson.edu
Financial aid: (864) 656-2280
Application deadline: 07/15
In-state tuition: full time: $18,666; part time: $697/credit hour
Out-of-state tuition: full time: $30,672
Room/board/expenses: $13,750
College-funded aid: Yes
International student aid: Yes
Full-time enrollment: 150
men: 61%; women: 39%;
minorities: 15%; international: 15%
Part-time enrollment: 296
men: 69%; women: 31%;
minorities: 20%; international: 4%
Acceptance rate (full time): 78%
Average GMAT (full time): 568
Average GMAT (part time): 588
Average GPA (full time): 3.24
Average age of entrants to full-time program: 27
Average months of prior work experience (full time): 45
TOEFL requirement: Yes
Minimum TOEFL score: N/A
Most popular departments:
entrepreneurship, general management, health care administration, marketing, quantitative analysis/statistics and operations research
Mean starting base salary for 2016 full-time graduates: $70,057
Employment location for 2016 class: Intl. N/A; N.E. N/A; M.A. 7%; S. 93%; M.W. N/A; S.W. N/A; W. N/A

Coastal Carolina University

PO Box 261954
Conway, SC 29528-6054
www.coastal.edu/admissions
Public
Admissions: (843) 349-2026
Email: admissions@coastal.edu
Financial aid: (843) 349-2313
Application deadline: 06/15
In-state tuition: full time: $555/credit hour; part time: $555/credit hour
Out-of-state tuition: full time: $1,006/credit hour
Room/board/expenses: $5,076
College-funded aid: Yes
International student aid: Yes
Average student indebtedness at graduation: $20,880
Full-time enrollment: 67
men: 58%; women: 42%;
minorities: 31%; international: 15%
Part-time enrollment: 30
men: 50%; women: 50%;
minorities: 13%; international: 3%
Acceptance rate (full time): 86%
Average GMAT (full time): 392
Average GMAT (part time): 477
Average GPA (full time): 3.40
Average age of entrants to full-time program: 25
TOEFL requirement: Yes
Minimum TOEFL score: 550
Mean starting base salary for 2016 full-time graduates: $41,000

College of Charleston

66 George Street
Charleston, SC 29424
www.mbacharleston.com/
Public
Admissions: (843) 953-8112
Email: mba@cofc.edu
Financial aid: (843) 953-5540
Application deadline: 05/01
In-state tuition: total program: $29,945 (full time); part time: N/A
Out-of-state tuition: total program: $29,945 (full time)
Room/board/expenses: $16,080
College-funded aid: Yes
International student aid: Yes
Average student indebtedness at graduation: $21,837
Full-time enrollment: 46
men: 50%; women: 50%;
minorities: 17%; international: 4%
Part-time enrollment: N/A
men: N/A; women: N/A;
minorities: N/A; international: N/A
Acceptance rate (full time): 61%
Average GMAT (full time): 540
Average GPA (full time): 3.28
Average age of entrants to full-time program: 27
Average months of prior work experience (full time): 55
TOEFL requirement: Yes
Minimum TOEFL score: N/A
Mean starting base salary for 2016 full-time graduates: $50,212
Employment location for 2016 class: Intl. N/A; N.E. 13%; M.A. 4%; S. 78%; M.W. 4%; S.W. N/A; W. N/A

Francis Marion University[1]

Box 100547
Florence, SC 29501
www.fmarion.edu/academics/mba
Public
Admissions: (843) 661-1281
Email: graduate@fmarion.edu
Financial aid: N/A
Tuition: N/A
Room/board/expenses: N/A
Enrollment: N/A

South Carolina State University

300 College Street NE
Orangeburg, SC 29117
www.scsu.edu/schoolofgraduatestudies.aspx
Public
Admissions: (803) 536-7133
Email: graduateschool@scsu.edu
Financial aid: (803) 536-7067
Application deadline: 06/15
In-state tuition: full time: $10,420; part time: $579/credit hour
Out-of-state tuition: full time: $20,500
Room/board/expenses: N/A
College-funded aid: Yes
International student aid: Yes
Full-time enrollment: 19
men: 42%; women: 58%;
minorities: 89%; international: 0%
Part-time enrollment: 10
men: 50%; women: 50%;
minorities: 100%; international: 0%
Acceptance rate (full time): 93%
Average age of entrants to full-time program: 23
TOEFL requirement: Yes
Minimum TOEFL score: 550

University of South Carolina (Moore)

1014 Greene Street
Columbia, SC 29208
moore.sc.edu/
Public
Admissions: (803) 777-4346
Email: gradinfo@moore.sc.edu
Financial aid: (803) 777-8134
Application deadline: rolling
In-state tuition: total program: $44,422 (full time); part time: $705/credit hour
Out-of-state tuition: total program: $72,860 (full time)
Room/board/expenses: $18,229
College-funded aid: Yes
International student aid: Yes
Average student indebtedness at graduation: $53,446
Full-time enrollment: 66
men: 62%; women: 38%;
minorities: 12%; international: 20%
Part-time enrollment: 446
men: 69%; women: 31%;
minorities: 20%; international: 2%
Acceptance rate (full time): 71%
Average GMAT (full time): 677
Average GMAT (part time): 624
Average GPA (full time): 3.26
Average age of entrants to full-time program: 27

Average months of prior work experience (full time): 43
TOEFL requirement: Yes
Minimum TOEFL score: 600
Mean starting base salary for 2016 full-time graduates: $93,356

Winthrop University[1]

Thurmond Building
Rock Hill, SC 29733
www.winthrop.edu/cba
Public
Admissions: (803) 323-2204
Email: gradschool@winthrop.edu
Financial aid: N/A
Tuition: N/A
Room/board/expenses: N/A
Enrollment: N/A

SOUTH DAKOTA

Black Hills State University[1]

1200 University Street
Spearfish, SD 57799
www.bhsu.edu/
Public
Admissions: (800) 255-2478
Email: BHSUGraduateStudies@bhsu.edu
Financial aid: N/A
Tuition: N/A
Room/board/expenses: N/A
Enrollment: N/A

University of South Dakota

414 E. Clark Street
Vermillion, SD 57069
www.usd.edu/mba
Public
Admissions: (605) 677-5232
Email: mba@usd.edu
Financial aid: (605) 677-5446
Application deadline: 06/01
In-state tuition: full time: $313/credit hour; part time: $442/credit hour
Out-of-state tuition: full time: $602/credit hour
Room/board/expenses: N/A
College-funded aid: Yes
International student aid: Yes
Average student indebtedness at graduation: $23,250
Full-time enrollment: 31
men: 68%; women: 32%;
minorities: 3%; international: 26%
Part-time enrollment: 248
men: 72%; women: 28%;
minorities: 6%; international: 6%
Acceptance rate (full time): 92%
Average GMAT (full time): 509
Average GMAT (part time): 552
Average GPA (full time): 3.20
Average age of entrants to full-time program: 26
Average months of prior work experience (full time): 43
TOEFL requirement: Yes
Minimum TOEFL score: 550
Most popular departments: general management, health care administration, marketing, production/operations management, other
Mean starting base salary for 2016 full-time graduates: $48,417
Employment location for 2016 class: Intl. 0%; N.E. 0%; M.A. 0%; S. 0%; M.W. 83%; S.W. 0%; W. 17%

TENNESSEE

Belmont University (Massey)

1900 Belmont Boulevard
Nashville, TN 37212
www.belmont.edu/business/graduatebusiness
Private
Admissions: (615) 460-6480
Email: masseyadmissions@belmont.edu
Financial aid: (615) 460-6403
Application deadline: 06/01
Tuition: total program: $54,570 (full time); $54,570 (part time)
Room/board/expenses: N/A
College-funded aid: Yes
International student aid: Yes
Full-time enrollment: 28
men: 46%; women: 54%;
minorities: 4%; international: 0%
Part-time enrollment: 116
men: 59%; women: 41%;
minorities: 17%; international: 2%
Acceptance rate (full time): 81%
Average GMAT (full time): 544
Average GMAT (part time): 557
Average GPA (full time): 3.45
Average age of entrants to full-time program: 23
TOEFL requirement: Yes
Minimum TOEFL score: 550
Most popular departments: entrepreneurship, finance, general management, health care administration, marketing
Mean starting base salary for 2016 full-time graduates: $53,000

East Tennessee State University[1]

PO Box 70699
Johnson City, TN 37614
www.etsu.edu/cbat
Public
Admissions: (423) 439-5314
Email: business@etsu.edu
Financial aid: N/A
Tuition: N/A
Room/board/expenses: N/A
Enrollment: N/A

Middle Tennessee State University[1]

PO Box 290
Murfreesboro, TN 37132
www.mtsu.edu
Public
Admissions: (615) 898-2840
Email: graduate@mtsu.edu
Financial aid: N/A
Tuition: N/A
Room/board/expenses: N/A
Enrollment: N/A

Tennessee State University[1]

330 N. 10th Avenue
Nashville, TN 37203
www.tnstate.edu/business
Public
Admissions: (615) 963-5145
Email: cobinfo@tnstate.edu
Financial aid: N/A
Tuition: N/A
Room/board/expenses: N/A
Enrollment: N/A

Tennessee Technological University

Box 5023
Cookeville, TN 38505
www.tntech.edu/mba
Public
Admissions: (931) 372-3600
Email: mbastudies@tntech.edu
Financial aid: (931) 372-3073
Application deadline: 07/01
In-state tuition: full time: $447/credit hour; part time: $447/credit hour
Out-of-state tuition: full time: $706/credit hour
Room/board/expenses: $25,600
College-funded aid: Yes
International student aid: Yes
Average student indebtedness at graduation: $10,473
Full-time enrollment: 45
men: 51%; women: 49%;
minorities: 7%; international: 27%
Part-time enrollment: 168
men: 70%; women: 30%;
minorities: 8%; international: 1%
Acceptance rate (full time): 51%
Average GMAT (full time): 472
Average GMAT (part time): 522
Average GPA (full time): 3.41
Average age of entrants to full-time program: 25
Average months of prior work experience (full time): 32
TOEFL requirement: Yes
Minimum TOEFL score: 550
Most popular departments: accounting, general management, human resources management, international business, management information systems

Union University

1050 Union University Drive
Jackson, TN 38305
www.uu.edu/academics/graduate/mba/
Private
Admissions: (731) 661-5341
Email: lpowell@uu.edu
Financial aid: (731) 661-5213
Application deadline: rolling
Tuition: full time: $555/credit hour; part time: $555/credit hour
Room/board/expenses: N/A
College-funded aid: Yes
International student aid: Yes
Full-time enrollment: N/A
men: N/A; women: N/A;
minorities: N/A; international: N/A
Part-time enrollment: 145
men: 55%; women: 45%;
minorities: 32%; international: 1%
TOEFL requirement: Yes
Minimum TOEFL score: 560

University of Memphis (Fogelman)

3675 Central Avenue
Memphis, TN 38152
fcbe.memphis.edu/
Public
Admissions: (901) 678-3721
Email: krishnan@memphis.edu
Financial aid: (901) 678-4825
Application deadline: 07/01
In-state tuition: full time: $596/credit hour; part time: $596/credit hour
Out-of-state tuition: full time: $1,084/credit hour
Room/board/expenses: N/A

College-funded aid: Yes
International student aid: Yes
Full-time enrollment: 48
men: 48%; women: 52%;
minorities: 52%; international: 0%
Part-time enrollment: 135
men: 67%; women: 33%;
minorities: 32%; international: 0%
Acceptance rate (full time): 68%
Average GMAT (full time): 465
Average GMAT (part time): 561
Average GPA (full time): 3.10
Average age of entrants to full-time program: 29
Average months of prior work experience (full time): 53
TOEFL requirement: Yes
Minimum TOEFL score: 550
Most popular departments: accounting, finance, general management, international business, management information systems

University of Tennessee-Chattanooga

615 McCallie Avenue
Chattanooga, TN 37403
www.utc.edu/Academic/Business/
Public
Admissions: (423) 425-4666
Email: bonny-clark@utc.edu
Financial aid: (423) 425-4677
Application deadline: rolling
In-state tuition: full time: N/A; part time: $450/credit hour
Out-of-state tuition: full time: N/A
Room/board/expenses: N/A
College-funded aid: Yes
International student aid: No
Full-time enrollment: N/A
men: N/A; women: N/A;
minorities: N/A; international: N/A
Part-time enrollment: 280
men: 53%; women: 48%;
minorities: 18%; international: 2%
Average GMAT (part time): 515
TOEFL requirement: Yes
Minimum TOEFL score: 550
Most popular departments: accounting, finance, general management, human resources management, marketing

University of Tennessee-Knoxville (Haslam)

504 Haslam Business Building
Knoxville, TN 37996-4150
mba.utk.edu
Public
Admissions: (865) 974-5033
Email: mba@utk.edu
Financial aid: (865) 974-3131
Application deadline: 02/01
In-state tuition: full time: $24,834; part time: N/A
Out-of-state tuition: full time: $43,252
Room/board/expenses: $16,000
College-funded aid: Yes
International student aid: Yes
Average student indebtedness at graduation: $36,378
Full-time enrollment: 133
men: 68%; women: 32%;
minorities: 10%; international: 29%

Part-time enrollment: N/A
men: N/A; women: N/A;
minorities: N/A; international: N/A
Acceptance rate (full time): 59%
Average GMAT (full time): 627
Average GPA (full time): 3.36
Average age of entrants to full-time program: 27
Average months of prior work experience (full time): 56
TOEFL requirement: Yes
Minimum TOEFL score: 600
Most popular departments: entrepreneurship, finance, marketing, supply chain management/logistics, other
Mean starting base salary for 2016 full-time graduates: $79,137
Employment location for 2016 class: Intl. 0%; N.E. 2%; M.A. 0%; S. 75%; M.W. 17%; S.W. 6%; W. 0%

University of Tennessee-Martin

103 Business Administration Building
Martin, TN 38238
www.utm.edu/departments/cbga/mba
Public
Admissions: (731) 881-7012
Email: jcunningham@utm.edu
Financial aid: (731) 881-7040
Application deadline: 07/31
In-state tuition: full time: $558/credit hour; part time: $558/credit hour
Out-of-state tuition: full time: $743/credit hour
Room/board/expenses: N/A
College-funded aid: Yes
International student aid: Yes
Full-time enrollment: 86
men: 60%; women: 40%;
minorities: 8%; international: 5%
Part-time enrollment: 8
men: 75%; women: 25%;
minorities: 0%; international: N/A
Acceptance rate (full time): 85%
Average GMAT (full time): 465
Average GPA (full time): 3.17
Average age of entrants to full-time program: 30
Average months of prior work experience (full time): 61
TOEFL requirement: Yes
Minimum TOEFL score: 525
Most popular departments: other

Vanderbilt University (Owen)

401 21st Avenue S
Nashville, TN 37203
www.owen.vanderbilt.edu
Private
Admissions: (615) 322-6469
Email: mba@owen.vanderbilt.edu
Financial aid: (615) 322-3591
Application deadline: 05/06
Tuition: full time: $52,368; part time: N/A
Room/board/expenses: $19,338
College-funded aid: Yes
International student aid: Yes
Average student indebtedness at graduation: $91,813
Full-time enrollment: 341
men: 72%; women: 28%;
minorities: 13%; international: 23%
Part-time enrollment: N/A
men: N/A; women: N/A;
minorities: N/A; international: N/A

Acceptance rate (full time): 46%
Average GMAT (full time): 691
Average GPA (full time): 3.40
Average age of entrants to full-time program: 28
Average months of prior work experience (full time): 63
TOEFL requirement: Yes
Minimum TOEFL score: N/A
Most popular departments: finance, health care administration, marketing, production/operations management, organizational behavior
Mean starting base salary for 2016 full-time graduates: $110,357
Employment location for 2016 class: Intl. 1%; N.E. 15%; M.A. 4%; S. 45%; M.W. 13%; S.W. 9%; W. 13%

TEXAS

Abilene Christian University[1]
ACU Box 29300
Abilene, TX 79699-9300
www.acu.edu/academics/coba/index.html
Private
Admissions: (800) 460-6228
Email: info@admissions.acu.edu
Financial aid: N/A
Tuition: N/A
Room/board/expenses: N/A
Enrollment: N/A

Baylor University (Hankamer)
1 Bear Place #98013
Waco, TX 76798-8013
www.baylor.edu/mba
Private
Admissions: (254) 710-3718
Email: mba_info@baylor.edu
Financial aid: (254) 710-2611
Application deadline: 06/15
Tuition: full time: $42,606; part time: N/A
Room/board/expenses: $19,062
College-funded aid: Yes
International student aid: Yes
Average student indebtedness at graduation: $51,000
Full-time enrollment: 90
men: 64%; women: 36%; minorities: 22%; international: 9%
Part-time enrollment: N/A
men: N/A; women: N/A; minorities: N/A; international: N/A
Acceptance rate (full time): 40%
Average GMAT (full time): 621
Average GPA (full time): 3.50
Average age of entrants to full-time program: 25
Average months of prior work experience (full time): 30
TOEFL requirement: Yes
Minimum TOEFL score: 600
Most popular departments: entrepreneurship, finance, health care administration, marketing, management information systems
Mean starting base salary for 2016 full-time graduates: $76,198
Employment location for 2016 class: Intl. 0%; N.E. 0%; M.A. 11%; S. 0%; M.W. 0%; S.W. 84%; W. 5%

Lamar University
4400 Martin Luther King Parkway
Beaumont, TX 77710
lamar.edu/mba
Public
Admissions: (409) 880-8888
Email: gradmissions@lamar.edu
Financial aid: (409) 880-7011
Application deadline: 07/31
In-state tuition: full time: $12,128; part time: $9,104
Out-of-state tuition: full time: $21,920
Room/board/expenses: N/A
College-funded aid: Yes
International student aid: Yes
Average student indebtedness at graduation: $32,118
Full-time enrollment: 204
men: 51%; women: 49%; minorities: 37%; international: 5%
Part-time enrollment: N/A
men: N/A; women: N/A; minorities: N/A; international: N/A
Acceptance rate (full time): 91%
Average GMAT (full time): 463
Average GPA (full time): 3.19
Average age of entrants to full-time program: 35
TOEFL requirement: Yes
Minimum TOEFL score: 550
Most popular departments: finance, health care administration, leadership, marketing, management information systems
Employment location for 2016 class: Intl. N/A; N.E. N/A; M.A. N/A; S. N/A; M.W. N/A; S.W. 100%; W. N/A

Midwestern State University
3410 Taft Boulevard
Wichita Falls, TX 76308
www.mwsu.edu/mba
Public
Admissions: (940) 397-4920
Email: graduateschool@mwsu.edu
Financial aid: (940) 397-4214
Application deadline: 08/01
In-state tuition: full time: $214/credit hour; part time: $214/credit hour
Out-of-state tuition: full time: $279/credit hour
Room/board/expenses: N/A
College-funded aid: Yes
International student aid: Yes
Full-time enrollment: 16
men: 50%; women: 50%; minorities: 0%; international: 50%
Part-time enrollment: 39
men: 49%; women: 51%; minorities: 23%; international: 10%
Acceptance rate (full time): 44%
Average GMAT (full time): 511
Average GMAT (part time): 511
Average GPA (full time): 3.33
TOEFL requirement: Yes
Minimum TOEFL score: N/A

Prairie View A&M University
PO Box 519; MS 2300
Prairie View, TX 77446
pvamu.edu/business
Public
Admissions: (936) 261-9215
Email: mba@pvamu.edu
Financial aid: (936) 261-1000
Application deadline: 06/01
In-state tuition: full time: $273/credit hour; part time: $273/credit hour
Out-of-state tuition: full time: $720/credit hour
Room/board/expenses: $14,140
College-funded aid: Yes
International student aid: Yes
Full-time enrollment: 81
men: 40%; women: 60%; minorities: 73%; international: 20%
Part-time enrollment: 157
men: 43%; women: 57%; minorities: 93%; international: 1%
Acceptance rate (full time): 93%
Average GPA (full time): 2.84
Average age of entrants to full-time program: 29
TOEFL requirement: Yes
Minimum TOEFL score: 500
Most popular departments: accounting, finance, general management, international business, management information systems

Rice University (Jones)
PO Box 2932
Houston, TX 77252-2932
business.rice.edu
Private
Admissions: (713) 348-4918
Email: ricemba@rice.edu
Financial aid: (713) 348-4958
Application deadline: rolling
Tuition: full time: $56,097; total program: $49,250 (part time)
Room/board/expenses: $24,473
College-funded aid: Yes
International student aid: Yes
Average student indebtedness at graduation: $59,713
Full-time enrollment: 226
men: 70%; women: 30%; minorities: 24%; international: 26%
Part-time enrollment: 310
men: 80%; women: 20%; minorities: 22%; international: 11%
Acceptance rate (full time): 27%
Average GMAT (full time): 690
Average GMAT (part time): 618
Average GPA (full time): 3.42
Average age of entrants to full-time program: 28
Average months of prior work experience (full time): 65
TOEFL requirement: Yes
Minimum TOEFL score: N/A
Most popular departments: consulting, entrepreneurship, finance, general management, other
Mean starting base salary for 2016 full-time graduates: $112,158

Sam Houston State University
PO Box 2056
Huntsville, TX 77341
www.shsu.edu/dept/graduate-admissions
Public
Admissions: (936) 294-1971
Email: graduate@shsu.edu
Financial aid: (936) 294-1724
Application deadline: 08/01

In-state tuition: full time: $286/credit hour; part time: $286/credit hour
Out-of-state tuition: full time: $694/credit hour
Room/board/expenses: $11,692
College-funded aid: Yes
International student aid: Yes
Average student indebtedness at graduation: $29,846
Full-time enrollment: 292
men: 56%; women: 44%; minorities: 34%; international: 5%
Part-time enrollment: N/A
men: N/A; women: N/A; minorities: N/A; international: N/A
Acceptance rate (full time): 76%
Average GMAT (full time): 536
Average GPA (full time): 3.35
Average age of entrants to full-time program: 32
Average months of prior work experience (full time): 83
TOEFL requirement: Yes
Minimum TOEFL score: 550
Most popular departments: economics, finance, general management

Southern Methodist University (Cox)
PO Box 750333
Dallas, TX 75275-0333
www.smu.edu/Cox/MBAPrograms
Private
Admissions: (214) 768-1214
Email: mbainfo@cox.smu.edu
Financial aid: (214) 768-2371
Application deadline: 05/02
Tuition: full time: $45,976; part time: $40,896
Room/board/expenses: $20,253
College-funded aid: Yes
International student aid: Yes
Full-time enrollment: 238
men: 65%; women: 35%; minorities: 15%; international: 21%
Part-time enrollment: 225
men: 72%; women: 28%; minorities: 26%; international: 6%
Acceptance rate (full time): 39%
Average GMAT (full time): 662
Average GMAT (part time): 596
Average GPA (full time): 3.31
Average age of entrants to full-time program: 27
Average months of prior work experience (full time): 53
TOEFL requirement: Yes
Minimum TOEFL score: 600
Most popular departments: entrepreneurship, finance, marketing, real estate, other
Mean starting base salary for 2016 full-time graduates: $96,587
Employment location for 2016 class: Intl. 3%; N.E. 4%; M.A. 1%; S. 4%; M.W. 7%; S.W. 71%; W. 9%

Stephen F. Austin State University[1]
PO Box 13004, SFA Station
Nacogdoches, TX 75962-3004
www.sfasu.edu/cob/
Public
Admissions: (936) 468-2807
Email: gschool@titan.sfasu.edu
Financial aid: N/A

Tuition: N/A
Room/board/expenses: N/A
Enrollment: N/A

St. Mary's University (Greehey)
1 Camino Santa Maria
San Antonio, TX 78228-8607
www.stmarytx.edu/academics/programs/mba-values/
Private
Admissions: (210) 436-3101
Email: kthornton@stmarytx.edu
Financial aid: (210) 436-3141
Application deadline: 07/01
Tuition: full time: $865/credit hour; part time: $865/credit hour
Room/board/expenses: $19,774
College-funded aid: Yes
International student aid: Yes
Full-time enrollment: 63
men: 60%; women: 40%; minorities: 37%; international: 13%
Part-time enrollment: 3
men: 33%; women: 67%; minorities: 33%; international: 0%
Acceptance rate (full time): 61%
Average GMAT (full time): 499
Average GMAT (part time): 551
Average GPA (full time): 3.17
Average age of entrants to full-time program: 27
TOEFL requirement: Yes
Minimum TOEFL score: 570
Most popular departments: general management

Texas A&M International University
5201 University Boulevard
Western Hemispheric Trade Center, Suite 203
Laredo, TX 78041-1900
www.tamiu.edu
Public
Admissions: (956) 326-3020
Email: graduatedmissions@tamiu.edu
Financial aid: (956) 326-2225
Application deadline: 04/30
In-state tuition: full time: $77/credit hour; part time: $77/credit hour
Out-of-state tuition: full time: $485/credit hour
Room/board/expenses: $10,934
College-funded aid: Yes
International student aid: Yes
Average student indebtedness at graduation: $15,653
Full-time enrollment: 83
men: 60%; women: 40%; minorities: 41%; international: 57%
Part-time enrollment: 179
men: 59%; women: 41%; minorities: 79%; international: 18%
Acceptance rate (full time): 97%
Average GMAT (full time): 440
Average GPA (full time): 3.28
Average age of entrants to full-time program: 25
Average months of prior work experience (full time): 39
TOEFL requirement: Yes
Minimum TOEFL score: 550
Most popular departments: accounting, finance, general management, international business, management information systems

Texas A&M University-College Station (Mays)

4117 TAMU
390 Wehner Building
College Station, TX 77843-4117
mays.tamu.edu/mbaprograms
Public
Admissions: (979) 845-4714
Email: mbaprograms@
mays.tamu.edu
Financial aid: (979) 845-3236
Application deadline: 04/15
In-state tuition: full time: $28,309;
part time: $59,000
Out-of-state tuition: full time:
$44,078
Room/board/expenses: $21,854
College-funded aid: Yes
International student aid: Yes
**Average student indebtedness at
graduation:** $41,157
Full-time enrollment: 139
men: 72%; women: 28%;
minorities: 20%; international:
33%
Part-time enrollment: 96
men: 77%; women: 23%;
minorities: 23%; international:
8%
Acceptance rate (full time): 27%
Average GMAT (full time): 649
Average GMAT (part time): 604
Average GPA (full time): 3.32
**Average age of entrants to full-
time program:** 27
**Average months of prior work
experience (full time):** 56
TOEFL requirement: Yes
Minimum TOEFL score: 600
Most popular departments:
entrepreneurship, finance,
marketing, supply chain
management/logistics,
quantitative analysis/statistics
and operations research
**Mean starting base salary for 2016
full-time graduates:** $103,299
**Employment location for 2016
class:** Intl. 2%; N.E. 7%; M.A. 0%;
S. 22%; M.W. 9%; S.W. 53%;
W. 7%

Texas A&M University-Commerce[1]

PO Box 3011
Commerce, TX 75429-3011
www.tamuc.edu
Public
Admissions: N/A
Financial aid: N/A
Tuition: N/A
Room/board/expenses: N/A
Enrollment: N/A

Texas A&M University-Corpus Christi

6300 Ocean Drive
Corpus Christi, TX 78412-5807
www.cob.tamucc.edu/
prstudents/graduate.html
Public
Admissions: (361) 825-2177
Email: gradweb@tamucc.edu
Financial aid: (361) 825-2338
Application deadline: 07/15
In-state tuition: full time: $208/
credit hour; part time: $213/
credit hour
Out-of-state tuition: full time:
$616/credit hour
Room/board/expenses: N/A
College-funded aid: Yes

International student aid: Yes
Full-time enrollment: N/A
men: N/A; women: N/A;
minorities: N/A; international: N/A
Part-time enrollment: 558
men: 54%; women: 46%;
minorities: 43%; international:
13%
TOEFL requirement: Yes
Minimum TOEFL score: 550
Most popular departments:
finance, health care
administration, international
business

Texas Christian University (Neeley)

PO Box 298540
Fort Worth, TX 76129
www.mba.tcu.edu
Private
Admissions: (817) 257-7531
Email: mbainfo@tcu.edu
Financial aid: (817) 257-7531
Application deadline: 11/01
Tuition: full time: $53,760; part
time: $38,340
Room/board/expenses: $19,700
College-funded aid: Yes
International student aid: Yes
Full-time enrollment: 92
men: 72%; women: 28%;
minorities: 32%; international:
10%
Part-time enrollment: 141
men: 74%; women: 26%;
minorities: 17%; international: 3%
Acceptance rate (full time): 55%
Average GMAT (full time): 641
Average GMAT (part time): 551
Average GPA (full time): 3.30
**Average age of entrants to full-
time program:** 27
**Average months of prior work
experience (full time):** 56
TOEFL requirement: Yes
Minimum TOEFL score: N/A
Most popular departments:
consulting, finance, health care
administration, marketing,
supply chain management/
logistics
**Mean starting base salary for 2016
full-time graduates:** $93,010
**Employment location for 2016
class:** Intl. 3%; N.E. 6%; M.A.
N/A; S. 6%; M.W. N/A; S.W. 72%;
W. 13%

Texas Southern University (Jones)

3100 Cleburne Avenue
Houston, TX 77004
www.tsu.edu/academics/
colleges_schools/Jesse_H_Jones_
School_of_Business/
Public
Admissions: (713) 313-7309
Email: haidern@tsu.edu
Financial aid: (713) 313-7480
Application deadline: 07/15
In-state tuition: full time: $7,556;
part time: $5,284
Out-of-state tuition: full time:
$14,000
Room/board/expenses: N/A
College-funded aid: Yes
International student aid: Yes
Full-time enrollment: 207
men: 53%; women: 47%;
minorities: 77%; international:
23%
Part-time enrollment: N/A
men: N/A; women: N/A;
minorities: N/A; international: N/A

Acceptance rate (full time): 59%
Average GMAT (full time): 335
Average GPA (full time): 3.11
**Average age of entrants to full-
time program:** 28
**Average months of prior work
experience (full time):** 63
TOEFL requirement: Yes
Minimum TOEFL score: 550
Most popular departments:
accounting, general
management, health care
administration, management
information systems, other

Texas State University (McCoy)

601 University Drive
San Marcos, TX 78666-4616
www.txstate.edu
Public
Admissions: (512) 245-3591
Email: gradcollege@txstate.edu
Financial aid: (512) 245-2315
Application deadline: 06/01
In-state tuition: total program:
$23,400 (full time); $23,400
(part time)
Out-of-state tuition: total
program: $40,500 (full time)
Room/board/expenses: N/A
College-funded aid: Yes
International student aid: Yes
Full-time enrollment: 28
men: 54%; women: 46%;
minorities: 54%; international:
4%
Part-time enrollment: 227
men: 53%; women: 47%;
minorities: 25%; international:
5%
Acceptance rate (full time): 58%
Average GMAT (full time): 520
Average GMAT (part time): 536
Average GPA (full time): 3.40
**Average age of entrants to full-
time program:** 25
**Average months of prior work
experience (full time):** 51
TOEFL requirement: Yes
Minimum TOEFL score: N/A
Most popular departments:
general management, health
care administration, human
resources management,
international business,
manufacturing and technology
management

Texas Tech University (Rawls)

PO Box 42101
Lubbock, TX 79409-2101
texastechmba.com
Public
Admissions: (806) 742-3184
Email: rawls.mba@ttu.edu
Financial aid: (806) 742-0454
Application deadline: 07/01
In-state tuition: full time: $315/
credit hour; part time: N/A
Out-of-state tuition: full time:
$723/credit hour
Room/board/expenses: N/A
College-funded aid: Yes
International student aid: Yes
**Average student indebtedness at
graduation:** $39,932
Full-time enrollment: 102
men: 62%; women: 38%;
minorities: 24%; international:
3%
Part-time enrollment: N/A
men: N/A; women: N/A;
minorities: N/A; international: N/A

Acceptance rate (full time): 66%
Average GMAT (full time): 595
Average GPA (full time): 3.21
**Average age of entrants to full-
time program:** 28
**Average months of prior work
experience (full time):** 77
TOEFL requirement: Yes
Minimum TOEFL score: 550
Most popular departments:
general management, health
care administration, other
**Mean starting base salary for 2016
full-time graduates:** $63,066
**Employment location for 2016
class:** Intl. N/A; N.E. 0%; M.A.
2%; S. 2%; M.W. 4%; S.W. 87%;
W. 4%

Texas Wesleyan University

1201 Wesleyan Street
Fort Worth, TX 76105
txwes.edu/
Private
Admissions: (817) 531-4422
Email: graduate@txwes.edu
Financial aid: (817) 531-4420
Application deadline: rolling
Tuition: full time: $788/credit
hour; part time: $788/credit hour
Room/board/expenses: $9,084
College-funded aid: No
Full-time enrollment: N/A
men: N/A; women: N/A;
minorities: N/A; international: N/A
Part-time enrollment: 40
men: 55%; women: 45%;
minorities: 20%; international:
63%
Average GMAT (part time): 450
TOEFL requirement: Yes
Minimum TOEFL score: 550
Most popular departments:
general management

University of Dallas[1]

1845 East Northgate Drive
Irving, TX 75062
www.udallas.edu/cob/
Private
Admissions: N/A
Email: admiss@udallas.edu
Financial aid: N/A
Tuition: N/A
Room/board/expenses: N/A
Enrollment: N/A

University of Houston (Bauer)

334 Melcher Hall, Suite 330
Houston, TX 77204-6021
www.bauer.uh.edu/graduate
Public
Admissions: (713) 743-0700
Email: mba@uh.edu
Financial aid: (713) 743-2062
Application deadline: 06/01
In-state tuition: full time: $24,082;
part time: $14,842
Out-of-state tuition: full time:
$39,322
Room/board/expenses: $17,884
College-funded aid: Yes
International student aid: Yes
Full-time enrollment: 88
men: 65%; women: 35%;
minorities: 27%; international:
32%
Part-time enrollment: 327
men: 69%; women: 31%;
minorities: 30%; international:
20%

Acceptance rate (full time): 49%
Average GMAT (full time): 616
Average GMAT (part time): 584
Average GPA (full time): 3.08
**Average age of entrants to full-
time program:** 28
**Average months of prior work
experience (full time):** 59
TOEFL requirement: Yes
Minimum TOEFL score: 603
**Mean starting base salary for 2016
full-time graduates:** $80,525
**Employment location for 2016
class:** Intl. 0%; N.E. 9%; M.A.
0%; S. 4%; M.W. 0%; S.W. 87%;
W. 0%

University of Houston-Clear Lake

2700 Bay Area Boulevard
Box 71
Houston, TX 77058
www.uhcl.edu/admissions
Public
Admissions: (281) 283-2500
Email: admissions@uhcl.edu
Financial aid: (281) 283-2480
Application deadline: 08/01
In-state tuition: full time: N/A; part
time: $438/credit hour
Out-of-state tuition: full time: N/A
Room/board/expenses: N/A
College-funded aid: Yes
International student aid: Yes
Full-time enrollment: N/A
men: N/A; women: N/A;
minorities: N/A; international: N/A
Part-time enrollment: 200
men: 56%; women: 44%;
minorities: 38%; international:
10%
Average GMAT (part time): 513
TOEFL requirement: Yes
Minimum TOEFL score: 550
Most popular departments:
finance, human resources
management, international
business, manufacturing and
technology management, other

University of Houston-Downtown

320 North Main Street
Houston, TX 77002
www.uhd.edu/admissions/Pages/
admissions-index.aspx
Public
Admissions: (713) 221-8093
Email: gradadmissions@uhd.edu
Financial aid: (713) 221-8041
Application deadline: 08/15
In-state tuition: full time: N/A; part
time: $428/credit hour
Out-of-state tuition: full time: N/A
Room/board/expenses: N/A
College-funded aid: Yes
International student aid: Yes
Full-time enrollment: N/A
men: N/A; women: N/A;
minorities: N/A; international: N/A
Part-time enrollment: 1,044
men: 46%; women: 54%;
minorities: 73%; international:
5%
Average GMAT (part time): 396
TOEFL requirement: Yes
Minimum TOEFL score: 550
Most popular departments:
finance, general management,
human resources management,
leadership, supply chain
management/logistics

University of Houston-Victoria

University West, Room 214
3007 N. Ben Wilson
Victoria, TX 77901
www.uhv.edu/business
Public
Admissions: (361) 570-4110
Email: admissions@uhv.edu
Financial aid: (361) 570-4131
Application deadline: rolling
In-state tuition: full time: $323/
credit hour; part time: $323/
credit hour
Out-of-state tuition: full time:
$731/credit hour
Room/board/expenses: $8,000
College-funded aid: Yes
International student aid: No
Average student indebtedness at
graduation: $31,000
Full-time enrollment: 146
men: 47%; women: 53%;
minorities: 39%; international:
2%
Part-time enrollment: 405
men: 54%; women: 46%;
minorities: 39%; international:
2%
Acceptance rate (full time): 98%
Average GMAT (part time): 439
Average age of entrants to full-
time program: 32
TOEFL requirement: Yes
Minimum TOEFL score: 500
Most popular departments:
accounting, entrepreneurship,
finance, general management,
international business

University of North Texas

1155 Union Circle, #311160
Denton, TX 76203-5017
www.cob.unt.edu
Public
Admissions: (940) 369-8977
Email: mbacob@unt.edu
Financial aid: (940) 565-2302
Application deadline: 06/15
In-state tuition: full time: $303/
credit hour; part time: $303/
credit hour
Out-of-state tuition: full time: $711/
credit hour
Room/board/expenses: $16,670
College-funded aid: Yes
International student aid: Yes
Average student indebtedness at
graduation: $29,867
Full-time enrollment: 210
men: 59%; women: 41%;
minorities: 25%; international:
25%
Part-time enrollment: 303
men: 56%; women: 44%;
minorities: 30%; international:
8%
Acceptance rate (full time): 86%
Average GMAT (full time): 523
Average GMAT (part time): 540
Average GPA (full time): 3.37
Average age of entrants to full-
time program: 27
Average months of prior work
experience (full time): 42
TOEFL requirement: Yes
Minimum TOEFL score: 550
Most popular departments:
accounting, finance, general
management, marketing,
organizational behavior
Mean starting base salary for 2016
full-time graduates: $70,036

University of St. Thomas-Houston

3800 Montrose Boulevard
Houston, TX 77006
www.stthom.edu/bschool
Private
Admissions: (713) 525-2100
Email: cameron@stthom.edu
Financial aid: (713) 525-2170
Application deadline: 07/15
Tuition: full time: $1,163/credit
hour; part time: $1,163/credit
hour
Room/board/expenses: $8,824
College-funded aid: Yes
International student aid: Yes
Full-time enrollment: 236
men: 47%; women: 53%;
minorities: 49%; international:
22%
Part-time enrollment: N/A
men: N/A; women: N/A;
minorities: N/A; international: N/A
Acceptance rate (full time): 97%
Average GMAT (full time): 448
Average GPA (full time): 2.90
TOEFL requirement: Yes
Minimum TOEFL score: N/A
Most popular departments:
finance, general management,
international business,
marketing, management
information systems

University of Texas-Arlington

UTA Box 19377
Arlington, TX 76019-0376
wweb.uta.edu/business/gradbiz
Public
Admissions: (817) 272-3004
Email: gradbiz@uta.edu
Financial aid: (817) 272-3561
Application deadline: 06/01
In-state tuition: full time: N/A; part
time: $7,540
Out-of-state tuition: full time: N/A
Room/board/expenses: N/A
College-funded aid: Yes
International student aid: Yes
Full-time enrollment: N/A
men: N/A; women: N/A;
minorities: N/A; international: N/A
Part-time enrollment: 466
men: 61%; women: 39%;
minorities: 26%; international:
40%
Average GMAT (part time): 496
TOEFL requirement: Yes
Minimum TOEFL score: 550
Most popular departments:
accounting, general
management, health care
administration, human resources
management, management
information systems

University of Texas-Austin (McCombs)

MBA Program
2110 Speedway, Stop B6004
Austin, TX 78712-1750
www.mccombs.utexas.edu/mba/
full-time
Public
Admissions: (512) 471-7698
Email: TexasMBA@
mccombs.utexas.edu
Financial aid: (512) 471-7698
Application deadline: 04/04
In-state tuition: full time: $34,296;
total program: $100,095 (part
time)

Out-of-state tuition: full time:
$50,296
Room/board/expenses: $19,660
College-funded aid: Yes
International student aid: Yes
Average student indebtedness at
graduation: $59,860
Full-time enrollment: 521
men: 66%; women: 34%;
minorities: 23%; international:
26%
Part-time enrollment: 459
men: 73%; women: 27%;
minorities: 33%; international:
9%
Acceptance rate (full time): 28%
Average GMAT (full time): 699
Average GMAT (part time): 634
Average GPA (full time): 3.42
Average age of entrants to full-
time program: 28
Average months of prior work
experience (full time): 66
TOEFL requirement: Yes
Minimum TOEFL score: 620
Most popular departments:
consulting, entrepreneurship,
finance, marketing, management
information systems
Mean starting base salary for 2016
full-time graduates: $113,481
Employment location for 2016
class: Intl. 2%; N.E. 6%; M.A.
4%; S. 4%; M.W. 4%; S.W. 64%;
W. 17%

University of Texas-Dallas

800 W. Campbell Road, SM 40
Richardson, TX 75080-3021
jindal.utdallas.edu/mba
Public
Admissions: (972) 883-5055
Email: mba@utdallas.edu
Financial aid: (972) 883-2941
Application deadline: 05/01
In-state tuition: full time: $14,005;
part time: $13,028
Out-of-state tuition: full time:
$29,026
Room/board/expenses: $15,000
College-funded aid: Yes
International student aid: Yes
Average student indebtedness at
graduation: $7,132
Full-time enrollment: 103
men: 69%; women: 31%;
minorities: 17%; international:
43%
Part-time enrollment: 728
men: 67%; women: 33%;
minorities: 34%; international:
22%
Acceptance rate (full time): 19%
Average GMAT (full time): 670
Average GMAT (part time): 640
Average GPA (full time): 3.50
Average age of entrants to full-
time program: 29
Average months of prior work
experience (full time): 61
TOEFL requirement: Yes
Minimum TOEFL score: 550
Most popular departments:
accounting, finance,
management information
systems, production/operations
management, supply chain
management/logistics
Mean starting base salary for 2016
full-time graduates: $86,644
Employment location for 2016
class: Intl. 0%; N.E. 2%; M.A.
0%; S. 0%; M.W. 2%; S.W. 74%;
W. 22%

University of Texas-El Paso

500 W. University Avenue
El Paso, TX 79968
mba.utep.edu
Public
Admissions: (915) 747-7726
Email: mba@utep.edu
Financial aid: (915) 747-5204
Application deadline: 11/15
In-state tuition: full time: $432/
credit hour; part time: $432/
credit hour
Out-of-state tuition: full time:
$917/credit hour
Room/board/expenses: $18,412
College-funded aid: Yes
International student aid: Yes
Average student indebtedness at
graduation: $27,325
Full-time enrollment: 31
men: 55%; women: 45%;
minorities: 68%; international:
10%
Part-time enrollment: 148
men: 53%; women: 47%;
minorities: 72%; international:
21%
Acceptance rate (full time): 72%
Average GMAT (full time): 512
Average GMAT (part time): 486
Average GPA (full time): 3.53
Average age of entrants to full-
time program: 24
Average months of prior work
experience (full time): 39
TOEFL requirement: Yes
Minimum TOEFL score: 600
Most popular departments:
finance, general management,
human resources management,
international business, marketing
Mean starting base salary for 2016
full-time graduates: $64,714
Employment location for 2016
class: Intl. N/A; N.E. N/A; M.A.
N/A; S. 14%; M.W. N/A; S.W. 71%;
W. 14%

University of Texas of the Permian Basin

4901 E. University
Odessa, TX 79762
www.utpb.edu/
Public
Admissions: (432) 552-2605
Email: Admissions@utpb.edu
Financial aid: (432) 552-2620
Application deadline: 07/15
In-state tuition: full time: $180/
credit hour; part time: $180/
credit hour
Out-of-state tuition: full time:
$229/credit hour
Room/board/expenses: $14,430
College-funded aid: Yes
International student aid: Yes
Average student indebtedness at
graduation: $18,634
Full-time enrollment: 27
men: 52%; women: 48%;
minorities: 59%; international:
7%
Part-time enrollment: 105
men: 45%; women: 55%;
minorities: 50%; international:
2%
Acceptance rate (full time): 55%
Average GMAT (part time): 411
Average age of entrants to full-
time program: 26
TOEFL requirement: Yes
Minimum TOEFL score: 550

Most popular departments:
accounting, ethics, finance,
public administration, other
Mean starting base salary for 2016
full-time graduates: $74,500
Employment location for 2016
class: Intl. N/A; N.E. N/A; M.A.
N/A; S. N/A; M.W. N/A; S.W.
100%; W. N/A

University of Texas-Rio Grande Valley

1201 W University Drive
Edinburg, TX 78539
www.utrgv.edu/graduate/
for-future-students/
how-to-apply/index.htm
Public
Admissions: (956) 665-3661
Financial aid: (888) 882-4026
Application deadline: 04/15
In-state tuition: full time: $6,608;
part time: $411/credit hour
Out-of-state tuition: full time:
$13,952
Room/board/expenses: $11,102
College-funded aid: Yes
International student aid: Yes
Full-time enrollment: 62
men: 63%; women: 37%;
minorities: 50%; international:
27%
Part-time enrollment: 224
men: 56%; women: 44%;
minorities: 67%; international:
5%
Acceptance rate (full time): 84%
Average age of entrants to full-
time program: 30
TOEFL requirement: Yes
Minimum TOEFL score: 550
Most popular departments:
accounting, finance, general
management, marketing,
management information
systems

University of Texas-San Antonio

1 UTSA Circle
San Antonio, TX 78249
www.graduateschool.utsa.edu
Public
Admissions: (210) 458-4331
Email: GraduateAdmissions@
utsa.edu
Financial aid: (210) 458-8000
Application deadline: 06/15
In-state tuition: full time: $338/
credit hour; part time: $338/
credit hour
Out-of-state tuition: full time:
$1,206/credit hour
Room/board/expenses: $15,054
College-funded aid: Yes
International student aid: Yes
Full-time enrollment: 70
men: 61%; women: 39%;
minorities: 40%; international:
17%
Part-time enrollment: 147
men: 71%; women: 29%;
minorities: 37%; international:
3%
Average GMAT (full time): 543
Average GMAT (part time): 521
Average GPA (full time): 3.31
Average age of entrants to full-
time program: 27
TOEFL requirement: Yes
Minimum TOEFL score: 550

Most popular departments: finance, health care administration, marketing, quantitative analysis/statistics and operations research, other
Mean starting base salary for 2016 full-time graduates: $51,496
Employment location for 2016 class: Intl. 14%; N.E. N/A; M.A. 14%; S. N/A; M.W. N/A; S.W. 71%; W. N/A

University of Texas-Tyler[1]
3900 University Boulevard
Tyler, TX 75799
www.uttyler.edu/cbt/
Public
Admissions: (903) 566-7360
Email: cbtinfo@uttyler.edu
Financial aid: N/A
Tuition: N/A
Room/board/expenses: N/A
Enrollment: N/A

West Texas A&M University
WTAMU Box 60768
Canyon, TX 79016
www.wtamu.edu/academics/online-mba.aspx
Public
Admissions: (806) 651-2501
Email: lmills@wtamu.edu
Financial aid: (806) 651-2059
Application deadline: rolling
In-state tuition: total program: $13,400 (full time); $13,900 (part time)
Out-of-state tuition: total program: $15,400 (full time)
Room/board/expenses: $15,000
College-funded aid: Yes
International student aid: Yes
Average student indebtedness at graduation: $18,500
Full-time enrollment: 345
men: 60%; women: 40%; minorities: 34%; international: 33%
Part-time enrollment: 865
men: 57%; women: 43%; minorities: 41%; international: 3%
Acceptance rate (full time): 72%
Average GMAT (full time): 540
Average GMAT (part time): 530
Average GPA (full time): 3.60
Average age of entrants to full-time program: 26
Average months of prior work experience (full time): 18
TOEFL requirement: Yes
Minimum TOEFL score: 525
Most popular departments: accounting, finance, health care administration, marketing, management information systems
Mean starting base salary for 2016 full-time graduates: $62,000
Employment location for 2016 class: Intl. 11%; N.E. 11%; M.A. 9%; S. 2%; M.W. 4%; S.W. 44%; W. 18%

UTAH

Brigham Young University (Marriott)
W-437 TNRB
Provo, UT 84602
mba.byu.edu
Private
Admissions: (801) 422-3500
Email: mba@byu.edu
Financial aid: (801) 422-5195
Application deadline: 05/01
Tuition: full time: $12,310; part time: N/A
Room/board/expenses: $20,552
College-funded aid: Yes
International student aid: Yes
Average student indebtedness at graduation: $38,355
Full-time enrollment: 325
men: 81%; women: 19%; minorities: 5%; international: 21%
Part-time enrollment: N/A
men: N/A; women: N/A; minorities: N/A; international: N/A
Acceptance rate (full time): 49%
Average GMAT (full time): 672
Average GPA (full time): 3.54
Average age of entrants to full-time program: 30
Average months of prior work experience (full time): 53
TOEFL requirement: Yes
Minimum TOEFL score: 590
Most popular departments: entrepreneurship, finance, human resources management, marketing, supply chain management/logistics
Mean starting base salary for 2016 full-time graduates: $105,374
Employment location for 2016 class: Intl. 5%; N.E. 8%; M.A. 1%; S. 5%; M.W. 16%; S.W. 19%; W. 47%

Southern Utah University
351 W. University Boulevard
Cedar City, UT 84720
www.suu.edu/business
Public
Admissions: (435) 586-7740
Email: adminfo@suu.edu
Financial aid: (435) 586-7735
Application deadline: 03/01
In-state tuition: total program: $13,679 (full time); part time: $466/credit hour
Out-of-state tuition: total program: $37,783 (full time)
Room/board/expenses: $9,900
College-funded aid: Yes
International student aid: No
Average student indebtedness at graduation: $26,350
Full-time enrollment: 51
men: 75%; women: 25%; minorities: 10%; international: 6%
Part-time enrollment: 13
men: 62%; women: 38%; minorities: N/A; international: N/A
Acceptance rate (full time): 86%
Average GMAT (full time): 580
Average GPA (full time): 3.40
Average age of entrants to full-time program: 32
TOEFL requirement: Yes
Minimum TOEFL score: 525

University of Utah (Eccles)
1655 E. Campus Center Drive
Room 1113
Salt Lake City, UT 84112-9301
eccles.utah.edu/programs/mba/
Public
Admissions: (801) 585-6291
Email: stephanie.geisler@eccles.utah.edu
Financial aid: (801) 585-6291
Application deadline: 05/01
In-state tuition: total program: $58,000 (full time); $58,800 (part time)
Out-of-state tuition: total program: $60,000 (full time)
Room/board/expenses: $17,500
College-funded aid: Yes
International student aid: Yes
Average student indebtedness at graduation: $40,335
Full-time enrollment: 136
men: 75%; women: 25%; minorities: 3%; international: 11%
Part-time enrollment: 293
men: 74%; women: 26%; minorities: N/A; international: N/A
Acceptance rate (full time): 54%
Average GMAT (full time): 629
Average GMAT (part time): 540
Average GPA (full time): 3.40
Average age of entrants to full-time program: 27
Average months of prior work experience (full time): 47
TOEFL requirement: Yes
Minimum TOEFL score: 600
Most popular departments: entrepreneurship, general management, health care administration, marketing, management information systems
Mean starting base salary for 2016 full-time graduates: $78,815
Employment location for 2016 class: Intl. 0%; N.E. 5%; M.A. 0%; S. 2%; M.W. 5%; S.W. 9%; W. 79%

Utah State University (Huntsman)[1]
3500 Old Main Hill
Logan, UT 84322-3500
www.huntsman.usu.edu/mba/
Public
Admissions: (435) 797-3624
Email: HuntsmanMBA@usu.edu
Financial aid: N/A
Tuition: N/A
Room/board/expenses: N/A
Enrollment: N/A

Utah Valley University[1]
800 W. University Parkway
Orem, UT 84058
www.uvu.edu/woodbury
Public
Admissions: (801) 863-8367
Financial aid: N/A
Tuition: N/A
Room/board/expenses: N/A
Enrollment: N/A

Weber State University (Goddard)
2750 N. University Park Boulevard, MC102
Layton, UT 84041-9099
weber.edu/mba
Public
Admissions: (801) 395-3528

Email: mba@weber.edu
Financial aid: (801) 626-7569
Application deadline: 05/01
In-state tuition: full time: N/A/credit hour; part time: $679/credit hour
Out-of-state tuition: full time: N/A/credit hour
Room/board/expenses: N/A
College-funded aid: Yes
International student aid: Yes
Full-time enrollment: N/A
men: N/A; women: N/A; minorities: N/A; international: N/A
Part-time enrollment: 257
men: 78%; women: 22%; minorities: N/A; international: N/A
Average GMAT (part time): 575
TOEFL requirement: Yes
Minimum TOEFL score: N/A

VERMONT

University of Vermont
55 Colchester Avenue
Burlington, VT 05405
www.uvm.edu/semba
Public
Admissions: (802) 656-1467
Email: semba@uvm.edu
Financial aid: (802) 656-5700
Application deadline: 07/15
In-state tuition: total program: $30,347 (full time); part time: N/A
Out-of-state tuition: total program: $51,516 (full time)
Room/board/expenses: $15,622
College-funded aid: Yes
International student aid: Yes
Average student indebtedness at graduation: $42,677
Full-time enrollment: 23
men: 48%; women: 52%; minorities: 9%; international: 0%
Part-time enrollment: N/A
men: N/A; women: N/A; minorities: N/A; international: N/A
Acceptance rate (full time): 83%
Average GMAT (full time): 589
Average GPA (full time): 3.50
Average age of entrants to full-time program: 30
Average months of prior work experience (full time): 84
TOEFL requirement: Yes
Minimum TOEFL score: 550
Most popular departments: entrepreneurship, other
Mean starting base salary for 2016 full-time graduates: $59,103
Employment location for 2016 class: Intl. N/A; N.E. 83%; M.A. N/A; S. 17%; M.W. N/A; S.W. N/A; W. N/A

VIRGINIA

College of William and Mary (Mason)
PO Box 8795
Williamsburg, VA 23187-8795
mason.wm.edu
Public
Admissions: (757) 221-2900
Email: admissions@mason.wm.edu
Financial aid: (757) 221-2944
Application deadline: 07/15
In-state tuition: full time: $31,992; part time: $800/credit hour
Out-of-state tuition: full time: $43,148
Room/board/expenses: $18,500
College-funded aid: Yes
International student aid: Yes

Average student indebtedness at graduation: $68,225
Full-time enrollment: 179
men: 63%; women: 37%; minorities: 17%; international: 40%
Part-time enrollment: 183
men: 63%; women: 37%; minorities: 30%; international: 1%
Acceptance rate (full time): 54%
Average GMAT (full time): 622
Average GMAT (part time): 673
Average GPA (full time): 3.30
Average age of entrants to full-time program: 28
Average months of prior work experience (full time): 58
TOEFL requirement: Yes
Minimum TOEFL score: N/A
Most popular departments: consulting, entrepreneurship, finance, general management, marketing
Mean starting base salary for 2016 full-time graduates: $87,480
Employment location for 2016 class: Intl. 6%; N.E. 11%; M.A. 66%; S. 6%; M.W. 0%; S.W. 4%; W. 8%

George Mason University
4400 University Drive
Fairfax, VA 22030
business.gmu.edu
Public
Admissions: (703) 993-2136
Email: mba@gmu.edu
Financial aid: (703) 993-2353
Application deadline: 04/01
In-state tuition: full time: $941/credit hour; part time: $914/credit hour
Out-of-state tuition: full time: $1,712/credit hour
Room/board/expenses: $23,620
College-funded aid: Yes
International student aid: Yes
Average student indebtedness at graduation: $40,730
Full-time enrollment: 40
men: 48%; women: 53%; minorities: 20%; international: 58%
Part-time enrollment: 245
men: 60%; women: 40%; minorities: 34%; international: 5%
Acceptance rate (full time): 75%
Average GMAT (part time): 560
Average GPA (full time): 3.23
Average age of entrants to full-time program: 24
Average months of prior work experience (full time): 10
TOEFL requirement: Yes
Minimum TOEFL score: N/A
Mean starting base salary for 2016 full-time graduates: $46,000

James Madison University
Showker Hall
Harrisonburg, VA 22807
www.jmu.edu/cob/mba
Public
Admissions: (540) 568-3058
Email: mccoynta@jmu.edu
Financial aid: (540) 568-3139
Application deadline: 07/01
In-state tuition: full time: N/A; part time: $500/credit hour
Out-of-state tuition: full time: N/A
Room/board/expenses: N/A

College-funded aid: Yes
International student aid: Yes
Full-time enrollment: N/A
men: N/A; women: N/A;
minorities: N/A; international: N/A
Part-time enrollment: 26
men: 50%; women: 50%;
minorities: 12%; international: 4%
Average GMAT (part time): 525
TOEFL requirement: Yes
Minimum TOEFL score: 570
Most popular departments:
entrepreneurship, general
management, leadership,
marketing, organizational
behavior

Longwood University[1]

201 High Street
Farmville, VA 23909
www.longwood.edu/business/
Public
Admissions: (877) 267-7883
Email: graduate@longwood.edu
Financial aid: N/A
Tuition: N/A
Room/board/expenses: N/A
Enrollment: N/A

Old Dominion University

1026 Constant Hall
Norfolk, VA 23529
odu.edu/mba
Public
Admissions: (757) 683-3585
Email: mbainfo@odu.edu
Financial aid: (757) 683-3683
Application deadline: 06/01
In-state tuition: full time: $478/
credit hour; part time: $478/
credit hour
Out-of-state tuition: full time:
$1,195/credit hour
Room/board/expenses: $18,615
College-funded aid: Yes
International student aid: Yes
Full-time enrollment: 18
men: 50%; women: 50%;
minorities: 17%; international:
28%
Part-time enrollment: 131
men: 56%; women: 44%;
minorities: 20%; international:
5%
Average GMAT (part time): 536
TOEFL requirement: Yes
Minimum TOEFL score: 550
Most popular departments:
entrepreneurship, general
management, health care
administration, public
administration, other

Radford University

PO Box 6956
Radford, VA 24142
www.radford.edu
Public
Admissions: (540) 831-6296
Email: gradcoll@radford.edu
Financial aid: (540) 831-5408
Application deadline: rolling
In-state tuition: full time: $328/
credit hour; part time: $328/
credit hour
Out-of-state tuition: full time:
$683/credit hour
Room/board/expenses: $19,930
College-funded aid: Yes
International student aid: Yes
Average student indebtedness at
graduation: $20,471

Full-time enrollment: 8
men: 50%; women: 50%;
minorities: 0%; international:
13%
Part-time enrollment: 33
men: 39%; women: 61%;
minorities: 6%; international:
12%
Acceptance rate (full time): 41%
Average GMAT (full time): 485
Average GMAT (part time): 473
Average GPA (full time): 3.25
Average age of entrants to full-
time program: 29
TOEFL requirement: Yes
Minimum TOEFL score: 550
Most popular departments:
general management
Employment location for 2016
class: Intl. N/A; N.E. N/A; M.A.
100%; S. N/A; M.W. N/A; S.W.
N/A; W. N/A

Shenandoah University (Byrd)

Halpin Harrison, Room 103
Winchester, VA 22601
www.su.edu/
Private
Admissions: (540) 665-4581
Email: admit@su.edu
Financial aid: (540) 665-4538
Application deadline: 05/01
Tuition: full time: $15,848; part
time: $846/credit hour
Room/board/expenses: $14,500
College-funded aid: Yes
International student aid: Yes
Average student indebtedness at
graduation: $76,146
Full-time enrollment: 49
men: 45%; women: 55%;
minorities: 22%; international:
35%
Part-time enrollment: 44
men: 50%; women: 50%;
minorities: 25%; international:
5%
Acceptance rate (full time): 56%
Average GPA (full time): 3.30
Average age of entrants to full-
time program: 27
TOEFL requirement: Yes
Minimum TOEFL score: 550

University of Richmond (Robins)

1 Gateway Road
Richmond, VA 23173
robins.richmond.edu/mba/
Private
Admissions: (804) 289-8553
Email: mba@richmond.edu
Financial aid: (804) 289-8438
Application deadline: rolling
Tuition: full time: N/A/credit hour;
part time: $1,410/credit hour
Room/board/expenses: N/A
College-funded aid: Yes
International student aid: Yes
Full-time enrollment: N/A
men: N/A; women: N/A;
minorities: N/A; international: N/A
Part-time enrollment: 88
men: 58%; women: 42%;
minorities: 16%; international: 1%
Average GMAT (part time): 614
TOEFL requirement: Yes
Minimum TOEFL score: 600

University of Virginia (Darden)

PO Box 6550
Charlottesville, VA 22906-6550
www.darden.virginia.edu
Public
Admissions: (434) 924-7281
Email: darden@virginia.edu
Financial aid: (434) 924-7739
Application deadline: 05/01
In-state tuition: full time: $61,182;
part time: N/A
Out-of-state tuition: full time:
$63,500
Room/board/expenses: $27,163
College-funded aid: Yes
International student aid: Yes
Average student indebtedness at
graduation: $106,710
Full-time enrollment: 678
men: 63%; women: 37%;
minorities: N/A; international: N/A
Part-time enrollment: N/A
men: N/A; women: N/A;
minorities: N/A; international: N/A
Acceptance rate (full time): 26%
Average GMAT (full time): 712
Average GPA (full time): 3.50
Average age of entrants to full-
time program: 27
Average months of prior work
experience (full time): 59
TOEFL requirement: No
Minimum TOEFL score: N/A
Most popular departments:
consulting, entrepreneurship,
finance, general management,
marketing
Mean starting base salary for 2016
full-time graduates: $122,806
Employment location for 2016
class: Intl. 9%; N.E. 31%; M.A.
19%; S. 12%; M.W. 7%; S.W. 9%;
W. 14%

Virginia Commonwealth University

301 W. Main Street
Richmond, VA 23284-4000
business.vcu.edu/
graduate-studies/
Public
Admissions: (804) 828-4622
Email: gsib@vcu.edu
Financial aid: (804) 828-6669
Application deadline: 07/01
In-state tuition: full time: $13,947;
part time: $605/credit hour
Out-of-state tuition: full time:
$25,450
Room/board/expenses: $20,685
College-funded aid: Yes
International student aid: Yes
Full-time enrollment: N/A
men: N/A; women: N/A;
minorities: N/A; international: N/A
Part-time enrollment: 141
men: 62%; women: 38%;
minorities: N/A; international: N/A
Average GMAT (part time): 546
TOEFL requirement: Yes
Minimum TOEFL score: 600
Most popular departments:
entrepreneurship, finance,
general management,
international business,
quantitative analysis/statistics
and operations research

Virginia Tech (Pamplin)

1044 Pamplin Hall (0209)
Blacksburg, VA 24061
www.mba.vt.edu
Public
Admissions: (703) 538-8410
Email: mba@vt.edu
Financial aid: (540) 231-5179
Application deadline: 08/01
In-state tuition: full time: N/A/
credit hour; part time: $766/
credit hour
Out-of-state tuition: full time: N/A/
credit hour
Room/board/expenses: N/A
College-funded aid: Yes
International student aid: Yes
Full-time enrollment: N/A
men: N/A; women: N/A;
minorities: N/A; international: N/A
Part-time enrollment: 163
men: 61%; women: 39%;
minorities: 33%; international:
1%
Average GMAT (part time): 626
TOEFL requirement: Yes
Minimum TOEFL score: 550
Most popular departments:
finance, general management,
international business,
management information
systems, technology

WASHINGTON

Eastern Washington University[1]

668 N. Riverpoint Boulevard
Suite A
Spokane, WA 99202-1677
www.ewu.edu/mba
Public
Admissions: (509) 828-1248
Email: mbaprogram@ewu.edu
Financial aid: N/A
Tuition: N/A
Room/board/expenses: N/A
Enrollment: N/A

Gonzaga University

502 E. Boone Avenue
Spokane, WA 99258-0009
www.gonzaga.edu/mba
Private
Admissions: (509) 313-4622
Email: chatman@gonzaga.edu
Financial aid: (509) 313-6581
Application deadline: 05/30
Tuition: full time: $955/credit
hour; part time: $955/credit hour
Room/board/expenses: $12,227
College-funded aid: Yes
International student aid: Yes
Full-time enrollment: 36
men: 53%; women: 47%;
minorities: 14%; international:
8%
Part-time enrollment: 121
men: 60%; women: 40%;
minorities: 24%; international:
7%
Acceptance rate (full time): 71%
Average GMAT (full time): 540
Average GMAT (part time): 540
Average GPA (full time): 3.47
Average age of entrants to full-
time program: 24
TOEFL requirement: Yes
Minimum TOEFL score: 570
Most popular departments:
accounting, entrepreneurship,
finance, marketing, tax

Pacific Lutheran University

Morken Center for Learning
and Technology, Room 176
Tacoma, WA 98447
www.plu.edu/mba
Private
Admissions: (253) 535-7252
Email: plumba@plu.edu
Financial aid: (253) 535-7134
Application deadline: rolling
Tuition: full time: $1,205/credit
hour; part time: $1,205/credit
hour
Room/board/expenses: $13,888
College-funded aid: Yes
International student aid: Yes
Average student indebtedness at
graduation: $34,650
Full-time enrollment: 48
men: 65%; women: 35%;
minorities: 29%; international:
6%
Part-time enrollment: 5
men: 40%; women: 60%;
minorities: 40%; international:
0%
Acceptance rate (full time): 88%
Average GMAT (full time): 510
Average GPA (full time): 3.35
Average age of entrants to full-
time program: 28
Average months of prior work
experience (full time): 82
TOEFL requirement: Yes
Minimum TOEFL score: 570
Most popular departments:
entrepreneurship, general
management, health care
administration, supply chain
management/logistics,
technology

Seattle Pacific University[1]

3307 Third Avenue W, Suite 201
Seattle, WA 98119-1950
www.spu.edu/sbe
Private
Admissions: (206) 281-2753
Email: drj@spu.edu
Financial aid: (206) 281-2469
Tuition: N/A
Room/board/expenses: N/A
Enrollment: N/A

Seattle University (Albers)

901 12th Avenue
PO Box 222000
Seattle, WA 98122-1090
www.seattleu.edu/albers/
gradoverview/
Private
Admissions: (206) 296-5708
Email: millardj@seattleu.edu
Financial aid: (206) 220-8020
Application deadline: 08/20
Tuition: full time: N/A; part time:
$835/credit hour
Room/board/expenses: N/A
College-funded aid: Yes
International student aid: Yes
Full-time enrollment: N/A
men: N/A; women: N/A;
minorities: N/A; international: N/A
Part-time enrollment: 581
men: 52%; women: 48%;
minorities: 24%; international:
27%
Average GMAT (part time): 591
TOEFL requirement: Yes
Minimum TOEFL score: 580

Most popular departments: accounting, finance, marketing, management information systems, quantitative analysis/statistics and operations research

University of Washington-Bothell

18115 Campus Way NW
Box 358533
Bothell, WA 98011
www.uwb.edu/mba
Public
Admissions: (425) 352-5394
Email: uwbmba@uw.edu
Financial aid: N/A
Application deadline: 04/15
In-state tuition: full time: N/A; part time: $23,592
Out-of-state tuition: full time: N/A
Room/board/expenses: N/A
College-funded aid: Yes
International student aid: Yes
Full-time enrollment: N/A
men: N/A; women: N/A;
minorities: N/A; international: N/A
Part-time enrollment: 109
men: 66%; women: 34%;
minorities: 30%; international: 2%
Average GMAT (part time): 529
TOEFL requirement: Yes
Minimum TOEFL score: 580
Most popular departments: consulting, entrepreneurship, human resources management, leadership, technology

University of Washington (Foster)

PO Box 353200
Seattle, WA 98195-3200
foster.uw.edu/academics/degree-programs/full-time-mba//
Public
Admissions: (206) 543-4661
Email: mba@uw.edu
Financial aid: (206) 543-4661
Application deadline: 03/15
In-state tuition: full time: $32,394; part time: $24,579
Out-of-state tuition: full time: $47,214
Room/board/expenses: $29,363
College-funded aid: Yes
International student aid: Yes
Average student indebtedness at graduation: $32,047
Full-time enrollment: 253
men: 62%; women: 38%;
minorities: 11%; international: 36%
Part-time enrollment: 377
men: 65%; women: 35%;
minorities: 26%; international: 5%
Acceptance rate (full time): 24%
Average GMAT (full time): 691
Average GMAT (part time): 623
Average GPA (full time): 3.38
Average age of entrants to full-time program: 29
Average months of prior work experience (full time): 72
TOEFL requirement: Yes
Minimum TOEFL score: 600
Most popular departments: consulting, entrepreneurship, finance, manufacturing and technology management, marketing
Mean starting base salary for 2016 full-time graduates: $111,847

Employment location for 2016 class: Intl. 1%; N.E. 1%; M.A. 0%; S. 1%; M.W. 2%; S.W. 1%; W. 94%

University of Washington-Tacoma (Milgard)

1900 Commerce Street
Box 358420
Tacoma, WA 98402
www.tacoma.uw.edu/milgard/mba/overview
Public
Admissions: (253) 692-5630
Email: uwtmba@uw.edu
Financial aid: (253) 692-4374
Application deadline: 06/01
In-state tuition: full time: N/A; part time: $1,022/credit hour
Out-of-state tuition: full time: N/A
Room/board/expenses: N/A
College-funded aid: Yes
International student aid: Yes
Full-time enrollment: N/A
men: N/A; women: N/A;
minorities: N/A; international: N/A
Part-time enrollment: 50
men: 62%; women: 38%;
minorities: 44%; international: 0%
Average GMAT (part time): 516
TOEFL requirement: Yes
Minimum TOEFL score: 580

Washington State University[1]

PO Box 644744
Pullman, WA 99164-4744
business.wsu.edu/graduate-programs/
Public
Admissions: (509) 335-7617
Email: mba@wsu.edu
Financial aid: (509) 335-9711
Tuition: N/A
Room/board/expenses: N/A
Enrollment: N/A

Western Washington University[1]

516 High Street, MS 9072
Bellingham, WA 98225-9072
www.cbe.wwu.edu/mba/
Public
Admissions: (360) 650-3898
Email: mba@wwu.edu
Financial aid: N/A
Tuition: N/A
Room/board/expenses: N/A
Enrollment: N/A

WEST VIRGINIA

Marshall University (Lewis)

1 John Marshall Drive
Huntington, WV 25755-2020
www.marshall.edu/lcob/
Public
Admissions: (800) 642-9842
Email: johnson73@marshall.edu
Financial aid: (800) 438-5390
Application deadline: rolling
In-state tuition: full time: $446/credit hour; part time: $446/credit hour
Out-of-state tuition: full time: $1,051/credit hour
Room/board/expenses: N/A
College-funded aid: Yes
International student aid: Yes

Full-time enrollment: 140
men: 71%; women: 29%;
minorities: N/A; international: N/A
Part-time enrollment: 41
men: 56%; women: 44%;
minorities: N/A; international: N/A
Acceptance rate (full time): 82%
Average GPA (full time): 3.10
Average age of entrants to full-time program: 25
TOEFL requirement: Yes
Minimum TOEFL score: N/A
Most popular departments: finance, general management, health care administration, human resources management, marketing

West Virginia University

PO Box 6027
Morgantown, WV 26506
www.be.wvu.edu
Public
Admissions: (304) 293-7811
Email: mba@wvu.edu
Financial aid: (304) 293-5242
Application deadline: 03/01
In-state tuition: full time: $777/credit hour; part time: N/A
Out-of-state tuition: full time: $1,778/credit hour
Room/board/expenses: $15,712
College-funded aid: Yes
International student aid: Yes
Average student indebtedness at graduation: $18,608
Full-time enrollment: 26
men: 58%; women: 42%;
minorities: 15%; international: 15%
Part-time enrollment: N/A
men: N/A; women: N/A;
minorities: N/A; international: N/A
Acceptance rate (full time): 49%
Average GMAT (full time): 609
Average GPA (full time): 3.49
Average age of entrants to full-time program: 24
Average months of prior work experience (full time): 32
TOEFL requirement: Yes
Minimum TOEFL score: 580
Most popular departments: finance, human resources management
Mean starting base salary for 2016 full-time graduates: $53,988
Employment location for 2016 class: Intl. N/A; N.E. 0%; M.A. 67%; S. 17%; M.W. 17%; S.W. N/A; W. N/A

WISCONSIN

Marquette University

PO Box 1881
Milwaukee, WI 53201-1881
www.marquette.edu/gsm
Private
Admissions: (414) 288-7145
Email: mba@Marquette.edu
Financial aid: (414) 288-7137
Application deadline: rolling
Tuition: full time: $1,075/credit hour; part time: $1,075/credit hour
Room/board/expenses: $17,718
College-funded aid: Yes
International student aid: Yes
Full-time enrollment: 121
men: 46%; women: 54%;
minorities: 8%; international: 45%

Part-time enrollment: 211
men: 72%; women: 28%;
minorities: 7%; international: 3%
Acceptance rate (full time): 78%
Average GMAT (full time): 598
Average GMAT (part time): 578
Average GPA (full time): 3.25
Average age of entrants to full-time program: 24
TOEFL requirement: Yes
Minimum TOEFL score: N/A
Most popular departments: accounting, finance, human resources management, international business

University of Wisconsin-Eau Claire

Schneider Hall 215
Eau Claire, WI 54702-4004
www.uwec.edu/academics/college-business/
Public
Admissions: (715) 836-5415
Email: uwecmba@uwec.edu
Financial aid: (715) 836-3373
Application deadline: 09/04
In-state tuition: full time: $675/credit hour; part time: $675/credit hour
Out-of-state tuition: full time: $675/credit hour
Room/board/expenses: N/A
College-funded aid: Yes
International student aid: Yes
Full-time enrollment: 13
men: 69%; women: 31%;
minorities: 0%; international: 0%
Part-time enrollment: 268
men: 55%; women: 45%;
minorities: 10%; international: 2%
Acceptance rate (full time): 0%
Average GMAT (part time): 551
TOEFL requirement: Yes
Minimum TOEFL score: 550
Most popular departments: accounting, general management, health care administration, marketing, management information systems

University of Wisconsin-La Crosse[1]

1725 State Street
La Crosse, WI 54601
www.uwlax.edu
Public
Admissions: (608) 785-8939
Email: admissions@uwlax.edu
Financial aid: (608) 785-8604
Tuition: N/A
Room/board/expenses: N/A
Enrollment: N/A

University of Wisconsin-Madison

975 University Avenue
Suite 4339
Madison, WI 53706-1323
wsb.wisc.edu/programs-degrees/
Public
Admissions: (608) 262-4000
Email: mba@wsb.wisc.edu
Financial aid: (608) 262-3060
Application deadline: 04/12
In-state tuition: full time: $17,109; part time: $19,276
Out-of-state tuition: full time: $33,379
Room/board/expenses: $18,242
College-funded aid: Yes
International student aid: Yes

Full-time enrollment: 196
men: 63%; women: 37%;
minorities: 16%; international: 21%
Part-time enrollment: 167
men: 68%; women: 32%;
minorities: 8%; international: 3%
Acceptance rate (full time): 78%
Average GMAT (full time): 669
Average GMAT (part time): 592
Average GPA (full time): 3.42
Average age of entrants to full-time program: 28
Average months of prior work experience (full time): 70
TOEFL requirement: Yes
Minimum TOEFL score: N/A
Most popular departments: finance, general management, marketing, production/operations management, real estate
Mean starting base salary for 2016 full-time graduates: $96,531
Employment location for 2016 class: Intl. 0%; N.E. 7%; M.A. 4%; S. 4%; M.W. 57%; S.W. 15%; W. 14%

University of Wisconsin-Milwaukee (Lubar)

PO Box 742
Milwaukee, WI 53201-9863
lubar.uwm.edu
Public
Admissions: (414) 229-5403
Email: mba-ms@uwm.edu
Financial aid: (414) 229-4541
Application deadline: rolling
In-state tuition: full time: $17,634; part time: $14,141
Out-of-state tuition: full time: $34,578
Room/board/expenses: $14,600
College-funded aid: Yes
International student aid: Yes
Full-time enrollment: 12
men: 17%; women: 83%;
minorities: 25%; international: 25%
Part-time enrollment: 400
men: 65%; women: 35%;
minorities: 16%; international: 12%
Acceptance rate (full time): 84%
Average GMAT (part time): 541
Average GPA (full time): 3.29
Average age of entrants to full-time program: 24
Average months of prior work experience (full time): 13
TOEFL requirement: Yes
Minimum TOEFL score: 550
Most popular departments: accounting, finance, general management, management information systems

University of Wisconsin-Oshkosh

800 Algoma Boulevard
Oshkosh, WI 54901
www.uwosh.edu/coba/
Public
Admissions: (800) 633-1430
Email: mba@uwosh.edu
Financial aid: (920) 424-3377
Application deadline: rolling
In-state tuition: full time: $758/credit hour; total program: $23,765 (part time)
Out-of-state tuition: full time: $1,266/credit hour
Room/board/expenses: N/A

College-funded aid: Yes
International student aid: Yes
Full-time enrollment: 12
men: 75%; women: 25%;
minorities: 0%; international: 25%
Part-time enrollment: 312
men: 62%; women: 38%;
minorities: 7%; international: 3%
Acceptance rate (full time): 100%
Average GMAT (part time): 590
Average GPA (full time): 3.11
Average age of entrants to full-time program: 40
Average months of prior work experience (full time): 186
TOEFL requirement: Yes
Minimum TOEFL score: 550
Most popular departments: health care administration, other

University of Wisconsin-Parkside

PO Box 2000
Kenosha, WI 53141-2000
uwp.edu/learn/programs/mbamasters.cfm
Public
Admissions: (262) 595-2243
Email: admissions@uwp.edu
Financial aid: (262) 595-2574
Application deadline: rolling
In-state tuition: full time: $497/credit hour; part time: $497/credit hour
Out-of-state tuition: full time: $1,010/credit hour
Room/board/expenses: $9,000

College-funded aid: Yes
International student aid: Yes
Full-time enrollment: 28
men: 46%; women: 54%;
minorities: 14%; international: 57%
Part-time enrollment: 68
men: 59%; women: 41%;
minorities: 29%; international: 0%
Acceptance rate (full time): 79%
Average GMAT (full time): 513
Average GMAT (part time): 393
Average GPA (full time): 3.47
Average age of entrants to full-time program: 26
Average months of prior work experience (full time): 18
TOEFL requirement: Yes
Minimum TOEFL score: 550

University of Wisconsin-River Falls

410 S. Third Street
River Falls, WI 54022-5001
www.uwrf.edu/mba
Public
Admissions: (715) 425-3335
Email: mbacbe@uwrf.edu
Financial aid: (715) 425-4111
Application deadline: rolling
In-state tuition: full time: $692/credit hour; part time: $692/credit hour
Out-of-state tuition: full time: $692/credit hour
Room/board/expenses: N/A
College-funded aid: Yes

International student aid: Yes
Average student indebtedness at graduation: $25,309
Full-time enrollment: 24
men: 67%; women: 33%;
minorities: 8%; international: 75%
Part-time enrollment: 68
men: 49%; women: 51%;
minorities: 6%; international: N/A
Acceptance rate (full time): 100%
Average GMAT (full time): 500
Average GMAT (part time): 427
Average GPA (full time): 2.60
Average age of entrants to full-time program: 24
TOEFL requirement: Yes
Minimum TOEFL score: 550

University of Wisconsin-Whitewater

800 W. Main Street
Whitewater, WI 53190
www.uww.edu/cobe
Public
Admissions: (262) 472-1945
Email: gradbus@uww.edu
Financial aid: (262) 472-1130
Application deadline: 07/15
In-state tuition: full time: $9,492; part time: $527/credit hour
Out-of-state tuition: full time: $19,018
Room/board/expenses: $6,900
College-funded aid: Yes
International student aid: Yes

Average student indebtedness at graduation: $8,000
Full-time enrollment: 76
men: 47%; women: 53%;
minorities: 21%; international: 9%
Part-time enrollment: 462
men: 60%; women: 40%;
minorities: 11%; international: 2%
Acceptance rate (full time): 70%
Average GMAT (full time): 460
Average GMAT (part time): 507
Average GPA (full time): 3.32
Average age of entrants to full-time program: 27
Average months of prior work experience (full time): 118
TOEFL requirement: Yes
Minimum TOEFL score: 550
Most popular departments: finance, general management, marketing, management information systems, supply chain management/logistics
Mean starting base salary for 2016 full-time graduates: $57,000
Employment location for 2016 class: Intl. 50%; N.E. N/A; M.A. N/A; S. N/A; M.W. 50%; S.W. N/A; W. N/A

WYOMING

University of Wyoming

PO Box 3275
Laramie, WY 82071-3275
www.uwyo.edu/mba/
Public
Admissions: (307) 766-2449
Email: tparmely@uwyo.edu

Financial aid: (307) 766-2116
Application deadline: 06/30
In-state tuition: full time: $595/credit hour; part time: $630/credit hour
Out-of-state tuition: full time: $906/credit hour
Room/board/expenses: $4,470
College-funded aid: Yes
International student aid: Yes
Full-time enrollment: 38
men: 79%; women: 21%;
minorities: N/A; international: N/A
Part-time enrollment: 88
men: 59%; women: 41%;
minorities: N/A; international: N/A
Acceptance rate (full time): 70%
Average GMAT (full time): 572
Average GMAT (part time): 600
Average GPA (full time): 3.24
Average age of entrants to full-time program: 25
Average months of prior work experience (full time): 18
TOEFL requirement: Yes
Minimum TOEFL score: N/A
Most popular departments: international business, other
Employment location for 2016 class: Intl. N/A; N.E. N/A; M.A. N/A; S. 11%; M.W. N/A; S.W. N/A; W. 89%

EDUCATION

Here you'll find information on 379 schools nationwide that offer doctoral programs in education. Two hundred fifty-six responded to the U.S. News survey, which was conducted in the fall of 2016 and early 2017. They provided information on matters of interest to applicants such as entrance requirements, enrollment, costs, location and specialties. Schools that did not respond to the survey have abbreviated entries.

KEY TO THE TERMINOLOGY

1. A school whose name has been footnoted with the numeral 1 did not return the U.S. News statistical survey; limited data appear in its entry.
N/A. Not available from the school or not applicable.
Admissions. The admissions office phone number.
Email. The address of the admissions office. If instead of an email address a website is listed, the website will automatically present an email screen programmed to reach the admissions office.
Financial aid. The financial aid office phone number.
Application deadline. For fall 2018 enrollment. "Rolling" means there is no deadline; the school acts on applications as they are received. "Varies" means deadlines vary according to department or whether applicants are U.S. citizens or foreign nationals.
Tuition. For the 2016-17 academic year. Includes fees.
Credit hour. The cost per credit hour for the 2016-17 academic year.
Room/board/expenses. For the 2016-17 academic year.
Enrollment. Full-time and part-time graduate-level enrollment at the education school for fall 2016.
Minorities. Full-time and part-time graduate-level minority enrollment percentage for fall 2016. It is the share of students who are black or African-American, Asian, American Indian or Alaska Native, Native Hawaiian or other Pacific Islander, Hispanic/Latino, or two or more races. The number of minority students was reported by each school.
Acceptance rate. Percentage of applicants who were accepted among those who applied for fall 2016 for both master's and doctoral programs.

Entrance test required. GRE means that scores on the Graduate Record Examination are required by some or all departments. GRE scores displayed are for both the master's and Ph.D. students and are only for those GRE exams taken by the fall 2016 entering students. MAT means that the Miller Analogies Test is required by some or all departments. GRE or MAT means that some or all departments require either the GRE or MAT.
Average GRE scores. Average verbal and quantitative scores for students who entered in fall 2016. Averages are based on the number of students who provided the school with scores. That number may be less than the total number of students who entered in fall 2016. (The GRE scores published in the ranking table refer to the scores of a school's entering doctoral students and may not be the same as the average GRE scores for the overall entering class printed in the directory.)
Total research assistantships. For the 2016-17 academic year.
Students reporting specialty. The percentage of graduate students, both full and part time, reporting a program specialization in fall 2016. If a school's figure is less than 50 percent, then its directory entry does not include this information or an enumeration of student specialties.
Student specialties. Proportion of students in the specialty-reporting population (not necessarily the entire student body) who are enrolled in a particular specialty. Numbers may not add up to 100 percent because of rounding or students enrolled in multiple specialties. The largest specialty areas in graduate education are listed.

ALABAMA

Alabama A&M University[1]
P. O. Box 998
Normal, AL 35762
www.aamu.edu/academics/gradstudies/pages/default.aspx
Public
Admissions: (256) 372-5266
Email: gradschool1@aamu.edu
Financial aid: N/A
Tuition: N/A
Room/board/expenses: N/A
Enrollment: N/A

Alabama State University[1]
915 S. Jackson Street
Montgomery, AL 36101
www.alasu.edu/Education/
Public
Admissions: (334) 229-4275
Financial aid: (334) 229-4324
Tuition: N/A
Room/board/expenses: N/A
Enrollment: N/A

Auburn University
3084 Haley Center
Auburn, AL 36849-5218
www.auburn.edu/
Public
Admissions: (334) 844-4700
Email: gradadm@auburn.edu
Financial aid: (334) 844-4634
Application deadline: rolling
In-state tuition: full time: $10,696; part time: $504/credit hour
Out-of-state tuition: full time: $28,840
Room/board/expenses: $19,662
Full-time enrollment: 457
doctoral students: 39%; master's students: 61%; education specialists: 1%; men: 30%; women: 70%; minorities: 28%; international: 7%
Part-time enrollment: 502
doctoral students: 53%; master's students: 39%; education specialists: 9%; men: 33%; women: 67%; minorities: 28%; international: 1%
Acceptance rate (master's): 64%
Acceptance rate (doctoral): 45%
Entrance test required: GRE
Avg. GRE (of all entering students with scores): quantitative: 147; verbal: 149
Research assistantships: 35
Students reporting specialty: 100%
Students specializing in: admin.: 9%; instructional media design: 1%; educational psych.: 7%; elementary: 3%; higher education admin.: 8%; secondary: 10%; special: 9%; counseling: 10%; technical (vocational): 6%; other: 35%

Samford University (Beeson)
800 Lakeshore Drive
Birmingham, AL 35229
samford.edu/education
Private
Admissions: (205) 726-2451
Email: lsennis@samford.edu
Financial aid: (205) 726-2905
Application deadline: 07/15
Tuition: full time: $789/credit hour; part time: $789/credit hour
Room/board/expenses: $1,100
Full-time enrollment: 223
doctoral students: 26%; master's students: 62%; education specialists: 12%; men: 28%; women: 72%; minorities: 34%; international: 1%
Part-time enrollment: 86
doctoral students: 83%; master's students: 17%; education specialists: 0%; men: 36%; women: 64%; minorities: 34%; international: 0%
Acceptance rate (master's): 65%
Acceptance rate (doctoral): 42%
Entrance test required: GRE
Avg. GRE (of all entering students with scores): quantitative: 146; verbal: 148
Research assistantships: 0
Students reporting specialty: 100%
Students specializing in: curriculum/instr.: 8%; admin.: 62%; policy: 6%; instructional media design: 4%; elementary: 7%; junior high: 11%; secondary: 11%; special: 1%; other: 1%

University of Alabama
Box 870231
Tuscaloosa, AL 35487-0231
graduate.ua.edu
Public
Admissions: (205) 348-5921
Email: gradschool@ua.edu
Financial aid: (205) 348-7949
Application deadline: rolling
In-state tuition: full time: $10,470; part time: N/A*
Out-of-state tuition: full time: $26,950
Room/board/expenses: $13,330
Full-time enrollment: 379
doctoral students: 55%; master's students: 42%; education specialists: 2%; men: 30%; women: 70%; minorities: 29%; international: 7%
Part-time enrollment: 533
doctoral students: 54%; master's students: 34%; education specialists: 12%; men: 28%; women: 72%; minorities: 26%; international: 4%
Acceptance rate (master's): 59%
Acceptance rate (doctoral): 52%
Entrance test required: GRE
Avg. GRE (of all entering students with scores): quantitative: 149; verbal: 151
Research assistantships: 73
Students reporting specialty: 100%
Students specializing in: admin.: 26%; evaluation/research/statistics: 3%; educational psych.: 12%; elementary: 4%;

higher education admin.: 15%; secondary: 13%; special: 6%; counseling: 3%; other: 22%

University of Alabama-Birmingham

1530 Third Avenue S, EB 217
Birmingham, AL 35294-1250
www.uab.edu/graduate
Public
Admissions: (205) 934-8227
Email: gradschool@uab.edu
Financial aid: (205) 934-8223
Application deadline: 07/01
In-state tuition: full time: $7,588;
part time: $396/credit hour
Out-of-state tuition: full time:
$17,294
Room/board/expenses: $14,409
Full-time enrollment: 184
doctoral students: 10%; master's
students: 89%; education
specialists: 1%; men: 24%;
women: 76%; minorities: 25%;
international: 7%
Part-time enrollment: 493
doctoral students: 12%; master's
students: 75%; education
specialists: 13%; men: 21%;
women: 79%; minorities: 30%;
international: 1%
Acceptance rate (master's): 91%
Acceptance rate (doctoral): 65%
Entrance test required: GRE
**Avg. GRE (of all entering students
with scores):** quantitative: 144;
verbal: 149
Research assistantships: 6
Students reporting specialty: 100%
Students specializing in: admin.:
15%; evaluation/research/
statistics: 3%; elementary: 2%;
secondary: 14%; special: 8%;
counseling: 12%; other: 46%

University of South Alabama[1]

UCOM 3600
Mobile, AL 36688
www.southalabama.edu/
Public
Admissions: N/A
Financial aid: N/A
Tuition: N/A
Room/board/expenses: N/A
Enrollment: N/A

ARIZONA

Arizona State University

PO Box 37100, MC 1252
Phoenix, AZ 85069-7100
www.asu.edu/graduate
Public
Admissions: (480) 965-6113
Email: gograd@asu.edu
Financial aid: (855) 278-5080
Application deadline: rolling
In-state tuition: full time: $11,506;
part time: $772/credit hour
Out-of-state tuition: full time:
$28,882
Room/board/expenses: $19,044
Full-time enrollment: 704
doctoral students: 20%;
master's students: 80%;
education specialists: N/A; men:
30%; women: 70%; minorities:
35%; international: 4%
Part-time enrollment: 1,803
doctoral students: 6%; master's
students: 94%; education
specialists: N/A; men: 16%;
women: 84%; minorities: 31%;
international: 3%
Acceptance rate (master's): 85%

Acceptance rate (doctoral): 20%
Entrance test required: GRE
**Avg. GRE (of all entering students
with scores):** quantitative: 150;
verbal: 157
Research assistantships: 59
Students reporting specialty: 100%
Students specializing in:
curriculum/instr.: 57%; admin.:
8%; policy: 2%; evaluation/
research/statistics: 0%;
instructional media design:
2%; educational psych:
0%; elementary: 4%; higher
education admin.: 6%;
secondary: 5%; special: 2%;
other: 13%

Grand Canyon University[1]

3300 W. Camelback Road
Phoenix, AZ 85017
www.gcu.edu
Private
Admissions: N/A
Financial aid: N/A
Tuition: N/A
Room/board/expenses: N/A
Enrollment: N/A

Northcentral University

2488 Historic Decatur Road
Suite 100
San Diego, CA 92106
www.ncu.edu
Private
Admissions: (866) 776-0331
Email: admissions@ncu.edu
Financial aid: (866) 776-0331
Application deadline: rolling
Tuition: full time: $15,984; part
time: $666/credit hour
Full-time enrollment: 2,175
doctoral students: 85%;
master's students: 12%;
education specialists: 3%; men:
26%; women: 74%; minorities:
34%; international: 0%
Part-time enrollment: 1,607
doctoral students: 55%;
master's students: 36%;
education specialists: 9%; men:
29%; women: 71%; minorities:
35%; international: 0%
Acceptance rate (master's): N/A
Acceptance rate (doctoral): N/A
Entrance test required: N/A
**Avg. GRE (of all entering students
with scores):** quantitative: N/A;
verbal: N/A
Students reporting specialty: 0%
Students specializing in: N/A

Northern Arizona University

PO Box 5774
Flagstaff, AZ 86011-5774
nau.edu/GradCol/Welcome/
Public
Admissions: (928) 523-4348
Email: gradadmissions@nau.edu
Financial aid: (928) 523-4951
Application deadline: rolling
In-state tuition: full time: $9,990;
part time: $444/credit hour
Out-of-state tuition: full time:
$21,976
Room/board/expenses: $15,332
Full-time enrollment: 605
doctoral students: 11%; master's
students: 85%; education
specialists: 4%; men: 28%;
women: 72%; minorities: 32%;
international: 5%

Part-time enrollment: 1,090
doctoral students: 15%; master's
students: 85%; education
specialists: 1%; men: 27%;
women: 73%; minorities: 34%;
international: 0%
Acceptance rate (master's): 87%
Acceptance rate (doctoral): 81%
Entrance test required: GRE
**Avg. GRE (of all entering students
with scores):** quantitative: 146;
verbal: 150
Students reporting specialty: 100%
Students specializing in:
curriculum/instr.: 3%; admin.:
44%; educational psych:
1%; educational tech.: 5%;
elementary: 7%; secondary:
0%; special: 6%; counseling:
18%; technical (vocational): 0%;
other: 16%

Prescott College

220 Grove Avenue
Prescott, AZ 86301
prescott.edu/learn/index.html
Private
Admissions: N/A
Financial aid: N/A
Application deadline: rolling
Tuition: full time: $796/credit
hour; part time: N/A
Room/board/expenses: $10,592
Full-time enrollment: 89
doctoral students: 26%;
master's students: 74%;
education specialists: N/A; men:
20%; women: 80%; minorities:
19%; international: 3%
Part-time enrollment: 251
doctoral students: 12%; master's
students: 88%; education
specialists: N/A; men: 25%;
women: 75%; minorities: 16%;
international: 2%
Acceptance rate (master's): 36%
Acceptance rate (doctoral): 90%
Entrance test required: N/A
**Avg. GRE (of all entering students
with scores):** quantitative: N/A;
verbal: N/A
Students reporting specialty: 0%
Students specializing in: N/A

University of Arizona

Box 210069
1430 E. Second Street
Tucson, AZ 85721-0069
grad.arizona.edu/admissions
Public
Admissions: (520) 626-8851
Email: gradadmissions@
grad.arizona.edu
Financial aid: (520) 621-5200
Application deadline: rolling
In-state tuition: full time: $12,422;
part time: $812/credit hour
Out-of-state tuition: full time:
$32,122
Room/board/expenses: $17,500
Full-time enrollment: 478
doctoral students: 38%;
master's students: 56%;
education specialists: 6%; men:
24%; women: 76%; minorities:
36%; international: 10%
Part-time enrollment: 278
doctoral students: 38%;
master's students: 56%;
education specialists: 5%; men:
24%; women: 76%; minorities:
34%; international: 5%
Acceptance rate (master's): 72%
Acceptance rate (doctoral): 73%
Entrance test required: GRE
**Avg. GRE (of all entering students
with scores):** quantitative: 150;
verbal: 154

Research assistantships: 30
Students reporting specialty: 100%
Students specializing in:
curriculum/instr.: 9%; admin.:
26%; policy: 26%; educational
psych: 5%; elementary: 2%;
higher education admin.: 26%;
junior high: 2%; secondary: 7%;
social/philosophical foundations:
5%; special: 17%; counseling:
15%; other: 2%

University of Phoenix[1]

1625 W. Fountainhead Parkway
Tempe, AZ 85282-2371
www.phoenix.edu/colleges_
divisions/education.html
Private
Admissions: N/A
Financial aid: N/A
Tuition: N/A
Room/board/expenses: N/A
Enrollment: N/A

ARKANSAS

Arkansas State University-Jonesboro

PO Box 10
State University, AR 72467
www.astate.edu/college/
graduate-school/
Public
Admissions: N/A
Financial aid: (870) 972-2310
Application deadline: rolling
In-state tuition: full time: $257/
credit hour; part time: $257/
credit hour
Out-of-state tuition: full time: $514/
credit hour
Room/board/expenses: N/A
Full-time enrollment: 135
doctoral students: 3%; master's
students: 61%; education
specialists: 36%; men: 34%;
women: 66%; minorities: N/A;
international: N/A
Part-time enrollment: 2,266
doctoral students: 3%; master's
students: 75%; education
specialists: 22%; men: 29%;
women: 71%; minorities: N/A;
international: N/A
Acceptance rate (master's): N/A
Acceptance rate (doctoral): N/A
Entrance test required: GRE
**Avg. GRE (of all entering students
with scores):** quantitative: N/A;
verbal: N/A
Students reporting specialty: 0%
Students specializing in: N/A

Harding University

Box 12234
Searcy, AR 72149
www.harding.edu/education/
grad.html/
Private
Admissions: (501) 279-4315
Email:
gradstudies@harding.edu
Financial aid: (501) 279-4081
Application deadline: rolling
Tuition: full time: $436/credit
hour; part time: $436/credit hour
Room/board/expenses: N/A
Full-time enrollment: 130
doctoral students: 0%; master's
students: 97%; education
specialists: 3%; men: 27%;
women: 73%; minorities: 12%;
international: 8%
Part-time enrollment: 537
doctoral students: 6%; master's
students: 92%; education

specialists: 3%; men: 19%;
women: 81%; minorities: 22%;
international: 0%
Acceptance rate (master's): 100%
Acceptance rate (doctoral): 100%
Entrance test required: GRE
**Avg. GRE (of all entering students
with scores):** quantitative: N/A;
verbal: N/A
Research assistantships: 0
Students reporting specialty: 100%
Students specializing in:
curriculum/instr.: 1%; admin.:
11%; instructional media design:
1%; elementary: 4%; junior high:
5%; secondary: 10%; counseling:
15%; other: 54%

University of Arkansas-Fayetteville

324 Graduate Education Building
Fayetteville, AR 72701
coehp.uark.edu
Public
Admissions: (479) 575-6247
Email: gradinfo@uark.edu
Financial aid: (479) 575-3276
Application deadline: rolling
In-state tuition: full time: $410/
credit hour; part time: $410/
credit hour
Out-of-state tuition: full time:
$1,047/credit hour
Room/board/expenses: $16,224
Full-time enrollment: 246
doctoral students: 77%; master's
students: 23%; education
specialists: 0%; men: 35%;
women: 65%; minorities: 3%;
international: 2%
Part-time enrollment: 209
doctoral students: 79%; master's
students: 19%; education
specialists: 2%; men: 60%;
women: 40%; minorities: 8%;
international: 1%
Acceptance rate (master's): 23%
Acceptance rate (doctoral): 17%
Entrance test required: GRE
**Avg. GRE (of all entering students
with scores):** quantitative: 147;
verbal: 151
Research assistantships: 41
Students reporting specialty: N/A
Students specializing in: N/A

University of Arkansas-Little Rock[1]

2801 S. University Avenue
Little Rock, AR 72204
ualr.edu/www/
Public
Admissions: N/A
Financial aid: N/A
Tuition: N/A
Room/board/expenses: N/A
Enrollment: N/A

CALIFORNIA

Alliant International University

1 Beach Street
San Francisco, CA 94133-1221
www.alliant.edu/
Private
Admissions: (866) 825-5426
Email: admissions@alliant.edu
Financial aid: (858) 635-4550
Application deadline: rolling
Tuition: full time: $648/credit
hour; part time: $648/credit hour
Room/board/expenses: $27,500

Full-time enrollment: 111
doctoral students: 15%; master's students: 85%; education specialists: 0%; men: 20%; women: 80%; minorities: N/A; international: N/A
Part-time enrollment: 317
doctoral students: 24%; master's students: 76%; education specialists: 0%; men: 35%; women: 65%; minorities: N/A; international: N/A
Acceptance rate (master's): N/A
Acceptance rate (doctoral): N/A
Entrance test required: N/A
Avg. GRE (of all entering students with scores): quantitative: N/A; verbal: N/A
Students reporting specialty: 100%
Students specializing in: admin.: 5%; educational psych: 6%; elementary: 2%; higher education admin.: 0%; special: 14%; counseling: 6%; other: 66%

Azusa Pacific University
PO Box 7000
Azusa, CA 91702
www.apu.edu
Private
Admissions: (800) 825-5278
Email: gpc@apu.edu
Financial aid: (800) 825-5278
Application deadline: 07/24
Tuition: full time: $672/credit hour; part time: $672/credit hour
Room/board/expenses: N/A
Full-time enrollment: 607
doctoral students: 4%; master's students: 80%; education specialists: 16%; men: 20%; women: 80%; minorities: 50%; international: 0%
Part-time enrollment: 395
doctoral students: 10%; master's students: 81%; education specialists: 9%; men: 27%; women: 73%; minorities: 42%; international: 0%
Acceptance rate (master's): 96%
Acceptance rate (doctoral): 93%
Entrance test required: GRE
Avg. GRE (of all entering students with scores): quantitative: N/A; verbal: N/A
Students reporting specialty: 100%
Students specializing in: admin.: 15%; educational psych: 12%; educational tech.: 2%; elementary: 15%; secondary: 13%; special: 25%; counseling: 17%; other: 3%

Brandman University[1]
16355 Laguna Canyon Road
Irvine, CA 92618
www.brandman.edu/education
Private
Admissions: (800) 746-0082
Email: soe@brandman.edu
Financial aid: N/A
Tuition: N/A
Room/board/expenses: N/A
Enrollment: N/A

California Lutheran University[1]
60 West Olsen Road
Thousand Oaks, CA 91360
www.callutheran.edu/
Private
Admissions: N/A
Financial aid: N/A
Tuition: N/A
Room/board/expenses: N/A
Enrollment: N/A

California State University-East Bay
25800 Carlos Bee Boulevard
Hayward, CA 94542
www.csueastbay.edu
Public
Admissions: (510) 885-7571
Email: gradadmission@csueastbay.edu
Financial aid: (510) 885-2784
Application deadline: 05/31
In-state tuition: full time: $7,830; part time: N/A
Out-of-state tuition: full time: $15,492
Room/board/expenses: $16,776
Full-time enrollment: 274
doctoral students: 9%; master's students: 91%; education specialists: N/A; men: 26%; women: 74%; minorities: 46%; international: 1%
Part-time enrollment: 148
doctoral students: 24%; master's students: 76%; education specialists: N/A; men: 27%; women: 73%; minorities: 56%; international: 3%
Acceptance rate (master's): 58%
Acceptance rate (doctoral): N/A
Entrance test required: GRE
Avg. GRE (of all entering students with scores): quantitative: N/A; verbal: N/A
Students reporting specialty: 0%
Students specializing in: N/A

California State University-Fresno[1]
5150 N. Maple
Fresno, CA 93740
www.fresnostate.edu
Public
Admissions: N/A
Financial aid: N/A
Tuition: N/A
Room/board/expenses: N/A
Enrollment: N/A

California State University-Fullerton[1]
800 N. State College Boulevard
Fullerton, CA 92831-3599
ed.fullerton.edu/
Public
Admissions: N/A
Financial aid: N/A
Tuition: N/A
Room/board/expenses: N/A
Enrollment: N/A

California State University-Long Beach[1]
1250 Bellflower Boulevard
Long Beach, CA 90840
www.ced.csulb.edu
Public
Admissions: (562) 985-4547
Email: nmcgloth@csulb.edu
Financial aid: (562) 985-8403
Tuition: N/A
Room/board/expenses: N/A
Enrollment: N/A

California State University-Los Angeles
5151 State University Drive
Los Angeles, CA 90032
calstatela.edu/academic/ccoe/
Public
Admissions: (323) 343-3844
Email: gradadm@calstatela.edu

Financial aid: (323) 343-5808
Application deadline: 05/31
In-state tuition: full time: $7,621; part time: $4,788
Out-of-state tuition: full time: $10,969
Room/board/expenses: $16,174
Full-time enrollment: 502
doctoral students: 9%; master's students: 91%; education specialists: 0%; men: 24%; women: 76%; minorities: N/A; international: N/A
Part-time enrollment: 208
doctoral students: 14%; master's students: 86%; education specialists: 0%; men: 25%; women: 75%; minorities: N/A; international: N/A
Acceptance rate (master's): 52%
Acceptance rate (doctoral): 61%
Entrance test required: GRE
Avg. GRE (of all entering students with scores): quantitative: N/A; verbal: N/A
Research assistantships: 0
Students reporting specialty: 100%
Students specializing in: curriculum/instr.: 6%; admin.: 4%; evaluation/research/statistics: 0%; instructional media design: 3%; educational psych: 6%; educational tech.: 3%; elementary: 3%; higher education admin.: 6%; junior high: 3%; secondary: 7%; social/philosophical foundations: 3%; special: 6%; counseling: 9%; technical (vocational): 0%; other: 49%

California State University-Northridge[1]
18111 Nordhoff Street
Northridge, CA 91330-8265
www.csun.edu/
Public
Admissions: N/A
Financial aid: N/A
Tuition: N/A
Room/board/expenses: N/A
Enrollment: N/A

California State University-Sacramento
6000 J Street
Sacramento, CA 95819-2694
www.csus.edu/
Public
Admissions: (916) 278-7766
Email: admissions@csus.edu
Financial aid: (916) 278-6554
Application deadline: 11/30
In-state tuition: full time: $8,166; part time: $5,334
Out-of-state tuition: full time: $14,862
Room/board/expenses: $18,004
Full-time enrollment: 471
doctoral students: 7%; master's students: 93%; education specialists: N/A; men: 25%; women: 75%; minorities: N/A; international: N/A
Part-time enrollment: 145
doctoral students: 9%; master's students: 91%; education specialists: N/A; men: 26%; women: 74%; minorities: N/A; international: N/A
Acceptance rate (master's): N/A
Acceptance rate (doctoral): N/A
Entrance test required: N/A
Avg. GRE (of all entering students with scores): quantitative: N/A; verbal: N/A

Research assistantships: 8
Students reporting specialty: 0%
Students specializing in: N/A

California State University-San Bernardino[1]
5500 University Parkway
San Bernardino, CA 92407
www.csusb.edu/
Public
Admissions: N/A
Financial aid: N/A
Tuition: N/A
Room/board/expenses: N/A
Enrollment: N/A

California State University-Stanislaus[1]
801 W. Monte Vista Avenue
Turlock, CA 95382
www.csustan.edu/
Public
Admissions: N/A
Financial aid: N/A
Tuition: N/A
Room/board/expenses: N/A
Enrollment: N/A

Chapman University
1 University Drive
Orange, CA 92866
www.chapman.edu/ces
Private
Admissions: (888) 282-7759
Email: admit@chapman.edu
Financial aid: (714) 997-6741
Application deadline: 04/15
Tuition: full time: $870/credit hour; part time: $870/credit hour
Room/board/expenses: $2,275
Full-time enrollment: 220
doctoral students: 5%; master's students: 80%; education specialists: 15%; men: 20%; women: 80%; minorities: N/A; international: N/A
Part-time enrollment: 209
doctoral students: 25%; master's students: 64%; education specialists: 11%; men: 23%; women: 77%; minorities: N/A; international: N/A
Acceptance rate (master's): 60%
Acceptance rate (doctoral): 50%
Entrance test required: GRE
Avg. GRE (of all entering students with scores): quantitative: 147; verbal: 152
Research assistantships: 20
Students reporting specialty: 100%
Students specializing in: curriculum/instr.: 5%; educational psych: 12%; elementary: 14%; secondary: 12%; special: 11%; counseling: 18%; other: 29%

Claremont Graduate University
150 E. 10th Street
Claremont, CA 91711
www.cgu.edu/pages/267.asp
Private
Admissions: (909) 621-8263
Email: admissions@cgu.edu
Financial aid: (909) 621-8337
Application deadline: N/A
Tuition: full time: $44,328; part time: $1,847/credit hour
Room/board/expenses: $26,000
Full-time enrollment: 71
doctoral students: 69%; master's students: 31%; education specialists: N/A;

men: 25%; women: 75%; minorities: 62%; international: 4%
Part-time enrollment: 277
doctoral students: 82%; master's students: 18%; education specialists: N/A; men: 27%; women: 73%; minorities: 52%; international: 3%
Acceptance rate (master's): 81%
Acceptance rate (doctoral): 67%
Entrance test required: GRE
Avg. GRE (of all entering students with scores): quantitative: 147; verbal: 153
Research assistantships: 14
Students reporting specialty: 100%
Students specializing in: curriculum/instr.: 1%; admin.: 14%; policy: 6%; educational psych: 1%; elementary: 5%; higher education admin.: 11%; secondary: 12%; special: 8%; other: 42%

Fielding Graduate University[1]
2020 De La Vina Street
Santa Barbara, CA 93105
www.fielding.edu/programs/education/default.aspx
Private
Admissions: (800) 340-1099
Email: admission@fielding.edu
Financial aid: (805) 898-4009
Tuition: N/A
Room/board/expenses: N/A
Enrollment: N/A

La Sierra University[1]
4700 Pierce Street
Riverside, CA 92515
lasierra.edu
Private
Admissions: N/A
Financial aid: N/A
Tuition: N/A
Room/board/expenses: N/A
Enrollment: N/A

Loyola Marymount University
1 LMU Drive
Los Angeles, CA 90045
soe.lmu.edu
Private
Admissions: (310) 338-7845
Email: soeinfo@lmu.edu
Financial aid: (310) 338-2753
Application deadline: 06/15
Tuition: full time: $1,167/credit hour; part time: $1,167/credit hour
Room/board/expenses: $23,262
Full-time enrollment: 814
doctoral students: 8%; master's students: 86%; education specialists: 7%; men: 23%; women: 77%; minorities: 64%; international: 5%
Part-time enrollment: 124
doctoral students: 0%; master's students: 99%; education specialists: 1%; men: 27%; women: 73%; minorities: 58%; international: 4%
Acceptance rate (master's): 33%
Acceptance rate (doctoral): 29%
Entrance test required: GRE
Avg. GRE (of all entering students with scores): quantitative: 152; verbal: 153
Research assistantships: 16
Students reporting specialty: 100%
Students specializing in: admin.: 9%; educational psych: 4%; elementary: 30%;

higher education admin.: 1%; secondary: 19%; special: 11%; counseling: 13%; other: 17%

Mills College
5000 MacArthur Boulevard
Oakland, CA 94613
www.mills.edu/
Private
Admissions: (510) 430-3309
Email: grad-studies@mills.edu
Financial aid: (510) 430-2000
Application deadline: 12/15
Tuition: full time: $33,667; part time: $2,032/credit hour
Room/board/expenses: $16,975
Full-time enrollment: 147
doctoral students: 13%; master's students: 87%; education specialists: N/A; men: 11%; women: 89%; minorities: 45%; international: 5%
Part-time enrollment: 55
doctoral students: 38%; master's students: 62%; education specialists: N/A; men: 24%; women: 76%; minorities: 58%; international: 0%
Acceptance rate (master's): 78%
Acceptance rate (doctoral): 85%
Entrance test required: N/A
Avg. GRE (of all entering students with scores): quantitative: N/A; verbal: N/A
Research assistantships: 8
Students reporting specialty: 100%
Students specializing in: admin.: 35%; elementary: 30%; secondary: 35%; other: 17%

Pepperdine University[1]
6100 Center Drive, Fifth Floor
Los Angeles, CA 90045-4301
gsep.pepperdine.edu/
Private
Admissions: (310) 568-5744
Email: barbara.moore@pepperdine.edu
Financial aid: (310) 568-2304
Tuition: N/A
Room/board/expenses: N/A
Enrollment: N/A

San Diego State University
5500 Campanile Drive
San Diego, CA 92182
www.sdsu.edu/
Public
Admissions: (619) 594-6336
Email: admmsions@mail.sdsu.edu
Financial aid: (619) 594-6323
Application deadline: 03/01
In-state tuition: full time: $8,350; part time: $5,221
Out-of-state tuition: full time: $372/credit hour
Room/board/expenses: $16,613
Full-time enrollment: 491
doctoral students: 8%; master's students: 80%; education specialists: 12%; men: 20%; women: 80%; minorities: 55%; international: 3%
Part-time enrollment: 313
doctoral students: 31%; master's students: 69%; education specialists: N/A; men: 29%; women: 71%; minorities: 52%; international: 5%
Acceptance rate (master's): 71%
Acceptance rate (doctoral): 54%
Entrance test required: GRE
Avg. GRE (of all entering students with scores): quantitative: 144; verbal: 148

Research assistantships: 24
Students reporting specialty: 100%
Students specializing in: curriculum/instr.: 6%; admin.: 11%; educational tech.: 0%; elementary: 13%; higher education admin.: 8%; secondary: 12%; social/philosophical foundations: 3%; special: 10%; counseling: 15%; other: 21%

San Francisco State University[1]
1600 Holloway Avenue
San Francisco, CA 94132
www.sfsu.edu/
Public
Admissions: N/A
Financial aid: N/A
Tuition: N/A
Room/board/expenses: N/A
Enrollment: N/A

Stanford University
485 Lasuen Mall
Stanford, CA 94305-3096
ed.stanford.edu
Private
Admissions: (650) 723-4794
Email: info@gse.stanford.edu
Financial aid: (650) 723-4794
Application deadline: N/A
Tuition: full time: $47,940; part time: N/A
Room/board/expenses: $24,780
Full-time enrollment: 339
doctoral students: 44%; master's students: 56%; education specialists: N/A; men: 32%; women: 68%; minorities: 42%; international: 18%
Part-time enrollment: N/A
doctoral students: N/A; master's students: N/A; education specialists: N/A; men: N/A; women: N/A; minorities: N/A; international: N/A
Acceptance rate (master's): 26%
Acceptance rate (doctoral): 6%
Entrance test required: GRE
Avg. GRE (of all entering students with scores): quantitative: 158; verbal: 161
Research assistantships: 434
Students reporting specialty: 100%
Students specializing in: curriculum/instr.: 9%; policy: 15%; evaluation/research/statistics: 12%; instructional media design: 8%; educational psych.: 7%; educational tech.: 6%; elementary: 8%; higher education admin.: 1%; secondary: 19%; social/philosophical foundations: 7%; other: 8%

St. Mary's College of California[1]
1928 St. Marys Road
Moraga, CA 94556
www.stmarys-ca.edu
Private
Admissions: N/A
Financial aid: N/A
Tuition: N/A
Room/board/expenses: N/A
Enrollment: N/A

Trident University International[1]
5757 Plaza Drive, #100
Cypress, CA 90630
Private
Admissions: N/A

Financial aid: N/A
Tuition: N/A
Room/board/expenses: N/A
Enrollment: N/A

University of California-Berkeley
1600 Tolman Hall, MC #1670
Berkeley, CA 94720-1670
gse.berkeley.edu
Public
Admissions: (510) 642-0841
Email: gse_info@berkeley.edu
Financial aid: (510) 643-1720
Application deadline: 12/01
In-state tuition: full time: $17,654; part time: N/A
Out-of-state tuition: full time: $32,756
Room/board/expenses: $25,664
Full-time enrollment: 303
doctoral students: 66%; master's students: 34%; education specialists: 0%; men: 27%; women: 73%; minorities: 43%; international: 13%
Part-time enrollment: N/A
doctoral students: N/A; master's students: N/A; education specialists: N/A; men: N/A; women: N/A; minorities: N/A; international: N/A
Acceptance rate (master's): 33%
Acceptance rate (doctoral): 8%
Entrance test required: GRE
Avg. GRE (of all entering students with scores): quantitative: 153; verbal: 156
Research assistantships: 86
Students reporting specialty: 100%
Students specializing in: admin.: 13%; policy: 7%; evaluation/research/statistics: 6%; educational psych.: 16%; elementary: 7%; secondary: 14%; social/philosophical foundations: 10%; special: 7%; other: 20%

University of California-Davis
School of Education
1 Shields Avenue
Davis, CA 95616
education.ucdavis.edu
Public
Admissions: (530) 752-5887
Email: eduadvising@ucdavis.edu
Financial aid: (530) 752-2396
Application deadline: N/A
In-state tuition: full time: $26,474; part time: $20,864
Out-of-state tuition: full time: $41,576
Room/board/expenses: $22,671
Full-time enrollment: 121
doctoral students: 96%; master's students: 4%; education specialists: 0%; men: 37%; women: 63%; minorities: 49%; international: 1%
Part-time enrollment: 124
doctoral students: 15%; master's students: 85%; education specialists: 0%; men: 31%; women: 69%; minorities: 47%; international: 0%
Acceptance rate (master's): 53%
Acceptance rate (doctoral): 35%
Entrance test required: GRE
Avg. GRE (of all entering students with scores): quantitative: 148; verbal: 154
Research assistantships: 143
Students reporting specialty: 100%
Students specializing in: curriculum/instr.: 33%; admin.: 17%; policy: 4%; evaluation/

research/statistics: 1%; educational psych.: 4%; elementary: 19%; higher education admin.: 17%; junior high: 41%; secondary: 22%; technical (vocational): 1%

University of California-Irvine
3200 Education
Irvine, CA 92697-5500
education.uci.edu
Public
Admissions: (949) 824-7465
Email: gseinfo@uci.edu
Financial aid: (949) 824-5337
Application deadline: rolling
In-state tuition: full time: $16,984; part time: $11,374
Out-of-state tuition: full time: $32,086
Room/board/expenses: $19,370
Full-time enrollment: 189
doctoral students: 41%; master's students: 59%; education specialists: N/A; men: 26%; women: 74%; minorities: 53%; international: 7%
Part-time enrollment: 1
doctoral students: N/A; master's students: 100%; education specialists: N/A; men: 100%; women: N/A; minorities: 100%; international: 0%
Acceptance rate (master's): 76%
Acceptance rate (doctoral): 18%
Entrance test required: GRE
Avg. GRE (of all entering students with scores): quantitative: 151; verbal: 153
Research assistantships: 38
Students reporting specialty: 100%
Students specializing in: other: 100%

University of California-Los Angeles
1009 Moore Hall, MB 951521
Los Angeles, CA 90095-1521
www.gseis.ucla.edu
Public
Admissions: (310) 825-8326
Email: info@gseis.ucla.edu
Financial aid: (310) 206-0400
Application deadline: 12/01
In-state tuition: full time: $16,425; part time: N/A
Out-of-state tuition: full time: $31,527
Room/board/expenses: $21,388
Full-time enrollment: 674
doctoral students: 54%; master's students: 46%; education specialists: 0%; men: 30%; women: 70%; minorities: 64%; international: 6%
Part-time enrollment: N/A
doctoral students: N/A; master's students: N/A; education specialists: N/A; men: N/A; women: N/A; minorities: N/A; international: N/A
Acceptance rate (master's): 50%
Acceptance rate (doctoral): 29%
Entrance test required: GRE
Avg. GRE (of all entering students with scores): quantitative: 150; verbal: 154
Research assistantships: 152
Students reporting specialty: 100%
Students specializing in: curriculum/instr.: 2%; admin.: 14%; policy: 18%; evaluation/research/statistics: 6%; instructional media design: 2%; educational psych.: 6%; elementary: 13%; higher education admin.: 14%;

secondary: 21%; social/philosophical foundations: 12%; special: 4%; counseling: 3%

University of California-Riverside
1207 Sproul Hall
Riverside, CA 92521
www.education.ucr.edu
Public
Admissions: (951) 827-6362
Email: edgrad@ucr.edu
Financial aid: (951) 827-3878
Application deadline: 06/01
In-state tuition: full time: $16,750; part time: N/A
Out-of-state tuition: full time: $31,852
Room/board/expenses: $16,550
Full-time enrollment: 239
doctoral students: 32%; master's students: 68%; education specialists: N/A; men: 24%; women: 76%; minorities: N/A; international: N/A
Part-time enrollment: N/A
doctoral students: N/A; master's students: N/A; education specialists: N/A; men: N/A; women: N/A; minorities: N/A; international: N/A
Acceptance rate (master's): 77%
Acceptance rate (doctoral): 22%
Entrance test required: GRE
Avg. GRE (of all entering students with scores): quantitative: 150; verbal: 152
Research assistantships: 14
Students reporting specialty: 100%
Students specializing in: curriculum/instr.: 0%; educational psych: 5%; elementary: 20%; higher education admin.: 10%; secondary: 35%; special: 11%; counseling: 9%; other: 9%

University of California-San Diego
9500 Gilman Drive
La Jolla, CA 92093
eds.ucsd.edu
Public
Admissions: (858) 534-2958
Email: gvanluit@ucsd.edu
Financial aid: (858) 534-3800
Application deadline: rolling
In-state tuition: full time: $16,631; part time: $11,021
Out-of-state tuition: full time: $31,733
Room/board/expenses: $18,395
Full-time enrollment: 147
doctoral students: 38%; master's students: 58%; education specialists: 4%; men: 30%; women: 70%; minorities: 54%; international: 0%
Part-time enrollment: N/A
doctoral students: N/A; master's students: N/A; education specialists: N/A; men: N/A; women: N/A; minorities: N/A; international: N/A
Acceptance rate (master's): 82%
Acceptance rate (doctoral): 27%
Entrance test required: GRE
Avg. GRE (of all entering students with scores): quantitative: 150; verbal: 153
Research assistantships: 7
Students reporting specialty: 100%
Students specializing in: curriculum/instr.: 30%; admin.: 29%; elementary: 26%; higher education admin.: 10%; junior high: 36%; secondary: 00%; special: 4%; other: 5%

University of California–Santa Barbara (Gevirtz)

Education Building
Santa Barbara, CA 93106-9490
www.education.ucsb.edu
Public
Admissions: (805) 893-2137
Email: sao@education.ucsb.edu
Financial aid: (805) 893-2432
Application deadline: N/A
In-state tuition: full time: $16,398;
part time: N/A
Out-of-state tuition: full time:
$31,500
Room/board/expenses: $20,766
Full-time enrollment: 273
doctoral students: 67%; master's
students: 30%; education
specialists: 3%; men: 25%;
women: 75%; minorities: 40%;
international: 7%
Part-time enrollment: N/A
doctoral students: N/A; master's
students: N/A; education
specialists: N/A; men: N/A;
women: N/A; minorities: N/A;
international: N/A
Acceptance rate (master's): 63%
Acceptance rate (doctoral): 17%
Entrance test required: GRE
**Avg. GRE (of all entering students
with scores):** quantitative: 151;
verbal: 155
Research assistantships: 32
Students reporting specialty: 100%
Students specializing in:
curriculum/instr.: 4%; policy:
3%; evaluation/research/
statistics: 0%; elementary:
13%; secondary: 13%; social/
philosophical foundations: 6%;
special: 5%; counseling: 24%;
other: 31%

University of California–Santa Cruz

1156 High Street
Santa Cruz, CA 95064
www.graddiv.ucsc.edu/
Public
Admissions: (831) 459-5905
Email: gradadm@ucsc.edu
Financial aid: (831) 459-2963
Application deadline: N/A
In-state tuition: full time: $18,414;
part time: $12,267
Out-of-state tuition: full time:
$33,516
Room/board/expenses: $23,544
Full-time enrollment: 110
doctoral students: 28%;
master's students: 72%;
education specialists: N/A; men:
28%; women: 72%; minorities:
37%; international: 4%
Part-time enrollment: 1
doctoral students: 100%;
master's students: 0%;
education specialists: N/A; men:
N/A; women: 100%; minorities:
0%; international: 0%
Acceptance rate (master's): 78%
Acceptance rate (doctoral): 42%
Entrance test required: GRE
**Avg. GRE (of all entering students
with scores):** quantitative: 149;
verbal: 154
Research assistantships: 6
Students reporting specialty: 100%
Students specializing in:
elementary: 31%; junior high:
39%; secondary: 39%; other:
31%

University of La Verne

1950 Third Street
La Verne, CA 91750
www.laverne.edu/academics/
education/
Private
Admissions: (877) 468-6858
Email: gradadmt@ulv.edu
Financial aid: (800) 649-0160
Application deadline: rolling
Tuition: full time: $710/credit hour;
part time: $710/credit hour
Room/board/expenses: N/A
Full-time enrollment: 426
doctoral students: 26%;
master's students: 74%;
education specialists: 0%; men:
19%; women: 81%; minorities:
72%; international: 1%
Part-time enrollment: 496
doctoral students: 11%; master's
students: 89%; education
specialists: 0%; men: 21%;
women: 79%; minorities: 78%;
international: 1%
Acceptance rate (master's): 52%
Acceptance rate (doctoral): 73%
Entrance test required: N/A
**Avg. GRE (of all entering students
with scores):** quantitative: N/A;
verbal: N/A
Students reporting specialty: 100%
Students specializing in: admin.:
18%; elementary: 12%;
secondary: 9%; special: 7%;
counseling: 24%; other: 31%

University of Redlands

PO Box 3080
Redlands, CA 92373
www.redlands.edu
Private
Admissions: (909) 748-8064
Email:
soeadmissions@redlands.edu
Financial aid: (909) 748-8047
Application deadline: 07/10
Tuition: full time: $695/credit
hour; part time: $695/credit hour
Room/board/expenses: N/A
Full-time enrollment: 626
doctoral students: 7%; master's
students: 92%; education
specialists: 2%; men: 30%;
women: 70%; minorities: N/A;
international: N/A
Part-time enrollment: 56
doctoral students: 30%;
master's students: 45%;
education specialists: 25%; men:
20%; women: 80%; minorities:
N/A; international: N/A
Acceptance rate (master's): N/A
Acceptance rate (doctoral): N/A
Entrance test required: N/A
**Avg. GRE (of all entering students
with scores):** quantitative: N/A;
verbal: N/A
Students reporting specialty: 0%
Students specializing in: N/A

University of San Diego

5998 Alcala Park
San Diego, CA 92110-2492
www.sandiego.edu/soles/
Private
Admissions: (619) 260-4524
Email: grads@sandiego.edu
Financial aid: (619) 260-2700
Application deadline: 06/30
Tuition: full time: $1,410/credit
hour; part time: $1,410/credit
hour
Room/board/expenses: $18,450
Full-time enrollment: 388
doctoral students: 12%; master's

students: 88%; education
specialists: N/A; men: 22%;
women: 78%; minorities: 40%;
international: 9%
Part-time enrollment: 405
doctoral students: 9%; master's
students: 91%; education
specialists: N/A; men: 21%;
women: 79%; minorities: 43%;
international: 1%
Acceptance rate (master's): 72%
Acceptance rate (doctoral): 49%
Entrance test required: GRE
**Avg. GRE (of all entering students
with scores):** quantitative: 150;
verbal: 154
Research assistantships: 12
Students reporting specialty: 100%
Students specializing in:
curriculum/instr.: 33%; admin.:
18%; instructional media
design: 3%; elementary: 7%;
higher education admin.: 17%;
secondary: 8%; special: 5%;
counseling: 6%; other: 17%

University of San Francisco

2130 Fulton Street
San Francisco, CA 94117-1080
www.usfca.edu
Private
Admissions: (415) 422-6563
Email: graduate@usfca.edu
Financial aid: (415) 422-2624
Application deadline: N/A
Tuition: full time: $1,130/credit
hour; part time: $1,130/credit
hour
Room/board/expenses: $5,400
Full-time enrollment: 796
doctoral students: 15%; master's
students: 85%; education
specialists: N/A; men: 22%;
women: 78%; minorities: 52%;
international: 8%
Part-time enrollment: 264
doctoral students: 33%;
master's students: 67%;
education specialists: N/A; men:
26%; women: 74%; minorities:
43%; international: 6%
Acceptance rate (master's): 81%
Acceptance rate (doctoral): 96%
Entrance test required: GRE
**Avg. GRE (of all entering students
with scores):** quantitative: N/A;
verbal: N/A
Students reporting specialty: 100%
Students specializing in:
curriculum/instr.: 4%; admin.:
3%; evaluation/research/
statistics: 7%; educational
tech.: 0%; elementary: 15%;
higher education admin.: 5%;
secondary: 10%; special: 4%;
counseling: 0%; other: 53%

University of Southern California (Rossier)

3470 Trousdale Parkway
Waite Phillips Hall
Los Angeles, CA 90089-0031
rossier.usc.edu
Private
Admissions: (213) 740-0224
Email: info@rossier.usc.edu
Financial aid: (213) 740-1111
Application deadline: 12/01
Tuition: full time: $1,733/credit
hour; part time: $1,733/credit
hour
Room/board/expenses: $19,600
Full-time enrollment: 614
doctoral students: 9%; master's
students: 91%; education

specialists: 0%; men: 24%;
women: 76%; minorities: 53%;
international: 9%
Part-time enrollment: 976
doctoral students: 59%;
master's students: 41%;
education specialists: 0%; men:
30%; women: 70%; minorities:
57%; international: 7%
Acceptance rate (master's): 69%
Acceptance rate (doctoral): 13%
Entrance test required: GRE
**Avg. GRE (of all entering students
with scores):** quantitative: 151;
verbal: 152
Research assistantships: 40
Students reporting specialty: 100%
Students specializing in:
curriculum/instr.: 5%; admin.:
13%; policy: 3%; instructional
media design: 2%; educational
psych: 9%; elementary: 14%;
higher education admin.: 16%;
secondary: 18%; special: 1%;
counseling: 4%; other: 16%

University of the Pacific[1]

3601 Pacific Avenue
Stockton, CA 95211
www.pacific.edu
Private
Admissions: N/A
Financial aid: N/A
Tuition: N/A
Room/board/expenses: N/A
Enrollment: N/A

COLORADO

Colorado State University

1588 Campus Delivery
Fort Collins, CO 80523-1588
www.soe.chhs.colostate.edu/
Public
Admissions: (970) 491-6909
Email: gradadmissions@
colostate.edu
Financial aid: (970) 491-6321
Application deadline: rolling
In-state tuition: full time: $10,192;
part time: $6,983
Out-of-state tuition: full time:
$24,168
Room/board/expenses: $15,116
Full-time enrollment: 133
doctoral students: 8%; master's
students: 92%; education
specialists: N/A; men: 36%;
women: 64%; minorities: 26%;
international: 6%
Part-time enrollment: 483
doctoral students: 40%;
master's students: 60%;
education specialists: N/A; men:
34%; women: 66%; minorities:
22%; international: 2%
Acceptance rate (master's): 29%
Acceptance rate (doctoral): 64%
Entrance test required: GRE
**Avg. GRE (of all entering students
with scores):** quantitative: 146;
verbal: 155
Research assistantships: 5
Students reporting specialty: 100%
Students specializing in:
curriculum/instr.: 20%; admin.:
11%; policy: 8%; evaluation/
research/statistics: 17%;
educational tech.: 1%; higher
education admin.: 35%; junior
high: 9%; secondary: 9%; social/
philosophical foundations: 5%;
counseling: 23%; technical
(vocational): 1%; other: 37%

University of Colorado–Boulder

Campus Box 249
Boulder, CO 80309-0249
www.colorado.edu/education
Public
Admissions: (303) 492-6555
Email: edadvise@colorado.edu
Financial aid: (303) 492-5091
Application deadline: 12/15
In-state tuition: full time: $12,610;
part time: $602/credit hour
Out-of-state tuition: full time:
$30,430
Room/board/expenses: $17,684
Full-time enrollment: 142
doctoral students: 56%;
master's students: 44%;
education specialists: N/A; men:
31%; women: 69%; minorities:
33%; international: 3%
Part-time enrollment: 213
doctoral students: 3%; master's
students: 97%; education
specialists: N/A; men: 15%;
women: 85%; minorities: 25%;
international: 1%
Acceptance rate (master's): 70%
Acceptance rate (doctoral): 17%
Entrance test required: GRE
**Avg. GRE (of all entering students
with scores):** quantitative: 155;
verbal: 161
Research assistantships: 105
Students reporting specialty: 100%
Students specializing in:
curriculum/instr.: 29%;
evaluation/research/statistics:
2%; educational psych:
7%; secondary: 8%; social/
philosophical foundations: 62%;
other: 91%

University of Colorado–Colorado Springs

PO Box 7150
Colorado Springs, CO 80933
www.uccs.edu/coe/index.html
Public
Admissions: (719) 255-4996
Email: education@uccs.edu
Financial aid: (719) 255-3460
Application deadline: 01/15
In-state tuition: full time: $555/
credit hour; part time: $638/
credit hour
Out-of-state tuition: full time:
$1,120/credit hour
Room/board/expenses: $18,920
Full-time enrollment: 131
doctoral students: 11%; master's
students: 89%; education
specialists: N/A; men: 31%;
women: 69%; minorities: 22%;
international: 2%
Part-time enrollment: 226
doctoral students: 16%; master's
students: 84%; education
specialists: N/A; men: 34%;
women: 66%; minorities: 26%;
international: 2%
Acceptance rate (master's): 85%
Acceptance rate (doctoral): 85%
Entrance test required: GRE
**Avg. GRE (of all entering students
with scores):** quantitative: 149;
verbal: 156
Research assistantships: 1
Students reporting specialty: 100%
Students specializing in:
curriculum/instr.: 20%; admin.:
23%; evaluation/research/
statistics: 13%; special: 5%;
counseling: 30%; other: 8%

University of Colorado-Denver

PO Box 173364
Campus Box 106
Denver, CO 80217-3364
www.ucdenver.edu/education
Public
Admissions: (303) 315-6300
Email: education@ucdenver.edu
Financial aid: (303) 315-1850
Application deadline: rolling
In-state tuition: full time: $373/credit hour; part time: $373/credit hour
Out-of-state tuition: full time: $1,243/credit hour
Room/board/expenses: $22,769
Full-time enrollment: 843
doctoral students: 20%; master's students: 75%; education specialists: 5%; men: 21%; women: 79%; minorities: 21%; international: 1%
Part-time enrollment: 464
doctoral students: 8%; master's students: 90%; education specialists: 2%; men: 16%; women: 84%; minorities: 16%; international: 2%
Acceptance rate (master's): 62%
Acceptance rate (doctoral): 75%
Entrance test required: GRE
Avg. GRE (of all entering students with scores): quantitative: N/A; verbal: N/A
Research assistantships: 45
Students reporting specialty: 100%
Students specializing in: curriculum/instr.: 6%; admin.: 18%; evaluation/research/statistics: 1%; instructional media design: 2%; educational psych: 6%; educational tech.: 7%; elementary: 19%; secondary: 12%; special: 10%; counseling: 8%; other: 32%

University of Denver (Morgridge)

Ruffatto Hall
1999 East Evans Avenue
Denver, CO 80208
morgridge.du.edu/
Private
Admissions: (303) 871-2509
Email: mce@du.edu
Financial aid: (303) 871-6291
Application deadline: 12/01
Tuition: full time: $1,258/credit hour; part time: $1,258/credit hour
Room/board/expenses: N/A
Full-time enrollment: 458
doctoral students: 26%; master's students: 60%; education specialists: 14%; men: 21%; women: 79%; minorities: 16%; international: 4%
Part-time enrollment: 357
doctoral students: 51%; master's students: 48%; education specialists: 0%; men: 22%; women: 78%; minorities: 15%; international: 5%
Acceptance rate (master's): 72%
Acceptance rate (doctoral): 52%
Entrance test required: GRE
Avg. GRE (of all entering students with scores): quantitative: 152; verbal: 154
Research assistantships: 26
Students reporting specialty: 100%
Students specializing in: curriculum/instr.: 7%; admin.: 13%; evaluation/research/statistics: 13%; other: 80%

University of Northern Colorado[1]

McKee 125
Greeley, CO 80639
www.unco.edu/grad/index.html
Public
Admissions: (970) 351-2831
Email: gradsch@unco.edu
Financial aid: (970) 351-2502
Tuition: N/A
Room/board/expenses: N/A
Enrollment: N/A

CONNECTICUT

Central Connecticut State University

1615 Stanley Street
New Britain, CT 06050
www.ccsu.edu/grad/
Public
Admissions: (860) 832-2350
Financial aid: (860) 832-2200
Application deadline: 06/01
In-state tuition: full time: $10,956; part time: $606/credit hour
Out-of-state tuition: full time: $22,561
Room/board/expenses: $14,689
Full-time enrollment: 212
doctoral students: 0%; master's students: 100%; education specialists: N/A; men: 24%; women: 76%; minorities: 25%; international: 3%
Part-time enrollment: 582
doctoral students: 8%; master's students: 92%; education specialists: N/A; men: 26%; women: 74%; minorities: 15%; international: 0%
Acceptance rate (master's): 69%
Acceptance rate (doctoral): N/A
Entrance test required: GRE
Avg. GRE (of all entering students with scores): quantitative: N/A; verbal: N/A
Students reporting specialty: 100%
Students specializing in: admin.: 9%; instructional media design: 4%; elementary: 0%; social/philosophical foundations: 1%; special: 16%; counseling: 21%; other: 48%

Southern Connecticut State University[1]

501 Crescent Street
New Haven, CT 06515
www.southernct.edu/
Public
Admissions: (203) 392-5240
Email: GradInfo@southernCT.edu
Financial aid: (203) 392-5222
Tuition: N/A
Room/board/expenses: N/A
Enrollment: N/A

University of Bridgeport

126 Park Avenue
Bridgeport, CT 06604
www.bridgeport.edu/
Private
Admissions: (203) 576-4552
Email: admit@bridgeport.edu
Financial aid: (203) 576-4568
Application deadline: rolling
Tuition: full time: $700/credit hour; part time: $700/credit hour
Room/board/expenses: $16,420
Full-time enrollment: 254
doctoral students: 7%; master's students: 82%; education

specialists: 11%; men: 34%; women: 66%; minorities: 26%; international: 2%
Part-time enrollment: 300
doctoral students: 10%; master's students: 48%; education specialists: 42%; men: 25%; women: 75%; minorities: 23%; international: 1%
Acceptance rate (master's): 44%
Acceptance rate (doctoral): 50%
Entrance test required: GRE
Avg. GRE (of all entering students with scores): quantitative: N/A; verbal: N/A
Students reporting specialty: 100%
Students specializing in: curriculum/instr.: 2%; admin.: 30%; elementary: 34%; secondary: 19%; counseling: 15%

University of Connecticut (Neag)

249 Glenbrook Road, Unit 3064
Storrs, CT 06269-3064
education.uconn.edu
Public
Admissions: (860) 486-3617
Email: gradschool@uconn.edu
Financial aid: (860) 486-2819
Application deadline: rolling
In-state tuition: full time: $16,178; part time: $763/credit hour
Out-of-state tuition: full time: $37,124
Room/board/expenses: $19,054
Full-time enrollment: 438
doctoral students: 25%; master's students: 75%; education specialists: N/A; men: 33%; women: 67%; minorities: 21%; international: 4%
Part-time enrollment: 131
doctoral students: 56%; master's students: 44%; education specialists: N/A; men: 27%; women: 73%; minorities: 19%; international: 1%
Acceptance rate (master's): 47%
Acceptance rate (doctoral): 43%
Entrance test required: GRE
Avg. GRE (of all entering students with scores): quantitative: 155; verbal: 157
Research assistantships: 103
Students reporting specialty: 100%
Students specializing in: curriculum/instr.: 5%; admin.: 18%; policy: 2%; evaluation/research/statistics: 5%; instructional media design: 3%; educational psych: 7%; educational tech.: 2%; elementary: 5%; higher education admin.: 5%; secondary: 16%; special: 18%; counseling: 7%; other: 8%

University of Hartford

200 Bloomfield Avenue
West Hartford, CT 06117
www.hartford.edu/enhp
Private
Admissions: (860) 768-4371
Email: gradstudy@hartford.edu
Financial aid: (860) 768-4296
Application deadline: rolling
Tuition: full time: N/A; part time: $570/credit hour
Room/board/expenses: N/A
Full-time enrollment: 90
doctoral students: 42%; master's students: 58%; education specialists: N/A; men: 26%; women: 74%; minorities: 26%; international: 0%

Part-time enrollment: 113
doctoral students: 32%; master's students: 68%; education specialists: N/A; men: 23%; women: 77%; minorities: 16%; international: 0%
Acceptance rate (master's): 84%
Acceptance rate (doctoral): 80%
Entrance test required: GRE
Avg. GRE (of all entering students with scores): quantitative: 145; verbal: 147
Research assistantships: 10
Students reporting specialty: 100%
Students specializing in: admin.: 16%; elementary: 11%; higher education admin.: 34%; special: 10%; other: 29%

Western Connecticut State University[1]

181 White Street
Danbury, CT 06810
www.wcsu.edu
Public
Admissions: (877) 837-9278
Email: admissions@wcsu.edu
Financial aid: N/A
Tuition: N/A
Room/board/expenses: N/A
Enrollment: N/A

DELAWARE

Delaware State University[1]

1200 N. DuPont Highway
Dover, DE 19901
www.desu.edu
Public
Admissions: N/A
Financial aid: N/A
Tuition: N/A
Room/board/expenses: N/A
Enrollment: N/A

University of Delaware

113 Willard Hall Education Building
Newark, DE 19716
www.education.udel.edu
Public
Admissions: (302) 831-2129
Email: marym@udel.edu
Financial aid: (302) 831-2129
Application deadline: N/A
In-state tuition: full time: $625/credit hour; part time: $625/credit hour
Out-of-state tuition: full time: $1,720/credit hour
Room/board/expenses: $17,062
Full-time enrollment: 95
doctoral students: 37%; master's students: 49%; education specialists: 14%; men: 15%; women: 85%; minorities: 17%; international: 25%
Part-time enrollment: 179
doctoral students: 51%; master's students: 49%; education specialists: 0%; men: 26%; women: 74%; minorities: 16%; international: 0%
Acceptance rate (master's): 71%
Acceptance rate (doctoral): 40%
Entrance test required: GRE
Avg. GRE (of all entering students with scores): quantitative: 152; verbal: 152
Research assistantships: 26
Students reporting specialty: 0%
Students specializing in: N/A

Wilmington University[1]

320 DuPont Highway
Wilmington, DE 19720
www.wilmu.edu
Private
Admissions: N/A
Financial aid: N/A
Tuition: N/A
Room/board/expenses: N/A
Enrollment: N/A

DISTRICT OF COLUMBIA

American University[1]

4400 Massachusetts Avenue NW
Washington, DC 20016-8030
www.american.edu/cas/seth/
Private
Admissions: N/A
Financial aid: N/A
Tuition: N/A
Room/board/expenses: N/A
Enrollment: N/A

The Catholic University of America

Cardinal Station
Washington, DC 20064
admissions.cua.edu/graduate/
Private
Admissions: (800) 673-2772
Email: cua-admissions@cua.edu
Financial aid: (202) 319-5307
Application deadline: 07/15
Tuition: full time: $43,450; part time: $1,710/credit hour
Room/board/expenses: $19,362
Full-time enrollment: 7
doctoral students: 0%; master's students: 100%; education specialists: 0%; men: 14%; women: 86%; minorities: 0%; international: 43%
Part-time enrollment: 21
doctoral students: 62%; master's students: 24%; education specialists: 14%; men: 38%; women: 62%; minorities: 24%; international: 0%
Acceptance rate (master's): 53%
Acceptance rate (doctoral): 33%
Entrance test required: GRE
Avg. GRE (of all entering students with scores): quantitative: 137; verbal: 143
Research assistantships: 0
Students reporting specialty: 100%
Students specializing in: educational psych: 11%; elementary: 18%; secondary: 11%; special: 14%; other: 46%

Gallaudet University

800 Florida Avenue NE
Washington, DC 20002-3695
gradschool.gallaudet.edu
Private
Admissions: (202) 651-5717
Email: graduate.school@gallaudet.edu
Financial aid: (202) 651-5290
Application deadline: 02/15
Tuition: full time: $17,100; part time: $950/credit hour
Room/board/expenses: $24,750
Full-time enrollment: 41
doctoral students: 0%; master's students: 68%; education specialists: 32%; men: 12%; women: 88%; minorities: 24%; international: 15%
Part-time enrollment: 31
doctoral students: 42%; master's students: 35%; education specialists: 23%; men: 19%; women: 81%; minorities: 28%; international: 3%

Acceptance rate (master's): 54%
Acceptance rate (doctoral): N/A
Entrance test required: GRE
Avg. GRE (of all entering students with scores): quantitative: N/A; verbal: N/A
Research assistantships: 0
Students reporting specialty: 100%
Students specializing in: special: 70%; counseling: 13%; other: 29%

George Washington University
2134 G Street NW
Washington, DC 20052
gsehd.gwu.edu
Private
Admissions: (202) 994-9283
Email: gsehdadm@gwu.edu
Financial aid: (202) 994-6820
Application deadline: rolling
Tuition: full time: $1,600/credit hour; part time: $1,600/credit hour
Room/board/expenses: $21,858
Full-time enrollment: 416
doctoral students: 22%; master's students: 76%; education specialists: 2%; men: 20%; women: 80%; minorities: 35%; international: 19%
Part-time enrollment: 910
doctoral students: 43%; master's students: 53%; education specialists: 4%; men: 25%; women: 75%; minorities: 38%; international: 3%
Acceptance rate (master's): 72%
Acceptance rate (doctoral): 59%
Entrance test required: GRE
Avg. GRE (of all entering students with scores): quantitative: 157; verbal: 161
Research assistantships: 25
Students reporting specialty: 100%
Students specializing in: curriculum/instr.: 5%; admin.: 22%; evaluation/research/statistics: 0%; instructional media design: 1%; educational tech.: 5%; elementary: 1%; higher education admin.: 7%; secondary: 2%; special: 15%; counseling: 31%; other: 9%

Howard University
2441 Fourth Street NW
Washington, DC 20059
howard.edu/schooleducation
Private
Admissions: (202) 806-7523
Email: hugsadmission@howard.edu
Financial aid: (202) 806-2820
Application deadline: rolling
Tuition: full time: $30,569; part time: $1,700/credit hour
Room/board/expenses: $25,587
Full-time enrollment: 137
doctoral students: 64%; master's students: 36%; education specialists: N/A; men: 24%; women: 76%; minorities: 55%; international: 31%
Part-time enrollment: 94
doctoral students: 76%; master's students: 24%; education specialists: N/A; men: 30%; women: 70%; minorities: 56%; international: 31%
Acceptance rate (master's): 81%
Acceptance rate (doctoral): 49%
Entrance test required: GRE
Avg. GRE (of all entering students with scores): quantitative: 142; verbal: 148
Research assistantships: 17

Students reporting specialty: 100%
Students specializing in: admin.: 34%; educational psych: 7%; elementary: 4%; secondary: 2%; special: 2%; counseling: 29%; other: 21%

FLORIDA

Barry University (Dominican)[1]
11300 N.E. Second Avenue
Miami Shores, FL 33161-6695
www.barry.edu/
Private
Admissions: N/A
Financial aid: N/A
Tuition: N/A
Room/board/expenses: N/A
Enrollment: N/A

Florida A&M University
Gore Education Center
Tallahassee, FL 32307
www.famu.edu/education/
Public
Admissions: (850) 599-3315
Email: adm@famu.edu
Financial aid: (850) 599-3730
Application deadline: 05/01
In-state tuition: full time: $406/credit hour; part time: $406/credit hour
Out-of-state tuition: full time: $1,022/credit hour
Room/board/expenses: $15,524
Full-time enrollment: 51
doctoral students: 22%; master's students: 78%; education specialists: N/A; men: 31%; women: 69%; minorities: 92%; international: 0%
Part-time enrollment: 71
doctoral students: 62%; master's students: 38%; education specialists: N/A; men: 34%; women: 66%; minorities: 99%; international: 0%
Acceptance rate (master's): 55%
Acceptance rate (doctoral): 12%
Entrance test required: GRE
Avg. GRE (of all entering students with scores): quantitative: 132; verbal: 140
Research assistantships: 0
Students reporting specialty: 100%
Students specializing in: curriculum/instr.: 7%; admin.: 57%; counseling: 22%; other: 13%

Florida Atlantic University
777 Glades Road
PO Box 3091
Boca Raton, FL 33431-0991
www.coe.fau.edu/menu.htm
Public
Admissions: (561) 297-3624
Email: gradadm@fau.edu
Financial aid: (561) 297-3131
Application deadline: rolling
In-state tuition: full time: $303/credit hour; part time: $303/credit hour
Out-of-state tuition: full time: $623/credit hour
Room/board/expenses: $17,814
Full-time enrollment: 316
doctoral students: 18%; master's students: 80%; education specialists: 1%; men: 26%; women: 74%; minorities: 39%; international: 4%
Part-time enrollment: 501
doctoral students: 33%;

master's students: 60%; education specialists: 7%; men: 26%; women: 74%; minorities: 39%; international: 1%
Acceptance rate (master's): 29%
Acceptance rate (doctoral): 35%
Entrance test required: GRE
Avg. GRE (of all entering students with scores): quantitative: 152; verbal: 149
Research assistantships: 50
Students reporting specialty: 100%
Students specializing in: curriculum/instr.: 15%; admin.: 40%; instructional media design: 0%; educational psych: 0%; elementary: 2%; social/philosophical foundations: 2%; special: 8%; counseling: 15%; technical (vocational): 2%; other: 15%

Florida Gulf Coast University[1]
10501 FGCU Boulevard, S
Fort Myers, FL 33965
coe.fgcu.edu/
Public
Admissions: N/A
Email: graduate@fgcu.edu
Financial aid: N/A
Tuition: N/A
Room/board/expenses: N/A
Enrollment: N/A

Florida Institute of Technology
150 W. University Boulevard
Melbourne, FL 32901
www.fit.edu
Private
Admissions: (800) 944-4348
Email: grad-admissions@fit.edu
Financial aid: (321) 674-8070
Application deadline: rolling
Tuition: full time: $1,241/credit hour; part time: $1,241/credit hour
Room/board/expenses: $17,810
Full-time enrollment: 36
doctoral students: 64%; master's students: 36%; education specialists: 0%; men: 47%; women: 53%; minorities: 17%; international: 44%
Part-time enrollment: 24
doctoral students: 50%; master's students: 50%; education specialists: 0%; men: 42%; women: 58%; minorities: 21%; international: 29%
Acceptance rate (master's): 41%
Acceptance rate (doctoral): 40%
Entrance test required: N/A
Avg. GRE (of all entering students with scores): quantitative: 153; verbal: 155
Students reporting specialty: 0%
Students specializing in: N/A

Florida International University
11200 S.W. Eighth Street
Miami, FL 33199
education.fiu.edu
Public
Admissions: (305) 348-7442
Email: gradadm@fiu.edu
Financial aid: (305) 348-7272
Application deadline: rolling
In-state tuition: full time: $11,334; part time: $456/credit hour
Out-of-state tuition: full time: $24,438
Room/board/expenses: $25,218

Full-time enrollment: 438
doctoral students: 9%; master's students: 86%; education specialists: 5%; men: 21%; women: 79%; minorities: 76%; international: 6%
Part-time enrollment: 536
doctoral students: 25%; master's students: 69%; education specialists: 6%; men: 20%; women: 80%; minorities: 82%; international: 2%
Acceptance rate (master's): 63%
Acceptance rate (doctoral): 31%
Entrance test required: GRE
Avg. GRE (of all entering students with scores): quantitative: 145; verbal: 148
Research assistantships: 7
Students reporting specialty: 100%
Students specializing in: curriculum/instr.: 18%; admin.: 23%; higher education admin.: 15%; special: 11%; counseling: 15%; other: 34%

Florida State University
Suite 1100 Stone Building
1114 W. Call Street
Tallahassee, FL 32306-4450
www.education.fsu.edu
Public
Admissions: (850) 644-6200
Email: admissions@fsu.edu
Financial aid: (850) 644-0539
Application deadline: 07/01
In-state tuition: full time: $404/credit hour; part time: $404/credit hour
Out-of-state tuition: full time: $1,035/credit hour
Room/board/expenses: $18,766
Full-time enrollment: 620
doctoral students: 41%; master's students: 47%; education specialists: 12%; men: 35%; women: 65%; minorities: 23%; international: 26%
Part-time enrollment: 411
doctoral students: 40%; master's students: 49%; education specialists: 12%; men: 30%; women: 70%; minorities: 29%; international: 7%
Acceptance rate (master's): 57%
Acceptance rate (doctoral): 38%
Entrance test required: GRE
Avg. GRE (of all entering students with scores): quantitative: 149; verbal: 152
Research assistantships: 127
Students reporting specialty: 100%
Students specializing in: curriculum/instr.: 24%; admin.: 16%; evaluation/research/statistics: 2%; instructional media design: 10%; educational psych: 9%; higher education admin.: 11%; secondary: 0%; social/philosophical foundations: 3%; counseling: 13%; other: 12%

Keiser University
1500 N.W. 49th Street
Fort Lauderdale, FL 33309
Private
Admissions: N/A
Financial aid: N/A
Application deadline: N/A
Tuition: full time: $23,280; part time: N/A
Room/board/expenses: N/A
Full-time enrollment: 352
doctoral students: 11%; master's students: 88%; education

specialists: 1%; men: 32%; women: 68%; minorities: N/A; international: N/A
Part-time enrollment: 493
doctoral students: 23%; master's students: 76%; education specialists: 0%; men: 25%; women: 75%; minorities: N/A; international: N/A
Acceptance rate (master's): N/A
Acceptance rate (doctoral): N/A
Entrance test required: N/A
Avg. GRE (of all entering students with scores): quantitative: N/A; verbal: N/A
Students reporting specialty: 0%
Students specializing in: N/A

Lynn University
3601 North Military Trail
Boca Raton, FL 33431
www.lynn.edu
Private
Admissions: (561) 237-7834
Email: admission@lynn.edu
Financial aid: (561) 237-7816
Application deadline: 08/14
Tuition: full time: $725/credit hour; part time: $725/credit hour
Room/board/expenses: N/A
Full-time enrollment: 93
doctoral students: 70%; master's students: 30%; education specialists: N/A; men: 26%; women: 74%; minorities: 28%; international: 4%
Part-time enrollment: 2
doctoral students: 50%; master's students: 50%; education specialists: N/A; men: 100%; women: N/A; minorities: 50%; international: 0%
Acceptance rate (master's): 94%
Acceptance rate (doctoral): 65%
Entrance test required: GRE
Avg. GRE (of all entering students with scores): quantitative: N/A; verbal: N/A
Students reporting specialty: 100%
Students specializing in: admin.: 92%; special: 8%

Nova Southeastern University (Fischler)
3301 College Avenue
Fort Lauderdale, FL 33314
www.schoolofed.nova.edu
Private
Admissions: (954) 262-8500
Email: admitteam@nova.edu
Financial aid: (954) 262-3380
Application deadline: 08/20
Tuition: full time: $940/credit hour; part time: $940/credit hour
Room/board/expenses: $12,080
Full-time enrollment: 1,836
doctoral students: 92%; master's students: 6%; education specialists: 1%; men: 22%; women: 78%; minorities: 71%; international: 0%
Part-time enrollment: 1,680
doctoral students: 36%; master's students: 48%; education specialists: 15%; men: 22%; women: 78%; minorities: 76%; international: 1%
Acceptance rate (master's): N/A
Acceptance rate (doctoral): N/A
Entrance test required: GRE
Avg. GRE (of all entering students with scores): quantitative: N/A; verbal: N/A
Students reporting specialty: 100%

Students specializing in: curriculum/instr.: 2%; admin.: 12%; instructional media design: 0%; elementary: 2%; secondary: 0%; special: 4%; other: 79%

University of Central Florida

4000 Central Florida Boulevard
Orlando, FL 32816-1250
education.ucf.edu/grad
Public
Admissions: (407) 823-5369
Email: edgrad@ucf.edu
Financial aid: (407) 823-2827
Application deadline: 01/15
In-state tuition: full time: $370/credit hour; part time: $370/credit hour
Out-of-state tuition: full time: $1,194/credit hour
Room/board/expenses: $15,886
Full-time enrollment: 671
doctoral students: 28%; master's students: 65%; education specialists: 7%; men: 24%; women: 76%; minorities: 33%; international: 5%
Part-time enrollment: 820
doctoral students: 9%; master's students: 89%; education specialists: 2%; men: 21%; women: 79%; minorities: 33%; international: 0%
Acceptance rate (master's): 58%
Acceptance rate (doctoral): 43%
Entrance test required: GRE
Avg. GRE (of all entering students with scores): quantitative: 149; verbal: 152
Research assistantships: 14
Students reporting specialty: 100%
Students specializing in: curriculum/instr.: 6%; admin.: 23%; evaluation/research/statistics: 0%; instructional media design: 6%; educational tech.: 1%; elementary: 4%; higher education admin.: 5%; junior high: 2%; secondary: 2%; special: 11%; counseling: 4%; technical (vocational): 3%; other: 34%

University of Florida

140 Norman Hall
PO Box 117040
Gainesville, FL 32611-7040
education.ufl.edu/
Public
Admissions: (352) 273-4376
Email: waldron@coe.ufl.edu
Financial aid: (352) 392-1275
Application deadline: rolling
In-state tuition: full time: $449/credit hour; part time: $449/credit hour
Out-of-state tuition: full time: $1,139/credit hour
Room/board/expenses: $17,150
Full-time enrollment: 534
doctoral students: 35%; master's students: 47%; education specialists: 19%; men: 18%; women: 82%; minorities: 22%; international: 21%
Part-time enrollment: 519
doctoral students: 52%; master's students: 41%; education specialists: 7%; men: 26%; women: 74%; minorities: 25%; international: 2%
Acceptance rate (master's): 52%
Acceptance rate (doctoral): 56%
Entrance test required: GRE
Avg. GRE (of all entering students with scores): quantitative: 152; verbal: 153

Research assistantships: 99
Students reporting specialty: 100%
Students specializing in: curriculum/instr.: 28%; admin.: 11%; evaluation/research/statistics: 2%; elementary: 8%; higher education admin.: 7%; special: 9%; counseling: 10%; other: 26%

University of Miami

PO Box 248212
Coral Gables, FL 33124
www.education.miami.edu
Private
Admissions: (305) 284-2167
Email: soegradadmissions@miami.edu
Financial aid: (305) 284-5212
Application deadline: rolling
Tuition: full time: $1,900/credit hour; part time: $1,900/credit hour
Room/board/expenses: $23,962
Full-time enrollment: 404
doctoral students: 29%; master's students: 71%; education specialists: 0%; men: 48%; women: 52%; minorities: 47%; international: 7%
Part-time enrollment: 85
doctoral students: 2%; master's students: 98%; education specialists: 0%; men: 28%; women: 72%; minorities: 62%; international: 7%
Acceptance rate (master's): 51%
Acceptance rate (doctoral): 26%
Entrance test required: GRE
Avg. GRE (of all entering students with scores): quantitative: 148; verbal: 150
Research assistantships: 38
Students reporting specialty: 100%
Students specializing in: admin.: 4%; evaluation/research/statistics: 2%; higher education admin.: 14%; special: 3%; other: 76%

University of North Florida[1]

1 UNF Drive
Jacksonville, FL 32224-2676
www.unf.edu/graduatestudies
Public
Admissions: (904) 620-1360
Email: graduatestudies@unf.edu
Financial aid: (904) 620-5555
Tuition: N/A
Room/board/expenses: N/A
Enrollment: N/A

University of South Florida

4202 E. Fowler Avenue
EDU 105
Tampa, FL 33620
www.grad.usf.edu
Public
Admissions: (813) 974-8800
Email: admissions@grad.usf.edu
Financial aid: (813) 974-4700
Application deadline: rolling
In-state tuition: full time: $431/credit hour; part time: $431/credit hour
Out-of-state tuition: full time: $877/credit hour
Room/board/expenses: $16,350
Full-time enrollment: 440
doctoral students: 40%; master's students: 57%; education specialists: 2%; men: 31%; women: 69%; minorities: 31%; international: 19%

Part-time enrollment: 710
doctoral students: 49%; master's students: 45%; education specialists: 6%; men: 26%; women: 74%; minorities: 28%; international: 4%
Acceptance rate (master's): 44%
Acceptance rate (doctoral): 70%
Entrance test required: GRE
Avg. GRE (of all entering students with scores): quantitative: 147; verbal: 150
Research assistantships: 6
Students reporting specialty: 100%
Students specializing in: admin.: 11%; evaluation/research/statistics: 3%; educational psych: 5%; educational tech.: 5%; elementary: 5%; higher education admin.: 6%; junior high: 1%; secondary: 11%; special: 9%; counseling: 6%; technical (vocational): 5%; other: 33%

University of West Florida[1]

11000 University Parkway
Pensacola, FL 32514-5750
uwf.edu
Public
Admissions: N/A
Financial aid: N/A
Tuition: N/A
Room/board/expenses: N/A
Enrollment: N/A

GEORGIA

Clark Atlanta University

223 James P. Brawley Drive SW
Atlanta, GA 30314
www.cau.edu/
Private
Admissions: (404) 880-6605
Email: cauadmissions@cau.edu
Financial aid: (404) 880-8992
Application deadline: rolling
Tuition: full time: $861/credit hour; part time: $861/credit hour
Room/board/expenses: $15,579
Full-time enrollment: 85
doctoral students: 39%; master's students: 59%; education specialists: 2%; men: 42%; women: 58%; minorities: 68%; international: 16%
Part-time enrollment: 48
doctoral students: 65%; master's students: 35%; education specialists: 0%; men: 42%; women: 58%; minorities: 88%; international: 4%
Acceptance rate (master's): 93%
Acceptance rate (doctoral): 86%
Entrance test required: GRE
Avg. GRE (of all entering students with scores): quantitative: N/A; verbal: N/A
Students reporting specialty: 100%
Students specializing in: admin.: 66%; secondary: 4%; special: 1%; counseling: 19%; other: 10%

Columbus State University

4225 University Avenue
Columbus, GA 31907
www.columbusstate.edu
Public
Admissions: (706) 507-8800
Email: esc@columbusstate.edu
Financial aid: (706) 507-8000
Application deadline: 06/30

In-state tuition: full time: $201/credit hour; part time: $201/credit hour
Out-of-state tuition: full time: $801/credit hour
Room/board/expenses: N/A
Full-time enrollment: 449
doctoral students: 8%; master's students: 44%; education specialists: 47%; men: 28%; women: 72%; minorities: 44%; international: 1%
Part-time enrollment: 436
doctoral students: 17%; master's students: 47%; education specialists: 36%; men: 25%; women: 75%; minorities: 48%; international: 1%
Acceptance rate (master's): 54%
Acceptance rate (doctoral): 55%
Entrance test required: GRE
Avg. GRE (of all entering students with scores): quantitative: 144; verbal: 148
Research assistantships: 2
Students reporting specialty: 100%
Students specializing in: curriculum/instr.: 6%; admin.: 50%; elementary: 5%; junior high: 3%; secondary: 10%; special: 15%; other: 11%

Georgia Southern University

U.S. Highway 301, S
P.O. Box 8033
Statesboro, GA 30460
cogs.georgiasouthern.edu/admission
Public
Admissions: (912) 478-5384
Email: GradAdmissions@georgiasouthern.edu
Financial aid: (912) 478-5413
Application deadline: 07/01
In-state tuition: full time: $302/credit hour; part time: $302/credit hour
Out-of-state tuition: full time: $1,130/credit hour
Room/board/expenses: $16,656
Full-time enrollment: 322
doctoral students: 8%; master's students: 73%; education specialists: 19%; men: 16%; women: 84%; minorities: 32%; international: 1%
Part-time enrollment: 900
doctoral students: 26%; master's students: 61%; education specialists: 13%; men: 21%; women: 79%; minorities: 30%; international: 0%
Acceptance rate (master's): 82%
Acceptance rate (doctoral): 50%
Entrance test required: GRE
Avg. GRE (of all entering students with scores): quantitative: 146; verbal: 150
Research assistantships: 2
Students reporting specialty: 100%
Students specializing in: curriculum/instr.: 12%; admin.: 11%; instructional media design: 12%; higher education admin.: 13%; junior high: 2%; secondary: 5%; counseling: 4%; other: 42%

Georgia State University

PO Box 3980
Atlanta, GA 30302-3980
education.gsu.edu/admissions/graduate-admissions/
Public
Admissions: (404) 413-8000
Email: educadmissions@gsu.edu
Financial aid: (404) 413-2400

Application deadline: 07/01
In-state tuition: full time: $382/credit hour; part time: $382/credit hour
Out-of-state tuition: full time: $1,243/credit hour
Room/board/expenses: $14,940
Full-time enrollment: 780
doctoral students: 26%; master's students: 73%; education specialists: 1%; men: 27%; women: 73%; minorities: 42%; international: 5%
Part-time enrollment: 393
doctoral students: 43%; master's students: 51%; education specialists: 6%; men: 32%; women: 68%; minorities: 46%; international: 1%
Acceptance rate (master's): 39%
Acceptance rate (doctoral): 17%
Entrance test required: GRE
Avg. GRE (of all entering students with scores): quantitative: 148; verbal: 152
Research assistantships: 326
Students reporting specialty: 100%
Students specializing in: curriculum/instr.: 2%; admin.: 8%; policy: 4%; evaluation/research/statistics: 1%; instructional media design: 4%; educational psych: 3%; elementary: 11%; junior high: 2%; secondary: 18%; social/philosophical foundations: 1%; special: 7%; counseling: 4%; technical (vocational): 1%; other: 35%

Kennesaw State University[1]

1000 Chastain Road
Campus Box 0123
Kennesaw, GA 30144
www.kennesaw.edu
Public
Admissions: N/A
Financial aid: N/A
Tuition: N/A
Room/board/expenses: N/A
Enrollment: N/A

Mercer University (Tift)[1]

1501 Mercer University Drive
Macon, GA 31207
education.mercer.edu
Private
Admissions: (678) 547-6422
Email: WOFFORD_TM@mercer.edu
Financial aid: (478) 301-2671
Tuition: N/A
Room/board/expenses: N/A
Enrollment: N/A

Piedmont College[1]

165 Central Avenue
PO Box 10
Demorest, GA 30535
www.piedmont.edu
Private
Admissions: N/A
Financial aid: N/A
Tuition: N/A
Room/board/expenses: N/A
Enrollment: N/A

University of Georgia

G-3 Aderhold Hall
Athens, GA 30602-7101
www.coe.uga.edu/
Public
Admissions: (706) 542-1739
Email: gradadm@uga.edu

Financial aid: (706) 542-6147
Application deadline: 07/01
In-state tuition: full time: $10,762;
part time: $354/credit hour
Out-of-state tuition: full time:
$26,360
Room/board/expenses: $13,126
Full-time enrollment: 930
doctoral students: 44%;
master's students: 55%;
education specialists: 2%; men:
30%; women: 70%; minorities:
21%; international: 19%
Part-time enrollment: 592
doctoral students: 41%; master's
students: 46%; education
specialists: 12%;
men: 26%; women: 74%;
minorities: 29%; international:
3%
Acceptance rate (master's): 51%
Acceptance rate (doctoral): 34%
Entrance test required: GRE
Avg. GRE (of all entering students
with scores): quantitative: 150;
verbal: 152
Research assistantships: 127
Students reporting specialty: 100%
Students specializing in: admin.:
2%; policy: 2%; evaluation/
research/statistics: 1%;
instructional media design:
2%; educational psych:
8%; educational tech.: 4%;
elementary: 8%; higher
education admin.: 3%; junior
high: 3%; secondary: 19%;
social/philosophical foundations:
0%; special: 4%; counseling:
18%; technical (vocational): 3%;
other: 22%

University of West Georgia

1601 Maple Street
Carrollton, GA 30118
www.westga.edu/academics/
gradstudies/
Public
Admissions: (678) 839-1394
Email: graduate@westga.edu
Financial aid: (678) 839-6421
Application deadline: 07/15
In-state tuition: full time: $7,278;
part time: $222/credit hour
Out-of-state tuition: full time:
$22,620
Room/board/expenses: N/A
Full-time enrollment: 321
doctoral students: 2%; master's
students: 78%; education
specialists: 20%; men: 17%;
women: 83%; minorities: 35%;
international: 2%
Part-time enrollment: 1,002
doctoral students: 10%; master's
students: 52%; education
specialists: 38%; men: 19%;
women: 81%; minorities: 35%;
international: 1%
Acceptance rate (master's): 70%
Acceptance rate (doctoral): N/A
Entrance test required: GRE
Avg. GRE (of all entering students
with scores): quantitative: 146;
verbal: 149
Students reporting specialty: 0%
Students specializing in: N/A

Valdosta State University[1]

1500 N. Patterson Street
Valdosta, GA 31698
www.valdosta.edu/
Public
Admissions: (229) 333-5694
Email: rlwaters@valdosta.edu
Financial aid: (229) 333-5935

Tuition: N/A
Room/board/expenses: N/A
Enrollment: N/A

HAWAII

University of Hawaii-Manoa

1776 University Avenue
Everly Hall 128
Honolulu, HI 96822
manoa.hawaii.edu/graduate/
content/prospective-students
Public
Admissions: (808) 956-8544
Email: graduate.education@
hawaii.edu
Financial aid: (808) 956-7251
Application deadline: rolling
In-state tuition: full time: $637/
credit hour; part time: $637/
credit hour
Out-of-state tuition: full time:
$1,532/credit hour
Room/board/expenses: $16,881
Full-time enrollment: 226
doctoral students: 12%; master's
students: 88%; education
specialists: N/A; men: 31%;
women: 69%; minorities: 68%;
international: 5%
Part-time enrollment: 540
doctoral students: 42%;
master's students: 58%;
education specialists: N/A; men:
27%; women: 73%; minorities:
70%; international: 2%
Acceptance rate (master's): 80%
Acceptance rate (doctoral): 66%
Entrance test required: GRE
Avg. GRE (of all entering students
with scores): quantitative: 148;
verbal: 150
Research assistantships: 38
Students reporting specialty: 100%
Students specializing in:
curriculum/instr.: 14%; admin.:
10%; policy: 0%; educational
psych: 7%; educational
tech.: 14%; elementary:
5%; secondary: 9%; social/
philosophical foundations: 5%;
special: 21%; other: 14%

IDAHO

Boise State University

1910 University Drive
Boise, ID 83725-1700
www.boisestate.edu/
Public
Admissions: (208) 426-3903
Email: gradcoll@boisestate.edu
Financial aid: (800) 824-7017
Application deadline: 03/01
In-state tuition: full time: $8,440;
part time: $382/credit hour
Out-of-state tuition: full time:
$22,890
Room/board/expenses: $12,344
Full-time enrollment: 113
doctoral students: 13%; master's
students: 85%; education
specialists: 2%; men: 25%;
women: 75%; minorities: 18%;
international: 6%
Part-time enrollment: 673
doctoral students: 13%; master's
students: 82%; education
specialists: 5%; men: 35%;
women: 65%; minorities: 7%;
international: 1%
Acceptance rate (master's): 58%
Acceptance rate (doctoral): 23%
Entrance test required: GRE
Avg. GRE (of all entering students
with scores): quantitative: 152;
verbal: 159

Research assistantships: 26
Students reporting specialty: 100%
Students specializing in:
curriculum/instr.: 5%; admin.:
5%; instructional media design:
22%; special: 2%; counseling:
3%; other: 82%

Idaho State University[1]

921 S. Eighth Avenue
Pocatello, ID 83209-8059
ed.isu.edu/
Public
Admissions: N/A
Financial aid: N/A
Tuition: N/A
Room/board/expenses: N/A
Enrollment: N/A

Northwest Nazarene University[1]

623 Holly Street
Nampa, ID 83686
www.nnu.edu
Private
Admissions: (208) 467-8341
Email: sblenker@nnu.edu
Financial aid: (208) 467-8424
Tuition: N/A
Room/board/expenses: N/A
Enrollment: N/A

University of Idaho

PO Box 443080
Moscow, ID 83844-3080
www.uidaho.edu/ed
Public
Admissions: (208) 885-4001
Email: graduateadmissions@
uidaho.edu
Financial aid: (208) 885-6312
Application deadline: 02/01
In-state tuition: full time: $8,530;
part time: $457/credit hour
Out-of-state tuition: full time:
$23,338
Room/board/expenses: $15,100
Full-time enrollment: 65
doctoral students: 43%;
master's students: 54%;
education specialists: 3%; men:
N/A; women: N/A; minorities: N/A;
international: N/A
Part-time enrollment: 228
doctoral students: 21%; master's
students: 59%; education
specialists: 20%; men: N/A;
women: N/A; minorities: N/A;
international: N/A
Acceptance rate (master's): N/A
Acceptance rate (doctoral): N/A
Entrance test required: GRE
Avg. GRE (of all entering students
with scores): quantitative: N/A;
verbal: N/A
Students reporting specialty: 0%
Students specializing in: N/A

ILLINOIS

Argosy University[1]

225 N. Michigan Avenue
Chicago, IL 60601
www.argosy.edu/colleges/
education/default.aspx
Private
Admissions: N/A
Financial aid: N/A
Tuition: N/A
Room/board/expenses: N/A
Enrollment: N/A

Aurora University[1]

347 S. Gladstone Avenue
Aurora, IL 60506-4892
www.aurora.edu
Private
Admissions: N/A
Financial aid: N/A
Tuition: N/A
Room/board/expenses: N/A
Enrollment: N/A

Benedictine University[1]

5700 College Road
Lisle, IL 60532
www.ben.edu
Private
Admissions: N/A
Financial aid: N/A
Tuition: N/A
Room/board/expenses: N/A
Enrollment: N/A

Chicago State University[1]

9501 S. King Drive
ED 320
Chicago, IL 60628
www.csu.edu/
Public
Admissions: N/A
Financial aid: N/A
Tuition: N/A
Room/board/expenses: N/A
Enrollment: N/A

Concordia University[1]

7400 Augusta Street
River Forest, IL 60305-1499
www.cuchicago.edu
Private
Admissions: N/A
Financial aid: N/A
Tuition: N/A
Room/board/expenses: N/A
Enrollment: N/A

DePaul University

1 E. Jackson Boulevard
Chicago, IL 60604-2287
education.depaul.edu
Private
Admissions: (773) 325-4405
Email: edgradadmissions@
depaul.edu
Financial aid: (312) 362-8610
Application deadline: rolling
Tuition: full time: $620/credit
hour; part time: $620/credit hour
Room/board/expenses: $16,041
Full-time enrollment: 630
doctoral students: 16%; master's
students: 84%; education
specialists: N/A; men: 26%;
women: 74%; minorities: 11%;
international: 4%
Part-time enrollment: 269
doctoral students: 29%;
master's students: 71%;
education specialists: N/A; men:
25%; women: 75%; minorities:
24%; international: 5%
Acceptance rate (master's): 75%
Acceptance rate (doctoral): 77%
Entrance test required: GRE
Avg. GRE (of all entering students
with scores): quantitative: 143;
verbal: 149
Research assistantships: 11
Students reporting specialty: 100%
Students specializing in:
curriculum/instr.: 7%;
admin.: 19%; elementary:
8%; secondary: 14%; social/
philosophical foundations: 2%;

special: 6%; counseling: 22%;
other: 21%

Governors State University

1 University Parkway
University Park, IL 60466
www.govst.edu
Public
Admissions: (708) 534-4490
Email: admissions@govst.edu
Financial aid: (708) 534-4480
Application deadline: 04/01
In-state tuition: full time: $7,368;
part time: $307/credit hour
Out-of-state tuition: full time:
$14,736
Room/board/expenses: $15,568
Full-time enrollment: 141
doctoral students: 30%;
master's students: 59%;
education specialists: 11%; men:
14%; women: 86%; minorities:
54%; international: 2%
Part-time enrollment: 347
doctoral students: 7%; master's
students: 90%; education
specialists: 3%; men: 22%;
women: 78%; minorities: 48%;
international: 1%
Acceptance rate (master's): 50%
Acceptance rate (doctoral): 34%
Entrance test required: GRE
Avg. GRE (of all entering students
with scores): quantitative: 147;
verbal: 150
Research assistantships: 19
Students reporting specialty: 100%
Students specializing in:
curriculum/instr.: 6%; admin.:
13%; counseling: 5%; other: 76%

Illinois Institute of Technology[1]

10 W. 33rd Street
Peristein Hall, Room 203
Chicago, IL 60616
admissions.iit.edu/graduate/
programs/armour-college-
engineering
Private
Admissions: (312) 567-3020
Financial aid: N/A
Tuition: N/A
Room/board/expenses: N/A
Enrollment: N/A

Illinois State University

Campus Box 5300
Normal, IL 61790-5300
www.illinoisstate.edu
Public
Admissions: (309) 438-2181
Email:
admissions@illinoisstate.edu
Financial aid: (309) 438-2231
Application deadline: rolling
In-state tuition: full time: $389/
credit hour; part time: $389/
credit hour
Out-of-state tuition: full time:
$808/credit hour
Room/board/expenses: $14,562
Full-time enrollment: 236
doctoral students: 21%; master's
students: 70%; education
specialists: 9%; men: 16%;
women: 84%; minorities: N/A;
international: N/A
Part-time enrollment: 605
doctoral students: 40%;
master's students: 51%;
education specialists: 9%;
men: 26%; women: 74%;
minorities: N/A; international: N/A

Acceptance rate (master's): 65%
Acceptance rate (doctoral): 84%
Entrance test required: GRE
Avg. GRE (of all entering students with scores): quantitative: 150; verbal: 151
Research assistantships: 99
Students reporting specialty: 100%
Students specializing in: curriculum/instr.: 12%; admin.: 28%; educational tech.: 1%; special: 11%; counseling: 5%; other: 43%

Lewis University[1]
One University Parkway
Romeoville, IL 60446
www.lewisu.edu/
Private
Admissions: N/A
Financial aid: N/A
Tuition: N/A
Room/board/expenses: N/A
Enrollment: N/A

Loyola University Chicago
820 N. Michigan Avenue
Chicago, IL 60611
www.luc.edu/education/
Private
Admissions: (312) 915-8907
Email: schleduc@luc.edu
Financial aid: (773) 508-7704
Application deadline: N/A
Tuition: full time: $949/credit hour; part time: $949/credit hour
Room/board/expenses: $26,407
Full-time enrollment: 424
doctoral students: 38%; master's students: 48%; education specialists: 15%; men: 23%; women: 77%; minorities: 39%; international: 4%
Part-time enrollment: 204
doctoral students: 27%; master's students: 72%; education specialists: 0%; men: 23%; women: 77%; minorities: 33%; international: 2%
Acceptance rate (master's): 73%
Acceptance rate (doctoral): 24%
Entrance test required: GRE
Avg. GRE (of all entering students with scores): quantitative: N/A; verbal: N/A
Research assistantships: 76
Students reporting specialty: 100%
Students specializing in: curriculum/instr.: 7%; admin.: 16%; policy: 3%; evaluation/research/statistics: 3%; educational psych: 3%; elementary: 3%; higher education admin.: 21%; secondary: 2%; social/philosophical foundations: 7%; special: 2%; counseling: 18%; other: 15%

National-Louis University
122 S. Michigan Avenue
Chicago, IL 60603
www.nl.edu
Private
Admissions: N/A
Financial aid: N/A
Application deadline: N/A
Tuition: full time: N/A; part time: N/A
Room/board/expenses: N/A
Full-time enrollment: 613
doctoral students: 4%; master's students: 89%; education

specialists: 7%; men: 25%; women: 75%; minorities: 31%; international: 0%
Part-time enrollment: 1,349
doctoral students: 15%; master's students: 77%; education specialists: 8%; men: 17%; women: 83%; minorities: 32%; international: 0%
Acceptance rate (master's): 98%
Acceptance rate (doctoral): 98%
Entrance test required: N/A
Avg. GRE (of all entering students with scores): quantitative: N/A; verbal: N/A
Students reporting specialty: 0%
Students specializing in: N/A

Northern Illinois University
321 Graham Hall
DeKalb, IL 60115
www.cedu.niu.edu/index.shtml/
Public
Admissions: (815) 753-0395
Email: gradsch@niu.edu
Financial aid: (815) 753-1395
Application deadline: 07/15
In-state tuition: full time: $10,874; part time: $988/credit hour
Out-of-state tuition: full time: $17,300
Room/board/expenses: $14,010
Full-time enrollment: 320
doctoral students: 21%; master's students: 79%; education specialists: N/A; men: 40%; women: 60%; minorities: 24%; international: 16%
Part-time enrollment: 882
doctoral students: 35%; master's students: 63%; education specialists: 3%; men: 28%; women: 72%; minorities: 22%; international: 2%
Acceptance rate (master's): 70%
Acceptance rate (doctoral): 51%
Entrance test required: GRE
Avg. GRE (of all entering students with scores): quantitative: 147; verbal: 149
Research assistantships: 33
Students reporting specialty: 100%
Students specializing in: curriculum/instr.: 10%; admin.: 25%; evaluation/research/statistics: 0%; instructional media design: 13%; educational psych: 2%; elementary: 0%; social/philosophical foundations: 0%; special: 7%; counseling: 13%; other: 29%

Northwestern University
2120 Campus Drive
Evanston, IL 60208
www.sesp.northwestern.edu
Private
Admissions: (847) 467-2789
Email: sesp@northwestern.edu
Financial aid: (847) 467-2789
Application deadline: rolling
Tuition: full time: $50,856; part time: $5,980/credit hour
Room/board/expenses: N/A
Full-time enrollment: 164
doctoral students: 39%; master's students: 61%; education specialists: N/A; men: 27%; women: 73%; minorities: N/A; international: N/A
Part-time enrollment: 132
doctoral students: N/A; master's students: 100%; education specialists: N/A; men: 26%; women: 74%; minorities: N/A; international: N/A

Acceptance rate (master's): 67%
Acceptance rate (doctoral): 8%
Entrance test required: GRE
Avg. GRE (of all entering students with scores): quantitative: 157; verbal: 161
Research assistantships: 28
Students reporting specialty: 100%
Students specializing in: elementary: 8%; higher education admin.: 17%; secondary: 12%; other: 62%

Roosevelt University
430 S. Michigan Avenue
Chicago, IL 60605
www.roosevelt.edu
Private
Admissions: (877) 277-5978
Email: admissions@roosevelt.edu
Financial aid: (866) 421-0935
Application deadline: rolling
Tuition: full time: $14,858; part time: $759/credit hour
Room/board/expenses: $800
Full-time enrollment: 73
doctoral students: 0%; master's students: 100%; education specialists: N/A; men: 22%; women: 78%; minorities: N/A; international: N/A
Part-time enrollment: 186
doctoral students: 13%; master's students: 87%; education specialists: N/A; men: 25%; women: 75%; minorities: N/A; international: N/A
Acceptance rate (master's): 58%
Acceptance rate (doctoral): N/A
Entrance test required: N/A
Avg. GRE (of all entering students with scores): quantitative: N/A; verbal: N/A
Students reporting specialty: 100%
Students specializing in: curriculum/instr.: 9%; admin.: 16%; elementary: 6%; higher education admin.: 9%; secondary: 7%; special: 1%; counseling: 13%; other: 41%

Southern Illinois University-Carbondale
Wham Building 115
Carbondale, IL 62901-4624
ehs.siu.edu/
Public
Admissions: (618) 536-7791
Email: gradschl@siu.edu
Financial aid: (618) 453-4334
Application deadline: rolling
In-state tuition: full time: $17,215; part time: $1,392/credit hour
Out-of-state tuition: full time: $36,948
Room/board/expenses: $17,675
Full-time enrollment: 466
doctoral students: 20%; master's students: 80%; education specialists: 0%; men: 29%; women: 71%; minorities: 31%; international: 16%
Part-time enrollment: 369
doctoral students: 37%; master's students: 63%; education specialists: 0%; men: 32%; women: 68%; minorities: 26%; international: 9%
Acceptance rate (master's): 43%
Acceptance rate (doctoral): 34%
Entrance test required: GRE
Avg. GRE (of all entering students with scores): quantitative: 150; verbal: 151
Research assistantships: 108
Students reporting specialty: 100%

Students specializing in: curriculum/instr.: 16%; admin.: 8%; educational psych: 0%; higher education admin.: 3%; secondary: 0%; special: 1%; counseling: 3%; other: 69%

Southern Illinois University-Edwardsville
Campus Box 1049
Edwardsville, IL 62026
www.siue.edu/education/
Public
Admissions: (618) 650-3770
Email: graduateadmissions@siue.edu
Financial aid: (618) 650-3880
Application deadline: rolling
In-state tuition: full time: $9,284; part time: $305/credit hour
Out-of-state tuition: full time: $20,264
Room/board/expenses: $13,764
Full-time enrollment: 52
doctoral students: 2%; master's students: 92%; education specialists: 6%; men: 21%; women: 79%; minorities: 27%; international: 8%
Part-time enrollment: 284
doctoral students: 6%; master's students: 77%; education specialists: 18%; men: 27%; women: 73%; minorities: 19%; international: 2%
Acceptance rate (master's): 70%
Acceptance rate (doctoral): 100%
Entrance test required: GRE
Avg. GRE (of all entering students with scores): quantitative: 149; verbal: 151
Research assistantships: 11
Students reporting specialty: 100%
Students specializing in: curriculum/instr.: 11%; admin.: 28%; educational tech.: 14%; higher education admin.: 17%; social/philosophical foundations: 6%; special: 8%; other: 16%

University of Illinois-Chicago
1040 W. Harrison Street
Chicago, IL 60607-7133
www.education.uic.edu
Public
Admissions: (312) 996-4532
Email: aelami2@uic.edu
Financial aid: (312) 996-3126
Application deadline: rolling
In-state tuition: full time: $14,566; part time: $10,740
Out-of-state tuition: full time: $26,806
Room/board/expenses: $17,958
Full-time enrollment: 120
doctoral students: 53%; master's students: 48%; education specialists: N/A; men: 28%; women: 73%; minorities: 50%; international: 13%
Part-time enrollment: 513
doctoral students: 47%; master's students: 53%; education specialists: N/A; men: 28%; women: 72%; minorities: 42%; international: 3%
Acceptance rate (master's): 76%
Acceptance rate (doctoral): 37%
Entrance test required: GRE
Avg. GRE (of all entering students with scores): quantitative: 150; verbal: 152
Research assistantships: 153
Students reporting specialty: 100%

Students specializing in: curriculum/instr.: 11%; admin.: 14%; policy: 3%; evaluation/research/statistics: 10%; educational psych: 13%; elementary: 0%; secondary: 5%; social/philosophical foundations: 4%; special: 19%; other: 20%

University of Illinois-Urbana-Champaign
1310 S. Sixth Street
Champaign, IL 61820
education.illinois.edu
Public
Admissions: (217) 333-2800
Email: saao@education.illinois.edu
Financial aid: (217) 333-2800
Application deadline: 04/01
In-state tuition: full time: $16,106; part time: $12,018
Out-of-state tuition: full time: $30,342
Room/board/expenses: $18,260
Full-time enrollment: 374
doctoral students: 67%; master's students: 33%; education specialists: N/A; men: 34%; women: 66%; minorities: 38%; international: 21%
Part-time enrollment: 430
doctoral students: 32%; master's students: 68%; education specialists: N/A; men: 30%; women: 70%; minorities: 28%; international: 6%
Acceptance rate (master's): 70%
Acceptance rate (doctoral): 25%
Entrance test required: GRE
Avg. GRE (of all entering students with scores): quantitative: N/A; verbal: N/A
Research assistantships: 120
Students reporting specialty: 100%
Students specializing in: curriculum/instr.: 16%; admin.: 21%; policy: 18%; evaluation/research/statistics: 3%; instructional media design: 7%; educational psych: 7%; educational tech.: 4%; elementary: 1%; higher education admin.: 11%; junior high: 6%; secondary: 3%; social/philosophical foundations: 19%; special: 8%; counseling: 2%; other: 21%

University of St. Francis
500 Wilcox Street
Joliet, IL 60435
www.stfrancis.edu/academics/college-of-education/
Private
Admissions: (800) 735-7500
Email: admissions@stfrancis.edu
Financial aid: (866) 890-8331
Application deadline: rolling
Tuition: full time: $739/credit hour; part time: $739/credit hour
Room/board/expenses: N/A
Full-time enrollment: 34
doctoral students: 24%; master's students: 76%; education specialists: N/A; men: 24%; women: 76%; minorities: 21%; international: 12%
Part-time enrollment: 420
doctoral students: 30%; master's students: 70%; education specialists: N/A; men: 25%; women: 75%; minorities: 20%; international: 0%
Acceptance rate (master's): 51%
Acceptance rate (doctoral): 33%
Entrance test required: N/A

Avg. GRE (of all entering students with scores): quantitative: N/A; verbal: N/A
Students reporting specialty: 100%
Students specializing in: curriculum/instr.: 38%; admin.: 50%; elementary: 0%; higher education admin.: 1%; special: 1%; other: 10%

Western Illinois University

1 University Circle
Macomb, IL 61455
www.wiu.edu
Public
Admissions: (309) 298-1806
Email: Grad-Office@wiu.edu
Financial aid: (309) 298-2446
Application deadline: rolling
In-state tuition: full time: $324/credit hour; part time: $324/credit hour
Out-of-state tuition: full time: $485/credit hour
Room/board/expenses: $4,790
Full-time enrollment: 108
doctoral students: 4%; master's students: 94%; education specialists: 3%; men: 29%; women: 71%; minorities: 20%; international: 4%
Part-time enrollment: 389
doctoral students: 10%; master's students: 78%; education specialists: 12%; men: 30%; women: 70%; minorities: 8%; international: 0%
Acceptance rate (master's): 72%
Acceptance rate (doctoral): 92%
Entrance test required: N/A
Avg. GRE (of all entering students with scores): quantitative: N/A; verbal: N/A
Research assistantships: 37
Students reporting specialty: 100%
Students specializing in: curriculum/instr.: 18%; admin.: 35%; special: 4%; counseling: 15%; other: 32%

INDIANA

Ball State University

2000 W. University Avenue
Muncie, IN 47306
cms.bsu.edu/academics/collegesanddepartments/gradschool
Public
Admissions: (765) 285-1297
Email: gradschool@bsu.edu
Financial aid: (765) 285-5600
Application deadline: 08/14
In-state tuition: full time: $394/credit hour; part time: $394/credit hour
Out-of-state tuition: full time: $1,078/credit hour
Room/board/expenses: $14,400
Full-time enrollment: 647
doctoral students: 11%; master's students: 89%; education specialists: 0%; men: 22%; women: 78%; minorities: 15%; international: 3%
Part-time enrollment: 2,456
doctoral students: 8%; master's students: 91%; education specialists: 1%; men: 20%; women: 80%; minorities: 16%; international: 2%
Acceptance rate (master's): 87%
Acceptance rate (doctoral): 57%
Entrance test required: GRE
Avg. GRE (of all entering students with scores): quantitative: 149; verbal: 151

Research assistantships: 13
Students reporting specialty: 100%
Students specializing in: curriculum/instr.: 2%; admin.: 16%; evaluation/research/statistics: 0%; educational psych: 5%; elementary: 4%; junior high: 0%; secondary: 1%; special: 69%; counseling: 1%; technical (vocational): 0%; other: 23%

Indiana State University

401 N. Seventh Street
Terre Haute, IN 47809
www.indstate.edu/education
Public
Admissions: (800) 444-4723
Email: grdstudy@indstate.edu
Financial aid: (800) 841-4744
Application deadline: rolling
In-state tuition: full time: $396/credit hour; part time: $396/credit hour
Out-of-state tuition: full time: $777/credit hour
Room/board/expenses: $12,805
Full-time enrollment: 285
doctoral students: 46%; master's students: 49%; education specialists: 5%; men: 31%; women: 69%; minorities: 19%; international: 9%
Part-time enrollment: 356
doctoral students: 62%; master's students: 26%; education specialists: 13%; men: 35%; women: 65%; minorities: 17%; international: 4%
Acceptance rate (master's): 33%
Acceptance rate (doctoral): 47%
Entrance test required: GRE
Avg. GRE (of all entering students with scores): quantitative: N/A; verbal: N/A
Research assistantships: 2
Students reporting specialty: 100%
Students specializing in: curriculum/instr.: 14%; admin.: 37%; educational tech.: 1%; elementary: 3%; higher education admin.: 12%; special: 5%; counseling: 10%; other: 18%

Indiana University-Bloomington

201 N. Rose Avenue
Bloomington, IN 47405-1006
education.indiana.edu/
Public
Admissions: (812) 856-8504
Email: educate@indiana.edu
Financial aid: (812) 855-3278
Application deadline: 01/01
In-state tuition: full time: $420/credit hour; part time: $420/credit hour
Out-of-state tuition: full time: $1,295/credit hour
Room/board/expenses: $20,332
Full-time enrollment: 366
doctoral students: 51%; master's students: 46%; education specialists: 3%; men: 29%; women: 71%; minorities: 21%; international: 29%
Part-time enrollment: 489
doctoral students: 58%; master's students: 40%; education specialists: 2%; men: 31%; women: 69%; minorities: 15%; international: 10%
Acceptance rate (master's): 53%
Acceptance rate (doctoral): 47%
Entrance test required: GRE

Avg. GRE (of all entering students with scores): quantitative: 150; verbal: 153
Research assistantships: 89
Students reporting specialty: 100%
Students specializing in: curriculum/instr.: 7%; admin.: 12%; policy: 5%; evaluation/research/statistics: 2%; instructional media design: 12%; educational psych: 10%; elementary: 1%; higher education admin.: 8%; secondary: 1%; special: 3%; counseling: 16%; other: 22%

Oakland City University

143 N. Lucretia Street
Oakland City, IN 47660
www.oak.edu
Private
Admissions: (812) 749-1378
Email: nmiller@oak.edu
Financial aid: (800) 737-5125
Application deadline: rolling
Tuition: full time: $410/credit hour; part time: $410/credit hour
Room/board/expenses: $800
Full-time enrollment: 27
doctoral students: 37%; master's students: 59%; education specialists: 4%; men: 52%; women: 48%; minorities: 26%; international: 0%
Part-time enrollment: 51
doctoral students: 73%; master's students: 27%; education specialists: 0%; men: 57%; women: 43%; minorities: 6%; international: 1%
Acceptance rate (master's): 100%
Acceptance rate (doctoral): 100%
Entrance test required: N/A
Avg. GRE (of all entering students with scores): quantitative: N/A; verbal: N/A
Students reporting specialty: 0%
Students specializing in: N/A

Purdue University-West Lafayette

100 N. University Street
West Lafayette, IN 47907-2098
www.education.purdue.edu/
Public
Admissions: (765) 494-2345
Email: education-gradoffice@purdue.edu
Financial aid: (765) 494-5050
Application deadline: rolling
In-state tuition: full time: $10,002; part time: $345/credit hour
Out-of-state tuition: full time: $28,804
Room/board/expenses: $12,820
Full-time enrollment: 137
doctoral students: 72%; master's students: 28%; education specialists: N/A; men: 24%; women: 76%; minorities: 18%; international: 44%
Part-time enrollment: 531
doctoral students: 22%; master's students: 78%; education specialists: 1%; men: 32%; women: 68%; minorities: 16%; international: 6%
Acceptance rate (master's): 84%
Acceptance rate (doctoral): 51%
Entrance test required: GRE
Avg. GRE (of all entering students with scores): quantitative: 152; verbal: 152
Research assistantships: 51
Students reporting specialty: 100%
Students specializing in: curriculum/instr.: 18%; admin.:

7%; educational psych: 9%; educational tech.: 34%; higher education admin.: 0%; social/philosophical foundations: 0%; special: 22%; counseling: 7%; technical (vocational): 2%

IOWA

Drake University

3206 University Avenue
Des Moines, IA 50311-4505
www.drake.edu/soe/
Private
Admissions: (515) 271-2552
Email: soegradadmission@drake.edu
Financial aid: (515) 271-3048
Application deadline: rolling
Tuition: full time: $475/credit hour; part time: $475/credit hour
Room/board/expenses: $10,600
Full-time enrollment: 75
doctoral students: 1%; master's students: 93%; education specialists: 5%; men: 19%; women: 81%; minorities: 5%; international: 3%
Part-time enrollment: 543
doctoral students: 15%; master's students: 80%; education specialists: 5%; men: 27%; women: 73%; minorities: 7%; international: 1%
Acceptance rate (master's): 80%
Acceptance rate (doctoral): 100%
Entrance test required: GRE
Avg. GRE (of all entering students with scores): quantitative: 150; verbal: 154
Research assistantships: 2
Students reporting specialty: 100%
Students specializing in: curriculum/instr.: 29%; admin.: 15%; elementary: 6%; higher education admin.: 13%; secondary: 7%; special: 2%; counseling: 5%; other: 23%

Iowa State University

1620 Lagomarcino Hall
Ames, IA 50011
www.grad-college.iastate.edu/
Public
Admissions: (515) 294-5836
Email: admissions@iastate.edu
Financial aid: (515) 294-2223
Application deadline: N/A
In-state tuition: full time: $8,474; part time: $471/credit hour
Out-of-state tuition: full time: $21,786
Room/board/expenses: $14,509
Full-time enrollment: 115
doctoral students: 26%; master's students: 74%; education specialists: N/A; men: 42%; women: 58%; minorities: 25%; international: 7%
Part-time enrollment: 189
doctoral students: 50%; master's students: 50%; education specialists: N/A; men: 30%; women: 70%; minorities: 11%; international: 6%
Acceptance rate (master's): 62%
Acceptance rate (doctoral): 48%
Entrance test required: GRE
Avg. GRE (of all entering students with scores): quantitative: 150; verbal: 153
Research assistantships: 32
Students reporting specialty: 100%
Students specializing in: curriculum/instr.: 9%; admin.: 13%; evaluation/research/statistics: 1%; educational psych: 0%; educational tech.: 14%;

higher education admin.: 33%; junior high: 3%; secondary: 3%; social/philosophical foundations: 3%; special: 2%; counseling: 20%; other: 2%

University of Iowa

Lindquist Center
Iowa City, IA 52242
www.education.uiowa.edu
Public
Admissions: (319) 335-5359
Email: edu-educationservices@uiowa.edu
Financial aid: (319) 335-1450
Application deadline: rolling
In-state tuition: full time: $580/credit hour; part time: $581/credit hour
Out-of-state tuition: full time: $1,560/credit hour
Room/board/expenses: $16,970
Full-time enrollment: 410
doctoral students: 66%; master's students: 34%; education specialists: 0%; men: 31%; women: 69%; minorities: 19%; international: 20%
Part-time enrollment: 180
doctoral students: 54%; master's students: 42%; education specialists: 4%; men: 43%; women: 57%; minorities: 8%; international: 8%
Acceptance rate (master's): 67%
Acceptance rate (doctoral): 45%
Entrance test required: GRE
Avg. GRE (of all entering students with scores): quantitative: 151; verbal: 152
Research assistantships: 190
Students reporting specialty: 100%
Students specializing in: admin.: 9%; evaluation/research/statistics: 11%; educational psych: 3%; elementary: 2%; higher education admin.: 11%; secondary: 22%; social/philosophical foundations: 5%; special: 9%; counseling: 9%; other: 21%

University of Northern Iowa

150 Schindler Education Center
Cedar Falls, IA 50614-0610
www.uni.edu/coe
Public
Admissions: (319) 273-2281
Email: admissions@uni.edu
Financial aid: (800) 772-2736
Application deadline: rolling
In-state tuition: full time: $9,803; part time: $478/credit hour
Out-of-state tuition: full time: $20,277
Room/board/expenses: $11,529
Full-time enrollment: 124
doctoral students: 10%; master's students: 77%; education specialists: 12%; men: 26%; women: 74%; minorities: 7%; international: 15%
Part-time enrollment: 375
doctoral students: 18%; master's students: 82%; education specialists: 0%; men: 29%; women: 71%; minorities: 6%; international: 6%
Acceptance rate (master's): 74%
Acceptance rate (doctoral): 69%
Entrance test required: GRE
Avg. GRE (of all entering students with scores): quantitative: 158; verbal: 154
Research assistantships: 25
Students reporting specialty: 100%

Students specializing in: curriculum/instr.: 4%; admin.: 31%; instructional media design: 6%; educational psych: 1%; elementary: 3%; social/philosophical foundations: 3%; special: 4%; counseling: 6%; other: 41%

KANSAS

Baker University[1]
PO Box 65
Baldwin City, KS 66006
www.bakeru.edu/
soe-prospective-students2
Private
Admissions: (913) 491-4432
Email: education@bakeru.edu
Financial aid: N/A
Tuition: N/A
Room/board/expenses: N/A
Enrollment: N/A

Kansas State University
006 Bluemont Hall
Manhattan, KS 66506
www.ksu.edu/
Public
Admissions: (785) 532-5765
Email: coegrads@ksu.edu
Financial aid: (785) 532-6420
Application deadline: rolling
In-state tuition: full time: $503/credit hour; part time: $503/credit hour
Out-of-state tuition: full time: $1,010/credit hour
Room/board/expenses: $12,370
Full-time enrollment: 228
doctoral students: 24%; master's students: 76%; education specialists: 0%; men: 39%; women: 61%; minorities: 20%; international: 9%
Part-time enrollment: 577
doctoral students: 24%; master's students: 76%; education specialists: 0%; men: 32%; women: 68%; minorities: 19%; international: 1%
Acceptance rate (master's): 94%
Acceptance rate (doctoral): 83%
Entrance test required: GRE
Avg. GRE (of all entering students with scores): quantitative: 148; verbal: 153
Research assistantships: 14
Students reporting specialty: 100%
Students specializing in: curriculum/instr.: 14%; admin.: 17%; evaluation/research/statistics: 0%; elementary: 5%; secondary: 0%; special: 3%; counseling: 34%; other: 31%

Southwestern College[1]
100 College Street
Winfield, KS 67156-2499
www.sckans.edu/
Private
Admissions: N/A
Financial aid: N/A
Tuition: N/A
Room/board/expenses: N/A
Enrollment: N/A

University of Kansas
217 Joseph R. Pearson Hall
Lawrence, KS 66045
www.soe.ku.edu
Public
Admissions: (785) 864-4510
Email: graduate@ku.edu
Financial aid: (785) 864-4700

Application deadline: rolling
In-state tuition: full time: $395/credit hour; part time: $395/credit hour
Out-of-state tuition: full time: $924/credit hour
Room/board/expenses: N/A
Full-time enrollment: 549
doctoral students: 63%; master's students: 35%; education specialists: 2%; men: 34%; women: 66%; minorities: 17%; international: 19%
Part-time enrollment: 791
doctoral students: 7%; master's students: 93%; education specialists: 0%; men: 20%; women: 80%; minorities: 14%; international: 1%
Acceptance rate (master's): 81%
Acceptance rate (doctoral): 46%
Entrance test required: GRE
Avg. GRE (of all entering students with scores): quantitative: 150; verbal: 154
Research assistantships: 62
Students reporting specialty: 100%
Students specializing in: curriculum/instr.: 29%; admin.: 13%; policy: 1%; evaluation/research/statistics: 3%; educational psych: 3%; educational tech.: 4%; higher education admin.: 8%; secondary: 1%; social/philosophical foundations: 2%; special: 28%; counseling: 5%; other: 5%

Wichita State University[1]
1845 N. Fairmount
Wichita, KS 67260-0131
www.wichita.edu
Public
Admissions: N/A
Financial aid: N/A
Tuition: N/A
Room/board/expenses: N/A
Enrollment: N/A

KENTUCKY

Eastern Kentucky University[1]
521 Lancaster Avenue
Richmond, KY 40475
www.eku.edu
Public
Admissions: N/A
Financial aid: N/A
Tuition: N/A
Room/board/expenses: N/A
Enrollment: N/A

Morehead State University[1]
Ginger Hall 100
Morehead, KY 40351
www.moreheadstate.edu/education/
Public
Admissions: N/A
Financial aid: N/A
Tuition: N/A
Room/board/expenses: N/A
Enrollment: N/A

Northern Kentucky University[1]
Nunn Drive
Highland Heights, KY 41099
www.nku.edu
Public
Admissions: N/A

Financial aid: N/A
Tuition: N/A
Room/board/expenses: N/A
Enrollment: N/A

Spalding University[1]
851 S. Fourth Street
Louisville, KY 40203
spalding.edu/
Private
Admissions: N/A
Financial aid: N/A
Tuition: N/A
Room/board/expenses: N/A
Enrollment: N/A

University of Kentucky
103 Dickey Hall
Lexington, KY 40506-0033
www.gradschool.uky.edu/
Public
Admissions: (859) 257-4905
Email: Brian.Jackson@uky.edu
Financial aid: (859) 257-3172
Application deadline: rolling
In-state tuition: full time: $15,208; part time: $648/credit hour
Out-of-state tuition: full time: $31,352
Room/board/expenses: $16,920
Full-time enrollment: 506
doctoral students: 46%; master's students: 48%; education specialists: 5%; men: 33%; women: 67%; minorities: 18%; international: 6%
Part-time enrollment: 254
doctoral students: 51%; master's students: 36%; education specialists: 13%; men: 37%; women: 63%; minorities: 14%; international: 0%
Acceptance rate (master's): 83%
Acceptance rate (doctoral): 49%
Entrance test required: GRE
Avg. GRE (of all entering students with scores): quantitative: 147; verbal: 148
Research assistantships: 38
Students reporting specialty: 100%
Students specializing in: curriculum/instr.: 0%; admin.: 13%; policy: 4%; evaluation/research/statistics: 22%; instructional media design: 1%; educational psych: 4%; educational tech.: 0%; higher education admin.: 3%; secondary: 6%; social/philosophical foundations: 0%; special: 5%; other: 43%

University of Louisville
Cardinal Boulevard and First Street
Louisville, KY 40292
www.louisville.edu/education
Public
Admissions: (502) 852-3101
Email: gradadm@louisville.edu
Financial aid: (502) 852-5511
Application deadline: rolling
In-state tuition: full time: $12,246; part time: $681/credit hour
Out-of-state tuition: full time: $25,486
Room/board/expenses: $14,762
Full-time enrollment: 585
doctoral students: 15%; master's students: 85%; education specialists: 0%; women: 46%; minorities: 26%; international: 2%
Part-time enrollment: 616
doctoral students: 19%; master's students: 74%; education specialists: 6%; men: 34%;

women: 66%; minorities: 22%; international: 0%
Acceptance rate (master's): 73%
Acceptance rate (doctoral): 38%
Entrance test required: GRE
Avg. GRE (of all entering students with scores): quantitative: 147; verbal: 151
Research assistantships: 45
Students reporting specialty: 100%
Students specializing in: curriculum/instr.: 3%; admin.: 11%; elementary: 3%; higher education admin.: 23%; special: 4%; counseling: 16%; other: 41%

University of the Cumberlands
7792 College Station Drive
Williamsburg, KY 40769
www.ucumberlands.edu
Private
Admissions: (606) 539-4530
Email: gradadm@ucumberlands.edu
Financial aid: (606) 539-4239
Application deadline: rolling
Tuition: full time: $315/credit hour; part time: $315/credit hour
Room/board/expenses: $9,450
Full-time enrollment: 1,672
doctoral students: 3%; master's students: 82%; education specialists: 16%; men: 26%; women: 74%; minorities: 4%; international: 0%
Part-time enrollment: 994
doctoral students: 8%; master's students: 84%; education specialists: 8%; men: 32%; women: 68%; minorities: 6%; international: 0%
Acceptance rate (master's): 90%
Acceptance rate (doctoral): 83%
Entrance test required: GRE
Avg. GRE (of all entering students with scores): quantitative: 146; verbal: 150
Research assistantships: 3
Students reporting specialty: 100%
Students specializing in: curriculum/instr.: 38%; admin.: 32%; policy: 19%; evaluation/research/statistics: 5%; educational tech.: 0%; elementary: 12%; higher education admin.: 20%; junior high: 4%; secondary: 24%; social/philosophical foundations: 5%; special: 13%

Western Kentucky University
1906 College Heights Boulevard
Bowling Green, KY 42101
www.wku.edu/cebs
Public
Admissions: (270) 745-2446
Email: graduate.studies@wku.edu
Financial aid: (270) 745-2755
Application deadline: rolling
In-state tuition: full time: $395/credit hour; part time: $395/credit hour
Out-of-state tuition: full time: $816/credit hour
Room/board/expenses: $11,520
Full-time enrollment: 165
doctoral students: 2%; master's students: 88%; education specialists: 10%; men: 13%; women: 87%; minorities: 8%; international: 4%
Part-time enrollment: 405
doctoral students: 8%; master's students: 89%; education specialists: 0%; men: 10%;

women: 81%; minorities: 7%; international: 0%
Acceptance rate (master's): 42%
Acceptance rate (doctoral): 100%
Entrance test required: GRE
Avg. GRE (of all entering students with scores): quantitative: 147; verbal: 152
Research assistantships: 28
Students reporting specialty: 100%
Students specializing in: admin.: 9%; educational psych: 6%; educational tech.: 10%; elementary: 11%; junior high: 4%; secondary: 6%; special: 9%; other: 44%

LOUISIANA

Grambling State University
GSU Box 4305
Grambling, LA 71245
www.gram.edu/
Public
Admissions: N/A
Financial aid: N/A
Application deadline: 07/01
In-state tuition: full time: $7,122; part time: $284/credit hour
Out-of-state tuition: full time: $16,145
Room/board/expenses: $18,346
Full-time enrollment: 9
doctoral students: 56%; master's students: 44%; education specialists: N/A; men: 44%; women: 56%; minorities: 56%; international: 44%
Part-time enrollment: 101
doctoral students: 60%; master's students: 40%; education specialists: N/A; men: 21%; women: 79%; minorities: 83%; international: 3%
Acceptance rate (master's): 30%
Acceptance rate (doctoral): 52%
Entrance test required: N/A
Avg. GRE (of all entering students with scores): quantitative: N/A; verbal: N/A
Students reporting specialty: 100%
Students specializing in: curriculum/instr.: 11%; secondary: 10%; special: 14%; other: 75%

Louisiana State University-Baton Rouge
223 Peabody Hall
Baton Rouge, LA 70803
www.lsu.edu/coe
Public
Admissions: (225) 578-2311
Email: graddeanoffice@lsu.edu
Financial aid: (225) 578-3103
Application deadline: rolling
In-state tuition: full time: $11,393; part time: $6,641
Out-of-state tuition: full time: $28,308
Room/board/expenses: $18,120
Full-time enrollment: 372
doctoral students: 22%; master's students: 78%; education specialists: 0%; men: 28%; women: 72%; minorities: 28%; international: 8%
Part-time enrollment: 353
doctoral students: 24%; master's students: 71%; education specialists: 5%; men: 18%; women: 82%; minorities: 29%; international: 1%
Acceptance rate (master's): 74%
Acceptance rate (doctoral): 64%

Entrance test required: GRE
Avg. GRE (of all entering students with scores): quantitative: 146; verbal: 151
Research assistantships: 50
Students reporting specialty: 100%
Students specializing in: curriculum/instr.: 12%; admin.: 10%; evaluation/research/statistics: 2%; educational psych: 3%; elementary: 2%; higher education admin.: 23%; secondary: 2%; special: 2%; counseling: 6%; other: 40%

Louisiana Tech University
PO Box 3163
Ruston, LA 71272-0001
www.latech.edu/education/
Public
Admissions: (318) 257-2924
Email: gschool@latech.edu
Financial aid: (318) 257-2641
Application deadline: 08/01
In-state tuition: full time: $7,293; part time: $5,942
Out-of-state tuition: full time: $16,383
Room/board/expenses: $9,516
Full-time enrollment: 251
doctoral students: 27%; master's students: 73%; education specialists: 0%; men: 32%; women: 68%; minorities: 28%; international: 2%
Part-time enrollment: 260
doctoral students: 23%; master's students: 77%; education specialists: 0%; men: 24%; women: 76%; minorities: 27%; international: 1%
Acceptance rate (master's): 75%
Acceptance rate (doctoral): 55%
Entrance test required: GRE
Avg. GRE (of all entering students with scores): quantitative: 147; verbal: 151
Research assistantships: 11
Students reporting specialty: 100%
Students specializing in: curriculum/instr.: 2%; admin.: 27%; elementary: 3%; junior high: 1%; secondary: 5%; special: 4%; counseling: 20%; other: 42%

Southeastern Louisiana University
SLU 10671
Hammond, LA 70402
www.southeastern.edu/
Public
Admissions: (800) 222-7358
Email: admissions@selu.edu
Financial aid: (985) 549-2244
Application deadline: 07/15
In-state tuition: full time: $8,369; part time: $465/credit hour
Out-of-state tuition: full time: $20,846
Room/board/expenses: $12,292
Full-time enrollment: 10
doctoral students: 20%; master's students: 80%; education specialists: N/A; men: N/A; women: 100%; minorities: 14%; international: 5%
Part-time enrollment: 168
doctoral students: 42%; master's students: 58%; education specialists: N/A; men: 16%; women: 84%; minorities: 28%; international: 0%
Acceptance rate (master's): 60%
Acceptance rate (doctoral): 50%
Entrance test required: GRE

Avg. GRE (of all entering students with scores): quantitative: 146; verbal: 146
Students reporting specialty: 100%
Students specializing in: curriculum/instr.: 7%; admin.: 46%; elementary: 2%; secondary: 15%; special: 10%; other: 20%

Southern University and A&M College[1]
JC Clark Admin. Building, 4th Floor
Baton Rouge, LA 70813
www.subr.edu/
Public
Admissions: N/A
Financial aid: N/A
Tuition: N/A
Room/board/expenses: N/A
Enrollment: N/A

University of Louisiana-Lafayette[1]
PO Drawer 44872
Lafayette, LA 70504-4872
www.louisiana.edu
Public
Admissions: N/A
Financial aid: N/A
Tuition: N/A
Room/board/expenses: N/A
Enrollment: N/A

University of Louisiana-Monroe
Walker Hall 2-37
Monroe, LA 71209-0001
www.ulm.edu/gradschool/index.html
Public
Admissions: (318) 342-1036
Email: gradadmissions@ulm.edu
Financial aid: (318) 342-5320
Application deadline: 07/31
In-state tuition: full time: $8,659; part time: $6,721
Out-of-state tuition: full time: $20,759
Room/board/expenses: $12,209
Full-time enrollment: 40
doctoral students: 18%; master's students: 83%; education specialists: 0%; men: 20%; women: 80%; minorities: 20%; international: 0%
Part-time enrollment: 156
doctoral students: 39%; master's students: 61%; education specialists: 0%; men: 17%; women: 83%; minorities: 30%; international: 0%
Acceptance rate (master's): 86%
Acceptance rate (doctoral): 71%
Entrance test required: GRE
Avg. GRE (of all entering students with scores): quantitative: 145; verbal: 151
Research assistantships: 7
Students reporting specialty: 100%
Students specializing in: curriculum/instr.: 37%; admin.: 11%; educational tech.: 5%; elementary: 15%; secondary: 10%; special: 9%; other: 23%

University of New Orleans
2000 Lakeshore Drive
New Orleans, LA 70148
www.uno.edu/index.aspx
Public
Admissions: (504) 280-6595
Email: pec@uno.edu
Financial aid: (504) 280-6603

Application deadline: 07/01
In-state tuition: full time: $8,298; part time: $5,562
Out-of-state tuition: full time: $21,737
Room/board/expenses: $14,284
Full-time enrollment: 102
doctoral students: 25%; master's students: 75%; education specialists: 0%; men: 20%; women: 80%; minorities: 28%; international: 6%
Part-time enrollment: 225
doctoral students: 36%; master's students: 64%; education specialists: 0%; men: 24%; women: 76%; minorities: 28%; international: 1%
Acceptance rate (master's): 55%
Acceptance rate (doctoral): 38%
Entrance test required: GRE
Avg. GRE (of all entering students with scores): quantitative: 146; verbal: 151
Students reporting specialty: 100%
Students specializing in: curriculum/instr.: 10%; admin.: 14%; elementary: 7%; higher education admin.: 10%; secondary: 10%; special: 12%; counseling: 25%; other: 11%

MAINE

University of Maine
Shibles Hall
Orono, ME 04469-5766
www.umaine.edu/edhd/
Public
Admissions: (207) 581-3219
Email: graduate@maine.edu
Financial aid: (207) 581-1324
Application deadline: rolling
In-state tuition: full time: $418/credit hour; part time: $418/credit hour
Out-of-state tuition: full time: $1,361/credit hour
Room/board/expenses: $13,594
Full-time enrollment: 125
doctoral students: 10%; master's students: 86%; education specialists: 4%; men: 23%; women: 77%; minorities: 11%; international: 4%
Part-time enrollment: 259
doctoral students: 18%; master's students: 65%; education specialists: 17%; men: 17%; women: 83%; minorities: 4%; international: 1%
Acceptance rate (master's): 95%
Acceptance rate (doctoral): 86%
Entrance test required: GRE
Avg. GRE (of all entering students with scores): quantitative: 148; verbal: 152
Students reporting specialty: 100%
Students specializing in: curriculum/instr.: 10%; admin.: 17%; educational tech.: 6%; higher education admin.: 7%; secondary: 0%; special: 22%; counseling: 5%; other: 35%

MARYLAND

Bowie State University
14000 Jericho Park Road
Bowie, MD 20715-9465
www.bowiestate.edu/academics-research/the-graduate-school/
Public
Admissions: (301) 860-3415
Email: gradadmissions@bowiestate.edu
Financial aid: (301) 860-3543
Application deadline: N/A

In-state tuition: full time: $399/credit hour; part time: $399/credit hour
Out-of-state tuition: full time: $688/credit hour
Room/board/expenses: $13,671
Full-time enrollment: 93
doctoral students: 9%; master's students: 91%; education specialists: 0%; men: 33%; women: 67%; minorities: N/A; international: N/A
Part-time enrollment: 83
doctoral students: 34%; master's students: 66%; education specialists: 0%; men: 34%; women: 66%; minorities: N/A; international: 1%
Acceptance rate (master's): 67%
Acceptance rate (doctoral): 100%
Entrance test required: GRE
Avg. GRE (of all entering students with scores): quantitative: N/A; verbal: N/A
Students reporting specialty: 0%
Students specializing in: N/A

Frostburg State University[1]
101 Braddock Road
Frostburg, MD 21532-2303
www.frostburg.edu/grad/
Public
Admissions: (301) 687-7053
Email: gradservices@frostburg.edu
Financial aid: N/A
Tuition: N/A
Room/board/expenses: N/A
Enrollment: N/A

Johns Hopkins University
2800 N. Charles Street
Baltimore, MD 21218
education.jhu.edu/admission/
Private
Admissions: (877) 548-7631
Email: soe.info@jhu.edu
Financial aid: (410) 516-9808
Application deadline: 04/01
Tuition: full time: $1,000/credit hour; part time: $740/credit hour
Room/board/expenses: N/A
Full-time enrollment: 367
doctoral students: 6%; master's students: 94%; education specialists: N/A; men: 24%; women: 76%; minorities: 45%; international: 5%
Part-time enrollment: 1,816
doctoral students: 12%; master's students: 88%; education specialists: N/A; men: 23%; women: 77%; minorities: 40%; international: 3%
Acceptance rate (master's): 76%
Acceptance rate (doctoral): 27%
Entrance test required: GRE
Avg. GRE (of all entering students with scores): quantitative: 162; verbal: 164
Students reporting specialty: 100%
Students specializing in: curriculum/instr.: 2%; admin.: 6%; evaluation/research/statistics: 1%; educational tech.: 3%; elementary: 21%; secondary: 30%; special: 4%; counseling: 10%; other: 31%

Morgan State University[1]
1700 E. Cold Spring Lane
Baltimore, MD 21251
www.morgan.edu/
Public
Admissions: N/A
Financial aid: N/A
Tuition: N/A
Room/board/expenses: N/A
Enrollment: N/A

Notre Dame of Maryland University[1]
4701 North Charles Street
Baltimore, MD 21210
www.ndm.edu
Private
Admissions: (410) 532-5317
Email: gradadm@ndm.edu
Financial aid: (410) 532-5369
Tuition: N/A
Room/board/expenses: N/A
Enrollment: N/A

Towson University
8000 York Road
Towson, MD 21252
grad.towson.edu
Public
Admissions: (410) 704-2501
Email: grads@towson.edu
Financial aid: (410) 704-4236
Application deadline: rolling
In-state tuition: full time: $379/credit hour; part time: $379/credit hour
Out-of-state tuition: full time: $785/credit hour
Room/board/expenses: $15,928
Full-time enrollment: 289
doctoral students: 21%; master's students: 79%; education specialists: N/A; men: 15%; women: 85%; minorities: 11%; international: 2%
Part-time enrollment: 952
doctoral students: 2%; master's students: 98%; education specialists: N/A; men: 15%; women: 85%; minorities: 14%; international: 0%
Acceptance rate (master's): 58%
Acceptance rate (doctoral): 38%
Entrance test required: GRE
Avg. GRE (of all entering students with scores): quantitative: 149; verbal: 152
Research assistantships: 1
Students reporting specialty: 100%
Students specializing in: admin.: 18%; instructional media design: 15%; educational psych: 3%; educational tech.: 2%; elementary: 3%; secondary: 5%; special: 14%; other: 41%

University of Maryland-College Park
3119 Benjamin Building
College Park, MD 20742-1121
www.education.umd.edu/GraduatePrograms
Public
Admissions: (301) 405-5609
Email: pdowdell@umd.edu
Financial aid: (301) 314-9000
Application deadline: rolling
In-state tuition: full time: $651/credit hour; part time: $651/credit hour
Out-of-state tuition: full time: $1,404/credit hour
Room/board/expenses: $15,562

Full-time enrollment: 553 doctoral students: 61%; master's students: 39%; education specialists: 0%; men: 25%; women: 75%; minorities: 32%; international: 13%
Part-time enrollment: 285 doctoral students: 14%; master's students: 86%; education specialists: 0%; men: 18%; women: 82%; minorities: 35%; international: 1%
Acceptance rate (master's): 58%
Acceptance rate (doctoral): 24%
Entrance test required: GRE
Avg. GRE (of all entering students with scores): quantitative: 154; verbal: 157
Research assistantships: 62
Students reporting specialty: 100%
Students specializing in: admin.: 7%; policy: 7%; evaluation/research/statistics: 6%; educational psych: 8%; elementary: 4%; higher education admin.: 5%; junior high: 5%; secondary: 35%; social/philosophical foundations: 1%; special: 9%; counseling: 14%; technical (vocational): 1%

University of Maryland-Eastern Shore[1]

1 Backbone Road
Princess Anne, MD 21853
www.umes.edu
Public
Admissions: N/A
Financial aid: N/A
Tuition: N/A
Room/board/expenses: N/A
Enrollment: N/A

MASSACHUSETTS

American International College

1000 State Street
Springfield, MA 01109
www.aic.edu
Private
Admissions: (413) 205-3703
Email: kerry.barnes@aic.edu
Financial aid: (413) 205-3280
Application deadline: rolling
Tuition: full time: $439/credit hour; part time: $439/credit hour
Room/board/expenses: $14,360
Full-time enrollment: 1,121 doctoral students: 6%; master's students: 94%; education specialists: 0%; men: 19%; women: 81%; minorities: 9%; international: 0%
Part-time enrollment: 71 doctoral students: 0%; master's students: 100%; education specialists: 0%; men: 28%; women: 72%; minorities: 8%; international: 0%
Acceptance rate (master's): 72%
Acceptance rate (doctoral): 52%
Entrance test required: N/A
Avg. GRE (of all entering students with scores): quantitative: N/A; verbal: N/A
Research assistantships: 0
Students reporting specialty: 100%
Students specializing in: admin.: 17%; elementary: 11%; junior high: 8%; secondary: 9%; special: 28%; counseling: 2%; other: 24%

Boston College (Lynch)

Campion Hall
Chestnut Hill, MA 02467-3813
www.bc.edu/schools/lsoe/gradadmission
Private
Admissions: (617) 552-4214
Email: gsoe@bc.edu
Financial aid: (617) 552-3300
Application deadline: 01/04
Tuition: full time: $1,364/credit hour; part time: $1,364/credit hour
Room/board/expenses: $22,491
Full-time enrollment: 481 doctoral students: 22%; master's students: 78%; education specialists: N/A; men: 19%; women: 81%; minorities: 23%; international: 17%
Part-time enrollment: 283 doctoral students: 37%; master's students: 63%; education specialists: N/A; men: 29%; women: 71%; minorities: 16%; international: 7%
Acceptance rate (master's): 82%
Acceptance rate (doctoral): 8%
Entrance test required: GRE
Avg. GRE (of all entering students with scores): quantitative: 152; verbal: 154
Research assistantships: 406
Students reporting specialty: 100%
Students specializing in: curriculum/instr.: 19%; admin.: 6%; evaluation/research/statistics: 8%; educational psych: 5%; elementary: 5%; higher education admin.: 16%; secondary: 3%; special: 7%; counseling: 27%; other: 4%

Boston University

2 Silber Way
Boston, MA 02215
www.bu.edu/sed
Private
Admissions: (617) 353-4237
Email: sedgrad@bu.edu
Financial aid: (617) 353-4238
Application deadline: rolling
Tuition: full time: $49,906; part time: $768/credit hour
Room/board/expenses: $18,516
Full-time enrollment: 235 doctoral students: 23%; master's students: 77%; education specialists: 0%; men: 23%; women: 77%; minorities: 19%; international: 17%
Part-time enrollment: 326 doctoral students: 13%; master's students: 86%; education specialists: 0%; men: 25%; women: 75%; minorities: 28%; international: 3%
Acceptance rate (master's): 65%
Acceptance rate (doctoral): 25%
Entrance test required: GRE
Avg. GRE (of all entering students with scores): quantitative: 156; verbal: 157
Research assistantships: 21
Students reporting specialty: 100%
Students specializing in: curriculum/instr.: 28%; admin.: 9%; elementary: 1%; higher education admin.: 9%; junior high: 10%; secondary: 10%; special: 6%; counseling: 14%; other: 24%

Cambridge College[1]

1000 Massachusetts Avenue
Cambridge, MA 02138
www.cambridgecollege.edu/
Private
Admissions: N/A
Financial aid: N/A
Tuition: N/A
Room/board/expenses: N/A
Enrollment: N/A

Harvard University

Appian Way
Cambridge, MA 02138
www.gse.harvard.edu
Private
Admissions: (617) 495-3414
Email: gseadmissions@harvard.edu
Financial aid: (617) 495-3416
Application deadline: 12/01
Tuition: full time: $48,726; part time: $26,222
Room/board/expenses: $23,850
Full-time enrollment: 794 doctoral students: 21%; master's students: 79%; education specialists: N/A; men: 25%; women: 75%; minorities: 31%; international: 20%
Part-time enrollment: 72 doctoral students: 3%; master's students: 97%; education specialists: N/A; men: 24%; women: 76%; minorities: 25%; international: 1%
Acceptance rate (master's): 50%
Acceptance rate (doctoral): 4%
Entrance test required: GRE
Avg. GRE (of all entering students with scores): quantitative: 156; verbal: 160
Research assistantships: 82
Students reporting specialty: 100%
Students specializing in: curriculum/instr.: 4%; admin.: 15%; policy: 25%; evaluation/research/statistics: 4%; higher education admin.: 7%; secondary: 6%; social/philosophical foundations: 5%; counseling: 6%; other: 41%

Lesley University[1]

29 Everett Street
Cambridge, MA 02138-2790
www.lesley.edu/soe.html
Private
Admissions: N/A
Financial aid: N/A
Tuition: N/A
Room/board/expenses: N/A
Enrollment: N/A

Northeastern University[1]

360 Huntington Avenue
50 Nightingale Hall
Boston, MA 02115
www.northeastern.edu/
Private
Admissions: N/A
Financial aid: N/A
Tuition: N/A
Room/board/expenses: N/A
Enrollment: N/A

Tufts University[1]

Paige Hall
12 Upper Campus Road
Medford, MA 02155
asegrad.tufts.edu/
Private
Admissions: (617) 627-3395
Email: gradadmissions@tufts.edu
Financial aid: (617) 627-2000

Tuition: N/A
Room/board/expenses: N/A
Enrollment: N/A

University of Massachusetts-Amherst

Furcolo Hall
813 N. Pleasant Street
Amherst, MA 01003-9308
www.umass.edu/education
Public
Admissions: (413) 545-0722
Email: gradadm@grad.umass.edu
Financial aid: (413) 545-0801
Application deadline: 01/02
In-state tuition: full time: $15,613; part time: $10,639
Out-of-state tuition: full time: $31,733
Room/board/expenses: $14,600
Full-time enrollment: 351 doctoral students: 49%; master's students: 38%; education specialists: 13%; men: 29%; women: 71%; minorities: 19%; international: 29%
Part-time enrollment: 198 doctoral students: 69%; master's students: 28%; education specialists: 4%; men: 31%; women: 69%; minorities: 18%; international: 3%
Acceptance rate (master's): 56%
Acceptance rate (doctoral): 49%
Entrance test required: GRE
Avg. GRE (of all entering students with scores): quantitative: 154; verbal: 154
Research assistantships: 155
Students reporting specialty: 100%
Students specializing in: curriculum/instr.: 23%; admin.: 6%; policy: 8%; evaluation/research/statistics: 5%; educational psych: 6%; educational tech.: 5%; elementary: 3%; higher education admin.: 13%; junior high: 2%; secondary: 7%; social/philosophical foundations: 6%; special: 5%; counseling: 13%; other: 4%

University of Massachusetts-Boston

100 Morrissey Boulevard
Boston, MA 02125-3393
www.umb.edu/academics/graduate
Public
Admissions: (617) 287-6400
Email: bos.gadm@umb.edu
Financial aid: (617) 287-6300
Application deadline: N/A
In-state tuition: full time: $16,863; part time: $702/credit hour
Out-of-state tuition: full time: $32,913
Room/board/expenses: $14,856
Full-time enrollment: 337 doctoral students: 15%; master's students: 84%; education specialists: 2%; men: 19%; women: 81%; minorities: 28%; international: 6%
Part-time enrollment: 440 doctoral students: 25%; master's students: 58%; education specialists: 17%; men: 27%; women: 73%; minorities: 32%; international: 2%
Acceptance rate (master's): 70%
Acceptance rate (doctoral): 37%
Entrance test required: GRE

Avg. GRE (of all entering students with scores): quantitative: 146; verbal: 151
Research assistantships: 57
Students reporting specialty: 100%
Students specializing in: admin.: 12%; evaluation/research/statistics: 1%; educational psych: 9%; elementary: 10%; higher education admin.: 8%; junior high: 15%; secondary: 7%; special: 6%; counseling: 9%; other: 22%

University of Massachusetts-Lowell

510 O'Leary Library
61 Wilder Street
Lowell, MA 01854
www.uml.edu
Public
Admissions: (978) 934-2373
Email: Graduate_Admissions@uml.edu
Financial aid: (978) 934-2000
Application deadline: 08/01
In-state tuition: full time: $795/credit hour; part time: $795/credit hour
Out-of-state tuition: full time: $1,436/credit hour
Room/board/expenses: $1,150
Full-time enrollment: 48 doctoral students: 17%; master's students: 83%; education specialists: 0%; men: 31%; women: 69%; minorities: 13%; international: 8%
Part-time enrollment: 323 doctoral students: 30%; master's students: 59%; education specialists: 12%; men: 24%; women: 76%; minorities: 8%; international: 1%
Acceptance rate (master's): 92%
Acceptance rate (doctoral): 92%
Entrance test required: GRE
Avg. GRE (of all entering students with scores): quantitative: 144; verbal: 154
Research assistantships: 3
Students reporting specialty: 100%
Students specializing in: curriculum/instr.: 25%; admin.: 12%; elementary: 3%; higher education admin.: 9%; secondary: 12%; special: 2%; other: 37%

MICHIGAN

Andrews University

8975 US-31
Berrien Springs, MI 49104-0103
www.andrews.edu/
Private
Admissions: (800) 253-2874
Email: enroll@andrews.edu
Financial aid: (269) 471-3334
Application deadline: 07/15
Tuition: full time: $1,218/credit hour; part time: $1,218/credit hour
Room/board/expenses: $16,580
Full-time enrollment: 132 doctoral students: 75%; master's students: 20%; education specialists: 5%; men: 37%; women: 63%; minorities: 29%; international: 32%
Part-time enrollment: 104 doctoral students: 50%; master's students: 41%; education specialists: 0%; men: 41%; women: 59%; minorities: 28%; international: 04%
Acceptance rate (master's): 92%
Acceptance rate (doctoral): 88%

Entrance test required: GRE
Avg. GRE (of all entering students with scores): quantitative: 154; verbal: 147
Research assistantships: 4
Students reporting specialty: 100%
Students specializing in: curriculum/instr.: 10%; admin.: 13%; educational psych: 14%; elementary: 2%; higher education admin.: 8%; secondary: 1%; special: 1%; counseling: 25%; other: 27%

Central Michigan University[1]
105 Warriner
Mount Pleasant, MI 48859
www.cmich.edu/
Public
Admissions: N/A
Financial aid: N/A
Tuition: N/A
Room/board/expenses: N/A
Enrollment: N/A

Eastern Michigan University
310 Porter Building
Ypsilanti, MI 48197
www.emich.edu/coe/
Public
Admissions: (734) 487-3400
Email: graduate.admissions@emich.edu
Financial aid: (734) 487-0455
Application deadline: rolling
In-state tuition: full time: $630/credit hour; part time: $630/credit hour
Out-of-state tuition: full time: $1,160/credit hour
Room/board/expenses: $13,154
Full-time enrollment: 185
doctoral students: 0%; master's students: 99%; education specialists: 1%; men: 12%; women: 88%; minorities: 18%; international: 9%
Part-time enrollment: 653
doctoral students: 20%; master's students: 74%; education specialists: 6%; men: 22%; women: 78%; minorities: 22%; international: 2%
Acceptance rate (master's): 56%
Acceptance rate (doctoral): 50%
Entrance test required: GRE
Avg. GRE (of all entering students with scores): quantitative: 147; verbal: 151
Research assistantships: 8
Students reporting specialty: 100%
Students specializing in: admin.: 16%; evaluation/research/statistics: 5%; instructional media design: 3%; educational psych: 0%; elementary: 3%; higher education admin.: 12%; secondary: 5%; social/philosophical foundations: 1%; special: 26%; counseling: 5%; other: 23%

Ferris State University
1349 Cramer Circle, Bishop 421
Big Rapids, MI 49307
www.ferris.edu/education/education/
Public
Admissions: N/A
Financial aid: (231) 591-2950
Application deadline: rolling
In-state tuition: full time: $542/credit hour; part time: $542/credit hour

Out-of-state tuition: full time: $813/credit hour
Room/board/expenses: $500
Full-time enrollment: 18
doctoral students: N/A; master's students: 100%; education specialists: N/A; men: 33%; women: 67%; minorities: N/A; international: N/A
Part-time enrollment: 71
doctoral students: N/A; master's students: 100%; education specialists: N/A; men: 37%; women: 63%; minorities: N/A; international: N/A
Acceptance rate (master's): 41%
Acceptance rate (doctoral): N/A
Entrance test required: N/A
Avg. GRE (of all entering students with scores): quantitative: N/A; verbal: N/A
Students reporting specialty: 0%
Students specializing in: N/A

Michigan State University
620 Farm Lane, Room 501
East Lansing, MI 48824-1034
education.msu.edu/
Public
Admissions: (517) 355-8332
Email: admis@msu.edu
Financial aid: (517) 353-5940
Application deadline: 12/01
In-state tuition: full time: $732/credit hour; part time: $732/credit hour
Out-of-state tuition: full time: $1,406/credit hour
Room/board/expenses: $12,103
Full-time enrollment: 916
doctoral students: 56%; master's students: 44%; education specialists: 1%; men: 34%; women: 66%; minorities: 17%; international: 12%
Part-time enrollment: 328
doctoral students: 13%; master's students: 85%; education specialists: 2%; men: 25%; women: 75%; minorities: 11%; international: 1%
Acceptance rate (master's): 39%
Acceptance rate (doctoral): 37%
Entrance test required: GRE
Avg. GRE (of all entering students with scores): quantitative: 152; verbal: 154
Research assistantships: 221
Students reporting specialty: 100%
Students specializing in: curriculum/instr.: 21%; admin.: 8%; policy: 3%; evaluation/research/statistics: 2%; educational psych: 2%; educational tech.: 8%; elementary: 16%; higher education admin.: 13%; secondary: 10%; social/philosophical foundations: 1%; special: 9%; counseling: 6%; technical (vocational): 0%; other: 8%

Oakland University
415 Pawley Hall
Rochester, MI 48309-4494
www.oakland.edu/grad
Public
Admissions: (248) 370-4855
Email: gradinfo@oakland.edu
Financial aid: (248) 370-2550
Application deadline: rolling
In-state tuition: full time: $16,338; part time: $680/credit hour
Out-of-state tuition: full time: $24,648
Room/board/expenses: $12,208

Full-time enrollment: 314
doctoral students: 10%; master's students: 90%; education specialists: 0%; men: 20%; women: 80%; minorities: 18%; international: 5%
Part-time enrollment: 587
doctoral students: 17%; master's students: 64%; education specialists: 19%; men: 19%; women: 81%; minorities: 16%; international: 1%
Acceptance rate (master's): 51%
Acceptance rate (doctoral): 34%
Entrance test required: N/A
Avg. GRE (of all entering students with scores): quantitative: N/A; verbal: N/A
Students reporting specialty: 100%
Students specializing in: curriculum/instr.: 1%; admin.: 21%; elementary: 5%; higher education admin.: 4%; secondary: 4%; special: 14%; counseling: 18%; other: 33%

University of Michigan-Ann Arbor
610 E. University Street
Ann Arbor, MI 48109-1259
www.soe.umich.edu/
Public
Admissions: (734) 615-1528
Email: ed.grad.admit@umich.edu
Financial aid: (734) 615-1528
Application deadline: N/A
In-state tuition: full time: $22,212; part time: $1,547/credit hour
Out-of-state tuition: full time: $44,550
Room/board/expenses: $21,566
Full-time enrollment: 409
doctoral students: 53%; master's students: 47%; education specialists: N/A; men: 28%; women: 72%; minorities: 29%; international: 9%
Part-time enrollment: 30
doctoral students: 37%; master's students: 63%; education specialists: N/A; men: 23%; women: 77%; minorities: 28%; international: 3%
Acceptance rate (master's): 82%
Acceptance rate (doctoral): 15%
Entrance test required: GRE
Avg. GRE (of all entering students with scores): quantitative: 147; verbal: 154
Research assistantships: 119
Students reporting specialty: 100%
Students specializing in: curriculum/instr.: 17%; admin.: 4%; policy: 4%; evaluation/research/statistics: 1%; educational psych: 7%; educational tech.: 2%; elementary: 8%; higher education admin.: 25%; secondary: 27%; social/philosophical foundations: 3%; other: 4%

University of Michigan-Dearborn[1]
19000 Hubbard Drive
Dearborn, MI 48126
www.soe.umd.umich.edu/
Public
Admissions: (313) 593-5006
Email: joanno@umd.umich.edu
Financial aid: (313) 593-5300
Tuition: N/A
Room/board/expenses: N/A
Enrollment: N/A

Wayne State University
5425 Gullen Mall
Detroit, MI 48202-3489
www.coe.wayne.edu/
Public
Admissions: (313) 577-1605
Email: gradadmissions@wayne.edu
Financial aid: (313) 577-2100
Application deadline: rolling
In-state tuition: full time: $614/credit hour; part time: $614/credit hour
Out-of-state tuition: full time: $1,331/credit hour
Room/board/expenses: $16,452
Full-time enrollment: 453
doctoral students: 28%; master's students: 69%; education specialists: 3%; men: 26%; women: 74%; minorities: 31%; international: 11%
Part-time enrollment: 883
doctoral students: 9%; master's students: 77%; education specialists: 14%; men: 28%; women: 72%; minorities: 39%; international: 1%
Acceptance rate (master's): 42%
Acceptance rate (doctoral): 13%
Entrance test required: GRE
Avg. GRE (of all entering students with scores): quantitative: 147; verbal: 151
Research assistantships: 12
Students reporting specialty: 100%
Students specializing in: curriculum/instr.: 5%; admin.: 13%; policy: 1%; evaluation/research/statistics: 3%; instructional media design: 9%; educational psych: 5%; elementary: 4%; secondary: 5%; special: 4%; counseling: 16%; technical (vocational): 1%; other: 36%

Western Michigan University
1903 W. Michigan Avenue
Kalamazoo, MI 49008-5229
wmich.edu/education
Public
Admissions: (269) 387-2000
Email: ask-wmu@wmich.edu
Financial aid: (269) 387-6000
Application deadline: rolling
In-state tuition: full time: $555/credit hour; part time: $555/credit hour
Out-of-state tuition: full time: $1,175/credit hour
Room/board/expenses: $14,120
Full-time enrollment: 687
doctoral students: 16%; master's students: 84%; education specialists: 0%; men: 29%; women: 71%; minorities: 23%; international: 13%
Part-time enrollment: 673
doctoral students: 24%; master's students: 74%; education specialists: 2%; men: 30%; women: 70%; minorities: 18%; international: 6%
Acceptance rate (master's): 71%
Acceptance rate (doctoral): 34%
Entrance test required: GRE
Avg. GRE (of all entering students with scores): quantitative: 148; verbal: 151
Research assistantships: 71
Students reporting specialty: 100%
Students specializing in: admin.: 16%; evaluation/research/statistics: 3%; educational tech.: 3%; higher education admin.:

5%; secondary: 1%; social/philosophical foundations: 0%; special: 6%; counseling: 14%; technical (vocational): 2%; other: 51%

MINNESOTA

Bethel University[1]
3900 Bethel Drive
St. Paul, MN 55112-6999
gs.bethel.edu
Private
Admissions: N/A
Financial aid: N/A
Tuition: N/A
Room/board/expenses: N/A
Enrollment: N/A

Capella University[1]
225 South 6th Street
Minneapolis, MN 55402
www.capella.edu
Private
Admissions: N/A
Financial aid: N/A
Tuition: N/A
Room/board/expenses: N/A
Enrollment: N/A

Hamline University[1]
1536 Hewitt Avenue
St. Paul, MN 55104-1284
www.hamline.edu
Private
Admissions: (651) 523-2900
Email: gradprog@hamline.edu
Financial aid: N/A
Tuition: N/A
Room/board/expenses: N/A
Enrollment: N/A

Minnesota State University-Mankato[1]
118 Armstrong Hall
Mankato, MN 56001
www.mnsu.edu
Public
Admissions: N/A
Financial aid: N/A
Tuition: N/A
Room/board/expenses: N/A
Enrollment: N/A

St. Cloud State University[1]
720 S. Fourth Avenue
St. Cloud, MN 56301
www.stcloudstate.edu
Public
Admissions: N/A
Financial aid: N/A
Tuition: N/A
Room/board/expenses: N/A
Enrollment: N/A

St. Mary's University of Minnesota
700 Terrace Heights
Winona, MN 55987-1700
www.smumn.edu
Private
Admissions: N/A
Email: tcadmission@smumn.edu
Financial aid: (612) 238-4566
Application deadline: rolling
Tuition: full time: N/A; part time: N/A
Room/board/expenses: N/A
Full-time enrollment: 1,008
doctoral students: 6%; master's students: 92%; education

specialists: 2%; men: 30%; women: 70%; minorities: 7%; international: 1%
Part-time enrollment: 506 doctoral students: 27%; master's students: 70%; education specialists: 3%; men: 29%; women: 71%; minorities: 5%; international: 1%
Acceptance rate (master's): N/A
Acceptance rate (doctoral): N/A
Entrance test required: N/A
Avg. GRE (of all entering students with scores): quantitative: N/A; verbal: N/A
Students reporting specialty: 100%
Students specializing in: curriculum/instr.: 4%; admin.: 28%; instructional media design: 5%; special: 14%; other: 48%

University of Minnesota-Duluth
1207 Ordean Court
Duluth, MN 55812
www.d.umn.edu/educ/academics/programs/MastersPrograms.html
Public
Admissions: (612) 625-3014
Email: gsquest@umn.edu
Financial aid: (218) 726-8000
Application deadline: 04/15
In-state tuition: full time: $660/credit hour; part time: $660/credit hour
Out-of-state tuition: full time: $1,046/credit hour
Room/board/expenses: $11,044
Full-time enrollment: 46 doctoral students: 13%; master's students: 87%; education specialists: N/A; men: 41%; women: 59%; minorities: 18%; international: 4%
Part-time enrollment: 53 doctoral students: 32%; master's students: 68%; education specialists: N/A; men: 34%; women: 66%; minorities: 28%; international: 2%
Acceptance rate (master's): 91%
Acceptance rate (doctoral): N/A
Entrance test required: GRE
Avg. GRE (of all entering students with scores): quantitative: N/A; verbal: N/A
Research assistantships: 1
Students reporting specialty: 100%
Students specializing in: admin.: 5%; other: 95%

University of Minnesota-Twin Cities
104 Burton Hall
178 Pillsbury Drive SE
Minneapolis, MN 55455
www.cehd.umn.edu
Public
Admissions: (612) 625-3339
Email: cehdinfo@umn.edu
Financial aid: (612) 624-1111
Application deadline: rolling
In-state tuition: full time: $17,367; part time: $1,353/credit hour
Out-of-state tuition: full time: $26,247
Room/board/expenses: $15,320
Full-time enrollment: 1,177 doctoral students: 40%; master's students: 60%; education specialists: 0%; men: 28%; women: 72%; minorities: 21%; international: 10%
Part-time enrollment: 491 doctoral students: 45%; master's students: 54%; education specialists: 1%; men:

31%; women: 69%; minorities: 21%; international: 5%
Acceptance rate (master's): 51%
Acceptance rate (doctoral): 28%
Entrance test required: GRE
Avg. GRE (of all entering students with scores): quantitative: 152; verbal: 156
Research assistantships: 292
Students reporting specialty: 100%
Students specializing in: curriculum/instr.: 10%; admin.: 3%; evaluation/research/statistics: 1%; educational psych: 4%; educational tech.: 2%; elementary: 4%; higher education admin.: 5%; secondary: 17%; social/philosophical foundations: 4%; special: 6%; counseling: 4%; other: 40%

University of St. Thomas
1000 LaSalle Avenue
Minneapolis, MN 55403
www.stthomas.edu/education
Private
Admissions: (651) 962-4550
Email: education@stthomas.edu
Financial aid: (651) 962-6550
Application deadline: rolling
Tuition: full time: $750/credit hour; part time: $750/credit hour
Room/board/expenses: $14,740
Full-time enrollment: 352 doctoral students: 12%; master's students: 76%; education specialists: 12%; men: 36%; women: 64%; minorities: 21%; international: 7%
Part-time enrollment: 277 doctoral students: 29%; master's students: 65%; education specialists: 7%; men: 33%; women: 67%; minorities: 13%; international: 2%
Acceptance rate (master's): 98%
Acceptance rate (doctoral): 83%
Entrance test required: N/A
Avg. GRE (of all entering students with scores): quantitative: N/A; verbal: N/A
Research assistantships: 3
Students reporting specialty: 100%
Students specializing in: curriculum/instr.: 3%; admin.: 26%; elementary: 4%; higher education admin.: 5%; secondary: 4%; special: 41%; other: 28%

Walden University[1]
155 Fifth Avenue, S
Minneapolis, MN 55401
www.waldenu.edu/acad-prog/index.html
Private
Admissions: N/A
Financial aid: N/A
Tuition: N/A
Room/board/expenses: N/A
Enrollment: N/A

MISSISSIPPI

Delta State University[1]
1003 W. Sunflower Road
Cleveland, MS 38733
deltastate.edu/pages/251.asp
Public
Admissions: (662) 846-4875
Email: grad-info@deltastate.edu
Financial aid: (662) 846-4670
Tuition: N/A
Room/board/expenses: N/A
Enrollment: N/A

Jackson State University[1]
1400 John R. Lynch Street
Administration Tower
Jackson, MS 39217
www.jsums.edu/
Public
Admissions: N/A
Financial aid: N/A
Tuition: N/A
Room/board/expenses: N/A
Enrollment: N/A

Mississippi College[1]
P.O. Box 4026
Clinton, MS 39058
www.mc.edu/
Private
Admissions: (601) 925-7617
Email: mdavis@mc.edu
Financial aid: (601) 925-3249
Tuition: N/A
Room/board/expenses: N/A
Enrollment: N/A

Mississippi State University
PO Box 9710
Mississippi State, MS 39762
www.educ.msstate.edu/
Public
Admissions: (662) 325-2224
Email: grad@grad.msstate.edu
Financial aid: (662) 325-2450
Application deadline: rolling
In-state tuition: full time: $7,780; part time: $426/credit hour
Out-of-state tuition: full time: $20,900
Room/board/expenses: $18,726
Full-time enrollment: 264 doctoral students: 25%; master's students: 69%; education specialists: 6%; men: 39%; women: 61%; minorities: 28%; international: 6%
Part-time enrollment: 458 doctoral students: 40%; master's students: 49%; education specialists: 10%; men: 27%; women: 73%; minorities: 37%; international: 0%
Acceptance rate (master's): 65%
Acceptance rate (doctoral): 52%
Entrance test required: GRE
Avg. GRE (of all entering students with scores): quantitative: 144; verbal: 146
Research assistantships: 11
Students reporting specialty: 100%
Students specializing in: curriculum/instr.: 5%; admin.: 24%; educational psych: 5%; educational tech.: 7%; elementary: 2%; junior high: 8%; secondary: 9%; special: 2%; counseling: 19%; technical (vocational): 0%; other: 18%

University of Mississippi
222 Guyton Hall
University, MS 38677
education.olemiss.edu
Public
Admissions: (662) 915-7226
Email: admissions@olemiss.edu
Financial aid: (662) 915-5788
Application deadline: 03/01
In-state tuition: full time: $425/credit hour; part time: $425/credit hour
Out-of-state tuition: full time: $1,217/credit hour
Room/board/expenses: $17,400

Full-time enrollment: 191 doctoral students: 18%; master's students: 73%; education specialists: 9%; men: 21%; women: 79%; minorities: 25%; international: 2%
Part-time enrollment: 412 doctoral students: 42%; master's students: 44%; education specialists: 14%; men: 27%; women: 73%; minorities: 39%; international: 1%
Acceptance rate (master's): 66%
Acceptance rate (doctoral): 70%
Entrance test required: GRE
Avg. GRE (of all entering students with scores): quantitative: 144; verbal: 147
Research assistantships: 22
Students reporting specialty: 100%
Students specializing in: curriculum/instr.: 8%; admin.: 21%; elementary: 14%; higher education admin.: 31%; secondary: 8%; special: 3%; counseling: 15%

University of Southern Mississippi
118 College Drive, Box 5023
Hattiesburg, MS 39406
www.usm.edu/graduate-school
Public
Admissions: (601) 266-5137
Financial aid: (601) 266-4774
Application deadline: N/A
In-state tuition: full time: $7,659; part time: $426/credit hour
Out-of-state tuition: full time: $16,529
Room/board/expenses: $219
Full-time enrollment: 146 doctoral students: 36%; master's students: 64%; education specialists: 0%; men: 29%; women: 71%; minorities: 32%; international: 10%
Part-time enrollment: 422 doctoral students: 49%; master's students: 47%; education specialists: 4%; men: 25%; women: 75%; minorities: 31%; international: 1%
Acceptance rate (master's): 29%
Acceptance rate (doctoral): 13%
Entrance test required: GRE
Avg. GRE (of all entering students with scores): quantitative: 144; verbal: 147
Students reporting specialty: 100%
Students specializing in: curriculum/instr.: 2%; admin.: 7%; instructional media design: 6%; higher education admin.: 12%; secondary: 2%; special: 10%; counseling: 7%; other: 54%

William Carey University
498 Tuscan Avenue
Hattiesburg, MS 39401-5499
www.wmcarey.edu/
Private
Admissions: (601) 318-6774
Email: alyssa.king@wmcarey.edu
Financial aid: (601) 318-6153
Application deadline: 08/18
Tuition: full time: $6,300; part time: $350/credit hour
Room/board/expenses: $10,575
Full-time enrollment: 579 doctoral students: 17%; master's students: 45%; education specialists: 38%; men: 22%; women: 78%; minorities: 36%; international: 0%

Part-time enrollment: 371 doctoral students: 3%; master's students: 77%; education specialists: 20%; men: 26%; women: 74%; minorities: 22%; international: 0%
Acceptance rate (master's): 100%
Acceptance rate (doctoral): 100%
Entrance test required: GRE
Avg. GRE (of all entering students with scores): quantitative: 132; verbal: 154
Research assistantships: 0
Students reporting specialty: 100%
Students specializing in: curriculum/instr.: 31%; admin.: 23%; elementary: 22%; higher education admin.: 6%; secondary: 9%; special: 10%

MISSOURI

Lindenwood University[1]
209 S. Kingshighway
St. Charles, MO 63301
www.lindenwood.edu
Private
Admissions: (636) 949-4933
Email: eveningadmissions@lindenwood.edu
Financial aid: (636) 949-4923
Tuition: N/A
Room/board/expenses: N/A
Enrollment: N/A

Maryville University of St. Louis
650 Maryville University Drive
St. Louis, MO 63141
maryville.edu
Private
Admissions: (314) 529-9350
Email: admissions@maryville.edu
Financial aid: (314) 529-9361
Application deadline: 08/15
Tuition: full time: $27,958; part time: $781/credit hour
Room/board/expenses: $12,488
Full-time enrollment: 10 doctoral students: N/A; master's students: 100%; education specialists: N/A; men: 10%; women: 90%; minorities: 17%; international: 17%
Part-time enrollment: 283 doctoral students: 83%; master's students: 17%; education specialists: N/A; men: 30%; women: 70%; minorities: 30%; international: 1%
Acceptance rate (master's): 100%
Acceptance rate (doctoral): 100%
Entrance test required: N/A
Avg. GRE (of all entering students with scores): quantitative: N/A; verbal: N/A
Students reporting specialty: 100%
Students specializing in: curriculum/instr.: 5%; admin.: 68%; elementary: 1%; higher education admin.: 17%; junior high: 0%; special: 2%; other: 7%

Missouri Baptist University[1]
1 College Park Drive
St. Louis, MO 63141
www.mobap.edu/academics/graduate-education-division/
Private
Admissions: N/A
Financial aid: N/A
Tuition: N/A
Room/board/expenses: N/A
Enrollment: N/A

Southwest Baptist University[1]

1600 University Avenue
Bolivar, MO 65613
sbuniv.edu/academics/graduate/
graduate-education.php
Private
Admissions: N/A
Financial aid: N/A
Tuition: N/A
Room/board/expenses: N/A
Enrollment: N/A

St. Louis University

3500 Lindell Boulevard
St. Louis, MO 63103-3412
www.slu.edu/x7039.xml
Private
Admissions: (314) 977-2500
Email: mwikete@slu.edu
Financial aid: (314) 977-2350
Application deadline: 07/01
Tuition: full time: $1,075/credit
hour; part time: $1,075/credit
hour
Room/board/expenses: $18,540
Full-time enrollment: 184
doctoral students: 85%;
master's students: 14%;
education specialists: 1%; men:
34%; women: 66%; minorities:
22%; international: 16%
Part-time enrollment: 50
doctoral students: 68%;
master's students: 30%;
education specialists: 2%; men:
30%; women: 70%; minorities:
16%; international: 4%
Acceptance rate (master's): 81%
Acceptance rate (doctoral): 80%
Entrance test required: GRE
**Avg. GRE (of all entering students
with scores):** quantitative: 145;
verbal: 147
Research assistantships: 0
Students reporting specialty: N/A
Students specializing in: N/A

University of Central Missouri

Lovinger 2190
Warrensburg, MO 64093
www.ucmo.edu/graduate
Public
Admissions: (660) 543-4897
Email: GradInfo@ucmo.edu
Financial aid: (660) 543-8266
Application deadline: rolling
In-state tuition: full time: $278/
credit hour; part time: $278/
credit hour
Out-of-state tuition: full time:
$557/credit hour
Room/board/expenses: $8,318
Full-time enrollment: 132
doctoral students: 0%; master's
students: 95%; education
specialists: 5%; men: 23%;
women: 77%; minorities: 13%;
international: 3%
Part-time enrollment: 721
doctoral students: 2%; master's
students: 76%; education
specialists: 21%; men: 20%;
women: 80%; minorities: 9%;
international: 0%
Acceptance rate (master's): N/A
Acceptance rate (doctoral): N/A
Entrance test required: GRE
**Avg. GRE (of all entering students
with scores):** quantitative: N/A;
verbal: N/A
Students reporting specialty: 100%
Students specializing in:
curriculum/instr.: 12%; admin.:
17%; instructional media

design: 13%; elementary: 6%;
higher education admin.: 8%;
secondary: 3%; special: 4%;
counseling: 1%; other: 36%

University of Missouri

118 Hill Hall
Columbia, MO 65211
education.missouri.edu
Public
Admissions: (573) 882-6311
Email: gradadmin@missouri.edu
Financial aid: (573) 882-7506
Application deadline: 07/01
In-state tuition: full time: $353/
credit hour; part time: $353/
credit hour
Out-of-state tuition: full time:
$966/credit hour
Room/board/expenses: $19,806
Full-time enrollment: 640
doctoral students: 51%; master's
students: 46%; education
specialists: 3%; men: 33%;
women: 67%; minorities: 16%;
international: 9%
Part-time enrollment: 733
doctoral students: 19%; master's
students: 71%; education
specialists: 10%; men: 35%;
women: 65%; minorities: 8%;
international: 2%
Acceptance rate (master's): 67%
Acceptance rate (doctoral): 22%
Entrance test required: GRE
**Avg. GRE (of all entering students
with scores):** quantitative: 150;
verbal: 153
Research assistantships: 110
Students reporting specialty: 100%
Students specializing in:
curriculum/instr.: 23%; admin.:
23%; policy: 1%; evaluation/
research/statistics: 1%;
instructional media design:
16%; educational psych: 3%;
educational tech.: 5%; special:
4%; counseling: 26%

University of Missouri-Kansas City

5100 Rockhill Road
Kansas City, MO 64110-2499
www.umkc.edu/
Public
Admissions: (816) 235-1111
Email: admit@umkc.edu
Financial aid: (816) 235-1154
Application deadline: 06/15
In-state tuition: full time: $359/
credit hour; part time: $359/
credit hour
Out-of-state tuition: full time:
$926/credit hour
Room/board/expenses: $14,808
Full-time enrollment: 136
doctoral students: 26%;
master's students: 71%;
education specialists: 3%; men:
24%; women: 76%; minorities:
26%; international: 8%
Part-time enrollment: 275
doctoral students: 19%; master's
students: 68%; education
specialists: 13%; men: 29%;
women: 71%; minorities: 26%;
international: 3%
Acceptance rate (master's): 44%
Acceptance rate (doctoral): 20%
Entrance test required: GRE
**Avg. GRE (of all entering students
with scores):** quantitative: 147;
verbal: 157
Research assistantships: 24
Students reporting specialty: 100%
Students specializing in:
curriculum/instr.: 22%; admin.:
20%; educational psych:

9%; secondary: 1%; social/
philosophical foundations: 0%;
special: 3%; counseling: 22%;
other: 23%

University of Missouri-St. Louis[1]

1 University Boulevard
St. Louis, MO 63121
coe.umsl.edu
Public
Admissions: (314) 516-5458
Email: gradadm@umsl.edu
Financial aid: (314) 516-5508
Tuition: N/A
Room/board/expenses: N/A
Enrollment: N/A

Washington University in St. Louis

1 Brookings Drive, Box 1183
St. Louis, MO 63130-4899
education.wustl.edu
Private
Admissions: (314) 935-6791
Email: rludy@wustl.edu
Financial aid: (314) 935-6880
Application deadline: N/A
Tuition: full time: $51,282; part
time: $2,040/credit hour
Room/board/expenses: N/A
Full-time enrollment: 25
doctoral students: 44%;
master's students: 56%;
education specialists: N/A; men:
24%; women: 76%; minorities:
19%; international: 19%
Part-time enrollment: 2
doctoral students: 0%; master's
students: 100%; education
specialists: N/A; men: 100%;
women: N/A; minorities: 33%;
international: 0%
Acceptance rate (master's): 74%
Acceptance rate (doctoral): 13%
Entrance test required: GRE
**Avg. GRE (of all entering students
with scores):** quantitative: 154;
verbal: 155
Research assistantships: 0
Students reporting specialty: 100%
Students specializing in: policy:
38%; elementary: 41%;
secondary: 21%

William Woods University

One University Avenue
Fulton, MO 65251
www.williamwoods.edu/
academics/graduate/
education_graduate/index.html
Private
Admissions: (800) 995-3159
Financial aid: (573) 592-1793
Application deadline: rolling
Tuition: full time: $325/credit
hour; part time: $325/credit hour
Room/board/expenses: $2,450
Full-time enrollment: 50
doctoral students: 0%; master's
students: 68%; education
specialists: 32%; men: 44%;
women: 56%; minorities: 8%;
international: 0%
Part-time enrollment: 903
doctoral students: 17%; master's
students: 54%; education
specialists: 29%; men: 38%;
women: 62%; minorities: 5%;
international: 0%
Acceptance rate (master's): 72%
Acceptance rate (doctoral): 65%
Entrance test required: N/A

**Avg. GRE (of all entering students
with scores):** quantitative: N/A;
verbal: N/A
Research assistantships: 20
Students reporting specialty: 100%
Students specializing in:
curriculum/instr.: 13%; admin.:
79%; instructional media design:
5%; other: 3%

MONTANA

Montana State University

215 Reid Hall
Bozeman, MT 59717
www.montana.edu/wwweduc/
Public
Admissions: (406) 994-4145
Email: gradstudy@montana.edu
Financial aid: (406) 994-2845
Application deadline: 04/01
In-state tuition: full time: $5,200;
part time: $267/credit hour
Out-of-state tuition: full time:
$16,200
Room/board/expenses: $9,850
Full-time enrollment: 173
doctoral students: 25%;
master's students: 75%;
education specialists: 0%; men:
35%; women: 65%; minorities:
4%; international: 5%
Part-time enrollment: 70
doctoral students: 57%; master's
students: 43%; education
specialists: 0%; men: 29%;
women: 71%; minorities: 9%;
international: 1%
Acceptance rate (master's): 83%
Acceptance rate (doctoral): 54%
Entrance test required: GRE
**Avg. GRE (of all entering students
with scores):** quantitative: 159;
verbal: 152
Research assistantships: 3
Students reporting specialty: 100%
Students specializing in:
curriculum/instr.: 23%;
admin.: 26%; higher education
admin.: 16%; secondary: 17%;
counseling: 2%; other: 21%

University of Montana

PJWEC Room 321
Missoula, MT 59812
www.coehs.umt.edu
Public
Admissions: (406) 243-2572
Email:
grad.school@umontana.edu
Financial aid: (406) 243-5373
Application deadline: rolling
In-state tuition: full time: $6,981;
part time: $215/credit hour
Out-of-state tuition: full time:
$16,472
Room/board/expenses: $14,076
Full-time enrollment: 361
doctoral students: 21%; master's
students: 78%; education
specialists: 1%; men: 30%;
women: 70%; minorities: N/A;
international: N/A
Part-time enrollment: N/A
doctoral students: N/A; master's
students: N/A; education
specialists: N/A; men: N/A;
women: N/A; minorities: N/A;
international: N/A
Acceptance rate (master's): 50%
Acceptance rate (doctoral): 74%
Entrance test required: GRE
**Avg. GRE (of all entering students
with scores):** quantitative: 149;
verbal: 153
Research assistantships: 5
Students reporting specialty: 100%

Students specializing in:
curriculum/instr.: 46%; admin.:
22%; counseling: 17%; other:
15%

NEBRASKA

College of St. Mary

7000 Mercy Road
Omaha, NE 68106
www.csm.edu
Private
Admissions: (800) 926-5534
Email: enroll@csm.edu
Financial aid: (402) 399-2415
Application deadline: rolling
Tuition: full time: $635/credit
hour; part time: $635/credit hour
Room/board/expenses: $12,656
Full-time enrollment: 85
doctoral students: 11%; master's
students: 89%; education
specialists: 0%; men: 7%;
women: 93%; minorities: 18%;
international: 0%
Part-time enrollment: 43
doctoral students: 67%; master's
students: 33%; education
specialists: 0%; men: 9%;
women: 91%; minorities: 6%;
international: 0%
Acceptance rate (master's): 79%
Acceptance rate (doctoral): 38%
Entrance test required: N/A
**Avg. GRE (of all entering students
with scores):** quantitative: N/A;
verbal: N/A
Research assistantships: 0
Students reporting specialty: 100%
Students specializing in:
curriculum/instr.: 6%; admin.:
28%; elementary: 24%;
secondary: 21%; special: 16%;
other: 4%

University of Nebraska-Lincoln

233 Mabel Lee Hall
Lincoln, NE 68588-0234
cehs.unl.edu
Public
Admissions: (402) 472-2878
Email: graduate@unl.edu
Financial aid: (402) 472-2030
Application deadline: rolling
In-state tuition: full time: $297/
credit hour; part time: $297/
credit hour
Out-of-state tuition: full time:
$850/credit hour
Room/board/expenses: $12,644
Full-time enrollment: 314
doctoral students: 44%;
master's students: 55%;
education specialists: 1%; men:
23%; women: 77%; minorities:
14%; international: 16%
Part-time enrollment: 526
doctoral students: 51%; master's
students: 48%; education
specialists: 1%; men: 31%;
women: 69%; minorities: 10%;
international: 3%
Acceptance rate (master's): 30%
Acceptance rate (doctoral): 26%
Entrance test required: GRE
**Avg. GRE (of all entering students
with scores):** quantitative: 150;
verbal: 152
Research assistantships: 154
Students reporting specialty: 100%
Students specializing in:
curriculum/instr.: 16%; admin.:
25%; evaluation/research/
statistics: 3%; instructional
media design: 2%; educational

psych: 14%; educational tech.: 1%; elementary: 8%; higher education admin.: 14%; secondary: 3%; special: 18%; counseling: 10%

University of Nebraska-Omaha[1]
6001 Dodge Street
Omaha, NE 68182
www.unomaha.edu
Public
Admissions: (402) 554-2936
Email: graduate@unomaha.edu
Financial aid: (402) 554-3408
Tuition: N/A
Room/board/expenses: N/A
Enrollment: N/A

NEVADA

University of Nevada-Las Vegas
4505 Maryland Parkway
Box 453001
Las Vegas, NV 89154-3001
www.unlv.edu/gradcollege/futurestudents
Public
Admissions: (702) 895-3320
Email: GradAdmissions@unlv.edu
Financial aid: (702) 895-3424
Application deadline: 06/01
In-state tuition: full time: $4,752; part time: $264/credit hour
Out-of-state tuition: full time: $18,662
Room/board/expenses: $16,170
Full-time enrollment: 594
doctoral students: 10%; master's students: 87%; education specialists: 3%; men: 24%; women: 76%; minorities: 44%; international: 2%
Part-time enrollment: 516
doctoral students: 29%; master's students: 69%; education specialists: 2%; men: 29%; women: 71%; minorities: 36%; international: 2%
Acceptance rate (master's): 71%
Acceptance rate (doctoral): 68%
Entrance test required: GRE
Avg. GRE (of all entering students with scores): quantitative: N/A; verbal: N/A
Research assistantships: 57
Students reporting specialty: 100%
Students specializing in: curriculum/instr.: 43%; policy: 0%; educational psych: 8%; higher education admin.: 7%; special: 26%; counseling: 7%; other: 9%

University of Nevada-Reno
MS278
Reno, NV 89557-0278
www.unr.edu/grad
Public
Admissions: (775) 784-6869
Email: gradadmissions@unr.edu
Financial aid: (775) 784-4666
Application deadline: rolling
In-state tuition: full time: $264/credit hour; part time: $264/credit hour
Out-of-state tuition: full time: $15,372
Room/board/expenses: $19,248
Full-time enrollment: 209
doctoral students: 19%; master's students: 81%; education specialists: N/A; men: 34%; women: 66%; minorities: 27%; international: 4%

Part-time enrollment: 306
doctoral students: 21%; master's students: 79%; education specialists: N/A; men: 30%; women: 70%; minorities: 28%; international: 2%
Acceptance rate (master's): 68%
Acceptance rate (doctoral): 82%
Entrance test required: GRE
Avg. GRE (of all entering students with scores): quantitative: 147; verbal: 154
Research assistantships: 10
Students reporting specialty: 100%
Students specializing in: curriculum/instr.: 0%; admin.: 14%; educational tech.: 2%; elementary: 13%; higher education admin.: 14%; secondary: 15%; social/philosophical foundations: 8%; special: 12%; counseling: 5%; other: 18%

NEW HAMPSHIRE

New England College[1]
98 Bridge Street
Henniker, NH 03242
www.nec.edu
Private
Admissions: (603) 428-2906
Email: graduateadmission@nec.edu
Financial aid: (603) 428-2226
Tuition: N/A
Room/board/expenses: N/A
Enrollment: N/A

Plymouth State University[1]
17 High Street, MSC 11
Plymouth, NH 03264
www.plymouth.edu/
Public
Admissions: N/A
Financial aid: N/A
Tuition: N/A
Room/board/expenses: N/A
Enrollment: N/A

Rivier University[1]
420 Main Street
Nashua, NH 03060
www.rivier.edu/
Private
Admissions: N/A
Financial aid: N/A
Tuition: N/A
Room/board/expenses: N/A
Enrollment: N/A

University of New Hampshire
Morrill Hall
Durham, NH 03824-3595
www.unh.edu/education/
Public
Admissions: (603) 862-3446
Email: goergia.kerns@unh.edu
Financial aid: (603) 862-3600
Application deadline: rolling
In-state tuition: full time: $15,920; part time: $770/credit hour
Out-of-state tuition: full time: $29,210
Room/board/expenses: $4,411
Full-time enrollment: 90
doctoral students: 36%; master's students: 64%; education specialists: 0%; men: 23%; women: 77%; minorities: 0%; international: 3%
Part-time enrollment: 165
doctoral students: 14%; master's students: 81%; education

---

specialists: 5%; men: 28%; women: 72%; minorities: 6%; international: 2%
Acceptance rate (master's): 88%
Acceptance rate (doctoral): 76%
Entrance test required: GRE
Avg. GRE (of all entering students with scores): quantitative: 148; verbal: 154
Research assistantships: 1
Students reporting specialty: 100%
Students specializing in: admin.: 4%; evaluation/research/statistics: 21%; elementary: 17%; secondary: 27%; special: 11%; counseling: 2%; other: 18%

NEW JERSEY

College of St. Elizabeth
2 Convent Road
Morristown, NJ 07960-6989
www.cse.edu
Private
Admissions: (800) 210-7900
Email: apply@cse.edu
Financial aid: (973) 290-4432
Application deadline: rolling
Tuition: full time: $1,001/credit hour; part time: $1,001/credit hour
Room/board/expenses: $13,494
Full-time enrollment: 20
doctoral students: 5%; master's students: 95%; education specialists: 0%; men: 30%; women: 70%; minorities: 20%; international: 0%
Part-time enrollment: 86
doctoral students: 58%; master's students: 42%; education specialists: 0%; men: 28%; women: 72%; minorities: 25%; international: 0%
Acceptance rate (master's): 55%
Acceptance rate (doctoral): 68%
Entrance test required: N/A
Avg. GRE (of all entering students with scores): quantitative: N/A; verbal: N/A
Students reporting specialty: 0%
Students specializing in: N/A

Kean University[1]
1000 Morris Avenue
Union, NJ 07083
www.kean.edu/
Public
Admissions: N/A
Financial aid: N/A
Tuition: N/A
Room/board/expenses: N/A
Enrollment: N/A

Montclair State University
1 Normal Avenue
Upper Montclair, NJ 07043
cehs.montclair.edu/
Public
Admissions: (973) 655-5147
Email: Graduate.School@montclair.edu
Application deadline: rolling
In-state tuition: full time: $581/credit hour; part time: $581/credit hour
Out-of-state tuition: full time: $879/credit hour
Room/board/expenses: N/A
Full-time enrollment: 643
doctoral students: 5%; master's students: 95%; education specialists: N/A; men: 27%; women: 73%; minorities: 27%; international: 4%

Part-time enrollment: 1,100
doctoral students: 10%; master's students: 90%; education specialists: N/A; men: 24%; women: 76%; minorities: 28%; international: 1%
Acceptance rate (master's): 69%
Acceptance rate (doctoral): 43%
Entrance test required: GRE
Avg. GRE (of all entering students with scores): quantitative: 145; verbal: 148
Research assistantships: 97
Students reporting specialty: 100%
Students specializing in: admin.: 21%; evaluation/research/statistics: 0%; special: 6%; counseling: 16%; other: 57%

Rowan University
201 Mullica Hill Road
Glassboro, NJ 08028
www.rowan.edu/
Public
Admissions: (856) 256-4747
Email: global@rowan.edu
Financial aid: (856) 256-5141
Application deadline: 07/01
In-state tuition: full time: $670/credit hour; part time: $670/credit hour
Out-of-state tuition: full time: $670/credit hour
Room/board/expenses: N/A
Full-time enrollment: 173
doctoral students: 6%; master's students: 80%; education specialists: 14%; men: 16%; women: 84%; minorities: 26%; international: 1%
Part-time enrollment: 527
doctoral students: 34%; master's students: 61%; education specialists: 5%; men: 21%; women: 79%; minorities: 19%; international: 1%
Acceptance rate (master's): 37%
Acceptance rate (doctoral): 61%
Entrance test required: GRE
Avg. GRE (of all entering students with scores): quantitative: 141; verbal: 141
Students reporting specialty: 100%
Students specializing in: admin.: 37%; educational psych: 6%; special: 9%; counseling: 8%; other: 51%

Rutgers, The State University of New Jersey- New Brunswick
10 Seminary Place
New Brunswick, NJ 08901-1183
www.gse.rutgers.edu
Public
Admissions: (732) 932-7711
Email: grad_help@gradadm.rutgers.edu
Financial aid: (848) 932-7057
Application deadline: 02/01
In-state tuition: full time: $19,655; part time: $689/credit hour
Out-of-state tuition: full time: $30,047
Room/board/expenses: $18,524
Full-time enrollment: 379
doctoral students: 10%; master's students: 90%; education specialists: N/A; men: 27%; women: 73%; minorities: 31%; international: 5%
Part-time enrollment: 420
doctoral students: 50%; master's students: 50%;

---

education specialists: N/A; men: 29%; women: 71%; minorities: 24%; international: 1%
Acceptance rate (master's): 67%
Acceptance rate (doctoral): 55%
Entrance test required: GRE
Avg. GRE (of all entering students with scores): quantitative: 149; verbal: 151
Research assistantships: 0
Students reporting specialty: 100%
Students specializing in: admin.: 10%; policy: 1%; evaluation/research/statistics: 2%; instructional media design: 3%; educational psych: 4%; educational tech.: 1%; elementary: 10%; higher education admin.: 7%; junior high: 3%; secondary: 23%; social/philosophical foundations: 5%; special: 29%; counseling: 4%; other: 14%

Seton Hall University[1]
400 S. Orange Avenue
South Orange, NJ 07079
www.shu.edu/academics/education/
Private
Admissions: N/A
Financial aid: N/A
Tuition: N/A
Room/board/expenses: N/A
Enrollment: N/A

St. Peter's University[1]
2641 Kennedy Boulevard
Jersey City, NJ 07306
www.saintpeters.edu/school-of-education/curriculum/graduate-programs/
Private
Admissions: N/A
Financial aid: N/A
Tuition: N/A
Room/board/expenses: N/A
Enrollment: N/A

NEW MEXICO

New Mexico State University
PO Box 30001, MSC 3AC
Las Cruces, NM 88003-8001
education.nmsu.edu
Public
Admissions: (575) 646-3121
Email: admissions@nmsu.edu
Financial aid: (575) 646-4105
Application deadline: N/A
In-state tuition: full time: $4,941; part time: $227/credit hour
Out-of-state tuition: full time: $15,107
Room/board/expenses: $13,050
Full-time enrollment: 277
doctoral students: 31%; master's students: 62%; education specialists: 7%; men: 23%; women: 77%; minorities: N/A; international: N/A
Part-time enrollment: 417
doctoral students: 32%; master's students: 65%; education specialists: 3%; men: 26%; women: 74%; minorities: N/A; international: N/A
Acceptance rate (master's): 45%
Acceptance rate (doctoral): 47%
Entrance test required: GRE
Avg. GRE (of all entering students with scores): quantitative: 144; verbal: 147
Research assistantships: 29
Students reporting specialty: 100%

Students specializing in: curriculum/instr.: 48%; admin.: 18%; educational psych: 4%; special: 17%; counseling: 9%; other: 6%

University of New Mexico

MSC05 3040
Albuquerque, NM 87131-0001
www.unm.edu
Public
Admissions: (505) 277-2447
Email: unmlobos@unm.edu
Financial aid: (505) 277-8900
Application deadline: rolling
In-state tuition: full time: $6,162; part time: $324/credit hour
Out-of-state tuition: full time: $17,309
Room/board/expenses: $15,794
Full-time enrollment: 336
doctoral students: 32%; master's students: 68%; education specialists: 1%; men: 35%; women: 65%; minorities: 43%; international: 17%
Part-time enrollment: 584
doctoral students: 36%; master's students: 57%; education specialists: 8%; men: 27%; women: 73%; minorities: 50%; international: 4%
Acceptance rate (master's): 75%
Acceptance rate (doctoral): 64%
Entrance test required: GRE
Avg. GRE (of all entering students with scores): quantitative: 147; verbal: 150
Research assistantships: 22
Students reporting specialty: 100%
Students specializing in: curriculum/instr.: 2%; admin.: 14%; educational psych: 3%; elementary: 8%; secondary: 6%; social/philosophical foundations: 19%; special: 15%; counseling: 9%; other: 24%

NEW YORK

Binghamton University-SUNY

PO Box 6000
Binghamton, NY 13902-6000
gse.binghamton.edu
Public
Admissions: (607) 777-2000
Email: gradadmission@binghamton.edu
Financial aid: (607) 777-2428
Application deadline: rolling
In-state tuition: full time: $453/credit hour; part time: $453/credit hour
Out-of-state tuition: full time: $925/credit hour
Room/board/expenses: N/A
Full-time enrollment: 101
doctoral students: 3%; master's students: 97%; education specialists: N/A; men: 28%; women: 72%; minorities: 11%; international: 2%
Part-time enrollment: 100
doctoral students: 47%; master's students: 53%; education specialists: N/A; men: 26%; women: 74%; minorities: 8%; international: 2%
Acceptance rate (master's): 83%
Acceptance rate (doctoral): 100%
Entrance test required: GRE
Avg. GRE (of all entering students with scores): quantitative: 150; verbal: 152
Research assistantships: 1

Students reporting specialty: 0%
Students specializing in: N/A

CUNY-Graduate Center[1]

365 Fifth Avenue
New York, NY 10016
www.gc.cuny.edu
Public
Admissions: (212) 817-7470
Email: admissions@gc.cuny.edu
Financial aid: (212) 817-7460
Tuition: N/A
Room/board/expenses: N/A
Enrollment: N/A

Dowling College[1]

Idle Hour Boulevard
Oakdale Long Island, NY 11769
www.dowling.edu/school-education/index.shtm
Private
Admissions: (631) 244-3303
Financial aid: (631) 244-3220
Tuition: N/A
Room/board/expenses: N/A
Enrollment: N/A

D'Youville College[1]

1 D'Youville Square
320 Porter Avenue
Buffalo, NY 14201-1084
www.dyc.edu/academics/education/index.asp
Private
Admissions: (716) 829-7676
Email: graduateadmissions@dyc.edu
Financial aid: (716) 829-7500
Tuition: N/A
Room/board/expenses: N/A
Enrollment: N/A

Fordham University

113 W. 60th Street
New York, NY 10023
www.fordham.edu/gse
Private
Admissions: (212) 636-6401
Email: gse_admiss@fordham.edu
Financial aid: (212) 636-7611
Application deadline: rolling
Tuition: full time: $1,340/credit hour; part time: $1,340/credit hour
Room/board/expenses: $24,197
Full-time enrollment: 147
doctoral students: 29%; master's students: 57%; education specialists: 14%; men: 16%; women: 84%; minorities: 41%; international: 5%
Part-time enrollment: 689
doctoral students: 41%; master's students: 55%; education specialists: 4%; men: 25%; women: 75%; minorities: 39%; international: 5%
Acceptance rate (master's): 73%
Acceptance rate (doctoral): 38%
Entrance test required: GRE
Avg. GRE (of all entering students with scores): quantitative: 167; verbal: 166
Research assistantships: 60
Students reporting specialty: 100%
Students specializing in: curriculum/instr.: 3%; admin.: 24%; educational psych: 0%; elementary: 12%; secondary: 11%; special: 5%; counseling: 32%; other: 12%

Hofstra University

Hagedorn Hall
Hempstead, NY 11549
www.hofstra.edu/graduate
Private
Admissions: (516) 463-4723
Email: graduateadmission@hofstra.edu
Financial aid: (516) 463-8000
Application deadline: rolling
Tuition: full time: $1,240/credit hour; part time: $1,240/credit hour
Room/board/expenses: $22,690
Full-time enrollment: 399
doctoral students: 10%; master's students: 90%; education specialists: N/A; men: 19%; women: 81%; minorities: 19%; international: 6%
Part-time enrollment: 373
doctoral students: 35%; master's students: 65%; education specialists: N/A; men: 27%; women: 73%; minorities: 24%; international: 1%
Acceptance rate (master's): 91%
Acceptance rate (doctoral): 74%
Entrance test required: GRE
Avg. GRE (of all entering students with scores): quantitative: 148; verbal: 149
Research assistantships: 21
Students reporting specialty: 100%
Students specializing in: curriculum/instr.: 1%; admin.: 8%; instructional media design: 0%; elementary: 3%; higher education admin.: 6%; junior high: 0%; secondary: 2%; special: 19%; other: 61%

LIU Post

720 Northern Boulevard
Brookville, NY 11548
www.liu.edu/post/Academics/schools/CEIS
Private
Admissions: (516) 299-3952
Email: post-enroll@liu.edu
Financial aid: (516) 299-4212
Application deadline: rolling
Tuition: full time: $1,178/credit hour; part time: $1,178/credit hour
Room/board/expenses: $13,426
Full-time enrollment: 317
doctoral students: 0%; master's students: 100%; education specialists: N/A; men: 16%; women: 84%; minorities: 18%; international: 4%
Part-time enrollment: 419
doctoral students: 26%; master's students: 74%; education specialists: N/A; men: 20%; women: 80%; minorities: 25%; international: 1%
Acceptance rate (master's): 69%
Acceptance rate (doctoral): 84%
Entrance test required: GRE
Avg. GRE (of all entering students with scores): quantitative: N/A; verbal: N/A
Students reporting specialty: 100%
Students specializing in: admin.: 29%; educational tech.: 7%; elementary: 7%; secondary: 5%; special: 17%; counseling: 11%; other: 25%

Manhattanville College[1]

2900 Purchase Street
Purchase, NY 10577
www.mville.edu/
Private
Admissions: (914) 323-3208
Email: polia@mville.edu
Financial aid: (914) 323-5376
Tuition: N/A
Room/board/expenses: N/A
Enrollment: N/A

New York University (Steinhardt)

82 Washington Square E
Fourth Floor
New York, NY 10003
www.steinhardt.nyu.edu/
Private
Admissions: (212) 998-5030
Email: steinhardt.gradadmission@nyu.edu
Financial aid: (212) 998-4444
Application deadline: rolling
Tuition: full time: $40,736; part time: $1,596/credit hour
Room/board/expenses: $34,304
Full-time enrollment: 899
doctoral students: 22%; master's students: 78%; education specialists: N/A; men: 17%; women: 83%; minorities: 32%; international: 26%
Part-time enrollment: 532
doctoral students: 12%; master's students: 88%; education specialists: N/A; men: 21%; women: 79%; minorities: 39%; international: 15%
Acceptance rate (master's): 67%
Acceptance rate (doctoral): 7%
Entrance test required: GRE
Avg. GRE (of all entering students with scores): quantitative: 152; verbal: 154
Research assistantships: 36
Students reporting specialty: 100%
Students specializing in: admin.: 4%; policy: 2%; evaluation/research/statistics: 12%; instructional media design: 6%; elementary: 2%; higher education admin.: 9%; secondary: 1%; social/philosophical foundations: 2%; special: 0%; counseling: 14%; other: 48%

The Sage Colleges[1]

65 1st Street
Troy, NY 12180
www.sage.edu/academics/education/
Private
Admissions: N/A
Financial aid: N/A
Tuition: N/A
Room/board/expenses: N/A
Enrollment: N/A

St. John's University

8000 Utopia Parkway
Queens, NY 11439
www.stjohns.edu/soe
Private
Admissions: (718) 990-2304
Email: graded@stjohns.edu
Financial aid: (718) 990-2000
Application deadline: 08/17
Tuition: full time: $1,170/credit hour; part time: $1,170/credit hour
Room/board/expenses: $2,836
Full-time enrollment: 253
doctoral students: 9%; master's

students: 89%; education specialists: 2%; men: 17%; women: 83%; minorities: 36%; international: 11%
Part-time enrollment: 1,099
doctoral students: 27%; master's students: 55%; education specialists: 18%; men: 29%; women: 71%; minorities: 42%; international: 2%
Acceptance rate (master's): 86%
Acceptance rate (doctoral): 93%
Entrance test required: GRE
Avg. GRE (of all entering students with scores): quantitative: N/A; verbal: N/A
Research assistantships: 0
Students reporting specialty: 100%
Students specializing in: curriculum/instr.: 9%; admin.: 23%; elementary: 2%; secondary: 8%; special: 17%; counseling: 4%; other: 39%

Syracuse University

230 Huntington Hall
Syracuse, NY 13244-2340
soe.syr.edu
Private
Admissions: (315) 443-2505
Email: gradrcrt@gwmail.syr.edu
Financial aid: (315) 443-1039
Application deadline: rolling
Tuition: full time: $26,776; part time: $1,443/credit hour
Room/board/expenses: $18,146
Full-time enrollment: 345
doctoral students: 33%; master's students: 67%; education specialists: N/A; men: 28%; women: 72%; minorities: 25%; international: 22%
Part-time enrollment: 146
doctoral students: 41%; master's students: 59%; education specialists: N/A; men: 34%; women: 66%; minorities: 22%; international: 0%
Acceptance rate (master's): 68%
Acceptance rate (doctoral): 33%
Entrance test required: GRE
Avg. GRE (of all entering students with scores): quantitative: 150; verbal: 152
Research assistantships: 23
Students reporting specialty: 100%
Students specializing in: curriculum/instr.: 13%; admin.: 14%; instructional media design: 9%; elementary: 14%; higher education admin.: 15%; secondary: 17%; social/philosophical foundations: 9%; special: 11%; counseling: 14%; other: 3%

Teachers College, Columbia University

525 W. 120th Street
New York, NY 10027
www.tc.columbia.edu/
Private
Admissions: (212) 678-3710
Email: tcinfo@tc.columbia.edu
Financial aid: (212) 678-3702
Application deadline: rolling
Tuition: full time: $1,512/credit hour; part time: $1,512/credit hour
Room/board/expenses: $22,849
Full-time enrollment: 1,674
doctoral students: 23%; master's students: 77%; education specialists: N/A; men: 19%; women: 81%; minorities: 31%; international: 29%
Part-time enrollment: 3,218
doctoral students: 28%;

master's students: 72%; education specialists: N/A; men: 24%; women: 76%; minorities: 36%; international: 17%
Acceptance rate (master's): 57%
Acceptance rate (doctoral): 11%
Entrance test required: GRE
Avg. GRE (of all entering students with scores): quantitative: 154; verbal: 156
Research assistantships: 153
Students reporting specialty: 100%
Students specializing in: curriculum/instr.: 4%; admin.: 4%; evaluation/research/statistics: 3%; instructional media design: 3%; elementary: 2%; higher education admin.: 2%; social/philosophical foundations: 3%; special: 5%; other: 76%

University at Albany-SUNY

1400 Washington Avenue, ED 212
Albany, NY 12222
www.albany.edu/education
Public
Admissions: (518) 442-3980
Email: graduate@uamail.albany.edu
Financial aid: (518) 442-5757
Application deadline: rolling
In-state tuition: full time: $10,870; part time: $453/credit hour
Out-of-state tuition: full time: $22,210
Room/board/expenses: $15,417
Full-time enrollment: 336
doctoral students: 25%; master's students: 70%; education specialists: 4%; men: 25%; women: 75%; minorities: 15%; international: 13%
Part-time enrollment: 516
doctoral students: 34%; master's students: 60%; education specialists: 7%; men: 23%; women: 77%; minorities: 12%; international: 5%
Acceptance rate (master's): 78%
Acceptance rate (doctoral): 35%
Entrance test required: GRE
Avg. GRE (of all entering students with scores): quantitative: N/A; verbal: N/A
Research assistantships: 70
Students reporting specialty: 100%
Students specializing in: curriculum/instr.: 13%; admin.: 6%; policy: 3%; evaluation/research/statistics: 2%; instructional media design: 4%; educational psych: 5%; educational tech.: 0%; elementary: 5%; higher education admin.: 6%; secondary: 5%; special: 9%; counseling: 5%; other: 29%

University at Buffalo-SUNY

367 Baldy Hall
Buffalo, NY 14260-1000
www.gse.buffalo.edu
Public
Admissions: (716) 645-2110
Email: gseinfo@buffalo.edu
Financial aid: (716) 645-8232
Application deadline: rolling
In-state tuition: full time: $13,052; part time: $453/credit hour
Out-of-state tuition: full time: $24,692
Room/board/expenses: $17,781
Full-time enrollment: 430
doctoral students: 38%; master's students: 62%;

education specialists: 0%; men: 23%; women: 77%; minorities: 9%; international: 13%
Part-time enrollment: 469
doctoral students: 47%; master's students: 53%; education specialists: 0%; men: 32%; women: 68%; minorities: 12%; international: 4%
Acceptance rate (master's): 75%
Acceptance rate (doctoral): 54%
Entrance test required: GRE
Avg. GRE (of all entering students with scores): quantitative: 149; verbal: 151
Research assistantships: 79
Students reporting specialty: 100%
Students specializing in: curriculum/instr.: 20%; admin.: 6%; policy: 1%; educational psych: 3%; educational tech.: 2%; elementary: 5%; higher education admin.: 10%; secondary: 7%; social/philosophical foundations: 3%; special: 1%; counseling: 10%; other: 34%

University of Rochester (Warner)[1]

2-147 Dewey Hall
Rochester, NY 14627
www.rochester.edu/warner/
Private
Admissions: N/A
Financial aid: N/A
Tuition: N/A
Room/board/expenses: N/A
Enrollment: N/A

Yeshiva University (Azrieli)[1]

245 Lexington Avenue
New York, NY 10016
www.yu.edu/azrieli/
Private
Admissions: N/A
Financial aid: N/A
Tuition: N/A
Room/board/expenses: N/A
Enrollment: N/A

NORTH CAROLINA

Appalachian State University

College of Education Building
Boone, NC 28608-2068
graduate.appstate.edu
Public
Admissions: (828) 262-2130
Email: ParsonDO@appstate.edu
Financial aid: (828) 262-2190
Application deadline: rolling
In-state tuition: full time: $4,744; part time: $260/credit hour
Out-of-state tuition: full time: $17,913
Room/board/expenses: $4,250
Full-time enrollment: 338
doctoral students: 2%; master's students: 97%; education specialists: 1%; men: 17%; women: 83%; minorities: 14%; international: 1%
Part-time enrollment: 421
doctoral students: 19%; master's students: 71%; education specialists: 11%; men: 22%; women: 78%; minorities: 12%; international: 0%
Acceptance rate (master's): 45%
Acceptance rate (doctoral): 82%
Entrance test required: GRE
Avg. GRE (of all entering students with scores): quantitative: 148; verbal: 151

Research assistantships: 48
Students reporting specialty: 100%
Students specializing in: curriculum/instr.: 5%; admin.: 24%; instructional media design: 9%; educational psych: 2%; educational tech.: 1%; elementary: 1%; higher education admin.: 10%; junior high: 0%; secondary: 0%; special: 1%; counseling: 15%; other: 32%

East Carolina University

E. Fifth Street
Greenville, NC 27858
www.ecu.edu/gradschool/
Public
Admissions: (252) 328-6012
Email: gradschool@ecu.edu
Financial aid: (252) 328-6610
Application deadline: rolling
In-state tuition: full time: $7,237; part time: $6,073
Out-of-state tuition: full time: $20,128
Room/board/expenses: $14,694
Full-time enrollment: 216
doctoral students: 35%; master's students: 65%; education specialists: 0%; men: 28%; women: 72%; minorities: 26%; international: 0%
Part-time enrollment: 854
doctoral students: 9%; master's students: 88%; education specialists: 3%; men: 18%; women: 82%; minorities: 20%; international: 1%
Acceptance rate (master's): 86%
Acceptance rate (doctoral): 89%
Entrance test required: GRE
Avg. GRE (of all entering students with scores): quantitative: 147; verbal: 151
Research assistantships: 44
Students reporting specialty: 100%
Students specializing in: curriculum/instr.: 0%; admin.: 36%; instructional media design: 15%; elementary: 1%; higher education admin.: 1%; junior high: 1%; special: 5%; counseling: 7%; other: 39%

Fayetteville State University[1]

1200 Murchison Road
Fayetteville, NC 28301
www.uncfsu.edu/
Public
Admissions: N/A
Financial aid: N/A
Tuition: N/A
Room/board/expenses: N/A
Enrollment: N/A

Gardner-Webb University

110 S. Main Street
Boiling Springs, NC 28017
www.gardner-webb.edu
Private
Admissions: (800) 492-4723
Email: gradschool@gardner-webb.edu
Financial aid: (704) 406-3271
Application deadline: rolling
Tuition: full time: $429/credit hour; part time: $429/credit hour
Room/board/expenses: N/A
Full-time enrollment: 10
doctoral students: 100%; master's students: 0%; education specialists: 0%;

men: 30%; women: 70%; minorities: 40%; international: 0%
Part-time enrollment: 717
doctoral students: 47%; master's students: 49%; education specialists: 4%; men: 23%; women: 77%; minorities: 39%; international: 0%
Acceptance rate (master's): 46%
Acceptance rate (doctoral): 40%
Entrance test required: GRE
Avg. GRE (of all entering students with scores): quantitative: N/A; verbal: N/A
Students reporting specialty: 100%
Students specializing in: curriculum/instr.: 32%; admin.: 57%; educational tech.: 1%; higher education admin.: 12%; counseling: 3%; other: 7%

North Carolina State University-Raleigh

Campus Box 7801
Raleigh, NC 27695-7801
ced.ncsu.edu/
Public
Admissions: (919) 515-2872
Email: graduate_admissions@ncsu.edu
Financial aid: (919) 515-3325
Application deadline: N/A
In-state tuition: full time: $11,872; part time: $6,172
Out-of-state tuition: full time: $26,394
Room/board/expenses: $18,133
Full-time enrollment: 355
doctoral students: 32%; master's students: 68%; education specialists: N/A; men: 25%; women: 75%; minorities: 29%; international: 5%
Part-time enrollment: 578
doctoral students: 41%; master's students: 59%; education specialists: N/A; men: 26%; women: 74%; minorities: 24%; international: 1%
Acceptance rate (master's): 43%
Acceptance rate (doctoral): 42%
Entrance test required: GRE
Avg. GRE (of all entering students with scores): quantitative: 150; verbal: 154
Research assistantships: 28
Students reporting specialty: 100%
Students specializing in: curriculum/instr.: 12%; admin.: 25%; policy: 9%; evaluation/research/statistics: 11%; instructional media design: 3%; educational psych: 2%; elementary: 4%; higher education admin.: 5%; junior high: 3%; secondary: 8%; special: 1%; counseling: 12%; technical (vocational): 1%; other: 5%

University of North Carolina-Chapel Hill

CB#3500
101 Peabody Hall
Chapel Hill, NC 27599-3500
soe.unc.edu
Public
Admissions: (919) 966-1346
Email: ed@unc.edu
Financial aid: (919) 966-1346
Application deadline: rolling
In-state tuition: full time: $11,606; part time: $9,195
Out-of-state tuition: full time: $28,817

Room/board/expenses: $24,666
Full-time enrollment: 305
doctoral students: 58%; master's students: 42%; education specialists: 0%; men: 27%; women: 73%; minorities: 30%; international: 16%
Part-time enrollment: 82
doctoral students: 29%; master's students: 71%; education specialists: 0%; men: 18%; women: 82%; minorities: 35%; international: 2%
Acceptance rate (master's): 61%
Acceptance rate (doctoral): 28%
Entrance test required: GRE
Avg. GRE (of all entering students with scores): quantitative: N/A; verbal: N/A
Research assistantships: 34
Students reporting specialty: 100%
Students specializing in: curriculum/instr.: 8%; admin.: 24%; policy: 4%; evaluation/research/statistics: 2%; educational psych: 14%; elementary: 2%; junior high: 0%; secondary: 3%; social/philosophical foundations: 9%; special: 5%; counseling: 5%; other: 24%

University of North Carolina-Charlotte

9201 University City Boulevard
Charlotte, NC 28223
education.uncc.edu/
Public
Admissions: (704) 687-3366
Email: gradadm@uncc.edu
Financial aid: (704) 687-5547
Application deadline: N/A
In-state tuition: full time: $7,278; part time: $6,215
Out-of-state tuition: full time: $20,449
Room/board/expenses: $12,523
Full-time enrollment: 236
doctoral students: 33%; master's students: 67%; education specialists: N/A; men: 19%; women: 81%; minorities: 27%; international: 5%
Part-time enrollment: 567
doctoral students: 25%; master's students: 75%; education specialists: N/A; men: 22%; women: 78%; minorities: 29%; international: 1%
Acceptance rate (master's): 82%
Acceptance rate (doctoral): 59%
Entrance test required: GRE
Avg. GRE (of all entering students with scores): quantitative: 148; verbal: 151
Research assistantships: 38
Students reporting specialty: 100%
Students specializing in: curriculum/instr.: 5%; admin.: 11%; instructional media design: 4%; elementary: 1%; special: 7%; counseling: 16%; other: 58%

University of North Carolina-Greensboro

School of Education Building
PO Box 26170
Greensboro, NC 27402-6170
grs.uncg.edu/
Public
Admissions: (336) 334-5596
Email: gradinquiry@uncg.edu
Financial aid: (336) 334-5702
Application deadline: rolling

In-state tuition: full time: $7,823; part time: $5,265
Out-of-state tuition: full time: $21,272
Room/board/expenses: $11,106
Full-time enrollment: 419 doctoral students: 39%; master's students: 57%; education specialists: 4%; men: 23%; women: 77%; minorities: 30%; international: 4%
Part-time enrollment: 410 doctoral students: 21%; master's students: 74%; education specialists: 5%; men: 19%; women: 81%; minorities: 26%; international: 1%
Acceptance rate (master's): 45%
Acceptance rate (doctoral): 31%
Entrance test required: GRE
Avg. GRE (of all entering students with scores): quantitative: 149; verbal: 154
Research assistantships: 12
Students reporting specialty: 100%
Students specializing in: curriculum/instr.: 20%; admin.: 17%; evaluation/research/ statistics: 5%; educational psych: 0%; elementary: 3%; higher education admin.: 6%; junior high: 1%; secondary: 2%; special: 9%; counseling: 10%; other: 33%

University of North Carolina–Wilmington
601 S. College Road
Wilmington, NC 28403
uncw.edu/gradschool/
Public
Admissions: (910) 962-7449
Email: harrisk@uncw.edu
Financial aid: (910) 962-3177
Application deadline: 06/15
In-state tuition: full time: $7,044; part time: N/A
Out-of-state tuition: full time: $19,263
Room/board/expenses: $2,550
Full-time enrollment: 179 doctoral students: 3%; master's students: 97%; education specialists: 0%; men: 25%; women: 75%; minorities: 25%; international: 0%
Part-time enrollment: 365 doctoral students: 27%; master's students: 73%; education specialists: 0%; men: 18%; women: 82%; minorities: 31%; international: 0%
Acceptance rate (master's): 74%
Acceptance rate (doctoral): 50%
Entrance test required: GRE
Avg. GRE (of all entering students with scores): quantitative: N/A; verbal: N/A
Research assistantships: 0
Students reporting specialty: 100%
Students specializing in: curriculum/instr.: 4%; admin.: 26%; instructional media design: 4%; elementary: 4%; higher education admin.: 8%; junior high: 4%; secondary: 4%; other: 45%

Western Carolina University
Killian Building, Room 204
Cullowhee, NC 28723
www.wcu.edu/
Public
Admissions: (828) 227-7398
Email: grad@wcu.edu

Financial aid: (828) 227-7290
Application deadline: rolling
In-state tuition: full time: $14,480; part time: $647/credit hour
Out-of-state tuition: full time: $24,887
Room/board/expenses: $12,981
Full-time enrollment: 29 doctoral students: 0%; master's students: 34%; education specialists: 66%; men: 17%; women: 83%; minorities: 13%; international: 0%
Part-time enrollment: 230 doctoral students: 13%; master's students: 86%; education specialists: 1%; men: 20%; women: 80%; minorities: 15%; international: 1%
Acceptance rate (master's): 89%
Acceptance rate (doctoral): 50%
Entrance test required: GRE
Avg. GRE (of all entering students with scores): quantitative: N/A; verbal: N/A
Research assistantships: 22
Students reporting specialty: 100%
Students specializing in: admin.: 12%; elementary: 7%; junior high: 2%; secondary: 6%; special: 45%; counseling: 6%; other: 22%

Wingate University[1]
220 North Camden Road
Wingate, NC 28174
www.wingate.edu/matthews/ grad-ed
Private
Admissions: N/A
Financial aid: N/A
Tuition: N/A
Room/board/expenses: N/A
Enrollment: N/A

NORTH DAKOTA

North Dakota State University
Box 6050, Department 2600
Fargo, ND 58108-6050
www.ndsu.edu/gradschool/
Public
Admissions: (701) 231-7033
Email: ndsu.grad.school@ndsu.edu
Financial aid: (701) 231-6200
Application deadline: rolling
In-state tuition: full time: $310/ credit hour; part time: $310/ credit hour
Out-of-state tuition: full time: $464/credit hour
Room/board/expenses: N/A
Full-time enrollment: 33 doctoral students: 18%; master's students: 79%; education specialists: 3%; men: 6%; women: 94%; minorities: 15%; international: 0%
Part-time enrollment: 247 doctoral students: 34%; master's students: 64%; education specialists: 2%; men: 24%; women: 76%; minorities: 6%; international: 1%
Acceptance rate (master's): 75%
Acceptance rate (doctoral): 48%
Entrance test required: N/A
Avg. GRE (of all entering students with scores): quantitative: N/A; verbal: N/A
Research assistantships: 2
Students reporting specialty: 100%
Students specializing in: curriculum/instr.: 18%; admin.: 30%; evaluation/research/

statistics: 12%; higher education admin.: 8%; secondary: 9%; counseling: 6%; other: 16%

University of North Dakota[1]
Box 7189
Grand Forks, ND 58202-7189
und.edu/
Public
Admissions: N/A
Financial aid: N/A
Tuition: N/A
Room/board/expenses: N/A
Enrollment: N/A

OHIO

Ashland University (Schar)[1]
401 College Avenue
Ashland, OH 44805
www.ashland.edu/coe/ graduate-programs
Private
Admissions: (419) 289-5738
Email: grad-admissions@ ashland.edu
Financial aid: (800) 882-1548
Tuition: N/A
Room/board/expenses: N/A
Enrollment: N/A

Bowling Green State University
444 Education Building
Bowling Green, OH 43403
www.bgsu.edu/education-and-human-development.html
Public
Admissions: (419) 372-2791
Email: gradapply@bgsu.edu
Financial aid: (419) 372-2651
Application deadline: rolling
In-state tuition: full time: $8,996; part time: $424/credit hour
Out-of-state tuition: full time: $14,648
Room/board/expenses: $13,006
Full-time enrollment: 307 doctoral students: 10%; master's students: 90%; education specialists: 0%; men: 26%; women: 74%; minorities: 15%; international: 9%
Part-time enrollment: 441 doctoral students: 16%; master's students: 79%; education specialists: 5%; men: 23%; women: 77%; minorities: 10%; international: 3%
Acceptance rate (master's): 55%
Acceptance rate (doctoral): 31%
Entrance test required: GRE
Avg. GRE (of all entering students with scores): quantitative: N/A; verbal: N/A
Research assistantships: 69
Students reporting specialty: 100%
Students specializing in: curriculum/instr.: 8%; admin.: 15%; instructional media design: 1%; educational tech.: 6%; higher education admin.: 4%; special: 10%; counseling: 13%; other: 52%

Cleveland State University
2121 Euclid Avenue, JH 210
Cleveland, OH 44115
www.csuohio.edu/cehs/
Public
Admissions: (216) 687-5599

Email: graduate.admissions@ csuohio.edu
Financial aid: (216) 687-5411
Application deadline: rolling
In-state tuition: full time: $13,876; part time: $531/credit hour
Out-of-state tuition: full time: $15,826
Room/board/expenses: $15,000
Full-time enrollment: 1,001 doctoral students: 8%; master's students: 92%; education specialists: N/A; men: 22%; women: 78%; minorities: 30%; international: 5%
Part-time enrollment: N/A doctoral students: N/A; master's students: N/A; education specialists: N/A; men: N/A; women: N/A; minorities: N/A; international: N/A
Acceptance rate (master's): 84%
Acceptance rate (doctoral): 36%
Entrance test required: GRE
Avg. GRE (of all entering students with scores): quantitative: 147; verbal: 150
Research assistantships: 37
Students reporting specialty: 100%
Students specializing in: curriculum/instr.: 30%; admin.: 19%; policy: 2%; evaluation/research/ statistics: 0%; educational tech.: 2%; elementary: 3%; higher education admin.: 1%; secondary: 1%; special: 13%; counseling: 5%; other: 46%

Kent State University
PO Box 5190
Kent, OH 44242-0001
www.ehhs.kent.edu
Public
Admissions: (330) 672-2576
Email: gradapps@kent.edu
Financial aid: (330) 672-2972
Application deadline: rolling
In-state tuition: full time: $9,090; part time: $505/credit hour
Out-of-state tuition: full time: $15,858
Room/board/expenses: $14,100
Full-time enrollment: 824 doctoral students: 38%; master's students: 59%; education specialists: 3%; men: 25%; women: 75%; minorities: 11%; international: 11%
Part-time enrollment: 445 doctoral students: 17%; master's students: 80%; education specialists: 3%; men: 25%; women: 75%; minorities: 11%; international: 4%
Acceptance rate (master's): 50%
Acceptance rate (doctoral): 42%
Entrance test required: GRE
Avg. GRE (of all entering students with scores): quantitative: 148; verbal: 150
Research assistantships: 83
Students reporting specialty: 100%
Students specializing in: curriculum/instr.: 6%; admin.: 3%; evaluation/research/ statistics: 2%; instructional media design: 4%; educational psych: 3%; elementary: 1%; higher education admin.: 11%; junior high: 0%; secondary: 1%; social/philosophical foundations: 3%; special: 6%; counseling: 8%; technical (vocational): 1%; other: 51%

Miami University
207 McGuffey Hall
Oxford, OH 45056
www.miami.muohio.edu/ graduate-studies/index.html
Public
Admissions: (513) 529-3734
Email: gradschool@muohio.edu
Financial aid: (513) 529-8734
Application deadline: rolling
In-state tuition: full time: $13,528; part time: $563/credit hour
Out-of-state tuition: full time: $30,242
Room/board/expenses: $3,286
Full-time enrollment: 150 doctoral students: 26%; master's students: 61%; education specialists: 13%; men: 27%; women: 73%; minorities: 22%; international: 16%
Part-time enrollment: 497 doctoral students: 14%; master's students: 86%; education specialists: 0%; men: 22%; women: 78%; minorities: 10%; international: 1%
Acceptance rate (master's): 84%
Acceptance rate (doctoral): 45%
Entrance test required: GRE
Avg. GRE (of all entering students with scores): quantitative: N/A; verbal: N/A
Research assistantships: 0
Students reporting specialty: 100%
Students specializing in: admin.: 36%; evaluation/research/ statistics: 4%; instructional media design: 0%; educational psych: 2%; educational tech.: 2%; higher education admin.: 7%; secondary: 41%; special: 9%

Ohio State University
1945 N. High Street
Columbus, OH 43210-1172
ehe.osu.edu/
Public
Admissions: (614) 292-9444
Email: domestic.grad@osu.edu
Financial aid: (614) 292-0300
Application deadline: 12/01
In-state tuition: full time: $12,638; part time: $723/credit hour
Out-of-state tuition: full time: $32,110
Room/board/expenses: $21,616
Full-time enrollment: 684 doctoral students: 59%; master's students: 39%; education specialists: 2%; men: 30%; women: 70%; minorities: 18%; international: 25%
Part-time enrollment: 220 doctoral students: 26%; master's students: 72%; education specialists: 2%; men: 26%; women: 74%; minorities: 14%; international: 1%
Acceptance rate (master's): 47%
Acceptance rate (doctoral): 41%
Entrance test required: GRE
Avg. GRE (of all entering students with scores): quantitative: 154; verbal: 155
Research assistantships: 67
Students reporting specialty: 100%
Students specializing in: curriculum/instr.: 23%; admin.: 11%; policy: 2%; evaluation/research/ statistics: 1%; educational psych: 2%; educational tech.: 6%; elementary: 2%; higher education admin.: 8%; junior high: 2%; secondary: 4%; social/ philosophical foundations: 2%;

special: 6%; counseling: 9%; technical (vocational): 11%; other: 13%

Ohio University
102L McCracken Hall
Athens, OH 45701-2979
www.ohio.edu/education/
Public
Admissions: (740) 593-2800
Email: graduate@ohio.edu
Financial aid: (740) 593-4141
Application deadline: rolling
In-state tuition: full time: $11,744; part time: $556/credit hour
Out-of-state tuition: full time: $21,208
Room/board/expenses: $16,004
Full-time enrollment: 274
doctoral students: 26%; master's students: 74%; education specialists: N/A; men: 36%; women: 64%; minorities: 15%; international: 22%
Part-time enrollment: 535
doctoral students: 22%; master's students: 78%; education specialists: N/A; men: 54%; women: 46%; minorities: 19%; international: 6%
Acceptance rate (master's): 60%
Acceptance rate (doctoral): 43%
Entrance test required: GRE
Avg. GRE (of all entering students with scores): quantitative: 145; verbal: 168
Research assistantships: 25
Students reporting specialty: 100%
Students specializing in: curriculum/instr.: 9%; admin.: 11%; evaluation/research/statistics: 2%; instructional media design: 0%; educational tech.: 7%; higher education admin.: 13%; junior high: 1%; secondary: 1%; special: 2%; counseling: 11%; other: 63%

University of Akron
302 Buchtel Common
Akron, OH 44325-4201
www.uakron.edu/admissions/graduate
Public
Admissions: (330) 972-7663
Email: gradschool@uakron.edu
Financial aid: (330) 972-5858
Application deadline: rolling
In-state tuition: full time: $430/credit hour; part time: $430/credit hour
Out-of-state tuition: full time: $735/credit hour
Room/board/expenses: $14,000
Full-time enrollment: 84
doctoral students: 10%; master's students: 90%; education specialists: N/A; men: 39%; women: 61%; minorities: 9%; international: 21%
Part-time enrollment: 173
doctoral students: 16%; master's students: 84%; education specialists: N/A; men: 24%; women: 76%; minorities: 18%; international: 2%
Acceptance rate (master's): 65%
Acceptance rate (doctoral): N/A
Entrance test required: GRE
Avg. GRE (of all entering students with scores): quantitative: 146; verbal: 148
Research assistantships: 3
Students reporting specialty: 100%
Students specializing in: admin.: 6%; evaluation/research/statistics: 10%; instructional media design: 14%; elementary:

4%; higher education admin.: 11%; junior high: 1%; secondary: 9%; special: 19%; technical (vocational): 1%; other: 26%

University of Cincinnati
PO Box 210002
Cincinnati, OH 45221-0002
www.cech.uc.edu
Public
Admissions: (513) 556-1427
Email: kendalce@ucmail.uc.edu
Financial aid: (513) 556-4170
Application deadline: rolling
In-state tuition: full time: $12,790; part time: $640/credit hour
Out-of-state tuition: full time: $24,532
Room/board/expenses: $16,570
Full-time enrollment: 216
doctoral students: 45%; master's students: 50%; education specialists: 6%; men: 21%; women: 79%; minorities: 19%; international: 8%
Part-time enrollment: 865
doctoral students: 9%; master's students: 90%; education specialists: 1%; men: 15%; women: 85%; minorities: 17%; international: 2%
Acceptance rate (master's): 71%
Acceptance rate (doctoral): 38%
Entrance test required: GRE
Avg. GRE (of all entering students with scores): quantitative: 148; verbal: 152
Research assistantships: 48
Students reporting specialty: 100%
Students specializing in: curriculum/instr.: 18%; admin.: 3%; policy: 0%; evaluation/research/statistics: 1%; instructional media design: 2%; elementary: 5%; higher education admin.: 1%; junior high: 5%; secondary: 7%; social/philosophical foundations: 3%; special: 6%; counseling: 1%; other: 61%

University of Dayton
300 College Park
Fitz Hall
Dayton, OH 45469-2969
www.udayton.edu/education/
Private
Admissions: (800) 837-7433
Email: gradadmission@udayton.edu
Financial aid: (800) 229-4338
Application deadline: rolling
Tuition: full time: $620/credit hour; part time: $620/credit hour
Room/board/expenses: N/A
Full-time enrollment: 257
doctoral students: 13%; master's students: 82%; education specialists: 5%; men: 28%; women: 72%; minorities: 10%; international: 10%
Part-time enrollment: 202
doctoral students: 10%; master's students: 85%; education specialists: 5%; men: 23%; women: 77%; minorities: 9%; international: 3%
Acceptance rate (master's): 41%
Acceptance rate (doctoral): 33%
Entrance test required: GRE
Avg. GRE (of all entering students with scores): quantitative: 148; verbal: 152
Research assistantships: 18
Students reporting specialty: 100%
Students specializing in: admin.: 45%; instructional media

design: 3%; elementary: 13%; higher education admin.: 3%; junior high: 2%; secondary: 1%; special: 11%; counseling: 16%; other: 14%

University of Toledo
2801 W. Bancroft Street
Toledo, OH 43606
www.utoledo.edu/education/index.html
Public
Admissions: (419) 530-5251
Email: deborah.andrews@utoledo.edu
Financial aid: (419) 530-8700
Application deadline: rolling
In-state tuition: full time: $548/credit hour; part time: $548/credit hour
Out-of-state tuition: full time: $978/credit hour
Room/board/expenses: $11,184
Full-time enrollment: 245
doctoral students: 23%; master's students: 71%; education specialists: 7%; men: 24%; women: 76%; minorities: 21%; international: 13%
Part-time enrollment: 431
doctoral students: 39%; master's students: 50%; education specialists: 11%; men: 26%; women: 74%; minorities: 18%; international: 4%
Acceptance rate (master's): 84%
Acceptance rate (doctoral): 60%
Entrance test required: GRE
Avg. GRE (of all entering students with scores): quantitative: N/A; verbal: N/A
Research assistantships: 26
Students reporting specialty: 100%
Students specializing in: curriculum/instr.: 15%; admin.: 2%; evaluation/research/statistics: 2%; educational psych: 8%; educational tech.: 6%; elementary: 9%; higher education admin.: 14%; junior high: 1%; secondary: 3%; social/philosophical foundations: 5%; special: 14%; counseling: 16%; technical (vocational): 2%; other: 8%

Youngstown State University[1]
1 University Plaza
Youngstown, OH 44555
bcoe.ysu.edu/bcoe
Public
Admissions: N/A
Financial aid: N/A
Tuition: N/A
Room/board/expenses: N/A
Enrollment: N/A

OKLAHOMA

Oklahoma State University
325 Willard Hall
Stillwater, OK 74078-4033
www.okstate.edu/education/
Public
Admissions: (405) 744-6368
Email: grad-i@okstate.edu
Financial aid: (405) 744-6604
Application deadline: rolling
In-state tuition: full time: $210/credit hour; part time: $210/credit hour
Out-of-state tuition: full time: $825/credit hour
Room/board/expenses: $12,720

Full-time enrollment: 306
doctoral students: 34%; master's students: 59%; education specialists: 7%; men: 33%; women: 67%; minorities: 29%; international: 3%
Part-time enrollment: 522
doctoral students: 40%; master's students: 42%; education specialists: 18%; men: 35%; women: 65%; minorities: 25%; international: 3%
Acceptance rate (master's): 85%
Acceptance rate (doctoral): 63%
Entrance test required: GRE
Avg. GRE (of all entering students with scores): quantitative: 148; verbal: 151
Research assistantships: 53
Students reporting specialty: 100%
Students specializing in: curriculum/instr.: 1%; admin.: 8%; policy: 7%; evaluation/research/statistics: 0%; educational psych: 2%; educational tech.: 3%; elementary: 1%; higher education admin.: 4%; secondary: 10%; social/philosophical foundations: 1%; special: 2%; counseling: 2%; technical (vocational): 2%; other: 62%

Oral Roberts University[1]
7777 S. Lewis Avenue
Tulsa, OK 74171
www.oru.edu/
Private
Admissions: (918) 495-6553
Email: gradedu@oru.edu
Financial aid: (918) 495-6602
Tuition: N/A
Room/board/expenses: N/A
Enrollment: N/A

University of Oklahoma (Rainbolt)
820 Van Vleet Oval, No. 100
Norman, OK 73019-2041
www.ou.edu/education
Public
Admissions: (405) 325-2252
Email: admrec@ou.edu
Financial aid: (405) 325-4521
Application deadline: rolling
In-state tuition: full time: $9,212; part time: $204/credit hour
Out-of-state tuition: full time: $23,315
Room/board/expenses: $18,201
Full-time enrollment: 542
doctoral students: 31%; master's students: 69%; education specialists: N/A; men: 29%; women: 71%; minorities: 31%; international: 4%
Part-time enrollment: 212
doctoral students: 63%; master's students: 37%; education specialists: N/A; men: 26%; women: 74%; minorities: 28%; international: 7%
Acceptance rate (master's): 71%
Acceptance rate (doctoral): 39%
Entrance test required: GRE
Avg. GRE (of all entering students with scores): quantitative: 146; verbal: 152
Research assistantships: 147
Students reporting specialty: 100%
Students specializing in: curriculum/instr.: 23%; admin.: 23%; evaluation/research/statistics: 5%; social/philosophical foundations: 3%; special: 10%; counseling: 7%; other: 27%

OREGON

George Fox University[1]
414 N. Meridian Street
Newberg, OR 97132
www.georgefox.edu
Private
Admissions: N/A
Financial aid: N/A
Tuition: N/A
Room/board/expenses: N/A
Enrollment: N/A

Lewis & Clark College
0615 S.W. Palatine Hill Road
Portland, OR 97219-7899
graduate.lclark.edu
Private
Admissions: (503) 768-6200
Email: gseadmit@lclark.edu
Financial aid: (503) 768-7090
Application deadline: rolling
Tuition: full time: $879/credit hour; part time: $879/credit hour
Room/board/expenses: $29,475
Full-time enrollment: 185
doctoral students: 1%; master's students: 82%; education specialists: 17%; men: 23%; women: 77%; minorities: 20%; international: 2%
Part-time enrollment: 78
doctoral students: 42%; master's students: 24%; education specialists: 33%; men: 27%; women: 73%; minorities: 14%; international: 1%
Acceptance rate (master's): 86%
Acceptance rate (doctoral): 80%
Entrance test required: GRE
Avg. GRE (of all entering students with scores): quantitative: N/A; verbal: N/A
Students reporting specialty: 100%
Students specializing in: curriculum/instr.: 2%; admin.: 36%; educational psych: 13%; elementary: 6%; higher education admin.: 9%; secondary: 14%; special: 1%; counseling: 15%; other: 13%

Oregon State University
104 Furman Hall
Corvallis, OR 97331-3502
education.oregonstate.edu/
Public
Admissions: (541) 737-4881
Email: graduate.school@oregonstate.edu
Financial aid: (541) 737-2241
Application deadline: 06/01
In-state tuition: full time: $13,801; part time: $450/credit hour
Out-of-state tuition: full time: $23,440
Room/board/expenses: $16,254
Full-time enrollment: 190
doctoral students: 16%; master's students: 84%; education specialists: N/A; men: 26%; women: 74%; minorities: 20%; international: 3%
Part-time enrollment: 265
doctoral students: 43%; master's students: 57%; education specialists: N/A; men: 26%; women: 74%; minorities: 24%; international: 1%
Acceptance rate (master's): 61%
Acceptance rate (doctoral): 47%
Entrance test required: GRE
Avg. GRE (of all entering students with scores): quantitative: N/A; verbal: N/A
Research assistantships: 7
Students reporting specialty: 100%

Students specializing in: elementary: 7%; higher education admin.: 8%; secondary: 16%; counseling: 39%; other: 30%

Portland State University

PO Box 751
Portland, OR 97207-0751
www.pdx.edu/education/home
Public
Admissions: (503) 725-3511
Email: adm@pdx.edu
Financial aid: (503) 725-3461
Application deadline: rolling
In-state tuition: full time: $11,253; part time: $368/credit hour
Out-of-state tuition: full time: $16,869
Room/board/expenses: $16,542
Full-time enrollment: 476
doctoral students: 6%; master's students: 94%; education specialists: N/A; men: 29%; women: 71%; minorities: 26%; international: 9%
Part-time enrollment: 587
doctoral students: 10%; master's students: 90%; education specialists: N/A; men: 21%; women: 79%; minorities: 19%; international: 7%
Acceptance rate (master's): 66%
Acceptance rate (doctoral): 63%
Entrance test required: N/A
Avg. GRE (of all entering students with scores): quantitative: N/A; verbal: N/A
Research assistantships: 5
Students reporting specialty: 0%
Students specializing in: N/A

University of Oregon

1215 University of Oregon
Eugene, OR 97403-1215
education.uoregon.edu/
Public
Admissions: (541) 346-5134
Email: gradsch@uoregon.edu
Financial aid: (541) 346-3221
Application deadline: rolling
In-state tuition: full time: $20,166; part time: $555/credit hour
Out-of-state tuition: full time: $27,102
Room/board/expenses: $15,058
Full-time enrollment: 445
doctoral students: 39%; master's students: 61%; education specialists: N/A; men: 24%; women: 76%; minorities: N/A; international: N/A
Part-time enrollment: 27
doctoral students: 26%; master's students: 74%; education specialists: N/A; men: N/A; women: 26%; minorities: N/A; international: N/A
Acceptance rate (master's): 50%
Acceptance rate (doctoral): 16%
Entrance test required: GRE
Avg. GRE (of all entering students with scores): quantitative: 149; verbal: 154
Research assistantships: 14
Students reporting specialty: 99%
Students specializing in: curriculum/instr.: 16%; admin.: 16%; policy: 9%; elementary: 9%; junior high: 7%; secondary: 7%; social/philosophical foundations: 3%; special: 15%; counseling: 7%; other: 33%

PENNSYLVANIA

Arcadia University

450 S. Easton Road
Glenside, PA 19038-3295
www.arcadia.edu/
Private
Admissions: (877) 272-2342
Email: admiss@arcadia.edu
Financial aid: (215) 572-2980
Application deadline: rolling
Tuition: full time: N/A; part time: $720/credit hour
Room/board/expenses: N/A
Full-time enrollment: 21
doctoral students: 0%; master's students: 100%; education specialists: 0%; men: 29%; women: 71%; minorities: 30%; international: 4%
Part-time enrollment: 287
doctoral students: 20%; master's students: 80%; education specialists: 0%; men: 21%; women: 79%; minorities: 22%; international: 1%
Acceptance rate (master's): 73%
Acceptance rate (doctoral): 81%
Entrance test required: N/A
Avg. GRE (of all entering students with scores): quantitative: N/A; verbal: N/A
Students reporting specialty: 100%
Students specializing in: admin.: 18%; junior high: 1%; secondary: 6%; special: 15%; other: 61%

Drexel University

3141 Chestnut Street
Philadelphia, PA 19104
goodwin.drexel.edu/soe
Private
Admissions: (215) 895-2400
Email: admissions@drexel.edu
Financial aid: (215) 895-1627
Application deadline: rolling
Tuition: full time: $1,192/credit hour; part time: $1,192/credit hour
Room/board/expenses: N/A
Full-time enrollment: 66
doctoral students: 27%; master's students: 73%; education specialists: N/A; men: 23%; women: 77%; minorities: 24%; international: 5%
Part-time enrollment: 718
doctoral students: 39%; master's students: 61%; education specialists: N/A; men: 25%; women: 75%; minorities: 28%; international: 2%
Acceptance rate (master's): 91%
Acceptance rate (doctoral): 74%
Entrance test required: GRE
Avg. GRE (of all entering students with scores): quantitative: 146; verbal: 149
Research assistantships: 19
Students reporting specialty: 100%
Students specializing in: curriculum/instr.: 3%; admin.: 40%; policy: 6%; evaluation/research/statistics: 3%; instructional media design: 3%; educational tech.: 6%; elementary: 15%; higher education admin.: 22%; secondary: 10%; social/philosophical foundations: 5%; special: 5%; counseling: 5%; other: 19%

Duquesne University

600 Forbes Avenue
Pittsburgh, PA 15282
www.duq.edu/education/
Private
Admissions: (412) 396-6093
Email: edinfo@duq.edu
Financial aid: (412) 396-6607
Application deadline: 08/25
Tuition: full time: $1,234/credit hour; part time: $1,234/credit hour
Room/board/expenses: $15,360
Full-time enrollment: 477
doctoral students: 46%; master's students: 54%; education specialists: N/A; men: 27%; women: 73%; minorities: 15%; international: 8%
Part-time enrollment: 44
doctoral students: 11%; master's students: 89%; education specialists: N/A; men: 25%; women: 75%; minorities: 13%; international: 26%
Acceptance rate (master's): 55%
Acceptance rate (doctoral): 36%
Entrance test required: GRE
Avg. GRE (of all entering students with scores): quantitative: 147; verbal: 149
Research assistantships: 49
Students reporting specialty: 100%
Students specializing in: curriculum/instr.: 0%; admin.: 4%; policy: 0%; educational psych: 19%; educational tech.: 12%; elementary: 5%; junior high: 5%; special: 5%; counseling: 37%; other: 18%

East Stroudsburg University of Pennsylvania

200 Prospect Street
East Stroudsburg, PA 18301-2999
www.esu.edu
Public
Admissions: (570) 422-3536
Email: grad@po-box.esu.edu
Financial aid: (570) 422-2800
Application deadline: 08/11
In-state tuition: full time: $483/credit hour; part time: $483/credit hour
Out-of-state tuition: full time: $725/credit hour
Room/board/expenses: $11,841
Full-time enrollment: 36
doctoral students: N/A; master's students: 97%; education specialists: 3%; men: 44%; women: 56%; minorities: 19%; international: 3%
Part-time enrollment: 212
doctoral students: 26%; master's students: 72%; education specialists: 2%; men: 25%; women: 75%; minorities: 10%; international: 0%
Acceptance rate (master's): 84%
Acceptance rate (doctoral): 83%
Entrance test required: GRE
Avg. GRE (of all entering students with scores): quantitative: N/A; verbal: N/A
Students reporting specialty: 100%
Students specializing in: admin.: 28%; instructional media design: 0%; elementary: 2%; secondary: 18%; special: 17%; technical (vocational): 2%; other: 31%

Immaculata University[1]

1145 King Road
Immaculata, PA 19345
www.immaculata.edu
Private
Admissions: N/A
Financial aid: N/A
Tuition: N/A
Room/board/expenses: N/A
Enrollment: N/A

Indiana University of Pennsylvania

104 Stouffer Hall
Indiana, PA 15705-1083
www.iup.edu/graduate
Public
Admissions: (724) 357-2222
Email: graduate-admissions@iup.edu
Financial aid: (724) 357-2218
Application deadline: rolling
In-state tuition: full time: $483/credit hour; part time: $483/credit hour
Out-of-state tuition: full time: $725/credit hour
Room/board/expenses: $15,014
Full-time enrollment: 290
doctoral students: 4%; master's students: 92%; education specialists: 4%; men: 20%; women: 80%; minorities: 10%; international: 4%
Part-time enrollment: 353
doctoral students: 65%; master's students: 34%; education specialists: 1%; men: 31%; women: 69%; minorities: 11%; international: 3%
Acceptance rate (master's): 44%
Acceptance rate (doctoral): 61%
Entrance test required: GRE
Avg. GRE (of all entering students with scores): quantitative: 147; verbal: 150
Research assistantships: 136
Students reporting specialty: 100%
Students specializing in: admin.: 18%; educational psych: 1%; elementary: 14%; special: 4%; counseling: 16%; other: 47%

Lehigh University

111 Research Drive
Bethlehem, PA 18015
coe.lehigh.edu/
Private
Admissions: (610) 758-3231
Email: ineduc@lehigh.edu
Financial aid: (610) 758-3181
Application deadline: rolling
Tuition: full time: $565/credit hour; part time: $565/credit hour
Room/board/expenses: $19,640
Full-time enrollment: 160
doctoral students: 41%; master's students: 52%; education specialists: 7%; men: 14%; women: 86%; minorities: 12%; international: 19%
Part-time enrollment: 289
doctoral students: 29%; master's students: 70%; education specialists: 1%; men: 27%; women: 73%; minorities: 11%; international: 5%
Acceptance rate (master's): 61%
Acceptance rate (doctoral): 18%
Entrance test required: GRE
Avg. GRE (of all entering students with scores): quantitative: 149; verbal: 154
Research assistantships: 43
Students reporting specialty: 100%
Students specializing in: admin.: 24%; instructional media

design: 11%; educational psych: 12%; educational tech.: 0%; elementary: 3%; secondary: 3%; special: 11%; counseling: 14%; other: 21%

Neumann University

1 Neumann Drive
Aston, PA 19014
www.neumann.edu
Private
Admissions: (610) 361-5208
Email: gradadultadmiss@neumann.edu
Financial aid: (610) 558-5521
Application deadline: rolling
Tuition: full time: $12,060; part time: $670/credit hour
Room/board/expenses: $13,590
Full-time enrollment: 79
doctoral students: 0%; master's students: 100%; education specialists: 0%; men: 20%; women: 80%; minorities: 25%; international: 1%
Part-time enrollment: 141
doctoral students: 30%; master's students: 70%; education specialists: N/A; men: 23%; women: 77%; minorities: 12%; international: 0%
Acceptance rate (master's): 43%
Acceptance rate (doctoral): 45%
Entrance test required: N/A
Avg. GRE (of all entering students with scores): quantitative: N/A; verbal: N/A
Students reporting specialty: 100%
Students specializing in: admin.: 100%

Pennsylvania State University-Harrisburg

777 W. Harrisburg Pike
Middletown, PA 17057
hbg.psu.edu/admissions/index.php
Public
Admissions: (717) 948-6250
Email: hbgadmit@psu.edu
Financial aid: (717) 948-6307
Application deadline: rolling
In-state tuition: full time: $20,772; part time: $826/credit hour
Out-of-state tuition: full time: $27,064
Room/board/expenses: $18,330
Full-time enrollment: 7
doctoral students: 29%; master's students: 71%; education specialists: N/A; men: 29%; women: 71%; minorities: 26%; international: 0%
Part-time enrollment: 75
doctoral students: 48%; master's students: 52%; education specialists: N/A; men: 15%; women: 85%; minorities: 9%; international: 0%
Acceptance rate (master's): 98%
Acceptance rate (doctoral): 100%
Entrance test required: GRE
Avg. GRE (of all entering students with scores): quantitative: N/A; verbal: N/A
Research assistantships: 1
Students reporting specialty: 100%
Students specializing in: curriculum/instr.: 67%; secondary: 13%; special: 11%; other: 24%

Pennsylvania State University-University Park

274 Chambers Building
University Park, PA 16802-3206
ed.psu.edu/graduate
Public
Admissions: (814) 865-1795
Email: l-gswww@lists.psu.edu
Financial aid: (814) 865-2514
Application deadline: rolling
In-state tuition: full time: $20,912;
part time: $832/credit hour
Out-of-state tuition: full time:
$35,214
Room/board/expenses: $18,140
Full-time enrollment: 576
doctoral students: 60%;
master's students: 40%;
education specialists: N/A; men:
28%; women: 72%; minorities:
19%; international: 27%
Part-time enrollment: 799
doctoral students: 24%;
master's students: 76%;
education specialists: N/A; men:
26%; women: 74%; minorities:
14%; international: 4%
Acceptance rate (master's): 54%
Acceptance rate (doctoral): 46%
Entrance test required: GRE
**Avg. GRE (of all entering students
with scores):** quantitative: 151;
verbal: 154
Research assistantships: 15
Students reporting specialty: 100%
Students specializing in:
curriculum/instr.: 16%; admin.:
18%; policy: 3%; evaluation/
research/statistics: 1%;
instructional media design:
6%; educational psych: 5%;
educational tech.: 1%; higher
education admin.: 12%; special:
16%; counseling: 8%; technical
(vocational): 7%; other: 8%

Robert Morris University

6001 University Boulevard
Moon Township, PA 15108-1189
www.rmu.edu
Private
Admissions: (412) 397-5200
Email: graduateadmissions@
rmu.edu
Financial aid: (412) 397-6260
Application deadline: rolling
Tuition: full time: N/A; part time:
$840/credit hour
Room/board/expenses: N/A
Full-time enrollment: N/A
doctoral students: N/A; master's
students: N/A; education
specialists: N/A; men: N/A;
women: N/A; minorities: N/A;
international: N/A
Part-time enrollment: 137
doctoral students: 54%;
master's students: 30%;
education specialists: 16%; men:
39%; women: 61%; minorities:
11%; international: 1%
Acceptance rate (master's): 79%
Acceptance rate (doctoral): 100%
Entrance test required: N/A
**Avg. GRE (of all entering students
with scores):** quantitative: N/A;
verbal: N/A
Research assistantships: 4
Students reporting specialty: 0%
Students specializing in: N/A

St. Joseph's University

5600 City Avenue
Philadelphia, PA 19131
www.sju.edu
Private
Admissions: (610) 660-1300
Financial aid: (610) 660-2000
Application deadline: rolling
Tuition: full time: $750/credit
hour; part time: N/A
Room/board/expenses: $460
Full-time enrollment: 157
doctoral students: 50%;
master's students: 50%;
education specialists: N/A; men:
29%; women: 71%; minorities:
27%; international: 8%
Part-time enrollment: 694
doctoral students: 0%; master's
students: 100%; education
specialists: N/A; men: 23%;
women: 77%; minorities: 17%;
international: 0%
Acceptance rate (master's): 80%
Acceptance rate (doctoral): 81%
Entrance test required: N/A
**Avg. GRE (of all entering students
with scores):** quantitative: N/A;
verbal: N/A
Students reporting specialty: 100%
Students specializing in: admin.:
42%; instructional media design:
4%; secondary: 12%; special:
30%; other: 12%

Temple University

OSS RA238
Philadelphia, PA 19122
education.temple.edu
Public
Admissions: (215) 204-0999
Email: educate@temple.edu
Financial aid: (215) 204-8760
Application deadline: 03/01
In-state tuition: full time: $877/
credit hour; part time: $877/
credit hour
Out-of-state tuition: full time:
$1,202/credit hour
Room/board/expenses: $20,318
Full-time enrollment: 470
doctoral students: 36%;
master's students: 57%;
education specialists: 7%; men:
27%; women: 73%; minorities:
28%; international: 8%
Part-time enrollment: 300
doctoral students: 25%;
master's students: 75%;
education specialists: 0%; men:
34%; women: 66%; minorities:
24%; international: 8%
Acceptance rate (master's): 46%
Acceptance rate (doctoral): 30%
Entrance test required: GRE
**Avg. GRE (of all entering students
with scores):** quantitative: 150;
verbal: 152
Research assistantships: 10
Students reporting specialty: 100%
Students specializing in:
curriculum/instr.: 10%; admin.:
9%; policy: 6%; educational
psych: 5%; educational tech.:
1%; elementary: 3%; higher
education admin.: 13%; junior
high: 2%; secondary: 4%;
special: 8%; counseling: 8%;
technical (vocational): 8%; other:
25%

University of Pennsylvania

3700 Walnut Street
Philadelphia, PA 19104-6216
www.gse.upenn.edu
Private
Admissions: (215) 898-6455
Email:
admissions@gse.upenn.edu
Financial aid: (215) 898-6455
Application deadline: rolling
Tuition: full time: $48,304; part
time: $1,509/credit hour
Room/board/expenses: $28,310
Full-time enrollment: 789
doctoral students: 13%; master's
students: 87%; education
specialists: N/A; men: 23%;
women: 77%; minorities: 29%;
international: 35%
Part-time enrollment: 250
doctoral students: 2%; master's
students: 98%; education
specialists: N/A; men: 27%;
women: 73%; minorities: 38%;
international: 10%
Acceptance rate (master's): 71%
Acceptance rate (doctoral): 5%
Entrance test required: GRE
**Avg. GRE (of all entering students
with scores):** quantitative: 156;
verbal: 156
Research assistantships: 101
Students reporting specialty: 100%
Students specializing in:
curriculum/instr.: 32%; admin.:
4%; policy: 9%; evaluation/
research/statistics: 5%;
educational psych: 5%;
educational tech.: 2%;
elementary: 3%; higher
education admin.: 10%; junior
high: 3%; secondary: 8%; social/
philosophical foundations: 4%;
special: 3%; counseling: 13%

University of Pittsburgh

5601 Wesley W
Posvar Hall
Pittsburgh, PA 15260
www.education.pitt.edu
Public
Admissions: (412) 648-2230
Email: soeinfo@pitt.edu
Financial aid: (412) 648-2230
Application deadline: rolling
In-state tuition: full time: $22,578;
part time: $877/credit hour
Out-of-state tuition: full time:
$36,734
Room/board/expenses: $4,601
Full-time enrollment: 496
doctoral students: 33%;
master's students: 67%;
education specialists: 0%; men:
28%; women: 72%; minorities:
16%; international: 23%
Part-time enrollment: 386
doctoral students: 50%;
master's students: 42%;
education specialists: 0%; men:
28%; women: 72%; minorities:
17%; international: 1%
Acceptance rate (master's): 86%
Acceptance rate (doctoral): 50%
Entrance test required: GRE
**Avg. GRE (of all entering students
with scores):** quantitative: 153;
verbal: 149
Research assistantships: 21
Students reporting specialty: 100%
Students specializing in: admin.:
12%; policy: 2%; evaluation/
research/statistics: 1%;
educational psych: 9%;
elementary: 5%; higher
education admin.: 10%;
secondary: 23%; social/
philosophical foundations: 9%;
special: 16%; other: 17%

Widener University[1]

1 University Place
Chester, PA 19013-5792
www.widener.edu
Private
Admissions: N/A
Financial aid: N/A
Tuition: N/A
Room/board/expenses: N/A
Enrollment: N/A

Wilkes University[1]

84 W. South Street
Wilkes-Barre, PA 18766
www.wilkes.edu
Private
Admissions: N/A
Financial aid: N/A
Tuition: N/A
Room/board/expenses: N/A
Enrollment: N/A

RHODE ISLAND

Johnson & Wales University

8 Abbott Park Place
Providence, RI 02903-3703
www.jwu.edu
Private
Admissions: N/A
Financial aid: N/A
Application deadline: rolling
Tuition: full time: $438/credit
hour; part time: $438/credit hour
Room/board/expenses: N/A
Full-time enrollment: 100
doctoral students: 57%; master's
students: 43%; education
specialists: N/A; men: 34%;
women: 66%; minorities: 21%;
international: 1%
Part-time enrollment: 1
doctoral students: 0%; master's
students: 100%; education
specialists: N/A; men: N/A;
women: 100%; minorities: 0%;
international: 0%
Acceptance rate (master's): 41%
Acceptance rate (doctoral): 50%
Entrance test required: GRE
**Avg. GRE (of all entering students
with scores):** quantitative: N/A;
verbal: N/A
Students reporting specialty: 0%
Students specializing in: N/A

University of Rhode Island-Rhode Island College (Feinstein)[1]

600 Mount Pleasant Avenue
Providence, RI 02908
www.uri.edu/prov
Public
Admissions: N/A
Financial aid: N/A
Tuition: N/A
Room/board/expenses: N/A
Enrollment: N/A

SOUTH CAROLINA

Clemson University

102 Tillman Hall
Clemson, SC 29634-0702
www.grad.clemson.edu
Public
Admissions: (864) 656-2661
Email: grdapp@clemson.edu
Financial aid: (864) 656-2280
Application deadline: rolling
In-state tuition: full time: $8,528;
part time: $471/credit hour
Out-of-state tuition: full time:
$16,970
Room/board/expenses: N/A
Full-time enrollment: 253
doctoral students: 25%;
master's students: 75%;
education specialists: N/A; men:
25%; women: 75%; minorities:
N/A; international: N/A
Part-time enrollment: 323
doctoral students: 31%; master's
students: 55%; education
specialists: 14%; men: 33%;
women: 67%; minorities: N/A;
international: N/A
Acceptance rate (master's): 67%
Acceptance rate (doctoral): 52%
Entrance test required: GRE
**Avg. GRE (of all entering students
with scores):** quantitative: 147;
verbal: 150
Research assistantships: 7
Students reporting specialty: 100%
Students specializing in:
curriculum/instr.: 7%; admin.:
22%; evaluation/research/
statistics: 2%; higher education
admin.: 22%; junior high: 5%;
secondary: 2%; special: 3%;
counseling: 17%; other: 19%

Columbia International University[1]

7435 Monticello Road
Columbia, SC 29203
www.ciu.edu/
Private
Admissions: N/A
Financial aid: N/A
Tuition: N/A
Room/board/expenses: N/A
Enrollment: N/A

South Carolina State University

PO Box 7298
300 College Street NE
Orangeburg, SC 29117
www.scsu.edu/
schoolofgraduatestudies.aspx
Public
Admissions: (803) 536-7133
Email: graduateschool@scsu.edu
Financial aid: (803) 536-7067
Application deadline: 06/15
In-state tuition: full time: $10,420;
part time: $579/credit hour
Out-of-state tuition: full time:
$20,500
Room/board/expenses: N/A
Full-time enrollment: 81
doctoral students: 5%; master's
students: 79%; education
specialists: 16%; men: 27%;
women: 73%; minorities: 95%;
international: 0%
Part-time enrollment: 109
doctoral students: 47%; master's
students: 33%; education
specialists: 20%; men: 26%;
women: 74%; minorities: 94%;
international: 0%
Acceptance rate (master's): 93%
Acceptance rate (doctoral): 100%
Entrance test required: GRE
**Avg. GRE (of all entering students
with scores):** quantitative: N/A;
verbal: N/A
Students reporting specialty: 100%
Students specializing in:
admin.: 47%; elementary: 7%;
secondary: 7%; special: 1%;
counseling: 27%; other: 11%

University of South Carolina

Wardlaw Building
Columbia, SC 29208
www.ed.sc.edu
Public
Admissions: (803) 777-4243
Email: gradapp@mailbox.sc.edu
Financial aid: (803) 777-8134
Application deadline: rolling
In-state tuition: full time: $13,198;
part time: $533/credit hour
Out-of-state tuition: full time:
$27,808
Room/board/expenses: $17,000
Full-time enrollment: 423
doctoral students: 19%; master's
students: 72%; education
specialists: 9%; men: 31%;
women: 69%; minorities: 21%;
international: 2%
Part-time enrollment: 856
doctoral students: 48%;
master's students: 50%;
education specialists: 3%; men:
25%; women: 75%; minorities:
24%; international: 1%
Acceptance rate (master's): 79%
Acceptance rate (doctoral): 52%
Entrance test required: GRE
**Avg. GRE (of all entering students
with scores):** quantitative: 148;
verbal: 151
Research assistantships: 6
Students reporting specialty: 100%
Students specializing in:
curriculum/instr.: 21%;
admin.: 30%; educational
psych: 3%; educational
tech.: 1%; elementary: 3%;
higher education admin.:
8%; secondary: 5%; social/
philosophical foundations: 1%;
special: 4%; counseling: 6%;
other: 19%

SOUTH DAKOTA

University of South Dakota

414 E. Clark Street
Vermillion, SD 57069
www.usd.edu/grad
Public
Admissions: (605) 677-6240
Email: grad@usd.edu
Financial aid: (605) 677-5446
Application deadline: rolling
In-state tuition: full time: $313/
credit hour; part time: $313/
credit hour
Out-of-state tuition: full time:
$602/credit hour
Room/board/expenses: $11,878
Full-time enrollment: 159
doctoral students: 13%; master's
students: 77%; education
specialists: 9%; men: 31%;
women: 69%; minorities: 13%;
international: 3%
Part-time enrollment: 325
doctoral students: 35%;
master's students: 45%;
education specialists: 20%; men:
34%; women: 66%; minorities:
10%; international: 1%
Acceptance rate (master's): 81%
Acceptance rate (doctoral): 48%
Entrance test required: GRE
**Avg. GRE (of all entering students
with scores):** quantitative: 147;
verbal: 150
Research assistantships: 1
Students reporting specialty: 100%
Students specializing in:
curriculum/instr.: 6%; admin.:
36%; instructional media
design: 1%; educational

psych: 16%; elementary: 4%;
higher education admin.: 15%;
secondary: 2%; special: 4%;
counseling: 6%; other: 10%

TENNESSEE

East Tennessee State University (Clemmer)

PO Box 70720
Johnson City, TN 37614-0720
www.etsu.edu/coe/
Public
Admissions: (423) 439-4221
Email: gradsch@etsu.edu
Financial aid: (423) 439-4300
Application deadline: rolling
In-state tuition: full time: $9,371;
part time: $444/credit hour
Out-of-state tuition: full time:
$23,627
Room/board/expenses: $15,542
Full-time enrollment: 255
doctoral students: 18%; master's
students: 82%; education
specialists: 0%; men: 40%;
women: 60%; minorities: 11%;
international: 8%
Part-time enrollment: 322
doctoral students: 54%;
master's students: 45%;
education specialists: 1%; men:
32%; women: 68%; minorities:
11%; international: 0%
Acceptance rate (master's): 85%
Acceptance rate (doctoral): 100%
Entrance test required: GRE
**Avg. GRE (of all entering students
with scores):** quantitative: 148;
verbal: 151
Research assistantships: 12
Students reporting specialty: 100%
Students specializing in: admin.:
39%; instructional media design:
7%; elementary: 2%; secondary:
2%; special: 2%; counseling:
12%; other: 36%

Lincoln Memorial University[1]

6965 Cumberland Gap Parkway
Harrogateq, TN 37752
www.lmunet.edu/
Private
Admissions: N/A
Financial aid: N/A
Tuition: N/A
Room/board/expenses: N/A
Enrollment: N/A

Lipscomb University[1]

3901 Granny White Pike
Nashville, TN 37204-3951
www.lipscomb.edu/
Private
Admissions: (615) 279-6067
Email: junior.high@lipscomb.edu
Financial aid: (615) 269-1791
Tuition: N/A
Room/board/expenses: N/A
Enrollment: N/A

Middle Tennessee State University[1]

1301 E. Main Street
CAB Room 205
Murfreesboro, TN 37132
www.mtsu.edu/education/
index.php
Public
Admissions: N/A
Financial aid: N/A
Tuition: N/A
Room/board/expenses: N/A
Enrollment: N/A

Tennessee State University[1]

3500 John A. Merritt Boulevard
Nashville, TN 37209-1561
www.tnstate.edu
Public
Admissions: N/A
Financial aid: N/A
Tuition: N/A
Room/board/expenses: N/A
Enrollment: N/A

Tennessee Technological University

Box 5012
Cookeville, TN 38505-0001
www.tntech.edu/
Public
Admissions: (931) 372-3233
Email: gradstudies@tntech.edu
Financial aid: (931) 372-3073
Application deadline: 07/01
In-state tuition: full time: $16,375;
part time: $534/credit hour
Out-of-state tuition: full time:
$38,155
Room/board/expenses: $16,850
Full-time enrollment: 121
doctoral students: 8%; master's
students: 84%; education
specialists: 7%; men: 31%;
women: 69%; minorities: 10%;
international: 2%
Part-time enrollment: 244
doctoral students: 11%; master's
students: 64%; education
specialists: 25%; men: 27%;
women: 73%; minorities: 11%;
international: 2%
Acceptance rate (master's): 58%
Acceptance rate (doctoral): 67%
Entrance test required: GRE
**Avg. GRE (of all entering students
with scores):** quantitative: N/A;
verbal: N/A
Research assistantships: 10
Students reporting specialty: 100%
Students specializing in:
curriculum/instr.: 19%; admin.:
10%; evaluation/research/
statistics: 10%; educational
psych: 3%; educational tech.:
5%; elementary: 6%; secondary:
11%; special: 4%; counseling:
15%; other: 16%

Trevecca Nazarene University[1]

333 Murfreesboro Road
Nashville, TN 37210
www.trevecca.edu/academics/
schools-colleges/education/
Private
Admissions: N/A
Financial aid: N/A
Tuition: N/A
Room/board/expenses: N/A
Enrollment: N/A

Union University[1]

1050 Union University Drive
Jackson, TN 38305
www.uu.edu/
Private
Admissions: (731) 661-5928
Email: crbrown@uu.edu
Financial aid: (731) 661-5015
Tuition: N/A
Room/board/expenses: N/A
Enrollment: N/A

University of Memphis

215 Ball Hall
Memphis, TN 38152-6015
memphis.edu/admissions.htm
Public
Admissions: (901) 678-2911
Email: admissions@memphis.edu
Financial aid: (901) 678-4825
Application deadline: rolling
In-state tuition: full time: $493/
credit hour; part time: $596/
credit hour
Out-of-state tuition: full time:
$990/credit hour
Room/board/expenses: $14,513
Full-time enrollment: 217
doctoral students: 32%;
master's students: 67%;
education specialists: 1%; men:
22%; women: 78%; minorities:
31%; international: 5%
Part-time enrollment: 555
doctoral students: 47%; master's
students: 48%; education
specialists: 5%; men: 28%;
women: 72%; minorities: 44%;
international: 1%
Acceptance rate (master's): N/A
Acceptance rate (doctoral): N/A
Entrance test required: GRE
**Avg. GRE (of all entering students
with scores):** quantitative: N/A;
verbal: N/A
Students reporting specialty: 100%
Students specializing in:
curriculum/instr.: 14%; admin.:
12%; policy: 1%; evaluation/
research/statistics: 2%;
instructional media design:
7%; educational psych: 3%;
elementary: 4%; higher
education admin.: 9%; junior
high: 0%; secondary: 9%;
special: 8%; counseling: 25%;
other: 9%

University of Tennessee-Chattanooga

615 McCallie Avenue
Chattanooga, TN 37403
www.utc.edu/graduate-school
Public
Admissions: (423) 425-5942
Email: joanne-romagni@utc.edu
Financial aid: (423) 425-4677
Application deadline: rolling
In-state tuition: full time: $9,876;
part time: $450/credit hour
Out-of-state tuition: full time:
$25,994
Room/board/expenses: $17,400
Full-time enrollment: 48
doctoral students: N/A; master's
students: 81%; education
specialists: 19%; men: 38%;
women: 63%; minorities: 23%;
international: 2%
Part-time enrollment: 81
doctoral students: N/A; master's
students: 80%; education
specialists: 20%; men: 20%;
women: 80%; minorities: 20%;
international: 0%
Acceptance rate (master's): 90%
Acceptance rate (doctoral): N/A
Entrance test required: GRE
**Avg. GRE (of all entering students
with scores):** quantitative: 145;
verbal: 151
Students reporting specialty: 100%
Students specializing in: admin.:
14%; elementary: 12%;
secondary: 45%; special: 9%;
other: 19%

University of Tennessee-Knoxville

335 Claxton Complex
Knoxville, TN 37996-3400
cehhs.utk.edu
Public
Admissions: (865) 974-3251
Email: nfox@utk.edu
Financial aid: (865) 974-3131
Application deadline: rolling
In-state tuition: full time: $12,834;
part time: $615/credit hour
Out-of-state tuition: full time:
$31,022
Room/board/expenses: $19,176
Full-time enrollment: 315
doctoral students: 33%;
master's students: 63%;
education specialists: 4%; men:
22%; women: 78%; minorities:
N/A; international: N/A
Part-time enrollment: 259
doctoral students: 58%;
master's students: 36%;
education specialists: 7%; men:
29%; women: 71%; minorities:
N/A; international: N/A
Acceptance rate (master's): 75%
Acceptance rate (doctoral): 51%
Entrance test required: GRE
**Avg. GRE (of all entering students
with scores):** quantitative: 150;
verbal: 154
Research assistantships: 77
Students reporting specialty: 100%
Students specializing in: admin.:
4%; policy: 4%; evaluation/
research/statistics: 2%;
educational psych: 5%;
educational tech.: 3%;
elementary: 13%; higher
education admin.: 5%; junior
high: 0%; secondary: 13%;
social/philosophical foundations:
0%; special: 11%; counseling:
8%; other: 31%

Vanderbilt University (Peabody)

PO Box 227
Nashville, TN 37203-9418
peabody.vanderbilt.edu
Private
Admissions: (615) 322-8410
Email: peabody.admissions@
vanderbilt.edu
Financial aid: (615) 322-8410
Application deadline: 12/31
Tuition: full time: $1,854/credit
hour; part time: $1,854/credit
hour
Room/board/expenses: $20,526
Full-time enrollment: 722
doctoral students: 25%;
master's students: 75%;
education specialists: N/A; men:
19%; women: 81%; minorities:
18%; international: 14%
Part-time enrollment: 164
doctoral students: 46%;
master's students: 54%;
education specialists: N/A; men:
36%; women: 64%; minorities:
21%; international: 1%
Acceptance rate (master's): 64%
Acceptance rate (doctoral): 5%
Entrance test required: GRE
**Avg. GRE (of all entering students
with scores):** quantitative: 155;
verbal: 157
Research assistantships: 210
Students reporting specialty: 100%
Students specializing in:
curriculum/instr.: 11%; admin.:
6%; policy: 15%; evaluation/
research/statistics: 14%;
elementary: 3%; higher
education admin.: 9%;

secondary: 5%; special: 16%; counseling: 10%; other: 12%

TEXAS

Baylor University
1 Bear Place, #97304
Waco, TX 76798-7304
www.baylor.edu/SOE/
Private
Admissions: (254) 710-3584
Email:
graduate_school@baylor.edu
Financial aid: (254) 710-2611
Application deadline: 02/01
Tuition: full time: $1,583/credit hour; part time: $1,583/credit hour
Room/board/expenses: $12,654
Full-time enrollment: 133
doctoral students: 26%; master's students: 60%; education specialists: 14%; men: 32%; women: 68%; minorities: 20%; international: 4%
Part-time enrollment: 41
doctoral students: 37%; master's students: 63%; education specialists: 0%; men: 32%; women: 68%; minorities: 29%; international: 0%
Acceptance rate (master's): 48%
Acceptance rate (doctoral): 36%
Entrance test required: GRE
Avg. GRE (of all entering students with scores): quantitative: 152; verbal: 154
Research assistantships: 52
Students reporting specialty: 100%
Students specializing in:
curriculum/instr.: 22%; educational psych: 37%; higher education admin.: 22%; other: 18%

Dallas Baptist University (Bush)
3000 Mountain Creek Parkway
Dallas, TX 75211-9299
www.dbu.edu
Private
Admissions: (214) 333-5360
Email: admiss@dbu.edu
Financial aid: (214) 333-5363
Application deadline: rolling
Tuition: full time: $856/credit hour; part time: $856/credit hour
Room/board/expenses: $11,925
Full-time enrollment: 151
doctoral students: 87%; master's students: 13%; education specialists: 0%; men: 32%; women: 68%; minorities: N/A; international: N/A
Part-time enrollment: 302
doctoral students: 0%; master's students: 100%; education specialists: 0%; men: 19%; women: 81%; minorities: N/A; international: N/A
Acceptance rate (master's): 75%
Acceptance rate (doctoral): 67%
Entrance test required: GRE
Avg. GRE (of all entering students with scores): quantitative: N/A; verbal: N/A
Research assistantships: 0
Students reporting specialty: 0%
Students specializing in: N/A

Lamar University
PO Box 10034
Lamar University Station
Beaumont, TX 77710
dept.lamar.edu/education/
Public
Admissions: (409) 880-8356

Email:
gradmissions@hal.lamar.edu
Financial aid: (409) 880-8450
Application deadline: rolling
In-state tuition: full time: $8,008; part time: $336/credit hour
Out-of-state tuition: full time: $15,352
Room/board/expenses: $13,598
Full-time enrollment: 24
doctoral students: 33%; master's students: 67%; education specialists: N/A; men: 29%; women: 71%; minorities: 48%; international: 16%
Part-time enrollment: 3,170
doctoral students: 7%; master's students: 93%; education specialists: N/A; men: 21%; women: 79%; minorities: 42%; international: 0%
Acceptance rate (master's): 85%
Acceptance rate (doctoral): 97%
Entrance test required: GRE
Avg. GRE (of all entering students with scores): quantitative: 142; verbal: 146
Students reporting specialty: 100%
Students specializing in:
curriculum/instr.: 5%; admin.: 27%; instructional media design: 5%; special: 5%; other: 57%

Prairie View A&M University[1]
PO Box 3089
Office of Admissions and Records
Prairie View, TX 77446-0188
www.pvamu.edu/
Public
Admissions: N/A
Financial aid: N/A
Tuition: N/A
Room/board/expenses: N/A
Enrollment: N/A

Sam Houston State University
PO Box 2119
Huntsville, TX 77341
www.shsu.edu/dept/
graduate-admissions/
Public
Admissions: (936) 294-1971
Email: graduate@shsu.edu
Financial aid: (936) 294-1724
Application deadline: 08/01
In-state tuition: full time: $286/credit hour; part time: $286/credit hour
Out-of-state tuition: full time: $694/credit hour
Room/board/expenses: $11,944
Full-time enrollment: 148
doctoral students: 9%; master's students: 78%; education specialists: 14%; men: 16%; women: 84%; minorities: 33%; international: 1%
Part-time enrollment: 995
doctoral students: 20%; master's students: 80%; education specialists: N/A; men: 17%; women: 83%; minorities: 44%; international: 0%
Acceptance rate (master's): 90%
Acceptance rate (doctoral): 49%
Entrance test required: GRE
Avg. GRE (of all entering students with scores): quantitative: 146; verbal: 151
Research assistantships: 14
Students reporting specialty: 100%
Students specializing in:
curriculum/instr.: 14%; admin.: 25%; evaluation/research/statistics: 0%; educational psych: 2%; educational tech.:

4%; higher education admin.: 4%; special: 6%; counseling: 17%; other: 28%

Southern Methodist University[1]
PO Box 750181
Dallas, TX 75275-0181
www.smu.edu/
Private
Admissions: N/A
Financial aid: N/A
Tuition: N/A
Room/board/expenses: N/A
Enrollment: N/A

Stephen F. Austin State University
PO Box 13024, SFA Station
Nacogdoches, TX 75962
www.sfasu.edu/graduate
Public
Admissions: (936) 468-2807
Email: gschool@sfasu.edu
Financial aid: (936) 468-2403
Application deadline: rolling
In-state tuition: full time: $272/credit hour; part time: $272/credit hour
Out-of-state tuition: full time: $680/credit hour
Room/board/expenses: $11,914
Full-time enrollment: 223
doctoral students: 10%; master's students: 90%; education specialists: N/A; men: 20%; women: 80%; minorities: 26%; international: 3%
Part-time enrollment: 745
doctoral students: 4%; master's students: 96%; education specialists: N/A; men: 21%; women: 79%; minorities: 31%; international: 0%
Acceptance rate (master's): 93%
Acceptance rate (doctoral): 80%
Entrance test required: GRE
Avg. GRE (of all entering students with scores): quantitative: N/A; verbal: N/A
Research assistantships: 24
Students reporting specialty: 100%
Students specializing in:
admin.: 36%; elementary: 6%; secondary: 4%; special: 18%; counseling: 2%; other: 34%

Tarleton State University
Box T-0350
Stephenville, TX 76402
www.tarleton.edu
Public
Admissions: N/A
Financial aid: (254) 968-9070
Application deadline: 08/21
In-state tuition: full time: $204/credit hour; part time: $204/credit hour
Out-of-state tuition: full time: $612/credit hour
Room/board/expenses: N/A
Full-time enrollment: 60
doctoral students: 28%; master's students: 72%; education specialists: N/A; men: 42%; women: 58%; minorities: 18%; international: 3%
Part-time enrollment: 383
doctoral students: 31%; master's students: 69%; education specialists: N/A; men: 26%; women: 74%; minorities: 29%; international: 0%
Acceptance rate (master's): 76%
Acceptance rate (doctoral): 58%

Entrance test required: GRE
Avg. GRE (of all entering students with scores): quantitative: N/A; verbal: N/A
Research assistantships: 6
Students reporting specialty: 100%
Students specializing in:
curriculum/instr.: 27%; admin.: 19%; evaluation/research/statistics: 2%; educational psych: 2%; other: 49%

Texas A&M University-College Station
4222 TAMUS
College Station, TX 77843-4222
www.cehd.tamu.edu/
Public
Admissions: (979) 845-1071
Email: admissions@tamu.edu
Financial aid: (979) 458-5311
Application deadline: N/A
In-state tuition: full time: $258/credit hour; part time: $258/credit hour
Out-of-state tuition: full time: $681/credit hour
Room/board/expenses: $18,732
Full-time enrollment: 679
doctoral students: 44%; master's students: 56%; education specialists: N/A; men: 29%; women: 71%; minorities: 28%; international: 24%
Part-time enrollment: 957
doctoral students: 28%; master's students: 72%; education specialists: N/A; men: 28%; women: 72%; minorities: 35%; international: 1%
Acceptance rate (master's): 79%
Acceptance rate (doctoral): 54%
Entrance test required: GRE
Avg. GRE (of all entering students with scores): quantitative: 151; verbal: 152
Research assistantships: 85
Students reporting specialty: 100%
Students specializing in:
curriculum/instr.: 27%; admin.: 12%; educational psych: 12%; educational tech.: 5%; counseling: 2%; other: 42%

Texas A&M University-Commerce[1]
PO Box 3011
Commerce, TX 75429-3011
www.tamuc.edu/
Public
Admissions: N/A
Financial aid: N/A
Tuition: N/A
Room/board/expenses: N/A
Enrollment: N/A

Texas A&M University-Corpus Christi
6300 Ocean Drive
Corpus Christi, TX 78412
gradcollege.tamucc.edu
Public
Admissions: (361) 825-2177
Email: gradweb@tamucc.edu
Financial aid: (361) 825-2300
Application deadline: 05/01
In-state tuition: full time: $4,328; part time: $2,742
Out-of-state tuition: full time: $11,672
Room/board/expenses: $12,443

Full-time enrollment: 147
doctoral students: 29%; master's students: 71%; education specialists: 0%; men: 18%; women: 82%; minorities: 46%; international: 12%
Part-time enrollment: 324
doctoral students: 28%; master's students: 72%; education specialists: 0%; men: 18%; women: 82%; minorities: 60%; international: 1%
Acceptance rate (master's): 81%
Acceptance rate (doctoral): 70%
Entrance test required: GRE
Avg. GRE (of all entering students with scores): quantitative: 148; verbal: 144
Research assistantships: 0
Students reporting specialty: 100%
Students specializing in:
curriculum/instr.: 13%; admin.: 22%; instructional media design: 5%; elementary: 4%; secondary: 5%; special: 6%; counseling: 32%; other: 14%

Texas A&M University-Kingsville
700 University Boulevard
Kingsville, TX 78363
www.tamuk.edu/grad/
Public
Admissions: (361) 593-2808
Email: GradSchool@tamuk.edu
Financial aid: (361) 593-2173
Application deadline: 07/15
In-state tuition: full time: $5,369; part time: $704/credit hour
Out-of-state tuition: full time: $12,713
Room/board/expenses: $14,393
Full-time enrollment: 162
doctoral students: 15%; master's students: 85%; education specialists: N/A; men: 22%; women: 78%; minorities: 82%; international: 5%
Part-time enrollment: 270
doctoral students: 34%; master's students: 66%; education specialists: N/A; men: 27%; women: 73%; minorities: 72%; international: 11%
Acceptance rate (master's): 88%
Acceptance rate (doctoral): 74%
Entrance test required: GRE
Avg. GRE (of all entering students with scores): quantitative: 146; verbal: 146
Students reporting specialty: 100%
Students specializing in: admin.: 13%; policy: 23%; educational tech.: 4%; elementary: 10%; higher education admin.: 9%; secondary: 10%; special: 5%; counseling: 25%

Texas Christian University
3000 Bellaire Drive N
Fort Worth, TX 76129
www.coe.tcu.edu
Private
Admissions: (817) 257-7661
Financial aid: (817) 257-7872
Application deadline: N/A
Tuition: full time: $1,480/credit hour; part time: $1,480/credit hour
Room/board/expenses: $18,460
Full-time enrollment: 189
doctoral students: 41%; master's students: 59%; education specialists: N/A; men: 20%; women: 80%; minorities: 31%; international: 4%

Part-time enrollment: 31
doctoral students: 61%; master's students: 39%; education specialists: N/A; men: 42%; women: 58%; minorities: 42%; international: 3%
Acceptance rate (master's): 91%
Acceptance rate (doctoral): 65%
Entrance test required: GRE
Avg. GRE (of all entering students with scores): quantitative: 147; verbal: 151
Research assistantships: 11
Students reporting specialty: 100%
Students specializing in: curriculum/instr.: 16%; admin.: 48%; higher education admin.: 16%; special: 4%; counseling: 25%; other: 8%

Texas Southern University[1]

3100 Cleburne Street
Houston, TX 77004
www.tsu.edu/academics/colleges_schools/The_Graduate_School/admissions.php
Public
Admissions: (713) 313-7435
Email: graduateadmissions@tsu.edu
Financial aid: (713) 313-7071
Tuition: N/A
Room/board/expenses: N/A
Enrollment: N/A

Texas State University

601 University Drive
San Marcos, TX 78666
www.txstate.edu
Public
Admissions: (512) 245-2581
Email: gradcollege@txstate.edu
Financial aid: (512) 245-2315
Application deadline: rolling
In-state tuition: full time: $7,253; part time: $308/credit hour
Out-of-state tuition: full time: $14,597
Room/board/expenses: $11,990
Full-time enrollment: 569
doctoral students: 10%; master's students: 80%; education specialists: 9%; men: 23%; women: 77%; minorities: 42%; international: 4%
Part-time enrollment: 573
doctoral students: 20%; master's students: 77%; education specialists: 3%; men: 26%; women: 74%; minorities: 40%; international: 1%
Acceptance rate (master's): 56%
Acceptance rate (doctoral): 43%
Entrance test required: GRE
Avg. GRE (of all entering students with scores): quantitative: 147; verbal: 150
Research assistantships: 65
Students reporting specialty: 100%
Students specializing in: admin.: 22%; instructional media design: 2%; educational psych: 6%; elementary: 13%; higher education admin.: 3%; secondary: 7%; special: 3%; other: 44%

Texas Tech University

Box 41071
Lubbock, TX 79409-1071
www.educ.ttu.edu/
Public
Admissions: (806) 742-2787
Email: graduate.admissions@ttu.edu

Financial aid: (806) 742-3681
Application deadline: 06/01
In-state tuition: full time: $285/credit hour; part time: $285/credit hour
Out-of-state tuition: full time: $693/credit hour
Room/board/expenses: $14,805
Full-time enrollment: 365
doctoral students: 46%; master's students: 54%; education specialists: N/A; men: 26%; women: 74%; minorities: 31%; international: 16%
Part-time enrollment: 893
doctoral students: 47%; master's students: 53%; education specialists: N/A; men: 25%; women: 75%; minorities: 34%; international: 4%
Acceptance rate (master's): 54%
Acceptance rate (doctoral): 51%
Entrance test required: GRE
Avg. GRE (of all entering students with scores): quantitative: 146; verbal: 150
Research assistantships: 85
Students reporting specialty: 100%
Students specializing in: curriculum/instr.: 21%; admin.: 6%; evaluation/research/statistics: 13%; instructional media design: 5%; educational psych: 5%; special: 26%; counseling: 12%; other: 12%

Texas Wesleyan University

1201 Wesleyan
Fort Worth, TX 76105
www.txwes.edu/
Private
Admissions: (817) 531-4422
Financial aid: (817) 531-4420
Application deadline: rolling
Tuition: full time: $542/credit hour; part time: $542/credit hour
Room/board/expenses: $13,684
Full-time enrollment: 24
doctoral students: 21%; master's students: 79%; education specialists: N/A; men: 21%; women: 79%; minorities: 29%; international: 21%
Part-time enrollment: 225
doctoral students: 38%; master's students: 62%; education specialists: N/A; men: 13%; women: 87%; minorities: 46%; international: 2%
Acceptance rate (master's): 79%
Acceptance rate (doctoral): 76%
Entrance test required: GRE
Avg. GRE (of all entering students with scores): quantitative: 143; verbal: 145
Students reporting specialty: 100%
Students specializing in: curriculum/instr.: 14%; admin.: 8%; educational psych: 48%; technical (vocational): 2%; other: 27%

Texas Woman's University[1]

PO Box 425769
Denton, TX 76204-5769
www.twu.edu/
Public
Admissions: N/A
Financial aid: N/A
Tuition: N/A
Room/board/expenses: N/A
Enrollment: N/A

University of Houston

3657 Cullen Boulevard, Room 214
Houston, TX 77204-5023
www.coe.uh.edu/
Public
Admissions: (713) 743-4997
Email: coegrad@uh.edu
Financial aid: (713) 743-1010
Application deadline: rolling
In-state tuition: full time: $8,578; part time: $422/credit hour
Out-of-state tuition: full time: $17,722
Room/board/expenses: $16,238
Full-time enrollment: 278
doctoral students: 50%; master's students: 50%; education specialists: N/A; men: 22%; women: 78%; minorities: 48%; international: 13%
Part-time enrollment: 323
doctoral students: 62%; master's students: 38%; education specialists: N/A; men: 28%; women: 72%; minorities: 49%; international: 2%
Acceptance rate (master's): 76%
Acceptance rate (doctoral): 31%
Entrance test required: GRE
Avg. GRE (of all entering students with scores): quantitative: 148; verbal: 152
Research assistantships: 54
Students reporting specialty: 100%
Students specializing in: curriculum/instr.: 26%; admin.: 27%; educational psych: 4%; higher education admin.: 10%; special: 2%; counseling: 14%; technical (vocational): 0%; other: 19%

University of Houston-Clear Lake[1]

2700 Bay Area Boulevard
Houston, TX 77058
www.uhcl.edu/
Public
Admissions: N/A
Financial aid: N/A
Tuition: N/A
Room/board/expenses: N/A
Enrollment: N/A

University of Mary Hardin-Baylor[1]

UMHB Box 8017
900 College Street
Belton, TX 76513
www.umhb.edu/
Private
Admissions: N/A
Financial aid: N/A
Tuition: N/A
Room/board/expenses: N/A
Enrollment: N/A

University of North Texas

1155 Union Circle, #311337
Denton, TX 76203-1337
tsgs.unt.edu/overview
Public
Admissions: (940) 565-2383
Email: gradsch@unt.edu
Financial aid: (940) 565-2302
Application deadline: 10/15
In-state tuition: full time: $303/credit hour; part time: $303/credit hour
Out-of-state tuition: full time: $710/credit hour
Room/board/expenses: $13,510
Full-time enrollment: 344
doctoral students: 27%; master's students: 73%; education

specialists: 0%; men: 30%; women: 70%; minorities: 33%; international: 10%
Part-time enrollment: 878
doctoral students: 35%; master's students: 65%; education specialists: 0%; men: 27%; women: 73%; minorities: 33%; international: 2%
Acceptance rate (master's): 31%
Acceptance rate (doctoral): 39%
Entrance test required: GRE
Avg. GRE (of all entering students with scores): quantitative: 148; verbal: 152
Research assistantships: 6
Students reporting specialty: 100%
Students specializing in: curriculum/instr.: 8%; admin.: 28%; policy: 10%; evaluation/research/statistics: 2%; educational psych: 7%; elementary: 1%; higher education admin.: 10%; junior high: 0%; secondary: 0%; social/philosophical foundations: 10%; special: 7%; counseling: 20%; other: 23%

University of Texas-Arlington

701 S. Nedderman Drive
Arlington, TX 76019
www.uta.edu
Public
Admissions: (817) 272-6287
Financial aid: (817) 272-3561
Application deadline: 06/15
In-state tuition: full time: $273/credit hour; part time: $273/credit hour
Out-of-state tuition: full time: $273/credit hour
Room/board/expenses: $14,791
Full-time enrollment: 1,190
doctoral students: 1%; master's students: 99%; education specialists: N/A; men: 21%; women: 79%; minorities: 44%; international: 1%
Part-time enrollment: 738
doctoral students: 8%; master's students: 92%; education specialists: N/A; men: 19%; women: 81%; minorities: 43%; international: 1%
Acceptance rate (master's): 65%
Acceptance rate (doctoral): 49%
Entrance test required: GRE
Avg. GRE (of all entering students with scores): quantitative: 147; verbal: 151
Research assistantships: 2
Students reporting specialty: 100%
Students specializing in: curriculum/instr.: 55%; admin.: 43%; educational psych: 1%; elementary: 2%; higher education admin.: 4%; junior high: 0%; secondary: 2%; counseling: 0%

University of Texas-Austin

1 University Station, D5000
Sanchez Building, Room 210
Austin, TX 78712
www.education.utexas.edu
Public
Admissions: (512) 475-7391
Email: residency@austin.utexas.edu
Financial aid: (512) 475-6282
Application deadline: rolling
In-state tuition: full time: $8,654; part time: $8,308
Out-of-state tuition: full time: $16,828

Room/board/expenses: $16,465
Full-time enrollment: 782
doctoral students: 57%; master's students: 43%; education specialists: 0%; men: 32%; women: 68%; minorities: 33%; international: 16%
Part-time enrollment: 268
doctoral students: 54%; master's students: 46%; education specialists: 0%; men: 39%; women: 61%; minorities: 42%; international: 3%
Acceptance rate (master's): 50%
Acceptance rate (doctoral): 27%
Entrance test required: GRE
Avg. GRE (of all entering students with scores): quantitative: 152; verbal: 154
Research assistantships: 256
Students reporting specialty: 100%
Students specializing in: curriculum/instr.: 28%; admin.: 8%; policy: 5%; evaluation/research/statistics: 3%; educational psych: 14%; educational tech.: 4%; higher education admin.: 12%; special: 13%; counseling: 3%; other: 15%

University of Texas-El Paso[1]

500 W. University Avenue
El Paso, TX 79968
www.utep.edu/
Public
Admissions: N/A
Financial aid: N/A
Tuition: N/A
Room/board/expenses: N/A
Enrollment: N/A

University of Texas-Rio Grande Valley

Marialice Shary Shivers Building
Edinburg, TX 78539-2999
www.utrgv.edu/cep/
Public
Admissions: N/A
Financial aid: (888) 882-4026
Application deadline: 04/15
In-state tuition: full time: $5,439; part time: $411/credit hour
Out-of-state tuition: full time: $12,783
Room/board/expenses: $11,772
Full-time enrollment: 91
doctoral students: 22%; master's students: 78%; education specialists: N/A; men: 21%; women: 79%; minorities: 80%; international: 8%
Part-time enrollment: 746
doctoral students: 15%; master's students: 85%; education specialists: N/A; men: 22%; women: 78%; minorities: 85%; international: 1%
Acceptance rate (master's): 87%
Acceptance rate (doctoral): 33%
Entrance test required: GRE
Avg. GRE (of all entering students with scores): quantitative: N/A; verbal: N/A
Research assistantships: 26
Students reporting specialty: 100%
Students specializing in: curriculum/instr.: 15%; admin.: 24%; educational tech.: 8%; elementary: 0%; secondary: 1%; special: 19%; counseling: 21%; other: 12%

University of Texas-San Antonio

1 UTSA Circle
San Antonio, TX 78249-0617
www.graduateschool.utsa.edu
Public
Admissions: (210) 458-4331
Email: graduateadmissions@usta.edu
Financial aid: (210) 458-8000
Application deadline: rolling
In-state tuition: full time: $288/credit hour; part time: $288/credit hour
Out-of-state tuition: full time: $1,155/credit hour
Room/board/expenses: $15,054
Full-time enrollment: 471
doctoral students: 8%; master's students: 92%; education specialists: N/A; men: 24%; women: 76%; minorities: 56%; international: 3%
Part-time enrollment: 954
doctoral students: 18%; master's students: 82%; education specialists: N/A; men: 22%; women: 78%; minorities: 63%; international: 1%
Acceptance rate (master's): 82%
Acceptance rate (doctoral): 57%
Entrance test required: GRE
Avg. GRE (of all entering students with scores): quantitative: 144; verbal: 150
Research assistantships: 99
Students reporting specialty: 100%
Students specializing in: curriculum/instr.: 4%; admin.: 19%; policy: 18%; educational psych.: 5%; educational tech.: 2%; elementary: 3%; higher education admin.: 5%; special: 5%; counseling: 8%; other: 50%

University of the Incarnate Word

4301 Broadway
San Antonio, TX 78209
www.uiw.edu
Private
Admissions: (210) 829-6005
Email: admis@uiwtx.edu
Financial aid: (210) 829-6008
Application deadline: rolling
Tuition: full time: $885/credit hour; part time: $885/credit hour
Room/board/expenses: N/A
Full-time enrollment: 33
doctoral students: 27%; master's students: 73%; education specialists: N/A; men: 39%; women: 61%; minorities: 64%; international: 15%
Part-time enrollment: 191
doctoral students: 74%; master's students: 26%; education specialists: N/A; men: 31%; women: 69%; minorities: 59%; international: 8%
Acceptance rate (master's): 73%
Acceptance rate (doctoral): 71%
Entrance test required: N/A
Avg. GRE (of all entering students with scores): quantitative: N/A; verbal: N/A
Research assistantships: 20
Students reporting specialty: 100%
Students specializing in: elementary: 4%; secondary: 1%; other: 96%

UTAH

Brigham Young University-Provo (McKay)

301 MCKB
Provo, UT 84602
www.byu.edu/gradstudies
Private
Admissions: (801) 422-4091
Email: admissions@byu.edu
Financial aid: (801) 422-4104
Application deadline: 02/01
Tuition: full time: $6,680; part time: $393/credit hour
Room/board/expenses: $15,712
Full-time enrollment: 219
doctoral students: 53%; master's students: 32%; education specialists: 16%; men: 45%; women: 55%; minorities: 12%; international: 6%
Part-time enrollment: 97
doctoral students: 10%; master's students: 87%; education specialists: 3%; men: 31%; women: 69%; minorities: 6%; international: 1%
Acceptance rate (master's): 50%
Acceptance rate (doctoral): 28%
Entrance test required: GRE
Avg. GRE (of all entering students with scores): quantitative: 151; verbal: 156
Research assistantships: 94
Students reporting specialty: 100%
Students specializing in: curriculum/instr.: 8%; admin.: 22%; evaluation/research/statistics: 6%; instructional media design: 25%; educational psych.: 10%; special: 3%; counseling: 11%; other: 15%

University of Utah

1721 E. Campus Center Drive
Salt Lake City, UT 84112-9251
admissions.utah.edu
Public
Admissions: (801) 581-7281
Email: admissions@utah.edu
Financial aid: (801) 581-6211
Application deadline: 04/01
In-state tuition: full time: $7,012; part time: $332/credit hour
Out-of-state tuition: full time: $22,155
Room/board/expenses: $14,846
Full-time enrollment: 444
doctoral students: 36%; master's students: 64%; education specialists: N/A; men: 27%; women: 73%; minorities: 21%; international: 1%
Part-time enrollment: 214
doctoral students: 44%; master's students: 56%; education specialists: N/A; men: 32%; women: 68%; minorities: 15%; international: 1%
Acceptance rate (master's): 65%
Acceptance rate (doctoral): 39%
Entrance test required: GRE
Avg. GRE (of all entering students with scores): quantitative: 150; verbal: 154
Research assistantships: 31
Students reporting specialty: 100%
Students specializing in: admin.: 15%; policy: 7%; instructional media design: 8%; educational psych.: 35%; elementary: 1%; higher education admin.: 16%; secondary: 2%; social/philosophical foundations: 15%; special: 13%; counseling: 5%

Utah State University

2800 Old Main Hill
Logan, UT 84322-2800
rgs.usu.edu/graduateschool
Public
Admissions: (435) 797-1189
Email: graduateschool@usu.edu
Financial aid: (435) 797-1455
Application deadline: rolling
In-state tuition: full time: $7,231; part time: $6,687
Out-of-state tuition: full time: $20,540
Room/board/expenses: $12,300
Full-time enrollment: 287
doctoral students: 34%; master's students: 60%; education specialists: 7%; men: 28%; women: 72%; minorities: 12%; international: 3%
Part-time enrollment: 527
doctoral students: 29%; master's students: 71%; education specialists: 0%; men: 36%; women: 64%; minorities: 8%; international: 2%
Acceptance rate (master's): 42%
Acceptance rate (doctoral): 25%
Entrance test required: GRE
Avg. GRE (of all entering students with scores): quantitative: 151; verbal: 154
Research assistantships: 95
Students reporting specialty: 100%
Students specializing in: curriculum/instr.: 11%; admin.: 5%; instructional media design: 18%; elementary: 4%; junior high: 0%; secondary: 5%; special: 6%; counseling: 14%; other: 38%

VERMONT

University of Vermont

309 Waterman Building
Burlington, VT 05405-0160
www.uvm.edu/~gradcoll
Public
Admissions: (802) 656-2699
Email: graduate.admissions@uvm.edu
Financial aid: (802) 656-3156
Application deadline: 02/01
In-state tuition: full time: $11,322; part time: $629/credit hour
Out-of-state tuition: full time: $28,620
Room/board/expenses: $16,014
Full-time enrollment: 137
doctoral students: 15%; master's students: 43%; education specialists: 42%; men: 31%; women: 69%; minorities: 9%; international: 7%
Part-time enrollment: 139
doctoral students: 37%; master's students: 22%; education specialists: 40%; men: 33%; women: 67%; minorities: 10%; international: 2%
Acceptance rate (master's): 42%
Acceptance rate (doctoral): 60%
Entrance test required: GRE
Avg. GRE (of all entering students with scores): quantitative: 150; verbal: 155
Research assistantships: 2
Students reporting specialty: 100%
Students specializing in: curriculum/instr.: 13%; admin.: 33%; higher education admin.: 11%; special: 12%; counseling: 19%; other: 12%

VIRGINIA

College of William and Mary

PO Box 8795
Williamsburg, VA 23187-8795
education.wm.edu/
Public
Admissions: (757) 221-2317
Email: GradEd@wm.edu
Financial aid: (757) 221-2317
Application deadline: 01/15
In-state tuition: full time: $14,814; part time: $500/credit hour
Out-of-state tuition: full time: $30,500
Room/board/expenses: $20,250
Full-time enrollment: 198
doctoral students: 24%; master's students: 76%; education specialists: 0%; men: 27%; women: 73%; minorities: 19%; international: 4%
Part-time enrollment: 165
doctoral students: 76%; master's students: 20%; education specialists: 4%; men: 30%; women: 70%; minorities: 24%; international: 1%
Acceptance rate (master's): 68%
Acceptance rate (doctoral): 57%
Entrance test required: GRE
Avg. GRE (of all entering students with scores): quantitative: 151; verbal: 156
Students reporting specialty: 100%
Students specializing in: curriculum/instr.: 3%; admin.: 2%; policy: 18%; educational tech.: 2%; elementary: 4%; higher education admin.: 15%; secondary: 7%; special: 1%; counseling: 14%; other: 35%

George Mason University

4400 University Drive, MSN 2F1
Fairfax, VA 22030-4444
cehd.gmu.edu
Public
Admissions: (703) 993-2892
Email: cehdgrad@gmu.edu
Financial aid: (703) 993-2353
Application deadline: rolling
In-state tuition: full time: $572/credit hour; part time: $572/credit hour
Out-of-state tuition: full time: $772/credit hour
Room/board/expenses: $23,620
Full-time enrollment: 378
doctoral students: 24%; master's students: 76%; education specialists: N/A; men: 16%; women: 84%; minorities: 32%; international: 9%
Part-time enrollment: 1,908
doctoral students: 13%; master's students: 87%; education specialists: N/A; men: 18%; women: 82%; minorities: 27%; international: 1%
Acceptance rate (master's): 89%
Acceptance rate (doctoral): 64%
Entrance test required: GRE
Avg. GRE (of all entering students with scores): quantitative: 150; verbal: 154
Research assistantships: 54
Students reporting specialty: 100%
Students specializing in: curriculum/instr.: 43%; admin.: 14%; educational psych.: 1%; special: 23%; counseling: 4%; other: 15%

Hampton University[1]

Graduate College
Hampton, VA 23668
www.hamptonu.edu/GraduateCollege/home.html
Private
Admissions: (757) 727-5454
Email: hugrad@hamptonu.edu
Financial aid: (757) 727-5332
Tuition: N/A
Room/board/expenses: N/A
Enrollment: N/A

Liberty University

1971 University Boulevard
Lynchburg, VA 24502
www.liberty.edu/academics/graduate
Private
Admissions: (800) 424-9596
Email: gradadmissions@liberty.edu
Financial aid: (434) 582-2270
Application deadline: rolling
Tuition: full time: $565/credit hour; part time: $615/credit hour
Room/board/expenses: N/A
Full-time enrollment: 1,757
doctoral students: 17%; master's students: 58%; education specialists: 25%; men: 23%; women: 77%; minorities: 25%; international: 0%
Part-time enrollment: 4,142
doctoral students: 19%; master's students: 73%; education specialists: 7%; men: 24%; women: 76%; minorities: 25%; international: 0%
Acceptance rate (master's): 50%
Acceptance rate (doctoral): 17%
Entrance test required: GRE
Avg. GRE (of all entering students with scores): quantitative: 147; verbal: 153
Students reporting specialty: 100%
Students specializing in: curriculum/instr.: 8%; admin.: 38%; instructional media design: 6%; elementary: 11%; junior high: 2%; secondary: 6%; special: 10%; counseling: 19%; other: 2%

Old Dominion University (Darden)

Education Building, Room 218
Norfolk, VA 23529
education.odu.edu
Public
Admissions: (757) 683-3685
Email: admit@odu.edu
Financial aid: (757) 683-3683
Application deadline: rolling
In-state tuition: full time: $478/credit hour; part time: $478/credit hour
Out-of-state tuition: full time: $1,195/credit hour
Room/board/expenses: $13,575
Full-time enrollment: 529
doctoral students: 15%; master's students: 83%; education specialists: 2%; men: 19%; women: 81%; minorities: 27%; international: 4%
Part-time enrollment: 794
doctoral students: 29%; master's students: 61%; education specialists: 10%; men: 25%; women: 75%; minorities: 28%; international: 1%
Acceptance rate (master's): 62%
Acceptance rate (doctoral): 71%
Entrance test required: GRE
Avg. GRE (of all entering students with scores): quantitative: 145; verbal: 149

Research assistantships: 24
Students reporting specialty: 100%
Students specializing in: admin.: 17%; instructional media design: 0%; educational tech.: 0%; elementary: 21%; secondary: 10%; social/philosophical foundations: 1%; special: 10%; counseling: 10%; technical (vocational): 17%; other: 20%

Regent University
1000 Regent University Drive
Virginia Beach, VA 23464
www.regent.edu/acad/schedu
Private
Admissions: (888) 713-1595
Email: education@regent.edu
Financial aid: (757) 352-4125
Application deadline: rolling
Tuition: full time: $575/credit hour; part time: $575/credit hour
Room/board/expenses: $15,705
Full-time enrollment: 80
doctoral students: 0%; master's students: 99%; education specialists: 1%; men: 28%; women: 73%; minorities: 38%; international: 1%
Part-time enrollment: 931
doctoral students: 21%; master's students: 63%; education specialists: 15%; men: 21%; women: 79%; minorities: 40%; international: 3%
Acceptance rate (master's): 53%
Acceptance rate (doctoral): 41%
Entrance test required: GRE
Avg. GRE (of all entering students with scores): quantitative: 146; verbal: 153
Research assistantships: 0
Students reporting specialty: 100%
Students specializing in: curriculum/instr.: 6%; admin.: 20%; educational psych: 1%; educational tech.: 1%; elementary: 0%; higher education admin.: 2%; special: 14%; other: 56%

Shenandoah University
1460 University Drive
Winchester, VA 22601
www.su.edu
Private
Admissions: (540) 665-4581
Email: admit@su.edu
Financial aid: (540) 665-4538
Application deadline: 05/01
Tuition: full time: $9,800; part time: $510/credit hour
Room/board/expenses: $14,590
Full-time enrollment: 34
doctoral students: 6%; master's students: 94%; education specialists: 0%; men: 21%; women: 79%; minorities: 20%; international: 7%
Part-time enrollment: 208
doctoral students: 36%; master's students: 64%; education specialists: 0%; men: 31%; women: 69%; minorities: 10%; international: 0%
Acceptance rate (master's): 100%
Acceptance rate (doctoral): 91%
Entrance test required: N/A
Avg. GRE (of all entering students with scores): quantitative: N/A; verbal: N/A
Research assistantships: 0
Students reporting specialty: 100%
Students specializing in: admin.: 27%; elementary: 3%; junior high: 0%; secondary: 1%; other: 86%

University of Virginia (Curry)
405 Emmet Street S
Charlottesville, VA 22903-2495
curry.virginia.edu
Public
Admissions: (434) 924-0742
Email: curry-admissions@virginia.edu
Financial aid: (434) 982-6000
Application deadline: N/A
In-state tuition: full time: $18,124; part time: $834/credit hour
Out-of-state tuition: full time: $27,916
Room/board/expenses: $21,173
Full-time enrollment: 589
doctoral students: 24%; master's students: 76%; education specialists: 0%; men: 24%; women: 76%; minorities: 19%; international: 4%
Part-time enrollment: 333
doctoral students: 19%; master's students: 76%; education specialists: 5%; men: 24%; women: 76%; minorities: 17%; international: 1%
Acceptance rate (master's): 57%
Acceptance rate (doctoral): 16%
Entrance test required: GRE
Avg. GRE (of all entering students with scores): quantitative: 153; verbal: 156
Research assistantships: 84
Students reporting specialty: 100%
Students specializing in: curriculum/instr.: 22%; admin.: 10%; policy: 1%; evaluation/research/statistics: 1%; educational psych: 3%; educational tech.: 0%; elementary: 7%; higher education admin.: 8%; secondary: 10%; social/philosophical foundations: 5%; special: 6%; counseling: 7%; other: 19%

Virginia Commonwealth University
1015 W. Main Street
PO Box 842020
Richmond, VA 23284-2020
www.soe.vcu.edu
Public
Admissions: (804) 828-3382
Email: kmcauley@vcu.edu
Financial aid: (804) 828-6181
Application deadline: 02/01
In-state tuition: full time: $12,994; part time: $605/credit hour
Out-of-state tuition: full time: $27,412
Room/board/expenses: $15,700
Full-time enrollment: 334
doctoral students: 15%; master's students: 83%; education specialists: 3%; men: 22%; women: 78%; minorities: N/A; international: N/A
Part-time enrollment: 329
doctoral students: 50%; master's students: 45%; education specialists: 5%; men: 25%; women: 75%; minorities: N/A; international: N/A
Acceptance rate (master's): 74%
Acceptance rate (doctoral): 65%
Entrance test required: GRE
Avg. GRE (of all entering students with scores): quantitative: 148; verbal: 151
Research assistantships: 18
Students reporting specialty: 100%
Students specializing in: curriculum/instr.: 5%; admin.:

15%; evaluation/research/statistics: 2%; instructional media design: 0%; educational psych: 2%; educational tech.: 0%; elementary: 17%; secondary: 6%; special: 13%; counseling: 9%; other: 30%

Virginia State University[1]
1 Hayden Drive
Petersburg, VA 23806
www.vsu.edu/
Public
Admissions: (804) 524-5985
Email: gradadmiss@vsu.edu
Financial aid: N/A
Tuition: N/A
Room/board/expenses: N/A
Enrollment: N/A

Virginia Tech
226 War Memorial Hall (0313)
Blacksburg, VA 24061
www.graduateschool.vt.edu/
Public
Admissions: (540) 231-6691
Email: grads@vt.edu
Financial aid: (540) 231-4558
Application deadline: rolling
In-state tuition: full time: $14,532; part time: $693/credit hour
Out-of-state tuition: full time: $27,160
Room/board/expenses: $14,342
Full-time enrollment: 353
doctoral students: 40%; master's students: 55%; education specialists: 5%; men: 26%; women: 74%; minorities: 20%; international: 11%
Part-time enrollment: 318
doctoral students: 49%; master's students: 40%; education specialists: 10%; men: 33%; women: 67%; minorities: 19%; international: 3%
Acceptance rate (master's): 75%
Acceptance rate (doctoral): 69%
Entrance test required: GRE
Avg. GRE (of all entering students with scores): quantitative: 150; verbal: 152
Research assistantships: 5
Students reporting specialty: 100%
Students specializing in: curriculum/instr.: 48%; admin.: 38%; evaluation/research/statistics: 2%; counseling: 7%; other: 4%

WASHINGTON

Seattle Pacific University[1]
3307 Third Avenue W
Seattle, WA 98119-1997
www.spu.edu
Private
Admissions: N/A
Financial aid: N/A
Tuition: N/A
Room/board/expenses: N/A
Enrollment: N/A

Seattle University[1]
901 12th Avenue
Seattle, WA 98122
www.seattleu.edu/education
Private
Admissions: (206) 296-2000
Email: grad-admissions@seattleu.edu
Financial aid: (206) 296-2000
Tuition: N/A

Room/board/expenses: N/A
Enrollment: N/A

University of Washington
PO Box 353600
206 Miller
Seattle, WA 98195-3600
education.uw.edu/home
Public
Admissions: (206) 543-7834
Email: edinfo@u.washington.edu
Financial aid: (206) 543-7834
Application deadline: N/A
In-state tuition: full time: $18,048; part time: $759/credit hour
Out-of-state tuition: full time: $31,650
Room/board/expenses: $19,011
Full-time enrollment: 627
doctoral students: 28%; master's students: 66%; education specialists: 6%; men: 23%; women: 77%; minorities: 33%; international: 10%
Part-time enrollment: 215
doctoral students: 24%; master's students: 76%; education specialists: 0%; men: 25%; women: 75%; minorities: 27%; international: 2%
Acceptance rate (master's): 67%
Acceptance rate (doctoral): 24%
Entrance test required: GRE
Avg. GRE (of all entering students with scores): quantitative: 152; verbal: 154
Research assistantships: 59
Students reporting specialty: 100%
Students specializing in: curriculum/instr.: 18%; admin.: 21%; policy: 19%; evaluation/research/statistics: 1%; educational psych: 12%; elementary: 8%; higher education admin.: 4%; secondary: 6%; social/philosophical foundations: 6%; special: 17%; counseling: 5%; other: 17%

Washington State University[1]
PO Box 642114
Pullman, WA 99164-2114
www.wsu.edu/
Public
Admissions: N/A
Financial aid: N/A
Tuition: N/A
Room/board/expenses: N/A
Enrollment: N/A

WEST VIRGINIA

Marshall University[1]
100 Angus E. Peyton Drive
South Charleston, WV 25303
www.marshall.edu/gsepd/
Public
Admissions: N/A
Financial aid: N/A
Tuition: N/A
Room/board/expenses: N/A
Enrollment: N/A

West Virginia University
802 Allen Hall
PO Box 6122
Morgantown, WV 26506-6122
www.wvu.edu
Public
Admissions: (304) 293-2124
Email: graded@mail.wvu.edu
Financial aid: (304) 293-1988

Application deadline: rolling
In-state tuition: full time: $9,594; part time: $429/credit hour
Out-of-state tuition: full time: $24,102
Room/board/expenses: $13,370
Full-time enrollment: 428
doctoral students: 19%; master's students: 81%; education specialists: 0%; men: 18%; women: 82%; minorities: N/A; international: N/A
Part-time enrollment: 325
doctoral students: 24%; master's students: 76%; education specialists: 0%; men: 16%; women: 84%; minorities: N/A; international: N/A
Acceptance rate (master's): 45%
Acceptance rate (doctoral): 40%
Entrance test required: GRE
Avg. GRE (of all entering students with scores): quantitative: 146; verbal: 150
Research assistantships: 30
Students reporting specialty: 0%
Students specializing in: N/A

WISCONSIN

Cardinal Stritch University
6801 N. Yates Road
Milwaukee, WI 53217
www.stritch.edu/
Private
Admissions: (414) 410-4042
Email: admissions@stritch.edu
Financial aid: (414) 410-4048
Application deadline: rolling
Tuition: full time: $665/credit hour; part time: $665/credit hour
Room/board/expenses: N/A
Full-time enrollment: 80
doctoral students: 13%; master's students: 88%; education specialists: N/A; men: 18%; women: 83%; minorities: 25%; international: 3%
Part-time enrollment: 420
doctoral students: 39%; master's students: 61%; education specialists: N/A; men: 33%; women: 67%; minorities: 24%; international: 2%
Acceptance rate (master's): 100%
Acceptance rate (doctoral): 100%
Entrance test required: N/A
Avg. GRE (of all entering students with scores): quantitative: N/A; verbal: N/A
Students reporting specialty: 100%
Students specializing in: admin.: 47%; elementary: 12%; secondary: 5%; special: 15%; other: 20%

Edgewood College
1000 Edgewood College Drive
Madison, WI 53711
www.edgewood.edu
Private
Admissions: (608) 663-3297
Email: gps@edgewood.edu
Financial aid: (608) 663-4300
Application deadline: rolling
Tuition: full time: $898/credit hour; part time: $898/credit hour
Room/board/expenses: N/A
Full-time enrollment: 137
doctoral students: 69%; master's students: 31%; education specialists: N/A; men: 34%; women: 66%; minorities: N/A; international: N/A
Part-time enrollment: 215
doctoral students: 29%; master's students: 71%;

education specialists: N/A; men: 30%; women: 70%; minorities: N/A; international: N/A
Acceptance rate (master's): N/A
Acceptance rate (doctoral): N/A
Entrance test required: N/A
Avg. GRE (of all entering students with scores): quantitative: N/A; verbal: N/A
Students reporting specialty: 0%
Students specializing in: N/A

Marian University[1]
45 S. National Ave
Fond du Lac, WI 54935-4699
www.marianuniversity.edu/
admission-financial-aid/
graduate-studies/
Private
Admissions: N/A
Email: admission@
marianuniversity.edu
Financial aid: N/A
Tuition: N/A
Room/board/expenses: N/A
Enrollment: N/A

Marquette University
Schroeder Complex, Box 1881
Milwaukee, WI 53201
www.grad.marquette.edu
Private
Admissions: (414) 288-7137
Email: mugs@marquette.edu
Financial aid: (414) 288-5325
Application deadline: rolling
Tuition: full time: $805/credit hour; part time: $805/credit hour
Room/board/expenses: $17,420

Full-time enrollment: 37
doctoral students: 3%; master's students: 97%; education specialists: N/A; men: 22%; women: 78%; minorities: 30%; international: 0%
Part-time enrollment: 86
doctoral students: 33%; master's students: 67%; education specialists: N/A; men: 40%; women: 60%; minorities: 11%; international: 0%
Acceptance rate (master's): 90%
Acceptance rate (doctoral): 75%
Entrance test required: GRE
Avg. GRE (of all entering students with scores): quantitative: 149; verbal: 152
Research assistantships: 5
Students reporting specialty: 100%
Students specializing in: admin.: 19%; policy: 21%; elementary: 7%; higher education admin.: 19%; junior high: 29%; secondary: 22%; social/philosophical foundations: 28%; counseling: 5%

University of Wisconsin-Madison
1000 Bascom Mall, Suite 377
Madison, WI 53706-1326
www.education.wisc.edu
Public
Admissions: (608) 262-2433
Email: gradadmiss@grad.wisc.edu
Financial aid: (608) 262-3060
Application deadline: rolling
In-state tuition: full time: $10,728; part time: $770/credit hour

Out-of-state tuition: full time: $24,054
Room/board/expenses: $18,864
Full-time enrollment: 801
doctoral students: 55%; master's students: 45%; education specialists: N/A; men: 30%; women: 70%; minorities: 23%; international: 15%
Part-time enrollment: 279
doctoral students: 49%; master's students: 51%; education specialists: N/A; men: 34%; women: 66%; minorities: 15%; international: 9%
Acceptance rate (master's): 37%
Acceptance rate (doctoral): 26%
Entrance test required: GRE
Avg. GRE (of all entering students with scores): quantitative: 152; verbal: 155
Research assistantships: 21
Students reporting specialty: 100%
Students specializing in: curriculum/instr.: 23%; admin.: 22%; policy: 7%; educational psych: 12%; secondary: 5%; special: 3%; counseling: 2%; other: 26%

University of Wisconsin-Milwaukee
PO Box 413
Milwaukee, WI 53201
www.graduateschool.uwm.edu
Public
Admissions: (414) 229-6560
Email: gradschool@uwm.edu
Financial aid: (414) 229-4541
Application deadline: rolling

In-state tuition: full time: $13,189; part time: $1,237/credit hour
Out-of-state tuition: full time: $26,227
Room/board/expenses: $13,894
Full-time enrollment: 258
doctoral students: 37%; master's students: 59%; education specialists: 4%; men: 25%; women: 75%; minorities: 27%; international: 4%
Part-time enrollment: 331
doctoral students: 18%; master's students: 79%; education specialists: 3%; men: 27%; women: 73%; minorities: 27%; international: 1%
Acceptance rate (master's): 59%
Acceptance rate (doctoral): 31%
Entrance test required: GRE
Avg. GRE (of all entering students with scores): quantitative: 150; verbal: 153
Research assistantships: 12
Students reporting specialty: 100%
Students specializing in: curriculum/instr.: 9%; admin.: 44%; educational psych: 34%; social/philosophical foundations: 5%; special: 5%; counseling: 0%; other: 3%

WYOMING

University of Wyoming
Department 3374
1000 E. University Avenue
Laramie, WY 82071
www.uwyo.edu/education/
Public
Admissions: (307) 766-5160

Email: admissions@uwyo.edu
Financial aid: (307) 766-2116
Application deadline: rolling
In-state tuition: full time: $241/credit hour; part time: $241/credit hour
Out-of-state tuition: full time: $721/credit hour
Room/board/expenses: $16,943
Full-time enrollment: 140
doctoral students: 26%; master's students: 74%; education specialists: N/A; men: 26%; women: 74%; minorities: 11%; international: 6%
Part-time enrollment: 363
doctoral students: 39%; master's students: 61%; education specialists: N/A; men: 33%; women: 67%; minorities: 8%; international: 1%
Acceptance rate (master's): 82%
Acceptance rate (doctoral): 70%
Entrance test required: GRE
Avg. GRE (of all entering students with scores): quantitative: 149; verbal: 156
Research assistantships: 19
Students reporting specialty: 100%
Students specializing in: curriculum/instr.: 4%; admin.: 6%; special: 1%; counseling: 14%; other: 78%

ENGINEERING

The engineering directory lists the country's 215 schools offering doctoral programs. One hundred ninety-eight schools responded to the U.S. News survey conducted in the fall of 2016 and early 2017. Information about entrance requirements, enrollment and costs is reported. Institutions that did not respond to the survey have abbreviated entries.

KEY TO THE TERMINOLOGY

1. A school footnoted with the numeral 1 did not return the U.S. News statistical survey; limited data appear in its entry.

N/A. Not available from the school or not applicable.

Admissions. The admissions office phone number.

Email. The address of the admissions office. If instead of an email address a website is listed, the website will automatically present an email screen programmed to reach the admissions office.

Financial aid. The financial aid office phone number.

Application deadline. For fall 2018 enrollment. "Rolling" means there is no deadline; the school acts on applications as they are received. "Varies" means deadlines vary according to department or whether applicants are U.S. citizens or foreign nationals.

Tuition. For the 2016-17 academic year. Includes fees.

Credit hour. The cost per credit hour for the 2016-17 academic year.

Room/board/expenses. For the 2016-17 academic year.

Enrollment. Full and part time for fall 2016. The total is the combination of master's and doctoral students if the school offers both degrees. Where available, the breakdown for men, women, minorities and international students is provided. Percentages for men and women may not add up to 100 because of rounding.

Minorities. For fall 2016, the percentage of students who are black or African-American, Asian, American Indian or Alaska Native, Native Hawaiian or other Pacific Islander, Hispanic/Latino, or two or more races. The minority numbers were reported by each school.

Acceptance rate. Percentage of applicants who were accepted for fall 2016, including both master's and doctoral degree programs.

GRE requirement. "Yes" means Graduate Record Examination scores are required by some or all departments.

Average GRE scores. Combined for both master's and doctoral degree students who entered in fall 2016. GRE scores displayed are for fall 2016 entering master's and Ph.D. students.

TOEFL requirement. "Yes" means that students from non-English-speaking countries must submit scores for the Test of English as a Foreign Language.

Minimum TOEFL score. The score listed is the minimum acceptable score for the paper TOEFL. (The computer-administered TOEFL is graded on a different scale.)

Total fellowships, teaching assistantships and research assistantships. The number of student appointments for the 2016-17 academic year. Students may hold multiple appointments and would therefore be counted more than once.

Student specialties. Proportion of master's and doctoral students, both full and part time, in the specialty-reporting population (not necessarily the entire student body) who were enrolled in a particular specialty in fall 2016. Specialty fields listed are aerospace/aeronautical/astronautical; biological/agricultural; architectural engineering; bioengineering/biomedical; chemical; civil; computer engineering; computer science; electrical/electronic/communications; engineering management; engineering science and physics; environmental/environmental health; industrial/manufacturing/systems; materials; mechanical; mining; nuclear; petroleum; and other. Numbers may not add up to 100 percent from rounding or because students are enrolled in multiple specialties.

ALABAMA

Auburn University (Ginn)
1301 Shelby Center
Auburn, AL 36849-5330
www.grad.auburn.edu
Public
Admissions: (334) 844-4700
Email: gradadm@auburn.edu
Financial aid: (334) 844-4367
Application deadline: rolling
In-state tuition: full time: $10,696; part time: $504/credit hour
Out-of-state tuition: full time: $28,840
Room/board/expenses: $19,762
Full-time enrollment: 565
men: 75%; women: 25%;
minorities: 3%; international: 83%
Part-time enrollment: 332
men: 81%; women: 19%;
minorities: 11%; international: 26%
Acceptance rate: 46%
GRE requirement: Yes
Avg. GRE: quantitative: 163
TOEFL requirement: Yes
Minimum TOEFL score: 550
Fellowships: 138
Teaching assistantships: 202
Research assistantships: 341
Students reporting specialty:
aerospace: 5%; agriculture: 3%; chemical: 10%; civil: 15%; computer science: 16%; electrical: 15%; industrial: 14%; materials: 5%; mechanical: 16%; other: 1%

Tuskegee University[1]
202 Engineering Building
Tuskegee, AL 36088-1920
www.tuskegee.edu
Private
Admissions: (334) 727-8500
Email: adm@tuskegee.edu
Financial aid: N/A
Tuition: N/A
Room/board/expenses: N/A
Enrollment: N/A

University of Alabama
Box 870200
Tuscaloosa, AL 35487-0200
www.coeweb.eng.ua.edu/
Public
Admissions: (205) 348-5921
Email: gradschool@ua.edu
Financial aid: (205) 348-2976
Application deadline: rolling
In-state tuition: full time: $10,470; part time: N/A
Out-of-state tuition: full time: $26,950
Room/board/expenses: $13,330
Full-time enrollment: 289
men: 81%; women: 19%;
minorities: 6%; international: 58%
Part-time enrollment: 84
men: 87%; women: 13%;
minorities: 13%; international: 15%
Acceptance rate: 43%
GRE requirement: Yes
Avg. GRE: quantitative: 160
TOEFL requirement: Yes
Minimum TOEFL score: 550
Fellowships: 0
Teaching assistantships: 79
Research assistantships: 118

Students reporting specialty:
aerospace: 18%; chemical: 6%; civil: 17%; computer science: 11%; electrical: 18%; materials: 9%; mechanical: 21%; other: 1%

University of Alabama-Birmingham
1720 2nd Avenue S, HOEN 100
Birmingham, AL 35294-4440
www.uab.edu/engineering
Public
Admissions: (205) 934-8227
Email: gradschool@uab.edu
Financial aid: (205) 934-8132
Application deadline: 03/01
In-state tuition: full time: $8,050; part time: $396/credit hour
Out-of-state tuition: full time: $17,756
Room/board/expenses: $10,225
Full-time enrollment: 134
men: 84%; women: 16%;
minorities: 18%; international: 52%
Part-time enrollment: 342
men: 77%; women: 23%;
minorities: 33%; international: 7%
Acceptance rate: 82%
GRE requirement: Yes
Avg. GRE: quantitative: 155
TOEFL requirement: Yes
Minimum TOEFL score: 550
Fellowships: 14
Teaching assistantships: 24
Research assistantships: 55
Students reporting specialty:
biomedical: 7%; civil: 6%; computer: 4%; electrical: 6%; management: 52%; materials: 7%; mechanical: 5%; other: 13%

University of Alabama-Huntsville
301 Sparkman Drive, EB 102
Huntsville, AL 35899
www.uah.edu
Public
Admissions: (256) 824-6198
Email: berkowd@uah.edu
Financial aid: (256) 824-6942
Application deadline: rolling
In-state tuition: full time: $9,834; part time: $566/credit hour
Out-of-state tuition: full time: $21,830
Room/board/expenses: $12,618
Full-time enrollment: 329
men: 75%; women: 25%;
minorities: 7%; international: 65%
Part-time enrollment: 452
men: 80%; women: 20%;
minorities: 13%; international: 8%
Acceptance rate: 71%
GRE requirement: Yes
Avg. GRE: quantitative: 157
TOEFL requirement: Yes
Minimum TOEFL score: 550
Fellowships: 0
Teaching assistantships: 90
Research assistantships: 83
Students reporting specialty:
aerospace: 7%; biomedical: 4%; chemical: 1%; civil: 3%; computer: 11%; computer science: 28%; electrical: 19%; industrial: 14%; materials: 1%; mechanical: 13%

ALASKA

University of Alaska-Fairbanks

PO Box 755960
Fairbanks, AK 99775-5960
www.uaf.edu/cem
Public
Admissions: (800) 478-1823
Email: admissions@uaf.edu
Financial aid: (888) 474-7256
Application deadline: 06/01
In-state tuition: full time: $533/credit hour; part time: $533/credit hour
Out-of-state tuition: full time: $1,088/credit hour
Room/board/expenses: $13,340
Full-time enrollment: 64
men: 77%; women: 23%;
minorities: 2%; international: 45%
Part-time enrollment: 42
men: 79%; women: 21%;
minorities: 26%; international: 21%
Acceptance rate: 32%
GRE requirement: Yes
Avg. GRE: quantitative: 158
TOEFL requirement: Yes
Minimum TOEFL score: N/A
Teaching assistantships: 34
Research assistantships: 26
Students reporting specialty:
civil: 9%; computer science: 2%;
electrical: 21%; management: 1%;
environmental: 5%; mechanical: 8%; mining: 3%; petroleum: 22%;
other: 29%

ARIZONA

Arizona State University (Fulton)

Box 879309
Tempe, AZ 85287-9309
engineering.asu.edu
Public
Admissions: (480) 965-6113
Email: gograd@asu.edu
Financial aid: (480) 965-3355
Application deadline: rolling
In-state tuition: full time: $12,306; part time: $1,037/credit hour
Out-of-state tuition: full time: $29,682
Room/board/expenses: $19,044
Full-time enrollment: 2,779
men: 77%; women: 23%;
minorities: 7%; international: 79%
Part-time enrollment: 857
men: 79%; women: 21%;
minorities: 23%; international: 34%
Acceptance rate: 47%
GRE requirement: Yes
Avg. GRE: quantitative: 162
TOEFL requirement: Yes
Minimum TOEFL score: 550
Fellowships: 372
Teaching assistantships: 299
Research assistantships: 649
Students reporting specialty:
aerospace: 2%; biomedical: 5%; chemical: 3%; civil: 6%;
computer: 7%; computer science: 26%; electrical: 22%;
environmental: 2%; industrial: 5%; materials: 4%; mechanical: 10%; other: 8%

University of Arizona

Civil Engineering Building
Room 100
Tucson, AZ 85721-0072
grad.arizona.edu
Public
Admissions: (520) 621-3471
Email: gradadmission@grad.arizona.edu
Financial aid: (520) 621-1858
Application deadline: 06/01

In-state tuition: full time: $11,372; part time: $812/credit hour
Out-of-state tuition: full time: $30,124
Room/board/expenses: $16,950
Full-time enrollment: 756
men: 77%; women: 23%;
minorities: 13%; international: 57%
Part-time enrollment: 325
men: 82%; women: 18%;
minorities: 27%; international: 13%
Acceptance rate: 47%
GRE requirement: Yes
Avg. GRE: quantitative: 162
TOEFL requirement: Yes
Minimum TOEFL score: 550
Fellowships: 120
Teaching assistantships: 108
Research assistantships: 216
Students reporting specialty:
aerospace: 3%; agriculture: 3%;
biomedical: 3%; chemical: 4%;
civil: 4%; computer science: 6%;
electrical: 27%; management: 3%;
environmental: 3%; industrial: 8%; materials: 4%; mechanical: 4%; mining: 4%; other: 27%

ARKANSAS

University of Arkansas-Fayetteville

Bell Engineering Center
Room 4183
Fayetteville, AR 72701
engineering.uark.edu/
Public
Admissions: (479) 575-4401
Email: gradinfo@uark.edu
Financial aid: (479) 575-3806
Application deadline: 08/01
In-state tuition: full time: $410/credit hour; part time: $410/credit hour
Out-of-state tuition: full time: $1,047/credit hour
Room/board/expenses: $13,086
Full-time enrollment: 340
men: 73%; women: 27%;
minorities: 9%; international: 62%
Part-time enrollment: 174
men: 80%; women: 20%;
minorities: 17%; international: 21%
Acceptance rate: 32%
GRE requirement: Yes
Avg. GRE: quantitative: 159
TOEFL requirement: Yes
Minimum TOEFL score: 550
Fellowships: 40
Teaching assistantships: 77
Research assistantships: 201
Students reporting specialty:
agriculture: 3%; biomedical: 6%; chemical: 8%; civil: 10%;
computer: 6%; computer science: 9%; electrical: 24%;
industrial: 10%; mechanical: 9%;
other: 15%

University of Arkansas-Little Rock[1]

2801 S. University Avenue
Little Rock, AR 72204
ualr.edu/eit/
Public
Admissions: (501) 569-3127
Email: admissions@ualr.edu
Financial aid: N/A
Tuition: N/A
Room/board/expenses: N/A
Enrollment: N/A

CALIFORNIA

California Institute of Technology

1200 E. California Boulevard
Pasadena, CA 91125-4400
www.gradoffice.caltech.edu
Private
Admissions: (626) 395-6346
Email: gradofc@its.caltech.edu
Financial aid: (626) 395-6346
Application deadline: 12/01
Tuition: full time: $47,451; part time: N/A
Room/board/expenses: $31,335
Full-time enrollment: 542
men: 76%; women: 24%;
minorities: N/A; international: N/A
Part-time enrollment: 1
men: 0%; women: 100%;
minorities: N/A; international: N/A
Acceptance rate: 9%
GRE requirement: Yes
Avg. GRE: quantitative: 169
TOEFL requirement: Yes
Minimum TOEFL score: N/A
Fellowships: 169
Teaching assistantships: 74
Research assistantships: 331
Students reporting specialty:
aerospace: 13%; biomedical: 2%; chemical: 9%; civil: 2%;
computer science: 7%; electrical: 27%; science and physics: 13%;
environmental: 6%; materials: 12%; mechanical: 9%

California State University-Long Beach

1250 Bellflower Boulevard
Long Beach, CA 90840-8306
www.csulb.edu/colleges/coe/
Public
Admissions: (562) 985-7772
Email: coe-gr@csulb.edu
Financial aid: (562) 985-8403
Application deadline: 04/01
In-state tuition: full time: $7,718; part time: $4,886
Out-of-state tuition: full time: $14,414
Room/board/expenses: $17,500
Full-time enrollment: 254
men: 78%; women: 22%;
minorities: 16%; international: 79%
Part-time enrollment: 349
men: 78%; women: 22%;
minorities: 34%; international: 44%
Acceptance rate: 21%
GRE requirement: Yes
Avg. GRE: quantitative: 158
TOEFL requirement: Yes
Minimum TOEFL score: 550
Fellowships: 6
Teaching assistantships: 4
Research assistantships: 160
Students reporting specialty:
aerospace: 10%; civil: 11%;
computer: 3%; computer science: 33%; electrical: 23%;
industrial: 3%; mechanical: 13%;
other: 4%

Naval Postgraduate School[1]

1 University Circle
Monterey, CA 93943-5001
www.nps.edu/Academics/Schools/GSEAS/
Public
Admissions: (831) 656-3093
Email: grad-ed@nps.edu
Financial aid: N/A
Tuition: N/A
Room/board/expenses: N/A
Enrollment: N/A

Northwestern Polytechnic University[1]

47671 Westinghouse Drive
Fremont, CA 94539
www.npu.edu
Private
Admissions: (510) 592-9688
Email: admission@npu.edu
Financial aid: N/A
Tuition: N/A
Room/board/expenses: N/A
Enrollment: N/A

San Diego State University

5500 Campanile Drive
San Diego, CA 92182
www.engineering.sdsu.edu
Public
Admissions: (619) 594-6336
Email: admissions@sdsu.edu
Financial aid: (619) 594-6323
Application deadline: 03/01
In-state tuition: full time: $8,350; part time: $5,518
Out-of-state tuition: full time: $372/credit hour
Room/board/expenses: $20,624
Full-time enrollment: 178
men: 72%; women: 28%;
minorities: 19%; international: 60%
Part-time enrollment: 234
men: 74%; women: 26%;
minorities: 23%; international: 44%
Acceptance rate: 47%
GRE requirement: Yes
Avg. GRE: quantitative: 157
TOEFL requirement: Yes
Minimum TOEFL score: 550
Teaching assistantships: 21
Students reporting specialty:
aerospace: 8%; biomedical: 5%; civil: 15%; computer: 36%;
science and physics: 6%;
environmental: 3%; industrial: 3%; mechanical: 24%

Santa Clara University

500 El Camino Real
Santa Clara, CA 95053-0583
www.scu.edu/engineering/graduate
Private
Admissions: (408) 554-4313
Email: gradengineer@scu.edu
Financial aid: (408) 551-1000
Application deadline: 04/07
Tuition: full time: $928/credit hour; part time: $928/credit hour
Room/board/expenses: N/A
Full-time enrollment: 448
men: 58%; women: 42%;
minorities: 15%; international: 74%
Part-time enrollment: 297
men: 63%; women: 37%;
minorities: 40%; international: 28%
Acceptance rate: 45%
GRE requirement: Yes
Avg. GRE: quantitative: 161
TOEFL requirement: Yes
Minimum TOEFL score: N/A
Teaching assistantships: 40
Research assistantships: 8
Students reporting specialty:
biomedical: 5%; civil: 2%;
computer: 53%; electrical: 16%; management: 11%;
environmental: 1%; mechanical: 11%; other: 1%

Northwestern Polytechnic University[1]

Stanford University

Huang Engineering Center
Stanford, CA 94305-4121
gradadmissions.stanford.edu
Private
Admissions: (866) 732-7472
Email: gradadmissions@stanford.edu
Financial aid: (650) 723-3058
Application deadline: N/A
Tuition: full time: $51,102; part time: N/A
Room/board/expenses: $29,748
Full-time enrollment: 3,486
men: 71%; women: 29%;
minorities: 25%; international: 44%
Part-time enrollment: 189
men: 83%; women: 17%;
minorities: 28%; international: 32%
Acceptance rate: 15%
GRE requirement: Yes
Avg. GRE: quantitative: 167
TOEFL requirement: Yes
Minimum TOEFL score: 575
Fellowships: 1,280
Teaching assistantships: 570
Research assistantships: 1,088
Students reporting specialty:
aerospace: 6%; biomedical: 5%; chemical: 4%; civil: 13%;
computer science: 7%;
electrical: 20%; management: 8%; materials: 6%; mechanical: 14%; petroleum: 1%; other: 6%

University of California-Berkeley

320 McLaughlin Hall, # 1700
Berkeley, CA 94720-1700
www.grad.berkeley.edu/
Public
Admissions: (510) 643-7462
Email: gradadm@berkeley.edu
Financial aid: (510) 664-9181
Application deadline: 01/06
In-state tuition: full time: $17,741; part time: N/A
Out-of-state tuition: full time: $32,843
Room/board/expenses: $22,518
Full-time enrollment: 1,940
men: 69%; women: 31%;
minorities: 23%; international: 45%
Part-time enrollment: 136
men: 63%; women: 37%;
minorities: 35%; international: 16%
Acceptance rate: 17%
GRE requirement: Yes
Avg. GRE: quantitative: 165
TOEFL requirement: Yes
Minimum TOEFL score: 570
Fellowships: 873
Teaching assistantships: 290
Research assistantships: 783
Students reporting specialty:
biomedical: 12%; chemical: 7%; civil: 17%; computer: 11%;
electrical: 17%; industrial: 7%;
materials: 6%; mechanical: 18%;
nuclear: 3%; other: 2%

University of California-Davis

1042 Kemper Hall
1 Shields Avenue
Davis, CA 95616-5294
engineering.ucdavis.edu
Public
Admissions: (530) 752-1473
Email: gradadmit@ucdavis.edu
Financial aid: (530) 752-8864
Application deadline: N/A
In-state tuition: full time: $13,237; part time: $7,027
Out-of-state tuition: full time: $28,339
Room/board/expenses: $22,671

Full-time enrollment: 1,054
men: 73%; women: 27%;
minorities: 18%; international:
48%
Part-time enrollment: 36
men: 58%; women: 42%;
minorities: 28%; international:
11%
Acceptance rate: 22%
GRE requirement: Yes
Avg. GRE: quantitative: 163
TOEFL requirement: Yes
Minimum TOEFL score: 550
Fellowships: 259
Teaching assistantships: 281
Research assistantships: 425
Students reporting specialty:
aerospace: 13%; agriculture:
5%; biomedical: 8%; chemical:
6%; civil: 18%; computer:
21%; computer science: 20%;
electrical: 21%; science and
physics: 0%; environmental: 18%;
materials: 5%; mechanical: 13%;
other: 3%

University of California-Irvine (Samueli)

305 EH 5200
Irvine, CA 92697-2700
www.engineering.uci.edu
Public
Admissions: (949) 824-8090
Email: gradengr@uci.edu
Financial aid: (949) 824-4889
Application deadline: 12/01
In-state tuition: full time: $17,164;
part time: $11,554
Out-of-state tuition: full time:
$32,266
Room/board/expenses: $19,370
Full-time enrollment: 1,378
men: 68%; women: 32%;
minorities: 14%; international:
67%
Part-time enrollment: 64
men: 77%; women: 23%;
minorities: 19%; international:
45%
Acceptance rate: 18%
GRE requirement: Yes
Avg. GRE: quantitative: 164
TOEFL requirement: Yes
Minimum TOEFL score: 550
Fellowships: 482
Teaching assistantships: 358
Research assistantships: 674
Students reporting specialty:
aerospace: 10%; biomedical:
9%; chemical: 6%; civil: 9%;
computer: 9%; computer
science: 34%;
electrical: 13%; management: 1%;
environmental: 3%; industrial: 1%;
materials: 5%; mechanical: 10%

University of California-Los Angeles (Samueli)

6426 Boelter Hall
Box 951601
Los Angeles, CA 90095-1601
www.engineer.ucla.edu
Public
Admissions: (310) 825-2514
Email: gradadm@seas.ucla.edu
Financial aid: (310) 206-0400
Application deadline: 12/01
In-state tuition: full time: $12,684;
part time: N/A
Out-of-state tuition: full time:
$27,786
Room/board/expenses: $20,640
Full-time enrollment: 2,187
men: 77%; women: 23%;
minorities: 24%; international:
56%

Part-time enrollment: N/A
men: N/A; women: N/A;
minorities: N/A; international: N/A
Acceptance rate: 27%
GRE requirement: Yes
Avg. GRE: quantitative: 166
TOEFL requirement: Yes
Minimum TOEFL score: 560
Fellowships: 740
Teaching assistantships: 747
Research assistantships: 1,387
Students reporting specialty:
aerospace: 4%; biomedical: 7%;
chemical: 5%; civil: 8%; computer
science: 16%; electrical: 28%;
materials: 9%; mechanical: 15%;
other: 9%

University of California-Merced

5200 North Lake Road
Merced, CA 95343
engineering.ucmerced.edu/
Public
Admissions: (202) 228-4400
Email:
engineering@ucmerced.edu
Financial aid: (209) 228-4405
Application deadline: 01/17
In-state tuition: full time: $12,931;
part time: $7,321
Out-of-state tuition: full time:
$28,033
Room/board/expenses: $18,076
Full-time enrollment: 170
men: 69%; women: 31%;
minorities: 20%; international:
58%
Part-time enrollment: 2
men: 100%; women: 0%;
minorities: 0%; international: 0%
Acceptance rate: 35%
GRE requirement: Yes
Avg. GRE: quantitative: 160
TOEFL requirement: Yes
Minimum TOEFL score: 550
Fellowships: 22
Teaching assistantships: 67
Research assistantships: 34
Students reporting specialty:
biomedical: 13%; computer
science: 34%; environmental:
28%; mechanical: 25%

University of California-Riverside (Bourns)

University Office Building
Riverside, CA 92521-0208
www.graddiv.ucr.edu
Public
Admissions: (951) 827-3313
Email: grdadmis@ucr.edu
Financial aid: (951) 827-3157
Application deadline: 01/05
In-state tuition: full time: $16,803;
part time: $11,193
Out-of-state tuition: full time:
$31,905
Room/board/expenses: $22,300
Full-time enrollment: 851
men: 73%; women: 27%;
minorities: 24%; international: 0%
Part-time enrollment: N/A
men: N/A; women: N/A;
minorities: N/A; international: N/A
Acceptance rate: 29%
GRE requirement: Yes
Avg. GRE: quantitative: 162
TOEFL requirement: Yes
Minimum TOEFL score: 550
Fellowships: 182
Teaching assistantships: 233
Research assistantships: 270
Students reporting specialty:
biomedical: 10%; chemical:
13%; computer: 4%; computer
science: 24%; electrical: 18%;
materials: 11%; mechanical: 9%;
other: 11%

University of California-San Diego (Jacobs)

9500 Gilman Drive
La Jolla, CA 92093-0403
www.jacobsschool.ucsd.edu
Public
Admissions: (858) 534-3555
Email: gradadmissions@ucsd.edu
Financial aid: (858) 534-4480
Application deadline: N/A
In-state tuition: full time: $13,085;
part time: $7,475
Out-of-state tuition: full time:
$28,187
Room/board/expenses: $21,941
Full-time enrollment: 2,496
men: 77%; women: 23%;
minorities: 17%; international:
65%
Part-time enrollment: 139
men: 79%; women: 21%;
minorities: 44%; international:
18%
Acceptance rate: 26%
GRE requirement: Yes
Avg. GRE: quantitative: 166
TOEFL requirement: Yes
Minimum TOEFL score: 550
Fellowships: 480
Teaching assistantships: 720
Research assistantships: 1,220
Students reporting specialty:
aerospace: 1%; biomedical:
9%; chemical: 3%; civil: 8%;
computer: 5%; computer
science: 27%; electrical: 22%;
science and physics: 2%;
materials: 8%; mechanical: 10%;
other: 4%

University of California-Santa Barbara

Harold Frank Hall 1038
Santa Barbara, CA 93106-5130
www.graddiv.ucsb.edu
Public
Admissions: (805) 893-2277
Email: gradadmissions@
graddiv.ucsb.edu
Financial aid: (805) 893-2432
Application deadline: N/A
In-state tuition: full time: $13,248;
part time: N/A
Out-of-state tuition: full time:
$28,350
Room/board/expenses: $20,517
Full-time enrollment: 721
men: 77%; women: 23%;
minorities: 13%; international:
50%
Part-time enrollment: N/A
men: N/A; women: N/A;
minorities: N/A; international: N/A
Acceptance rate: 14%
GRE requirement: Yes
Avg. GRE: quantitative: 165
TOEFL requirement: Yes
Minimum TOEFL score: 550
Fellowships: 202
Teaching assistantships: 166
Research assistantships: 378
Students reporting specialty:
chemical: 12%; computer
science: 22%; electrical: 34%;
management: 4%; materials:
19%; mechanical: 9%

University of California-Santa Cruz (Baskin)

1156 High Street
Santa Cruz, CA 95064
ga.soe.ucsc.edu/
Public
Admissions: (831) 459-5905
Email:
soegradadm@soe.ucsc.edu

Financial aid: (831) 459-2963
Application deadline: N/A
In-state tuition: full time: $17,751;
part time: $12,141
Out-of-state tuition: full time:
$32,853
Room/board/expenses: $23,544
Full-time enrollment: 537
men: 75%; women: 25%;
minorities: 14%; international:
55%
Part-time enrollment: 53
men: 81%; women: 19%;
minorities: 21%; international:
40%
Acceptance rate: 39%
GRE requirement: Yes
Avg. GRE: quantitative: 164
TOEFL requirement: Yes
Minimum TOEFL score: 570
Fellowships: 100
Teaching assistantships: 407
Research assistantships: 335
Students reporting specialty:
biomedical: 9%; computer:
24%; computer science: 33%;
electrical: 18%; management: 2%;
other: 14%

University of Southern California (Viterbi)

University Park
Olin Hall 200
Los Angeles, CA 90089-1450
viterbi.usc.edu
Private
Admissions: (213) 740-4530
Email: viterbi.gradadmission@
usc.edu
Financial aid: (213) 740-0119
Application deadline: 01/15
Tuition: full time: $30,375; part
time: $1,845/credit hour
Room/board/expenses: $19,600
Full-time enrollment: 3,888
men: 71%; women: 29%;
minorities: 9%; international: 83%
Part-time enrollment: 1,609
men: 72%; women: 28%;
minorities: 20%; international:
57%
Acceptance rate: 20%
GRE requirement: Yes
Avg. GRE: quantitative: 166
TOEFL requirement: Yes
Minimum TOEFL score: N/A
Fellowships: 324
Teaching assistantships: 716
Research assistantships: 1,078
Students reporting specialty:
aerospace: 5%; biomedical:
4%; chemical: 3%; civil: 5%;
computer: 2%; computer
science: 41%; electrical: 22%;
management: 2%; environmental:
1%; industrial: 4%; materials: 3%;
mechanical: 6%; petroleum: 3%

COLORADO

Colorado School of Mines

1500 Illinois Street
Golden, CO 80401-1887
gradschool.mines.edu
Public
Admissions: (303) 273-3247
Email: grad-app@mines.edu
Financial aid: (303) 273-3207
Application deadline: 06/01
In-state tuition: full time: $17,842;
part time: $872/credit hour
Out-of-state tuition: full time:
$36,172
Room/board/expenses: $19,800
Full-time enrollment: 1,077
men: 70%; women: 30%;
minorities: 11%; international:
34%

Part-time enrollment: 150
men: 77%; women: 23%;
minorities: 23%; international: 9%
Acceptance rate: 44%
GRE requirement: Yes
Avg. GRE: quantitative: 160
TOEFL requirement: Yes
Minimum TOEFL score: 550
Fellowships: 63
Teaching assistantships: 154
Research assistantships: 476
Students reporting specialty:
chemical: 5%; civil: 6%; computer
science: 4%; electrical: 4%;
management: 4%; science and
physics: 1%; environmental:
2%; materials: 5%; mechanical:
11%; mining: 5%; nuclear: 2%;
petroleum: 8%; other: 44%

Colorado State University

Campus Delivery 1301
Fort Collins, CO 80523-1301
graduateschool.colostate.edu
Public
Admissions: (970) 491-6817
Email: gradschool@colostate.edu
Financial aid: (970) 491-6321
Application deadline: 04/01
In-state tuition: full time: $13,875;
part time: $847/credit hour
Out-of-state tuition: full time:
$27,850
Room/board/expenses: $16,016
Full-time enrollment: 371
men: 74%; women: 26%;
minorities: 5%; international: 55%
Part-time enrollment: 436
men: 75%; women: 25%;
minorities: 7%; international: 50%
Acceptance rate: 47%
GRE requirement: Yes
Avg. GRE: quantitative: 167
TOEFL requirement: Yes
Minimum TOEFL score: 550
Fellowships: 76
Teaching assistantships: 81
Research assistantships: 257
Students reporting specialty:
biomedical: 5%; chemical:
5%; civil: 31%; electrical: 31%;
industrial: 1%; mechanical: 16%;
other: 10%

University of Colorado-Boulder

422 UCB
Boulder, CO 80309-0422
www.colorado.edu/engineering
Public
Admissions: (303) 492-6694
Email: apply@colorado.edu
Financial aid: (303) 492-5091
Application deadline: N/A
In-state tuition: full time: $15,884;
part time: $11,186
Out-of-state tuition: full time:
$33,038
Room/board/expenses: $25,712
Full-time enrollment: 1,688
men: 72%; women: 28%;
minorities: 9%; international: 44%
Part-time enrollment: 212
men: 81%; women: 19%;
minorities: 23%; international: 9%
Acceptance rate: 27%
GRE requirement: Yes
Avg. GRE: quantitative: 162
TOEFL requirement: Yes
Minimum TOEFL score: N/A
Fellowships: 77
Teaching assistantships: 160
Research assistantships: 519
Students reporting specialty:
aerospace: 15%; architectural:
2%; chemical: 6%; civil: 11%;
computer science: 15%;
electrical: 18%; management: 9%;
environmental: 1%; materials:
2%; mechanical: 10%; other: 11%

University of Colorado-Colorado Springs

1420 Austin Bluffs Parkway
Colorado Springs, CO 80918
www.uccs.edu
Public
Admissions: (719) 255-3383
Email: go@uccs.edu
Financial aid: (719) 255-3460
Application deadline: 06/01
In-state tuition: full time: $680/credit hour; part time: $763/credit hour
Out-of-state tuition: full time: $1,195/credit hour
Room/board/expenses: $18,920
Full-time enrollment: 39
men: 79%; women: 21%; minorities: 8%; international: 72%
Part-time enrollment: 253
men: 81%; women: 19%; minorities: 21%; international: 25%
Acceptance rate: 53%
GRE requirement: Yes
Avg. GRE: quantitative: 154
TOEFL requirement: Yes
Minimum TOEFL score: N/A
Teaching assistantships: 2
Research assistantships: 14
Students reporting specialty:
computer science: 28%; electrical: 23%; management: 28%; mechanical: 9%; other: 11%

University of Colorado-Denver

PO Box 173364
Campus Box 104
Denver, CO 80217-3364
www.ucdenver.edu/
Public
Admissions: (303) 556-2704
Email: admissions@ucdenver.edu
Financial aid: (303) 556-2886
Application deadline: rolling
In-state tuition: full time: $18,429; part time: $571/credit hour
Out-of-state tuition: full time: $40,749
Room/board/expenses: N/A
Full-time enrollment: 323
men: 72%; women: 28%; minorities: 15%; international: 50%
Part-time enrollment: 129
men: 78%; women: 22%; minorities: 14%; international: 21%
Acceptance rate: 56%
GRE requirement: No
Avg. GRE: quantitative: N/A
TOEFL requirement: Yes
Minimum TOEFL score: N/A
Fellowships: 0
Teaching assistantships: 24
Research assistantships: 76
Students reporting specialty:
biomedical: 13%; civil: 28%; computer science: 22%; electrical: 15%; science and physics: 11%; mechanical: 11%

University of Denver

2135 E. Wesley Avenue
Denver, CO 80208
ritchieschool.du.edu/
Private
Admissions: (303) 871-2427
Email: Ashley.Sherman@du.edu
Financial aid: (303) 871-4020
Application deadline: 02/01
Tuition: full time: $30,447; part time: $1,258/credit hour
Room/board/expenses: $15,930
Full-time enrollment: 162
men: 78%; women: 22%; minorities: 9%; international: 64%

Part-time enrollment: 30
men: 73%; women: 27%; minorities: 27%; international: 13%
Acceptance rate: 62%
GRE requirement: Yes
Avg. GRE: quantitative: 157
TOEFL requirement: Yes
Minimum TOEFL score: 550
Fellowships: 0
Teaching assistantships: 39
Research assistantships: 25
Students reporting specialty:
biomedical: 5%; computer: 11%; computer science: 24%; electrical: 25%; industrial: 13%; materials: 6%; mechanical: 12%; other: 4%

CONNECTICUT

University of Bridgeport

221 University Avenue
Bridgeport, CT 06604
www.bridgeport.edu/sed
Private
Admissions: (203) 576-4552
Email: admit@bridgeport.edu
Financial aid: (203) 576-4568
Application deadline: rolling
Tuition: full time: $830/credit hour; part time: $830/credit hour
Room/board/expenses: $16,420
Full-time enrollment: 833
men: 76%; women: 24%; minorities: 2%; international: 96%
Part-time enrollment: 259
men: 81%; women: 19%; minorities: 12%; international: 78%
Acceptance rate: 60%
GRE requirement: No
Avg. GRE: quantitative: N/A
TOEFL requirement: Yes
Minimum TOEFL score: 550
Teaching assistantships: 44
Research assistantships: 54
Students reporting specialty:
biomedical: 7%; computer: 4%; computer science: 40%; electrical: 21%; management: 13%; mechanical: 16%

University of Connecticut

261 Glenbrook Road, Unit 3237
Storrs, CT 06269-3237
www.uconn.edu
Public
Admissions: (860) 486-0974
Email: gradadmissions@uconn.edu
Financial aid: (860) 486-2819
Application deadline: rolling
In-state tuition: full time: $13,726; part time: $763/credit hour
Out-of-state tuition: full time: $34,762
Room/board/expenses: $22,529
Full-time enrollment: 624
men: 68%; women: 32%; minorities: 9%; international: 67%
Part-time enrollment: 217
men: 82%; women: 18%; minorities: 20%; international: 0%
Acceptance rate: 26%
GRE requirement: Yes
Avg. GRE: quantitative: 163
TOEFL requirement: Yes
Minimum TOEFL score: 550
Fellowships: 266
Teaching assistantships: 85
Research assistantships: 309
Students reporting specialty:
biomedical: 13%; chemical: 6%; civil: 9%; computer: 16%; computer science: 16%; electrical: 17%; environmental: 5%; materials: 11%; mechanical: 18%; other: 6%

Yale University

226 Dunham Lab
10 Hillhouse Avenue
New Haven, CT 06520
www.seas.yale.edu
Private
Admissions: (203) 432-2771
Email: graduate.admissions@yale.edu
Financial aid: (203) 432-2739
Application deadline: 01/02
Tuition: full time: $39,800; part time: $4,975/credit hour
Room/board/expenses: $28,700
Full-time enrollment: 299
men: 67%; women: 33%; minorities: N/A; international: N/A
Part-time enrollment: 1
men: 100%; women: 0%; minorities: N/A; international: N/A
Acceptance rate: 18%
GRE requirement: Yes
Avg. GRE: quantitative: 168
TOEFL requirement: Yes
Minimum TOEFL score: 600
Fellowships: 100
Teaching assistantships: 169
Research assistantships: 149
Students reporting specialty:
biomedical: 25%; chemical: 23%; computer science: 20%; electrical: 17%; mechanical: 14%; other: 0%

DELAWARE

University of Delaware

102 DuPont Hall
Newark, DE 19716-3101
www.ongr.udel.edu
Public
Admissions: (302) 831-2129
Email: gradadmissions@udel.edu
Financial aid: (302) 831-8189
Application deadline: N/A
In-state tuition: full time: $1,720/credit hour; part time: $1,720/credit hour
Out-of-state tuition: full time: $1,720/credit hour
Room/board/expenses: $15,640
Full-time enrollment: 806
men: 73%; women: 27%; minorities: 11%; international: 58%
Part-time enrollment: 125
men: 84%; women: 16%; minorities: 18%; international: 17%
Acceptance rate: 36%
GRE requirement: Yes
Avg. GRE: quantitative: 169
TOEFL requirement: Yes
Minimum TOEFL score: 570
Fellowships: 30
Teaching assistantships: 62
Research assistantships: 408
Students reporting specialty:
biomedical: 4%; chemical: 15%; civil: 12%; computer: 30%; computer science: 16%; electrical: 30%; environmental: 12%; materials: 9%; mechanical: 10%; other: 4%

DISTRICT OF COLUMBIA

The Catholic University of America

620 Michigan Avenue NE
Washington, DC 20064
admissions.cua.edu/graduate/
Private
Admissions: (800) 673-2772
Email: cua-admissions@cua.edu
Financial aid: (202) 319-5307
Application deadline: 07/15
Tuition: full time: $42,940; part time: $1,710/credit hour
Room/board/expenses: $19,302

Full-time enrollment: 70
men: 74%; women: 26%; minorities: 10%; international: 77%
Part-time enrollment: 104
men: 73%; women: 27%; minorities: 24%; international: 48%
Acceptance rate: 68%
GRE requirement: No
Avg. GRE: quantitative: 151
TOEFL requirement: Yes
Minimum TOEFL score: 580
Fellowships: 4
Teaching assistantships: 31
Research assistantships: 43
Students reporting specialty:
biomedical: 13%; civil: 24%; computer science: 16%; electrical: 15%; management: 14%; materials: 7%; mechanical: 11%

George Washington University

Science and Engineering Hall
800 22nd Street NW
Washington, DC 20052
www.seas.gwu.edu/
Private
Admissions: (202) 994-8675
Email: engineering@gwu.edu
Financial aid: (202) 994-6822
Application deadline: 01/15
Tuition: full time: $1,690/credit hour; part time: $1,690/credit hour
Room/board/expenses: $29,925
Full-time enrollment: 750
men: 75%; women: 25%; minorities: 6%; international: 85%
Part-time enrollment: 1,063
men: 71%; women: 29%; minorities: 34%; international: 15%
Acceptance rate: 45%
GRE requirement: Yes
Avg. GRE: quantitative: 163
TOEFL requirement: Yes
Minimum TOEFL score: 550
Fellowships: 99
Teaching assistantships: 114
Research assistantships: 82
Students reporting specialty:
biomedical: 3%; civil: 3%; computer: 2%; computer science: 24%; electrical: 12%; management: 48%; mechanical: 8%

Howard University

2300 Sixth Street, NW
Washington, DC 20059
www.gs.howard.edu
Private
Admissions: (202) 806-4676
Email: hugsadmissions@howard.edu
Financial aid: (202) 806-2747
Application deadline: 01/15
Tuition: full time: $32,798; part time: $1,700/credit hour
Room/board/expenses: $22,062
Full-time enrollment: 73
men: 62%; women: 38%; minorities: 41%; international: 55%
Part-time enrollment: 25
men: 84%; women: 16%; minorities: 56%; international: 40%
Acceptance rate: 75%
GRE requirement: Yes
Avg. GRE: quantitative: 152
TOEFL requirement: Yes
Minimum TOEFL score: 550
Fellowships: 1
Teaching assistantships: 5
Research assistantships: 4
Students reporting specialty:
chemical: 8%; civil: 15%;

computer science: 20%; electrical: 35%; mechanical: 12%; other: 9%

FLORIDA

Embry-Riddle Aeronautical University

600 S. Clyde Morris Boulevard
Daytona Beach, FL 32114
daytonabeach.erau.edu/admissions/index.html
Private
Admissions: (800) 388-3728
Email: graduate.admissions@erau.edu
Financial aid: (855) 661-7968
Application deadline: rolling
Tuition: full time: $1,358/credit hour; part time: $1,358/credit hour
Room/board/expenses: $16,684
Full-time enrollment: 268
men: 79%; women: 21%; minorities: 10%; international: 60%
Part-time enrollment: 72
men: 78%; women: 22%; minorities: 13%; international: 36%
Acceptance rate: 38%
GRE requirement: Yes
Avg. GRE: quantitative: 157
TOEFL requirement: Yes
Minimum TOEFL score: 550
Fellowships: 48
Teaching assistantships: 71
Research assistantships: 25
Students reporting specialty:
aerospace: 41%; civil: 1%; computer science: 3%; electrical: 9%; science and physics: 11%; mechanical: 18%; other: 17%

Florida A&M University-Florida State University

2525 Pottsdamer Street
Tallahassee, FL 32310
www.eng.famu.fsu.edu
Public
Admissions: (850) 410-6423
Email: perry@eng.fsu.edu
Financial aid: (850) 410-6423
Application deadline: 03/01
In-state tuition: full time: $404/credit hour; part time: $404/credit hour
Out-of-state tuition: full time: $1,005/credit hour
Room/board/expenses: $18,766
Full-time enrollment: 329
men: 80%; women: 20%; minorities: 17%; international: 57%
Part-time enrollment: N/A
men: N/A; women: N/A; minorities: N/A; international: N/A
Acceptance rate: 46%
GRE requirement: Yes
Avg. GRE: quantitative: 157
TOEFL requirement: Yes
Minimum TOEFL score: 550
Fellowships: 20
Teaching assistantships: 79
Research assistantships: 123
Students reporting specialty:
biomedical: 3%; chemical: 11%; civil: 18%; electrical: 28%; industrial: 15%; mechanical: 24%

Florida Atlantic University

777 Glades Road
Boca Raton, FL 33431-0991
www.eng.fau.edu
Public
Admissions: (561) 297-3642

Email: graduatecollege@fau.edu
Financial aid: (561) 297-3530
Application deadline: rolling
In-state tuition: full time: $370/credit hour; part time: $370/credit hour
Out-of-state tuition: full time: $1,025/credit hour
Room/board/expenses: $15,880
Full-time enrollment: 182
men: 75%; women: 25%; minorities: 17%; international: 55%
Part-time enrollment: 200
men: 81%; women: 20%; minorities: 39%; international: 18%
Acceptance rate: 45%
GRE requirement: Yes
Avg. GRE: quantitative: 155
TOEFL requirement: Yes
Minimum TOEFL score: 550
Fellowships: 10
Teaching assistantships: 35
Research assistantships: 61
Students reporting specialty: biomedical: 5%; civil: 9%; computer: 12%; computer science: 29%; electrical: 11%; mechanical: 17%; other: 17%

Florida Institute of Technology
150 W. University Boulevard
Melbourne, FL 32901-6975
www.fit.edu
Private
Admissions: (800) 944-4348
Email: grad-admissions@fit.edu
Financial aid: (321) 674-8070
Application deadline: rolling
Tuition: full time: $1,241/credit hour; part time: $1,241/credit hour
Room/board/expenses: $17,810
Full-time enrollment: 574
men: 74%; women: 26%; minorities: 5%; international: 77%
Part-time enrollment: 313
men: 81%; women: 19%; minorities: 17%; international: 41%
Acceptance rate: 37%
GRE requirement: Yes
Avg. GRE: quantitative: 146
TOEFL requirement: Yes
Minimum TOEFL score: 550
Fellowships: 1
Teaching assistantships: 65
Research assistantships: 82
Students reporting specialty: aerospace: 8%; biomedical: 4%; chemical: 1%; civil: 4%; computer: 8%; computer science: 31%; electrical: 15%; management: 12%; mechanical: 10%; other: 7%

Florida International University
10555 W. Flagler Street
Miami, FL 33174
cec.fiu.edu
Public
Admissions: (305) 348-7861
Email: gradadm@fiu.edu
Financial aid: (305) 348-7272
Application deadline: 02/15
In-state tuition: full time: $11,334; part time: $456/credit hour
Out-of-state tuition: full time: $24,438
Room/board/expenses: $25,218
Full-time enrollment: 560
men: 72%; women: 28%; minorities: 29%; international: 63%
Part-time enrollment: 322
men: 79%; women: 21%; minorities: 64%; international: 24%

Acceptance rate: 47%
GRE requirement: Yes
Avg. GRE: quantitative: 156
TOEFL requirement: Yes
Minimum TOEFL score: 550
Fellowships: 44
Teaching assistantships: 98
Research assistantships: 140
Students reporting specialty: biomedical: 6%; civil: 11%; computer: 6%; computer science: 27%; electrical: 17%; management: 14%; environmental: 1%; materials: 3%; mechanical: 6%; other: 9%

University of Central Florida
4000 Central Florida Boulevard
Orlando, FL 32816-2993
www.cecs.ucf.edu/future-students/admissions-graduate-students/
Public
Admissions: (407) 823-2455
Email: gradengr@ucf.edu
Financial aid: (407) 823-2827
Application deadline: 07/15
In-state tuition: full time: $370/credit hour; part time: $370/credit hour
Out-of-state tuition: full time: $1,194/credit hour
Room/board/expenses: $15,886
Full-time enrollment: 954
men: 79%; women: 21%; minorities: 14%; international: 65%
Part-time enrollment: 473
men: 75%; women: 25%; minorities: 43%; international: 0%
Acceptance rate: 48%
GRE requirement: Yes
Avg. GRE: quantitative: 160
TOEFL requirement: Yes
Minimum TOEFL score: 550
Fellowships: 54
Teaching assistantships: 155
Research assistantships: 252
Students reporting specialty: aerospace: 3%; biomedical: 0%; civil: 11%; computer: 8%; computer science: 25%; electrical: 15%; management: 5%; environmental: 3%; industrial: 9%; materials: 4%; mechanical: 13%; other: 3%

University of Florida
300 Weil Hall
Gainesville, FL 32611-6550
www.eng.ufl.edu
Public
Admissions: (352) 392-0943
Email: admissions@eng.ufl.edu
Financial aid: (352) 392-0943
Application deadline: 06/01
In-state tuition: full time: $12,737; part time: $531/credit hour
Out-of-state tuition: full time: $30,130
Room/board/expenses: $17,150
Full-time enrollment: 2,503
men: 75%; women: 25%; minorities: 9%; international: 74%
Part-time enrollment: 564
men: 76%; women: 24%; minorities: 20%; international: 29%
Acceptance rate: 46%
GRE requirement: Yes
Avg. GRE: quantitative: 163
TOEFL requirement: Yes
Minimum TOEFL score: 550
Fellowships: 174
Teaching assistantships: 115
Research assistantships: 702
Students reporting specialty: aerospace: 3%; agriculture: 1%; biomedical: 6%; chemical: 6%; civil: 6%; computer: 4%; computer science: 24%;

electrical: 18%; environmental: 5%; industrial: 5%; materials: 8%; mechanical: 12%; nuclear: 1%

University of Miami
1251 Memorial Drive
Coral Gables, FL 33146
www.miami.edu/engineering
Private
Admissions: (305) 284-2942
Email: gradadm.eng@miami.edu
Financial aid: (305) 284-5212
Application deadline: 12/01
Tuition: full time: $1,900/credit hour; part time: $1,900/credit hour
Room/board/expenses: $21,392
Full-time enrollment: 217
men: 73%; women: 27%; minorities: 22%; international: 58%
Part-time enrollment: 17
men: 94%; women: 6%; minorities: 47%; international: 29%
Acceptance rate: 63%
GRE requirement: Yes
Avg. GRE: quantitative: 159
TOEFL requirement: Yes
Minimum TOEFL score: 550
Fellowships: 6
Teaching assistantships: 33
Research assistantships: 60
Students reporting specialty: architectural: 2%; biomedical: 26%; civil: 12%; computer science: 6%; electrical: 16%; industrial: 23%; mechanical: 16%

University of South Florida
4202 E. Fowler Avenue, ENB118
Tampa, FL 33620
www.usf.edu/admissions/
Public
Admissions: (813) 974-3350
Email: admissions@grad.usf.edu
Financial aid: (813) 974-4700
Application deadline: 02/15
In-state tuition: full time: $10,502; part time: $432/credit hour
Out-of-state tuition: full time: $21,200
Room/board/expenses: $16,350
Full-time enrollment: 1,076
men: 78%; women: 22%; minorities: 8%; international: 78%
Part-time enrollment: 140
men: 78%; women: 22%; minorities: 41%; international: 0%
Acceptance rate: 47%
GRE requirement: Yes
Avg. GRE: quantitative: 158
TOEFL requirement: Yes
Minimum TOEFL score: 550
Fellowships: 62
Teaching assistantships: 221
Research assistantships: 210
Students reporting specialty: biomedical: 4%; chemical: 3%; civil: 11%; computer: 8%; computer science: 15%; electrical: 31%; management: 10%; science and physics: 1%; environmental: 4%; industrial: 6%; materials: 2%; mechanical: 10%; other: 2%

GEORGIA

Georgia Institute of Technology
225 North Avenue
Atlanta, GA 30332-0360
www.gradadmiss.gatech.edu/
Public
Admissions: (404) 894-1610
Email: gradstudies@gatech.edu
Financial aid: (404) 894-4160
Application deadline: rolling

In-state tuition: full time: $15,652; part time: $2,761
Out-of-state tuition: full time: $30,072
Room/board/expenses: $17,840
Full-time enrollment: 4,181
men: 76%; women: 24%; minorities: 15%; international: 58%
Part-time enrollment: 4,669
men: 86%; women: 14%; minorities: 28%; international: 24%
Acceptance rate: 33%
GRE requirement: Yes
Avg. GRE: quantitative: 164
TOEFL requirement: Yes
Minimum TOEFL score: 550
Fellowships: 1,025
Teaching assistantships: 572
Research assistantships: 1,926
Students reporting specialty: aerospace: 6%; biomedical: 3%; chemical: 2%; civil: 4%; computer science: 54%; electrical: 13%; science and physics: 0%; environmental: 1%; industrial: 5%; materials: 2%; mechanical: 9%; nuclear: 1%; other: 1%

University of Georgia
Paul D. Coverdell Center
Athens, GA 30602
grad.uga.edu
Public
Admissions: (706) 542-1739
Email: gradadm@uga.edu
Financial aid: (706) 542-6147
Application deadline: 07/01
In-state tuition: full time: $15,879; part time: $354/credit hour
Out-of-state tuition: full time: $39,276
Room/board/expenses: $13,126
Full-time enrollment: 99
men: 68%; women: 32%; minorities: 3%; international: 59%
Part-time enrollment: 8
men: 50%; women: 50%; minorities: 25%; international: 25%
Acceptance rate: 33%
GRE requirement: Yes
Avg. GRE: quantitative: 160
TOEFL requirement: Yes
Minimum TOEFL score: 550
Fellowships: 0
Teaching assistantships: 15
Research assistantships: 107
Students reporting specialty: agriculture: 29%; science and physics: 64%; environmental: 7%

HAWAII

University of Hawaii-Manoa[1]
2540 Dole Street
Holmes Hall 240
Honolulu, HI 96822
www.eng.hawaii.edu/current-students/graduate-students
Public
Admissions: (808) 956-8544
Email: gradadm@hawaii.edu
Financial aid: (808) 956-7251
Tuition: N/A
Room/board/expenses: N/A
Enrollment: N/A

IDAHO

Boise State University
1910 University Drive
Boise, ID 83725
graduatecollege.boisestate.edu
Public
Admissions: (208) 426-3903
Email: gradcollege@boisestate.edu
Financial aid: (208) 426-1664

Application deadline: rolling
In-state tuition: full time: $8,440; part time: $382/credit hour
Out-of-state tuition: full time: $22,890
Room/board/expenses: $12,344
Full-time enrollment: 120
men: 71%; women: 29%; minorities: 10%; international: 44%
Part-time enrollment: 73
men: 78%; women: 22%; minorities: 12%; international: 36%
Acceptance rate: 39%
GRE requirement: Yes
Avg. GRE: quantitative: 160
TOEFL requirement: Yes
Minimum TOEFL score: 550
Fellowships: 4
Teaching assistantships: 24
Research assistantships: 67
Students reporting specialty: civil: 10%; computer: 1%; computer science: 28%; electrical: 23%; materials: 25%; mechanical: 6%; other: 7%

Idaho State University[1]
921 S. Eighth Street, MS 8060
Pocatello, ID 83209-8060
www.isu.edu/cse
Public
Admissions: (208) 282-2150
Email: graddean@isu.edu
Financial aid: N/A
Tuition: N/A
Room/board/expenses: N/A
Enrollment: N/A

University of Idaho[1]
PO Box 441011
Moscow, ID 83844-1011
www.engr.uidaho.edu/
Public
Admissions: (208) 885-4001
Email: gadms@uidaho.edu
Financial aid: N/A
Tuition: N/A
Room/board/expenses: N/A
Enrollment: N/A

ILLINOIS

Illinois Institute of Technology (Armour)
10 W. 33rd Street
Perlstein Hall, Suite 224
Chicago, IL 60616
www.iit.edu/engineering
Private
Admissions: (312) 567-3020
Email: gradstu@iit.edu
Financial aid: (312) 567-7219
Application deadline: 01/01
Tuition: full time: $1,400/credit hour; part time: $1,400/credit hour
Room/board/expenses: $17,895
Full-time enrollment: 1,569
men: 77%; women: 23%; minorities: 3%; international: 92%
Part-time enrollment: 316
men: 75%; women: 25%; minorities: 9%; international: 65%
Acceptance rate: 71%
GRE requirement: Yes
Avg. GRE: quantitative: 160
TOEFL requirement: Yes
Minimum TOEFL score: 550
Fellowships: 30
Teaching assistantships: 92
Research assistantships: 245
Students reporting specialty: aerospace: 10%; agriculture: 0%; architectural: 1%; biomedical: 3%; chemical: 5%; civil: 9%; computer: 6%; computer science: 45%; electrical: 20%; environmental: 1%; industrial: 1%; materials: 2%; mechanical: 10%

Northwestern University (McCormick)

2145 Sheridan Road
Evanston, IL 60208
www.tgs.northwestern.edu/
Private
Admissions: (847) 491-5279
Email: tgs@northwestern.edu
Financial aid: (847) 491-8495
Application deadline: N/A
Tuition: full time: $50,754; part time: $5,980/credit hour
Room/board/expenses: $22,590
Full-time enrollment: 1,732
men: 68%; women: 32%;
minorities: 15%; international: 55%
Part-time enrollment: 356
men: 67%; women: 33%;
minorities: 16%; international: 54%
Acceptance rate: 23%
GRE requirement: Yes
Avg. GRE: quantitative: 166
TOEFL requirement: Yes
Minimum TOEFL score: 550
Fellowships: 212
Teaching assistantships: 85
Research assistantships: 557
Students reporting specialty:
biomedical: 8%; chemical: 10%; civil: 4%; computer: 4%; computer science: 8%; electrical: 7%; management: 3%; science and physics: 3%; environmental: 2%; industrial: 3%; materials: 12%; mechanical: 8%; other: 28%

Southern Illinois University-Carbondale

900 S. Normal Avenue
Mailcode 4716
Carbondale, IL 62901-6603
gradschool.siuc.edu/
Public
Admissions: (618) 536-7791
Email: gradschl@siu.edu
Financial aid: (618) 453-4334
Application deadline: rolling
In-state tuition: full time: $439/credit hour; part time: $439/credit hour
Out-of-state tuition: full time: $1,096/credit hour
Room/board/expenses: $17,675
Full-time enrollment: 186
men: 81%; women: 19%;
minorities: 5%; international: 88%
Part-time enrollment: 105
men: 84%; women: 16%;
minorities: 2%; international: 68%
Acceptance rate: 58%
GRE requirement: Yes
Avg. GRE: quantitative: 159
TOEFL requirement: Yes
Minimum TOEFL score: 550
Fellowships: 14
Teaching assistantships: 232
Research assistantships: 96
Students reporting specialty:
biomedical: 1%; civil: 11%; computer: 55%; electrical: 55%; science and physics: 16%; environmental: 11%; mechanical: 14%; mining: 2%

University of Illinois-Chicago

851 S. Morgan Street
Chicago, IL 60607-7043
www.uic.edu/
Public
Admissions: (312) 996-5133
Email: uicgrad@uic.edu
Financial aid: (312) 996-3126
Application deadline: 05/15
In-state tuition: full time: $19,852; part time: $14,646

Out-of-state tuition: full time: $32,092
Room/board/expenses: $18,373
Full-time enrollment: 1,222
men: 75%; women: 25%;
minorities: 9%; international: 81%
Part-time enrollment: 206
men: 79%; women: 21%;
minorities: 28%; international: 33%
Acceptance rate: 16%
GRE requirement: Yes
Avg. GRE: quantitative: 160
TOEFL requirement: Yes
Minimum TOEFL score: 550
Fellowships: 18
Teaching assistantships: 258
Research assistantships: 215
Students reporting specialty:
biomedical: 12%; chemical: 5%; civil: 9%; computer science: 19%; electrical: 19%; industrial: 11%; materials: 1%; mechanical: 21%; other: 3%

University of Illinois-Urbana-Champaign

1308 W. Green
Urbana, IL 61801
engineering.illinois.edu
Public
Admissions: (217) 333-0035
Email: engineering@illinois.edu
Financial aid: (217) 333-0100
Application deadline: N/A
In-state tuition: full time: $21,496; part time: N/A
Out-of-state tuition: full time: $36,290
Room/board/expenses: $15,008
Full-time enrollment: 3,472
men: 76%; women: 24%;
minorities: 12%; international: 66%
Part-time enrollment: 334
men: 80%; women: 20%;
minorities: 26%; international: 26%
Acceptance rate: 30%
GRE requirement: Yes
Avg. GRE: quantitative: 166
TOEFL requirement: Yes
Minimum TOEFL score: 610
Fellowships: 264
Teaching assistantships: 913
Research assistantships: 1,316
Students reporting specialty:
aerospace: 5%; agriculture: 2%; biomedical: 3%; chemical: 3%; civil: 16%; computer: 15%; computer science: 19%; electrical: 15%; science and physics: 8%; environmental: 3%; industrial: 6%; materials: 5%; mechanical: 11%; nuclear: 3%

INDIANA

Indiana University-Purdue University-Indianapolis

799 W. Michigan Street, ET 219
Indianapolis, IN 46202-5160
engr.iupui.edu
Public
Admissions: (317) 278-4960
Email: etinfo@iupui.edu
Financial aid: N/A
Application deadline: 06/01
In-state tuition: full time: $381/credit hour; part time: $381/credit hour
Out-of-state tuition: full time: $1,090/credit hour
Room/board/expenses: $2,880
Full-time enrollment: 304
men: 81%; women: 19%;
minorities: 3%; international: 86%

Part-time enrollment: 57
men: 93%; women: 7%;
minorities: 26%; international: 12%
Acceptance rate: 72%
GRE requirement: Yes
Avg. GRE: quantitative: 158
TOEFL requirement: Yes
Minimum TOEFL score: 550
Fellowships: 4
Teaching assistantships: 24
Research assistantships: 62
Students reporting specialty:
biomedical: 7%; computer: 17%; electrical: 25%; mechanical: 50%

Purdue University-West Lafayette

701 W. Stadium Avenue
Suite 3000 ARMS
West Lafayette, IN 47907-2045
engineering.purdue.edu
Public
Admissions: (765) 494-2600
Email: gradinfo@purdue.edu
Financial aid: (765) 494-2598
Application deadline: rolling
In-state tuition: full time: $11,126; part time: $329/credit hour
Out-of-state tuition: full time: $29,928
Room/board/expenses: $13,030
Full-time enrollment: 3,037
men: 77%; women: 23%;
minorities: 8%; international: 71%
Part-time enrollment: 707
men: 81%; women: 19%;
minorities: 18%; international: 20%
Acceptance rate: 31%
GRE requirement: Yes
Avg. GRE: quantitative: 164
TOEFL requirement: Yes
Minimum TOEFL score: 550
Fellowships: 356
Teaching assistantships: 600
Research assistantships: 1,452
Students reporting specialty:
aerospace: 14%; agriculture: 3%; biomedical: 3%; chemical: 4%; civil: 10%; computer: 4%; computer science: 9%; electrical: 14%; industrial: 8%; materials: 4%; mechanical: 15%; nuclear: 1%; other: 12%

University of Notre Dame

257 Fitzpatrick Hall of Engineering
Notre Dame, IN 46556
www.nd.edu
Private
Admissions: (574) 631-7706
Email: gradad@nd.edu
Financial aid: (574) 631-7706
Application deadline: rolling
Tuition: full time: $49,050; part time: $2,725/credit hour
Room/board/expenses: $20,595
Full-time enrollment: 513
men: 74%; women: 26%;
minorities: 9%; international: 53%
Part-time enrollment: 7
men: 86%; women: 14%;
minorities: 29%; international: 43%
Acceptance rate: 21%
GRE requirement: Yes
Avg. GRE: quantitative: 163
TOEFL requirement: Yes
Minimum TOEFL score: N/A
Fellowships: 54
Teaching assistantships: 47
Research assistantships: 373
Students reporting specialty:
aerospace: 23%; chemical: 14%; civil: 18%; computer science: 24%; electrical: 21%

IOWA

Iowa State University

4100 Marston Hall
Ames, IA 50011-1130
www.engineering.iastate.edu/
Public
Admissions: (800) 262-3810
Email: grad_admissions@iastate.edu
Financial aid: (515) 294-2223
Application deadline: 02/01
In-state tuition: full time: $11,107; part time: $543/credit hour
Out-of-state tuition: full time: $24,361
Room/board/expenses: $12,591
Full-time enrollment: 1,337
men: 79%; women: 21%;
minorities: 7%; international: 58%
Part-time enrollment: N/A
men: N/A; women: N/A;
minorities: N/A; international: N/A
Acceptance rate: 18%
GRE requirement: Yes
Avg. GRE: quantitative: 167
TOEFL requirement: Yes
Minimum TOEFL score: 550
Fellowships: 9
Teaching assistantships: 260
Research assistantships: 619
Students reporting specialty:
aerospace: 7%; agriculture: 4%; chemical: 5%; civil: 15%; computer: 9%; electrical: 15%; management: 2%; environmental: 0%; industrial: 9%; materials: 5%; mechanical: 17%; other: 10%

University of Iowa

3100 Seamans Center
Iowa City, IA 52242-1527
www.uiowa.edu/admissions/graduate/index.html
Public
Admissions: (319) 335-1525
Email: admissions@uiowa.edu
Financial aid: (319) 335-1450
Application deadline: rolling
In-state tuition: full time: $11,894; part time: N/A
Out-of-state tuition: full time: $29,498
Room/board/expenses: $15,960
Full-time enrollment: 321
men: 79%; women: 21%;
minorities: 6%; international: 59%
Part-time enrollment: 77
men: 81%; women: 19%;
minorities: 9%; international: 39%
Acceptance rate: 22%
GRE requirement: Yes
Avg. GRE: quantitative: 161
TOEFL requirement: Yes
Minimum TOEFL score: 550
Fellowships: 23
Teaching assistantships: 91
Research assistantships: 241
Students reporting specialty:
biomedical: 17%; chemical: 8%; civil: 17%; computer science: 25%; electrical: 16%; industrial: 5%; mechanical: 12%

KANSAS

Kansas State University

1046 Rathbone Hall
Manhattan, KS 66506-5201
www.engg.ksu.edu/
Public
Admissions: (785) 532-6191
Email: grad@ksu.edu
Financial aid: (785) 532-6420
Application deadline: rolling
In-state tuition: full time: $403/credit hour; part time: $403/credit hour
Out-of-state tuition: full time: $910/credit hour
Room/board/expenses: $9,706

Full-time enrollment: 283
men: 73%; women: 27%;
minorities: 11%; international: 69%
Part-time enrollment: 192
men: 84%; women: 16%;
minorities: 24%; international: 14%
Acceptance rate: 37%
GRE requirement: Yes
Avg. GRE: quantitative: 162
TOEFL requirement: Yes
Minimum TOEFL score: 550
Fellowships: 18
Teaching assistantships: 114
Research assistantships: 141
Students reporting specialty: N/A

University of Kansas

1 Eaton Hall
1520 W. 15th Street
Lawrence, KS 66045-7621
www.engr.ku.edu
Public
Admissions: (785) 864-3881
Email: kuengrgrad@ku.edu
Financial aid: (785) 864-4423
Application deadline: 12/15
In-state tuition: full time: $395/credit hour; part time: $395/credit hour
Out-of-state tuition: full time: $924/credit hour
Room/board/expenses: $13,604
Full-time enrollment: 398
men: 75%; women: 25%;
minorities: 7%; international: 62%
Part-time enrollment: 242
men: 79%; women: 21%;
minorities: 14%; international: 24%
Acceptance rate: 44%
GRE requirement: Yes
Avg. GRE: quantitative: 161
TOEFL requirement: Yes
Minimum TOEFL score: N/A
Fellowships: 109
Teaching assistantships: 117
Research assistantships: 156
Students reporting specialty:
aerospace: 7%; architectural: 1%; biomedical: 7%; chemical: 5%; civil: 21%; computer: 1%; computer science: 11%; electrical: 12%; management: 14%; environmental: 3%; mechanical: 7%; petroleum: 6%; other: 9%

Wichita State University

1845 N. Fairmount
Wichita, KS 67260-0044
www.wichita.edu/engineering
Public
Admissions: (316) 978-3095
Email: jordan.oleson@wichita.edu
Financial aid: (010) 970-0400
Application deadline: rolling
In-state tuition: full time: $287/credit hour; part time: $287/credit hour
Out-of-state tuition: full time: $706/credit hour
Room/board/expenses: $13,890
Full-time enrollment: 321
men: 81%; women: 19%;
minorities: 5%; international: 89%
Part-time enrollment: 322
men: 86%; women: 14%;
minorities: 19%; international: 51%
Acceptance rate: 47%
GRE requirement: Yes
Avg. GRE: quantitative: 155
TOEFL requirement: Yes
Minimum TOEFL score: 550
Students reporting specialty:
aerospace: 19%; computer science: 14%; electrical: 15%; management: 5%; industrial: 25%; mechanical: 14%; other: 9%

KENTUCKY

University of Kentucky
351 Ralph G. Anderson Building
Lexington, KY 40506-0503
www.engr.uky.edu
Public
Admissions: (859) 257-4905
Email: grad.admit@uky.edu
Financial aid: (859) 257-3172
Application deadline: 07/13
In-state tuition: full time: $12,236;
part time: $648/credit hour
Out-of-state tuition: full time:
$28,380
Room/board/expenses: $11,722
Full-time enrollment: 394
men: 79%; women: 21%;
minorities: 5%; international: 60%
Part-time enrollment: 80
men: 89%; women: 11%;
minorities: 11%; international:
23%
Acceptance rate: 44%
GRE requirement: Yes
Avg. GRE: quantitative: 160
TOEFL requirement: Yes
Minimum TOEFL score: 550
Fellowships: 15
Teaching assistantships: 88
Research assistantships: 188
Students reporting specialty:
agriculture: 5%; biomedical:
5%; chemical: 8%; civil: 14%;
computer science: 20%;
electrical: 14%; industrial: 3%;
materials: 6%; mechanical: 20%;
mining: 4%

University of Louisville (Speed)
2301 S. Third Street
Louisville, KY 40292
louisville.edu/speed
Public
Admissions: (502) 852-6278
Email: gradadm@louisville.edu
Financial aid: (502) 852-6278
Application deadline: rolling
In-state tuition: full time: $12,492;
part time: $681/credit hour
Out-of-state tuition: full time:
$25,732
Room/board/expenses: $14,762
Full-time enrollment: 375
men: 78%; women: 22%;
minorities: 9%; international: 45%
Part-time enrollment: 247
men: 85%; women: 15%;
minorities: 18%; international:
21%
Acceptance rate: 37%
GRE requirement: Yes
Avg. GRE: quantitative: 157
TOEFL requirement: Yes
Minimum TOEFL score: 550
Fellowships: 23
Teaching assistantships: 47
Research assistantships: 57
Students reporting specialty:
biomedical: 4%; chemical:
7%; civil: 8%; computer:
4%; computer science: 18%;
electrical: 12%; management:
19%; industrial: 12%; mechanical:
15%

LOUISIANA

Louisiana State University-Baton Rouge
3304 Patrick F. Taylor Building
Baton Rouge, LA 70803
www.lsu.edu/eng
Public
Admissions: (225) 578-1641
Email: graddeanoffice@lsu.edu
Financial aid: (225) 578-3103
Application deadline: 05/15
In-state tuition: full time: $11,393;
part time: $6,641
Out-of-state tuition: full time:
$28,308
Room/board/expenses: $18,120
Full-time enrollment: 506
men: 75%; women: 25%;
minorities: 5%; international: 78%
Part-time enrollment: 113
men: 79%; women: 21%;
minorities: 26%; international:
16%
Acceptance rate: 36%
GRE requirement: Yes
Avg. GRE: quantitative: 159
TOEFL requirement: Yes
Minimum TOEFL score: 550
Fellowships: 28
Teaching assistantships: 125
Research assistantships: 218
Students reporting specialty:
agriculture: 1%; chemical: 9%;
civil: 15%; computer science:
14%; electrical: 16%; science
and physics: 10%; industrial: 2%;
mechanical: 10%; petroleum: 11%;
other: 12%

Louisiana Tech University
PO Box 10348
Ruston, LA 71272
www.coes.latech.edu/
grad-programs/index.php
Public
Admissions: (318) 257-2924
Email: gschool@latech.edu
Financial aid: (318) 257-2641
Application deadline: 08/01
In-state tuition: full time: $7,503;
part time: $6,152
Out-of-state tuition: full time:
$16,593
Room/board/expenses: $9,516
Full-time enrollment: 209
men: 74%; women: 26%;
minorities: 8%; international: 70%
Part-time enrollment: 74
men: 72%; women: 28%;
minorities: 19%; international:
20%
Acceptance rate: 43%
GRE requirement: Yes
Avg. GRE: quantitative: 157
TOEFL requirement: Yes
Minimum TOEFL score: 550
Fellowships: 13
Teaching assistantships: 53
Research assistantships: 67
Students reporting specialty:
biomedical: 13%; chemical:
6%; civil: 10%; computer
science: 12%; electrical: 11%;
management: 27%; science
and physics: 3%; industrial: 1%;
mechanical: 8%; other: 38%

Tulane University
201 Lindy Boggs Building
New Orleans, LA 70118
tulane.edu/sse/academics/
graduate/index.cfm
Private
Admissions: (504) 865-5764
Email: segrad@tulane.edu
Financial aid: (504) 865-5764
Application deadline: rolling
Tuition: full time: $51,010; part
time: $2,768/credit hour
Room/board/expenses: $18,800
Full-time enrollment: 103
men: 65%; women: 35%;
minorities: 13%; international:
45%
Part-time enrollment: N/A
men: N/A; women: N/A;
minorities: N/A; international: N/A
Acceptance rate: 57%
GRE requirement: Yes
Avg. GRE: quantitative: 161
TOEFL requirement: Yes
Minimum TOEFL score: N/A

Fellowships: 22
Teaching assistantships: 27
Research assistantships: 61
Students reporting specialty: N/A

University of Louisiana-Lafayette
PO Box 42251
Lafayette, LA 70504
engineering.louisiana.edu/
Public
Admissions: (337) 482-6467
Email: gradschool@louisiana.edu
Financial aid: (337) 482-6506
Application deadline: rolling
In-state tuition: full time: $9,420;
part time: $525/credit hour
Out-of-state tuition: full time:
$23,148
Room/board/expenses: $14,212
Full-time enrollment: 229
men: 78%; women: 22%;
minorities: 6%; international: 72%
Part-time enrollment: 49
men: 78%; women: 22%;
minorities: 16%; international:
43%
Acceptance rate: 28%
GRE requirement: Yes
Avg. GRE: quantitative: N/A
TOEFL requirement: Yes
Minimum TOEFL score: N/A
Students reporting specialty:
chemical: 8%; civil: 8%;
computer: 26%; computer
science: 28%; mechanical: 9%;
petroleum: 21%

University of New Orleans
2000 Lakeshore Drive
New Orleans, LA 70148
www.uno.edu
Public
Admissions: (504) 280-6595
Email: pec@uno.edu
Financial aid: (504) 280-6603
Application deadline: 07/01
In-state tuition: full time: $8,298;
part time: $5,562
Out-of-state tuition: full time:
$21,737
Room/board/expenses: $14,284
Full-time enrollment: 97
men: 77%; women: 23%;
minorities: 3%; international: 60%
Part-time enrollment: 70
men: 81%; women: 19%;
minorities: 11%; international: 21%
Acceptance rate: 38%
GRE requirement: Yes
Avg. GRE: quantitative: 156
TOEFL requirement: Yes
Minimum TOEFL score: 550
Students reporting specialty: N/A

MAINE

University of Maine
Advanced Manufacturing Center
Orono, ME 04469
www.engineering.umaine.edu/
Public
Admissions: (207) 581-3291
Email: graduate@maine.edu
Financial aid: (207) 581-1324
Application deadline: rolling
In-state tuition: full time: $418/
credit hour; part time: $418/
credit hour
Out-of-state tuition: full time:
$1,361/credit hour
Room/board/expenses: $13,594
Full-time enrollment: 156
men: 80%; women: 20%;
minorities: 8%; international: 44%
Part-time enrollment: 27
men: 85%; women: 15%;
minorities: 11%; international: 7%
Acceptance rate: 69%

GRE requirement: Yes
Avg. GRE: quantitative: 157
TOEFL requirement: Yes
Minimum TOEFL score: N/A
Fellowships: 3
Teaching assistantships: 18
Research assistantships: 37
Students reporting specialty:
biomedical: 4%; chemical:
10%; civil: 20%; computer:
3%; computer science: 13%;
electrical: 9%; science and
physics: 1%; mechanical: 18%;
other: 21%

MARYLAND

Johns Hopkins University (Whiting)
3400 N. Charles Street
Baltimore, MD 21218
engineering.jhu.edu/
graduate-studies
Private
Admissions: (410) 516-7125
Email: graduateadmissions@
jhu.edu
Financial aid: (410) 516-8028
Application deadline: N/A
Tuition: full time: $50,910; part
time: $1,680/credit hour
Room/board/expenses: $18,245
Full-time enrollment: 1,522
men: 70%; women: 30%;
minorities: 15%; international:
57%
Part-time enrollment: 2,170
men: 76%; women: 24%;
minorities: 19%; international: 3%
Acceptance rate: 35%
GRE requirement: Yes
Avg. GRE: quantitative: 166
TOEFL requirement: Yes
Minimum TOEFL score: 600
Fellowships: 196
Teaching assistantships: 75
Research assistantships: 563
Students reporting specialty:
aerospace: 2%; biomedical: 8%;
chemical: 4%; civil: 2%; computer
science: 18%; electrical: 12%;
management: 3%; science and
physics: 1%; environmental: 8%;
materials: 3%; mechanical: 7%;
other: 33%

Morgan State University (Mitchell)
1700 E. Coldspring Lane
Baltimore, MD 21251
morgan.edu/Prospective_Grad_
Students.html
Public
Admissions: (443) 885-3185
Email:
mark.garrison@morgan.edu
Financial aid: (443) 885-3170
Application deadline: 05/01
In-state tuition: full time: $393/
credit hour; part time: $393/
credit hour
Out-of-state tuition: full time:
$770/credit hour
Room/board/expenses: $15,310
Full-time enrollment: 93
men: 67%; women: 33%;
minorities: 65%; international:
28%
Part-time enrollment: 21
men: 90%; women: 10%;
minorities: 71%; international:
14%
Acceptance rate: 82%
GRE requirement: Yes
Avg. GRE: quantitative: 153
TOEFL requirement: Yes
Minimum TOEFL score: 550
Students reporting specialty: N/A

University of Maryland-Baltimore County
1000 Hilltop Circle
Baltimore, MD 21250
www.umbc.edu/gradschool/
Public
Admissions: (410) 455-2537
Email: umbcgrad@umbc.edu
Financial aid: (410) 455-2387
Application deadline: N/A
In-state tuition: full time: $603/
credit hour; part time: $603/
credit hour
Out-of-state tuition: full time:
$997/credit hour
Room/board/expenses: $20,592
Full-time enrollment: 572
men: 64%; women: 36%;
minorities: 14%; international:
68%
Part-time enrollment: 551
men: 72%; women: 28%;
minorities: 36%; international:
11%
Acceptance rate: 50%
GRE requirement: Yes
Avg. GRE: quantitative: 157
TOEFL requirement: Yes
Minimum TOEFL score: 550
Fellowships: 3
Teaching assistantships: 79
Research assistantships: 131
Students reporting specialty:
chemical: 3%; computer:
4%; computer science: 28%;
electrical: 8%; management: 5%;
mechanical: 7%; other: 45%

University of Maryland-College Park (Clark)
3110 Jeong H. Kim Engineering
Building
College Park, MD 20742-2831
www.eng.umd.edu
Public
Admissions: (301) 405-0376
Email: gradschool@umd.edu
Financial aid: (301) 314-9000
Application deadline: N/A
In-state tuition: full time: $14,558;
part time: $651/credit hour
Out-of-state tuition: full time:
$29,618
Room/board/expenses: $20,636
Full-time enrollment: 1,792
men: 77%; women: 23%;
minorities: 12%; international:
65%
Part-time enrollment: 579
men: 84%; women: 16%;
minorities: 38%; international: 8%
Acceptance rate: 34%
GRE requirement: Yes
Avg. GRE: quantitative: 164
TOEFL requirement: Yes
Minimum TOEFL score: 574
Fellowships: 209
Teaching assistantships: 219
Research assistantships: 742
Students reporting specialty:
aerospace: 8%; biomedical:
4%; chemical: 4%; civil: 13%;
computer science: 10%;
electrical: 19%; materials: 3%;
mechanical: 13%; other: 27%

MASSACHUSETTS

Boston University
44 Cummington Street
Boston, MA 02215
www.bu.edu/eng
Private
Admissions: (617) 353-9760
Email: enggrad@bu.edu
Financial aid: (617) 353-9760
Application deadline: 12/15

Tuition: full time: $49,886; part time: $1,537/credit hour
Room/board/expenses: $20,291
Full-time enrollment: 930
men: 69%; women: 31%; minorities: 13%; international: 56%
Part-time enrollment: 191
men: 73%; women: 27%; minorities: 14%; international: 51%
Acceptance rate: 28%
GRE requirement: Yes
Avg. GRE: quantitative: 164
TOEFL requirement: Yes
Minimum TOEFL score: 550
Fellowships: 127
Teaching assistantships: 99
Research assistantships: 358
Students reporting specialty: biomedical: 24%; computer: 12%; computer science: 12%; electrical: 19%; industrial: 5%; materials: 6%; mechanical: 16%; other: 6%

Harvard University

29 Oxford Street
Room 217A, Pierce Hall
Cambridge, MA 02138
www.gsas.harvard.edu
Private
Admissions: (617) 495-5315
Email: admiss@fas.harvard.edu
Financial aid: (617) 495-5396
Application deadline: 12/15
Tuition: full time: $47,014; part time: N/A
Room/board/expenses: $28,150
Full-time enrollment: 459
men: 71%; women: 29%; minorities: 16%; international: 49%
Part-time enrollment: 19
men: 63%; women: 37%; minorities: 26%; international: 47%
Acceptance rate: 11%
GRE requirement: Yes
Avg. GRE: quantitative: 166
TOEFL requirement: Yes
Minimum TOEFL score: N/A
Fellowships: 86
Teaching assistantships: 106
Research assistantships: 258
Students reporting specialty: biomedical: 10%; computer science: 31%; electrical: 8%; environmental: 5%; materials: 8%; mechanical: 4%; other: 35%

Massachusetts Institute of Technology

77 Massachusetts Avenue
Room 1-206
Cambridge, MA 02139-4307
gradadmissions.mit.edu/
Private
Admissions: (617) 253-3400
Email: mitgrad@mit.edu
Financial aid: (617) 253-4971
Application deadline: N/A
Tuition: full time: $48,452; part time: N/A
Room/board/expenses: $34,771
Full-time enrollment: 3,112
men: 71%; women: 29%; minorities: 21%; international: 44%
Part-time enrollment: 12
men: 75%; women: 25%; minorities: 17%; international: 0%
Acceptance rate: 13%
GRE requirement: Yes
Avg. GRE: quantitative: 166
Minimum TOEFL score: N/A
Fellowships: 568
Teaching assistantships: 329
Research assistantships: 1,649
Students reporting specialty: aerospace: 7%; biomedical: 8%; chemical: 7%; civil: 4%; computer

---

science: 16%; electrical: 12%; management: 10%; environmental: 2%; materials: 5%; mechanical: 18%; nuclear: 4%; other: 7%

Northeastern University

130 Snell Engineering Center
Boston, MA 02115-5000
www.coe.neu.edu/gse
Private
Admissions: (617) 373-2711
Email: grad-eng@coe.neu.edu
Financial aid: (617) 373-3190
Application deadline: 01/15
Tuition: full time: $1,471/credit hour; part time: $1,471/credit hour
Room/board/expenses: $19,960
Full-time enrollment: 4,040
men: 69%; women: 31%; minorities: 3%; international: 89%
Part-time enrollment: 219
men: 80%; women: 20%; minorities: 20%; international: 8%
Acceptance rate: 42%
GRE requirement: Yes
Avg. GRE: quantitative: 162
TOEFL requirement: Yes
Minimum TOEFL score: 550
Fellowships: 80
Teaching assistantships: 134
Research assistantships: 358
Students reporting specialty: biomedical: 2%; chemical: 3%; civil: 5%; computer: 2%; computer science: 20%; electrical: 11%; management: 12%; industrial: 10%; mechanical: 8%; other: 29%

Tufts University

Anderson Hall
Medford, MA 02155
asegrad.tufts.edu/
Private
Admissions: (617) 627-3395
Email: gradadmissions@tufts.edu
Financial aid: (617) 627-2000
Application deadline: 01/15
Tuition: full time: $51,364; part time: $5,052/credit hour
Room/board/expenses: $21,322
Full-time enrollment: 544
men: 61%; women: 39%; minorities: 17%; international: 38%
Part-time enrollment: 144
men: 73%; women: 27%; minorities: 17%; international: 6%
Acceptance rate: 42%
GRE requirement: Yes
Avg. GRE: quantitative: 162
TOEFL requirement: Yes
Minimum TOEFL score: 600
Fellowships: 13
Teaching assistantships: 60
Research assistantships: 163
Students reporting specialty: biomedical: 12%; chemical: 6%; civil: 5%; computer science: 14%; electrical: 13%; management: 34%; environmental: 7%; mechanical: 10%

University of Massachusetts-Amherst

Room 125, Marston Hall
Amherst, MA 01003
www.umass.edu/gradschool
Public
Admissions: (413) 545-0722
Email: gradadm@grad.umass.edu
Financial aid: (413) 545-0801
Application deadline: 02/01
In-state tuition: full time: $16,443; part time: $1,905/credit hour
Out-of-state tuition: full time: $32,563

Room/board/expenses: $14,897
Full-time enrollment: 983
men: 69%; women: 31%; minorities: 7%; international: 66%
Part-time enrollment: N/A
men: N/A; women: N/A; minorities: N/A; international: N/A
Acceptance rate: 33%
GRE requirement: Yes
Avg. GRE: quantitative: 163
TOEFL requirement: Yes
Minimum TOEFL score: 550
Fellowships: 89
Teaching assistantships: 70
Research assistantships: 431
Students reporting specialty: chemical: 6%; civil: 12%; computer science: 32%; electrical: 27%; management: 2%; environmental: 0%; industrial: 3%; materials: 10%; mechanical: 9%

University of Massachusetts-Dartmouth

285 Old Westport Road
North Dartmouth, MA 02747-2300
www.umassd.edu/graduate
Public
Admissions: (508) 999-8604
Email: graduate@umassd.edu
Financial aid: (508) 999-8643
Application deadline: 02/15
In-state tuition: full time: $15,399; part time: $625/credit hour
Out-of-state tuition: full time: $27,473
Room/board/expenses: $15,324
Full-time enrollment: 191
men: 74%; women: 26%; minorities: 5%; international: 74%
Part-time enrollment: 108
men: 81%; women: 19%; minorities: 11%; international: 48%
Acceptance rate: 69%
GRE requirement: Yes
Avg. GRE: quantitative: 155
TOEFL requirement: Yes
Minimum TOEFL score: 550
Fellowships: 24
Teaching assistantships: 29
Research assistantships: 37
Students reporting specialty: biomedical: 7%; civil: 3%; computer: 7%; computer science: 41%; electrical: 19%; science and physics: 10%; mechanical: 10%; other: 4%

University of Massachusetts-Lowell (Francis)

1 University Avenue
Lowell, MA 01854
www.uml.edu/grad
Public
Admissions: (978) 934-2390
Email: graduate_school@uml.edu
Financial aid: (978) 934-4226
Application deadline: rolling
In-state tuition: full time: $14,629; part time: $795/credit hour
Out-of-state tuition: full time: $26,178
Room/board/expenses: $13,573
Full-time enrollment: 547
men: 71%; women: 29%; minorities: 5%; international: 73%
Part-time enrollment: 436
men: 81%; women: 19%; minorities: 25%; international: 15%
Acceptance rate: 63%
GRE requirement: Yes
Avg. GRE: quantitative: 158
TOEFL requirement: Yes
Minimum TOEFL score: 550
Fellowships: 3

Teaching assistantships: 130
Research assistantships: 176
Students reporting specialty: biomedical: 13%; chemical: 5%; civil: 9%; computer: 11%; computer science: 19%; electrical: 15%; management: 1%; materials: 10%; mechanical: 12%; nuclear: 1%; other: 4%

Worcester Polytechnic Institute

100 Institute Road
Worcester, MA 01609-2280
grad.wpi.edu/
Private
Admissions: (508) 831-5301
Email: grad@wpi.edu
Financial aid: (508) 831-5469
Application deadline: rolling
Tuition: full time: $25,404; part time: $1,408/credit hour
Room/board/expenses: $23,707
Full-time enrollment: 455
men: 75%; women: 25%; minorities: 5%; international: 66%
Part-time enrollment: 748
men: 81%; women: 19%; minorities: 19%; international: 21%
Acceptance rate: 54%
GRE requirement: Yes
Avg. GRE: quantitative: 164
TOEFL requirement: Yes
Minimum TOEFL score: 563
Fellowships: 13
Teaching assistantships: 92
Research assistantships: 128
Students reporting specialty: aerospace: 2%; biomedical: 4%; chemical: 2%; civil: 3%; computer science: 11%; electrical: 19%; environmental: 1%; industrial: 3%; materials: 7%; mechanical: 13%; other: 35%

MICHIGAN

Lawrence Technological University

21000 W. Ten Mile Road
Southfield, MI 48075
www.ltu.edu
Private
Admissions: (248) 204-3160
Email: admissions@ltu.edu
Financial aid: (248) 204-2126
Application deadline: rolling
Tuition: full time: $15,018; part time: $7,584
Room/board/expenses: $15,808
Full-time enrollment: 21
men: 67%; women: 33%; minorities: 5%; international: 62%
Part-time enrollment: 562
men: 86%; women: 14%; minorities: 4%; international: 78%
Acceptance rate: 41%
GRE requirement: No
Avg. GRE: quantitative: N/A
TOEFL requirement: Yes
Minimum TOEFL score: 550
Fellowships: 0
Teaching assistantships: 0
Research assistantships: 2
Students reporting specialty: architectural: 2%; biomedical: 1%; civil: 10%; electrical: 14%; management: 9%; industrial: 10%; mechanical: 31%; other: 24%

Michigan State University

428 S.Shaw Lane
3410 Engineering Building
East Lansing, MI 48824
www.egr.msu.edu
Public
Admissions: (517) 355-8332

Email: egrgrad@egr.msu.edu
Financial aid: (517) 353-5940
Application deadline: 12/31
In-state tuition: full time: $706/credit hour; part time: $706/credit hour
Out-of-state tuition: full time: $1,386/credit hour
Room/board/expenses: $14,578
Full-time enrollment: 735
men: 78%; women: 22%; minorities: 8%; international: 63%
Part-time enrollment: N/A
men: N/A; women: N/A; minorities: N/A; international: N/A
Acceptance rate: 9%
GRE requirement: Yes
Avg. GRE: quantitative: 162
TOEFL requirement: Yes
Minimum TOEFL score: 550
Fellowships: 102
Teaching assistantships: 308
Research assistantships: 662
Students reporting specialty: agriculture: 5%; biomedical: 0%; chemical: 9%; civil: 12%; computer science: 19%; electrical: 25%; environmental: 5%; materials: 6%; mechanical: 18%; other: 1%

Michigan Technological University

1400 Townsend Drive
Houghton, MI 49931-1295
www.mtu.edu/gradschool/
Public
Admissions: (906) 487-2327
Email: gradadms@mtu.edu
Financial aid: (906) 487-2622
Application deadline: rolling
In-state tuition: full time: $18,725; part time: $1,027/credit hour
Out-of-state tuition: full time: $18,725
Room/board/expenses: $14,355
Full-time enrollment: 807
men: 80%; women: 20%; minorities: 2%; international: 79%
Part-time enrollment: 201
men: 80%; women: 20%; minorities: 10%; international: 40%
Acceptance rate: 25%
GRE requirement: Yes
Avg. GRE: quantitative: 162
TOEFL requirement: Yes
Minimum TOEFL score: 550
Fellowships: 48
Teaching assistantships: 100
Research assistantships: 134
Students reporting specialty: biomedical: 4%; chemical: 4%; civil: 7%; computer: 3%; computer science: 5%; electrical: 21%; environmental: 8%; materials: 4%; mechanical: 38%; mining: 0%; other: 6%

Oakland University

2200 Squirrel Road
Rochester, MI 48309
oakland.edu/secs/
Public
Admissions: (248) 370-2700
Email: gradinfo@oakland.edu
Financial aid: (248) 370-2550
Application deadline: 07/15
In-state tuition: full time: $680/credit hour; part time: $680/credit hour
Out-of-state tuition: full time: $1,027/credit hour
Room/board/expenses: $12,274
Full-time enrollment: 292
men: 67%; women: 33%; minorities: 9%; international: 65%

Part-time enrollment: 380
men: 84%; women: 16%;
minorities: 15%; international:
22%
Acceptance rate: 33%
Avg. GRE: quantitative: N/A
TOEFL requirement: Yes
Minimum TOEFL score: 550
Fellowships: 0
Teaching assistantships: 34
Research assistantships: 50
Students reporting specialty:
computer: 23%; computer
science: 14%; electrical: 11%;
management: 13%; industrial: 8%;
mechanical: 28%; other: 3%

University of
Detroit Mercy
4001 W. McNichols
Detroit, MI 48221-3038
www.udmercy.edu
Private
Admissions: (313) 993-1592
Email: admissions@udmercy.edu
Financial aid: (313) 993-3350
Application deadline: rolling
Tuition: full time: $1,565/credit
hour; part time: $1,565/credit
hour
Room/board/expenses: N/A
Full-time enrollment: 89
men: 88%; women: 12%;
minorities: 6%; international: 84%
Part-time enrollment: 74
men: 84%; women: 16%;
minorities: 14%; international:
49%
Acceptance rate: 90%
GRE requirement: No
Avg. GRE: quantitative: N/A
TOEFL requirement: No
Minimum TOEFL score: N/A
Fellowships: 0
Teaching assistantships: 7
Research assistantships: 1
Students reporting specialty: civil:
13%; computer: 12%; computer
science: 21%; electrical: 2%;
management: 7%; environmental:
2%; mechanical: 21%; other: 23%

University of
Michigan-Ann Arbor
Robert H. Lurie Engineering
Center
Ann Arbor, MI 48109-2102
www.engin.umich.edu/college/
academics/grad
Public
Admissions: (734) 647-7077
Email: coe-grad-ed@umich.edu
Financial aid: (734) 647-7077
Application deadline: rolling
In-state tuition: full time: $24,633;
part time: $1,317/credit hour
Out-of-state tuition: full time:
$46,163
Room/board/expenses: $21,788
Full-time enrollment: 3,248
men: 76%; women: 24%;
minorities: 12%; international:
60%
Part-time enrollment: 322
men: 81%; women: 19%;
minorities: 12%; international:
33%
Acceptance rate: 27%
GRE requirement: Yes
Avg. GRE: quantitative: 166
TOEFL requirement: Yes
Minimum TOEFL score: N/A
Teaching assistantships: 319
Research assistantships: 970
Students reporting specialty:
aerospace: 6%; biomedical: 6%;
chemical: 4%; civil: 4%; computer
science: 9%; electrical: 22%;
environmental: 2%; industrial:
6%; materials: 5%; mechanical:
15%; nuclear: 4%; other: 20%

University of
Michigan-Dearborn
4901 Evergreen Road
Dearborn, MI 48128
umdearborn.edu/cecs
Public
Admissions: (313) 593-1494
Email: umdgrad@umd.umich.edu
Financial aid: (313) 593-5300
Application deadline: 08/01
In-state tuition: full time: $659/
credit hour; part time: $659/
credit hour
Out-of-state tuition: full time:
$1,156/credit hour
Room/board/expenses: $12,728
Full-time enrollment: 394
men: 81%; women: 19%;
minorities: 2%; international: 94%
Part-time enrollment: 844
men: 81%; women: 19%;
minorities: 20%; international:
25%
Acceptance rate: 53%
GRE requirement: Yes
Avg. GRE: quantitative: 158
TOEFL requirement: Yes
Minimum TOEFL score: 560
Teaching assistantships: 22
Research assistantships: 29
Students reporting specialty:
biomedical: 0%; computer: 4%;
computer science: 7%; electrical:
13%; management: 11%;
industrial: 13%; mechanical: 24%;
other: 28%

Wayne State
University
5050 Anthony Wayne Drive
Detroit, MI 48202
engineering.wayne.edu
Public
Admissions: (313) 577-4723
Email:
gradadmissions@wayne.edu
Financial aid: (313) 577-2100
Application deadline: 06/01
In-state tuition: full time: $713/
credit hour; part time: $713/
credit hour
Out-of-state tuition: full time:
$1,430/credit hour
Room/board/expenses: $16,452
Full-time enrollment: 1,206
men: 82%; women: 18%;
minorities: 4%; international: 86%
Part-time enrollment: 384
men: 80%; women: 20%;
minorities: 17%; international:
36%
Acceptance rate: 43%
GRE requirement: Yes
Avg. GRE: quantitative: 156
TOEFL requirement: Yes
Minimum TOEFL score: 550
Fellowships: 20
Teaching assistantships: 114
Research assistantships: 69
Students reporting specialty:
biomedical: 8%; chemical:
3%; civil: 6%; computer:
3%; computer science: 10%;
electrical: 15%; management: 5%;
industrial: 24%; materials: 2%;
mechanical: 23%; other: 3%

Western Michigan
University
1903 W. Michigan Avenue
Kalamazoo, MI 49008-5314
wmich.edu/engineer
Public
Admissions: (269) 387-2000
Email: ask-wmu@wmich.edu
Financial aid: (269) 387-6000
Application deadline: rolling
In-state tuition: full time: $555/
credit hour; part time: $555/
credit hour

Out-of-state tuition: full time:
$1,175/credit hour
Room/board/expenses: $14,120
Full-time enrollment: 455
men: 80%; women: 20%;
minorities: 3%; international: 85%
Part-time enrollment: 181
men: 85%; women: 15%;
minorities: 7%; international: 60%
Acceptance rate: 55%
GRE requirement: Yes
Avg. GRE: quantitative: 154
TOEFL requirement: Yes
Minimum TOEFL score: 550
Teaching assistantships: 85
Research assistantships: 29
Students reporting specialty:
aerospace: 2%; chemical:
2%; civil: 10%; computer:
2%; computer science: 14%;
electrical: 17%; management: 8%;
industrial: 23%; mechanical: 17%;
other: 7%

MINNESOTA

Mayo Graduate
School[1]
200 First Street SW
Rochester, MN 55905
www.mayo.edu/mgs/
Private
Admissions: N/A
Financial aid: N/A
Tuition: N/A
Room/board/expenses: N/A
Enrollment: N/A

University of
Minnesota-Twin Cities
117 Pleasant Street SE
Minneapolis, MN 55455
www.cse.umn.edu
Public
Admissions: (612) 625-3014
Email: gsquest@umn.edu
Financial aid: (612) 624-1111
Application deadline: 12/15
In-state tuition: full time: $17,934;
part time: $1,353/credit hour
Out-of-state tuition: full time:
$26,814
Room/board/expenses: $16,230
Full-time enrollment: 1,583
men: 76%; women: 24%;
minorities: N/A; international: N/A
Part-time enrollment: 340
men: 80%; women: 20%;
minorities: N/A; international: N/A
Acceptance rate: 30%
GRE requirement: Yes
Avg. GRE: quantitative: 164
TOEFL requirement: Yes
Minimum TOEFL score: 550
Fellowships: 221
Teaching assistantships: 361
Research assistantships: 616
Students reporting specialty:
aerospace: 5%; biomedical: 9%;
chemical: 7%; civil: 7%; computer
science: 16%; electrical: 24%;
management: 2%; industrial: 4%;
materials: 4%; mechanical: 14%;
other: 8%

MISSISSIPPI

Jackson State
University
1400 John R. Lynch Street
Jackson, MS 39217
www.jsums.edu/
Public
Admissions: (601) 979-2455
Email: graduate@jsums.edu
Financial aid: (601) 979-2227
Application deadline: 03/01
In-state tuition: full time: $7,141;
part time: $298/credit hour

Out-of-state tuition: full time:
$17,614
Room/board/expenses: $11,008
Full-time enrollment: 69
men: 71%; women: 29%;
minorities: 38%; international:
57%
Part-time enrollment: 40
men: 75%; women: 25%;
minorities: 50%; international:
30%
Acceptance rate: 66%
GRE requirement: Yes
Avg. GRE: quantitative: N/A
TOEFL requirement: Yes
Minimum TOEFL score: N/A
Students reporting specialty:
computer science: 17%; other:
83%

Mississippi State
University (Bagley)
PO Box 9544
Mississippi State, MS 39762
www.bagley.msstate.edu/
Public
Email:
gradapps@grad.msstate.edu
Financial aid: (662) 325-2450
Application deadline: 07/01
In-state tuition: full time: $7,670;
part time: $426/credit hour
Out-of-state tuition: full time:
$20,790
Room/board/expenses: $18,726
Full-time enrollment: 359
men: 74%; women: 26%;
minorities: 9%; international: 52%
Part-time enrollment: 306
men: 80%; women: 20%;
minorities: 22%; international:
10%
Acceptance rate: 43%
GRE requirement: Yes
Avg. GRE: quantitative: 158
TOEFL requirement: Yes
Minimum TOEFL score: 477
Fellowships: 55
Teaching assistantships: 70
Research assistantships: 203
Students reporting specialty:
aerospace: 12%; agriculture: 4%;
biomedical: 3%; chemical: 2%;
civil: 12%; computer science: 9%;
electrical: 10%; industrial: 13%;
mechanical: 17%; other: 18%

University of
Mississippi
Brevard Hall, Room 227
University, MS 38677-1848
www.engineering.olemiss.edu/
Public
Admissions: (662) 915-7474
Email: gschool@olemiss.edu
Financial aid: (800) 891-4596
Application deadline: 04/01
In-state tuition: full time: $7,644;
part time: $425/credit hour
Out-of-state tuition: full time:
$21,912
Room/board/expenses: $17,260
Full-time enrollment: 116
men: 77%; women: 23%;
minorities: 8%; international: 59%
Part-time enrollment: 22
men: 95%; women: 5%;
minorities: 18%; international:
14%
Acceptance rate: 29%
GRE requirement: Yes
Avg. GRE: quantitative: 156
TOEFL requirement: Yes
Minimum TOEFL score: N/A
Fellowships: 3
Teaching assistantships: 74
Research assistantships: 24
Students reporting specialty:
chemical: 9%; civil: 13%;
computer science: 28%;

electrical: 14%; mechanical:
12%; other: 23%

University of
Southern Mississippi[1]
118 College Drive, #5050
Hattiesburg, MS 39406
www.usm.edu/graduate-school
Public
Admissions: (601) 266-4369
Financial aid: N/A
Tuition: N/A
Room/board/expenses: N/A
Enrollment: N/A

MISSOURI

Missouri University of
Science & Technology
500 W. 16th Street, 110 ERL
Rolla, MO 65409-0840
www.mst.edu
Public
Admissions: (800) 522-0938
Email: admissions@mst.edu
Financial aid: (800) 522-0938
Application deadline: 07/01
In-state tuition: full time: $10,537;
part time: $387/credit hour
Out-of-state tuition: full time:
$27,015
Room/board/expenses: $14,076
Full-time enrollment: 811
men: 81%; women: 19%;
minorities: 4%; international: 71%
Part-time enrollment: 316
men: 83%; women: 17%;
minorities: 14%; international:
35%
Acceptance rate: 53%
GRE requirement: Yes
Avg. GRE: quantitative: 156
TOEFL requirement: Yes
Minimum TOEFL score: N/A
Students reporting specialty:
aerospace: 5%; chemical:
6%; civil: 8%; computer:
3%; computer science: 8%;
electrical: 15%; management: 9%;
environmental: 1%; industrial:
7%; materials: 3%; mechanical:
11%; mining: 3%; nuclear: 4%;
petroleum: 7%; other: 10%

St. Louis
University (Parks)
3450 Lindell Boulevard
St. Louis, MO 63103
parks.slu.edu/grad
Private
Admissions: (314) 977-8306
Email: parksgraduateprograms@
slu.edu
Financial aid: (314) 977-2350
Application deadline: 06/30
Tuition: full time: $1,075/credit
hour; part time: $1,075/credit
hour
Room/board/expenses: $18,540
Full-time enrollment: 86
men: 67%; women: 33%;
minorities: 14%; international:
36%
Part-time enrollment: 18
men: 89%; women: 11%;
minorities: 28%; international:
11%
Acceptance rate: 68%
GRE requirement: Yes
Avg. GRE: quantitative: 159
TOEFL requirement: Yes
Minimum TOEFL score: 550
Fellowships: 7
Teaching assistantships: 0
Research assistantships: 18
Students reporting specialty:
aerospace: 15%; biomedical:
19%; civil: 19%; computer: 5%;
electrical: 5%; mechanical: 15%;
other: 21%

University of Missouri

W1025 Thomas and
Nell Lafferre Hall
Columbia, MO 65211
www.missouri.edu/
Public
Admissions: (573) 882-7786
Email: gradadmin@missouri.edu
Financial aid: (573) 882-2751
Application deadline: 02/15
In-state tuition: full time: $9,324;
part time: $483/credit hour
Out-of-state tuition: full time:
$19,823
Room/board/expenses: $18,806
Full-time enrollment: 613
men: 78%; women: 22%;
minorities: 4%; international: 77%
Part-time enrollment: N/A
men: N/A; women: N/A;
minorities: N/A; international: N/A
Acceptance rate: 23%
GRE requirement: Yes
Avg. GRE: quantitative: 161
TOEFL requirement: Yes
Minimum TOEFL score: N/A
Fellowships: 17
Teaching assistantships: 116
Research assistantships: 178
Students reporting specialty:
biomedical: 8%; chemical:
6%; civil: 12%; computer:
23%; computer science: 20%;
electrical: 23%; science and
physics: 2%; industrial: 5%;
mechanical: 18%; nuclear: 4%

University of Missouri-Kansas City

534 R. H. Flarsheim Hall
5100 Rockhill Road
Kansas City, MO 64110-2499
www.umkc.edu/sce
Public
Admissions: (816) 235-1111
Email: graduate@umkc.edu
Financial aid: (816) 235-1154
Application deadline: rolling
In-state tuition: full time: $359/
credit hour; part time: $359/
credit hour
Out-of-state tuition: full time:
$926/credit hour
Room/board/expenses: $14,808
Full-time enrollment: 481
men: 68%; women: 32%;
minorities: 1%; international: 94%
Part-time enrollment: 273
men: 81%; women: 19%;
minorities: 9%; international: 68%
Acceptance rate: 40%
GRE requirement: Yes
Avg. GRE: quantitative: N/A
TOEFL requirement: Yes
Minimum TOEFL score: 550
Teaching assistantships: 43
Research assistantships: 30
Students reporting specialty: N/A

Washington University in St. Louis

1 Brookings Drive
Campus Box 1100
St. Louis, MO 63130
www.engineering.wustl.edu/
Private
Admissions: (314) 935-4446
Email:
engineeringgradadmissions@
wustl.edu
Financial aid: (314) 935-5900
Application deadline: 01/15
Tuition: full time: $49,300; part
time: $2,040/credit hour
Room/board/expenses: $22,700
Full-time enrollment: 899
men: 71%; women: 29%;
minorities: 10%; international:
64%

Part-time enrollment: 357
men: 79%; women: 21%;
minorities: 22%; international:
11%
Acceptance rate: 40%
GRE requirement: Yes
Avg. GRE: quantitative: 165
TOEFL requirement: Yes
Minimum TOEFL score: 550
Fellowships: 32
Research assistantships: 345
Students reporting specialty:
aerospace: 4%; biomedical:
13%; computer: 3%; computer
science: 15%; electrical: 17%;
management: 1%; environmental:
10%; industrial: 2%; materials:
2%; mechanical: 15%; other: 19%

MONTANA

Montana State University

212 Roberts Hall
PO Box 173820
Bozeman, MT 59717-3820
www.montana.edu/wwwdg
Public
Admissions: (406) 994-4145
Email: gradstudy@montana.edu
Financial aid: (406) 994-2845
Application deadline: 08/28
In-state tuition: full time: $9,510;
part time: $267/credit hour
Out-of-state tuition: full time:
$25,808
Room/board/expenses: $15,180
Full-time enrollment: 78
men: 78%; women: 22%;
minorities: 5%; international: 31%
Part-time enrollment: 134
men: 76%; women: 24%;
minorities: 4%; international: 27%
Acceptance rate: 30%
GRE requirement: Yes
Avg. GRE: quantitative: 158
TOEFL requirement: Yes
Minimum TOEFL score: 580
Fellowships: 0
Teaching assistantships: 66
Research assistantships: 73
Students reporting specialty:
chemical: 19%; civil: 23%;
computer science: 22%;
electrical: 14%; mechanical: 21%;
other: 0%

NEBRASKA

University of Nebraska-Lincoln

114 Othmer Hall
Lincoln, NE 68588-0642
www.engineering.unl.edu/
graduate-programs
Public
Admissions: (402) 472-2875
Email: graduate@unl.edu
Financial aid: (402) 472-2030
Application deadline: rolling
In-state tuition: full time: $411/
credit hour; part time: $411/
credit hour
Out-of-state tuition: full time:
$1,098/credit hour
Room/board/expenses: $13,734
Full-time enrollment: 535
men: 80%; women: 20%;
minorities: 5%; international: 65%
Part-time enrollment: 109
men: 87%; women: 13%;
minorities: 14%; international:
31%
Acceptance rate: 34%
GRE requirement: Yes
Avg. GRE: quantitative: 161
TOEFL requirement: Yes
Minimum TOEFL score: 550
Fellowships: 4
Teaching assistantships: 133
Research assistantships: 304

Students reporting specialty:
agriculture: 6%; architectural:
8%; biomedical: 2%; chemical:
3%; civil: 15%; computer:
4%; computer science: 17%;
electrical: 15%; management: 5%;
environmental: 2%; materials:
5%; mechanical: 14%; other: 4%

NEVADA

University of Nevada-Las Vegas (Hughes)

4505 Maryland Parkway
Box 544005
Las Vegas, NV 89154-4005
www.unlv.edu/engineering
Public
Admissions: (702) 895-3320
Email: gradcollege@unlv.edu
Financial aid: (702) 895-3424
Application deadline: 08/01
In-state tuition: full time: $9,726;
part time: $276/credit hour
Out-of-state tuition: full time:
$23,636
Room/board/expenses: $14,857
Full-time enrollment: 200
men: 75%; women: 26%;
minorities: 18%; international:
52%
Part-time enrollment: 58
men: 84%; women: 16%;
minorities: 40%; international:
16%
Acceptance rate: 60%
GRE requirement: Yes
Avg. GRE: quantitative: 157
TOEFL requirement: Yes
Minimum TOEFL score: 550
Fellowships: 2
Teaching assistantships: 96
Research assistantships: 86
Students reporting specialty:
biomedical: 7%; civil: 24%;
computer science: 22%;
electrical: 19%; mechanical: 24%;
nuclear: 1%; other: 2%

University of Nevada-Reno

Mail Stop 0256
Reno, NV 89557-0256
www.unr.edu/grad/admissions
Public
Admissions: (775) 784-6869
Email: gradadmissions@unr.edu
Financial aid: (775) 784-4666
Application deadline: rolling
In-state tuition: full time: $371/
credit hour; part time: $371/
credit hour
Out-of-state tuition: full time:
$1,289/credit hour
Room/board/expenses: $20,100
Full-time enrollment: 227
men: 77%; women: 23%;
minorities: 12%; international:
69%
Part-time enrollment: 67
men: 87%; women: 13%;
minorities: 19%; international:
30%
Acceptance rate: 43%
GRE requirement: Yes
Avg. GRE: quantitative: 162
TOEFL requirement: Yes
Minimum TOEFL score: 550
Teaching assistantships: 84
Research assistantships: 128
Students reporting specialty:
biomedical: 4%; chemical:
4%; civil: 27%; computer:
33%; computer science: 33%;
electrical: 8%; environmental:
26%; materials: 9%; mechanical:
16%

Dartmouth College (Thayer)

14 Engineering Drive
Hanover, NH 03755
engineering.dartmouth.edu
Private
Admissions: (603) 646-2606
Email: engineering.admissions@
dartmouth.edu
Financial aid: (603) 646-3844
Application deadline: 01/01
Tuition: full time: $50,398; part
time: N/A
Room/board/expenses: $26,610
Full-time enrollment: 313
men: 71%; women: 29%;
minorities: 9%; international: 65%
Part-time enrollment: N/A
men: N/A; women: N/A;
minorities: N/A; international: N/A
Acceptance rate: 19%
GRE requirement: Yes
Avg. GRE: quantitative: 164
TOEFL requirement: Yes
Minimum TOEFL score: 600
Fellowships: 40
Teaching assistantships: 23
Research assistantships: 98
Students reporting specialty:
computer science: 32%; science
and physics: 68%

University of New Hampshire

Kingsbury Hall
33 College Road
Durham, NH 03824
www.gradschool.unh.edu/
Public
Admissions: (603) 862-3000
Email: grad.school@unh.edu
Financial aid: (603) 862-3600
Application deadline: 02/15
In-state tuition: full time: $15,920;
part time: $770/credit hour
Out-of-state tuition: full time:
$29,210
Room/board/expenses: $16,760
Full-time enrollment: 121
men: 73%; women: 27%;
minorities: 6%; international: 59%
Part-time enrollment: 145
men: 81%; women: 19%;
minorities: 5%; international: 32%
Acceptance rate: 62%
GRE requirement: Yes
Avg. GRE: quantitative: 160
TOEFL requirement: Yes
Minimum TOEFL score: 550
Students reporting specialty: N/A

New Jersey Institute of Technology

University Heights
Newark, NJ 07102-1982
www.njit.edu/
Public
Admissions: (973) 596-3300
Email: admissions@njit.edu
Financial aid: (973) 596-3479
Application deadline: 06/01
In-state tuition: full time: $21,814;
part time: $1,034/credit hour
Out-of-state tuition: full time:
$30,898
Room/board/expenses: $18,700
Full-time enrollment: 1,662
men: 73%; women: 27%;
minorities: 8%; international: 86%
Part-time enrollment: 788
men: 77%; women: 23%;
minorities: 51%; international: 6%
Acceptance rate: 51%
GRE requirement: Yes
Avg. GRE: quantitative: 159
TOEFL requirement: Yes
Minimum TOEFL score: 550

Fellowships: 1
Teaching assistantships: 107
Research assistantships: 94
Students reporting specialty:
biomedical: 5%; chemical:
4%; civil: 11%; computer:
2%; computer science: 43%;
electrical: 13%; management:
6%; science and physics: 0%;
environmental: 1%; industrial:
4%; materials: 2%; mechanical:
5%; other: 5%

Princeton University

C230 Engineering Quadrangle
Princeton, NJ 08544-5263
www.princeton.edu/engineering/
Private
Admissions: (609) 258-3034
Email: gsadmit@princeton.edu
Financial aid: (609) 258-3037
Application deadline: N/A
Tuition: full time: $47,220; part
time: N/A
Room/board/expenses: $29,400
Full-time enrollment: 615
men: 74%; women: 26%;
minorities: 12%; international:
56%
Part-time enrollment: N/A
men: N/A; women: N/A;
minorities: N/A; international: N/A
Acceptance rate: 13%
GRE requirement: Yes
Avg. GRE: quantitative: 167
TOEFL requirement: Yes
Minimum TOEFL score: N/A
Fellowships: 178
Teaching assistantships: 151
Research assistantships: 273
Students reporting specialty:
aerospace: 16%; chemical: 16%;
civil: 9%; computer science: 23%;
electrical: 27%; environmental:
9%; mechanical: 16%; other: 9%

Rutgers, The State University of New Jersey-New Brunswick

98 Brett Road
Piscataway, NJ 08854-8058
gradstudy.rutgers.edu
Public
Admissions: (732) 932-7711
Email: gradadm@rci.rutgers.edu
Financial aid: (848) 932-7057
Application deadline: rolling
In-state tuition: full time: $18,633;
part time: $889/credit hour
Out-of-state tuition: full time:
$30,225
Room/board/expenses: $18,765
Full-time enrollment: 864
men: 75%; women: 25%;
minorities: 8%; international: 79%
Part-time enrollment: 531
men: 73%; women: 27%;
minorities: 15%; international:
61%
Acceptance rate: 23%
GRE requirement: Yes
Avg. GRE: quantitative: 163
TOEFL requirement: Yes
Minimum TOEFL score: 550
Fellowships: 101
Teaching assistantships: 181
Research assistantships: 203
Students reporting specialty:
biomedical: 7%; chemical: 15%;
civil: 9%; computer science: 22%;
electrical: 25%; industrial: 7%;
materials: 4%; mechanical: 11%;
other: 1%

Stevens Institute of Technology (Schaefer)

Castle Point on Hudson
Hoboken, NJ 07030
www.stevens.edu/ses/index.php
Private
Admissions: (201) 216-5197
Email:
gradadmissions@stevens.edu
Financial aid: (201) 216-8143
Application deadline: 06/01
Tuition: full time: $34,514; part
time: $1,501/credit hour
Room/board/expenses: $16,150
Full-time enrollment: 1,494
men: 73%; women: 27%;
minorities: 3%; international: 89%
Part-time enrollment: 547
men: 78%; women: 22%;
minorities: 19%; international: 2%
Acceptance rate: 56%
GRE requirement: Yes
Avg. GRE: quantitative: 161
TOEFL requirement: Yes
Minimum TOEFL score: 537
Students reporting specialty: N/A

NEW MEXICO

New Mexico Institute of Mining and Technology

801 Leroy Place
Socorro, NM 87801
www.nmt.edu
Public
Admissions: (575) 835-5513
Email: graduate@nmt.edu
Financial aid: (575) 835-5333
Application deadline: 01/06
In-state tuition: full time: $6,101;
part time: $339/credit hour
Out-of-state tuition: full time:
$20,181
Room/board/expenses: $13,874
Full-time enrollment: 150
men: 80%; women: 20%;
minorities: 21%; international:
44%
Part-time enrollment: 65
men: 78%; women: 22%;
minorities: 20%; international: 8%
Acceptance rate: 53%
GRE requirement: Yes
Avg. GRE: quantitative: 157
TOEFL requirement: Yes
Minimum TOEFL score: N/A
Fellowships: 2
Teaching assistantships: 35
Research assistantships: 42
Students reporting specialty:
computer science: 17%;
electrical: 5%; management: 5%;
environmental: 3%; materials:
14%; mechanical: 26%; mining:
13%; petroleum: 17%

New Mexico State University

PO Box 30001, Department 3449
Las Cruces, NM 88003
www.nmsu.edu
Public
Admissions: (575) 646-3121
Email: admissions@nmsu.edu
Financial aid: (505) 646-4105
Application deadline: rolling
In-state tuition: full time: $4,941;
part time: $227/credit hour
Out-of-state tuition: full time:
$15,107
Room/board/expenses: $13,050
Full-time enrollment: 297
men: 78%; women: 22%;
minorities: N/A; international: N/A
Part-time enrollment: 182
men: 74%; women: 26%;
minorities: N/A; international: N/A
Acceptance rate: 48%
GRE requirement:

Avg. GRE: quantitative: 157
TOEFL requirement: Yes
Minimum TOEFL score: 550
Fellowships: 2
Teaching assistantships: 119
Research assistantships: 109
Students reporting specialty:
aerospace: 1%; chemical:
8%; civil: 13%; computer
science: 19%; electrical: 24%;
environmental: 1%; industrial:
27%; mechanical: 7%

University of New Mexico

MSC 01 1140
1 University of New Mexico
Albuquerque, NM 87131
grad.unm.edu/
Public
Admissions: (505) 277-8900
Email: unmlobos@unm.edu
Financial aid: (505) 277-8900
Application deadline: 07/15
In-state tuition: full time: $261/
credit hour; part time: $261/
credit hour
Out-of-state tuition: full time:
$880/credit hour
Room/board/expenses: $15,794
Full-time enrollment: 787
men: 81%; women: 19%;
minorities: 20%; international:
37%
Part-time enrollment: N/A
men: N/A; women: N/A;
minorities: N/A; international: N/A
Acceptance rate: 44%
GRE requirement: Yes
Avg. GRE: quantitative: 145
TOEFL requirement: Yes
Minimum TOEFL score: 550
Fellowships: 5
Teaching assistantships: 28
Research assistantships: 336
Students reporting specialty:
biomedical: 2%; chemical:
7%; civil: 14%; computer:
8%; computer science: 18%;
electrical: 26%; industrial: 1%;
mechanical: 12%; nuclear: 5%;
other: 7%

NEW YORK

Alfred University-New York State College of Ceramics (Inamori)

2 Pine Street
Alfred, NY 14802-1296
nyscc.alfred.edu
Public
Admissions: (800) 541-9229
Email: admwww@alfred.edu
Financial aid: (607) 871-2159
Application deadline: rolling
In-state tuition: full time: $23,490;
part time: $810/credit hour
Out-of-state tuition: full time:
$23,490
Room/board/expenses: $15,546
Full-time enrollment: 25
men: 76%; women: 24%;
minorities: N/A; international: N/A
Part-time enrollment: 19
men: 79%; women: 21%;
minorities: N/A; international: N/A
Acceptance rate: 66%
GRE requirement: No
Avg. GRE: quantitative: N/A
TOEFL requirement: Yes
Minimum TOEFL score: N/A
Fellowships: 1
Teaching assistantships: 8
Research assistantships: 11
Students reporting specialty: N/A

Binghamton University-SUNY (Watson)

PO Box 6000
Binghamton, NY 13902-6000
www.binghamton.edu/watson/
Public
Admissions: (607) 777-2151
Email: gradsch@binghamton.edu
Financial aid: (607) 777-2428
Application deadline: rolling
In-state tuition: full time: $13,115;
part time: $453/credit hour
Out-of-state tuition: full time:
$24,455
Room/board/expenses: $18,086
Full-time enrollment: 784
men: 75%; women: 25%;
minorities: 9%; international: 81%
Part-time enrollment: 401
men: 79%; women: 21%;
minorities: 11%; international:
59%
Acceptance rate: 57%
GRE requirement: Yes
Avg. GRE: quantitative: 160
TOEFL requirement: Yes
Minimum TOEFL score: 550
Fellowships: 5
Teaching assistantships: 111
Research assistantships: 138
Students reporting specialty:
biomedical: 6%; computer
science: 37%; electrical: 18%;
industrial: 26%; materials: 2%;
mechanical: 8%; other: 4%

Clarkson University

8 Clarkson Avenue
Box 5700
Potsdam, NY 13699
graduate.clarkson.edu/
engineering/
Private
Admissions: (315) 268-3802
Email: graduate@clarkson.edu
Financial aid: (315) 268-7929
Application deadline: rolling
Tuition: full time: $1,300/credit
hour; part time: $1,300/credit
hour
Room/board/expenses: $14,200
Full-time enrollment: 191
men: 77%; women: 23%;
minorities: 7%; international: 57%
Part-time enrollment: 104
men: 84%; women: 16%;
minorities: 10%; international: 1%
Acceptance rate: 68%
GRE requirement: Yes
Avg. GRE: quantitative: 162
TOEFL requirement: Yes
Minimum TOEFL score: 550
Fellowships: 5
Teaching assistantships: 47
Research assistantships: 61
Students reporting specialty:
chemical: 8%; civil: 11%;
electrical: 23%; management:
9%; science and physics: 2%;
environmental: 6%; materials:
2%; mechanical: 35%; other: 3%

Columbia University (Fu Foundation)

500 W. 120th Street
Room 510, Mudd
New York, NY 10027
www.engineering.columbia.edu
Private
Admissions: (212) 854-6438
Email:
seasgradmit@columbia.edu
Financial aid: (212) 854-6438
Application deadline: 02/15
Tuition: full time: $49,775; part
time: $1,858/credit hour
Room/board/expenses: $27,846

Full-time enrollment: 2,048
men: 69%; women: 31%;
minorities: 10%; international:
77%
Part-time enrollment: 1,302
men: 69%; women: 31%;
minorities: 10%; international:
69%
Acceptance rate: 24%
GRE requirement: Yes
Avg. GRE: quantitative: 167
TOEFL requirement: Yes
Minimum TOEFL score: 590
Fellowships: 130
Teaching assistantships: 142
Research assistantships: 376
Students reporting specialty:
biomedical: 5%; chemical:
6%; civil: 7%; computer:
2%; computer science: 17%;
electrical: 15%; management:
4%; science and physics: 2%;
environmental: 4%; industrial:
20%; materials: 3%; mechanical:
8%; other: 8%

Cornell University

242 Carpenter Hall
Ithaca, NY 14853
www.engineering.cornell.edu
Private
Admissions: (607) 255-5820
Email: engr_grad@cornell.edu
Financial aid: (607) 255-5820
Application deadline: rolling
Tuition: full time: $29,585; part
time: $2,113/credit hour
Room/board/expenses: $25,152
Full-time enrollment: 1,968
men: 67%; women: 33%;
minorities: 16%; international:
58%
Part-time enrollment: 101
men: 75%; women: 25%;
minorities: 30%; international: 2%
Acceptance rate: 27%
GRE requirement: Yes
Avg. GRE: quantitative: 165
TOEFL requirement: Yes
Minimum TOEFL score: N/A
Fellowships: 421
Teaching assistantships: 256
Research assistantships: 445
Students reporting specialty:
aerospace: 2%; agriculture:
2%; biomedical: 9%; chemical:
8%; civil: 5%; computer:
14%; computer science: 18%;
management: 2%; science and
physics: 4%; industrial: 10%;
materials: 5%; mechanical: 8%;
other: 13%

CUNY-City College (Grove)

Convent Avenue at 138th Street
New York, NY 10031
www.ccny.cuny.edu/admissions
Public
Admissions: (212) 650-6977
Email: graduateadmissions@
ccny.cuny.edu
Financial aid: (212) 650-6656
Application deadline: 05/01
In-state tuition: full time: $12,147;
part time: $505/credit hour
Out-of-state tuition: full time:
$870/credit hour
Room/board/expenses: $28,755
Full-time enrollment: 330
men: 68%; women: 32%;
minorities: 29%; international:
49%
Part-time enrollment: 213
men: 81%; women: 19%;
minorities: 61%; international:
14%
Acceptance rate: 58%
GRE requirement: Yes
Avg. GRE: quantitative: 157
TOEFL requirement: Yes

Minimum TOEFL score: 550
Fellowships: 23
Teaching assistantships: 50
Research assistantships: 142
Students reporting specialty:
biomedical: 10%; chemical:
10%; civil: 24%; computer
science: 21%; electrical: 20%;
environmental: 3%; mechanical:
14%

New York University (Tandon)

6 MetroTech Center
Brooklyn, NY 11201
engineering.nyu.edu/
Private
Admissions: (646) 997-3200
Email: engineering.gradinfo@
nyu.edu
Financial aid: (646) 997-3182
Application deadline: 02/15
Tuition: full time: $1,646/credit
hour; part time: $1,646/credit
hour
Room/board/expenses: $29,740
Full-time enrollment: 2,219
men: 74%; women: 26%;
minorities: 5%; international: 89%
Part-time enrollment: 466
men: 70%; women: 30%;
minorities: 32%; international:
33%
Acceptance rate: 34%
GRE requirement: Yes
Avg. GRE: quantitative: 164
TOEFL requirement: Yes
Minimum TOEFL score: 550
Fellowships: 40
Teaching assistantships: 69
Research assistantships: 191
Students reporting specialty:
biomedical: 3%; chemical:
2%; civil: 11%; computer:
8%; computer science: 25%;
electrical: 21%; management:
17%; environmental: 1%;
industrial: 6%; mechanical: 5%;
other: 1%

Rensselaer Polytechnic Institute

Jonsson Engineering Center 3004
Troy, NY 12180-3590
www.rpi.edu
Private
Admissions: (518) 276-6216
Email: admissions@rpi.edu
Financial aid: (518) 276-6813
Application deadline: 01/02
Tuition: full time: $52,137; part
time: $2,060/credit hour
Room/board/expenses: $16,633
Full-time enrollment: 543
men: 77%; women: 23%;
minorities: 11%; international:
56%
Part-time enrollment: 103
men: 82%; women: 18%;
minorities: 13%; international: 6%
Acceptance rate: 27%
GRE requirement: Yes
Avg. GRE: quantitative: 164
TOEFL requirement: Yes
Minimum TOEFL score: N/A
Fellowships: 52
Teaching assistantships: 190
Research assistantships: 265
Students reporting specialty:
aerospace: 5%; biomedical:
8%; chemical: 11%; civil: 2%;
computer: 2%; computer
science: 14%; electrical: 15%;
management: 2%; science and
physics: 0%; environmental: 1%;
industrial: 3%; materials: 8%;
mechanical: 24%; nuclear: 4%;
other: 1%

Rochester Institute of Technology (Gleason)
77 Lomb Memorial Drive
Rochester, NY 14623
www.rit.edu
Private
Admissions: (585) 475-2229
Email: gradinfo@rit.edu
Financial aid: (585) 475-2186
Application deadline: rolling
Tuition: full time: $42,078; part time: $1,742/credit hour
Room/board/expenses: $14,300
Full-time enrollment: 1,005
men: 76%; women: 24%;
minorities: 4%; international: 81%
Part-time enrollment: 192
men: 85%; women: 15%;
minorities: 10%; international: 31%
Acceptance rate: 38%
GRE requirement: No
Avg. GRE: quantitative: 160
TOEFL requirement: Yes
Minimum TOEFL score: 550
Fellowships: 3
Teaching assistantships: 62
Research assistantships: 104
Students reporting specialty:
computer: 6%; computer science: 41%; electrical: 21%; management: 2%; science and physics: 3%; industrial: 5%; mechanical: 14%; other: 17%

Stony Brook University-SUNY
Engineering Room 100
Stony Brook, NY 11794-2200
www.grad.stonybrook.edu
Public
Admissions: (631) 632-7035
Email: gradadmissions@stonybrook.edu
Financial aid: (631) 632-6840
Application deadline: N/A
In-state tuition: full time: $12,532; part time: $453/credit hour
Out-of-state tuition: full time: $23,872
Room/board/expenses: $19,136
Full-time enrollment: 1,222
men: 71%; women: 29%;
minorities: 10%; international: 78%
Part-time enrollment: 281
men: 74%; women: 26%;
minorities: 12%; international: 65%
Acceptance rate: 37%
GRE requirement: Yes
Avg. GRE: quantitative: 165
TOEFL requirement: Yes
Minimum TOEFL score: N/A
Fellowships: 11
Teaching assistantships: 216
Research assistantships: 253
Students reporting specialty:
biomedical: 5%; chemical: 0%; civil: 0%; computer: 5%; computer science: 34%; electrical: 8%; materials: 9%; mechanical: 10%; other: 29%

SUNY College of Environmental Science and Forestry
227 Bray Hall
Syracuse, NY 13210
www.esf.edu/
Public
Admissions: (315) 470-6599
Email: esfgrad@esf.edu
Financial aid: (315) 470-6673
Application deadline: 01/15
In-state tuition: full time: $12,310; part time: $453/credit hour
Out-of-state tuition: full time: $23,650
Room/board/expenses: $12,415

Full-time enrollment: 48
men: 54%; women: 46%;
minorities: 6%; international: 63%
Part-time enrollment: 41
men: 63%; women: 37%;
minorities: 10%; international: 39%
Acceptance rate: 58%
GRE requirement: Yes
Avg. GRE: quantitative: N/A
TOEFL requirement: Yes
Minimum TOEFL score: 550
Fellowships: 4
Teaching assistantships: 77
Students reporting specialty:
chemical: 51%; environmental: 49%

Syracuse University
223 Link Hall
Syracuse, NY 13244-1240
eng-cs.syr.edu/
Private
Admissions: (315) 443-1044
Email: topgrads@syr.edu
Financial aid: (315) 443-1513
Application deadline: rolling
Tuition: full time: $27,636; part time: $1,443/credit hour
Room/board/expenses: $17,286
Full-time enrollment: 883
men: 76%; women: 24%;
minorities: 4%; international: 87%
Part-time enrollment: 207
men: 81%; women: 19%;
minorities: 15%; international: 32%
Acceptance rate: 39%
GRE requirement: Yes
Avg. GRE: quantitative: 162
TOEFL requirement: Yes
Minimum TOEFL score: 550
Fellowships: 28
Teaching assistantships: 73
Research assistantships: 76
Students reporting specialty:
aerospace: 15%; biomedical: 5%; chemical: 5%; civil: 10%; computer: 18%; computer science: 19%; electrical: 6%; management: 5%; environmental: 2%; mechanical: 15%; other: 14%

University at Buffalo-SUNY
208 Davis Hall
Buffalo, NY 14260-1900
www.eng.buffalo.edu
Public
Admissions: (716) 645-2771
Email: seasgrad@buffalo.edu
Financial aid: (716) 645-2450
Application deadline: rolling
In-state tuition: full time: $13,347; part time: $453/credit hour
Out-of-state tuition: full time: $24,687
Room/board/expenses: $17,781
Full-time enrollment: 1,564
men: 77%; women: 23%;
minorities: 4%; international: 85%
Part-time enrollment: 295
men: 78%; women: 22%;
minorities: 9%; international: 63%
Acceptance rate: 33%
GRE requirement: Yes
Avg. GRE: quantitative: 162
TOEFL requirement: Yes
Minimum TOEFL score: N/A
Fellowships: 26
Teaching assistantships: 183
Research assistantships: 238
Students reporting specialty:
aerospace: 2%; biomedical: 5%; chemical: 8%; civil: 0%; computer science: 32%; electrical: 10%; science and physics: 1%; industrial: 14%; mechanical: 10%

University of Rochester
Lattimore Hall, Box 270076
Rochester, NY 14627-0076
www.Hajim.rochester.edu
Private
Admissions: (585) 275-2059
Email: graduate.admissions@rochester.edu
Financial aid: (585) 275-3226
Application deadline: N/A
Tuition: full time: $1,538/credit hour; part time: $1,538/credit hour
Room/board/expenses: $15,530
Full-time enrollment: 568
men: 76%; women: 24%;
minorities: 9%; international: 63%
Part-time enrollment: 22
men: 68%; women: 32%;
minorities: 0%; international: 27%
Acceptance rate: 38%
GRE requirement: Yes
Avg. GRE: quantitative: 165
TOEFL requirement: Yes
Minimum TOEFL score: 587
Fellowships: 63
Teaching assistantships: 198
Research assistantships: 258
Students reporting specialty:
biomedical: 11%; chemical: 8%; computer science: 16%; electrical: 21%; materials: 7%; mechanical: 7%; other: 31%

NORTH CAROLINA

Duke University (Pratt)
305 Teer Building
Durham, NC 27708-0271
www.pratt.duke.edu
Private
Admissions: (919) 684-3913
Email: grad-admissions@duke.edu
Financial aid: (919) 681-1552
Application deadline: 12/15
Tuition: full time: $54,339; part time: $2,875/credit hour
Room/board/expenses: $25,864
Full-time enrollment: 1,019
men: 66%; women: 34%;
minorities: 14%; international: 57%
Part-time enrollment: 74
men: 84%; women: 16%;
minorities: 23%; international: 4%
Acceptance rate: 27%
GRE requirement: Yes
Avg. GRE: quantitative: 164
TOEFL requirement: Yes
Minimum TOEFL score: 577
Fellowships: 163
Teaching assistantships: 16
Research assistantships: 347
Students reporting specialty:
biomedical: 21%; civil: 6%; computer science: 9%; electrical: 20%; management: 27%; mechanical: 10%; other: 7%

North Carolina A&T State University
1601 E. Market Street
651 McNair Hall
Greensboro, NC 27411
www.ncat.edu/tgc/admissions/
Public
Admissions: (336) 285-2366
Email: grad@ncat.edu
Financial aid: (336) 334-7973
Application deadline: 10/16
In-state tuition: full time: $7,447; part time: $253/credit hour
Out-of-state tuition: full time: $19,852
Room/board/expenses: $11,203
Full-time enrollment: 219
men: 64%; women: 36%;
minorities: 52%; international: 37%

Part-time enrollment: 86
men: 72%; women: 28%;
minorities: 44%; international: 41%
Acceptance rate: 79%
GRE requirement: Yes
Avg. GRE: quantitative: 154
TOEFL requirement: Yes
Minimum TOEFL score: 550
Fellowships: 15
Teaching assistantships: 100
Research assistantships: 50
Students reporting specialty:
biomedical: 6%; chemical: 3%; civil: 6%; computer science: 21%; electrical: 17%; industrial: 20%; mechanical: 12%; other: 16%

North Carolina State University
PO Box 7901
Raleigh, NC 27695
www.engr.ncsu.edu/
Public
Admissions: (919) 515-2872
Email: graduate-school@ncsu.edu
Financial aid: (919) 515-2866
Application deadline: 06/25
In-state tuition: full time: $11,572; part time: $9,550
Out-of-state tuition: full time: $26,094
Room/board/expenses: $19,919
Full-time enrollment: 2,795
men: 77%; women: 23%;
minorities: 5%; international: 70%
Part-time enrollment: 508
men: 81%; women: 19%;
minorities: 18%; international: 14%
Acceptance rate: 15%
GRE requirement: Yes
Avg. GRE: quantitative: 164
TOEFL requirement: Yes
Minimum TOEFL score: 550
Fellowships: 282
Teaching assistantships: 329
Research assistantships: 869
Students reporting specialty:
aerospace: 3%; agriculture: 2%; biomedical: 3%; chemical: 5%; civil: 8%; computer: 6%; computer science: 21%; electrical: 19%; environmental: 1%; industrial: 6%; materials: 4%; mechanical: 9%; nuclear: 3%; other: 8%

University of North Carolina-Chapel Hill
CB #7431, 166 Rosenau Hall
Chapel Hill, NC 27599-7431
www.sph.unc.edu/envr
Public
Admissions: (919) 966-3844
Email: wharper@email.unc.edu
Financial aid: (919) 966-3844
Application deadline: rolling
In-state tuition: full time: $12,467; part time: $876/credit hour
Out-of-state tuition: full time: $28,921
Room/board/expenses: $24,666
Full-time enrollment: 88
men: 40%; women: 60%;
minorities: 15%; international: 26%
Part-time enrollment: 2
men: 0%; women: 100%;
minorities: 50%; international: 0%
Acceptance rate: 35%
GRE requirement: Yes
Avg. GRE: quantitative: 159
TOEFL requirement: Yes
Minimum TOEFL score: 550
Fellowships: 10
Teaching assistantships: 11
Research assistantships: 35

Students reporting specialty:
environmental: 100%

University of North Carolina-Charlotte (Lee)
Duke Centennial Hall
9201 University City Boulevard
Charlotte, NC 28223-0001
graduateschool.uncc.edu
Public
Admissions: (704) 687-5503
Email: gradadm@uncc.edu
Financial aid: (704) 687-5504
Application deadline: rolling
In-state tuition: full time: $9,078; part time: $8,015
Out-of-state tuition: full time: $22,249
Room/board/expenses: $13,170
Full-time enrollment: 445
men: 79%; women: 21%;
minorities: 3%; international: 80%
Part-time enrollment: 185
men: 80%; women: 20%;
minorities: 17%; international: 33%
Acceptance rate: 57%
GRE requirement: Yes
Avg. GRE: quantitative: 152
TOEFL requirement: Yes
Minimum TOEFL score: 557
Fellowships: 5
Teaching assistantships: 105
Research assistantships: 129
Students reporting specialty:
civil: 6%; electrical: 37%; management: 12%; environmental: 9%; mechanical: 26%; other: 10%

NORTH DAKOTA

North Dakota State University
NDSU Dept. 2450
PO Box 6050
Fargo, ND 58108-6050
www.ndsu.nodak.edu/ndsu/cea/
Public
Admissions: (701) 231-7033
Email: ndsu.grad.school@ndsu.edu
Financial aid: (701) 231-7533
Application deadline: rolling
In-state tuition: full time: $338/credit hour; part time: $338/credit hour
Out-of-state tuition: full time: $904/credit hour
Room/board/expenses: $10,898
Full-time enrollment: 57
men: 79%; women: 21%;
minorities: 68%; international: 0%
Part-time enrollment: 106
men: 82%; women: 18%;
minorities: 59%; international: 0%
Acceptance rate: 29%
GRE requirement: Yes
Avg. GRE: quantitative: 151
TOEFL requirement: Yes
Minimum TOEFL score: 525
Fellowships: 5
Teaching assistantships: 62
Research assistantships: 76
Students reporting specialty:
agriculture: 10%; civil: 23%; electrical: 36%; environmental: 2%; industrial: 13%; mechanical: 16%

University of North Dakota
243 Centennial Drive, Stop 8155
Grand Forks, ND 58202-8155
und.edu/
Public
Admissions: (701) 777-2945
Email: questions@gradschool.und.edu

Financial aid: (701) 777-3121
Application deadline: rolling
In-state tuition: full time: N/A; part time: N/A
Out-of-state tuition: full time: N/A
Room/board/expenses: N/A
Full-time enrollment: 165
men: 78%; women: 22%;
minorities: 26%; international: 0%
Part-time enrollment: N/A
men: N/A; women: N/A;
minorities: N/A; international: N/A
GRE requirement: Yes
Avg. GRE: quantitative: 150
TOEFL requirement: Yes
Minimum TOEFL score: 525
Fellowships: 2
Teaching assistantships: 8
Research assistantships: 9
Students reporting specialty:
chemical: 13%; civil: 15%;
electrical: 23%; management:
8%; mechanical: 15%; petroleum:
10%; other: 16%

OHIO

Air Force Institute of Technology[1]
AFIT/RRA
2950 P Street
Wright Patterson AFB, OH 45433
www.afit.edu
Public
Admissions: (800) 211-5097
Email: counselors@afit.edu
Financial aid: N/A
Tuition: N/A
Room/board/expenses: N/A
Enrollment: N/A

Case Western Reserve University
500 Nord Hall
10900 Euclid Avenue
Cleveland, OH 44106-7220
gradstudies.case.edu
Private
Admissions: (216) 368-4390
Email: gradstudies@case.edu
Financial aid: (216) 368-4530
Application deadline: rolling
Tuition: full time: $42,610; part time: $1,774/credit hour
Room/board/expenses: $17,524
Full-time enrollment: 632
men: 73%; women: 27%;
minorities: 10%; international: 64%
Part-time enrollment: 70
men: 70%; women: 30%;
minorities: 13%; international: 40%
Acceptance rate: 34%
GRE requirement: Yes
Avg. GRE: quantitative: 164
TOEFL requirement: Yes
Minimum TOEFL score: 577
Fellowships: 35
Teaching assistantships: 32
Research assistantships: 258
Students reporting specialty:
aerospace: 2%; biomedical:
19%; chemical: 19%; civil:
3%; computer: 5%; computer
science: 7%; electrical: 17%;
management: 10%; materials:
6%; mechanical: 13%; other: 1%

Cleveland State University (Washkewicz)
2121 Euclid Avenue, FH 104
Cleveland, OH 44115-2425
www.csuohio.edu/engineering/
Public
Admissions: (216) 687-5599
Email: allin1@csuohio.edu
Financial aid: (216) 687-5594
Application deadline: 07/01

In-state tuition: full time: $531/credit hour; part time: $531/credit hour
Out-of-state tuition: full time: $999/credit hour
Room/board/expenses: $16,270
Full-time enrollment: 391
men: 81%; women: 19%;
minorities: 4%; international: 83%
Part-time enrollment: 265
men: 80%; women: 20%;
minorities: 10%; international: 47%
Acceptance rate: 40%
GRE requirement: Yes
Avg. GRE: quantitative: 158
TOEFL requirement: Yes
Minimum TOEFL score: 550
Fellowships: 0
Teaching assistantships: 62
Research assistantships: 57
Students reporting specialty:
biomedical: 7%; chemical:
7%; civil: 10%; computer
science: 11%; electrical: 43%;
environmental: 3%; mechanical:
15%; other: 4%

Ohio State University
2070 Neil Avenue
Columbus, OH 43210-1278
engineering.osu.edu/graduate/admissions
Public
Admissions: (614) 292-9444
Email: gpadmissions@osu.edu
Financial aid: (614) 292-0300
Application deadline: rolling
In-state tuition: full time: $12,935; part time: $746/credit hour
Out-of-state tuition: full time: $33,383
Room/board/expenses: $15,654
Full-time enrollment: 1,709
men: 77%; women: 23%;
minorities: 6%; international: 65%
Part-time enrollment: 140
men: 81%; women: 19%;
minorities: 14%; international: 21%
Acceptance rate: 17%
GRE requirement: Yes
Avg. GRE: quantitative: 164
TOEFL requirement: Yes
Minimum TOEFL score: 550
Fellowships: 115
Teaching assistantships: 258
Research assistantships: 764
Students reporting specialty:
aerospace: 3%; agriculture:
3%; biomedical: 4%; chemical:
6%; civil: 6%; computer: 16%;
electrical: 25%; management:
1%; environmental: 1%; industrial:
8%; materials: 10%; mechanical:
16%; nuclear: 2%

Ohio University (Russ)
150 Stocker Center
Athens, OH 45701
www.ohio.edu/engineering
Public
Admissions: (740) 593-2800
Email: graduate@ohio.edu
Financial aid: (740) 593-4141
Application deadline: rolling
In-state tuition: full time: $9,810; part time: $505/credit hour
Out-of-state tuition: full time: $17,802
Room/board/expenses: $12,438
Full-time enrollment: 286
men: 76%; women: 24%;
minorities: 6%; international: 63%
Part-time enrollment: 318
men: 86%; women: 14%;
minorities: 22%; international: 7%
Acceptance rate: 39%
GRE requirement: Yes
Avg. GRE: quantitative: 161
TOEFL requirement: Yes
Minimum TOEFL score: 500

Fellowships: 8
Teaching assistantships: 139
Research assistantships: 152
Students reporting specialty:
biomedical: 2%; chemical: 9%;
civil: 23%; computer science: 5%;
electrical: 22%; management:
23%; industrial: 8%; mechanical:
8%

University of Akron
201 ASEC
Akron, OH 44325-3901
www.uakron.edu/gradsch/
Public
Admissions: (330) 972-7663
Email: gradsch@uakron.edu
Financial aid: (330) 972-7663
Application deadline: rolling
In-state tuition: full time: $442/credit hour; part time: $442/credit hour
Out-of-state tuition: full time: $748/credit hour
Room/board/expenses: $15,313
Full-time enrollment: 359
men: 75%; women: 25%;
minorities: 3%; international: 84%
Part-time enrollment: 74
men: 81%; women: 19%;
minorities: 7%; international: 28%
Acceptance rate: 70%
GRE requirement: Yes
Avg. GRE: quantitative: 160
TOEFL requirement: Yes
Minimum TOEFL score: 550
Fellowships: 2
Teaching assistantships: 119
Research assistantships: 182
Students reporting specialty:
biomedical: 8%; chemical:
19%; civil: 21%; computer: 1%;
electrical: 19%; management: 3%;
mechanical: 28%; other: 2%

University of Cincinnati
PO Box 210077
Cincinnati, OH 45221-0077
www.ceas.uc.edu
Public
Admissions: (513) 556-6347
Email: engrgrad@uc.edu
Financial aid: (513) 556-3647
Application deadline: 03/31
In-state tuition: full time: $17,756; part time: $640/credit hour
Out-of-state tuition: full time: $29,498
Room/board/expenses: $17,625
Full-time enrollment: 757
men: 76%; women: 24%;
minorities: 4%; international: 71%
Part-time enrollment: 25
men: 100%; women: 0%;
minorities: 8%; international: 0%
Acceptance rate: 19%
GRE requirement: Yes
Avg. GRE: quantitative: 161
TOEFL requirement: Yes
Minimum TOEFL score: 580
Fellowships: 35
Teaching assistantships: 150
Research assistantships: 373
Students reporting specialty:
aerospace: 17%; biomedical:
3%; chemical: 4%; civil: 6%;
computer: 7%; computer
science: 10%; electrical: 10%;
environmental: 7%; materials:
10%; mechanical: 24%

University of Dayton
300 College Park
Dayton, OH 45469-0254
www.udayton.edu/apply
Private
Admissions: (937) 229-4411
Email: gradadmission@udayton.edu
Financial aid: (937) 229-4411

Application deadline: rolling
Tuition: full time: $970/credit hour; part time: $970/credit hour
Room/board/expenses: $15,506
Full-time enrollment: 491
men: 80%; women: 20%;
minorities: 8%; international: 58%
Part-time enrollment: 118
men: 79%; women: 21%;
minorities: 9%; international: 21%
Acceptance rate: 17%
GRE requirement: Yes
Avg. GRE: quantitative: 157
TOEFL requirement: Yes
Minimum TOEFL score: 550
Fellowships: 0
Teaching assistantships: 40
Research assistantships: 74
Students reporting specialty:
aerospace: 6%; biomedical:
0%; chemical: 5%; civil: 7%;
computer: 2%; electrical: 24%;
management: 10%; materials:
10%; mechanical: 17%; other: 18%

University of Toledo
2801 W. Bancroft
Toledo, OH 43606
www.eng.utoledo.edu/coe/grad_studies/
Public
Admissions: (419) 530-4723
Email: gradoff@eng.utoledo.edu
Financial aid: (419) 530-5812
Application deadline: rolling
In-state tuition: full time: $9,874; part time: $549/credit hour
Out-of-state tuition: full time: $17,627
Room/board/expenses: $15,600
Full-time enrollment: 256
men: 81%; women: 19%;
minorities: 2%; international: 88%
Part-time enrollment: 125
men: 82%; women: 18%;
minorities: 5%; international: 54%
Acceptance rate: 41%
GRE requirement: Yes
Avg. GRE: quantitative: 159
TOEFL requirement: Yes
Minimum TOEFL score: 550
Fellowships: 1
Teaching assistantships: 119
Research assistantships: 78
Students reporting specialty:
biomedical: 9%; chemical: 9%;
civil: 15%; computer science:
14%; electrical: 21%; industrial:
3%; mechanical: 23%; other: 7%

Wright State University
3640 Colonel Glenn Highway
Dayton, OH 45435
wright.edu/graduate-school
Public
Admissions: (937) 775-3734
Email: wsugrad@wright.edu
Financial aid: (937) 775-5405
Application deadline: rolling
In-state tuition: full time: $13,476; part time: $622/credit hour
Out-of-state tuition: full time: $22,892
Room/board/expenses: $14,800
Full-time enrollment: 815
men: 72%; women: 28%;
minorities: 4%; international: 73%
Part-time enrollment: 219
men: 77%; women: 23%;
minorities: 9%; international: 52%
Acceptance rate: 46%
GRE requirement: Yes
Avg. GRE: quantitative: 156
TOEFL requirement: Yes
Minimum TOEFL score: N/A
Fellowships: 0
Teaching assistantships: 29
Research assistantships: 151
Students reporting specialty:
aerospace: 1%; biomedical:
4%; computer: 5%; computer

science: 30%; electrical: 30%;
industrial: 8%; materials: 1%;
mechanical: 11%; other: 11%

OKLAHOMA

Oklahoma State University
201 ATRC
Stillwater, OK 74078-0535
gradcollege.okstate.edu
Public
Admissions: (405) 744-6368
Email: grad-i@okstate.edu
Financial aid: (405) 744-6604
Application deadline: 02/01
In-state tuition: full time: $209/credit hour; part time: $209/credit hour
Out-of-state tuition: full time: $825/credit hour
Room/board/expenses: $14,530
Full-time enrollment: 407
men: 79%; women: 21%;
minorities: 4%; international: 83%
Part-time enrollment: 211
men: 82%; women: 18%;
minorities: 17%; international: 0%
Acceptance rate: 36%
GRE requirement: Yes
Avg. GRE: quantitative: 160
TOEFL requirement: Yes
Minimum TOEFL score: 500
Fellowships: 29
Teaching assistantships: 111
Research assistantships: 162
Students reporting specialty:
aerospace: 17%; agriculture:
5%; chemical: 6%; civil: 12%;
computer: 16%; computer
science: 13%; electrical:
16%; management: 18%;
environmental: 1%; industrial:
21%; materials: 3%; mechanical:
17%; petroleum: 1%

University of Oklahoma
202 W. Boyd, CEC 107
Norman, OK 73019
www.ou.edu/admissions
Public
Admissions: (405) 325-6765
Email: gradadm@ou.edu
Financial aid: (405) 325-4521
Application deadline: rolling
In-state tuition: full time: $204/credit hour; part time: $204/credit hour
Out-of-state tuition: full time: $791/credit hour
Room/board/expenses: $18,201
Full-time enrollment: 443
men: 75%; women: 25%;
minorities: 8%; international: 68%
Part-time enrollment: 267
men: 76%; women: 24%;
minorities: 18%; international: 47%
Acceptance rate: 33%
GRE requirement: Yes
Avg. GRE: quantitative: 161
TOEFL requirement: Yes
Minimum TOEFL score: N/A
Fellowships: 27
Teaching assistantships: 133
Research assistantships: 248
Students reporting specialty:
aerospace: 2%; biomedical: 3%;
chemical: 5%; civil: 7%; computer
science: 12%; electrical: 23%;
science and physics: 1%;
environmental: 3%; industrial:
10%; mechanical: 5%; petroleum:
18%; other: 16%

University of Tulsa

800 S. Tucker Drive
Tulsa, OK 74104-3189
utulsa.edu
Private
Admissions: (918) 631-2336
Email: grad@utulsa.edu
Financial aid: (918) 631-2526
Application deadline: rolling
Tuition: full time: $1,235/credit
hour; part time: $1,235/credit
hour
Room/board/expenses: $15,628
Full-time enrollment: 230
men: 82%; women: 18%;
minorities: 3%; international: 64%
Part-time enrollment: 14
men: 93%; women: 7%;
minorities: 7%; international: 0%
Acceptance rate: 26%
GRE requirement: Yes
Avg. GRE: quantitative: 163
TOEFL requirement: Yes
Minimum TOEFL score: 550
Fellowships: 10
Teaching assistantships: 43
Research assistantships: 95
Students reporting specialty:
chemical: 10%; computer:
7%; computer science: 23%;
electrical: 4%; mechanical: 21%;
petroleum: 35%

OREGON

Oregon Health and Science University[1]

3181 S.W. Sam Jackson
Park Road, MC: L102GS
Portland, OR 97239
www.ohsu.edu/som/graduate
Public
Admissions: (503) 494-6222
Email: somgrad@ohsu.edu
Financial aid: N/A
Tuition: N/A
Room/board/expenses: N/A
Enrollment: N/A

Oregon State University

101 Covell Hall
Corvallis, OR 97331-2409
engineering.oregonstate.edu/
Public
Admissions: (541) 737-4881
Email: graduate.school@
oregonstate.edu
Financial aid: (541) 737-2241
Application deadline: 01/15
In-state tuition: full time: $15,781;
part time: $505/credit hour
Out-of-state tuition: full time:
$25,420
Room/board/expenses: $16,254
Full-time enrollment: 1,061
men: 77%; women: 23%;
minorities: 9%; international: 59%
Part-time enrollment: 187
men: 72%; women: 28%;
minorities: 12%; international:
36%
Acceptance rate: 22%
GRE requirement: Yes
Avg. GRE: quantitative: 160
TOEFL requirement: Yes
Minimum TOEFL score: 600
Fellowships: 31
Teaching assistantships: 272
Research assistantships: 396
Students reporting specialty:
agriculture: 1%; biomedical:
0%; chemical: 7%; civil: 13%;
computer science: 19%;
electrical: 19%; environmental:
3%; industrial: 8%; materials: 3%;
mechanical: 13%; nuclear: 5%;
other: 9%

Portland State University (Maseeh)

PO Box 751
Portland, OR 97207
www.pdx.edu/cecs
Public
Admissions: (503) 725-5525
Email: askadm@pdx.edu
Financial aid: (503) 725-3461
Application deadline: rolling
In-state tuition: full time: $12,630;
part time: $419/credit hour
Out-of-state tuition: full time:
$18,219
Room/board/expenses: $16,542
Full-time enrollment: 410
men: 72%; women: 28%;
minorities: 6%; international: 74%
Part-time enrollment: 372
men: 72%; women: 28%;
minorities: 21%; international:
28%
Acceptance rate: 41%
GRE requirement: Yes
Avg. GRE: quantitative: N/A
TOEFL requirement: Yes
Minimum TOEFL score: 550
Teaching assistantships: 60
Research assistantships: 54
Students reporting specialty: civil:
13%; computer science: 20%;
electrical: 41%; management:
16%; mechanical: 10%

PENNSYLVANIA

Carnegie Mellon University

5000 Forbes Avenue
Pittsburgh, PA 15213
www.cit.cmu.edu/
Private
Admissions: (412) 268-2478
Financial aid: (412) 268-2482
Application deadline: 01/31
Tuition: full time: $43,790; part
time: $1,791/credit hour
Room/board/expenses: $27,795
Full-time enrollment: 3,537
men: 70%; women: 30%;
minorities: 9%; international: 76%
Part-time enrollment: 200
men: 70%; women: 30%;
minorities: 16%; international:
53%
Acceptance rate: 20%
GRE requirement: Yes
Avg. GRE: quantitative: 166
TOEFL requirement: Yes
Minimum TOEFL score: N/A
Fellowships: 437
Teaching assistantships: 136
Research assistantships: 1,112
Students reporting specialty:
biomedical: 3%; chemical: 5%;
civil: 6%; computer science: 37%;
electrical: 20%; materials: 3%;
mechanical: 0%; other: 18%

Drexel University

3141 Chestnut Street
Philadelphia, PA 19104
www.drexel.edu/engineering
Private
Admissions: (215) 895-6700
Email: enroll@drexel.edu
Financial aid: (215) 895-1600
Application deadline: 09/01
Tuition: full time: $1,192/credit
hour; part time: $1,192/credit
hour
Room/board/expenses: N/A
Full-time enrollment: 796
men: 70%; women: 30%;
minorities: 14%; international:
48%
Part-time enrollment: 398
men: 80%; women: 20%;
minorities: 24%; international: 4%
Acceptance rate: 54%
GRE requirement: Yes

Avg. GRE: quantitative: 160
TOEFL requirement: Yes
Minimum TOEFL score: N/A
Fellowships: 179
Teaching assistantships: 90
Research assistantships: 140
Students reporting specialty:
architectural: 2%; biomedical:
18%; chemical: 6%; civil: 5%;
computer: 7%; computer
science: 9%; electrical: 17%;
environmental: 4%; materials:
7%; mechanical: 15%; other: 17%

Lehigh University (Rossin)

19 Memorial Drive W
Bethlehem, PA 18015
www.lehigh.edu/engineering
Private
Admissions: (610) 758-6310
Email: graduate.engineering@
lehigh.edu
Financial aid: (610) 758-3181
Application deadline: 01/15
Tuition: full time: $1,420/credit
hour; part time: $1,420/credit
hour
Room/board/expenses: $12,675
Full-time enrollment: 697
men: 72%; women: 28%;
minorities: 6%; international: 74%
Part-time enrollment: 132
men: 73%; women: 27%;
minorities: 20%; international: 8%
Acceptance rate: 32%
GRE requirement: Yes
Avg. GRE: quantitative: 165
TOEFL requirement: Yes
Minimum TOEFL score: N/A
Fellowships: 26
Teaching assistantships: 68
Research assistantships: 185
Students reporting specialty:
biomedical: 2%; chemical:
10%; civil: 8%; computer:
1%; computer science: 4%;
electrical: 11%; management: 1%;
environmental: 2%; industrial:
24%; materials: 7%; mechanical:
23%; other: 6%

Pennsylvania State University-University Park

101 Hammond Building
University Park, PA 16802
www.gradschool.psu.edu
Public
Admissions: (814) 865-1795
Email: gswww@psu.edu
Financial aid: (814) 865-6301
Application deadline: rolling
In-state tuition: full time: $22,242;
part time: $887/credit hour
Out-of-state tuition: full time:
$36,598
Room/board/expenses: $14,330
Full-time enrollment: 1,609
men: 76%; women: 24%;
minorities: 6%; international: 68%
Part-time enrollment: 420
men: 81%; women: 19%;
minorities: 10%; international:
28%
Acceptance rate: 21%
GRE requirement: Yes
Avg. GRE: quantitative: 163
TOEFL requirement: Yes
Minimum TOEFL score: 550
Fellowships: 64
Teaching assistantships: 348
Research assistantships: 692
Students reporting specialty:
aerospace: 6%; agriculture: 1%;
architectural: 6%; biomedical:
4%; chemical: 6%; civil: 5%;
computer: 9%; electrical: 11%;
science and physics: 4%;

environmental: 2%; industrial:
11%; materials: 7%; mechanical:
13%; nuclear: 4%; other: 10%

Philadelphia University[1]

4201 Henry Avenue
Philadelphia, PA 19144
www.philau.edu
Private
Admissions: (215) 951-2943
Email: gradadm@philau.edu
Financial aid: N/A
Tuition: N/A
Room/board/expenses: N/A
Enrollment: N/A

Temple University

1947 N. 12th Street
Philadelphia, PA 19122
engineering.temple.edu/
Public
Admissions: (215) 204-7800
Email: gradengr@temple.edu
Financial aid: (215) 204-2244
Application deadline: 03/01
In-state tuition: full time: $995/
credit hour; part time: $995/
credit hour
Out-of-state tuition: full time:
$1,319/credit hour
Room/board/expenses: $20,586
Full-time enrollment: 221
men: 71%; women: 29%;
minorities: 9%; international: 71%
Part-time enrollment: 84
men: 85%; women: 15%;
minorities: 29%; international:
11%
Acceptance rate: 52%
GRE requirement: Yes
Avg. GRE: quantitative: 159
TOEFL requirement: Yes
Minimum TOEFL score: 550
Fellowships: 13
Teaching assistantships: 66
Research assistantships: 49
Students reporting specialty:
biomedical: 13%; civil: 7%;
computer science: 35%;
electrical: 18%; management: 9%;
environmental: 7%; mechanical:
10%; other: 1%

University of Pennsylvania

107 Towne Building
Philadelphia, PA 19104
www.seas.upenn.edu/grad
Private
Admissions: (215) 898-4542
Email:
gradstudies@seas.upenn.edu
Financial aid: (215) 898-1988
Application deadline: 12/15
Tuition: full time: $32,286; part
time: $6,044/credit hour
Room/board/expenses: $20,555
Full-time enrollment: 1,674
men: 69%; women: 31%;
minorities: 17%; international:
56%
Part-time enrollment: N/A
men: N/A; women: N/A;
minorities: N/A; international: N/A
Acceptance rate: 23%
GRE requirement: Yes
Avg. GRE: quantitative: 165
TOEFL requirement: Yes
Minimum TOEFL score: N/A
Fellowships: 145
Research assistantships: 371
Students reporting specialty:
biomedical: 17%; chemical:
7%; computer: 3%; computer
science: 26%; electrical: 11%;
industrial: 8%; materials: 7%;
mechanical: 12%; other: 10%

University of Pittsburgh (Swanson)

109 Benedum Hall
Pittsburgh, PA 15261
www.engineering.pitt.edu
Public
Admissions: (412) 624-9800
Email: ssoeadm@pitt.edu
Financial aid: (412) 624-7488
Application deadline: 03/01
In-state tuition: full time: $25,792;
part time: $1,184/credit hour
Out-of-state tuition: full time:
$42,052
Room/board/expenses: $21,651
Full-time enrollment: 799
men: 73%; women: 27%;
minorities: 10%; international:
66%
Part-time enrollment: 230
men: 78%; women: 22%;
minorities: 13%; international:
13%
Acceptance rate: 37%
GRE requirement: Yes
Avg. GRE: quantitative: 162
TOEFL requirement: Yes
Minimum TOEFL score: 550
Fellowships: 87
Teaching assistantships: 166
Research assistantships: 258
Students reporting specialty:
biomedical: 19%; chemical:
10%; civil: 14%; computer: 0%;
computer science: 8%; electrical:
17%; industrial: 8%; materials:
5%; mechanical: 16%; nuclear:
0%; petroleum: 2%; other: 1%

Villanova University[1]

800 E. Lancaster Avenue
Villanova, PA 19085
www.villanova.edu
Private
Admissions: N/A
Email: engineering.grad@
villanova.edu
Financial aid: N/A
Tuition: N/A
Room/board/expenses: N/A
Enrollment: N/A

RHODE ISLAND

Brown University

Box D
Providence, RI 02912
www.brown.edu/academics/
gradschool
Private
Admissions: (401) 863-2600
Email: Admission_Graduate@
brown.edu
Financial aid: (401) 863-2721
Application deadline: rolling
Tuition: full time: $51,366; part
time: $13,698
Room/board/expenses: $17,550
Full-time enrollment: 415
men: 72%; women: 28%;
minorities: 9%; international: 62%
Part-time enrollment: 12
men: 58%; women: 42%;
minorities: 17%; international: 8%
Acceptance rate: 25%
GRE requirement: Yes
Avg. GRE: quantitative: 165
TOEFL requirement: Yes
Minimum TOEFL score: N/A
Fellowships: 64
Teaching assistantships: 32
Research assistantships: 124
Students reporting specialty:
biomedical: 16%; chemical:
3%; computer: 11%; computer
science: 39%; electrical: 3%;
management: 7%; materials: 7%;
mechanical: 13%

DIRECTORY

University of Rhode Island
102 Bliss Hall
Kingston, RI 02881
www.uri.edu/gsadmis/
Public
Admissions: (401) 874-2872
Email: urigrad@etal.uri.edu
Financial aid: (401) 874-2314
Application deadline: N/A
In-state tuition: full time: $13,362; part time: $655/credit hour
Out-of-state tuition: full time: $25,772
Room/board/expenses: $18,050
Full-time enrollment: 125
men: 77%; women: 23%; minorities: 6%; international: 58%
Part-time enrollment: 76
men: 83%; women: 17%; minorities: 18%; international: 8%
Acceptance rate: 63%
Avg. GRE: quantitative: N/A
TOEFL requirement: Yes
Minimum TOEFL score: 550
Fellowships: 0
Teaching assistantships: 28
Research assistantships: 43
Students reporting specialty: chemical: 14%; civil: 16%; electrical: 22%; industrial: 8%; mechanical: 20%; other: 20%

SOUTH CAROLINA

Clemson University
Room 109, Riggs Hall
Clemson, SC 29634-0901
www.grad.clemson.edu/
Public
Admissions: (864) 656-4172
Email: grdapp@clemson.edu
Financial aid: (864) 656-2280
Application deadline: rolling
In-state tuition: full time: $11,434; part time: $697/credit hour
Out-of-state tuition: full time: $22,588
Room/board/expenses: $15,754
Full-time enrollment: 1,165
men: 72%; women: 28%; minorities: 5%; international: 65%
Part-time enrollment: 250
men: 79%; women: 21%; minorities: 12%; international: 37%
Acceptance rate: 32%
GRE requirement: Yes
Avg. GRE: quantitative: 158
TOEFL requirement: Yes
Minimum TOEFL score: N/A
Fellowships: 83
Teaching assistantships: 300
Research assistantships: 510
Students reporting specialty: biomedical: 7%; chemical: 3%; civil: 9%; computer: 4%; computer science: 18%; electrical: 10%; environmental: 7%; industrial: 11%; materials: 4%; mechanical: 12%; other: 14%

University of South Carolina
Swearingen Engineering Center
Columbia, SC 29208
www.cec.sc.edu
Public
Admissions: (803) 777-4243
Email: gradapp@mailbox.sc.edu
Financial aid: (803) 777-8134
Application deadline: 12/01
In-state tuition: full time: $13,950; part time: $533/credit hour
Out-of-state tuition: full time: $28,560
Room/board/expenses: $10,759
Full-time enrollment: 465
men: 77%; women: 23%; minorities: 10%; international: 64%

Part-time enrollment: 122
men: 82%; women: 18%; minorities: 14%; international: 18%
Acceptance rate: 47%
GRE requirement: Yes
Avg. GRE: quantitative: 156
TOEFL requirement: Yes
Minimum TOEFL score: 570
Fellowships: 41
Teaching assistantships: 112
Research assistantships: 198
Students reporting specialty: aerospace: 3%; biomedical: 4%; chemical: 11%; civil: 12%; computer science: 29%; electrical: 13%; management: 5%; mechanical: 17%; nuclear: 4%

SOUTH DAKOTA

South Dakota School of Mines and Technology
501 E. St. Joseph Street
Rapid City, SD 57701-3995
www.sdsmt.edu/
Public
Admissions: (605) 394-2341
Email: graduate.admissions@sdsmt.edu
Financial aid: (605) 394-2400
Application deadline: rolling
In-state tuition: full time: $318/credit hour; part time: $318/credit hour
Out-of-state tuition: full time: $639/credit hour
Room/board/expenses: $12,920
Full-time enrollment: 171
men: 70%; women: 30%; minorities: 11%; international: 40%
Part-time enrollment: 142
men: 74%; women: 26%; minorities: 18%; international: 17%
Acceptance rate: 46%
GRE requirement: Yes
Avg. GRE: quantitative: 158
TOEFL requirement: Yes
Minimum TOEFL score: 520
Fellowships: 26
Teaching assistantships: 44
Research assistantships: 123
Students reporting specialty: biomedical: 5%; chemical: 11%; civil: 11%; computer science: 4%; electrical: 3%; management: 15%; industrial: 8%; materials: 8%; mechanical: 6%; mining: 13%; other: 17%

South Dakota State University
CEH 201, Box 2219
Brookings, SD 57007-0096
www.sdstate.edu/
Public
Admissions: (605) 688-4181
Email: gradschl@adm.sdstate.edu
Financial aid: (605) 688-4695
Application deadline: 04/15
In-state tuition: full time: $313/credit hour; part time: $313/credit hour
Out-of-state tuition: full time: $692/credit hour
Room/board/expenses: $8,884
Full-time enrollment: 313
men: 73%; women: 27%; minorities: 2%; international: 76%
Part-time enrollment: N/A
men: N/A; women: N/A; minorities: N/A; international: N/A
Acceptance rate: 50%
GRE requirement: No
Avg. GRE: quantitative: N/A
TOEFL requirement: Yes
Minimum TOEFL score: 527
Fellowships: 3

Teaching assistantships: 89
Research assistantships: 77
Students reporting specialty: agriculture: 9%; civil: 17%; computer science: 16%; electrical: 18%; management: 4%; mechanical: 11%; other: 29%

University of South Dakota
414 E Clark Street
Vermillion, SD 57069
www.usd.edu/
Public
Admissions: (605) 658-6140
Email: grad@usd.edu
Financial aid: (605) 658-6250
Application deadline: rolling
In-state tuition: full time: $313/credit hour; part time: $313/credit hour
Out-of-state tuition: full time: $602/credit hour
Room/board/expenses: $9,000
Full-time enrollment: 14
men: 86%; women: 14%; minorities: 0%; international: 21%
Part-time enrollment: N/A
men: N/A; women: N/A; minorities: N/A; international: N/A
Acceptance rate: 25%
GRE requirement: Yes
Avg. GRE: quantitative: 159
TOEFL requirement: Yes
Minimum TOEFL score: N/A
Fellowships: 0
Teaching assistantships: 0
Research assistantships: 13
Students reporting specialty: biomedical: 100%

TENNESSEE

Tennessee State University
3500 John Merritt Boulevard
Nashville, TN 37209-1651
www.tnstate.edu/
Public
Admissions: (615) 963-5107
Email: gradschool@tnstate.edu
Financial aid: (615) 963-7548
Application deadline: 06/01
In-state tuition: full time: $461/credit hour; part time: $461/credit hour
Out-of-state tuition: full time: $1,043/credit hour
Room/board/expenses: $12,129
Full-time enrollment: 40
men: 75%; women: 25%; minorities: 23%; international: 70%
Part-time enrollment: 24
men: 58%; women: 42%; minorities: 13%; international: 54%
Avg. GRE: quantitative: N/A
TOEFL requirement: Yes
Minimum TOEFL score: 525
Students reporting specialty: N/A

Tennessee Technological University
N. Dixie Avenue
Cookeville, TN 38505
www.tntech.edu/engineering
Public
Admissions: (931) 372-3233
Email: gradstudies@tntech.edu
Financial aid: (931) 372-3073
Application deadline: 07/01
In-state tuition: full time: $10,371; part time: $534/credit hour
Out-of-state tuition: full time: $23,871
Room/board/expenses: $16,000

Full-time enrollment: 124
men: 77%; women: 23%; minorities: 4%; international: 62%
Part-time enrollment: 86
men: 79%; women: 21%; minorities: 8%; international: 40%
Acceptance rate: 34%
GRE requirement: Yes
Avg. GRE: quantitative: 157
TOEFL requirement: Yes
Minimum TOEFL score: 550
Fellowships: 3
Teaching assistantships: 61
Research assistantships: 65
Students reporting specialty: chemical: 14%; civil: 12%; computer science: 15%; electrical: 28%; mechanical: 31%

University of Memphis (Herff)
201 Engineering Administration Building
Memphis, TN 38152
memphis.edu/herff/index.php
Public
Admissions: (901) 678-2111
Email: recruitment@memphis.edu
Financial aid: (901) 678-3687
Application deadline: 07/01
In-state tuition: full time: $10,463; part time: $597/credit hour
Out-of-state tuition: full time: $19,247
Room/board/expenses: $15,656
Full-time enrollment: 161
men: 70%; women: 30%; minorities: 12%; international: 76%
Part-time enrollment: 110
men: 78%; women: 22%; minorities: 20%; international: 45%
Acceptance rate: 53%
GRE requirement: Yes
Avg. GRE: quantitative: 159
TOEFL requirement: Yes
Minimum TOEFL score: 550
Fellowships: 19
Teaching assistantships: 27
Research assistantships: 67
Students reporting specialty: biomedical: 10%; civil: 10%; computer: 6%; computer science: 32%; electrical: 6%; mechanical: 3%; other: 34%

University of Tennessee-Chattanooga
615 McCallie Avenue
Chattanooga, TN 37403
www.utc.edu/college-engineering-computer-science/
Public
Admissions: (423) 425-4666
Email: Ethan-Carver@utc.edu
Financial aid: (423) 425-4677
Application deadline: 07/31
In-state tuition: full time: $8,100; part time: $450/credit hour
Out-of-state tuition: full time: $25,994
Room/board/expenses: $17,400
Full-time enrollment: 60
men: 73%; women: 27%; minorities: 22%; international: 57%
Part-time enrollment: 117
men: 74%; women: 26%; minorities: 28%; international: 9%
Acceptance rate: 88%
GRE requirement: Yes
Avg. GRE: quantitative: 155
TOEFL requirement: Yes
Minimum TOEFL score: 550
Teaching assistantships: 20
Research assistantships: 45
Students reporting specialty: chemical: 4%; civil: 2%; computer science: 28%; electrical: 14%;

management: 34%; industrial: 13%; mechanical: 5%

University of Tennessee-Knoxville
124 Perkins Hall
Knoxville, TN 37996-2000
graduateadmissions.utk.edu/
Public
Admissions: (865) 974-3251
Email: graduateadmissions@utk.edu
Financial aid: (865) 974-3131
Application deadline: 02/01
In-state tuition: full time: $12,834; part time: $615/credit hour
Out-of-state tuition: full time: $31,252
Room/board/expenses: $20,840
Full-time enrollment: 869
men: 77%; women: 23%; minorities: 8%; international: 46%
Part-time enrollment: 249
men: 82%; women: 18%; minorities: 12%; international: 10%
Acceptance rate: 35%
GRE requirement: Yes
Avg. GRE: quantitative: 160
TOEFL requirement: Yes
Minimum TOEFL score: 550
Fellowships: 76
Teaching assistantships: 215
Research assistantships: 550
Students reporting specialty: aerospace: 3%; agriculture: 1%; biomedical: 3%; chemical: 5%; civil: 13%; computer: 3%; computer science: 7%; electrical: 14%; science and physics: 1%; environmental: 2%; industrial: 14%; materials: 8%; mechanical: 9%; nuclear: 11%; other: 6%

Vanderbilt University
VU Station B 351826
2301 Vanderbilt Place
Nashville, TN 37235
engineering.vanderbilt.edu
Private
Admissions: (615) 322-0236
Email: apply@vanderbilt.edu
Financial aid: (615) 322-3591
Application deadline: 12/15
Tuition: full time: $1,854/credit hour; part time: $1,854/credit hour
Room/board/expenses: $24,098
Full-time enrollment: 497
men: 70%; women: 30%; minorities: 10%; international: 43%
Part-time enrollment: 17
men: 59%; women: 41%; minorities: 6%; international: 29%
Acceptance rate: 15%
GRE requirement: Yes
Avg. GRE: quantitative: 163
TOEFL requirement: Yes
Minimum TOEFL score: 570
Fellowships: 50
Teaching assistantships: 111
Research assistantships: 217
Students reporting specialty: biomedical: 16%; chemical: 10%; civil: 10%; computer science: 20%; electrical: 20%; environmental: 9%; materials: 5%; mechanical: 13%

TEXAS

Baylor University
One Bear Place, #97356
Waco, TX 76798
www.ecs.baylor.edu/
Private
Admissions: (254) 710-4060
Email: Graduate_Admissions@baylor.edu
Financial aid: (254) 710-2611

Application deadline: 02/15
Tuition: full time: $31,170; part time: $1,583/credit hour
Room/board/expenses: $10,226
Full-time enrollment: 100
men: 84%; women: 16%; minorities: 13%; international: 39%
Part-time enrollment: N/A
men: N/A; women: N/A; minorities: N/A; international: N/A
Acceptance rate: 50%
GRE requirement: Yes
Avg. GRE: quantitative: 162
TOEFL requirement: Yes
Minimum TOEFL score: 550
Teaching assistantships: 43
Research assistantships: 43
Students reporting specialty:
biomedical: 8%; computer science: 13%; electrical: 42%; mechanical: 31%; other: 6%

Lamar University

4400 Martin Luther King Boulevard
Beaumont, TX 77710
dept.lamar.edu/engineering/coe/
Public
Admissions: (409) 880-8888
Email: admissions@hal.lamar.edu
Financial aid: (409) 880-8450
Application deadline: rolling
In-state tuition: full time: $8,008; part time: $336/credit hour
Out-of-state tuition: full time: $15,352
Room/board/expenses: $13,598
Full-time enrollment: 331
men: 87%; women: 13%; minorities: 3%; international: 93%
Part-time enrollment: 183
men: 88%; women: 12%; minorities: 6%; international: 91%
Acceptance rate: 62%
GRE requirement: Yes
Avg. GRE: quantitative: 158
TOEFL requirement: Yes
Minimum TOEFL score: 550
Fellowships: 0
Teaching assistantships: 13
Research assistantships: 86
Students reporting specialty:
chemical: 18%; civil: 8%; electrical: 16%; environmental: 4%; industrial: 33%; mechanical: 22%

Prairie View A&M University

PO Box 519, MS 2500
Prairie View, TX 77446
www.pvamu.edu
Public
Admissions: (936) 261-3518
Email: graduateadmissions@pvamu.edu
Financial aid: (936) 261-1000
Application deadline: 06/01
In-state tuition: full time: $273/credit hour; part time: $273/credit hour
Out-of-state tuition: full time: $720/credit hour
Room/board/expenses: $14,140
Full-time enrollment: 171
men: 74%; women: 26%; minorities: 38%; international: 55%
Part-time enrollment: 50
men: 66%; women: 34%; minorities: 48%; international: 42%
Acceptance rate: 92%
GRE requirement: Yes
Avg. GRE: quantitative: 158
TOEFL requirement: Yes
Minimum TOEFL score: 500
Students reporting specialty:
computer science: 32%; electrical: 30%; mechanical: 38%

Rice University (Brown)

PO Box 1892, MS 364
Houston, TX 77251-1892
engr.rice.edu
Private
Admissions: (713) 348-4002
Email: graduate@rice.edu
Financial aid: (713) 348-4958
Application deadline: N/A
Tuition: full time: $43,765; part time: $2,402/credit hour
Room/board/expenses: N/A
Full-time enrollment: 896
men: 71%; women: 29%; minorities: 11%; international: 65%
Part-time enrollment: 53
men: 60%; women: 40%; minorities: 19%; international: 66%
Acceptance rate: 24%
GRE requirement: Yes
Avg. GRE: quantitative: 166
TOEFL requirement: Yes
Minimum TOEFL score: 600
Fellowships: 268
Teaching assistantships: 52
Research assistantships: 361
Students reporting specialty:
biomedical: 14%; chemical: 13%; civil: 3%; computer science: 17%; electrical: 20%; environmental: 3%; materials: 9%; mechanical: 6%; other: 15%

Southern Methodist University (Lyle)

3145 Dyer Street
Dallas, TX 75275-0335
www.smu.edu/lyle
Private
Admissions: (214) 768-3913
Email: msaloma@lyle.smu.edu
Financial aid: (214) 768-1501
Application deadline: 07/01
Tuition: full time: $1,165/credit hour; part time: $1,165/credit hour
Room/board/expenses: $24,775
Full-time enrollment: 588
men: 75%; women: 25%; minorities: 11%; international: 80%
Part-time enrollment: 527
men: 72%; women: 28%; minorities: 34%; international: 15%
Acceptance rate: 67%
GRE requirement: Yes
Avg. GRE: quantitative: 159
TOEFL requirement: Yes
Minimum TOEFL score: 550
Fellowships: 0
Teaching assistantships: 54
Research assistantships: 66
Students reporting specialty: civil: 3%; computer: 1%; computer science: 14%; electrical: 33%; management: 14%; environmental: 3%; industrial: 8%; mechanical: 7%; other: 17%

Texas A&M University-College Station

7607 Eastmark Drive, Suite 230
College Station, TX 77843-3126
engineering.tamu.edu/graduate
Public
Admissions: (979) 845-7200
Email: gradengineer@tamu.edu
Financial aid: (979) 845-3236
Application deadline: rolling
In-state tuition: full time: $258/credit hour; part time: $258/credit hour
Out-of-state tuition: full time: $681/credit hour
Room/board/expenses: $18,732

Full-time enrollment: 2,873
men: 78%; women: 22%; minorities: 10%; international: 71%
Part-time enrollment: 596
men: 81%; women: 19%; minorities: 20%; international: 42%
Acceptance rate: 23%
GRE requirement: Yes
Avg. GRE: quantitative: 164
TOEFL requirement: Yes
Minimum TOEFL score: 550
Fellowships: 378
Teaching assistantships: 436
Research assistantships: 1,180
Students reporting specialty:
aerospace: 3%; agriculture: 2%; biomedical: 3%; chemical: 6%; civil: 11%; computer science: 9%; electrical: 21%; industrial: 8%; materials: 4%; mechanical: 13%; nuclear: 4%; petroleum: 12%; other: 3%

Texas A&M University-Kingsville (Dotterweich)

MSC 188
Kingsville, TX 78363
www.tamuk.edu/grad/
Public
Admissions: (361) 593-2808
Email: GradSchool@tamuk.edu
Financial aid: (361) 593-2173
Application deadline: 07/15
In-state tuition: full time: $5,369; part time: $704/credit hour
Out-of-state tuition: full time: $12,713
Room/board/expenses: $14,393
Full-time enrollment: 1,179
men: 80%; women: 20%; minorities: 2%; international: 96%
Part-time enrollment: 349
men: 81%; women: 19%; minorities: 8%; international: 87%
Acceptance rate: 72%
GRE requirement: Yes
Avg. GRE: quantitative: 154
TOEFL requirement: Yes
Minimum TOEFL score: 550
Students reporting specialty:
chemical: 2%; civil: 7%; computer science: 32%; electrical: 27%; environmental: 4%; industrial: 7%; mechanical: 12%; petroleum: 1%; other: 8%

Texas State University[1]

601 University Drive
San Marcos, TX 78666
www.engineering.txstate.edu/
Public
Admissions: N/A
Financial aid: N/A
Tuition: N/A
Room/board/expenses: N/A
Enrollment: N/A

Texas Tech University (Whitacre)

Box 43103
Lubbock, TX 79409-3103
www.depts.ttu.edu/coe/
Public
Admissions: (806) 742-2787
Email: graduate.admissions@ttu.edu
Financial aid: (806) 742-3681
Application deadline: 06/01
In-state tuition: full time: $315/credit hour; part time: $315/credit hour
Out-of-state tuition: full time: $723/credit hour
Room/board/expenses: $14,805

Full-time enrollment: 663
men: 76%; women: 24%; minorities: 8%; international: 78%
Part-time enrollment: 233
men: 82%; women: 18%; minorities: 20%; international: 31%
Acceptance rate: 34%
GRE requirement: Yes
Avg. GRE: quantitative: 159
TOEFL requirement: Yes
Minimum TOEFL score: 550
Fellowships: 0
Teaching assistantships: 96
Research assistantships: 173
Students reporting specialty:
biomedical: 1%; chemical: 11%; civil: 11%; computer science: 12%; environmental: 2%; industrial: 21%; mechanical: 14%; petroleum: 9%; other: 2%

University of Houston (Cullen)

E421 Engineering Building 2
Houston, TX 77204-4007
www.egr.uh.edu
Public
Admissions: (713) 743-4200
Email: grad-admit@egr.uh.edu
Financial aid: (713) 743-1010
Application deadline: 02/01
In-state tuition: full time: $442/credit hour; part time: $442/credit hour
Out-of-state tuition: full time: $950/credit hour
Room/board/expenses: $16,248
Full-time enrollment: 1,076
men: 74%; women: 26%; minorities: 9%; international: 82%
Part-time enrollment: 372
men: 78%; women: 22%; minorities: 22%; international: 54%
Acceptance rate: 32%
GRE requirement: Yes
Avg. GRE: quantitative: 161
TOEFL requirement: Yes
Minimum TOEFL score: 550
Fellowships: 579
Teaching assistantships: 99
Research assistantships: 394
Students reporting specialty:
aerospace: 1%; biomedical: 4%; chemical: 9%; civil: 6%; computer: 5%; computer science: 14%; electrical: 16%; environmental: 13%; materials: 4%; mechanical: 11%; petroleum: 9%; other: 6%

University of North Texas

1155 Union Circle, #310440
Denton, TX 76203-5017
tsgs.unt.edu/overview
Public
Admissions: (940) 565-2383
Email: gradsch@unt.edu
Financial aid: (940) 565-2302
Application deadline: 06/15
In-state tuition: full time: $228/credit hour; part time: $228/credit hour
Out-of-state tuition: full time: $838/credit hour
Room/board/expenses: $13,336
Full-time enrollment: 428
men: 72%; women: 28%; minorities: 4%; international: 88%
Part-time enrollment: 147
men: 79%; women: 21%; minorities: 19%; international: 59%
Acceptance rate: 47%
GRE requirement: Yes
Avg. GRE: quantitative: 159
TOEFL requirement: Yes
Minimum TOEFL score: 550

Fellowships: 0
Teaching assistantships: 63
Research assistantships: 77
Students reporting specialty: N/A

University of Texas-Arlington

UTA Box 19019
Arlington, TX 76019
www.uta.edu/engineering/
Public
Admissions: (817) 272-6287
Financial aid: (817) 272-3561
Application deadline: 06/15
In-state tuition: full time: $8,858; part time: $6,595
Out-of-state tuition: full time: $17,680
Room/board/expenses: $14,791
Full-time enrollment: 2,528
men: 78%; women: 22%; minorities: 3%; international: 92%
Part-time enrollment: 718
men: 81%; women: 19%; minorities: 18%; international: 60%
Acceptance rate: 49%
GRE requirement: Yes
Avg. GRE: quantitative: 158
TOEFL requirement: Yes
Minimum TOEFL score: 550
Fellowships: 387
Teaching assistantships: 367
Research assistantships: 136
Students reporting specialty:
aerospace: 4%; biomedical: 4%; civil: 17%; computer: 2%; computer science: 23%; electrical: 12%; management: 3%; industrial: 15%; materials: 2%; mechanical: 18%

University of Texas-Austin (Cockrell)

301 E. Dean Keeton Street
Stop C2100
Austin, TX 78712-2100
www.engr.utexas.edu/
Public
Admissions: (512) 475-7391
Email: gradus@austin.utexas.edu
Financial aid: (512) 475-6282
Application deadline: rolling
In-state tuition: full time: $9,850; part time: N/A
Out-of-state tuition: full time: $18,030
Room/board/expenses: $18,810
Full-time enrollment: 1,986
men: 79%; women: 21%; minorities: 11%; international: 61%
Part-time enrollment: 376
men: 78%; women: 22%; minorities: 30%; international: 20%
Acceptance rate: 16%
GRE requirement: Yes
Avg. GRE: quantitative: 165
TOEFL requirement: Yes
Minimum TOEFL score: 550
Fellowships: 782
Teaching assistantships: 471
Research assistantships: 948
Students reporting specialty:
aerospace: 6%; biomedical: 4%; chemical: 8%; civil: 14%; computer: 14%; computer science: 9%; electrical: 12%; management: 3%; environmental: 2%; industrial: 3%; materials: 2%; mechanical: 13%; petroleum: 8%

University of Texas-Dallas (Jonsson)

800 W. Campbell Road
Mail Station EC32
Richardson, TX 75080-0021
www.utdallas.edu
Public

Admissions: (972) 883-2270
Email: interest@utdallas.edu
Financial aid: (972) 883-2941
Application deadline: 05/01
In-state tuition: full time: $12,418; part time: N/A
Out-of-state tuition: full time: $24,150
Room/board/expenses: $15,590
Full-time enrollment: 1,892
men: 71%; women: 29%; minorities: 5%; international: 88%
Part-time enrollment: 516
men: 74%; women: 26%; minorities: 9%; international: 73%
Acceptance rate: 22%
GRE requirement: Yes
Avg. GRE: quantitative: 162
TOEFL requirement: Yes
Minimum TOEFL score: 550
Fellowships: 39
Teaching assistantships: 208
Research assistantships: 326
Students reporting specialty: biomedical: 4%; computer: 4%; computer science: 45%; electrical: 31%; management: 4%; materials: 3%; mechanical: 8%; other: 2%

University of Texas-El Paso[1]
500 W. University Avenue
El Paso, TX 79968
www.utep.edu/graduate
Public
Admissions: (915) 747-5491
Email: gradschool@utep.edu
Financial aid: (915) 747-5204
Tuition: N/A
Room/board/expenses: N/A
Enrollment: N/A

University of Texas Health Science Center-San Antonio[1]
One UTSA Circle
San Antonio, TX 78249
engineering2.utsa.edu/
Public
Admissions: (210) 567-3709
Email: gsbs@uthscsa.edu
Financial aid: N/A
Tuition: N/A
Room/board/expenses: N/A
Enrollment: N/A

University of Texas-San Antonio
1 UTSA Circle
San Antonio, TX 78249-0665
graduateschool.utsa.edu/
Public
Admissions: (210) 458-4330
Email: GraduateAdmissions@utsa.edu
Financial aid: (210) 458-8000
Application deadline: 02/01
In-state tuition: full time: $288/credit hour; part time: $288/credit hour
Out-of-state tuition: full time: $1,115/credit hour
Room/board/expenses: $15,054
Full-time enrollment: 369
men: 72%; women: 28%; minorities: 20%; international: 64%
Part-time enrollment: 262
men: 78%; women: 22%; minorities: 37%; international: 26%
Acceptance rate: 60%
GRE requirement: Yes
Avg. GRE: quantitative: 156
TOEFL requirement: Yes
Minimum TOEFL score: 550
Fellowships: 64
Teaching assistantships: 85

Research assistantships: 67
Students reporting specialty: biomedical: 10%; civil: 10%; computer: 6%; computer science: 21%; electrical: 28%; environmental: 4%; industrial: 4%; materials: 1%; mechanical: 16%

UTAH

Brigham Young University (Fulton)
270 CB
Provo, UT 84602
www.byu.edu/gradstudies
Private
Admissions: (801) 422-4091
Email: gradstudies@byu.edu
Financial aid: (801) 422-8153
Application deadline: 12/15
Tuition: full time: $6,680; part time: $393/credit hour
Room/board/expenses: $19,568
Full-time enrollment: 410
men: 88%; women: 12%; minorities: 4%; international: 16%
Part-time enrollment: N/A
men: N/A; women: N/A; minorities: N/A; international: N/A
Acceptance rate: 62%
GRE requirement: Yes
Avg. GRE: quantitative: 162
TOEFL requirement: Yes
Minimum TOEFL score: 580
Fellowships: 26
Teaching assistantships: 235
Research assistantships: 780
Students reporting specialty: chemical: 13%; civil: 14%; computer science: 20%; electrical: 24%; mechanical: 29%

University of Utah
72 S. Central Campus Drive
1650 WEB
Salt Lake City, UT 84112-9200
www.utah.edu
Public
Admissions: (801) 585-1994
Email: admissions@sa.utah.edu
Financial aid: (801) 581-6211
Application deadline: 01/01
In-state tuition: full time: $9,384; part time: $6,725
Out-of-state tuition: full time: $23,500
Room/board/expenses: $14,846
Full-time enrollment: 985
men: 78%; women: 22%; minorities: 8%; international: 51%
Part-time enrollment: 274
men: 84%; women: 16%; minorities: 14%; international: 26%
Acceptance rate: 35%
GRE requirement: Yes
Avg. GRE: quantitative: 161
TOEFL requirement: Yes
Minimum TOEFL score: 550
Fellowships: 74
Teaching assistantships: 171
Research assistantships: 494
Students reporting specialty: biomedical: 13%; chemical: 7%; civil: 8%; computer science: 28%; electrical: 17%; materials: 2%; mechanical: 17%; mining: 1%; nuclear: 1%; petroleum: 2%; other: 4%

Utah State University
4100 Old Main Hill
Logan, UT 84322-4100
www.engineering.usu.edu/
Public
Admissions: (435) 797-8185
Email: graduateschool@usu.edu
Financial aid: (435) 797-0173
Application deadline: rolling

In-state tuition: full time: $6,886; part time: $5,861
Out-of-state tuition: full time: $19,683
Room/board/expenses: $12,420
Full-time enrollment: 191
men: 81%; women: 19%; minorities: 4%; international: 42%
Part-time enrollment: 192
men: 83%; women: 17%; minorities: 6%; international: 49%
Acceptance rate: 41%
GRE requirement: Yes
Avg. GRE: quantitative: N/A
TOEFL requirement: Yes
Minimum TOEFL score: 550
Fellowships: 15
Teaching assistantships: 52
Research assistantships: 183
Students reporting specialty: aerospace: 7%; agriculture: 7%; civil: 23%; computer: 3%; computer science: 24%; electrical: 15%; mechanical: 17%; other: 3%

VERMONT

University of Vermont
109 Votey Hall
Burlington, VT 05405
www.cems.uvm.edu
Public
Admissions: (802) 656-2699
Email: graduate.admissions@uvm.edu
Financial aid: (802) 656-5700
Application deadline: 02/01
In-state tuition: full time: $629/credit hour; part time: $629/credit hour
Out-of-state tuition: full time: $1,590/credit hour
Room/board/expenses: $15,622
Full-time enrollment: 76
men: 76%; women: 24%; minorities: 1%; international: 46%
Part-time enrollment: 26
men: 96%; women: 4%; minorities: 8%; international: 15%
Acceptance rate: 59%
GRE requirement: Yes
Avg. GRE: quantitative: 162
TOEFL requirement: Yes
Minimum TOEFL score: N/A
Fellowships: 1
Teaching assistantships: 25
Research assistantships: 35
Students reporting specialty: N/A

VIRGINIA

George Mason University (Volgenau)
4400 University Drive, MS4A3
Fairfax, VA 22030-4444
www2.gmu.edu/admissions-aid/how-apply/graduate
Public
Admissions: (703) 993-9700
Email: masongrad@gmu.edu
Financial aid: (703) 993-2353
Application deadline: 03/15
In-state tuition: full time: $16,124; part time: $671/credit hour
Out-of-state tuition: full time: $32,402
Room/board/expenses: $23,620
Full-time enrollment: 812
men: 69%; women: 31%; minorities: 10%; international: 75%
Part-time enrollment: 899
men: 76%; women: 24%; minorities: 35%; international: 10%
Acceptance rate: 74%
GRE requirement: Yes
Avg. GRE: quantitative: 159
TOEFL requirement: Yes
Minimum TOEFL score: 570
Fellowships: 0

Teaching assistantships: 175
Research assistantships: 88
Students reporting specialty: biomedical: 1%; civil: 6%; computer: 4%; computer science: 30%; electrical: 33%; industrial: 8%; other: 18%

Old Dominion University (Batten)
1105 Engineering Systems Building
Norfolk, VA 23529
www.odu.edu/admission/graduate
Public
Admissions: (757) 683-3685
Email: gradadmit@odu.edu
Financial aid: (757) 683-3689
Application deadline: rolling
In-state tuition: full time: $478/credit hour; part time: $478/credit hour
Out-of-state tuition: full time: $1,195/credit hour
Room/board/expenses: $16,324
Full-time enrollment: 157
men: 72%; women: 28%; minorities: 14%; international: 53%
Part-time enrollment: 569
men: 78%; women: 22%; minorities: 25%; international: 15%
Acceptance rate: 82%
Avg. GRE: quantitative: 157
TOEFL requirement: Yes
Minimum TOEFL score: 550
Fellowships: 10
Teaching assistantships: 68
Research assistantships: 305
Students reporting specialty: aerospace: 2%; biomedical: 1%; civil: 7%; computer: 9%; electrical: 9%; management: 37%; environmental: 6%; industrial: 3%; mechanical: 7%; other: 31%

University of Virginia
Thornton Hall
Charlottesville, VA 22904-4246
www.seas.virginia.edu/
Public
Admissions: (434) 924-8659
Email: seas-grad-admission@virginia.edu
Financial aid: (434) 924-8659
Application deadline: 01/15
In-state tuition: full time: $19,034; part time: $816/credit hour
Out-of-state tuition: full time: $28,934
Room/board/expenses: $21,173
Full-time enrollment: 743
men: 72%; women: 28%; minorities: 11%; international: 55%
Part-time enrollment: 43
men: 47%; women: 53%; minorities: 21%; international: 0%
Acceptance rate: 29%
GRE requirement: Yes
Avg. GRE: quantitative: 164
TOEFL requirement: Yes
Minimum TOEFL score: 600
Fellowships: 254
Teaching assistantships: 155
Research assistantships: 451
Students reporting specialty: biomedical: 10%; chemical: 6%; civil: 8%; computer: 6%; computer science: 15%; electrical: 18%; science and physics: 2%; industrial: 11%; materials: 10%; mechanical: 13%

Virginia Commonwealth University
PO Box 843068
Richmond, VA 23284-3068
www.egr.vcu.edu/
Public
Admissions: (804) 828-9306
Email: gradengr@vcu.edu
Financial aid: (804) 828-9306
Application deadline: 06/01
In-state tuition: full time: $10,485; part time: $499/credit hour
Out-of-state tuition: full time: $22,351
Room/board/expenses: $19,986
Full-time enrollment: 200
men: 74%; women: 27%; minorities: 16%; international: 48%
Part-time enrollment: 46
men: 83%; women: 17%; minorities: 15%; international: 20%
Acceptance rate: 60%
GRE requirement: Yes
Avg. GRE: quantitative: 159
TOEFL requirement: Yes
Minimum TOEFL score: 550
Fellowships: 17
Teaching assistantships: 83
Research assistantships: 65
Students reporting specialty: biomedical: 21%; chemical: 11%; computer: 22%; computer science: 19%; electrical: 22%; mechanical: 28%; nuclear: 26%

Virginia Tech
3046 Torgersen Hall
Blacksburg, VA 24061-0217
www.graduateschool.vt.edu
Public
Admissions: (540) 231-8636
Email: grads@vt.edu
Financial aid: (540) 231-5179
Application deadline: rolling
In-state tuition: full time: $17,532; part time: $692/credit hour
Out-of-state tuition: full time: $30,644
Room/board/expenses: $12,700
Full-time enrollment: 1,947
men: 75%; women: 25%; minorities: 10%; international: 62%
Part-time enrollment: 391
men: 82%; women: 18%; minorities: 14%; international: 36%
Acceptance rate: 19%
GRE requirement: Yes
Avg. GRE: quantitative: 162
TOEFL requirement: Yes
Minimum TOEFL score: 550
Fellowships: 126
Teaching assistantships: 460
Research assistantships: 876
Students reporting specialty: aerospace: 7%; agriculture: 2%; biomedical: 2%; chemical: 2%; civil: 14%; computer: 9%; computer science: 11%; electrical: 17%; science and physics: 3%; environmental: 2%; industrial: 9%; materials: 3%; mechanical: 14%; mining: 1%; nuclear: 0%; other: 2%

WASHINGTON

University of Washington
371 Loew Hall, Box 352180
Seattle, WA 98195-2180
www.engr.washington.edu
Public
Admissions: (206) 685-2630
Email: uwgrad@uw.edu
Financial aid: (206) 543-6101

Application deadline: N/A
In-state tuition: full time: $17,976; part time: $806/credit hour
Out-of-state tuition: full time: $31,212
Room/board/expenses: $19,011
Full-time enrollment: 1,590 men: 69%; women: 31%; minorities: 16%; international: 46%
Part-time enrollment: 826 men: 74%; women: 26%; minorities: 31%; international: 12%
Acceptance rate: 28%
GRE requirement: Yes
Avg. GRE: quantitative: 163
TOEFL requirement: Yes
Minimum TOEFL score: 580
Fellowships: 155
Teaching assistantships: 268
Research assistantships: 667
Students reporting specialty: aerospace: 10%; biomedical: 7%; chemical: 5%; civil: 16%; computer: 16%; electrical: 15%; industrial: 4%; materials: 5%; mechanical: 13%; other: 9%

Washington State University

PO Box 642714
Pullman, WA 99164-2714
www.vcea.wsu.edu
Public
Admissions: (509) 335-1446
Email: gradsch@wsu.edu
Financial aid: (509) 335-9711
Application deadline: 01/10
In-state tuition: full time: $12,753; part time: $589/credit hour
Out-of-state tuition: full time: $26,185
Room/board/expenses: $8,017
Full-time enrollment: 568 men: 73%; women: 27%; minorities: 8%; international: 70%
Part-time enrollment: 195 men: 74%; women: 26%; minorities: 27%; international: 20%
Acceptance rate: 24%
GRE requirement: Yes

Avg. GRE: quantitative: 161
TOEFL requirement: Yes
Minimum TOEFL score: 550
Fellowships: 32
Teaching assistantships: 92
Research assistantships: 223
Students reporting specialty: agriculture: 11%; biomedical: 1%; chemical: 7%; civil: 11%; computer: 1%; computer science: 14%; electrical: 14%; management: 11%; science and physics: 0%; environmental: 2%; materials: 9%; mechanical: 18%

WEST VIRGINIA

West Virginia University (Statler)

PO Box 6070
Morgantown, WV 26506-6070
www.statler.wvu.edu
Public
Admissions: (304) 293-2121
Email: graduateadmissions@mail.wvu.edu
Financial aid: (304) 293-5242
Application deadline: 05/01
In-state tuition: full time: $10,242; part time: $569/credit hour
Out-of-state tuition: full time: $25,056
Room/board/expenses: $12,870
Full-time enrollment: 560 men: 77%; women: 23%; minorities: 4%; international: 60%
Part-time enrollment: 141 men: 81%; women: 19%; minorities: 13%; international: 21%
Acceptance rate: 47%
GRE requirement: Yes
Avg. GRE: quantitative: 157
TOEFL requirement: Yes
Minimum TOEFL score: 550
Fellowships: 16
Teaching assistantships: 77
Research assistantships: 246
Students reporting specialty: aerospace: 5%; chemical: 7%; civil: 9%; computer: 2%; computer science: 12%; electrical: 13%; industrial: 6%;

materials: 2%; mechanical: 13%; mining: 3%; petroleum: 6%; other: 23%

WISCONSIN

Marquette University

PO Box 1881
Milwaukee, WI 53201-1881
www.grad.marquette.edu
Private
Admissions: (414) 288-7137
Email: mugs@mu.edu
Financial aid: (414) 288-5325
Application deadline: rolling
Tuition: full time: $1,075/credit hour; part time: $1,075/credit hour
Room/board/expenses: $17,406
Full-time enrollment: 113 men: 77%; women: 23%; minorities: 13%; international: 36%
Part-time enrollment: 80 men: 80%; women: 20%; minorities: 11%; international: 16%
Acceptance rate: 61%
GRE requirement: Yes
Avg. GRE: quantitative: 159
TOEFL requirement: Yes
Minimum TOEFL score: N/A
Fellowships: 8
Teaching assistantships: 29
Research assistantships: 62
Students reporting specialty: biomedical: 24%; civil: 17%; electrical: 25%; mechanical: 30%; other: 3%

University of Wisconsin-Madison

2610 Engineering Hall
Madison, WI 53706
www.engr.wisc.edu/
Public
Admissions: (608) 262-2433
Email: gradadmiss@bascom.wisc.edu
Financial aid: (608) 262-3060
Application deadline: N/A

In-state tuition: full time: $13,157; part time: $791/credit hour
Out-of-state tuition: full time: $26,484
Room/board/expenses: $19,098
Full-time enrollment: 1,460 men: 78%; women: 22%; minorities: 9%; international: 56%
Part-time enrollment: 361 men: 77%; women: 23%; minorities: 12%; international: 28%
Acceptance rate: 20%
GRE requirement: Yes
Avg. GRE: quantitative: 164
TOEFL requirement: Yes
Minimum TOEFL score: 580
Fellowships: 68
Teaching assistantships: 282
Research assistantships: 818
Students reporting specialty: agriculture: 2%; biomedical: 5%; chemical: 6%; civil: 8%; computer science: 20%; electrical: 17%; science and physics: 9%; environmental: 2%; industrial: 7%; materials: 6%; mechanical: 12%; nuclear: 5%

University of Wisconsin-Milwaukee

PO Box 784
Milwaukee, WI 53201-0784
www.uwm.edu/CEAS
Public
Admissions: (414) 229-6169
Email: bwarras@uwm.edu
Financial aid: (414) 229-4541
Application deadline: rolling
In-state tuition: full time: $11,764; part time: $1,237/credit hour
Out-of-state tuition: full time: $25,036
Room/board/expenses: $13,150
Full-time enrollment: 348 men: 72%; women: 28%; minorities: 5%; international: 82%
Part-time enrollment: 78 men: 81%; women: 19%; minorities: 24%; international: 0%
Acceptance rate: 50%
GRE requirement: Yes
Avg. GRE: quantitative: 158

TOEFL requirement: Yes
Minimum TOEFL score: 520
Fellowships: 46
Teaching assistantships: 117
Research assistantships: 52
Students reporting specialty: biomedical: 7%; civil: 13%; computer science: 19%; electrical: 27%; industrial: 9%; materials: 8%; mechanical: 17%

WYOMING

University of Wyoming

Dept. 3295
1000 E. University Avenue
Laramie, WY 82071
www.uwyo.edu/ceas/
Public
Admissions: (307) 766-5160
Email: why-wyo@uwyo.edu
Financial aid: (307) 766-2116
Application deadline: rolling
In-state tuition: full time: $241/credit hour; part time: $241/credit hour
Out-of-state tuition: full time: $721/credit hour
Room/board/expenses: $16,943
Full-time enrollment: 209 men: 78%; women: 22%; minorities: 4%; international: 64%
Part-time enrollment: 53 men: 75%; women: 25%; minorities: 8%; international: 53%
Acceptance rate: 45%
GRE requirement: Yes
Avg. GRE: quantitative: 161
TOEFL requirement: Yes
Minimum TOEFL score: 550
Fellowships: 28
Teaching assistantships: 39
Research assistantships: 157
Students reporting specialty: architectural: 3%; chemical: 12%; civil: 18%; computer science: 9%; electrical: 13%; mechanical: 18%; petroleum: 16%; other: 12%

LAW

The law directory lists the 204 schools in the country offering the J.D. degree that were fully or provisionally accredited by the American Bar Association in August 2016. One hundred ninety-three schools responded to the U.S. News survey conducted in the fall of 2016 and early 2017, and their data are reported here. Nonresponders have abbreviated entries.

KEY TO THE TERMINOLOGY

1. A school whose name is footnoted with the numeral 1 did not return the U.S. News statistical survey; limited data appear in its entry.

N/A. Not available from the school or not applicable.

Admissions. The admissions office phone number.

Email. The address of the admissions office. If instead of an email address a website is listed, the website will automatically present an email screen programmed to reach the admissions office.

Financial aid. The financial aid office phone number.

Application deadline. For fall 2018 enrollment. "Rolling" means there is no deadline; the school acts on applications as they are received. "Varies" means deadlines vary according to department or whether applicants are U.S. citizens or foreign nationals.

Tuition. For the 2016-17 academic year. Includes fees.

Credit hour. The cost per credit hour for the 2016-17 academic year.

Room/board/expenses. For the 2016-17 academic year.

Median grant. The median value of grants to full-time students enrolled in 2016-17. This is calculated for all full-time students (not just those in the first year) who received grants and scholarships from internal sources.

Average law school indebtedness. For 2016 graduates, the average law school debt for those taking out at least one educational loan while in school.

Enrollment. Full and part time, fall 2016. Gender figure is for full and part time.

Minorities. For fall 2016, the percentage of full-time and part-time U.S. students who are black or African-American, Asian, American Indian or Alaska Native, Native Hawaiian or other Pacific Islander, Hispanic/ Latino, or two or more races.

Acceptance rate. Percentage of applicants who were accepted for the fall 2016 full-time J.D. program.

Midrange Law School Admission Test (LSAT) score. For full-time students who entered in fall 2016. The first number is the 25th percentile test score for the class; the second, the 75th percentile.

Midrange undergraduate grade-point average. For full-time students who entered in fall 2016. The first number is the 25th percentile GPA for the class; the second is the 75th percentile.

Midrange of full-time private sector starting salaries. For the 2015 graduating class, the starting salary is for those employed full time in the private sector in law firms, business, industry or other jobs. The first number is the starting salary at the 25th percentile of the graduating class; the second number is the starting salary at the 75th percentile. When a school has the same salary at the 25th and 75th percentiles, it means that the starting salaries for private sector jobs were the same for a large proportion of the class.

Job classifications. For 2015 graduates, this represents the breakdown for the following types of employment: in law firms, business and industry (legal and nonlegal), government, public interest, judicial clerkship, academia and unknown. Numbers may not add up to 100 percent because of rounding.

Employment locations. For the 2015 graduating class. Abbreviations: **Intl.**, international; **N.E.**, New England (Conn., Maine, Mass., N.H., R.I., Vt.); **M.A.**, Middle Atlantic (N.J., N.Y., Pa.); **S.A.**, South Atlantic (Del., D.C., Fla., Ga., Md., N.C., S.C., Va., W.Va.); **E.N.C.**, East North Central (Ill., Ind., Mich., Ohio, Wis.); **W.N.C.**, West North Central (Iowa, Kan., Minn., Mo., Neb., N.D., S.D.); **E.S.C.**, East South Central (Ala., Ky., Miss., Tenn.); **W.S.C.**, West South Central (Ark., La., Okla., Texas); **Mt.**, Mountain (Ariz., Colo., Idaho, Mont., Nev., N.M., Utah, Wyo.); **Pac.**, Pacific (Alaska, Calif., Hawaii, Ore., Wash.).

ALABAMA

Faulkner University (Jones)
5345 Atlanta Highway
Montgomery, AL 36109
www.faulkner.edu/law
Private
Admissions: (334) 386-7190
Email: jbradley@faulkner.edu
Financial aid: (334) 386-7293
Application deadline: 07/15
Tuition: full time: $37,370; part time: N/A
Room/board/expenses: $28,400
Median grant: $11,220
Average student indebtedness at graduation: $18,434
Enrollment: full time: 245; part time: 3
men: 50%; women: 50%; minorities: 42%
Midrange LSAT (full time): 142-148
Midrange undergraduate GPA (full time): 2.50-3.44
Midrange of full-time private-sector salaries of 2015 grads: $50,000-$100,000
2015 grads employed in: law firms: 54%; business and industry: 12%; government: 23%; public interest: 1%; judicial clerk: 4%; academia: 2%; unknown: 5%
Employment location for 2015 class: Intl. 0%; N.E. 0%; M.A. 0%; E.N.C. 2%; W.N.C. 0%; S.A. 15%; E.S.C. 63%; W.S.C. 2%; Mt. 0%; Pac. 0%; unknown 1%

Samford University (Cumberland)
800 Lakeshore Drive
Birmingham, AL 35229
samford.edu/cumberlandlaw/
Private
Admissions: (205) 726-2702
Email: lawadm@samford.edu
Financial aid: (205) 726-2905
Application deadline: 06/01
Tuition: full time: $37,146; part time: $21,916
Room/board/expenses: $16,274
Median grant: $13,500
Average student indebtedness at graduation: $127,611
Enrollment: full time: 408; part time: 26
men: 52%; women: 48%; minorities: 17%
Acceptance rate (full time): 68%
Midrange LSAT (full time): 149-155
Midrange undergraduate GPA (full time): 2.92-3.59
Midrange of full-time private-sector salaries of 2015 grads: $42,500-$70,000
2015 grads employed in: law firms: 58%; business and industry: 22%; government: 10%; public interest: 2%; judicial clerk: 9%; academia: 0%; unknown: 0%
Employment location for 2015 class: Intl. 1%; N.E. 0%; M.A. 1%; E.N.C. 0%; W.N.C. 1%; S.A. 19%; E.S.C. 74%; W.S.C. 3%; Mt. 0%; Pac. 0%; unknown 0%

University of Alabama
Box 870382
Tuscaloosa, AL 35487
www.law.ua.edu
Public
Admissions: (205) 348-5440
Email: admissions@law.ua.edu
Financial aid: (205) 348-6756
Application deadline: rolling
In-state tuition: full time: $23,055; part time: N/A
Out-of-state tuition: full time: $39,115
Room/board/expenses: $19,056
Median grant: $15,100
Average student indebtedness at graduation: $75,577
Enrollment: full time: 408; part time: 1
men: 55%; women: 45%; minorities: 21%
Acceptance rate (full time): 31%
Midrange LSAT (full time): 157-165
Midrange undergraduate GPA (full time): 3.45-3.92
Midrange of full-time private-sector salaries of 2015 grads: $50,000-$90,000
2015 grads employed in: law firms: 50%; business and industry: 15%; government: 10%; public interest: 4%; judicial clerk: 18%; academia: 3%; unknown: 0%
Employment location for 2015 class: Intl. 1%; N.E. 0%; M.A. 1%; E.N.C. 1%; W.N.C. 2%; S.A. 16%; E.S.C. 63%; W.S.C. 13%; Mt. 1%; Pac. 1%; unknown 0%

ARIZONA

Arizona State University (O'Connor)
Mail Code 9520
111 E. Taylor Street
Phoenix, AZ 85004-4467
www.law.asu.edu
Public
Admissions: (480) 965-1474
Email: law.admissions@asu.edu
Financial aid: (480) 965-1474
Application deadline: 03/01
In-state tuition: full time: $27,226; part time: N/A
Out-of-state tuition: full time: $43,896
Room/board/expenses: $21,710
Median grant: $25,000
Average student indebtedness at graduation: $97,780
Enrollment: full time: 718; part time: N/A
men: 58%; women: 42%; minorities: 27%
Acceptance rate (full time): 42%
Midrange LSAT (full time): 158-163
Midrange undergraduate GPA (full time): 3.34-3.80
Midrange of full-time private-sector salaries of 2015 grads: $70,000-$115,000
2015 grads employed in: law firms: 48%; business and industry: 20%; government: 19%; public interest: 1%; judicial clerk: 9%; academia: 1%; unknown: 0%

Employment location for 2015 class: Intl. 0%; N.E. 0%; M.A. 1%; E.N.C. 1%; W.N.C. 2%; S.A. 3%; E.S.C. 0%; W.S.C. 1%; Mt. 84%; Pac. 7%; unknown 0%

Arizona Summit Law School[1]

One North Central Avenue
Phoenix, AZ 85004
www.azsummitlaw.edu/
Private
Admissions: (602) 682-6800
Email: admissions@AZSummitLaw.edu
Financial aid: () -
Tuition: N/A
Room/board/expenses: N/A
Enrollment: N/A

University of Arizona (Rogers)

PO Box 210176
Tucson, AZ 85721-0176
www.law.arizona.edu
Public
Admissions: (520) 621-7666
Email: admissions@law.arizona.edu
Financial aid: (520) 626-1832
Application deadline: 07/15
In-state tuition: full time: $25,525; part time: N/A
Out-of-state tuition: full time: $30,025
Room/board/expenses: $21,050
Median grant: $19,750
Average student indebtedness at graduation: $84,601
Enrollment: full time: 364; part time: 4
men: 60%; women: 40%; minorities: 31%
Acceptance rate (full time): 34%
Midrange LSAT (full time): 155-163
Midrange undergraduate GPA (full time): 3.19-3.75
Midrange of full-time private-sector salaries of 2015 grads: $80,000-$125,000
2015 grads employed in: law firms: 46%; business and industry: 8%; government: 15%; public interest: 5%; judicial clerk: 16%; academia: 9%; unknown: 0%
Employment location for 2015 class: Intl. 5%; N.E. 0%; M.A. 5%; E.N.C. 2%; W.N.C. 0%; S.A. 5%; E.S.C. 0%; W.S.C. 2%; Mt. 66%; Pac. 14%; unknown 1%

ARKANSAS

University of Arkansas-Fayetteville

Robert A. Leflar Law Center
Fayetteville, AR 72701
law.uark.edu/
Public
Admissions: (479) 575-3102
Email: jkmiller@uark.edu
Financial aid: (479) 575-3806
Application deadline: 04/15
In-state tuition: full time: $15,704; part time: N/A
Out-of-state tuition: full time: $33,372
Room/board/expenses: $16,224
Median grant: $8,000
Average student indebtedness at graduation: $67,758

Enrollment: full time: 352; part time: N/A
men: 59%; women: 41%; minorities: 18%
Acceptance rate (full time): 54%
Midrange LSAT (full time): 151-157
Midrange undergraduate GPA (full time): 3.19-3.71
Midrange of full-time private-sector salaries of 2015 grads: $50,000-$75,000
2015 grads employed in: law firms: 62%; business and industry: 17%; government: 15%; public interest: 2%; judicial clerk: 4%; academia: 1%; unknown: 0%
Employment location for 2015 class: Intl. 0%; N.E. 0%; M.A. 2%; E.N.C. 0%; W.N.C. 4%; S.A. 3%; E.S.C. 3%; W.S.C. 83%; Mt. 2%; Pac. 1%; unknown 3%

University of Arkansas-Little Rock (Bowen)

1201 McMath Avenue
Little Rock, AR 72202-5142
ualr.edu/law/
Public
Admissions: (501) 324-9903
Email: lawadmissions@ualr.edu
Financial aid: (501) 569-3035
Application deadline: 03/15
In-state tuition: full time: $15,121; part time: $10,605
Out-of-state tuition: full time: $30,676
Room/board/expenses: $16,571
Median grant: $6,400
Average student indebtedness at graduation: $65,931
Enrollment: full time: 293; part time: 101
men: 54%; women: 46%; minorities: 14%
Acceptance rate (full time): 55%
Midrange LSAT (full time): 148-155
Midrange undergraduate GPA (full time): 3.10-3.50
Midrange of full-time private-sector salaries of 2015 grads: $65,000-$75,000
2015 grads employed in: law firms: 38%; business and industry: 20%; government: 25%; public interest: 5%; judicial clerk: 8%; academia: 1%; unknown: 3%
Employment location for 2015 class: Intl. 1%; N.E. 0%; M.A. 2%; E.N.C. 0%; W.N.C. 4%; S.A. 0%; E.S.C. 0%; W.S.C. 80%; Mt. 5%; Pac. 1%; unknown 2%

CALIFORNIA

California Western School of Law

225 Cedar Street
San Diego, CA 92101-3090
www.cwsl.edu
Private
Admissions: (619) 525-1402
Email: admissions@cwsl.edu
Financial aid: (619) 525-7060
Application deadline: 04/01
Tuition: full time: $48,900; part time: $34,300
Room/board/expenses: $24,792
Median grant: $23,280
Average student indebtedness at graduation: $147,302

Enrollment: full time: 565; part time: 75
men: 40%; women: 60%; minorities: 42%
Acceptance rate (full time): 70%
Midrange LSAT (full time): 146-152
Midrange undergraduate GPA (full time): 2.80-3.40
Midrange of full-time private-sector salaries of 2015 grads: $53,500-$75,000
2015 grads employed in: law firms: 60%; business and industry: 15%; government: 11%; public interest: 8%; judicial clerk: 2%; academia: 3%; unknown: 1%
Employment location for 2015 class: Intl. 1%; N.E. 0%; M.A. 1%; E.N.C. 0%; W.N.C. 1%; S.A. 3%; E.S.C. 1%; W.S.C. 1%; Mt. 4%; Pac. 86%; unknown 3%

Chapman University (Fowler)

1 University Drive
Orange, CA 92866
www.chapman.edu/law
Private
Admissions: (714) 628-2500
Email: lawadmission@chapman.edu
Financial aid: (714) 628-2510
Application deadline: 04/16
Tuition: full time: $50,178; part time: $40,062
Room/board/expenses: $28,307
Median grant: $38,520
Average student indebtedness at graduation: $144,409
Enrollment: full time: 453; part time: 26
men: 46%; women: 54%; minorities: 41%
Acceptance rate (full time): 52%
Midrange LSAT (full time): 152-157
Midrange undergraduate GPA (full time): 3.03-3.48
Midrange of full-time private-sector salaries of 2015 grads: $42,375-$74,250
2015 grads employed in: law firms: 67%; business and industry: 24%; government: 6%; public interest: 4%; judicial clerk: 0%; academia: 0%; unknown: 0%
Employment location for 2015 class: Intl. 0%; N.E. 0%; M.A. 1%; E.N.C. 0%; W.N.C. 0%; S.A. 1%; E.S.C. 0%; W.S.C. 2%; Mt. 3%; Pac. 93%; unknown 0%

Golden Gate University

536 Mission Street
San Francisco, CA 94105
www.law.ggu.edu
Private
Admissions: (415) 442-6630
Email: lawadmit@ggu.edu
Financial aid: (415) 442-6635
Application deadline: 04/15
Tuition: full time: $48,500; part time: $35,700
Room/board/expenses: $26,898
Median grant: $20,000
Average student indebtedness at graduation: $161,809
Enrollment: full time: 260; part time: 94
men: 42%; women: 58%; minorities: 53%
Acceptance rate (full time): 65%
Midrange LSAT (full time): 146-152
Midrange undergraduate GPA (full time): 2.52-3.32

Midrange of full-time private-sector salaries of 2015 grads: $33,000-$70,000
2015 grads employed in: law firms: 51%; business and industry: 21%; government: 17%; public interest: 10%; judicial clerk: 0%; academia: 1%; unknown: 0%
Employment location for 2015 class: Intl. 0%; N.E. 0%; M.A. 0%; E.N.C. 0%; W.N.C. 1%; S.A. 2%; E.S.C. 1%; W.S.C. 2%; Mt. 5%; Pac. 90%; unknown 0%

Loyola Marymount University

919 Albany Street
Los Angeles, CA 90015-1211
www.lls.edu
Private
Admissions: (213) 736-1074
Email: Admissions@lls.edu
Financial aid: (213) 736-1140
Application deadline: 02/01
Tuition: full time: $52,760; part time: $35,312
Room/board/expenses: $30,942
Median grant: $32,000
Average student indebtedness at graduation: $146,494
Enrollment: full time: 771; part time: 167
men: 44%; women: 56%; minorities: 41%
Acceptance rate (full time): 41%
Midrange LSAT (full time): 157-161
Midrange undergraduate GPA (full time): 3.21-3.68
Midrange of full-time private-sector salaries of 2015 grads: $60,000-$90,000
2015 grads employed in: law firms: 69%; business and industry: 18%; government: 5%; public interest: 4%; judicial clerk: 4%; academia: 0%; unknown: 0%
Employment location for 2015 class: Intl. 0%; N.E. 0%; M.A. 1%; E.N.C. 0%; W.N.C. 0%; S.A. 1%; E.S.C. 0%; W.S.C. 1%; Mt. 0%; Pac. 95%; unknown 0%

Pepperdine University

24255 Pacific Coast Highway
Malibu, CA 90263
law.pepperdine.edu
Private
Admissions: (310) 506-4631
Email: lawadmis@pepperdine.edu
Financial aid: (310) 506-4633
Application deadline: 04/01
Tuition: full time: $51,200; part time: N/A
Room/board/expenses: $27,600
Median grant: $25,000
Average student indebtedness at graduation: $154,475
Enrollment: full time: 585; part time: 13
men: 47%; women: 53%; minorities: 33%
Acceptance rate (full time): 47%
Midrange of full-time private-sector salaries of 2015 grads: $51,000-$86,500
2015 grads employed in: law firms: 51%; business and industry: 19%; government: 9%; public interest: 2%; judicial clerk: 7%; academia: 11%; unknown: 0%

Employment location for 2015 class: Intl. 2%; N.E. 1%; M.A. 1%; E.N.C. 2%; W.N.C. 1%; S.A. 4%; E.S.C. 2%; W.S.C. 5%; Mt. 6%; Pac. 78%; unknown 0%

Santa Clara University

500 El Camino Real
Santa Clara, CA 95053-0421
www.scu.edu/law
Private
Admissions: (408) 554-4800
Email: lawadmissions@scu.edu
Financial aid: (408) 554-5048
Application deadline: 02/15
Tuition: full time: $1,688/credit hour; part time: $1,688/credit hour
Room/board/expenses: $24,416
Median grant: $20,000
Average student indebtedness at graduation: $149,940
Enrollment: full time: 537; part time: 121
men: 47%; women: 53%; minorities: 46%
Acceptance rate (full time): 71%
Midrange LSAT (full time): 151-157
Midrange undergraduate GPA (full time): 2.93-3.40
Midrange of full-time private-sector salaries of 2015 grads: $65,780-$160,000
2015 grads employed in: law firms: 57%; business and industry: 31%; government: 9%; public interest: 1%; judicial clerk: 0%; academia: 2%; unknown: 0%
Employment location for 2015 class: Intl. 0%; N.E. 1%; M.A. 1%; E.N.C. 1%; W.N.C. 0%; S.A. 2%; E.S.C. 0%; W.S.C. 1%; Mt. 3%; Pac. 93%; unknown 0%

Southwestern Law School

3050 Wilshire Boulevard
Los Angeles, CA 90010-1106
www.swlaw.edu
Private
Admissions: (213) 738-6834
Email: admissions@swlaw.edu
Financial aid: (213) 738-6719
Application deadline: 04/01
Tuition: full time: $50,090; part time: $33,470
Room/board/expenses: $30,042
Median grant: $19,700
Enrollment: full time: 607; part time: 258
men: 44%; women: 56%; minorities: 48%
Acceptance rate (full time): 51%
Midrange LSAT (full time): 150-155
Midrange undergraduate GPA (full time): 2.99-3.44
Midrange of full-time private-sector salaries of 2015 grads: $47,000-$75,000
2015 grads employed in: law firms: 63%; business and industry: 27%; government: 2%; public interest: 3%; judicial clerk: 1%; academia: 2%; unknown: 0%
Employment location for 2015 class: Intl. 0%; N.E. 0%; M.A. 0%; E.N.C. 0%; W.N.C. 0%; S.A. 0%; E.S.C. 0%; W.S.C. 0%; Mt. 0%; Pac. 97%; unknown 1%

Stanford University

Crown Quadrangle
559 Nathan Abbott Way
Stanford, CA 94305-8610
law.stanford.edu
Private
Admissions: (650) 723-4985
Email:
admissions@law.stanford.edu
Financial aid: (650) 723-9247
Application deadline: 02/01
Tuition: full time: $58,236; part
time: N/A
Room/board/expenses: $30,933
Median grant: $24,163
Average student indebtedness at
graduation: $137,625
Enrollment: full time: 579; part
time: N/A
men: 51%; women: 49%;
minorities: 35%
Acceptance rate (full time): 11%
Midrange LSAT (full time): 168-173
Midrange undergraduate GPA (full
time): 3.75-3.95
Midrange of full-time private-sector
salaries of 2015 grads: $160,000-
$160,000
2015 grads employed in: law firms:
55%; business and industry:
7%; government: 3%; public
interest: 7%; judicial clerk: 27%;
academia: 1%; unknown: 0%
Employment location for 2015 class:
Intl. 1%; N.E. 3%; M.A. 19%;
E.N.C. 4%; W.N.C. 1%; S.A. 15%;
E.S.C. 1%; W.S.C. 7%; Mt. 2%;
Pac. 47%; unknown 0%

Thomas Jefferson School of Law

1155 Island Avenue
San Diego, CA 92101
www.tjsl.edu
Private
Admissions: (619) 297-9700
Email: admissions@tjsl.edu
Financial aid: (619) 961-4271
Application deadline: 08/01
Tuition: full time: $47,600; part
time: $35,700
Room/board/expenses: $27,150
Median grant: $10,500
Average student indebtedness at
graduation: $182,411
Enrollment: full time: 436; part
time: 136
men: 43%; women: 57%;
minorities: 56%
Acceptance rate (full time): 83%
Midrange LSAT (full time): 140-147
Midrange undergraduate GPA (full
time): 2.66-3.14
Midrange of full-time private-sector
salaries of 2015 grads: $40,000-
$70,000
2015 grads employed in: law firms:
61%; business and industry:
23%; government: 8%; public
interest: 1%; judicial clerk: 2%;
academia: 4%; unknown: 0%
Employment location for 2015 class:
Intl. 0%; N.E. 0%; M.A. 3%;
E.N.C. 0%; W.N.C. 0%; S.A. 1%;
E.S.C. 0%; W.S.C. 4%; Mt. 7%;
Pac. 85%; unknown 0%

University of California-Berkeley

Boalt Hall
Berkeley, CA 94720-7200
www.law.berkeley.edu
Public
Admissions: (510) 642-2274

Email: admissions@
law.berkeley.edu
Financial aid: (510) 642-1563
Application deadline: 02/01
In-state tuition: full time: $48,703;
part time: N/A
Out-of-state tuition: full time:
$52,654
Room/board/expenses: $30,526
Median grant: $20,000
Average student indebtedness at
graduation: $145,260
Enrollment: full time: 925; part
time: 1
men: 42%; women: 58%;
minorities: 37%
Acceptance rate (full time): 23%
Midrange of full-time private-sector
salaries of 2015 grads: $150,000-
$160,000
2015 grads employed in: law firms:
61%; business and industry:
2%; government: 6%; public
interest: 15%; judicial clerk: 14%;
academia: 1%; unknown: 0%
Employment location for 2015 class:
Intl. 1%; N.E. 2%; M.A. 14%;
E.N.C. 2%; W.N.C. 1%; S.A. 8%;
E.S.C. 2%; W.S.C. 2%; Mt. 3%;
Pac. 65%; unknown 0%

University of California-Davis

400 Mrak Hall Drive
Davis, CA 95616-5201
www.law.ucdavis.edu/jd
Public
Admissions: (530) 752-6477
Email:
admissions@law.ucdavis.edu
Financial aid: (530) 752-6573
Application deadline: 03/15
In-state tuition: full time: $47,409;
part time: N/A
Out-of-state tuition: full time:
$56,660
Room/board/expenses: $22,518
Median grant: $32,500
Average student indebtedness at
graduation: $103,811
Enrollment: full time: 505; part
time: N/A
men: 47%; women: 53%;
minorities: 42%
Acceptance rate (full time): 33%
Midrange LSAT (full time): 158-164
Midrange undergraduate GPA (full
time): 3.31-3.72
Midrange of full-time private-sector
salaries of 2015 grads: $80,000-
$145,000
2015 grads employed in: law firms:
55%; business and industry:
10%; government: 16%; public
interest: 8%; judicial clerk: 3%;
academia: 7%; unknown: 0%
Employment location for 2015 class:
Intl. 1%; N.E. 0%; M.A. 2%;
E.N.C. 0%; W.N.C. 0%; S.A. 2%;
E.S.C. 0%; W.S.C. 0%; Mt. 2%;
Pac. 93%; unknown 0%

University of California (Hastings)

200 McAllister Street
San Francisco, CA 94102
www.uchastings.edu
Public
Admissions: (415) 565-4623
Email:
admissions@uchastings.edu
Financial aid: (415) 565-4624
Application deadline: 03/01

In-state tuition: full time: $44,218;
part time: N/A
Out-of-state tuition: full time:
$50,218
Room/board/expenses: $26,508
Median grant: $14,500
Average student indebtedness at
graduation: $137,157
Enrollment: full time: 930; part
time: 3
men: 44%; women: 56%;
minorities: 39%
Acceptance rate (full time): 47%
Midrange LSAT (full time): 156-161
Midrange undergraduate GPA (full
time): 3.18-3.64
Midrange of full-time private-sector
salaries of 2015 grads: $75,000-
$160,000
2015 grads employed in: law firms:
59%; business and industry:
15%; government: 11%; public
interest: 8%; judicial clerk: 3%;
academia: 2%; unknown: 0%
Employment location for 2015
class: Intl. 0%; N.E. 0%; M.A. 2%;
E.N.C. 1%; W.N.C. 0%; S.A. 2%;
E.S.C. 0%; W.S.C. 0%; Mt. 1%;
Pac. 93%; unknown 0%

University of California-Irvine

401 East Peltason Drive
Suite 1000
Irvine, CA 92697-8000
www.law.uci.edu/
Public
Admissions: (949) 824-4545
Email: lawadmit@law.uci.edu
Financial aid: (949) 824-8080
Application deadline: 03/01
In-state tuition: full time: $44,819;
part time: N/A
Out-of-state tuition: full time:
$51,313
Room/board/expenses: $27,504
Median grant: $25,000
Average student indebtedness at
graduation: $100,408
Enrollment: full time: 356; part
time: N/A
men: 48%; women: 52%;
minorities: 45%
Acceptance rate (full time): 27%
Midrange LSAT (full time): 160-165
Midrange undergraduate GPA (full
time): 3.32-3.68
Midrange of full-time private-sector
salaries of 2015 grads: $75,000-
$160,000
2015 grads employed in: law firms:
38%; business and industry:
3%; government: 21%; public
interest: 19%; judicial clerk: 17%;
academia: 1%; unknown: 0%
Employment location for 2015
class: Intl. 0%; N.E. 2%; M.A. 6%;
E.N.C. 2%; W.N.C. 1%; S.A. 5%;
E.S.C. 1%; W.S.C. 1%; Mt. 2%;
Pac. 76%; unknown 0%

University of California-Los Angeles

71 Dodd Hall
PO Box 951445
Los Angeles, CA 90095-1445
www.ucla.edu
Public
Admissions: (310) 825-2260
Email: admissions@law.ucla.edu
Financial aid: (310) 825-2459
Application deadline: 02/01
In-state tuition: full time: $45,338;
part time: N/A

Out-of-state tuition: full time:
$51,832
Room/board/expenses: $26,899
Median grant: $21,000
Average student indebtedness at
graduation: $118,291
Enrollment: full time: 979; part
time: N/A
men: 50%; women: 50%;
minorities: 33%
Acceptance rate (full time): 28%
Midrange LSAT (full time): 163-168
Midrange undergraduate GPA (full
time): 3.49-3.84
Midrange of full-time private-sector
salaries of 2015 grads: $90,000-
$160,000
2015 grads employed in: law firms:
66%; business and industry:
10%; government: 6%; public
interest: 9%; judicial clerk: 7%;
academia: 2%; unknown: 0%
Employment location for 2015
class: Intl. 2%; N.E. 1%; M.A. 4%;
E.N.C. 1%; W.N.C. 0%; S.A. 3%;
E.S.C. 0%; W.S.C. 1%; Mt. 3%;
Pac. 86%; unknown 0%

University of La Verne[1]

320 E. D Street
Ontario, CA 91764
law.laverne.edu
Private
Admissions: (909) 460-2006
Email: lawadm@laverne.edu
Tuition: N/A
Room/board/expenses: N/A
Enrollment: N/A

University of San Diego

5998 Alcala Park
San Diego, CA 92110-2492
www.law.sandiego.edu
Private
Admissions: (619) 260-4528
Email: jdinfo@SanDiego.edu
Financial aid: (619) 260-4570
Application deadline: rolling
Tuition: full time: $50,201; part
time: $37,191
Room/board/expenses: $21,652
Median grant: $25,500
Average student indebtedness at
graduation: $127,693
Enrollment: full time: 598; part
time: 98
men: 51%; women: 49%;
minorities: 33%
Acceptance rate (full time): 40%
Midrange LSAT (full time): 155-160
Midrange undergraduate GPA (full
time): 3.22-3.67
Midrange of full-time private-sector
salaries of 2015 grads: $65,000-
$100,000
2015 grads employed in: law firms:
65%; business and industry:
18%; government: 9%; public
interest: 3%; judicial clerk: 4%;
academia: 1%; unknown: 0%
Employment location for 2015 class:
Intl. 0%; N.E. 0%; M.A. 0%;
E.N.C. 0%; W.N.C. 0%; S.A. 1%;
E.S.C. 0%; W.S.C. 0%; Mt. 2%;
Pac. 89%; unknown 9%

University of San Francisco

2130 Fulton Street
San Francisco, CA 94117-1080
www.usfca.edu/law
Private
Admissions: (415) 422-6586

Email:
lawadmissions@usfca.edu
Financial aid: (415) 422-6210
Application deadline: 02/01
Tuition: full time: $48,220; part
time: $1,720/credit hour
Room/board/expenses: $31,518
Median grant: $26,879
Average student indebtedness at
graduation: $167,671
Enrollment: full time: 425; part
time: 99
men: 45%; women: 55%;
minorities: 54%
Acceptance rate (full time): 64%
Midrange LSAT (full time): 148-154
Midrange undergraduate GPA (full
time): 2.74-3.37
Midrange of full-time private-sector
salaries of 2015 grads: $58,500-
$100,000
2015 grads employed in: law firms:
54%; business and industry:
26%; government: 15%; public
interest: 3%; judicial clerk: 1%;
academia: 1%; unknown: 0%
Employment location for 2015
class: Intl. 3%; N.E. 1%; M.A. 3%;
E.N.C. 1%; W.N.C. 0%; S.A. 1%;
E.S.C. 1%; W.S.C. 0%; Mt. 3%;
Pac. 88%; unknown 0%

University of Southern California (Gould)

699 Exposition Boulevard
Los Angeles, CA 90089-0071
gould.usc.edu
Private
Admissions: (213) 740-2523
Email: admissions@law.usc.edu
Financial aid: (213) 740-6314
Application deadline: 04/01
Tuition: full time: $60,339; part
time: N/A
Room/board/expenses: $22,978
Median grant: $30,000
Average student indebtedness at
graduation: $140,745
Enrollment: full time: 649; part
time: N/A
men: 51%; women: 49%;
minorities: 36%
Acceptance rate (full time): 30%
Midrange LSAT (full time): 162-166
Midrange undergraduate GPA (full
time): 3.56-3.85
Midrange of full-time private-sector
salaries of 2015 grads: $75,000-
$160,000
2015 grads employed in: law firms:
65%; business and industry:
11%; government: 10%; public
interest: 9%; judicial clerk: 6%;
academia: 1%; unknown: 0%
Employment location for 2015
class: Intl. 2%; N.E. 0%; M.A. 2%;
E.N.C. 2%; W.N.C. 1%; S.A. 2%;
E.S.C. 1%; W.S.C. 1%; Mt. 1%;
Pac. 90%; unknown 0%

University of the Pacific (McGeorge)

3200 Fifth Avenue
Sacramento, CA 95817
www.mcgeorge.edu
Private
Admissions: (916) 739-7105
Email: mcgeorge@pacific.edu
Financial aid: (916) 739-7158
Application deadline: 04/01
Tuition: full time: $49,820; part
time: $33,120
Room/board/expenses: $25,350
Median grant: $13,046

Average student indebtedness at graduation: $144,431
Enrollment: full time: 357; part time: 115
men: 46%; women: 54%; minorities: 30%
Acceptance rate (full time): 71%
Midrange LSAT (full time): 149-155
Midrange undergraduate GPA (full time): 3.01-3.46
Midrange of full-time private-sector salaries of 2015 grads: $55,000-$77,000
2015 grads employed in: law firms: 52%; business and industry: 12%; government: 25%; public interest: 10%; judicial clerk: 1%; academia: 1%; unknown: 0%
Employment location for 2015 class: Intl. 2%; N.E. 1%; M.A. 0%; E.N.C. 0%; W.N.C. 0%; S.A. 2%; E.S.C. 0%; W.S.C. 1%; Mt. 2%; Pac. 92%; unknown 0%

Western State College of Law at Argosy University

1 Banting
Irvine, CA 92618
www.wsulaw.edu
Private
Admissions: (714) 459-1101
Email: adm@wsulaw.edu
Financial aid: (714) 459-1120
Application deadline: rolling
Tuition: full time: $43,350; part time: $29,150
Room/board/expenses: $31,385
Median grant: $21,430
Average student indebtedness at graduation: $119,382
Enrollment: full time: 225; part time: 125
men: 47%; women: 53%; minorities: 59%
Acceptance rate (full time): 61%
Midrange LSAT (full time): 145-150
Midrange undergraduate GPA (full time): 2.84-3.26
Midrange of full-time private-sector salaries of 2015 grads: $46,000-$67,500
2015 grads employed in: law firms: 64%; business and industry: 21%; government: 9%; public interest: 3%; judicial clerk: %; academia: 4%; unknown: 0%
Employment location for 2015 class: Intl. N/A; N.E. 1%; M.A. 1%; E.N.C. N/A; W.N.C. N/A; S.A. 3%; E.S.C. N/A; W.S.C. N/A; Mt. N/A; Pac. 3%; unknown 1%

Whittier College

3333 Harbor Boulevard
Costa Mesa, CA 92626-1501
www.law.whittier.edu
Private
Admissions: (800) 808-8188
Email: info@law.whittier.edu
Financial aid: (714) 444-4141
Application deadline: rolling
Tuition: full time: $45,350; part time: $30,400
Room/board/expenses: $32,136
Median grant: $18,000
Average student indebtedness at graduation: $179,056
Enrollment: full time: 275; part time: 116
men: 40%; women: 60%; minorities: 59%
Acceptance rate (full time): 69%
Midrange LSAT (full time): 144-149

Midrange undergraduate GPA (full time): 2.61-3.08
Midrange of full-time private-sector salaries of 2015 grads: $40,000-$65,000
2015 grads employed in: law firms: 61%; business and industry: 23%; government: 6%; public interest: 5%; judicial clerk: 0%; academia: 5%; unknown: 0%
Employment location for 2015 class: Intl. 0%; N.E. 0%; M.A. 0%; E.N.C. 0%; W.N.C. 0%; S.A. 0%; E.S.C. 0%; W.S.C. 1%; Mt. 2%; Pac. 96%; unknown 1%

COLORADO

University of Colorado-Boulder

Box 401
Boulder, CO 80309-0401
www.colorado.edu/law/
Public
Admissions: (303) 492-7203
Email: law.admissions@colorado.edu
Financial aid: (303) 492-0647
Application deadline: 03/15
In-state tuition: full time: $31,831; part time: N/A
Out-of-state tuition: full time: $38,623
Room/board/expenses: $19,430
Median grant: $11,000
Average student indebtedness at graduation: $100,499
Enrollment: full time: 523; part time: 6
men: 50%; women: 50%; minorities: 19%
Acceptance rate (full time): 34%
Midrange LSAT (full time): 156-164
Midrange undergraduate GPA (full time): 3.37-3.79
Midrange of full-time private-sector salaries of 2015 grads: $55,750-$110,000
2015 grads employed in: law firms: 29%; business and industry: 14%; government: 14%; public interest: 15%; judicial clerk: 24%; academia: 4%; unknown: 0%
Employment location for 2015 class: Intl. 0%; N.E. 1%; M.A. 3%; E.N.C. 1%; W.N.C. 1%; S.A. 4%; E.S.C. 0%; W.S.C. 1%; Mt. 87%; Pac. 3%; unknown 0%

University of Denver (Sturm)

2255 E. Evans Avenue
Denver, CO 80208
www.law.du.edu
Private
Admissions: (303) 871-6135
Email: admissions@law.du.edu
Financial aid: (303) 871-6362
Application deadline: rolling
Tuition: full time: $46,720; part time: $34,292
Room/board/expenses: $17,204
Median grant: $22,500
Average student indebtedness at graduation: $150,055
Enrollment: full time: 673; part time: 107
men: 48%; women: 52%; minorities: 21%
Acceptance rate (full time): 53%
Midrange LSAT (full time): 154-159
Midrange undergraduate GPA (full time): 3.13-3.60

Midrange of full-time private-sector salaries of 2015 grads: $59,750-$100,000
2015 grads employed in: law firms: 39%; business and industry: 19%; government: 19%; public interest: 3%; judicial clerk: 17%; academia: 3%; unknown: 0%
Employment location for 2015 class: Intl. 1%; N.E. 0%; M.A. 0%; E.N.C. 1%; W.N.C. 1%; S.A. 3%; E.S.C. 0%; W.S.C. 2%; Mt. 87%; Pac. 3%; unknown 0%

CONNECTICUT

Quinnipiac University

275 Mount Carmel Avenue
Hamden, CT 06518
law.qu.edu
Private
Admissions: (203) 582-3400
Email: law@qu.edu
Financial aid: (203) 582-3405
Application deadline: rolling
Tuition: full time: $48,085; part time: $33,895
Room/board/expenses: $19,658
Median grant: $30,000
Average student indebtedness at graduation: $101,371
Enrollment: full time: 215; part time: 63
men: 47%; women: 53%; minorities: 17%
Acceptance rate (full time): 54%
Midrange LSAT (full time): 150-155
Midrange undergraduate GPA (full time): 3.13-3.73
Midrange of full-time private-sector salaries of 2015 grads: $50,000-$83,000
2015 grads employed in: law firms: 58%; business and industry: 22%; government: 10%; public interest: 4%; judicial clerk: 5%; academia: 1%; unknown: 0%
Employment location for 2015 class: Intl. 0%; N.E. 76%; M.A. 12%; E.N.C. 2%; W.N.C. 0%; S.A. 6%; E.S.C. 0%; W.S.C. 0%; Mt. 1%; Pac. 1%; unknown 0%

University of Connecticut

55 Elizabeth Street
Hartford, CT 06105-2296
www.law.uconn.edu
Public
Admissions: (860) 570-5100
Email: law.admissions@uconn.edu
Financial aid: (000) 570-5147
Application deadline: 04/01
In-state tuition: full time: $28,634; part time: $20,202
Out-of-state tuition: full time: $58,802
Room/board/expenses: $17,520
Median grant: $11,000
Average student indebtedness at graduation: $72,042
Enrollment: full time: 287; part time: 104
men: 52%; women: 48%; minorities: 24%
Acceptance rate (full time): 49%
Midrange LSAT (full time): 154-159
Midrange undergraduate GPA (full time): 3.10-3.65
Midrange of full-time private-sector salaries of 2015 grads: $60,000-$105,000
2015 grads employed in: law firms: 43%; business and industry:

25%; government: 14%; public interest: 5%; judicial clerk: 13%; academia: 0%; unknown: 0%
Employment location for 2015 class: Intl. 1%; N.E. 81%; M.A. 10%; E.N.C. 0%; W.N.C. 0%; S.A. 6%; E.S.C. 1%; W.S.C. N/A; Mt. 0%; Pac. 1%; unknown 0%

Yale University

PO Box 208215
New Haven, CT 06520-8215
www.law.yale.edu
Private
Admissions: (203) 432-4995
Email: admissions.law@yale.edu
Financial aid: (203) 432-1688
Application deadline: 02/28
Tuition: full time: $59,865; part time: N/A
Room/board/expenses: $20,364
Median grant: $26,491
Average student indebtedness at graduation: $121,815
Enrollment: full time: 632; part time: 1
men: 52%; women: 48%; minorities: 33%
Acceptance rate (full time): 9%
Midrange LSAT (full time): 170-175
Midrange undergraduate GPA (full time): 3.79-3.97
Midrange of full-time private-sector salaries of 2015 grads: $160,000-$160,000
2015 grads employed in: law firms: 42%; business and industry: 4%; government: 6%; public interest: 9%; judicial clerk: 39%; academia: 1%; unknown: 0%
Employment location for 2015 class: Intl. 3%; N.E. 8%; M.A. 37%; E.N.C. 6%; W.N.C. 0%; S.A. 21%; E.S.C. 3%; W.S.C. 3%; Mt. 3%; Pac. 16%; unknown 0%

DELAWARE

Widener University Delaware

Wilmington, DE 19803-0406
delawarelaw.widener.edu
Private
Admissions: (302) 477-2703
Email: delawarelaw@widener.edu
Financial aid: (302) 477-2272
Application deadline: 05/15
Tuition: full time: $1,452/credit hour; part time: $1,452/credit hour
Room/board/expenses: $21,620
Median grant: $16,462
Average student indebtedness at graduation: $135,151
Enrollment: full time: 266; part time: 137
men: 48%; women: 52%; minorities: 24%
Acceptance rate (full time): 67%
Midrange LSAT (full time): 146-150
Midrange undergraduate GPA (full time): 2.81-3.36
Midrange of full-time private-sector salaries of 2015 grads: $52,250-$75,000
2015 grads employed in: law firms: 38%; business and industry: 22%; government: 14%; public interest: 1%; judicial clerk: 24%; academia: 1%; unknown: 0%
Employment location for 2015 class: Intl. 0%; N.E. 1%; M.A. 63%; E.N.C. 0%; W.N.C. 0%; S.A.

34%; E.S.C. 0%; W.S.C. 1%; Mt. 0%; Pac. 1%; unknown 0%

DISTRICT OF COLUMBIA

American University (Washington)

4801 Massachusetts Avenue NW
Washington, DC 20016-8192
www.wcl.american.edu
Private
Admissions: (202) 274-4101
Email: wcladmit@wcl.american.edu
Financial aid: (202) 274-4040
Application deadline: 03/01
Tuition: full time: $53,016; part time: $37,011
Room/board/expenses: $23,688
Median grant: $15,000
Average student indebtedness at graduation: $164,194
Enrollment: full time: 1,035; part time: 242
men: 38%; women: 62%; minorities: 39%
Acceptance rate (full time): 54%
Midrange LSAT (full time): 152-159
Midrange undergraduate GPA (full time): 3.16-3.60
Midrange of full-time private-sector salaries of 2015 grads: $75,000-$160,000
2015 grads employed in: law firms: 29%; business and industry: 14%; government: 24%; public interest: 17%; judicial clerk: 15%; academia: 2%; unknown: 0%
Employment location for 2015 class: Intl. 3%; N.E. 1%; M.A. 13%; E.N.C. 2%; W.N.C. 1%; S.A. 71%; E.S.C. 1%; W.S.C. 2%; Mt. 0%; Pac. 5%; unknown 0%

The Catholic University of America

3600 John McCormack Road NE
Washington, DC 20064
www.law.edu
Private
Admissions: (202) 319-5151
Email: admissions@law.edu
Financial aid: (202) 319-5143
Application deadline: 06/30
Tuition: full time: $48,020; part time: $36,200
Room/board/expenses: $24,644
Median grant: $16,000
Average student indebtedness at graduation: $133,917
Enrollment: full time: 261; part time: 119
men: 49%; women: 51%; minorities: 18%
Acceptance rate (full time): 52%
Midrange LSAT (full time): 150-155
Midrange undergraduate GPA (full time): 3.12-3.51
Midrange of full-time private-sector salaries of 2015 grads: $52,000-$160,000
2015 grads employed in: law firms: 32%; business and industry: 16%; government: 29%; public interest: 8%; judicial clerk: 13%; academia: 3%; unknown: 0%
Employment location for 2015 class: Intl. 1%; N.E. 3%; M.A. 10%; E.N.C. 2%; W.N.C. 0%; S.A. 83%; E.S.C. 0%; W.S.C. 0%; Mt. 0%; Pac. 2%; unknown 0%

Georgetown University

600 New Jersey Avenue NW
Washington, DC 20001-2075
www.law.georgetown.edu
Private
Admissions: (202) 662-9015
Email:
lawadmis@georgetown.edu
Financial aid: (202) 662-9210
Application deadline: 03/01
Tuition: full time: $57,576; part time: $39,064
Room/board/expenses: $27,924
Median grant: $20,000
Average student indebtedness at graduation: $166,027
Enrollment: full time: 1,721; part time: 242
men: 51%; women: 49%; minorities: 19%
Acceptance rate (full time): 26%
Midrange LSAT (full time): 162-168
Midrange undergraduate GPA (full time): 3.53-3.86
Midrange of full-time private-sector salaries of 2015 grads: $160,000-$160,000
2015 grads employed in: law firms: 52%; business and industry: 8%; government: 15%; public interest: 16%; judicial clerk: 8%; academia: 1%; unknown: 0%
Employment location for 2015 class: Intl. 2%; N.E. 3%; M.A. 28%; E.N.C. 2%; W.N.C. 1%; S.A. 49%; E.S.C. 0%; W.S.C. 2%; Mt. 1%; Pac. 10%; unknown 1%

George Washington University

2000 H Street NW
Washington, DC 20052
www.law.gwu.edu
Private
Admissions: (202) 994-7235
Email: jdadmit@law.gwu.edu
Financial aid: (202) 994-6592
Application deadline: 03/01
Tuition: full time: $56,244; part time: $1,980/credit hour
Room/board/expenses: $26,656
Median grant: $17,000
Average student indebtedness at graduation: $145,240
Enrollment: full time: 1,460; part time: 209
men: 46%; women: 54%; minorities: 26%
Acceptance rate (full time): 40%
Midrange LSAT (full time): 159-166
Midrange undergraduate GPA (full time): 3.35-3.80
Midrange of full-time private-sector salaries of 2015 grads: $138,750-$160,000
2015 grads employed in: law firms: 51%; business and industry: 12%; government: 19%; public interest: 10%; judicial clerk: 7%; academia: 1%; unknown: 0%
Employment location for 2015 class: Intl. 2%; N.E. 1%; M.A. 17%; E.N.C. 1%; W.N.C. 0%; S.A. 68%; E.S.C. 0%; W.S.C. 2%; Mt. 1%; Pac. 5%; unknown 0%

Howard University

2900 Van Ness Street NW
Washington, DC 20008
www.law.howard.edu
Private
Admissions: (202) 806-8009
Email:
admissions@law.howard.edu
Financial aid: (202) 806-8005
Application deadline: 03/15
Tuition: full time: $37,534; part time: N/A
Room/board/expenses: $23,512
Median grant: $16,000
Average student indebtedness at graduation: $50,920
Enrollment: full time: 395; part time: 1
men: 30%; women: 70%; minorities: 94%
Acceptance rate (full time): 39%
Midrange LSAT (full time): 148-153
Midrange undergraduate GPA (full time): 2.98-3.46
Midrange of full-time private-sector salaries of 2015 grads: $55,875-$160,000
2015 grads employed in: law firms: 27%; business and industry: 12%; government: 31%; public interest: 6%; judicial clerk: 19%; academia: 1%; unknown: 0%
Employment location for 2015 class: Intl. 0%; N.E. 5%; M.A. 19%; E.N.C. 2%; W.N.C. 1%; S.A. 58%; E.S.C. 4%; W.S.C. 4%; Mt. 0%; Pac. 7%; unknown 1%

University of the District of Columbia (Clarke)

4200 Connecticut Avenue NW
Building 38 & 52
Washington, DC 20008
www.law.udc.edu
Public
Admissions: (202) 274-7341
Email: tajira.mccoy@udc.edu
Financial aid: (202) 274-7337
Application deadline: 08/01
In-state tuition: full time: $13,260; part time: $379/credit hour
Out-of-state tuition: full time: $24,428
Room/board/expenses: $26,200
Median grant: $8,500
Average student indebtedness at graduation: $105,330
Enrollment: full time: 139; part time: 135
men: 39%; women: 61%; minorities: 66%
Acceptance rate (full time): 44%
Midrange LSAT (full time): 145-149
Midrange undergraduate GPA (full time): 2.76-3.24
Midrange of full-time private-sector salaries of 2015 grads: $50,000-$75,000
2015 grads employed in: law firms: 25%; business and industry: 33%; government: 27%; public interest: 8%; judicial clerk: 6%; academia: 0%; unknown: 0%
Employment location for 2015 class: Intl. 0%; N.E. 2%; M.A. 8%; E.N.C. 0%; W.N.C. 0%; S.A. 83%; E.S.C. 2%; W.S.C. 0%; Mt. 0%; Pac. 4%; unknown 2%

FLORIDA

Ave Maria School of Law

1025 Commons Circle
Naples, FL 34119
www.avemarialaw.edu
Private
Admissions: (239) 687-5420
Email: info@avemarialaw.edu
Financial aid: (239) 687-5335
Application deadline: 07/15
Tuition: full time: $41,706; part time: N/A
Room/board/expenses: $23,834
Median grant: $16,000
Average student indebtedness at graduation: $152,476
Enrollment: full time: 240; part time: 8
men: 48%; women: 52%; minorities: 31%
Acceptance rate (full time): 54%
Midrange LSAT (full time): 143-151
Midrange undergraduate GPA (full time): 2.84-3.38
Midrange of full-time private-sector salaries of 2015 grads: $48,500-$72,500
2015 grads employed in: law firms: 52%; business and industry: 17%; government: 23%; public interest: 5%; judicial clerk: 0%; academia: 3%; unknown: 0%
Employment location for 2015 class: Intl. 0%; N.E. 0%; M.A. 8%; E.N.C. 5%; W.N.C. 3%; S.A. 70%; E.S.C. 6%; W.S.C. 5%; Mt. 2%; Pac. 2%; unknown 0%

Barry University

6441 E. Colonial Drive
Orlando, FL 32807
www.barry.edu/law/
Private
Admissions: (321) 206-5657
Email: lawadmissions@barry.edu
Financial aid: (321) 206-5621
Application deadline: 05/01
Tuition: full time: $35,844; part time: $27,070
Room/board/expenses: $26,000
Median grant: $11,000
Average student indebtedness at graduation: $151,479
Enrollment: full time: 431; part time: 188
men: 43%; women: 57%; minorities: 48%
Acceptance rate (full time): 58%
Midrange LSAT (full time): 146-151
Midrange undergraduate GPA (full time): 2.59-3.32
Midrange of full-time private-sector salaries of 2015 grads: N/A-N/A
2015 grads employed in: law firms: 49%; business and industry: 25%; government: 21%; public interest: 3%; judicial clerk: 1%; academia: 1%; unknown: 0%
Employment location for 2015 class: Intl. 1%; N.E. N/A; M.A. 4%; E.N.C. 1%; W.N.C. N/A; S.A. 88%; E.S.C. N/A; W.S.C. 2%; Mt. 3%; Pac. 2%; unknown 0%

Florida A&M University

201 Beggs Avenue
Orlando, FL 32801
law.famu.edu/
Public
Admissions: (407) 254-3286
Email: famulaw.admissions@famu.edu
Financial aid: (407) 254-3232
Application deadline: 05/31
In-state tuition: full time: $14,132; part time: $10,029
Out-of-state tuition: full time: $34,035
Room/board/expenses: $28,770
Median grant: $5,158
Average student indebtedness at graduation: $20,500
Enrollment: full time: 311; part time: 142
men: 40%; women: 60%; minorities: 71%
Acceptance rate (full time): 53%
Midrange LSAT (full time): 143-148
Midrange undergraduate GPA (full time): 2.80-3.32
Midrange of full-time private-sector salaries of 2015 grads: $40,000-$64,250
2015 grads employed in: law firms: 51%; business and industry: 27%; government: 10%; public interest: 5%; judicial clerk: 3%; academia: 4%; unknown: 0%
Employment location for 2015 class: Intl. 0%; N.E. 0%; M.A. 1%; E.N.C. 1%; W.N.C. 0%; S.A. 93%; E.S.C. 2%; W.S.C. 1%; Mt. 0%; Pac. 3%; unknown 0%

Florida Coastal School of Law

8787 Baypine Road
Jacksonville, FL 32256
www.fcsl.edu
Private
Admissions: (904) 680-7710
Email: admissions@fcsl.edu
Financial aid: (904) 680-7717
Application deadline: 08/01
Tuition: full time: $46,068; part time: $37,362
Room/board/expenses: $19,476
Median grant: $12,500
Average student indebtedness at graduation: $158,878
Enrollment: full time: 580; part time: 75
men: 44%; women: 56%; minorities: 43%
Acceptance rate (full time): 60%
Midrange LSAT (full time): 141-149
Midrange undergraduate GPA (full time): 2.56-3.26
Midrange of full-time private-sector salaries of 2015 grads: $40,000-$60,000
2015 grads employed in: law firms: 48%; business and industry: 21%; government: 18%; public interest: 8%; judicial clerk: 2%; academia: 3%; unknown: 0%
Employment location for 2015 class: Intl. 0%; N.E. 2%; M.A. 2%; E.N.C. 2%; W.N.C. 0%; S.A. 82%; E.S.C. 2%; W.S.C. 5%; Mt. 2%; Pac. 1%; unknown 0%

Florida International University

Modesto A. Maidique Campus
RDB 2015
Miami, FL 33199
law.fiu.edu
Public
Admissions: (305) 348-8006
Email: lawadmit@fiu.edu
Financial aid: (305) 348-8006
Application deadline: 07/01
In-state tuition: full time: $21,806; part time: $14,900

Out-of-state tuition: full time: $36,050
Room/board/expenses: $25,918
Median grant: $5,000
Average student indebtedness at graduation: $93,838
Enrollment: full time: 391; part time: 86
men: 48%; women: 52%; minorities: 63%
Acceptance rate (full time): 29%
Midrange LSAT (full time): 152-157
Midrange undergraduate GPA (full time): 3.07-3.79
Midrange of full-time private-sector salaries of 2015 grads: N/A-N/A
2015 grads employed in: law firms: %; business and industry: %; government: %; public interest: %; judicial clerk: %; academia: %; unknown: %
Employment location for 2015 class: Intl. N/A; N.E. N/A; M.A. N/A; E.N.C. N/A; W.N.C. N/A; S.A. N/A; E.S.C. N/A; W.S.C. N/A; Mt. N/A; Pac. N/A; unknown N/A

Florida State University

425 W. Jefferson Street
Tallahassee, FL 32306-1601
www.law.fsu.edu
Public
Admissions: (850) 644-3787
Email: admissions@law.fsu.edu
Financial aid: (850) 644-7338
Application deadline: 07/15
In-state tuition: full time: $20,683; part time: N/A
Out-of-state tuition: full time: $40,695
Room/board/expenses: $17,190
Median grant: $10,500
Average student indebtedness at graduation: $88,732
Enrollment: full time: 537; part time: 39
men: 54%; women: 46%; minorities: 29%
Acceptance rate (full time): 34%
Midrange LSAT (full time): 157-160
Midrange undergraduate GPA (full time): 3.32-3.72
Midrange of full-time private-sector salaries of 2015 grads: $52,000-$75,000
2015 grads employed in: law firms: 45%; business and industry: 14%; government: 28%; public interest: 4%; judicial clerk: 8%; academia: 2%; unknown: 0%
Employment location for 2015 class: Intl. 0%; N.E. 0%; M.A. 5%; E.N.C. 1%; W.N.C. 0%; S.A. 87%; E.S.C. 2%; W.S.C. 1%; Mt. 0%; Pac. 2%; unknown 0%

Nova Southeastern University (Broad)

3305 College Avenue
Fort Lauderdale, FL 33314-7721
www.law.nova.edu
Private
Admissions: (954) 262-6119
Email: law-admissions@nova.edu
Financial aid: (954) 262-7412
Application deadline: 05/01
Tuition: full time: $38,910; part time: $29,415
Room/board/expenses: $28,553
Median grant: $10,000
Average student indebtedness at graduation: $147,879

Enrollment: full time: 553; part time: 161
men: 44%; women: 56%; minorities: 49%
Acceptance rate (full time): 50%
Midrange LSAT (full time): 146–152
Midrange undergraduate GPA (full time): 2.87–3.35
Midrange of full-time private-sector salaries of 2015 grads: $49,500–$65,000
2015 grads employed in: law firms: 65%; business and industry: 19%; government: 9%; public interest: 4%; judicial clerk: 0%; academia: 3%; unknown: 0%
Employment location for 2015 class: Intl. 0%; N.E. 0%; M.A. 3%; E.N.C. 0%; W.N.C. 0%; S.A. 94%; E.S.C. 0%; W.S.C. 1%; Mt. 1%; Pac. 0%; unknown 0%

Stetson University
1401 61st Street S
Gulfport, FL 33707
www.law.stetson.edu
Private
Admissions: (727) 562-7802
Email: lawadmit@law.stetson.edu
Financial aid: (727) 562-7813
Application deadline: 05/15
Tuition: full time: $41,454; part time: $28,720
Room/board/expenses: $15,748
Median grant: $13,000
Average student indebtedness at graduation: $128,703
Enrollment: full time: 682; part time: 133
men: 50%; women: 50%; minorities: 27%
Acceptance rate (full time): 52%
Midrange LSAT (full time): 152–156
Midrange undergraduate GPA (full time): 3.08–3.59
Midrange of full-time private-sector salaries of 2015 grads: N/A–N/A
2015 grads employed in: law firms: 49%; business and industry: 23%; government: 18%; public interest: 5%; judicial clerk: 3%; academia: 2%; unknown: 0%
Employment location for 2015 class: Intl. 0%; N.E. 0%; M.A. 2%; E.N.C. 1%; W.N.C. 0%; S.A. 91%; E.S.C. 2%; W.S.C. 1%; Mt. 0%; Pac. 2%; unknown 0%

St. Thomas University[1]
16401 N.W. 37th Avenue
Miami Gardens, FL 33054
www.stu.edu
Private
Admissions: (305) 623-2310
Email: admitme@stu.edu
Financial aid: (305) 474-2409
Tuition: N/A
Room/board/expenses: N/A
Enrollment: N/A

University of Florida (Levin)
PO Box 117620
Gainesville, FL 32611-7620
www.law.ufl.edu
Public
Admissions: (352) 273-0890
Email: admissions@law.ufl.edu
Financial aid: (352) 273-0628
Application deadline: 07/15
In-state tuition: full time: $22,299; part time: N/A

Out-of-state tuition: full time: $38,904
Room/board/expenses: $17,790
Median grant: $6,400
Average student indebtedness at graduation: $82,480
Enrollment: full time: 969; part time: N/A
men: 56%; women: 44%; minorities: 33%
Acceptance rate (full time): 36%
Midrange LSAT (full time): 156–161
Midrange undergraduate GPA (full time): 3.33–3.77
Midrange of full-time private-sector salaries of 2015 grads: $60,000–$99,000
2015 grads employed in: law firms: 64%; business and industry: 8%; government: 20%; public interest: 0%; judicial clerk: 7%; academia: 1%; unknown: 0%
Employment location for 2015 class: Intl. 0%; N.E. 0%; M.A. 2%; E.N.C. 0%; W.N.C. 0%; S.A. 94%; E.S.C. 0%; W.S.C. 0%; Mt. 0%; Pac. 2%; unknown 1%

University of Miami
PO Box 248087
Coral Gables, FL 33124-8087
www.law.miami.edu
Private
Admissions: (305) 284-2795
Email: admissions@law.miami.edu
Financial aid: (305) 284-6000
Application deadline: 07/31
Tuition: full time: $49,042; part time: $1,715/credit hour
Room/board/expenses: $28,592
Median grant: $28,161
Average student indebtedness at graduation: $149,580
Enrollment: full time: 895; part time: 21
men: 53%; women: 47%; minorities: 43%
Acceptance rate (full time): 58%
Midrange LSAT (full time): 155–160
Midrange undergraduate GPA (full time): 3.17–3.59
Midrange of full-time private-sector salaries of 2015 grads: $60,000–$104,000
2015 grads employed in: law firms: 59%; business and industry: 21%; government: 10%; public interest: 4%; judicial clerk: 4%; academia: 2%; unknown: 0%
Employment location for 2015 class: Intl. 1%; N.E. 1%; M.A. 6%; E.N.C. 2%; W.N.C. 1%; S.A. 83%; E.S.C. 1%; W.S.C. 2%; Mt. 2%; Pac. 1%; unknown 0%

GEORGIA

Atlanta's John Marshall Law School[1]
1422 W. Peachtree Street, NW
Atlanta, GA 30309
www.johnmarshall.edu
Private
Admissions: (404) 872-3593
Email: admissions@johnmarshall.edu
Tuition: N/A
Room/board/expenses: N/A
Enrollment: N/A

Emory University
1301 Clifton Road
Atlanta, GA 30322-2770
www.law.emory.edu
Private
Admissions: (404) 727-6802
Email: jdadmission@emory.edu
Financial aid: (404) 727-6039
Application deadline: 03/01
Tuition: full time: $53,350; part time: N/A
Room/board/expenses: $23,682
Median grant: $24,000
Average student indebtedness at graduation: $120,804
Enrollment: full time: 872; part time: N/A
men: 51%; women: 49%; minorities: 30%
Acceptance rate (full time): 37%
Midrange LSAT (full time): 157–166
Midrange undergraduate GPA (full time): 3.40–3.87
Midrange of full-time private-sector salaries of 2015 grads: $80,000–$160,000
2015 grads employed in: law firms: 53%; business and industry: 9%; government: 18%; public interest: 9%; judicial clerk: 6%; academia: 5%; unknown: 0%
Employment location for 2015 class: Intl. 2%; N.E. 1%; M.A. 11%; E.N.C. 1%; W.N.C. 1%; S.A. 72%; E.S.C. 5%; W.S.C. 2%; Mt. 2%; Pac. 3%; unknown 0%

Georgia State University
PO Box 4049
Atlanta, GA 30302-4049
law.gsu.edu
Public
Admissions: (404) 651-2048
Email: lawadmissions@gsu.edu
Financial aid: (404) 651-2227
Application deadline: 03/15
In-state tuition: full time: $16,858; part time: $13,204
Out-of-state tuition: full time: $36,456
Room/board/expenses: $15,438
Median grant: $6,000
Average student indebtedness at graduation: $64,384
Enrollment: full time: 453; part time: 179
men: 51%; women: 49%; minorities: 27%
Acceptance rate (full time): 28%
Midrange LSAT (full time): 155–160
Midrange undergraduate GPA (full time): 3.21–3.62
Midrange of full-time private-sector salaries of 2015 grads: $60,000–$120,000
2015 grads employed in: law firms: 63%; business and industry: 18%; government: 8%; public interest: 4%; judicial clerk: 4%; academia: 3%; unknown: 0%
Employment location for 2015 class: Intl. 1%; N.E. 0%; M.A. 1%; E.N.C. 1%; W.N.C. 1%; S.A. 92%; E.S.C. 2%; W.S.C. 1%; Mt. 1%; Pac. 1%; unknown 0%

Mercer University (George)
1021 Georgia Avenue
Macon, GA 31207-0001
www.law.mercer.edu
Private
Admissions: (478) 301-2605
Email: admissions@law.mercer.edu
Financial aid: (478) 301-5902
Application deadline: 03/15
Tuition: full time: $37,962; part time: N/A
Room/board/expenses: $21,338
Median grant: $12,500
Average student indebtedness at graduation: $135,300
Enrollment: full time: 389; part time: N/A
men: 48%; women: 52%; minorities: 23%
Acceptance rate (full time): 59%
Midrange LSAT (full time): 149–153
Midrange undergraduate GPA (full time): 3.00–3.52
Midrange of full-time private-sector salaries of 2015 grads: $45,000–$65,000
2015 grads employed in: law firms: 54%; business and industry: 6%; government: 20%; public interest: 2%; judicial clerk: 17%; academia: 1%; unknown: 0%
Employment location for 2015 class: Intl. 0%; N.E. 1%; M.A. 0%; E.N.C. 0%; W.N.C. 0%; S.A. 91%; E.S.C. 1%; W.S.C. 1%; Mt. 2%; Pac. 2%; unknown 0%

University of Georgia
225 Herty Drive
Athens, GA 30602
www.law.uga.edu
Public
Admissions: (706) 542-7060
Email: ugajd@uga.edu
Financial aid: (706) 542-6147
Application deadline: 06/01
In-state tuition: full time: $19,488; part time: N/A
Out-of-state tuition: full time: $37,536
Room/board/expenses: $17,008
Median grant: $7,500
Average student indebtedness at graduation: $82,199
Enrollment: full time: 566; part time: N/A
men: 53%; women: 47%; minorities: 17%
Acceptance rate (full time): 30%
Midrange LSAT (full time): 155–160
Midrange undergraduate GPA (full time): 3.21–3.62
Midrange of full-time private-sector salaries of 2015 grads: $72,500–$135,000
2015 grads employed in: law firms: 55%; business and industry: 9%; government: 10%; public interest: 8%; judicial clerk: 14%; academia: 2%; unknown: 1%
Employment location for 2015 class: Intl. 1%; N.E. 1%; M.A. 3%; E.N.C. 1%; W.N.C. 1%; S.A. 82%; E.S.C. 4%; W.S.C. 4%; Mt. 2%; Pac. 1%; unknown 0%

HAWAII

University of Hawaii-Manoa (Richardson)
2515 Dole Street
Honolulu, HI 96822-2328
www.law.hawaii.edu/
Public
Admissions: (808) 956-5557

Email: lawadm@hawaii.edu
Financial aid: (808) 956-5502
Application deadline: 07/01
In-state tuition: full time: $23,142; part time: $933/credit hour
Out-of-state tuition: full time: $46,566
Room/board/expenses: $19,793
Median grant: $4,000
Average student indebtedness at graduation: $82,510
Enrollment: full time: 241; part time: 65
men: 52%; women: 48%; minorities: 71%
Acceptance rate (full time): 49%
Midrange LSAT (full time): 150–156
Midrange undergraduate GPA (full time): 3.04–3.64
Midrange of full-time private-sector salaries of 2015 grads: $50,000–$68,750
2015 grads employed in: law firms: 29%; business and industry: 14%; government: 20%; public interest: 8%; judicial clerk: 28%; academia: %; unknown: 0%
Employment location for 2015 class: Intl. 1%; N.E. 0%; M.A. 0%; E.N.C. 0%; W.N.C. 0%; S.A. 3%; E.S.C. 0%; W.S.C. 2%; Mt. 1%; Pac. 92%; unknown 0%

IDAHO

Concordia University[1]
501 West Front Street
Boise, ID 83702
law.cu-portland.edu/
Private
Admissions: (208) 639-5440
Email: lawadmission@cu-portland.edu
Financial aid: () -
Tuition: N/A
Room/board/expenses: N/A
Enrollment: N/A

University of Idaho
875 Perimeter Drive, MS2321
Moscow, ID 83844-2321
www.uidaho.edu/law/admissions
Public
Admissions: (208) 885-2300
Email: lawadmit@uidaho.edu
Financial aid: (208) 885-6312
Application deadline: 03/15
In-state tuition: full time: $18,664; part time: N/A
Out-of-state tuition: full time: $33,472
Room/board/expenses: $16,318
Median grant: $7,000
Average student indebtedness at graduation: $86,022
Enrollment: full time: 295; part time: 3
men: 57%; women: 43%; minorities: 24%
Acceptance rate (full time): 55%
Midrange LSAT (full time): 148–154
Midrange undergraduate GPA (full time): 2.87–3.55
Midrange of full-time private-sector salaries of 2015 grads: $50,000–$50,000
2015 grads employed in: law firms: 37%; business and industry: 11%; government: 16%; public interest: 1%; judicial clerk: 28%; academia: 6%; unknown: 1%

Employment location for 2015 class:
Intl. 0%; N.E. 0%; M.A. 0%;
E.N.C. 0%; W.N.C. 0%; S.A. 3%;
E.S.C. 0%; W.S.C. 2%; Mt. 70%;
Pac. 24%; unknown 0%

ILLINOIS

DePaul University
25 E. Jackson Boulevard
Chicago, IL 60604
www.law.depaul.edu
Private
Admissions: (312) 362-6831
Email: lawinfo@depaul.edu
Financial aid: (312) 362-8610
Application deadline: 03/01
Tuition: full time: $46,300; part
time: $30,245
Room/board/expenses: $22,598
Median grant: $18,000
Average student indebtedness at
graduation: $126,446
Enrollment: full time: 586; part
time: 141
men: 42%; women: 58%;
minorities: 27%
Acceptance rate (full time): 72%
Midrange LSAT (full time): 149-154
Midrange undergraduate GPA (full
time): 2.81-3.39
Midrange of full-time private-sector
salaries of 2015 grads: $50,000-
$85,000
2015 grads employed in: law firms:
56%; business and industry:
25%; government: 11%; public
interest: 7%; judicial clerk: 0%;
academia: 0%; unknown: 0%
Employment location for 2015
class: Intl. 0%; N.E. 0%; M.A. 3%;
E.N.C. 86%; W.N.C. 0%; S.A.
5%; E.S.C. 0%; W.S.C. 2%; Mt.
1%; Pac. 2%; unknown 0%

Illinois Institute of Technology (Chicago-Kent)
565 W. Adams Street
Chicago, IL 60661-3691
www.kentlaw.iit.edu/
Private
Admissions: (312) 906-5020
Email:
admissions@kentlaw.iit.edu
Financial aid: (312) 906-5180
Application deadline: 03/15
Tuition: full time: $46,822; part
time: $34,210
Room/board/expenses: $18,843
Median grant: $23,900
Average student indebtedness at
graduation: $107,688
Enrollment: full time: 607; part
time: 131
men: 51%; women: 49%;
minorities: 31%
Acceptance rate (full time): 66%
Midrange LSAT (full time): 152-158
Midrange undergraduate GPA (full
time): 3.05-3.61
Midrange of full-time private-sector
salaries of 2015 grads: $51,000-
$90,500
2015 grads employed in: law firms:
52%; business and industry:
33%; government: 10%; public
interest: 4%; judicial clerk: 1%;
academia: 0%; unknown: 0%
Employment location for 2015
class: Intl. 1%; N.E. 0%; M.A. 2%;
E.N.C. 84%; W.N.C. 0%; S.A.
4%; E.S.C. 0%; W.S.C. 0%; Mt.
2%; Pac. 4%; unknown 3%

The John Marshall Law School
315 S. Plymouth Court
Chicago, IL 60604
www.jmls.edu
Private
Admissions: (800) 537-4280
Email: admission@jmls.edu
Financial aid: (800) 537-4280
Application deadline: 04/01
Tuition: full time: $46,470; part
time: $32,610
Room/board/expenses: $24,082
Median grant: $16,000
Average student indebtedness at
graduation: $158,888
Enrollment: full time: 671; part
time: 267
men: 49%; women: 51%;
minorities: 38%
Acceptance rate (full time): 66%
Midrange LSAT (full time): 145-151
Midrange undergraduate GPA (full
time): 2.79-3.38
Midrange of full-time private-sector
salaries of 2015 grads: N/A-N/A
2015 grads employed in: law firms:
56%; business and industry:
25%; government: 11%; public
interest: 3%; judicial clerk: 5%;
academia: 0%; unknown: 0%
Employment location for 2015 class:
Intl. 0%; N.E. 0%; M.A. 3%;
E.N.C. 89%; W.N.C. 1%; S.A. 2%;
E.S.C. 1%; W.S.C. 2%; Mt. 1%;
Pac. 2%; unknown 0%

Loyola University Chicago
25 E. Pearson Street
Chicago, IL 60611
www.luc.edu/law/
Private
Admissions: (312) 915-7170
Email: law-admissions@luc.edu
Financial aid: (312) 915-7170
Application deadline: 04/01
Tuition: full time: $47,416; part
time: $35,492
Room/board/expenses: $23,303
Median grant: $20,000
Average student indebtedness at
graduation: $88,588
Enrollment: full time: 590; part
time: 86
men: 46%; women: 54%;
minorities: 27%
Acceptance rate (full time): 56%
Midrange LSAT (full time): 154-160
Midrange undergraduate GPA (full
time): 3.05-3.54
Midrange of full-time private-sector
salaries of 2015 grads: $51,500-
$120,000
2015 grads employed in: law firms:
52%; business and industry:
30%; government: 7%; public
interest: 6%; judicial clerk: 4%;
academia: 1%; unknown: 0%
Employment location for 2015
class: Intl. 0%; N.E. 0%; M.A. 2%;
E.N.C. 85%; W.N.C. 1%; S.A. 4%;
E.S.C. 1%; W.S.C. 1%; Mt. 1%;
Pac. 4%; unknown 0%

Northern Illinois University
Swen Parson Hall, Room 276
De Kalb, IL 60115
niu.edu/law
Public
Admissions: (815) 753-8595
Email: law-admit@niu.edu
Financial aid: (815) 753-8595
Application deadline: 04/01
In-state tuition: full time: $22,130;
part time: $914/credit hour
Out-of-state tuition: full time:
$38,385
Room/board/expenses: $19,130
Median grant: $8,127
Average student indebtedness at
graduation: $86,899
Enrollment: full time: 254; part
time: 11
men: 52%; women: 48%;
minorities: 27%
Acceptance rate (full time): 63%
Midrange LSAT (full time): 145-151
Midrange undergraduate GPA (full
time): 2.79-3.33
Midrange of full-time private-sector
salaries of 2015 grads: $42,500-
$57,000
2015 grads employed in: law firms:
51%; business and industry:
12%; government: 27%; public
interest: 5%; judicial clerk: 3%;
academia: 2%; unknown: 0%
Employment location for 2015 class:
Intl. 0%; N.E. 0%; M.A. 0%;
E.N.C. 95%; W.N.C. 2%; S.A.
0%; E.S.C. 1%; W.S.C. 0%; Mt.
1%; Pac. 0%; unknown 0%

Northwestern University (Pritzker)
375 E. Chicago Avenue
Chicago, IL 60611
www.law.northwestern.edu
Private
Admissions: (312) 503-8465
Email: admissions@
law.northwestern.edu
Financial aid: (312) 503-8465
Application deadline: 02/15
Tuition: full time: $59,850; part
time: N/A
Room/board/expenses: $21,384
Median grant: $27,000
Average student indebtedness at
graduation: $154,923
Enrollment: full time: 661; part
time: 3
men: 52%; women: 48%;
minorities: 32%
Acceptance rate (full time): 18%
Midrange LSAT (full time): 163-170
Midrange undergraduate GPA (full
time): 3.43-3.89
Midrange of full-time private-sector
salaries of 2015 grads: $149,250-
$160,000
2015 grads employed in: law firms:
74%; business and industry:
9%; government: 3%; public
interest: 4%; judicial clerk: 10%;
academia: 0%; unknown: 0%
Employment location for 2015 class:
Intl. 3%; N.E. 2%; M.A. 19%;
E.N.C. 42%; W.N.C. 3%; S.A.
9%; E.S.C. 1%; W.S.C. 3%; Mt.
1%; Pac. 17%; unknown 0%

Southern Illinois University-Carbondale
Lesar Law Building
Carbondale, IL 62901
www.law.siu.edu
Public
Admissions: (800) 739-9187
Email: lawadmit@siu.edu
Financial aid: (618) 453-4334
Application deadline: 08/01
In-state tuition: full time: $20,833;
part time: N/A
Out-of-state tuition: full time:
$43,922

Room/board/expenses: $17,725
Median grant: $5,000
Average student indebtedness at
graduation: $87,634
Enrollment: full time: 330; part
time: 3
men: 62%; women: 38%;
minorities: 26%
Acceptance rate (full time): 70%
Midrange LSAT (full time): 145-150
Midrange undergraduate GPA (full
time): 2.55-3.27
Midrange of full-time private-sector
salaries of 2015 grads: $45,000-
$63,000
2015 grads employed in: law firms:
49%; business and industry:
24%; government: 21%; public
interest: 2%; judicial clerk: 2%;
academia: 1%; unknown: 0%
Employment location for 2015
class: Intl. 0%; N.E. 0%; M.A. 1%;
E.N.C. 61%; W.N.C. 13%; S.A.
6%; E.S.C. 7%; W.S.C. 2%; Mt.
1%; Pac. 4%; unknown 0%

University of Chicago
1111 E. 60th Street
Chicago, IL 60637
www.law.uchicago.edu
Private
Admissions: (773) 702-9484
Email: admissions@law.
uchicago.edu
Financial aid: (773) 702-9484
Application deadline: 03/01
Tuition: full time: $59,541; part
time: N/A/credit hour
Room/board/expenses: $27,471
Median grant: $20,000
Average student indebtedness at
graduation: $134,148
Enrollment: full time: 603; part
time: N/A
men: 56%; women: 44%;
minorities: 30%
Acceptance rate (full time): 21%
Midrange LSAT (full time): 166-172
Midrange undergraduate GPA (full
time): 3.73-3.95
Midrange of full-time private-sector
salaries of 2015 grads: $160,000-
$160,000
2015 grads employed in: law firms:
70%; business and industry:
3%; government: 2%; public
interest: 7%; judicial clerk: 18%;
academia: 0%; unknown: 0%
Employment location for 2015 class:
Intl. 2%; N.E. 1%; M.A. 24%;
E.N.C. 38%; W.N.C. 3%; S.A.
10%; E.S.C. 2%; W.S.C. 7%; Mt.
3%; Pac. 11%; unknown 0%

University of Illinois-Urbana-Champaign
504 E. Pennsylvania Avenue
Champaign, IL 61820
www.law.illinois.edu
Public
Admissions: (217) 244-6415
Email:
law-admissions@illinois.edu
Financial aid: (217) 244-6415
Application deadline: 03/15
In-state tuition: full time: $41,332;
part time: N/A
Out-of-state tuition: full time:
$49,082
Room/board/expenses: $18,260
Median grant: $30,000
Average student indebtedness at
graduation: $99,782

Enrollment: full time: 435; part
time: N/A
men: 60%; women: 40%;
minorities: 27%
Acceptance rate (full time): 46%
Midrange LSAT (full time): 154-162
Midrange undergraduate GPA (full
time): 3.32-3.70
Midrange of full-time private-sector
salaries of 2015 grads: $65,000-
$160,000
2015 grads employed in: law firms:
56%; business and industry:
14%; government: 17%; public
interest: 3%; judicial clerk: 7%;
academia: 4%; unknown: 0%
Employment location for 2015
class: Intl. 2%; N.E. 1%; M.A. 3%;
E.N.C. 75%; W.N.C. 3%; S.A. 6%;
E.S.C. 2%; W.S.C. 3%; Mt. 2%;
Pac. 3%; unknown 0%

INDIANA

Indiana University-Bloomington (Maurer)
211 S. Indiana Avenue
Bloomington, IN 47405-1001
www.law.indiana.edu
Public
Admissions: (812) 855-4765
Email: lawadmis@indiana.edu
Financial aid: (812) 855-7746
Application deadline: 07/15
In-state tuition: full time: $32,551;
part time: N/A/credit hour
Out-of-state tuition: full time:
$53,301
Room/board/expenses: $18,344
Median grant: $23,600
Average student indebtedness at
graduation: $99,895
Enrollment: full time: 525; part
time: N/A
men: 55%; women: 45%;
minorities: 22%
Acceptance rate (full time): 42%
Midrange LSAT (full time): 153-163
Midrange undergraduate GPA (full
time): 3.36-3.82
Midrange of full-time private-sector
salaries of 2015 grads: $55,000-
$115,000
2015 grads employed in: law firms:
49%; business and industry:
17%; government: 15%; public
interest: 5%; judicial clerk: 11%;
academia: 4%; unknown: 0%
Employment location for 2015
class: Intl. 3%; N.E. 1%; M.A. 8%;
E.N.C. 60%; W.N.C. 1%; S.A.
12%; E.S.C. 2%; W.S.C. 0%; Mt.
4%; Pac. 7%; unknown 2%

Indiana University-Indianapolis (McKinney)
530 W. New York Street
Indianapolis, IN 46202-3225
mckinneylaw.iu.edu
Public
Admissions: (317) 274-2459
Email: pkkinney@iupui.edu
Financial aid: (317) 278-2880
Application deadline: 07/31
In-state tuition: full time: $26,379;
part time: $20,030
Out-of-state tuition: full time:
$45,227
Room/board/expenses: $18,786
Median grant: $13,073
Average student indebtedness at
graduation: $105,065

Enrollment: full time: 564; part time: 240
men: 51%; women: 49%; minorities: 19%
Acceptance rate (full time): 55%
Midrange LSAT (full time): 150-157
Midrange undergraduate GPA (full time): 3.21-3.64
Midrange of full-time private-sector salaries of 2015 grads: $52,000-$95,000
2015 grads employed in: law firms: 48%; business and industry: 20%; government: 23%; public interest: 3%; judicial clerk: 3%; academia: 3%; unknown: 0%
Employment location for 2015 class: Intl. 0%; N.E. 0%; M.A. 0%; E.N.C. 93%; W.N.C. 0%; S.A. 3%; E.S.C. 0%; W.S.C. 1%; Mt. 0%; Pac. 3%; unknown 0%

University of Notre Dame

PO Box 780
Notre Dame, IN 46556-0780
law.nd.edu
Private
Admissions: (574) 631-6626
Email: lawadmit@nd.edu
Financial aid: (574) 631-6626
Application deadline: 03/15
Tuition: full time: $54,297; part time: N/A
Room/board/expenses: $20,250
Median grant: $21,000
Average student indebtedness at graduation: $123,924
Enrollment: full time: 599; part time: N/A
men: 56%; women: 44%; minorities: 26%
Acceptance rate (full time): 30%
Midrange LSAT (full time): 158-165
Midrange undergraduate GPA (full time): 3.41-3.82
Midrange of full-time private-sector salaries of 2015 grads: $80,250-$160,000
2015 grads employed in: law firms: 55%; business and industry: 8%; government: 16%; public interest: 7%; judicial clerk: 13%; academia: 1%; unknown: 0%
Employment location for 2015 class: Intl. 0%; N.E. 1%; M.A. 13%; E.N.C. 48%; W.N.C. 4%; S.A. 16%; E.S.C. 3%; W.S.C. 4%; Mt. 5%; Pac. 5%; unknown 0%

Valparaiso University

656 S. Greenwich Street
Wesemann Hall
Valparaiso, IN 46383
www.valpo.edu/law
Private
Admissions: (219) 465-7821
Email: law.admissions@valpo.edu
Financial aid: (219) 465-7818
Application deadline: 05/01
Tuition: full time: $40,372; part time: $24,672
Room/board/expenses: $15,650
Median grant: $19,725
Average student indebtedness at graduation: $136,765
Enrollment: full time: 328; part time: 18
men: 48%; women: 52%; minorities: 30%
Acceptance rate (full time): 59%
Midrange LSAT (full time): 145-151
Midrange undergraduate GPA (full time): 2.69-3.36

Midrange of full-time private-sector salaries of 2015 grads: $57,500-$77,500
2015 grads employed in: law firms: 58%; business and industry: 20%; government: 11%; public interest: 4%; judicial clerk: 3%; academia: 3%; unknown: 0%
Employment location for 2015 class: Intl. 0%; N.E. 0%; M.A. 1%; E.N.C. 84%; W.N.C. 1%; S.A. 6%; E.S.C. 2%; W.S.C. 1%; Mt. 2%; Pac. 2%; unknown 0%

IOWA

Drake University

2507 University Avenue
Des Moines, IA 50311
www.drake.edu/law
Private
Admissions: (515) 271-2782
Email: lawadmit@drake.edu
Financial aid: (515) 271-2782
Application deadline: 04/01
Tuition: full time: $39,642; part time: $1,363/credit hour
Room/board/expenses: $21,010
Median grant: $19,380
Average student indebtedness at graduation: $112,893
Enrollment: full time: 310; part time: 7
men: 49%; women: 51%; minorities: 10%
Acceptance rate (full time): 62%
Midrange LSAT (full time): 150-156
Midrange undergraduate GPA (full time): 3.00-3.62
Midrange of full-time private-sector salaries of 2015 grads: $45,375-$71,750
2015 grads employed in: law firms: 61%; business and industry: 11%; government: 16%; public interest: 5%; judicial clerk: 6%; academia: 2%; unknown: 0%
Employment location for 2015 class: Intl. 0%; N.E. 0%; M.A. 0%; E.N.C. 6%; W.N.C. 85%; S.A. 1%; E.S.C. 0%; W.S.C. 2%; Mt. 4%; Pac. 2%; unknown 0%

University of Iowa

320 Melrose Avenue
Iowa City, IA 52242
law.uiowa.edu
Public
Admissions: (319) 335-9095
Email: law-admissions@uiowa.edu
Financial aid: (319) 335-9142
Application deadline: 05/01
In-state tuition: full time: $24,930; part time: N/A
Out-of-state tuition: full time: $43,214
Room/board/expenses: $17,760
Median grant: $22,348
Average student indebtedness at graduation: $74,128
Enrollment: full time: 420; part time: 3
men: 56%; women: 44%; minorities: 21%
Acceptance rate (full time): 46%
Midrange LSAT (full time): 157-163
Midrange undergraduate GPA (full time): 3.44-3.79
Midrange of full-time private-sector salaries of 2015 grads: $60,000-$110,000

2015 grads employed in: law firms: 48%; business and industry: 14%; government: 9%; public interest: 5%; judicial clerk: 22%; academia: 1%; unknown: 0%
Employment location for 2015 class: Intl. 1%; N.E. 1%; M.A. 4%; E.N.C. 14%; W.N.C. 60%; S.A. 8%; E.S.C. 1%; W.S.C. 3%; Mt. 5%; Pac. 4%; unknown 0%

KANSAS

University of Kansas

Green Hall
1535 W. 15th Street
Lawrence, KS 66045-7608
www.law.ku.edu
Public
Admissions: (866) 220-3654
Email: admitlaw@ku.edu
Financial aid: (785) 864-4700
Application deadline: 04/01
In-state tuition: full time: $21,617; part time: N/A
Out-of-state tuition: full time: $36,958
Room/board/expenses: $15,492
Median grant: $13,100
Average student indebtedness at graduation: $88,809
Enrollment: full time: 351; part time: N/A
men: 58%; women: 42%; minorities: 14%
Acceptance rate (full time): 57%
Midrange LSAT (full time): 151-159
Midrange undergraduate GPA (full time): 3.17-3.70
Midrange of full-time private-sector salaries of 2015 grads: $55,000-$80,000
2015 grads employed in: law firms: 53%; business and industry: 16%; government: 20%; public interest: 1%; judicial clerk: 7%; academia: 3%; unknown: 0%
Employment location for 2015 class: Intl. 0%; N.E. 1%; M.A. 2%; E.N.C. 2%; W.N.C. 76%; S.A. 7%; E.S.C. 2%; W.S.C. 2%; Mt. 7%; Pac. 1%; unknown 0%

Washburn University

1700 S.W. College Avenue
Topeka, KS 66621
washburnlaw.edu
Public
Admissions: (785) 670-1185
Email: admissions@washburnlaw.edu
Financial aid: (785) 670-1151
Application deadline: 04/01
In-state tuition: full time: $20,950; part time: N/A
Out-of-state tuition: full time: $32,695
Room/board/expenses: $16,171
Median grant: $16,412
Average student indebtedness at graduation: $81,528
Enrollment: full time: 293; part time: 7
men: 59%; women: 41%; minorities: 14%
Acceptance rate (full time): 61%
Midrange LSAT (full time): 149-155
Midrange undergraduate GPA (full time): 2.88-3.71
Midrange of full-time private-sector salaries of 2015 grads: $50,000-$72,000

2015 grads employed in: law firms: 53%; business and industry: 21%; government: 17%; public interest: 5%; judicial clerk: 2%; academia: 2%; unknown: 0%
Employment location for 2015 class: Intl. 0%; N.E. 0%; M.A. 0%; E.N.C. 1%; W.N.C. 80%; S.A. 3%; E.S.C. 0%; W.S.C. 6%; Mt. 7%; Pac. 3%; unknown 1%

KENTUCKY

Northern Kentucky University (Chase)

Nunn Hall
Highland Heights, KY 41099
chaselaw.nku.edu
Public
Admissions: (859) 572-5841
Email: chaseadmissions@nku.edu
Financial aid: (859) 572-6437
Application deadline: rolling
In-state tuition: full time: $18,870; part time: $15,994
Out-of-state tuition: full time: $30,284
Room/board/expenses: $15,442
Median grant: $13,595
Average student indebtedness at graduation: $74,190
Enrollment: full time: 274; part time: 133
men: 52%; women: 48%; minorities: 10%
Acceptance rate (full time): 78%
Midrange LSAT (full time): 145-151
Midrange undergraduate GPA (full time): 2.94-3.53
Midrange of full-time private-sector salaries of 2015 grads: $42,000-$65,000
2015 grads employed in: law firms: 41%; business and industry: 31%; government: 17%; public interest: 5%; judicial clerk: 3%; academia: 3%; unknown: 0%
Employment location for 2015 class: Intl. 0%; N.E. 0%; M.A. 0%; E.N.C. 51%; W.N.C. 1%; S.A. 2%; E.S.C. 44%; W.S.C. 0%; Mt. 1%; Pac. 1%; unknown 0%

University of Kentucky

209 Law Building
Lexington, KY 40506-0048
www.law.uky.edu
Public
Admissions: (859) 218-1699
Email: uklawadmissions@uky.edu
Financial aid: (860) 257-0172
Application deadline: 03/15
In-state tuition: full time: $22,700; part time: N/A
Out-of-state tuition: full time: $44,320
Room/board/expenses: $15,832
Median grant: $6,000
Average student indebtedness at graduation: $59,163
Enrollment: full time: 396; part time: N/A
men: 53%; women: 47%; minorities: 13%
Acceptance rate (full time): 66%
Midrange LSAT (full time): 151-157
Midrange undergraduate GPA (full time): 3.24-3.74
Midrange of full-time private-sector salaries of 2015 grads: $45,000-$97,000

2015 grads employed in: law firms: 45%; business and industry: 14%; government: 13%; public interest: 6%; judicial clerk: 22%; academia: 1%; unknown: 0%
Employment location for 2015 class: Intl. 2%; N.E. 0%; M.A. 1%; E.N.C. 6%; W.N.C. 1%; S.A. 16%; E.S.C. 70%; W.S.C. 2%; Mt. 3%; Pac. 1%; unknown 0%

University of Louisville (Brandeis)

2301 S. Third Street
Louisville, KY 40292
www.louisville.edu/law
Public
Admissions: (502) 852-6365
Email: lawadmissions@louisville.edu
Financial aid: (502) 852-5511
Application deadline: 04/15
In-state tuition: full time: $21,292; part time: $17,092
Out-of-state tuition: full time: $39,498
Room/board/expenses: $18,820
Median grant: $9,500
Average student indebtedness at graduation: $99,581
Enrollment: full time: 284; part time: 13
men: 56%; women: 44%; minorities: 13%
Acceptance rate (full time): 69%
Midrange LSAT (full time): 150-155
Midrange undergraduate GPA (full time): 2.95-3.47
Midrange of full-time private-sector salaries of 2015 grads: $40,000-$70,000
2015 grads employed in: law firms: 45%; business and industry: 19%; government: 19%; public interest: 8%; judicial clerk: 6%; academia: 3%; unknown: 0%
Employment location for 2015 class: Intl. 0%; N.E. 0%; M.A. 0%; E.N.C. 7%; W.N.C. 1%; S.A. 11%; E.S.C. 81%; W.S.C. 1%; Mt. 0%; Pac. 0%; unknown 0%

LOUISIANA

Louisiana State University-Baton Rouge (Hebert)

400 Paul M. Hebert Law Center
Baton Rouge, LA 70803
www.law.lsu.edu
Public
Admissions: (225) 578-8646
Email: admissions@law.lsu.edu
Financial aid: (225) 578-3103
Application deadline: 06/01
In-state tuition: full time: $22,520; part time: N/A
Out-of-state tuition: full time: $37,960
Room/board/expenses: $23,514
Median grant: $10,000
Average student indebtedness at graduation: $83,919
Enrollment: full time: 539; part time: 11
men: 55%; women: 45%; minorities: 15%
Acceptance rate (full time): 60%
Midrange LSAT (full time): 152-158
Midrange undergraduate GPA (full time): 3.08-3.66
Midrange of full-time private-sector salaries of 2015 grads: $60,000-$98,000

2015 grads employed in: law firms: 53%; business and industry: 12%; government: 14%; public interest: 4%; judicial clerk: 13%; academia: 2%; unknown: 0%
Employment location for 2015 class: Intl. 2%; N.E. 0%; M.A. 2%; E.N.C. 1%; W.N.C. 0%; S.A. 7%; E.S.C. 1%; W.S.C. 85%; Mt. 2%; Pac. 1%; unknown 0%

Loyola University New Orleans

7214 St. Charles Avenue
PO Box 901
New Orleans, LA 70118
law.loyno.edu/
Private
Admissions: (504) 861-5575
Email: ladmit@loyno.edu
Financial aid: (504) 865-3231
Application deadline: 08/01
Tuition: full time: $43,410; part time: $32,910
Room/board/expenses: $22,262
Median grant: $24,000
Average student indebtedness at graduation: $39,138
Enrollment: full time: 370; part time: 99
men: 47%; women: 53%; minorities: 30%
Acceptance rate (full time): 87%
Midrange LSAT (full time): 146-153
Midrange undergraduate GPA (full time): 2.92-3.46
Midrange of full-time private-sector salaries of 2015 grads: $50,000-$80,000
2015 grads employed in: law firms: 55%; business and industry: 22%; government: 7%; public interest: 4%; judicial clerk: 9%; academia: 3%; unknown: 0%
Employment location for 2015 class: Intl. 0%; N.E. 0%; M.A. 3%; E.N.C. 1%; W.N.C. 1%; S.A. 5%; E.S.C. 3%; W.S.C. 81%; Mt. 2%; Pac. 3%; unknown 0%

Southern University Law Center

PO Box 9294
Baton Rouge, LA 70813
www.sulc.edu/index_v3.htm
Public
Admissions: (225) 771-5340
Email: Admission@sulc.edu
Financial aid: (225) 771-2141
Application deadline: 02/28
In-state tuition: full time: $14,956; part time: $13,200
Out-of-state tuition: full time: $26,556
Room/board/expenses: $18,703
Median grant: $3,800
Average student indebtedness at graduation: $89,552
Enrollment: full time: 394; part time: 166
men: 44%; women: 56%; minorities: 65%
Acceptance rate (full time): 68%
Midrange LSAT (full time): 142-146
Midrange undergraduate GPA (full time): 2.68-3.28
Midrange of full-time private-sector salaries of 2015 grads: $38,500-$52,500
2015 grads employed in: law firms: 34%; business and industry: 21%; government: 17%; public interest: 5%; judicial clerk: 7%; academia: 6%; unknown: 9%

Employment location for 2015 class: Intl. 0%; N.E. 0%; M.A. 0%; E.N.C. 3%; W.N.C. 0%; S.A. 11%; E.S.C. 3%; W.S.C. 77%; Mt. 0%; Pac. 0%; unknown 6%

Tulane University

6329 Freret Street
John Giffen Weinmann Hall
New Orleans, LA 70118-6231
www.tulane.edu
Private
Admissions: (504) 865-5930
Email: admissions@law.tulane.edu
Financial aid: (504) 865-5931
Application deadline: rolling
Tuition: full time: $52,554; part time: N/A
Room/board/expenses: $22,344
Median grant: $25,000
Average student indebtedness at graduation: $139,508
Enrollment: full time: 553; part time: 1
men: 54%; women: 46%; minorities: 18%
Acceptance rate (full time): 57%
Midrange LSAT (full time): 155-160
Midrange undergraduate GPA (full time): 3.22-3.62
Midrange of full-time private-sector salaries of 2015 grads: $60,000-$160,000
2015 grads employed in: law firms: 54%; business and industry: 18%; government: 13%; public interest: 3%; judicial clerk: 10%; academia: 3%; unknown: 0%
Employment location for 2015 class: Intl. 2%; N.E. 0%; M.A. 13%; E.N.C. 2%; W.N.C. 1%; S.A. 11%; E.S.C. 1%; W.S.C. 57%; Mt. 1%; Pac. 11%; unknown 0%

MAINE

University of Maine

246 Deering Avenue
Portland, ME 04102
mainelaw.maine.edu
Public
Admissions: (207) 780-4341
Email: lawadmissions@maine.edu
Financial aid: (207) 780-5250
Application deadline: 07/31
In-state tuition: full time: $23,560; part time: N/A
Out-of-state tuition: full time: $34,630
Room/board/expenses: $14,980
Median grant: $8,000
Average student indebtedness at graduation: $89,513
Enrollment: full time: 219; part time: 15
men: 50%; women: 50%; minorities: 9%
Acceptance rate (full time): 66%
Midrange LSAT (full time): 147-155
Midrange undergraduate GPA (full time): 2.96-3.46
Midrange of full-time private-sector salaries of 2015 grads: $37,450-$72,000
2015 grads employed in: law firms: 43%; business and industry: 20%; government: 12%; public interest: 10%; judicial clerk: 10%; academia: 5%; unknown: 0%

Employment location for 2015 class: Intl. 2%; N.E. 85%; M.A. 2%; E.N.C. 2%; W.N.C. 2%; S.A. 2%; E.S.C. 2%; W.S.C. 3%; Mt. 0%; Pac. 2%; unknown 0%

MARYLAND

University of Baltimore

1420 N. Charles Street
Baltimore, MD 21201-5779
law.ubalt.edu
Public
Admissions: (410) 837-4459
Email: lawadmissions@ubalt.edu
Financial aid: (410) 837-4763
Application deadline: 08/01
In-state tuition: full time: $30,144; part time: $22,502
Out-of-state tuition: full time: $43,972
Room/board/expenses: $19,950
Median grant: $10,000
Average student indebtedness at graduation: $108,328
Enrollment: full time: 444; part time: 247
men: 50%; women: 50%; minorities: 31%
Acceptance rate (full time): 61%
Midrange LSAT (full time): 150-155
Midrange undergraduate GPA (full time): 2.81-3.49
Midrange of full-time private-sector salaries of 2015 grads: $50,500-$80,000
2015 grads employed in: law firms: 34%; business and industry: 16%; government: 17%; public interest: 4%; judicial clerk: 28%; academia: 2%; unknown: 0%
Employment location for 2015 class: Intl. 0%; N.E. 0%; M.A. 3%; E.N.C. 0%; W.N.C. 0%; S.A. 95%; E.S.C. 0%; W.S.C. 0%; Mt. 0%; Pac. 0%; unknown 0%

University of Maryland (Carey)

500 W. Baltimore Street
Baltimore, MD 21201-1786
www.law.umaryland.edu
Public
Admissions: (410) 706-3492
Email: admissions@law.umaryland.edu
Financial aid: (410) 706-0873
Application deadline: 04/01
In-state tuition: full time: $31,380; part time: $21,237
Out-of-state tuition: full time: $45,399
Room/board/expenses: $23,075
Median grant: $8,596
Average student indebtedness at graduation: $113,927
Enrollment: full time: 506; part time: 112
men: 49%; women: 51%; minorities: 33%
Acceptance rate (full time): 55%
Midrange LSAT (full time): 155-159
Midrange undergraduate GPA (full time): 3.30-3.66
Midrange of full-time private-sector salaries of 2015 grads: $50,000-$115,000
2015 grads employed in: law firms: 26%; business and industry: 17%; government: 20%; public interest: 5%; judicial clerk: 28%; academia: 4%; unknown: 0%

Employment location for 2015 class: Intl. 0%; N.E. 1%; M.A. 7%; E.N.C. 1%; W.N.C. 0%; S.A. 85%; E.S.C. 0%; W.S.C. 1%; Mt. 2%; Pac. 3%; unknown 0%

MASSACHUSETTS

Boston College

885 Centre Street
Newton, MA 02459-1154
www.bc.edu/law
Private
Admissions: (617) 552-4351
Email: bclawadm@bc.edu
Financial aid: (617) 552-4243
Application deadline: 03/31
Tuition: full time: $50,620; part time: N/A
Room/board/expenses: $19,360
Median grant: $20,000
Average student indebtedness at graduation: $108,873
Enrollment: full time: 723; part time: 1
men: 54%; women: 46%; minorities: 25%
Acceptance rate (full time): 37%
Midrange LSAT (full time): 161-163
Midrange undergraduate GPA (full time): 3.32-3.65
Midrange of full-time private-sector salaries of 2015 grads: $85,000-$160,000
2015 grads employed in: law firms: 58%; business and industry: 12%; government: 10%; public interest: 5%; judicial clerk: 12%; academia: 3%; unknown: 0%
Employment location for 2015 class: Intl. 0%; N.E. 63%; M.A. 19%; E.N.C. 3%; W.N.C. 1%; S.A. 7%; E.S.C. 0%; W.S.C. 2%; Mt. 0%; Pac. 4%; unknown 0%

Boston University

765 Commonwealth Avenue
Boston, MA 02215
www.bu.edu/law/
Private
Admissions: (617) 353-3100
Email: bulawadm@bu.edu
Financial aid: (617) 353-3160
Application deadline: 04/01
Tuition: full time: $51,210; part time: N/A
Room/board/expenses: $18,902
Median grant: $20,000
Average student indebtedness at graduation: $104,755
Enrollment: full time: 710; part time: N/A
men: 47%; women: 53%; minorities: 28%
Acceptance rate (full time): 29%
Midrange LSAT (full time): 161-165
Midrange undergraduate GPA (full time): 3.52-3.77
Midrange of full-time private-sector salaries of 2015 grads: $74,750-$160,000
2015 grads employed in: law firms: 56%; business and industry: 10%; government: 18%; public interest: 9%; judicial clerk: 6%; academia: 2%; unknown: 0%
Employment location for 2015 class: Intl. 2%; N.E. 59%; M.A. 20%; E.N.C. 3%; W.N.C. 1%; S.A. 10%; E.S.C. 1%; W.S.C. 1%; Mt. 2%; Pac. 3%; unknown 0%

Harvard University

1563 Massachusetts Avenue
Cambridge, MA 02138
hls.harvard.edu/
Private
Admissions: (617) 495-3109
Email: jdadmiss@law.harvard.edu
Financial aid: (617) 495-4606
Application deadline: 02/01
Tuition: full time: $60,638; part time: N/A
Room/board/expenses: $27,962
Median grant: $21,670
Average student indebtedness at graduation: $153,172
Enrollment: full time: 1,771; part time: N/A
men: 51%; women: 49%; minorities: 32%
Acceptance rate (full time): 17%
Midrange LSAT (full time): 170-175
Midrange undergraduate GPA (full time): 3.76-3.94
Midrange of full-time private-sector salaries of 2015 grads: $160,000-$160,000
2015 grads employed in: law firms: 56%; business and industry: 5%; government: 4%; public interest: 11%; judicial clerk: 23%; academia: 1%; unknown: 0%
Employment location for 2015 class: Intl. 3%; N.E. 12%; M.A. 36%; E.N.C. 6%; W.N.C. 1%; S.A. 17%; E.S.C. 2%; W.S.C. 5%; Mt. 3%; Pac. 16%; unknown 0%

New England Law Boston

154 Stuart Street
Boston, MA 02116
www.nesl.edu
Private
Admissions: (617) 422-7210
Email: admit@nesl.edu
Financial aid: (617) 422-7232
Application deadline: 03/15
Tuition: full time: $47,054; part time: $35,330
Room/board/expenses: $19,980
Median grant: $28,186
Enrollment: full time: 437; part time: 185
men: 43%; women: 57%; minorities: 28%
Acceptance rate (full time): 70%
Midrange LSAT (full time): 146-153
Midrange undergraduate GPA (full time): 2.93-3.50
Midrange of full-time private-sector salaries of 2015 grads: $50,000-$70,000
2015 grads employed in: law firms: 47%; business and industry: 26%; government: 12%; public interest: 6%; judicial clerk: 7%; academia: 3%; unknown: 0%
Employment location for 2015 class: Intl. 0%; N.E. 69%; M.A. 16%; E.N.C. 1%; W.N.C. 0%; S.A. 5%; E.S.C. 0%; W.S.C. 2%; Mt. 0%; Pac. 4%; unknown 0%

Northeastern University

360 Huntington Avenue
Boston, MA 02115
www.northeastern.edu/law
Private
Admissions: (617) 373-2395
Email: lawadmissions@northeastern.edu
Financial aid: (617) 373-4620

Application deadline: rolling
Tuition: full time: $47,790; part time: N/A
Room/board/expenses: $19,599
Median grant: $27,000
Average student indebtedness at graduation: $111,410
Enrollment: full time: 486; part time: N/A
men: 37%; women: 63%; minorities: 33%
Acceptance rate (full time): 38%
Midrange LSAT (full time): 154-163
Midrange undergraduate GPA (full time): 3.30-3.69
Midrange of full-time private-sector salaries of 2015 grads: $60,000-$160,000
2015 grads employed in: law firms: 31%; business and industry: 20%; government: 14%; public interest: 17%; judicial clerk: 17%; academia: 1%; unknown: 1%
Employment location for 2015 class: Intl. 0%; N.E. 65%; M.A. 12%; E.N.C. 3%; W.N.C. 0%; S.A. 7%; E.S.C. 0%; W.S.C. 1%; Mt. 2%; Pac. 7%; unknown 1%

Suffolk University

120 Tremont Street
Boston, MA 02108
www.suffolk.edu/law
Private
Admissions: (617) 573-8144
Email: lawadm@suffolk.edu
Financial aid: (617) 573-8470
Application deadline: 04/01
Tuition: full time: $46,042; part time: $34,530
Room/board/expenses: $15,811
Median grant: $15,962
Average student indebtedness at graduation: $135,272
Enrollment: full time: 724; part time: 346
men: 46%; women: 54%; minorities: 22%
Acceptance rate (full time): 65%
Midrange LSAT (full time): 146-153
Midrange undergraduate GPA (full time): 2.96-3.52
Midrange of full-time private-sector salaries of 2015 grads: $50,000-$90,000
2015 grads employed in: law firms: 41%; business and industry: 34%; government: 15%; public interest: 3%; judicial clerk: 5%; academia: 2%; unknown: 0%
Employment location for 2015 class: Intl. 1%; N.E. 85%; M.A. 4%; E.N.C. 1%; W.N.C. 0%; S.A. 4%; E.S.C. 0%; W.S.C. 1%; Mt. 1%; Pac. 3%; unknown 0%

University of Massachusetts-Dartmouth

333 Faunce Corner Road
North Dartmouth, MA 02747
umassd.edu/law/admissions
Public
Admissions: (508) 985-1110
Email: lawadmissions@umassd.edu
Financial aid: (508) 985-1112
Application deadline: 06/30
In-state tuition: full time: $26,466; part time: $19,968
Out-of-state tuition: full time: $34,618
Room/board/expenses: $19,492
Median grant: $8,000

Average student indebtedness at graduation: $98,730
Enrollment: full time: 123; part time: 63
men: 45%; women: 55%; minorities: 26%
Acceptance rate (full time): 61%
Midrange LSAT (full time): 146-153
Midrange undergraduate GPA (full time): 2.75-3.35
Midrange of full-time private-sector salaries of 2015 grads: $60,000-$120,000
2015 grads employed in: law firms: 35%; business and industry: 26%; government: 28%; public interest: 4%; judicial clerk: 2%; academia: 4%; unknown: 0%
Employment location for 2015 class: Intl. 0%; N.E. 91%; M.A. 2%; E.N.C. 0%; W.N.C. 0%; S.A. 0%; E.S.C. 0%; W.S.C. 4%; Mt. 2%; Pac. 0%; unknown 0%

Western New England University

1215 Wilbraham Road
Springfield, MA 01119-2684
www.law.wne.edu
Private
Admissions: (413) 782-1406
Email: admissions@law.wne.edu
Financial aid: (413) 796-2080
Application deadline: 03/15
Tuition: full time: $40,954; part time: $30,298
Room/board/expenses: $21,848
Median grant: $19,910
Average student indebtedness at graduation: $121,367
Enrollment: full time: 174; part time: 95
men: 43%; women: 57%; minorities: 28%
Acceptance rate (full time): 56%
Midrange LSAT (full time): 146-150
Midrange undergraduate GPA (full time): 2.76-3.45
Midrange of full-time private-sector salaries of 2015 grads: $50,000-$65,000
2015 grads employed in: law firms: 45%; business and industry: 22%; government: 14%; public interest: 11%; judicial clerk: 7%; academia: 1%; unknown: 0%
Employment location for 2015 class: Intl. 0%; N.E. 73%; M.A. 19%; E.N.C. 0%; W.N.C. 3%; S.A. 1%; E.S.C. 0%; W.S.C. 1%; Mt. 3%; Pac. 0%; unknown 0%

MICHIGAN

Michigan State University

648 N. Shaw Lane, Room 368
East Lansing, MI 48824-1300
www.law.msu.edu
Private
Admissions: (517) 432-0222
Email: law@law.msu.edu
Financial aid: (517) 432-6810
Application deadline: 04/30
Tuition: full time: $41,528; part time: $1,432/credit hour
Room/board/expenses: $16,150
Median grant: $26,462
Average student indebtedness at graduation: $91,014

Enrollment: full time: 678; part time: 82
men: 50%; women: 50%; minorities: 22%
Acceptance rate (full time): 44%
Midrange LSAT (full time): 150-156
Midrange undergraduate GPA (full time): 3.19-3.72
Midrange of full-time private-sector salaries of 2015 grads: $50,000-$74,000
2015 grads employed in: law firms: 41%; business and industry: 25%; government: 10%; public interest: 7%; judicial clerk: 8%; academia: 7%; unknown: 0%
Employment location for 2015 class: Intl. 3%; N.E. 1%; M.A. 6%; E.N.C. 63%; W.N.C. 2%; S.A. 10%; E.S.C. 1%; W.S.C. 4%; Mt. 5%; Pac. 4%; unknown 0%

University of Detroit Mercy

651 E. Jefferson Avenue
Detroit, MI 48226
www.law.udmercy.edu
Private
Admissions: (313) 596-0264
Email: udmlawao@udmercy.edu
Financial aid: (313) 596-0213
Application deadline: 05/01
Tuition: full time: $40,532; part time: $32,447
Room/board/expenses: $25,132
Median grant: $3,582
Average student indebtedness at graduation: $152,000
Enrollment: full time: 453; part time: 93
men: 43%; women: 57%; minorities: 14%
Acceptance rate (full time): 57%
Midrange LSAT (full time): 149-156
Midrange undergraduate GPA (full time): 2.95-3.45
Midrange of full-time private-sector salaries of 2015 grads: $45,000-$88,000
2015 grads employed in: law firms: 57%; business and industry: 22%; government: 11%; public interest: 3%; judicial clerk: 6%; academia: 2%; unknown: 0%
Employment location for 2015 class: Intl. 28%; N.E. 0%; M.A. 1%; E.N.C. 67%; W.N.C. 0%; S.A. 1%; E.S.C. 0%; W.S.C. 2%; Mt. 0%; Pac. 1%; unknown 0%

University of Michigan-Ann Arbor

625 S. State Street
Ann Arbor, MI 48109-1215
www.law.umich.edu/
Public
Admissions: (734) 764-0537
Email: law.jd.admissions@umich.edu
Financial aid: (734) 764-5289
Application deadline: 02/15
In-state tuition: full time: $55,012; part time: N/A
Out-of-state tuition: full time: $58,012
Room/board/expenses: $19,010
Median grant: $17,500
Average student indebtedness at graduation: $146,309
Enrollment: full time: 929; part time: 4
men: 53%; women: 47%; minorities: 22%

Acceptance rate (full time): 24%
Midrange LSAT (full time): 164-169
Midrange undergraduate GPA (full time): 3.56-3.87
Midrange of full-time private-sector salaries of 2015 grads: $125,000-$160,000
2015 grads employed in: law firms: 58%; business and industry: 4%; government: 11%; public interest: 9%; judicial clerk: 18%; academia: 1%; unknown: 0%
Employment location for 2015 class: Intl. 3%; N.E. 3%; M.A. 25%; E.N.C. 27%; W.N.C. 2%; S.A. 16%; E.S.C. 1%; W.S.C. 7%; Mt. 2%; Pac. 15%; unknown 0%

Wayne State University

471 W. Palmer Street
Detroit, MI 48202
www.law.wayne.edu
Public
Admissions: (313) 577-3937
Email: lawinquire@wayne.edu
Financial aid: (313) 577-3049
Application deadline: 07/01
In-state tuition: full time: $30,727; part time: $16,654
Out-of-state tuition: full time: $33,509
Room/board/expenses: $21,990
Median grant: $20,996
Average student indebtedness at graduation: $81,738
Enrollment: full time: 373; part time: 49
men: 58%; women: 42%; minorities: 14%
Acceptance rate (full time): 55%
Midrange LSAT (full time): 152-159
Midrange undergraduate GPA (full time): 3.32-3.67
Midrange of full-time private-sector salaries of 2015 grads: $52,000-$100,000
2015 grads employed in: law firms: 60%; business and industry: 19%; government: 8%; public interest: 3%; judicial clerk: 6%; academia: 3%; unknown: 1%
Employment location for 2015 class: Intl. 1%; N.E. 0%; M.A. 1%; E.N.C. 89%; W.N.C. 0%; S.A. 0%; E.S.C. 0%; W.S.C. 0%; Mt. 0%; Pac. 1%; unknown 8%

Western Michigan University Thomas M. Cooley Law School

300 S. Capitol Avenue
Lansing, MI 48933
www.cooley.edu
Private
Admissions: (517) 371-5140
Email: admissions@cooley.edu
Financial aid: (517) 371-5140
Application deadline: 09/01
Tuition: full time: $50,790; part time: $29,790
Room/board/expenses: $17,714
Median grant: $15,581
Enrollment: full time: 185; part time: 1,024
men: 43%; women: 57%; minorities: 42%
Acceptance rate (full time): 79%
Midrange LSAT (full time): 139-148
Midrange undergraduate GPA (full time): 2.53-3.17

Midrange of full-time private-sector salaries of 2015 grads: $38,000-$62,400
2015 grads employed in: law firms: 42%; business and industry: 31%; government: 16%; public interest: 2%; judicial clerk: 5%; academia: 3%; unknown: 0%
Employment location for 2015 class: Intl. 1%; N.E. 0%; M.A. 5%; E.N.C. 64%; W.N.C. 1%; S.A. 18%; E.S.C. 2%; W.S.C. 3%; Mt. 2%; Pac. 2%; unknown 0%

MINNESOTA

Mitchell Hamline School of Law

875 Summit Avenue
St. Paul, MN 55105
mitchellhamline.edu/
Private
Admissions: (651) 290-6476
Email: admissions@mitchellhamline.edu
Financial aid: (651) 290-6403
Application deadline: 08/01
Tuition: full time: $40,930; part time: $29,680
Room/board/expenses: $19,450
Median grant: $20,117
Average student indebtedness at graduation: $100,603
Enrollment: full time: 478; part time: 510
men: 49%; women: 51%; minorities: 20%
Acceptance rate (full time): 85%
Midrange LSAT (full time): 146-155
Midrange undergraduate GPA (full time): 3.03-3.53
Midrange of full-time private-sector salaries of 2015 grads: $50,000-$82,500
2015 grads employed in: law firms: 34%; business and industry: 32%; government: 9%; public interest: 7%; judicial clerk: 16%; academia: 1%; unknown: 2%
Employment location for 2015 class: Intl. 1%; N.E. 0%; M.A. 1%; E.N.C. 5%; W.N.C. 82%; S.A. 2%; E.S.C. 0%; W.S.C. 1%; Mt. 1%; Pac. 2%; unknown 5%

University of Minnesota

229 19th Avenue S
Minneapolis, MN 55455
www.law.umn.edu
Public
Admissions: (612) 625-3487
Email: jdadmissions@umn.edu
Financial aid: (612) 625-0750
Application deadline: 07/15
In-state tuition: full time: $43,244; part time: N/A
Out-of-state tuition: full time: $51,590
Room/board/expenses: $17,020
Median grant: $25,000
Average student indebtedness at graduation: $106,436
Enrollment: full time: 555; part time: 22
men: 55%; women: 45%; minorities: 18%
Acceptance rate (full time): 45%
Midrange LSAT (full time): 159-166
Midrange undergraduate GPA (full time): 3.48-3.87
Midrange of full-time private-sector salaries of 2015 grads: $97,500-$135,000

2015 grads employed in: law firms: 42%; business and industry: 13%; government: 14%; public interest: 8%; judicial clerk: 21%; academia: 2%; unknown: 0%
Employment location for 2015 class: Intl. 4%; N.E. 1%; M.A. 7%; E.N.C. 9%; W.N.C. 61%; S.A. 8%; E.S.C. 0%; W.S.C. 2%; Mt. 3%; Pac. 5%; unknown 0%

University of St. Thomas

MSL 411, 1000 LaSalle Avenue
Minneapolis, MN 55403-2015
www.stthomas.edu/law
Private
Admissions: (651) 962-4895
Email: lawschool@stthomas.edu
Financial aid: (651) 962-6550
Application deadline: 08/01
Tuition: full time: $39,077; part time: N/A
Room/board/expenses: $20,197
Median grant: $25,791
Average student indebtedness at graduation: $100,805
Enrollment: full time: 359; part time: 6
men: 48%; women: 52%; minorities: 15%
Acceptance rate (full time): 71%
Midrange LSAT (full time): 149-156
Midrange undergraduate GPA (full time): 3.15-3.62
Midrange of full-time private-sector salaries of 2015 grads: $51,000-$85,000
2015 grads employed in: law firms: 37%; business and industry: 27%; government: 9%; public interest: 3%; judicial clerk: 22%; academia: 3%; unknown: 0%
Employment location for 2015 class: Intl. 0%; N.E. 0%; M.A. 4%; E.N.C. 2%; W.N.C. 89%; S.A. 1%; E.S.C. 0%; W.S.C. 0%; Mt. 2%; Pac. 2%; unknown 0%

MISSISSIPPI

Mississippi College

151 E. Griffith Street
Jackson, MS 39201
www.law.mc.edu
Private
Admissions: (601) 925-7152
Email: mcopelan@mc.edu
Financial aid: (601) 925-7110
Application deadline: 07/15
Tuition: full time: $33,630; part time: $1,068/credit hour
Room/board/expenses: $23,025
Median grant: $17,000
Average student indebtedness at graduation: $119,000
Enrollment: full time: 366; part time: 7
men: 55%; women: 45%; minorities: 24%
Acceptance rate (full time): 65%
Midrange LSAT (full time): 144-149
Midrange undergraduate GPA (full time): 2.75-3.34
Midrange of full-time private-sector salaries of 2015 grads: $47,000-$80,000
2015 grads employed in: law firms: 51%; business and industry: 11%; government: 23%; public interest: 2%; judicial clerk: 9%; academia: 0%; unknown: 4%

Employment location for 2015 class: Intl. 1%; N.E. 1%; M.A. 2%; E.N.C. 1%; W.N.C. 1%; S.A. 4%; E.S.C. 73%; W.S.C. 16%; Mt. 1%; Pac. 1%; unknown 0%

University of Mississippi

PO Box 1848
University, MS 38677
law.olemiss.edu
Public
Admissions: (662) 915-6910
Email: lawmiss@olemiss.edu
Financial aid: (800) 891-4569
Application deadline: 03/15
In-state tuition: full time: $15,336; part time: N/A/credit hour
Out-of-state tuition: full time: $33,712
Room/board/expenses: $17,260
Median grant: $12,000
Average student indebtedness at graduation: $67,539
Enrollment: full time: 363; part time: N/A
men: 56%; women: 44%; minorities: 23%
Acceptance rate (full time): 45%
Midrange LSAT (full time): 150-157
Midrange undergraduate GPA (full time): 3.18-3.61
Midrange of full-time private-sector salaries of 2015 grads: $45,000-$58,000
2015 grads employed in: law firms: 50%; business and industry: 16%; government: 11%; public interest: 2%; judicial clerk: 20%; academia: 1%; unknown: 0%
Employment location for 2015 class: Intl. 0%; N.E. 1%; M.A. 1%; E.N.C. 3%; W.N.C. 1%; S.A. 14%; E.S.C. 70%; W.S.C. 7%; Mt. 2%; Pac. 1%; unknown 0%

MISSOURI

St. Louis University

100 N. Tucker
St. Louis, MO 63101
law.slu.edu
Private
Admissions: (314) 977-2800
Email: admissions@law.slu.edu
Financial aid: (314) 977-3369
Application deadline: rolling
Tuition: full time: $40,145; part time: $29,235
Room/board/expenses: $18,540
Median grant: $21,000
Average student indebtedness at graduation: $117,335
Enrollment: full time: 447; part time: 69
men: 48%; women: 52%; minorities: 18%
Acceptance rate (full time): 65%
Midrange LSAT (full time): 151-158
Midrange undergraduate GPA (full time): 3.15-3.66
Midrange of full-time private-sector salaries of 2015 grads: $50,000-$120,000
2015 grads employed in: law firms: 49%; business and industry: 26%; government: 13%; public interest: 6%; judicial clerk: 4%; academia: 1%; unknown: 0%
Employment location for 2015 class: Intl. 0%; N.E. 0%; M.A. 0%; E.N.C. 17%; W.N.C. 70%; S.A. 4%; E.S.C. 2%; W.S.C. 3%; Mt. 1%; Pac. 3%; unknown 0%

University of Missouri

203 Hulston Hall
Columbia, MO 65211-4300
law.missouri.edu/
Public
Admissions: (573) 882-6042
Email: mulawadmissions@missouri.edu
Financial aid: (573) 882-1383
Application deadline: 03/15
In-state tuition: full time: $20,918; part time: N/A
Out-of-state tuition: full time: $38,672
Room/board/expenses: $12,366
Median grant: $12,750
Average student indebtedness at graduation: $80,138
Enrollment: full time: 300; part time: 11
men: 60%; women: 40%; minorities: 18%
Acceptance rate (full time): 55%
Midrange LSAT (full time): 153-160
Midrange undergraduate GPA (full time): 3.17-3.72
Midrange of full-time private-sector salaries of 2015 grads: $50,000-$85,000
2015 grads employed in: law firms: 47%; business and industry: 17%; government: 17%; public interest: 4%; judicial clerk: 11%; academia: 2%; unknown: 1%
Employment location for 2015 class: Intl. N/A; N.E. N/A; M.A. N/A; E.N.C. 5%; W.N.C. 87%; S.A. 2%; E.S.C. 1%; W.S.C. N/A; Mt. 1%; Pac. 4%; unknown N/A

University of Missouri-Kansas City

500 East 52nd Street
Kansas City, MO 64110
www.law.umkc.edu
Public
Admissions: (816) 235-1644
Email: law@umkc.edu
Financial aid: (816) 235-1154
Application deadline: 03/01
In-state tuition: full time: $18,647; part time: $11,360
Out-of-state tuition: full time: $35,456
Room/board/expenses: $16,568
Median grant: $5,000
Average student indebtedness at graduation: $93,678
Enrollment: full time: 373; part time: 43
men: 56%; women: 44%; minorities: 17%
Acceptance rate (full time): 55%
Midrange LSAT (full time): 149-154
Midrange undergraduate GPA (full time): 3.08-3.64
Midrange of full-time private-sector salaries of 2015 grads: $45,000-$75,000
2015 grads employed in: law firms: 48%; business and industry: 23%; government: 18%; public interest: 3%; judicial clerk: 8%; academia: 0%; unknown: 0%
Employment location for 2015 class: Intl. 0%; N.E. 0%; M.A. 1%; E.N.C. 2%; W.N.C. 89%; S.A. 1%; E.S.C. 1%; W.S.C. 2%; Mt. 3%; Pac. 2%; unknown 0%

Washington University in St. Louis

1 Brookings Drive, Box 1120
St. Louis, MO 63130
www.law.wustl.edu
Private
Admissions: (314) 935-4525
Email: applylaw@wustl.edu
Financial aid: (314) 935-4605
Application deadline: 08/15
Tuition: full time: $53,506; part time: N/A
Room/board/expenses: $23,611
Median grant: $35,000
Average student indebtedness at graduation: $93,768
Enrollment: full time: 701; part time: 4
men: 53%; women: 47%; minorities: 25%
Acceptance rate (full time): 32%
Midrange LSAT (full time): 160-169
Midrange undergraduate GPA (full time): 3.15-3.81
Midrange of full-time private-sector salaries of 2015 grads: $70,000-$160,000
2015 grads employed in: law firms: 55%; business and industry: 18%; government: 10%; public interest: 7%; judicial clerk: 9%; academia: 2%; unknown: 0%
Employment location for 2015 class: Intl. 5%; N.E. 2%; M.A. 16%; E.N.C. 13%; W.N.C. 34%; S.A. 11%; E.S.C. 0%; W.S.C. 6%; Mt. 3%; Pac. 10%; unknown 0%

MONTANA

University of Montana

32 Campus Drive
Missoula, MT 59812
www.umt.edu/law
Public
Admissions: (406) 243-2396
Email: sarah.pepe@umontana.edu
Financial aid: (406) 243-5524
Application deadline: 03/15
In-state tuition: full time: $11,451; part time: N/A
Out-of-state tuition: full time: $30,850
Room/board/expenses: $15,726
Median grant: $3,000
Average student indebtedness at graduation: $75,470
Enrollment: full time: 230; part time: N/A
men: 49%; women: 51%; minorities: 11%
Acceptance rate (full time): 59%
Midrange LSAT (full time): 151-158
Midrange undergraduate GPA (full time): 3.04-3.65
Midrange of full-time private-sector salaries of 2015 grads: $52,000-$60,000
2015 grads employed in: law firms: 37%; business and industry: 15%; government: 11%; public interest: 5%; judicial clerk: 32%; academia: 0%; unknown: 0%
Employment location for 2015 class: Intl. 0%; N.E. 0%; M.A. 0%; E.N.C. 0%; W.N.C. 0%; S.A. 3%; E.S.C. 0%; W.S.C. 2%; Mt. 94%; Pac. 2%; unknown 0%

Creighton University

2500 California Plaza
Omaha, NE 68178
law.creighton.edu/
Private
Admissions: (402) 280-2872
Email: lawadmit@creighton.edu
Financial aid: (402) 280-2352
Application deadline: 07/01
Tuition: full time: $37,522; part time: $1,195/credit hour
Room/board/expenses: $19,300
Median grant: $20,000
Average student indebtedness at graduation: $130,145
Enrollment: full time: 299; part time: 8
men: 57%; women: 43%; minorities: 21%
Acceptance rate (full time): 74%
Midrange LSAT (full time): 149-155
Midrange undergraduate GPA (full time): 3.02-3.55
Midrange of full-time private-sector salaries of 2015 grads: $43,500-$82,000
2015 grads employed in: law firms: 43%; business and industry: 22%; government: 19%; public interest: 3%; judicial clerk: 10%; academia: 3%; unknown: 0%
Employment location for 2015 class: Intl. 0%; N.E. 0%; M.A. 1%; E.N.C. 5%; W.N.C. 72%; S.A. 4%; E.S.C. 0%; W.S.C. 1%; Mt. 16%; Pac. 1%; unknown 0%

University of Nebraska-Lincoln

PO Box 830902
Lincoln, NE 68583-0902
law.unl.edu
Public
Admissions: (402) 472-8333
Email: lawadm@unl.edu
Financial aid: (402) 472-8333
Application deadline: 03/01
In-state tuition: full time: $15,036; part time: $354/credit hour
Out-of-state tuition: full time: $34,192
Room/board/expenses: $16,424
Median grant: $14,721
Average student indebtedness at graduation: $62,888
Enrollment: full time: 328; part time: 6
men: 51%; women: 49%; minorities: 8%
Acceptance rate (full time): 58%
Midrange LSAT (full time): 153-159
Midrange undergraduate GPA (full time): 3.40-3.92
Midrange of full-time private-sector salaries of 2015 grads: $50,000-$65,000
2015 grads employed in: law firms: 53%; business and industry: 21%; government: 13%; public interest: 5%; judicial clerk: 6%; academia: 2%; unknown: 0%
Employment location for 2015 class: Intl. 0%; N.E. 1%; M.A. 0%; E.N.C. 4%; W.N.C. 85%; S.A. 2%; E.S.C. 1%; W.S.C. 1%; Mt. 3%; Pac. 4%; unknown 0%

NEVADA

University of Nevada-Las Vegas

4505 S. Maryland Parkway
Box 451003
Las Vegas, NV 89154-1003
www.law.unlv.edu/
Public
Admissions: (702) 895-2440
Email: eric.eden@law.unlv.edu
Financial aid: (702) 895-4107
Application deadline: 06/01
In-state tuition: full time: $26,749;
part time: $20,225
Out-of-state tuition: full time:
$38,649
Room/board/expenses: $21,372
Median grant: $12,450
**Average student indebtedness at
graduation:** $97,361
Enrollment: full time: 286; part
time: 93
men: 54%; women: 46%;
minorities: 34%
Acceptance rate (full time): 35%
Midrange LSAT (full time): 153-160
**Midrange undergraduate GPA (full
time):** 3.21-3.71
**Midrange of full-time private-sector
salaries of 2015 grads:** $67,500-
$85,000
2015 grads employed in: law firms:
53%; business and industry:
11%; government: 8%; public
interest: 4%; judicial clerk: 24%;
academia: 0%; unknown: 0%
**Employment location for 2015
class:** Intl. 1%; N.E. 0%; M.A. 2%;
E.N.C. 0%; W.N.C. 0%; S.A. 0%;
E.S.C. 0%; W.S.C. 1%; Mt. 92%;
Pac. 5%; unknown 0%

NEW HAMPSHIRE

University of New Hampshire School of Law

2 White Street
Concord, NH 03301
www.law.unh.edu
Public
Admissions: (603) 513-5300
Email: admissions@law.unh.edu
Financial aid: (603) 228-1541
Application deadline: 04/01
In-state tuition: full time: $37,388;
part time: $0/credit hour
Out-of-state tuition: full time:
$41,388
Room/board/expenses: $20,877
Median grant: $21,000
**Average student indebtedness at
graduation:** $95,650
Enrollment: full time: 206; part
time: 1
men: 57%; women: 43%;
minorities: 13%
Acceptance rate (full time): 52%
Midrange LSAT (full time): 154-159
**Midrange undergraduate GPA (full
time):** 3.06-3.68
**Midrange of full-time private-sector
salaries of 2015 grads:** $48,000-
$88,000
2015 grads employed in: law firms:
59%; business and industry:
24%; government: 8%; public
interest: 6%; judicial clerk: 0%;
academia: 0%; unknown: 0%
Employment location for 2015 class:
Intl. 0%; N.E. 68%; M.A. 11%;
E.N.C. 0%; W.N.C. 0%; S.A. 8%;
E.S.C. 0%; W.S.C. 2%; Mt. 5%;
Pac. 6%; unknown 0%

NEW JERSEY

Rutgers, The State University of New Jersey

Camden and Newark, NJ
law.rutgers.edu/
Public
Admissions: N/A
Email:
admissions@law.rutgers.edu
Financial aid: N/A
Application deadline: 08/01
In-state tuition: full time: $27,269;
part time: $22,908
Out-of-state tuition: full time:
$39,683
Room/board/expenses: $18,195
Median grant: $15,000
**Average student indebtedness at
graduation:** $56,173
Enrollment: full time: 873; part
time: 237
men: 57%; women: 43%;
minorities: 31%
Acceptance rate (full time): 56%
Midrange LSAT (full time): 152-157
**Midrange undergraduate GPA (full
time):** 3.11-3.65
**Midrange of full-time private-sector
salaries of 2015 grads:** $55,000-
$120,000
2015 grads employed in: law firms:
28%; business and industry:
17%; government: 7%; public
interest: 4%; judicial clerk: 43%;
academia: 1%; unknown: 0%
Employment location for 2015 class:
Intl. 0%; N.E. 1%; M.A. 95%;
E.N.C. 0%; W.N.C. 0%; S.A. 3%;
E.S.C. 1%; W.S.C. 0%; Mt. 1%;
Pac. 0%; unknown 0%

Seton Hall University

1 Newark Center
Newark, NJ 07102-5210
law.shu.edu
Private
Admissions: (888) 415-7271
Email: admitme@shu.edu
Financial aid: (973) 642-8850
Application deadline: 04/01
Tuition: full time: $52,022; part
time: $39,226
Room/board/expenses: $22,344
Median grant: $25,000
**Average student indebtedness at
graduation:** $125,300
Enrollment: full time: 353; part
time: 156
men: 56%; women: 44%;
minorities: 26%
Acceptance rate (full time): 53%
Midrange LSAT (full time): 154-160
**Midrange undergraduate GPA (full
time):** 3.09-3.72
**Midrange of full-time private-sector
salaries of 2015 grads:** $70,000-
$130,000
2015 grads employed in: law firms:
28%; business and industry:
12%; government: 4%; public
interest: 1%; judicial clerk: 55%;
academia: 1%; unknown: 0%
Employment location for 2015 class:
Intl. 1%; N.E. 0%; M.A. 94%;
E.N.C. 1%; W.N.C. 1%; S.A. 0%;
E.S.C. 0%; W.S.C. 0%; Mt. 1%;
Pac. 2%; unknown 0%

NEW MEXICO

University of New Mexico

1117 Stanford Drive NE
MSC11 6070
Albuquerque, NM 87131-0001
lawschool.unm.edu
Public
Admissions: (505) 277-0958
Email: admissions@law.unm.edu
Financial aid: (505) 277-9035
Application deadline: 03/01
In-state tuition: full time: $16,761;
part time: N/A
Out-of-state tuition: full time:
$35,816
Room/board/expenses: $15,834
Median grant: $4,000
**Average student indebtedness at
graduation:** $75,277
Enrollment: full time: 338; part
time: N/A
men: 47%; women: 53%;
minorities: 49%
Acceptance rate (full time): 43%
Midrange LSAT (full time): 150-157
**Midrange undergraduate GPA (full
time):** 3.20-3.67
**Midrange of full-time private-sector
salaries of 2015 grads:** $56,000-
$70,000
2015 grads employed in: law firms:
46%; business and industry:
11%; government: 29%; public
interest: 8%; judicial clerk: 5%;
academia: 0%; unknown: 2%
**Employment location for 2015
class:** Intl. 0%; N.E. 0%; M.A. 1%;
E.N.C. 1%; W.N.C. 1%; S.A. 2%;
E.S.C. 0%; W.S.C. 3%; Mt. 89%;
Pac. 1%; unknown 2%

NEW YORK

Albany Law School

80 New Scotland Avenue
Albany, NY 12208-3494
www.albanylaw.edu
Private
Admissions: (518) 445-2326
Email:
admissions@albanylaw.edu
Financial aid: (518) 445-2357
Application deadline: 06/01
Tuition: full time: $44,696; part
time: $33,560
Room/board/expenses: $15,970
Median grant: $18,000
**Average student indebtedness at
graduation:** $107,185
Enrollment: full time: 342; part
time: 38
men: 50%; women: 50%;
minorities: 17%
Acceptance rate (full time): 57%
Midrange LSAT (full time): 149-154
**Midrange undergraduate GPA (full
time):** 3.01-3.55
**Midrange of full-time private-sector
salaries of 2015 grads:** $50,000-
$83,000
2015 grads employed in: law firms:
49%; business and industry:
11%; government: 23%; public
interest: 6%; judicial clerk: 7%;
academia: 3%; unknown: 0%
Employment location for 2015 class:
Intl. 0%; N.E. 4%; M.A. 91%;
E.N.C. 1%; W.N.C. 0%; S.A. 3%;
E.S.C. 0%; W.S.C. 1%; Mt. 0%;
Pac. 1%; unknown 0%

Brooklyn Law School

250 Joralemon Street
Brooklyn, NY 11201
www.brooklaw.edu
Private
Admissions: (718) 780-7906
Email: admitq@brooklaw.edu
Financial aid: (718) 780-7915
Application deadline: 05/15
Tuition: full time: $1,526/credit
hour; part time: $1,526/credit
hour
Room/board/expenses: $24,399
Median grant: $24,783
**Average student indebtedness at
graduation:** $117,581
Enrollment: full time: 814; part
time: 284
men: 49%; women: 51%;
minorities: 29%
Acceptance rate (full time): 52%
Midrange LSAT (full time): 154-159
**Midrange undergraduate GPA (full
time):** 3.12-3.55
**Midrange of full-time private-sector
salaries of 2015 grads:** $79,000-
$160,000
2015 grads employed in: law firms:
49%; business and industry:
15%; government: 18%; public
interest: 10%; judicial clerk: 6%;
academia: 1%; unknown: 1%
Employment location for 2015 class:
Intl. 0%; N.E. 1%; M.A. 94%;
E.N.C. 0%; W.N.C. 0%; S.A. 2%;
E.S.C. 0%; W.S.C. 0%; Mt. 0%;
Pac. 1%; unknown 1%

Columbia University

435 W. 116th Street
New York, NY 10027
www.law.columbia.edu
Private
Admissions: (212) 854-2670
Email:
admissions@law.columbia.edu
Financial aid: (212) 854-7730
Application deadline: 02/15
Tuition: full time: $65,260; part
time: N/A
Room/board/expenses: $23,313
Median grant: $20,000
**Average student indebtedness at
graduation:** $159,769
Enrollment: full time: 1,234; part
time: N/A
men: 52%; women: 48%;
minorities: 32%
Acceptance rate (full time): 20%
Midrange LSAT (full time): 168-174
**Midrange undergraduate GPA (full
time):** 3.56-3.81
**Midrange of full-time private-sector
salaries of 2015 grads:** $160,000-
$160,000
2015 grads employed in: law firms:
78%; business and industry: 3%;
government: 5%; public interest:
7%; judicial clerk: 7%; academia:
0%; unknown: 0%
Employment location for 2015 class:
Intl. 2%; N.E. 1%; M.A. 78%;
E.N.C. 1%; W.N.C. 0%; S.A. 8%;
E.S.C. 0%; W.S.C. 1%; Mt. 1%;
Pac. 7%; unknown 0%

Cornell University

Myron Taylor Hall
Ithaca, NY 14853-4901
www.lawschool.cornell.edu
Private
Admissions: (607) 255-5141
Email: jdadmissions@cornell.edu
Financial aid: (607) 255-5141
Application deadline: 02/01

CUNY

2 Court Square
Long Island City, NY 11101-4356
www.law.cuny.edu/
Public
Admissions: (718) 340-4210
Email: admissions@law.cuny.edu
Financial aid: (718) 340-4284
Application deadline: 06/15
In-state tuition: full time: $14,663;
part time: $13,726
Out-of-state tuition: full time:
$23,983
Room/board/expenses: $20,379
Median grant: $5,000
**Average student indebtedness at
graduation:** $78,523
Enrollment: full time: 339; part
time: 95
men: 38%; women: 62%;
minorities: 53%
Acceptance rate (full time): 49%
Midrange LSAT (full time): 149-156
**Midrange undergraduate GPA (full
time):** 2.96-3.58
**Midrange of full-time private-sector
salaries of 2015 grads:** $35,000-
$82,500
2015 grads employed in: law firms:
16%; business and industry:
8%; government: 33%; public
interest: 36%; judicial clerk: 6%;
academia: 2%; unknown: 0%
Employment location for 2015 class:
Intl. 0%; N.E. 1%; M.A. 88%;
E.N.C. 0%; W.N.C. 0%; S.A. 3%;
E.S.C. 0%; W.S.C. 4%; Mt. 0%;
Pac. 2%; unknown 0%

Fordham University

150 W. 62nd Street
New York, NY 10023-7485
law.fordham.edu
Private
Admissions: (212) 636-6810
Email: lawadmissions@law.
fordham.edu
Financial aid: (212) 636-6815
Application deadline: 03/31
Tuition: full time: $56,146; part
time: $42,196
Room/board/expenses: $25,578
Median grant: $15,000
**Average student indebtedness at
graduation:** $110,320

Column 5 top (continued from Brooklyn):
Tuition: full time: $61,485; part
time: N/A
Room/board/expenses: $23,436
Median grant: $22,000
**Average student indebtedness at
graduation:** $158,128
Enrollment: full time: 605; part
time: N/A
men: 58%; women: 42%;
minorities: 39%
Acceptance rate (full time): 24%
Midrange LSAT (full time): 163-168
**Midrange undergraduate GPA (full
time):** 3.60-3.81
**Midrange of full-time private-sector
salaries of 2015 grads:** $160,000-
$160,000
2015 grads employed in: law firms:
72%; business and industry:
2%; government: 12%; public
interest: 3%; judicial clerk: 10%;
academia: 1%; unknown: 0%
Employment location for 2015 class:
Intl. 6%; N.E. 5%; M.A. 57%;
E.N.C. 2%; W.N.C. 2%; S.A. 10%;
E.S.C. 2%; W.S.C. 2%; Mt. 3%;
Pac. 9%; unknown 2%

Enrollment: full time: 993; part time: 169
men: 49%; women: 51%; minorities: 28%
Acceptance rate (full time): 38%
Midrange LSAT (full time): 160-165
Midrange undergraduate GPA (full time): 3.38-3.68
Midrange of full-time private-sector salaries of 2015 grads: $80,000-$160,000
2015 grads employed in: law firms: 61%; business and industry: 19%; government: 8%; public interest: 4%; judicial clerk: 6%; academia: 3%; unknown: 0%
Employment location for 2015 class: Intl. 3%; N.E. 3%; M.A. 89%; E.N.C. 0%; W.N.C. 0%; S.A. 1%; E.S.C. 0%; W.S.C. 0%; Mt. 0%; Pac. 3%; unknown 0%

Hofstra University (Deane)

121 Hofstra University
Hempstead, NY 11549
law.hofstra.edu
Private
Admissions: (516) 463-5916
Email: lawadmissions@hofstra.edu
Financial aid: (516) 463-5916
Application deadline: 04/15
Tuition: full time: $55,860; part time: $41,830
Room/board/expenses: $25,206
Median grant: $30,000
Average student indebtedness at graduation: $142,261
Enrollment: full time: 695; part time: 24
men: 46%; women: 54%; minorities: 27%
Acceptance rate (full time): 58%
Midrange LSAT (full time): 146-154
Midrange undergraduate GPA (full time): 3.08-3.60
Midrange of full-time private-sector salaries of 2015 grads: $50,000-$75,000
2015 grads employed in: law firms: 59%; business and industry: 11%; government: 16%; public interest: 8%; judicial clerk: 4%; academia: 0%; unknown: 3%
Employment location for 2015 class: Intl. 1%; N.E. 2%; M.A. 91%; E.N.C. 1%; W.N.C. 0%; S.A. 2%; E.S.C. 0%; W.S.C. 1%; Mt. 0%; Pac. 0%; unknown 2%

New York Law School

185 W. Broadway
New York, NY 10013-2960
www.nyls.edu
Private
Admissions: (212) 431-2888
Email: admissions@nyls.edu
Financial aid: (212) 431-2828
Application deadline: 07/01
Tuition: full time: $49,240; part time: $37,880
Room/board/expenses: $23,663
Median grant: $20,000
Average student indebtedness at graduation: $157,568
Enrollment: full time: 621; part time: 242
men: 43%; women: 57%; minorities: 34%
Acceptance rate (full time): 58%

Midrange LSAT (full time): 149-155
Midrange undergraduate GPA (full time): 3.01-3.54
Midrange of full-time private-sector salaries of 2015 grads: $69,000-$160,000
2015 grads employed in: law firms: 42%; business and industry: 31%; government: 15%; public interest: 5%; judicial clerk: 6%; academia: 1%; unknown: 0%
Employment location for 2015 class: Intl. 0%; N.E. 8%; M.A. 81%; E.N.C. 0%; W.N.C. 0%; S.A. 3%; E.S.C. 0%; W.S.C. 1%; Mt. 0%; Pac. 1%; unknown 6%

New York University

40 Washington Square S
New York, NY 10012
www.law.nyu.edu
Private
Admissions: (212) 998-6060
Email: law.moreinfo@nyu.edu
Financial aid: (212) 998-6050
Application deadline: 02/15
Tuition: full time: $61,622; part time: N/A
Room/board/expenses: $27,720
Median grant: $20,000
Average student indebtedness at graduation: $167,646
Enrollment: full time: 1,369; part time: N/A
men: 49%; women: 51%; minorities: 30%
Acceptance rate (full time): 30%
Midrange LSAT (full time): 166-171
Midrange undergraduate GPA (full time): 3.65-3.89
Midrange of full-time private-sector salaries of 2015 grads: $160,000-$160,000
2015 grads employed in: law firms: 68%; business and industry: 4%; government: 6%; public interest: 14%; judicial clerk: 8%; academia: 0%; unknown: 0%
Employment location for 2015 class: Intl. 1%; N.E. 2%; M.A. 75%; E.N.C. 1%; W.N.C. 0%; S.A. 10%; E.S.C. 1%; W.S.C. 1%; Mt. 0%; Pac. 8%; unknown 0%

Pace University

78 N. Broadway
White Plains, NY 10603
www.law.pace.edu
Private
Admissions: (914) 422-4210
Email: admissions@law.pace.edu
Financial aid: (914) 422-4050
Application deadline: 06/01
Tuition: full time: $46,284; part time: $34,716
Room/board/expenses: $19,362
Median grant: $24,000
Average student indebtedness at graduation: $124,317
Enrollment: full time: 485; part time: 48
men: 46%; women: 54%; minorities: 28%
Acceptance rate (full time): 60%
Midrange LSAT (full time): 148-153
Midrange undergraduate GPA (full time): 2.99-3.58
Midrange of full-time private-sector salaries of 2015 grads: $57,500-$90,000

2015 grads employed in: law firms: 47%; business and industry: 19%; government: 14%; public interest: 9%; judicial clerk: 8%; academia: 0%; unknown: 4%
Employment location for 2015 class: Intl. 0%; N.E. 8%; M.A. 81%; E.N.C. 0%; W.N.C. 0%; S.A. 3%; E.S.C. 0%; W.S.C. 1%; Mt. 0%; Pac. 1%; unknown 6%

St. John's University

8000 Utopia Parkway
Jamaica, NY 11439
www.law.stjohns.edu/
Private
Admissions: (718) 990-6474
Email: lawinfo@stjohns.edu
Financial aid: (718) 990-1485
Application deadline: 04/15
Tuition: full time: $55,150; part time: $41,380
Room/board/expenses: $25,703
Median grant: $40,000
Average student indebtedness at graduation: $117,572
Enrollment: full time: 591; part time: 114
men: 52%; women: 48%; minorities: 27%
Acceptance rate (full time): 44%
Midrange LSAT (full time): 154-160
Midrange undergraduate GPA (full time): 3.21-3.75
Midrange of full-time private-sector salaries of 2015 grads: $60,000-$102,500
2015 grads employed in: law firms: 57%; business and industry: 17%; government: 18%; public interest: 3%; judicial clerk: 4%; academia: 1%; unknown: 0%
Employment location for 2015 class: Intl. 1%; N.E. 2%; M.A. 91%; E.N.C. 0%; W.N.C. 0%; S.A. 3%; E.S.C. 0%; W.S.C. 1%; Mt. 1%; Pac. 1%; unknown 0%

Syracuse University

950 Irving Avenue, Suite 408
Syracuse, NY 13244-6070
www.law.syr.edu
Private
Admissions: (315) 443-1962
Email: admissions@law.syr.edu
Financial aid: (315) 443-1963
Application deadline: 07/01
Tuition: full time: $48,552; part time: $40,712
Room/board/expenses: $19,148
Median grant: $25,000
Average student indebtedness at graduation: $117,127
Enrollment: full time: 534; part time: 5
men: 53%; women: 47%; minorities: 20%
Acceptance rate (full time): 51%
Midrange LSAT (full time): 152-157
Midrange undergraduate GPA (full time): 3.12-3.58
Midrange of full-time private-sector salaries of 2015 grads: $53,000-$87,000
2015 grads employed in: law firms: 50%; business and industry: 17%; government: 16%; public interest: 5%; judicial clerk: 10%; academia: 1%; unknown: 0%

Employment location for 2015 class: Intl. 1%; N.E. 4%; M.A. 62%; E.N.C. 3%; W.N.C. 0%; S.A. 19%; E.S.C. 1%; W.S.C. 1%; Mt. 3%; Pac. 6%; unknown 0%

Touro College (Fuchsberg)

225 Eastview Drive
Central Islip, NY 11722
www.tourolaw.edu
Private
Admissions: (631) 761-7010
Email: admissions@tourolaw.edu
Financial aid: (631) 761-7020
Application deadline: 08/01
Tuition: full time: $47,320; part time: $35,340
Room/board/expenses: $23,620
Median grant: $13,000
Enrollment: full time: 302; part time: 156
men: 45%; women: 55%; minorities: 34%
Acceptance rate (full time): 55%
Midrange LSAT (full time): 146-150
Midrange undergraduate GPA (full time): 2.74-3.33
Midrange of full-time private-sector salaries of 2015 grads: $50,000-$75,000
2015 grads employed in: law firms: 54%; business and industry: 17%; government: 19%; public interest: 2%; judicial clerk: 6%; academia: 1%; unknown: 0%
Employment location for 2015 class: Intl. 1%; N.E. 1%; M.A. 96%; E.N.C. 0%; W.N.C. 0%; S.A. 1%; E.S.C. 0%; W.S.C. 0%; Mt. 1%; Pac. 0%; unknown 0%

University at Buffalo-SUNY

John Lord O'Brian Hall
Buffalo, NY 14260
www.law.buffalo.edu
Public
Admissions: (716) 645-2907
Email: law-admissions@buffalo.edu
Financial aid: (716) 645-7324
Application deadline: 03/01
In-state tuition: full time: $27,979; part time: N/A
Out-of-state tuition: full time: $45,249
Room/board/expenses: $21,193
Median grant: $7,000
Average student indebtedness at graduation: $90,546
Enrollment: full time: 451; part time: 4
men: 50%; women: 50%; minorities: 17%
Acceptance rate (full time): 51%
Midrange LSAT (full time): 150-157
Midrange undergraduate GPA (full time): 3.13-3.70
Midrange of full-time private-sector salaries of 2015 grads: $50,000-$76,000
2015 grads employed in: law firms: 54%; business and industry: 16%; government: 13%; public interest: 9%; judicial clerk: 5%; academia: 2%; unknown: 0%
Employment location for 2015 class: Intl. 1%; N.E. 1%; M.A. 92%; E.N.C. 1%; W.N.C. 0%; S.A. 2%; E.S.C. 0%; W.S.C. 0%; Mt. 1%; Pac. 2%; unknown 0%

Yeshiva University (Cardozo)

55 Fifth Avenue
New York, NY 10003
www.cardozo.yu.edu
Private
Admissions: (212) 790-0274
Email: lawinfo@yu.edu
Financial aid: (212) 790-0392
Application deadline: 04/01
Tuition: full time: $56,796; part time: $56,796
Room/board/expenses: $27,413
Median grant: $30,000
Average student indebtedness at graduation: $118,764
Enrollment: full time: 803; part time: 78
men: 48%; women: 52%; minorities: 25%
Acceptance rate (full time): 54%
Midrange LSAT (full time): 159-162
Midrange undergraduate GPA (full time): 3.15-3.70
Midrange of full-time private-sector salaries of 2015 grads: $52,000-$111,250
2015 grads employed in: law firms: 53%; business and industry: 23%; government: 12%; public interest: 7%; judicial clerk: 5%; academia: 0%; unknown: 0%
Employment location for 2015 class: Intl. 0%; N.E. 1%; M.A. 93%; E.N.C. 1%; W.N.C. 0%; S.A. 3%; E.S.C. 0%; W.S.C. 0%; Mt. 1%; Pac. 1%; unknown 0%

NORTH CAROLINA

Campbell University

225 Hillsborough Street
Suite 401
Raleigh, NC 27603
www.law.campbell.edu
Private
Admissions: (919) 865-5989
Email: lawadmissions@campbell.edu
Financial aid: (919) 865-5990
Application deadline: 05/01
Tuition: full time: $39,300; part time: $19,650
Room/board/expenses: $26,970
Median grant: $12,500
Average student indebtedness at graduation: $131,894
Enrollment: full time: 380; part time: 30
men: 52%; women: 48%; minorities: 13%
Acceptance rate (full time): 61%
Midrange LSAT (full time): 150-156
Midrange undergraduate GPA (full time): 2.96-3.56
Midrange of full-time private-sector salaries of 2015 grads: $50,000-$70,000
2015 grads employed in: law firms: 50%; business and industry: 24%; government: 19%; public interest: 1%; judicial clerk: 4%; academia: 3%; unknown: 0%
Employment location for 2015 class: Intl. 0%; N.E. 0%; M.A. 2%; E.N.C. 2%; W.N.C. 0%; S.A. 89%; E.S.C. 2%; W.S.C. 1%; Mt. 1%; Pac. 0%; unknown 4%

Charlotte School of Law[1]

201 S. College Street
Suite 400
Charlotte, NC 28244
www.charlottelaw.edu/
Private
Admissions: (704) 971-8500
Email:
admissions@charlottelaw.edu
Financial aid: (704) 971-8386
Tuition: N/A
Room/board/expenses: N/A
Enrollment: N/A

Duke University

210 Science Drive
Box 90362
Durham, NC 27708-0362
www.law.duke.edu
Private
Admissions: (919) 613-7020
Email: admissions@law.duke.edu
Financial aid: (919) 613-7026
Application deadline: 02/15
Tuition: full time: $59,912; part
time: N/A
Room/board/expenses: $19,868
Median grant: $22,500
**Average student indebtedness at
graduation:** $137,829
Enrollment: full time: 676; part
time: N/A
men: 58%; women: 42%;
minorities: 24%
Acceptance rate (full time): 20%
Midrange LSAT (full time): 167-170
**Midrange undergraduate GPA (full
time):** 3.59-3.84
**Midrange of full-time private-sector
salaries of 2015 grads:** $135,000-
$160,000
2015 grads employed in: law firms:
73%; business and industry:
4%; government: 3%; public
interest: 2%; judicial clerk: 16%;
academia: 1%; unknown: 0%
Employment location for 2015 class:
Intl. 4%; N.E. 2%; M.A. 36%;
E.N.C. 3%; W.N.C. 1%; S.A. 35%;
E.S.C. 2%; W.S.C. 6%; Mt. 2%;
Pac. 7%; unknown 0%

Elon University

201 N. Greene Street
Greensboro, NC 27401
law.elon.edu
Private
Admissions: (336) 279-9200
Email: lawadmissions@elon.edu
Financial aid: (336) 278-2000
Application deadline: 08/01
Tuition: full time: $33,334; part
time: N/A
Room/board/expenses: $29,060
Median grant: $15,000
**Average student indebtedness at
graduation:** $153,347
Enrollment: full time: 333; part
time: N/A
men: 43%; women: 57%;
minorities: 26%
Acceptance rate (full time): 45%
Midrange LSAT (full time): 145-152
**Midrange undergraduate GPA (full
time):** 2.92-3.48
**Midrange of full-time private-sector
salaries of 2015 grads:** $40,000-
$58,500
2015 grads employed in: law firms:
53%; business and industry:

22%; government: 9%; public
interest: 7%; judicial clerk: 7%;
academia: 2%; unknown: 0%
**Employment location for 2015
class:** Intl. 0%; N.E. 0%; M.A.
3%; E.N.C. 2%; W.N.C. 0%; S.A.
90%; E.S.C. 0%; W.S.C. 3%; Mt.
2%; Pac. 0%; unknown 0%

North Carolina Central University

640 Nelson Street
Durham, NC 27707
law.nccu.edu
Public
Admissions: (919) 530-5243
Email: recruiter@nccu.edu
Financial aid: (919) 530-6365
Application deadline: 03/31
In-state tuition: full time: $18,020;
part time: $18,020
Out-of-state tuition: full time:
$40,438
Room/board/expenses: $21,000
Median grant: $8,541
**Average student indebtedness at
graduation:** $60,479
Enrollment: full time: 423; part
time: 96
men: 38%; women: 62%;
minorities: 69%
Acceptance rate (full time): 52%
Midrange LSAT (full time): 141-148
**Midrange undergraduate GPA (full
time):** 3.05-3.52
**Midrange of full-time private-sector
salaries of 2015 grads:** N/A-N/A
2015 grads employed in: law firms:
38%; business and industry:
30%; government: 17%; public
interest: 5%; judicial clerk: 2%;
academia: 4%; unknown: 3%
**Employment location for 2015
class:** Intl. 0%; N.E. 1%; M.A. 6%;
E.N.C. 0%; W.N.C. 0%; S.A. 77%;
E.S.C. 0%; W.S.C. 3%; Mt. 4%;
Pac. 1%; unknown 0%

University of North Carolina-Chapel Hill

Van Hecke-Wettach Hall
CB No. 3380
Chapel Hill, NC 27599-3380
www.law.unc.edu
Public
Admissions: (919) 962-5109
Email: law_admissions@unc.edu
Financial aid: (919) 962-8396
Application deadline: 08/01
In-state tuition: full time: $23,551;
part time: N/A
Out-of-state tuition: full time:
$40,182
Room/board/expenses: $20,400
Median grant: $14,000
**Average student indebtedness at
graduation:** $95,365
Enrollment: full time: 634; part
time: N/A
men: 51%; women: 49%;
minorities: 24%
Acceptance rate (full time): 44%
Midrange LSAT (full time): 158-163
**Midrange undergraduate GPA (full
time):** 3.31-3.70
**Midrange of full-time private-sector
salaries of 2015 grads:** $57,000-
$160,000

2015 grads employed in: law firms:
49%; business and industry:
16%; government: 16%; public
interest: 6%; judicial clerk: 9%;
academia: 4%; unknown: 0%
**Employment location for 2015
class:** Intl. 0%; N.E. 3%; M.A. 9%;
E.N.C. 4%; W.N.C. 1%; S.A. 74%;
E.S.C. 1%; W.S.C. 3%; Mt. 2%;
Pac. 2%; unknown 0%

Wake Forest University

Reynolda Station
PO Box 7206
Winston-Salem, NC 27109
www.law.wfu.edu
Private
Admissions: (336) 758-5437
Email: lawadmissions@wfu.edu
Financial aid: (336) 758-5437
Application deadline: 03/15
Tuition: full time: $44,220; part
time: N/A
Room/board/expenses: $21,912
Median grant: $25,000
**Average student indebtedness at
graduation:** $105,090
Enrollment: full time: 467; part
time: 23
men: 51%; women: 49%;
minorities: 20%
Acceptance rate (full time): 45%
Midrange LSAT (full time): 156-162
**Midrange undergraduate GPA (full
time):** 3.35-3.70
**Midrange of full-time private-sector
salaries of 2015 grads:** $51,500-
$102,500
2015 grads employed in: law firms:
53%; business and industry:
18%; government: 13%; public
interest: 6%; judicial clerk: 5%;
academia: 5%; unknown: 0%
Employment location for 2015 class:
Intl. N/A; N.E. 2%; M.A. 11%;
E.N.C. 3%; W.N.C. 2%; S.A. 72%;
E.S.C. 4%; W.S.C. 4%; Mt. 1%;
Pac. 2%; unknown N/A

University of North Dakota

215 Centennial Drive
Stop 9003
Grand Forks, ND 58202
www.law.und.edu
Public
Admissions: (701) 777-2260
Email: benjamin.hoffman@
law.und.edu
Financial aid: (701) 777-3121
Application deadline: 07/15
In-state tuition: full time: $11,434;
part time: N/A
Out-of-state tuition: full time:
$25,423
Room/board/expenses: $16,553
Median grant: $3,500
**Average student indebtedness at
graduation:** $66,917
Enrollment: full time: 234; part
time: N/A
men: 49%; women: 51%;
minorities: 11%
Acceptance rate (full time): 64%
**Midrange of full-time private-sector
salaries of 2015 grads:** $40,000-
$58,500
2015 grads employed in: law firms:
46%; business and industry:
8%; government: 19%; public
interest: 2%; judicial clerk: 24%;
academia: 2%; unknown: 0%

Employment location for 2015 class:
Intl. 3%; N.E. N/A; M.A. 2%;
E.N.C. 2%; W.N.C. 81%; S.A. N/A;
E.S.C. N/A; W.S.C. N/A; Mt. 8%;
Pac. 3%; unknown N/A

Capital University

303 E. Broad Street
Columbus, OH 43215-3200
www.law.capital.edu
Private
Admissions: (614) 236-6310
Email:
admissions@law.capital.edu
Financial aid: (614) 236-6350
Application deadline: 08/01
Tuition: full time: $1,220/credit
hour; part time: $1,220/credit
hour
Room/board/expenses: $18,899
Median grant: $17,000
**Average student indebtedness at
graduation:** $35,079
Enrollment: full time: 240; part
time: 138
men: 56%; women: 44%;
minorities: 23%
Acceptance rate (full time): 81%
Midrange LSAT (full time): 145-153
**Midrange undergraduate GPA (full
time):** 2.94-3.50
**Midrange of full-time private-sector
salaries of 2015 grads:** $50,000-
$80,000
2015 grads employed in: law firms:
50%; business and industry:
27%; government: 21%; public
interest: 1%; judicial clerk: 0%;
academia: 1%; unknown: 0%
**Employment location for 2015
class:** Intl. 0%; N.E. 0%; M.A. 1%;
E.N.C. 91%; W.N.C. 1%; S.A. 5%;
E.S.C. 1%; W.S.C. 0%; Mt. 2%;
Pac. 0%; unknown 0%

Case Western Reserve University

11075 E. Boulevard
Cleveland, OH 44106-7148
www.law.case.edu
Private
Admissions: (800) 756-0036
Email: lawadmissions@case.edu
Financial aid: (877) 889-4279
Application deadline: 04/01
Tuition: full time: $49,634; part
time: $2,066/credit hour
Room/board/expenses: $23,574
Median grant: $33,233
**Average student indebtedness at
graduation:** $102,370
Enrollment: full time: 421; part
time: N/A
men: 49%; women: 51%;
minorities: 18%
Acceptance rate (full time): 43%
Midrange LSAT (full time): 155-161
**Midrange undergraduate GPA (full
time):** 3.25-3.69
**Midrange of full-time private-sector
salaries of 2015 grads:** $55,000-
$110,000
2015 grads employed in: law firms:
50%; business and industry:
24%; government: 15%; public
interest: 6%; judicial clerk: 3%;
academia: 1%; unknown: 1%
Employment location for 2015 class:
Intl. 5%; N.E. 3%; M.A. 13%;
E.N.C. 64%; W.N.C. 2%; S.A.
9%; E.S.C. 1%; W.S.C. 2%; Mt.
1%; Pac. 1%; unknown 0%

Cleveland State University (Cleveland-Marshall)

2121 Euclid Avenue, LB 138
Cleveland, OH 44115-2214
www.law.csuohio.edu
Public
Admissions: (216) 687-2304
Email:
law.admissions@csuohio.edu
Financial aid: (216) 687-2304
Application deadline: 05/01
In-state tuition: full time: $27,209;
part time: $21,977
Out-of-state tuition: full time:
$37,430
Room/board/expenses: $19,486
Median grant: $9,282
**Average student indebtedness at
graduation:** $29,051
Enrollment: full time: 249; part
time: 87
men: 51%; women: 49%;
minorities: 15%
Acceptance rate (full time): 57%
Midrange LSAT (full time): 150-156
**Midrange undergraduate GPA (full
time):** 3.10-3.51
**Midrange of full-time private-sector
salaries of 2015 grads:** $45,000-
$105,000
2015 grads employed in: law firms:
44%; business and industry:
34%; government: 16%; public
interest: 3%; judicial clerk: 2%;
academia: 1%; unknown: 0%
**Employment location for 2015
class:** Intl. 0%; N.E. 1%; M.A. 0%;
E.N.C. 91%; W.N.C. 1%; S.A. 4%;
E.S.C. 0%; W.S.C. 0%; Mt. 1%;
Pac. 0%; unknown 0%

Ohio Northern University (Pettit)

525 S. Main Street
Ada, OH 45810-1599
www.law.onu.edu
Private
Admissions: (419) 772-2211
Email: lawadmissions@onu.edu
Financial aid: (419) 772-2272
Application deadline: 08/01
Tuition: full time: $26,940; part
time: N/A
Room/board/expenses: $21,479
Median grant: $18,500
**Average student indebtedness at
graduation:** $104,284
Enrollment: full time: 173; part
time: N/A
men: 51%; women: 49%;
minorities: 23%
Acceptance rate (full time): 59%
Midrange LSAT (full time): 143-152
**Midrange undergraduate GPA (full
time):** 2.98-3.61
**Midrange of full-time private-sector
salaries of 2015 grads:** $45,000-
$75,000
2015 grads employed in: law firms:
44%; business and industry:
24%; government: 14%; public
interest: 2%; judicial clerk: 4%;
academia: 2%; unknown: 10%
Employment location for 2015 class:
Intl. 2%; N.E. 0%; M.A. 24%;
E.N.C. 50%; W.N.C. 4%; S.A.
10%; E.S.C. 4%; W.S.C. 2%; Mt.
0%; Pac. 0%; unknown 0%

Ohio State University (Moritz)
55 W. 12th Avenue
Columbus, OH 43210
www.moritzlaw.osu.edu
Public
Admissions: (614) 292-8810
Email: lawadmit@osu.edu
Financial aid: (614) 292-8807
Application deadline: 03/31
In-state tuition: full time: $29,668; part time: N/A
Out-of-state tuition: full time: $44,620
Room/board/expenses: $20,028
Median grant: $13,000
Average student indebtedness at graduation: $88,301
Enrollment: full time: 505; part time: N/A
men: 51%; women: 49%; minorities: 20%
Acceptance rate (full time): 49%
Midrange LSAT (full time): 156-161
Midrange undergraduate GPA (full time): 3.43-3.79
Midrange of full-time private-sector salaries of 2015 grads: $59,000-$105,000
2015 grads employed in: law firms: 42%; business and industry: 27%; government: 18%; public interest: 4%; judicial clerk: 5%; academia: 3%; unknown: 0%
Employment location for 2015 class: Intl. 0%; N.E. 1%; M.A. 4%; E.N.C. 84%; W.N.C. N/A; S.A. 5%; E.S.C. N/A; W.S.C. 3%; Mt. 2%; Pac. 2%; unknown 0%

University of Akron
C. Blake McDowell Law Center
Akron, OH 44325-2901
www.uakron.edu/law
Public
Admissions: (800) 425-7668
Email: lawadmissions@uakron.edu
Financial aid: (800) 621-3847
Application deadline: 03/31
In-state tuition: full time: $24,214; part time: $14,819
Out-of-state tuition: full time: $24,314
Room/board/expenses: $16,524
Median grant: $8,750
Average student indebtedness at graduation: $82,854
Enrollment: full time: 290; part time: 144
men: 54%; women: 46%; minorities: 13%
Acceptance rate (full time): 52%
Midrange LSAT (full time): 149-154
Midrange undergraduate GPA (full time): 3.06-3.55
Midrange of full-time private-sector salaries of 2015 grads: $48,000-$75,000
2015 grads employed in: law firms: 50%; business and industry: 26%; government: 18%; public interest: 2%; judicial clerk: 2%; academia: 1%; unknown: 0%
Employment location for 2015 class: Intl. 0%; N.E. 0%; M.A. 6%; E.N.C. 87%; W.N.C. 0%; S.A. 2%; E.S.C. 2%; W.S.C. 1%; Mt. 0%; Pac. 2%; unknown 0%

University of Cincinnati
PO Box 210040
Cincinnati, OH 45221-0040
www.law.uc.edu
Public
Admissions: (513) 556-6805
Email: admissions@law.uc.edu
Financial aid: (513) 556-0078
Application deadline: 03/15
In-state tuition: full time: $24,010; part time: N/A
Out-of-state tuition: full time: $29,010
Room/board/expenses: $19,268
Median grant: $10,000
Average student indebtedness at graduation: $75,512
Enrollment: full time: 286; part time: 3
men: 54%; women: 46%; minorities: 18%
Acceptance rate (full time): 53%
Midrange LSAT (full time): 153-158
Midrange undergraduate GPA (full time): 3.24-3.76
Midrange of full-time private-sector salaries of 2015 grads: $52,000-$110,000
2015 grads employed in: law firms: 49%; business and industry: 19%; government: 18%; public interest: 11%; judicial clerk: 3%; academia: 0%; unknown: 0%
Employment location for 2015 class: Intl. 0%; N.E. 0%; M.A. 1%; E.N.C. 81%; W.N.C. 1%; S.A. 4%; E.S.C. 5%; W.S.C. 0%; Mt. 2%; Pac. 5%; unknown 0%

University of Dayton
300 College Park
Dayton, OH 45469-2772
www.udayton.edu/law
Private
Admissions: (937) 229-3555
Email: lawinfo@udayton.edu
Financial aid: (937) 229-3555
Application deadline: 05/01
Tuition: full time: $33,391; part time: N/A
Room/board/expenses: $17,500
Median grant: $12,000
Average student indebtedness at graduation: $108,724
Enrollment: full time: 266; part time: N/A
men: 51%; women: 49%; minorities: 23%
Acceptance rate (full time): 60%
Midrange LSAT (full time): 145-152
Midrange undergraduate GPA (full time): 2.83-3.41
Midrange of full-time private-sector salaries of 2015 grads: $50,000-$85,000
2015 grads employed in: law firms: 44%; business and industry: 27%; government: 21%; public interest: 3%; judicial clerk: 3%; academia: 3%; unknown: 0%
Employment location for 2015 class: Intl. 0%; N.E. 0%; M.A. 3%; E.N.C. 77%; W.N.C. 1%; S.A. 8%; E.S.C. 7%; W.S.C. 3%; Mt. 0%; Pac. 1%; unknown 0%

University of Toledo
2801 W. Bancroft
Toledo, OH 43606
www.utoledo.edu/law/admissions
Public
Admissions: (419) 530-4131
Email: law.admissions@utoledo.edu
Financial aid: (419) 530-4712
Application deadline: 08/01
In-state tuition: full time: $19,612; part time: $817/credit hour
Out-of-state tuition: full time: $31,161
Room/board/expenses: $19,320
Median grant: $10,295
Average student indebtedness at graduation: $85,649
Enrollment: full time: 179; part time: 45
men: 54%; women: 46%; minorities: 14%
Acceptance rate (full time): 59%
Midrange LSAT (full time): 149-154
Midrange undergraduate GPA (full time): 3.02-3.60
Midrange of full-time private-sector salaries of 2015 grads: $40,000-$73,000
2015 grads employed in: law firms: 36%; business and industry: 18%; government: 24%; public interest: 11%; judicial clerk: 7%; academia: 3%; unknown: 0%
Employment location for 2015 class: Intl. 2%; N.E. 1%; M.A. 2%; E.N.C. 79%; W.N.C. 0%; S.A. 9%; E.S.C. 1%; W.S.C. 4%; Mt. 0%; Pac. 2%; unknown 0%

OKLAHOMA

Oklahoma City University
2501 N. Blackwelder Avenue
Oklahoma City, OK 73106-1493
www.law.okcu.edu
Private
Admissions: (866) 529-6281
Email: lawquestions@okcu.edu
Financial aid: (800) 633-7242
Application deadline: 08/01
Tuition: full time: $1,065/credit hour; part time: $1,065/credit hour
Room/board/expenses: $23,642
Median grant: $14,000
Average student indebtedness at graduation: $102,024
Enrollment: full time: 357; part time: 53
men: 51%; women: 49%; minorities: 33%
Acceptance rate (full time): 68%
Midrange LSAT (full time): 144-151
Midrange undergraduate GPA (full time): 2.68-3.39
Midrange of full-time private-sector salaries of 2015 grads: $47,000-$65,000
2015 grads employed in: law firms: 50%; business and industry: 30%; government: 11%; public interest: 7%; judicial clerk: 1%; academia: 1%; unknown: 0%
Employment location for 2015 class: Intl. 0%; N.E. 0%; M.A. 0%; E.N.C. 0%; W.N.C. 2%; S.A. 0%; E.S.C. 1%; W.S.C. 92%; Mt. 3%; Pac. 2%; unknown 0%

University of Oklahoma
Andrew M. Coats Hall
300 Timberdell Road
Norman, OK 73019-5081
www.law.ou.edu
Public
Admissions: (405) 325-4728
Email: admissions@law.ou.edu
Financial aid: (405) 325-4521
Application deadline: 03/15
In-state tuition: full time: $19,973; part time: N/A
Out-of-state tuition: full time: $30,398
Room/board/expenses: $17,110
Median grant: $7,250
Average student indebtedness at graduation: $83,433
Enrollment: full time: 505; part time: N/A
men: 57%; women: 43%; minorities: 22%
Acceptance rate (full time): 50%
Midrange LSAT (full time): 154-159
Midrange undergraduate GPA (full time): 3.17-3.74
Midrange of full-time private-sector salaries of 2015 grads: $50,000-$90,000
2015 grads employed in: law firms: 59%; business and industry: 15%; government: 19%; public interest: 4%; judicial clerk: 1%; academia: 1%; unknown: 0%
Employment location for 2015 class: Intl. 0%; N.E. 0%; M.A. 0%; E.N.C. 2%; W.N.C. 4%; S.A. 4%; E.S.C. 0%; W.S.C. 86%; Mt. 3%; Pac. 1%; unknown 0%

University of Tulsa
3120 E. Fourth Place
Tulsa, OK 74104
law.utulsa.edu
Private
Admissions: (918) 631-2709
Email: lawadmissions@utulsa.edu
Financial aid: (918) 631-2526
Application deadline: 07/31
Tuition: full time: $38,030; part time: N/A
Room/board/expenses: $19,560
Median grant: $22,500
Average student indebtedness at graduation: $76,988
Enrollment: full time: 231; part time: 30
men: 54%; women: 46%; minorities: 26%
Acceptance rate (full time): 39%
Midrange LSAT (full time): 151-157
Midrange undergraduate GPA (full time): 3.11-3.65
Midrange of full-time private-sector salaries of 2015 grads: $52,500-$75,000
2015 grads employed in: law firms: 58%; business and industry: 22%; government: 8%; public interest: 8%; judicial clerk: 1%; academia: 2%; unknown: 0%
Employment location for 2015 class: Intl. 0%; N.E. 0%; M.A. 0%; E.N.C. 0%; W.N.C. 7%; S.A. 3%; E.S.C. 1%; W.S.C. 85%; Mt. 1%; Pac. 2%; unknown 0%

OREGON

Lewis & Clark College (Northwestern)
10015 S.W. Terwilliger Boulevard
Portland, OR 97219
law.lclark.edu
Private
Admissions: (503) 768-6613
Email: lawadmss@lclark.edu
Financial aid: (503) 768-7090
Application deadline: 03/15
Tuition: full time: $43,290; part time: $32,476
Room/board/expenses: $26,800
Median grant: $17,804
Average student indebtedness at graduation: $139,624
Enrollment: full time: 452; part time: 132
men: 49%; women: 51%; minorities: 22%
Acceptance rate (full time): 59%
Midrange LSAT (full time): 154-161
Midrange undergraduate GPA (full time): 3.06-3.62
Midrange of full-time private-sector salaries of 2015 grads: $44,150-$75,250
2015 grads employed in: law firms: 31%; business and industry: 19%; government: 20%; public interest: 13%; judicial clerk: 17%; academia: 1%; unknown: 0%
Employment location for 2015 class: Intl. 1%; N.E. 1%; M.A. 2%; E.N.C. 3%; W.N.C. 3%; S.A. 6%; E.S.C. 1%; W.S.C. 2%; Mt. 3%; Pac. 78%; unknown 0%

University of Oregon
1221 University of Oregon
Eugene, OR 97403-1221
www.law.uoregon.edu
Public
Admissions: (541) 346-3846
Email: admissions@law.uoregon.edu
Financial aid: (800) 760-6953
Application deadline: 03/01
In-state tuition: full time: $32,474; part time: N/A
Out-of-state tuition: full time: $40,394
Room/board/expenses: $15,058
Median grant: $16,000
Average student indebtedness at graduation: $17,834
Enrollment: full time: 334; part time: N/A
men: 52%; women: 48%; minorities: 18%
Acceptance rate (full time): 54%
Midrange LSAT (full time): 154-159
Midrange undergraduate GPA (full time): 3.20-3.64
Midrange of full-time private-sector salaries of 2015 grads: $59,500-$115,000
2015 grads employed in: law firms: 38%; business and industry: 14%; government: 16%; public interest: 6%; judicial clerk: 17%; academia: 4%; unknown: 4%
Employment location for 2015 class: Intl. 1%; N.E. 1%; M.A. 2%; E.N.C. 0%; W.N.C. 1%; S.A. 3%; E.S.C. 0%; W.S.C. 1%; Mt. 9%; Pac. 81%; unknown 2%

Willamette University (Collins)

245 Winter Street SE
Salem, OR 97301
www.willamette.edu/law
Private
Admissions: (503) 370-6282
Email: law-admission@
willamette.edu
Financial aid: (503) 370-6273
Application deadline: rolling
Tuition: full time: $41,245; part
time: $28,440
Room/board/expenses: $21,030
Median grant: $15,000
**Average student indebtedness at
graduation:** $148,429
Enrollment: full time: 277; part
time: 15
men: 50%; women: 50%;
minorities: 18%
Acceptance rate (full time): 75%
Midrange LSAT (full time): 149-156
**Midrange undergraduate GPA (full
time):** 2.75-3.65
**Midrange of full-time private-sector
salaries of 2015 grads:** N/A
2015 grads employed in: law firms:
49%; business and industry:
14%; government: 10%; public
interest: 4%; judicial clerk: 17%;
academia: 1%; unknown: 5%
Employment location for 2015 class:
Intl: 0%; N.E. 0%; M.A. 0%;
E.N.C. 0%; W.N.C. 1%; S.A. 0%;
E.S.C. 0%; W.S.C. 2%; Mt. 5%;
Pac. 91%; unknown 0%

PENNSYLVANIA

Drexel University (Kline)

3320 Market Street, Suite 400
Philadelphia, PA 19104
www.drexel.edu/law/admissions/
overview/
Private
Admissions: (215) 895-1529
Email:
lawadmissions@drexel.edu
Financial aid: (215) 895-1044
Application deadline: 08/01
Tuition: full time: $1,422/credit
hour; part time: N/A/credit hour
Room/board/expenses: $23,380
Median grant: $25,000
**Average student indebtedness at
graduation:** $96,402
Enrollment: full time: 374; part
time: 12
men: 48%; women: 52%;
minorities: 17%
Acceptance rate (full time): 52%
Midrange LSAT (full time): 152-156
**Midrange undergraduate GPA (full
time):** 3.04-3.56
**Midrange of full-time private-sector
salaries of 2015 grads:** $53,000-
$80,000
2015 grads employed in: law firms:
41%; business and industry:
21%; government: 13%; public
interest: 1%; judicial clerk: 24%;
academia: 0%; unknown: 0%
Employment location for 2015 class:
Intl. 1%; N.E. 0%; M.A. 84%;
E.N.C. 1%; W.N.C. 0%; S.A. 12%;
E.S.C. 0%; W.S.C. 0%; Mt. 0%;
Pac. 2%; unknown 0%

Duquesne University

600 Forbes Avenue
Pittsburgh, PA 15282
www.duq.edu/law
Private
Admissions: (412) 396-6296
Email: lawadmissions@duq.edu
Financial aid: (412) 396-6607
Application deadline: 03/01
Tuition: full time: $41,276; part
time: $31,914
Room/board/expenses: $15,460
Median grant: $20,000
**Average student indebtedness at
graduation:** $108,414
Enrollment: full time: 301; part
time: 88
men: 47%; women: 53%;
minorities: 7%
Acceptance rate (full time): 63%
Midrange LSAT (full time): 150-155
**Midrange undergraduate GPA (full
time):** 3.14-3.63
**Midrange of full-time private-sector
salaries of 2015 grads:** $53,500-
$80,000
2015 grads employed in: law firms:
47%; business and industry:
34%; government: 9%; public
interest: 2%; judicial clerk: 8%;
academia: 1%; unknown: 0%
Employment location for 2015 class:
Intl. 0%; N.E. 0%; M.A. 91%;
E.N.C. 1%; W.N.C. 0%; S.A. 7%;
E.S.C. 0%; W.S.C. 1%; Mt. 0%;
Pac. 0%; unknown 0%

Pennsylvania State University-Carlisle (Dickinson)

150 S. College Street
Carlisle, PA 17013
dickinsonlaw.psu.edu
Public
Admissions: (717) 240-5207
Email: dickinsonlaw@psu.edu
Financial aid: (717) 240-5207
Application deadline: 06/30
In-state tuition: full time: $46,854;
part time: N/A
Out-of-state tuition: full time:
$46,854
Room/board/expenses: $20,802
Median grant: $35,112
**Average student indebtedness at
graduation:** $109,828
Enrollment: full time: 184; part
time: N/A
men: 55%; women: 45%;
minorities: 21%
Acceptance rate (full time): 36%
Midrange LSAT (full time): 156-160
**Midrange undergraduate GPA (full
time):** 3.07-3.71
**Midrange of full-time private-sector
salaries of 2015 grads:** $45,500-
$75,000
2015 grads employed in: law firms:
38%; business and industry:
20%; government: 22%; public
interest: 4%; judicial clerk: 16%;
academia: %; unknown: 0%
**Employment location for 2015
class:** Intl. 2%; N.E. 0%; M.A.
71%; E.N.C. 0%; W.N.C. 0%; S.A.
24%; E.S.C. 2%; W.S.C. 0%; Mt.
0%; Pac. 0%; unknown 0%

Pennsylvania State University-University Park

Lewis Katz Building
University Park, PA 16802
pennstatelaw.psu.edu
Public
Admissions: (800) 840-1122
Email: admissions@
pennstatelaw.psu.edu
Financial aid: (814) 863-0469
Application deadline: 03/31
In-state tuition: full time: $47,174;
part time: N/A
Out-of-state tuition: full time:
$47,174
Room/board/expenses: $22,776
Median grant: $28,700
**Average student indebtedness at
graduation:** $117,692
Enrollment: full time: 402; part
time: N/A
men: 56%; women: 44%;
minorities: 21%
Acceptance rate (full time): 40%
Midrange LSAT (full time): 156-159
**Midrange undergraduate GPA (full
time):** 3.15-3.69
**Midrange of full-time private-sector
salaries of 2015 grads:** $50,000-
$100,000
2015 grads employed in: law firms:
45%; business and industry:
16%; government: 18%; public
interest: 4%; judicial clerk: 12%;
academia: 5%; unknown: 0%
Employment location for 2015 class:
Intl. 4%; N.E. 3%; M.A. 42%;
E.N.C. 1%; W.N.C. 0%; S.A. 28%;
E.S.C. 1%; W.S.C. 7%; Mt. 7%;
Pac. 8%; unknown 0%

Temple University (Beasley)

1719 N. Broad Street
Philadelphia, PA 19122
www.law.temple.edu
Public
Admissions: (800) 560-1428
Email: lawadmis@temple.edu
Financial aid: (800) 560-1428
Application deadline: 03/01
In-state tuition: full time: $24,786;
part time: $20,018
Out-of-state tuition: full time:
$37,500
Room/board/expenses: $22,488
Median grant: $15,000
**Average student indebtedness at
graduation:** $86,937
Enrollment: full time: 534; part
time: 153
men: 49%; women: 51%;
minorities: 28%
Acceptance rate (full time): 42%
Midrange LSAT (full time): 156-162
**Midrange undergraduate GPA (full
time):** 3.27-3.72
**Midrange of full-time private-sector
salaries of 2015 grads:** $65,000-
$120,000
2015 grads employed in: law firms:
43%; business and industry:
15%; government: 15%; public
interest: 9%; judicial clerk: 15%;
academia: 1%; unknown: 0%
Employment location for 2015 class:
Intl. 1%, N.E. 0%; M.A. 80%;
E.N.C. 1%; W.N.C. 0%; S.A. 7%;
E.S.C. 0%; W.S.C. 0%; Mt. 0%;
Pac. 0%; unknown 0%

University of Pennsylvania

3501 Sansom Street
Philadelphia, PA 19104-6204
www.law.upenn.edu
Private
Admissions: (215) 898-7400
Email: contactadmissions@
law.upenn.edu
Financial aid: (215) 898-7400
Application deadline: 03/01
Tuition: full time: $60,988; part
time: N/A
Room/board/expenses: $23,852
Median grant: $20,000
**Average student indebtedness at
graduation:** $156,725
Enrollment: full time: 749; part
time: N/A
men: 54%; women: 46%;
minorities: 29%
Acceptance rate (full time): 17%
Midrange LSAT (full time): 163-170
**Midrange undergraduate GPA (full
time):** 3.57-3.95
**Midrange of full-time private-sector
salaries of 2015 grads:** $160,000-
$160,000
2015 grads employed in: law firms:
72%; business and industry:
5%; government: 2%; public
interest: 7%; judicial clerk: 14%;
academia: 0%; unknown: 0%
Employment location for 2015 class:
Intl. 1%; N.E. 1%; M.A. 64%;
E.N.C. 3%, W.N.C. 0%, S.A. 17%;
E.S.C. 1%; W.S.C. 6%; Mt. 1%;
Pac. 5%; unknown 0%

University of Pittsburgh

3900 Forbes Avenue
Pittsburgh, PA 15260
www.law.pitt.edu
Public
Admissions: (412) 648-1805
Email: admitlaw@pitt.edu
Financial aid: (412) 648-1415
Application deadline: 04/01
In-state tuition: full time: $33,152;
part time: $1,219/credit hour
Out-of-state tuition: full time:
$41,332
Room/board/expenses: $18,976
Median grant: $15,000
**Average student indebtedness at
graduation:** $103,990
Enrollment: full time: 413; part
time: 1
men: 54%; women: 46%;
minorities: 19%
Acceptance rate (full time): 36%
Midrange LSAT (full time): 152-159
**Midrange undergraduate GPA (full
time):** 3.12-3.64
**Midrange of full-time private-sector
salaries of 2015 grads:** $50,000-
$82,000
2015 grads employed in: law firms:
44%; business and industry:
32%; government: 6%; public
interest: 2%; judicial clerk: 15%;
academia: 1%; unknown: 0%
Employment location for 2015 class:
Intl. 1%; N.E. 1%; M.A. 79%;
E.N.C. 2%; W.N.C. 1%; S.A. 7%;
E.S.C. 1%; W.S.C. 1%; Mt. 3%;
Pac. 4%; unknown 0%

Villanova University

299 N. Spring Mill Road
Villanova, PA 19085
www1.villanova.edu/villanova/
law.html
Private
Admissions: (610) 519-7010
Email: admissions@
law.villanova.edu
Financial aid: (610) 519-7015
Application deadline: 04/01
Tuition: full time: $43,895; part
time: N/A
Room/board/expenses: $22,732
Median grant: $32,000
**Average student indebtedness at
graduation:** $99,736
Enrollment: full time: 540; part
time: N/A
men: 50%; women: 50%;
minorities: 19%
Acceptance rate (full time): 43%
Midrange LSAT (full time): 153-159
**Midrange undergraduate GPA (full
time):** 3.24-3.70
**Midrange of full-time private-sector
salaries of 2015 grads:** $55,000-
$120,000
2015 grads employed in: law firms:
47%; business and industry:
20%; government: 9%; public
interest: 2%; judicial clerk: 21%;
academia: 1%; unknown: 0%
Employment location for 2015 class:
Intl. 1%; N.E. 6%; M.A. 78%;
F.N.C. 0%; W.N.C. 1%; S.A. 12%;
E.S.C. 0%; W.S.C. 0%; Mt. 0%;
Pac. 2%; unknown 0%

Widener University (Commonwealth)

3800 Vartan Way
Harrisburg, PA 17110
commonwealthlaw.widener.edu
Private
Admissions: (717) 541-3903
Email: admitcwlaw@widener.edu
Financial aid: (717) 541-1924
Application deadline: 05/01
Tuition: full time: $1,438/credit
hour; part time: $1,438/credit
hour
Room/board/expenses: $21,628
Median grant: $10,000
**Average student indebtedness at
graduation:** $129,016
Enrollment: full time: 184; part
time: 69
men: 54%; women: 46%;
minorities: 17%
Acceptance rate (full time): 68%
Midrange LSAT (full time): 145-149
**Midrange undergraduate GPA (full
time):** 2.87-3.40
**Midrange of full-time private-sector
salaries of 2015 grads:** $45,000-
$55,000
2015 grads employed in: law firms:
40%; business and industry:
16%; government: 16%; public
interest: 3%; judicial clerk: 24%;
academia: 1%; unknown: 0%
Employment location for 2015 class:
Intl. 0%; N.E. 0%; M.A. 93%;
E.N.C. 0%; W.N.C. 0%; S.A. 4%;
E.S.C. 0%; W.S.C. 0%; Mt. 0%;
Pac. 3%; unknown 0%

PUERTO RICO

Inter-American University[1]
PO Box 70351
San Juan, PR 00936-8351
www.metro.inter.edu
Private
Admissions: (787) 765-1270
Financial aid: N/A
Tuition: N/A
Room/board/expenses: N/A
Enrollment: N/A

Pontifical Catholic University of Puerto Rico[1]
2250 Avenida Las Americas
Suite 584
Ponce, PR 00717-0777
www.pucpr.edu
Private
Admissions: (787) 841-2000
Email: admisiones@pucpr.edu
Financial aid: N/A
Tuition: N/A
Room/board/expenses: N/A
Enrollment: N/A

University of Puerto Rico[1]
PO Box 23303
Estacion Universidad
Rio Piedras, PR 00931-3302
www.upr.edu
Public
Admissions: (787) 764-0000
Email: admisiones@upr.edu
Financial aid: N/A
Tuition: N/A
Room/board/expenses: N/A
Enrollment: N/A

RHODE ISLAND

Roger Williams University
10 Metacom Avenue
Bristol, RI 02809-5171
law.rwu.edu
Private
Admissions: (401) 254-4555
Email: Admissions@rwu.edu
Financial aid: (401) 254-4510
Application deadline: 04/18
Tuition: full time: $34,742; part time: N/A
Room/board/expenses: $17,450
Median grant: $16,896
Average student indebtedness at graduation: $126,334
Enrollment: full time: 423; part time: N/A
men: 48%; women: 52%; minorities: 25%
Acceptance rate (full time): 69%
Midrange LSAT (full time): 145-153
Midrange undergraduate GPA (full time): 2.83-3.47
Midrange of full-time private-sector salaries of 2015 grads: $45,000-$71,000
2015 grads employed in: law firms: 40%; business and industry: 18%; government: 12%; public interest: 9%; judicial clerk: 19%; academia: 1%; unknown: 2%
Employment location for 2015 class: Intl. 0%; N.E. 70%; M.A. 20%; E.N.C. 0%; W.N.C. 1%; S.A. 4%; E.S.C. 0%; W.S.C. 0%; Mt. 2%; Pac. 1%; unknown 0%

SOUTH CAROLINA

Charleston School of Law
PO Box 535
Charleston, SC 29402
www.charlestonlaw.edu
Private
Admissions: (843) 377-2143
Email: info@charlestonlaw.edu
Financial aid: (843) 377-1102
Application deadline: 03/01
Tuition: full time: $40,716; part time: $32,738
Room/board/expenses: $22,603
Median grant: $12,000
Average student indebtedness at graduation: $137,345
Enrollment: full time: 363; part time: 53
men: 46%; women: 54%; minorities: 24%
Acceptance rate (full time): 78%
Midrange LSAT (full time): 142-149
Midrange undergraduate GPA (full time): 2.70-3.32
Midrange of full-time private-sector salaries of 2015 grads: $40,000-$50,000
2015 grads employed in: law firms: 57%; business and industry: 16%; government: 8%; public interest: 4%; judicial clerk: 11%; academia: 5%; unknown: 0%
Employment location for 2015 class: Intl. 1%; N.E. 0%; M.A. 3%; E.N.C. 2%; W.N.C. 1%; S.A. 89%; E.S.C. 1%; W.S.C. 0%; Mt. 1%; Pac. 2%; unknown 0%

University of South Carolina
701 S. Main Street
Columbia, SC 29208
www.law.sc.edu/admissions
Public
Admissions: (803) 777-6605
Email: usclaw@law.sc.edu
Financial aid: (803) 777-6605
Application deadline: 03/01
In-state tuition: full time: $25,994; part time: N/A
Out-of-state tuition: full time: $51,050
Room/board/expenses: $18,229
Median grant: $21,206
Average student indebtedness at graduation: $89,388
Enrollment: full time: 607; part time: N/A
men: 56%; women: 44%; minorities: 19%
Acceptance rate (full time): 58%
Midrange undergraduate GPA (full time): 3.17-3.64
Midrange of full-time private-sector salaries of 2015 grads: $55,000-$105,000
2015 grads employed in: law firms: 36%; business and industry: 18%; government: 20%; public interest: 2%; judicial clerk: 21%; academia: 2%; unknown: 1%
Employment location for 2015 class: Intl. 0%; N.E. 1%; M.A. 1%; E.N.C. 0%; W.N.C. 0%; S.A. 94%; E.S.C. 0%; W.S.C. 1%; Mt. 1%; Pac. 2%; unknown N/A

SOUTH DAKOTA

University of South Dakota
414 E. Clark Street
Vermillion, SD 57069-2390
www.usd.edu/law
Public
Admissions: (605) 677-6358
Email: law@usd.edu
Financial aid: (605) 677-5446
Application deadline: 07/01
In-state tuition: full time: $14,501; part time: $450/credit hour
Out-of-state tuition: full time: $32,487
Room/board/expenses: $14,364
Median grant: $1,169
Average student indebtedness at graduation: $56,609
Enrollment: full time: 196; part time: 3
men: 59%; women: 41%; minorities: 13%
Acceptance rate (full time): 61%
Midrange LSAT (full time): 144-152
Midrange undergraduate GPA (full time): 3.04-3.66
Midrange of full-time private-sector salaries of 2015 grads: $42,000-$66,000
2015 grads employed in: law firms: 38%; business and industry: 15%; government: 13%; public interest: 4%; judicial clerk: 27%; academia: 2%; unknown: 0%
Employment location for 2015 class: Intl. 0%; N.E. 0%; M.A. 0%; E.N.C. 6%; W.N.C. 90%; S.A. 0%; E.S.C. 0%; W.S.C. 0%; Mt. 2%; Pac. 0%; unknown 0%

TENNESSEE

Belmont University
1900 Belmont Boulevard
Nashville, TN 37212
www.belmont.edu/law/
Private
Admissions: (615) 460-8400
Email: law@belmont.edu
Financial aid: (615) 460-6403
Application deadline: rolling
Tuition: full time: $40,900; part time: N/A
Room/board/expenses: $24,950
Median grant: $28,605
Average student indebtedness at graduation: $40,677
Enrollment: full time: 260; part time: N/A
men: 46%; women: 54%; minorities: 13%
Acceptance rate (full time): 60%
Midrange LSAT (full time): 152-158
Midrange undergraduate GPA (full time): 3.19-3.67
Midrange of full-time private-sector salaries of 2015 grads: $53,000-$67,000
2015 grads employed in: law firms: 40%; business and industry: 38%; government: 14%; public interest: 3%; judicial clerk: 5%; academia: 0%; unknown: 0%
Employment location for 2015 class: Intl. 0%; N.E. 0%; M.A. 0%; E.N.C. 0%; W.N.C. 1%; S.A. 1%; E.S.C. 97%; W.S.C. 0%; Mt. 0%; Pac. 0%; unknown 0%

Lincoln Memorial University
601 West Summit Hill Drive
Knoxville, TN 37902
law.lmunet.edu
Private
Admissions: (865) 545-5304
Email: Law.admissions@LMUnet.edu
Financial aid: (423) 869-6465
Application deadline: 07/15
Tuition: full time: $1,125/credit hour; part time: $1,125/credit hour
Room/board/expenses: $22,060
Median grant: $20,924
Average student indebtedness at graduation: $89,779
Enrollment: full time: 105; part time: 29
men: 54%; women: 46%; minorities: 13%
Acceptance rate (full time): 69%
Midrange LSAT (full time): 146-152
Midrange undergraduate GPA (full time): 2.72-3.38
Midrange of full-time private-sector salaries of 2015 grads: N/A-N/A
2015 grads employed in: law firms: 33%; business and industry: 29%; government: 21%; public interest: 0%; judicial clerk: 8%; academia: 8%; unknown: 0%
Employment location for 2015 class: Intl. 0%; N.E. 4%; M.A. N/A; E.N.C. N/A; W.N.C. N/A; S.A. 4%; E.S.C. 79%; W.S.C. N/A; Mt. N/A; Pac. N/A; unknown N/A

University of Memphis (Humphreys)
1 North Front Street
Memphis, TN 38103-2189
www.memphis.edu/law
Public
Admissions: (901) 678-5403
Email: lawadmissions@memphis.edu
Financial aid: (901) 678-3737
Application deadline: 03/15
In-state tuition: full time: $18,763; part time: $899/credit hour
Out-of-state tuition: full time: $25,968
Room/board/expenses: $17,576
Median grant: $7,860
Average student indebtedness at graduation: $76,997
Enrollment: full time: 308; part time: 17
men: 55%; women: 45%; minorities: 25%
Acceptance rate (full time): 55%
Midrange LSAT (full time): 149-154
Midrange undergraduate GPA (full time): 3.01-3.54
Midrange of full-time private-sector salaries of 2015 grads: $42,000-$73,500
2015 grads employed in: law firms: 66%; business and industry: 9%; government: 11%; public interest: 3%; judicial clerk: 6%; academia: 3%; unknown: 2%
Employment location for 2015 class: Intl. 0%; N.E. 0%; M.A. 0%; E.N.C. 2%; W.N.C. 0%; S.A. 1%; E.S.C. 87%; W.S.C. 5%; Mt. 2%; Pac. 2%; unknown 0%

University of Tennessee-Knoxville
1505 W. Cumberland Avenue
Knoxville, TN 37996-1810
www.law.utk.edu
Public
Admissions: (865) 974-4131
Email: lawadmit@utk.edu
Financial aid: (865) 974-4131
Application deadline: 03/01
In-state tuition: full time: $19,308; part time: N/A
Out-of-state tuition: full time: $37,982
Room/board/expenses: $20,998
Median grant: $10,000
Average student indebtedness at graduation: $80,445
Enrollment: full time: 333; part time: N/A
men: 56%; women: 44%; minorities: 17%
Acceptance rate (full time): 36%
Midrange LSAT (full time): 154-160
Midrange undergraduate GPA (full time): 3.30-3.77
Midrange of full-time private-sector salaries of 2015 grads: $47,500-$109,500
2015 grads employed in: law firms: 56%; business and industry: 20%; government: 9%; public interest: 4%; judicial clerk: 9%; academia: 2%; unknown: 0%
Employment location for 2015 class: Intl. 1%; N.E. 0%; M.A. 1%; E.N.C. 2%; W.N.C. 1%; S.A. 14%; E.S.C. 77%; W.S.C. 4%; Mt. 0%; Pac. 1%; unknown 0%

Vanderbilt University
131 21st Avenue S
Nashville, TN 37203-1181
law.vanderbilt.edu/
Private
Admissions: (615) 322-6452
Email: admissions@law.vanderbilt.edu
Financial aid: (615) 322-6452
Application deadline: 04/01
Tuition: full time: $53,150; part time: N/A/credit hour
Room/board/expenses: $24,910
Median grant: $20,000
Average student indebtedness at graduation: $127,434
Enrollment: full time: 572; part time: N/A
men: 49%; women: 51%; minorities: 22%
Acceptance rate (full time): 32%
Midrange LSAT (full time): 162-168
Midrange undergraduate GPA (full time): 3.50-3.85
Midrange of full-time private-sector salaries of 2015 grads: $110,000-$160,000
2015 grads employed in: law firms: 52%; business and industry: 12%; government: 9%; public interest: 9%; judicial clerk: 16%; academia: 1%; unknown: 0%
Employment location for 2015 class: Intl. 2%; N.E. 1%; M.A. 16%; E.N.C. 9%; W.N.C. 5%; S.A. 20%; E.S.C. 26%; W.S.C. 12%; Mt. 4%; Pac. 5%; unknown 0%

TEXAS

Baylor University

1114 S. University Parks Drive
1 Bear Place, # 97288
Waco, TX 76798-7288
www.baylor.edu/law/
Private
Admissions: (254) 710-4842
Email:
jenny_branson@baylor.edu
Financial aid: (254) 710-2611
Application deadline: 07/15
Tuition: full time: $57,752; part
time: $1,391/credit hour
Room/board/expenses: $20,418
Median grant: $24,000
**Average student indebtedness at
graduation:** $144,732
Enrollment: full time: 363; part
time: 2
men: 48%; women: 52%;
minorities: 24%
Acceptance rate (full time): 33%
Midrange LSAT (full time): 155-161
**Midrange undergraduate GPA (full
time):** 3.29-3.76
**Midrange of full-time private-sector
salaries of 2015 grads:** $65,000-
$100,000
2015 grads employed in: law firms:
71%; business and industry:
7%; government: 12%; public
interest: 1%; judicial clerk: 6%;
academia: 3%; unknown: 0%
Employment location for 2015 class:
Intl: 0%; N.E. 0%; M.A. 0%;
E.N.C. 0%; W.N.C. 0%; S.A. 1%;
E.S.C. 0%; W.S.C. 96%; Mt. 2%;
Pac. 1%; unknown 0%

South Texas College of Law Houston

1303 San Jacinto Street
Houston, TX 77002-7006
www.stcl.edu
Private
Admissions: (713) 646-1810
Email: admissions@stcl.edu
Financial aid: (713) 646-1820
Application deadline: 03/15
Tuition: full time: $30,600; part
time: $20,600
Room/board/expenses: $19,104
Median grant: $3,687
**Average student indebtedness at
graduation:** $38,717
Enrollment: full time: 732; part
time: 237
men: 54%; women: 46%;
minorities: 39%
Acceptance rate (full time): 61%
Midrange LSAT (full time): 148-154
**Midrange undergraduate GPA (full
time):** 2.82-3.33
**Midrange of full-time private-sector
salaries of 2015 grads:** $55,000-
$90,000
2015 grads employed in: law firms:
63%; business and industry:
14%; government: 10%; public
interest: 2%; judicial clerk: 1%;
academia: 0%; unknown: 9%
Employment location for 2015 class:
Intl. 1%; N.E. 0%; M.A. 0%;
E.N.C. 1%; W.N.C. 0%; S.A. 0%;
E.S.C. 0%; W.S.C. 60%; Mt. 0%;
Pac. 0%; unknown 38%

Southern Methodist University (Dedman)

PO Box 750116
Dallas, TX 75275-0116
www.law.smu.edu
Private
Admissions: (214) 768-2540
Email: lawadmit@mail.smu.edu
Financial aid: (214) 768-4119
Application deadline: 04/15
Tuition: full time: $51,096; part
time: $38,323
Room/board/expenses: $29,370
Median grant: $23,000
**Average student indebtedness at
graduation:** $126,172
Enrollment: full time: 620; part
time: 121
men: 50%; women: 50%;
minorities: 22%
Acceptance rate (full time): 47%
Midrange LSAT (full time): 155-163
**Midrange undergraduate GPA (full
time):** 3.39-3.78
**Midrange of full-time private-sector
salaries of 2015 grads:** $67,500-
$154,000
2015 grads employed in: law firms:
66%; business and industry:
19%; government: 9%; public
interest: 1%; judicial clerk: 5%;
academia: 1%; unknown: %
**Employment location for 2015
class:** Intl. 0%; N.E. N/A; M.A. 1%;
E.N.C. 0%; W.N.C. 0%; S.A. 2%;
E.S.C. N/A; W.S.C. 94%; Mt. 0%;
Pac. 1%; unknown N/A

St. Mary's University

1 Camino Santa Maria
San Antonio, TX 78228-8602
law.stmarytx.edu
Private
Admissions: (210) 436-3523
Email:
lawadmissions@stmarytx.edu
Financial aid: (210) 431-6743
Application deadline: 03/01
Tuition: full time: $35,240; part
time: $23,350
Room/board/expenses: $19,472
Median grant: $5,246
**Average student indebtedness at
graduation:** $118,583
Enrollment: full time: 557; part
time: 170
men: 55%; women: 45%;
minorities: 56%
Acceptance rate (full time): 66%
Midrange LSAT (full time): 147-152
**Midrange undergraduate GPA (full
time):** 2.71-3.34
**Midrange of full-time private-sector
salaries of 2015 grads:** $55,000-
$85,000
2015 grads employed in: law firms:
58%; business and industry:
17%; government: 17%; public
interest: 4%; judicial clerk: 1%;
academia: 2%; unknown: 0%
Employment location for 2015 class:
Intl. 1%; N.E. 1%; M.A. 0%; E.N.C.
0%; W.N.C. 0%; S.A. 1%; E.S.C.
0%; W.S.C. 96%; Mt. 1%; Pac.
1%; unknown 0%

Texas A&M University

1515 Commerce Street
Fort Worth, TX 76102
law.tamu.edu/
Public
Admissions: (817) 212-4040
Email: law-admissions@
law.tamu.edu

Financial aid: (817) 212-4090
Application deadline: 07/01
In-state tuition: full time: $28,000;
part time: $22,000
Out-of-state tuition: full time:
$33,668
Room/board/expenses: $28,188
Median grant: $19,000
**Average student indebtedness at
graduation:** $115,405
Enrollment: full time: 355; part
time: 129
men: 50%; women: 50%;
minorities: 24%
Acceptance rate (full time): 25%
Midrange LSAT (full time): 155-158
**Midrange undergraduate GPA (full
time):** 3.17-3.60
**Midrange of full-time private-sector
salaries of 2015 grads:** $50,000-
$80,000
2015 grads employed in: law firms:
58%; business and industry:
23%; government: 14%; public
interest: 2%; judicial clerk: 2%;
academia: 1%; unknown: 1%
**Employment location for 2015
class:** Intl. 0%; N.E. 0%; M.A. 1%;
E.N.C. 0%; W.N.C. 0%; S.A. 1%;
E.S.C. 0%; W.S.C. 96%; Mt. 1%;
Pac. 0%; unknown 2%

Texas Southern University (Marshall)[1]

3100 Cleburne Street
Houston, TX 77004
www.tsulaw.edu
Public
Admissions: (713) 313-7114
Email: lawadmit@tsulaw.edu
Tuition: N/A
Room/board/expenses: N/A
Enrollment: N/A

Texas Tech University

1802 Hartford Avenue
Lubbock, TX 79409-0004
www.law.ttu.edu
Public
Admissions: (806) 834-5024
Email: admissions.law@ttu.edu
Financial aid: (806) 834-3875
Application deadline: 03/01
In-state tuition: full time: $23,668;
part time: N/A
Out-of-state tuition: full time:
$35,008
Room/board/expenses: $16,060
Median grant: $6,680
**Average student indebtedness at
graduation:** $80,087
Enrollment: full time: 517; part
time: 1
men: 55%; women: 45%;
minorities: 26%
Acceptance rate (full time): 53%
Midrange LSAT (full time): 151-156
**Midrange undergraduate GPA (full
time):** 3.03-3.56
**Midrange of full-time private-sector
salaries of 2015 grads:** $54,532-
$86,013
2015 grads employed in: law firms:
63%; business and industry:
10%; government: 16%; public
interest: 3%; judicial clerk: 6%;
academia: 2%; unknown: 0%
Employment location for 2015 class:
Intl. 0%; N.E. 0%; M.A. 0%;
E.N.C. 0%; W.N.C. 0%; S.A. 1%;
E.S.C. 1%; W.S.C. 91%; Mt. 6%;
Pac. 1%; unknown 0%

University of Houston

4604 Calhoun Road
Houston, TX 77204-6060
www.law.uh.edu
Public
Admissions: (713) 743-2280
Email: lawadmissions@uh.edu
Financial aid: (713) 743-2269
Application deadline: 02/15
In-state tuition: full time: $30,401;
part time: $20,911
Out-of-state tuition: full time:
$45,219
Room/board/expenses: $19,484
Median grant: $7,500
**Average student indebtedness at
graduation:** $97,246
Enrollment: full time: 610; part
time: 100
men: 54%; women: 46%;
minorities: 39%
Acceptance rate (full time): 35%
Midrange LSAT (full time): 156-162
**Midrange undergraduate GPA (full
time):** 3.26-3.70
**Midrange of full-time private-sector
salaries of 2015 grads:** $65,000-
$160,000
2015 grads employed in: law firms:
63%; business and industry:
22%; government: 7%; public
interest: 5%; judicial clerk: 2%;
academia: 1%; unknown: 0%
Employment location for 2015 class:
Intl. 1%; N.E. 1%; M.A. 1%; E.N.C.
1%; W.N.C. 0%; S.A. 1%; E.S.C.
1%; W.S.C. 95%; Mt. 0%; Pac.
1%; unknown 0%

University of Texas-Austin

727 E. Dean Keeton Street
Austin, TX 78705-3299
law.utexas.edu/
Public
Admissions: (512) 232-1200
Email:
admissions@law.utexas.edu
Financial aid: (512) 232-1130
Application deadline: 03/01
In-state tuition: full time: $33,995;
part time: N/A
Out-of-state tuition: full time:
$50,480
Room/board/expenses: $19,354
Median grant: $13,000
**Average student indebtedness at
graduation:** $103,417
Enrollment: full time: 898; part
time: 6
men: 56%; women: 44%;
minorities: 31%
Acceptance rate (full time): 27%
Midrange LSAT (full time): 162-168
**Midrange undergraduate GPA (full
time):** 3.41-3.84
**Midrange of full-time private-sector
salaries of 2015 grads:** $100,000-
$160,000
2015 grads employed in: law firms:
58%; business and industry:
8%; government: 12%; public
interest: 7%; judicial clerk: 15%;
academia: 1%; unknown: 0%
**Employment location for 2015
class:** Intl. 1%; N.E. 0%; M.A. 3%;
E.N.C. 2%; W.N.C. 1%; S.A. 4%;
E.S.C. 1%; W.S.C. 83%; Mt. 1%;
Pac. 3%; unknown 0%

UTAH

Brigham Young University (Clark)

243 JRCB
Provo, UT 84602-8000
www.law.byu.edu
Private
Admissions: (801) 422-7871
Email: admissions@law.byu.edu
Financial aid: (801) 422-6386
Application deadline: rolling
Tuition: full time: $12,310; part
time: N/A
Room/board/expenses: $20,352
Median grant: $3,934
**Average student indebtedness at
graduation:** $58,133
Enrollment: full time: 390; part
time: 12
men: 63%; women: 37%;
minorities: 16%
Acceptance rate (full time): 44%
Midrange LSAT (full time): 157-164
**Midrange undergraduate GPA (full
time):** 3.55-3.89
**Midrange of full-time private-sector
salaries of 2015 grads:** $65,000-
$107,000
2015 grads employed in: law firms:
44%; business and industry:
17%; government: 15%; public
interest: 5%; judicial clerk: 15%;
academia: 3%; unknown: 0%
**Employment location for 2015
class:** Intl. 2%; N.E. 0%; M.A. 1%;
E.N.C. 2%; W.N.C. 0%; S.A. 6%;
E.S.C. 0%; W.S.C. 4%; Mt. 72%;
Pac. 13%; unknown 1%

University of Utah (Quinney)

383 South University Street
Salt Lake City, UT 84112
www.law.utah.edu
Public
Admissions: (801) 581-7479
Email: admissions@law.utah.edu
Financial aid: (801) 585-6461
Application deadline: 02/15
In-state tuition: full time: $26,758;
part time: N/A
Out-of-state tuition: full time:
$50,816
Room/board/expenses: $18,208
Median grant: $7,365
**Average student indebtedness at
graduation:** $91,982
Enrollment: full time: 292; part
time: 12
men: 58%; women: 42%;
minorities: 12%
Acceptance rate (full time): 49%
Midrange LSAT (full time): 156-161
**Midrange undergraduate GPA (full
time):** 3.33-3.70
**Midrange of full-time private-sector
salaries of 2015 grads:** $52,000-
$100,000
2015 grads employed in: law firms:
45%; business and industry:
20%; government: 12%; public
interest: 7%; judicial clerk: 15%;
academia: 1%; unknown: 0%
**Employment location for 2015
class:** Intl. 0%; N.E. 0%; M.A. 1%;
E.N.C. 1%; W.N.C. 0%; S.A. 1%;
E.S.C. 0%; W.S.C. 3%; Mt. 95%;
Pac. 0%; unknown 0%

VERMONT

Vermont Law School
Chelsea Street
South Royalton, VT 05068-0096
www.vermontlaw.edu
Private
Admissions: (888) 277-5985
Email: admiss@vermontlaw.edu
Financial aid: (888) 277-5985
Application deadline: 04/15
Tuition: full time: $47,998; part time: $1,691/credit hour
Room/board/expenses: $24,934
Median grant: $20,000
Average student indebtedness at graduation: $52,682
Enrollment: full time: 383; part time: N/A
men: 43%; women: 57%; minorities: 21%
Acceptance rate (full time): 81%
Midrange of full-time private-sector salaries of 2015 grads: $47,000-$72,000
2015 grads employed in: law firms: 28%; business and industry: 22%; government: 14%; public interest: 14%; judicial clerk: 22%; academia: 0%; unknown: %
Employment location for 2015 class: Intl. 1%; N.E. 37%; M.A. 17%; E.N.C. 2%; W.N.C. 2%; S.A. 16%; E.S.C. 1%; W.S.C. 2%; Mt. 8%; Pac. 13%; unknown 0%

VIRGINIA

Appalachian School of Law
1169 Edgewater Drive
Grundy, VA 24614-2825
www.asl.edu
Private
Admissions: (800) 244-1303
Email: aslinfo@asl.edu
Financial aid: (276) 244-1211
Application deadline: rolling
Tuition: full time: $31,525; part time: N/A
Room/board/expenses: $20,400
Median grant: $13,000
Enrollment: full time: 94; part time: N/A
men: 63%; women: 37%; minorities: 12%
Acceptance rate (full time): 28%
Midrange of full-time private-sector salaries of 2015 grads: N/A-N/A
2015 grads employed in: law firms: N/A; business and industry: N/A; government: N/A; public interest: N/A; judicial clerk: N/A; academia: N/A; unknown: N/A
Employment location for 2015 class: Intl. N/A; N.E. N/A; M.A. N/A; E.N.C. N/A; W.N.C. N/A; S.A. N/A; E.S.C. N/A; W.S.C. N/A; Mt. N/A; Pac. N/A; unknown N/A

College of William and Mary (Marshall-Wythe)
PO Box 8795
Williamsburg, VA 23187-8795
law.wm.edu/
Public
Admissions: (757) 221-3785
Email: lawadm@wm.edu
Financial aid: (757) 221-2420
Application deadline: 03/01
In-state tuition: full time: $32,000; part time: N/A
Out-of-state tuition: full time: $41,000
Room/board/expenses: $18,250
Median grant: $12,000
Average student indebtedness at graduation: $90,028
Enrollment: full time: 633; part time: N/A
men: 45%; women: 55%; minorities: 17%
Acceptance rate (full time): 41%
Midrange LSAT (full time): 157-164
Midrange undergraduate GPA (full time): 3.49-3.88
Midrange of full-time private-sector salaries of 2015 grads: $75,000-$145,000
2015 grads employed in: law firms: 43%; business and industry: 12%; government: 16%; public interest: 6%; judicial clerk: 20%; academia: 3%; unknown: 0%
Employment location for 2015 class: Intl. 1%; N.E. 1%; M.A. 20%; E.N.C. 1%; W.N.C. 1%; S.A. 60%; E.S.C. 4%; W.S.C. 3%; Mt. 3%; Pac. 5%; unknown 0%

George Mason University
3301 Fairfax Drive
Arlington, VA 22201-4426
www.law.gmu.edu
Public
Admissions: (703) 993-8010
Email: lawadmit@gmu.edu
Financial aid: (703) 993-2353
Application deadline: 04/01
In-state tuition: full time: $25,351; part time: $905/credit hour
Out-of-state tuition: full time: $40,737
Room/board/expenses: $23,908
Median grant: $12,000
Average student indebtedness at graduation: $118,056
Enrollment: full time: 365; part time: 153
men: 56%; women: 44%; minorities: 23%
Acceptance rate (full time): 26%
Midrange LSAT (full time): 158-164
Midrange undergraduate GPA (full time): 3.35-3.75
Midrange of full-time private-sector salaries of 2015 grads: $56,950-$102,719
2015 grads employed in: law firms: 41%; business and industry: 16%; government: 23%; public interest: 4%; judicial clerk: 10%; academia: 5%; unknown: 0%
Employment location for 2015 class: Intl. 1%; N.E. 0%; M.A. 5%; E.N.C. 1%; W.N.C. 2%; S.A. 84%; E.S.C. 0%; W.S.C. 1%; Mt. 3%; Pac. 3%; unknown 0%

Liberty University
1971 University Boulevard
Lynchburg, VA 24515
law.liberty.edu
Private
Admissions: (434) 592-5300
Email: lawadmissions@liberty.edu
Financial aid: (434) 592-5300
Application deadline: 07/01
Tuition: full time: $32,302; part time: N/A
Room/board/expenses: $16,800
Median grant: $19,500
Average student indebtedness at graduation: $73,857
Enrollment: full time: 167; part time: 1
men: 60%; women: 40%; minorities: 17%
Acceptance rate (full time): 51%
Midrange LSAT (full time): 150-155
Midrange undergraduate GPA (full time): 2.90-3.80
Midrange of full-time private-sector salaries of 2015 grads: $50,000-$65,000
2015 grads employed in: law firms: 54%; business and industry: 7%; government: 17%; public interest: 10%; judicial clerk: 10%; academia: 2%; unknown: 0%
Employment location for 2015 class: Intl. 0%; N.E. 2%; M.A. 2%; E.N.C. 7%; W.N.C. 5%; S.A. 63%; E.S.C. 10%; W.S.C. 5%; Mt. 0%; Pac. 5%; unknown 0%

Regent University
1000 Regent University Drive
Virginia Beach, VA 23464-9880
www.regent.edu/law/admissions
Private
Admissions: (757) 352-4132
Email: lawschool@regent.edu
Financial aid: (757) 352-5137
Application deadline: 06/01
Tuition: full time: $1,140/credit hour; part time: $1,140/credit hour
Room/board/expenses: $22,180
Median grant: $15,000
Average student indebtedness at graduation: $124,221
Enrollment: full time: 193; part time: 29
men: 41%; women: 59%; minorities: 25%
Acceptance rate (full time): 45%
Midrange LSAT (full time): 149-154
Midrange undergraduate GPA (full time): 3.08-3.66
Midrange of full-time private-sector salaries of 2015 grads: $45,000-$65,000
2015 grads employed in: law firms: 43%; business and industry: 15%; government: 15%; public interest: 11%; judicial clerk: 11%; academia: 4%; unknown: 0%
Employment location for 2015 class: Intl. 0%; N.E. 0%; M.A. 3%; E.N.C. 5%; W.N.C. 3%; S.A. 73%; E.S.C. 2%; W.S.C. 5%; Mt. 5%; Pac. 2%; unknown 0%

University of Richmond
28 Westhampton Way
Richmond, VA 23173
law.richmond.edu
Private
Admissions: (804) 289-8189
Email: mrahman@richmond.edu
Financial aid: (804) 289-8438
Application deadline: 03/01
Tuition: full time: $41,500; part time: $2,310/credit hour
Room/board/expenses: $16,440
Median grant: $25,000
Average student indebtedness at graduation: $104,624
Enrollment: full time: 440; part time: 5
men: 49%; women: 51%; minorities: 12%
Acceptance rate (full time): 31%
Midrange LSAT (full time): 154-163
Midrange undergraduate GPA (full time): 3.23-3.68

Midrange of full-time private-sector salaries of 2015 grads: $52,000-$85,000
2015 grads employed in: law firms: 44%; business and industry: 18%; government: 11%; public interest: 5%; judicial clerk: 21%; academia: 1%; unknown: 1%
Employment location for 2015 class: Intl. 2%; N.E. 0%; M.A. 7%; E.N.C. 1%; W.N.C. 0%; S.A. 83%; E.S.C. 1%; W.S.C. 2%; Mt. 0%; Pac. 4%; unknown 0%

University of Virginia
580 Massie Road
Charlottesville, VA 22903-1738
www.law.virginia.edu
Public
Admissions: (434) 924-7351
Email: lawadmit@virginia.edu
Financial aid: (434) 924-7805
Application deadline: 03/05
In-state tuition: full time: $56,300; part time: N/A
Out-of-state tuition: full time: $59,300
Room/board/expenses: $18,828
Median grant: $25,000
Average student indebtedness at graduation: $155,177
Enrollment: full time: 893; part time: N/A
men: 57%; women: 43%; minorities: 21%
Acceptance rate (full time): 20%
Midrange LSAT (full time): 164-170
Midrange undergraduate GPA (full time): 3.48-3.94
Midrange of full-time private-sector salaries of 2015 grads: $145,000-$160,000
2015 grads employed in: law firms: 64%; business and industry: 4%; government: 10%; public interest: 3%; judicial clerk: 19%; academia: 1%; unknown: 0%
Employment location for 2015 class: Intl. 1%; N.E. 3%; M.A. 24%; E.N.C. 4%; W.N.C. 2%; S.A. 43%; E.S.C. 3%; W.S.C. 7%; Mt. 3%; Pac. 11%; unknown 0%

Washington and Lee University
Sydney Lewis Hall
Lexington, VA 24450-0303
law.wlu.edu
Private
Admissions: (540) 458-8503
Email: lawadm@wlu.edu
Financial aid: (540) 458-8032
Application deadline: 07/01
Tuition: full time: $47,437; part time: N/A
Room/board/expenses: $18,123
Median grant: $25,000
Average student indebtedness at graduation: $105,426
Enrollment: full time: 329; part time: N/A
men: 55%; women: 45%; minorities: 20%
Acceptance rate (full time): 47%
Midrange LSAT (full time): 155-161
Midrange undergraduate GPA (full time): 3.16-3.67
Midrange of full-time private-sector salaries of 2015 grads: $62,500-$120,000
2015 grads employed in: law firms: 50%; business and industry: 11%; government: 11%; public interest: 9%; judicial clerk: 19%; academia: 1%; unknown: 0%

WASHINGTON

Gonzaga University
PO Box 3528
Spokane, WA 99220-3528
www.law.gonzaga.edu
Private
Admissions: (800) 793-1710
Email: admissions@lawschool.gonzaga.edu
Financial aid: (800) 448-2138
Application deadline: 04/15
Tuition: full time: $37,245; part time: N/A
Room/board/expenses: $18,514
Median grant: $18,000
Average student indebtedness at graduation: $109,692
Enrollment: full time: 305; part time: 2
men: 55%; women: 45%; minorities: 16%
Acceptance rate (full time): 57%
Midrange LSAT (full time): 151-155
Midrange undergraduate GPA (full time): 3.01-3.42
Midrange of full-time private-sector salaries of 2015 grads: $50,000-$78,000
2015 grads employed in: law firms: 54%; business and industry: 13%; government: 14%; public interest: 10%; judicial clerk: 9%; academia: %; unknown: 0%
Employment location for 2015 class: Intl. 0%; N.E. 1%; M.A. 2%; E.N.C. 0%; W.N.C. 0%; S.A. 6%; E.S.C. 0%; W.S.C. 1%; Mt. 25%; Pac. 65%; unknown 0%

Seattle University
901 12th Avenue
Seattle, WA 98122-1090
law.seattleu.edu/
Private
Admissions: (206) 398-4200
Email: lawadmis@seattleu.edu
Financial aid: (206) 398-4250
Application deadline: 03/01
Tuition: full time: $43,582; part time: $30,510
Room/board/expenses: $25,019
Median grant: $15,000
Average student indebtedness at graduation: $139,745
Enrollment: full time: 520; part time: 134
men: 43%; women: 57%; minorities: 32%
Acceptance rate (full time): 65%
Midrange LSAT (full time): 151-158
Midrange undergraduate GPA (full time): 3.13-3.52
Midrange of full-time private-sector salaries of 2015 grads: $55,000-$92,500
2015 grads employed in: law firms: 46%; business and industry: 18%; government: 17%; public interest: 9%; judicial clerk: 9%; academia: 2%; unknown: %
Employment location for 2015 class: Intl. 1%; N.E. 0%; M.A. 1%; E.N.C. 1%; W.N.C. 0%; S.A. 2%; E.S.C. 0%; W.S.C. 1%; Mt. 3%; Pac. 93%; unknown 0%

University of Washington

Campus Box 353020
Seattle, WA 98195-3020
www.law.washington.edu
Public
Admissions: (206) 543-4078
Email: lawadm@uw.edu
Financial aid: (206) 543-4078
Application deadline: 03/15
In-state tuition: full time: $32,721; part time: N/A
Out-of-state tuition: full time: $44,112
Room/board/expenses: $19,011
Median grant: $12,162
Average student indebtedness at graduation: $120,554
Enrollment: full time: 500; part time: N/A
men: 52%; women: 48%; minorities: 28%
Acceptance rate (full time): 27%
Midrange LSAT (full time): 157-165
Midrange undergraduate GPA (full time): 3.43-3.80
Midrange of full-time private-sector salaries of 2015 grads: $65,000-$125,000
2015 grads employed in: law firms: 54%; business and industry: 10%; government: 18%; public interest: 6%; judicial clerk: 11%; academia: 0%; unknown: 0%
Employment location for 2015 class: Intl. 2%; N.E. 0%; M.A. 1%; E.N.C. 0%; W.N.C. 0%; S.A. 1%; E.S.C. 0%; W.S.C. 1%; Mt. 5%; Pac. 89%; unknown 0%

WEST VIRGINIA

West Virginia University

PO Box 6130
Morgantown, WV 26506-6130
www.law.wvu.edu/
Public
Admissions: (304) 293-5304
Email: wvulaw.admissions@mail.wvu.edu
Financial aid: (304) 293-5302
Application deadline: 03/01
In-state tuition: full time: $20,916; part time: $1,162/credit hour
Out-of-state tuition: full time: $37,674
Room/board/expenses: $16,790
Median grant: $17,784
Average student indebtedness at graduation: $82,683
Enrollment: full time: 302; part time: 3
men: 57%; women: 43%; minorities: 10%
Acceptance rate (full time): 60%
Midrange LSAT (full time): 151-156
Midrange undergraduate GPA (full time): 3.06-3.60
Midrange of full-time private-sector salaries of 2015 grads: $55,000-$75,000
2015 grads employed in: law firms: 50%; business and industry: 13%; government: 11%; public interest: 3%; judicial clerk: 19%; academia: 4%; unknown: 0%
Employment location for 2015 class: Intl. 0%; N.E. 0%; M.A. 5%; E.N.C. 3%; W.N.C. 1%; S.A. 85%; E.S.C. 0%; W.S.C. 2%; Mt. 5%; Pac. 0%; unknown 0%

WISCONSIN

Marquette University

Eckstein Hall
PO Box 1881
Milwaukee, WI 53201-1881
law.marquette.edu
Private
Admissions: (414) 288-6767
Email: law.admission@marquette.edu
Financial aid: (414) 288-7390
Application deadline: 04/01
Tuition: full time: $43,530; part time: $1,725/credit hour
Room/board/expenses: $20,558
Median grant: $8,000
Average student indebtedness at graduation: $142,601
Enrollment: full time: 513; part time: 62
men: 59%; women: 41%; minorities: 18%
Acceptance rate (full time): 68%
Midrange LSAT (full time): 149-156
Midrange undergraduate GPA (full time): 3.08-3.54
Midrange of full-time private-sector salaries of 2015 grads: $50,000-$93,750
2015 grads employed in: law firms: 54%; business and industry: 20%; government: 12%; public interest: 7%; judicial clerk: 4%; academia: 4%; unknown: 0%
Employment location for 2015 class: Intl. 0%; N.E. 2%; M.A. 1%; E.N.C. 86%; W.N.C. 2%; S.A. 4%; E.S.C. 0%; W.S.C. 3%; Mt. 2%; Pac. 1%; unknown 0%

University of Wisconsin-Madison

975 Bascom Mall
Madison, WI 53706-1399
law.wisc.edu
Public
Admissions: (608) 262-5914
Email: admissions@law.wisc.edu
Financial aid: (608) 262-5914
Application deadline: 04/01
In-state tuition: full time: $21,450; part time: $941/credit hour
Out-of-state tuition: full time: $40,147
Room/board/expenses: $19,706
Median grant: $15,679
Average student indebtedness at graduation: $77,555
Enrollment: full time: 481; part time: 24
men: 52%; women: 48%; minorities: 22%
Acceptance rate (full time): 46%
Midrange LSAT (full time): 156-163
Midrange undergraduate GPA (full time): 3.30-3.72
Midrange of full-time private-sector salaries of 2015 grads: $55,000-$120,000
2015 grads employed in: law firms: 45%; business and industry: 16%; government: 24%; public interest: 8%; judicial clerk: 5%; academia: 2%; unknown: 0%
Employment location for 2015 class: Intl. 1%; N.E. 2%; M.A. 3%; E.N.C. 73%; W.N.C. 9%; S.A. 5%; E.S.C. 1%; W.S.C. 1%; Mt. 4%; Pac. 4%; unknown 0%

WYOMING

University of Wyoming

Department 3035
1000 E. University Avenue
Laramie, WY 82071
www.uwyo.edu/law/
Public
Admissions: (307) 766-6416
Email: lawadmis@uwyo.edu
Financial aid: (307) 766-2116
Application deadline: 06/08
In-state tuition: full time: $15,758; part time: N/A
Out-of-state tuition: full time: $32,590
Room/board/expenses: $17,075
Median grant: $6,000
Average student indebtedness at graduation: $90,231
Enrollment: full time: 231; part time: N/A
men: 53%; women: 47%; minorities: 14%
Acceptance rate (full time): 58%
Midrange LSAT (full time): 150-157
Midrange undergraduate GPA (full time): 3.25-3.65
Midrange of full-time private-sector salaries of 2015 grads: $50,000-$62,500
2015 grads employed in: law firms: 55%; business and industry: 17%; government: 6%; public interest: 9%; judicial clerk: 9%; academia: 3%; unknown: 0%
Employment location for 2015 class: Intl. 0%; N.E. 0%; M.A. 0%; E.N.C. 0%; W.N.C. 5%; S.A. 2%; E.S.C. 0%; W.S.C. 0%; Mt. 72%; Pac. 5%; unknown 17%

MEDICINE

This directory lists the 140 schools offering M.D. degrees that were accredited by the Liaison Committee on Medical Education in 2016 plus the 30 schools that offer D.O. degrees and were accredited by the American Osteopathic Association in 2016. Of those, a total of 118 M.D.-granting and D.O.-granting schools responded to the U.S. News survey, conducted in the fall of 2016 and early 2017. Their data are reported below. Schools that did not respond have abbreviated entries.

KEY TO THE TERMINOLOGY

1. A school whose name is footnoted with the numeral 1 did not return the U.S. News statistical survey; limited data appear in its entry.

N/A. Not available from the school or not applicable.

Admissions. The admissions office phone number.

Email. The address of the admissions office. If instead of an email address a website is listed, the website will automatically present an email screen programmed to reach the admissions office.

Financial aid. The financial aid office phone number.

Application deadline. For fall 2018 enrollment.

Tuition. For the 2016-17 academic year. Includes fees.

Room/board/expenses. For the 2016-17 academic year.

Students receiving grants. The percentage of the entire student body during the 2015-16 academic year that received grants or scholarships.

Average indebtedness. For 2015 graduates who incurred medical school-related debt.

Enrollment. Total doctor of medicine (M.D.) or doctor of osteopathy (D.O.) degree program enrollment for fall 2016.

Minorities. For fall 2016, percentage of U.S. students who fall in one of these groups: black or African-American, Asian, American Indian or Alaska Native, Native Hawaiian or other Pacific Islander, Hispanic/Latino, or two or more races. The number of minority students was reported by the school.

Underrepresented minorities. For fall 2016, percentage of U.S. students who are black or African-American, American Indian or Alaska Native, Native Hawaiian or other Pacific Islander, Hispanic/Latino, or two or more races. (This category is used only for medical schools. The underrepresented minority count was reported by the school.)

Acceptance rate. Percentage of applicants who were accepted for fall 2016 to an M.D. or D.O. degree program.

Median new Medical College Admission Test (MCAT) total score. For M.D. or D.O. students who entered the medical or osteopathic program in the fall of 2016. Separate scores for each of the test's four sections are reported to test-takers on a scale of 118 to 132. The total score is the sum of the four scores and ranges from 472 to 528.

Median undergraduate grade point average (GPA). For M.D. or D.O. students who entered in the fall of 2016.

Most popular undergraduate majors. For students who entered in the fall of 2016. The main areas are biological sciences, including microbiology; physical sciences, including chemistry; nonsciences, including the humanities; and other, including double majors, mixed disciplines, and other health professions like nursing and pharmacy.

Graduates entering primary care specialties. This is the three-year average percentage of all medical or osteopathic school graduates entering primary care residencies in the fields of family practice, general pediatrics or general internal medicine during 2014, 2015, 2016.

ALABAMA

University of Alabama-Birmingham
Medical Student Services
VH Suite 100
Birmingham, AL 35294-0019
www.uab.edu/medicine/home
Public
Admissions: (205) 934-2433
Email: medschool@uab.edu
Financial aid: (205) 934-8223
Application deadline: 11/01
In-state tuition: $29,144
Out-of-state tuition: $64,214
Room/board/expenses: $21,760
Percent receiving grants: 44%
Average student indebtedness at graduation: $108,690
Enrollment: 792
men: 55%; women: 45%; minorities: 23%; underrepresented minorities: 16%; in state: 91%
Acceptance rate: 7%
Median New MCAT total score: 507
Median GPA: 3.77
Most popular undergraduate majors: biological sciences: 54%; physical sciences: 19%; nonsciences: 9%; other: 18%
Percent of graduates entering primary care specialties: 42.0%

University of South Alabama[1]
307 University Boulevard
170 CSAB
Mobile, AL 36688
www.usahealthsystem.com/com
Public
Admissions: (251) 460-7176
Financial aid: N/A
Tuition: N/A
Room/board/expenses: N/A
Enrollment: N/A

ARIZONA

University of Arizona
1501 N. Campbell Avenue
Tucson, AZ 85724
www.medicine.arizona.edu/
Public
Admissions: (520) 626-6214
Email: admissions@medicine.arizona.edu
Financial aid: (520) 626-7145
Application deadline: 11/01
In-state tuition: $31,641
Out-of-state tuition: $53,315
Room/board/expenses: $13,300
Percent receiving grants: 80%
Average student indebtedness at graduation: $163,049
Enrollment: 511
men: 48%; women: 52%; minorities: 43%; underrepresented minorities: 26%; in state: 72%
Acceptance rate: 3%
Median New MCAT total score: 505
Median GPA: 3.66
Most popular undergraduate majors: biological sciences: 45%; physical sciences: 14%; nonsciences: 9%; other: 32%
Percent of graduates entering primary care specialties: 37.5%

ARKANSAS

University of Arkansas for Medical Sciences[1]
4301 W. Markham Street, Slot 551
Little Rock, AR 72205
www.uams.edu
Public
Admissions: (501) 686-5354
Email: southtomg@uams.edu
Financial aid: (501) 686-5451
Tuition: N/A
Room/board/expenses: N/A
Enrollment: N/A

CALIFORNIA

California Northstate University[1]
9700 W. Taron Drive
Elk Grove, CA 95757
Private
Admissions: (916) 686-7300
Email: COMadmissions@cnsu.edu
Financial aid: N/A
Tuition: N/A
Room/board/expenses: N/A
Enrollment: N/A

Loma Linda University[1]
24851 Circle Drive
Loma Linda, CA 92350
www.llu.edu/medicine/index.page
Private
Admissions: (909) 558-4467
Email: admissions.sm@llu.edu
Financial aid: N/A
Tuition: N/A
Room/board/expenses: N/A
Enrollment: N/A

Stanford University
300 Pasteur Drive, Suite M121
Stanford, CA 94305
med.stanford.edu
Private
Admissions: (650) 723-6861
Email: mdadmissions@stanford.edu
Financial aid: (650) 723-6958
Application deadline: 10/02
Tuition: $55,314
Room/board/expenses: $30,368
Percent receiving grants: 71%
Average student indebtedness at graduation: $122,611
Enrollment: 487
men: 50%; women: 50%; minorities: 61%; underrepresented minorities: 18%; in state: 40%
Acceptance rate: 2%
Median New MCAT total score: 518
Median GPA: 3.90
Most popular undergraduate majors: biological sciences: 46%; physical sciences: 22%; nonsciences: 10%; other: 22%
Percent of graduates entering primary care specialties: 33.0%

University of California-Davis
4610 X Street
Sacramento, CA 95817
www.ucdmc.ucdavis.edu/medschool/
Public

Admissions: (916) 734-4800
Email:
medadmsinfo@ucdavis.edu
Financial aid: (916) 734-4120
Application deadline: 10/01
In-state tuition: $38,698
Out-of-state tuition: $50,943
Room/board/expenses: $16,075
Percent receiving grants: 95%
Average student indebtedness at
graduation: $153,418
Enrollment: 438
men: 42%; women:
58%; minorities: 68%;
underrepresented minorities:
33%; in state: 100%
Acceptance rate: 3%
Median New MCAT total score:
506
Median GPA: 3.64
Most popular undergraduate
majors: biological sciences:
55%; physical sciences: 16%;
nonsciences: 10%; other: 19%
Percent of graduates entering
primary care specialties: 52.4%

University of
California-Irvine
252 Irvine Hall
Irvine, CA 92697-3950
www.som.uci.edu
Public
Admissions: (949) 824-5388
Email: medadmit@uci.edu
Financial aid: (949) 824-6476
Application deadline: 11/01
In-state tuition: $38,707
Out-of-state tuition: $50,952
Room/board/expenses: $12,450
Percent receiving grants: 59%
Average student indebtedness at
graduation: $159,161
Enrollment: 410
men: 47%; women:
53%; minorities: 54%;
underrepresented minorities:
21%; in state: 96%
Acceptance rate: 4%
Median New MCAT total score: 511
Median GPA: 3.70
Most popular undergraduate
majors: biological sciences:
37%; physical sciences: 18%;
nonsciences: 8%; other: 37%
Percent of graduates entering
primary care specialties: 36.0%

University of
California-
Los Angeles (Geffen)
885 Tiverton Drive
Los Angeles, CA 90095
medschool.ucla.edu/
apply-admissions
Public
Admissions: (310) 825-8447
Email: somadmiss@
mednet.ucla.edu
Financial aid: (310) 825-4181
Application deadline: 10/17
In-state tuition: $37,924
Out-of-state tuition: $50,169
Room/board/expenses: $18,500
Percent receiving grants: 91%
Average student indebtedness at
graduation: $117,590
Enrollment: 737
men: 49%; women:
51%; minorities: 66%;
underrepresented minorities:
37%; in state: 82%
Acceptance rate: 3%
Median New MCAT total score:
505
Median GPA: 3.72

Most popular undergraduate
majors: biological sciences:
52%; physical sciences: 20%;
nonsciences: 19%; other: 9%
Percent of graduates entering
primary care specialties: 50.0%

University of
California-Riverside[1]
900 University Avenue
Riverside, CA 92521
medschool.ucr.edu/admissions/
Private
Admissions: (951) 827-7353
Email: medadmissions@ucr.edu
Financial aid: N/A
Tuition: N/A
Room/board/expenses: N/A
Enrollment: N/A

University of
California-San Diego
9500 Gilman Drive
La Jolla, CA 92093-0602
meded.ucsd.edu/
Public
Admissions: (858) 534-3880
Email: somadmissions@ucsd.edu
Financial aid: (858) 534-4664
Application deadline: 11/01
In-state tuition: $37,798
Out-of-state tuition: $50,043
Room/board/expenses: $12,510
Percent receiving grants: 61%
Average student indebtedness at
graduation: $98,750
Enrollment: 507
men: 50%; women:
50%; minorities: 52%;
underrepresented minorities:
17%; in state: 90%
Acceptance rate: 3%
Median New MCAT total score: 517
Median GPA: 3.82
Most popular undergraduate
majors: biological sciences:
60%; physical sciences: 18%;
nonsciences: 17%; other: 5%
Percent of graduates entering
primary care specialties: 45.2%

University of
California-
San Francisco
513 Parnassus Avenue
Room S224
San Francisco, CA 94143-0410
medschool.ucsf.edu/
Public
Admissions: (415) 476-4044
Email: admissions@
medsch.ucsf.edu
Financial aid: (415) 476-4181
Application deadline: 10/15
In-state tuition: $38,519
Out-of-state tuition: $50,764
Room/board/expenses: $26,380
Percent receiving grants: 82%
Average student indebtedness at
graduation: $139,457
Enrollment: 633
men: 48%; women:
52%; minorities: 58%;
underrepresented minorities:
33%; in state: 92%
Acceptance rate: 3%
Median New MCAT total score: 514
Median GPA: 3.84
Most popular undergraduate
majors: biological sciences:
54%; physical sciences: 0%;
nonsciences: 16%; other: 21%
Percent of graduates entering
primary care specialties: 42.5%

University of
Southern California
(Keck)
1975 Zonal Avenue, KAM 500
Los Angeles, CA 90033
www.usc.edu/keck
Private
Admissions: (323) 442-2552
Email: medadmit@usc.edu
Financial aid: (213) 740-5462
Application deadline: 11/01
Tuition: $61,689
Room/board/expenses: $20,167
Percent receiving grants: 44%
Average student indebtedness at
graduation: $220,614
Enrollment: 762
men: 53%; women:
47%; minorities: 56%;
underrepresented minorities:
20%; in state: 78%
Acceptance rate: 5%
Median New MCAT total score: 512
Median GPA: 3.70
Most popular undergraduate
majors: biological sciences:
49%; physical sciences: 21%;
nonsciences: 20%; other: 10%
Percent of graduates entering
primary care specialties: 38.5%

COLORADO

University of Colorado
13001 E. 17th Place, MS C290
Aurora, CO 80045
medschool.ucdenver.edu/
admissions
Public
Admissions: (303) 724-8025
Email: somadmin@ucdenver.edu
Financial aid: (303) 724-8039
Application deadline: 12/15
In-state tuition: $37,142
Out-of-state tuition: $63,098
Room/board/expenses: $20,910
Percent receiving grants: 38%
Average student indebtedness at
graduation: $182,055
Enrollment: 697
men: 54%; women:
46%; minorities: 39%;
underrepresented minorities:
23%; in state: 76%
Acceptance rate: 4%
Median New MCAT total score: 511
Median GPA: 3.71
Most popular undergraduate
majors: biological sciences:
43%; physical sciences: 27%;
nonsciences: 12%; other: 18%
Percent of graduates entering
primary care specialties: 41.2%

CONNECTICUT

Quinnipiac University[1]
275 Mt. Carmel Avenue
Hamden, CT 06518
Private
Admissions: N/A
Financial aid: N/A
Tuition: N/A
Room/board/expenses: N/A
Enrollment: N/A

University of
Connecticut
263 Farmington Avenue
Farmington, CT 06030-1905
medicine.uconn.edu
Public
Admissions: (860) 679-4713
Email: admissions@uchc.edu
Financial aid: (860) 679-1364
Application deadline: 11/15

In-state tuition: $36,714
Out-of-state tuition: $67,922
Room/board/expenses: $23,290
Percent receiving grants: 54%
Average student indebtedness at
graduation: $148,575
Enrollment: 403
men: 49%; women:
51%; minorities: 39%;
underrepresented minorities:
20%; in state: 92%
Acceptance rate: 7%
Median New MCAT total score:
509
Median GPA: 3.77
Most popular undergraduate
majors: biological sciences:
35%; physical sciences: 15%;
nonsciences: 13%; other: 37%
Percent of graduates entering
primary care specialties: 49.0%

Yale University
333 Cedar Street
PO Box 208055
New Haven, CT 06520-8055
medicine.yale.edu
Private
Admissions: (203) 785-2643
Email: medical.admissions@
yale.edu
Financial aid: (203) 785-2645
Application deadline: 10/15
Tuition: $58,644
Room/board/expenses: $13,297
Percent receiving grants: 52%
Average student indebtedness at
graduation: $119,281
Enrollment: 411
men: 53%; women:
47%; minorities: 51%;
underrepresented minorities:
22%; in state: 7%
Acceptance rate: 6%
Median New MCAT total score: 517
Median GPA: 3.82
Most popular undergraduate
majors: biological sciences:
44%; physical sciences: 35%;
nonsciences: 15%; other: 6%
Percent of graduates entering
primary care specialties: 35.0%

DISTRICT OF COLUMBIA

Georgetown
University
3900 Reservoir Road NW
Med-Dent Building
Washington, DC 20007
som.georgetown.edu/
Private
Admissions: (202) 687-1154
Email: medicaladmissions@
georgetown.edu
Financial aid: (202) 687-1693
Application deadline: 11/06
Tuition: $58,246
Room/board/expenses: $19,250
Percent receiving grants: 50%
Average student indebtedness at
graduation: $212,553
Enrollment: 785
men: 47%; women:
53%; minorities: 27%;
underrepresented minorities:
13%; in state: 3%
Acceptance rate: 2%
Median New MCAT total score: 512
Median GPA: 3.63
Most popular undergraduate
majors: biological sciences:
53%; physical sciences: 15%;
nonsciences: 15%; other: 17%
Percent of graduates entering
primary care specialties: 34.0%

George Washington
University
2300 Eye Street NW, Room 708W
Washington, DC 20037
smhs.gwu.edu
Private
Admissions: (202) 994-3506
Email: medadmit@gwu.edu
Financial aid: (202) 994-2960
Application deadline: 11/15
Tuition: $57,258
Room/board/expenses: $14,670
Average student indebtedness at
graduation: $201,981
Enrollment: 725
men: 42%; women:
58%; minorities: 43%;
underrepresented minorities:
20%; in state: 0%
Acceptance rate: 3%
Median New MCAT total score: 511
Median GPA: 3.70
Most popular undergraduate
majors: biological sciences:
43%; physical sciences: 13%;
nonsciences: 30%; other: 14%
Percent of graduates entering
primary care specialties: 39.0%

Howard University
520 W. Street NW
Washington, DC 20059
healthsciences.howard.edu
Private
Admissions: (202) 806-6279
Email:
hucmadmissions@howard.edu
Financial aid: (202) 806-4338
Application deadline: 12/15
Tuition: $50,782
Room/board/expenses: $18,030
Percent receiving grants: 50%
Average student indebtedness at
graduation: $187,042
Enrollment: 453
men: 49%; women:
51%; minorities: 88%;
underrepresented minorities:
74%; in state: 0%
Acceptance rate: 3%
Median New MCAT total score:
502
Median GPA: 3.38
Most popular undergraduate
majors: biological sciences:
46%; physical sciences: 11%;
nonsciences: 12%; other: 31%
Percent of graduates entering
primary care specialties: 41.0%

FLORIDA

Florida Atlantic
University[1]
777 Glades Road
Boca Raton, FL 33431
Private
Admissions: N/A
Financial aid: N/A
Tuition: N/A
Room/board/expenses: N/A
Enrollment: N/A

Florida International
University (Wertheim)[1]
11200 SW 8th Street
Miami, FL 33199
medicine.fiu.edu/
Public
Admissions: (305) 348-0644
Email: med.admissions@fiu.edu
Financial aid: N/A
Tuition: N/A
Room/board/expenses: N/A
Enrollment: N/A

Florida State University

1115 W. Call Street
Tallahassee, FL 32306-4300
www.med.fsu.edu/
Public
Admissions: (850) 644-7904
Email: medadmissions@
med.fsu.edu
Financial aid: (850) 645-7270
Application deadline: 12/01
In-state tuition: $26,370
Out-of-state tuition: $59,276
Room/board/expenses: $15,104
Percent receiving grants: 31%
Average student indebtedness at graduation: $150,008
Enrollment: 479
men: 49%; women: 51%; minorities: 40%; underrepresented minorities: 29%; in state: 100%
Acceptance rate: 3%
Median New MCAT total score: 505
Median GPA: 3.71
Most popular undergraduate majors: biological sciences: 64%; physical sciences: 19%; nonsciences: 3%; other: 14%
Percent of graduates entering primary care specialties: 44.2%

University of Central Florida

6850 Lake Nona Boulevard
Orlando, FL 32827
med.ucf.edu/
Public
Admissions: (407) 266-1350
Email: mdadmissions@ucf.edu
Financial aid: (407) 266-1000
Application deadline: 11/15
In-state tuition: $29,680
Out-of-state tuition: $31,063
Room/board/expenses: $13,650
Percent receiving grants: 100%
Average student indebtedness at graduation: $138,728
Enrollment: 479
men: 51%; women: 49%; minorities: N/A; underrepresented minorities: N/A; in state: 73%
Acceptance rate: 5%
Median New MCAT total score: 511
Median GPA: 3.69
Most popular undergraduate majors: biological sciences: 60%; physical sciences: 20%; nonsciences: 5%; other: 15%
Percent of graduates entering primary care specialties: 34.0%

University of Florida

Box 100216 UFHSC
Gainesville, FL 32610-0216
www.med.ufl.edu
Public
Admissions: (352) 273-7990
Email: med-admissions@ufl.edu
Financial aid: (352) 273-7939
Application deadline: 12/01
In-state tuition: $37,129
Out-of-state tuition: $49,385
Room/board/expenses: $14,020
Percent receiving grants: 72%
Average student indebtedness at graduation: $150,126
Enrollment: 550
men: 50%; women: 50%; minorities: 37%; underrepresented minorities: 26%; in state: 95%
Acceptance rate: 5%
Median New MCAT total score: 513
Median GPA: 3.86

Most popular undergraduate majors: biological sciences: 61%; physical sciences: 13%; nonsciences: 16%; other: 10%
Percent of graduates entering primary care specialties: 36.0%

University of Miami (Miller)

1120 N.W. 14th Street
Miami, FL 33136
www.med.miami.edu
Private
Admissions: (305) 243-3234
Email:
med.admissions@miami.edu
Financial aid: (305) 243-6211
Application deadline: 12/01
Tuition: $38,515
Room/board/expenses: $17,500
Percent receiving grants: 35%
Average student indebtedness at graduation: $183,947
Enrollment: 806
men: 53%; women: 47%; minorities: 44%; underrepresented minorities: 22%; in state: 50%
Acceptance rate: 4%
Median New MCAT total score: 512
Median GPA: 3.71
Most popular undergraduate majors: biological sciences: 51%; physical sciences: 19%; nonsciences: 9%; other: 21%
Percent of graduates entering primary care specialties: 39.0%

University of South Florida

12901 Bruce B. Downs Boulevard
MDC 2
Tampa, FL 33612
health.usf.edu/medicine/
mdprogram/mdadmissions
Public
Admissions: (813) 974-2266
Email: md-admissions@
health.usf.edu
Financial aid: (813) 974-8961
Application deadline: 11/15
In-state tuition: $33,726
Out-of-state tuition: $54,915
Room/board/expenses: $12,750
Percent receiving grants: 58%
Average student indebtedness at graduation: $148,306
Enrollment: 707
men: 56%; women: 44%; minorities: 44%; underrepresented minorities: 16%; in state: 66%
Acceptance rate: 5%
Median New MCAT total score: 513
Median GPA: 3.57
Most popular undergraduate majors: biological sciences: 51%; physical sciences: 24%; nonsciences: 11%; other: 14%
Percent of graduates entering primary care specialties: 45.0%

GEORGIA

Augusta University

1120 15th Street
Augusta, GA 30912-4750
www.augusta.edu/mcg/
admissions/
Public
Admissions: (706) 721-3186
Email: stdadmin@augusta.edu
Financial aid: (706) 737-1524
Application deadline: 11/01
In-state tuition: $33,195
Out-of-state tuition: $61,553
Room/board/expenses: $22,566
Percent receiving grants: 25%

Average student indebtedness at graduation: $157,053
Enrollment: 916
men: 53%; women: 47%; minorities: 40%; underrepresented minorities: 18%; in state: 96%
Acceptance rate: 13%
Median New MCAT total score: 509
Median GPA: 3.70
Most popular undergraduate majors: biological sciences: 56%; physical sciences: 26%; nonsciences: 1%; other: 17%
Percent of graduates entering primary care specialties: 44.0%

Emory University

100 Woodruff Circle NE
Atlanta, GA 30322
www.med.emory.edu
Private
Admissions: (404) 727-5660
Email: medadmiss@emory.edu
Financial aid: (404) 727-5683
Application deadline: 10/15
Tuition: $51,100
Room/board/expenses: $23,970
Percent receiving grants: 47%
Average student indebtedness at graduation: $146,658
Enrollment: 575
men: 43%; women: 57%; minorities: 33%; underrepresented minorities: 14%; in state: 33%
Acceptance rate: 5%
Median New MCAT total score: 514
Median GPA: 3.70
Most popular undergraduate majors: biological sciences: 41%; physical sciences: 21%; nonsciences: 19%; other: 19%
Percent of graduates entering primary care specialties: 37.7%

Mercer University[1]

1550 College Street
Macon, GA 31207
medicine.mercer.edu
Private
Admissions: (478) 301-5425
Email:
admissions@med.mercer.edu
Financial aid: (478) 301-2539
Tuition: N/A
Room/board/expenses: N/A
Enrollment: N/A

Morehouse School of Medicine[1]

720 Westview Drive SW
Atlanta, GA 30310
www.msm.edu
Private
Admissions: (404) 752-1650
Email: mdadmissions@msm.edu
Financial aid: (404) 752-1655
Tuition: N/A
Room/board/expenses: N/A
Enrollment: N/A

HAWAII

University of Hawaii-Manoa (Burns)

651 Ilalo Street
Honolulu, HI 96813
jabsom.hawaii.edu
Public
Admissions: (808) 692-0892
Email: medadmin@hawaii.edu
Financial aid: (808) 692-1002
Application deadline: 11/01
In-state tuition: $37,422

Out-of-state tuition: $72,078
Room/board/expenses: $15,926
Percent receiving grants: 77%
Average student indebtedness at graduation: $160,000
Enrollment: 270
men: 50%; women: 50%; minorities: 86%; underrepresented minorities: 36%; in state: 86%
Acceptance rate: 5%
Median New MCAT total score: 509
Median GPA: 3.67
Most popular undergraduate majors: biological sciences: 54%; physical sciences: 10%; nonsciences: 6%; other: 30%
Percent of graduates entering primary care specialties: 52.3%

ILLINOIS

Loyola University Chicago (Stritch)[1]

2160 S. First Avenue, Building 120
Maywood, IL 60153
www.meddean.luc.edu/
Private
Admissions: (708) 216-3229
Email:
ssom-admissions@lumc.edu
Financial aid: N/A
Tuition: N/A
Room/board/expenses: N/A
Enrollment: N/A

Northwestern University (Feinberg)

420 E. Superior Street
Rubloff Building, 12th Floor
Chicago, IL 60611
www.feinberg.northwestern.edu
Private
Admissions: (312) 503-8206
Email: med-admissions@
northwestern.edu
Financial aid: (312) 503-8722
Application deadline: 10/15
Tuition: $60,680
Room/board/expenses: $18,282
Percent receiving grants: 40%
Average student indebtedness at graduation: $162,437
Enrollment: 648
men: 55%; women: 45%; minorities: 51%; underrepresented minorities: 20%; in state: 19%
Acceptance rate: 7%
Median New MCAT total score: 518
Median GPA: 3.87
Most popular undergraduate majors: biological sciences: 34%; physical sciences: 28%; nonsciences: 12%; other: 26%
Percent of graduates entering primary care specialties: 38.5%

Rosalind Franklin University of Medicine and Science[1]

3333 Green Bay Road
North Chicago, IL 60064
www.rosalindfranklin.edu/cms/
Private
Admissions: (847) 578-3204
Email: cms.admissions@
rosalindfranklin.edu
Financial aid: N/A
Tuition: N/A
Room/board/expenses: N/A
Enrollment: N/A

Rush University

600 S. Paulina Street
Chicago, IL 60612
www.rushu.rush.edu/
rush-medical-college
Private
Admissions: N/A
Email:
RMC_Admissions@rush.edu
Financial aid: (312) 942-6256
Application deadline: 11/01
Tuition: $51,306
Room/board/expenses: $0
Percent receiving grants: 53%
Average student indebtedness at graduation: $201,571
Enrollment: 515
men: 50%; women: 50%; minorities: 41%; underrepresented minorities: 15%; in state: 45%
Acceptance rate: 5%
Median New MCAT total score: 511
Median GPA: 3.68
Most popular undergraduate majors: biological sciences: 63%; physical sciences: 6%; nonsciences: 17%; other: 14%
Percent of graduates entering primary care specialties: 43.0%

Southern Illinois University-Springfield[1]

801 N. Rutledge
PO Box 19620
Springfield, IL 62794-9620
www.siumed.edu/
Public
Admissions: (217) 545-6013
Email: admissions@siumed.edu
Financial aid: N/A
Tuition: N/A
Room/board/expenses: N/A
Enrollment: N/A

University of Chicago (Pritzker)

5841 S. Maryland Avenue
MC 1000
Chicago, IL 60637-5416
pritzker.uchicago.edu
Private
Admissions: (773) 702-1937
Email: pritzkeradmissions@
bsd.uchicago.edu
Financial aid: (773) 702-1938
Application deadline: 10/15
Tuition: $57,050
Room/board/expenses: $16,800
Percent receiving grants: 87%
Average student indebtedness at graduation: $119,830
Enrollment: 362
men: 51%; women: 49%; minorities: 43%; underrepresented minorities: 23%; in state: 22%
Acceptance rate: 4%
Median New MCAT total score: 520
Median GPA: 3.88
Most popular undergraduate majors: biological sciences: 40%; physical sciences: 21%; nonsciences: 16%; other: 23%
Percent of graduates entering primary care specialties: 38.0%

University of Illinois

1853 W. Polk Street
M/C 784
Chicago, IL 60612
www.medicine.uic.edu
Public
Admissions: (312) 996-5635
Email: medadmit@uic.edu
Financial aid: (312) 413-0127

Application deadline: 11/01
In-state tuition: $40,678
Out-of-state tuition: $77,678
Room/board/expenses: $14,464
Percent receiving grants: 48%
Average student indebtedness at graduation: $208,579
Enrollment: 1,336
men: 53%; women: 47%; minorities: 55%; underrepresented minorities: 38%; in state: 75%
Acceptance rate: 8%
Median New MCAT total score: 511
Median GPA: 3.68
Most popular undergraduate majors: biological sciences: 62%; physical sciences: 4%; nonsciences: 18%; other: 16%
Percent of graduates entering primary care specialties: 46.0%

INDIANA

Indiana University-Indianapolis

340 W. 10th Street
Suite 6200
Indianapolis, IN 46202
www.medicine.iu.edu
Public
Admissions: (317) 274-3772
Email: inmedadm@iupui.edu
Financial aid: (317) 274-1967
Application deadline: 11/17
In-state tuition: $34,484
Out-of-state tuition: $57,438
Room/board/expenses: $11,860
Percent receiving grants: 34%
Average student indebtedness at graduation: $184,843
Enrollment: 1,395
men: 56%; women: 44%; minorities: 35%; underrepresented minorities: 21%; in state: 78%
Acceptance rate: 8%
Median New MCAT total score: 509
Median GPA: 3.80
Most popular undergraduate majors: biological sciences: 40%; physical sciences: 18%; nonsciences: 4%; other: 38%
Percent of graduates entering primary care specialties: 40.0%

IOWA

University of Iowa (Carver)

200 CMAB
Iowa City, IA 52242-1101
www.medicine.uiowa.edu
Public
Admissions: (319) 335-8052
Email: medical-admissions@uiowa.edu
Financial aid: (319) 335-8059
Application deadline: 11/01
In-state tuition: $36,071
Out-of-state tuition: $54,003
Room/board/expenses: $11,160
Percent receiving grants: 60%
Average student indebtedness at graduation: $146,207
Enrollment: 603
men: 56%; women: 44%; minorities: 26%; underrepresented minorities: 13%; in state: 68%
Acceptance rate: 7%
Median New MCAT total score: 511
Median GPA: 3.74
Most popular undergraduate majors: biological sciences: 59%; physical sciences: 11%; nonsciences: 13%; other: 17%

Percent of graduates entering primary care specialties: 41.0%

KANSAS

University of Kansas Medical Center

3901 Rainbow Boulevard
Kansas City, KS 66160
medicine.kumc.edu
Public
Admissions: (913) 588-5280
Email: premedinfo@kumc.edu
Financial aid: (913) 588-5170
Application deadline: 10/16
In-state tuition: $36,211
Out-of-state tuition: $63,471
Room/board/expenses: $16,544
Percent receiving grants: 87%
Average student indebtedness at graduation: $155,241
Enrollment: 843
men: 54%; women: 46%; minorities: 24%; underrepresented minorities: 16%; in state: 92%
Acceptance rate: 7%
Median New MCAT total score: 508
Median GPA: 3.82
Most popular undergraduate majors: biological sciences: 53%; physical sciences: 23%; nonsciences: 10%; other: 14%
Percent of graduates entering primary care specialties: 45.0%

KENTUCKY

University of Kentucky

800 Rose Street, MN-104
Lexington, KY 40536-0298
www.med.uky.edu
Public
Admissions: (859) 323-6161
Email: kymedap@uky.edu
Financial aid: (859) 257-1652
Application deadline: 11/01
In-state tuition: $37,716
Out-of-state tuition: $65,861
Room/board/expenses: $15,000
Percent receiving grants: 40%
Average student indebtedness at graduation: $203,590
Enrollment: 547
men: 57%; women: 43%; minorities: 18%; underrepresented minorities: 9%; in state: 62%
Acceptance rate: 7%
Median New MCAT total score: 511
Median GPA: 3.75
Most popular undergraduate majors: biological sciences: 54%; physical sciences: 21%; nonsciences: 7%; other: 18%
Percent of graduates entering primary care specialties: 38.0%

University of Louisville

Abell Administration Center
H.S.C.
Louisville, KY 40202
www.louisville.edu
Public
Admissions: (502) 852-5193
Email: medadm@louisville.edu
Financial aid: (502) 852-5187
Application deadline: 10/15
In-state tuition: $39,133
Out-of-state tuition: $59,043
Room/board/expenses: $10,576
Percent receiving grants: 32%
Average student indebtedness at graduation: $181,605

men: 56%; women: 44%; minorities: 23%; underrepresented minorities: 11%; in state: 76%
Acceptance rate: 7%
Median New MCAT total score: 507
Median GPA: 3.70
Most popular undergraduate majors: biological sciences: 49%; physical sciences: 24%; nonsciences: 14%; other: 13%
Percent of graduates entering primary care specialties: 40.7%

LOUISIANA

Louisiana State University Health Sciences Center-New Orleans[1]

Admissions Office
1901 Perdido Street
New Orleans, LA 70112-1393
www.medschool.lsuhsc.edu/
Public
Admissions: (504) 568-6262
Email: ms-admissions@lsuhsc.edu
Financial aid: N/A
Tuition: N/A
Room/board/expenses: N/A
Enrollment: N/A

Louisiana State University Health Sciences Center-Shreveport[1]

PO Box 33932
1501 Kings Highway
Shreveport, LA 71130-3932
www.lsuhscshreveport.edu/Education/SchoolofMedicine.aspx
Public
Admissions: (318) 675-5190
Email: shvadm@lsuhsc.edu
Financial aid: N/A
Tuition: N/A
Room/board/expenses: N/A
Enrollment: N/A

Tulane University[1]

1430 Tulane Avenue, SL67
New Orleans, LA 70112-2699
tulane.edu/som/
Private
Admissions: (504) 988-5187
Email: medsch@tulane.edu
Financial aid: N/A
Tuition: N/A
Room/board/expenses: N/A
Enrollment: N/A

MARYLAND

Johns Hopkins University

733 N. Broadway
Baltimore, MD 21205
www.hopkinsmedicine.org
Private
Admissions: (410) 955-3182
Email: somadmiss@jhmi.edu
Financial aid: (410) 955-1324
Application deadline: 10/15
Tuition: $55,266
Room/board/expenses: $19,272
Percent receiving grants: 54%
Average student indebtedness at graduation: $113,684
Enrollment: 471
men: 49%; women: 51%; minorities: 49%; underrepresented minorities: 15%; in state: 17%

Acceptance rate: 6%
Median New MCAT total score: 518
Median GPA: 3.90
Most popular undergraduate majors: biological sciences: 51%; physical sciences: 27%; nonsciences: 14%; other: 8%
Percent of graduates entering primary care specialties: 30.0%

Uniformed Services University of the Health Sciences (Hebert)[1]

4301 Jones Bridge Road
Bethesda, MD 20814
www.usuhs.edu
Public
Admissions: (800) 772-1743
Email: admissions@usuhs.edu
Financial aid: N/A
Tuition: N/A
Room/board/expenses: N/A
Enrollment: N/A

University of Maryland

655 W. Baltimore Street
Room 14-029
Baltimore, MD 21201-1559
medschool.umaryland.edu
Public
Admissions: (410) 706-7478
Email: admissions@som.umaryland.edu
Financial aid: (410) 706-7347
Application deadline: 11/01
In-state tuition: $37,273
Out-of-state tuition: $63,139
Room/board/expenses: $21,500
Percent receiving grants: 70%
Average student indebtedness at graduation: $157,155
Enrollment: 638
men: 40%; women: 60%; minorities: 40%; underrepresented minorities: 12%; in state: 87%
Acceptance rate: 7%
Median New MCAT total score: 511
Median GPA: 3.79
Most popular undergraduate majors: biological sciences: 52%; physical sciences: 14%; nonsciences: 16%; other: 18%
Percent of graduates entering primary care specialties: 40.0%

MASSACHUSETTS

Boston University

72 E. Concord Street, L-103
Boston, MA 02118
www.bumc.bu.edu
Private
Admissions: (617) 638-4630
Email: medadms@bu.edu
Financial aid: (617) 638-5130
Application deadline: 11/01
Tuition: $58,198
Room/board/expenses: $13,511
Percent receiving grants: 68%
Average student indebtedness at graduation: $193,676
Enrollment: 698
men: 48%; women: 52%; minorities: 47%; underrepresented minorities: 19%; in state: 24%
Acceptance rate: 7%
Median New MCAT total score: 515
Median GPA: 3.75
Most popular undergraduate majors: biological sciences: 40%; physical sciences: 17%; nonsciences: 9%; other: 34%
Percent of graduates entering primary care specialties: 41.0%

Harvard University

25 Shattuck Street
Boston, MA 02115-6092
hms.harvard.edu
Private
Admissions: (617) 432-1550
Email: admissions_office@hms.harvard.edu
Financial aid: (617) 432-0449
Application deadline: 10/23
Tuition: $59,731
Room/board/expenses: $17,485
Percent receiving grants: 65%
Average student indebtedness at graduation: $101,478
Enrollment: 720
men: 47%; women: 53%; minorities: 49%; underrepresented minorities: 21%; in state: N/A
Acceptance rate: 3%
Median New MCAT total score: 517
Median GPA: 3.91
Most popular undergraduate majors: biological sciences: 49%; physical sciences: 22%; nonsciences: 16%; other: 13%
Percent of graduates entering primary care specialties: 36.0%

Tufts University

136 Harrison Avenue
Boston, MA 02111
medicine.tufts.edu/
Private
Admissions: (617) 636-6571
Email: med-admissions@tufts.edu
Financial aid: (617) 636-6574
Application deadline: 11/01
Tuition: $60,258
Room/board/expenses: $14,620
Percent receiving grants: 35%
Average student indebtedness at graduation: $205,322
Enrollment: 846
men: 46%; women: 54%; minorities: 36%; underrepresented minorities: 16%; in state: 29%
Acceptance rate: 6%
Median New MCAT total score: 511
Median GPA: 3.67
Most popular undergraduate majors: biological sciences: 59%; physical sciences: 9%; nonsciences: 14%; other: 18%
Percent of graduates entering primary care specialties: 45.6%

University of Massachusetts-Worcester

55 Lake Avenue N
Worcester, MA 01655
www.umassmed.edu
Public
Admissions: (508) 856-2323
Email: admissions@umassmed.edu
Financial aid: (508) 856-2265
Application deadline: 10/15
In-state tuition: $35,657
Out-of-state tuition: $61,457
Room/board/expenses: $13,909
Percent receiving grants: 37%
Average student indebtedness at graduation: $138,479
Enrollment: 543
men: 46%; women: 54%; minorities: 31%; underrepresented minorities: 8%; in state: 93%
Acceptance rate: 8%
Median New MCAT total score: 510
Median GPA: 3.70

Most popular undergraduate majors: biological sciences: 39%; physical sciences: 19%; nonsciences: 13%; other: 29%
Percent of graduates entering primary care specialties: 52.9%

MICHIGAN

Central Michigan University[1]
1200 S. Franklin Street
Mt Pleasant, MI 48859
Private
Admissions: N/A
Financial aid: N/A
Tuition: N/A
Room/board/expenses: N/A
Enrollment: N/A

Michigan State University (College of Human Medicine)
15 Michigan Street NE
Grand Rapids, MI 49503
mdaadmissions.msu.edu
Public
Admissions: (517) 353-9620
Email: MDadmissions@msu.edu
Financial aid: (517) 353-5940
Application deadline: 11/01
In-state tuition: $44,259
Out-of-state tuition: $87,213
Room/board/expenses: $14,616
Percent receiving grants: 37%
Average student indebtedness at graduation: $254,164
Enrollment: 831
men: 47%; women: 53%; minorities: 35%; underrepresented minorities: 19%; in state: 83%
Acceptance rate: 4%
Median New MCAT total score: 506
Median GPA: 3.64
Most popular undergraduate majors: biological sciences: 53%; physical sciences: 30%; nonsciences: 13%; other: 4%
Percent of graduates entering primary care specialties: 44.6%

Oakland University[1]
2200 N. Squirrel
Rochester, MI 48309
Private
Admissions: N/A
Financial aid: N/A
Tuition: N/A
Room/board/expenses: N/A
Enrollment: N/A

University of Michigan-Ann Arbor
1301 Catherine Road
Ann Arbor, MI 48109-0624
medicine.umich.edu/md-admissions
Public
Admissions: (734) 936-7253
Email: umichmedadmiss@umich.edu
Financial aid: (734) 763-4147
Application deadline: 09/30
In-state tuition: $34,378
Out-of-state tuition: $52,708
Room/board/expenses: $24,815
Percent receiving grants: 56%
Average student indebtedness at graduation: $124,091
Enrollment: 719
men: 47%; women: 53%; minorities: 27%; underrepresented minorities: 9%; in state: 53%

Acceptance rate: 6%
Median New MCAT total score: 514
Median GPA: 3.82
Most popular undergraduate majors: biological sciences: 30%; physical sciences: 33%; nonsciences: 12%; other: 25%
Percent of graduates entering primary care specialties: 46.1%

Wayne State University
540 E. Canfield
Detroit, MI 48201
admissions.med.wayne.edu/
Public
Admissions: (313) 577-1466
Email: mdadmissions@wayne.edu
Financial aid: (313) 577-3049
Application deadline: 12/15
In-state tuition: $33,930
Out-of-state tuition: $68,347
Room/board/expenses: $11,700
Percent receiving grants: 70%
Average student indebtedness at graduation: $160,859
Enrollment: 1,188
men: 57%; women: 43%; minorities: 31%; underrepresented minorities: 10%; in state: 78%
Acceptance rate: 12%
Median New MCAT total score: 508
Median GPA: 3.65
Most popular undergraduate majors: biological sciences: 54%; physical sciences: 19%; nonsciences: 11%; other: 16%
Percent of graduates entering primary care specialties: N/A

Western Michigan University[1]
1000 Oakland Drive
Kalamazoo, MI 49008
Private
Admissions: N/A
Financial aid: N/A
Tuition: N/A
Room/board/expenses: N/A
Enrollment: N/A

MINNESOTA

Mayo Clinic School of Medicine
200 First Street SW
Rochester, MN 55905
www.mayo.edu/mms/
Private
Admissions: (507) 284-3671
Email: medschooladmissions@mayo.edu
Financial aid: (507) 284-4839
Application deadline: 10/01
Tuition: $49,900
Room/board/expenses: $18,048
Percent receiving grants: 91%
Average student indebtedness at graduation: $69,695
Enrollment: 207
men: 46%; women: 54%; minorities: 42%; underrepresented minorities: 16%; in state: 10%
Acceptance rate: 2%
Median New MCAT total score: 513
Median GPA: 3.80
Most popular undergraduate majors: biological sciences: 55%; physical sciences: 22%; nonsciences: 10%; other: 13%
Percent of graduates entering primary care specialties: 37.0%

University of Minnesota
420 Delaware Street SE
MMC 293
Minneapolis, MN 55455
www.med.umn.edu
Public
Admissions: (612) 625-7977
Email: meded@umn.edu
Financial aid: (612) 625-4998
Application deadline: 11/15
In-state tuition: $39,694
Out-of-state tuition: $54,619
Room/board/expenses: $15,400
Percent receiving grants: 62%
Average student indebtedness at graduation: $173,800
Enrollment: 982
men: 51%; women: 49%; minorities: 22%; underrepresented minorities: 12%; in state: 92%
Acceptance rate: 6%
Median New MCAT total score: 508
Median GPA: 3.73
Most popular undergraduate majors: biological sciences: 45%; physical sciences: 20%; nonsciences: 16%; other: 19%
Percent of graduates entering primary care specialties: 49.7%

MISSISSIPPI

University of Mississippi[1]
2500 N. State Street
Jackson, MS 39216-4505
www.umc.edu/som/
Public
Admissions: (601) 984-5010
Email: AdmitMD@umc.edu
Financial aid: N/A
Tuition: N/A
Room/board/expenses: N/A
Enrollment: N/A

MISSOURI

St. Louis University
1402 S. Grand Boulevard
St. Louis, MO 63104
medschool.slu.edu
Private
Admissions: (314) 977-9870
Email: slumd@slu.edu
Financial aid: (314) 977-9840
Application deadline: 12/15
Tuition: $52,340
Room/board/expenses: $12,600
Percent receiving grants: 69%
Average student indebtedness at graduation: $191,966
Enrollment: 727
men: 51%; women: 49%; minorities: 42%; underrepresented minorities: 10%; in state: 37%
Acceptance rate: 7%
Median New MCAT total score: 512
Median GPA: 3.90
Most popular undergraduate majors: biological sciences: 53%; physical sciences: 19%; nonsciences: 7%; other: 21%
Percent of graduates entering primary care specialties: 47.1%

University of Missouri
One Hospital Drive
Columbia, MO 65212
medicine.missouri.edu
Public
Admissions: (573) 882-9219
Email: MizzouMed@missouri.edu
Financial aid: (573) 882-2923
Application deadline: 10/15

In-state tuition: $30,550
Out-of-state tuition: $59,314
Room/board/expenses: $11,320
Percent receiving grants: 62%
Average student indebtedness at graduation: $153,398
Enrollment: 417
men: 54%; women: 46%; minorities: 21%; underrepresented minorities: 9%; in state: 81%
Acceptance rate: 8%
Median New MCAT total score: 508
Median GPA: 3.84
Most popular undergraduate majors: biological sciences: 38%; physical sciences: 27%; nonsciences: 8%; other: 27%
Percent of graduates entering primary care specialties: 42.7%

University of Missouri-Kansas City[1]
2411 Holmes
Kansas City, MO 64108
www.med.umkc.edu
Public
Admissions: (816) 235-1870
Email: medicine@umkc.edu
Financial aid: N/A
Tuition: N/A
Room/board/expenses: N/A
Enrollment: N/A

Washington University in St. Louis
660 S. Euclid Avenue
St. Louis, MO 63110
mdadmissions.wustl.edu
Private
Admissions: (314) 362-6858
Email: wumscoa@wustl.edu
Financial aid: (314) 362-6845
Application deadline: 12/01
Tuition: $60,798
Room/board/expenses: $12,768
Percent receiving grants: 69%
Average student indebtedness at graduation: $84,758
Enrollment: 507
men: 48%; women: 52%; minorities: 42%; underrepresented minorities: 13%; in state: 10%
Acceptance rate: 9%
Median New MCAT total score: 521
Median GPA: 3.85
Most popular undergraduate majors: biological sciences: 49%; physical sciences: 21%; nonsciences: 11%; other: 19%
Percent of graduates entering primary care specialties: 35.0%

NEBRASKA

Creighton University
2500 California Plaza
Omaha, NE 68178
medicine.creighton.edu
Private
Admissions: (402) 280-2799
Email: medadmissions@creighton.edu
Financial aid: (402) 280-2731
Application deadline: 11/01
Tuition: $55,888
Room/board/expenses: $16,200
Average student indebtedness at graduation: $205,066
Enrollment: 618
men: 51%; women: 49%; minorities: N/A; underrepresented minorities: N/A; in state: 7%
Acceptance rate: 5%

Median New MCAT total score: 507
Median GPA: 3.76
Most popular undergraduate majors: biological sciences: 38%; physical sciences: 12%; nonsciences: 10%; other: 40%
Percent of graduates entering primary care specialties: 35.0%

University of Nebraska Medical Center
985527 Nebraska Medical Center
Omaha, NE 68198-5527
www.unmc.edu/com/admissions.htm
Public
Admissions: (402) 559-2259
Email: COMadmissions@unmc.edu
Financial aid: (402) 559-4199
Application deadline: 11/01
In-state tuition: $32,985
Out-of-state tuition: $76,405
Room/board/expenses: $18,900
Percent receiving grants: 50%
Average student indebtedness at graduation: $162,638
Enrollment: 509
men: 59%; women: 41%; minorities: 16%; underrepresented minorities: 7%; in state: 86%
Acceptance rate: 9%
Median New MCAT total score: 509
Median GPA: 3.73
Most popular undergraduate majors: biological sciences: N/A; physical sciences: N/A; nonsciences: N/A; other: N/A
Percent of graduates entering primary care specialties: 54.0%

NEVADA

University of Nevada
Pennington Building, Mailstop 357
Reno, NV 89557-0357
med.unr.edu
Public
Admissions: (775) 784-6063
Email: asa@med.unr.edu
Financial aid: (775) 682-8358
Application deadline: 10/15
In-state tuition: $31,216
Out-of-state tuition: $60,566
Room/board/expenses: $15,500
Percent receiving grants: 84%
Average student indebtedness at graduation: $135,788
Enrollment: 273
men: 55%; women: 45%; minorities: N/A; underrepresented minorities: N/A; in state: 92%
Acceptance rate: 38%
Median New MCAT total score: 507
Median GPA: 3.65
Most popular undergraduate majors: biological sciences: 35%; physical sciences: 26%; nonsciences: 10%; other: 29%
Percent of graduates entering primary care specialties: 39.3%

NEW HAMPSHIRE

Dartmouth College (Geisel)
1 Rope Ferry Road
Hanover, NH 03755-1404
geiselmed.dartmouth.edu
Private
Admissions: (603) 650-1505
Email: geisel.admissions@dartmouth.edu

Financial aid: (603) 650-1111
Application deadline: 11/01
Tuition: $61,753
Room/board/expenses: $11,250
Percent receiving grants: 59%
Average student indebtedness at graduation: $160,439
Enrollment: 365
men: 42%; women: 58%; minorities: 45%; underrepresented minorities: 26%; in state: 5%
Acceptance rate: 4%
Median New MCAT total score: 512
Median GPA: 3.69
Most popular undergraduate majors: biological sciences: 48%; physical sciences: 20%; nonsciences: 5%; other: 27%
Percent of graduates entering primary care specialties: 43.8%

NEW JERSEY

Rutgers New Jersey Medical School-Newark

185 S. Orange Avenue
Newark, NJ 07101-1709
www.njms.rutgers.edu
Public
Admissions: (973) 972-4631
Email: njmsadmiss@njms.rutgers.edu
Financial aid: (973) 972-4376
Application deadline: 12/01
In-state tuition: $41,878
Out-of-state tuition: $63,212
Room/board/expenses: $17,870
Percent receiving grants: 39%
Average student indebtedness at graduation: $177,217
Enrollment: 738
men: 58%; women: 42%; minorities: 63%; underrepresented minorities: 21%; in state: 97%
Acceptance rate: 9%
Median New MCAT total score: 511
Median GPA: 3.69
Most popular undergraduate majors: biological sciences: 42%; physical sciences: 16%; nonsciences: 9%; other: 33%
Percent of graduates entering primary care specialties: 35.0%

Rutgers Robert Wood Johnson Medical School-New Brunswick

125 Paterson Street
New Brunswick, NJ 08903-0019
rwjms.rutgers.edu/education/admission/index.html
Public
Admissions: (732) 235-4576
Email: rwjapadm@rwjms.rutgers.edu
Financial aid: (732) 235-4689
Application deadline: 12/01
In-state tuition: $43,021
Out-of-state tuition: $64,355
Room/board/expenses: $14,160
Percent receiving grants: 22%
Average student indebtedness at graduation: $154,255
Enrollment: 683
men: 44%; women: 56%; minorities: 43%; underrepresented minorities: 13%; in state: 95%
Acceptance rate: 7%
Median New MCAT total score: 510
Median GPA: 3.65

Most popular undergraduate majors: biological sciences: 55%; physical sciences: 9%; nonsciences: 14%; other: 22%
Percent of graduates entering primary care specialties: 38.0%

NEW MEXICO

University of New Mexico

Reginald Heber Fitz Hall
Room 107
Albuquerque, NM 87131
som.unm.edu
Public
Admissions: (505) 272-4766
Email: somadmissions@salud.unm.edu
Financial aid: (505) 272-8008
Application deadline: 11/01
In-state tuition: $10,270
Out-of-state tuition: $48,852
Room/board/expenses: $15,958
Percent receiving grants: 87%
Average student indebtedness at graduation: $126,783
Enrollment: 420
men: 50%; women: 50%; minorities: 55%; underrepresented minorities: 46%; in state: 96%
Acceptance rate: 8%
Median New MCAT total score: 505
Median GPA: 3.71
Most popular undergraduate majors: biological sciences: 39%; physical sciences: 25%; nonsciences: 15%; other: 21%
Percent of graduates entering primary care specialties: 49.6%

NEW YORK

Albany Medical College[1]

47 New Scotland Avenue
Albany, NY 12208
www.amc.edu/Academic/
Private
Admissions: (518) 262-5521
Email: admissions@mail.amc.edu
Financial aid: N/A
Tuition: N/A
Room/board/expenses: N/A
Enrollment: N/A

Columbia University

630 W. 168th Street
New York, NY 10032
ps.columbia.edu
Private
Admissions: (212) 305-3595
Email: psadmissions@cumc.columbia.edu
Financial aid: (212) 305-4100
Application deadline: 10/15
Tuition: $63,890
Room/board/expenses: $17,478
Percent receiving grants: 64%
Average student indebtedness at graduation: $113,367
Enrollment: 660
men: 50%; women: 50%; minorities: 40%; underrepresented minorities: 22%; in state: 29%
Acceptance rate: 4%
Median New MCAT total score: 520
Median GPA: 3.87
Most popular undergraduate majors: biological sciences: 41%; physical sciences: 11%; nonsciences: 27%; other: 21%
Percent of graduates entering primary care specialties: 33.4%

Cornell University (Weill)

1300 York Avenue
New York, NY 10065
www.weill.cornell.edu
Private
Admissions: (212) 746-1067
Email: wcmc-admissions@med.cornell.edu
Financial aid: (212) 746-1066
Application deadline: 10/15
Tuition: $56,335
Room/board/expenses: $13,195
Percent receiving grants: 71%
Average student indebtedness at graduation: $149,055
Enrollment: 409
men: 52%; women: 48%; minorities: 43%; underrepresented minorities: 18%; in state: 28%
Acceptance rate: 5%
Median New MCAT total score: 518
Median GPA: 3.84
Most popular undergraduate majors: biological sciences: 35%; physical sciences: 16%; nonsciences: 14%; other: 35%
Percent of graduates entering primary care specialties: 40.0%

Hofstra University

500 Hofstra University
Hempstead, NY 11549
medicine.hofstra.edu
Private
Admissions: (516) 463-7519
Email: medicine.admissions@hofstra.edu
Financial aid: (516) 463-7523
Application deadline: 11/01
Tuition: $49,500
Room/board/expenses: $21,025
Percent receiving grants: 77%
Enrollment: 362
men: 53%; women: 47%; minorities: 44%; underrepresented minorities: 20%; in state: 52%
Acceptance rate: 6%
Median New MCAT total score: 514
Median GPA: 3.74
Most popular undergraduate majors: biological sciences: 46%; physical sciences: 24%; nonsciences: 15%; other: 15%
Percent of graduates entering primary care specialties: 45.0%

Icahn School of Medicine at Mount Sinai

1 Gustave L. Levy Place
PO Box 1217
New York, NY 10029
www.icahn.mssm.edu
Private
Admissions: (212) 241-6696
Email: admissions@mssm.edu
Financial aid: (212) 241-5245
Application deadline: 10/15
Tuition: $54,731
Room/board/expenses: $12,917
Percent receiving grants: 44%
Average student indebtedness at graduation: $144,824
Enrollment: 561
men: 50%; women: 50%; minorities: 45%; underrepresented minorities: 19%; in state: 33%
Acceptance rate: 7%
Median New MCAT total score: 518
Median GPA: 3.77
Most popular undergraduate majors: biological sciences: 29%; physical sciences: 18%; nonsciences: 29%; other: 24%

Percent of graduates entering primary care specialties: 38.5%

New York Medical College

40 Sunshine Cottage Road
Valhalla, NY 10595
www.nymc.edu
Private
Admissions: (914) 594-4507
Email: mdadmit@nymc.edu
Financial aid: (914) 594-4491
Application deadline: 01/31
Tuition: $54,746
Room/board/expenses: $19,789
Percent receiving grants: 41%
Average student indebtedness at graduation: $226,749
Enrollment: 844
men: 49%; women: 51%; minorities: 45%; underrepresented minorities: 22%; in state: 35%
Acceptance rate: 6%
Median New MCAT total score: 511
Median GPA: 3.60
Most popular undergraduate majors: biological sciences: 40%; physical sciences: 13%; nonsciences: 14%; other: 33%
Percent of graduates entering primary care specialties: 40.0%

New York University (Langone)

550 First Avenue
New York, NY 10016
school.med.nyu.edu
Private
Admissions: (212) 263-5290
Email: admissions@nyumc.org
Financial aid: (212) 263-5286
Application deadline: 10/15
Tuition: $55,110
Room/board/expenses: $14,832
Percent receiving grants: 40%
Average student indebtedness at graduation: $147,952
Enrollment: 571
men: 53%; women: 47%; minorities: 46%; underrepresented minorities: 22%; in state: 34%
Acceptance rate: 5%
Median New MCAT total score: 520
Median GPA: 3.91
Most popular undergraduate majors: biological sciences: 35%; physical sciences: 26%; nonsciences: 20%; other: 19%
Percent of graduates entering primary care specialties: 39.0%

Stony Brook University-SUNY

Office of Admissions
Health Science Center, L4
Stony Brook, NY 11794-8434
medicine.stonybrookmedicine.edu/
Public
Admissions: (631) 444-2113
Email: somadmissions@stonybrookmedicine.edu
Financial aid: (631) 444-2341
Application deadline: 12/01
In-state tuition: $43,176
Out-of-state tuition: $68,176
Room/board/expenses: $11,750
Percent receiving grants: 23%
Average student indebtedness at graduation: $166,610
Enrollment: 522
men: 54%; women: 46%; minorities: 44%; underrepresented minorities: 11%; in state: 92%

Acceptance rate: 8%
Median New MCAT total score: 511
Median GPA: 3.70
Most popular undergraduate majors: biological sciences: 62%; physical sciences: 11%; nonsciences: 20%; other: 7%
Percent of graduates entering primary care specialties: 32.3%

SUNY Downstate Medical Center[1]

450 Clarkson Avenue
Box 60
Brooklyn, NY 11203
www.downstate.edu/college_of_medicine/
Public
Admissions: (718) 270-2446
Email: medadmissions@downstate.edu
Financial aid: N/A
Tuition: N/A
Room/board/expenses: N/A
Enrollment: N/A

SUNY-Syracuse[1]

766 Irving Avenue
Syracuse, NY 13210
www.upstate.edu/com/
Public
Admissions: (315) 464-4570
Email: admiss@upstate.edu
Financial aid: N/A
Tuition: N/A
Room/board/expenses: N/A
Enrollment: N/A

University at Buffalo-SUNY (Jacobs)

155 Biomedical Education Building
Buffalo, NY 14214
medicine.buffalo.edu
Public
Admissions: (716) 829-3466
Email: jjrosso@buffalo.edu
Financial aid: (716) 645-2993
Application deadline: 11/15
In-state tuition: $42,709
Out-of-state tuition: $67,709
Room/board/expenses: $15,006
Percent receiving grants: 26%
Average student indebtedness at graduation: $155,635
Enrollment: 579
men: 53%; women: 47%; minorities: 29%; underrepresented minorities: 20%; in state: 97%
Acceptance rate: 7%
Median New MCAT total score: 509
Median GPA: 3.75
Most popular undergraduate majors: biological sciences: 38%; physical sciences: 19%; nonsciences: 27%; other: 16%
Percent of graduates entering primary care specialties: 43.0%

University of Rochester

601 Elmwood Avenue
Box 706
Rochester, NY 14642
www.urmc.rochester.edu/education/md/admissions
Private
Admissions: (585) 275-4539
Email: mdadmish@urmc.rochester.edu
Financial aid: (585) 275-4523
Application deadline: 10/15
Tuition: $54,830
Room/board/expenses: $17,000
Percent receiving grants: 53%

Average student indebtedness at graduation: $130,512
Enrollment: 431
men: 48%; women: 52%; minorities: 44%; underrepresented minorities: 20%; in state: 49%
Acceptance rate: 4%
Median New MCAT total score: 512
Median GPA: 3.71
Most popular undergraduate majors: biological sciences: 46%; physical sciences: 14%; nonsciences: 13%; other: 27%
Percent of graduates entering primary care specialties: 36.8%

Yeshiva University (Einstein)
1300 Morris Park Avenue
Bronx, NY 10461
www.einstein.yu.edu
Private
Admissions: (718) 430-2106
Email: admissions@einstein.yu.edu
Financial aid: (718) 862-1813
Application deadline: 10/15
Tuition: $55,394
Room/board/expenses: $17,350
Percent receiving grants: 44%
Average student indebtedness at graduation: $161,506
Enrollment: 762
men: 53%; women: 47%; minorities: 32%; underrepresented minorities: 12%; in state: 43%
Acceptance rate: 4%
Median New MCAT total score: 515
Median GPA: 3.82
Most popular undergraduate majors: biological sciences: 39%; physical sciences: 19%; nonsciences: 14%; other: 28%
Percent of graduates entering primary care specialties: 45.0%

Duke University
DUMC 3710
Durham, NC 27710
dukemed.duke.edu
Private
Admissions: (919) 684-2985
Email: medadm@mc.duke.edu
Financial aid: (919) 684-6649
Application deadline: 10/15
Tuition: $59,072
Room/board/expenses: $16,258
Percent receiving grants: 69%
Average student indebtedness at graduation: $118,579
Enrollment: 478
men: 51%; women: 49%; minorities: 49%; underrepresented minorities: 17%; in state: 12%
Acceptance rate: 4%
Median New MCAT total score: 513
Median GPA: 3.80
Most popular undergraduate majors: biological sciences: 41%; physical sciences: 33%; nonsciences: 16%; other: 10%
Percent of graduates entering primary care specialties: 30.0%

East Carolina University (Brody)
600 Moye Boulevard
Greenville, NC 27834
www.ecu.edu/bsomadmissions
Public
Admissions: (252) 744-2202
Email: somadmissions@ecu.edu
Financial aid: (252) 328-6610

Application deadline: 11/01
In-state tuition: $22,716
Out-of-state tuition: N/A
Room/board/expenses: $14,775
Percent receiving grants: 80%
Average student indebtedness at graduation: $112,692
Enrollment: 315
men: 50%; women: 50%; minorities: N/A; underrepresented minorities: N/A; in state: 100%
Acceptance rate: 13%
Median New MCAT total score: 506
Median GPA: 3.65
Most popular undergraduate majors: biological sciences: 50%; physical sciences: 9%; nonsciences: 8%; other: 33%
Percent of graduates entering primary care specialties: 61.0%

University of North Carolina-Chapel Hill
CB #7000, 4030 Bondurant Hall
Chapel Hill, NC 27599-7000
www.med.unc.edu/admit/
Public
Admissions: (919) 962-8331
Email: admissions@med.unc.edu
Financial aid: (919) 962-6117
Application deadline: 10/15
In-state tuition: $26,782
Out-of-state tuition: $53,661
Room/board/expenses: $34,672
Percent receiving grants: 87%
Enrollment: 834
men: 49%; women: 51%; minorities: 37%; underrepresented minorities: 33%; in state: 80%
Acceptance rate: 4%
Median New MCAT total score: 509
Median GPA: 3.76
Most popular undergraduate majors: biological sciences: 43%; physical sciences: 19%; nonsciences: 6%; other: 32%
Percent of graduates entering primary care specialties: 61.0%

Wake Forest University
Medical Center Boulevard
Winston-Salem, NC 27157
www.wakehealth.edu/school/md-program
Private
Admissions: (336) 716-4264
Email: medadmit@wakehealth.edu
Financial aid: (336) 713-2725
Application deadline: 11/01
Tuition: $53,354
Room/board/expenses: $24,838
Percent receiving grants: 55%
Average student indebtedness at graduation: $185,620
Enrollment: 479
men: 50%; women: 50%; minorities: 34%; underrepresented minorities: 18%; in state: 32%
Acceptance rate: 3%
Median New MCAT total score: 508
Median GPA: 3.58
Most popular undergraduate majors: biological sciences: 41%; physical sciences: 19%; nonsciences: 24%; other: 16%
Percent of graduates entering primary care specialties: 35.9%

University of North Dakota[1]
501 N. Columbia Road, Stop 9037
Grand Forks, ND 58202-9037
www.med.und.nodak.edu
Public
Admissions: (701) 777-4221
Financial aid: N/A
Tuition: N/A
Room/board/expenses: N/A
Enrollment: N/A

Case Western Reserve University
10900 Euclid Avenue
Cleveland, OH 44106
case.edu/medicine
Private
Admissions: (216) 368-3450
Email: casemed-admissions@case.edu
Financial aid: (216) 368-3666
Application deadline: 11/01
Tuition: $61,386
Room/board/expenses: $21,972
Percent receiving grants: 59%
Average student indebtedness at graduation: $165,341
Enrollment: 896
men: 50%; women: 50%; minorities: 41%; underrepresented minorities: 11%; in state: 20%
Acceptance rate: 8%
Median New MCAT total score: 517
Median GPA: 3.76
Most popular undergraduate majors: biological sciences: 24%; physical sciences: 40%; nonsciences: 15%; other: 21%
Percent of graduates entering primary care specialties: 32.9%

Northeast Ohio Medical University[1]
4209 State Route 44
PO Box 95
Rootstown, OH 44272-0095
www.neomed.edu/
Public
Admissions: (330) 325-6270
Email: admission@neomed.edu
Financial aid: N/A
Tuition: N/A
Room/board/expenses: N/A
Enrollment: N/A

Ohio State University
200 Meiling Hall
370 W. Ninth Avenue
Columbus, OH 43210-1238
medicine.osu.edu
Public
Admissions: (614) 292-7137
Email: medicine@osu.edu
Financial aid: (614) 688-4955
Application deadline: 11/01
In-state tuition: $31,687
Out-of-state tuition: $37,345
Room/board/expenses: $10,810
Percent receiving grants: 80%
Average student indebtedness at graduation: $168,656
Enrollment: 770
men: 50%; women: 50%; minorities: 47%; underrepresented minorities: 25%; in state: 86%
Acceptance rate: 6%
Median New MCAT total score: 514
Median GPA: 3.80

Most popular undergraduate majors: biological sciences: 42%; physical sciences: 28%; nonsciences: 4%; other: 26%
Percent of graduates entering primary care specialties: 42.9%

University of Cincinnati
231 Albert Sabin Way
Cincinnati, OH 45267-0552
www.med.uc.edu
Public
Admissions: (513) 558-7314
Email: MDAdmissions@uc.edu
Financial aid: (513) 558-5991
Application deadline: 11/17
In-state tuition: $30,631
Out-of-state tuition: $48,895
Room/board/expenses: $19,030
Percent receiving grants: 40%
Average student indebtedness at graduation: $182,941
Enrollment: 678
men: 51%; women: 49%; minorities: 32%; underrepresented minorities: 15%; in state: 91%
Acceptance rate: 9%
Median New MCAT total score: 513
Median GPA: 3.76
Most popular undergraduate majors: biological sciences: 48%; physical sciences: 29%; nonsciences: 7%; other: 16%
Percent of graduates entering primary care specialties: 38.6%

University of Toledo
3000 Arlington Avenue
Toledo, OH 43614
www.utoledo.edu/med/md/
Public
Admissions: (419) 383-4229
Email: medadmissions@utoledo.edu
Financial aid: (419) 530-5812
Application deadline: 11/01
In-state tuition: $34,378
Out-of-state tuition: $64,884
Room/board/expenses: $13,146
Percent receiving grants: 18%
Average student indebtedness at graduation: $186,836
Enrollment: 695
men: 56%; women: 44%; minorities: 19%; underrepresented minorities: 5%; in state: 93%
Acceptance rate: 8%
Median New MCAT total score: 511
Median GPA: 3.60
Most popular undergraduate majors: biological sciences: 73%; physical sciences: 6%; nonsciences: 7%; other: 14%
Percent of graduates entering primary care specialties: 40.0%

Wright State University (Boonshoft)
3640 Colonel Glenn Highway
Dayton, OH 45435-0001
medicine.wright.edu/
Public
Admissions: (937) 775-2934
Email: som_saa@wright.edu
Financial aid: (937) 775-2934
Application deadline: 12/01
In-state tuition: $37,200
Out-of-state tuition: $54,152
Room/board/expenses: $13,116
Percent receiving grants: 38%
Average student indebtedness at graduation: $176,857

Enrollment: 443
men: 48%; women: 52%; minorities: N/A; underrepresented minorities: N/A; in state: 91%
Acceptance rate: 6%
Median New MCAT total score: 502
Median GPA: 3.88
Most popular undergraduate majors: biological sciences: N/A; physical sciences: N/A; nonsciences: N/A; other: N/A
Percent of graduates entering primary care specialties: 47.7%

University of Oklahoma
PO Box 26901, BMSB 357
Oklahoma City, OK 73126
www.medicine.ouhsc.edu
Public
Admissions: (405) 271-2331
Email: adminmed@ouhsc.edu
Financial aid: (405) 271-2118
Application deadline: 10/15
In-state tuition: $27,430
Out-of-state tuition: $58,244
Room/board/expenses: $20,926
Percent receiving grants: 49%
Average student indebtedness at graduation: $150,258
Enrollment: 644
men: 58%; women: 42%; minorities: 31%; underrepresented minorities: 16%; in state: 92%
Acceptance rate: 10%
Median New MCAT total score: 508
Median GPA: 3.74
Most popular undergraduate majors: biological sciences: 48%; physical sciences: 25%; nonsciences: 17%; other: 10%
Percent of graduates entering primary care specialties: 41.1%

Oregon Health and Science University
2730 S.W. Moody Avenue, CL5MD
Portland, OR 97201-3098
www.ohsu.edu/xd
Public
Admissions: (503) 494-2998
Financial aid: (503) 494-7800
Application deadline: 10/15
In-state tuition: $46,112
Out-of-state tuition: $63,415
Room/board/expenses: $16,016
Percent receiving grants: 95%
Average student indebtedness at graduation: $217,162
Enrollment: 578
men: 48%; women: 52%; minorities: 25%; underrepresented minorities: 12%; in state: 73%
Acceptance rate: 3%
Median New MCAT total score: 509
Median GPA: 3.69
Most popular undergraduate majors: biological sciences: 43%; physical sciences: 7%; nonsciences: 20%; other: 30%
Percent of graduates entering primary care specialties: 46.3%

PENNSYLVANIA

The Commonwealth Medical College[1]
525 Pine Street
Scranton, PA 18509
www.tcmc.edu/
Private
Admissions: N/A
Email: admissions@tcmc.edu
Financial aid: N/A
Tuition: N/A
Room/board/expenses: N/A
Enrollment: N/A

Drexel University
2900 Queen Lane
Philadelphia, PA 19129
www.drexel.edu/medicine
Private
Admissions: (215) 991-8202
Email: Medadmis@drexel.edu
Financial aid: (215) 991-8210
Application deadline: 12/01
Tuition: $56,292
Room/board/expenses: N/A
Percent receiving grants: 8%
Average student indebtedness at graduation: $235,449
Enrollment: 1,059
men: 50%; women:
50%; minorities: 45%;
underrepresented minorities:
14%; in state: 34%
Acceptance rate: 6%
Median New MCAT total score: 511
Median GPA: 3.68
Most popular undergraduate majors: biological sciences:
N/A; physical sciences: N/A;
nonsciences: N/A; other: N/A
Percent of graduates entering primary care specialties: 40.3%

Pennsylvania State University College of Medicine[1]
500 University Drive
Hershey, PA 17033
med.psu.edu/web/college/home
Public
Admissions: (717) 531-8755
Email: StudentAdmissions@hmc.psu.edu
Financial aid: N/A
Tuition: N/A
Room/board/expenses: N/A
Enrollment: N/A

Temple University (Katz)
3500 N. Broad Street
MERB 1140
Philadelphia, PA 19140
medicine.temple.edu
Private
Admissions: (215) 707-3656
Email:
medadmissions@temple.edu
Financial aid: (215) 707-0749
Application deadline: 12/15
Tuition: $50,691
Room/board/expenses: $13,833
Percent receiving grants: 67%
Average student indebtedness at graduation: $209,758
Enrollment: 870
men: 54%; women:
46%; minorities: 39%;
underrepresented minorities:
18%; in state: 56%
Acceptance rate: 5%
Median New MCAT total score: 511
Median GPA: 3.73

Most popular undergraduate majors: biological sciences:
57%; physical sciences: 20%;
nonsciences: 13%; other: 10%
Percent of graduates entering primary care specialties: 44.0%

Thomas Jefferson University (Kimmel)
1025 Walnut Street, Room 100
Philadelphia, PA 19107-5083
www.tju.edu
Private
Admissions: (215) 955-6983
Email: jmc.admissions@jefferson.edu
Financial aid: (215) 955-2867
Application deadline: 11/15
Tuition: $55,247
Room/board/expenses: $17,391
Percent receiving grants: 48%
Average student indebtedness at graduation: $179,745
Enrollment: 1,070
men: 50%; women:
50%; minorities: 32%;
underrepresented minorities:
10%; in state: 45%
Acceptance rate: 4%
Median New MCAT total score: 511
Median GPA: 3.72
Most popular undergraduate majors: biological sciences:
46%; physical sciences: 8%;
nonsciences: 14%; other: 32%
Percent of graduates entering primary care specialties: 42.9%

University of Pennsylvania (Perelman)
3400 Civic Center Boulevard
Philadelphia, PA 19104-5162
www.med.upenn.edu
Private
Admissions: (215) 898-8001
Email:
admiss@mail.med.upenn.edu
Financial aid: (215) 573-3423
Application deadline: 10/15
Tuition: $58,809
Room/board/expenses: $22,220
Percent receiving grants: 75%
Average student indebtedness at graduation: $121,668
Enrollment: 629
men: 54%; women:
46%; minorities: 49%;
underrepresented minorities:
26%; in state: 25%
Acceptance rate: 5%
Median New MCAT total score: 517
Median GPA: 3.86
Most popular undergraduate majors: biological sciences:
45%; physical sciences: 20%;
nonsciences: 32%; other: 3%
Percent of graduates entering primary care specialties: 38.0%

University of Pittsburgh
401 Scaife Hall
Pittsburgh, PA 15261
www.medschool.pitt.edu
Public
Admissions: (412) 648-9891
Email: admissions@medschool.pitt.edu
Financial aid: (412) 648-9891
Application deadline: 10/15
In-state tuition: $53,382
Out-of-state tuition: $54,908
Room/board/expenses: $17,388
Percent receiving grants: 56%
Average student indebtedness at graduation: $142,689

Enrollment: 601
men: 53%; women:
47%; minorities: 41%;
underrepresented minorities:
17%; in state: 29%
Acceptance rate: 6%
Median New MCAT total score: 514
Median GPA: 3.82
Most popular undergraduate majors: biological sciences:
38%; physical sciences: 19%;
nonsciences: 13%; other: 30%
Percent of graduates entering primary care specialties: 42.0%

PUERTO RICO

Ponce School of Medicine[1]
PO Box 7004
Ponce, PR 00732
www.psm.edu
Private
Admissions: (787) 840-2575
Email: admissions@psm.edu
Financial aid: N/A
Tuition: N/A
Room/board/expenses: N/A
Enrollment: N/A

San Juan Bautista School of Medicine[1]
PO Box 4968
Caguas, PR 00726-4968
www.sanjuanbautista.edu
Private
Admissions: (787) 743-3038
Email: admissions@sanjuanbautista.edu
Financial aid: N/A
Tuition: N/A
Room/board/expenses: N/A
Enrollment: N/A

Universidad Central del Caribe[1]
PO Box 60-327
Bayamon, PR 00960-6032
www.uccaribe.edu/medicine/
Private
Admissions: (787) 798-3001
Email: admissions@uccaribe.edu
Financial aid: N/A
Tuition: N/A
Room/board/expenses: N/A
Enrollment: N/A

University of Puerto Rico School of Medicine[1]
PO Box 365067
San Juan, PR 00936-5067
www.md.rcm.upr.edu/
Public
Admissions: (787) 758-2525
Financial aid: N/A
Tuition: N/A
Room/board/expenses: N/A
Enrollment: N/A

RHODE ISLAND

Brown University (Alpert)
222 Richmond Street, Box G-M
Providence, RI 02912-9706
med.brown.edu
Private
Admissions: (401) 863-2149
Email: medschool_admissions@brown.edu
Financial aid: (401) 863-1142
Application deadline: 11/01
Tuition: $60,028
Room/board/expenses: $18,634

Percent receiving grants: 52%
Average student indebtedness at graduation: $131,988
Enrollment: 544
men: 49%; women:
51%; minorities: 53%;
underrepresented minorities:
24%; in state: 10%
Acceptance rate: 3%
Median New MCAT total score: 514
Median GPA: 3.78
Most popular undergraduate majors: biological sciences:
45%; physical sciences: 8%;
nonsciences: 33%; other: 14%
Percent of graduates entering primary care specialties: 42.0%

SOUTH CAROLINA

Medical University of South Carolina
96 Jonathan Lucas Street
Suite 601
Charleston, SC 29425
www.musc.edu/com
Public
Admissions: (843) 792-2055
Email: taylorwl@musc.edu
Financial aid: (843) 792-2536
Application deadline: 11/01
In-state tuition: $35,662
Out-of-state tuition: $62,126
Room/board/expenses: $13,340
Percent receiving grants: 49%
Average student indebtedness at graduation: $190,033
Enrollment: 731
men: 58%; women:
42%; minorities: 27%;
underrepresented minorities:
20%; in state: 84%
Acceptance rate: 12%
Median New MCAT total score: 508
Median GPA: 3.70
Most popular undergraduate majors: biological sciences:
56%; physical sciences: 10%;
nonsciences: 10%; other: 24%
Percent of graduates entering primary care specialties: 34.3%

University of South Carolina[1]
6311 Garners Ferry Road
Columbia, SC 29208
www.med.sc.edu
Public
Admissions: (803) 216-3625
Email: admissions@uscmed.sc.edu
Financial aid: N/A
Tuition: N/A
Room/board/expenses: N/A
Enrollment: N/A

University of South Carolina-Greenville[1]
607 Grove Road
Greenville, SC 29605
Private
Admissions: N/A
Financial aid: N/A
Tuition: N/A
Room/board/expenses: N/A
Enrollment: N/A

SOUTH DAKOTA

University of South Dakota (Sanford)
1400 W. 22nd Street
Sioux Falls, SD 57105
www.usd.edu/medstudentaffairs
Public
Admissions: (605) 658-6302
Email: md@usd.edu
Financial aid: (605) 658-6303
Application deadline: 11/01
In-state tuition: $31,703
Out-of-state tuition: $72,971
Room/board/expenses: $17,652
Percent receiving grants: 80%
Average student indebtedness at graduation: $160,439
Enrollment: 258
men: 55%; women:
45%; minorities: 7%;
underrepresented minorities:
4%; in state: 87%
Acceptance rate: 11%
Median New MCAT total score: 509
Median GPA: 3.84
Most popular undergraduate majors: biological sciences:
48%; physical sciences: 12%;
nonsciences: 19%; other: 21%
Percent of graduates entering primary care specialties: 38.9%

TENNESSEE

East Tennessee State University (Quillen)
PO Box 70694
Johnson City, TN 37614
www.etsu.edu/com
Public
Admissions: (423) 439-2033
Email: sacom@etsu.edu
Financial aid: (423) 439-2035
Application deadline: 11/15
In-state tuition: $35,145
Out-of-state tuition: $67,267
Room/board/expenses: $11,407
Average student indebtedness at graduation: $184,284
Enrollment: 283
men: 57%; women:
43%; minorities: 14%;
underrepresented minorities:
6%; in state: 95%
Acceptance rate: 6%
Median New MCAT total score: 504
Median GPA: 3.82
Most popular undergraduate majors: biological sciences:
55%; physical sciences: 25%;
nonsciences: 7%; other: 13%
Percent of graduates entering primary care specialties: 44.1%

Meharry Medical College[1]
1005 D. B. Todd Jr. Boulevard
Nashville, TN 37208
www.mmc.edu/education/som/
Private
Admissions: (615) 327-6223
Email: admissions@mmc.edu
Financial aid: N/A
Tuition: N/A
Room/board/expenses: N/A
Enrollment: N/A

University of Tennessee Health Science Center

910 Madison Avenue, Suite 1002
Memphis, TN 38163
www.uthsc.edu/Medicine
Public
Admissions: (901) 448-5559
Email: diharris@uthsc.edu
Financial aid: (901) 448-5568
Application deadline: 11/15
In-state tuition: $36,880
Out-of-state tuition: $69,310
Room/board/expenses: $19,948
Percent receiving grants: 50%
Average student indebtedness at graduation: $178,183
Enrollment: 674
men: 59%; women: 41%; minorities: 27%; underrepresented minorities: 12%; in state: 95%
Acceptance rate: 12%
Median New MCAT total score: 509
Median GPA: 3.70
Most popular undergraduate majors: biological sciences: 36%; physical sciences: 20%; nonsciences: 13%; other: 31%
Percent of graduates entering primary care specialties: 50.0%

Vanderbilt University

1211 22nd Avenue S
and 201 Light Hall
Nashville, TN 37232-2104
medschool.vanderbilt.edu/
Private
Admissions: (615) 322-2145
Email: mdadmissions@vanderbilt.edu
Financial aid: (615) 322-2145
Application deadline: 11/01
Tuition: $53,604
Room/board/expenses: $19,548
Percent receiving grants: 70%
Average student indebtedness at graduation: $127,184
Enrollment: 384
men: 56%; women: 44%; minorities: 38%; underrepresented minorities: 23%; in state: 18%
Acceptance rate: 4%
Median New MCAT total score: 520
Median GPA: 3.87
Most popular undergraduate majors: biological sciences: 38%; physical sciences: 25%; nonsciences: 8%; other: 29%
Percent of graduates entering primary care specialties: 32.5%

TEXAS

Baylor College of Medicine

1 Baylor Plaza
Houston, TX 77030
www.bcm.edu
Private
Admissions: (713) 798-4842
Email: admissions@bcm.tmc.edu
Financial aid: (713) 798-4612
Application deadline: 11/01
Tuition: $19,563
Room/board/expenses: $28,860
Percent receiving grants: 60%
Average student indebtedness at graduation: $99,882

Enrollment: 718
men: 51%; women: 49%; minorities: 56%; underrepresented minorities: 17%; in state: 87%
Acceptance rate: 4%
Median New MCAT total score: 515
Median GPA: 3.86
Most popular undergraduate majors: biological sciences: 26%; physical sciences: 22%; nonsciences: 4%; other: 48%
Percent of graduates entering primary care specialties: 49.0%

Texas A&M Health Science Center

8447 State Highway 47
Bryan, TX 77807-3260
medicine.tamhsc.edu
Public
Admissions: (979) 436-0237
Email: admissions@medicine.tamhsc.edu
Financial aid: (979) 436-0199
Application deadline: 10/01
In-state tuition: $17,591
Out-of-state tuition: $30,691
Room/board/expenses: $17,322
Percent receiving grants: 78%
Average student indebtedness at graduation: $128,797
Enrollment: 786
men: 52%; women: 48%; minorities: 52%; underrepresented minorities: 17%; in state: 90%
Acceptance rate: 9%
Median New MCAT total score: 509
Median GPA: 3.69
Most popular undergraduate majors: biological sciences: 49%; physical sciences: 17%; nonsciences: 4%; other: 30%
Percent of graduates entering primary care specialties: 41.0%

Texas Tech University-El Paso[1]

5001 El Paso Drive
El Paso, TX 79905
elpaso.ttuhsc.edu/som/
Private
Admissions: (915) 215-4410
Email: fostersom.admissions@ttuhsc.edu
Financial aid: (915) 215-4923
Tuition: N/A
Room/board/expenses: N/A
Enrollment: N/A

Texas Tech University Health Sciences Center

3601 Fourth Street
Lubbock, TX 79430
www.ttuhsc.edu/som/
Public
Admissions: (806) 743-2297
Email: somadm@ttuhsc.edu
Financial aid: (806) 743-3025
Application deadline: 10/01
In-state tuition: $17,925
Out-of-state tuition: $31,025
Room/board/expenses: $15,290
Percent receiving grants: 72%
Average student indebtedness at graduation: $129,454

Enrollment: 690
men: 55%; women: 45%; minorities: 39%; underrepresented minorities: 14%; in state: 91%
Acceptance rate: 10%
Median New MCAT total score: 507
Median GPA: 3.73
Most popular undergraduate majors: biological sciences: 46%; physical sciences: 21%; nonsciences: 6%; other: 27%
Percent of graduates entering primary care specialties: 48.0%

University of Texas Health Science Center-Houston

6431 Fannin Street
MSB G. 400
Houston, TX 77030
med.uth.edu
Public
Admissions: (713) 500-5160
Email: ms.admissions@uth.tmc.edu
Financial aid: (713) 500-3860
Application deadline: 09/29
In-state tuition: $20,796
Out-of-state tuition: $31,396
Room/board/expenses: $16,230
Percent receiving grants: 30%
Average student indebtedness at graduation: $117,381
Enrollment: 968
men: 54%; women: 46%; minorities: 48%; underrepresented minorities: 24%; in state: 94%
Acceptance rate: 14%
Median New MCAT total score: 509
Median GPA: 3.78
Most popular undergraduate majors: biological sciences: 52%; physical sciences: 25%; nonsciences: 11%; other: 12%
Percent of graduates entering primary care specialties: 34.3%

University of Texas Health Science Center-San Antonio

7703 Floyd Curl Drive
San Antonio, TX 78229-3900
som.uthscsa.edu
Public
Admissions: (210) 567-6080
Email: medadmissions@uthscsa.edu
Financial aid: (210) 567-2635
Application deadline: 09/29
In-state tuition: $18,813
Out-of-state tuition: $33,220
Room/board/expenses: N/A
Percent receiving grants: 55%
Average student indebtedness at graduation: $120,529
Enrollment: 854
men: 53%; women: 47%; minorities: 48%; underrepresented minorities: 30%; in state: 90%
Acceptance rate: 9%
Median New MCAT total score: 505
Median GPA: 3.77
Most popular undergraduate majors: biological sciences: 51%; physical sciences: 18%; nonsciences: 9%; other: 22%

Percent of graduates entering primary care specialties: 35.3%

University of Texas Medical Branch-Galveston[1]

301 University Boulevard
Galveston, TX 77555-0133
www.som.utmb.edu/
Public
Admissions: (409) 772-6958
Email: somadmis@utmb.edu
Financial aid: N/A
Tuition: N/A
Room/board/expenses: N/A
Enrollment: N/A

University of Texas Southwestern Medical Center

5323 Harry Hines Boulevard
Dallas, TX 75390
www.utsouthwestern.edu/
Public
Admissions: (214) 648-5617
Email: admissions@utsouthwestern.edu
Financial aid: (214) 648-6490
Application deadline: 10/01
In-state tuition: $19,923
Out-of-state tuition: $33,023
Room/board/expenses: $12,965
Percent receiving grants: 52%
Average student indebtedness at graduation: $109,350
Enrollment: 939
men: 53%; women: 47%; minorities: 53%; underrepresented minorities: 18%; in state: 85%
Acceptance rate: 8%
Median New MCAT total score: 513
Median GPA: 3.85
Most popular undergraduate majors: biological sciences: 48%; physical sciences: 24%; nonsciences: 8%; other: 20%
Percent of graduates entering primary care specialties: 46.0%

UTAH

University of Utah

30 N. 1900 E
Salt Lake City, UT 84132-2101
medicine.utah.edu
Public
Admissions: (801) 581-7498
Email: deans.admissions@hsc.utah.edu
Financial aid: (801) 581-6499
Application deadline: 11/01
In-state tuition: $37,502
Out-of-state tuition: $70,002
Room/board/expenses: $9,936
Percent receiving grants: 68%
Average student indebtedness at graduation: $166,985
Enrollment: 440
men: 54%; women: 46%; minorities: 20%; underrepresented minorities: 8%; in state: 80%
Acceptance rate: 4%
Median New MCAT total score: 509
Median GPA: 3.70
Most popular undergraduate majors: biological sciences: 52%; physical sciences: 13%; nonsciences: 6%; other: 29%

Percent of graduates entering primary care specialties: 35.2%

VERMONT

University of Vermont

E-126 Given Building
89 Beaumont Avenue
Burlington, VT 05405
www.uvm.edu/medicine/admissions/
Public
Admissions: (802) 656-2154
Email: medadmissions@uvm.edu
Financial aid: (802) 656-5700
Application deadline: 11/15
In-state tuition: $37,208
Out-of-state tuition: $62,448
Room/board/expenses: $10,752
Percent receiving grants: 48%
Average student indebtedness at graduation: $183,092
Enrollment: 469
men: 50%; women: 50%; minorities: 30%; underrepresented minorities: 14%; in state: 27%
Acceptance rate: 5%
Median New MCAT total score: 510
Median GPA: 3.73
Most popular undergraduate majors: biological sciences: 41%; physical sciences: 19%; nonsciences: 20%; other: 20%
Percent of graduates entering primary care specialties: 40.0%

VIRGINIA

Eastern Virginia Medical School

721 Fairfax Avenue
PO Box 1980
Norfolk, VA 23501-1980
www.evms.edu
Public
Admissions: (757) 446-5812
Email: evms_admissions@evms.edu
Financial aid: (757) 446-5804
Application deadline: 11/15
In-state tuition: $33,368
Out-of-state tuition: $58,554
Room/board/expenses: $14,733
Percent receiving grants: 28%
Average student indebtedness at graduation: $213,283
Enrollment: 593
men: 57%; women: 43%; minorities: 38%; underrepresented minorities: 12%; in state: 51%
Acceptance rate: 5%
Median New MCAT total score: 510
Median GPA: 3.60
Most popular undergraduate majors: biological sciences: 50%; physical sciences: 18%; nonsciences: 11%; other: 21%
Percent of graduates entering primary care specialties: 54.6%

University of Virginia

PO Box 800793
McKim Hall
Charlottesville, VA 22908-0793
med.virginia.edu/admissions/
Public
Admissions: (434) 924-5571
Email: SOMADM@virginia.edu
Financial aid: (434) 924-0033
Application deadline: 11/01
In-state tuition: $48,114

Out-of-state tuition: $58,238
Room/board/expenses: $21,528
Percent receiving grants: 65%
Average student indebtedness at
graduation: $125,094
Enrollment: 650
men: 54%; women:
46%; minorities: 43%;
underrepresented minorities:
26%; in state: 50%
Acceptance rate: 10%
Median New MCAT total score: 517
Median GPA: 3.88
Most popular undergraduate
majors: biological sciences:
42%; physical sciences: 20%;
nonsciences: 12%; other: 26%
Percent of graduates entering
primary care specialties: 38.0%

Virginia Commonwealth University

PO Box 980565
Richmond, VA 23298-0565
www.medschool.vcu.edu
Public
Admissions: (804) 828-9629
Email: somume@vcuhealth.org
Financial aid: (804) 828-4006
Application deadline: 10/15
In-state tuition: $32,453
Out-of-state tuition: $49,653
Room/board/expenses: $14,834
Percent receiving grants: 41%
Average student indebtedness at
graduation: $159,288
Enrollment: 848
men: 53%; women:
47%; minorities: 44%;
underrepresented minorities:
13%; in state: 52%
Acceptance rate: 4%
Median GPA: 3.60

Most popular undergraduate
majors: biological sciences:
28%; physical sciences: 12%;
nonsciences: 5%; other: 55%
Percent of graduates entering
primary care specialties: 45.5%

Virginia Tech Carilion School of Medicine[1]

2 Riverside Circle
Roanoke, VA 24016
www.vtc.vt.edu/
Public
Admissions: (540) 526-2560
Email: VTCAdmissions2015@
carilionclinic.org
Financial aid: N/A
Tuition: N/A
Room/board/expenses: N/A
Enrollment: N/A

WASHINGTON

University of Washington

PO Box 356350
Seattle, WA 98195
www.uwmedicine.org/admissions
Public
Admissions: (206) 543-7212
Email: askuwsom@uw.edu
Financial aid: (206) 685-9229
Application deadline: 10/15
In-state tuition: $34,933
Out-of-state tuition: $64,387
Room/board/expenses: $16,890
Percent receiving grants: 70%
Average student indebtedness at
graduation: $153,494

Enrollment: 1,022
men: 45%; women:
55%; minorities: N/A;
underrepresented minorities:
N/A; in state: 93%
Acceptance rate: 4%
Median New MCAT total score:
506
Median GPA: 3.69
Most popular undergraduate
majors: biological sciences:
46%; physical sciences: 14%;
nonsciences: 14%; other: 26%
Percent of graduates entering
primary care specialties: 53.0%

WEST VIRGINIA

Marshall University (Edwards)

1600 Medical Center Drive
Huntington, WV 25701-3655
musom.marshall.edu
Public
Admissions: (800) 544-8514
Email: warren@marshall.edu
Financial aid: (304) 691-8739
Application deadline: 11/01
In-state tuition: $21,104
Out-of-state tuition: $50,074
Room/board/expenses: $14,560
Percent receiving grants: 66%
Average student indebtedness at
graduation: $190,345
Enrollment: 306
men: 61%; women:
39%; minorities: 23%;
underrepresented minorities:
10%; in state: 75%
Acceptance rate: 7%
Median New MCAT total score:
500
Median GPA: 3.56

Most popular undergraduate
majors: biological sciences:
44%; physical sciences: 30%;
nonsciences: 6%; other: 20%
Percent of graduates entering
primary care specialties: 50.2%

West Virginia University

1 Medical Center Drive
Morgantown, WV 26506-9111
medicine.hsc.wvu.edu/students
Public
Admissions: (304) 293-1439
Email: medadmissions@
hsc.wvu.edu
Financial aid: (304) 293-3706
Application deadline: 11/01
In-state tuition: $30,348
Out-of-state tuition: $58,914
Room/board/expenses: $16,458
Percent receiving grants: 51%
Average student indebtedness at
graduation: $154,798
Enrollment: 441
men: 51%; women:
49%; minorities: 21%;
underrepresented minorities:
10%; in state: 57%
Acceptance rate: 4%
Median New MCAT total score:
507
Median GPA: 3.72
Most popular undergraduate
majors: biological sciences:
37%; physical sciences: 24%;
nonsciences: 3%; other: 36%
Percent of graduates entering
primary care specialties: 49.0%

WISCONSIN

Medical College of Wisconsin[1]

8701 Watertown Plank Road
Milwaukee, WI 53226
www.mcw.edu/medical-school/
Private
Admissions: (414) 955-8246
Email: medschool@mcw.edu
Financial aid: (414) 955-8208
Tuition: N/A
Room/board/expenses: N/A
Enrollment: N/A

University of Wisconsin-Madison

750 Highland Avenue
Madison, WI 53705-2221
www.med.wisc.edu/education
Public
Admissions: (608) 263-4925
Email: medadmissions@med.
wisc.edu
Financial aid: (608) 262-3060
Application deadline: 11/01
In-state tuition: $29,865
Out-of-state tuition: $39,761
Room/board/expenses: $23,242
Percent receiving grants: 36%
Average student indebtedness at
graduation: $144,334
Enrollment: 725
men: 50%; women:
50%; minorities: 29%;
underrepresented minorities:
12%; in state: 73%
Acceptance rate: 5%
Median New MCAT total score: 512
Median GPA: 3.77
Most popular undergraduate
majors: biological sciences:
50%; physical sciences: 28%;
nonsciences: 8%; other: 14%
Percent of graduates entering
primary care specialties: 40.1%

INSTITUTIONS THAT GRANT THE DOCTOR OF OSTEOPATHIC MEDICINE (D.O.) DEGREE

ALABAMA

Alabama College of Osteopathic Medicine[1]
445 Health Sciences Boulevard
Dothan, AL 36303
Private
Admissions: N/A
Financial aid: N/A
Tuition: N/A
Room/board/expenses: N/A
Enrollment: N/A

ARIZONA

A.T. Still University of Health Sciences-Mesa[1]
5850 E. Still Circle
Mesa, AZ 85206
www.atsu.edu/soma/index.htm
Private
Admissions: (866) 626-2878
Email: admissions@atsu.edu
Financial aid: N/A
Tuition: N/A
Room/board/expenses: N/A
Enrollment: N/A

Midwestern University[1]
19555 N. 59th Avenue
Glendale, AZ 85308
www.midwestern.edu
Private
Admissions: (623) 572-3215
Email: admissaz@midwestern.edu
Financial aid: N/A
Tuition: N/A
Room/board/expenses: N/A
Enrollment: N/A

CALIFORNIA

Touro University-California
1310 Club Drive
Vallejo, CA 94592
www.tu.edu
Private
Admissions: (707) 638-5270
Email: steven.davis@tu.edu
Financial aid: (707) 638-5280
Application deadline: 03/15
Tuition: $51,725
Room/board/expenses: $17,550
Percent receiving grants: 5%
Enrollment: 545
men: 55%; women: 45%; minorities: N/A; underrepresented minorities: N/A; in state: 77%
Acceptance rate: 6%
Median GPA: 3.57
Most popular undergraduate majors: biological sciences: N/A; physical sciences: N/A; nonsciences: N/A; other: N/A
Percent of graduates entering primary-care specialties: 56.0%

Western University of Health Sciences
309 E. Second Street
Pomona, CA 91766-1854
prospective.westernu.edu/
Private
Admissions: (909) 469-5335
Email: admissions@westernu.edu
Financial aid: (909) 469-5560
Application deadline: 02/01

Tuition: $54,970
Room/board/expenses: $18,923
Percent receiving grants: 10%
Average student indebtedness at graduation: $235,004
Enrollment: 1,301
men: 52%; women: 48%; minorities: 44%; underrepresented minorities: 15%; in state: 71%
Acceptance rate: 6%
Median New MCAT total score: 505
Median GPA: 3.57
Most popular undergraduate majors: biological sciences: 63%; physical sciences: 11%; nonsciences: 7%; other: 19%
Percent of graduates entering primary-care specialties: 55.0%

COLORADO

Rocky Vista University
8401 S. Chambers Road
Parker, CO 80134
www.rvu.edu
Private
Admissions: (720) 875-2800
Email: admissions@rvu.edu
Financial aid: (720) 875-2800
Application deadline: 03/15
Tuition: $52,024
Room/board/expenses: $17,050
Percent receiving grants: 23%
Average student indebtedness at graduation: $251,768
Enrollment: 641
men: 54%; women: 46%; minorities: 16%; underrepresented minorities: 7%; in state: 41%
Acceptance rate: 7%
Median New MCAT total score: 504
Median GPA: 3.66
Most popular undergraduate majors: biological sciences: 57%; physical sciences: 12%; nonsciences: 10%; other: 21%
Percent of graduates entering primary-care specialties: 46.0%

FLORIDA

Nova Southeastern University
3200 S. University Drive
Fort Lauderdale, FL 33328
osteopathic.nova.edu
Private
Admissions: (954) 262-1101
Email: hpdops@nova.edu
Financial aid: (954) 262-7439
Application deadline: 03/01
Tuition: $52,399
Room/board/expenses: $25,501
Percent receiving grants: 9%
Average student indebtedness at graduation: $259,422
Enrollment: 1,009
men: 55%; women: 45%; minorities: 51%; underrepresented minorities: 25%; in state: 60%
Acceptance rate: 8%
Median New MCAT total score: 505
Median GPA: 3.59
Most popular undergraduate majors: biological sciences: 50%; physical sciences: 12%; nonsciences: 9%; other: 29%
Percent of graduates entering primary-care specialties: 52.0%

ILLINOIS

Midwestern University[1]
555 31st Street
Downers Grove, IL 60515
www.midwestern.edu
Private
Admissions: (630) 515-6171
Email: admissil@midwestern.edu
Financial aid: N/A
Tuition: N/A
Room/board/expenses: N/A
Enrollment: N/A

INDIANA

Marian University College of Osteopathic Medicine[1]
3200 Cold Spring Road
Indianapolis, IN 46222
Private
Admissions: N/A
Financial aid: N/A
Tuition: N/A
Room/board/expenses: N/A
Enrollment: N/A

IOWA

Des Moines University[1]
3200 Grand Avenue
Des Moines, IA 50312
www.dmu.edu/do/
Private
Admissions: (515) 271-1499
Email: doadmit@dmu.edu
Financial aid: N/A
Tuition: N/A
Room/board/expenses: N/A
Enrollment: N/A

KENTUCKY

University of Pikeville
147 Sycamore Street
Pikeville, KY 41501
www.upike.edu
Private
Admissions: (606) 218-5409
Email: kycomadmissions@upike.edu
Financial aid: (606) 218-5407
Application deadline: 02/01
Tuition: $42,975
Room/board/expenses: $0
Percent receiving grants: 17%
Average student indebtedness at graduation: $162,397
Enrollment: 527
men: 58%; women: 42%; minorities: 10%; underrepresented minorities: 7%; in state: 42%
Acceptance rate: 7%
Median New MCAT total score: 500
Median GPA: 3.50
Most popular undergraduate majors: biological sciences: 79%; physical sciences: 7%; nonsciences: 10%; other: 4%
Percent of graduates entering primary-care specialties: 76.3%

MAINE

University of New England
11 Hills Beach Road
Biddeford, ME 04005
www.une.edu/com/
Private
Admissions: (800) 477-4863
Email: gradadmissions2@une.edu
Financial aid: (207) 602-2342
Application deadline: 02/01
Tuition: $54,555
Room/board/expenses: $12,500
Percent receiving grants: 22%
Average student indebtedness at graduation: $233,282
Enrollment: 700
men: 51%; women: 49%; minorities: 18%; underrepresented minorities: 8%; in state: 13%
Acceptance rate: 9%
Median New MCAT total score: 504
Median GPA: 3.64
Most popular undergraduate majors: biological sciences: 42%; physical sciences: 18%; nonsciences: 16%; other: 24%
Percent of graduates entering primary-care specialties: 60.0%

MICHIGAN

Michigan State University (College of Osteopathic Medicine)
A308 E. Fee Hall
East Lansing, MI 48824
www.com.msu.edu
Public
Admissions: (517) 353-7740
Email: com.admissions@hc.msu.edu
Financial aid: (517) 353-5940
Application deadline: 12/15
In-state tuition: $44,259
Out-of-state tuition: $86,948
Room/board/expenses: $17,661
Percent receiving grants: 37%
Average student indebtedness at graduation: $232,172
Enrollment: 1,263
men: 57%; women: 43%; minorities: 22%; underrepresented minorities: 7%; in state: 85%
Acceptance rate: 9%
Median New MCAT total score: 503
Median GPA: 3.62
Most popular undergraduate majors: biological sciences: 22%; physical sciences: 8%; nonsciences: 1%; other: 69%
Percent of graduates entering primary-care specialties: 76.0%

MISSISSIPPI

William Carey University College of Osteopathic Medicine[1]
498 Tuscan Avenue
Hattiesburg, MS 39401
www.wmcarey.edu/departments/college-osteopathic-medicine
Private
Admissions: (601) 318-6235
Email: wcucom@wmcarey.edu
Financial aid: N/A
Tuition: N/A

Room/board/expenses: N/A
Enrollment: N/A

MISSOURI

A.T. Still University of Health Sciences-Kirksville[1]
800 W. Jefferson Street
Kirksville, MO 63501
www.atsu.edu/kcom/index.htm
Private
Admissions: (866) 626-2878
Email: admissions@atsu.edu
Financial aid: N/A
Tuition: N/A
Room/board/expenses: N/A
Enrollment: N/A

Kansas City University of Medicine and Biosciences
1750 Independence Avenue
Kansas City, MO 64106-1453
www.kcumb.edu/
Private
Admissions: (800) 234-4847
Email: admissions@kcumb.edu
Financial aid: (816) 654-7175
Application deadline: 03/01
Tuition: $44,595
Room/board/expenses: $24,475
Percent receiving grants: 27%
Average student indebtedness at graduation: $228,896
Enrollment: 1,056
men: 58%; women: 42%; minorities: 28%; underrepresented minorities: 6%; in state: 17%
Acceptance rate: 9%
Median New MCAT total score: 506
Median GPA: 3.64
Most popular undergraduate majors: biological sciences: 50%; physical sciences: 10%; nonsciences: 5%; other: 35%
Percent of graduates entering primary-care specialties: 58.0%

NEW JERSEY

Rowan University
1 Medical Center Drive
Stratford, NJ 08084-1501
www.rowan.edu/som
Public
Admissions: (856) 566-7050
Email: somadm@rowan.edu
Financial aid: (856) 566-6008
Application deadline: 02/01
In-state tuition: $44,705
Out-of-state tuition: $67,796
Room/board/expenses: $15,500
Percent receiving grants: 0%
Average student indebtedness at graduation: $183,347
Enrollment: 676
men: 54%; women: 46%; minorities: 57%; underrepresented minorities: 19%; in state: 86%
Acceptance rate: 10%
Median New MCAT total score: 503
Median GPA: 3.62
Most popular undergraduate majors: biological sciences: 42%; physical sciences: 26%; nonsciences: 11%; other: 21%

More @ usnews.com/grad

Percent of graduates entering primary-care specialties: 76.3%

NEW YORK

New York Institute of Technology[1]

Old Westbury
Northern Boulevard
Long Island, NY 11568
www.nyit.edu
Private
Admissions: (516) 686-3747
Email: comadm@nyit.edu
Financial aid: N/A
Tuition: N/A
Room/board/expenses: N/A
Enrollment: N/A

Touro College of Osteopathic Medicine

230 W. 125th Street
New York, NY 10027
www.tourocom.touro.edu
Private
Admissions: (212) 851-2569
Email: admissions.tourocom@touro.edu
Financial aid: (212) 851-1199
Application deadline: 04/01
Tuition: $50,270
Room/board/expenses: $27,460
Percent receiving grants: 1%
Average student indebtedness at graduation: $213,149
Enrollment: 961
men: 53%; women: 47%; minorities: 49%; underrepresented minorities: 14%; in state: 37%
Acceptance rate: 8%
Median New MCAT total score: 504
Median GPA: 3.43
Most popular undergraduate majors: biological sciences: 50%; physical sciences: 12%; nonsciences: 16%; other: 22%
Percent of graduates entering primary-care specialties: 52.0%

NORTH CAROLINA

Campbell University (Wallace)[1]

4350 U.S. 421 S
Lillington, NC 27546
Private
Admissions: N/A
Financial aid: N/A
Tuition: N/A
Room/board/expenses: N/A
Enrollment: N/A

OHIO

Ohio University

Grosvenor Hall
Athens, OH 45701
www.ohio.edu/medicine
Public
Admissions: (740) 593-4313
Email: ou-hcom@ohio.edu

Financial aid: (740) 593-2158
Application deadline: 02/01
In-state tuition: $35,584
Out-of-state tuition: $49,722
Room/board/expenses: $15,386
Percent receiving grants: 33%
Average student indebtedness at graduation: $200,876
Enrollment: 815
men: 53%; women: 47%; minorities: 24%; underrepresented minorities: 16%; in state: 99%
Acceptance rate: 7%
Median New MCAT total score: 502
Median GPA: 3.59
Most popular undergraduate majors: biological sciences: 65%; physical sciences: 18%; nonsciences: 7%; other: 10%
Percent of graduates entering primary-care specialties: 52.5%

OKLAHOMA

Oklahoma State University

1111 W. 17th Street
Tulsa, OK 74107-1898
healthsciences.okstate.edu
Public
Admissions: (918) 561-8277
Email: lindsey.yoder@okstate.edu
Financial aid: (918) 561-8278
Application deadline: 02/28
In-state tuition: $25,486
Out-of-state tuition: $49,277
Room/board/expenses: $18,000
Percent receiving grants: 24%
Average student indebtedness at graduation: $195,829
Enrollment: 446
men: 59%; women: 41%; minorities: 34%; underrepresented minorities: 24%; in state: 91%
Acceptance rate: 14%
Median New MCAT total score: 501
Median GPA: 3.73
Most popular undergraduate majors: biological sciences: 56%; physical sciences: 18%; nonsciences: 11%; other: 15%
Percent of graduates entering primary-care specialties: 57.9%

PENNSYLVANIA

Lake Erie College of Osteopathic Medicine

1858 W. Grandview Boulevard
Erie, PA 16509
www.lecom.edu
Private
Admissions: (814) 866-6641
Email: admissions@lecom.edu
Financial aid: (814) 866-6641
Application deadline: 04/01
Tuition: $33,055
Room/board/expenses: $14,500
Percent receiving grants: 35%
Average student indebtedness at graduation: $194,609

Enrollment: 2,275
men: 59%; women: 41%; minorities: 30%; underrepresented minorities: 9%; in state: 37%
Acceptance rate: 8%
Median New MCAT total score: 502
Median GPA: 3.55
Most popular undergraduate majors: biological sciences: 71%; physical sciences: 12%; nonsciences: 10%; other: 7%
Percent of graduates entering primary-care specialties: 66.7%

Philadelphia College of Osteopathic Medicine[1]

4170 City Avenue
Philadelphia, PA 19131
www.pcom.edu
Private
Admissions: (800) 999-6998
Email: admissions@pcom.edu
Financial aid: N/A
Tuition: N/A
Room/board/expenses: N/A
Enrollment: N/A

TENNESSEE

Lincoln Memorial University (DeBusk)

6965 Cumberland Gap Parkway
Harrogate, TN 37752
www.lmunet.edu/academics/schools/debusk-college-of-osteopathic-medicine/do/admissions
Private
Admissions: (423) 869-7090
Email: dcomadmissions@lmunet.edu
Financial aid: (423) 869-7107
Application deadline: 03/15
Tuition: $47,880
Room/board/expenses: $14,650
Percent receiving grants: 3%
Enrollment: 949
men: 61%; women: 39%; minorities: 28%; underrepresented minorities: 11%; in state: 26%
Acceptance rate: 9%
Median New MCAT total score: 501
Median GPA: 3.45
Most popular undergraduate majors: biological sciences: N/A; physical sciences: N/A; nonsciences: N/A; other: N/A
Percent of graduates entering primary-care specialties: 78.8%

TEXAS

University of North Texas Health Science Center

3500 Camp Bowie Boulevard
Fort Worth, TX 76107-2699
www.unthsc.edu
Public
Admissions: (800) 535-8266

Email: TCOMAdmissions@unthsc.edu
Financial aid: (817) 735-2505
Application deadline: 09/29
In-state tuition: $19,068
Out-of-state tuition: $34,756
Room/board/expenses: $16,588
Percent receiving grants: 75%
Average student indebtedness at graduation: $147,899
Enrollment: 916
men: 54%; women: 46%; minorities: 46%; underrepresented minorities: 16%; in state: 95%
Acceptance rate: 13%
Median New MCAT total score: 504
Median GPA: 3.70
Most popular undergraduate majors: biological sciences: 71%; physical sciences: 8%; nonsciences: 3%; other: 18%
Percent of graduates entering primary-care specialties: 60.0%

VIRGINIA

Edward Via College of Osteopathic Medicine-Virginia, Carolinas, and Auburn

2265 Kraft Drive
Blacksburg, VA 24060
www.vcom.edu
Private
Admissions: (540) 231-6138
Email: admissions@vcom.vt.edu
Financial aid: (540) 231-6021
Application deadline: 03/01
Tuition: $43,800
Room/board/expenses: N/A
Percent receiving grants: 27%
Enrollment: 1,708
men: 49%; women: 51%; minorities: 30%; underrepresented minorities: 14%; in state: 39%
Acceptance rate: 12%
Median New MCAT total score: 500
Median GPA: 3.60
Most popular undergraduate majors: biological sciences: 59%; physical sciences: 14%; nonsciences: 8%; other: 19%
Percent of graduates entering primary-care specialties: 69.0%

Liberty University College of Osteopathic Medicine[1]

306 Liberty View Lane
Lynchburg, VA 24502
Private
Admissions: N/A
Financial aid: N/A
Tuition: N/A
Room/board/expenses: N/A
Enrollment: N/A

WASHINGTON

Pacific Northwest University of Health Sciences

200 University Parkway
Yakima, WA 98901
www.pnwu.edu/
Private
Admissions: (509) 249-7888
Email: admission@pnwu.edu
Financial aid: (509) 249-7888
Application deadline: 02/01
Tuition: $51,500
Room/board/expenses: $13,230
Percent receiving grants: 11%
Average student indebtedness at graduation: $254,117
Enrollment: 569
men: 52%; women: 48%; minorities: 28%; underrepresented minorities: 14%; in state: 49%
Acceptance rate: 6%
Median New MCAT total score: 503
Median GPA: 3.49
Most popular undergraduate majors: biological sciences: 63%; physical sciences: 3%; nonsciences: 9%; other: 25%
Percent of graduates entering primary-care specialties: 53.0%

WEST VIRGINIA

West Virginia School of Osteopathic Medicine

400 N. Lee Street
Lewisburg, WV 24901
www.wvsom.edu
Public
Admissions: (800) 356-7836
Email: admissions@osteo.wvsom.edu
Financial aid: (304) 647-6369
Application deadline: 02/15
In-state tuition: $21,650
Out-of-state tuition: $51,400
Room/board/expenses: $14,980
Percent receiving grants: 16%
Average student indebtedness at graduation: $227,032
Enrollment: 847
men: 51%; women: 49%; minorities: 26%; underrepresented minorities: 9%; in state: 27%
Acceptance rate: 7%
Median New MCAT total score: 496
Median GPA: 3.50
Most popular undergraduate majors: biological sciences: 51%; physical sciences: 11%; nonsciences: 12%; other: 26%
Percent of graduates entering primary-care specialties: 70.3%

NURSING

Here you'll find information on the 532 nursing schools with master's or doctoral programs accredited by either the Commission on Collegiate Nursing Education or the Accreditation Commission for Education in Nursing. Two hundred ninety-two schools that offer at least master's degrees responded to the U.S. News survey, which was conducted in the fall of 2016 and early 2017. Nursing schools or programs that did not respond have abbreviated entries.

KEY TO THE TERMINOLOGY

1. A school whose name has been footnoted with the numeral 1 did not return the U.S. News statistical survey; limited data appear in its entry.
N/A. Not available from the school or not applicable.
Admissions. The admissions office phone number.
Email. The address of the admissions office. If instead of an email address a website is listed, the website will automatically present an email screen programmed to reach the admissions office.
Financial aid. The financial aid office phone number.
Application deadline. "Rolling" means there is no deadline; the school acts on applications as they are received. "Varies" means deadlines vary according to department or whether applicants are U.S. citizens or foreign nationals.
Degrees offered. Master's, Ph.D. and Doctor of Nursing Practice (DNP)
Tuition. For the 2016-17 academic year for master's, Ph.D. and Doctor of Nursing Practice programs. Doesn't include fees.
Credit hour. The cost per credit hour for the 2016-17 academic year.
Room/board/expenses. For the 2016-17 academic year.
Enrollment. Full-time and part-time, including master's, Ph.D. and DNP candidates, for fall 2016.

Minorities. Full-time and part-time master's, Ph.D., and DNP minority enrollment percentage for fall 2016. Reflects the share of students who are black or African-American, Asian, American Indian or Alaska Native, Native Hawaiian or other Pacific Islander, Hispanic/Latino, or two or more races. The minority numbers were reported by each school.
Acceptance rates. Percentage of applicants who were accepted among those who applied for fall 2016 admission to master's, Ph.D. or DNP nursing programs.
Nursing programs offered in 2016-17. Areas of specialization include administration, case management, clinical nurse leader, clinical nurse specialist, community health/public health, education, forensic nursing, generalist, health management & policy, health care systems, informatics, nurse anesthesia, nurse-midwifery, nurse practitioner, adult-gerontology acute care nurse practitioner, adult-gerontology primary care nurse practitioner, adult nurse practitioner, family nurse practitioner, pediatric primary care nurse practitioner, psychiatric-mental health nurse practitioner–across the lifespan, research, school nursing, other majors, combined nurse practitioner/clinical nurse specialist, dual majors.

ALABAMA

Auburn University
102 Miller Hall
Auburn University, AL 36849
www.auburn.edu/academic/nursing/
Public
Admissions: (334) 844-4700
Email: gradadm@auburn.edu
Financial aid: (334) 844-4634
Application deadline: N/A
Degrees offered: master's
In-state tuition: full time: $9,072, part time: $504/credit hour
Out-of-state tuition: full time: $27,216
Room/board/expenses: $12,898
Full-time enrollment: 2
men: 50%; women: 50%;
minorities: 0%; international: 0%
Part-time enrollment: 124
men: 10%; women: 90%;
minorities: 20%; international: 0%
Acceptance rate (master's): 63%
Specialties offered: education; nurse practitioner; nurse practitioner: family; dual majors

Auburn University-Montgomery[1]
PO Box 244023
Montgomery, AL 36124
Public
Admissions: N/A
Financial aid: N/A
Tuition: N/A
Room/board/expenses: N/A
Enrollment: N/A

Jacksonville State University
700 Pelham Road N
Jacksonville, AL 36265-1602
www.jsu.edu/nursing/index.html
Public
Admissions: (256) 782-5268
Email: info@jsu.edu
Financial aid: (256) 782-5006
Application deadline: N/A
Degrees offered: master's
In-state tuition: full time: $371/credit hour, part time: $371/credit hour
Out-of-state tuition: full time: $742/credit hour
Room/board/expenses: $7,128
Full-time enrollment: 11
men: 0%; women: 100%;
minorities: 55%; international: 0%
Part-time enrollment: 34
men: 9%; women: 91%;
minorities: 50%; international: 0%
Acceptance rate (master's): 80%
Specialties offered: community health/public health; education; other majors

Samford University
800 Lakeshore Drive
Birmingham, AL 35229
www.samford.edu/nursing/
Private
Admissions: (205) 726-2047
Email: amaddox@samford.edu
Financial aid: (205) 726-2905
Application deadline: 6/1
Degrees offered: master's, DNP
Tuition: full time: $809/credit hour, part time: $809/credit hour (master's); full time: $809/credit hour, part time: $809/credit hour (DNP)
Room/board/expenses: N/A
Full-time enrollment: 268 (master's); 13 (DNP)
men: 25%; women: 75%;
minorities: 16%; international: 0%
Part-time enrollment: N/A (master's); 63 (DNP)
men: 6%; women: 94%;
minorities: 16%; international: 0%
Acceptance rate (master's): 43%
Acceptance rate (DNP): 74%
Specialties offered: administration; education; health management & policy health care systems; nurse anesthesia; nurse practitioner; nurse practitioner: family

Spring Hill College[1]
4000 Dauphin Street
Mobile, AL 36608
Private
Admissions: N/A
Financial aid: N/A
Tuition: N/A
Room/board/expenses: N/A
Enrollment: N/A

Troy University-Montgomery
College View Building
Troy, AL 35082
www.troy.edu/healthandhumanservices
Public
Admissions: (800) 551-9716
Email: admit@troy.edu
Financial aid: (800) 414-5756
Application deadline: 3/1
Degrees offered: master's, DNP
In-state tuition: full time: $494/credit hour, part time: $494/credit hour (master's); full time: $494/credit hour, part time: $494/credit hour (DNP)
Out-of-state tuition: full time: $494/credit hour (master's); full time: $494/credit hour (DNP)
Room/board/expenses: N/A
Full-time enrollment: 85 (master's); 10 (DNP)
men: 15%; women: 85%;
minorities: 24%; international: 0%
Part-time enrollment: 151 (master's); 50 (DNP)
men: 10%; women: 90%;
minorities: 28%; international: 0%

Acceptance rate (master's): 98%
Acceptance rate (DNP): 97%
Specialties offered: informatics;
nurse practitioner: family

University of Alabama

Box 870358
Tuscaloosa, AL 35487
nursing.ua.edu/index.html
Public
Admissions: (205) 348-5921
Email: gradschool@ua.edu
Financial aid: (205) 348-6756
Application deadline: 4/1
Degrees offered: master's, DNP
In-state tuition: full time: $367/
credit hour, part time: $367/
credit hour (master's); full time:
$367/credit hour, part time:
$367/credit hour (DNP)
Out-of-state tuition: full time:
$367/credit hour (master's); full
time: $367/credit hour (DNP)
Room/board/expenses: N/A
Full-time enrollment: 81
(master's); 55 (DNP)
men: 10%; women: 90%;
minorities: 32%; international:
0%
Part-time enrollment: 51
(master's); 122 (DNP)
men: 17%; women: 83%;
minorities: 35%; international:
0%
Acceptance rate (master's): 43%
Acceptance rate (DNP): 46%
Specialties offered:
administration; case
management; clinical nurse
leader; nurse practitioner;
nurse practitioner: family; nurse
practitioner: psychiatric-mental
health, across the lifespan; dual
majors

University of Alabama-Birmingham

1530 Third Avenue S
Birmingham, AL 35294-1210
www.uab.edu/nursing/home/
Public
Admissions: (205) 975-7529
Email: sonstudaffairs@uab.edu
Financial aid: (205) 934-8223
Application deadline: 9/1
Degrees offered: master's, Ph.D.,
DNP
In-state tuition: full time: $510/
credit hour, part time: $510/
credit hour (master's); full time:
$510/credit hour, part time:
$510/credit hour (DNP)
Out-of-state tuition: full time:
$510/credit hour (master's); full
time: $1,203/credit hour (Ph.D.);
full time: $510/credit hour (DNP)
Room/board/expenses: $5,400
(master's); $5,400 (Ph.D.);
$5,400 (DNP)
Full-time enrollment: 261
(master's); 13 (Ph.D.); 13 (DNP)
men: 24%; women: 76%;
minorities: 21%; international:
1%
Part-time enrollment: 1,191
(master's); 23 (Ph.D.); 183
(DNP)
men: 11%; women: 89%;
minorities: 24%; international:
0%
Acceptance rate (master's): 60%
Acceptance rate (Ph.D.): 70%
Acceptance rate (DNP): 100%

Specialties offered:
administration; clinical nurse
leader; education; informatics;
nurse anesthesia; neonatal;
nurse practitioner: nurse
practitioner: adult-gerontology
acute care; nurse practitioner:
adult-gerontology primary care;
nurse practitioner: family; nurse
practitioner: pediatric primary
care; nurse practitioner:
psychiatric-mental health,
across the lifespan; research;
women's health; other majors;
dual majors

University of Alabama-Huntsville

301 Sparkman Drive
Huntsville, AL 35899
uah.edu/nursing
Public
Admissions: (256) 824-6198
Email: deangrad@uah.edu
Financial aid: (256) 824-6650
Application deadline: 4/1
Degrees offered: master's, DNP
In-state tuition: full time: $702/
credit hour, part time: $702/
credit hour (master's); full time:
$381/credit hour, part time:
$381/credit hour (DNP)
Out-of-state tuition: full time:
$1,530/credit hour (master's);
full time: $381/credit hour (DNP)
Room/board/expenses: N/A
Full-time enrollment: 159
(master's); 37 (DNP)
men: 15%; women: 85%;
minorities: 23%; international:
0%
Part-time enrollment: 150
(master's); 70 (DNP)
men: 16%; women: 84%;
minorities: 16%; international:
0%
Acceptance rate (master's): 88%
Acceptance rate (DNP): 94%
Specialties offered:
administration; nurse
practitioner; nurse practitioner:
adult-gerontology acute care;
nurse practitioner: family

University of Mobile

5735 College Parkway
Mobile, AL 36613-2842
www.umobile.edu/Academics/
AcademicAreas/SchoolofNursing.
aspx#.VFKIM01ATIU
Private
Admissions: (251) 442-2343
Email: measter@umobile.edu
Financial aid: (251) 442-2239
Application deadline: N/A
Degrees offered: master's
Tuition: full time: $510/credit
hour, part time: $510/credit hour
Room/board/expenses: N/A
Full-time enrollment: 4
men: 0%; women: 100%;
minorities: 75%; international:
0%
Part-time enrollment: 6
men: 0%; women: 100%;
minorities: 67%; international:
0%
Specialties offered:
administration; education

University of North Alabama[1]

223 Stevens Hall
Florence, AL 35632
Public
Admissions: N/A
Financial aid: N/A
Tuition: N/A
Room/board/expenses: N/A
Enrollment: N/A

University of South Alabama[1]

5721 USA Drive N, Room 3068
Mobile, AL 36688-0002
Public
Admissions: N/A
Financial aid: N/A
Tuition: N/A
Room/board/expenses: N/A
Enrollment: N/A

ALASKA

University of Alaska-Anchorage[1]

3211 Providence Drive
Anchorage, AK 99508-8030
Public
Admissions: N/A
Financial aid: N/A
Tuition: N/A
Room/board/expenses: N/A
Enrollment: N/A

ARIZONA

Arizona State University

500 N. Third Street
Phoenix, AZ 85004
nursingandhealth.asu.edu/
Public
Admissions: (480) 727-0262
Email: Michael.Mobley@asu.edu
Financial aid: (855) 278-5080
Application deadline: 3/31
Degrees offered: master's, Ph.D.,
DNP
In-state tuition: full time: $12,580,
part time: $898/credit hour
(master's); full time: $15,080,
part time: $1,077/credit hour
(Ph.D.); full time: $15,080, part
time: $1,077/credit hour (DNP)
Out-of-state tuition: full time:
$22,632 (master's); full time:
$25,132 (Ph.D.); full time:
$25,132 (DNP)
Room/board/expenses: $12,132
(master's); $12,132 (Ph.D.);
$12,132 (DNP)
Full-time enrollment: 12
(master's); 13 (Ph.D.); 143 (DNP)
men: 13%; women: 87%;
minorities: 32%; international:
4%
Part-time enrollment: 13
(master's); 23 (Ph.D.); 81 (DNP)
men: 15%; women: 85%;
minorities: 32%; international:
0%
Acceptance rate (master's): 100%
Acceptance rate (Ph.D.): 33%
Acceptance rate (DNP): 56%
Specialties offered: education;
neonatal; nurse practitioner;
nurse practitioner: adult-
gerontology primary care;
nurse practitioner: family; nurse
practitioner: pediatric primary
care; nurse practitioner:
psychiatric-mental health,

across the lifespan; research;
women's health; other majors

Brookline College[1]

2445 W Dunlap Avenue
Suite 100
Phoenix, AZ 85021
Private
Admissions: N/A
Financial aid: N/A
Tuition: N/A
Room/board/expenses: N/A
Enrollment: N/A

Grand Canyon University[1]

3300 West Camelback Road
Phoenix, AZ 85061
Private
Admissions: N/A
Financial aid: N/A
Tuition: N/A
Room/board/expenses: N/A
Enrollment: N/A

Northern Arizona University

NAU Box 15035
Flagstaff, AZ 86011
nau.edu/GradCol/; nau.edu/chhs/
nursing/
Public
Admissions: (920) 523-4348
Email: gradadmissions@nau.edu
Financial aid: (055) 028-6333
Application deadline: 3/15
Degrees offered: master's, DNP
In-state tuition: full time: $458/
credit hour, part time: $458/
credit hour (master's); full time:
$458/credit hour, part time:
$458/credit hour (DNP)
Out-of-state tuition: full time:
$1,157/credit hour (master's); full
time: $1,157/credit hour (DNP)
Room/board/expenses: N/A
Full-time enrollment: 34
(master's); N/A (DNP)
men: 29%; women: 71%;
minorities: 6%; international: 0%
Part-time enrollment: 131
(master's); 8 (DNP)
men: 17%; women: 83%;
minorities: 28%; international:
0%
Acceptance rate (master's): 96%
Acceptance rate (DNP): 100%
Specialties offered: generalist;
nurse practitioner; nurse
practitioner: family

University of Arizona

1305 N. Martin Avenue
Tucson, AZ 85721-0203
www.nursing.arizona.edu/
Public
Admissions: (520) 626-3808
Email: studentaffairs@
nursing.arizona.edu
Financial aid: (520) 621-1858
Application deadline: 12/15
Degrees offered: master's, Ph.D.,
DNP
In-state tuition: full time: $812/
credit hour, part time: $812/
credit hour (master's); full time:
$812/credit hour, part time:
$812/credit hour (Ph.D.); full
time: $975/credit hour, part
time: $975/credit hour (DNP)

Out-of-state tuition: full time:
$1,729/credit hour (master's);
full time: $1,729/credit hour
(Ph.D.); full time: $975/credit
hour (DNP)
Room/board/expenses: N/A
Full-time enrollment: 142
(master's); 55 (Ph.D.); 271
(DNP)
men: 17%; women: 83%;
minorities: 43%; international:
0%
Part-time enrollment: 258
(master's); 25 (Ph.D.); 93 (DNP)
men: 13%; women: 87%;
minorities: 36%; international:
0%
Acceptance rate (master's): 66%
Acceptance rate (Ph.D.): 77%
Acceptance rate (DNP): 54%
Specialties offered: generalist;
nurse anesthesia; nurse
practitioner; nurse practitioner:
adult-gerontology acute care;
nurse practitioner: family; nurse
practitioner: pediatric primary
care; nurse practitioner:
psychiatric-mental health,
across the lifespan; research;
other majors

University of Phoenix[1]

4615 E. Elwood Street
Phoenix, AZ 85040
Private
Admissions: N/A
Financial aid: N/A
Tuition: N/A
Room/board/expenses: N/A
Enrollment: N/A

ARKANSAS

Arkansas State University-Jonesboro[1]

P.O. Box 910
State University, AR 72467
www.astate.edu/college/conhp/
Public
Admissions: (870) 972-2031
Email: www.astate.edu/college/
graduate-school/
Financial aid: (870) 972-2310
Tuition: N/A
Room/board/expenses: N/A
Enrollment: N/A

Arkansas Tech University[1]

Dean Hall 224
402 West O Street
Russellville, AR 72801
www.muw.edu/nslp
Public
Admissions: (662) 329-7142
Email: www.muw.edu/
graduates/admission
Financial aid: (662) 329-7145
Tuition: N/A
Room/board/expenses: N/A
Enrollment: N/A

University of Arkansas

606 N. Razorback Road
Fayetteville, AR 72701
nurs.uark.edu/
Public
Admissions: (479) 575-6247
Email: gradinfo@uark.edu
Financial aid: (479) 575-3806
Application deadline: N/A
Degrees offered: master's, DNP

In-state tuition: full time: $410/ credit hour, part time: $410/ credit hour (master's); full time: $410/credit hour, part time: $410/credit hour (DNP)
Out-of-state tuition: full time: $1,047/credit hour (master's); full time: $1,047/credit hour (DNP)
Room/board/expenses: $20,664 (master's); $20,664 (DNP)
Full-time enrollment: 1 (master's); 37 (DNP)
men: 3%; women: 97%; minorities: 3%; international: 0%
Part-time enrollment: 10 (master's); 46 (DNP)
men: 9%; women: 91%; minorities: 18%; international: 0%
Acceptance rate (DNP): 63%
Specialties offered: clinical nurse specialist; education; nurse practitioner: adult-gerontology acute care; nurse practitioner: family

University of Arkansas for Medical Sciences[1]

4301 W. Markham Street
Slot 529
Little Rock, AR 72205-7199
Public
Admissions: N/A
Financial aid: N/A
Tuition: N/A
Room/board/expenses: N/A
Enrollment: N/A

University of Central Arkansas

201 Donaghey Avenue
Conway, AR 72035
Public
Admissions: (501) 450-3120
Email: rschlosser@uca.edu
Financial aid: (501) 450-3410
Application deadline: 4/1
Degrees offered: master's, DNP
In-state tuition: full time: $255/ credit hour, part time: $255/ credit hour (master's); full time: $255/credit hour, part time: $255/credit hour (DNP)
Out-of-state tuition: full time: $510/credit hour (master's); full time: $510/credit hour (DNP)
Room/board/expenses: $6,248 (master's); $6,248 (DNP)
Full-time enrollment: 1 (master's); N/A (DNP)
men: 0%; women: 100%; minorities: 0%; international: 100%
Part-time enrollment: 146 (master's); 16 (DNP)
men: 10%; women: 90%; minorities: 18%; international: 0%
Acceptance rate (master's): 71%
Acceptance rate (DNP): 100%
Specialties offered: clinical nurse leader; education; nurse practitioner: adult-gerontology primary care; nurse practitioner: family

Azusa Pacific University[1]

Graduate Center
Azusa, CA 91702-7000
Private
Admissions: N/A
Financial aid: N/A
Tuition: N/A
Room/board/expenses: N/A
Enrollment: N/A

Brandman University

16355 Laguna Canyon Road
Irvine, CA 92618
www.brandman.edu/
Private
Admissions: (800) 746-0082
Email: adminfo@brandman.edu
Financial aid: (800) 746-0082
Application deadline: 8/15
Degrees offered: DNP
Tuition: full time: $1,095/credit hour, part time: $1,095/credit hour
Room/board/expenses: N/A
Full-time enrollment: 189
men: 24%; women: 76%; minorities: 68%; international: 0%
Part-time enrollment: 21
men: 14%; women: 86%; minorities: 62%; international: 0%
Acceptance rate (DNP): 100%
Specialties offered: nurse practitioner; nurse practitioner: adult-gerontology acute care; nurse practitioner: family; nurse practitioner: psychiatric-mental health, across the lifespan

California Baptist University

8432 Magnolia Avenue
Riverside, CA 92506
www.calbaptist.edu/academics/ schools-colleges/school-nursing/
Private
Admissions: (951) 343-4336
Email: asonke@calbaptist.edu
Financial aid: (951) 343-4236
Application deadline: 8/1
Degrees offered: master's, DNP
Tuition: full time: $768/credit hour, part time: $768/credit hour (master's); full time: $1,200/ credit hour, part time: $1,200/ credit hour (DNP)
Room/board/expenses: $10,840 (master's); N/A (DNP)
Full-time enrollment: 98 (master's); N/A (DNP)
men: 17%; women: 83%; minorities: 61%; international: 0%
Part-time enrollment: 149 (master's); 7 (DNP)
men: 22%; women: 78%; minorities: 54%; international: 2%
Acceptance rate (master's): 57%
Acceptance rate (DNP): 31%
Specialties offered: clinical nurse specialist; education; health management & policy health care systems; nurse practitioner: family

California State University-Chico

400 W. First Street
Chico, CA 95929-0200
www.csuchico.edu/nurs
Public
Admissions: (530) 898-6880
Email: graduatestudies@ csuchico.edu
Financial aid: (530) 898-6451
Application deadline: 3/1
Degrees offered: master's
In-state tuition: full time: $8,310, part time: $5,478
Out-of-state tuition: full time: $17,238
Room/board/expenses: $11,206
Full-time enrollment:
men: N/A; women: N/A; minorities: N/A; international: N/A
Part-time enrollment: 11
men: 27%; women: 73%; minorities: 18%; international: 0%
Acceptance rate (master's): 100%
Specialties offered: administration; education

California State University-Dominguez Hills

1000 East Victoria Street
Carson, CA 90747
www4.csudh.edu/son/
Public
Admissions: (310) 243-2110
Email: admit@csudh.edu
Financial aid: (310) 243-3691
Application deadline: 5/31
Degrees offered: master's
In-state tuition: full time: $6,738, part time: $3,906
Out-of-state tuition: full time: $9,714
Room/board/expenses: $25,920
Full-time enrollment: 14
men: 0%; women: 100%; minorities: 57%; international: 0%
Part-time enrollment: 271
men: 12%; women: 88%; minorities: 61%; international: 1%
Acceptance rate (master's): 86%
Specialties offered: administration; clinical nurse specialist; education; nurse practitioner; nurse practitioner: family

California State University-Fresno[1]

2345 E. San Ramon Avenue
Fresno, CA 93740-8031
Public
Admissions: N/A
Financial aid: N/A
Tuition: N/A
Room/board/expenses: N/A
Enrollment: N/A

California State University-Fullerton

800 N. State College Boulevard
Fullerton, CA 92834
nursing.fullerton.edu
Public
Admissions: (657) 278-3336
Email: nursing@fullerton.edu
Financial aid: (657) 278-3125
Application deadline: N/A

Degrees offered: master's, DNP
In-state tuition: full time: $6,738, part time: $3,906 (master's); full time: $14,340, part time: N/A (DNP)
Out-of-state tuition: full time: N/A (master's); full time: N/A (DNP)
Room/board/expenses: $13,882 (master's); $13,882 (DNP)
Full-time enrollment: 125 (master's); 51 (DNP)
men: 27%; women: 73%; minorities: 57%; international: 0%
Part-time enrollment: 62 (master's); N/A (DNP)
men: 11%; women: 89%; minorities: 65%; international: 0%
Acceptance rate (master's): 32%
Acceptance rate (DNP): 66%
Specialties offered: administration; education; nurse anesthesia; nurse-midwifery; school nursing; women's health

California State University-Long Beach[1]

1250 Bellflower Boulevard
Long Beach, CA 90840
Public
Admissions: N/A
Financial aid: N/A
Tuition: N/A
Room/board/expenses: N/A
Enrollment: N/A

California State University-Los Angeles

5151 State University Drive
Los Angeles, CA 90032-8171
www.calstatela.edu/academic/ hhs/nursing
Public
Admissions: (323) 343-3901
Email: admission@calstatela.edu
Financial aid: (323) 343-6260
Application deadline: 11/30
Degrees offered: master's, DNP
In-state tuition: full time: $7,610, part time: $4,780 (master's); full time: N/A, part time: N/A (DNP)
Out-of-state tuition: full time: $16,538 (master's); full time: N/A (DNP)
Room/board/expenses: $12,750 (master's); N/A (DNP)
Full-time enrollment: 184 (master's); N/A (DNP)
men: 14%; women: 86%; minorities: 57%; international: 0%
Part-time enrollment: 35 (master's); N/A (DNP)
men: 17%; women: 83%; minorities: 29%; international: 0%
Acceptance rate (master's): 52%
Specialties offered: education; nurse practitioner: adult-gerontology acute care; nurse practitioner: adult-gerontology primary care; nurse practitioner: family; nurse practitioner: psychiatric-mental health, across the lifespan

California State University-Sacramento

6000 J Street
Sacramento, CA 95819-6096
www.csus.edu/hhs/nrs/index.html
Public
Admissions: (916) 278-7766
Email: admissions@csus.edu
Financial aid: (916) 278-1000
Application deadline: 3/1
Degrees offered: master's
In-state tuition: full time: $6,738, part time: $3,906
Out-of-state tuition: full time: $11,946
Room/board/expenses: N/A
Full-time enrollment: 70
men: 16%; women: 84%; minorities: 39%; international: 0%
Part-time enrollment: 45
men: 13%; women: 87%; minorities: 40%; international: 0%
Acceptance rate (master's): 84%
Specialties offered: N/A

California State University-San Bernardino[1]

5500 University Parkway
San Bernadino, CA 92407
Public
Admissions: N/A
Financial aid: N/A
Tuition: N/A
Room/board/expenses: N/A
Enrollment: N/A

California State University-San Marcos[1]

333 S. Twin Oaks Valley Road
San Marcos, CA 92096
Public
Admissions: N/A
Financial aid: N/A
Tuition: N/A
Room/board/expenses: N/A
Enrollment: N/A

California State University-Stanislaus[1]

One University Circle
Turlock, CA 95382
Public
Admissions: N/A
Financial aid: N/A
Tuition: N/A
Room/board/expenses: N/A
Enrollment: N/A

Charles R. Drew University of Medicine and Science[1]

1731 E. 120th Street
Los Angeles, CA 90059
Private
Admissions: N/A
Financial aid: N/A
Tuition: N/A
Room/board/expenses: N/A
Enrollment: N/A

Fresno Pacific University[1]

5 River Park Place West
Suite 303
Fresno, CA 93720
Private
Admissions: N/A
Financial aid: N/A
Tuition: N/A
Room/board/expenses: N/A
Enrollment: N/A

Holy Names University

3500 Mountain Boulevard
Oakland, CA 94619
www.hnu.edu/academics/
nursing-programs/ms-nursing
Private
Admissions: (510) 592-6943
Email: admissions@hnu.edu
Financial aid: (510) 436-1327
Application deadline: N/A
Degrees offered: master's
Tuition: full time: $1,023/credit
hour, part time: $1,023/credit
hour
Room/board/expenses: $12,822
Full-time enrollment: 28
men: 18%; women: 82%;
minorities: 82%; international:
0%
Part-time enrollment: 52
men: 4%; women: 96%;
minorities: 75%; international:
0%
Acceptance rate (master's): 64%
Specialties offered:
administration; case
management; education;
informatics; nurse practitioner;
nurse practitioner: family

Loma Linda University[1]

School of Nursing
Admissions Office
Loma Linda, CA 92350
Private
Admissions: N/A
Financial aid: N/A
Tuition: N/A
Room/board/expenses: N/A
Enrollment: N/A

Mount Saint Mary's University[1]

10 Chester Place
Los Angeles, CA 90007
Private
Admissions: N/A
Financial aid: N/A
Tuition: N/A
Room/board/expenses: N/A
Enrollment: N/A

Point Loma Nazarene University

3900 Lomaland Drive
San Diego, CA 92106
www.pointloma.edu/experience/
academics/schools-departments/
school-nursing
Private
Admissions: (619) 563-2846
Email: gradinfo@pointloma.edu
Financial aid: (619) 849-2495
Application deadline: N/A
Degrees offered: master's
Tuition: full time: $755/credit
hour, part time: $755/credit hour
Room/board/expenses: N/A

Full-time enrollment: 45
men: 11%; women: 89%;
minorities: 44%; international:
2%
Part-time enrollment: 23
men: 13%; women: 87%;
minorities: 65%; international:
0%
Acceptance rate (master's): 93%
Specialties offered: clinical nurse
specialist; generalist

Samuel Merritt University

3100 Summit Street
3rd Floor
Oakland, CA 94609
www.samuelmerritt.edu/nursing
Private
Admissions: (510) 869-1550
Email: admission@
samuelmerritt.edu
Financial aid: (510) 869-1529
Application deadline: 12/1
Degrees offered: master's, DNP
Tuition: full time: $1,289/credit
hour, part time: $1,289/credit
hour (master's); full time: $1,117/
credit hour, part time: $1,117/
credit hour (DNP)
Room/board/expenses: N/A
Full-time enrollment: 537
(master's); 24 (DNP)
men: 20%; women: 80%;
minorities: 67%; international:
0%
Part-time enrollment: 51
(master's); 9 (DNP)
men: 23%; women: 77%;
minorities: 47%; international:
0%
Acceptance rate (master's): 48%
Acceptance rate (DNP): 50%
Specialties offered: case
management; nurse anesthesia;
nurse practitioner; nurse
practitioner: family

San Diego State University[1]

Hardy Tower, Room 58
San Diego, CA 92182-4158
Public
Admissions: N/A
Financial aid: N/A
Tuition: N/A
Room/board/expenses: N/A
Enrollment: N/A

San Francisco State University[1]

Burk Hall, Room 371
San Francisco, CA 94132
Public
Admissions: N/A
Financial aid: N/A
Tuition: N/A
Room/board/expenses: N/A
Enrollment: N/A

San Jose State University

Health Building 420
San Jose, CA 95192-0057
www.sjsu.edu/nursing/
Public
Admissions: (408) 283-7500
Email: graduate@sjsu.edu
Financial aid: (408) 283-7500
Application deadline: 4/1
Degrees offered: master's, DNP

In-state tuition: full time: $4,342,
part time: $2,926 (master's); full
time: N/A, part time: N/A (DNP)
Out-of-state tuition: full time:
$8,806 (master's); full time:
N/A (DNP)
Room/board/expenses: N/A
Full-time enrollment: 1 (master's);
N/A (DNP)
men: 0%; women: 100%;
minorities: 100%; international:
0%
Part-time enrollment: 25
(master's) N/A (DNP)
men: 12%; women: 88%;
minorities: 60%; international:
0%
Acceptance rate (master's): 57%
Specialties offered:
administration; education

Sonoma State University[1]

1801 E.Cotati Avenue
Rohnert Park, CA 94928
Public
Admissions: N/A
Financial aid: N/A
Tuition: N/A
Room/board/expenses: N/A
Enrollment: N/A

United States University[1]

830 Bay Boulevard
Chula Vista, CA 91911
Private
Admissions: N/A
Financial aid: N/A
Tuition: N/A
Room/board/expenses: N/A
Enrollment: N/A

University of California-Davis

4610 X Street, Suite 4202
Sacramento, CA 95817
www.ucdmc.ucdavis.edu/
nursing/
Public
Admissions: (916) 734-2145
Email: hs-bettyirenemooreson@
ucdavis.edu
Financial aid: (916) 734-4120
Application deadline: 1/15
Degrees offered: master's, Ph.D.
In-state tuition: full time: $21,750,
part time: N/A (master's); full
time: $11,220, part time: $5,610
Out-of-state tuition: full time:
$33,995 (master's); full time:
$26,322
Room/board/expenses: $14,467
(master's); $14,467
Full-time enrollment: 97
(master's); 31
men: 22%; women: 78%;
minorities: 55%; international:
0%
Part-time enrollment: N/A
(master's);
men: N/A; women: N/A;
minorities: N/A; international:
N/A
Acceptance rate (master's): 31%
Acceptance rate (Ph.D.): 41%
Specialties offered: nurse
practitioner; nurse practitioner:
family; other majors

University of California-Irvine

252 Berk Hall
Irvine, CA 92697
www.nursing.uci.edu/
Public
Admissions: (949) 824-1514
Email: gnsao@uci.edu
Financial aid: (949) 824-8262
Application deadline: 2/1
Degrees offered: master's, Ph.D.
In-state tuition: full time: $21,750,
part time: N/A (master's); full
time: $11,220, part time: $5,610
Out-of-state tuition: full time:
$33,995 (master's); full time:
$26,322
Room/board/expenses: $12,617
(master's); $12,617
Full-time enrollment: 32
(master's); 10
men: 10%; women: 90%;
minorities: 76%; international:
0%
Part-time enrollment: N/A
(master's);
men: N/A; women: N/A;
minorities: N/A; international:
N/A
Acceptance rate (master's): 49%
Acceptance rate (Ph.D.): 38%
Specialties offered: community
health/public health; nurse
practitioner: adult-gerontology
primary care; nurse
practitioner: family

University of California-Los Angeles

700 Tiverton Avenue
Factor Building 2-256
Los Angeles, CA 90095
nursing.ucla.edu
Public
Admissions: (310) 825-9193
Email: rflenoy@sonnet.ucla.edu
Financial aid: (310) 825-2583
Application deadline: 12/1
Degrees offered: master's, Ph.D.
In-state tuition: full time: $21,750,
part time: N/A (master's); full
time: $11,220, part time: N/A
Out-of-state tuition: full time:
$33,995 (master's); full time:
$26,322
Room/board/expenses: $14,502
(master's); $14,502
Full-time enrollment: 352
(master's); 59
men: 12%; women: 88%;
minorities: 58%; international:
3%
Part-time enrollment: N/A
(master's);
men: N/A; women: N/A;
minorities: N/A; international:
N/A
Acceptance rate (master's): 46%
Acceptance rate (Ph.D.): 57%
Specialties offered: clinical
nurse leader; clinical nurse
specialist; generalist; nurse
practitioner; nurse practitioner:
adult-gerontology acute care;
nurse practitioner: adult-
gerontology primary care;
nurse practitioner: family; nurse
practitioner: pediatric primary
care; research; combined
nurse practitioner/clinical nurse
specialist; dual majors

University of California-San Francisco[1]

2 Koret Way
San Francisco, CA 94143
nursing.ucsf.edu/
Public
Admissions: (415) 476-4801
Email: judy.martin-holland@
ucsf.edu
Financial aid: (415) 476-4181
Tuition: N/A
Room/board/expenses: N/A
Enrollment: N/A

University of San Diego

5998 Alcala Park
San Diego, CA 92110
www.sandiego.edu/nursing
Private
Admissions: (619) 260-4524
Email: grads@sandiego.edu
Financial aid: (616) 260-2700
Application deadline: 11/1
Degrees offered: master's, Ph.D.,
DNP
Tuition: full time: $1,425/credit
hour, part time: $1,425/credit
hour (master's); full time: $1,455/
credit hour, part time: $1,455/
credit hour (Ph.D.); full time:
$1,455/credit hour, part time:
$1,455/credit hour (DNP)
Room/board/expenses: $12,000
(master's); $12,000 (Ph.D.);
$12,000 (DNP)
Full-time enrollment: 155
(master's); 36 (Ph.D.); 64 (DNP)
men: 16%; women: 84%;
minorities: 51%; international:
2%
Part-time enrollment: 47
(master's); 32 (Ph.D.); 9 (DNP)
men: 11%; women: 89%;
minorities: 48%; international:
2%
Acceptance rate (master's): 22%
Acceptance rate (Ph.D.): 33%
Acceptance rate (DNP): 53%
Specialties offered:
administration; clinical nurse
leader; clinical nurse specialist;
informatics; nurse practitioner;
nurse practitioner: adult-
gerontology primary care;
nurse practitioner: family; nurse
practitioner: pediatric primary
care; nurse practitioner:
psychiatric-mental health,
across the lifespan; research

University of San Francisco

2130 Fulton Street
San Francisco, CA 94117-1080
www.usfca.edu/nursing/
Private
Admissions: (415) 422-6681
Email: nursing@usfca.edu
Financial aid: (415) 422-2624
Application deadline: 5/15
Degrees offered: master's, DNP
Tuition: full time: $1,295/credit
hour, part time: $1,295/credit
hour (master's); full time: $1,295/
credit hour, part time: $1,295/
credit hour (DNP)
Room/board/expenses: N/A

Full-time enrollment: 409
(master's); 111 (DNP)
men: 15%; women: 85%;
minorities: N/A; international:
N/A
Part-time enrollment: 157
(master's); 83 (DNP)
men: 15%; women: 85%;
minorities: N/A; international:
N/A
Acceptance rate (master's): 32%
Acceptance rate (DNP): 92%
Specialties offered:
administration; clinical nurse
leader; community health/
public health; informatics; nurse
practitioner; nurse practitioner:
family; nurse practitioner:
psychiatric-mental health,
across the lifespan

Vanguard University of Southern California

55 Fair Drive
Costa Mesa, CA 92626
Private
Admissions: N/A
Financial aid: N/A
Application deadline: N/A
Degrees offered: master's
Tuition: full time: $575/credit
hour, part time: $575/credit
hour/credit hour/credit hour
Room/board/expenses: $15,960
Full-time enrollment:
men: N/A; women: N/A;
minorities: N/A; international:
N/A
Part-time enrollment: 23
men: 0%; women: 100%;
minorities: 65%; international:
0%
Acceptance rate (master's): 46%
Specialties offered:
administration; clinical nurse
specialist; education

West Coast University[1]

1477 S. Manchester Avenue
Anaheim, CA 92802
Private
Admissions: N/A
Financial aid: N/A
Tuition: N/A
Room/board/expenses: N/A
Enrollment: N/A

Western University of Health Sciences

309 E. Second Street
Pomona, CA 91766-1854
www.westernu.edu/nursing/
Private
Admissions: (909) 469-5335
Email:
admissions@westernu.edu
Financial aid: (909) 469-5350
Application deadline: N/A
Degrees offered: master's, DNP
Tuition: full time: $852/credit
hour, part time: $852/credit
hour (master's); full time: $1,114/
credit hour, part time: $1,114/
credit hour (DNP)
Room/board/expenses: N/A
Full-time enrollment: 263
(master's); 38 (DNP)
men: 15%; women: 85%;
minorities: 51%; international:
0%

Part-time enrollment: N/A
(master's); N/A (DNP)
men: N/A; women: N/A;
minorities: N/A; international:
N/A
Acceptance rate (master's): 30%
Specialties offered:
administration; clinical nurse
leader; nurse practitioner;
nurse practitioner: family; other
majors

COLORADO

American Sentinel University[1]

2260 South Xanadu Way
Suite 310
Aurora, CO 80014
www.americansentinel.edu/
nursing
Private
Admissions: (866) 922-5690
Email: admissions@
AmericanSentinel.edu
Financial aid: (800) 729-2427
Tuition: N/A
Room/board/expenses: N/A
Enrollment: N/A

Aspen University[1]

720 South Colorado Boulevard
Denver, CO 80246
Private
Admissions: N/A
Financial aid: N/A
Tuition: N/A
Room/board/expenses: N/A
Enrollment: N/A

Colorado Mesa University

1100 North Avenue, M 142
Grand Junction, CO 81501
www.coloradomesa.edu/
Public
Admissions: (970) 248-1875
Email: admissions@
coloradomesa.edu
Financial aid: (970) 248-1396
Application deadline: N/A
Degrees offered: master's, DNP
In-state tuition: full time: $455/
credit hour, part time: $455/
credit hour (master's); full time:
$455/credit hour, part time:
$455/credit hour (DNP)
Out-of-state tuition: full time:
$455/credit hour (master's); full
time: $455/credit hour (DNP)
Room/board/expenses: N/A
Full-time enrollment: 10
(master's); 13 (DNP)
men: 13%; women: 87%;
minorities: 26%; international:
0%
Part-time enrollment: 11
(master's); 10 (DNP)
men: 5%; women: 95%;
minorities: 0%; international: 5%
Acceptance rate (master's): 100%
Acceptance rate (DNP): 100%
Specialties offered: clinical nurse
specialist; education; nurse
practitioner: family

Colorado State University-Pueblo[1]

2200 Bonforte Boulevard
Pueblo, CO 81001
ceeps.colostate-pueblo.edu/
nursing/
Public

Admissions: (719) 549-2462
Financial aid: (719) 549-2753
Tuition: N/A
Room/board/expenses: N/A
Enrollment: N/A

Regis University

3333 Regis Boulevard, G-8
Denver, CO 80221
regis.edu/RHCHP/Schools/
Loretto-Heights-School-of-
Nursing.aspx
Private
Admissions: (303) 458-4344
Email: healthcare@regis.edu
Financial aid: (303) 458-4126
Application deadline: 5/1
Degrees offered: master's, DNP
Tuition: full time: $620/credit
hour, part time: $620/credit
hour (master's); full time: $840/
credit hour, part time: $840/
credit hour (DNP)
Room/board/expenses: N/A
Full-time enrollment: 246
(master's); 11 (DNP)
men: 7%; women: 93%;
minorities: 16%; international:
0%
Part-time enrollment: 102
(master's); 18 (DNP)
men: 9%; women: 91%;
minorities: 22%; international:
0%
Acceptance rate (master's): 90%
Acceptance rate (DNP): 97%
Specialties offered:
administration; education;
generalist; neonatal; nurse
practitioner; nurse practitioner:
adult-gerontology acute care;
nurse practitioner: family

University of Colorado Anschutz Medical Campus

13120 E. 19th Avenue
Aurora, CO 80045
www.ucdenver.edu/academics/
colleges/nursing/Pages/default.
aspx
Public
Admissions: (303) 724-1450
Email:
shane.hoon@ucdenver.edu
Financial aid: (303) 724-8048
Application deadline: 2/15*
Degrees offered: master's, Ph.D.,
DNP
In-state tuition: full time: $610/
credit hour, part time: $610/
credit hour (master's); full time:
$575/credit hour, part time:
$575/credit hour (Ph.D.); full
time: $610/credit hour, part
time: $610/credit hour (DNP)
Out-of-state tuition: full time:
$1,020/credit hour (master's);
full time: $1,020/credit hour
(Ph.D.); full time: $1,020/credit
hour (DNP)
Room/board/expenses: N/A
Full-time enrollment: 497
(master's); 47 (Ph.D.); 36 (DNP)
men: 11%; women: 89%;
minorities: 19%; international:
0%
Part-time enrollment: 118
(master's); 1 (Ph.D.); 45 (DNP)
men: 12%; women: 88%;
minorities: 20%; international:
0%
Acceptance rate (master's): 38%
Acceptance rate (Ph.D.): 77%
Acceptance rate (DNP): 71%

Specialties offered:
administration; clinical
nurse specialist; community
health/public health; health
management & policy health
care systems; informatics;
nurse-midwifery; nurse
practitioner; nurse practitioner:
adult-gerontology acute care;
nurse practitioner: adult-
gerontology primary care;
nurse practitioner: adult; nurse
practitioner: family; nurse
practitioner: pediatric primary
care; nurse practitioner:
psychiatric-mental health,
across the lifespan; women's
health; other majors; dual
majors

University of Colorado-Colorado Springs

1420 Austin Bluffs Parkway
Colorado Springs, CO 80933
www.uccs.edu/bethel/index.html
Public
Admissions: (719) 255-4424
Email: bethel@uccs.edu
Financial aid: (719) 255-3460
Application deadline: 3/15
Degrees offered: master's, DNP
In-state tuition: full time: $680/
credit hour, part time: $763/
credit hour (master's); full time:
$680/credit hour, part time:
$763/credit hour (DNP)
Out-of-state tuition: full time:
$771/credit hour (master's); full
time: $771/credit hour (DNP)
Room/board/expenses: $12,200
(master's); $12,200 (DNP)
Full-time enrollment: 6 (master's);
6 (DNP)
men: 0%; women: 100%;
minorities: 17%; international:
0%
Part-time enrollment: 167
(master's); 20 (DNP)
men: 10%; women: 90%;
minorities: 22%; international:
0%
Acceptance rate (master's): 57%
Acceptance rate (DNP): 43%
Specialties offered: education;
nurse practitioner; nurse
practitioner: adult-gerontology
primary care; nurse
practitioner: family; nurse
practitioner: psychiatric-mental
health, across the lifespan

University of Northern Colorado[1]

Gunter 3080
PO Box 125
Greeley, CO 80639
Public
Admissions: N/A
Email: gradsch@unco.edu
Financial aid: N/A
Tuition: N/A
Room/board/expenses: N/A
Enrollment: N/A

CONNECTICUT

Fairfield University

1073 North Benson Road
Fairfield, CT 06824
www.fairfield.edu/egan
Private
Admissions: (203) 254-4184

Email: gradadmis@fairfield.edu
Financial aid: (203) 254-4125
Application deadline: 8/1
Degrees offered: master's, DNP
Tuition: full time: $850/credit
hour, part time: $850/credit
hour (master's); full time: $950/
credit hour, part time: $950/
credit hour (DNP)
Room/board/expenses: N/A
Full-time enrollment: N/A
(master's); 43 (DNP)
men: 19%; women: 81%;
minorities: 28%; international:
2%
Part-time enrollment: 91
(master's); 82 (DNP)
men: 10%; women: 90%;
minorities: 19%; international:
1%
Acceptance rate (master's): 66%
Acceptance rate (DNP): 50%
Specialties offered: clinical nurse
leader; nurse anesthesia; nurse-
midwifery; nurse practitioner;
nurse practitioner: family; nurse
practitioner: psychiatric-mental
health, across the lifespan;
other majors

Quinnipiac University[1]

275 Mount Carmel Avenue
Hamden, CT 06518
www.quinnipiac.edu/nursing
Private
Admissions: (203) 582-8672
Email: graduate@quinnipiac.edu
Financial aid: (203) 582-8588
Tuition: N/A
Room/board/expenses: N/A
Enrollment: N/A

Sacred Heart University

5151 Park Avenue
Fairfield, CT 06825-1000
sacredheart.edu/academics/
collegeofhealthprofessions/
academicprograms/nursing/
Private
Admissions: (203) 365-4827
Email: gradstudies@
sacredheart.edu
Financial aid: (203) 371-7980
Application deadline: N/A
Degrees offered: master's, DNP
Tuition: full time: N/A, part time:
$795/credit hour (master's); full
time: N/A, part time: $950/credit
hour (DNP)
Room/board/expenses: N/A
Full-time enrollment: 15
(master's); 1 (DNP)
men: 13%; women: 88%;
minorities: 19%; international:
0%
Part-time enrollment: 743
(master's); 34 (DNP)
men: 7%; women: 93%;
minorities: 20%; international:
0%
Acceptance rate (master's): 82%
Acceptance rate (DNP): 91%
Specialties offered:
administration; clinical nurse
leader; education; nurse
practitioner; nurse practitioner:
family

Southern Connecticut State University

501 Crescent Street
New Haven, CT 06515
www.southernct.edu/
gradadmissions/
Public
Admissions: N/A
Email: GradAdmissions@
SouthernCT.edu
Financial aid: (203) 392-5222
Application deadline: N/A
Degrees offered: master's
In-state tuition: full time: $11,219,
part time: $574/credit hour
Out-of-state tuition: full time:
$24,019
Room/board/expenses: N/A
Full-time enrollment: 12
men: 8%; women: 92%;
minorities: 33%; international:
0%
Part-time enrollment: 56
men: 14%; women: 86%;
minorities: 21%; international:
0%
Acceptance rate (master's): 11%
Specialties offered: clinical
nurse leader; education; nurse
practitioner

University of Connecticut

231 Glen Brook Road
Storrs, CT 06269-2026
nursing.uconn.edu/
Public
Admissions: (860) 486-1937
Email: nursingadmissions@
uconn.edu
Financial aid: (860) 486-2819
Application deadline: 2/1
Degrees offered: master's, Ph.D.,
DNP
In-state tuition: full time: $13,726,
part time: $763/credit hour
(master's); full time: $13,726,
part time: $763/credit hour
(Ph.D.); full time: $13,726, part
time: $763/credit hour (DNP)
Out-of-state tuition: full time:
$34,762 (master's); full time:
$34,762 (Ph.D.); full time:
$34,762 (DNP)
Room/board/expenses: $11,888
(master's); $11,888 (Ph.D.);
$11,888 (DNP)
Full-time enrollment: 31
(master's); 23 (Ph.D.); 15 (DNP)
men: 12%; women: 88%;
minorities: 23%; international:
3%
Part-time enrollment: 92
(master's); 9 (Ph.D.); 40 (DNP)
men: 10%; women: 90%;
minorities: 23%; international:
0%
Acceptance rate (master's): 57%
Acceptance rate (Ph.D.): 70%
Acceptance rate (DNP): 100%
Specialties offered: clinical nurse
leader; education; neonatal;
nurse practitioner; nurse
practitioner: adult-gerontology
acute care; nurse practitioner:
adult-gerontology primary
care; nurse practitioner: family;
research; other majors

University of Hartford

200 Bloomfield Avenue
West Hartford, CT 06117
www.hartford.edu/enhp
Private
Admissions: (860) 768-4371
Email: gradstudy@hartford.edu
Financial aid: (860) 768-4296
Application deadline: N/A
Degrees offered: master's
Tuition: full time: N/A, part time:
$590/credit hour
Room/board/expenses: N/A
Full-time enrollment:
men: N/A; women: N/A;
minorities: N/A; international:
N/A
Part-time enrollment: 106
men: 9%; women: 91%;
minorities: 25%; international:
0%
Acceptance rate (master's): 87%
Specialties offered:
administration; community
health/public health; education

University of St. Joseph

1678 Asylum Avenue
West Hartford, CT 06117
www.usj.edu/
Private
Admissions: (860) 231-5216
Email: Graduate@usj.edu
Financial aid: (860) 231-5223
Application deadline: 3/1
Degrees offered: master's, DNP
Tuition: full time: $755/credit
hour, part time: $755/credit hour
(master's); full time: N/A, part
time: $810/credit hour (DNP)
Room/board/expenses: N/A
Full-time enrollment: 2 (master's);
1 (DNP)
men: 0%; women: 100%;
minorities: 33%; international:
0%
Part-time enrollment: 130
(master's); 13 (DNP)
men: 8%; women: 92%;
minorities: 28%; international:
0%
Acceptance rate (master's): 46%
Acceptance rate (DNP): 38%
Specialties offered: education;
nurse practitioner; nurse
practitioner: family; nurse
practitioner: psychiatric-mental
health, across the lifespan

Western Connecticut State University[1]

181 White Street
Danbury, CT 06810
www.wcsu.edu/nursing/graduate/
Public
Admissions: N/A
Financial aid: N/A
Tuition: N/A
Room/board/expenses: N/A
Enrollment: N/A

Yale University

400 West Campus Drive
Orange, CT 06477
nursing.yale.edu
Private
Admissions: (203) 737-1793
Email: sourav.guha@yale.edu
Financial aid: (203) 737-1700
Application deadline: 11/1
Degrees offered: master's, Ph.D.,
DNP

Tuition: full time: $37,932, part
time: $25,216 (master's); full
time: N/A/credit hour, part time:
N/A/credit hour (Ph.D.); full time:
N/A, part time: $25,216 (DNP)
Room/board/expenses: N/A
Full-time enrollment: 285
(master's); 12 (Ph.D.); N/A (DNP)
men: 15%; women: 85%;
minorities: 17%; international: 1%
Part-time enrollment: 12
(master's); N/A (Ph.D.); 48 (DNP)
men: 23%; women: 77%;
minorities: 28%; international:
3%
Acceptance rate (master's): 37%
Acceptance rate (Ph.D.): 43%
Acceptance rate (DNP): 63%
Specialties offered: community
health/public health; health
management & policy health
care systems; nurse-midwifery;
nurse practitioner; nurse
practitioner: adult-gerontology
acute care; nurse practitioner:
adult-gerontology primary care;
nurse practitioner: family; nurse
practitioner: pediatric primary
care; nurse practitioner:
psychiatric-mental health,
across the lifespan; research;
women's health; dual majors

DELAWARE

Wesley College[1]

120 N. State Street
Dover, DE 19901
www.wesley.edu
Private
Admissions: (302) 736-2400
Email: admissions@wesley.edu
Financial aid: (302) 736-2483
Tuition: N/A
Room/board/expenses: N/A
Enrollment: N/A

Wilmington University[1]

320 N. DuPont Highway
New Castle, DE 19720-6491
Private
Admissions: N/A
Financial aid: N/A
Tuition: N/A
Room/board/expenses: N/A
Enrollment: N/A

DISTRICT OF COLUMBIA

The Catholic University of America

620 Michigan Avenue NE
Washington, DC 20064
nursing.cua.edu/
Private
Admissions: (800) 673-2772
Email: cua-admissions@cua.edu
Financial aid: (202) 319-5307
Application deadline: 7/15
Degrees offered: master's, Ph.D.,
DNP
Tuition: full time: $42,850,
part time: $1,710/credit hour
(master's); full time: $42,850,
part time: $1,710/credit hour
(Ph.D.); full time: $42,850, part
time: $1,710/credit hour (DNP)
Room/board/expenses: $16,372
(master's); $16,372 (Ph.D.);
$16,372 (DNP)

Full-time enrollment: 17
(master's); 4 (Ph.D.); 2 (DNP)
men: 9%; women: 91%;
minorities: 35%; international:
26%
Part-time enrollment: 100
(master's); 80 (Ph.D.); 33 (DNP)
men: 8%; women: 92%;
minorities: 34%; international:
3%
Acceptance rate (master's): 71%
Acceptance rate (Ph.D.): 61%
Acceptance rate (DNP): 79%
Specialties offered: nurse
practitioner; nurse practitioner:
adult-gerontology primary care;
nurse practitioner: family; nurse
practitioner: pediatric primary
care

Georgetown University

3700 Reservoir Road NW
Washington, DC 20057
nhs.georgetown.edu/nursing
Private
Admissions: (202) 687-1561
Email: ka584@georgetown.edu
Financial aid: (202) 687-4547
Application deadline: 1/15
Degrees offered: master's, DNP
Tuition: full time: $1,928/credit
hour, part time: $1,928/credit
hour (master's); full time: N/A,
part time: $1,928/credit hour
(DNP)
Room/board/expenses: N/A
Full-time enrollment: 214
(master's); N/A (DNP)
men: 16%; women: 84%;
minorities: 25%; international:
3%
Part-time enrollment: 603
(master's); 30 (DNP)
men: 7%; women: 93%;
minorities: 23%; international:
2%
Acceptance rate (master's): 43%
Acceptance rate (DNP): 88%
Specialties offered: clinical nurse
leader; nurse anesthesia; nurse-
midwifery; nurse practitioner:
adult-gerontology acute care;
nurse practitioner: family;
women's health

George Washington University

900 23rd Street NW
Washington, DC 20037
nursing.gwu.edu
Private
Admissions: (202) 994-8429
Email: sonadmit@gwu.edu
Financial aid: (202) 994-6822
Application deadline: 2/15
Degrees offered: master's, DNP
Tuition: full time: $1,155/credit
hour, part time: $1,155/credit
hour (master's); full time: $1,155/
credit hour, part time: $1,155/
credit hour (DNP)
Room/board/expenses: N/A
Full-time enrollment: 48
(master's); 3 (DNP)
men: 8%; women: 92%;
minorities: 39%; international:
0%
Part-time enrollment: 406
(master's); 84 (DNP)
men: 10%; women: 90%;
minorities: 30%; international:
0%

Acceptance rate (master's): 65%
Acceptance rate (DNP): 74%
Specialties offered:
administration; education;
nurse-midwifery; nurse
practitioner; nurse practitioner:
adult-gerontology primary care;
nurse practitioner: family; other
majors

Howard University

516 Bryan Street NW
Washington, DC 20059
healthsciences.howard.edu/
education/schools-and-
academics/nursing-allied-health
Private
Admissions: (202) 806-5021
Email:
tammi.damas@howard.edu
Financial aid: (202) 806-2820
Application deadline: 7/1
Degrees offered: master's
Tuition: full time: $31,309, part
time: $1,700/credit hour
Room/board/expenses: $13,822
Full-time enrollment: 1
men: 100%; women: 0%;
minorities: 0%; international:
100%
Part-time enrollment: 17
men: 12%; women: 88%;
minorities: 100%; international:
0%
Acceptance rate (master's): 100%
Specialties offered: education;
nurse practitioner: family

FLORIDA

Barry University

11300 NE Second Avenue
Miami Shores, FL 33161-6695
Private
Admissions: N/A
Financial aid: N/A
Application deadline: N/A
Degrees offered: master's, Ph.D.,
DNP
Tuition: full time: N/A, part time:
N/A (master's); full time: N/A,
part time: N/A (Ph.D.); full time:
N/A, part time: N/A (DNP)
Room/board/expenses: N/A
Full-time enrollment: 146
(master's); 60 (Ph.D.); 65 (DNP)
men: 23%; women: 77%;
minorities: 54%; international:
3%
Part-time enrollment: 202
(master's); 58 (Ph.D.); 7 (DNP)
men: 7%; women: 93%;
minorities: 66%; international:
1%
Specialties offered: N/A

Florida A&M University[1]

103 Ware-Rhaney Building
Tallahassee, FL 32307
Public
Admissions: N/A
Financial aid: N/A
Tuition: N/A
Room/board/expenses: N/A
Enrollment: N/A

Florida Atlantic University (Lynn)

777 Glades Road
Boca Raton, FL 33431
nursing.fau.edu/
Public

Admissions: (561) 297-2428
Email: nbarragan@fau.edu
Financial aid: (561) 297-3530
Application deadline: 6/1
Degrees offered: master's, Ph.D., DNP
In-state tuition: full time: $304/credit hour, part time: $304/credit hour (master's); full time: $304/credit hour, part time: $304/credit hour (Ph.D.); full time: $304/credit hour, part time: $304/credit hour (DNP)
Out-of-state tuition: full time: $928/credit hour (master's); full time: $928/credit hour (Ph.D.); full time: $928/credit hour (DNP)
Room/board/expenses: $10,518 (master's); $10,518 (Ph.D.); $10,518 (DNP)
Full-time enrollment: 10 (master's); 15 (Ph.D.), 64 (DNP) men: 9%; women: 91%; minorities: 46%; international: 12%
Part-time enrollment: 379 (master's); 30 (Ph.D.), 35 (DNP) men: 4%; women: 96%; minorities: 53%; international: 0%
Acceptance rate (master's): 79%
Acceptance rate (Ph.D.): 100%
Acceptance rate (DNP): 61%
Specialties offered: administration; clinical nurse leader; education; nurse practitioner; nurse practitioner: adult-gerontology primary care; nurse practitioner: family; research; other majors

Florida Gulf Coast University

10501 FGCU Boulevard S
Fort Myers, FL 33965
www.fgcu.edu/CHPSW/Nursing/index.html
Public
Admissions: (239) 590-7988
Email: graduate@fgcu.edu
Financial aid: (239) 590-7920
Application deadline: 3/1
Degrees offered: master's, DNP
In-state tuition: full time: $374/credit hour, part time: $374/credit hour (master's); full time: $374/credit hour, part time: $374/credit hour (DNP)
Out-of-state tuition: full time: $1,301/credit hour (master's); full time: $1,301/credit hour (DNP)
Room/board/expenses: $10,000 (master's); $10,000 (DNP)
Full-time enrollment: 38 (master's); 18 (DNP) men: 38%; women: 63%; minorities: 34%; international: 2%
Part-time enrollment: 8 (master's); 3 (DNP) men: 9%; women: 91%; minorities: 18%; international: 0%
Acceptance rate (master's): 36%
Acceptance rate (DNP): 83%
Specialties offered: education; nurse anesthesia; nurse practitioner: nurse practitioner: family

Florida International University

11200 SW 8th Street, AHC3
Miami, FL 33199
cnhs.fiu.edu/nursing/graduate/index.html
Public
Admissions: (305) 348-7733
Email: gordony@fiu.edu
Financial aid: (305) 348-2333
Application deadline: 2/15
Degrees offered: master's, Ph.D., DNP
In-state tuition: full time: $628/credit hour, part time: N/A (master's); full time: $456/credit hour, part time: N/A (Ph.D.); full time: $628/credit hour, part time: N/A (DNP)
Out-of-state tuition: full time: $1,133/credit hour (master's); full time: $1,002/credit hour (Ph.D.); full time: $1,133/credit hour (DNP)
Room/board/expenses: N/A
Full-time enrollment: 208 (master's); 6 (Ph.D.), 101 (DNP) men: 30%; women: 70%; minorities: 76%; international: 2%
Part-time enrollment: 63 (master's); 14 (Ph.D.), 20 (DNP) men: 25%; women: 75%; minorities: 87%; international: 3%
Acceptance rate (master's): 53%
Acceptance rate (Ph.D.): 50%
Acceptance rate (DNP): 54%
Specialties offered: nurse anesthesia; nurse practitioner; nurse practitioner: adult-gerontology primary care; nurse practitioner: family; nurse practitioner: pediatric primary care; nurse practitioner: psychiatric-mental health, across the lifespan; research

Florida Southern College[1]

111 Lake Hollingsworth Drive
Lakeland, FL 33801-5698
www.flsouthern.edu/home.aspx
Private
Admissions: (863) 680-4131
Email: adm@flsouthern.edu
Financial aid: (863) 680-4140
Tuition: N/A
Room/board/expenses: N/A
Enrollment: N/A

Florida State University

102 Vivian M. Duxbury Hall
Tallahassee, FL 32306-4310
nursing.fsu.edu/
Public
Admissions: (850) 644-1328
Email: jfinney@admin.fsu.edu
Financial aid: (850) 644-0539
Application deadline: 4/15
Degrees offered: master's, DNP
In-state tuition: full time: $544/credit hour, part time: $544/credit hour (master's); full time: $479/credit hour, part time: $479/credit hour (DNP)
Out-of-state tuition: full time: $1,175/credit hour (master's); full time: $1,111/credit hour (DNP)
Room/board/expenses: N/A

Full-time enrollment: N/A (master's); 74 (DNP) men: 8%; women: 92%; minorities: 28%; international: 0%
Part-time enrollment: 23 (master's); 2 (DNP) men: 8%; women: 92%; minorities: 16%; international: 0%
Acceptance rate (master's): 86%
Acceptance rate (DNP): 74%
Specialties offered: education; nurse practitioner; nurse practitioner: family; other majors

Jacksonville University

2800 University Boulevard N
Jacksonville, FL 32211
www.ju.edu/chs/Nursing/Pages/default.aspx
Private
Admissions: (904) 256-7280
Email: web@ju.edu
Financial aid: (904) 256-7080
Application deadline: N/A
Degrees offered: master's, DNP
Tuition: full time: $565/credit hour, part time: $565/credit hour (master's); full time: $600/credit hour, part time: $600/credit hour (DNP)
Room/board/expenses: N/A
Full-time enrollment: 212 (master's); 27 (DNP) men: 10%; women: 90%; minorities: 31%; international: 0%
Part-time enrollment: 305 (master's); 65 (DNP) men: 13%; women: 87%; minorities: 40%; international: 0%
Acceptance rate (master's): 51%
Acceptance rate (DNP): 71%
Specialties offered: administration; education; emergency; informatics; nurse practitioner: adult-gerontology acute care; nurse practitioner: family; nurse practitioner: psychiatric-mental health, across the lifespan; dual majors

Keiser University[1]

1900 W. Commercial Boulevard
Suite 100
Fort Lauderdale, FL 33309
www.keiseruniversity.edu/
Private
Admissions: (954) 351-4040
Email: ryounkins@keiseruniversity.edu
Financial aid: N/A
Tuition: N/A
Room/board/expenses: N/A
Enrollment: N/A

Nova Southeastern University[1]

3200 S. University Drive
Fort Lauderdale, FL 33328
www.nova.edu/nursing
Private
Admissions: (954) 262-1975
Email: www.nova.edu/nursing
Financial aid: (954) 262-3380
Tuition: N/A
Room/board/expenses: N/A
Enrollment: N/A

Pensacola Christian College[1]

250 Brent Lane
Pensacola, FL 32523-9160
Admissions: N/A
Financial aid: N/A
Tuition: N/A
Room/board/expenses: N/A
Enrollment: N/A

University of Central Florida

12201 Research Parkway
Suite 300
Orlando, FL 32826-3298
www.nursing.ucf.edu/
Public
Admissions: (407) 823-2766
Email: gradnurse@ucf.edu
Financial aid: (407) 823-2827
Application deadline: 2/16
Degrees offered: master's, Ph.D., DNP
In-state tuition: full time: $327/credit hour, part time: $327/credit hour (master's); full time: $327/credit hour, part time: $327/credit hour (Ph.D.); full time: $327/credit hour, part time: $327/credit hour (DNP)
Out-of-state tuition: full time: $1,152/credit hour (master's); full time: $1,152/credit hour (Ph.D.); full time: $1,152/credit hour (DNP)
Room/board/expenses: $9,764 (master's); $9,764 (Ph.D.); $9,758 (DNP)
Full-time enrollment: 37 (master's); 8 (Ph.D.), 7 (DNP) men: 12%; women: 88%; minorities: 33%; international: 0%
Part-time enrollment: 228 (master's); 11 (Ph.D.), 39 (DNP) men: 12%; women: 88%; minorities: 27%; international: 0%
Acceptance rate (master's): 43%
Acceptance rate (Ph.D.): 67%
Acceptance rate (DNP): 27%
Specialties offered: administration; clinical nurse specialist; education; nurse practitioner; nurse practitioner: adult-gerontology acute care; nurse practitioner: adult-gerontology primary care; nurse practitioner: family; research; other majors

University of Florida

PO Box 100197
Gainesville, FL 32610-0197
nursing.ufl.edu/
Public
Admissions: (352) 273-6409
Email: kimcurry@ufl.edu
Financial aid: (352) 273-6115
Application deadline: 3/1
Degrees offered: Ph.D., DNP
In-state tuition: full time: $531/credit hour, part time: $531/credit hour (Ph.D.); full time: $531/credit hour, part time: $531/credit hour (DNP)
Out-of-state tuition: full time: $1,255/credit hour (Ph.D.); full time: $1,255/credit hour (DNP)
Room/board/expenses: $17,150 (Ph.D.); $17,150 (DNP)

Full-time enrollment: 24 (Ph.D.); 122 (DNP) men: 10%; women: 90%; minorities: 22%; international: 3%
Part-time enrollment: 12 (Ph.D.); 136 (DNP) men: 11%; women: 89%; minorities: 19%; international: 1%
Acceptance rate (Ph.D.): 65%
Acceptance rate (DNP): 50%
Specialties offered: nurse-midwifery; nurse practitioner; nurse practitioner: adult-gerontology acute care; nurse practitioner: adult-gerontology primary care; nurse practitioner: family; nurse practitioner: pediatric primary care; nurse practitioner: psychiatric-mental health, across the lifespan; research; other majors

University of Miami

5030 Brunson Drive
Coral Gables, FL 33146
www.miami.edu/sonhs/
Private
Admissions: (305) 284-4325
Email: sonhs@miami.edu
Financial aid: (305) 284-2270
Application deadline: 4/1
Degrees offered: master's, Ph.D., DNP
Tuition: full time: $44,400, part time: $26,640 (master's); full time: $1,900/credit hour, part time: $1,900/credit hour (Ph.D.); full time: $50,000, part time: $25,000 (DNP)
Room/board/expenses: $24,101 (master's); $24,101 (Ph.D.); $24,101 (DNP)
Full-time enrollment: 47 (master's); 23 (Ph.D.), 56 (DNP) men: 21%; women: 79%; minorities: 60%; international: 4%
Part-time enrollment: 110 (master's); N/A (Ph.D.), 47 (DNP) men: 12%; women: 88%; minorities: 71%; international: 0%
Acceptance rate (master's): 38%
Acceptance rate (Ph.D.): 28%
Acceptance rate (DNP): 41%
Specialties offered: informatics; nurse anesthesia; nurse practitioner; nurse practitioner: adult-gerontology acute care; nurse practitioner: adult-gerontology primary care; nurse practitioner: family; nurse practitioner: psychiatric-mental health, across the lifespan; research

University of North Florida

1 UNF Drive
Jacksonville, FL 32224
www.unf.edu/brooks/nursing/
Public
Admissions: (904) 620-1360
Email: graduateschool@unf.edu
Financial aid: (904) 620-5555
Application deadline: N/A
Degrees offered: DNP
In-state tuition: full time: $436/credit hour, part time: $436/credit hour
Out-of-state tuition: full time: $1,017/credit hour

Room/board/expenses: $9,602
Full-time enrollment: 23 60
men: 17%; women: 83%;
minorities: 24%; international:
1%
Part-time enrollment: 1 123
men: 19%; women: 81%;
minorities: 42%; international:
1%
Acceptance rate (DNP): 59%
Specialties offered:
administration; nurse
practitioner; nurse practitioner:
family; nurse practitioner:
psychiatric-mental health,
across the lifespan; other
majors

University of South Florida

12901 Bruce B. Downs
Boulevard
Tampa, FL 33612-4766
health.usf.edu/nursing/index.htm
Public
Admissions: (813) 974-2191
Email: jford2@health.usf.edu
Financial aid: (813) 974-4700
Application deadline: 2/15
Degrees offered: master's, Ph.D.,
DNP
In-state tuition: full time: $348/
credit hour, part time: $348/
credit hour (master's); full time:
$348/credit hour, part time:
$348/credit hour (Ph.D.); full
time: $348/credit hour, part
time: $348/credit hour (DNP)
Out-of-state tuition: full time:
$772/credit hour (master's); full
time: $772/credit hour (Ph.D.);
full time: $772/credit hour (DNP)
Room/board/expenses: $11,050
(master's); $11,050 (Ph.D.);
$11,050 (DNP)
Full-time enrollment: 101
(master's); 16 (Ph.D.); 77 (DNP)
men: 22%; women: 78%;
minorities: 36%; international:
2%
Part-time enrollment: 535
(master's); 6 (Ph.D.); 80 (DNP)
men: 13%; women: 87%;
minorities: 33%; international:
1%
Acceptance rate (master's): 39%
Acceptance rate (Ph.D.): 75%
Acceptance rate (DNP): 56%
Specialties offered: community
health/public health; education;
nurse anesthesia; nurse
practitioner; nurse practitioner:
adult-gerontology acute care;
nurse practitioner: adult-
gerontology primary care; nurse
practitioner: family; nurse
practitioner: pediatric primary
care; dual majors

University of Tampa

401 W. Kennedy Boulevard
Tampa, FL 33606-1490
www.ut.edu/nursing/
Private
Admissions: (813) 253-6211
Email: admissions@ut.edu
Financial aid: (813) 253-6219
Application deadline: N/A
Degrees offered: master's
Tuition: full time: $588/credit
hour, part time: $588/credit
hour
Room/board/expenses: $10,196

Full-time enrollment: 4
men: 0%; women: 100%;
minorities: 0%; international: 0%
Part-time enrollment: 160
men: 11%; women: 89%;
minorities: 14%; international:
1%
Acceptance rate (master's): 64%
Specialties offered: nurse
practitioner: adult-gerontology
primary care; nurse
practitioner: family

University of West Florida

Building 37
11000 University Parkway
Pensacola, FL 32514
uwf.edu/coh/departments/
school-of-nursing/graduate-
programs/master-of-science-in-
nursing/
Public
Admissions: (850) 473-7764
Email: msnnursing@uwf.edu
Financial aid: (850) 474-2400
Application deadline: N/A
Degrees offered: master's
In-state tuition: full time: $336/
credit hour, part time: $336/
credit hour
Out-of-state tuition: full time:
$964/credit hour
Room/board/expenses: N/A
Full-time enrollment: 69
men: 7%; women: 93%;
minorities: 28%; international:
0%
Part-time enrollment: 22
men: 14%; women: 86%;
minorities: 36%; international:
0%
Acceptance rate (master's): 68%
Specialties offered:
administration; education

GEORGIA

Albany State University[1]

504 College Drive
Albany, GA 31705
Public
Admissions: N/A
Financial aid: N/A
Tuition: N/A
Room/board/expenses: N/A
Enrollment: N/A

Armstrong State University[1]

11935 Abercorn Street
Savannah, GA 31419
Public
Admissions: N/A
Financial aid: N/A
Tuition: N/A
Room/board/expenses: N/A
Enrollment: N/A

Augusta University

1120 15th Street
Augusta, GA 30912
www.augusta.edu/nursing
Public
Admissions: (706) 737-1632
Email: admissions@augusta.edu
Financial aid: (706) 667-4199
Application deadline: 2/1
Degrees offered: master's, Ph.D.,
DNP

In-state tuition: full time: $576/
credit hour, part time: $549/
credit hour (master's); full time:
$391/credit hour, part time:
$391/credit hour (Ph.D.); full
time: $430/credit hour, part
time: $430/credit hour (DNP)
Out-of-state tuition: full time:
$1,275/credit hour (master's);
full time: $1,092/credit hour
(Ph.D.); full time: $1,132/credit
hour (DNP)
Room/board/expenses: $9,835
(master's); $9,835 (Ph.D.);
$9,835 (DNP)
Full-time enrollment: 328
(master's); 17 (Ph.D.); 86 (DNP)
men: 20%; women: 80%;
minorities: 26%; international:
0%
Part-time enrollment: N/A
(master's); 4 (Ph.D.); 85 (DNP)
men: 13%; women: 87%;
minorities: 27%; international:
0%
Acceptance rate (master's): 44%
Acceptance rate (Ph.D.): 83%
Acceptance rate (DNP): 65%
Specialties offered: clinical nurse
leader; nurse anesthesia; nurse
practitioner; nurse practitioner:
adult-gerontology acute care;
nurse practitioner; nurse
practitioner: pediatric primary
care; nurse practitioner:
psychiatric-mental health,
across the lifespan; research

Brenau University[1]

500 Washington Street SE
Gainesville, GA 30501
www.brenau.edu/healthsciences/
department-of-nursing/
Private
Admissions: (770) 534-6100
Email: admissions@brenau.edu
Financial aid: (770) 534-6152
Tuition: N/A
Room/board/expenses: N/A
Enrollment: N/A

Clayton State University

2000 Clayton State Boulevard
Morrow, GA 30260
www.clayton.edu/health/nursing
Public
Admissions: (578) 466-4108
Email:
elizabethtaylor@clayton.edu
Financial aid: (678) 466-4185
Application deadline: 11/15
Degrees offered: master's
In-state tuition: full time: $385/
credit hour, part time: $385/
credit hour
Out-of-state tuition: full time:
$385/credit hour
Room/board/expenses: N/A
Full-time enrollment: 22
men: 0%; women: 100%;
minorities: 73%; international:
5%
Part-time enrollment: 38
men: 11%; women: 89%;
minorities: 84%; international:
3%
Acceptance rate (master's): 24%
Specialties offered: education;
nurse practitioner: family

Columbus State University[1]

308 Illges Hall
Columbus, GA 31907
Public
Admissions: N/A
Financial aid: N/A
Tuition: N/A
Room/board/expenses: N/A
Enrollment: N/A

Emory University

1520 Clifton Road, NE
Atlanta, GA 30322-4207
www.nursing.emory.edu/
Private
Admissions: (404) 727-6524
Email:
nursingquestions@emory.edu
Financial aid: (404) 712-8456
Application deadline: 3/15
Degrees offered: master's, Ph.D.,
DNP
Tuition: full time: $1,817/credit
hour, part time: $1,817/credit
hour (master's); full time:
$39,800, part time: $2,211/credit
hour (Ph.D.); full time: $1,817/
credit hour, part time: $1,817/
credit hour (DNP)
Room/board/expenses: N/A
Full-time enrollment: 268
(master's); 34 (Ph.D.); 3 (DNP)
men: 12%; women: 88%;
minorities: 30%; international:
2%
Part-time enrollment: 46
(master's); N/A (Ph.D.); 18 (DNP)
men: 6%; women: 94%;
minorities: 42%; international:
2%
Acceptance rate (master's): 56%
Acceptance rate (Ph.D.): 29%
Acceptance rate (DNP): 57%
Specialties offered: emergency;
health management & policy
health care systems; nurse
anesthesia; nurse-midwifery;
neonatal; nurse practitioner;
nurse practitioner: adult-
gerontology acute care;
nurse practitioner: adult-
gerontology primary care;
nurse practitioner: family; nurse
practitioner: pediatric primary
care; women's health; other
majors; dual majors

Georgia College & State University

Campus Box 63
Milledgeville, GA 31061
www.gcsu.edu/health/nursing
Public
Admissions: (478) 445-6289
Email: grad-admit@gcsu.edu
Financial aid: (478) 445-5149
Application deadline: 1/10
Degrees offered: master's, DNP
In-state tuition: full time: $373/
credit hour, part time: $373/
credit hour (master's); full time:
$373/credit hour, part time:
$373/credit hour (DNP)
Out-of-state tuition: full time:
$373/credit hour (master's); full
time: $373/credit hour (DNP)
Room/board/expenses: N/A
Full-time enrollment: 70
(master's); 18 (DNP)
men: 7%; women: 93%;
minorities: 34%; international:
0%

Part-time enrollment: 27
(master's); 6 (DNP)
men: 12%; women: 88%;
minorities: 36%; international:
0%
Acceptance rate (master's): 90%
Acceptance rate (DNP): 88%
Specialties offered: education;
nurse practitioner: family; nurse
practitioner: psychiatric-mental
health, across the lifespan

Georgia Southern University

PO Box 8158
Statesboro, GA 30460
chhs.georgiasouthern.edu/
nursing/
Public
Admissions: (912) 478-5384
Email: gradadmissions@
georgiasouthern.edu
Financial aid: (912) 478-5413
Application deadline: 4/1
Degrees offered: master's, DNP
In-state tuition: full time: N/A, part
time: N/A (master's); full time:
$462/credit hour, part time:
N/A (DNP)
Out-of-state tuition: full time: N/A
(master's); full time: $462/credit
hour (DNP)
Room/board/expenses: N/A
Full-time enrollment: N/A
(master's); 90 (DNP)
men: 10%; women: 90%;
minorities: 33%; international:
0%
Part-time enrollment: N/A
(master's); N/A (DNP)
men: N/A; women: N/A;
minorities: N/A; international:
N/A
Acceptance rate (DNP): 89%
Specialties offered: nurse
practitioner; nurse practitioner:
family; nurse practitioner:
psychiatric-mental health,
across the lifespan; other
majors

Georgia Southwestern State University

800 Georgia Southwestern State
University Drive
Americus, GA 31709
gsw.edu/Academics/Schools-
and-Departments/School-of-
Nursing/index
Admissions: (229) 931-4206
Email: graduateadmissions@
gsw.edu
Financial aid: (229) 928-1378
Application deadline: 2/15
Degrees offered: master's
Room/board/expenses: N/A
Full-time enrollment: 12
men: 0%; women: 100%;
minorities: 42%; international:
0%
Part-time enrollment: 82
men: 12%; women: 88%;
minorities: 33%; international:
0%
Acceptance rate (master's): 58%
Specialties offered:
administration; education;
informatics; nurse practitioner:
family

Georgia State University

PO Box 3995
Atlanta, GA 30302-3995
snhp.gsu.edu
Public
Admissions: (404) 413-2500
Email: admissions@gsu.edu
Financial aid: (404) 413-2600
Application deadline: 2/1
Degrees offered: master's, Ph.D., DNP
In-state tuition: full time: $388/credit hour, part time: $388/credit hour (master's); full time: $388/credit hour, part time: $388/credit hour (Ph.D.); full time: $382/credit hour, part time: $382/credit hour (DNP)
Out-of-state tuition: full time: $1,249/credit hour (master's); full time: $1,249/credit hour (Ph.D.); full time: $1,243/credit hour (DNP)
Room/board/expenses: $14,160 (master's); $14,160 (Ph.D.); $13,342 (DNP)
Full-time enrollment: 73 (master's); 6 (Ph.D.); 8 (DNP) men: 7%; women: 93%; minorities: 44%; international: 3%
Part-time enrollment: 150 (master's); 15 (Ph.D.); 12 (DNP) men: 11%; women: 89%; minorities: 51%; international: 0%
Acceptance rate (master's): 67%
Acceptance rate (Ph.D.): 43%
Acceptance rate (DNP): 88%
Specialties offered: administration; clinical nurse specialist; informatics; nurse practitioner; nurse practitioner: adult-gerontology acute care; nurse practitioner: adult-gerontology primary care; nurse practitioner: adult; nurse practitioner: family; nurse practitioner: pediatric primary care; nurse practitioner: psychiatric-mental health, across the lifespan

Kennesaw State University[1]

1000 Chastain Road
Kennesaw, GA 30144-5591
Public
Admissions: N/A
Financial aid: N/A
Tuition: N/A
Room/board/expenses: N/A
Enrollment: N/A

Mercer University

3001 Mercer University Drive
Atlanta, GA 30341
nursing.mercer.edu/
Private
Admissions: (678) 547-6700
Email: nursingadmissions@mercer.edu
Financial aid: (678) 547-6467
Application deadline: 3/1
Degrees offered: master's, Ph.D., DNP
Tuition: full time: $33,375, part time: $1,125/credit hour (master's); full time: $32,210, part time: $1,188/credit hour (Ph.D.); full time: $21,000, part time: $1,165/credit hour (DNP)

Room/board/expenses: $9,000 (master's); N/A (Ph.D.); N/A (DNP)
Full-time enrollment: 46 (master's); 9 (Ph.D.); 14 (DNP) men: 6%; women: 94%; minorities: 59%; international: 1%
Part-time enrollment: 23 (master's); 19 (Ph.D.); N/A (DNP) men: 5%; women: 95%; minorities: 36%; international: 0%
Acceptance rate (master's): 52%
Acceptance rate (Ph.D.): 53%
Acceptance rate (DNP): 64%
Specialties offered: nurse practitioner: adult-gerontology acute care; nurse practitioner: family

South University[1]

709 Mall Boulevard
Savannah, GA 31406
Private
Admissions: N/A
Financial aid: N/A
Tuition: N/A
Room/board/expenses: N/A
Enrollment: N/A

Thomas University[1]

1501 Millpond Road
Thomasville, GA 31792
Private
Admissions: N/A
Financial aid: N/A
Tuition: N/A
Room/board/expenses: N/A
Enrollment: N/A

University of North Georgia[1]

82 College Circle
Dahlonega, GA 30597
Public
Admissions: N/A
Financial aid: N/A
Tuition: N/A
Room/board/expenses: N/A
Enrollment: N/A

University of West Georgia[1]

1601 Maple Street
Carrollton, GA 30118
nursing.westga.edu/index.php
Public
Admissions: (678) 839-1390
Email: tziglar@westga.edu
Financial aid: (678) 839-6421
Tuition: N/A
Room/board/expenses: N/A
Enrollment: N/A

Valdosta State University[1]

S. Walter Martin Hall
Valdosta, GA 31698-0130
Public
Admissions: N/A
Financial aid: N/A
Tuition: N/A
Room/board/expenses: N/A
Enrollment: N/A

HAWAII

Hawaii Pacific University

45-045 Kamehameha Highway
Kaneohe, HI 96744
www.hpu.edu
Private
Admissions: (808) 236-5847
Email: DKNIGHT@HPU.EDU
Financial aid: (808) 544-0253
Application deadline: 4/15
Degrees offered: master's
Tuition: full time: $1,330/credit hour, part time: $1,330/credit hour
Room/board/expenses: $13,898
Full-time enrollment: 40 men: 23%; women: 78%; minorities: 53%; international: 8%
Part-time enrollment: 12 men: 17%; women: 83%; minorities: 58%; international: 8%
Acceptance rate (master's): 59%
Specialties offered: nurse practitioner; nurse practitioner: adult-gerontology acute care; nurse practitioner: family; dual majors

University of Hawaii-Hilo[1]

200 W. Kawili Street
Hilo, HI 96720
Public
Admissions: N/A
Financial aid: N/A
Tuition: N/A
Room/board/expenses: N/A
Enrollment: N/A

University of Hawaii-Manoa

2528 McCarthy Mall
Webster Hall
Honolulu, HI 96822
www.nursing.hawaii.edu/home
Public
Admissions: (808) 956-8544
Email: graduate.education@hawaii.edu
Financial aid: (808) 956-7251
Application deadline: 1/5
Degrees offered: master's, Ph.D., DNP
In-state tuition: full time: $1,001/credit hour, part time: $1,001/credit hour (master's); full time: $1,001/credit hour, part time: $1,001/credit hour (Ph.D.); full time: $1,001/credit hour, part time: $1,001/credit hour (DNP)
Out-of-state tuition: full time: $1,896/credit hour (master's); full time: $1,896/credit hour (Ph.D.); full time: $1,896/credit hour (DNP)
Room/board/expenses: $15,512 (master's); $15,512 (Ph.D.); $15,512 (DNP)
Full-time enrollment: 73 (master's); 10 (Ph.D.); 60 (DNP) men: 17%; women: 83%; minorities: 76%; international: 1%
Part-time enrollment: 45 (master's); 22 (Ph.D.); 6 (DNP) men: 14%; women: 86%; minorities: 66%; international: 1%
Acceptance rate (master's): 64%

Acceptance rate (DNP): 22%
Specialties offered: clinical nurse specialist; community health/public health; nurse practitioner; nurse practitioner: adult-gerontology primary care; nurse practitioner: family; other majors

IDAHO

Boise State University[1]

1910 University Drive
Boise, ID 82537-1840
hs.boisestate.edu/nursing/news/
Public
Admissions: (208) 426-3903
Email: gradcoll@boisestate.edu
Financial aid: (800) 824-7017
Tuition: N/A
Room/board/expenses: N/A
Enrollment: N/A

Idaho State University

921 S, 8th Avenue, Stop 8101
Pocatello, ID 83209-8101
www.isu.edu/nursing
Public
Admissions: (208) 282-4346
Email: profnurs@isu.edu
Financial aid: (208) 282-2756
Application deadline: N/A
Degrees offered: master's, Ph.D., DNP
In-state tuition: full time: $8,502, part time: N/A (master's); full time: $8,502, part time: $426/credit hour (Ph.D.); full time: $8,502, part time: $426/credit hour (DNP)
Out-of-state tuition: full time: N/A (master's); full time: N/A (Ph.D.); full time: N/A (DNP)
Room/board/expenses: N/A
Full-time enrollment: N/A (master's); 11 (Ph.D.); 44 (DNP) men: 16%; women: 84%; minorities: 7%; international: 0%
Part-time enrollment: N/A (master's); 3 (Ph.D.); 4 (DNP) men: 29%; women: 71%; minorities: 14%; international: 0%
Acceptance rate (Ph.D.): 100%
Acceptance rate (DNP): 43%
Specialties offered: education; nurse practitioner: family; nurse practitioner: psychiatric-mental health, across the lifespan; research

Northwest Nazarene University[1]

623 S. University Boulevard
Nampa, ID 83686
Private
Admissions: N/A
Financial aid: N/A
Tuition: N/A
Room/board/expenses: N/A
Enrollment: N/A

ILLINOIS

Aurora University[1]

347 S. Gladstone Avenue
Aurora, IL 60506
Private
Admissions: N/A
Financial aid: N/A
Tuition: N/A
Room/board/expenses: N/A
Enrollment: N/A

Benedictine University[1]

5700 College Road
Lisle, IL 60532
ben.edu/college-of-education-and-health-services/nursing-health/faculty-staff.cfm
Private
Admissions: (630) 366-2981
Email: online.ben.edu/msn/masters-in-nursing
Financial aid: (630) 829-6415
Tuition: N/A
Room/board/expenses: N/A
Enrollment: N/A

Blessing-Rieman College of Nursing[1]

PO Box 7005
Quincy, IL 62305-7005
Private
Admissions: (217) 228-5520
Email: admissions@brcn.edu
Financial aid: (217) 228-5520
Tuition: N/A
Room/board/expenses: N/A
Enrollment: N/A

Bradley University

1501 W. Bradley Avenue
Peoria, IL 61625
www.bradley.edu/academic/gradschool/
Private
Admissions: (309) 677-2375
Email: klcarroll@bradley.edu
Financial aid: (309) 677-3089
Application deadline: 8/7
Degrees offered: master's, DNP
Tuition: full time: $850/credit hour, part time: $850/credit hour (master's); full time: $850/credit hour, part time: $850/credit hour (DNP)
Room/board/expenses: $10,010 (master's); N/A (DNP)
Full-time enrollment: 115 (master's); 2 (DNP) men: 10%; women: 90%; minorities: 2%; international: 1%
Part-time enrollment: 103 (master's); 161 (DNP) men: 14%; women: 86%; minorities: 2%; international: 3%
Acceptance rate (master's): 85%
Acceptance rate (DNP): 95%
Specialties offered: administration; education; nurse practitioner: family

Chamberlain College of Nursing

3005 Highland Parkway
Downers Grove, IL 60515
www.chamberlain.edu
Private
Admissions: (888) 556-8226
Financial aid: (888) 556-8226
Application deadline: N/A
Degrees offered: master's, DNP
Tuition: full time: $15,960, part time: $665/credit hour (master's); full time: $13,500, part time: $750/credit hour (DNP)
Room/board/expenses: N/A
Full-time enrollment: 6,389 (master's); 569 (DNP) men: 10%; women: 90%; minorities: 33%; international: 0%

Part-time enrollment: 2,611 (master's); 305 (DNP) men: 9%; women: 91%; minorities: 32%; international: 0%
Acceptance rate (master's): 95%
Acceptance rate (DNP): 99%
Specialties offered: administration; education; health management & policy health care systems; informatics; nurse practitioner; nurse practitioner: family

DePaul University

990 W. Fullerton Avenue
Chicago, IL 60613
csh.depaul.edu/departments/ nursing/
Private
Admissions: (773) 325-7315
Email: graddepaul@depaul.edu
Financial aid: (312) 362-8610
Application deadline: N/A
Degrees offered: master's, DNP
Tuition: full time: $695/credit hour, part time: $695/credit hour (master's); full time: $695/ credit hour, part time: $695/ credit hour (DNP)
Room/board/expenses: N/A
Full-time enrollment: 253 (master's); 66 (DNP) men: 15%; women: 85%; minorities: 8%; international: 1%
Part-time enrollment: 17 (master's); 27 (DNP) men: 27%; women: 73%; minorities: 23%; international: 2%
Acceptance rate (master's): 56%
Acceptance rate (DNP): 100%
Specialties offered: generalist; nurse anesthesia; nurse practitioner; nurse practitioner: adult-gerontology primary care; nurse practitioner: family

Elmhurst College[1]

190 Prospect Avenue
Elmhurst, IL 60126
Private
Admissions: N/A
Financial aid: N/A
Tuition: N/A
Room/board/expenses: N/A
Enrollment: N/A

Governors State University

1 University Parkway
University Park, IL 60484
www.govst.edu/
Public
Admissions: (708) 534-4490
Email: admissions@govst.edu
Financial aid: (708) 534-4480
Application deadline: N/A
Degrees offered: master's, DNP
In-state tuition: full time: $7,368, part time: $307/credit hour (master's); full time: $16,632, part time: $309/credit hour (DNP)
Out-of-state tuition: full time: $14,736 (master's); full time: $23,760 (DNP)
Room/board/expenses: $9,868 (master's); $9,868 (DNP)
Full-time enrollment: 2 (master's); 7 (DNP) men: 0%; women: 100%; minorities: 56%; international: 0%

Part-time enrollment: 162 (master's); 15 (DNP) men: 16%; women: 84%; minorities: 68%; international: 0%
Acceptance rate (master's): 92%
Acceptance rate (DNP): 100%
Specialties offered: administration; clinical nurse specialist; nurse practitioner: family

Illinois State University

Campus Box 5810
Normal, IL 61790-5810
nursing.illinoisstate.edu/
Public
Admissions: (309) 438-2181
Email: admissions@ilstu.edu
Financial aid: (309) 438-2231
Application deadline: 2/1
Degrees offered: master's, Ph.D., DNP
In-state tuition: full time: $389/ credit hour, part time: $389/ credit hour (master's); full time: $389/credit hour, part time: $389/credit hour (Ph.D.); full time: $389/credit hour, part time: $389/credit hour (DNP)
Out-of-state tuition: full time: $808/credit hour (master's); full time: $808/credit hour (Ph.D.); full time: $808/credit hour (DNP)
Room/board/expenses: $5,334 (master's); $5,334 (Ph.D.); $5,334 (DNP)
Full-time enrollment: 7 (master's); N/A (Ph.D.); N/A (DNP) men: 0%; women: 100%; minorities: N/A; international: N/A
Part-time enrollment: 79 (master's); 22 (Ph.D.); 10 (DNP) men: 11%; women: 89%; minorities: N/A; international: N/A
Acceptance rate (master's): 83%
Acceptance rate (Ph.D.): 100%
Acceptance rate (DNP): 100%
Specialties offered: administration; research

Lewis University

One University Parkway
Romeoville, IL 60446
www.lewisu.edu/academics/ nursing/
Private
Admissions: (815) 836-5610
Email: grad@lewisu.edu
Financial aid: (815) 836-5263
Application deadline: 6/1
Degrees offered: master's, DNP
Tuition: full time: $770/credit hour, part time: $770/credit hour (master's); full time: $770/credit hour, part time: $770/credit hour (DNP)
Room/board/expenses: $10,320 (master's); $10,320 (DNP)
Full-time enrollment: 13 (master's); 1 (DNP) men: 7%; women: 93%; minorities: 21%; international: 0%
Part-time enrollment: 375 (master's); 23 (DNP) men: 7%; women: 93%; minorities: 25%; international: 0%
Acceptance rate (master's): 70%
Acceptance rate (DNP): 73%

Specialties offered: administration; clinical nurse specialist; education; nurse practitioner; nurse practitioner: adult-gerontology acute care; nurse practitioner: adult-gerontology primary care; nurse practitioner: family; school nursing; other majors; dual majors

Loyola University Chicago

6525 North Sheridan Road
Chicago, IL 60626-5385
www.luc.edu/nursing
Private
Admissions: (312) 915-8902
Email: gradapp@luc.edu
Financial aid: (773) 508-7704
Application deadline: 6/1
Degrees offered: master's, Ph.D., DNP
Tuition: full time: $1,081/credit hour, part time: $1,081/credit hour (master's); full time: $1,081/ credit hour, part time: $1,081/ credit hour (Ph.D.); full time: $1,081/credit hour, part time: $1,081/credit hour (DNP)
Room/board/expenses: $11,500 (master's); $11,500 (Ph.D.); $11,500 (DNP)
Full-time enrollment: 148 (master's); 25 (Ph.D.); 16 (DNP) men: 5%; women: 95%; minorities: 25%; international: 2%
Part-time enrollment: 197 (master's); 6 (Ph.D.); 20 (DNP) men: 5%; women: 95%; minorities: 30%; international: 0%
Acceptance rate (master's): 76%
Acceptance rate (Ph.D.): 90%
Acceptance rate (DNP): 100%
Specialties offered: clinical nurse specialist; health management & policy health care systems; informatics; nurse practitioner; nurse practitioner: adult-gerontology acute care; nurse practitioner: adult-gerontology primary care; nurse practitioner: family; research; women's health; other majors; dual majors

McKendree University

701 College Road
Lebanon, IL 62254
mckendree.edu/academics/info/ nursing-health/nursing/index.php
Private
Admissions: (618) 537-6576
Email: graduate@mckendree.edu
Financial aid: (618) 537-6828
Application deadline: N/A
Degrees offered: master's, DNP
Tuition: full time: $440/credit hour, part time: $440/credit hour (master's); full time: $540/ credit hour, part time: $540/ credit hour (DNP)
Room/board/expenses: N/A
Full-time enrollment: 2 (master's); N/A (DNP) men: 0%; women: 100%; minorities: 50%; international: 0%
Part-time enrollment: 73 (master's); 10 (DNP) men: 10%; women: 90%; minorities: 12%; international: 0%

Acceptance rate (master's): 81%
Acceptance rate (DNP): 100%
Specialties offered: administration; education; other majors; dual majors

Millikin University

1184 W. Main Street
Decatur, IL 62522-2084
www.millikin.edu/graduate-nursing
Private
Admissions: (217) 424-6210
Email: admis@millikin.edu
Financial aid: (217) 424-6317
Application deadline: N/A
Degrees offered: master's, DNP
Tuition: full time: N/A, part time: N/A (master's); full time: N/A, part time: N/A (DNP)
Room/board/expenses: N/A
Full-time enrollment: 12 (master's); 20 (DNP) men: N/A; women: N/A; minorities: N/A; international: N/A
Part-time enrollment: 4 (master's); 19 (DNP) men: N/A; women: N/A; minorities: N/A; international: N/A
Acceptance rate (master's): 65%
Acceptance rate (DNP): 32%
Specialties offered: education; nurse anesthesia

Northern Illinois University[1]

1240 Normal Road
DeKalb, IL 60115
Public
Admissions: N/A
Financial aid: N/A
Tuition: N/A
Room/board/expenses: N/A
Enrollment: N/A

North Park University[1]

3225 W. Foster Avenue
Chicago, IL 60625-4895
Private
Admissions: N/A
Financial aid: N/A
Tuition: N/A
Room/board/expenses: N/A
Enrollment: N/A

Olivet Nazarene University[1]

3601 Algonquin Road
Rolling Meadows, IL 60008
Private
Admissions: N/A
Financial aid: N/A
Tuition: N/A
Room/board/expenses: N/A
Enrollment: N/A

Resurrection University[1]

1431 N. Claremont Avenue
Chicago, IL 60622-'
Private
Admissions: N/A
Financial aid: N/A
Tuition: N/A
Room/board/expenses: N/A
Enrollment: N/A

Rush University

600 S. Paulina, Suite 1080
Chicago, IL 60612-3873
www.rushu.rush.edu/college-nursing
Private
Admissions: (312) 942-7110
Email: jennifer_thorndyke@ rush.edu
Financial aid: (312) 942-6523
Application deadline: 1/4
Degrees offered: master's, Ph.D., DNP
Tuition: full time: $995/credit hour, part time: $995/credit hour (master's); full time: $1,050/credit hour, part time: $1,050/credit hour (Ph.D.); full time: $1,050/credit hour, part time: $1,050/credit hour (DNP)
Room/board/expenses: N/A
Full-time enrollment: 280 (master's); 3 (Ph.D.); 99 (DNP) men: 14%; women: 86%; minorities: 28%; international: 0%
Part-time enrollment: 49 (master's); 22 (Ph.D.); 635 (DNP) men: 9%; women: 91%; minorities: 22%; international: 0%
Acceptance rate (master's): 30%
Acceptance rate (Ph.D.): 60%
Acceptance rate (DNP): 60%
Specialties offered: administration; clinical nurse leader; clinical nurse specialist; community health/public health; generalist; health management & policy health care systems; nurse anesthesia; neonatal; nurse practitioner; nurse practitioner: adult-gerontology acute care; nurse practitioner: adult-gerontology primary care; nurse practitioner: family; nurse practitioner: pediatric primary care; nurse practitioner: psychiatric-mental health, across the lifespan; research; other majors

Southern Illinois University-Edwardsville

Campus Box 1066
Edwardsville, IL 62026-1066
www.siue.edu/nursing/
Public
Admissions: (618) 650-3705
Email: tburrel@siue.edu
Financial aid: (618) 650-3880
Application deadline: N/A
Degrees offered: master's, DNP
In-state tuition: full time: $305/ credit hour, part time: $305/ credit hour (master's); full time: $650/credit hour, part time: $650/credit hour (DNP)
Out-of-state tuition: full time: $763/credit hour (master's); full time: $650/credit hour (DNP)
Room/board/expenses: N/A
Full-time enrollment: 20 (master's); 85 (DNP) men: 34%; women: 66%; minorities: 14%; international: 2%
Part-time enrollment: 120 (master's); 29 (DNP) men: 9%; women: 91%; minorities: 13%; international: 0%
Acceptance rate (master's): 94%

Acceptance rate (DNP): 57%
Specialties offered: administration; education; nurse anesthesia; nurse practitioner; nurse practitioner: family

St. Anthony College of Nursing[1]

5658 E. State Street
Rockford, IL 61108-2468
sacn.edu
Private
Admissions: (815) 395-5091
Email: msn@sacn.edu
Financial aid: (815) 395-5089
Tuition: N/A
Room/board/expenses: N/A
Enrollment: N/A

St. Francis Medical Center

511 NE Greenleaf
Peoria, IL 61603
www.sfmccon.edu/
Private
Admissions: (309) 655-6362
Email: janice.farquharson@osfhealthcare.org
Financial aid: (309) 655-4119
Application deadline: 4/1
Degrees offered: master's, DNP
Tuition: full time: $7,700, part time: $625/credit hour (master's); full time: $7,700, part time: $625/credit hour (DNP)
Room/board/expenses: $3,500 (master's); $3,500 (DNP)
Full-time enrollment: 12 (master's); N/A (DNP)
men: 0%; women: 100%;
minorities: 8%; international: 0%
Part-time enrollment: 218 (master's); 25 (DNP)
men: 14%; women: 86%;
minorities: 9%; international: 0%
Acceptance rate (master's): 88%
Acceptance rate (DNP): 100%
Specialties offered: administration; clinical nurse specialist; education; neonatal; nurse practitioner; nurse practitioner: adult-gerontology primary care; nurse practitioner: family; nurse practitioner: psychiatric-mental health, across the lifespan

St. Xavier University

3700 W. 103rd Street
Chicago, IL 60655
www.sxu.edu/academics/colleges_schools/son/index.asp
Private
Admissions: (773) 298-3096
Email: graduateadmission@sxu.edu
Financial aid: (773) 298-3070
Application deadline: 6/1
Degrees offered: master's
Tuition: full time: $895/credit hour, part time: $895/credit hour
Room/board/expenses: $11,520
Full-time enrollment: 190
men: 12%; women: 88%;
minorities: 24%; international: N/A
Part-time enrollment: 83
men: 7%; women: 93%;
minorities: 28%; international: N/A
Acceptance rate (master's): 77%
Specialties offered: administration; clinical nurse

leader; education; nurse practitioner; nurse practitioner: family; dual majors

University of Illinois-Chicago

845 South Damen Avenue
MC 802
Chicago, IL 60612
nursing.uic.edu
Public
Admissions: (312) 996-7800
Email: conapply@uic.edu
Financial aid: (312) 996-3126
Application deadline: 1/15
Degrees offered: master's, Ph.D., DNP
In-state tuition: full time: $20,120, part time: $13,414 (master's); full time: $20,120, part time: $13,414 (Ph.D.); full time: $22,250, part time: $14,834 (DNP)
Out-of-state tuition: full time: $32,360 (master's); full time: $32,360 (Ph.D.); full time: $34,720 (DNP)
Room/board/expenses: $11,712 (master's); $11,712 (Ph.D.); N/A (DNP)
Full-time enrollment: 277 (master's); 38 (Ph.D.); 172 (DNP)
men: 9%; women: 91%;
minorities: 30%; international: 6%
Part-time enrollment: 99 (master's); 27 (Ph.D.); 230 (DNP)
men: 10%; women: 90%;
minorities: 34%; international: 0%
Acceptance rate (master's): 51%
Acceptance rate (Ph.D.): 89%
Acceptance rate (DNP): 95%
Specialties offered: administration; clinical nurse leader; community health; public health; generalist; health management & policy health care systems; informatics; nurse-midwifery; neonatal; nurse practitioner; nurse practitioner: adult-gerontology acute care; nurse practitioner: adult-gerontology primary care; nurse practitioner: family; nurse practitioner: pediatric primary care; nurse practitioner: psychiatric-mental health, across the lifespan; research; school nursing; women's health; other majors

University of St. Francis

500 Wilcox Street
Joliet, IL 60435
www.stfrancis.edu/academics/college-of-nursing
Private
Admissions: (800) 735-7500
Email: admissions@stfrancis.edu
Financial aid: (866) 890-8331
Application deadline: N/A
Degrees offered: master's, DNP
Tuition: full time: $770/credit hour, part time: $770/credit hour (master's); full time: $780/credit hour, part time: $780/credit hour (DNP)
Room/board/expenses: N/A

Full-time enrollment: 68 (master's); 15 (DNP)
men: 4%; women: 96%;
minorities: 37%; international: 0%
Part-time enrollment: 289 (master's); 8 (DNP)
men: 11%; women: 89%;
minorities: 33%; international: 0%
Acceptance rate (master's): 41%
Acceptance rate (DNP): 25%
Specialties offered: administration; education; nurse practitioner: family; nurse practitioner: psychiatric-mental health, across the lifespan

INDIANA

Ball State University

2000 W. University Avenue
Muncie, IN 47306
www.bsu.edu/nursing
Public
Admissions: (765) 285-9130
Email: nursing@bsu.edu
Financial aid: (765) 285-5600
Application deadline: 2/9
Degrees offered: master's, DNP
In-state tuition: full time: N/A, part time: N/A (master's); full time: N/A, part time: N/A (DNP)
Out-of-state tuition: full time: N/A (master's); full time: N/A (DNP)
Room/board/expenses: N/A
Full-time enrollment: N/A (master's); N/A (DNP)
men: N/A; women: N/A;
minorities: N/A; international: N/A
Part-time enrollment: 315 (master's); 6 (DNP)
men: 7%; women: 93%;
minorities: 7%; international: 0%
Specialties offered: administration; education; nurse practitioner; nurse practitioner: family

Bethel College[1]

1001 Bethel Circle
Mishawaka, IN 46545
Private
Admissions: N/A
Financial aid: N/A
Tuition: N/A
Room/board/expenses: N/A
Enrollment: N/A

Goshen College

1700 South Main Street
Goshen, IN 46526
www.goshen.edu/
Private
Admissions: (574) 535-7535
Email: admissions@goshen.edu
Financial aid: (574) 535-7525
Application deadline: N/A
Degrees offered: master's
Tuition: full time: $650/credit hour, part time: $650/credit hour
Room/board/expenses: N/A
Full-time enrollment: 57
men: 11%; women: 89%;
minorities: 16%; international: 2%
Part-time enrollment: 1
men: 0%; women: 100%;
minorities: 100%; international: 0%
Acceptance rate (master's): 53%

Specialties offered: nurse practitioner: family

Indiana State University

749 Chestnut Street
Terre Haute, IN 47809-1937
www.indstate.edu/health/department/son
Public
Admissions: (812) 237-3005
Email: Patricia.yeager@indstate.edu
Financial aid: (812) 237-2215
Application deadline: N/A
Degrees offered: master's, DNP
In-state tuition: full time: $396/credit hour, part time: $396/credit hour (master's); full time: $396/credit hour, part time: $396/credit hour (DNP)
Out-of-state tuition: full time: $499/credit hour (master's); full time: $499/credit hour (DNP)
Room/board/expenses: N/A
Full-time enrollment: N/A (master's); N/A (DNP)
men: N/A; women: N/A;
minorities: N/A; international: N/A
Part-time enrollment: 255 (master's); 32 (DNP)
men: 7%; women: 93%;
minorities: 18%; international: 0%
Acceptance rate (master's): 78%
Acceptance rate (DNP): 100%
Specialties offered: education; nurse practitioner: family

Indiana University East[1]

2325 Chester Boulevard
Richmond, IN 47374
www.iue.edu/nursing/msn
Public
Admissions: N/A
Financial aid: N/A
Tuition: N/A
Room/board/expenses: N/A
Enrollment: N/A

Indiana University-Kokomo[1]

2300 S. Washington Street
Kokomo, IN 46904
Public
Admissions: N/A
Financial aid: N/A
Tuition: N/A
Room/board/expenses: N/A
Enrollment: N/A

Indiana University-Purdue University-Indianapolis

1111 Middle Drive
Indianapolis, IN 46202-5107
nursing.iu.edu
Public
Admissions: (317) 274-0003
Email: tlabney@iu.edu
Financial aid: (317) 274-5920
Application deadline: 2/15
Degrees offered: master's, Ph.D., DNP
In-state tuition: full time: $519/credit hour, part time: $519/credit hour (master's); full time: $519/credit hour, part time:

$519/credit hour (Ph.D.); full time: $1,000/credit hour, part time: $1,000/credit hour (DNP)
Out-of-state tuition: full time: $1,499/credit hour (master's); full time: $1,499/credit hour (Ph.D.); full time: $1,000/credit hour (DNP)
Room/board/expenses: $10,909 (master's); $10,909 (Ph.D.); $10,909 (DNP)
Full-time enrollment: 21 (master's); 12 (Ph.D.); 11 (DNP)
men: 9%; women: 91%;
minorities: 14%; international: 0%
Part-time enrollment: 238 (master's); 28 (Ph.D.); 19 (DNP)
men: 12%; women: 88%;
minorities: 13%; international: 2%
Acceptance rate (master's): 77%
Acceptance rate (Ph.D.): 57%
Acceptance rate (DNP): 50%
Specialties offered: administration; clinical nurse specialist; education; nurse practitioner; nurse practitioner: adult-gerontology acute care; nurse practitioner: adult-gerontology primary care; nurse practitioner: family; nurse practitioner: pediatric primary care; nurse practitioner: psychiatric-mental health, across the lifespan

Indiana University-South Bend

1700 Mishawaka Avenue
South Bend, IN 46634
www.iusb.edu/nursing/index.php
Public
Admissions: (557) 520-4839
Email: admissions@iusb.edu
Financial aid: (574) 520-4357
Application deadline: 10/3
Degrees offered: master's
In-state tuition: full time: $342/credit hour, part time: $342/credit hour
Out-of-state tuition: full time: $996/credit hour
Room/board/expenses: N/A
Full-time enrollment:
men: N/A; women: N/A;
minorities: N/A; international: N/A
Part-time enrollment: 29
men: 0%; women: 100%;
minorities: 21%; international: 0%
Specialties offered: nurse practitioner: family

Indiana Wesleyan University[1]

4201 S. Washington Street
Marion, IN 46953
Private
Admissions: N/A
Financial aid: N/A
Tuition: N/A
Room/board/expenses: N/A
Enrollment: N/A

Purdue University-Calumet[1]

2200 169th Street
Hammond, IN 46323
Public
Admissions: N/A
Financial aid: N/A

Tuition: N/A
Room/board/expenses: N/A
Enrollment: N/A

Purdue University-West Lafayette

502 N. University Street
West Lafayette, IN 47907
www.purdue.edu/hhs/nur/
Public
Admissions: (765) 494-9116
Email: gradinfo@purdue.edu
Financial aid: (765) 494-5050
Application deadline: 4/1
Degrees offered: master's, Ph.D., DNP
In-state tuition: full time: $10,002, part time: $348/credit hour (master's); full time: N/A, part time: N/A (Ph.D.); full time: $725/credit hour, part time: $725/credit hour (DNP)
Out-of-state tuition: full time: $28,804 (master's); full time: N/A (Ph.D.); full time: $950/credit hour (DNP)
Room/board/expenses: N/A
Full-time enrollment: 44 (master's); N/A (Ph.D.); N/A (DNP)
men: 7%; women: 93%; minorities: 14%; international: 2%
Part-time enrollment: 13 (master's); N/A (Ph.D.); 22 (DNP)
men: 3%; women: 97%; minorities: 11%; international: 3%
Acceptance rate (master's): 85%
Acceptance rate (DNP): 100%
Specialties offered: nurse practitioner; nurse practitioner: adult-gerontology primary care; nurse practitioner: family; nurse practitioner: pediatric primary care

University of Indianapolis

1400 East Hanna Avenue
Indianapolis, IN 46227
uindy.edu/nursing
Private
Admissions: (317) 788-3216
Financial aid: (317) 788-3217
Application deadline: 4/15
Degrees offered: master's, DNP
Tuition: full time: $692/credit hour, part time: $692/credit hour (master's); full time: $692/credit hour, part time: $692/credit hour (DNP)
Room/board/expenses: N/A
Full-time enrollment: 12 (master's); N/A (DNP)
men: 0%; women: 100%; minorities: 8%; international: 0%
Part-time enrollment: 254 (master's); 19 (DNP)
men: 7%; women: 93%; minorities: 10%; international: 0%
Acceptance rate (master's): 51%
Acceptance rate (DNP): 63%
Specialties offered: administration; education; neonatal; nurse practitioner; nurse practitioner: adult-gerontology primary care; nurse practitioner: family

University of Saint Francis[1]

2701 Spring Street
Fort Wayne, IN 46808
nursing.sf.edu/
Private
Admissions: (260) 399-8000
Email: gradschool@sf.edu
Financial aid: (260) 399-8000
Tuition: N/A
Room/board/expenses: N/A
Enrollment: N/A

University of Southern Indiana

8600 University Boulevard
Evansville, IN 47712-3596
www.usi.edu/health/nursing
Public
Admissions: (812) 465-7140
Email: graduate.studies@usi.edu
Financial aid: (812) 465-1026
Application deadline: 2/1
Degrees offered: master's, DNP
In-state tuition: full time: $354/credit hour, part time: $354/credit hour (master's); full time: $354/credit hour, part time: $354/credit hour (DNP)
Out-of-state tuition: full time: $354/credit hour (master's); full time: $354/credit hour (DNP)
Room/board/expenses: $8,896 (master's); $8,896 (DNP)
Full-time enrollment: 97 (master's); 4 (DNP)
men: 17%; women: 83%; minorities: 8%; international: 3%
Part-time enrollment: 286 (master's); 35 (DNP)
men: 12%; women: 88%; minorities: 9%; international: 0%
Acceptance rate (master's): 54%
Acceptance rate (DNP): 83%
Specialties offered: administration; clinical nurse specialist; education; nurse practitioner; nurse practitioner: adult-gerontology acute care; nurse practitioner: adult-gerontology primary care; nurse practitioner: family; nurse practitioner: psychiatric-mental health, across the lifespan

Valparaiso University[1]

LeBien Hall 103
Valparaiso, IN 46383
valpo.edu/nursing
Private
Admissions: (219) 464-5313
Email: graduate.school@valpo.edu
Financial aid: (219) 464-5015
Tuition: N/A
Room/board/expenses: N/A
Enrollment: N/A

IOWA

Allen College

1825 Logan Avenue
Waterloo, IA 50703
www.allencollege.edu/academic-programs.aspx
Private
Admissions: (319) 226-2014
Email: admissions@allencollege.edu
Financial aid: (319) 226-2515
Application deadline: N/A
Degrees offered: master's, DNP

Tuition: full time: $797/credit hour, part time: $797/credit hour (master's); full time: $797/credit hour, part time: $797/credit hour (DNP)
Room/board/expenses: $7,281 (master's); $7,281 (DNP)
Full-time enrollment: 31 (master's); 1 (DNP)
men: 9%; women: 91%; minorities: 0%; international: 6%
Part-time enrollment: 177 (master's); 6 (DNP)
men: 13%; women: 87%; minorities: 6%; international: 1%
Acceptance rate (master's): 41%
Acceptance rate (DNP): 8%
Specialties offered: administration; community health/public health; education; informatics; nurse practitioner; nurse practitioner: adult-gerontology acute care; nurse practitioner: adult-gerontology primary care; nurse practitioner: family; nurse practitioner: psychiatric-mental health, across the lifespan; dual majors

Briar Cliff University[1]

3303 Rebecca Street
Sioux City, IA 51104
Private
Admissions: N/A
Financial aid: N/A
Tuition: N/A
Room/board/expenses: N/A
Enrollment: N/A

Clarke University

1550 Clarke Drive
Dubuque, IA 52001
www.clarke.edu/page.aspx?id=22047
Private
Admissions: (563) 588-6432
Email: admissions@clarke.edu
Financial aid: (563) 588-6327
Application deadline: 2/1
Degrees offered: DNP
Tuition: full time: $825/credit hour, part time: $825/credit hour
Room/board/expenses: N/A
Full-time enrollment: 64
men: 2%; women: 98%; minorities: 3%; international: 0%
Part-time enrollment: 4
men: 0%; women: 100%; minorities: 0%; international: 0%
Acceptance rate (DNP): 97%
Specialties offered: nurse practitioner; nurse practitioner: family; other majors

Grand View University[1]

1200 Grandview Avenue
Des Moines, IA 50316
Private
Admissions: N/A
Financial aid: N/A
Tuition: N/A
Room/board/expenses: N/A
Enrollment: N/A

Kaplan University[1]

1801 East Kimberly Road, Suite 1
Davenport, IA 52807
Private
Admissions: N/A
Financial aid: N/A
Tuition: N/A

Room/board/expenses: N/A
Enrollment: N/A

Mount Mercy University

1330 Elmhurst Drive NE
Cedar Rapids, IA 52402
www.mtmercy.edu/master-science-nursing
Private
Admissions: (319) 363-1323
Email: tom@mtmercy.edu
Financial aid: (319) 363-8213
Application deadline: N/A
Degrees offered: master's
Tuition: full time: $583/credit hour, part time: $583/credit hour
Room/board/expenses: N/A
Full-time enrollment: 38
men: 3%; women: 97%; minorities: 5%; international: 3%
Part-time enrollment: 8
men: 13%; women: 88%; minorities: 25%; international: 0%
Specialties offered: administration; community health/public health; education

University of Iowa

50 Newton Road
101 College of Nursing Building
Iowa City, IA 52242-1121
www.nursing.uiowa.edu/
Public
Admissions: (319) 335-1525
Email: gradmail@uiowa.edu
Financial aid: (319) 335-1450
Application deadline: 2/1
Degrees offered: master's, Ph.D., DNP
In-state tuition: full time: N/A, part time: $12,110 (master's); full time: $8,856, part time: $5,904 (Ph.D.); full time: $21,021, part time: $15,015 (DNP)
Out-of-state tuition: full time: N/A (master's); full time: $26,460 (Ph.D.); full time: $39,517 (DNP)
Room/board/expenses: $15,960 (master's); $15,960 (Ph.D.); $15,960 (DNP)
Full-time enrollment: N/A (master's); 16 (Ph.D.); 145 (DNP)
men: 13%; women: 87%; minorities: 16%; international: 2%
Part-time enrollment: 16 (master's); 7 (Ph.D.); 56 (DNP)
men: 15%; women: 85%; minorities: 8%; international: 0%
Acceptance rate (master's): 100%
Acceptance rate (Ph.D.): 92%
Acceptance rate (DNP): 60%
Specialties offered: administration; clinical nurse leader; health management & policy health care systems; nurse anesthesia; nurse practitioner; nurse practitioner: adult-gerontology acute care; nurse practitioner: adult-gerontology primary care; nurse practitioner: family; nurse practitioner: pediatric primary care; nurse practitioner: psychiatric-mental health, across the lifespan; research; other majors

Room/board/expenses: N/A
Enrollment: N/A

KANSAS

Fort Hays State University[1]

600 Park Street
Hays, KS 67601-4099
Public
Admissions: N/A
Financial aid: N/A
Tuition: N/A
Room/board/expenses: N/A
Enrollment: N/A

MidAmerica Nazarene University[1]

2030 E. College Way
Olathe, KS 66062
Private
Admissions: N/A
Financial aid: N/A
Tuition: N/A
Room/board/expenses: N/A
Enrollment: N/A

Pittsburg State University

1701 S. Broadway
Pittsburg, KS 66762
Public
Admissions: N/A
Financial aid: N/A
Application deadline: N/A
Degrees offered: master's, DNP
In-state tuition: full time: $6,218, part time: $259/credit hour (master's); full time: $396/credit hour, part time: $396/credit hour (DNP)
Out-of-state tuition: full time: $16,302 (master's); full time: $396/credit hour (DNP)
Room/board/expenses: $7,572 (master's); $7,572 (DNP)
Full-time enrollment: N/A (master's); N/A (DNP)
men: N/A; women: N/A; minorities: N/A; international: N/A
Part-time enrollment: 5 (master's); 35 (DNP)
men: 15%; women: 85%; minorities: 33%; international: 0%
Acceptance rate (DNP): 88%
Specialties offered: N/A

University of Kansas

Mail Stop 2029
3901 Rainbow Boulevard
Kansas City, KS 66160
nursing.kumc.edu
Public
Admissions: (913) 588-1619
Email: soninfo@kumc.edu
Financial aid: (913) 588-5170
Application deadline: 12/1
Degrees offered: master's, Ph.D., DNP
In-state tuition: full time: $637/credit hour, part time: $637/credit hour (master's); full time: $637/credit hour, part time: $637/credit hour (Ph.D.); full time: $637/credit hour, part time: $637/credit hour (DNP)
Out-of-state tuition: full time: $637/credit hour (master's); full time: $637/credit hour (Ph.D.); full time: $637/credit hour (DNP)
Room/board/expenses: N/A

Full-time enrollment: N/A
(master's); 11 (Ph.D.); 30 (DNP)
men: 2%; women: 98%;
minorities: 15%; international:
0%
Part-time enrollment: 70
(master's); 15 (Ph.D.); 172 (DNP)
men: 10%; women: 90%;
minorities: 16%; international:
0%
Acceptance rate (master's): 100%
Acceptance rate (Ph.D.): 100%
Acceptance rate (DNP): 100%
Specialties offered:
administration; clinical nurse
specialist; community health/
public health; informatics;
nurse-midwifery; nurse
practitioner; nurse practitioner:
adult-gerontology primary care;
nurse practitioner: family; nurse
practitioner: psychiatric-mental
health, across the lifespan;
research

University of Saint Mary[1]
4100 S. 4th Street
Leavenworth, KS 66048
Admissions: N/A
Financial aid: N/A
Tuition: N/A
Room/board/expenses: N/A
Enrollment: N/A

Washburn University-Topeka[1]
1700 S.W. College Avenue
Topeka, KS 66621-1117
www.washburn.edu/sonuk
Public
Admissions: (785) 670-1525
Email:
shirley.dinkel@washburn.edu
Financial aid: (785) 670-2773
Tuition: N/A
Room/board/expenses: N/A
Enrollment: N/A

Wichita State University[1]
1845 Fairmount
Wichita, KS 67260-0041
Public
Admissions: N/A
Financial aid: N/A
Tuition: N/A
Room/board/expenses: N/A
Enrollment: N/A

KENTUCKY

Bellarmine University[1]
2001 Newburg Road
Louisville, KY 40205
www.bellarmine.edu/lansing/
nursing/
Private
Admissions: (502) 272-7200
Email: admissionsoffice@
bellarmine.edu
Financial aid: (502) 272-7300
Tuition: N/A
Room/board/expenses: N/A
Enrollment: N/A

Eastern Kentucky University[1]
521 Lancaster Avenue
Rowlett Building 223
Richmond, KY 40475
bsn-gn.eku.edu
Public
Admissions: (859) 622-1742
Email:
jerry.pogatshnick@eku.edu
Financial aid: (859) 622-2361
Tuition: N/A
Room/board/expenses: N/A
Enrollment: N/A

Frontier Nursing University
PO Box 528
Hyden, KY 41749
www.frontier.edu/
Private
Admissions: (606) 672-2312
Email: admissionscounselor@
frontier.edu
Financial aid: (859) 899-2524
Application deadline: N/A
Degrees offered: master's, DNP
Tuition: full time: $550/credit
hour, part time: $550/credit
hour (master's); full time: $580/
credit hour, part time: N/A (DNP)
Room/board/expenses: N/A
Full-time enrollment: 1,343
(master's); 117 (DNP)
men: 5%; women: 95%;
minorities: 19%; international:
0%
Part-time enrollment: 220
(master's); 18 (DNP)
men: 6%; women: 94%;
minorities: 17%; international:
0%
Acceptance rate (master's): 50%
Acceptance rate (DNP): 96%
Specialties offered: nurse-
midwifery; nurse practitioner;
nurse practitioner: family; nurse
practitioner: psychiatric-mental
health, across the lifespan

Murray State University[1]
121 Mason Hall
Murray, KY 42071
www.murraystate.edu/nursing.
aspx
Public
Admissions: (270) 809-3779
Email:
msu.graduateadmissions@
murraystate.edu
Financial aid: (270) 809-2546
Tuition: N/A
Room/board/expenses: N/A
Enrollment: N/A

Northern Kentucky University[1]
Nunn Drive
Highland Heights, KY 41099
healthprofessions.nku.edu/
Public
Admissions: (859) 572-6934
Email: graduate@nku.edu
Financial aid: (859) 572-5143
Tuition: N/A
Room/board/expenses: N/A
Enrollment: N/A

Spalding University[1]
851 S. Fourth Street
Louisville, KY 40203-2188
Private
Admissions: N/A
Financial aid: N/A
Tuition: N/A
Room/board/expenses: N/A
Enrollment: N/A

University of Kentucky
315 College of Nursing Building
Lexington, KY 40536-0232
www.uky.edu/nursing
Public
Admissions: (859) 323-5108
Email: conss@uky.edu
Financial aid: (859) 257-3172
Application deadline: 2/15
Degrees offered: Ph.D., DNP
In-state tuition: full time: $12,236,
part time: $648/credit hour
(Ph.D.); full time: $15,956, part
time: $855/credit hour (DNP)
Out-of-state tuition: full time:
$28,380 (Ph.D.); full time:
$39,208 (Ph.D.); N/A (DNP)
Room/board/expenses: N/A
(Ph.D.); N/A (DNP)
Full-time enrollment: 34 (Ph.D.);
109 (DNP)
men: 11%; women: 89%;
minorities: 10%; international:
5%
Part-time enrollment: 7 (Ph.D.);
124 (DNP)
men: 10%; women: 90%;
minorities: 9%; international: 0%
Acceptance rate (Ph.D.): 71%
Acceptance rate (DNP): 72%
Specialties offered: clinical nurse
specialist; health management
& policy health care systems;
nurse practitioner; nurse
practitioner: adult-gerontology
acute care; nurse practitioner:
adult-gerontology primary care;
nurse practitioner: family; nurse
practitioner: pediatric primary
care; nurse practitioner:
psychiatric-mental health,
across the lifespan; research

University of Louisville
555 S. Floyd Street
Louisville, KY 40292
louisville.edu/nursing/
Public
Admissions: (502) 852-3101
Email: gradadm@louisville.edu
Financial aid: (502) 852-5511
Application deadline: 10/1
Degrees offered: master's, Ph.D.,
DNP
In-state tuition: full time: $12,246,
part time: $681/credit hour
(master's); full time: $12,246,
part time: $681/credit hour
(Ph.D.); full time: $12,246, part
time: $681/credit hour (DNP)
Out-of-state tuition: full time:
$25,486 (master's); full time:
$25,486 (Ph.D.); full time:
$25,486 (DNP)
Room/board/expenses: $8,130
(master's); $8,130 (Ph.D.);
$8,130 (DNP)
Full-time enrollment: 79
(master's); 14 (Ph.D.); 41 (DNP)
men: 11%; women: 89%;
minorities: 17%; international:
3%

Part-time enrollment: 6
(master's); 5 (Ph.D.); 9 (DNP)
men: 10%; women: 90%;
minorities: 5%; international: 0%
Acceptance rate (master's): 20%
Acceptance rate (Ph.D.): 71%
Acceptance rate (DNP): 94%
Specialties offered: education;
generalist; neonatal; nurse
practitioner: adult-gerontology
acute care; nurse practitioner:
adult-gerontology primary care;
nurse practitioner: family; nurse
practitioner: psychiatric-mental
health, across the lifespan; dual
majors

Western Kentucky University
1906 College Heights Boulevard
#11036
Bowling Green, KY 42101-1036
www.wku.edu/nursing/index.php
Public
Admissions: (270) 745-2446
Email: graduate.admissions@
wku.edu
Financial aid: (270) 745-2755
Application deadline: 4/1
Degrees offered: master's, DNP
In-state tuition: full time: $679/
credit hour, part time: $679/
credit hour (master's); full time:
$643/credit hour, part time:
$643/credit hour (DNP)
Out-of-state tuition: full time:
$679/credit hour (master's); full
time: $833/credit hour (DNP)
Room/board/expenses: N/A
Full-time enrollment: 9 (master's);
23 (DNP)
men: 19%; women: 81%;
minorities: 13%; international:
0%
Part-time enrollment: 62
(master's); 49 (DNP)
men: 9%; women: 91%;
minorities: 5%; international: 0%
Acceptance rate (master's): 56%
Acceptance rate (DNP): 68%
Specialties offered:
administration; education; nurse
practitioner; nurse practitioner:
family; nurse practitioner:
psychiatric-mental health,
across the lifespan; other
majors

LOUISIANA

Grambling State University[1]
1 Cole Street
Grambling, LA 71245
Public
Admissions: N/A
Financial aid: N/A
Tuition: N/A
Room/board/expenses: N/A
Enrollment: N/A

Louisiana State University Health Sciences Center[1]
1900 Gravier Street
New Orleans, LA 70112
nursing.lsuhsc.edu/default.aspx
Public
Admissions: N/A
Financial aid: N/A
Tuition: N/A

Room/board/expenses: N/A
Enrollment: N/A

Loyola University New Orleans
6363 St. Charles Avenue
New Orleans, LA 70118
gps.loyno.edu/nursing
Private
Admissions: (866) 789-9809
Email: nursing@loyno.edu
Financial aid: (504) 865-3231
Application deadline: 7/15
Degrees offered: master's, DNP
Tuition: full time: $818/credit
hour, part time: $818/credit hour
(master's); full time: $818/credit
hour, part time: $818/credit
hour (DNP)
Room/board/expenses: N/A
Full-time enrollment: 188
(master's); 69 (DNP)
men: 7%; women: 93%;
minorities: 30%; international:
0%
Part-time enrollment: 58
(master's); 11 (DNP)
men: 9%; women: 91%;
minorities: 22%; international:
0%
Acceptance rate (master's): 81%
Acceptance rate (DNP): 85%
Specialties offered:
administration; education; nurse
practitioner; nurse practitioner:
family

McNeese State University
Box 90415 MSU
Lake Charles, LA 70609
www.mcneese.edu/nursing/
graduate
Public
Admissions: (337) 475-5504
Email:
admissions@mcneese.edu
Financial aid: (337) 475-5068
Application deadline: N/A
Degrees offered: master's
In-state tuition: full time: N/A,
part time: N/A
Out-of-state tuition: full time: N/A
Room/board/expenses: N/A
Full-time enrollment: 13
men: 23%; women: 77%;
minorities: N/A; international:
N/A
Part-time enrollment: 152
men: 24%; women: 76%;
minorities: N/A; international:
N/A
Specialties offered:
administration; education; nurse
practitioner; nurse practitioner:
psychiatric-mental health,
across the lifespan

Nicholls State University[1]
161 Betsy Cheramie Ayo Hall
Thibodaux, LA 70310
Admissions: N/A
Financial aid: N/A
Tuition: N/A
Room/board/expenses: N/A
Enrollment: N/A

Northwestern State University of Louisiana

1800 Line Avenue
Shreveport, LA 71101-4653
nsula.edu/academics/nursing-allied-health/
Public
Admissions: (318) 357-6171
Email: belle@nsula.edu
Financial aid: (318) 357-5961
Application deadline: 7/6
Degrees offered: master's, DNP
In-state tuition: full time: $475/credit hour, part time: $475/credit hour (master's); full time: $475/credit hour, part time: $475/credit hour (DNP)
Out-of-state tuition: full time: $475/credit hour (master's); full time: $475/credit hour (DNP)
Room/board/expenses: N/A
Full-time enrollment: 12 (master's); N/A (DNP)
men: 8%; women: 92%; minorities: 8%; international: 0%
Part-time enrollment: 217 (master's); 22 (DNP)
men: 12%; women: 88%; minorities: 15%; international: 0%
Acceptance rate (master's): 99%
Acceptance rate (DNP): 100%
Specialties offered: administration; education; nurse practitioner; nurse practitioner: adult-gerontology acute care; nurse practitioner: adult-gerontology primary care; nurse practitioner: family; nurse practitioner: pediatric primary care; women's health

Our Lady of the Lake College[1]

7434 Perkins Road
Baton Rouge, LA 70808
Private
Admissions: N/A
Financial aid: N/A
Tuition: N/A
Room/board/expenses: N/A
Enrollment: N/A

Southeastern Louisiana University

SLU Box 10835
Hammond, LA 70402
www.southeastern.edu/acad_research/depts/nurs/index.html
Public
Admissions: (800) 222-7358
Email: admissions@southeastern.edu
Financial aid: (985) 549-2244
Application deadline: 7/15
Degrees offered: master's, DNP
In-state tuition: full time: $6,540, part time: $465/credit hour (master's); full time: N/A, part time: N/A (DNP)
Out-of-state tuition: full time: $19,017 (master's); full time: N/A (DNP)
Room/board/expenses: $9,072 (master's); N/A (DNP)
Full-time enrollment: 27 (master's); 12 (DNP)
men: 15%; women: 85%; minorities: 21%; international: 0%

Part-time enrollment: 98 (master's); 23 (DNP)
men: 13%; women: 87%; minorities: 16%; international: 0%
Acceptance rate (master's): 58%
Acceptance rate (DNP): 100%
Specialties offered: administration; education; nurse practitioner; nurse practitioner: family; nurse practitioner: psychiatric-mental health, across the lifespan

Southern University and A&M College[1]

PO Box 11784
Baton Rouge, LA 70813
Public
Admissions: N/A
Financial aid: N/A
Tuition: N/A
Room/board/expenses: N/A
Enrollment: N/A

University of Louisiana-Lafayette

411 E. Saint Mary Boulevard
Lafayette, LA 70503
www.louisiana.edu/
Public
Admissions: (337) 482-6965
Email: gradschool@louisiana.edu
Financial aid: (337) 482-6506
Application deadline: 6/30
Degrees offered: master's, DNP
In-state tuition: full time: $5,511, part time: $525/credit hour (master's); full time: $5,511, part time: $525/credit hour (DNP)
Out-of-state tuition: full time: $19,239 (master's); full time: $19,239 (DNP)
Room/board/expenses: $9,073 (master's); $9,073 (DNP)
Full-time enrollment: 26 (master's); 7 (DNP)
men: 6%; women: 94%; minorities: 9%; international: 0%
Part-time enrollment: 114 (master's); 12 (DNP)
men: 13%; women: 87%; minorities: 10%; international: 0%
Acceptance rate (master's): 48%
Acceptance rate (DNP): 36%
Specialties offered: education; nurse practitioner; nurse practitioner: family; nurse practitioner: psychiatric-mental health, across the lifespan

MAINE

Husson University

1 College Circle
Bangor, ME 04401
www.husson.edu/school-of-nursing
Private
Admissions: (207) 992-4994
Email: graduateschool@husson.edu
Financial aid: (207) 973-1090
Application deadline: 3/30
Degrees offered: master's
Tuition: full time: $560/credit hour, part time: $560/credit hour
Room/board/expenses: $10,000
Full-time enrollment:
men: N/A; women: N/A; minorities: N/A; international: N/A

Part-time enrollment: 60
men: 13%; women: 87%; minorities: 7%; international: 0%
Acceptance rate (master's): 67%
Specialties offered: nurse practitioner; nurse practitioner: family

St. Joseph's College[1]

278 Whites Bridge Road
Standish, ME 04084-5263
Private
Admissions: N/A
Financial aid: N/A
Tuition: N/A
Room/board/expenses: N/A
Enrollment: N/A

University of Maine

5724 Dunn Hall
Orono, ME 04469-5724
www.umaine.edu/nursing/
Public
Admissions: (207) 581-3291
Email: graduate@maine.edu
Financial aid: (207) 581-1324
Application deadline: N/A
Degrees offered: master's, Ph.D.
In-state tuition: full time: $418/credit hour, part time: $418/credit hour (master's); full time: $418/credit hour, part time: $418/credit hour
Out-of-state tuition: full time: $648/credit hour (master's); full time: $648/credit hour
Room/board/expenses: $12,428 (master's); $12,428
Full-time enrollment: N/A (master's);
men: N/A; women: N/A; minorities: N/A; international: N/A
Part-time enrollment: 35 (master's); 5
men: 15%; women: 85%; minorities: N/A; international: N/A
Acceptance rate (master's): 56%
Acceptance rate (Ph.D.): 100%
Specialties offered: education; nurse practitioner; nurse practitioner: pediatric primary care; other majors

University of Southern Maine

96 Falmouth Street
Portland, ME 04104-9300
usm.maine.edu/nursing
Public
Admissions: N/A
Financial aid: (207) 780-5250
Application deadline: N/A
Degrees offered: master's, DNP
In-state tuition: full time: N/A, part time: N/A (master's); full time: N/A, part time: N/A (DNP)
Out-of-state tuition: full time: N/A (master's); full time: N/A (DNP)
Room/board/expenses: N/A
Full-time enrollment: 148 (master's); N/A (DNP)
men: 16%; women: 84%; minorities: 4%; international: 0%
Part-time enrollment: 75 (master's); 4 (DNP)
men: 19%; women: 81%; minorities: 6%; international: 0%
Acceptance rate (master's): 42%
Acceptance rate (DNP): 83%
Specialties offered: education; nurse practitioner; nurse practitioner: adult-gerontology

primary care; nurse practitioner: family; nurse practitioner: psychiatric-mental health, across the lifespan

MARYLAND

Bowie State University

14000 Jericho Park Road
Bowie, MD 20715-9465
Public
Admissions: (301) 860-3415
Email: aisaac@bowiestate.edu
Financial aid: (301) 860-4543
Application deadline: N/A
Degrees offered: master's
In-state tuition: full time: $9,576, part time: $7,182
Out-of-state tuition: full time: $16,512
Room/board/expenses: $12,860
Full-time enrollment: 57
men: N/A; women: N/A; minorities: 86%; international: 0%
Part-time enrollment: 62
men: N/A; women: N/A; minorities: 87%; international: 0%
Specialties offered: N/A

Coppin State University (Fuld)[1]

2500 W. North Avenue
Baltimore, MD 21216-3698
Public
Admissions: N/A
Financial aid: N/A
Tuition: N/A
Room/board/expenses: N/A
Enrollment: N/A

Johns Hopkins University

525 N. Wolfe Street
Baltimore, MD 21205-2100
nursing.jhu.edu
Private
Admissions: (410) 955-7548
Email: jhuson@jhu.edu
Financial aid: (410) 955-9840
Application deadline: 1/1
Degrees offered: master's, Ph.D., DNP
Tuition: full time: $37,056, part time: $1,544/credit hour (master's); full time: $41,360, part time: $2,297/credit hour (Ph.D.); full time: $37,306, part time: $1,622/credit hour (DNP)
Room/board/expenses: $13,140 (master's); $13,140 (Ph.D.); $13,140 (DNP)
Full-time enrollment: 396 (master's); 49 (Ph.D.); 9 (DNP)
men: 14%; women: 86%; minorities: 34%; international: 5%
Part-time enrollment: 251 (master's); N/A (Ph.D.); 48 (DNP)
men: 8%; women: 92%; minorities: 30%; international: 4%
Acceptance rate (master's): 67%
Acceptance rate (Ph.D.): 49%
Acceptance rate (DNP): 62%
Specialties offered: administration; clinical nurse specialist; community health/public health; generalist; health management & policy; health care systems; nurse practitioner; nurse practitioner:

adult-gerontology acute care; nurse practitioner: adult-gerontology primary care; nurse practitioner: family; nurse practitioner: pediatric primary care; nurse practitioner: psychiatric-mental health, across the lifespan; research; dual majors

Morgan State University[1]

Jenkins Building, Room 308
1700 E. Cold Spring Lane
Baltimore, MD 21251
Public
Admissions: N/A
Financial aid: N/A
Tuition: N/A
Room/board/expenses: N/A
Enrollment: N/A

Notre Dame of Maryland University

4701 North Charles Street
Baltimore, MD 21210
www.ndm.edu/academics/school-of-nursing/
Private
Admissions: (410) 532-5108
Email: gradadm@ndm.edu
Financial aid: (410) 532-5735
Application deadline: N/A
Degrees offered: master's
Tuition: full time: $650/credit hour, part time: $650/credit hour
Room/board/expenses: N/A
Full-time enrollment:
men: N/A; women: N/A; minorities: N/A; international: N/A
Part-time enrollment: 96
men: 0%; women: 100%; minorities: 57%; international: 0%
Acceptance rate (master's): 91%
Specialties offered: administration; education

Salisbury University

1101 Camden Avenue
Salisbury, MD 21801
www.salisbury.edu/nursing/
Public
Admissions: (410) 677-0047
Email: graduateadmissions@salisbury.edu
Financial aid: (410) 543-6165
Application deadline: 3/1
Degrees offered: master's, DNP
In-state tuition: full time: $640/credit hour, part time: $640/credit hour (master's); full time: $640/credit hour, part time: $640/credit hour (DNP)
Out-of-state tuition: full time: $807/credit hour (master's); full time: $807/credit hour (DNP)
Room/board/expenses: N/A
Full-time enrollment: N/A (master's); 28 (DNP)
men: 11%; women: 89%; minorities: 25%; international: 0%
Part-time enrollment: 1 (master's); 5 (DNP)
men: N/A; women: 100%; minorities: 0%; international: 0%
Acceptance rate (DNP): 58%
Specialties offered: community health/public health; education; health management & policy

health care systems; nurse practitioner; nurse practitioner: family

Stevenson University

10945 Boulevard Circle
Owings Mills, MD 21117
www.stevenson.edu/graduate-professional-studies/graduate-programs/nursing/
Private
Admissions: (443) 352-4030
Email:
amreynolds@stevenson.edu
Financial aid: (443) 334-3200
Application deadline: N/A
Degrees offered: master's
Tuition: full time: $625/credit hour, part time: $625/credit hour
Room/board/expenses: N/A
Full-time enrollment:
men: N/A; women: N/A; minorities: N/A; international: N/A
Part-time enrollment: 189
men: 4%; women: 96%; minorities: 32%; international: 0%
Acceptance rate (master's): 75%
Specialties offered:
administration; education; other majors

Towson University[1]

8000 York Road
Towson, MD 21252
Public
Admissions: N/A
Financial aid: N/A
Tuition: N/A
Room/board/expenses: N/A
Enrollment: N/A

Uniformed Services University of the Health Sciences

4301 Jones Bridge Road
Bethesda, MD 20814
www.usuhs.edu/gsn
Public
Admissions: (301) 295-1055
Email:
terry.malavakis@usuhs.edu
Financial aid: N/A
Application deadline: 8/15
Degrees offered: master's, Ph.D., DNP
In-state tuition: full time: N/A/credit hour, part time: N/A/credit hour (master's); full time: N/A/credit hour, part time: N/A/credit hour (Ph.D.); full time: N/A/credit hour, part time: N/A/credit hour (DNP)
Out-of-state tuition: full time: N/A/credit hour (master's); full time: N/A/credit hour (Ph.D.); full time: N/A/credit hour (DNP)
Room/board/expenses: N/A
Full-time enrollment: N/A (master's); 10 (Ph.D.); 152 (DNP)
men: 48%; women: 52%; minorities: 26%; international: 0%
Part-time enrollment: N/A (master's); 7 (Ph.D.); N/A (DNP)
men: 0%; women: 100%; minorities: 29%; international: 0%
Acceptance rate (Ph.D.): 67%
Acceptance rate (DNP): 59%
Specialties offered: clinical nurse specialist; nurse anesthesia;

nurse practitioner; nurse practitioner: family; nurse practitioner: psychiatric-mental health, across the lifespan; research; women's health

University of Maryland–Baltimore

Suite 516
Baltimore, MD 21201-1579
www.nursing.umaryland.edu
Public
Admissions: (410) 706-2326
Email: admissions@
son.umaryland.edu
Financial aid: (410) 706-7347
Application deadline: N/A
Degrees offered: master's, Ph.D., DNP
In-state tuition: full time: $724/credit hour, part time: $724/credit hour (master's); full time: $732/credit hour, part time: $732/credit hour (Ph.D.); full time: $732/credit hour, part time: $732/credit hour (DNP)
Out-of-state tuition: full time: $1,324/credit hour (master's); full time: $1,324/credit hour (Ph.D.); full time: $1,324/credit hour (DNP)
Room/board/expenses: N/A
Full-time enrollment: 242 (master's); 19 (Ph.D.); 194 (DNP)
men: 11%; women: 89%; minorities: 42%; international: 3%
Part-time enrollment: 261 (master's); 21 (Ph.D.); 171 (DNP)
men: 9%; women: 91%; minorities: 39%; international: 1%
Acceptance rate (master's): 48%
Acceptance rate (Ph.D.): 82%
Acceptance rate (DNP): 35%
Specialties offered:
administration; clinical nurse leader; clinical nurse specialist; community health/public health; informatics; nurse anesthesia; neonatal; nurse practitioner; nurse practitioner: adult-gerontology acute care; nurse practitioner: adult-gerontology primary care; nurse practitioner: adult; nurse practitioner: family; nurse practitioner: pediatric primary care; nurse practitioner: psychiatric-mental health, across the lifespan; research; school nursing; combined nurse practitioner/clinical nurse specialist

MASSACHUSETTS

American International College[1]

1000 State Street
Springfield, MA 01109
Private
Admissions: N/A
Financial aid: N/A
Tuition: N/A
Room/board/expenses: N/A
Enrollment: N/A

Boston College

140 Commonwealth Avenue
Chestnut Hill, MA 02467
www.bc.edu/nursing
Private
Admissions: (617) 552-4745
Email: sean.sendall@bc.edu

Financial aid: (617) 552-4745
Application deadline: N/A
Degrees offered: master's, Ph.D.
Tuition: full time: $1,298/credit hour, part time: $1,298/credit hour (master's); full time: $1,298/credit hour, part time: $1,298/credit hour
Room/board/expenses: N/A
Full-time enrollment: 170 (master's); 18
men: 14%; women: 86%; minorities: 14%; international: 0%
Part-time enrollment: 64 (master's); 6
men: 10%; women: 90%; minorities: 17%; international: 0%
Acceptance rate (master's): 52%
Acceptance rate (Ph.D.): 53%
Specialties offered: nurse anesthesia; nurse practitioner; nurse practitioner: adult-gerontology primary care; nurse practitioner: family; nurse practitioner: pediatric primary care; nurse practitioner: psychiatric-mental health, across the lifespan; women's health

Curry College[1]

1071 Blue Hill Avenue
Milton, MA 02186
Private
Admissions: N/A
Financial aid: N/A
Tuition: N/A
Room/board/expenses: N/A
Enrollment: N/A

Elms College[1]

291 Springfield Street
Chicopee, MA 01013
Private
Admissions: N/A
Financial aid: N/A
Tuition: N/A
Room/board/expenses: N/A
Enrollment: N/A

Emmanuel College[1]

400 The Fenway
Boston, MA 02115
Private
Admissions: N/A
Financial aid: N/A
Tuition: N/A
Room/board/expenses: N/A
Enrollment: N/A

Endicott College[1]

376 Hale Street
Beverly, MA 01915
Private
Admissions: N/A
Financial aid: N/A
Tuition: N/A
Room/board/expenses: N/A
Enrollment: N/A

Fitchburg State University

160 Pearl Street
Fitchburg, MA 01420-2697
fitchburgstate.edu/academics/academic-departments/department-homepage-nursing/
Public
Admissions: (800) 705-9692

Email: admissions@
fitchburgsatte.edu
Financial aid: (978) 665-3156
Application deadline: N/A
Degrees offered: master's
In-state tuition: full time: $167/credit hour, part time: $167/credit hour
Out-of-state tuition: full time: $167/credit hour
Room/board/expenses: N/A
Full-time enrollment: 2
men: 0%; women: 100%; minorities: 50%; international: 0%
Part-time enrollment: 35
men: 6%; women: 94%; minorities: 11%; international: 0%
Acceptance rate (master's): 100%
Specialties offered: N/A

Framingham State University[1]

100 State Street
Framingham, MA 01701
framingham.edu/academics/graduate-studies/graduate-degree-programs/msn-education
Public
Admissions: (508) 626-4501
Email:
ddonovan@framingham.edu
Financial aid: (508) 626-4534
Tuition: N/A
Room/board/expenses: N/A
Enrollment: N/A

MCPHS University[1]

179 Longwood Avenue
Boston, MA 02115
www.mcphs.edu/academics/schools/school%20of%20nursing
Private
Admissions: N/A
Financial aid: N/A
Tuition: N/A
Room/board/expenses: N/A
Enrollment: N/A

MGH Institute of Health Professions

36 1st Avenue
Boston, MA 02129
www.mghihp.edu/school-nursing
Private
Admissions: (617) 726-6069
Email: admissions@mghihp.edu
Financial aid: (617) 726-9549
Application deadline: 1/1
Degrees offered: master's, DNP
Tuition: full time: $54,765, part time: $1,217/credit hour (master's); full time: $1,136/credit hour, part time: $1,136/credit hour (DNP)
Room/board/expenses: N/A
Full-time enrollment: 276 (master's); 6 (DNP)
men: 14%; women: 86%; minorities: 22%; international: N/A
Part-time enrollment: 28 (master's); 44 (DNP)
men: 15%; women: 85%; minorities: 19%; international: N/A
Acceptance rate (master's): 55%
Acceptance rate (DNP): 83%
Specialties offered: nurse practitioner: adult-gerontology acute care; nurse practitioner: adult-gerontology primary care; nurse practitioner: family; nurse

practitioner: pediatric primary care; nurse practitioner: psychiatric-mental health, across the lifespan; women's health; other majors

Northeastern University

123 Behrakis Health Sciences Center
Boston, MA 02115
www.northeastern.edu/bouve/nursing/
Private
Admissions: (617) 373-2708
Email: bouvegrad@neu.edu
Financial aid: (617) 373-5899
Application deadline: N/A
Degrees offered: master's, Ph.D., DNP
Tuition: full time: $1,338/credit hour, part time: $1,338/credit hour (master's); full time: $1,338/credit hour, part time: $1,338/credit hour (Ph.D.); full time: $1,338/credit hour, part time: $1,338/credit hour (DNP)
Room/board/expenses: $21,600 (master's); $21,600 (Ph.D.); N/A (DNP)
Full-time enrollment: 225 (master's); 15 (Ph.D.); 99 (DNP)
men: 32%; women: 68%; minorities: N/A; international: N/A
Part-time enrollment: 106 (master's); 4 (Ph.D.); 43 (DNP)
men: 12%; women: 88%; minorities: N/A; international: N/A
Acceptance rate (master's): 100%
Acceptance rate (Ph.D.): 100%
Acceptance rate (DNP): 40%
Specialties offered:
administration; informatics; nurse anesthesia; neonatal; nurse practitioner; nurse practitioner: adult-gerontology acute care; nurse practitioner: adult-gerontology primary care; nurse practitioner: family; nurse practitioner: pediatric primary care; nurse practitioner: psychiatric-mental health, across the lifespan; research; school nursing; dual majors

Regis College[1]

235 Wellesley Street
Weston, MA 02493
Private
Admissions: N/A
Financial aid: N/A
Tuition: N/A
Room/board/expenses: N/A
Enrollment: N/A

Salem State University–South Campus[1]

352 Lafayette Street
Salem, MA 01970
Public
Admissions: N/A
Financial aid: N/A
Tuition: N/A
Room/board/expenses: N/A
Enrollment: N/A

Simmons College

300 The Fenway
Boston, MA 02115
www.simmons.edu/academics/
schools/school-of-nursing-and-
health-sciences
Private
Admissions: (617) 521-2605
Email: snhs@simmons.edu
Financial aid: (617) 521-2001
Application deadline: 12/1
Degrees offered: master's, DNP
Tuition: full time: $1,315/credit
hour, part time: $1,315/credit
hour (master's); full time:
$1,300/credit hour, part time:
$1,300/credit hour (DNP)
Room/board/expenses: N/A
Full-time enrollment: 221
(master's); N/A (DNP)
men: 8%; women: 92%;
minorities: 22%; international:
0%
Part-time enrollment: 1,001
(master's); 39 (DNP)
men: 5%; women: 95%;
minorities: 22%; international:
0%
Acceptance rate (master's): 71%
Acceptance rate (DNP): 97%
Specialties offered: nurse
practitioner; nurse practitioner:
family

University of Massachusetts-Amherst

Arnold House
Amherst, MA 01003-9304
www.umass.edu/nursing
Public
Admissions: (413) 545-0722
Email:
gradadm@grad.umass.edu
Financial aid: (413) 545-0356
Application deadline: 12/15
Degrees offered: master's, Ph.D.,
DNP
In-state tuition: full time: $750/
credit hour, part time: $750/
credit hour (master's); full time:
$12,782, part time: $110/credit
hour (Ph.D.); full time: $750/
credit hour, part time: $750/
credit hour (DNP)
Out-of-state tuition: full time:
$750/credit hour (master's); full
time: $28,000 (Ph.D.); full time:
$750/credit hour (DNP)
Room/board/expenses: N/A
(master's); $3,400 (Ph.D.); N/A
(DNP)
Full-time enrollment: N/A
(master's); 14 (Ph.D.); 86 (DNP)
men: 13%; women: 87%;
minorities: 23%; international:
3%
Part-time enrollment: 37
(master's); 37 (Ph.D.); 129
(DNP)
men: 11%; women: 89%;
minorities: 24%; international:
3%
Acceptance rate (master's): 89%
Acceptance rate (Ph.D.): 75%
Acceptance rate (DNP): 66%
Specialties offered: clinical
nurse leader; community
health/public health; nurse
practitioner; nurse practitioner:
adult-gerontology primary care;
nurse practitioner: family; nurse
practitioner: psychiatric-mental
health, across the lifespan;
research

University of Massachusetts-Boston

100 Morrissey Boulevard
Boston, MA 02125-3393
www.umb.edu/academics/cnhs
Public
Admissions: (617) 287-6400
Email: Peggy.Patel@umb.edu
Financial aid: (617) 287-6300
Application deadline: 3/15
Degrees offered: master's, Ph.D.,
DNP
In-state tuition: full time: $703/
credit hour, part time: $703/
credit hour (master's); full time:
$703/credit hour, part time:
$703/credit hour (Ph.D.); full
time: $703/credit hour, part
time: $703/credit hour (DNP)
Out-of-state tuition: full time:
$1,371/credit hour (master's);
full time: $1,371/credit hour
(Ph.D.); full time: $1,371/credit
hour (DNP)
Room/board/expenses: N/A
Full-time enrollment: 49
(master's); 17 (Ph.D.); N/A (DNP)
men: 12%; women: 88%;
minorities: 18%; international:
18%
Part-time enrollment: 119
(master's); 25 (Ph.D.); 39 (DNP)
men: 8%; women: 92%;
minorities: 28%; international:
2%
Acceptance rate (master's): 80%
Acceptance rate (Ph.D.): 43%
Acceptance rate (DNP): 81%
Specialties offered: clinical nurse
specialist; nurse practitioner;
adult-gerontology primary care;
nurse practitioner: family

University of Massachusetts-Dartmouth

285 Old Westport Road
Dartmouth, MA 02747-2300
www.umassd.edu/nursing
Public
Admissions: (508) 999-8604
Email: graduate@umassd.edu
Financial aid: (508) 999-8643
Application deadline: 3/15
Degrees offered: master's, Ph.D.,
DNP
In-state tuition: full time: $14,994,
part time: $625/credit hour
(master's); full time: $14,994,
part time: $625/credit hour
(Ph.D.); full time: $14,994, part
time: $625/credit hour (DNP)
Out-of-state tuition: full time:
$27,068 (master's); full time:
$27,068 (Ph.D.); full time:
$27,068 (DNP)
Room/board/expenses: $12,470
(master's); $12,470 (Ph.D.);
$12,470 (DNP)
Full-time enrollment: N/A
(master's); 26 (Ph.D.); N/A
(DNP)
men: 8%; women: 92%;
minorities: 12%; international:
0%
Part-time enrollment: 20
(master's); N/A (Ph.D.); 61 (DNP)
men: 12%; women: 88%;
minorities: 19%; international:
0%
Acceptance rate (master's): 92%
Acceptance rate (Ph.D.): 100%
Acceptance rate (DNP): 95%

Specialties offered:
administration; community
health/public health; education;
generalist; nurse practitioner;
nurse practitioner: adult-
gerontology primary care

University of Massachusetts-Lowell

3 Solomont Way
Lowell, MA 01854-512
www.uml.edu/health-sciences/
Nursing/
Public
Admissions: (978) 934-2373
Email: Graduate_Admissions@
uml.edu
Financial aid: (978) 934-2000
Application deadline: 4/1
Degrees offered: master's, Ph.D.,
DNP
In-state tuition: full time: $14,304,
part time: $795/credit hour
(master's); full time: $14,304,
part time: $795/credit hour
(Ph.D.); full time: $14,304, part
time: $795/credit hour (DNP)
Out-of-state tuition: full time:
$25,853 (master's); full time:
$25,853 (Ph.D.); full time:
$25,853 (DNP)
Room/board/expenses: $12,073
(master's); $12,073 (Ph.D.);
$12,073 (DNP)
Full-time enrollment: 22
(master's); 2 (Ph.D.); N/A (DNP)
men: 13%; women: 88%;
minorities: 33%; international:
4%
Part-time enrollment: 48
(master's); 24 (Ph.D.); 21 (DNP)
men: 12%; women: 88%;
minorities: 25%; international:
0%
Acceptance rate (master's): 70%
Acceptance rate (Ph.D.): 100%
Acceptance rate (DNP): 100%
Specialties offered: nurse
practitioner; nurse practitioner:
adult-gerontology primary care;
nurse practitioner: family

University of Massachusetts-Worcester

55 Lake Avenue N
Worcester, MA 01655
www.umassmed.edu
Public
Admissions: (508) 856-3488
Email: gsnadmissions@
umassmed.edu
Financial aid: (508) 856-2265
Application deadline: 12/1
Degrees offered: master's, Ph.D.,
DNP
In-state tuition: full time: $550/
credit hour, part time: $550/
credit hour (master's); full time:
$550/credit hour, part time:
$550/credit hour (Ph.D.); full
time: $550/credit hour, part
time: $550/credit hour (DNP)
Out-of-state tuition: full time:
$825/credit hour (master's); full
time: $825/credit hour (Ph.D.);
full time: $825/credit hour (DNP)
Room/board/expenses: N/A
Full-time enrollment: 63
(master's); 15 (Ph.D.); 73 (DNP)
men: 15%; women: 85%;
minorities: 17%; international: 1%
Part-time enrollment: N/A
(master's); 11 (Ph.D.); 16 (DNP)

men: 4%; women: 96%;
minorities: 19%; international:
0%
Acceptance rate (Ph.D.): 73%
Acceptance rate (DNP): 72%
Specialties offered: education;
nurse practitioner; nurse
practitioner: adult-gerontology
acute care; nurse practitioner:
adult-gerontology primary
care; nurse practitioner: family;
research

Worcester State University

486 Chandler Street
Worcester, MA 01602
www.worcester.edu/
Graduate-Programs
Public
Admissions: (508) 929-8127
Email: gradadmissions@
worcester.edu
Financial aid: (508) 929-8056
Application deadline: 6/15
Degrees offered: master's
In-state tuition: full time: $150/
credit hour, part time: $150/
credit hour
Out-of-state tuition: full time:
$150/credit hour
Room/board/expenses: N/A
Full-time enrollment: 1
men: 0%; women: 100%;
minorities: 0%; international: 0%
Part-time enrollment: 133
men: 5%; women: 95%;
minorities: 34%; international:
0%
Acceptance rate (master's): 100%
Specialties offered: community
health/public health; education

MICHIGAN

Davenport University[1]

6191 Kraft Avenue SE
Grand Rapids, MI 49512
Private
Admissions: N/A
Financial aid: N/A
Tuition: N/A
Room/board/expenses: N/A
Enrollment: N/A

Eastern Michigan University[1]

3111 Marshall Building
Ypsilanti, MI 48197
Public
Admissions: N/A
Financial aid: N/A
Tuition: N/A
Room/board/expenses: N/A
Enrollment: N/A

Ferris State University

200 Ferris Drive
Big Rapids, MI 49307
www.ferris.edu/HTMLS/colleges/
alliedhe/Nursing/homepage.htm
Public
Admissions: (800) 433-7747
Financial aid: (231) 591-2110
Application deadline: N/A
Degrees offered: master's
In-state tuition: full time: $542/
credit hour, part time: $542/
credit hour
Out-of-state tuition: full time:
$813/credit hour
Room/board/expenses: N/A

Full-time enrollment: 4
men: 25%; women: 75%;
minorities: 0%; international: 0%
Part-time enrollment: 93
men: 8%; women: 92%;
minorities: 12%; international:
0%
Acceptance rate (master's): 60%
Specialties offered:
administration; education;
informatics

Grand Valley State University[1]

301 Michigan Street NE
Grand Rapids, MI 49503-3314
www.gvsu/kcon
Public
Admissions: (616) 331-2025
Email: admissions@gvsu.edu
Financial aid: (616) 331-3234
Tuition: N/A
Room/board/expenses: N/A
Enrollment: N/A

Madonna University

36600 Schoolcraft Road
Livonia, MI 48150-1253
www.madonna.edu/academics/
departments/nursing-graduate/
Private
Admissions: (734) 432-5667
Email: grad@madonna.edu
Financial aid: (734) 432-5663
Application deadline: 1/2
Degrees offered: master's, DNP
Tuition: full time: $795/credit
hour, part time: $795/credit hour
(master's); full time: $795/credit
hour, part time: $795/credit
hour (DNP)
Room/board/expenses: $9,550
(master's); $9,550 (DNP)
Full-time enrollment: 1 (master's);
N/A (DNP)
men: 100%; women: 0%;
minorities: 0%; international: 0%
Part-time enrollment: 240
(master's); 23 (DNP)
men: 11%; women: 89%;
minorities: 19%; international:
1%
Acceptance rate (master's): 73%
Acceptance rate (DNP): 33%
Specialties offered:
administration; nurse
practitioner; nurse practitioner:
adult-gerontology acute care;
nurse practitioner: adult-
gerontology primary care; other
majors; dual majors

Michigan State University

1335 Bogue Street
East Lansing, MI 48823
nursing.msu.edu
Public
Admissions: (517) 353-4827
Email: nurse@hc.msu.edu
Financial aid: (517) 353-5940
Application deadline: N/A
Degrees offered: master's, Ph.D.,
DNP
In-state tuition: full time: $699/
credit hour, part time: $699/
credit hour (master's); full time:
$699/credit hour, part time:
$699/credit hour (Ph.D.); full
time: $699/credit hour, part
time: $699/credit hour (DNP)
Out-of-state tuition: full time:
$1,373/credit hour (master's);

full time: $1,373/credit hour
(Ph.D.); full time: $1,373/credit
hour (DNP)
Room/board/expenses: $10,696
(master's); $10,696 (Ph.D.);
$10,696 (DNP)
Full-time enrollment: 72
(master's); 14 (Ph.D.); 11 (DNP)
men: 16%; women: 84%;
minorities: 8%; international: 5%
Part-time enrollment: 102
(master's); N/A (Ph.D.); 5 (DNP)
men: 10%; women: 90%;
minorities: 11%; international:
0%
Acceptance rate (master's): 43%
Acceptance rate (Ph.D.): 50%
Acceptance rate (DNP): 100%
Specialties offered: clinical
nurse specialist; nurse
anesthesia; nurse practitioner;
nurse practitioner: adult-
gerontology primary care; nurse
practitioner: family

Oakland University
428 O'Dowd Hall
Rochester, MI 48309-4401
www.oakland.edu/nursing
Public
Admissions: (248) 370-2558
Email: gradmail@oakland.edu
Financial aid: (248) 370-2550
Application deadline: N/A
Degrees offered: master's, DNP
In-state tuition: full time: $16,338,
part time: $681/credit hour
(master's); full time: $16,338,
part time: $681/credit hour
(DNP)
Out-of-state tuition: full time:
$24,648 (master's); full time:
$24,648 (DNP)
Room/board/expenses: $9,620
(master's); $9,620 (DNP)
Full-time enrollment: 143
(master's); 4 (DNP)
men: 18%; women: 82%;
minorities: 5%; international: 1%
Part-time enrollment: 29
(master's); 21 (DNP)
men: 12%; women: 88%;
minorities: 18%; international:
0%
Acceptance rate (master's): 20%
Acceptance rate (DNP): 60%
Specialties offered: nurse
anesthesia; nurse practitioner;
nurse practitioner: adult-
gerontology acute care; nurse
practitioner: adult-gerontology
primary care; nurse practitioner:
adult; nurse practitioner: family;
nurse practitioner: pediatric
primary care

Saginaw Valley State University
7400 Bay Road
University Center, MI 48710
www.svsu.edu/nursing/
Public
Admissions: (989) 964-6096
Email: gradadm@svsu.edu
Financial aid: (989) 964-4103
Application deadline: N/A
Degrees offered: master's, DNP
In-state tuition: full time: $536/
credit hour, part time: $536/
credit hour (master's); full time:
$590/credit hour, part time:
$590/credit hour (DNP)

Out-of-state tuition: full time:
$1,022/credit hour (master's);
full time: $1,081/credit hour
(DNP)
Room/board/expenses: N/A
Full-time enrollment: 10
(master's); N/A (DNP)
men: 20%; women: 80%;
minorities: 10%; international:
10%
Part-time enrollment: 54
(master's); 44 (DNP)
men: 13%; women: 87%;
minorities: 12%; international:
0%
Acceptance rate (master's): 95%
Acceptance rate (DNP): 100%
Specialties offered:
administration; clinical nurse
leader; education; nurse
practitioner: family

Spring Arbor University[1]
106 E. Main Street
Spring Arbor, MI 49283
Private
Admissions: N/A
Financial aid: N/A
Tuition: N/A
Room/board/expenses: N/A
Enrollment: N/A

University of Detroit Mercy
4001 W. McNichols Road
Detroit, MI 48221-3038
healthprofessions.udmercy.edu/
programs/nursing/index.htm
Private
Admissions: (313) 993-1245
Email: admissions@udmercy.edu
Financial aid: (313) 993-3350
Application deadline: N/A
Degrees offered: master's, DNP
Tuition: full time: $955/credit
hour, part time: $955/credit
hour (master's); full time: $955/
credit hour, part time: $955/
credit hour (DNP)
Room/board/expenses: N/A
Full-time enrollment: 76
(master's); N/A (DNP)
men: 24%; women: 76%;
minorities: 18%; international:
4%
Part-time enrollment: 130
(master's); 14 (DNP)
men: 10%; women: 90%;
minorities: 28%; international:
3%
Acceptance rate (master's): 99%
Acceptance rate (DNP): 100%
Specialties offered: clinical nurse
leader; clinical nurse specialist;
education; health management
& policy health care systems;
nurse anesthesia; nurse
practitioner; nurse practitioner:
family

University of Michigan-Ann Arbor
400 N. Ingalls
Ann Arbor, MI 48109-0482
nursing.umich.edu/
Public
Admissions: (734) 763-5237
Email:
umsn-mastersadmissions@
med.umich.edu
Financial aid: (734) 764-3972
Application deadline: 1/11

Degrees offered: master's, Ph.D.,
DNP
In-state tuition: full time: $21,390,
part time: $1,189/credit hour
(master's); full time: $21,390,
part time: $1,189/credit hour
(Ph.D.); full time: $21,390, part
time: $1,189/credit hour (DNP)
Out-of-state tuition: full time:
$43,982 (master's); full time:
$43,982 (Ph.D.); full time:
$43,982 (DNP)
Room/board/expenses: $14,676
(master's); $14,676 (Ph.D.);
$14,676 (DNP)
Full-time enrollment: 192
(master's); 37 (Ph.D.); 35 (DNP)
men: 14%; women: 86%;
minorities: 17%; international:
5%
Part-time enrollment: 121
(master's); 1 (Ph.D.); 19 (DNP)
men: 10%; women: 90%;
minorities: 15%; international:
1%
Acceptance rate (master's): 50%
Acceptance rate (Ph.D.): 36%
Acceptance rate (DNP): 56%
Specialties offered:
administration; clinical nurse
specialist; health management
& policy health care systems;
informatics; nurse-midwifery;
nurse practitioner; nurse
practitioner: adult-gerontology
acute care; nurse practitioner:
adult-gerontology primary
care; nurse practitioner: adult;
nurse practitioner: family; nurse
practitioner: pediatric primary
care; dual majors

University of Michigan-Flint
303 E. Kearsley Street
Flint, MI 48502-1950
www.umflint.edu/nursing
Public
Admissions: (810) 762-3171
Email: graduate@umflint.edu
Financial aid: (810) 762-3444
Application deadline: 8/1
Degrees offered: master's, DNP
In-state tuition: full time: $9,959,
part time: $553/credit hour
(master's); full time: $9,959, part
time: $553/credit hour (DNP)
Out-of-state tuition: full time:
$14,922 (master's); full time:
$14,922 (DNP)
Room/board/expenses: $8,706
(master's); $8,706 (DNP)
Full-time enrollment: 47
(master's); 118 (DNP)
men: 11%; women: 89%;
minorities: 25%; international:
1%
Part-time enrollment: 2
(master's); 96 (DNP)
men: 17%; women: 83%;
minorities: 23%; international:
0%
Acceptance rate (DNP): 84%
Specialties offered: nurse
anesthesia; nurse practitioner;
nurse practitioner: adult-
gerontology acute care;
nurse practitioner: adult-
gerontology primary care;
nurse practitioner: family; nurse
practitioner: psychiatric-mental
health, across the lifespan

Wayne State University
5557 Cass Avenue
Detroit, MI 48202
nursing.wayne.edu/
Public
Admissions: (313) 577-8141
Email:
gradadmissions@wayne.edu
Financial aid: (313) 577-2100
Application deadline: 1/31
Degrees offered: master's, Ph.D.,
DNP
In-state tuition: full time: $838/
credit hour, part time: $838/
credit hour (master's); full time:
$838/credit hour, part time:
$838/credit hour (Ph.D.); full
time: $838/credit hour, part
time: $838/credit hour (DNP)
Out-of-state tuition: full time:
$1,555/credit hour (master's);
full time: $1,555/credit hour
(Ph.D.); full time: $1,555/credit
hour (DNP)
Room/board/expenses: $9,134
(master's); $9,134 (Ph.D.);
$9,134 (DNP)
Full-time enrollment: 62
(master's); 24 (Ph.D.); 51 (DNP)
men: 4%; women: 96%;
minorities: 26%; international:
11%
Part-time enrollment: 90
(master's); 5 (Ph.D.); 51 (DNP)
men: 15%; women: 85%;
minorities: 25%; international:
3%
Acceptance rate (master's): 39%
Acceptance rate (Ph.D.): 35%
Acceptance rate (DNP): 44%
Specialties offered: community
health/public health; education;
nurse-midwifery; neonatal;
nurse practitioner; nurse
practitioner: adult-gerontology
acute care; nurse practitioner:
adult-gerontology primary care;
nurse practitioner: family; nurse
practitioner: pediatric primary
care; nurse practitioner:
psychiatric-mental health,
across the lifespan; research;
other majors

Western Michigan University[1]
1903 West Michigan Avenue
Kalamazoo, MI 49008-5200
wmich.edu/nursing
Public
Admissions: (269) 387-2000
Email: ask-wmu@wmich.edu
Financial aid: (269) 387-6000
Tuition: N/A
Room/board/expenses: N/A
Enrollment: N/A

MINNESOTA

Augsburg College[1]
2211 Riverside Avenue S
Minneapolis, MN 55454
Private
Admissions: N/A
Financial aid: N/A
Tuition: N/A
Room/board/expenses: N/A
Enrollment: N/A

Bethel University[1]
3900 Bethel Drive
St. Paul, MN 55112
Private
Admissions: N/A
Financial aid: N/A
Tuition: N/A
Room/board/expenses: N/A
Enrollment: N/A

Capella University[1]
225 S 6th Street, 9th Floor
Minneapolis, MN 55402
Private
Admissions: N/A
Financial aid: N/A
Tuition: N/A
Room/board/expenses: N/A
Enrollment: N/A

College of St. Scholastica
1200 Kenwood Avenue
Duluth, MN 55811
www.css.edu/academics/
school-of-nursing.html
Private
Admissions: (218) 733-2240
Email: geoadmin@css.edu
Financial aid: (218) 723-6725
Application deadline: 12/15
Degrees offered: DNP
Tuition: full time: $810/credit
hour, part time: $810/credit hour
Room/board/expenses: N/A
Full-time enrollment: 1 153
men: 22%; women: 78%;
minorities: 16%; international:
0%
Part-time enrollment: 3 4
men: 29%; women: 71%;
minorities: 14%; international:
0%
Acceptance rate (DNP): 82%
Specialties offered: informatics;
nurse practitioner; nurse
practitioner: adult-gerontology
primary care; nurse
practitioner: family; nurse
practitioner: psychiatric-mental
health, across the lifespan

Metropolitan State University[1]
730 Hennepin Avenue
Minneapolis, MN 55403-1897
Public
Admissions: N/A
Financial aid: N/A
Tuition: N/A
Room/board/expenses: N/A
Enrollment: N/A

Minnesota State University-Mankato[1]
College of Graduate Studies and
Research
Mankato, MN 56001
ahn.mnsu.edu/nursing/
Public
Admissions: N/A
Financial aid: N/A
Tuition: N/A
Room/board/expenses: N/A
Enrollment: N/A

Minnesota State University-Moorhead

1104 Seventh Avenue South
Moorhead, MN 56563
www.mnstate.edu/graduate-nursing/
Public
Admissions: (218) 477-2134
Email: graduate@mnstate.edu
Financial aid: (218) 477-2251
Application deadline: N/A
Degrees offered: master's
In-state tuition: full time: $485/credit hour, part time: $485/credit hour
Out-of-state tuition: full time: $915/credit hour
Room/board/expenses: N/A
Full-time enrollment: 4
men: N/A; women: N/A; minorities: N/A; international: N/A
Part-time enrollment: 45
men: N/A; women: N/A; minorities: N/A; international: N/A
Acceptance rate (master's): 100%
Specialties offered: administration; education

St. Catherine University

2004 Randolph Avenue
Mail #F-22
St. Paul, MN 55105-1794
www2.stkate.edu/nursing/home
Private
Admissions: (651) 690-6933
Email: graduate_study@stkate.edu
Financial aid: (651) 690-6607
Application deadline: N/A
Degrees offered: master's, DNP
Tuition: full time: $782/credit hour, part time: $782/credit hour (master's); full time: $978/credit hour, part time: $978/credit hour (DNP)
Room/board/expenses: N/A
Full-time enrollment: 182 (master's); 10 (DNP)
men: 9%; women: 91%; minorities: 19%; international: 1%
Part-time enrollment: 9 (master's); 19 (DNP)
men: 11%; women: 89%; minorities: 11%; international: 0%
Acceptance rate (master's): 95%
Acceptance rate (DNP): 100%
Specialties offered: education; generalist; nurse practitioner; nurse practitioner: adult-gerontology primary care; nurse practitioner: pediatric primary care

University of Minnesota-Twin Cities

308 Harvard Street SE
Minneapolis, MN 55455
www.nursing.umn.edu/
Public
Admissions: (612) 625-7980
Email: sonstudentinfo@umn.edu
Financial aid: (612) 624-4138
Application deadline: 3/1
Degrees offered: Ph.D., DNP
In-state tuition: full time: $17,334, part time: $1,353/credit hour (Ph.D.); full time: $17,527, part time: $974/credit hour (DNP)

Out-of-state tuition: full time: $26,214 (Ph.D.); full time: $17,697 (DNP)
Room/board/expenses: $12,320 (Ph.D.); $12,320 (DNP)
Full-time enrollment: 30 (Ph.D.); 320 (DNP)
men: 11%; women: 89%; minorities: 21%; international: 1%
Part-time enrollment: 10 (Ph.D.); 34 (DNP)
men: 9%; women: 91%; minorities: 16%; international: 0%
Acceptance rate (Ph.D.): 56%
Acceptance rate (DNP): 66%
Specialties offered: administration; clinical nurse specialist; community health; public health; informatics; nurse anesthesia; nurse-midwifery; nurse practitioner; nurse practitioner: adult-gerontology primary care; nurse practitioner: family; nurse practitioner: pediatric primary care; nurse practitioner: psychiatric-mental health, across the lifespan; research; women's health; other majors

Walden University[1]

100 Washington Avenue S
Suite 900
Minneapolis, MN 55401
Private
Admissions: N/A
Financial aid: N/A
Tuition: N/A
Room/board/expenses: N/A
Enrollment: N/A

Winona State University-Rochester[1]

859 30th Avenue SE
Rochester, MN 55904
Public
Admissions: N/A
Financial aid: N/A
Tuition: N/A
Room/board/expenses: N/A
Enrollment: N/A

MISSISSIPPI

Alcorn State University

15 Campus Drive
Natchez, MS 39122-8399
www.alcorn.edu/
Public
Admissions: N/A
Email: ebarnes@alcorn.edu
Financial aid: (601) 877-6190
Application deadline: 12/15
Degrees offered: master's
In-state tuition: full time: $364/credit hour, part time: $364/credit hour
Out-of-state tuition: full time: $364/credit hour
Room/board/expenses: $6,858
Full-time enrollment: 29
men: N/A; women: N/A; minorities: 83%; international: 0%
Part-time enrollment: 1
men: N/A; women: N/A; minorities: 0%; international: 0%
Acceptance rate (master's): 74%
Specialties offered: education; nurse practitioner: family

Delta State University

PO Box 3343
1003 West Sunflower Road
Cleveland, MS 38733
www.deltastate.edu/school-of-nursing/
Public
Admissions: (662) 846-4700
Email: grad-info@deltastate.edu
Financial aid: (662) 846-4670
Application deadline: 2/1
Degrees offered: master's, DNP
In-state tuition: full time: $6,298, part time: $350/credit hour (master's); full time: $6,298, part time: $350/credit hour (DNP)
Out-of-state tuition: full time: $6,298 (master's); full time: $6,298 (DNP)
Room/board/expenses: N/A
Full-time enrollment: 20 (master's); 14 (DNP)
men: 9%; women: 91%; minorities: 24%; international: 0%
Part-time enrollment: 3 (master's); 2 (DNP)
men: 0%; women: 100%; minorities: 40%; international: 0%
Acceptance rate (master's): 72%
Acceptance rate (DNP): 100%
Specialties offered: nurse practitioner: family

Mississippi University for Women

1100 College Street
MUW-910
Columbus, MS 39701-5800
www.muw.edu/nslp
Public
Admissions: (662) 329-7142
Financial aid: (662) 329-7145
Application deadline: 2/1
Degrees offered: master's, DNP
In-state tuition: full time: N/A, part time: N/A (master's); full time: N/A, part time: N/A (DNP)
Out-of-state tuition: full time: N/A (master's); full time: N/A (DNP)
Room/board/expenses: N/A
Full-time enrollment: 30 (master's); 12 (DNP)
men: 5%; women: 95%; minorities: 10%; international: 0%
Part-time enrollment: 1 (master's); 1 (DNP)
men: 0%; women: 100%; minorities: 0%; international: 0%
Acceptance rate (master's): 36%
Acceptance rate (DNP): 100%
Specialties offered: nurse practitioner; nurse practitioner: family

University of Mississippi Medical Center[1]

2500 N. State Street
Jackson, MS 39216-4505
Public
Admissions: N/A
Financial aid: N/A
Tuition: N/A
Room/board/expenses: N/A
Enrollment: N/A

University of Southern Mississippi

118 College Drive
PO Box 5095
Hattiesburg, MS 39406-5095
www.usm.edu/nursing
Public
Admissions: (601) 266-4369
Email: Karen.Coats@usm.edu
Financial aid: (601) 266-4813
Application deadline: 3/1
Degrees offered: master's, Ph.D., DNP
In-state tuition: full time: $11,488, part time: $7,560 (master's); full time: $11,488, part time: $7,560 (Ph.D.); full time: $11,488, part time: $7,560 (DNP)
Out-of-state tuition: full time: $24,793 (master's); full time: $24,793 (Ph.D.); full time: $24,793 (DNP)
Room/board/expenses: $8,719 (master's); $8,719 (Ph.D.); $8,719 (DNP)
Full-time enrollment: 100 (master's); 12 (Ph.D.); 68 (DNP)
men: 28%; women: 72%; minorities: 22%; international: 0%
Part-time enrollment: 51 (master's); 15 (Ph.D.); 2 (DNP)
men: 10%; women: 90%; minorities: 35%; international: 0%
Acceptance rate (master's): 75%
Acceptance rate (Ph.D.): 100%
Acceptance rate (DNP): 100%
Specialties offered: nurse anesthesia; nurse practitioner; nurse practitioner: family; nurse practitioner: psychiatric-mental health, across the lifespan; research; other majors

William Carey University

498 Tuscan Avenue
Hattiesburg, MS 39401
www.wmcarey.edu/schools/school-nursing
Private
Admissions: (601) 318-6103
Email: admissions@wmcarey.edu
Financial aid: (601) 318-6153
Application deadline: N/A
Degrees offered: master's, Ph.D.
Tuition: full time: $370/credit hour, part time: $370/credit hour (master's); full time: $500/credit hour, part time: $500/credit hour
Room/board/expenses: $4,200 (master's); $4,200
Full-time enrollment: 47 (master's); 38
men: 6%; women: 94%; minorities: 57%; international: 0%
Part-time enrollment: 23 (master's); 34
men: 11%; women: 89%; minorities: 37%; international: 0%
Acceptance rate (master's): 89%
Acceptance rate (Ph.D.): 89%
Specialties offered: education; generalist; dual majors

MISSOURI

Central Methodist University[1]

411 Central Methodist Square
Fayette, MO 65248
Private
Admissions: N/A
Financial aid: N/A
Tuition: N/A
Room/board/expenses: N/A
Enrollment: N/A

Cox College[1]

1423 N. Jefferson Avenue
Springfield, MO 65802
Private
Admissions: N/A
Financial aid: N/A
Tuition: N/A
Room/board/expenses: N/A
Enrollment: N/A

Goldfarb School of Nursing at Barnes-Jewish College[1]

4483 Duncan Avenue
St. Louis, MO 63110
Private
Admissions: N/A
Financial aid: N/A
Tuition: N/A
Room/board/expenses: N/A
Enrollment: N/A

Graceland University

1401 W. Truman Road
Independence, MO 64050-3434
www.graceland.edu/admissions/
Private
Admissions: N/A
Email: admissions@graceland.edu
Financial aid: (641) 784-5117
Application deadline: N/A
Degrees offered: master's, DNP
Tuition: full time: $735/credit hour, part time: $735/credit hour (master's); full time: $825/credit hour, part time: $825/credit hour (DNP)
Room/board/expenses: N/A
Full-time enrollment: 250 (master's); 12 (DNP)
men: 11%; women: 89%; minorities: 15%; international: 1%
Part-time enrollment: 269 (master's); 14 (DNP)
men: 14%; women: 86%; minorities: 12%; international: 0%
Acceptance rate (master's): 89%
Acceptance rate (DNP): 100%
Specialties offered: education; nurse practitioner: adult-gerontology acute care; nurse practitioner: family

Maryville University of St. Louis

650 Maryville University Drive
St. Louis, MO 63141
www.maryville.edu/hp/nursing/
Private
Admissions: (314) 529-9350
Email: admissions@maryville.edu
Financial aid: (314) 529-9360
Application deadline: N/A
Degrees offered: master's

DIRECTORY

Tuition: full time: $781/credit hour, part time: N/A
Room/board/expenses: N/A
Full-time enrollment: 8
men: 0%; women: 100%; minorities: 25%; international: 25%
Part-time enrollment: 115
men: 10%; women: 90%; minorities: 11%; international: 1%
Acceptance rate (master's): 62%
Specialties offered: nurse practitioner; nurse practitioner: adult-gerontology acute care; nurse practitioner: adult-gerontology primary care; nurse practitioner: adult; nurse practitioner: family; nurse practitioner: pediatric primary care

Missouri State University

Professional Building, Suite 300
Springfield, MO 65897
www.missouristate.edu/nursing/
Public
Admissions: (417) 836-5310
Email: GraduateAdmissions@missouristate.edu
Financial aid: (417) 836-5262
Application deadline: 12/1
Degrees offered: master's, DNP
In-state tuition: full time: $315/credit hour, part time: $315/credit hour (master's); full time: $315/credit hour, part time: $315/credit hour (DNP)
Out-of-state tuition: full time: $315/credit hour (master's); full time: $315/credit hour (DNP)
Room/board/expenses: N/A
Full-time enrollment: N/A (master's); 34 (DNP)
men: 12%; women: 88%; minorities: 0%; international: 0%
Part-time enrollment: 15 (master's); 18 (DNP)
men: 3%; women: 97%; minorities: 21%; international: 0%
Acceptance rate (master's): 100%
Acceptance rate (DNP): 76%
Specialties offered: education; nurse practitioner: family

Missouri Western State University[1]

4525 Downs Drive
Murphy Hall, Room 309
St. Joseph, MO 64507
Public
Admissions: N/A
Financial aid: N/A
Tuition: N/A
Room/board/expenses: N/A
Enrollment: N/A

Research College of Nursing[1]

2525 E. Meyer Boulevard
Kansas City, MO 64132
Private
Admissions: N/A
Financial aid: N/A
Tuition: N/A
Room/board/expenses: N/A
Enrollment: N/A

Saint Luke's College of Health Sciences[1]

624 Westport Road
Kansas City, MO 64111
Admissions: N/A
Financial aid: N/A
Tuition: N/A
Room/board/expenses: N/A
Enrollment: N/A

Southeast Missouri State University[1]

1 University Plaza
Cape Girardeau, MO 63701
semo.edu/nursing
Public
Admissions: (573) 651-2590
Email: admissions@semo.edu
Financial aid: (573) 651-2253
Tuition: N/A
Room/board/expenses: N/A
Enrollment: N/A

Southwest Baptist University[1]

1600 University Avenue
Bolivar, MO 65613
Private
Admissions: N/A
Financial aid: N/A
Tuition: N/A
Room/board/expenses: N/A
Enrollment: N/A

St. Louis University

3525 Caroline Mall
St. Louis, MO 63104-1099
nursing.slu.edu
Private
Admissions: (314) 977-2500
Email: admission@slu.edu
Financial aid: (314) 977-2350
Application deadline: N/A
Degrees offered: master's, Ph.D., DNP
Tuition: full time: $1,105/credit hour, part time: $1,105/credit hour (master's); full time: $1,105/credit hour, part time: $1,105/credit hour (Ph.D.); full time: $1,105/credit hour, part time: $1,105/credit hour (DNP)
Room/board/expenses: N/A
Full-time enrollment: 217 (master's); 39 (Ph.D.); 31 (DNP)
men: 17%; women: 83%; minorities: 19%; international: 8%
Part-time enrollment: 201 (master's); 4 (Ph.D.); 18 (DNP)
men: 13%; women: 87%; minorities: 20%; international: 1%
Acceptance rate (master's): 73%
Acceptance rate (Ph.D.): 87%
Acceptance rate (DNP): 81%
Specialties offered: clinical nurse leader; nurse practitioner; nurse practitioner: adult-gerontology acute care; nurse practitioner: adult-gerontology primary care; nurse practitioner: family; nurse practitioner: pediatric primary care; nurse practitioner: psychiatric-mental health, across the lifespan

University of Central Missouri

UHC 106A
Warrensburg, MO 64093
www.ucmo.edu/nursing
Public
Admissions: (660) 543-4897
Email: GradInfo@ucmo.edu
Financial aid: (660) 543-8266
Application deadline: N/A
Degrees offered: master's
In-state tuition: full time: $278/credit hour, part time: $278/credit hour
Out-of-state tuition: full time: $557/credit hour
Full-time enrollment:
men: N/A; women: N/A; minorities: N/A; international: N/A
Part-time enrollment: 163
men: 7%; women: 93%; minorities: 8%; international: 0%
Acceptance rate (master's): 72%
Specialties offered: education; nurse practitioner; nurse practitioner: family

University of Missouri

S235 School of Nursing
Columbia, MO 65211
nursing.missouri.edu
Public
Admissions: (573) 882-0277
Email: nursing@missouri.edu
Financial aid: (573) 882-7506
Application deadline: 3/1
Degrees offered: master's, Ph.D., DNP
In-state tuition: full time: $422/credit hour, part time: $422/credit hour (master's); full time: $422/credit hour, part time: $422/credit hour (Ph.D.); full time: $422/credit hour, part time: $422/credit hour (DNP)
Out-of-state tuition: full time: $422/credit hour (master's); full time: $422/credit hour (Ph.D.); full time: $422/credit hour (DNP)
Room/board/expenses: N/A
Full-time enrollment: 2 (master's); 36 (Ph.D.); 32 (DNP)
men: 7%; women: 93%; minorities: 16%; international: 9%
Part-time enrollment: 35 (master's); 11 (Ph.D.); 172 (DNP)
men: 6%; women: 94%; minorities: 11%; international: 2%
Acceptance rate (master's): 100%
Acceptance rate (Ph.D.): 60%
Acceptance rate (DNP): 84%
Specialties offered: administration; clinical nurse specialist; education; generalist; nurse practitioner; nurse practitioner: family; nurse practitioner: pediatric primary care; nurse practitioner: psychiatric-mental health, across the lifespan; research; other majors; combined nurse practitioner/clinical nurse specialist; dual majors

University of Missouri-Kansas City

2464 Charlotte
Kansas City, MO 64108
www.umkc.edu/nursing
Public
Admissions: (816) 235-1111
Email: admit@umkc.edu
Financial aid: (816) 235-1154
Application deadline: 12/15
Degrees offered: master's, Ph.D., DNP
In-state tuition: full time: $450/credit hour, part time: $450/credit hour (master's); full time: $450/credit hour, part time: $450/credit hour (Ph.D.); full time: $450/credit hour, part time: $450/credit hour (DNP)
Out-of-state tuition: full time: $450/credit hour (master's); full time: $450/credit hour (Ph.D.); full time: $450/credit hour (DNP)
Room/board/expenses: N/A
Full-time enrollment: 23 (master's); 3 (Ph.D.); 65 (DNP)
men: 18%; women: 82%; minorities: 15%; international: 0%
Part-time enrollment: 155 (master's); 43 (Ph.D.); 106 (DNP)
men: 8%; women: 92%; minorities: 18%; international: 0%
Acceptance rate (master's): 84%
Acceptance rate (Ph.D.): 82%
Acceptance rate (DNP): 88%
Specialties offered: education; nurse anesthesia; neonatal; nurse practitioner; nurse practitioner: adult-gerontology primary care; nurse practitioner: family; nurse practitioner: pediatric primary care; nurse practitioner: psychiatric-mental health, across the lifespan; research; women's health

University of Missouri-St. Louis

One University Boulevard
St. Louis, MO 63121
www.umsl.edu/divisions/nursing/
Public
Admissions: (314) 516-5458
Email: gradadm@umsl.edu
Financial aid: (314) 516-5526
Application deadline: 1/15
Degrees offered: Ph.D., DNP
In-state tuition: full time: $445/credit hour, part time: $445/credit hour (Ph.D.); full time: $445/credit hour, part time: $445/credit hour (DNP)
Out-of-state tuition: full time: $1,091/credit hour (Ph.D.); full time: $1,091/credit hour (DNP)
Room/board/expenses: $11,396 (Ph.D.); $11,396 (DNP)
Full-time enrollment: 4 (Ph.D.); 25 (DNP)
men: 3%; women: 97%; minorities: 7%; international: 0%
Part-time enrollment: 107 22 (Ph.D.); 67 (DNP)
men: 2%; women: 98%; minorities: 17%; international: 1%
Acceptance rate (Ph.D.): 75%
Acceptance rate (DNP): 93%
Specialties offered: community health/public health; education; nurse practitioner; nurse practitioner: adult-gerontology primary care; nurse practitioner: family; nurse practitioner: pediatric primary care; nurse practitioner: psychiatric-mental health, across the lifespan; research; women's health; other majors

Webster University

470 E. Lockwood Avenue
Saint Louis, MO 63119
www.webster.edu/arts-and-sciences/academics/nursing/
Private
Admissions: (800) 753-6765
Email: admit@webster.edu
Financial aid: (800) 983-4623
Application deadline: N/A
Degrees offered: master's
Tuition: full time: $705/credit hour, part time: $705/credit hour
Room/board/expenses: $11,190
Full-time enrollment: 1
men: N/A; women: 100%; minorities: 0%; international: 0%
Part-time enrollment: 131
men: 4%; women: 96%; minorities: 17%; international: 0%
Acceptance rate (master's): 84%
Specialties offered: education; other majors

MONTANA

Montana State University

PO Box 173560
Bozeman, MT 59717-3560
www.montana.edu/nursing
Public
Admissions: (406) 994-2452
Email: admissions@montana.edu
Financial aid: (406) 994-2845
Application deadline: 2/15
Degrees offered: master's, DNP
In-state tuition: full time: $267/credit hour, part time: $267/credit hour (master's); full time: $267/credit hour, part time: $267/credit hour (DNP)
Out-of-state tuition: full time: $934/credit hour (master's); full time: $934/credit hour (DNP)
Room/board/expenses: N/A
Full-time enrollment: N/A (master's); 44 (DNP)
men: 5%; women: 95%; minorities: 9%; international: 0%
Part-time enrollment: 15 (master's); 41 (DNP)
men: 14%; women: 86%; minorities: 9%; international: 0%
Acceptance rate (master's): 100%
Acceptance rate (DNP): 39%
Specialties offered: clinical nurse leader; education; nurse practitioner; nurse practitioner: family; nurse practitioner: psychiatric-mental health, across the lifespan

NEBRASKA

Bryan College of Health Sciences[1]

5035 Everett Street
Lincoln, NE 68506
Private
Admissions: N/A
Financial aid: N/A
Tuition: N/A
Room/board/expenses: N/A
Enrollment: N/A

Clarkson College
101 S. 42nd Street
Omaha, NE 68131-2715
www.clarksoncollege.edu/about/
Private
Admissions: (402) 552-2796
Email: Admissions@
clarksoncollege.edu
Financial aid: (402) 552-3470
Application deadline: 11/1
Degrees offered: master's, DNP
Tuition: full time: $556/credit
hour, part time: $556/credit
hour (master's); full time: $783/
credit hour, part time: $783/
credit hour (DNP)
Room/board/expenses: N/A
Full-time enrollment: 244
(master's); N/A (DNP)
men: 14%; women: 86%;
minorities: 7%; international: 0%
Part-time enrollment: 284
(master's); 4 (DNP)
men: 14%; women: 86%;
minorities: 9%; international: 0%
Acceptance rate (master's): 44%
Acceptance rate (DNP): 25%
Specialties offered:
administration; education; nurse
anesthesia; nurse practitioner;
nurse practitioner: adult-
gerontology primary care; nurse
practitioner: family

College of St. Mary[1]
7000 Mercy Road
Omaha, NE 68106
Private
Admissions: N/A
Financial aid: N/A
Tuition: N/A
Room/board/expenses: N/A
Enrollment: N/A

Creighton University
2500 California Plaza
Omaha, NE 68178
nursing.creighton.edu/
Private
Admissions: (402) 280-2703
Email: nursing@creighton.edu
Financial aid: (402) 280-2731
Application deadline: N/A
Degrees offered: master's, DNP
Tuition: full time: $820/credit
hour, part time: $820/credit
hour (master's); full time: $820/
credit hour, part time: $820/
credit hour (DNP)
Room/board/expenses: N/A
Full-time enrollment: 7 (master's);
117 (DNP)
men: 10%; women: 90%;
minorities: 12%; international:
1%
Part-time enrollment: 44
(master's); 198 (DNP)
men: 5%; women: 95%;
minorities: 10%; international:
0%
Acceptance rate (master's): 63%
Acceptance rate (DNP): 76%
Specialties offered:
administration; clinical nurse
leader; neonatal; nurse
practitioner: adult-gerontology
acute care; nurse practitioner:
adult-gerontology primary care;
nurse practitioner: family; nurse
practitioner: psychiatric-mental
health, across the lifespan;
other majors

Nebraska Methodist College
720 N. 87th Street
Omaha, NE 68114
www.methodistcollege.edu/
Private
Admissions: (402) 354-7202
Email: admissions@
methodistcollege.edu
Financial aid: (402) 354-7225
Application deadline: N/A
Degrees offered: master's, DNP
Tuition: full time: $719/credit
hour, part time: $719/credit hour
(master's); full time: $793/credit
hour, part time: $793/credit
hour (DNP)
Room/board/expenses: $7,464
(master's); $7,464 (DNP)
Full-time enrollment: 88
(master's); 41 (DNP)
men: 4%; women: 96%;
minorities: 13%; international:
1%
Part-time enrollment: 22
(master's); 5 (DNP)
men: 4%; women: 96%;
minorities: 7%; international: 0%
Acceptance rate (master's): 61%
Acceptance rate (DNP): 28%
Specialties offered:
administration; clinical
nurse specialist; education;
informatics; nurse practitioner;
nurse practitioner: family

Nebraska Wesleyan University
5000 Saint Paul Avenue
Lincoln, NE 68504
Private
Admissions: N/A
Financial aid: (402) 465-2167
Application deadline: N/A
Degrees offered: master's
Tuition: full time: $400/credit
hour, part time: $400/credit
hour
Room/board/expenses: $9,600
Full-time enrollment: 77
men: 5%; women: 95%;
minorities: N/A; international:
N/A
Part-time enrollment: 12
men: 33%; women: 67%;
minorities: N/A; international:
N/A
Acceptance rate (master's): 100%
Specialties offered:
administration; education; other
majors; dual majors

University of Nebraska Medical Center
985330 Nebraska Medical
Center
Omaha, NE 68198-5330
www.unmc.edu/nursing/
Public
Admissions: (402) 559-6639
Email: rolee.kelly@unmc.edu
Financial aid: (402) 559-4911
Application deadline: 2/1
Degrees offered: master's, Ph.D.,
DNP
In-state tuition: full time: $459/
credit hour, part time: $459/
credit hour (master's); full time:
$459/credit hour, part time:
$459/credit hour (Ph.D.); full
time: $459/credit hour, part
time: $459/credit hour (DNP)

Out-of-state tuition: full time:
$957/credit hour (master's); full
time: $957/credit hour (Ph.D.);
full time: $957/credit hour (DNP)
Room/board/expenses: N/A
Full-time enrollment: 138
(master's); 15 (Ph.D.); 87 (DNP)
men: 8%; women: 92%;
minorities: 14%; international:
1%
Part-time enrollment: 128
(master's); 7 (Ph.D.); 27 (DNP)
men: 6%; women: 94%;
minorities: 10%; international:
0%
Acceptance rate (master's): 59%
Acceptance rate (Ph.D.): 83%
Acceptance rate (DNP): 77%
Specialties offered:
administration; clinical nurse
specialist; education; nurse
practitioner; nurse practitioner:
adult-gerontology acute care;
nurse practitioner: adult-
gerontology primary care;
nurse practitioner: family; nurse
practitioner: pediatric primary
care; nurse practitioner:
psychiatric-mental health,
across the lifespan; research;
women's health

NEVADA

University of Nevada-Las Vegas[1]
4505 Maryland Parkway
Las Vegas, NV 89154-3018
Public
Admissions: N/A
Financial aid: N/A
Tuition: N/A
Room/board/expenses: N/A
Enrollment: N/A

University of Nevada-Reno
1664 North Virginia Street
Reno, NV 89557-0042
Public
Admissions: N/A
Financial aid: N/A
Application deadline: N/A
Degrees offered: master's, DNP
In-state tuition: full time: $550/
credit hour, part time: $550/
credit hour (master's); full time:
$550/credit hour, part time:
$550/credit hour (DNP)
Out-of-state tuition: full time:
$36,000 (master's); full time:
$26,000 (DNP)
Room/board/expenses: N/A
Full-time enrollment: 24
(master's); 8 (DNP)
men: 28%; women: 72%;
minorities: 38%; international:
0%
Part-time enrollment: 69
(master's); 26 (DNP)
men: 12%; women: 88%;
minorities: 17%; international:
0%
Acceptance rate (master's): 67%
Acceptance rate (DNP): 78%
Specialties offered: clinical
nurse leader; education; nurse
practitioner; nurse practitioner:
adult-gerontology acute care;
nurse practitioner: family; nurse
practitioner: psychiatric-mental
health, across the lifespan; dual
majors

NEW HAMPSHIRE

Franklin Pierce University[1]
40 University Drive
Rindge, NH 03461
Private
Admissions: N/A
Financial aid: N/A
Tuition: N/A
Room/board/expenses: N/A
Enrollment: N/A

Rivier University
420 S. Main Street
Nashua, NH 03060
www.rivier.edu/academics.
aspx?menu=76&id=521
Private
Admissions: (603) 897-8507
Email: admissions@rivier.edu
Financial aid: (603) 897-8510
Application deadline: N/A
Degrees offered: master's, DNP
Tuition: full time: N/A, part time:
N/A (master's); full time: N/A,
part time: N/A (DNP)
Room/board/expenses: N/A
Full-time enrollment: 8 (master's);
N/A (DNP)
men: 13%; women: 88%;
minorities: 25%; international:
0%
Part-time enrollment: 322
(master's); N/A (DNP)
men: 7%; women: 93%;
minorities: 8%; international: 0%
Acceptance rate (master's): 90%
Specialties offered: community
health/public health; education;
nurse practitioner; nurse
practitioner: adult-gerontology
primary care; nurse
practitioner: family; nurse
practitioner: psychiatric-mental
health, across the lifespan;
other majors

Southern New Hampshire University[1]
2500 North River Road
Manchester, NH 03106
Private
Admissions: N/A
Financial aid: N/A
Tuition: N/A
Room/board/expenses: N/A
Enrollment: N/A

University of New Hampshire[1]
Hewitt Hall
4 Library Way
Durham, NH 03824-3563
Public
Admissions: N/A
Financial aid: N/A
Tuition: N/A
Room/board/expenses: N/A
Enrollment: N/A

NEW JERSEY

College of New Jersey[1]
PO Box 7718
Ewing, NJ 08628-0718
Public
Admissions: N/A
Financial aid: N/A
Tuition: N/A
Room/board/expenses: N/A
Enrollment: N/A

College of St. Elizabeth[1]
2 Convent Road
Morristown, NJ 07960
Private
Admissions: N/A
Financial aid: N/A
Tuition: N/A
Room/board/expenses: N/A
Enrollment: N/A

Fairleigh Dickinson University
1000 River Road
H-DH4-02
Teaneck, NJ 07666
www.fdu.edu/
Private
Admissions: (201) 692-7308
Email: admissions@fdu.edu
Financial aid: (201) 692-2363
Application deadline: 5/1
Degrees offered: master's, DNP
Tuition: full time: $1,256/credit
hour, part time: $1,256/credit
hour (master's); full time: $1,310/
credit hour, part time: $1,310/
credit hour (DNP)
Room/board/expenses: $13,521
(master's); $13,521 (DNP)
Full-time enrollment: 3 (master's);
2 (DNP)
men: 0%; women: 100%;
minorities: 20%; international:
60%
Part-time enrollment: 316
(master's); 72 (DNP)
men: 8%; women: 92%;
minorities: 51%; international:
0%
Acceptance rate (master's): 86%
Acceptance rate (DNP): 100%
Specialties offered: nurse
practitioner: adult-gerontology
primary care; nurse
practitioner: family; nurse
practitioner: psychiatric-mental
health, across the lifespan

Felician University
262 South Main Street
Lodi, NJ 07644
felician.edu/
Private
Admissions: (201) 355-1465
Email: admissions@felician.edu
Financial aid: (201) 559-6036
Application deadline: 8/25
Degrees offered: master's, DNP
Tuition: full time: $1,000/credit
hour, part time: $1,000/credit
hour (master's); full time:
$1,000/credit hour, part time:
$1,000/credit hour (DNP)
Room/board/expenses: $12,380
(master's); $12,380 (DNP)
Full-time enrollment: 1 (master's);
N/A (DNP)
men: 0%; women: 100%;
minorities: 100%; international:
0%
Part-time enrollment: 115
(master's); 13 (DNP)
men: 5%; women: 95%;
minorities: 47%; international:
0%
Acceptance rate (master's): 76%
Acceptance rate (DNP): 83%
Specialties offered:
administration; education;
nurse practitioner: adult-
gerontology primary care; nurse
practitioner: family

Kean University[1]

1000 Morris Avenue
Union, NJ 07083
www.kean.edu/academics/
college-natural-applied-health-
sciences/school-nursing
Public
Admissions: N/A
Financial aid: N/A
Tuition: N/A
Room/board/expenses: N/A
Enrollment: N/A

Monmouth University

400 Cedar Avenue
West Long Branch, NJ 07764
www.monmouth.edu/school-of-
nursing-health/department-of-
nursing.aspx
Private
Admissions: (732) 571-3452
Email: gradadm@monmouth.edu
Financial aid: (732) 571-3463
Application deadline: 7/15
Degrees offered: master's, DNP
Tuition: full time: $1,098/credit
hour, part time: $1,098/credit
hour (master's); full time: $1,098/
credit hour, part time: $1,098/
credit hour (DNP)
Room/board/expenses: N/A
Full-time enrollment: 2 (master's);
N/A (DNP)
men: 0%; women: 100%;
minorities: 0%; international: 0%
Part-time enrollment: 256
(master's); 17 (DNP)
men: 9%; women: 91%;
minorities: 36%; international:
1%
Acceptance rate (master's): 87%
Acceptance rate (DNP): 89%
Specialties offered:
administration; education; nurse
practitioner; nurse practitioner:
adult-gerontology primary care;
nurse practitioner: family; nurse
practitioner: psychiatric-mental
health, across the lifespan;
school nursing

Ramapo College of New Jersey[1]

505 Ramapo Valley Road
Mahwah, NJ 07430
Public
Admissions: N/A
Financial aid: N/A
Tuition: N/A
Room/board/expenses: N/A
Enrollment: N/A

Rowan University

201 Mullica Hill Road
Glassboro, NJ 08028
Admissions: N/A
Financial aid: N/A
Application deadline: N/A
Degrees offered: master's
Room/board/expenses: N/A
Full-time enrollment:
men: N/A; women: N/A;
minorities: N/A; international:
N/A
Part-time enrollment: 165
men: 18%; women: 82%;
minorities: 42%; international:
0%
Acceptance rate (master's): 90%
Specialties offered: clinical nurse
leader; nurse practitioner: adult-
gerontology acute care; nurse
practitioner: family

Rutgers University-Newark

180 University Avenue
Newark, NJ 07102
nursing.rutgers.edu
Public
Admissions: (973) 353-5293
Email:
snRecruiter@sn.rutgers.edu
Financial aid: (973) 972-7030
Application deadline: 4/1
Degrees offered: master's, Ph.D.,
DNP
In-state tuition: full time: $806/
credit hour, part time: $806/
credit hour (master's); full time:
$806/credit hour, part time:
$806/credit hour (Ph.D.); full
time: $806/credit hour, part
time: $806/credit hour (DNP)
Out-of-state tuition: full time:
$1,169/credit hour (master's);
full time: $1,169/credit hour
(Ph.D.); full time: $1,169/credit
hour (DNP)
Room/board/expenses: $11,730
(master's); $11,730 (Ph.D.);
$11,730 (DNP)
Full-time enrollment: 3 (master's);
6 (Ph.D.); 143 (DNP)
men: 15%; women: 85%;
minorities: 49%; international:
1%
Part-time enrollment: 165
(master's); 11 (Ph.D.); 340 (DNP)
men: 14%; women: 86%;
minorities: 54%; international:
1%
Acceptance rate (master's): 78%
Acceptance rate (Ph.D.): 80%
Acceptance rate (DNP): 46%
Specialties offered: clinical
nurse leader; education;
emergency; health management
& policy health care systems;
informatics; nurse anesthesia;
nurse-midwifery; nurse
practitioner; nurse practitioner:
adult-gerontology acute care;
nurse practitioner: adult-
gerontology primary care;
nurse practitioner: adult; nurse
practitioner: family; nurse
practitioner: pediatric primary
care; nurse practitioner:
psychiatric-mental health,
across the lifespan; research;
school nursing; women's health;
other majors

Seton Hall University

400 S. Orange Avenue
South Orange, NJ 07079
www.shu.edu/search.
cfm?q=College%20of%20Nursing
Private
Admissions: (973) 761-9107
Email: thehall@shu.edu
Financial aid: (800) 222-7183
Application deadline: 4/1
Degrees offered: master's, Ph.D.,
DNP
Tuition: full time: $1,171/credit
hour, part time: $1,171/credit
hour (master's); full time: N/A,
part time: N/A (Ph.D.); full time:
N/A, part time: N/A (DNP)
Room/board/expenses: N/A
Full-time enrollment: 39
(master's); N/A (Ph.D.); N/A
(DNP)
men: 15%; women: 85%;
minorities: 10%; international:
0%

Part-time enrollment: 124

(master's); 31 (Ph.D.); 30 (DNP)
men: 16%; women: 84%;
minorities: 30%; international:
0%
Acceptance rate (master's): 78%
Acceptance rate (Ph.D.): 100%
Acceptance rate (DNP): 67%
Specialties offered:
administration; case
management; clinical nurse
leader; nurse practitioner; nurse
practitioner: adult-gerontology
acute care; nurse practitioner:
adult-gerontology primary care;
nurse practitioner: pediatric
primary care; research; school
nursing; dual majors

Stockton University[1]

PO Box 195
Pomona, NJ 08240
Public
Admissions: N/A
Financial aid: N/A
Tuition: N/A
Room/board/expenses: N/A
Enrollment: N/A

St. Peter's University[1]

Hudson Terrace
Englewood Cliffs, NJ 07632
Private
Admissions: N/A
Financial aid: N/A
Tuition: N/A
Room/board/expenses: N/A
Enrollment: N/A

Thomas Edison State College[1]

101 West State Street
Trenton, NJ 08608
Public
Admissions: N/A
Financial aid: N/A
Tuition: N/A
Room/board/expenses: N/A
Enrollment: N/A

William Paterson University of New Jersey

300 Pompton Road
Wayne, NJ 07470
www.wpunj.edu/admissions/
graduate/about-us/index.html
Public
Admissions: (973) 720-3641
Email: graduate@wpunj.edu
Financial aid: (973) 720-3945
Application deadline: 6/1
Degrees offered: master's, DNP
In-state tuition: full time: N/A, part
time: N/A (master's); full time:
N/A, part time: N/A (DNP)
Out-of-state tuition: full time: N/A
(master's); full time: N/A (DNP)
Room/board/expenses: N/A
Full-time enrollment: 2 (master's);
N/A (DNP)
men: 0%; women: 100%;
minorities: 0%; international: 0%
Part-time enrollment: 125
(master's); 22 (DNP)
men: 9%; women: 91%;
minorities: 50%; international:
1%
Acceptance rate (master's): 12%
Acceptance rate (DNP): 70%

Specialties offered:

administration; education; nurse
practitioner: adult-gerontology
acute care; nurse practitioner:
adult-gerontology primary care;
nurse practitioner: family

NEW MEXICO

Eastern New Mexico University[1]

1500 S Avenue K
Portales, NM 88130
Admissions: N/A
Financial aid: N/A
Tuition: N/A
Room/board/expenses: N/A
Enrollment: N/A

New Mexico State University

PO Box 30001, MSC 3185
Las Cruces, NM 88003-8001
schoolofnursing.nmsu.edu
Public
Admissions: (575) 646-3812
Email: nursing@nmsu.edu
Financial aid: (575) 646-4105
Application deadline: 2/1
Degrees offered: master's, Ph.D.,
DNP
In-state tuition: full time: $4,088,
part time: $227/credit hour
(master's); full time: $4,088, part
time: $227/credit hour (Ph.D.);
full time: $4,088, part time:
$227/credit hour (DNP)
Out-of-state tuition: full time:
$14,254 (master's); full time:
$14,254 (Ph.D.); full time:
$14,254 (DNP)
Room/board/expenses: $7,988
(master's); $7,988 (Ph.D.);
$7,988 (DNP)
Full-time enrollment: 2 (master's);
1 (Ph.D.); 16 (DNP)
men: 0%; women: 100%;
minorities: N/A; international:
N/A
Part-time enrollment: 11
(master's); 21 (Ph.D.); 44 (DNP)
men: 21%; women: 79%;
minorities: N/A; international:
N/A
Acceptance rate (master's): 89%
Acceptance rate (Ph.D.): 100%
Acceptance rate (DNP): 84%
Specialties offered:
administration; nurse
practitioner: family; nurse
practitioner: psychiatric-mental
health, across the lifespan

University of New Mexico[1]

MSC09 5350
Albuquerque, NM 87131-0001
Public
Admissions: N/A
Financial aid: N/A
Tuition: N/A
Room/board/expenses: N/A
Enrollment: N/A

NEW YORK

Adelphi University

1 South Avenue
Garden City, NY 11530
admissions.adelphi.edu/
Private
Admissions: (800) 233-5744

Email: admissions@adelphi.edu
Financial aid: (516) 877-3080
Application deadline: 1/15
Degrees offered: master's, Ph.D.
Tuition: full time: N/A, part time:
$1,165/credit hour (master's);
full time: $23,120, part time:
$1,290/credit hour
Room/board/expenses: N/A
Full-time enrollment: N/A
(master's); 14
men: 0%; women: 100%;
minorities: 43%; international:
0%
Part-time enrollment: 151
(master's); 26
men: 11%; women: 89%;
minorities: 63%; international:
1%
Acceptance rate (master's): 73%
Acceptance rate (Ph.D.): 78%
Specialties offered:
administration; education; nurse
practitioner: adult-gerontology
primary care

American University of Beirut

3 Dag Hammarskjold Plaza
New York, NY 10017
aub.edu.lb/~webson
Private
Admissions: (961) 137-4374
Email: admissions@aub.edu.lb
Financial aid: (961) 137-4374
Application deadline: 4/1
Degrees offered: master's
Tuition: full time: $786/credit
hour, part time: $786/credit hour
Room/board/expenses: $13,821
Full-time enrollment: 6
men: 0%; women: 100%;
minorities: 100%; international:
0%
Part-time enrollment: 49
men: 16%; women: 84%;
minorities: 100%; international:
0%
Acceptance rate (master's): 92%
Specialties offered:
administration; community
health/public health; other
majors

Binghamton University-SUNY

P.O. Box 6000
Binghamton, NY 13902-6000
www.binghamton.edu/dson
Public
Admissions: (607) 777-2151
Email: gradadmission@
binghamton.edu
Financial aid: (607) 777-2428
Application deadline: 4/15
Degrees offered: master's, Ph.D.,
DNP
In-state tuition: full time: $10,870,
part time: $453/credit hour
(master's); full time: $10,870,
part time: $453/credit hour
(Ph.D.); full time: $24,390, part
time: $1,016/credit hour (DNP)
Out-of-state tuition: full time:
$22,210 (master's); full time:
$22,210 (Ph.D.); full time:
$42,880 (DNP)
Room/board/expenses: N/A
Full-time enrollment: 83
(master's); 8 (Ph.D.); 1 (DNP)
men: 21%; women: 79%;
minorities: 14%; international:
13%

Part-time enrollment: 73 (master's); 17 (Ph.D.); 11 (DNP) men: 11%; women: 89%; minorities: 16%; international: 2%
Acceptance rate (master's): 94%
Acceptance rate (Ph.D.): 85%
Acceptance rate (DNP): 100%
Specialties offered: administration; clinical nurse specialist; community health/public health; education; nurse practitioner; nurse practitioner: adult-gerontology primary care; nurse practitioner: family; nurse practitioner: psychiatric-mental health, across the lifespan; other majors

College of Mount St. Vincent[1]
6301 Riverdale Avenue
Riverdale, NY 10471
Private
Admissions: N/A
Financial aid: N/A
Tuition: N/A
Room/board/expenses: N/A
Enrollment: N/A

College of New Rochelle[1]
29 Castle Place
New Rochelle, NY 10805-2308
www.cnr.edu/web/school-of-nuring
Private
Admissions: (914) 654-5085
Email: kcavanagh@cnr.edu
Financial aid: (914) 654-5225
Tuition: N/A
Room/board/expenses: N/A
Enrollment: N/A

Columbia University
630 West 168th Street
Mailbox 6
New York, NY 10032
nursing.columbia.edu/
Private
Admissions: (212) 305-5756
Email: nursing@columbia.edu
Financial aid: (212) 305-8147
Application deadline: 1/4
Degrees offered: master's, Ph.D., DNP
Tuition: full time: $1,450/credit hour, part time: $1,450/credit hour (master's); full time: $1,874/credit hour, part time: $1,874/credit hour (Ph.D.); full time: $1,874/credit hour, part time: $1,874/credit hour (DNP)
Room/board/expenses: $24,000 (master's); $24,000 (Ph.D.); $24,000 (DNP)
Full-time enrollment: 340 (master's); 22 (Ph.D.); 18 (DNP) men: 13%; women: 87%; minorities: 39%; international: 3%
Part-time enrollment: 314 (master's); N/A (Ph.D.); 34 (DNP) men: 10%; women: 90%; minorities: 45%; international: 1%
Acceptance rate (master's): 35%
Acceptance rate (Ph.D.): 52%
Acceptance rate (DNP): 51%
Specialties offered: generalist; nurse anesthesia; nurse-midwifery; nurse practitioner; nurse practitioner: adult-

gerontology acute care; nurse practitioner: adult-gerontology primary care; nurse practitioner: family; nurse practitioner: pediatric primary care; nurse practitioner: psychiatric-mental health, across the lifespan; research

CUNY-Hunter College
695 Park Avenue
New York, NY 10065
www.hunter.cuny.edu/nursing
Public
Admissions: (212) 396-6049
Email: gradadmissions@hunter.cuny.edu
Financial aid: (212) 772-4820
Application deadline: 4/1
Degrees offered: master's, DNP
In-state tuition: full time: $11,130, part time: $475/credit hour (master's); full time: $13,370, part time: $560/credit hour (DNP)
Out-of-state tuition: full time: $20,880 (master's); full time: $21,840 (DNP)
Room/board/expenses: N/A
Full-time enrollment: 18 (master's); 10 (DNP) men: 25%; women: 75%; minorities: 46%; international: 0%
Part-time enrollment: 539 (master's); 29 (DNP) men: 15%; women: 85%; minorities: 53%; international: 3%
Acceptance rate (master's): 45%
Acceptance rate (DNP): 94%
Specialties offered: administration; clinical nurse specialist; community health/public health; nurse practitioner; nurse practitioner: adult-gerontology primary care; nurse practitioner: psychiatric-mental health, across the lifespan; dual majors

CUNY-Lehman College[1]
250 Bedford Park Boulevard
West Bronx, NY 10468-1589
Public
Admissions: N/A
Financial aid: N/A
Tuition: N/A
Room/board/expenses: N/A
Enrollment: N/A

CUNY-Staten Island[1]
2800 Victory Boulevard
Building 55, Room 203
Staten Island, NY 10314
Public
Admissions: N/A
Financial aid: N/A
Tuition: N/A
Room/board/expenses: N/A
Enrollment: N/A

Daemen College[1]
4380 Main Street
Amherst, NY 14226
www.daemen.edu/
Private
Admissions: N/A
Financial aid: N/A
Tuition: N/A
Room/board/expenses: N/A
Enrollment: N/A

Dominican College
470 Western Highway
Orangeburg, NY 10962
www.dc.edu/graduate-nursing
Private
Admissions: (845) 848-7800
Email: admissions@dc.edu
Financial aid: (845) 848-7818
Application deadline: 5/1
Degrees offered: master's, DNP
Tuition: full time: N/A, part time: $868/credit hour (master's); full time: N/A, part time: $940/credit hour (DNP)
Room/board/expenses: N/A
Full-time enrollment: 21 (master's); 3 (DNP) men: 17%; women: 83%; minorities: 54%; international: 4%
Part-time enrollment: 59 (master's); 16 (DNP) men: 15%; women: 85%; minorities: 37%; international: 0%
Acceptance rate (master's): 42%
Acceptance rate (DNP): 100%
Specialties offered: nurse practitioner; nurse practitioner: family

D'Youville College
320 Porter Avenue
Buffalo, NY 14201-9985
www.dyc.edu/academics/nursing/
Private
Admissions: (800) 777-3921
Email: graduateadmissions@dyc.edu
Financial aid: (716) 829-7500
Application deadline: N/A
Degrees offered: master's, DNP
Tuition: full time: $910/credit hour, part time: $910/credit hour (master's); full time: $990/credit hour, part time: $990/credit hour (DNP)
Room/board/expenses: $11,570 (master's); $11,570 (DNP)
Full-time enrollment: 101 (master's); 4 (DNP) men: 10%; women: 90%; minorities: 10%; international: 13%
Part-time enrollment: 142 (master's); 6 (DNP) men: 9%; women: 91%; minorities: 14%; international: 28%
Acceptance rate (master's): 58%
Acceptance rate (DNP): 38%
Specialties offered: nurse practitioner: family; nurse practitioner: psychiatric-mental health, across the lifespan

Excelsior College[1]
7 Columbia Circle
Albany, NY 12203-5159
Private
Admissions: N/A
Financial aid: N/A
Tuition: N/A
Room/board/expenses: N/A
Enrollment: N/A

Keuka College[1]
141 Central Avenue
Keuka Park, NY 14478
asap.keuka.edu/programs/ms-nursing/
Private
Admissions: N/A
Financial aid: N/A

Tuition: N/A
Room/board/expenses: N/A
Enrollment: N/A

Le Moyne College
1419 Salt Springs Road
Syracuse, NY 13214-1301
www.lemoyne.edu/nursing
Private
Admissions: (315) 445-5444
Email: nursing@lemoyne.edu
Financial aid: (315) 445-4400
Application deadline: 4/1
Degrees offered: master's
Tuition: full time: $861/credit hour, part time: $861/credit hour
Room/board/expenses: N/A
Full-time enrollment: 21 men: 24%; women: 76%; minorities: 10%; international: 0%
Part-time enrollment: 54 men: 17%; women: 83%; minorities: 15%; international: 2%
Acceptance rate (master's): 93%
Specialties offered: administration; education; informatics; nurse practitioner; nurse practitioner: family

LIU Brooklyn
1 University Plaza
Brooklyn, NY 11201
www.liu.edu/brooklyn/
Private
Admissions: (718) 488-1555
Email: bkly-admissions@liu.edu
Financial aid: (718) 488-1618
Application deadline: N/A
Degrees offered: master's
Tuition: full time: $1,178/credit hour, part time: $1,178/credit hour
Room/board/expenses: N/A
Full-time enrollment: men: N/A; women: N/A; minorities: N/A; international: N/A
Part-time enrollment: 188 men: 9%; women: 91%; minorities: 63%; international: 1%
Acceptance rate (master's): 55%
Specialties offered: education; nurse practitioner; nurse practitioner: adult; nurse practitioner: family

LIU Post
720 Northern Boulevard
Brookville, NY 11548
liu.edu/post/nursing
Private
Admissions: (516) 299-4000
Email: post-enroll@liu.edu
Financial aid: (516) 299-2323
Application deadline: N/A
Degrees offered: master's
Tuition: full time: $1,178/credit hour, part time: $1,178/credit hour
Room/board/expenses: $13,426
Full-time enrollment: men: N/A; women: N/A; minorities: N/A; international: N/A
Part-time enrollment: 117 men: 15%; women: 85%; minorities: 55%; international: 0%
Acceptance rate (master's): 43%
Specialties offered: education; nurse practitioner: family

Mercy College
555 Broadway
Dobbs Ferry, NY 10522
www.mercy.edu/health-and-natural-sciences/
Private
Admissions: (877) 637-2946
Email: admissions@mercy.edu
Financial aid: (877) 637-2946
Application deadline: N/A
Degrees offered: master's
Tuition: full time: $842/credit hour, part time: $842/credit hour
Room/board/expenses: $13,700
Full-time enrollment: 1 men: N/A; women: 100%; minorities: 0%; international: N/A
Part-time enrollment: 161 men: 4%; women: 96%; minorities: 69%; international: N/A
Acceptance rate (master's): 80%
Specialties offered: administration; education

Molloy College
1000 Hempstead Avenue
Rockville, NY 11571-5002
www.molloy.edu/academics/graduate-programs/graduate-nursing
Private
Admissions: (516) 323-4014
Email: admissions@molloy.edu
Financial aid: (516) 323-4200
Application deadline: 4/15
Degrees offered: master's, Ph.D., DNP
Tuition: full time: $1,065/credit hour, part time: $1,065/credit hour (master's); full time: $1,195/credit hour, part time: $1,195/credit hour (Ph.D.); full time: $1,195/credit hour, part time: $1,195/credit hour (DNP)
Room/board/expenses: N/A
Full-time enrollment: 19 (master's); N/A (Ph.D.); N/A (DNP) men: 11%; women: 89%; minorities: 63%; international: 11%
Part-time enrollment: 488 (master's); 30 (Ph.D.); 24 (DNP) men: 8%; women: 92%; minorities: 57%; international: 0%
Acceptance rate (master's): 55%
Acceptance rate (Ph.D.): 86%
Acceptance rate (DNP): 80%
Specialties offered: administration; clinical nurse specialist; education; informatics; nurse practitioner; nurse practitioner: adult-gerontology primary care; nurse practitioner: family; nurse practitioner: pediatric primary care; nurse practitioner: psychiatric-mental health, across the lifespan; other majors; dual majors

Mount St. Mary College[1]
330 Powell Avenue
Newburgh, NY 12550
www.msmc.edu/Academics/Graduate_Programs/Master_of_Science_in_Nursing
Private
Admissions: (845) 569-3225

Email: graduateadmissions@ msmc.edu
Financial aid: (845) 569-3394
Tuition: N/A
Room/board/expenses: N/A
Enrollment: N/A

New York University (Meyers)

726 Broadway, 10th Floor
New York, NY 10003
www.nursing.nyu.edu
Private
Admissions: (212) 998-5317
Email: admissions.nursing@ nyu.edu
Financial aid: (212) 998-4444
Application deadline: N/A
Degrees offered: master's, Ph.D., DNP
Tuition: full time: $41,576, part time: $21,200 (master's); full time: $41,576, part time: $21,200 (Ph.D.); full time: $41,576, part time: $21,200 (DNP)
Room/board/expenses: $25,170 (master's); $25,170 (Ph.D.); $25,170 (DNP)
Full-time enrollment: 42 (master's); 19 (Ph.D.); N/A (DNP) men: 8%; women: 92%; minorities: 36%; international: 13%
Part-time enrollment: 551 (master's); 19 (Ph.D.); 42 (DNP) men: 10%; women: 90%; minorities: 37%; international: 3%
Acceptance rate (master's): 68%
Acceptance rate (Ph.D.): 47%
Acceptance rate (DNP): 51%
Specialties offered: administration; education; informatics; nurse-midwifery; nurse practitioner; nurse practitioner: adult-gerontology acute care; nurse practitioner: adult-gerontology primary care; nurse practitioner: family; nurse practitioner: pediatric primary care; nurse practitioner: psychiatric-mental health, across the lifespan; research; dual majors

Pace University

861 Bedford Road
Pleasantville, NY 10570
www.pace.edu/college-health-professions/department/lienhard-school-nursing
Private
Admissions: (212) 346-1531
Email: graduateadmission@ pace.edu
Financial aid: (212) 346-1309
Application deadline: 3/1
Degrees offered: master's, DNP
Tuition: full time: $1,190/credit hour, part time: $1,190/credit hour (master's); full time: N/A, part time: $18,920 (DNP)
Room/board/expenses: N/A
Full-time enrollment: N/A (master's); N/A (DNP) men: N/A; women: N/A; minorities: N/A; international: N/A
Part-time enrollment: 361 (master's); 22 (DNP) men: 6%; women: 94%; minorities: 51%; international: 0%
Acceptance rate (master's): 73%
Acceptance rate (DNP): 100%

Specialties offered: clinical nurse leader; nurse practitioner: adult-gerontology acute care; nurse practitioner: family

Roberts Wesleyan College

2301 Westside Drive
Rochester, NY 14624
www.roberts.edu/graduate-nursing-programs.aspx
Private
Admissions: (585) 594-6686
Email: gradnursing@roberts.edu
Financial aid: (585) 594-6668
Application deadline: N/A
Degrees offered: master's
Tuition: full time: $789/credit hour, part time: N/A
Room/board/expenses: N/A
Full-time enrollment: 65 men: 5%; women: 95%; minorities: 29%; international: 6%
Part-time enrollment: men: N/A; women: N/A; minorities: N/A; international: N/A
Acceptance rate (master's): 46%
Specialties offered: administration; education

The Sage Colleges[1]

65 1st Street
Troy, NY 12180
Private
Admissions: N/A
Financial aid: N/A
Tuition: N/A
Room/board/expenses: N/A
Enrollment: N/A

St. John Fisher College

3690 East Avenue
Rochester, NY 14618
www.sjfc.edu/academics/nursing/about/index.dot
Private
Admissions: (585) 385-8161
Email: grad@sjfc.edu
Financial aid: (585) 385-8042
Application deadline: N/A
Degrees offered: master's, DNP
Tuition: full time: $885/credit hour, part time: $885/credit hour (master's); full time: $1,235/credit hour, part time: $1,235/credit hour (DNP)
Room/board/expenses: N/A
Full-time enrollment: 5 (master's); 10 (DNP) men: 0%; women: 100%; minorities: 33%; international: 0%
Part-time enrollment: 153 (master's); 14 (DNP) men: 10%; women: 90%; minorities: 14%; international: 0%
Acceptance rate (master's): 45%
Acceptance rate (DNP): 63%
Specialties offered: clinical nurse specialist; nurse practitioner; nurse practitioner: adult-gerontology acute care; nurse practitioner: adult-gerontology primary care; nurse practitioner: family; nurse practitioner: psychiatric-mental health, across the lifespan

St. Joseph's College[1]

206 Prospect Avenue
Syracuse, NY 13203
Private
Admissions: N/A
Financial aid: N/A
Tuition: N/A
Room/board/expenses: N/A
Enrollment: N/A

Stony Brook University-SUNY

Health Science Center
Stony Brook, NY 11794-8240
nursing.stonybrookmedicine.edu/
Public
Admissions: (631) 444-3554
Email: Karen.Allard@stonybrook.edu
Financial aid: (631) 444-2111
Application deadline: 1/19
Degrees offered: master's, DNP
In-state tuition: full time: $10,870, part time: $453/credit hour (master's); full time: $24,390, part time: $1,016/credit hour (DNP)
Out-of-state tuition: full time: $22,210 (master's); full time: $42,880 (DNP)
Room/board/expenses: $9,194 (master's); $9,194 (DNP)
Full-time enrollment: 10 (master's); 26 (DNP) men: 11%; women: 89%; minorities: 33%; international: 8%
Part-time enrollment: 787 (master's); 22 (DNP) men: 11%; women: 89%; minorities: 32%; international: 4%
Acceptance rate (master's): 61%
Acceptance rate (DNP): 69%
Specialties offered: education; nurse-midwifery; neonatal; nurse practitioner; nurse practitioner: adult-gerontology primary care; nurse practitioner: family; nurse practitioner: pediatric primary care; nurse practitioner: psychiatric-mental health, across the lifespan; women's health; other majors

SUNY Downstate Medical Center

450 Clarkson Avenue, Box 22
Brooklyn, NY 11203-2098
www.downstate.edu
Public
Admissions: (718) 270-4744
Email: admissions@downstate.edu
Financial aid: (718) 270-2488
Application deadline: 11/30
Degrees offered: master's
In-state tuition: full time: $10,870, part time: $453/credit hour
Out-of-state tuition: full time: $11,105
Room/board/expenses: N/A
Full-time enrollment: 157 men: 18%; women: 82%; minorities: 64%; international: 1%
Part-time enrollment: 41 men: 15%; women: 85%; minorities: 63%; international: 0%
Acceptance rate (master's): 41%
Specialties offered: clinical nurse specialist; nurse anesthesia; nurse-midwifery; nurse

practitioner; nurse practitioner: family; women's health

SUNY Empire State College[1]

111 West Avenue
Saratoga Springs, NY 12866
Admissions: N/A
Financial aid: N/A
Tuition: N/A
Room/board/expenses: N/A
Enrollment: N/A

SUNY Polytechnic Institute

PO Box 3050
Utica, NY 13504
sunypoly.edu/graduate-admissions/
Public
Admissions: (315) 792-7347
Email: graduate@sunypoly.edu
Financial aid: (315) 792-7210
Application deadline: 7/1
Degrees offered: master's
In-state tuition: full time: $453/credit hour, part time: $453/credit hour
Out-of-state tuition: full time: $925/credit hour
Room/board/expenses: $12,778
Full-time enrollment: 48 men: 15%; women: 85%; minorities: 17%; international: 0%
Part-time enrollment: 157 men: 6%; women: 94%; minorities: 11%; international: 0%
Acceptance rate (master's): 43%
Specialties offered: education; nurse practitioner: family

SUNY Upstate Medical Center[1]

750 East Adams Street
Syracuse, NY 13210-2375
Public
Admissions: N/A
Financial aid: N/A
Tuition: N/A
Room/board/expenses: N/A
Enrollment: N/A

University at Buffalo-SUNY

103 Wende Hall
3435 Main Street
Buffalo, NY 14214
nursing.buffalo.edu
Public
Admissions: (716) 829-2537
Email: nursing@buffalo.edu
Financial aid: (716) 645-8232
Application deadline: 1/1
Degrees offered: master's, Ph.D., DNP
In-state tuition: full time: $13,337, part time: $453/credit hour (master's); full time: $1,337, part time: $453/credit hour (Ph.D.); full time: $24,390, part time: $1,016/credit hour (DNP)
Out-of-state tuition: full time: $24,687 (master's); full time: $24,687 (Ph.D.); full time: $42,880 (DNP)
Room/board/expenses: $15,260 (master's); $15,260 (Ph.D.); $15,260 (DNP)
Full-time enrollment: N/A (master's); 8 (Ph.D.); 75 (DNP)

men: 36%; women: 64%; minorities: 16%; international: 5%
Part-time enrollment: 8 (master's); 17 (Ph.D.); 94 (DNP) men: 12%; women: 88%; minorities: 19%; international: 2%
Acceptance rate (master's): 67%
Acceptance rate (Ph.D.): 58%
Acceptance rate (DNP): 71%
Specialties offered: administration; nurse anesthesia; nurse practitioner; nurse practitioner: adult-gerontology primary care; nurse practitioner: family; nurse practitioner: psychiatric-mental health, across the lifespan; research

University of Rochester

601 Elmwood Avenue, Box SON
Rochester, NY 14642
son.rochester.edu/
Private
Admissions: (585) 275-2375
Email: son_admissions@urmc.rochester.edu
Financial aid: (585) 275-3226
Application deadline: 1/3
Degrees offered: master's, Ph.D., DNP
Tuition: full time: $25,200, part time: $1,400/credit hour (master's); full time: $25,200, part time: $1,400/credit hour (Ph.D.); full time: $25,200, part time: $1,400/credit hour (DNP)
Room/board/expenses: $15,530 (master's); $15,530 (Ph.D.); $15,530 (DNP)
Full-time enrollment: 7 (master's); 11 (Ph.D.); N/A (DNP) men: 6%; women: 94%; minorities: 39%; international: 22%
Part-time enrollment: 221 (master's); 1 (Ph.D.); 21 (DNP) men: 17%; women: 83%; minorities: 13%; international: N/A
Acceptance rate (master's): 80%
Acceptance rate (Ph.D.): 50%
Acceptance rate (DNP): 100%
Specialties offered: clinical nurse leader; education; health management & policy health care systems; neonatal; nurse practitioner; nurse practitioner: adult-gerontology acute care; nurse practitioner: adult-gerontology primary care; nurse practitioner: family; nurse practitioner: pediatric primary care; nurse practitioner: psychiatric-mental health, across the lifespan; research

Wagner College[1]

1 Campus Road
Staten Island, NY 10301
Private
Admissions: N/A
Financial aid: N/A
Tuition: N/A
Room/board/expenses: N/A
Enrollment: N/A

NORTH CAROLINA

Duke University

Box 3322 Medical Center
Durham, NC 27710-3322
nursing.duke.edu
Private
Admissions: (877) 415-3853
Email: SONAdmissions@
dm.duke.edu
Financial aid: (877) 344-4680
Application deadline: 12/1
Degrees offered: master's, Ph.D.,
DNP
Tuition: full time: $1,639/credit
hour, part time: $1,639/credit
hour (master's); full time:
$52,925, part time: $2,875/
credit hour (Ph.D.); full time:
$1,639/credit hour, part time:
$1,639/credit hour (DNP)
Room/board/expenses: $17,736
(master's); $17,736 (Ph.D.);
$17,304 (DNP)
Full-time enrollment: 82
(master's); 37 (Ph.D.); 76 (DNP)
men: 14%; women: 86%;
minorities: 20%; international:
8%
Part-time enrollment: 404
(master's); N/A (Ph.D.); 157
(DNP)
men: 11%; women: 89%;
minorities: 22%; international:
1%
Acceptance rate (master's): 51%
Acceptance rate (Ph.D.): 52%
Acceptance rate (DNP): 42%
Specialties offered:
administration; case
management; education; health
management & policy health
care systems; informatics;
nurse anesthesia; neonatal;
nurse practitioner; nurse
practitioner: adult-gerontology
acute care; nurse practitioner:
adult-gerontology primary care;
nurse practitioner: family; nurse
practitioner: pediatric primary
care; research; women's health;
other majors; dual majors

East Carolina University

Library, Allied Health and
Nursing Building
Greenville, NC 27858
www.ecu.edu/nursing/
Public
Admissions: (252) 744-6477
Email: gradnurs@ecu.edu
Financial aid: (252) 328-6610
Application deadline: 3/15
Degrees offered: master's, Ph.D.,
DNP
In-state tuition: full time: $353/
credit hour, part time: $353/
credit hour (master's); full time:
$6,906, part time: $343/credit
hour (Ph.D.); full time: $353/
credit hour, part time: $353/
credit hour (DNP)
Out-of-state tuition: full time:
$985/credit hour (master's); full
time: $19,797 (Ph.D.); full time:
$985/credit hour (DNP)
Room/board/expenses: $9,935
(master's); $9,935 (Ph.D.);
$9,935 (DNP)
Full-time enrollment: 63
(master's); 5 (Ph.D.); 89 (DNP)
men: 10%; women: 90%;
minorities: 21%; international:
0%

Part-time enrollment: 289
(master's); 30 (Ph.D.); 76 (DNP)
men: 7%; women: 93%;
minorities: 18%; international:
0%
Acceptance rate (master's): 64%
Acceptance rate (Ph.D.): 52%
Acceptance rate (DNP): 58%
Specialties offered:
administration; clinical nurse
specialist; education; nurse
anesthesia; nurse-midwifery;
neonatal; nurse practitioner;
nurse practitioner: adult-
gerontology primary care; nurse
practitioner: family

Gardner-Webb University

PO Box 7286
Boiling Springs, NC 28017
gardner-webb.edu/academic-
programs-and-resources/
colleges-and-schools/health-
sciences/schools-and-
departments/hunt-school-of-
nursing/graduate-programs/index
Private
Admissions: (704) 406-4490
Email: gradschool@gardner-
webb.edu
Financial aid: (704) 406-4247
Application deadline: N/A
Degrees offered: master's, DNP
Tuition: full time: $453/credit
hour, part time: $453/credit
hour (master's); full time: $749/
credit hour, part time: $749/
credit hour (DNP)
Room/board/expenses: N/A
Full-time enrollment: 127
(master's); 38 (DNP)
men: 7%; women: 93%;
minorities: 11%; international:
0%
Part-time enrollment: 49
(master's); 5 (DNP)
men: 2%; women: 98%;
minorities: 19%; international:
0%
Acceptance rate (master's): 42%
Acceptance rate (DNP): 69%
Specialties offered:
administration; education; nurse
practitioner: family; dual majors

Lenoir-Rhyne University

625 7th Avenue NE
Hickory, NC 28601
www.lr.edu/
Private
Admissions: (828) 328-7111
Financial aid: N/A
Application deadline: N/A
Degrees offered: master's
Tuition: full time: $550/credit
hour, part time: $550/credit
hour
Room/board/expenses: N/A
Full-time enrollment: 7
men: N/A; women: N/A;
minorities: 43%; international:
0%
Part-time enrollment: 61
men: N/A; women: N/A;
minorities: 8%; international: 0%
Acceptance rate (master's): 72%
Specialties offered:
administration; education

Queens University of Charlotte

1900 Selwyn Avenue
Charlotte, NC 28274
www.queens.edu/
Private
Admissions: (704) 337-2314
Email: PSONAdmissions@
queens.edu
Financial aid: (704) 688-2713
Application deadline: N/A
Degrees offered: master's
Tuition: full time: $490/credit
hour, part time: $490/credit
hour
Room/board/expenses: N/A
Full-time enrollment: 102
men: 5%; women: 95%;
minorities: 40%; international:
0%
Part-time enrollment: 11
men: 0%; women: 100%;
minorities: 18%; international:
0%
Acceptance rate (master's): 98%
Specialties offered:
administration; clinical nurse
leader; education

University of North Carolina-Chapel Hill

Carrington Hall, CB #7460
Chapel Hill, NC 27599-7460
nursing.unc.edu/
Public
Admissions: (919) 843-6391
Email: nursing@unc.edu
Financial aid: (919) 962-8396
Application deadline: 1/12
Degrees offered: master's, Ph.D.,
DNP
In-state tuition: full time: $14,929,
part time: $11,216 (master's); full
time: $9,643, part time: $7,232
(Ph.D.); full time: $14,929, part
time: $11,216 (DNP)
Out-of-state tuition: full time:
$32,154 (master's); full time:
$26,854 (Ph.D.); full time:
$32,154 (DNP)
Room/board/expenses: $17,510
(master's); $17,510 (Ph.D.);
$17,510 (DNP)
Full-time enrollment: 167
(master's); 41 (Ph.D.); 66 (DNP)
men: 11%; women: 89%;
minorities: 34%; international:
5%
Part-time enrollment: 67
(master's); N/A (Ph.D.); 10
(DNP)
men: 4%; women: 96%;
minorities: 32%; international:
0%
Acceptance rate (master's): 34%
Acceptance rate (Ph.D.): 25%
Acceptance rate (DNP): 42%
Specialties offered:
administration; clinical nurse
leader; education; informatics;
nurse practitioner: adult-
gerontology primary care;
nurse practitioner: family; nurse
practitioner: pediatric primary
care; nurse practitioner:
psychiatric-mental health,
across the lifespan; other
majors; dual majors

University of North Carolina-Charlotte

9201 University City Boulevard
Charlotte, NC 28223-0001
nursing.uncc.edu
Public
Admissions: (704) 687-5503
Email:
graduateschool@uncc.edu
Financial aid: (704) 687-7010
Application deadline: 2/2
Degrees offered: master's, DNP
In-state tuition: full time: $4,252,
part time: $2,126 (master's); full
time: $4,252, part time: $3,190
(DNP)
Out-of-state tuition: full time:
$17,422 (master's); full time:
$17,424 (DNP)
Room/board/expenses: N/A
Full-time enrollment: 126
(master's); 15 (DNP)
men: 26%; women: 74%;
minorities: 20%; international:
0%
Part-time enrollment: 77
(master's); 4 (DNP)
men: 6%; women: 94%;
minorities: 22%; international:
0%
Acceptance rate (master's): 40%
Acceptance rate (DNP): 86%
Specialties offered:
administration; community
health/public health; education;
nurse anesthesia; nurse
practitioner: adult-gerontology
acute care; nurse practitioner:
family

University of North Carolina-Greensboro

PO Box 26170
Greensboro, NC 27402-6170
nursing.uncg.edu
Public
Admissions: (336) 334-5596
Email: gradinquiry@uncg.edu
Financial aid: (336) 334-5702
Application deadline: 5/15
Degrees offered: master's, Ph.D.,
DNP
In-state tuition: full time: $4,514,
part time: $250/credit hour
(master's); full time: $5,117, part
time: $639/credit hour (Ph.D.);
full time: $4,514, part time:
$250/credit hour (DNP)
Out-of-state tuition: full time:
$16,381 (master's); full time:
$18,566 (Ph.D.); full time:
$16,381 (DNP)
Room/board/expenses: $8,000
(master's); $8,000 (Ph.D.);
$8,000 (DNP)
Full-time enrollment: 40
(master's); 40 (Ph.D.); 159
(DNP)
men: 29%; women: 71%;
minorities: 21%; international:
3%
Part-time enrollment: 68
(master's); 3 (Ph.D.); N/A (DNP)
men: 34%; women: 66%;
minorities: 51%; international:
1%
Acceptance rate (master's): 68%
Acceptance rate (Ph.D.): 64%
Acceptance rate (DNP): 55%
Specialties offered:
administration; education; nurse
anesthesia; nurse practitioner:

adult-gerontology primary care;
research; dual majors

University of North Carolina-Pembroke

One University Drive
Pembroke, NC 28372-1510
www.uncp.edu/nursing
Public
Admissions: (910) 521-6271
Email: grad@uncp.edu
Financial aid: (910) 521-6255
Application deadline: 5/15
Degrees offered: master's
In-state tuition: full time: $3,639,
part time: $1,819
Out-of-state tuition: full time:
$13,896
Room/board/expenses: $8,572
Full-time enrollment: 21
men: 19%; women: 81%;
minorities: 43%; international:
0%
Part-time enrollment: 18
men: 0%; women: 100%;
minorities: 50%; international:
0%
Acceptance rate (master's): 100%
Specialties offered: case
management; clinical nurse
leader; education

University of North Carolina-Wilmington

601 S. College Road
Wilmington, NC 28403-5995
uncw.edu/oss/
nursingmasters.html
Public
Admissions: (910) 962-7449
Email: harrisk@uncw.edu
Financial aid: (910) 962-3117
Application deadline: 2/1
Degrees offered: master's, DNP
In-state tuition: full time: $494/
credit hour, part time: $370/
credit hour (master's); full time:
$284/credit hour, part time:
$284/credit hour (DNP)
Out-of-state tuition: full time:
$1,851/credit hour (master's); full
time: $1,765/credit hour (DNP)
Room/board/expenses: N/A
Full-time enrollment: 81
(master's); N/A (DNP)
men: 16%; women: 84%;
minorities: 9%; international: 0%
Part-time enrollment: 64
(master's); 7 (DNP)
men: 10%; women: 90%;
minorities: 21%; international:
0%
Acceptance rate (master's): 49%
Acceptance rate (DNP): 100%
Specialties offered: education;
nurse practitioner: family

Western Carolina University-Cullowhee[1]

1459 Sand Hill Road
Candler, NC 28715
nursing.wcu.edu
Public
Admissions: N/A
Financial aid: N/A
Tuition: N/A
Room/board/expenses: N/A
Enrollment: N/A

Winston-Salem State University

601 S. Martin Luther King Jr. Drive
Winston-Salem, NC 27110
www.wssu.edu/school-health-sciences/departments/nursing/msn/default.aspx
Public
Admissions: (336) 750-2078
Email: admissions@wssu.edu
Financial aid: (336) 750-3296
Application deadline: 2/15
Degrees offered: master's, DNP
In-state tuition: full time: N/A, part time: N/A (master's); full time: N/A, part time: N/A (DNP)
Out-of-state tuition: full time: N/A (master's); full time: N/A (DNP)
Room/board/expenses: N/A
Full-time enrollment: 57 (master's); 20 (DNP)
men: 19%; women: 81%; minorities: 70%; international: 0%
Part-time enrollment: 21 (master's); 4 (DNP)
men: 0%; women: 100%; minorities: 52%; international: 0%
Acceptance rate (master's): 56%
Acceptance rate (DNP): 86%
Specialties offered: education; nurse practitioner: family

NORTH DAKOTA

North Dakota State University

NDSU Department 2820
Fargo, ND 58108
www.ndsu.edu/nursing/
Public
Admissions: N/A
Financial aid: N/A
Application deadline: N/A
Degrees offered: DNP
In-state tuition: full time: $8,521, part time: $376/credit hour
Out-of-state tuition: full time: $22,750
Room/board/expenses: $7,918
Full-time enrollment: 45
men: 13%; women: 87%; minorities: 9%; international: 0%
Part-time enrollment: 1 2
men: 33%; women: 67%; minorities: 0%; international: 0%
Acceptance rate (DNP): 37%
Specialties offered: education; nurse practitioner; nurse practitioner: family

University of Mary[1]

7500 University Drive
Bismarck, ND 58504-9652
Private
Admissions: (701) 355-8030
Email: marauder@umary.edu
Financial aid: (701) 355-8142
Tuition: N/A
Room/board/expenses: N/A
Enrollment: N/A

University of North Dakota[1]

Box 9025
Grand Forks, ND 58202
nursing.und.edu/
Public
Admissions: (701) 777-4535
Email: questions@gradschool.und.edu
Financial aid: (701) 777-3092
Tuition: N/A
Room/board/expenses: N/A
Enrollment: N/A

OHIO

Ashland University[1]

401 College Avenue
Ashland, OH 44805
Admissions: N/A
Financial aid: N/A
Tuition: N/A
Room/board/expenses: N/A
Enrollment: N/A

Capital University[1]

1 College and Main
Columbus, OH 43209-2394
Private
Admissions: N/A
Financial aid: N/A
Tuition: N/A
Room/board/expenses: N/A
Enrollment: N/A

Case Western Reserve University

10900 Euclid Avenue
Cleveland, OH 44106-4904
nursing.case.edu/
Private
Admissions: (216) 368-2529
Email: admissionsfpb@case.edu
Financial aid: (216) 368-0517
Application deadline: 3/1
Degrees offered: master's, Ph.D., DNP
Tuition: full time: $1,952/credit hour, part time: $1,952/credit hour (master's); full time: $1,774/credit hour, part time: $1,774/credit hour (Ph.D.); full time: $1,952/credit hour, part time: $1,952/credit hour (DNP)
Room/board/expenses: $26,721 (master's); $26,721 (Ph.D.); $6,240 (DNP)
Full-time enrollment: 137 (master's); 53 (Ph.D.); 75 (DNP)
men: 18%; women: 82%; minorities: 20%; international: 10%
Part-time enrollment: 164 (master's); 7 (Ph.D.); 56 (DNP)
men: 17%; women: 83%; minorities: 17%; international: 1%
Acceptance rate (master's): 64%
Acceptance rate (Ph.D.): 57%
Acceptance rate (DNP): 87%
Specialties offered: administration; education; generalist; nurse anesthesia; nurse-midwifery; neonatal; nurse practitioner; nurse practitioner: adult-gerontology acute care; nurse practitioner: adult-gerontology primary care; nurse practitioner: family; nurse practitioner: pediatric primary care; nurse practitioner: psychiatric-mental health, across the lifespan; research; women's health; other majors; dual majors

Cedarville University

251 N. Main Street
Cedarville, OH 45314
www.cedarville.edu/Academics/Nursing.aspx
Private
Admissions: (800) 233-2784
Email: admiss@cedarville.edu
Financial aid: (937) 766-7866
Application deadline: N/A
Degrees offered: master's
Tuition: full time: $552/credit hour, part time: $552/credit hour
Room/board/expenses: $6,880
Full-time enrollment: 16
men: 13%; women: 88%; minorities: 13%; international: 0%
Part-time enrollment: 57
men: 11%; women: 89%; minorities: 32%; international: 0%
Acceptance rate (master's): 97%
Specialties offered: community health/public health; education; nurse practitioner: family

Cleveland State University

2121 Euclid Avenue, RT 1416
Cleveland, OH 44115-2214
www.csuohio.edu/nursing
Public
Admissions: (216) 687-5411
Email: graduate.admissions@csuohio.edu
Financial aid: (216) 687-5411
Application deadline: 3/1
Degrees offered: master's
In-state tuition: full time: $531/credit hour, part time: $531/credit hour
Out-of-state tuition: full time: $541/credit hour
Room/board/expenses: N/A
Full-time enrollment:
men: N/A; women: N/A; minorities: N/A; international: N/A
Part-time enrollment: 54 2
men: 5%; women: 95%; minorities: 30%; international: 0%
Acceptance rate (master's): 91%
Specialties offered: clinical nurse leader; education; other majors

Franciscan University of Steubenville

1235 University Boulevard
Steubenville, OH 43952
www.franciscan.edu/
Private
Admissions: (740) 284-5249
Email: gradadmissions@franciscan.edu
Financial aid: (740) 284-5216
Application deadline: 7/1
Degrees offered: master's
Tuition: full time: $500/credit hour, part time: $500/credit hour
Room/board/expenses: N/A
Full-time enrollment: 13
men: 15%; women: 85%; minorities: 15%; international: 0%
Part-time enrollment: 56
men: 18%; women: 82%; minorities: 0%; international: 0%
Acceptance rate (master's): 92%
Specialties offered: nurse practitioner

Kent State University

P.O. Box 5190
Henderson Hall
Kent, OH 44242
www.kent.edu/nursing
Public
Admissions: (330) 672-7911
Email: nursing@kent.edu
Financial aid: (330) 672-2972
Application deadline: 3/1
Degrees offered: master's, Ph.D., DNP
In-state tuition: full time: $505/credit hour, part time: $505/credit hour (master's); full time: $505/credit hour, part time: $505/credit hour (Ph.D.); full time: $505/credit hour, part time: $505/credit hour (DNP)
Out-of-state tuition: full time: $881/credit hour (master's); full time: $881/credit hour (Ph.D.); full time: $881/credit hour (DNP)
Room/board/expenses: $10,720 (master's); $10,720 (Ph.D.); $10,720 (DNP)
Full-time enrollment: 89 (master's); 27 (Ph.D.); 1 (DNP)
men: 18%; women: 82%; minorities: 12%; international: 15%
Part-time enrollment: 391 (master's); 10 (Ph.D.); 18 (DNP)
men: 13%; women: 87%; minorities: 11%; international: 0%
Acceptance rate (master's): 88%
Acceptance rate (Ph.D.): 100%
Acceptance rate (DNP): 50%
Specialties offered: clinical nurse specialist; education; health management & policy health care systems; nurse practitioner; nurse practitioner: adult-gerontology acute care; nurse practitioner: adult-gerontology primary care; nurse practitioner: family; nurse practitioner: pediatric primary care; nurse practitioner: psychiatric-mental health, across the lifespan; women's health; dual majors

Lourdes University

6832 Convent Boulevard
Sylvania, OH 43560
www.lourdes.edu/
Private
Admissions: (419) 517-8908
Email: gradschool@lourdes.edu
Financial aid: (419) 824-3732
Application deadline: 1/12
Degrees offered: master's
Tuition: full time: $650/credit hour, part time: $650/credit hour
Room/board/expenses: $9,400
Full-time enrollment: 70
men: 16%; women: 84%; minorities: 16%; international: 0%
Part-time enrollment: 22
men: 5%; women: 95%; minorities: 27%; international: 0%
Specialties offered: clinical nurse leader; education; nurse anesthesia

Malone University[1]

515 25th Street NW
Canton, OH 44709
www.malone.edu/academics/snhs/
Private
Admissions: (330) 471-8145
Email: admissions@malone.edu
Financial aid: (330) 471-8159
Tuition: N/A
Room/board/expenses: N/A
Enrollment: N/A

Mount Carmel College of Nursing[1]

127 S. Davis Avenue
Columbus, OH 43222
Private
Admissions: N/A
Financial aid: N/A
Tuition: N/A
Room/board/expenses: N/A
Enrollment: N/A

Mount St. Joseph University

5701 Delhi Road
Cincinati, OH 45233
www.msj.edu/academics/divisions-departments/division-of-health-sciences/
Private
Admissions: (513) 244-4531
Email: admission@msj.edu
Financial aid: (513) 244-4418
Application deadline: N/A
Degrees offered: master's, DNP
Tuition: full time: $610/credit hour, part time: $610/credit hour (master's); full time: $635/credit hour, part time: $635/credit hour (DNP)
Room/board/expenses: $9,000 (master's); $9,000 (DNP)
Full-time enrollment: 85 (master's); N/A (DNP)
men: 18%; women: 82%; minorities: 26%; international: 0%
Part-time enrollment: 109 (master's); 38 (DNP)
men: 7%; women: 93%; minorities: 3%; international: 0%
Acceptance rate (master's): 94%
Acceptance rate (DNP): 100%
Specialties offered: administration; clinical nurse leader; education; generalist; nurse practitioner

Ohio State University

1585 Neil Avenue
Columbus, OH 43210
nursing.osu.edu/
Public
Admissions: (614) 292-4041
Email: nursing@osu.edu
Financial aid: (614) 292-8595
Application deadline: 1/15
Degrees offered: master's, Ph.D., DNP
In-state tuition: full time: $723/credit hour, part time: $723/credit hour (master's); full time: $723/credit hour, part time: $723/credit hour (Ph.D.); full time: $723/credit hour, part time: $723/credit hour (DNP)
Out-of-state tuition: full time: $1,940/credit hour (master's); full time: $1,940/credit hour (Ph.D.); full time: $723/credit hour (DNP)

Room/board/expenses: $814 (master's); $814 (Ph.D.); $814 (DNP)
Full-time enrollment: 531 (master's); 20 (Ph.D.); 18 (DNP) men: 15%; women: 85%; minorities: 18%; international: 1%
Part-time enrollment: 155 (master's); 4 (Ph.D.); 64 (DNP) men: 13%; women: 87%; minorities: 11%; international: 1%
Acceptance rate (master's): 58%
Acceptance rate (Ph.D.): 43%
Acceptance rate (DNP): 91%
Specialties offered: administration; clinical nurse leader; clinical nurse specialist; health management & policy health care systems; nurse-midwifery; neonatal; nurse practitioner: adult-gerontology acute care; nurse practitioner: adult-gerontology primary care; nurse practitioner: family; nurse practitioner: pediatric primary care; nurse practitioner: psychiatric-mental health, across the lifespan; research; women's health; other majors; dual majors

Ohio University
Grover Center E365
Athens, OH 45701-2979
www.ohio.edu/
Public
Admissions: (740) 593-4100
Email: admissions@ohio.edu
Financial aid: (740) 593-4141
Application deadline: 12/1
Degrees offered: master's
In-state tuition: full time: $504/credit hour, part time: $504/credit hour/credit hour/credit hour
Out-of-state tuition: full time: $596/credit hour/credit hour/credit hour
Room/board/expenses: N/A
Full-time enrollment: 4 men: 0%; women: 100%; minorities: 0%; international: 50%
Part-time enrollment: 250 men: 11%; women: 89%; minorities: 10%; international: 0%
Acceptance rate (master's): 42%
Specialties offered: administration; education; nurse practitioner: family

Otterbein University[1]
1 Otterbein College
Westerville, OH 43081
www.otterbein.edu/
Private
Admissions: (614) 823-1108
Email: mmoffitt@otterbein.edu
Financial aid: N/A
Tuition: N/A
Room/board/expenses: N/A
Enrollment: N/A

University of Akron[1]
209 Carroll Street
Akron, OH 44325-3701
Public
Admissions: N/A
Financial aid: N/A
Tuition: N/A

Room/board/expenses: N/A
Enrollment: N/A

University of Cincinnati
3110 Vine Street (ML 0038)
Cincinnati, OH 45221-0038
nursing.uc.edu/
Public
Admissions: (513) 558-3600
Email: nursing1@uc.edu
Financial aid: (513) 556-9171
Application deadline: 2/15
Degrees offered: master's, Ph.D., DNP
In-state tuition: full time: $14,668, part time: $724/credit hour (master's); full time: $14,468, part time: $724/credit hour (Ph.D.); full time: $14,468, part time: $724/credit hour (DNP)
Out-of-state tuition: full time: $26,210 (master's); full time: $26,210 (Ph.D.); full time: $26,210 (DNP)
Room/board/expenses: N/A
Full-time enrollment: 166 (master's); 21 (Ph.D.); 36 (DNP) men: 20%; women: 80%; minorities: 17%; international: 2%
Part-time enrollment: 1,075 (master's); 5 (Ph.D.); 46 (DNP) men: 13%; women: 87%; minorities: 20%; international: 0%
Acceptance rate (master's): 64%
Acceptance rate (Ph.D.): 80%
Acceptance rate (DNP): 77%
Specialties offered: administration; nurse anesthesia; nurse-midwifery; neonatal; nurse practitioner; nurse practitioner: adult-gerontology acute care; nurse practitioner: adult-gerontology primary care; nurse practitioner: family; nurse practitioner: pediatric primary care; nurse practitioner: psychiatric-mental health, across the lifespan; research; women's health; other majors

University of Toledo
3000 Arlington Avenue, MS1026
Toledo, OH 43614
utoledo.edu/nursing/index.html
Public
Admissions: (419) 383-5841
Email: admitnurse@utoledo.edu
Financial aid: (419) 383-3600
Application deadline: 12/16
Degrees offered: master's, DNP
In-state tuition: full time: $13,166, part time: $549/credit hour (master's); full time: $16,560, part time: $690/credit hour (DNP)
Out-of-state tuition: full time: $23,502 (master's); full time: $23,785 (DNP)
Room/board/expenses: $11,070 (master's); $11,070 (DNP)
Full-time enrollment: 104 (master's); 11 (DNP) men: 10%; women: 90%; minorities: 2%; international: 0%
Part-time enrollment: 110 (master's); 27 (DNP) men: 2%; women: 98%; minorities: 1%; international: 0%
Acceptance rate (master's): 92%
Acceptance rate (DNP): 26%

Specialties offered: clinical nurse leader; education; nurse practitioner; nurse practitioner: adult-gerontology primary care; nurse practitioner: adult; nurse practitioner: family; nurse practitioner: pediatric primary care; nurse practitioner: psychiatric-mental health, across the lifespan

Urbana University[1]
101 Miller Hall
Springfield, OH 45505
www.urbana.edu/academics/college-of-professional-applied-studies.html
Private
Admissions: (937) 772-9200
Email: admissions@urbana.edu
Financial aid: N/A
Tuition: N/A
Room/board/expenses: N/A
Enrollment: N/A

Ursuline College
2550 Lander Road
Pepper Pike, OH 44124
www.ursuline.edu
Private
Admissions: (440) 449-4200
Email: graduateadmissions@ursuline.edu
Financial aid: (440) 449-4200
Application deadline: 12/31
Degrees offered: master's, DNP
Tuition: full time: $1,052/credit hour, part time: $1,052/credit hour (master's); full time: $1,052/credit hour, part time: $1,052/credit hour (DNP)
Room/board/expenses: $9,490 (master's); $9,490 (DNP)
Full-time enrollment: 148 (master's); 12 (DNP) men: 6%; women: 94%; minorities: 25%; international: 1%
Part-time enrollment: 104 (master's); 1 (DNP) men: 5%; women: 95%; minorities: 24%; international: 1%
Acceptance rate (master's): 97%
Acceptance rate (DNP): 100%
Specialties offered: clinical nurse specialist; nurse practitioner; nurse practitioner: adult-gerontology acute care; nurse practitioner: adult-gerontology primary care; nurse practitioner: family; nurse practitioner: psychiatric-mental health, across the lifespan

Walsh University[1]
Aultman Health Science Center
100 2020 East Maple Street
North Canton, OH 44720
Private
Admissions: N/A
Financial aid: N/A
Tuition: N/A
Room/board/expenses: N/A
Enrollment: N/A

Wright State University
3640 Colonel Glenn Highway
Dayton, OH 45435-0001
nursing.wright.edu
Public
Admissions: (937) 775-2953

Email: wsugrad@wright.edu
Financial aid: (937) 775-5405
Application deadline: 8/28
Degrees offered: master's, DNP
In-state tuition: full time: $13,476, part time: $622/credit hour (master's); full time: $15,820, part time: $733/credit hour (DNP)
Out-of-state tuition: full time: $22,892 (master's); full time: $25,280 (DNP)
Room/board/expenses: $11,376 (master's); $11,376 (DNP)
Full-time enrollment: 118 (master's); 11 (DNP) men: 13%; women: 87%; minorities: 18%; international: 1%
Part-time enrollment: 90 (master's); 8 (DNP) men: 13%; women: 87%; minorities: 15%; international: 0%
Acceptance rate (master's): 45%
Acceptance rate (DNP): 0%
Specialties offered: administration; clinical nurse specialist; education; neonatal; nurse practitioner; nurse practitioner: adult-gerontology acute care; nurse practitioner: family; nurse practitioner: pediatric primary care; nurse practitioner: psychiatric-mental health, across the lifespan; school nursing; other majors

Xavier University
119 Cohen Center
Cincinnati, OH 45207
www.xavier.edu/nursing
Private
Admissions: (513) 745-3301
Email: xuadmit@xavier.edu
Financial aid: (513) 745-3142
Application deadline: 1/15
Degrees offered: master's, DNP
Tuition: full time: N/A, part time: N/A (master's); full time: N/A, part time: N/A (DNP)
Room/board/expenses: N/A
Full-time enrollment: 85 (master's); N/A (DNP) men: 14%; women: 86%; minorities: 18%; international: 0%
Part-time enrollment: 146 (master's); 22 (DNP) men: 4%; women: 96%; minorities: 10%; international: 0%
Acceptance rate (master's): 52%
Acceptance rate (DNP): 12%
Specialties offered: administration; clinical nurse leader; education; generalist; informatics; nurse practitioner: family; other majors

Youngstown State University[1]
1 University Plaza
Youngstown, OH 44555
Public
Admissions: N/A
Financial aid: N/A
Tuition: N/A
Room/board/expenses: N/A
Enrollment: N/A

Northeastern State University[1]
600 N. Grand Avenue
Tahlequah, OK 74464
academics.nsuok.edu/healthprofessions/DegreePrograms/Graduate/NursingEducationMSN.aspx
Public
Admissions: (918) 444-2093
Email: graduatecollege@nsuok.edu
Financial aid: (918) 444-3456
Tuition: N/A
Room/board/expenses: N/A
Enrollment: N/A

Oklahoma Baptist University[1]
111 Harrison Avenue
Oklahoma City, OK 73104
Private
Admissions: N/A
Financial aid: N/A
Tuition: N/A
Room/board/expenses: N/A
Enrollment: N/A

Oklahoma City University
2501 N. Blackwelder
Oklahoma City, OK 73106
Private
Admissions: (405) 208-5094
Email: gadmissions@okcu.edu
Financial aid: (405) 208-5848
Application deadline: N/A
Degrees offered: master's, Ph.D., DNP
Tuition: full time: $10,620, part time: $7,080 (master's); full time: $11,940, part time: $5,970 (Ph.D.); full time: $11,940, part time: $5,970 (DNP)
Room/board/expenses: $9,682 (master's); $9,682 (Ph.D.); $9,682 (DNP)
Full-time enrollment: 4 (master's); 13 (Ph.D.); 17 (DNP) men: 21%; women: 79%; minorities: 9%; international: 38%
Part-time enrollment: 15 (master's); 18 (Ph.D.); 79 (DNP) men: 6%; women: 94%; minorities: 13%; international: 0%
Acceptance rate (master's): 88%
Acceptance rate (Ph.D.): 100%
Acceptance rate (DNP): 80%
Specialties offered: administration; clinical nurse leader; education; nurse practitioner; nurse practitioner: adult-gerontology acute care; nurse practitioner: family

Oklahoma Wesleyan University[1]
2201 Silver Lake Road
Bartlesville, OK 74006
Admissions: N/A
Financial aid: N/A
Tuition: N/A
Room/board/expenses: N/A
Enrollment: N/A

Southern Nazarene University[1]
6729 N.W. 39th Expressway
Bethany, OK 73008-2605
Private
Admissions: N/A
Financial aid: N/A
Tuition: N/A
Room/board/expenses: N/A
Enrollment: N/A

University of Central Oklahoma
100 N University Drive, Box 187
Edmond, OK 73034
www.uco.edu/em/index-freshman.asp
Admissions: (405) 974-2727
Email: onestop@uco.edu
Financial aid: (405) 974-2727
Application deadline: N/A
Degrees offered: master's
Room/board/expenses: $7,800
Full-time enrollment: 18
men: 11%; women: 89%;
minorities: 17%; international: 39%
Part-time enrollment: 14
men: 7%; women: 93%;
minorities: 14%; international: 36%
Acceptance rate (master's): 100%
Specialties offered: education; generalist

University of Oklahoma Health Sciences Center
PO Box 26901
Oklahoma City, OK 73190
nursing.ouhsc.edu
Public
Admissions: (405) 271-2428
Email: Nursing@OUHSC.edu
Financial aid: (405) 271-2118
Application deadline: 3/1
Degrees offered: master's, Ph.D., DNP
In-state tuition: full time: $272/credit hour, part time: $272/credit hour (master's); full time: $204/credit hour, part time: $204/credit hour (Ph.D.); full time: $468/credit hour, part time: $468/credit hour (DNP)
Out-of-state tuition: full time: $877/credit hour (master's); full time: $792/credit hour (Ph.D.); full time: $1,125/credit hour (DNP)
Room/board/expenses: $20,926 (master's); $20,926 (Ph.D.); $20,926 (DNP)
Full-time enrollment: 49 (master's); 6 (Ph.D.); 5 (DNP)
men: 12%; women: 88%;
minorities: 23%; international: 0%
Part-time enrollment: 161 (master's); 5 (Ph.D.); 17 (DNP)
men: 11%; women: 89%;
minorities: 25%; international: 1%
Acceptance rate (master's): 43%
Acceptance rate (Ph.D.): 100%
Acceptance rate (DNP): 93%
Specialties offered: administration; clinical nurse specialist; education; nurse practitioner: family

OREGON

Oregon Health and Science University
3455 S.W. US Veterans Hospital Road, SN-ADM
Portland, OR 97239-2941
www.ohsu.edu/xd/education/schools/school-of-nursing/
Public
Admissions: (503) 494-7725
Email: proginfo@ohsu.edu
Financial aid: (503) 494-7800
Application deadline: 1/4
Degrees offered: master's, Ph.D., DNP
In-state tuition: full time: $583/credit hour, part time: $583/credit hour (master's); full time: $572/credit hour, part time: $572/credit hour (Ph.D.); full time: $572/credit hour, part time: $572/credit hour (DNP)
Out-of-state tuition: full time: $755/credit hour (master's); full time: $740/credit hour (Ph.D.); full time: $740/credit hour (DNP)
Room/board/expenses: N/A
Full-time enrollment: 156 (master's); 20 (Ph.D.); 29 (DNP)
men: 15%; women: 85%;
minorities: 20%; international: 2%
Part-time enrollment: 27 (master's); 6 (Ph.D.); 12 (DNP)
men: 16%; women: 84%;
minorities: 13%; international: 4%
Acceptance rate (master's): 40%
Acceptance rate (Ph.D.): 41%
Acceptance rate (DNP): 58%
Specialties offered: education; generalist; health management & policy health care systems; nurse anesthesia; nurse-midwifery; nurse practitioner; nurse practitioner: adult-gerontology acute care; nurse practitioner: family; nurse practitioner: pediatric primary care; nurse practitioner: psychiatric-mental health, across the lifespan; research; other majors

University of Portland
5000 N. Willamette Boulevard
MSC 153
Portland, OR 97203
nursing.up.edu/
Private
Admissions: (503) 943-7107
Email: gradschl@up.edu
Financial aid: (503) 943-7311
Application deadline: 1/15
Degrees offered: master's, DNP
Tuition: full time: N/A, part time: N/A (master's); full time: $1,170/credit hour, part time: $1,170/credit hour (DNP)
Room/board/expenses: N/A
Full-time enrollment: 5 (master's); 30 (DNP)
men: 9%; women: 91%;
minorities: 9%; international: 0%
Part-time enrollment: N/A (master's); N/A (DNP)
men: N/A; women: N/A;
minorities: N/A; international: N/A
Acceptance rate (DNP): 25%
Specialties offered: clinical nurse leader; education; nurse practitioner; nurse practitioner: family

PENNSYLVANIA

Alvernia University[1]
400 St. Bernardine Street
Reading, PA 19607
Private
Admissions: N/A
Financial aid: N/A
Tuition: N/A
Room/board/expenses: N/A
Enrollment: N/A

Bloomsburg University of Pennsylvania[1]
3109 McCormick Center for Human Services
Bloomsburg, PA 17815-1301
Public
Admissions: N/A
Financial aid: N/A
Tuition: N/A
Room/board/expenses: N/A
Enrollment: N/A

California University of Pennsylvania
250 University Avenue
California, PA 15419
www.calu.edu/academics/online-programs/nursing-administration/index.htm
Public
Admissions: (866) 595-6348
Email: msonline@calu.edu
Financial aid: (724) 938-4415
Application deadline: N/A
Degrees offered: master's
In-state tuition: full time: $483/credit hour, part time: $483/credit hour
Out-of-state tuition: full time: $493/credit hour
Room/board/expenses: N/A
Full-time enrollment: 97
men: 14%; women: 86%;
minorities: 10%; international: 0%
Part-time enrollment:
men: N/A; women: N/A;
minorities: N/A; international: N/A
Acceptance rate (master's): 72%
Specialties offered: administration; dual majors

Carlow University[1]
3333 Fifth Avenue
Pittsburgh, PA 15213
Private
Admissions: N/A
Financial aid: N/A
Tuition: N/A
Room/board/expenses: N/A
Enrollment: N/A

Cedar Crest College
100 College Drive
Allentown, PA 18104
www.cedarcrest.edu/ca/academics/nursing/index.shtm
Private
Admissions: (610) 606-4666
Email: sage@cedarcrest.edu
Financial aid: (610) 606-4666
Application deadline: N/A
Degrees offered: master's
Tuition: full time: $772/credit hour, part time: $772/credit hour
Room/board/expenses: N/A
Full-time enrollment:
men: N/A; women: N/A;
minorities: N/A; international: N/A

Part-time enrollment: 11
men: 18%; women: 82%;
minorities: 0%; international: 0%
Acceptance rate (master's): 57%
Specialties offered: administration; education

Chatham University
Woodland Road
Pittsburgh, PA 15232
www.chatham.edu
Private
Admissions: (412) 365-1139
Email: abecher@chatham.edu
Financial aid: (412) 365-2781
Application deadline: N/A
Degrees offered: master's, DNP
Tuition: full time: $903/credit hour, part time: $903/credit hour (master's); full time: $903/credit hour, part time: $903/credit hour (DNP)
Room/board/expenses: N/A
Full-time enrollment: 13 (master's); 46 (DNP)
men: 19%; women: 81%;
minorities: 36%; international: 19%
Part-time enrollment: 6 (master's); 65 (DNP)
men: 15%; women: 85%;
minorities: 34%; international: 0%
Acceptance rate (master's): 100%
Acceptance rate (DNP): 100%
Specialties offered: education; informatics; other majors

Clarion University - Edinboro University
840 Wood Street
Clarion, PA 16214
www.clarion.edu/dnp
Public
Admissions: (814) 393-2337
Email: gradstudies@clarion.edu
Financial aid: (814) 393-2315
Application deadline: N/A
Degrees offered: master's, DNP
In-state tuition: full time: $531/credit hour, part time: $574/credit hour (master's); full time: N/A, part time: $628/credit hour (DNP)
Out-of-state tuition: full time: $531/credit hour (master's); full time: N/A (DNP)
Room/board/expenses: N/A
Full-time enrollment: 7 (master's); N/A (DNP)
men: 14%; women: 86%;
minorities: 0%; international: 0%
Part-time enrollment: 90 (master's); 15 (DNP)
men: 11%; women: 89%;
minorities: 7%; international: 0%
Acceptance rate (master's): 90%
Acceptance rate (DNP): 100%
Specialties offered: nurse practitioner: family

DeSales University
2755 Station Avenue
Center Valley, PA 18034-9568
www.desales.edu/nursing
Private
Admissions: (610) 282-1100
Email: gradadmissions@desales.edu
Financial aid: (610) 282-1100
Application deadline: N/A
Degrees offered: master's, DNP

Tuition: full time: N/A, part time: N/A (master's); full time: N/A, part time: N/A (DNP)
Room/board/expenses: N/A
Full-time enrollment: 7 (master's); 21 (DNP)
men: 7%; women: 93%;
minorities: 4%; international: 4%
Part-time enrollment: 111 (master's); N/A (DNP)
men: 12%; women: 88%;
minorities: 8%; international: 0%
Acceptance rate (master's): 68%
Acceptance rate (DNP): 58%
Specialties offered: administration; clinical nurse specialist; health management & policy health care systems; nurse practitioner; nurse practitioner: adult-gerontology acute care; nurse practitioner: family; nurse practitioner: psychiatric-mental health, across the lifespan; dual majors

Drexel University
Bellet Building
Philadelphia, PA 19102-1192
www.drexel.edu/cnhp/academics/graduate/gradNursing/
Private
Admissions: (215) 895-6172
Email: randall.c.deike@drexel.edu
Financial aid: (215) 571-4545
Application deadline: 5/1
Degrees offered: master's, Ph.D., DNP
Tuition: full time: $913/credit hour, part time: $913/credit hour (master's); full time: $886/credit hour, part time: $886/credit hour (Ph.D.); full time: $925/credit hour, part time: $925/credit hour (DNP)
Room/board/expenses: N/A
Full-time enrollment: 35 (master's); 3 (Ph.D.); N/A (DNP)
men: 24%; women: 76%;
minorities: 0%; international: 0%
Part-time enrollment: 1,200 (master's); N/A (Ph.D.); 85 (DNP)
men: 10%; women: 90%;
minorities: 21%; international: 2%
Acceptance rate (master's): 53%
Acceptance rate (Ph.D.): 100%
Acceptance rate (DNP): 74%
Specialties offered: administration; clinical nurse leader; education; nurse anesthesia; nurse practitioner; nurse practitioner: adult-gerontology acute care; nurse practitioner: adult-gerontology primary care; nurse practitioner: adult; nurse practitioner: family; nurse practitioner: pediatric primary care; nurse practitioner: psychiatric-mental health, across the lifespan; other majors

Duquesne University
600 Forbes Avenue
Pittsburgh, PA 15282-1760
www.duq.edu/academics/schools/nursing
Private
Admissions: (412) 396-6550
Email: nursing@duq.edu
Financial aid: (412) 396-6607
Application deadline: 3/1

Degrees offered: master's, Ph.D., DNP
Tuition: full time: $1,264/credit hour, part time: $1,264/credit hour (master's); full time: $1,264/credit hour, part time: $1,264/credit hour (Ph.D.); full time: $1,264/credit hour, part time: $1,264/credit hour (DNP)
Room/board/expenses: N/A (master's); $1,264 (Ph.D.); N/A (DNP)
Full-time enrollment: 95 (master's); 45 (Ph.D.); 13 (DNP) men: 10%; women: 90%; minorities: 16%; international: 2%
Part-time enrollment: 60 (master's); 14 (Ph.D.); N/A (DNP) men: 7%; women: 93%; minorities: 23%; international: 0%
Acceptance rate (master's): 79%
Acceptance rate (Ph.D.): 50%
Acceptance rate (DNP): 100%
Specialties offered: education; nurse practitioner; nurse practitioner: family

Gannon University[1]
109 University Square
Erie, PA 16541
www.gannon.edu/
Private
Admissions: N/A
Financial aid: N/A
Tuition: N/A
Room/board/expenses: N/A
Enrollment: N/A

Gwynedd Mercy University
1325 Sumneytown Pike
Gwynedd Valley, PA 19437
www.gmercyu.edu/academics/programs/doctor-nursing-practice
Private
Admissions: (215) 646-7300
Email: roski.j@gmercyu.edu
Financial aid: (215) 646-7300
Application deadline: 3/3
Degrees offered: master's, DNP
Tuition: full time: $800/credit hour, part time: $800/credit hour (master's); full time: $900/credit hour, part time: $900/credit hour (DNP)
Room/board/expenses: N/A
Full-time enrollment: 19 (master's); N/A (DNP) men: N/A; women: N/A; minorities: 63%; international: 0%
Part-time enrollment: 114 (master's); 6 (DNP) men: 8%; women: 92%; minorities: 47%; international: 0%
Acceptance rate (master's): 58%
Specialties offered: clinical nurse specialist; nurse practitioner: adult-gerontology primary care; nurse practitioner: pediatric primary care

Holy Family University[1]
9801 Frankford Avenue
Philadelphia, PA 19114
www.holyfamily.edu/choosing-holy-family-u/academics/schools-of-study/philadelphia-sch
Private
Admissions: (267) 341-3327

Email: gradstudy@holyfamily.edu
Financial aid: (267) 341-3233
Tuition: N/A
Room/board/expenses: N/A
Enrollment: N/A

Immaculata University[1]
1145 King Road
Immaculata, PA 19345-0500
Private
Admissions: N/A
Financial aid: N/A
Tuition: N/A
Room/board/expenses: N/A
Enrollment: N/A

Indiana University of Pennsylvania
Johnson Hall, Room 210/1010 Oakland Avenue
Indiana, PA 15705
www.iup.edu/rn-alliedhealth/
Public
Admissions: (724) 357-2222
Email: graduate-admissions@iup.edu
Financial aid: (724) 357-2218
Application deadline: N/A
Degrees offered: master's, Ph.D.
In-state tuition: full time: $508/credit hour, part time: $508/credit hour (master's); full time: $534/credit hour, part time: $534/credit hour
Out-of-state tuition: full time: $763/credit hour (master's); full time: $801/credit hour
Room/board/expenses: $12,246 (master's); $12,246
Full-time enrollment: 31 (master's); men: 19%; women: 81%; minorities: 0%; international: 94%
Part-time enrollment: 45 (master's); 53 men: 11%; women: 89%; minorities: 11%; international: 7%
Acceptance rate (master's): 69%
Acceptance rate (Ph.D.): 55%
Specialties offered: administration; education

La Roche College
9000 Babcock Boulevard
Pittsburgh, PA 15237-5898
www.laroche.edu/Academics/Academic_Divisions/Education_and_Nursing_Division/NURSING/D
Private
Admissions: (412) 536-1266
Financial aid: (412) 536-1125
Application deadline: N/A
Degrees offered: master's
Tuition: full time: $700/credit hour, part time: $700/credit hour
Room/board/expenses: N/A
Full-time enrollment: 18 men: 11%; women: 89%; minorities: 6%; international: 0%
Part-time enrollment: 8 men: 13%; women: 88%; minorities: 0%; international: 25%
Acceptance rate (master's): 83%
Specialties offered: administration; education

La Salle University
1900 W. Olney Avenue
Philadelphia, PA 19141-1199
www.lasalle.edu/snhs/
Private
Admissions: (215) 951-1322
Email: dillonp@lasalle.edu
Financial aid: (215) 951-1070
Application deadline: N/A
Degrees offered: master's, DNP
Tuition: full time: $895/credit hour, part time: $895/credit hour (master's); full time: $955/credit hour, part time: $955/credit hour (DNP)
Room/board/expenses: N/A
Full-time enrollment: 2 (master's); N/A (DNP) men: 50%; women: 50%; minorities: 0%; international: 50%
Part-time enrollment: 330 (master's); 31 (DNP) men: 18%; women: 82%; minorities: 28%; international: 1%
Acceptance rate (master's): 67%
Acceptance rate (DNP): 56%
Specialties offered: administration; clinical nurse leader; clinical nurse specialist; community health/public health; nurse anesthesia; nurse practitioner; nurse practitioner: adult-gerontology primary care; nurse practitioner: family; school nursing

Mansfield University of Pennsylvania[1]
G24 South Hall
Mansfield, PA 16933
Public
Admissions: N/A
Financial aid: N/A
Tuition: N/A
Room/board/expenses: N/A
Enrollment: N/A

Millersville University of Pennsylvania[1]
127 Caputo Hall
Millersville, PA 17551
Public
Admissions: N/A
Financial aid: N/A
Tuition: N/A
Room/board/expenses: N/A
Enrollment: N/A

Misericordia University[1]
301 Lake Street
Dallas, PA 18612
Private
Admissions: N/A
Financial aid: N/A
Tuition: N/A
Room/board/expenses: N/A
Enrollment: N/A

Moravian College
1200 Main Street
Bethlehem, PA 18018
moravian.edu/nursing
Private
Admissions: (800) 441-3191
Email: admission@moravian.edu
Financial aid: (610) 861-1330
Application deadline: 4/1
Degrees offered: master's

Tuition: full time: $846/credit hour, part time: $846/credit hour
Room/board/expenses: N/A
Full-time enrollment: 1 men: 0%; women: 100%; minorities: 0%; international: 0%
Part-time enrollment: 64 men: 8%; women: 92%; minorities: 8%; international: 0%
Acceptance rate (master's): 68%
Specialties offered: administration; clinical nurse leader; education; nurse practitioner; nurse practitioner: adult-gerontology acute care; nurse practitioner: adult-gerontology primary care

Neumann University[1]
1 Neumann Drive
Aston, PA 19014-1298
Private
Admissions: N/A
Financial aid: N/A
Tuition: N/A
Room/board/expenses: N/A
Enrollment: N/A

Pennsylvania State University-University Park
201 Nursing Sciences Building
University Park, PA 16802-1589
www.nursing.psu.edu/
Public
Admissions: (814) 863-1795
Email: nursgrad@psu.edu
Financial aid: (814) 865-6301
Application deadline: 2/15
Degrees offered: master's, Ph.D., DNP
In-state tuition: full time: $16,640, part time: $832/credit hour (master's); full time: $19,964, part time: $832/credit hour (Ph.D.); full time: $16,420, part time: $821/credit hour (DNP)
Out-of-state tuition: full time: $28,560 (master's); full time: $34,266 (Ph.D.); full time: $16,420 (DNP)
Room/board/expenses: $12,490 (master's); $12,490 (Ph.D.); $12,490 (DNP)
Full-time enrollment: 51 (master's); 6 (Ph.D.); 4 (DNP) men: 15%; women: 85%; minorities: 8%; international: 7%
Part-time enrollment: 100 (master's); 9 (Ph.D.); 26 (DNP) men: 13%; women: 87%; minorities: 16%; international: 1%
Acceptance rate (master's): 45%
Acceptance rate (Ph.D.): 60%
Acceptance rate (DNP): 65%
Specialties offered: administration; education; nurse practitioner; nurse practitioner: adult-gerontology acute care; nurse practitioner: adult-gerontology primary care; nurse practitioner: family; research; other majors; dual majors

Robert Morris University
6001 University Boulevard
Moon Township, PA 15108
snhs.rmu.edu/OurPrograms/GraduateDegrees
Private

Admissions: (800) 762-0097
Email: graduateadmissionsoffice@rmu.edu
Financial aid: (412) 397-6250
Application deadline: 5/1
Degrees offered: master's, DNP
Tuition: full time: N/A, part time: $565/credit hour (master's); full time: $27,375, part time: $925/credit hour (DNP)
Room/board/expenses: N/A (master's); N/A (DNP) men: N/A; women: N/A; minorities: N/A; international: N/A
Part-time enrollment: 27 (master's); 203 (DNP) men: 16%; women: 84%; minorities: 7%; international: 0%
Acceptance rate (master's): 69%
Acceptance rate (DNP): 63%
Specialties offered: education; generalist; nurse practitioner; nurse practitioner: adult-gerontology primary care; nurse practitioner: adult; nurse practitioner: family; nurse practitioner: psychiatric-mental health, across the lifespan

Temple University
1801 N. Broad Street
Philadelphia, PA 19122
cph.temple.edu/nursing/home
Public
Admissions: (215) 707-4618
Email: tunurse@temple.edu
Financial aid: (215) 204-2244
Application deadline: 2/15
Degrees offered: DNP
In-state tuition: full time: $906/credit hour, part time: $906/credit hour
Out-of-state tuition: full time: $1,246/credit hour
Room/board/expenses: $14,348
Full-time enrollment: 11 men: 0%; women: 100%; minorities: 36%; international: 0%
Part-time enrollment: 50 men: 20%; women: 80%; minorities: 56%; international: 0%
Acceptance rate (DNP): 80%
Specialties offered: nurse practitioner: adult-gerontology primary care; nurse practitioner: family

Thomas Jefferson University
901 Walnut Street, 8th Floor
Philadelphia, PA 19107
www.jefferson.edu/nursing
Private
Admissions: (215) 503-1040
Email: erin.finn@jefferson.edu
Financial aid: (215) 955-2867
Application deadline: 2/15
Degrees offered: master's, DNP
Tuition: full time: N/A, part time: N/A (master's); full time: N/A, part time: N/A (DNP)
Room/board/expenses: N/A
Full-time enrollment: 50 (master's); 23 (DNP) men: 17%; women: 83%; minorities: 24%; international: 0%

Part-time enrollment: 425 (master's); 51 (DNP) men: 18%; women: 82%; minorities: 21%; international: 0%
Specialties offered: clinical nurse specialist; community health/public health; informatics; nurse anesthesia; neonatal; nurse practitioner; nurse practitioner: adult-gerontology acute care; nurse practitioner: adult-gerontology primary care; nurse practitioner: family; nurse practitioner: pediatric primary care; women's health; combined nurse practitioner/clinical nurse specialist; dual majors

University of Pennsylvania
420 Guardian Drive
Philadelphia, PA 19104-6096
www.nursing.upenn.edu
Private
Admissions: (215) 898-4271
Email: admissions@nursing.upenn.edu
Financial aid: (215) 898-8191
Application deadline: 6/30
Degrees offered: master's, Ph.D., DNP
Tuition: full time: $39,552, part time: $1,657/credit hour (master's); full time: $32,286, part time: $1,996/credit hour (Ph.D.); full time: $32,286, part time: $1,657/credit hour (DNP)
Room/board/expenses: $28,310 (master's); $28,310 (Ph.D.); $28,310 (DNP)
Full-time enrollment: 183 (master's); 61 (Ph.D.); 17 (DNP) men: 11%; women: 89%; minorities: 27%; international: 5%
Part-time enrollment: 431 (master's); 4 (Ph.D.); N/A (DNP) men: 11%; women: 89%; minorities: 31%; international: 0%
Acceptance rate (master's): 56%
Acceptance rate (Ph.D.): 35%
Acceptance rate (DNP): 73%
Specialties offered: administration; clinical nurse specialist; nurse anesthesia; nurse-midwifery; neonatal; nurse practitioner; nurse practitioner: adult-gerontology acute care; nurse practitioner: adult-gerontology primary care; nurse practitioner: family; nurse practitioner: pediatric primary care; nurse practitioner: psychiatric-mental health, across the lifespan; women's health; other majors; dual majors

University of Pittsburgh
Victoria Building
Pittsburgh, PA 15261
www.nursing.pitt.edu/
Public
Admissions: (412) 624-6910
Email: sao50@pitt.edu
Financial aid: (412) 624-7488
Application deadline: 5/1
Degrees offered: master's, Ph.D., DNP
In-state tuition: full time: $850/credit hour, part time: $1,039/credit hour (master's); full time: $850/credit hour, part time: $1,039/credit hour (Ph.D.); full time: $850/credit hour, part time: $1,039/credit hour (DNP)
Out-of-state tuition: full time: $988/credit hour (master's); full time: $988/credit hour (Ph.D.); full time: $988/credit hour (DNP)
Room/board/expenses: N/A
Full-time enrollment: 136 (master's); 27 (Ph.D.); 44 (DNP) men: 21%; women: 79%; minorities: 11%; international: 6%
Part-time enrollment: 47 (master's); 4 (Ph.D.); 94 (DNP) men: 19%; women: 81%; minorities: 6%; international: 0%
Acceptance rate (master's): 32%
Acceptance rate (Ph.D.): 35%
Acceptance rate (DNP): 53%
Specialties offered: administration; clinical nurse leader; clinical nurse specialist; informatics; nurse anesthesia; nurse-midwifery; neonatal; nurse practitioner; nurse practitioner: adult-gerontology acute care; nurse practitioner: adult-gerontology primary care; nurse practitioner: adult; nurse practitioner: family; nurse practitioner: pediatric primary care; nurse practitioner: psychiatric-mental health, across the lifespan; research; other majors

University of Scranton
800 Linden Street
Scranton, PA 18510
www.scranton.edu/nursing
Private
Admissions: (570) 941-4416
Email: caitlyn.hollingshead@scranton.edu
Financial aid: (570) 941-7700
Application deadline: N/A
Degrees offered: master's, DNP
Tuition: full time: $965/credit hour, part time: $965/credit hour (master's); full time: $772/credit hour, part time: $772/credit hour (DNP)
Room/board/expenses: N/A
Full-time enrollment: 48 (master's); 9 (DNP) men: 37%; women: 63%; minorities: 28%; international: 0%
Part-time enrollment: 35 (master's); 1 (DNP) men: 8%; women: 92%; minorities: 8%; international: 3%
Acceptance rate (master's): 51%
Acceptance rate (DNP): 100%
Specialties offered: clinical nurse specialist; nurse anesthesia; nurse practitioner; nurse practitioner: adult-gerontology primary care; nurse practitioner: family

Villanova University
800 Lancaster Avenue
Villanova, PA 19085
www1.villanova.edu/villanova/nursing.html
Private
Admissions: (610) 519-4934
Email: marguerite.schlag@villanova.edu
Financial aid: (610) 519-4010
Application deadline: N/A

Degrees offered: master's, Ph.D., DNP
Tuition: full time: $862/credit hour, part time: $862/credit hour (master's); full time: $1,081/credit hour, part time: $1,081/credit hour (Ph.D.); full time: $1,375/credit hour, part time: $1,375/credit hour (DNP)
Room/board/expenses: $17,620 (master's); $17,620 (Ph.D.); $17,260 (DNP)
Full-time enrollment: 141 (master's); 61 (Ph.D.); 13 (DNP) men: 10%; women: 90%; minorities: 10%; international: 7%
Part-time enrollment: 126 (master's); 3 (Ph.D.); 4 (DNP) men: 14%; women: 86%; minorities: 10%; international: 0%
Acceptance rate (master's): 61%
Acceptance rate (Ph.D.): 43%
Acceptance rate (DNP): 100%
Specialties offered: education; nurse anesthesia; nurse practitioner; nurse practitioner: adult-gerontology primary care; nurse practitioner: family; nurse practitioner: pediatric primary care; research

Waynesburg University[1]
51 West College Street
Waynesburg, PA 15370
www.waynesburg.edu/graduate/graduate-majors/nursing
Private
Admissions: (724) 743-7612
Email: sstoneci@waynesburg.edu
Financial aid: (724) 852-3208
Tuition: N/A
Room/board/expenses: N/A
Enrollment: N/A

West Chester University of Pennsylvania[1]
222 Sturzebecker Health Sciences Center
West Chester, PA 19383
Public
Admissions: N/A
Financial aid: N/A
Tuition: N/A
Room/board/expenses: N/A
Enrollment: N/A

Widener University[1]
One University Place
Chester, PA 19013-5892
Private
Admissions: N/A
Financial aid: N/A
Tuition: N/A
Room/board/expenses: N/A
Enrollment: N/A

Wilkes University[1]
109 S. Franklin Street
Wilkes-Barre, PA 18766
wilkes.edu/academics/colleges/school-of-nursing/index.aspx
Private
Admissions: (800) 945-5378
Email: GraduateStudies@wilkes.edu
Financial aid: (570) 408-2000
Tuition: N/A

Room/board/expenses: N/A
Enrollment: N/A

York College of Pennsylvania[1]
York College of Pennsylvania
York, PA 17405
Private
Admissions: N/A
Financial aid: N/A
Tuition: N/A
Room/board/expenses: N/A
Enrollment: N/A

PUERTO RICO

Universidad del Turabo[1]
P.O. Box 3030
Gurabo, PR 00778-3030
Private
Admissions: N/A
Financial aid: N/A
Tuition: N/A
Room/board/expenses: N/A
Enrollment: N/A

University of Puerto Rico[1]
Box 365067
San Juan, PR 00936-5067
Public
Admissions: N/A
Financial aid: N/A
Tuition: N/A
Room/board/expenses: N/A
Enrollment: N/A

RHODE ISLAND

Rhode Island College[1]
600 Mount Pleasant Avenue
Providence, RI 02908-1991
www.ric.edu/nursing/
Public
Admissions: N/A
Financial aid: (401) 456-8033
Tuition: N/A
Room/board/expenses: N/A
Enrollment: N/A

University of Rhode Island
White Hall
Kingston, RI 02881-2021
web.uri.edu/nursing/
Public
Admissions: (401) 874-2872
Email: gradadm@etal.uri.edu
Financial aid: (401) 874-9500
Application deadline: 2/15
Degrees offered: master's, Ph.D., DNP
In-state tuition: full time: $11,796, part time: $655/credit hour (master's); full time: $11,796, part time: $655/credit hour (Ph.D.); full time: $11,796, part time: $655/credit hour (DNP)
Out-of-state tuition: full time: $24,206 (master's); full time: $24,206 (Ph.D.); full time: $24,206 (DNP)
Room/board/expenses: N/A
Full-time enrollment: 24 (master's); 2 (Ph.D.); 11 (DNP) men: 8%; women: 92%; minorities: 22%; international: 5%

Part-time enrollment: 46 (master's); 16 (Ph.D.); 19 (DNP) men: 10%; women: 90%; minorities: 11%; international: 1%
Acceptance rate (master's): 68%
Acceptance rate (Ph.D.): 50%
Acceptance rate (DNP): 100%
Specialties offered: education; nurse practitioner; nurse practitioner: adult-gerontology acute care; nurse practitioner: adult-gerontology primary care; nurse practitioner: family; research; combined nurse practitioner/clinical nurse specialist

SOUTH CAROLINA

Charleston Southern University
9200 University Boulevard
North Charleston, SC 29406
www.csuniv.edu
Private
Admissions: (843) 863-7054
Email: jrhoton@csuniv.edu
Financial aid: (843) 863-4707
Application deadline: N/A
Degrees offered: master's
Tuition: full time: N/A, part time: N/A
Room/board/expenses: N/A
Full-time enrollment: 10 men: 20%; women: 80%; minorities: 20%; international: 0%
Part-time enrollment: men: N/A; women: N/A; minorities: N/A; international: N/A
Acceptance rate (master's): 100%
Specialties offered: administration; education

Clemson University[1]
524 Edwards Hall
Clemson, SC 29634
www.clemson.edu/hehd/departments/nursing/
Public
Admissions: (864) 656-3195
Email: grdapp@clemson.edu
Financial aid: (864) 656-2280
Tuition: N/A
Room/board/expenses: N/A
Enrollment: N/A

Francis Marion University
Frank B. Lee Nursing Building
Florence, SC 29502-0547
www.fmarion.edu/
Public
Admissions: (843) 661-1231
Email: pwilson@fmarion.edu
Financial aid: (843) 661-1190
Application deadline: 7/15
Degrees offered: master's
In-state tuition: full time: $15,668, part time: $783/credit hour/credit hour
Out-of-state tuition: full time: $31,336/credit hour/credit hour
Room/board/expenses: N/A
Full-time enrollment: 26 men: 12%; women: 88%; minorities: 19%; international: 0%
Part-time enrollment: 61 men: 18%; women: 82%; minorities: 20%; international: 0%
Acceptance rate (master's): 100%

Specialties offered: education; nurse practitioner: family; dual majors

Lander University[1]
320 Stanley Avenue
Greenwood, SC 29649-2099
Admissions: N/A
Financial aid: N/A
Tuition: N/A
Room/board/expenses: N/A
Enrollment: N/A

Medical University of South Carolina
99 Jonathan Lucas Street
MSC 160
Charleston, SC 29425
musc.edu/nursing
Public
Admissions: (843) 792-7408
Email: hudsonly@musc.edu
Financial aid: (843) 792-2536
Application deadline: 3/15
Degrees offered: master's, Ph.D., DNP
In-state tuition: full time: $24,348, part time: $835/credit hour (master's); full time: $24,348, part time: $835/credit hour (Ph.D.); full time: $24,348, part time: $835/credit hour (DNP)
Out-of-state tuition: full time: $28,659 (master's); full time: $28,659 (Ph.D.); full time: $28,659 (DNP)
Room/board/expenses: N/A
Full-time enrollment: 14 (master's); 14 (Ph.D.); 148 (DNP) men: 9%; women: 91%; minorities: 20%; international: 0%
Part-time enrollment: 12 (master's); 34 (Ph.D.); 66 (DNP) men: 7%; women: 93%; minorities: 29%; international: 0%
Acceptance rate (master's): 25%
Acceptance rate (Ph.D.): 83%
Acceptance rate (DNP): 85%
Specialties offered: administration; generalist; nurse practitioner; nurse practitioner: adult-gerontology primary care; nurse practitioner: family; nurse practitioner: pediatric primary care; nurse practitioner: psychiatric-mental health, across the lifespan; research

University of South Carolina
1601 Greene Street
Columbia, SC 29208-0001
www.sc.edu/nursing
Public
Admissions: (803) 777-7412
Email: ribara@mailbox.sc.edu
Financial aid: (803) 777-8134
Application deadline: 4/1
Degrees offered: master's, Ph.D., DNP
In-state tuition: full time: $731/credit hour, part time: $731/credit hour (master's); full time: $533/credit hour, part time: $533/credit hour (Ph.D.); full time: $731/credit hour, part time: $731/credit hour (DNP)
Out-of-state tuition: full time: $1,340/credit hour (master's); full time: $1,142/credit hour

(Ph.D.); full time: $1,340/credit hour (DNP)
Room/board/expenses: N/A
Full-time enrollment: 132 (master's); 7 (Ph.D.); 25 (DNP) men: 7%; women: 93%; minorities: 21%; international: 1%
Part-time enrollment: 216 (master's); 7 (Ph.D.); 64 (DNP) men: 10%; women: 90%; minorities: 20%; international: 0%
Acceptance rate (master's): 66%
Acceptance rate (Ph.D.): 45%
Acceptance rate (DNP): 57%
Specialties offered: administration; nurse practitioner; nurse practitioner: adult-gerontology acute care; nurse practitioner: family; nurse practitioner: psychiatric-mental health, across the lifespan; research

University of South Carolina Upstate[1]
800 University Way
Spartanburg, SC 29303
Admissions: N/A
Financial aid: N/A
Tuition: N/A
Room/board/expenses: N/A
Enrollment: N/A

SOUTH DAKOTA

Mount Marty College
1105 West 8th Street
Yankton, SD 57078-3725
www.mtmc.edu/
Admissions: (855) 686-2789
Email: mmcadmit@mtmc.edu
Financial aid: (605) 668-1589
Application deadline: 3/1
Degrees offered: master's
Room/board/expenses: N/A
Full-time enrollment: 20 men: 10%; women: 90%; minorities: 0%; international: 0%
Part-time enrollment: 7 men: 0%; women: 100%; minorities: 0%; international: 0%
Acceptance rate (master's): 82%
Specialties offered: nurse practitioner: family

National American University[1]
925 29th Street SE
Watertown, SD 57201
www.national.edu/programs/school-nursing
Private
Admissions: (877) 398-0118
Email: graduateadmissions@national.edu
Financial aid: (855) 459-3629
Tuition: N/A
Room/board/expenses: N/A
Enrollment: N/A

South Dakota State University
SNF 217
Brookings, SD 57007
www.sdstate.edu/nurs/index.cfm
Public
Admissions: (605) 688-4101
Email: sdsu_gradschool@sdstate.edu
Financial aid: (800) 952-3541

Application deadline: 3/15
Degrees offered: master's, Ph.D., DNP
In-state tuition: full time: $313/credit hour, part time: $313/credit hour (master's); full time: $313/credit hour, part time: $313/credit hour (Ph.D.); full time: $313/credit hour, part time: $313/credit hour (DNP)
Out-of-state tuition: full time: $602/credit hour (master's); full time: $602/credit hour (Ph.D.); full time: $602/credit hour (DNP)
Room/board/expenses: $9,965 (master's); $9,965 (Ph.D.); $9,965 (DNP)
Full-time enrollment: 18 (master's); 3 (Ph.D.); 31 (DNP) men: 8%; women: 92%; minorities: 2%; international: N/A
Part-time enrollment: 74 (master's); 15 (Ph.D.); 76 (DNP) men: 9%; women: 91%; minorities: 6%; international: N/A
Acceptance rate (master's): 83%
Acceptance rate (Ph.D.): 100%
Acceptance rate (DNP): 84%
Specialties offered: administration; clinical nurse leader; clinical nurse specialist; education; neonatal; nurse practitioner; nurse practitioner: family; nurse practitioner: pediatric primary care; nurse practitioner: psychiatric-mental health, across the lifespan; research

TENNESSEE

Aquinas College[1]
4210 Harding Pike
Nashville, TN 37205
Private
Admissions: N/A
Financial aid: N/A
Tuition: N/A
Room/board/expenses: N/A
Enrollment: N/A

Belmont University
1900 Belmont Boulevard
Nashville, TN 37212-3757
www.belmont.edu/gradnursing/
Private
Admissions: (615) 460-6107
Email: bill.nichols@belmont.edu
Financial aid: (615) 460-6403
Application deadline: 5/1
Degrees offered: master's, DNP
Tuition: full time: $1,185/credit hour, part time: $1,185/credit hour (master's); full time: $22,880, part time: $1,275/credit hour (DNP)
Room/board/expenses: N/A
Full-time enrollment: 17 (master's); 37 (DNP) men: 11%; women: 89%; minorities: 13%; international: 0%
Part-time enrollment: 35 (master's); N/A (DNP) men: 11%; women: 89%; minorities: 14%; international: 0%
Acceptance rate (master's): 59%
Acceptance rate (DNP): 69%
Specialties offered: nurse practitioner; nurse practitioner: family

Carson-Newman University
1646 Russell Avenue
Jefferson City, TN 71883
www.cn.edu/
Private
Admissions: (865) 471-3471
Email: adult@cn.edu
Financial aid: (800) 678-9061
Application deadline: 3/15
Degrees offered: master's
Tuition: full time: $600/credit hour, part time: $600/credit hour
Room/board/expenses: N/A
Full-time enrollment: 46 men: N/A; women: N/A; minorities: N/A; international: N/A
Part-time enrollment: 1 men: N/A; women: N/A; minorities: N/A; international: N/A
Specialties offered: education; nurse practitioner: family

East Tennessee State University
Campus Box 70617
Johnson City, TN 37614-0617
www.etsu.edu/nursing
Public
Admissions: (423) 439-4221
Email: gradsch@etsu.edu
Financial aid: (423) 439-4300
Application deadline: 2/1
Degrees offered: master's, Ph.D., DNP
In-state tuition: full time: $531/credit hour, part time: $531/credit hour (master's); full time: $531/credit hour, part time: $531/credit hour (Ph.D.); full time: $531/credit hour, part time: $531/credit hour (DNP)
Out-of-state tuition: full time: $1,323/credit hour (master's); full time: $1,323/credit hour (Ph.D.); full time: $1,323/credit hour (DNP)
Room/board/expenses: $5,000 (master's); $5,000 (Ph.D.); $5,000 (DNP)
Full-time enrollment: 42 (master's); 1 (Ph.D.); 41 (DNP) men: 18%; women: 82%; minorities: 10%; international: 0%
Part-time enrollment: 250 (master's); 23 (Ph.D.); 29 (DNP) men: 12%; women: 88%; minorities: 8%; international: 0%
Acceptance rate (master's): 85%
Acceptance rate (Ph.D.): 50%
Acceptance rate (DNP): 61%
Specialties offered: administration; clinical nurse leader; education; nurse practitioner; nurse practitioner: adult-gerontology primary care; nurse practitioner: family; nurse practitioner: psychiatric-mental health, across the lifespan; research

King University[1]
1350 King College Road
Bristol, TN 37620
Private
Admissions: N/A
Financial aid: N/A
Tuition: N/A
Room/board/expenses: N/A
Enrollment: N/A

Lincoln Memorial University[1]
6965 Cumberland Gap Parkway
Harrogate, TN 37752
Private
Admissions: N/A
Financial aid: N/A
Tuition: N/A
Room/board/expenses: N/A
Enrollment: N/A

Southern Adventist University[1]
PO Box 370
Collegedale, TN 37315
Private
Admissions: N/A
Financial aid: N/A
Tuition: N/A
Room/board/expenses: N/A
Enrollment: N/A

Tennessee Board of Regents[1]
1415 Murfreesboro Road
Suite 350
Nashville, TN 37217-2833
Public
Admissions: N/A
Financial aid: N/A
Tuition: N/A
Room/board/expenses: N/A
Enrollment: N/A

Tennessee State University[1]
3500 John A. Merritt Boulevard
Box 9590
Nashville, TN 37209-1561
Public
Admissions: N/A
Financial aid: N/A
Tuition: N/A
Room/board/expenses: N/A
Enrollment: N/A

Union University
1050 Union University Drive
Jackson, TN 38305
www.uu.edu/academics/son/
Private
Admissions: (731) 661-6545
Email: nursingadmissions@uu.edu
Financial aid: (731) 661-5015
Application deadline: 1/15
Degrees offered: master's, DNP
Tuition: full time: $572/credit hour, part time: $572/credit hour (master's); full time: $875/credit hour, part time: $875/credit hour (DNP)
Room/board/expenses: N/A
Full-time enrollment: 84 (master's); 123 (DNP) men: 28%; women: 72%; minorities: 17%; international: 0%
Part-time enrollment: 17 (master's); 18 (DNP) men: 6%; women: 94%; minorities: 11%; international: 0%
Acceptance rate (master's): 55%
Acceptance rate (DNP): 30%
Specialties offered: administration; education; nurse anesthesia; nurse practitioner; nurse practitioner: adult-gerontology primary care; nurse practitioner: family; nurse practitioner: pediatric primary

care; nurse practitioner: psychiatric–mental health, across the lifespan

University of Memphis (Loewenberg)

610 Goodman
Memphis, TN 38152
www.memphis.edu/nursing/
Public
Admissions: (901) 678-5255
Financial aid: (901) 678-4825
Application deadline: 2/15
Degrees offered: master's
In-state tuition: full time: $27,416, part time: $27,416
Out-of-state tuition: full time: $49,864
Room/board/expenses: $3,350
Full-time enrollment: 45
men: 11%; women: 89%; minorities: 33%; international: 0%
Part-time enrollment: 239
men: 10%; women: 90%; minorities: 35%; international: 0%
Acceptance rate (master's): 38%
Specialties offered: administration; education; nurse practitioner: family; other majors

University of Tennessee–Chattanooga[1]

615 McCallie Avenue
Chattanooga, TN 37403
www.utc.edu/nursing/
Public
Admissions: (423) 425-4666
Email: gsadmin@utc.edu
Financial aid: (423) 425-4677
Tuition: N/A
Room/board/expenses: N/A
Enrollment: N/A

University of Tennessee Health Science Center[1]

877 Madison Avenue
Memphis, TN 38163
Public
Admissions: N/A
Financial aid: N/A
Tuition: N/A
Room/board/expenses: N/A
Enrollment: N/A

University of Tennessee–Knoxville

1200 Volunteer Boulevard
Knoxville, TN 37996-4180
nursing.utk.edu
Public
Admissions: (865) 974-3251
Email: gradschool@utk.edu
Financial aid: (865) 974-1111
Application deadline: 2/1
Degrees offered: master's, Ph.D., DNP
In-state tuition: full time: $615/credit hour, part time: $615/credit hour (master's); full time: $615/credit hour, part time: $615/credit hour (Ph.D.); full time: $615/credit hour, part time: $615/credit hour (DNP)
Out-of-state tuition: full time: $1,626/credit hour (master's);

full time: $1,626/credit hour (Ph.D.); full time: $1,626/credit hour (DNP)
Room/board/expenses: N/A
Full-time enrollment: 114
(master's); 7 (Ph.D.); N/A (DNP)
men: 19%; women: 81%; minorities: 8%; international: 0%
Part-time enrollment: 19
(master's); 23 (Ph.D.); 18 (DNP)
men: 15%; women: 85%; minorities: 10%; international: 0%
Acceptance rate (master's): 48%
Acceptance rate (Ph.D.): 85%
Acceptance rate (DNP): 57%
Specialties offered: administration; health management & policy health care systems; nurse anesthesia; nurse practitioner: nurse practitioner: family; nurse practitioner: pediatric primary care; nurse practitioner: psychiatric–mental health, across the lifespan; research

Vanderbilt University

464 21st Avenue South
Nashville, TN 37240
www.nursing.vanderbilt.edu/
Private
Admissions: (615) 322-3800
Email: vusn-admissions@vanderbilt.edu
Financial aid: (615) 322-8986
Application deadline: 9/15
Degrees offered: master's, Ph.D., DNP
Tuition: full time: $1,359/credit hour, part time: $1,359/credit hour (master's); full time: $1,854/credit hour, part time: $1,854/credit hour (Ph.D.); full time: $1,359/credit hour, part time: $1,359/credit hour (DNP)
Room/board/expenses: N/A
Full-time enrollment: 432
(master's); 24 (Ph.D.); 37 (DNP)
men: 13%; women: 87%; minorities: 18%; international: 0%
Part-time enrollment: 201
(master's); 6 (Ph.D.); 138 (DNP)
men: 6%; women: 94%; minorities: 17%; international: 0%
Acceptance rate (master's): 67%
Acceptance rate (Ph.D.): 27%
Acceptance rate (DNP): 82%
Specialties offered: administration; informatics; nurse-midwifery; neonatal; nurse practitioner; nurse practitioner: adult-gerontology acute care; nurse practitioner: adult-gerontology primary care; nurse practitioner: family; nurse practitioner: pediatric primary care; nurse practitioner: psychiatric–mental health, across the lifespan; women's health; other majors; dual majors

TEXAS

Angelo State University

ASU Station 10902
San Angelo, TX 76909-0902
www.angelo.edu/dept/nursing/
Public
Admissions: (325) 942-2169

Email: graduate.school@angelo.edu
Financial aid: (325) 942-2246
Application deadline: 4/1
Degrees offered: master's
In-state tuition: full time: $480/credit hour, part time: $480/credit hour
Out-of-state tuition: full time: $812/credit hour
Room/board/expenses: N/A
Full-time enrollment: 37
men: 19%; women: 81%; minorities: 27%; international: 0%
Part-time enrollment: 49
men: 12%; women: 88%; minorities: 22%; international: 0%
Acceptance rate (master's): 56%
Specialties offered: education; nurse practitioner; nurse practitioner: family

Baylor University

3700 Worth Street
Dallas, TX 75246
www.baylor.edu/nursing/nursing_grad/
Private
Admissions: (214) 820-3361
Email: bu_nursing@baylor.edu
Financial aid: (214) 820-4143
Application deadline: N/A
Degrees offered: master's, DNP
Tuition: full time: $1,583/credit hour, part time: $1,583/credit hour (master's); full time: $1,583/credit hour, part time: $1,583/credit hour (DNP)
Room/board/expenses: N/A
(master's); $12,786 (DNP)
Full-time enrollment: 12
(master's); 39 (DNP)
men: 8%; women: 92%; minorities: 33%; international: 0%
Part-time enrollment: 2
(master's); 6 (DNP)
men: 0%; women: 100%; minorities: 63%; international: 0%
Acceptance rate (master's): 57%
Acceptance rate (DNP): 59%
Specialties offered: administration; nurse-midwifery; neonatal; nurse practitioner; nurse practitioner: family

Hardin-Simmons University[1]

2149 Hickory Street
Abilene, TX 79601
Private
Admissions: N/A
Financial aid: N/A
Tuition: N/A
Room/board/expenses: N/A
Enrollment: N/A

Lamar University

4400 Martin Luther King Boulevard
Beaumont, TX 77710
artssciences.lamar.edu/nursing/
Public
Admissions: (409) 880-8890
Email: gradmissions@lamar.edu
Financial aid: (409) 880-7011
Application deadline: N/A
Degrees offered: master's
In-state tuition: full time: N/A, part time: $318/credit hour

Out-of-state tuition: full time: N/A
Room/board/expenses: N/A
Full-time enrollment:
men: N/A; women: N/A; minorities: N/A; international: N/A
Part-time enrollment: 81
men: 11%; women: 89%; minorities: 52%; international: 0%
Acceptance rate (master's): 94%
Specialties offered: administration; education; dual majors

Lubbock Christian University

5601 19th Street
Lubbock, TX 79407
www.lcu.edu/admissions/graduate/nursing
Private
Admissions: (806) 720-7599
Email: patricia.moulton@lcu.edu
Financial aid: (806) 720-7178
Application deadline: N/A
Degrees offered: master's
Tuition: full time: $426/credit hour, part time: $426/credit hour
Room/board/expenses: N/A
Full-time enrollment: 70
men: 23%; women: 77%; minorities: 33%; international: 10%
Part-time enrollment: 50
men: N/A; women: N/A; minorities: N/A; international: N/A
Acceptance rate (master's): 89%
Specialties offered: education; nurse practitioner; nurse practitioner: family

McMurry University (Shelton)[1]

2149 Hickory Street
Abilene, TX 79601
Private
Admissions: N/A
Financial aid: N/A
Tuition: N/A
Room/board/expenses: N/A
Enrollment: N/A

Midwestern State University

3410 Taft Boulevard
Wichita Falls, TX 76308
www.mwsu.edu/academics/hs2/nursing/index
Public
Admissions: (940) 397-4920
Email: graduateschool@mwsu.edu
Financial aid: (940) 397-4214
Application deadline: 4/1
Degrees offered: master's
In-state tuition: full time: $214/credit hour, part time: $214/credit hour
Out-of-state tuition: full time: $279/credit hour
Room/board/expenses: N/A
Full-time enrollment: 96
men: 16%; women: 84%; minorities: 27%; international: 0%
Part-time enrollment:
men: N/A; women: N/A; minorities: N/A; international: N/A
Acceptance rate (master's): 34%

Specialties offered: nurse practitioner: family; nurse practitioner: psychiatric–mental health, across the lifespan

Patty Hanks Shelton School of Nursing[1]

2149 Hickory Street
Abilene, TX 79601
Private
Admissions: N/A
Financial aid: N/A
Tuition: N/A
Room/board/expenses: N/A
Enrollment: N/A

Prairie View A&M University

6436 Fannin Street
Houston, TX 77030
www.pvamu.edu/nursing/
Public
Admissions: (713) 797-7000
Email: graduatenursing@pvamu.edu
Financial aid: (936) 261-1000
Application deadline: 6/1
Degrees offered: master's, DNP
In-state tuition: full time: $273/credit hour, part time: $273/credit hour (master's); full time: $273/credit hour, part time: $273/credit hour (DNP)
Out-of-state tuition: full time: $720/credit hour (master's); full time: $720/credit hour (DNP)
Room/board/expenses: $8,754 (master's); $8,754 (DNP)
Full-time enrollment: 71
(master's); 3 (DNP)
men: 12%; women: 88%; minorities: 91%; international: 3%
Part-time enrollment: 49
(master's); 8 (DNP)
men: 9%; women: 91%; minorities: 91%; international: 5%
Acceptance rate (master's): 97%
Acceptance rate (DNP): 100%
Specialties offered: administration; education; generalist; nurse practitioner

Tarleton State University

Nursing Building, Room 301
Stephenville, TX 76402
www.tarleton.edu/nursing/
Public
Admissions: N/A
Financial aid: (254) 968-9070
Application deadline: 8/22
Degrees offered: master's
In-state tuition: full time: $204/credit hour, part time: $204/credit hour
Out-of-state tuition: full time: $612/credit hour
Room/board/expenses: N/A
Full-time enrollment: 2
men: 0%; women: 100%; minorities: 50%; international: 0%
Part-time enrollment: 14
men: 14%; women: 86%; minorities: 43%; international: 14%
Acceptance rate (master's): 100%
Specialties offered: administration; education

Texas A&M University-Texarkana[1]

7101 University Avenue
Texarkana, TX 75503
Public
Admissions: N/A
Financial aid: N/A
Tuition: N/A
Room/board/expenses: N/A
Enrollment: N/A

Texas A&M Health Science Center

8447 State Highway 47
Bryan, TX 77807
nursing.tamhsc.edu/
Admissions: (979) 436-0110
Email:
CONadmissions@tamhsc.edu
Financial aid: (979) 845-3236
Application deadline: 1/15
Degrees offered: master's
Room/board/expenses: N/A
Full-time enrollment: 14
men: 7%; women: 93%;
minorities: 14%; international:
0%
Part-time enrollment: 39
men: 15%; women: 85%;
minorities: 21%; international:
0%
Acceptance rate (master's): 33%
Specialties offered: education;
nurse practitioner: family

Texas A&M International University[1]

5201 University Boulevard
Laredo, TX 78041
Public
Admissions: N/A
Financial aid: N/A
Tuition: N/A
Room/board/expenses: N/A
Enrollment: N/A

Texas A&M University-Corpus Christi

6300 Ocean Drive, Unit 5805
Corpus Christi, TX 78412
conhs.tamucc.edu
Public
Admissions: (361) 825-2177
Email: gradweb@tamucc.edu
Financial aid: (361) 825-2338
Application deadline: 4/1
Degrees offered: master's, DNP
In-state tuition: full time: $372/
credit hour, part time: $372/
credit hour (master's); full time:
$372/credit hour, part time:
$372/credit hour (DNP)
Out-of-state tuition: full time:
$780/credit hour (master's); full
time: $780/credit hour (DNP)
Room/board/expenses: N/A
Full-time enrollment: N/A
(master's); N/A (DNP)
men: N/A; women: N/A;
minorities: N/A; international:
N/A
Part-time enrollment: 511
(master's); 10 (DNP)
men: 16%; women: 84%;
minorities: 50%; international:
0%
Acceptance rate (master's): 41%
Acceptance rate (DNP): 77%

Texas Christian University

2800 W. Bowie Street
Fort Worth, TX 76019
www.harriscollege.tcu.edu
Private
Admissions: (817) 257-6726
Email: m.allred@tcu.edu
Financial aid: (817) 257-7858
Application deadline: N/A
Degrees offered: master's, DNP
Tuition: full time: $1,480/credit
hour, part time: $1,480/credit
hour (master's); full time: $1,480/
credit hour, part time: $1,480/
credit hour (DNP)
Room/board/expenses: N/A
Full-time enrollment: 46
(master's); 213 (DNP)
men: 32%; women: 68%;
minorities: 22%; international:
0%
Part-time enrollment: 14
(master's); 13 (DNP)
men: 7%; women: 93%;
minorities: 26%; international:
0%
Acceptance rate (master's): 82%
Acceptance rate (DNP): 45%
Specialties offered:
administration; clinical nurse
leader; clinical nurse specialist;
education; generalist; nurse
anesthesia; nurse practitioner:
family

Texas State University

1555 University Drive
Round Rock, TX 78665
www.nursing.txstate.edu/
Public
Admissions: (512) 245-2581
Email: gradcollege@txstate.edu
Financial aid: (512) 245-2315
Application deadline: 1/15
Degrees offered: master's
In-state tuition: full time: $6,166,
part time: $308/credit hour
Out-of-state tuition: full time:
$14,327
Room/board/expenses: $8,100
Full-time enrollment: 71
men: 13%; women: 87%;
minorities: 37%; international:
1%
Part-time enrollment:
men: N/A; women: N/A;
minorities: N/A; international:
N/A
Acceptance rate (master's): 40%
Specialties offered: nurse
practitioner; nurse practitioner:
family

Texas Tech University Health Sciences Center

3601 4th Street, MS 6264
Lubbock, TX 79430
www.ttuhsc.edu/son
Public
Admissions: (800) 851-8240
Email: songrad@ttuhsc.edu
Financial aid: (806) 743-3025
Application deadline: 2/15
Degrees offered: master's, DNP

In-state tuition: full time: $3,060,
part time: $340/credit hour
(master's); full time: $3,060, part
time: $340/credit hour (DNP)
Out-of-state tuition: full time:
$8,505 (master's); full time:
$8,505 (DNP)
Room/board/expenses: N/A
Full-time enrollment: 11
(master's); 41 (DNP)
men: 15%; women: 85%;
minorities: 23%; international:
0%
Part-time enrollment: 552
(master's); 12 (DNP)
men: 16%; women: 84%;
minorities: 35%; international:
0%
Acceptance rate (master's): 42%
Acceptance rate (DNP): 75%
Specialties offered:
administration; education;
informatics; nurse-midwifery;
nurse practitioner; nurse
practitioner: adult-gerontology
acute care; nurse practitioner:
family; nurse practitioner:
pediatric primary care; nurse
practitioner: psychiatric-mental
health, across the lifespan

Texas Woman's University

PO Box 425498
Denton, TX 76204-5498
www.twu.edu
Public
Admissions: (940) 898-3188
Email: admissions@twu.edu
Financial aid: (940) 898-3064
Application deadline: 3/15
Degrees offered: master's, Ph.D.,
DNP
In-state tuition: full time: $306/
credit hour, part time: $306/
credit hour (master's); full time:
$331/credit hour, part time:
$331/credit hour (Ph.D.); full
time: $331/credit hour, part
time: $331/credit hour (DNP)
Out-of-state tuition: full time:
$714/credit hour (master's); full
time: $739/credit hour (Ph.D.);
full time: $739/credit hour (DNP)
Room/board/expenses: $7,578
(master's); $7,578 (Ph.D.);
$7,578 (DNP)
Full-time enrollment: 15
(master's); 3 (Ph.D.); 6 (DNP)
men: 8%; women: 92%;
minorities: 50%; international:
29%
Part-time enrollment: 754
(master's); 105 (Ph.D.); 46
(DNP)
men: 7%; women: 93%;
minorities: 57%; international:
2%
Acceptance rate (master's): 69%
Acceptance rate (Ph.D.): 39%
Acceptance rate (DNP): 91%
Specialties offered:
administration; clinical nurse
leader; education; health
management & policy health
care systems; informatics;
nurse practitioner; nurse
practitioner: adult-gerontology
acute care; nurse practitioner:
adult-gerontology primary
care; nurse practitioner: adult;
nurse practitioner: family; nurse
practitioner: pediatric primary
care; other majors

University of Houston[1]

3007 N. Ben Wilson
Victoria, TX 77901
Public
Admissions: N/A
Financial aid: N/A
Tuition: N/A
Room/board/expenses: N/A
Enrollment: N/A

University of Mary Hardin-Baylor[1]

900 College Street
Belton, TX 76513
umhb.edu/nursing
Private
Admissions: N/A
Financial aid: (254) 295-4515
Tuition: N/A
Room/board/expenses: N/A
Enrollment: N/A

University of Texas-Arlington

411 S. Nedderman Drive
PO Box 19407
Arlington, TX 76019
www.uta.edu/nursing
Public
Admissions: (817) 272-2776
Email: nursing@uta.edu
Financial aid: N/A
Application deadline: 5/1
Degrees offered: master's, Ph.D.,
DNP
In-state tuition: full time: $4,207,
part time: $1,840 (master's); full
time: $4,207, part time: $1,840
(Ph.D.); full time: $4,207, part
time: $1,840 (DNP)
Out-of-state tuition: full time:
$10,171 (master's); full time:
$10,171 (Ph.D.); full time: $10,171
(DNP)
Room/board/expenses: $9,222
(master's); $9,222 (Ph.D.);
$9,222 (DNP)
Full-time enrollment: 2,294
(master's); 22 (Ph.D.); 28 (DNP)
men: 11%; women: 89%;
minorities: 46%; international:
1%
Part-time enrollment: 731
(master's); 9 (Ph.D.); 14 (DNP)
men: 10%; women: 90%;
minorities: 47%; international:
0%
Acceptance rate (master's): 53%
Acceptance rate (Ph.D.): 30%
Acceptance rate (DNP): 39%
Specialties offered:
administration; education;
neonatal; nurse practitioner;
nurse practitioner: adult-
gerontology acute care; nurse
practitioner: adult-gerontology
primary care; nurse practitioner:
family; nurse practitioner:
pediatric primary care; nurse
practitioner: psychiatric-mental
health, across the lifespan;
research; other majors

University of Texas-Austin

1710 Red River
Austin, TX 78701
www.nursing.utexas.edu
Public
Admissions: (512) 471-7927
Email: tdemchuk@
mail.nur.utexas.edu
Financial aid: (512) 475-6282

University of Houston[1]

Application deadline: 10/1
Degrees offered: master's, Ph.D.,
DNP
In-state tuition: full time: $11,919,
part time: $4,306 (master's); full
time: $11,919, part time: $4,306
(Ph.D.); full time: $18,000, part
time: $9,000 (DNP)
Out-of-state tuition: full time:
$21,749 (master's); full time:
$21,749 (Ph.D.); full time:
$18,000 (DNP)
Room/board/expenses: $13,200
(master's); $13,200 (Ph.D.);
$13,200 (DNP)
Full-time enrollment: 197
(master's); 30 (Ph.D.); 25 (DNP)
men: 13%; women: 87%;
minorities: 31%; international:
2%
Part-time enrollment: 34
(master's); 10 (Ph.D.); 2 (DNP)
men: 22%; women: 78%;
minorities: 35%; international:
0%
Acceptance rate (master's): 52%
Acceptance rate (Ph.D.): 89%
Acceptance rate (DNP): 94%
Specialties offered:
administration; clinical nurse
specialist; nurse practitioner;
nurse practitioner: family; nurse
practitioner: pediatric primary
care; nurse practitioner:
psychiatric-mental health,
across the lifespan; research;
other majors

University of Texas-El Paso[1]

500 W. University Avenue
El Paso, TX 79902
nursing.utep.edu/
Public
Admissions: (915) 747-5491
Email: gradschool@utep.edu
Financial aid: (915) 747-5204
Tuition: N/A
Room/board/expenses: N/A
Enrollment: N/A

University of Texas Health Science Center-Houston

6901 Bertner Avenue
Houston, TX 77030
nursing.uth.edu/
Public
Admissions: (713) 500-2101
Email: soninfo@uth.tmc.edu
Financial aid: (713) 500-3860
Application deadline: 3/1
Degrees offered: master's, Ph.D.,
DNP
In-state tuition: full time: $256/
credit hour, part time: $256/
credit hour (master's); full time:
$256/credit hour, part time:
$256/credit hour (Ph.D.); full
time: $256/credit hour, part
time: $256/credit hour (DNP)
Out-of-state tuition: full time:
$1,010/credit hour (master's);
full time: $1,010/credit hour
(Ph.D.); full time: $1,010/credit
hour (DNP)
Room/board/expenses: N/A
Full-time enrollment: 136
(master's); 10 (Ph.D.); 62 (DNP)
men: 20%; women: 80%;
minorities: 52%; international:
1%

Part-time enrollment: 479 (master's); 36 (Ph.D.); 91 (DNP) men: 14%; women: 86%; minorities: 59%; international: 0%
Acceptance rate (master's): 73%
Acceptance rate (Ph.D.): 83%
Acceptance rate (DNP): 84%
Specialties offered: administration; education; emergency; informatics; nurse anesthesia; nurse practitioner; nurse practitioner: adult-gerontology acute care; nurse practitioner: adult-gerontology primary care; nurse practitioner: family; nurse practitioner: psychiatric-mental health, across the lifespan; research; dual majors

University of Texas Health Science Center-San Antonio
7703 Floyd Curl Drive
San Antonio, TX 78229-3900
nursing.uthscsa.edu
Public
Admissions: (210) 567-5805
Email: SONAdmissions@ uthscsa.edu
Financial aid: (210) 567-2635
Application deadline: 2/17
Degrees offered: master's, Ph.D., DNP
In-state tuition: full time: $6,581, part time: $4,935 (master's); full time: $6,581, part time: $4,935 (Ph.D.); full time: $6,581, part time: $4,935 (DNP)
Out-of-state tuition: full time: $18,293 (master's); full time: $18,293 (Ph.D.); full time: $18,293 (DNP)
Room/board/expenses: $18,563 (master's); $18,563 (Ph.D.); $18,563 (DNP)
Full-time enrollment: 93 (master's); 8 (Ph.D.); 8 (DNP) men: 17%; women: 83%; minorities: 54%; international: 6%
Part-time enrollment: 97 (master's); 16 (Ph.D.); 25 (DNP) men: 21%; women: 79%; minorities: 62%; international: 0%
Acceptance rate (master's): 73%
Acceptance rate (Ph.D.): 58%
Acceptance rate (DNP): 88%
Specialties offered: administration; clinical nurse leader; education; nurse practitioner; nurse practitioner: adult-gerontology primary care; nurse practitioner: family; nurse practitioner: pediatric primary care; nurse practitioner: psychiatric-mental health, across the lifespan

University of Texas Medical Branch-Galveston
301 University Boulevard
Galveston, TX 77555-1132
nursing.utmb.edu/
Public
Admissions: (409) 772-8205
Email: dpearro@utmb.edu
Financial aid: (409) 772-1215
Application deadline: 1/15
Degrees offered: master's, Ph.D., DNP

In-state tuition: full time: $285/ credit hour, part time: $285/ credit hour (master's); full time: $285/credit hour, part time: $285/credit hour (Ph.D.); full time: $285/credit hour, part time: $285/credit hour (DNP)
Out-of-state tuition: full time: $693/credit hour (master's); full time: $693/credit hour (Ph.D.); full time: $693/credit hour (DNP)
Room/board/expenses: $14,424 (master's); $14,424 (Ph.D.); $14,424 (DNP)
Full-time enrollment: 43 (master's); 16 (Ph.D.); N/A (DNP) men: N/A; women: 100%; minorities: 49%; international: 0%
Part-time enrollment: 488 (master's); 22 (Ph.D.); 42 (DNP) men: 13%; women: 87%; minorities: 52%; international: 1%
Acceptance rate (master's): 20%
Acceptance rate (Ph.D.): 20%
Acceptance rate (DNP): 28%
Specialties offered: administration; clinical nurse leader; education; neonatal; nurse practitioner; nurse practitioner: adult-gerontology primary care; nurse practitioner: family; research

University of Texas-Rio Grande Valley
Marialice Shary Shivers Building
1201 W. University Drive
Edinburg, TX 78539-2999
www.utrgv.edu/en-us/academics/ colleges/health-affairs
Public
Admissions: (956) 665-3661
Email: gradcollege@utrgv.edu
Financial aid: (956) 665-3491
Application deadline: 4/1
Degrees offered: master's
In-state tuition: full time: $7,169, part time: $303/credit hour
Out-of-state tuition: full time: $14,962
Room/board/expenses: N/A
Full-time enrollment: 31 men: 42%; women: 58%; minorities: 90%; international: 3%
Part-time enrollment: 91 men: 12%; women: 88%; minorities: 85%; international: 0%
Acceptance rate (master's): 84%
Specialties offered: administration; education; nurse practitioner; nurse practitioner: family; nurse practitioner: psychiatric-mental health, across the lifespan

University of Texas-Tyler
3900 University Boulevard
Tyler, TX 75799
www.uttyler.edu/nursing/college/
Public
Admissions: (903) 566-7457
Email: ogs@uttyler.edu
Financial aid: (903) 566-7183
Application deadline: 2/15
Degrees offered: master's, Ph.D., DNP
In-state tuition: full time: $744/ credit hour, part time: $744/ credit hour (master's); full time:

$787/credit hour, part time: $787/credit hour (Ph.D.); full time: $787/credit hour, part time: $787/credit hour (DNP)
Out-of-state tuition: full time: $1,155/credit hour (master's); full time: $1,195/credit hour (Ph.D.); full time: $1,195/credit hour (DNP)
Room/board/expenses: N/A
Full-time enrollment: 108 (master's); 28 (Ph.D.); N/A (DNP) men: 12%; women: 88%; minorities: 35%; international: N/A
Part-time enrollment: 247 (master's); 47 (Ph.D.); 10 (DNP) men: 16%; women: 84%; minorities: 40%; international: N/A
Acceptance rate (master's): 54%
Acceptance rate (Ph.D.): 41%
Acceptance rate (DNP): 86%
Specialties offered: administration; education; nurse practitioner: family; research

University of the Incarnate Word
4301 Broadway
San Antonio, TX 78209
uiw.edu/nursing/
Private
Admissions: (210) 829-6005
Email: admis@uiwtx.edu
Financial aid: (210) 829-6008
Application deadline: N/A
Degrees offered: master's, DNP
Tuition: full time: $885/credit hour, part time: $885/credit hour (master's); full time: $875/ credit hour, part time: $875/ credit hour (DNP)
Room/board/expenses: N/A
Full-time enrollment: 6 (master's); 4 (DNP) men: 20%; women: 80%; minorities: 70%; international: 0%
Part-time enrollment: 20 (master's); 54 (DNP) men: 16%; women: 84%; minorities: 72%; international: 3%
Acceptance rate (master's): 80%
Acceptance rate (DNP): 100%
Specialties offered: clinical nurse leader; clinical nurse specialist; nurse practitioner: family; nurse practitioner: psychiatric-mental health, across the lifespan

Wayland Baptist University[1]
8300 Pat Booker Road
Live Oak, TX 78233
Private
Admissions: N/A
Financial aid: N/A
Tuition: N/A
Room/board/expenses: N/A
Enrollment: N/A

West Texas A&M University[1]
Killgore Research Center
Room 102
Canyon, TX 79016
Public
Admissions: N/A
Financial aid: N/A
Tuition: N/A

Room/board/expenses: N/A
Enrollment: N/A

UTAH

Brigham Young University
400 SWKT
Provo, UT 84602
nursing.byu.edu
Private
Admissions: (801) 422-4091
Email: graduatestudies@byu.edu
Financial aid: (801) 422-4104
Application deadline: 12/1
Degrees offered: master's
Tuition: full time: $393/credit hour, part time: $393/credit hour
Room/board/expenses: $15,000
Full-time enrollment: 29 men: 28%; women: 72%; minorities: 3%; international: 0%
Part-time enrollment: men: N/A; women: N/A; minorities: N/A; international: N/A
Acceptance rate (master's): 30%
Specialties offered: nurse practitioner; nurse practitioner: family

Rocky Mountain University of Health Professions
122 E. 1700 S
Provo, UT 84606
rmuohp.edu/
Admissions: (801) 734-6800
Email: admissions@rmuohp.edu
Financial aid: (801) 734-6764
Application deadline: 7/24
Degrees offered: DNP
Room/board/expenses: N/A
Full-time enrollment: 55 men: 31%; women: 69%; minorities: 35%; international: 0%
Part-time enrollment: men: N/A; women: N/A; minorities: N/A; international: N/A
Acceptance rate (DNP): 100%
Specialties offered: nurse practitioner: family

University of Utah
10 South 2000 East
Salt Lake City, UT 84112
nursing.utah.edu
Public
Admissions: (801) 581-3414
Email: info@nurs.utah.edu
Financial aid: (801) 585-1671
Application deadline: 1/15
Degrees offered: master's, Ph.D., DNP
In-state tuition: full time: $15,402, part time: $12,486 (master's); full time: $15,402, part time: $12,486 (Ph.D.); full time: $17,345, part time: N/A (DNP)
Out-of-state tuition: full time: $38,116 (master's); full time: $30,545 (Ph.D.); full time: $43,757 (DNP)
Room/board/expenses: $9,936 (master's); $9,936 (Ph.D.); $9,936 (DNP)

Room/board/expenses: N/A
Enrollment: N/A

Full-time enrollment: 15 (master's); 22 (Ph.D.); 204 (DNP) men: 21%; women: 79%; minorities: 15%; international: 3%
Part-time enrollment: 13 (master's); 22 (Ph.D.); 16 (DNP) men: 14%; women: 86%; minorities: 14%; international: 0%
Acceptance rate (master's): 90%
Acceptance rate (Ph.D.): 59%
Acceptance rate (DNP): 50%
Specialties offered: case management; education; health management & policy health care systems; informatics; nurse-midwifery; neonatal; nurse practitioner; nurse practitioner: adult-gerontology acute care; nurse practitioner: adult-gerontology primary care; nurse practitioner: family; nurse practitioner: psychiatric-mental health, across the lifespan; research; women's health; other majors; dual majors

Utah Valley University[1]
800 W. University Parkway
Orem, UT 84058
Public
Admissions: N/A
Financial aid: N/A
Tuition: N/A
Room/board/expenses: N/A
Enrollment: N/A

Weber State University[1]
3875 Stadium Way
Department 3903
Ogden, UT 84408
weber.edu/nursing
Public
Admissions: (801) 626-6753
Email: rholt@weber.edu
Financial aid: N/A
Tuition: N/A
Room/board/expenses: N/A
Enrollment: N/A

Western Governors University[1]
4001 S. 700 E
Salt Lake City, UT 84107
Private
Admissions: N/A
Financial aid: N/A
Tuition: N/A
Room/board/expenses: N/A
Enrollment: N/A

Westminster College[1]
1840 S. 1300 E
Salt Lake City, UT 84105
Private
Admissions: N/A
Financial aid: N/A
Tuition: N/A
Room/board/expenses: N/A
Enrollment: N/A

VERMONT

Norwich University[1]
158 Harmon Drive
Northfield, VT 05663
online.norwich.edu/degree-programs/masters/master-science-nursing/overview
Private
Admissions: (800) 460-5597
Email: msn@online.norwich.edu
Financial aid: (802) 485-2969
Tuition: N/A
Room/board/expenses: N/A
Enrollment: N/A

University of Vermont
216 Rowell Building
Burlington, VT 05405
www.uvm.edu/~cnhs/nursing/
Public
Admissions: (802) 656-3858
Email: cnhsgrad@uvm.edu
Financial aid: (802) 656-5700
Application deadline: N/A
Degrees offered: master's, DNP
In-state tuition: full time: $629/credit hour, part time: $629/credit hour (master's); full time: $629/credit hour, part time: $629/credit hour (DNP)
Out-of-state tuition: full time: $1,130/credit hour (master's); full time: $1,130/credit hour (DNP)
Room/board/expenses: $9,992 (master's); N/A (DNP)
Full-time enrollment: 19 (master's); 48 (DNP) men: 16%; women: 84%; minorities: 6%; international: 0%
Part-time enrollment: 8 (master's); 19 (DNP) men: 15%; women: 85%; minorities: 0%; international: 0%
Acceptance rate (master's): 80%
Acceptance rate (DNP): 45%
Specialties offered: clinical nurse leader; nurse practitioner; nurse practitioner: adult-gerontology primary care; nurse practitioner: family

VIRGINIA

Eastern Mennonite University[1]
1200 Park Road
Harrisonburg, VA 22802
Private
Admissions: N/A
Financial aid: N/A
Tuition: N/A
Room/board/expenses: N/A
Enrollment: N/A

George Mason University
4400 University Drive
Fairfax, VA 22030-4444
chhs.gmu.edu/nursing/index.cfm
Public
Admissions: (703) 993-2400
Email: admissions@gmu.edu
Financial aid: (703) 993-2353
Application deadline: 2/1
Degrees offered: master's, Ph.D., DNP
In-state tuition: full time: $647/credit hour, part time: $647/credit hour (master's); full time: $647/credit hour, part time:
$647/credit hour (Ph.D.); full time: $647/credit hour, part time: $647/credit hour (DNP)
Out-of-state tuition: full time: $1,425/credit hour (master's); full time: $1,425/credit hour (Ph.D.); full time: $1,425/credit hour (DNP)
Room/board/expenses: $16,862 (master's); $16,862 (Ph.D.); $16,862 (DNP)
Full-time enrollment: 24 (master's); 7 (Ph.D.); 27 (DNP) men: 19%; women: 81%; minorities: 47%; international: 10%
Part-time enrollment: 89 (master's); 16 (Ph.D.); 55 (DNP) men: 11%; women: 89%; minorities: 41%; international: 1%
Acceptance rate (master's): 86%
Acceptance rate (Ph.D.): 17%
Acceptance rate (DNP): 95%
Specialties offered: administration; education; nurse practitioner; nurse practitioner: adult-gerontology primary care; nurse practitioner: family; nurse practitioner: psychiatric-mental health, across the lifespan; research

Hampton University[1]
100 E. Queen Street
Hampton, VA 23668
Private
Admissions: N/A
Financial aid: N/A
Tuition: N/A
Room/board/expenses: N/A
Enrollment: N/A

James Madison University
MSC 4305
Harrisonburg, VA 22807
jmu.edu/nursing
Public
Admissions: N/A
Email: walshmd@jmu.edu
Financial aid: (540) 568-7820
Application deadline: N/A
Degrees offered: master's, DNP
In-state tuition: full time: $538/credit hour, part time: $538/credit hour (master's); full time: $538/credit hour, part time: $538/credit hour (DNP)
Out-of-state tuition: full time: $1,269/credit hour (master's); full time: $1,269/credit hour (DNP)
Room/board/expenses: N/A
Full-time enrollment: 17 (master's); N/A (DNP) men: 18%; women: 82%; minorities: 18%; international: 0%
Part-time enrollment: 60 (master's); 25 (DNP) men: 8%; women: 92%; minorities: 4%; international: 0%
Acceptance rate (master's): 66%
Acceptance rate (DNP): 100%
Specialties offered: administration; clinical nurse leader; nurse-midwifery; nurse practitioner: adult-gerontology primary care; nurse practitioner: family

Jefferson College of Health Sciences[1]
101 Elm Avenue SE
Roanoke, VA 24013
Private
Admissions: N/A
Financial aid: N/A
Tuition: N/A
Room/board/expenses: N/A
Enrollment: N/A

Liberty University
1971 University Boulevard
Lynchburg, VA 24502
www.liberty.edu/academics/arts-sciences/nursing/index.cfm?PID=188
Private
Admissions: (800) 424-9596
Email: gradadmissions@liberty.edu
Financial aid: (434) 582-2270
Application deadline: N/A
Degrees offered: master's, DNP
Tuition: full time: $565/credit hour, part time: $615/credit hour (master's); full time: $570/credit hour, part time: $570/credit hour (DNP)
Room/board/expenses: N/A
Full-time enrollment: 57 (master's); 60 (DNP) men: 7%; women: 93%; minorities: 18%; international: 0%
Part-time enrollment: 498 (master's); 4 (DNP) men: 12%; women: 88%; minorities: 16%; international: 0%
Acceptance rate (master's): 36%
Acceptance rate (DNP): 29%
Specialties offered: administration; education; nurse practitioner; nurse practitioner: family

Lynchburg College
1501 Lakeside Drive
Lynchburg, VA 24501
www.lynchburg.edu/graduate/online-master-of-science-in-nursing/
Private
Admissions: (800) 426-8101
Email: admissions@lynchburg.edu
Financial aid: (434) 544-8230
Application deadline: N/A
Degrees offered: master's
Tuition: full time: $490/credit hour, part time: $490/credit hour
Room/board/expenses: N/A
Full-time enrollment: men: N/A; women: N/A; minorities: N/A; international: N/A
Part-time enrollment: 23 men: 9%; women: 91%; minorities: 9%; international: 9%
Acceptance rate (master's): 100%
Specialties offered: clinical nurse leader

Marymount University
2807 N. Glebe Road
Arlington, VA 22207-4299
www.marymount.edu/Academics/Malek-School-of-Health-Professions
Private
Admissions: (703) 284-5901

Email: grad.admissions@marymount.edu
Financial aid: (703) 284-1530
Application deadline: 5/1
Degrees offered: master's, DNP
Tuition: full time: $940/credit hour, part time: $940/credit hour (master's); full time: $940/credit hour, part time: $940/credit hour (DNP)
Room/board/expenses: N/A
Full-time enrollment: 13 (master's); N/A (DNP) men: 15%; women: 85%; minorities: 31%; international: 0%
Part-time enrollment: 38 (master's); 14 (DNP) men: 8%; women: 92%; minorities: 38%; international: 2%
Acceptance rate (master's): 63%
Acceptance rate (DNP): 100%
Specialties offered: nurse practitioner; nurse practitioner: family

Old Dominion University[1]
Office of Admissions
Norfolk, VA 23529-0500
Public
Admissions: N/A
Financial aid: N/A
Tuition: N/A
Room/board/expenses: N/A
Enrollment: N/A

Radford University[1]
PO Box 6964, Radford Station
Radford, VA 24142
Public
Admissions: N/A
Financial aid: N/A
Tuition: N/A
Room/board/expenses: N/A
Enrollment: N/A

Shenandoah University
1460 University Drive
Winchester, VA 22601
www.su.edu/nursing/
Private
Admissions: (540) 665-4581
Email: admit@su.edu
Financial aid: (540) 665-4538
Application deadline: 4/15
Degrees offered: master's, DNP
Tuition: full time: $846/credit hour, part time: $846/credit hour (master's); full time: $846/credit hour, part time: $846/credit hour (DNP)
Room/board/expenses: $9,990 (master's); $9,990 (DNP)
Full-time enrollment: 24 (master's); 2 (DNP) men: 8%; women: 92%; minorities: 23%; international: 12%
Part-time enrollment: 30 (master's); 5 (DNP) men: 9%; women: 91%; minorities: 20%; international: 0%
Acceptance rate (master's): 85%
Acceptance rate (DNP): 100%
Specialties offered: health management & policy health care systems; nurse-midwifery; nurse practitioner; nurse practitioner: family; nurse

practitioner: psychiatric-mental health, across the lifespan

University of Virginia
PO Box 800826
Charlottesville, VA 22908-0926
www.nursing.virginia.edu/
Public
Admissions: (434) 924-0067
Email: seid@virginia.edu
Financial aid: (434) 924-0067
Application deadline: 11/1
Degrees offered: master's, Ph.D., DNP
In-state tuition: full time: $15,450, part time: $834/credit hour (master's); full time: $15,026, part time: N/A (Ph.D.); full time: $15,450, part time: $834/credit hour (DNP)
Out-of-state tuition: full time: $25,242 (master's); full time: $25,168 (Ph.D.); full time: $25,242 (DNP)
Room/board/expenses: N/A
Full-time enrollment: 110 (master's); 27 (Ph.D.); 29 (DNP) men: 17%; women: 83%; minorities: 27%; international: 4%
Part-time enrollment: 124 (master's); 12 (Ph.D.); 48 (DNP) men: 15%; women: 85%; minorities: 20%; international: 0%
Acceptance rate (master's): 59%
Acceptance rate (Ph.D.): 59%
Acceptance rate (DNP): 75%
Specialties offered: clinical nurse leader; clinical nurse specialist; community health/public health; health management & policy health care systems; nurse practitioner; nurse practitioner: adult-gerontology acute care; nurse practitioner: family; nurse practitioner: pediatric primary care; nurse practitioner: psychiatric-mental health, across the lifespan; research; combined nurse practitioner/clinical nurse specialist

Virginia Commonwealth University
1100 E. Leigh Street
Richmond, VA 23298
www.nursing.vcu.edu
Public
Admissions: (804) 828-0727
Email: VCU_Nurse@vcu.edu
Financial aid: (804) 828-6181
Application deadline: 2/1
Degrees offered: master's, Ph.D., DNP
In-state tuition: full time: $14,523, part time: $598/credit hour (master's); full time: $10,485, part time: $499/credit hour (Ph.D.); full time: $14,700, part time: $700/credit hour (DNP)
Out-of-state tuition: full time: $30,894 (master's); full time: $22,351 (Ph.D.); full time: $14,700 (DNP)
Room/board/expenses: N/A
Full-time enrollment: 40 (master's); 20 (Ph.D.); 2 (DNP) men: 6%; women: 94%; minorities: 19%; international: 1%

...e enrollment: 175 (...ster's); 12 (Ph.D.); 19 (DNP) ...en: 6%; women: 94%; minorities: 21%; international: 1%
Acceptance rate (master's): 60%
Acceptance rate (Ph.D.): 85%
Acceptance rate (DNP): 81%
Specialties offered: administration; nurse practitioner; nurse practitioner: adult-gerontology acute care; nurse practitioner: adult-gerontology primary care; nurse practitioner: family; nurse practitioner: psychiatric-mental health, across the lifespan

WASHINGTON

Gonzaga University
502 E. Boone Avenue
Spokane, WA 99258-0038
www.gonzaga.edu/SNHP
Private
Admissions: (509) 313-6239
Email: burdette@gonzaga.edu
Financial aid: (800) 793-1716
Application deadline: 12/12
Degrees offered: master's, DNP
Tuition: full time: $975/credit hour, part time: $975/credit hour (master's); full time: $975/credit hour, part time: $975/credit hour (DNP)
Room/board/expenses: N/A
Full-time enrollment: 418 (master's); 47 (DNP) men: 18%; women: 82%; minorities: 14%; international: 0%
Part-time enrollment: 182 (master's); 83 (DNP) men: 13%; women: 87%; minorities: 17%; international: 0%
Acceptance rate (master's): 54%
Acceptance rate (DNP): 52%
Specialties offered: administration; nurse anesthesia; nurse practitioner; nurse practitioner: family; nurse practitioner: psychiatric-mental health, across the lifespan; other majors

Pacific Lutheran University
121st and Park Avenue
Tacoma, WA 98447-0029
www.plu.edu/nursing
Private
Admissions: (253) 535-8570
Email: gradadmission@plu.edu
Financial aid: (253) 535-7164
Application deadline: 1/15
Degrees offered: master's, DNP
Tuition: full time: $1,000/credit hour, part time: $1,000/credit hour (master's); full time: $1,115/credit hour, part time: $1,115/credit hour (DNP)
Room/board/expenses: $8,500 (master's); $8,000 (DNP)
Full-time enrollment: 45 (master's); 17 (DNP) men: 19%; women: 81%; minorities: 23%; international: 3%
Part-time enrollment: N/A (master's); 12 (DNP) men: 17%; women: 83%; minorities: 17%; international: 8%
Acceptance rate (master's): 31%
Acceptance rate (DNP): 91%
Specialties offered: clinical nurse leader; generalist; nurse practitioner; nurse practitioner: family; nurse practitioner: psychiatric-mental health, across the lifespan; dual majors

Seattle Pacific University[1]
3307 Third Avenue W
Seattle, WA 98119-1922
Private
Admissions: N/A
Financial aid: N/A
Tuition: N/A
Room/board/expenses: N/A
Enrollment: N/A

Seattle University
901 12th Avenue
Seattle, WA 98122-4340
www.seattleu.edu/nursing
Private
Admissions: (206) 220-8010
Email: grad-admissions@seattleu.edu
Financial aid: (206) 220-8020
Application deadline: 1/11
Degrees offered: master's, DNP
Tuition: full time: $775/credit hour, part time: $775/credit hour (master's); full time: $796/credit hour, part time: $796/credit hour (DNP)
Room/board/expenses: N/A
Full-time enrollment: 190 (master's); 20 (DNP) men: 14%; women: 86%; minorities: 20%; international: 0%
Part-time enrollment: N/A (master's); 5 (DNP) men: 20%; women: 80%; minorities: 20%; international: 0%
Acceptance rate (master's): 18%
Acceptance rate (DNP): 76%
Specialties offered: community health/public health; nurse-midwifery; nurse practitioner; nurse practitioner: adult-gerontology acute care; nurse practitioner: adult-gerontology primary care; nurse practitioner: family; nurse practitioner: psychiatric-mental health, across the lifespan

University of Washington
PO Box 357260
Seattle, WA 98195
nursing.uw.edu/
Public
Admissions: (206) 543-8736
Email: sonsas@uw.edu
Financial aid: (206) 543-6107
Application deadline: 1/15
Degrees offered: master's, Ph.D., DNP
In-state tuition: full time: $25,575, part time: $21,921 (master's); full time: $17,031, part time: $14,598 (Ph.D.); full time: $25,575, part time: $21,921 (DNP)
Out-of-state tuition: full time: $39,048 (master's); full time: $30,267 (Ph.D.); full time: $39,048 (DNP)
Room/board/expenses: $14,625 (master's); $14,625 (Ph.D.); $14,625 (DNP)
Full-time enrollment: 18 (master's); 49 (Ph.D.); 244 (DNP) men: N/A; women: N/A; minorities: 30%; international: 8%
Part-time enrollment: 51 (master's); 12 (Ph.D.); 59 (DNP) men: N/A; women: N/A; minorities: 41%; international: 2%
Acceptance rate (master's): 83%
Acceptance rate (Ph.D.): 54%
Acceptance rate (DNP): 55%
Specialties offered: clinical nurse specialist; community health/public health; informatics; nurse-midwifery; nurse practitioner; nurse practitioner: adult-gerontology acute care; nurse practitioner: adult-gerontology primary care; nurse practitioner: family; nurse practitioner: pediatric primary care; nurse practitioner: psychiatric-mental health, across the lifespan; research

Washington State University
P.O. Box 1495
Spokane, WA 99210-1495
nursing.wsu.edu
Public
Admissions: (509) 324-7279
Email: anita.hunter@wsu.edu
Financial aid: (509) 335-9711
Application deadline: 1/10
Degrees offered: master's, Ph.D., DNP
In-state tuition: full time: $17,792, part time: $890/credit hour (master's); full time: $17,792, part time: $890/credit hour (Ph.D.); full time: $17,792, part time: $890/credit hour (DNP)
Out-of-state tuition: full time: $32,814 (master's); full time: $32,814 (Ph.D.); full time: $32,814 (DNP)
Room/board/expenses: $11,356 (master's); $11,356 (Ph.D.); $11,356 (DNP)
Full-time enrollment: 2 (master's); 12 (Ph.D.); 57 (DNP) men: 25%; women: 75%; minorities: 20%; international: 3%
Part-time enrollment: 29 (master's); 20 (Ph.D.); 86 (DNP) men: 10%; women: 90%; minorities: 23%; international: 1%
Acceptance rate (master's): 71%
Acceptance rate (Ph.D.): 86%
Acceptance rate (DNP): 61%
Specialties offered: administration; community health/public health; education; health management & policy health care systems; nurse practitioner; nurse practitioner: family; nurse practitioner: psychiatric-mental health, across the lifespan; research

WEST VIRGINIA

Marshall University[1]
100 Angus E. Peyton Drive
South Charleston, WV 25303
Public
Admissions: N/A
Financial aid: N/A
Tuition: N/A
Room/board/expenses: N/A
Enrollment: N/A

West Virginia University
One Medical Drive
PO Box 9600
Morgantown, WV 26506-9600
nursing.hsc.wvu.edu/
Public
Admissions: (304) 293-5908
Email: mmmichael@hsc.wvu.edu
Financial aid: (304) 293-3706
Application deadline: 2/1
Degrees offered: master's, Ph.D., DNP
In-state tuition: full time: $9,558, part time: $531/credit hour (master's); full time: $9,558, part time: $531/credit hour (Ph.D.); full time: $9,558, part time: $531/credit hour (DNP)
Out-of-state tuition: full time: $23,796 (master's); full time: $23,796 (Ph.D.); full time: $23,796 (DNP)
Room/board/expenses: N/A
Full-time enrollment: 14 (master's); N/A (Ph.D.); 16 (DNP) men: 3%; women: 97%; minorities: 3%; international: 0%
Part-time enrollment: 63 (master's); 15 (Ph.D.); 52 (DNP) men: 10%; women: 90%; minorities: 3%; international: 0%
Acceptance rate (master's): 91%
Acceptance rate (Ph.D.): 100%
Acceptance rate (DNP): 78%
Specialties offered: neonatal; nurse practitioner; nurse practitioner: family; nurse practitioner: pediatric primary care

West Virginia Wesleyan College[1]
59 College Avenue
Buckhannon, WV 26201
Private
Admissions: N/A
Financial aid: N/A
Tuition: N/A
Room/board/expenses: N/A
Enrollment: N/A

Wheeling Jesuit University[1]
316 Washington Avenue
Wheeling, WV 26003
Private
Admissions: (304) 243-2359
Email: adulted@wju.edu
Financial aid: (304) 243-2304
Tuition: N/A
Room/board/expenses: N/A
Enrollment: N/A

WISCONSIN

Alverno College
300 S. 43 Street
Milwaukee, WI 53234-3922
www.alverno.edu/academics/academicdepartments/joannmcgrathschoolofnursing
Private
Admissions: (800) 933-3401
Email: admissions@alverno.edu
Financial aid: (414) 382-6046
Application deadline: N/A
Degrees offered: master's
Tuition: full time: $967/credit hour, part time: N/A
Room/board/expenses: N/A
Full-time enrollment: 95 men: 6%; women: 94%; minorities: 20%; international: 1%
Part-time enrollment: 96 men: 7%; women: 93%; minorities: 27%; international: 0%
Acceptance rate (master's): 100%
Specialties offered: clinical nurse specialist; nurse practitioner; nurse practitioner: family; nurse practitioner: psychiatric-mental health, across the lifespan

Bellin College[1]
3201 Eaton Road
Green Bay, WI 54311
Private
Admissions: N/A
Financial aid: N/A
Tuition: N/A
Room/board/expenses: N/A
Enrollment: N/A

Cardinal Stritch University[1]
6801 N. Yates Road
Milwaukee, WI 53217-3985
Private
Admissions: N/A
Financial aid: N/A
Tuition: N/A
Room/board/expenses: N/A
Enrollment: N/A

Columbia College of Nursing[1]
4425 N. Port Washington Road
Glendale, WI 53212
Admissions: N/A
Financial aid: N/A
Tuition: N/A
Room/board/expenses: N/A
Enrollment: N/A

Concordia University
12800 N. Lake Shore Drive
Mequon, WI 53097
www.cuw.edu/Programs/nursing/index.html
Private
Admissions: (262) 243-4590
Email: michelle.hoffman@cuw.edu
Financial aid: (262) 243-4569
Application deadline: 5/1
Degrees offered: master's, DNP
Tuition: full time: $682/credit hour, part time: $682/credit hour (master's); full time: $751/credit hour, part time: $751/credit hour (DNP)
Room/board/expenses: N/A
Full-time enrollment: 221 (master's); N/A (DNP) men: 9%; women: 91%; minorities: 12%; international: 0%
Part-time enrollment: 418 (master's); 54 (DNP) men: 8%; women: 92%; minorities: 14%; international: 0%
Acceptance rate (master's): 84%
Acceptance rate (DNP): 91%
Specialties offered: education; nurse practitioner; nurse practitioner: adult-gerontology primary care; nurse practitioner: family

Edgewood College[1]
1000 Edgewood College Drive
Madison, WI 53711
Private
Admissions: (608) 663-2294
Email:
admissions@edgewood.edu
Financial aid: (608) 663-4300
Tuition: N/A
Room/board/expenses: N/A
Enrollment: N/A

Herzing University-Milwaukee[1]
525 North 6th Street
Milwaukee, WI 53203
Private
Admissions: N/A
Financial aid: N/A
Tuition: N/A
Room/board/expenses: N/A
Enrollment: N/A

Marian University[1]
45 S. National Avenue
Fond du Lac, WI 54935-4699
www.marianuniversity.edu/
nursing/
Private
Admissions: (800) 262-7426
Email: admission@
marianuniversity.edu
Financial aid: (920) 923-7614
Tuition: N/A
Room/board/expenses: N/A
Enrollment: N/A

Marquette University
PO Box 1881
Milwaukee, WI 53201-1881
www.marquette.edu/nursing/
index.shtml
Private
Admissions: (414) 288-7137
Email: gradadmit@mu.edu
Financial aid: (414) 288-5325
Application deadline: 2/15
Degrees offered: master's, Ph.D.,
DNP
Tuition: full time: $1,075/credit
hour, part time: $1,075/credit
hour (master's); full time: $1,075/

credit hour, part time: $1,075/
credit hour (Ph.D.); full time:
$1,075/credit hour, part time:
$1,075/credit hour (DNP)
Room/board/expenses: $13,770
(master's); $13,770 (Ph.D.);
$13,050 (DNP)
Full-time enrollment: 149
(master's); 5 (Ph.D.); 11 (DNP)
men: 15%; women: 85%;
minorities: 11%; international: 1%
Part-time enrollment: 133
(master's); 24 (Ph.D.); 19 (DNP)
men: 11%; women: 89%;
minorities: 7%; international: 2%
Acceptance rate (master's): 57%
Acceptance rate (Ph.D.): 75%
Acceptance rate (DNP): 92%
Specialties offered:
administration; clinical nurse
leader; clinical nurse specialist;
generalist; nurse-midwifery;
nurse practitioner: nurse
practitioner: adult-gerontology
acute care; nurse practitioner:
adult-gerontology primary care;
nurse practitioner: pediatric
primary care; other majors

University of Wisconsin-Eau Claire
Nursing 127
Eau Claire, WI 54702-4004
www.uwec.edu/CONHS/index.
htm
Public
Admissions: (715) 836-5415
Email: admissions@uwec.edu
Financial aid: (715) 836-3373
Application deadline: 1/4
Degrees offered: master's, DNP
In-state tuition: full time: $7,641,
part time: $425/credit hour
(master's); full time: $13,200,
part time: $425/credit hour
(DNP)
Out-of-state tuition: full time:
$16,771 (master's); full time:
$23,100 (DNP)
Room/board/expenses: $6,984
(master's); $6,984 (DNP)

Full-time enrollment: N/A
(master's); 25 (DNP)
men: 16%; women: 84%;
minorities: 0%; international: 0%
Part-time enrollment: 5
(master's); 53 (DNP)
men: 3%; women: 97%;
minorities: 7%; international: 0%
Acceptance rate (master's): 100%
Acceptance rate (DNP): 61%
Specialties offered:
administration; clinical nurse
specialist; education; nurse
practitioner; nurse practitioner:
adult-gerontology primary care;
nurse practitioner: family

University of Wisconsin-Green Bay[1]
2420 Nicolet Drive
Green Bay, WI 54311-7001
Admissions: N/A
Financial aid: N/A
Tuition: N/A
Room/board/expenses: N/A
Enrollment: N/A

University of Wisconsin-Madison
600 Highland Avenue
Madison, WI 53792-2455
www.son.wisc.edu/
Public
Admissions: (608) 263-5180
Email: gradadmit@son.wisc.edu
Financial aid: (608) 262-3060
Application deadline: 2/1
Degrees offered: Ph.D., DNP
In-state tuition: full time: $10,728,
part time: $670/credit hour
(Ph.D.); full time: $13,048, part
time: $816/credit hour (DNP)
Out-of-state tuition: full time:
$24,054 (Ph.D.); full time:
$27,254 (DNP)
Room/board/expenses: $10,842
(Ph.D.); $11,420 (DNP)
Full-time enrollment: 22 (Ph.D.);
54 (DNP)
men: 13%; women: 87%;
minorities: 16%; international:
16%

Part-time enrollment: 2 (Ph.D.);
56 (DNP)
men: 14%; women: 86%;
minorities: 10%; international:
2%
Acceptance rate (Ph.D.): 57%
Acceptance rate (DNP): 54%
Specialties offered: clinical nurse
specialist; education; nurse
practitioner; nurse practitioner:
adult-gerontology acute care;
nurse practitioner: adult-
gerontology primary care; nurse
practitioner: pediatric primary
care; nurse practitioner:
psychiatric-mental health,
across the lifespan

University of Wisconsin-Milwaukee
1921 E. Hartford Avenue
Milwaukee, WI 53201
www.uwm.edu/nursing
Public
Admissions: (414) 229-2494
Email: rjens@uwm.edu
Financial aid: (414) 229-4541
Application deadline: 2/1
Degrees offered: master's, Ph.D.,
DNP
In-state tuition: full time: $11,789,
part time: $1,237/credit hour
(master's); full time: $11,789,
part time: $1,237/credit hour
(Ph.D.); full time: $11,789, part
time: $1,237/credit hour (DNP)
Out-of-state tuition: full time:
$24,824 (master's); full time:
$24,824 (Ph.D.); full time:
$24,824 (DNP)
Room/board/expenses: $9,315
(master's); $9,315 (Ph.D.);
$9,315 (DNP)
Full-time enrollment: 84
(master's); 37 (Ph.D.); 22 (DNP)
men: 10%; women: 90%;
minorities: 18%; international:
7%
Part-time enrollment: 7
(master's); 46 (Ph.D.); 129
(DNP)
men: 13%; women: 87%;
minorities: 19%; international:
3%

Acceptance rate (master's): 73%
Acceptance rate (Ph.D.): 68%
Acceptance rate (DNP): 94%
Specialties offered:
administration; clinical nurse
leader; clinical nurse specialist;
community health/public health;
generalist; health management
& policy health care systems;
informatics; nurse practitioner;
nurse practitioner: family;
research; dual majors

University of Wisconsin-Oshkosh[1]
800 Algoma Boulevard
Oshkosh, WI 54901
con.uwosh.edu/
Public
Admissions: (920) 424-1223
Email: gradschool@uwosh.edu
Financial aid: (920) 424-3377
Tuition: N/A
Room/board/expenses: N/A
Enrollment: N/A

Viterbo University[1]
900 Viterbo Drive
La Crosse, WI 54601
Private
Admissions: N/A
Financial aid: N/A
Tuition: N/A
Room/board/expenses: N/A
Enrollment: N/A

WYOMING

University of Wyoming[1]
Dept. 3065
Laramie, WY 82071
Public
Admissions: N/A
Financial aid: N/A
Tuition: N/A
Room/board/expenses: N/A
Enrollment: N/A

EDUCATION

More @ usnews.com/grad

ENGINEERING

378